1983/84 FICTION WRITER'S MARKET

Edited by
Jean M. Fredette

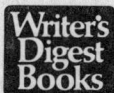

Writer's Digest Books

Cincinnati, Ohio

International Standard Serial Number 0275-2123
International Standard Book Number 0-89879-108-1

Book Design by Carol Buchanan

Acknowledgments

The editor of *Fiction Writer's Market* gratefully acknowledges the following publishers, authors and agents for granting permission to reprint their articles and book excerpts:

Richard Balkin, "Sample Book Publishing Agreement; Guidelines for Publishers and Authors," Dustbooks, Copyright © Richard Balkin, 1982.

Lawrence Block, "It Takes More Than Talent," *Writer's Yearbook 1981*. Copyright © *Writer's Yearbook*.

John Braine, "Dialogue," from *Writing a Novel*, Coward, McCann & Geoghegan, Inc. Copyright © 1974 by John Braine (Bingley) LTD.

Hallie and Whit Burnett, "Style: The Manner of Telling," from *Fiction Writer's Handbook*, by Hallie and Whit Burnett. Copyright © 1975 by Hallie Burnett. Reprinted by permission of Harper & Row, Publishers, Inc.

Dorothy Salisbury Davis, "Background and Atmosphere," from *The Mystery Writer's Handbook*, by The Mystery Writers of America, Writer's Digest Books. Copyright © 1976, Mystery Writers of America.

Dianne Doubtfire, "Characterization; Creating Imaginary Characters," *The Craft of Novel-Writing*. Revised edition published by Allison & Busby Limited (Schocken Books). Copyright © by Dianne Doubtfire 1978, 1981.

Roberta Gellis, "Researching the Historical Novel," from *Affaire de Coeur*, September/October 1982, Barbara N. Keenan, publisher.

Anne Gisonny, "Formulas for Writing the Romantic Novel," from *How to Write a Romance*, by Kathryn Falk. Reprinted with permission of Denise Marcil Agency (316 W. 82nd St., New York NY 10024).

Annette Grant, "John Cheever," from *Writers at Work: The Paris Review Interviews*, fifth series, edited by George Plimpton. Copyright © 1981 by The Paris Review, Inc. Reprinted by permission of Viking Penguin Inc.

Francine du Plessix Gray, "I Write for Revenge Against Reality," from *New York Times Book Review*. Reprinted by permission of the author and Georges Borchardt, Inc. Copyright © 1982 by Francine du Plessix Gray.

Stephen King, "The Last Waltz—Horror and Morality, Horror and Magic," from *Danse Macabre* by Stephen King. Copyright © 1981 by Stephen King. Reprinted with permission of Everest House, Publishers.

Dean R. Koontz, "Read, Read, Read," from *How to Write Best Selling Fiction*, Writer's Digest Books. Copyright © 1981 by Dean R. Koontz.

Rega Kramer McCarty, "Using Symbols as a Shortcut to Meaning," *WDS Forum* March/April 1981. Copyright © 1981 by Writer's Digest School.

James McKimmey, "All's Well That Ends Well," *Writer's Digest*, June 1982. Copyright © *Writer's Digest*.

Wright Morris, "Of Memory, Emotion and Imagination," from *Earthly Delights, Unearthly Adornments*, by Wright Morris. Copyright © 1978 by Wright Morris. Reprinted by permission of Harper & Row, Publishers, Inc.

Colleen Reece, "Just a Bunch of Words: How to Develop Believable Characters," *Writer's Digest*, November 1981. Copyright © *Writer's Digest*.

Paul R. Reynolds, "Revising the First Draft," from *The Writing and Selling of Fiction*, Newly Revised, by Paul R. Reynolds. Copyright © 1965, 1980 by Paul R. Reynolds. Reprinted by permission of William Morrow & Company.

Table of contents

Foreword

The statistics on writers and their publishing successes are not always encouraging: Seventy thousand stated their professions as writers in the 1980 US Census; many thousand others consider writing their interest, avocation, hobby or even obsession; approximately one-half of all would-be writers are working on short stories or novels; and about 40,000 books are published each year in the commercial publishing industry, only 15% of which, at the most, is fiction.

We're here to help you beat those great odds—with the third edition of *Fiction Writer's Market*.

Last year with copies of our '82/'83 edition, we enclosed surveys asking you, our readers/writers, for recommendations for improvement in our book—information or articles you would like to see in *Fiction Writer's Market* to assist you in your writing and publishing efforts. Many of you graciously obliged with suggestions and requests.

You asked for additional fiction markets—and in this new edition we have brought you more than 450 new opportunities, 250 more than last year, far exceeding the number of publishers and publications that went out of business or for other reasons are no longer listed in the book. We have thoroughly updated the listing information in all sections. We have also developed a larger, more comphrensive list of agents handling fiction who do not charge a reading or pre-publication fee.

In the surveys you also said you were curious to learn more about the publishing industry. Therefore this year we have 15 expanded close-ups, interviews with people at work in all areas of the publishing world. You will meet a reader/researcher with a commercial publication, a one-woman small press, a literary agent and the president of a large commercial publishing house, each with a different perspective—and tips for the fiction writer—based on his/her own experiences.

At your request—and even insistence—*Fiction Writer's Market '83/'84* again offers the category index, a section we did not include last year. We agree with the importance of this index and feel it will help shortcut your endeavors to see your work in print.

You also expressed an interest in current information on selected writing technique topics. We solicited original articles by individuals with that particular expertise: How to write a book proposal; how to use viewpoint in your story; how to market your children's story; and how to—and how not to—write and submit a short story to a magazine.

We are grateful for your helpful suggestions. But we'd like to hear more. We continually seek to improve each edition, so we ask you to let us know how you feel about our book and what subjects you would like us to touch on in the future. Tell us, too, of the problems you have had in your publishing pursuits. But please, if a reply is requested, enclose a self-addressed stamped envelope.

We appreciate that fiction writing is not easy. Even Ernest Hemingway agreed. When asked to explain how to start a novel, the old master responded, "First, you defrost the refrigerator." Such distractions and procrastination are inherent in all writers. Instead we urge you to forego your stalling techniques, read and study the text and markets that follow—and begin your story or novel at once.

—*Jean M. Fredette*

It takes more than talent

by Lawrence Block

It continues to astonish me what a widespread and enduring fantasy Being A Writer is for the population at large. It's a rare day when I don't encounter some misguided chap who expresses the desire to trade places with me. And it's on those not-so-rare days when everything goes wrong, when the words won't come but the rejections fly thick and fast, when the bank account has gone dry again and editors don't bother lying about the check's being in the mail, that otherwise sane folks tell me how much they envy me.

"I wish I had your self-discipline," they will say, generally saying so on a day when I have the backbone of a threadworm. "I envy you the imagination to keep coming up with ideas." Or they may envy me my education, which was an unremarkable one, or they will say they wish they knew my formula for writing success, as though I had somehow unearthed an alchemist's secret for transmuting the dross of nouns and verbs into the shimmering gold of fiction.

Nobody ever says, "I wish I had your talent."

And I find that fascinating. I don't think artists in other media get the same response. I doubt somehow that people kept grabbing Picasso by the shoulder and telling him how they envied his self-discipline, standing in front of the easel day after day. I don't suppose Caruso had to listen to that kind of crap, either. Actors and singers in particular seem to be plagued by people who think talent is all there is to it, that they have been given a gift that allows them to stand up there in front of the microphone and show

---

Lawrence Block, *author of more than 100 books, specializes in mystery and suspense fiction. His novel* Deadly Honeymoon *was made into a movie, and film rights have been purchased for several of his other books. His novel* Ariel *was a Book-of-the-Month Club selection, and his short fiction has appeared in major mystery and suspense magazines. Block's monthly columns on fiction for* Writer's Digest *are compiled in* Telling Lies for Fun and Profit. *His latest novels are* A Stab in the Dark *and* Eight Million Ways to Die.

their stuff. The hours of training and practice, the essential will and tenacity, are somehow discounted.

With writing, it's the talent that's apt to be discounted. There are times when I resent this. The unspoken premise in "I wish I had your self-discipline" is that anyone with my self-discipline could do what I do, that a persistent chimpanzee could match me book for book if he could just sit still long enough and work the space bar with his nonopposable thumb. My ego doesn't much like to hear this sort of thing.

And yet I have to admit that there are times when I think these people are onto something. It strikes me now and then that talent may be one of the least important variables in the writing business. People without a superabundance of talent succeed anyhow. People with tons of talent never get anywhere. It happens all the time.

The truth fairy

And it happens, I guess, in every field of creative endeavor. For years I subscribed to the popular myth that talent will out sooner or later, that all people with genuine ability in a particular field will ultimately achieve success in that field. I'll tell you, you would be better off believing in the tooth fairy. All over America are singers and actors and painters and composers and sculptors and yes, writers, blessed with a sufficient talent but born, as Thomas G. would put it, to blush unseen, and waste their sweetness on the desert air.

If talent's not the answer, what *does* it take? Why do some of us succeed while others do not? Is it just a matter of luck?

I'll tell you this much. Luck doesn't hurt. And simple luck has a great deal to do with the fate of an individual submission. When you mail off a story to a magazine, elements that have nothing whatsoever to do with the quality of that story will play a part in determining whether or not it sells. The editor's mood when he reads it is a factor, and one you have no way of controlling. The state of the magazine's inventory is another. Competition being what it is, I would go so far as to say that every time you manage to sell an unsolicited submission to a magazine, you have been lucky.

But I also think that luck tends to average out over a period of time. The writer who sells his first story to the first editor who sees it is a lucky writer indeed, but that first sale provides no guarantee of a second sale. Luck runs hot and cold, and nobody is lucky all the time.

Thy will to be done

What does it take, then, to succeed at freelance writing? What, besides talent and luck, helps determine who makes it and who doesn't?

It seems to me that will is enormously important. There are any number of jobs a person can pretty much fall into, but I don't believe writing is one of them. Every once in a while somebody does become a writer apparently by accident, but such persons rarely remain writers for long. In order to get into this business and in order to stay in it, you generally have to desire it with a passion bordering on desperation.

And the intensity of that desire doesn't seem to have anything to do with talent. A couple of summers ago I taught a seven-day seminar at Antioch College. One of my students was head and shoulders above the others. She was a middle-aged woman who had spent all her life on a farm, raising children and helping her husband with the farm work, and she had as good an eye and ear for rural settings as I have yet encountered. Her prose was clear and clean, her dialogue was excellent, and her stories and sketches absolutely sparkled. It was immediately evident to me that she was the one person in the seminar who had more than enough ability to succeed as a professional writer.

She also had something to write about. She knew that she wanted to write fiction that derived from what she knew—life in the rural Midwest. Some of us know that we want to be writers without having the faintest idea what we shall write about—I was certainly in that category—but this woman had no problems on that score.

What she did want was reassurance. Could I assure her that her prospects were good? Could I tell her it was not unrealistic to hope to make sales writing the sort of stories she had in mind? Because if such expectations were unwarranted, she explained, then she didn't want to go on wasting her time writing.

I spent quite a bit of time telling her how good she was, but even as I did so I wondered if perhaps *I* was wasting *my* time. Oh, she had talent, all right. And there were any number of ways in which she could ultimately exploit her background and turn it into successful and commercially viable fiction. But her question suggested to me that she would never achieve her goal because she didn't want it badly enough.

Because for almost everyone the road to writing success goes through some very rocky territory indeed. If she was that worried in advance that the time she spent writing might turn out to have been wasted, how could one expect her to rise above the inevitable rejections and disappointments that just plain come with the territory?

Perhaps I should not even have encouraged her. There's an old story about a young man who cornered a world-famous violinist and begged to be allowed to play for him. If the master offered him encouragement, he would devote his life to music. But, if his talent was not equal to his calling, he wanted to know ahead of time so he could avoid wasting his life. He played, and the great violinist shook his head. "You lack the fire," he said.

Decades later the two met again, and the would-be violinist, now a prosperous businessman, recalled their previous meeting. "You changed my entire life," he explained. "It was a bitter disappointment, giving up music, but I forced myself to accept your judgment. Thus, instead of becoming a fourth-rate musician, I've had a good life in the world of commerce. But tell me, how could you tell so readily that I lacked the fire?"

"Oh, I hardly listed when you played," the old master said. "That's what I tell everyone who plays for me—that they lack the fire."

"But that's unforgivable!" the businessman cried. "How could you do that? You altered the entire course of my life. Perhaps I could have been another Kreisler, another Heifetz—"

The old man shook his head again. "You don't understand," he said. "If you had the fire, you would have paid no attention to me."

Reading the will

Perhaps my student had the fire. I have had no contact with her since the seminar, so I can't say whether or not she has continued to write, or if she has had any success with it. But it wouldn't surprise me to learn that she has given up. Not everyone has the will. Not everyone cares that much about writing stories and getting them published.

Will is every bit as important for those of who have had a taste of success. Several years ago a woman of my acquaintance decided to try her hand at writing. She showed me a couple of chapters of an erotic novel she had written and I was immediately impressed by her ability. She was a natural stylist, readily able to assume the general style of any literary genre. While she tended to minimize this talent, insisting it was simple mimicry, that's what stylistic ability generally consists of at the outset of one's career.

She abandoned the erotic novel, finding it an uncomfortable genre, and took the time to read half a dozen gothics. Then, in rather rapid succession, she wrote and sold two gothics. After that she wrote a hundred or so pages of an unsuccessful mystery novel, and after that she didn't write a thing.

She had the talent, and she had enough success to make it clear that a career as a freelance writer was available to her. She had, too, enough drive and self-discipline to produce those two books and get them published. But, ultimately, being a writer was just not important to her. She had drifted into it largely as a result of association with other writers, and she drifted out of it when it proved insufficiently rewarding.

I suspect my friend has something in common with the phenomenon of one-book authors. The common wisdom holds that such writers had only one book in them, that having gotten it out of their systems they had nothing further to say. I think it might be more accurate to say that they had a very strong desire to write a particular book but no real desire to become a writer per se. Having written that book, their hunger was slaked.

Fair enough. Some people climb one mountain and complete one marathon and let it go at that. Others define themselves as mountain climbers or marathoners and go on climbing or running as long as they have breath in their bodies.

And some of us go on writing.

Self-help

I have a feeling that the tendency to perceive oneself as a writer is a somewhat different matter from simple will. I think, too, that it plays a big part in determining who makes it as a writer and who does not. In my own case, I decided (or recognized; it may have been more a matter of recognition than decision) that I was going to be a writer when I was in the 11th grade. A teacher's offhand remark put the idea in my head, but once planted it grew like a weed. I had no idea how I would go about becoming a writer or what I would write about, but I somehow knew it was what I was going to do.

I am quite certain that this self-definition had a lot to do with the development of my career. I submitted my earliest efforts to magazines, and while they came back like swallows to Capistrano, and with better cause, I took this in stride. The day came when an editor suggested a rewrite, and then another day came when he bought the story.

That was not the end of rejection and disappointment. Sometimes it seems more like the beginning, and the end is not yet in sight. But through it all I have never been able to shake that perception of self as a writer. It has kept me chained to this bloody desk for more years than I care to number, and it has made it impossible for me to entertain seriously the idea of doing anything else for very long.

That recognition of self as a writer can happen at any age. Consider another friend of mine, who awoke eight or nine years ago to the idea of becoming a writer. He was at the time editing a scientific trade journal for little money and less glory, and he had lately become friendly with several of us who wrote fiction for a living. One weekend he realized two things—that he wanted the sort of life we were leading, and that such a life was attainable.

Monday morning he called in sick and rolled a sheet of paper into his typewriter. By the time his wife got home from her job he had eight or ten pages of a novel written. He called in sick Tuesday and did another chunk of the book. Same thing Wednesday.

Thursday he got up bright and early, ate as hearty a breakfast as the next condemned man, and went to his office. A couple of hours later my phone rang. "I just quit my job," he said. "The book's coming along nicely and I want to stay with it."

I don't remember what I said. Probably something along the lines of yeah-but-how-are-you-gonna-make-a-living?

"No problem," he said. "I'm a writer now."

I wasn't convinced of the truth of either of those sentences, but even so I figured his downside risk was limited. After all, his wife was working, they didn't have any kids, their basic overhead was low and the job he had quit hadn't been much. After a little token breastbeating at having encouraged him to persist in his folly, I gave a shrug that would have gladdened a Frenchman's heart and went on about my business, such as it was.

Couple of weeks later he presented me with something like 250 pages of manuscript. Would I be so kind? Ahem. I took it home. I sat down with it. I started to read.

Page for page and line for line, his book was as bad a piece of writing as I have ever been confronted with, and that covers a lot of ground. It was not publishable, but that's the least of it. It was not rewritable, either, nor was it readable. Nor, alas, could it have been described as promising. There was nothing promising about it. No one could in good conscience read that manuscript and encourage its author to try writing anything more ambitious than a laundry list.

I was aghast. My friend had quit a job to produce this? Well, he had better get another in a hurry. Assuming he could find someone fool enough to hire him.

I didn't have the guts to say any of this. Instead I passed the buck—and the manuscript with it—to my agent. When his judgment echoed mine we tried to figure out what to tell the author. We decided to stall, and while we did so my friend told me he was half-way through Novel Number Two.

The second book was much better. It was still nothing you would be tempted to call good, but it was written in a language readily identifiable as English. My friend finished it, gave it to me and then to my agent, and went on to the third book.

The second book didn't sell. The third did, though, and the fourth and fifth. They were not wildly successful. They were published as hardcover mysteries, had reasonably positive reviews and mediocre sales, and did not go into paperback. One got nominated for an award but failed to win.

Bard of the bar

The story could stop right there and it wouldn't be the worst story ever told, either But there's more. My friend went on to write several more mysteries and these did not sell. There was a market slump about that time, and hardcover mysteries were suddenly about as much in demand as legionnaire's disease. My friend wrote three or four in a row and couldn't get arrested.

By this time he was single again, and broke. He took a job tending bar and wrote days. After a while he quit writing mysteries that nobody wanted and began doing the preliminary research for a large-scale adventure novel that would capitalize on his interests and areas of expertise. He spent a lot of time on research and more on plot development, and then he went on to spend a great deal more time writing and rewriting. Then the book came out, had a six-figure paperback sale and a six-figure movie sale, touched one or two of the bestseller lists briefly, and must have earned him something like—what? Half a million? I don't know, and it's not really important, because this article isn't about money. It's about writing, and the set of mind necessary to make a go of it.

At first glance, the story's point seems obvious enough. My friend had the will to succeed, the drive to keep going in the face of discouragement and rejection. He had, too, a perception of himself as a writer that refused to fade. In addition, he had a single-mindedness of purpose that enabled him to take chances. Quitting his job on the basis of a few days' production was probably ill-advised, and I certainly would not recommend it to anyone in a similar situation, but perhaps it was essential for him. Suppose he had worked nights and weekends on that first book, taking a year or so to produce an unsalable manuscript. Would he have been as quick to plunge in again and write books two and three?

When, after having sold several books, he found himself incapable of supporting himself by writing, he might have tried to find a job rather like the one he had left. Instead he deliberately sought out a subsistence job, undemanding part-time work that let him pay the rent while he went on writing. Again, he was taking a chance instead of playing it safe.

It's worth noting, though, that the chances he took were sane ones. If he was walking a tightrope, he was not doing so without a net. If he had failed at the beginning, the worst thing that could have happened is that he would have had to find another job. If his big adventure novel had failed, he would have had to go on tending bar, or look for something with more long-range promise. But no one was going to starve because he wanted to be a writer.

This talk of starving puts me in mind of another attitude that's important if one is to be comfortable as a freelance writer. You have to have a pretty high threshold for financial insecurity. If a regular pay check is emotionally essential to you, perhaps you would be well advised to stay with a regular job.

I was very fortunate in that respect. I started writing so early in life that my ordinary expenses were extremely low. The last job I held before taking up writing fulltime was in a literary agency, where my base pay was $60 a week before taxes. That doesn't sound like much money now, and it wasn't much money then, either.

My low standard of living made the small sums of money I could earn writing more significant than they would have been otherwise. If I went home from the office and wrote a 3,000-word pulp story and sold it for a cent a word, that was half a week's income right there. And, once I left the job, I didn't have to hit the bestseller list in order to match my previous income. Before very long I had a standing assignment writing a book a month for a paperback publisher. The pay was $600 a book, which was more than double what my salary had been.

All of this was helpful early on. As I grew older and acquired a wife and children and a higher standard of living, what helped keep me from going crazy was a temperament that took financial insecurity for granted. This is not to say that I find poverty a treat, or that I am not aggravated by slow-pay publishers and inconvenienced by the stretches of financial hardship that seem to be an inescapable part of the writing life. Sometimes a pile of bills and dunning letters can paralyze just about anyone. But most of the time my writing goes on independent of my solvency or lack thereof.

This is true of most of the people I know who function successfully as freelance writers. But not everyone is so constituted. I know a number of established professional writers who simply lack the temperament required for fulltime freelancing. They continue to hold 40-hour-a-week jobs, jobs they often profess to hate, simply because they are not comfortable without the security of a regular pay check. In several cases, there's no question but that they could earn more if they gave up their jobs. And they know this, but some of them have found out fulltime self-employment cuts their writing production to the bone because they can't work effectively when burdened with all that anxiety.

It has always seemed to me, on the other hand, that writing is infinitely more secure than any employment could hope to be. All my friends who hold jobs could conceivably be fired. Who can fire me? Even a tenured college professor could one day see his college go out of business, and then where would he be? I, meanwhile, can go on writing for a variety of publishers, adapting to changes in the marketplace, and all without a care for compulsory retirement rules or other abominations,

Of course, I can't look forward to a pension, and I have to pay my own medical insurance, and I don't get any fringe benefits or sick leave or paid vacations. Nor am I guaranteed a day's pay just by showing up for work in the morning; if I don't produce anything, neither do I earn anything. I can generally accept all that. But not everybody can.

Writing and hating

There's another essential quality in the writer's temperament, and it seems on the surface so obvious that I came close to overlooking it altogether. Quite simply, you have to like the work.

By this I don't mean that the physical act of sitting at a typewriter has to be enjoyable in and of itself. Most writers hate the process, to one extent or another, and everybody hates it now and then. (This is an anomaly of writing, and an interesting one at that. Most of the painters I know enjoy the act of painting, and almost every musician I have known loves to play so much that he goes on doing it after his day's work is done. But writers often hate writing.)

What a writer must enjoy, or at least be able to tolerate, is the utterly solitary nature of the work. When all is said and done, writing is a matter of sitting alone at a desk, staring more often than not at a blank wall, and turning thoughts into words and putting the words on paper.

I know a man who freelanced for a while some years ago. He started off working at home, then rented a hotel room so he would have an office to go to. That structured his days somewhat, but it didn't really help because he still couldn't take the solitude. He gave up the hotel room and rented space in an office so that there would be other people working around him. He enjoyed that more but it cut into his productivity because he preferred interacting with the other people to concentrating on his own work. He stopped freelancing and got a job, and he has been gainfully employed every since. He has published books now and then, writing them at night and on weekends, and periodically he tells me how much he hates his job and how he longs to quit it and write fulltime, but that's nonsense. He would go nuts without a job to go to.

Even if you're the sort who finds solitude comfortable, I think it's very important for writers to make sure they have sufficient human contact when they're not working to compensate for the lack thereof during their working hours. We can't be alone all the time, nor can we expect our families to fill our needs in this area. The isolated writer loses touch with the world. He forgets what people are like. He uses up his writing source material and fails to replenish it.

In my own case, I have found that I need the occasional company of other writers. There are simply things about writing that people who are not in the business cannot share. The company of my fellows is stimulating. There's a certain amount of cross-pollination in such social intercourse, and a few hours in another writer's company serves to reinforce my perception of myself as a writer.

At the same time, I definitely require the company of people who are *not* writers. An exclusive diet of shop talk is an unbalanced one. Besides, one wants to be occasionally exposed to reality, if only in small doses. As a friend of mine, herself a writer, says, "People who spend the most meaningful hours of their lives in the exclusive company of imaginary people are apt to be a little strange."

And that's the final requisite of the writer's temperament. We're every last one of us a little strange, a wee bit different.

And *vive la difference*.

Still just writing

by Anne Tyler

While I was painting the downstairs hall I thought of a novel to write. Really I just thought of a character; he more or less wandered into my mind, wearing a beard and a broad-brimmed leather hat. I figured that if I sat down and organized this character on paper, a novel would grow up around him. But it was March and the children's spring vacation began the next day, so I waited.

After spring vacation the children went back to school, but the dog got worms. It was a little complicated at the vet's and I lost a day. By then it was Thursday; Friday is the only day I can buy the groceries, pick up new cedar chips for the gerbils, scrub the bathrooms. I waited till Monday. Still, that left me four good weeks in April to block out the novel.

By May I was ready to start actually writing, but I had to do it in patches. There was the follow-up treatment at the vet, and then a half-day spent trailing the dog with a specimen tin so the lab could be sure the treatment had really worked. There were visits from the washing machine repairman and the Davey tree man, not to mention briefer interruptions by the meter reader, five Jehovah's Witnesses, and two Mormons. People telephoned wanting to sell me permanent light bulbs and waterproof basements. An Iranian cousin of my husband's had a baby; the cousin's uncle died; then the cousin's mother decided to go home to Iran and needed to know where to buy a black American coat before she left. There *are* no black American coats; don't Americans wear mourning? I told her no, but I checked around at all the department stores anyway because she didn't speak

Anne Tyler graduated at 19 from Duke University, where she twice won the Anne Flexner Award for creative writing. Since then her stories have appeared in The New Yorker and Harper's and many other magazines. She is the author of nine novels, among them Earthly Possessions, Searching for Caleb, and her most recent work and bestseller, The Dinner at Homesick Restaurant.

English. Then I wrote chapters one and two. I had planned to work till 3:30 every day, but it was a month of early quittings: once for the children's dental appointment, once for the cat's rabies shot, once for our older daughter's orthopedist, and twice for her gymnastic meets. Sitting on the bleachers in the school gymnasium, I told myself I could always use this in a novel someplace, but I couldn't really picture writing a novel about 20 little girls in leotards trying to walk the length of a wooden beam without falling off. By the time I'd written chapter three, it was Memorial Day and the children were home again.

Characters on hold

I knew I shouldn't expect anything from June. School was finished then and camp hadn't yet begun. I put the novel away. I closed down my mind and planted some herbs and played cribbage with the children. Then on the 25th, we drove one child to a sleep-away camp in Virginia and entered the other in a day camp, and I was ready to start work again. First I had to take my car in for repairs and the mechanics lost it, but I didn't get diverted. I sat in the garage on a folding chair while they hunted my car all one afternoon, and I hummed a calming tune and tried to remember what I'd planned to do next in my novel. Or even what the novel was about, for that matter. My character wandered in again in his beard and his broad-brimmed hat. He looked a little pale and knuckly, like someone scrabbling at a cliff edge so as not to fall away entirely.

I had high hopes for July, but it began with a four-day weekend, and on Monday night we had a long-distance call from our daughter's camp in Virginia. She was seriously ill in a Charlottesville hospital. We left our youngest with friends and drove three hours in a torrent of rain. We found our daughter frightened and crying, and another child (the only other child I knew in all of Virginia) equally frightened and crying down in the emergency room with possible appendicitis, so I spent that night alternating between a chair in the pediatric wing and a chair in the emergency room. By morning, it had begun to seem that our daughter's illness was typhoid fever. We loaded her into the car and took her back to Baltimore, where her doctor put her on drugs and prescribed a long bed-rest. She lay in bed six days, looking wretched and calling for fluids and cold cloths. On the seventh day she got up her same old healthy self, and the illness was declared to be not typhoid fever after all but a simple virus, and we shipped her back to Virginia on the evening train. The next day I was free to start writing again but sat, instead, on the couch in my study, staring blankly at the wall.

Part-time creativity

I could draw some conclusions here about the effect that being a woman/wife/mother has upon my writing, except that I am married to a writer who is also a man/husband/father. He published his first novel while he was a medical student in Iran; then he came to America to finish his training. His writing fell by the wayside, for a long while. You can't be on call in the emergency room for 20 hours and write a novel during the other four. Now he's a child psychiatrist, fulltime, and he writes his novels in the odd moments here and there—when he's not preparing a lecture, when he's not on the phone with a patient, when he's not attending classes at the psychoanalytic institute. He writes in Persian, still, in those black-and-white speckled composition books. Sometimes one of the children will interrupt him in English and he will answer in Persian, and they'll say, "What?" and he'll look up blankly, and it seems a sheet has to fall from in front of his eyes before he remembers where he is and switches to English. Often, I wonder what he would be doing now if he didn't have a family to support. He cares deeply about his writing and he's very good at it, but every morning at 5:30 he gets up and puts on a suit and tie and drives in the dark to the hospital. Both of us, in different ways, seem to be hewing our creative time in small, hard chips from our living time.

Drained and drawn

Occasionally, I take a day off. I go to a friend's house for lunch, or weed the garden, or rearrange the linen closet. I notice that at the end of one of these days, when my husband asks me what I've been doing, I tend to exaggerate any hardships I may have encountered. ("A pickup nearly sideswiped me on Greenspring Avenue. I stood in line an hour just trying to buy the children some flip-flops.") It seems sinful to have lounged around so. Also, it seems sinful that I have more choice than my husband as to whether or not to undertake any given piece of work. I can refuse to do an article if it doesn't appeal to me, refuse to change a short story, refuse to hurry a book any faster than it wants to go—all luxuries. My husband, on the other hand, is forced to rise and go off to that hospital every blessed weekday of his life. *His* luxury is that no one expects him to drop all else for two weeks when a child has chicken pox. The only person who has no luxuries at all, it seems to me, is the woman writer who is the sole support of her children. I often think about how she must manage. I think that if I were in that position, I'd have to find a job involving manual labor. I have spent so long erecting partitions around the part of me that writes—learning how to close the door on it when ordinary life intervenes, how to close the door on ordinary life when it's time to start writing again—that I'm not sure I could fit the two parts of me back together now.

Before we had children I worked in a library. It was a boring job, but I tend to like doing boring things. I would sit on a stool alphabetizing Russian catalogue cards and listening to the other librarians talking around me. It made me think of my adolescence, which was spent listening to the tobacco stringers while I handed tobacco. At night I'd go home from the library and write. I never wrote what the librarians said, exactly, but having those voices in my ears all day helped me summon up my own characters' voices. Then our first baby came along—an insomniac. I quit work and stayed home all day with her and walked her all night. Even if I had found the time to write, I wouldn't have had the insides. I felt drained; too much care and feeling were being drawn out of me. And the only voices I heard now were by appointment—people who came to dinner, or invited us to dinner, and who therefore felt they had to make deliberate conversation. That's one thing writers never have, and I still miss it: the easy-going, on-again-off-again, gossipy murmurs of people working alongside each other all day.

Free and useful

I enjoyed tending infants (though I've much preferred the later ages), but it was hard to be solely, continually in their company and not to be able to write. And I couldn't think of any alternative. I know it must be possible to have a child raised beautifully by a housekeeper, but every such child I've run into has seemed dulled and doesn't use words well. So I figured I'd better stick it out. As it happened, it wasn't that long—five years, from the time our first daughter was born till our second started nursery school and left me with my mornings free. But while I was going through it I thought it would be a lot longer. I couldn't imagine any end to it. I felt that everything I wanted to write was somehow coagulating in my veins and making me fidgety and slow. Then after a while I didn't have anything to write anyhow, but I still had the fidgets. I felt useless, no matter how many diapers I washed or strollers I pushed. The only way I could explain my life to myself was to imagine that I was living in a very small commune. I had spent my childhood in a commune, or what would nowadays be called a commune, and I was used to the idea of division of labor. What we had here, I told myself, was a perfectly sensible arrangement: One member was the liaison with the outside world, bringing in money; another was the caretaker, reading the Little Bear books to the children and repairing the electrical switches. This second member might have less physical freedom, but she had much more freedom to arrange her own work schedule. I must have sat down a dozen times a week and very carefully, consciously thought it all through. Often, I was merely trying to convince myself that I really did pull my own weight.

Strung up

This Iranian cousin who just had the baby: She sits home now and cries a lot. She was working on her master's degree and is used to being out in the world more. "Never mind," I tell her, "you'll soon be out again. This stage doesn't last long."

"How long?" she asks.

"Oh . . . three years, if you just have the one."

"Three years!"

I can see she's appalled. Her baby is beautiful, very dark and Persian; and what's more, he sleeps—something I've rarely seen a baby do. What I'm trying to say to her (but of course, she'll agree without really hearing me) is that he's worth it. It seems to me that since I've had children, I've grown richer and deeper. They may have slowed down my writing for a while, but when I did write, I had more of a self to speak from. After all, who else in the world do you *have* to love, no matter what? Who else can you absolutely not give up on? My life seems more intricate. Also more dangerous.

After the children started school, I put up the partitions in my mind. I would rush around in the morning braiding their hair, packing their lunches; then the second they were gone I would grow quiet and climb the stairs to my study. Sometimes a child would come home early and I would feel a little tug between the two parts of me; I'd be absent-minded and short-tempered. Then gradually I learned to make the transition more easily. It feels like a sort of string that I tell myself to loosen. When the children come home, I drop the string and close the study door and that's the end of it. It doesn't always work perfectly, of course. There are times when it doesn't work at all: If a child is sick, for instance, I can't possibly drop the children's end of the string, and I've learned not to try. It's easier just to stop writing for a while. Or if they're home but otherwise occupied, I no longer attempt to sneak off to my study to finish that one last page; I know that instantly, as if by magic, assorted little people will be pounding on my door requiring Band-Aids, tetanus shots, and a complete summation of the facts of life.

Last spring, I bought a midget tape recorder to make notes on. I'd noticed that my best ideas came while I was running the vacuum cleaner, but I was always losing them. I thought this little recorder would help. I carried it around in my shirt pocket. But I was ignoring the partitions, is what it was; I was letting one half of my life intrude upon the other. A child would be talking about her day at school and suddenly I'd whip out the tape recorder and tell it, "Get Morgan out of that cocktail party; he's not the type to drink." "Huh?" the child would say. Both halves began to seem ludicrous, unsynchronized. I took the recorder back to Radio Shack.

Faith and adaptation

A few years ago, my parents went to the Gaza Strip to work for the American Friends Service Committee. It was a lifelong dream of my father's to do something with the AFSC as soon as all his children were grown, and he'd been actively preparing for it for years. But almost as soon as they got there, my mother fell ill with a mysterious fever that neither the Arab nor the Israeli hospitals could diagnose. My parents had to come home for her treatment, and since they'd sublet their house in North Carolina, they had to live with us. For four months, they stayed here—but only on a week-to-week basis, not knowing when they were going back, or whether they were going back at all, or how serious my mother's illness was. It was hard for her, of course, but it should have been especially hard in another way for my father, who had simply to hang in suspended animation for four months while my mother was whisked in and out of hospitals. However, I believe he was as pleased with life as he always is. He whistled Mozart and puttered around insulating our windows. He went on long walks collecting firewood. He strolled over to the meetinghouse and gave a talk on the plight of the Arab refugees. "Now that we seem to have a little time," he told my mother, "why not visit the boys?" and during one of her outpatient periods he took her on a gigantic cross-country trip to see all my brothers and any other relatives they happened upon. Then my mother decided she ought to go to a faith healer. (She wouldn't usually do such a thing, but she was desperate.) "Oh. Okay," my father said, and he took her to a faith healer, whistling all the way. And when the faith healer didn't work, my mother said, "I think this is psychosomatic. Let's go back to Gaza." My father said, "Okay," and reserved two seats on the next plane over. The children and I went to see them the following summer: My mother's fever was utterly gone, and my father drove us down the Strip, weaving a little Renault among the tents and camels, cheerfully whistling Mozart.

I hold this entire, rambling set of events in my head at all times, and remind myself of it almost daily. It seems to me that the way my father lives (infinitely adapting, and looking around him with a smile to say, "Oh! So *this* is where I am!") is also the way to slip gracefully through a choppy life of writing novels, plastering the dining room ceiling, and presiding at slumber parties. I have learned, bit by bit, to accept a school snow-closing as an unexpected holiday, an excuse to play 17 rounds of Parcheesi instead of typing up a short story. When there's a midweek visitation of uncles from Iran (hordes of great, bald, yellow men calling for their glasses of tea, sleeping on guest beds, couches, two armchairs pushed together, and discarded crib mattresses), I have decided that I might as well listen to what they have to say, and work on my novel tomorrow instead. I smile at the uncles out of a kind of clear, swept space inside me. What this takes, of course, is a sense of limitless time, but I'm getting that. My life is beginning to seem unusually long. And there's a danger to it: I could wind up as passive as a piece of wood on a wave. But I try to walk a middle line.

Wait for heaven

I was standing in the schoolyard waiting for a child when another mother came up to me. "Have you found work yet?" she asked. "Or are you still just writing?"

Now, how am I supposed to answer that?

I could take offense, come to think of it. Maybe the reason I didn't is that I halfway share her attitude. They're *paying* me for this? For just writing down untruthful stories? I'd better look around for more permanent employment. For I do consider writing to be a finite job. I expect that any day now, I will have said all I have to say; I'll have used up all my characters, and then I'll be free to get on with my real life. When I make a note of new ideas on index cards, I imagine I'm clearing out my head, and that soon it will be empty and spacious. I file the cards in a little blue box, and I can picture myself using the final card one day—ah! through at last!—and throwing the blue box away. I'm like a dentist who continually fights tooth decay, working toward the time when he's conquered it altogether and done himself out of a job. But my head keeps loading up again; the little blue box stays crowded and messy. Even when I feel I have no ideas at all, and can't possibly start the next chapter, I have a sense of something still bottled in me, trying to get out.

People have always seemed funny and strange to me, and touching in unexpected ways. I can't shake off a sort of mist of irony that hangs over whatever I see. Probably that's what I'm trying to put across when I write; I may believe that I'm the one person who holds this view of things. And I'm always hurt when a reader says that I choose only bizarre or eccentric people to write about. It's not a matter of choice; it just seems to me that even the most ordinary person, in real life, will turn out to have something unusual at his center. I like to think that I might meet up with one of my past characters at the very next street corner. The odd thing is, sometimes I have. And if I were remotely religious, I'd believe that a little gathering of my characters would be waiting for me in heaven when I died. "*Then* what happened?" I'd ask them. "How have things worked out, since the last time I saw you?"

Eudora's legacy

I think I was born with the impression that what happened in books was much more reasonable, and interesting, and *real*, in some ways, than what happened in life. I hated childhood, and spent it sitting behind a book waiting for adulthood to arrive. When I ran out of books I made up my own. At night, when I couldn't sleep, I made up stories in the dark. Most of my plots involved girls going west in covered wagons. I was truly furious that I'd been born too late to go west in a covered wagon.

I know a poet who says that in order to be a writer, you have to have had rheumatic fever in your childhood. I've never had rheumatic fever, but I believe that any kind of setting-apart situation will do as well. In my case, it was emerging from that commune— really an experimental Quaker community in the wilderness—and trying to fit into the outside world. I was eleven. I had never used a telephone and could strike a match on the soles of my bare feet. All the children in my new school looked very peculiar to me, and I certainly must have looked peculiar to them. I am still surprised, to this day, to find myself where I am. My life is so streamlined and full of modern conveniences. How did I get here? I have given up hope, by now, of ever losing my sense of distance; in fact, I seem to have come to cherish it. Neither I nor any of my brothers can stand being out among a crowd of people for any length of time at all.

I spent my adolescence planning to be an artist, not a writer. After all, books had to be about major events, and none had ever happened to me. All I knew were tobacco workers, stringing the leaves I handed them and talking up a storm. Then I found a book of Eudora Welty's short stories in the high school library. She was writing about Edna Earle, who was so slow-witted she could sit all day just pondering how the tail of the *C* got through the loop of the *L* on the Coca-Cola sign. Why, I knew Edna Earle. You mean you could *write* about such people? I have always meant to send Eudora Welty a thank-you note, but I imagine she would find it a little strange.

The write of passage

I wanted to go to Swarthmore College, but my parents suggested Duke instead, where I had a full scholarship, because my three brothers were coming along right behind me and it was more important for boys to get a good education than for girls. That was the first and last time that my being female was ever a serious issue. I still don't think it was just, but I can't say it ruined my life. After all, Duke had Reynolds Price, who turned out to be the only person I ever knew who could actually teach writing. It all worked out, in the end.

I believe that for many writers, the hardest time is that dead spot after college (where they're wonder-children, made much of) and before their first published work. Luckily, I didn't notice that part; I was so vague about what I wanted to do that I could hardly chafe at not yet doing it. I went to graduate school in Russian studies; I scrubbed decks on a boat in Maine; I got a job ordering books from the Soviet Union. Writing was something that crept in around the edges. For a while I lived in New York, where I became addicted to riding any kind of train or subway, and while I rode I often felt I was nothing but an enormous eye, taking things in and turning them over and sorting them out. But who would I tell them to, once I'd sorted them? I have never had more than three or four close friends, at any period of my life; and anyway, I don't talk well. I am the kind of person who wakes up at four in the morning and suddenly thinks of what she should have said yesterday at lunch. For me, writing something down was the only road out.

Rewarding routines and rituals

You would think, since I waited so long and so hopefully for adulthood, that it would prove to be a disappointment. Actually, I figure it was worth the wait. I like everything about it but the paperwork—the income tax and protesting the Sears bill and renewing the Triple-A membership. I always did count on having a husband and children, and here they are. I'm surprised to find myself a writer but have fitted it in fairly well, I think. The only real trouble that writing has ever brought me is an occasional sense of being invaded by the outside world. Why do people imagine that writers, having chosen the most private of professions, should be any good at performing in public, or should have the slightest desire to tell their secrets to interveiwers from ladies' magazines? I feel I am only holding myself together by being extremely firm and decisive about what I will do and what I will not do. I will write my books and raise the children. Anything else just fritters me away. I know this makes me seem narrow, but in fact, I *am* narrow. I like routine and rituals and I hate leaving home; I have a sense of digging my heels in. I refuse to drive on freeways. I dread our annual vacation. Yet I'm continually prepared for travel: It is physically impossible for me to buy any necessity without buying a travel-sized version as well. I have a little toilet kit, with soap and a nightgown, forever packed and ready to go. How do you explain that?

As the outside world grows less dependable, I keep buttressing my inside world, where people go on meaning well and surprising other people with little touches of grace. There are days when I sink into my novel like a pool and emerge feeling blank and bemused and used up. Then I drift over to the schoolyard, and there's this mother wondering if I'm doing anything halfway useful yet. Am I working? Have I found a job? No, I tell her.

I'm still just writing.

> 66 *I think a lot of what stops women writing is not lack of talent . . . . It's fear. And, it's lack of confidence. I've seen people with equal amounts of talent, and the thing that meant one went on and the other stopped was the attitude toward themselves and their confidence and anxiety and fear. Sometimes that's what has to be worked on. Then you can work on the novel . . . If you have the confidence in writing, you can do that, and if you don't, you can't.*
> —*Margaret Atwood* 99

I write for revenge against reality

by Francine du Plessix Gray

A nightmare recurs since childhood:

Facing a friend, I struggle for words and emit no sound. I have an urgent message to share but am struck dumb, my jaw is clamped shut as in a metal vise, I gasp for breath and can not set my tongue free. At the dream's end my friend has fled and I am locked into the solitude of silence.

The severe stutter I had as a child, my father's impatience and swiftness of tongue, his constant interruption of me when I tried to speak?

Or perhaps another incident which also has to do with the threat of the Father and the general quirkiness of my French education: One day when I was 9 I was assigned my first free composition. From infancy I had been tutored at home in Paris by a tyrannical governess, the two of us traveling once a week to a correspondence school whose Gallically rigid assignments (memorization of Asian capitals and Latin verbs, codifying of sentence parts) were hardly conducive to a fertile imagination. "Write a Story About Anything You Wish," Central Bureau suddenly ordered. Filled with excitement and terror by this freedom, I began as a severe minimalist:

"The little girl was forbidden by her parents to walk alone to the lake at the other end of the long lawn. But she wished to visit a luminous green-eyed frog who would offer her the key to freedom. One day she disobeyed her parents and walked to the lake and immediately drowned." (The End)

"Pathetic dribble!" the Father stormed on his daily visit to my study room. "You dare call that a story! What will become of you if you can't ever finish anything!"

Francine du Plessix Gray is the acclaimed author of Divine Disobedience, Hawaii: The Sugar-Coated Fortress, Lovers and Tyrants, *and her latest novel* World Without End. *Her work has appeared in* The New York Times Magazine, The New Yorker, *the* New York Review of Books *and other publications.*

It was a warm May evening of 1939, the year before he died in the Resistance. The love of my life (my father was himself an occasional scribbler) was warning me that I should never write again. I still remember the hours I spent honing those meager sentences, the square white china inkwell into which I squeezed the rubber filler of a Waterman pen, the awkwardness of ink-stained fingers as I struggled to shape my letters (I was born left-handed and had been forced to use my right), the tears, the sense that my writing was doomed to be sloppy, abortive, good for naught.

So it may have begun, the central torment of my life, my simultaneous need to commit fantasies to paper and the terror that accompanies that need, the leaden slowness of the words' arrival, my struggle with the clamped metal jaws of mouth and mind. An affliction deepened by that infatuation with the written word that possesses most solitary children. For books had been the only companions of my childhood prison, particularly such stirring tales of naval adventure as *Captains Courageous* or *Two Years Before the Mast*, which fueled dreams of running away to sea and never being seen again.

Then came the war, the flight to America, the need to learn a new language. English was learned as a means of survival and became a lover to be seduced and conquered as swiftly as possible, to be caressed and rolled on the tongue in a continuous ecstasy of union. English words, from the time I was 11 on, were my medium of joy and liberation. I fondled them by memorizing 20 lines of Blake when 10 had been assigned; I wooed them so assiduously that I won the Lower School Spelling Bee within 10 months of having come to the United States. (I was the only foreign scholarship student at the Spence School; shortly after the contest a delegation of Spence parents descended on my mother, who was supporting us by designing hats at Henri Bendel's, to verify that we were true emigrés and not usurpers from Brooklyn).

I continued to court my new tongue by struggling for A's in English, by being elected editor of the school paper, which a predecessor had artfully named Il Spenceroso. Omens of a "literary gift" continued to accrete—a prize in Bryn Mawr's Freshman Essay Contest, the Creative Writing Award at Barnard for three stories of a strictly autobiographical nature. Such portents brought no security. I fled from myself by being a compulsive talker, a bureaucrat, polemicist, hack journalist. I had taken no more than two courses in literature beyond Freshman English, thinking I was smartass enough to learn it for myself. One of the other courses had been a creative writing class that earned me a C—for first-person fictions about situations I knew nothing about—I seemed always to be a middle-aged alcoholic actor seeking salvation in a Bowery church. After that fiasco I had sought refuge in rigor and formalism—physics, philosophy, medieval history. There was a curious furtiveness about the way I continued to carry on my love affair with literature. I copied entire paragraphs from Henry James or T.S. Eliot into private notebooks out of sheer delectation in the texture of their prose. In a stretch of a few solitary vacation weeks I would memorize 200 lines of Marvell for the pleasure of speaking them to myself during nights of insomnia. Why all this reluctance and covertness?

"You're writing pure junk," Charles Olson had stormed at me during a summer workshop at Black Mountain when I'd handed him my prize-winning college stories. "If you want to be a writer keep it to a journal." The giant walrus rising from his chair, 6 feet 7 inches of him towering. " . . . AND ABOVE ALL DON'T TRY TO PUBLISH ANYTHING FOR 10 YEARS!" Another paternal figure had censored me into silence, perhaps this time for the best.

Personal epiphany

I followed Big Charles's advice. I kept my journal in New Orleans where I dallied as if I had ten lives to squander, drinking half a bottle of gin at night as I followed a jazz clarinetist on the rounds of Bourbon Street. I remained faithful to my secret vice in the dawns of New York when I worked the night shift at United Press, writing World in Briefs about Elks' Meetings and watermelon-eating contests in Alabama. I remained loyal to my journal through a myriad of failed aspirations while flirting with the thought of entering Harvard's Department of Architecture, of going to Union Theological Seminary for a degree in divinity. I persevered with it when I moved to Paris to earn my living as a fashion reporter, dallying with a succession of consummate narcissists to whom I eventually gave their literary due. I continued to write it when I fulfilled one of my life's earliest dreams and spent five years as a painter of meticulously naturalistic landscapes and still lifes.

By then I was married and had two children. And since I lived in deep country and in relative solitude, encompassed by domestic duties, the journal became increasingly voluminous, angry, introspective. The nomad, denied flight and forced to turn inward, was beginning to explode. One day when I was 33, after I'd cooked and smiled for a bevy of weekend guests whom I never wished to see again, I felt an immense void, great powerlessness, the deepest loneliness I'd ever know. I wept for some hours, took out a notebook, started rewriting one of the three stories that had won me my Barnard prize. It was the one about my governess. It was published a short time later in *The New Yorker*, one year past the deadline Charles Olson had set me. It was to become, 12 years and two books of nonfiction later, the first chapter of *Lovers and Tyrants*. The process of finishing that book was as complex and lengthy as it was painful. It entailed a solid and delicate psychoanalysis which forced me to accept my father's death. Epiphany achieved, I was able to write the novel's three last chapters—my first genuine attempt at fiction—in a mere six months. I may have had to bury my father to set my tongue free.

Minus narcissism

And yet what kind of writer have I become, six years and two novels later? Few scribblers I know have struggled so hard for so little. I am too many things I do not wish to be—a Jane of all trades shuttling back and forth between scant fiction, voluminous reporting, innumerable and unmemorable literary essays. I feel honored by yet undeserving of the appellation "novelist." I am merely a craftsperson, a cabinetmaker of texts and occasionally, I hope, a witness to our times. My terror of fictional invention has denied me that activity which from childhood has been the most furtively longed for, which has proved to be (when I finally began to tackle it) the most deeply satisfying.

Might I remain brainwashed, along with many of my generation, by the notion that fiction is the noblest, the most "creative" of all genres of prose? No avocation has better clarified that issue or my identity as a writer than the business of teaching. I stress to young colleagues that some of the greatest masterpieces of our time have been works of nonfiction or hybrid forms which defy classification—James Agee's *Let Us Now Praise Famous Men*, Edmund Wilson's criticism, Peter Hanke's *A Sorrow Beyond Dreams*, all of Roland Barth's work. I urge them to shake loose from the peculiarly American fixation on novel-writing. I tell them that the obsession to write The Great American Novel might have done more harm to generations of Americans than all the marijuana in Mexico. The syllabus for the course I taught at Yale last fall sums it all up:

THE WRITING OF THE TEXT: This is a seminar in the reading and writing of literature which I hope can remain untainted by the word "creative." It is dedicated to the premise that a distinction between "fiction" and "nonfiction" is potentially harmful to many aspiring writers who will progress more fruitfully if they are encouraged to think of their writing as pure "text" without worrying about what "form" or "genre" it will fall into.

Reading Assignments: F. Scott Fitzgerald's "Crack-Up," Max Frisch's *Sketchbooks*, Flaubert's *Dictionary of Accepted Ideas*, Elizabeth Hardwick's *Sleepless Nights*, Boris Pasternak's *Safe Conduct*, William Gass's *On Being Blue*, Maureen Howard's *Facts of Life*.

The first thing we must do when we set out to write, I also tell my classes, is to shed all narcissism. My own decades of fear came from my anxiety that my early drafts were ugly, sloppy, not promising enough. We must persevere and scrawl atrocities, persevere dreadful draft after dreadful draft in an unhindered stream of consciousness, persevere, if need be, in Breton's technique of automatic writing, of mindless trance. And within that morass of words there may be an ironic turn of phrase, a dislocation that gives us a key to the voice, the tone, the structure we're struggling to find. I am a witness to the lateness of my own vocation, the hesitation and terrors that still haunt all my beginnings, the painful slowness with which I proceed through a minimum of four drafts in both fiction and nonfiction.

Faith in the surprise

Question:

Why do I go on writing, seeing the continuing anguish of the act, the dissatisfaction I feel toward most results?

Flannery O'Connor said it best: "I write because I don't know what I think until I read what I say."

I write out of a desire for revenge against reality, to destroy forever the stuttering powerless child I once was, to gain the love and attention that silenced child never had, to allay the dissatisfaction I still have with myself, to be something other than what I am. I write out of hate, out of a desire for revenge against all the men who have oppressed and humiliated me.

I also write out of love and gratitude for a mother and stepfather who made me feel worthy by hoarding every scrap of correspondence I ever sent them; love and gratitude for a husband of exquisite severity who still edits every final draft that leaves my typewriter. I write out of an infantile dread of ever disappointing them again.

I write because in the act of creation there comes that mysterious, abundant sense of being both parent and child; I am giving birth to an Other and simultaneously being reborn as child in the playground of creation.

I write on while continuing to despair that I can't ever achieve the inventiveness, irreverence, complexity of my favorite contemporary authors—Milan Kunderea, Italo Calvino, Günter Grass, Salman Rushdie, to name only the foreign ones. they are certain enough of their readers' love (or indifferent enough to it, since the great Indifferents are the great Seducers) to indulge in that shrewd teasing and misguiding of the reader, that ironic obliqueness which is the marrow of the best modernist work. It is not only my lesser gift that is at fault. Behind my impulsive cataloguing, my Slavic unleashing of emotion, my Quaker earnestness to inform my readers guilelessly of all I know, there still lurks the lonely, stuttering child too terrified of losing the reader's love to take the necessary risks.

Yet I remain sustained by a definition of faith once offered me by Ivan Illich: "Faith is a readiness for the Surprise." I write because I have faith in the possibility that I can eventually surprise myself. I am still occasionally plagued by that recurring nightmare of my jaw being clamped shut, my mouth frozen in silence. But I wake up from it with less dread, with the hope that some day my tongue will loosen and emit a surprising new sound which even I, at first, shall not be able to understand.

Of memory, emotion and imagination

by Wright Morris

The small creatures of this world, and not a few of the large ones, are only at their ease under something. The cat crawls into the culvert, the infant under the table, screened off by the cloth that hangs like a curtain. In the Moldavanka ghetto of Odessa we have this self-portrait of Isaac Babel:

> As a boy I was given to lying. It was all due to reading. My imagination was always on fire. I read in class, during recess, on the way home, at night—under the dinner table, hidden by the folds of cloth that reached down to the floor. Reading made me miss all the important doings of this world.

In these few words much light is shed on the subject of fiction and the imagination. Not all writers burn with this fire, but many have their beginnings under something. Far from Odessa, in the Platte Valley of Nebraska, street culverts, piano boxes, the seats of wagons and buggies, railroad trestles, low bridges, the dark caves under front porches were all favored places of concealment. With Br'er Fox I shared the instinct to lie low. Seated in dust as fine as talcum, my lap and hands overlaid with a pattern of shadows, I peered out at the world through the holes between the slats. A train passed, a tethered cow mooed, a woman collected clothespins in the hammock of her apron, thunder crackled, rain puffed dust in the road, the bell tinkled on the Jewel's Tea Wagon as it crossed the tracks.

Wright Morris is a writer of 20 novels, short stories, and critical essays. He has been compared to Sherwood Anderson in his treatment of the quality of American life in such novels as My Uncle Dudley, The Man Who Was There, Works of Love, Deep Sleep *and* Life Among the Cannibals. *Morris, a recipient of the Common Health Award for Distinguished Service in Literature, recalls his early life in his most recent and highly acclaimed work,* Will's Boy, A Memoir.

One reason I see it all so clearly is that I have so often put it into writing. Perhaps it is the writing I remember, the vibrant image I have made of the memory impression. A memory for just such details is thought to be characteristic of the writer, but the fiction is already at work in what he remembers. No deception is intended, but he wants to see clearly what is invariably, intrinsically vague. So he imagines. Image-making is indivisibly a part of remembering.

Not so long ago I returned to the town I was born in, to the house I associated with my childhood. There were several, but *this* house was the house with the porch. From the concealment of this porch I saw the train pass, I heard the cow moo and the thunder crackle, I watched the rain puff the dust in the road. To my puzzlement it proved to be a stoop less than a foot off the ground. A cat or a small dog might have crawled beneath it, but not a child. Brooding on this mystery, I began to recall under-the-porch furnishings I had conveniently forgotten. There had been a pair of stilts, a scooter made from a fruit crate and a skate, a sled known as a Flexible Flyer Junior Racer, the wheels of a dismantled tricycle. Not this porch. *That* porch indeed, had been five steps up from the walk to the porch, where a chain swing creaked and banged the clapboards. There *had* been a crosshatching of slats at one end, but the view had been blocked by the second-floor windows of a neighboring house. How was that possible? That porch was on a steep hill in the bluffs of Omaha, and not in the flatness of the Platte Valley. It had been a superior porch for concealment and spying, and my imagination had shifted the scenery to suit the needs of fiction and emotion. I had substituted this more accommodating porch (with no loss in the quality of the dust, and a gain in furnishings and the height of the ceiling) for the one that my hometown had been lacking. I badly *wanted* that porch, and my imagination had obliged.

Indelible impressions

If I attempt to distinguish between fiction and memory, and press my nose to memory's glass to see more clearly, the remembered image grows more illusive, like the details in a Pointillist painting. I recognize it, more than I see it. The recognition is a fabric of emotion, as immaterial as music. In this defect of memory do we have the emergence of imagination? If we remember both vibrantly and accurately—a documentary image rather than an impression—the imaginative faculty would be blocked, lacking the stimulus necessary to fill in what is empty or create what is missing. This faculty of artful lying is image-making, and not always confined to fiction writers. Precisely where memory is frail and emotion is strong, imagination takes fire.

One memory that is clear is that of a reader who took special pains to praise my memory, as evident in my fiction. He cited specific details from a number of novels: the white hairs from a mare's tail, a bent skate key, the cracked chimney of a lamp, a salvaged ball of tinfoil, and so on. I had heard this before. What led me to question it on that occasion? One novel in question, *Ceremony in Lone Tree*, was an assembly of parts from my own fictive archive. In the opening chapter, entitled "The Scene," many of these stray, unclaimed pieces found their ultimate and appropriate place. Somewhere in the past, memory had done its work, recording details from a variety of sources. From that album of objects and places I had selected the pieces appropriate to the fiction. Artifacts were jumbled with sensations. The cracked lamp of the chimney, in one place, gave rise to the smell of singed hair in another. That in turn to the fragrance of freshly dampened clothes, and the scorched smell of the iron. Fiction writers are often obsessed with a sense of place, and perhaps I am somewhat more obsessed than others. Most places have for me, in James' phrase, a sense of their own, a mystic meaning to give out.

To the extent one thing is almost like another, we are able to grasp, to reaffirm, both things. The overlapping of accumulated impressions gives depth and mystery to our experience with time. We have Proust's theme and variations on the inexhaustible Madeleine. The impressions of childhood, indelibly imprinted on a mind open and eager for sensations before it is cunningly attuned to ego satisfactions and evasions, are the ideal circumstances for the nature destined to be an image-maker. Adult impressions accumulate like the yearly fall of leaves, providing both protection and compost, waiting for the moment that the seedbed will sprout with its new growth. It will prove to be more than the writer had in mind, and much of it will be new.

For the American writer, more than most, repossession may be an act of re-creation. What was once there may have been little enough—or what was once there may have been obliterated. The furnishing of the mind with artifacts and symbols that began with Walt Whitman is increasingly a matter of salvage. The shortage of appropriately *saturated* artifacts is part of the deprivation felt by the younger generation. We all may miss, but hardly grow to cherish, what is felt to be intentionally obsolescent, instant *kitsch*.

The imagination fueled

In the craft of image-making there is much to be said for the slow grower. The less culture-shaped child, accumulating experience before he does art, when stimulated by the images of art will have recourse to his own unique resources. From Twain through Faulkner this has been a characteristic American experience. Those favored by a more cultivated background (like Henry James, or Edith Wharton) are felt to be less American. This is a narrow but telling distinction. The mind of James was shaped by the images of culture, rather than the rawer materials of experience. It is the purpose of culture to produce such minds, but a democratic culture has not evolved an appropriate use or place for them. Within the scope of a century, since Whitman, native raw materials have lost their rawness, and most writers of fiction have their beginnings as readers of fiction. It is the written image that now shapes the writer in his effort to become his own image-maker.

The observant child who grows up with paintings, the reflective child who grows up with books, is already at an artful remove from the natural surroundings of objects and places. Later he may well experience a confusion of impressions. What was *real*? What had been imagined by somebody else? This is a tiresome but durable dilemma. Young Isaac Babel assures us that his imagination was enflamed by what he read, not by what he saw, but what he wrote tells us otherwise. He was pollinated from both sources. From the reading he received the emotional charge that fueled his feverish imagination. To a remarkable degree art produces art, and writing produces writers. Lack of originality in most image-makers has its roots in this imprinting. Only those with a very pronounced talent manage to depart from what they have received, and image what is their own. The cave painter also fell under this persuasion once he had a ceiling of images to inspire him, drawing what he beheld on the walls of the cave rather than the confusion and disorder of the hunt. We know that mimicry is crucial to learning, but those who learn it too early, or too well, may end up as duplicators, not image-makers. Image-making as distinct from likeness-making is illustrated in the description of a well-known public figure as one who has "a face like the bottom of a foot." This seemingly far-fetched comparison is an inspired piece of image-making: an original, not a duplication.

Beyond the visible

In his more buoyant moments the fiction writer knows that there is fiction quite beyond his conception, and his practice, but implicit in the nature of image-making. Of all this he has glimpses just beyond his grasping, teasingly beckoning and elusive. These glimpses go far to explain his romantic readiness for audacious gestures and strident manifestoes—as well as his irksome suspicion that he is in chains. The captivity of custom is so comprehensive the bonds that bind him also free and support him. He is aware of the world behind the Looking Glass but seems powerless to step through it. Space probers and great image-makers occupy the same void.

Almost a century ago Twain greeted his readers:

NOTICE

Persons attempting to find a motive in this narrative will be prosecuted; persons attempting to find a moral in it will be banished; persons attempting to find a plot in it will be shot.

At the risk of being banished, few American writers have felt it safe to depart from the vernacular. All writers fell under the spell of the visible world, but only American writers had at their disposal a language seamlessly welded to their material—indeed, seemed to be the material itself, fraying away at the fringe of the immediate present.

. . . Whatever may have been the case in years gone by, the true use for the imaginative faculty of modern times is to give ultimate vivification to facts, to science, and to common lives, endowing them with glows and glories and final illustriousness which belong to every real thing, and to real things only. Without that ultimate vivification—which the poet or other artist alone can give—reality would seem incomplete, and science, democracy, and life itself, finally in vain.

So Walt Whitman, in a loving all-embracing, backward glance.

---

66 *We build character in the stream of the world but talent in solitude.*
—Goethe 99

Some very good masters

by Richard Yates

It must have been the movies of the 1930s more than any other influence that got me into the habit of thinking like a writer. I wasn't a bookish child; reading was such hard work for me that I avoided it whenever possible. But I wasn't exactly the rough-and-ready type either, and so the movies filled a double need: They gave me an awful lot of cheap story material and a good place to hide.

When I was about 14, I started submitting movie-haunted stories to my English teachers, as if to prove there was *something* I could do, but it wasn't until three or four years later that reading, both fiction and poetry, began to sweep the movies into a dark and vaguely shameful corner of my mind, where they have remained ever since. I almost never go to a movie now, and have been known to explain loftily, if not quite at the top of my lungs, that this is because movies are for children.

At 20, fresh out of the Army and surfeited with Thomas Wolfe, I embarked on a long binge of Ernest Hemingway that entailed embarrassingly frequent attempts to talk and act like characters in the early Hemingway books. And I was hooked on T.S. Eliot at the same time, which made for an uncomfortable set of mannerisms.

But F. Scott Fitzgerald's *The Great Gatsby* turned out to be the most nourishing novel I read, in much the same way that my discovery of John Keats some years earlier made most other English lyric poets seem insubstantial.

Realistic, revealing dialogue

Like certain of Keats's poems, Fitzgerald's novel is a short piece of work that gains

Richard Yates, former publicity writer, ghostwriter, screenwriter, teacher of creative writing and recipient of literary grants and awards, is the author of Revolutionary Road *and* The Easter Parade, *among other novels. A lecturer and contributor to major publications, Yates' most recent work is* Liars in Love, *a collection of short stories.*

range as it gathers momentum, until the end of it leaves you with a stunning illumination of the world. And the best part of this for an apprentice writer is that the novel can be seen not only as a miracle of talent but as a triumph of technique, suggesting at least a hope that you might be able to figure out how it's done.

You can figure out the important part of it almost at once: Every line of dialogue in *Gatsby* serves to reveal more about the speaker than the speaker might care to have revealed. The author never permits his use of dialogue to become merely "realistic," with people exchanging flat, information-laden sentences, but contrives time and again to catch all his characters, however subtly, in the very act of giving themselves away.

An especially pure concentration of that skill occurs in the talk at the awful little party in Myrtle Wilson's apartment—the party that provides Nick Carraway with a well-earned observation that has always struck me as an eloquent statement of every storyteller's quandary and delight:

"Yet high over the city our line of yellow windows must have contributed their share of human secrecy to the casual watcher in the darkening streets, and I was him too, looking up and wondering. I was within and without, simultaneously enchanted and repelled by the inexhaustible variety of life."

I had never understood what Eliot meant by the curious phrase "objective correlative" until the scene in *Gatsby* where the almost comically sinister Meyer Wolfshiem, who has just been introduced, displays his cuff links and explains that they are "the finest specimens of human molars."

Get it? Got it. *That's* what Eliot meant.

Or the heap of custom-made shirts into which Daisy Buchanan weeps "stormily" during her first visit to Jay Gatsby's house ("They're such beautiful shirts . . . It makes me sad because I've never seen such—such beautiful shirts before.")

Or the homely entries in Gatsby's boyhood "Schedule" and "Resolves," which his father carefully reads aloud to Nick, as if for Nick's own use and profit, after Gatsby is dead.

The Great Gatsby, along with most of Fitzgerald's other work, was my formal introduction to the craft.

In 1951, when I was 25, the Veteran's Adminstration bailed me out of gainful employment with a disability pension for a rapidly healing case of TB, and so for the next two and a half years I lived in Europe with nothing to do but write short stories and try to make each one better than the last. I learned a lot. Being allowed to write fulltime was very instructive in itself, and I also learned how rich the American language can be when most of it must be dredged up from memory.

Three of those stories were sold to magazines before I came home, and there were five more sales over the next few years. But suddenly I was 29, earning my living as a freelance public-relations writer—an activity I can recommend to no one—and it was increasingly clear that I had better write a novel soon.

That was when *Madame Bovary* took command. I had read it before but hadn't studied it the way I'd studied *Gatsby* and other books; now it seemed ideally suited to serve as a guide, if not a model, for the novel that was taking shape in my mind. I wanted *that* kind of balance and quiet resonance on every page, that kind of foreboding mixed with comedy, that kind of inexorable destiny in the heart of a lonely, romantic girl. And all of it, of course, would have to be done with an F. Scott Fitzgerald kind of freshness and grace.

Fate as the villain

Like many other readers, I have always felt that the first 70 pages of *Madame Bovary* aren't as good as they could have been, but from the moment Charles and Emma are invited to the society dance, Flaubert lets everything start to roll.

And talk about "objective correlatives"!

● When Charles finds a green silk cigar case in the dust of a road newly trampled by heroic-looking horsemen, and when Emma later hides it away from him for her own use as a source of voluptuous daydreams.

● When Rodolphe has his farewell letter to Emma delivered at the bottom of a gift basket of apricots, and when Charles then unwittingly drives her over the edge of a nervous breakdown by thrusting one of those apricots under her nose and saying, "Smell that fragrance!"

● When the pharamacist's young apprentice Justin, who is hopelessly in love with Emma, is cruelly reprimanded by his employer, in her presence, for possessing an illustrated marriage manual *and* for messing around with the jar of arsenic. Wow.

Another thing I have always liked about both *Gatsby* and *Bovary* is that there are no villains in either one. The force of evil is felt in these novels but is never personified—neither novelist is willing to let us off that easily. Tom and Daisy Buchanan might have been blamed for Jay Gatsby's death, but Fitzgerald prevents us from seeing it that way by having Nick say, in his own final judgment, that they were simply "careless people." Charles Bovary might have every right to hold Rodolphe responsible for Emma's eventual suicide, but when he accidentally meets the man afterward he ways, "I don't blame you . . . Fate is to blame."

Here are some of the other writers without whose work I might never have put together a halfway decent book of my own: Dickens, Tolstoy, Dostoyevsky, Chekhov, Conrad, Joyce, E.M. Forster, Katherine Mansfield, Sinclair Lewis, Ring Lardner, Dylan Thomas, J.D. Salinger, James Jones.

It would be easy to extend this list to twice its length by bringing it up to the present day, but I have come to distrust any such list as sounding like the membership roster of a private club, or like the breathless final results of some popularity contest.

Time is everything. I am 55 now, and my first grandchild is expected in June. It has been many years since I was a young man, let alone an apprentice writer. But the eager, fearful, self-hectoring spirit of the beginner is slow to fade. With my 8th book just begun—and with deep regret for the desolate wastes of time that have kept it from being my 10th or 12th—I feel I haven't really started yet. And I suppose this rather ludicrous condition will persist, for better or worse, until my time runs out.

> 66   *Talent is extremely common. What is rare is the willingness to endure*
> *the life of a writer.*
> —*Kurt Vonnegut, Jr.* 99

Read, read, read

by Dean R. Koontz

Every writer needs to be well-read. I now refer you to the following list of authors. If you have read novels by only one-fifth of them, your chances of writing successful popular mainstream fiction are very small indeed. If you have read half of these authors, you are beginning to form an idea of what modern popular fiction *is*, but you still have a lot to learn. If you have read at least 70 percent of these authors, and if you have any talent of your own, you are probably ready to write salable fiction. Works by the people listed below have *defined* modern popular fiction; if you are serious about wanting to be a writer, you not only should read these authors, but you will desperately *want* to read them in order to learn from them.

Warning! If you want to be a mystery novelist, that does not mean that you should read only mysteries. Regardless of the type of fiction you write (or wish to write), you should read every kind of popular fiction you can get your hands on, both mainstream and genre. The more you broaden your interests as a reader, the more you will simultaneously broaden your perspective and your talent *as a writer*. I know a few authors who read only one kind of fiction, the kind they write themselves; in every case, this provincialism is evident in the author's work, and none of these writers is very successful in the marketplace.

Warning! This list of recommended authors isn't complete by any means. I purposely have not mentioned classic wordsmiths like Dickens, Trollope, and Melville, for I assume that anyone who wishes to write popular fiction is aware of the need to familiarize himself with the work of authors who have proven themselves to be artists of lasting

Dean R. Koontz won an Atlantic Monthly *fiction award at age 20 and has been writing ever since. His recent books* The Vision *and* Whispers *each earned six-figure paperback advances; and his newest novel* Phantoms *is expected in early 1983. Koontz's books have sold more than 25 million copies in 14 languages.*

stature. The list mainly comprises the names of contemporary novelists. I have not listed authors who have published only one or two books, not even if those books were awfully good, for I have tried to direct you toward those writers who not only have published good material but have had an effect upon the development of modern popular fiction. Finally, the list is incomplete because I am bound to have overlooked a dozen or two names that should have been included. Once you have read the people I recommend, for God's sake don't stop! Your need to read some fiction every day should be almost like a drug dependency.

Read, read, read!

Richard Adams. *Watership Down*, *The Plague Dogs*, *The Girl in a Swing*. Adams is primarily a fantasist, uneven in his plotting from one book to another, but always a superb stylist. *Watership Down* is the one "must read" of his books; it is a tightly structured and emotionally involving saga unlike any other book you have ever read.

Catherine Aird. Aird is a superb mystery novelist whose work shows breakthrough potential. Her novels include *A Late Phoenix*, *The Religious Body*, *The Stately Home Murder*, *His Burial Too*, and *Some Die Eloquent*.

Brian Aldiss. Aldiss is primarily a science fiction writer, although he has published several mainstream novels, at least two of which have been major bestsellers in Britain and modestly successful over here. I recommend Aldiss because reading him is a sure way to stretch your imagination, get your idea pump working, and further your appreciation of well-polished, literate prose. Among Aldiss' many books are *The Dark Light Years*, *The Long Afternoon of Earth*, *Frankenstein Unbound*, *Greybeard*, *The Hand-Reared Boy* and *An Island Called Moreau*.

Eric Ambler. Ambler, a stylish writer of espionage novels, made large contributions to the definition of the modern spy story. *A Coffin for Dimitrios*, *State of Siege*, and *Passage of Arms* are a few of his books.

Kingsley Amis. Amis is a one-of-a-kind writer who should be read because: 1) he knows how to tell a story; 2) he is a fine stylist; 3) he can teach you how to write with both humor and suspense at the same time. His books include *Lucky Jim*, *The Green Man*, and *I Want It Now*.

Poul Anderson. Anderson writes both historical novels and science fiction novels, primarily the latter, but he often combines the two forms. He is a fine adventure writer who, with better direction from a caring agent and an imaginative editor, might well have been an extremely popular author of mainstream historical novels. Some of his many books include *Brainwave*, *Tau Zero*, *Shield*, *The Corridors of Time*, and *The High Crusade*.

Isaac Asimov. Asimov has pretty much abandoned fiction in favor of nonfiction, but in his prime he wrote a few science fiction classics, including *The Naked Sun* and *The Caves of Steel*, that helped shape the field.

Desmond Bagley. Bagley is considerably more popular in the rest of the world than he is in the US, largely because his US publishers have never done a very good job of packaging and promoting his books. He writes thrillers with a real flair, in a literate style that puts many thriller writers to shame. His books include *Running Blind*, *The Tightrope Men*, and the stunning *The Enemy*, which was a huge bestseller in many other countries.

Alfred Bester. Bester has had as much impact on the science fiction field as any writer, excluding Robert Heinlein. His two most famous novels—*The Demolished Man* and *The Stars My Destination*—are packed with more ideas and excitement than any dozen other novels, and they have had a great impact on other writers in the SF genre.

Ray Bradbury. The one and only. Bradbury's publishers—Doubleday, Knopf,

Ballantine, Bantam—have always insisted on pinning the SCIENCE FICTION WRIT-ER label on him. In reality, Bradbury is at times a fantasist, at times a grisly-horror writer, at times a fable-maker, at times a straight mainstream author, and only very seldom a science fiction writer. His one science fiction novel, *Fahrenheit 451*, is a classic in the field. His horror-fantasy novel, *Something Wicked This Way Comes*, is simply one of the ten best stories of its kind ever written. Bradbury's forte is the short story, and there are many collections of his short fiction in print: *Long After Midnight*, *The October Country*, *The Martian Chronicles*, *The Golden Apples of the Sun*, *R Is for Rocket*, *A Medicine for Melancholy*, *The Illustrated Man*, and several others.

Gary Brandner. His *The Howling* was the basis for one of the best horror movies ever made. *Walkers*, another horror novel, has several fresh ideas that any horror novelist would envy. He has great potential.

John Brunner. Brunner is a good, craftsmanlike science fiction writer who has published dozens of adventure novels in the field. Now and again, he outdoes himself and produces books that are as good as anything SF has to offer: *The Whole Man*, *The Squares of the City*, *Stand on Zanzibar*, and *The Long Result*.

W. R. Burnett. A few decades ago, Burnett helped to define hard-boiled fiction and created an archetype with novels like *Little Caesar*.

James M. Cain. Some time ago I decided to collect rare, first-edition novels by American writers who seemed, to me at least, to have written breakthrough books, artists who created forms and characters and stories that would last. I started with James M. Cain, who almost single-handedly created the hard, lean prose style that formed the basis of modern American writing. In novels like *The Postman Always Rings Twice*, *Double Indemnity*, *Serenade*, and *Mildred Pierce*, Cain painted a picture of certain American cultural groups, social strata, and psychological patterns that was revolutionary in his time; his work *still* stands as a vital and unique vision. For the most part he shaped his art in the form of *thrillers*.

Today, almost 50 years after it was first published, *The Postman Always Rings Twice* is as readable and poignant and relevant as it was when it first saw print. Indeed, *Postman* reads as if it were written last week! Cain was so in touch with the people about whom he wrote, so intimately familiar with the fears and desires of the masses in the 1920s and 1930s, that he seems to have known not only how the common man and woman talked and thought at that time, but also how they would talk and think for decades to come. I am not aware of another American writer of our century whose books have been so utterly untouched by the passage of so many years, as have Cain's.

When I started to collect first editions of Cain's work a couple of years ago, those books sold for just a few dollars, even in fine or mint condition with dust jacket, even in spite of their rarity. Although they now command prices three times that high, they are relatively cheap compared to what they will surely bring in ten or fifteen years. A large collection of Cain's letters and original manuscripts recently sold for more than $20,000, though the man who had put together the collection had spent less than $1,000 to do so. Cain's value as a novelist is clearly becoming generally recognized among those who love books enough to collect and cherish them.

The academic world has always shunned James M. Cain, but that has nothing to do with whether or not he will ultimately occupy a permanent shelf in the library of American literature. Yes, Cain wrote some thrillers—just as Mark Twain wrote some adventure stories, just as Poe wrote some horror stories—but within the framework of suspense fiction, Cain said something important about the way people of his time and place lived, thought, dreamed, and died. Cain has lasted this long and will last much longer because the masses still read him. He conned us with entertainment while he subtly made his thematic points. Today, all of Cain's works are available in paperback editions. At least three of his books are being made into movies as I write this. Nearly every writer I know has read and greatly admires Cain's books. Several years ago, James M. Cain died, but because of his wonderful novels, he is still very much alive and will continue to live for a long, long time to come.

I strongly recommend you read *all* of Cain to see how the simplest genre ideas can be transformed into fresh, compelling mainstream fiction.

Raymond Chandler. I also collect first-edition copies of Raymond Chandler's novels—*The Long Goodbye*, *The Big Sleep*, *The Lady in the Lake*, *The Little Sister*, *The High Window*, *Farewell My Lovely*. Thus far, Chandler has been written off by the academic community as a mere detective story writer. In truth, no novelist of his period painted a better or more vivid picture of American culture, especially the sleazy and lonely aspects of it, than did Chandler. No writer has ever surpassed Chandler's evocation of Southern California. He made Los Angeles his, as surely as Dickens laid claim to London. Today, decades after his novels were written, they still sell very well indeed, year in and year out, because in addition to saying something important about the human condition, Raymond Chandler made an effort to *entertain*.

I recommend that you read every word Chandler wrote. His plotting is sometimes weak, but from reading him you will learn everything you need to know about pace, characterization, mood, background, and *style*. My God, what style!

Agatha Christie. I must admit I'm not a Christie fan. But she was one of the half dozen most important influences on the modern mystery novel, and you could do worse than to read her *Death on the Nile*, *And Then There Were None*, *Murder in the Calais Coach*, and *The Murder of Roger Ackroyd*.

Mary Higgins Clark. Clark's books often suffer from too many coincidences in the plots, and she is not a glittering stylist. However, *A Stranger Is Watching* and *The Cradle Will Fall* possess such marvelous, fast-paced, ambitiously complicated plots that the reader is willing to forgive her a few flaws.

James Clavell. Clavell is a consummate adventure novelist. He established himself with *King Rat*, took a giant step with *Tai-Pan* (his best book to date), and set sales records with *Shogun*. His latest, *Noble House*, will probably firmly establish him as one of the two or three bestselling authors of the decade.

Richard Condon. The one and only. He writes curious books that contain a large measure of suspense, an almost equally large measure of extremely dry humor, and a healthy dollop of social commentary. If you don't like Condon, you hate him. If you do like him, you *love* him. There is no middle ground. Some of his best novels are *The Manchurian Candidate*, *Any God Will Do*, *Mile High*, and *Winter Kills*.

Edwin Corley. I said that most of the people in this list helped to shape the direction of modern fiction. I cannot pretend that Corley has done anything of the sort. He has enjoyed his share of successes, but he has never been a top-of-the-list bestseller, and he has not really broken any important new ground with his fiction. But dammit, I *like* his stuff. He has one of those easy-reading styles that lifts you up and sweeps you along and . . . well . . . *delights* you. I recommend you read him with the idea of acquiring some of his smoothness. And while you're studying his style, he'll never fail to entertain you. Try *The Jesus Factor*, *Air Force One*, *Sargasso*, *Siege*, and *Long Shots*.

Michael Crichton. Crichton is unpredictable. He has written mainstream-science fiction—*The Andromeda Strain* and *The Terminal Man*—one mainstream-historical-caper novel titled *The Great Train Robbery*, one African adventure-science fiction piece titled *Congo*, and a slew of taut thrillers under the name "John Lange." He has proved to be a good screenwriter and an even better director—*Westworld*, *The Great Train Robbery*. The only thing that isn't unpredictable about him is the quality of his novels: They're always great fun. Crichton is a slick writer rather than a stylish one. His characters are too thinly drawn for mainstream. Yet he *is* a mainstream writer by virtue of his background, his heavy thematic structures, and his extremely fresh and inventive plots.

Samuel R. Delany. Delany burst upon the science fiction field in the early 1960s, dazzling fans and critics alike, and scooping up armfuls of awards. Rightly so. His early books like *Babel-17*, *The Jewels of Aptor*, *The Einstein Intersection*, *Nova*, *Empire Star*, *Captives of the Flame*, *The Towers of Toron*, *The City of a Thousand Suns*, and *The Ballad of Beta-2* were beautifully intricate, crammed full of startling and memorable images, filled with characters who were sharply drawn yet as mysterious as the shadowy reflection one sees in a bronzed mirror. By reading Delany's early works you can not only learn how to write the very best kind of science fiction, but you can also learn how to write, period. Recently, Delany seems to have forsaken the average reader in an attempt to cater to academe, and his latest novels are pedantic and sometimes unreadable. In his youth, he wrote better than anyone in his genre.

Philip K. Dick. The one and only. No one writes like Dick. His style is so personal, so different that it defies imitation. *The Eye in the Sky*, *The Three Stigmata of Palmer Eldritch*, *Do Androids Dream of Electric Sheep?* (recently retitled *Blade Runner*), *Clans of the Alphane Moon*, *The Martian Time-Slip*, *Solar Lottery*, *Now Wait for Last Year*, *The Man in the High Castle*, *A Scanner Darkly*, *Ubik*, and many other Philip K. Dick novels are one-of-a-kind, mind-expanding examples of the lengths to which popular fiction can be stretched while retaining its popularity. His 1962 novel *The Man in the High Castle* is certainly one of the dozen best science fiction novels ever written.

Gordon R. Dickson. He is a fine writer of science fiction and adventure. Try *None But Man*, *Dorsai*, *The Alien Way*, and *Timestorm*.

Thomas Disch. Disch began his career as a science fiction writer and still occasionally produces a novel in that field. He also does work outside of SF—such as *Black Alice* in collaboration with John Sladek and the bestselling *Clara Reeve* under a pseudonym. Disch's books are so cynical and downbeat that they are sometimes unintentionally amusing; but when he is good he is very, very good. His writing is literate and often dazzling. SF: *On Wings of Song*, *The Genocides*, and *Camp Concentration*.

Stanley Ellin. Ellin is a winner of many awards for his mystery fiction. His books are ingeniously plotted, and his characters are real. Try *House of Cards*, *The Eighth Circle*, and *The Big Night*, among others.

Harlan Ellison. Ellison is a short story writer, but I believe I should include him in this list. He may have won more Hugos and Nebula Awards than any other science fiction writer, and he is one of the few to cross genres and win an Edgar Award from the Mystery Writers of America as well. I find his work uneven, but it is also often brilliant, and it is never, ever boring. There are many collections of his short fiction on the market: *Alone Against Tomorrow*, *Deathbird Stories*, *Shatterday*, *The Beast That Shouted Love at the Heart of the World*, *Approaching Oblivion*, and others. He is a key figure in the SF-fantasy-horror fields.

Paul Erdman. Erdman isn't a stylist, and he isn't a creator of deep, thoroughly revealed characters. But he is one hell of a storyteller. He knows *exactly* how to shape a plot, and his imagination is so fertile that he is always two steps ahead of his readers. He also manages to take an often dull subject—international finance—and make it not only interesting but gripping. His well-deserved bestsellers—*The Billion-Dollar Sure Thing*,

The Silver Bears, *The Crash of '79*—are superb examples of how background material should be integrated into a novel.

Philip José Farmer. Farmer is another key figure in the science fiction world and a marvelous adventure story writer. In his early days he shocked the SF field with his sexually daring—though never sexually explicit—stories. Later he created the "Riverworld" books, which embody one of the most intriguing backgrounds any SF writer has ever devised. His many books include *To Your Scattered Bodies Go*, *The Fabulous Riverboat*, *The Dark Design*, *Dare*, *The Maker of Universes*, *The Gates of Creation*, *A Private Cosmos*, *Behind the Walls of Terra*, *Inside-Out* and *The Wind Whales of Ishmael*.

Edna Ferber. Her novels seem a bit dated now, but she is still worth reading if you want to know how American fiction got to its present state. Try *Show Boat*, *Giant*, and *Saratoga Trunk*. Winner of a Pulitzer Prize for fiction, Ferber was an excellent storyteller and had an admirable talent for in-depth characterization.

Dick Francis. For years Francis' US publisher insisted on fixing the MYSTERY WRITER label to his books, thus condemning him to no better than modest sales. In fact, he ceased being a strictly genre writer at least 16 or 17 books ago. The quality of his characterizations and the richness of his backgrounds, which are always combined with sharply drawn thematic structures, put his books leagues above most mystery novels. He is very much in the mainstream, and his new American publisher, G.P. Putnam's Sons, seems at least somewhat aware of this, for they have given his latest novel, *Reflex*, bestseller promotion and advertising. A few of his other novels are *Bonecrack*, *High Stakes*, *Blood Sport*, *In the Frame*, *Enquiry*, *Slayride*, and *Whip Hand*.

William Goldman. Goldman is the famous screenwriter—*Butch Cassidy and the Sundance Kid*, *All the President's Men*, and many others—but he also has had quite a career as a novelist. His early books were solidly mainstream and of the highest quality. *The Temple of Gold*, *Soldier in the Rain*, and *Boys and Girls Together* are novels that virtually any writer would be delighted to have written. Later, he tried his hand at thrillers that he lifted into the mainstream largely by virtue of his splendid characterizations and his thematic purposes. *No Way To Treat a Lady* is a clever, gripping, and entirely successful little tour de force. His other thrillers are generally flawed but nevertheless well worth reading. Try *Magic* and *Marathon Man*.

Arthur Hailey. Hailey is a master of background. His characters are usually little more than adequately drawn, but his plots tick away like fine Swiss watches, and his backgrounds are splendidly drawn. You should read *Hotel*, *Airport*, *Wheels*, *The Moneychangers*, *The Final Diagnosis*, and *Overload*.

Adam Hall. This is the pen name for novelist Ellston Trevor. As "Adam Hall," Trevor has helped to shape the modern mainstream spy story in a long series of very well-crafted books including *The Quiller Memorandum*, *The Ninth Directive*, *The Tango Briefing*, and *The Cobra Manifesto*.

William Hallahan. Hallahan's first two books—*The Dead of Winter* and *The Ross Forgery*—were published as mysteries and pretty much sank without a trace. Then he produced *The Search for Joseph Tully*, which many believe to be one of the finest and most original occult novels of the past 20 years. I am one of those many. After *Tully*, Hallahan gave us *Catch Me: Kill Me*, a thoughtful suspense novel which, for me at least, seemed uneven. Next came *The Keeper of the Children*, another occult novel with some wonderfully evocative scenes but with some less wonderful stuff at the end which gave it an uneven tone again. His latest, *The Trade*, is squarely on target, a mainstream thriller of real power. With *The Search for Joseph Tully*, Hallahan had a truly profound effect upon many authors of supernatural novels, and with each successive book, his colleagues have become increasingly sure that eventually he will go all the way to the top of the bestseller lists.

Dashiell Hammett. Hammett was perhaps the hardest of the hard-boiled writers working in the 1930s and 1940s. His prose is so spare, so completely trimmed of all fat, that it sometimes looks childishly simple. Be warned: His prose is *never* simple. It is stripped down, often cold, but it always carries an enormous load of meaning and purpose. Hammett is an American original, a one-of-a-kind writer who has inspired thousands of cheap imitations. As with James M. Cain and Raymond Chandler, there is an excellent chance that Hammett's novels will withstand the test of time and will be read long after most of us now living are dead and gone. You should read every one of Hammett's books: *Red Harvest*, *The Dain Curse*, *The Maltese Falcon*, *The Glass Key*, and *The Thin Man*.

Harry Harrison. Harrison is a fine craftsman who writes highly entertaining science fiction adventure stories like *Deathworld*, *Deathworld-2*, *Deathworld-3*, *The Plague from Space*, and *The Daleth Effect*. He also manages to pull off the difficult trick of writing hilariously funny science fiction like *Bill, the Galactic Hero*. And finally, he can be as serious and "meaningful" as any writer in the field, as witness his prophetic novel about overpopulation, *Make Room! Make Room!*.

Robert Heinlein. The one and only. If there is any single author who defines science fiction, it is Robert Heinlein. He is surely the most widely read science fiction author of all time, for his books long ago began to break out of the straight science fiction market to tap a vein of the mainstream audience. By virtue of his amazing skill at background, his fresh plotting, and his powerful thematic structures, his books have usually been solidly in the mainstream in spite of their futuristic settings and science fictional concerns. His characters are sometimes thinly drawn but always very colorful and memorable. And when he *does* give us well-rounded characters, they are as real and as fascinating as any fictional human beings can ever be. They are usually individualists, strong and clever and determined and *moral* people who know how to get things done; they are people you can respect, and their triumphs somehow stir and move you. There are other writers who are every bit as entertaining as Mr. Heinlein, and there are other writers who have written a greater number of fine books than he has, and there are other novelists who are better stylists than Heinlein. But there is no other writer whose work has *exhilarated* me as often and to such an extent as has Heinlein. His books are nearly always, at the core, about liberty, freedom, and the sanctity of the individual. His books have great spirit, and I recommend the following: *The Moon Is a Harsh Mistress*, *Stranger in a Strange Land*, *Orphans of the Sky*, *Farnham's Freehold*, *The Puppet Masters*, *Revolt in 2000*, *Starship Troopers*, *Methuselah's Children*, *Double Star*, *The Day After Tomorrow*, *Podkayne of Mars*, *The Unpleasant Profession of Jonathan Hoag*, *The Green Hills of Earth*, *Glory Road*, and *Assignment in Eternity*. Heinlein has also written the most successful series of SF novels for young adults ever produced, and all of them will entertain adults every bit as much as they entertain adolescents. Try *Citizen of the Galaxy*, *Red Planet*, *Tunnel in the Sky*, *The Star Beast*, and *Between Planets*. You should be warned that some of Heinlein's more recent works are burdened down by excess dialogue and sermonizing. Later books like *Time Enough for Love* and *The Number of the Beast* should be saved for last, after you have read all of his other marvelous novels.

Frank Herbert. Herbert is another science fiction writer who has broken out into the mainstream, in part because of his thematic vision and his care with background material. *Dune* is one of the most successful SF novels of all time. Try it and its sequels,

Dune Messiah, *Children of Dune*, and *God-Emperor of Dune*, as well as non-Dune novels like *The Heaven Makers* and *Dragon in the Sea*.

James Herbert. Herbert is a much-underrated horror novelist who is good enough to lift his work into the mainstream. Try *The Spear*, *The Fog*, *The Dark*, and others.

Jack Higgins. Higgins is actually Harry Patterson. Try some of his novels—*The Keys of Hell*, *Night Judgment at Simos*, *In the Hour Before Midnight* and by all means read *Solo*, *The Eagle Has Landed*, and *Storm Warning*.

Patricia Highsmith. Her mystery novels have helped define the field, and her *Strangers on a Train* is a classic.

Evan Hunter. Hunter is one of the most underrated novelists of the past 25 years. His style is literate and as smooth as glass. He has written everything from serious and ambitious mainstream fiction like *The Blackboard Jungle* to comedy capers like *The Horse's Head* to seriocomic mysteries. For years his career was hampered, I believe, by poor agenting, but he seems to be on his way back to prominence with his most recent novel, *Love, Dad*, which received bestseller promotion. Few writers are better at characterization than Hunter, and no writer I know of is equal to him in the creation of mood. Such books as *Last Summer*, *Come Winter*, and *Nobody Knew They Were There* are superb evocations of various moods, times, places, and psychological states. In addition to the books I've already mentioned, don't miss *Streets of Gold*, *Strangers When We Meet*, *Mothers and Daughters*, and *Sons*. (See the entry for "Ed McBain" later in this list.)

Hammond Innes. Innes' work helps to define the modern adventure story. He is a literate writer who never fails to entertain. I especially recommend *Gale Warning*, *Air Bridge*, *The Wreck of the Mary Deare*, and *The Naked Land*.

John Irving. Irving manages to write moving and very meaningful, ambitious novels without ever forgetting that readability is essential. He is embraced by academe but has not yet allowed it to corrupt him. Try *Setting Free the Bears* and especially *The World According to Garp*.

Shirley Jackson. Jackson was an elegant writer, and at least two of her works have had profound influence upon writers of mainstream supernatural fiction. Try *The Haunting of Hill House* and *We Have Always Lived in the Castle*.

Rona Jaffe. Let's get a couple of things straight: Jaffe is not a consummate stylist, and she is not a creator of tight and clever plots. But she *is* an excellent storyteller nonetheless. Her characters are real, modern, and sympathetic. Her books always have thematic purpose. She writes dialogue that rings true. She succeeds routinely where so many writers of "women's fiction" fail miserably. Try her ground-breaking *The Best of Everything* and *Class Reunion*.

John Jakes. Jakes started one of the biggest trends in recent publishing history with his American Bicentennial Series, including *The Bastard*, *The Rebels*, *The Furies*, and *The Americans*. He has scores of imitators hanging on his coattails.

Harry Kemelman. Kemelman's series of mysteries, all featuring Rabbi David Small as the lead character, manages to break out of the genre classification by virtue of characterization, background, and thematic purpose all far more richly developed than genre fiction requires. Try *Friday the Rabbi Slept Late* and all the other books in the series.

Stephen King. It is vitally important that the new writer sample King's work. Even if he weren't as good as he is, he should be read because he probably sold more books during the past decade than any other novelist. Try *'Salem's Lot*, *The Shining*, *The Stand*, *The Dead Zone*, and *Firestarter*.

James Kirkwood. He is co-author of the smash Broadway hit, *A Chorus Line*, and other plays. His novels are unique, funny, suspenseful, and stylish. Try *P.S. Your Cat Is Dead*, *Some Kind of Hero*, *Hit Me with a Rainbow*, and *Good Times/Bad Times*.

C.M. Kornbluth. Kornbluth was a science fiction writer with a special, dark vision. Most of his best work is in short story and novelette length. His *The Syndic* is a fine novel, and his collaborations with Frederik Pohl are among the field's short list of genuine classics. Those collaborations include *Gladiator-at-Law* and *The Space Merchants*. Kornbluth's work has had a strong influence on many modern SF writers.

Louis L'Amour. If you want to write genre Westerns, or if you want to write mainstream novels with Western backgrounds, you must read L'Amour's Western novels. Try: *Shalako*, *Over on the Dry Side*, or any of his other eighty-plus novels.

Keith Laumer. Laumer is an excellent writer of science fiction adventure. He's not the most brilliant characterizer to put pen to paper, and there are a few other weaknesses in his work, but he *is* a master storyteller. *A Plague of Demons*, *The Other Side of Time*, *A Trace of Memory*, *The Monitors*, *Worlds of the Imperium*, and many of his other novels are solid entertainments. (Note: Retief is a series character appearing in a number of Laumer's books. These Retief stories, while popular, do not represent his best work.)

Fritz Leiber. He is a superb stylist, a literate writer whose prose has both color and clarity. He writes both science fiction and fantasy, though he is at his best when dealing with the latter. Try *The Big Time*, *The Wanderer*, *Our Lady of Darkness*, *Swords in the Mist*, *Swords Against Deviltry*, and *Conjure Wife* among others.

Elmore Leonard. Leonard has written some excellent Westerns, including *Valdez Is Coming* and *Hombre*. However, these days he is writing very tight, very tough contemporary thrillers, generally with Detroit settings. *Nobody* writes about street types better than Leonard. At his best, Leonard is sort of a cross between James M. Cain, Dashiell Hammett, and George Higgins, though the quality that makes him Elmore Leonard is something that resists comparison. By all means, read *Fifty-Two Pickup*, *Unknown Man No. 89*, *City Primeval*, *The Switch*, *Mr. Majestyk*, and his other novels. Someday, a smart publisher is going to go to Leonard's agent, offer an obscene amount of money, and ask for the *ultimate* novel about street types, small-time hoods, and big city corruption; the result is going to be a huge bestseller. At least that's what *should* happen; but remember, imaginative publishers are few and far between.

Ira Levin. The one and only. With a surprisingly short list of credits, Ira Levin has established himself as *the* writer of contemporary terror stories. *A Kiss Before Dying* is one of the most brilliantly plotted thrillers ever written. It contains several surprises, one of which is so startling that most readers are quite literally catapulted right up out of their chairs. That surprise, by the way, does not come at the end of the book, as you might expect, but at about the one-third mark, at the end of Part One. When you suddenly realize how Levin has been deceiving you, the rest of *A Kiss Before Dying* becomes unputdownable, for you can't wait to see what *else* he might be able to pull off. Of course *Rosemary's Baby* is the book that single-handedly revived the supernatural novel as a viable modern form. The prose in that book is so stylish and the plot is so exquisitely designed that I could easily spend 50 or 60 pages discussing it here; unfortunately, I do not have the space to do so. I can only say that *Rosemary's Baby* is a must-read book for anyone seriously attempting to write popular fiction of *any* kind. *The Stepford Wives*, while good, is far less successful than Levin's first two novels, and *This Perfect Day*, a science fiction story, is less than perfect. But with *The Boys from Brazil*, Levin gets back on track. This is another flawlessly plotted story from page one right down to the wonderfully chilling, one-page scene at the end. Levin is a playwright as well as a novelist—*Death Trap*, currently running on Broadway, has totted up the largest number of performances of any thriller ever produced in the New York Theater. When you read his novels, keep his playwriting career in mind, for you will see its effect on his transitions, on his dialogue, and on the sweet simplicity of his scene structure.

Robert Ludlum. No writer of recent years has made as much of a splash in the mainstream thriller market as Ludlum. His relentlessly fast-paced books often give short shrift to character development, but they are never short of thematic purpose and are rich in background detail. And most important of all, Ludlum never tries to write like anyone else; his style is very much his own and, like it or hate it, you must admire its individuality. I highly recommend that you read *The Scarlatti Inheritance*, *The Bourne Identity*, *The Matarese Circle*, and other Ludlum novels.

Gregory McDonald. When McDonald writes about his series character, Fletch, he is very good indeed. *Fletch* and *Confess, Fletch*, and *Fletch's Fortune* are marvelous, and you ought to read them to see how the best dialogue is written. When McDonald writes about other characters, he does so with mixed results, so I suggest you stick to the Fletch books—and have one hell of a good time!

John D. MacDonald. The one and only. MacDonald is often called "the best suspense novelist of our time," but he is far, far more than *just* a suspense novelist. Personally, I would even go so far as to say that he is *the* best American writer of his generation, or that at least there is no one better, and I would not stand alone in making that assessment, either. MacDonald's best-known books—his series featuring Travis McGee—are superbly plotted, filled with brilliantly drawn characters and riveting action, enhanced by exceedingly well-rendered backgrounds, and infused with thematic purpose of the best sort. Nevertheless, the McGee books are in many ways less powerful and less fascinating than MacDonald's other work. A couple of dozen of his non-McGee novels—*The Damned*; *Cry Hard, Cry Fast*; *Slam the Big Door, Cancel All Our Vows*; *Where Is Janice Gentry?*; *One Monday We Killed Them All*; *April Evil*; *The Brass Cupcake*; *A Key to the Suite*; *The Last One Left*; *On the Run*; *The Girl, the Gold Watch & Everything*; *Deadly Welcome*; *A Bullet for Cinderella*; *Contrary Pleasure*; *The Crossroads*; and many others—are so good that they have become standards by which a great many writers measure their own work. I know of no writer more universally admired by other writers than is John D. MacDonald. Even the academic-literary crowd admits a sort of shame-faced fascination with MacDonald's fiction (shame-faced because really cultured, lit'ry folks aren't *supposed* to like that kind of stuff.) MacDonald is one of the few living American writers about whom I would say, unequivocally, "He will be widely read a hundred years from now." I have read every one of his novels at least twice, and I recommend that you do the same. If you are perceptive and talented, you will learn everything you need to know about writing fiction by studying his example. And you will be so well entertained in the process that you won't for a moment look upon that study as work. Virtually every book MacDonald wrote is a *must-read* title for the would-be novelist.

Ross Macdonald. He has influenced the modern detective story with his Lew Archer series, and he is one of the few mystery novelists to escape the genre trap after writing many novels that were consigned to that oblivion. He is now published as a mainstream author, and all of his old books have found a wider audience. You should read his crisply written, very atmospheric books, including *The Chill*, *The Ivory Grin*, *The Zebra-Striped Hearse*, and *The Moving Target*.

Helen MacInnes. She is one of the few women who can write major mainstream-thriller novels that appeal equally to men and women. Her greatest strengths are plotting and background. Try *The Double Image*, *While Still We Live*, *Agent in Place*, and others.

Alistair MacLean. No author has done more to define the modern mainstream adventure story than MacLean. By the time he had written just three novels, publishers were boldly using his name to promote lesser storytellers; bookstands were cluttered with novels bearing such banners as BETTER THAN ALISTAIR MACLEAN and MORE RIVETING THAN ALISTAIR MACLEAN and THIS BOOK MAKES THE NOVELS OF ALISTAIR MACLEAN SEEM DULL. Of course none of those claims was true. In his prime, MacLean was at the top of the heap; no one could touch him. For examples of how the adventure story can be lifted into the mainstream and sold to a wide audience, you could do no better than *The Guns of Navarone*, *Force 10 from Navarone*, *H.M.S. Ulysses*, *Where Eagles Dare*, *Ice Station Zebra*, *When Eight Bells Toll*, *South by Java Head*, *Fear is the Key*, *The Secret Ways*, and others. I would suggest starting with those books I have named, for a number of MacLean's recent novels are considerably less successful as art and as entertainment.

Dan J. Marlowe. Marlowe has written some fine, tightly plotted suspense novels that have won him a couple of awards, and he is well worth your attention. You should read *One Endless Hour*, *Four for the Money*, and *Never Live Twice*. Most of Marlowe's work is, unfortunately, out of print, but I suspect it may be coming back into the bookstores soon, as publishers start seeking what they call "men's action fiction."

Richard Matheson. Matheson is a key figure in the fantasy-horror field. He is usually labeled SCIENCE FICTION WRITER, but most of his work doesn't really fit into that genre. Two of his novels have had great influence on modern mainstream-horror writers, and you should read both of them: *I Am Legend* and *The Shrinking Man*. (If you've seen the grotesque Lily Tomlin film in which Matheson's book is trashed, do not get the idea that you know what the story is about.) *The Shrinking Man* is a perfect example of how stylish prose, thematic purpose, and a well-drawn central character can lift a book out of the genre pit, into the mainstream.

Ed McBain. This is the pen name for Evan Hunter, who was discussed earlier in this list. Under the McBain pseudonym, Hunter has written a shelfful of police procedural novels with a continuing cast of characters. These mysteries include *Jigsaw*, *Shotgun*, *Fuzz*, *Ax*, *King's Ransom*, *See Them Die*, *Cophater*, and *Pusher* plus many others. Mystery-suspense aficionados consider these books—the 87th Precinct Series—to be among the best police procedurals ever written. Other McBain books, outside the 87th Precinct milieu, are worthy of carrying the Evan Hunter by-line. I strongly suggest you read *Guns* and *Goldilocks* after you've gone through the 87th Precinct line-up.

Robert Merle. This French author has struck big several times in the US market and deservedly so. His works are stylish, well characterized and freshly plotted. Try *The Day of the Dolphin*, one of the first of a wave of techno-terror stories, and *Malevil*.

C.L. Moore. She's a much underrated science fiction writer. She was one of the first women to seize a piece of that male-dominated genre and make it her own. *Judgment Night* and *Doomsday Morning*.

Larry Niven. He is one of the better hard-science writers in the SF genre. His influence in the field has been greater than many of his colleagues realize. To fully understand modern SF, you should read Niven's work, including *Protector*, *Ringworld*, *Ringworld Engineers*, and *World of Ptaavs*. Niven enjoyed a major mainstream bestseller, *Lucifer's Hammer*, which was co-authored by another good hard-science SF author, Jerry Pournelle.

Andre Norton. Most of her science fiction novels were written for young adults, but they are suitable for grown-ups, too. I recommend sampling at least a couple of her books, so that you can see what most science fiction fans grew up reading and loving before they moved on to more ambitious authors. She does what she does quite well. Try

Moon of Three Rings, *Star Gate*, *The Zero Stone*, *Lord of Thunder*, *Star Hunter*, *Victory on Janus*, or any of her other books.

Belva Plain. Just when everyone said that massive family saga novels had peaked and would be in disfavor with readers for a few years, Plain came along with *Evergreen* and confounded all of the experts. Her *Random Winds* was also a bestseller. Reading her will give you a feel for the current requirements of this kind of novel.

Frederik Pohl. He is a key figure in science fiction, both as an author and as an editor. His collaborations with C.M. Kornbluth (listed earlier) are classics in the field. His other books—notably *Gateway*, *The Age of the Pussyfoot*, *A Plague of Pythons*, and *Man Plus*—have won awards within the genre and are superior examples of science fiction storytelling.

Mario Puzo. *The Godfather* is a minor American classic, and his influence on the publishing industry has been enormous. He is a fine writer, and he is at his best when writing what he apparently thinks of as ''strictly commercial'' books.

Ayn Rand. Rand was not just a popular mainstream writer; she was a major figure in American literature, a fact which will probably not be fully recognized for at least another 20 years. Her two most famous novels are *Atlas Shrugged* and *The Fountainhead*, which can best be described as ''fiction of ideas,'' although that does not mean they are dull. Far from it! Rand's books read like thrillers, but they are crammed full of philosophy. *This* is an author to read if you have doubts about how to integrate thematic content into your story line. American critics have treated Rand with indifference and even hostility because her political assumptions were alien to them; her philosophy was libertarian, and her books stress the need for individual freedom at virtually any cost. But if current trends in politics and philosophy continue, Rand may eventually be seen as a prophet. In any event, she was a superior storyteller.

Willo Davis Roberts. She was one of the best Gothic novelists at the height of that craze. She wrote some good mysteries. She has done fine novels for young adults. Now she is on the verge of major mainstream success. Read *Destiny's Woman*.

Lawrence Sanders. Sanders has taken the detective story and lifted it out of the genre pit. In fact he hasn't merely lifted it out, he's *thrown* it with considerable force. In books like *The First Deadly Sin*, *The Second Deadly Sin*, and *The Sixth Commandment* he has shown a talent for characterization and a plotting skill that have put him on all the bestseller lists. His first novel, *The Anderson Tapes*, was a thriller told in an experimental style and is a true tour de force.

Dorothy Sayers. Here is an author who had a style so unique that imitating it would lead only to hilarity. She managed to blend suspense and humor in a fashion so stylish that she lifted the mystery novel to new heights. Most readers feel that she is an acquired taste, but once the taste is acquired, you will always be hungry for her books. Try *Clouds of Witness*, *The Unpleasantness at the Bellona Club*, *The Dawson Pedigree (Unnatural Death)*, *Hangman's Holiday*, *Busman's Honeymoon*, and all her other titles. With the books of Dorothy Sayers, the mystery novel began to come of age; she is of historical importance to the genre. Besides, her stories are as much fun today as they were when she began writing them in the 1920s, and virtually all of them are still in print.

Irwin Shaw. His short stories are acclaimed in academe, and many of them are very good indeed. But it is in his novel-length fiction that he speaks to the average reader, and it is this work that I find worth recommending to you. (Of course the academic community dislikes Shaw's novels, for they are not elitist.) He is a very stylish writer who creates characters as real and believable as any others in modern American fiction. Try *Nightwork* and *Rich Man, Poor Man* and *The Young Lions* and *Top of the Hill*.

Nevil Shute. Here is another British author who helped to define the parameters of the modern adventure story. But Shute is much more than an adventure novelist; he is very good at background and characterization. A real find if you've never read his work. I suggest you try *Most Secret*, *The Rainbow and the Rose*, and *On the Beach*, among others.

Robert Silverberg. He is a major figure in the science fiction field. In his early days, he ground out a phenomenal number of novels—literally hundreds of them—and wisely invested his money. Later in his career, he began writing more ambitious books which, while working within the confines of the genre, were nevertheless dazzling and of lasting importance. A few of his books have transcended the science fiction genre, and all of the following are well worth your time: *Downward to the Earth*, *Dying Inside*, *The Book of Skulls*, *Up the Line*, *Nightwings*, *Thorns*, and *Lord Valentine's Castle*.

Clifford Simak. He's another science fiction writer whose work has defined the field. Try such classics as *City*, *Time and Again*, *They Walked Like Men*, and *All Flesh Is Grass*.

Maj Sjowall and Per Wahloo. I am listing this Swedish husband-and-wife team as a single entry, for their best and most famous work was written in collaboration. Their psychological mysteries are highly regarded and have enjoyed worldwide popularity. Their writing is crisp, moody, and enriched with strong thematic purpose. Try *The Laughing Policeman*, *The Abominable Man*, *Cop Killer*, and others.

Cordwainer Smith. This science fiction writer did not produce a large body of work, but his stories have had a lasting effect on the genre. He is so stylish that sometimes he risks seeming mannered, but never falls into that pit. Read *The Planet Buyers*, *The Underpeople*, and the short story collection titled *You Will Never Be the Same*, plus any other Cordwainer Smith works that you can get your hands on.

Richard Stark. This is Donald Westlake's pseudonym. The Stark books are among the most tightly structured, lightning-paced novels ever produced by an American writer. Most of them are built around the same anti-hero, a man known only as Parker. This is the hard-boiled school of writing, given a modern tone, brought into the America of the 1960s and 1970s. If you have never read the Stark novels, I envy you the hours of first-rate entertainment that lie ahead of you. Some of the Stark books are: *Slayground*, *Deadly Edge*, *Point Blank!*, *The Split*, *The Rare Coin Score*, *The Sour Lemon Score*, *The Black Ice Score*, *The Jugger*, and *Butcher's Moon*. Most of the Stark novels have been out of print too long, and I imagine that some enterprising publisher will finally remember them before too many more years go by. In the meantime, if you cannot find them in your bookstore, it is well worth haunting used-book emporiums and searching through stacks of mouldering paperbacks in order to put together a collection of these gems. Stark will teach you plotting and mood and the value of economy in language.

Rex Stout. Stout's long list of Nero Wolfe novels is a gold mine for anyone looking to be entertained. Furthermore, these are landmark novels in the mystery genre. The writing is economical. It is also some of the most highly polished prose anyone has ever produced inside the genre. Stout was also a fine characterizer, and his story people—especially Archie Goodwin, Nero Wolfe, and some of the other regulars in the series—are always sympathetic and convincing. A few of his many titles are *The Doorbell Rang*, *Death of a Doxy*, *The Father Hunt*, *The Mother Hunt*, *Too Many Clients*, *Triple Jeopardy*, and *Where There's a Will*.

Theodore Sturgeon. The one and only. This man is truly an American original. His viewpoint is unique. His stories are unique. And his sensitivity is more than unique; it is devastating. Sturgeon is primarily a science fiction writer, if you would believe the publishers who routinely label him as such, but I think he easily qualifies as a mainstream author. The characters in his books are so real we can hear them talking while we read the page. More than most writers in the SF genre, Sturgeon is aware of the need for thematic structure. His concerns are not the hardware of most science fiction stories; he's not interested in spaceships and time machines and such stuff. Sturgeon's material is human emotion—love, hate, love, greed, love, jealousy, love, and love again—and he can translate *feeling* to the printed page better than anyone else in the genre and better than nine out of ten writers who *aren't* in the genre. You *must* read *More Than Human*, *The Dreaming Jewels*, *The Cosmic Rape*, and such story collections as *Caviar*, *E Pluribus Unicorn*, and *Sturgeon in Orbit*. This is not so much a writer who has defined modern fiction as a writer who has shown us what the genre could be if more of its writers cared enough and had enough talent to elevate it out of its pulp traditions. Sturgeon also wrote one of the finest psychological horror novels ever to see print. The title is *Some of Your Blood*, and it should have had the impact on the American public that Levin's *Rosemary's Baby* had. Find it, read it, enjoy.

Ross Thomas. Thomas is a fine mainstream thriller writer who is a favorite among aficionados of the form. His work is polished, erudite, and compelling. Try *The Cold War Swap*, *The Singapore Wink*, *The Mordida Man*, *A Chinaman's Chance*, *The Eighth Dwarf*, and others.

J.R.R. Tolkien. This is *the* writer of fantasy in our century. His magnificent *Lord of the Rings* trilogy has sold many millions of copies and is even more popular today than it was when it was first published. Tolkien's prose is so polished it shines. His characters are deeply drawn, and his backgrounds are so vividly detailed that they seem more real than the world in which we actually live. Tolkien is another author whose awareness of the need for thematic structure has elevated his work to the highest levels that fiction can attain.

Jack Vance. Vance has written both mysteries and science fiction novels, but it is his SF for which he is famous. He has won many awards in that genre, and virtually all of his many science fiction books are still in print. Try *The Dying Earth*, *Big Planet*, *Emphyrio*, and others.

A.E. van Vogt. He is another key figure in the science fiction field. Some of his work seems dated now, but most of it is still as readable, fascinating, and mysterious as it was when it first saw print. Van Vogt is not much of a stylist. He is not adept at characterization. But he plots like a demon, and he has an ability to create mood and delineate futuristic backgrounds that earns him a lasting place in the SF field. Try such classics as *The Weapons Shops of Isher*, *Slan*, *The Players of Null-A*, *The World of Null-A*.

Gore Vidal. His use of language is as close to faultless as anyone could reasonably expect a writer to get. He creates characters as real as those you meet on the street. (In fact, considering some of the people I've been meeting on the street lately, Vidal's characters are even more real than that!) He never sets pen to paper without a clear thematic purpose. And he is a storyteller first-class. Sometimes I find his political opinions to be distinctly elitist and perhaps even anti-human, but somehow that never gets in the way of his story. *Messiah* is one of the finest novels about religion and about Americans' attitudes toward death that I have ever read. *Burr*, *1876*, and *Creation* are first-rate historical novels.

Kurt Vonnegut. Here is another American original. No one writes like Vonnegut, and no one should even try. Only Vonnegut can do what Vonnegut does so well. Nevertheless, because he is one of the most widely read of modern writers, you ought to be familiar with his work. Try *Player Piano*, *The Sirens of Titan*, *Slaughterhouse Five*,

Breakfast of Champions, and others.

Joseph Wambaugh. Wambaugh is a police detective who eventually gave up his badge to be a full-time writer. No one has ever written more realistically about the day-to-day lives of modern American police officers. Wambaugh is a born storyteller, and you would do well to study the ways in which he inserts large amounts of background material into a novel. Read *The New Centurions*, *The Blue Knight*, *The Black Marble*, and others. As an added bonus, Wambaugh can be quite funny.

Donald Westlake. Westlake stands alone as master of the comic suspense novel. His most recent books have been weak, but many of his others—*The Fugitive Pigeon*, *God Save the Mark*, *The Hot Rock*, *Adios Scheherazade*, *Cops and Robbers*—have never been equalled. Earlier in this list, I discussed Westlake's alter-ego, Richard Stark, and perhaps it is worth comparing the two sides of Westlake's talent. In my opinion, and in that of many other writers I know, even though the Donald Westlake books are wonderful, they are not quite as successful in artistic terms as the Stark novels. This might be because comedy seems inherently less important than serious fiction. Whatever the reason, when you read a Donald Westlake novel and then read a Richard Stark novel, you kind of wish that Westlake had spent more time on the hard-boiled stuff. And *then* you start wishing that he set his sights even higher at some point in his career, for he is such a fine writer that he might well have become a major mainstream author if he had at some point made up his mind to break out of the genres.

Colin Wilson. This British author has written books of philosophy and some of the best studies of the occult ever done. He is also a novelist with a rather dense but uncannily affecting style. Just to broaden your horizons, I recommend you read *The Mind Parasites*, *Lingard*, and *The Glass Cage*.

Gene Wolfe. Wolfe is a science fiction writer and a fantasist who is gradually becoming one of the half-dozen most important writers in his field. He's a fine stylist. Try *The Fifth Head of Cerberus*, *The Shadow of the Torturer*, and *The Claw of the Conciliator*.

Cornell Woolrich. Although he apparently died believing that his life's work had been shallow and worthless, Woolrich has had enormous influence upon mystery and suspense writers. His style is usually slick and colorful, in spite of occasional slips into the melodramatic pulp tradition from which he originally came. His plotting is fresh. His characters are real, and his understanding of their psychology is always deep. He is historically important in his field. Try *The Bride Wore Black*, *The Black Angel*, and *Deadline at Dawn*, among others.

Herman Wouk. It is true that his prose seldom sings. Nevertheless, I am a great fan of Wouk's, for his characters come alive, and his work is brimming with compassion. He's no slouch at plotting, either! *The Caine Mutiny*, *The Winds of War*, *Marjorie Morningstar*, and *Youngblood Hawke* will grab and hold you from first page to last. Wouk is always acutely aware of the need for good fiction to go beyond entertainment, and the thematic structures of some of his books are complex and amazing to behold. Sometimes, in the middle of a Wouk novel, I wonder if the critical consensus—that he is a good pop novelist but little more—might be woefully wrong; perhaps he will turn out to be our Dickens. If he *does* last, it will be his keen eye for character and his compassion that will earn him immortality.

Roger Zelazny. Zelazny is a science fiction writer, but he clearly could have written anything he chose to write. In his early days he wrote such stylish, poetic novelettes and novellas as "The Keys to December," "A Rose for Ecclesiastes," "The Furies," "The Graveyard Heart," "For a Breath I Tarry," "This Moment of the Storm," "This

Mortal Mountain,'' and "He Who Shapes.'' His earliest novels were also poetic, over-flowing with brilliant imagery: *The Dream Master*, *This Immortal*, and *Lord of Light*. Many of his later books have been unpretentious adventure novels—such as the *Nine Princes in Amber* series. Other things—like *Doorways in the Sand*, *Today We Choose Faces*, and *Jack of Shadows*—are not so easily categorized within the subgenres of science fiction. I recommend that you read his early works first. He has had considerable influence upon his field.

Although I am sure I have inadvertently left out a dozen or two dozen important authors, this should get you started on your quest toward being a writer. Perhaps your name will appear on the next list of this sort that I compose, in the revised edition of *How to Write Best-Selling Fiction*, five or ten years from now. I truly hope so. Good luck.

> **66** *When I was young the study house was the most important place in my life. Now the library has taken over. When I come to a new place, my first question is, 'Is there a library here?' I cannot imagine myself living in a town or a village without a library. The book and the library are as important in my life as bread and love.*
> **—Isaac Bashevis Singer** **99**

Researching the historical novel

by Roberta Gellis

For many people, research is a frightening and depressing word. It sounds heavy and laborious, and, worse yet, one often does not know where to start.

Personally, I have always enjoyed research. You invariably find all sorts of unexpected, delightful and interesting tidbits when delving into the past, and once the techniques of discovery are familiar, research is simple. The first step, prenatal or even in the preconception stage, is to decide what and how much you wish to discover.

To start, it is necessary to define the subject. There are three main types of historical fiction: (1) the historical costume drama, in which historical events play no part at all or are barely mentioned and no real effort is made to depict cultural and emotional attitudes accurately; (2) the historical romance, in which historical events are a loose framework around fictional characters who live their own lives and have adventures that may or may not pertain to history; (3) the historical novel, in which the characters were real people, the plot and action of the book are fixed on the historical events, and the cultural and emotional attitudes and mores are shown with all the accuracy possible considering the lapse of time and lack of information. All shadings between these types also exist, however. For example, the books I have published under my own name fall between the second and third groups, whereas *The Love Token*, published under the pseudonym Priscilla Hamilton, is a straight costume drama. Edith Pargeter's *Marriage of Megotta*, and Mary Renault's "Alexander" novels are probably as close to the third as one can get and still be gripping stories rather than bad textbooks.

Roberta Gellis was well schooled in history, foreign languages and medieval literature before she started writing 23 years ago. Since then she has published numerous historical romances, many of which are set in the medieval period, including her successful series, The Roselynde Chronicles. Gellis has also written two science fiction novels under the pseudonym of Max Daniels.

Oldies but goodies

Of course, in order to do research for historical fiction, one must first decide which type to write. I must emphasize, however, that whether you plan to write a costume drama or a serious historical novel, accuracy is of essential importance. Readers who concentrate on historical fiction soon pick up a surprising fund of information. When such readers find a gross mistake, it jolts them and they lose what is called "the suspension of disbelief"; that is, they can no longer accept the fictional world in which you are trying to involve them. And this is as true for the costume drama as for the other types.

To give a brief example: A friend of mine, who is not a historian but is an avid reader of historical fiction, was reading a costume drama set in 1630 by the author. A few pages along, the heroine was presented to James I and his wife, Anne of Denmark. At that point my friend said she lost contact with the story. Although she finished it, she claimed she could not enjoy it properly and resolved not to buy another book by that author. It so happened that she knew from other novels that James I had died in 1625 and his wife in 1619. Although she had found the story interesting up to that point and she knew the events being described were not true, she could no longer believe in the book—and she felt she could not trust the author.

Naturally, if you intend to write costume drama, no major research is needed. It is very easy to avoid gross errors of this kind. Many desk dictionaries have the dates of births and deaths of important individuals and any encyclopedia would surely have such information. Some dictionaires, *Webster's Collegiate*, for example, also have a section on forms of address as has the *Information Please Almanac*. Even better is *Whitaker's Almanac*, a British publication. I have come across used copies of this work in book sales, and many libraries keep a current copy on the shelf.

Thus, an author dealing with the English nobility or the clergy can use the proper title for such characters. For a costume drama the three sources mentioned—a good dictionary, a good encyclopedia, and an almanac—are probably sufficient if they are consulted with intelligence. Moreover, all of these sources are reasonably inexpensive, particularly if purchased second hand; so an author can have them immediately available. Almost every book sale I have attended has old copies of dictionaires and almanacs, and I have seen old sets of encyclopedias for as little $5 to $25. This is an advantage of historical research—the older the almanac or encyclopedia the better.

Pick the period

For the past six or seven years, the market has been flooded with costume dramas. When this happens—as it happened in the past with gothic romance—the reader's taste becomes more refined. If the quality of the work does not improve, the taste becomes sated. Many of us have seen the result of satiation in the demise of the gothic romance, a fate it did not deserve because this genre can be delightful if properly handled. It still remains popular in England today. Wisely, to avoid such a fate for the historical romance, publishers are growing more selective in the material they accept. Thus it may be necessary for authors to delve a little more deeply into actual historical events and personalities. But the research need not be onerous.

For those who have never written historical fiction or who have written costume drama and wish to add more historical facts and a more genuine atmosphere to their work, I offer a pleasant and easy method of obtaining information. For a first attempt at a research historical work, choose a limited period of time that contains one or two great climactic events—a great battle with far-reaching results is a convenient device. Such a choice simplifies the research, gives adequate scope for individual adventures for the heroine or the hero, and limits the amount of historical explanation one must give the reader. If the battle has a name (and most have), you are immediately provided with a specific word to look up in encyclopedias and the indexes of historical texts and biographies to pinpoint which books will be useful for your purposes.

It may seem more romantic to sweep from country to country around the world, but if you want to provide any "verisimilitude to an otherwise bald and unconvincing narrative" that means maps, antique guide books, and complicated calculations on travel times by horse, cart, or foot on land and by sail or oar-driven vessels by sea. However, if sweep you must, there are books to help you, from atlases with maps and descriptions for every time period to books on the daily life of people in weird and wonderful places in all eras of history.

The place to start is with a relatively simple book on world history. Or, if you are confining your work to a single country, use a general history of that country. Any college or high school text will do. It isn't necessary to read the whole book, of course; you only need to cover a period of about 50-100 years, which might be one or a few chapters. This is not really part of the research; the only purpose of this initial reading is to pick up an overall view of events and to discover the names of the most important people of the period. With these people true research begins.

Wealthy information

Once you have a list of names—a half dozen or less—a brief check may be made in any good encyclopedia, such as *The Encyclopedia Britannica*. For biographical, geographical, and historical articles, the 9th or 11th editions are greatly preferred over more recent ones. I am not familiar with the 12th or 13th editions, but the 14th and 15th place greater emphasis on scientific and technological subjects and on very recent history. There is a limit to the length of any encyclopedia, even the *Britannica*. What has been deleted or condensed are the biographical articles about persons before the 19th century and related frills, such as the colored plates of the historical uniforms. A similar problem exists with *The Encyclopedia Americana*. It emphasize science and technology, but there are good articles on biography and particularly good sections on costume.

There are far better capsule biographies, however, in *The Dictionary of National Biography* (commonly called the *DNB*) for British people and *The Dictionary of American Biography* (the *DAB*) for Americans. These volumes contain rather long selections, and for important people, the article may be as much as five to ten pages of small print in double column text.

The *DNB* and *DAB* also include many people of great interest who are not important enough to be mentioned in an encyclopedia. Another valuable asset of the *DNB* and *DAB* are their indexes, which provide the dates during which the persons listed lived. There one can garner a complete cast of real characters to support the fictional hero and heroine. But for preliminary work you are only trying to choose one or two people who had the longest and most interesting lives, preferably a king or queen or a government official. The next step is to obtain scholarly biographies of these persons.

Biographies provide a multitude of information. Not only will you estabilsh the history of the period, but you find discussions on the manners and mores of the time, descriptions of clothing, palaces, and homes, the food eaten during that period, and the methods by which they traveled. Often there will be quotations from letters or diaries, expense accounts—bills, lists of expenses for food, jewels, furniture, clothing and charity events.

Here is an example of the wealth of general information that can be found in a biography. In Amy Kelly's *Eleanor of Aquitaine*, there is a delightful description of women's garments from a most exasperated Abbot Bernard of the great Abbey of Clairvaux:

"Fie," he says, "on a beauty that is put on in the morning and taken off at night." The garments of the court ladies are fashioned from the finest tissues of wool or silk. A costly fur between two layers of rich stuffs forms the lining and border of their cloaks. Their arms are loaded with bracelets; from their ears hang pendants enshrining precious stones. For head dress they have a kerchief of fine linen, which they drape about their necks and shoulders, allowing one corner to fall over the left arm . . . Gotten up in this way, they walk with mincing steps, their necks thrust forward; and furnished and adorned as only temples should be, they drag after them a tail of precious stuff that raises a cloud of dust.

Enduring emotions

Historical research not only provides information for descriptions of personal items, but places or settings as well. From the same source, we have a vivid picture of London in the 12th century.

"Across the river from the royal quarters the London wall formed three sides of an old town, but crumbled away before the traffic of the river, where streets ended in docks and wharves, cook shops and wine shops along the Strand. A hearty smell of fish, wool, and beer rose from the waterside, and the calls of boatmen and eel-wives filled the air with babel. The ancient bridge, with its jumble of narrow houses, gathered swarms of smacks and wherries about its landing stairs. Along the wharves, the shipping of the north countries, of Flanders, and Rouen, of Nantes and La Rochelle, even of Syria, lay in haven, their oars banked, their colored sails furled against the wintry fury of the sea . . ."
" . . Whereas Paris swarmed with students and resounded with their irresponsible levity, London thronged with burghers—merchants, shippers, money changers, masters of guilds—who went soberly, but with a cheerful and properous air from their rich homes to their profitable stalls and warehouses upon the Strand. The town houses of bishops and nobles were of princely elegance and wide hospitality."

In addition to the simple description of the city, we learn that London was not defended by walls on the river side, an interesting fact if it is necessary to describe the defense of the city. We learn that a bridge, which is called ancient as early as 1154, existed, and that houses were built on it. We discover that food was sold in shops and peddled on the street in this period, and that trade goods came from as far away as the Middle East. Such material can be stretched to provide a fascinating background for historical fiction—and even more can be discovered by careful examination of detail.

The procedures of travel were very different in past times. Here is a brief quote that depicts the details vividly.

"The royal household, from chamberlain to scullion, often numbered at least 200 souls, equipped with chapel, bed furnishings, kitchen utensils, plates, treasures, garments, vestments, documents, and all services thereunto pertaining . . . . When [King Henry's] orders came at last, the cortege made off with an infernal clamor and commotion . . . . The queen, when not riding herself, made these journeys with her household and the royal children in litters or in barrel-topped wains, safe from rain but not from the abysses of roads often hardly wider than a bridle path."

Clothes change, cities change, methods of travel change, but people's emotions—although their motives and the causes that bring forth these emotions differ—change very little, as proven in letters and diaries. For example, there is a letter with great feeling 700 years ago to the Pope from Queen Eleanor, who described herself in one as "Queen, by the wrath of God, of England"

"The kings and princes of the earth have conspired against my son, the anointed of the Lord. One keeps him in chains while another ravages his lands; one holds him by the heels while another flays him. And while this goes on, the sword of St. Peter reposes in its scabbard. Three times you have promised to send legates, and they have not been sent . . . . My posterity has been snatched from me . . . . The young king and the County of Brittany sleep in the dust. Their unhappy mother is forced to live on, ceaselessly tormented by their memory . . . . I have lost the staff of my age, the light of my eyes, my Richard."

Special editions

Of course, the use of material gleaned from a biography need not be restricted to the particular person about whom the biography was written—except, naturally, exact quotations from letters and diaries. Thus when I say that I read biographies as the first serious step in researching a novel, I do not mean that I intend to write a novel about the person whose biography I read. Within the framework provided, "typical" people can be invented upon whose actions there are fewer restrictions so that an author can be free—without taking liberties.

For example, when the provisions of the Magna Carta were being negotiated, King John was at Windsor and the rebel barons were in London, 30 miles away. There were, of course, no telephones, no radios, no telegraphs, not even a postal service in the early 13th century. Thus a man—or, perhaps, many men—rode horseback between Windsor and London carrying copies of provisional forms of the agreement until a final version was adopted. The names of these messengers have not come down to us. Thus I do no violence to history if my fictional hero is said to have been one of these messengers.

At this point, the hopeful novelist may feel that enough is known for the purposes of the type of book to be written, but for those who wish to learn more toward the serious historical novel rather than the costume drama, there is another stage of depth to research on a historical novel. A scholarly biography has a great deal to offer. At the end of such a book will be a bibliography, listing the source material on which the biography was built. Some of this source material is beyond the reach or the patience of a novelist, since it is in manuscript form, in libraries in foreign countries, in ancient or foreign languages, but much will be of value, particularly references to published letters and diaries.

Most reference books beyond the simple biographies will probably be expensive. Thus further research is best conducted through a library where, as an additional advantage, the assistance of a librarian is available. In small libraries, however, sometimes the librarian is not professionally trained, or may have the time to assist someone who is doing somewhat esoteric research.

If this should be true for your library, there is no need to despair; there are many books available to help you work efficiently on your own. Look in the subject section of the library card catalogue under Library, use of, Research, or Writing. Books such as Cook's *New Library Key* or Morse's *Concise Guide to Library Research*, give a wide variety of sources, classified by subject, that will help you find the reference works you need.

Even if the library in your area is small, it may be able to supply the books you want through an interloan system. If there is a college or university in your area, be sure to inquire whether persons who are not students are permitted to use its resources.

And for those few who intend to do very serious work, there are even special libraries, solely devoted to a particular subject. It is not difficult to discover whether there is a special library devoted to the subject of your interest. There is a book—or, rather, there are several books that list libraries, their locations, and the subjects in which they specialize.

Chronicles of uncommon customs

A final step necessary in providing realism in historical fiction is an accurate depiction of the customs of the times, the clothes people wore, the food they ate, and the level of technology in their society. By technology I do not mean television and computers, of course, but whether or not, for example, they had scissors or saddles or carriages rather than springless carts.

Occasionally some information on these specific details can be obtained from biographics. We did learn, for example, that Queen Eleanor traveled in a barrel-topped wain—springless—but she is not likely to have needed to use scissors; her maids would probably have performed any tasks requiring them. Thus it is easier in general to have a source that treats such information directly.

Among the myriad books covering historical customs and data, the most useful and direct is the *Everyday Life* series, by a variety of authors. These books treat every period from prehistoric times to the 19th century and such varied cultures as those of ancient Egypt, Rome, Greece, Byzantium, Aztec, Viking and English. They discuss every aspect of life from food and clothing to common customs.

Beyond the aforementioned materials there are more esoteric sources, such as chronicles, periodicals, and newspapers of the period under study, collections of published and unpublished scholarly dissertations, and original and published legal, diplomatic, and testamentary documents, found only in very large public or university libraries or in special libraries. Most sources of this type are more suited to the scholarly biography rather than even very serious historical novels, however, and require more in-depth research than necessary for historical fiction.

Researchers' bibliography

For those who would like to establish a very basic library for historical research, I suggest the following books as essential:

Reference Books: A Brief Guide (published by Enoch Pratt Free Library, 400 Cathedral St., Baltimore MD 21201).

Webster's New International Dictionary, unabridged, 2nd ed.

Webster's Biographical Dictionary (any edition).

The Encyclopedia Britannica (or Americana).

Muir's Historical Atlas: Ancient, Medieval, and Modern; *The Penguin Atlas of Ancient History*; and *The Penguin Atlas of Medieval History*.

Costume Through the Ages, by James Laver; and *European Costume*, by Doreen Yarwood.

The Everyday Life series of books (B.T. Batsford, Ltd. London), by various authors. Check the list of books available and choose the country and period best suited to your own work.

Never lead with a dead dog

by Nancy McCarthy

Slightly apprehensive, I sat down gingerly in the only empty chair and inspected my new office. The prevailing decor theme was mustard yellow—more properly, manila—the color of the hundreds of unopened manuscript envelopes that dominated the room. They were everywhere, towering stacks of them—on the desk, the file cabinets, the coffee table, even the chairs.

It was my first day as the new fiction editor at *Woman's World*. My predecessor had been ill for weeks and in her absence, submissions had been accumulating, unread. Now, the piles seemed to have developed a life of their own, shifting impatiently, as though tired of waiting to be opened, an impression that was reinforced when a few slipped off a stack and settled around my feet, as if they'd decided to demand attention by nipping at my ankles.

All a little nervous making, and not just because of the manila towers. I'd never been a fiction editor before and nothing in my past experience as an international journalist had prepared me to choose the kind of fiction this new weekly magazine for women had decided to run—light, wholesome, undemanding stories built around a romantic plotline and ending happily with the big fadeout clinch. Gooey stuff. Sort of Love Boat, without the waves and portholes.

Still, I'd been going broke writing a novel of my own, the job was offered to me when I most needed one and so, in pursuit of romantic illusions, I settled in and began to read . . . and read and read and read.

Nancy McCarthy is the fiction editor at Woman's World *Magazine. Previously as an international journalist she wrote for newspapers, TV and films in Indonesia, Iran, London and New York. McCarthy spends her weekends working on a novel.*

Dead ducks and daddies

After a few weeks of this it was with a growing sense of disquiet that I began to realize I was seeing a disproportionately large number of manuscripts that involved a dead dog. A lot of them were headed in the general direction of: I-saw-the-dead-dog-on-the-road-this-made-me-think-about-my-own-life. Since there's no way a dead dog can be incorporated successfully into a light romance, even one stiffening canine was one too many for us, but dozens were turning up. What were all those people out there doing writing about dead dogs, anyway?

Without really wanting to spend a lot of time finding an answer to that question, I did realize that as a new magazine, we couldn't expect readers and writers to be all that familiar with our needs. Clearly, guidelines would have to be written and sent back with every rejection. And, Rule One in the guidelines, I resolved, would be:

Never, under any circumstances whatsoever, lead with a dead dog.

Then one day I began to read a manuscript that showed real promise. Well written, it opened with a gently evocative description of this adorable little four-year-old girl wandering around the barnyard carrying her pet duck, while her mother calls to her from the kitchen. But then as I read on I began to realize with mounting horror what the story was all about. Turns out the child's father has died and no one's been able to tell the little girl. Now the mother and the grandparents are all bent out of shape because they think the duck's dying, see, and the little girl won't let go of it. They figure when the duck kicks off, the little kid's going to start asking a lot of questions like ''what's happening here?'' and ''by the way, where's daddy?'' and they can't deal with this at all.

Neither could I.

I knew I couldn't bear to read any more of the piece, but I did want to find out how it all worked out in the end so I snuck a peek at the last page. I never did get what they told the little girl, but sure enough, the duck died.

As I was mailing that one back I decided that in view of this new twist in animal mortality, the dimensions of the guidelines would have to be expanded. Rule One became:

Never lead with a dead dog/dying duck.

Cat flambé

After that I redoubled my efforts to let writers know what we wanted, paying special attention to those who had already been published in the magazine.

One writer, who'd managed, during an experimental stage of the magazine, to sell us a cryptically brooding piece that never was used, couldn't seem to understand our new requirements.

After I'd written him a lengthy explanation, he asked for further amplification. Okay. I wrote again. He said he still didn't quite see, I explained once more, and it went on and on. Finally, after a couple of months of heavy communicating, he sent in a new submission with a sunny cover letter telling me he'd read all the recent issues, finally understood our needs and had written the enclosed story just for us.

I was delighted. This was what real editors did, right? Gently coax promising talent along in the right direction. And the story looked as though it might be right; it had a title that suggested exactly the sort of fluffy pink glow we wanted.

So this was his lead, which I will paraphrase but only slightly as I will remember it forever: ''He grabbed the cat, poured kerosene over it, lit a match to set it on fire and then swung it once around his head by the tail to get the flames going . . .''

I was tempted not to mail that one back. Instead I toyed with the idea of writing the author a note that began . . . "The editor grabbed the manuscript, poured kerosene over it, lit a match to set it on fire and swung it once around her head to get the flames going . . ."

I didn't though. I just mailed it back with the usual rejection slip. However, as I sealed the envelope I was already adding to the the guidelines again. Rule One had now become:

Never lead with a dead dog/dying duck/flaming cat.

By then I'd figured out why writers seemed to be so devoted to writing about these poor miserable dead things, or about lonely old women in nursing homes, or cancer. They're all used as a shortcut to evoke an intended emotional response on the cheap.

We all know that when a beloved pet dies, it's a very sad event. We want our reader to feel very sad, so we throw in a really recognizable downer and that removes any obligation to create effective emotion within the true structure of the story. In effect, the dead dog becomes a kind of literary laugh track, in reverse.

It's enough to keep you up nights, wondering if the cheap and quick manipulation of superficial emotion that is characterized by TV soaps and situation comedies has penetrated the national consciousness so thoroughly that real emotion has become unrecognizable and almost extinct.

Trite and tried

All right, those are mistakes novice writers make. But even experienced professionals don't seem to understand that when a magazine states its range of interests, that's what the magazine wants.

I am continually amazed at the number of writers—good, solid, working professionals—who, after learning we wanted light romance, would still submit something totally unsuitable with a letter that inevitably begins, "I know this isn't what you asked for but I thought . . ."

You can write the master work on bicycles, a story so splendid it ought to be set to music, and if you submit it to a magazine that wants only stories about typewriters, you will get it back. This is a law, but writers prefer to believe an editor will be so moved by the brilliance and eloquence of their submission that requirements will be abandoned. That doesn't happen. Believe it.

When I mail out our guidelines that tell you I'm looking for light romantic fiction with realistic and contemporary plots, I do not want to open my mail and find myself reading—and I swear to God this truly happened—the story of Iris and Rico, frogs in love.

Of course, there are submissions that do meet guidelines but still don't stand much of a chance because they're based on themes so familiar and trite it would take exceptional treatment to make them usable.

The great classic, and I'll bet I've read a thousand of them, is the city-mouse, country-mouse encounter. In these, a frayed and harrassed housewife, struggling with kids and bills, gets a chance to meet her former best friend after 20 years or so. The best friend has gone out into the big world and made it. But when she returns to East Boondock, elegantly and expensively dressed, she inevitably dives into the white wine and then confesses with sobs that her life is shallow, shallow, shallow, and oh, what she wouldn't give for the chance to wipe a runny nose. Interestingly, this story always ends right here. The glamorous one never hangs around much longer. However much she might wail, she always beats it right back to the big city, leaving the frumpy housewife with a new appreciation of her bills, kids and life with good old Joe.

Another favorite is the high school reunion. Here, after having hungered for years for the captain of the football team, our heroine runs into him at the big party and discovers he has turned into a loathsome slob who drinks and paws women. Once again, she sees how lucky she is to have good old Joe.

This theme only worked once for me, and we did buy the story. In it, the woman discovers, with rue, that her former lover would have been just as terrific a husband as the one she's got. She doesn't do anything rash, but she does understand the situation.

On somewhat the same track, another popular theme has a celebrity returning to his home town, where the girl he left behind is still waiting. He is always a pro football player, TV anchorman or movie star and if I were any of the above, I'd think very carefully before making the trek back home again. There may be a lot of resentment waiting. At least there is in the stories I see. Again the woman who has idolized the returning hero for years finds out he is an utter toad and once more goes home gratefully to . . . you guessed it, good old Joe.

Morals majority

After reading so many of these, you begin to develop a fair amount of sympathy for good old Joe. He never seems to be desired because he's charming and attractive, only because he's all that's left. The bird in the hand philosophy of wedded bliss.

Of course it's not fair to suggest that these themes typify the collective national consciousness. Still, it's rare to see a story that has anything positive to say about glittering material wealth, or great fame, beauty or success. I sense a strong streak of suspicion about living life in the fast lane, and I've wondered if that might not be some sort of vestigial Puritanism. Or, it may be that beginning writers feel a story isn't a story unless there's a moral lurking in it somewhere and the simplistic ones come most easily to mind.

There are a lot more themes that receive more than their fair share of recycling, but I'll mention just a few. Sibling rivalry is a hardy perennial, usually with the good sister and the bad apple fighting it out over the same man. Moving, with a husband who fails to understand his wife's attachment to the house, while she fails to see his need to accept the promotion, is a regular contender. And there's always the woman who travels to a foreign country, falls in love with a native and then is usually convinced she's better off back home with that nice young man who manages the supermarket. (She'll marry him, of course, and he'll turn up in later stories as good old Joe.)

Incidentally, if I were struggling to break into the fiction field, I would avoid, like the plague, any story idea that incorporates a foreign character. Dialogue that demands an accent for credibility is hard to write and always looks faintly comedic—"Your eyes are ze collair of ze sky." But even more importantly—and this ought to be a phrase every beginning writer paints in foot-high letters on the wall just above the typewriter—the unfamiliar is always unconvincing.

That doesn't apply only to foreign settings. If a character runs a plant store, you'd better learn the difference between a ficus and a philodendron; if a story revolves around a real estate deal, you have to find out about mortgage points and closings; and if computers are part of the plot, you really have to get to know your floppy discs.

Changing roils

By the way, with very few exceptions all these comments apply equally to men and women. You'd expect, or at least I did, that men and women would have dramatically different ways of handling the delicate area of love. They don't. In fact if bylines were masked out on the stories I see, in most cases I wouldn't be able to identify the sex of the author. And, we've frequently bought first person stories written by women from a masculine point of view and vice versa.

The one general distinction I've found is that men do handle descriptions of action events a lot better, probably because until recently women who were physically active weren't regarded as exactly nice. As a result we're less able to describe spontaneously what it really feels like to throw a hard punch or even fall out of a tree. And that may be why women have a tendency to gravitate toward essay constructions in which all thought and feeling is conveyed with virtually no accompanying action. A lot of these begin where most women start their day—in the kitchen.

Which brings me to the most common mistake beginning writers who are women make, one that I find most interesting.

There is a terrific roil going on out there. Women are changing. And not just those living in big cities either. Ninety per cent of the stories we get reflect a growing awareness and some turmoil over this shift in established values. It's very exciting to listen in on internal dialogues as women struggle with entrenched, conditioned ideas and re-evaluate them.

But, however much drama is derived from the stuff of ordinary life, ordinary life is not automatically drama. It's rare for stories about self-realization to become good fiction.

So then what does make good fiction? Well, the characters have to really be there— living, breathing, moving through a drama that has a definite beginning, middle and end. Beyond that, the fine points of creative writing can be learned if anyone wants to work at it. Creative writing courses, and a number of good books on writing fiction, abound.

Editors, unfortunately, aren't able to help writers polish their work. Perhaps in the more leisurely days of publishing it was possible for an editor to embark on a lengthy correspondence with a number of talented beginners. It's certainly not anymore. Not at least, for me, because those towering manila piles build up every week.

So I will have to get back to them now, and leave you with a couple of final caveats. In romantic fiction, the most frequently misspelled word in the English language is "exhilarate." And, no bit of dialogue in a story is ever improved by the addition of the word "shucks."

---

66   *The short story is the glancing form of fiction that seems to be right for the nervousness and restlessness of contemporary life.*

V.S. Pritchett   99

On writing the short story

by Adela Rogers St. Johns

It has always puzzled me a little that people think they can just write. I know of no other profession or trade where some initial study and practice and apprenticeship are not regarded as requisite, inescapable, inevitable, and even compulsory. The singer must learn to sing, the composer must study the laws of harmony, the actor goes to summer stock, vaudeville, or on the road—and we had better actors when more time was spent at this, there are few such artists as Helen Hayes or Katharine Cornell or Charles Laughton who have not served a term of practice. The violinist spends a lifetime, beginning in childhood and continuing. I shall never forget spending a few days with Jascha Heifetz and his wife and realizing that even then, when he was acknowledged the greatest artist in the world in his field, he worked four and five hours a day with his accompanist. Doctors—lawyers—painters—all work to learn their trade.

But I have met very few people who didn't think they could write a good book if they just had the time.

Every man knows his own business plus writing.

What they mean, of course, is that their life is an interesting story, or they have observed in their lives things that would make interesting stories, and this is completely true. But it isn't all or enough.

I am also amazed at how easily discouraged the young folks are today. If they receive a couple of rejections they are a little too inclined to say, "Ah—that proves what I've always thought, they don't really want good stories," or, "I guess I haven't any tal-

---

Adela Rogers St. Johns' career as a reporter and writer has spanned more than six decades. She has taught short story writing at Stephens College and the University of California "on the theory that accomplishment in the subject taught was equivalent to the degrees I didn't have." Her latest of many books, No Good-Byes: My Search Into Life Beyond Death, *was published by McGraw-Hill in 1981.*

ent.'' They have not yet learned their scales or practiced more than a few pieces. They must not be so ready to give up. Maupassant, under the guidance and tutelage of Flaubert, wrote a hundred short stories before one was submitted for sale. His complete works amounted to over 200 short stories, and the majority of them are good and they became classics and he the founder, really, of the modern school.

If you are willing to study the works of the masters you will improve and learn. I know this, I have seen it.

Nobody but a fool would start a tough prospecting trek if he'd been convinced there wasn't any more gold in them thar hills—and fools cannot write short stories. Oddballs, crackpots, and madmen, yes. Fools, no.

Nor is anyone apt to succeed at anything if he starts on the premise that his best is too good, so he won't strain the last tissue to give it.

Short story writing is a tough racket. Like a doctor's, or pro football, or the FBI, or being President of the United States. The difference between being able to write, learning to write—which anybody can do—and being a writer is guts, stamina, discipline, endurance, dedication, the ability to absorb punishment, and working at it 24 hours a day, always conscious of it, always having it going on inside no matter what is happening outside, when you're awake and when you're asleep, because it keeps going on and often you wake up with a scene, a character, a solution for a plot tangle or a way to shorten your telling that you didn't have when you closed your eyes.

What is a short story?

A short story is a story that can be adequately and even superbly told *short*.
There are no other rules.
Absolutely none.

Today the short means anywhere from 3,000 to 7,000 words, preferably 4 to 5,000. But, this does not include short shorts, of which I am too old a dog to learn the new trick.

When I say there are no rules about short stories, I make one exception. The rule is they should be good. Rich. Filled with temperament and desire to tell them.

Otherwise the story may be about anything.

Any kind of people young or old, black, white, brown or yellow, good or bad, rich or poor, short or tall, lean or fat, funny or solemn, pagans or true believers, sick or well, smart or stupid, poets or peasants, dogs or cats.

As long as they are people the writer knows.

The story may cover centuries or minutes. Continents and the air above them and the water underneath and even trips to the moon, though I don't recommend any more of those right now. Or it may take place on a park bench.

It may be told in the first or third person, and as to grammar, it has to some degree ceased to exist if the story is best told by ignoring the rules of grammar to give it reality and flavor, as witness Runyon and Lardner and often Sherwood Anderson.

Adventure. Science Fiction. Love. Teenage. Lavender and Old Lace. New Yorker. Mood. Detective. Ghost. Character. War. Religious.

These at least are a few of the kinds of short stories there are.

With a thousand thousand variations therefrom.

They may bring tears, laughter, furious indignation, curiosity—as long as they bring something to the reader.

There is only one thing they must possess. One quality that must be common to them all. Whether they are serious as Theodore Dreiser or as amusing as James Thurber. One factor without which no art can make them succeed:

Entertainment.

James Farley, the greatest campaign manager of all time, once told me that there was only one quality a candidate for office must have. He must be electable.

A short story must be readable.

Willy-nilly whether or not, it must entertain.

Next to the sonnet, I believe a short story—a superior short story—is the most difficult and precarious of all things to write, the most demanding of all forms to follow. It has to burn with a pure, gemlike flame. True, a novel takes longer, but it has to be easier doing. You can stop to explain.

In the short story you have to be right the first time. Every word must count, not just the right word but the only right word. Half the sentences in a good short story could be made into whole chapters in a novel, they must do the work of whole chapters. "You men! You filthy, dirty pigs! You're all the same, all of you. Pigs! Pigs!" Sadie Thompson said in "Rain." A Russian novelist would make eight chapters out of that sentence. Maugham made those 15 words do it. Made your hair stand up. But I think Somerset Maugham would admit that it was harder to bring "Rain" to its amazing perfection than to write *Of Human Bondage*.

Those who have tried know.

A writer has to make a short story complete in itself.

The action must all be there, whether it is told in a sentence of flashback or is part of the narrative. So that when the idea presents itself it is necessary to find out whether the idea will and can be told in the length in which a short story is publishable.

There should be one story, plus a minor plot. No more. For the reader will wish to follow your character closely. If it's a fine character to love or hate there is hardly enough time as it is. Stick to the point. Keep the reader's interest focused on that character.

Paul Gallico gave us a perfect recipe for a good short story, which "McKabe" is. One third hero worship, or strong emotion. One third from life, the killing of Legs Diamond. One third method, how to put it on paper, that urge to imitate a specific story by Kipling. Two thirds, you see, is emotion—urge—desire. Observe also please that all these things were and are available to anybody anywhere anytime.

All it takes after that is reaction. Response. Recognition. Susceptibility to drama. Keeping the soul and heart and mind and eyes and ears wide open all the time. All the time.

Whatever the approach, it is essential to illuminated writing that it is written to be read. Before it can be read, it must be sold. Therefore, as good or bad soil in which that germ of an idea is planted and grows, it dawned upon me that selling a short story has to be considered first, which is perhaps only natural in an age of salesmanship.

Great stories not only sell once but go on and on in every field and medium where storytelling exists. They also do for the reputation and standing of a writer what a grand-slam home run in the ninth inning of the last game of the World Series with the score tied does for a hitter. They become classics.

A short story writer

Writing short stories is a profession so pleasant, so rewarding, so extraordinary in the kind of life it not only enables but forces you to live that I want to recommend that those who have a spark of talent or the faintest conception of what a story is should spend some time and work and study trying to see if they can make it theirs. If they do not succeed, if they can write but aren't writers, if they have ideas but are among the few who can't learn to write, they can probably go into radio or television or advertising, as so many failures in the field of creative writing have done. Those are well-paid and exciting jobs, if the aspirant possesses a strong heart, steady nerves, and a thick hide. They are potent and powerful in their influence upon the world today, and the training and discipline of trying to write short stories will benefit everybody concerned.

Talent makes it easier, and I would say that the majority of successful professional writers had some story talent to begin with. But not all. A number of writers didn't have it. But they were impelled by a strong inner urge which took its place.

The things that are most devotedly to be wished for are:

A nose for a story. Without that—oh dear!

A writer's memory.

A great, abiding, never failing interest in people.

A set of quick and violent reactions to things and people.

A real stamina, not an ability to endure discipline but to build *self-discipline*, so that you can wrap it up.

Without these it would be better not to try to learn the things that anybody can learn. Like writing, and vocabulary, and plotting and such.

Work is essential. Study is, in my opinion, necessary.

Genius, like everything else, is known by its fruits. Story writing becomes an art, as do all other creative processes, by love, hard work, interest, aspiration, hope, and prayer.

Anybody can learn to write.

If he will read, work, keep at it, study, write and write and write and cut and cut and cut.

Temperament

For years I have treasured the finest definition of artistic temperament I've ever heard, given me by a great actress, Alla Nazimova. "You know those little Chinese bells they have in the doorways?" she said. "They are not what we call bells, they are panels of delicate glass, hung very lightly by silk cords. The merest breath of wind makes them tinkle, they respond to a stir of air you have not felt at all. That is the artistic temperament. It finds itself depressed or exalted, dark or illumined, and does not even know why. As you think back, it may be a letter, a paragraph or picture in the newspaper, a tone of voice of someone you love, a bird's song you didn't know you heard, a memory drifting across your soul. People without this sensitivity may be like the big brass gongs outside the temple, they must be hit with a great padded hammer to make any sound at all. But the little glass bells will give you music in response to a sigh, they will dance to a breath of spring. And they will break if the storm is too great—but not often. They are much stronger than you think, but they are sensitive."

Don't be ashamed of a lot of artistic temperament.

Without some of it, no one is likely to succeed as a short story writer. It isn't necessary to put on displays of it and get in other people's hair about it. However, between you and me, sometimes it helps. If it is on the level—nobody worth bothering about is impressed by a phony pose—I have found that other people, once they understand it, are both sympathetic and respectful. The average citizen knows that the artist—and a good short story writer must have some artistry in him, he is a creator—has that sensitive nature which really does make things hit harder.

Temperament is important.

Like fire, it has to be handled wisely or it can consume instead of warm and heat and produce birth.

For all good short story writers—all storytellers—possess some degree of that artistic or erratic temperament which is composed of never failing sensitivity far beyond the average, or how could they see and feel so much more than others do? Of burning passion, of great warmth, of high voltage of all emotions. These can backfire, and yet they are absolutely essential, and to attempt to deny them, discredit them, overlook them is, I believe, the most dangerous process of all.

That creative temperament must be recognized as the gift of the gods—which it most definitely is—and safeguarded in every way possible.

I do not believe those who can write short stories and have them read by millions are just like the people who deliver the laundry or sit behind typewriters in offices or sell you life insurance or doughnuts or even take care of you when you are sick. To my mind the most important job in the world is teaching, I know myself to be a frustrated schoolteacher, but I am not just like a schoolteacher or I would have been one and not fought my way to be a short story writer. I do not say short story writers—any kinds of storytellers—are better or greater or more important or worthwhile. I do say they are different, that they have been given a sensitive and peculiar gift, and that while some of them may have the gigantic soul strength and gusto and vitality and love of Ernest Hemingway, a lot of them don't.

A thoroughbred race horse can carry just so much weight and no more.

The artistic creative temperament can swim upstream just so far and hard—and no more.

This is one of the reasons we do not have as many good writers as we used to have, and the demand for stories comes from every direction.

Have temperament if you want to know how to write and sell short stories. Have it, use it, foster it, tune in to it. Dive head first. Rejoice and sing. Skip among the hills and dance in the meadows and, having absorbed and loved and hated and lived and suffered today in this world, tomorrow begin to remold it nearer to the heart's desire.

Let me say here that I have never in my life known a short story writer who was any good at all who wasn't temperamental. It's impossible. It may be that fairy enchantment of Mary Roberts Rinehart. Or the simple, endearing Hirman Holiday quality of Paul Gallico. Or the distinguished touchy brilliance of Edna Ferber. Or the strange where-am-I vagueness of William Faulkner.

Memory

I wish I could write that word here in letters of fire nine feet high, like a sign in Times Square.

In my reporting days I interviewed many of the leading figures of our world. If I had to pick one characteristic they had in common, it would be a good memory.

I do not mean a memory like the professor's, or even the actor's. A writer's memory is different from all others. Unconscious, subconscious, subliminal, the heart's core, the inner-most recess of the mind, a tape recorder, a wax disc, a filing system, and it never, never, never stops. This is a gift, an intrinsic part, an inborn trait of nature, an essential of the inwardness without which I myself would hesitate to encourage anyone to try to become a short story writer. A professional short story writer.

Memory is a gift, but I also know that once you are made aware of it and of its vital consequence, it is possible to begin to stimulate it, turn it on, keep it on, see that it registers, emphasize its recordings for a time until it becomes automatic, as it should and must be.

All your knowledge of human nature records as memory. When you start to plot, that memory works. If you are not deeply, constantly, always interested in human beings, don't attempt to be a writer. You don't have to like them all. But you have to be interested in them all. Then you will take in and keep the memory of what they do. Say. How they look.

Naturally, experience helps in all this. The years give you rich stocks, from which you clip coupons. But it is also true, I sincerely believe, that the childhood record is deeply engraved and very clear. Children are more impressed by what they see and hear, by the people they know, their confines are narrower, therefore they have a file cabinet of memories, too.

All from life, life, life.

Don't you see? It is all from life, and your memory is your recorder of dialogue, of gestures, of incidents, of business day after day. A professional writer could not possibly make them all up if that were the way to do it, which it isn't. You do not photograph. You sketch them all deep into your memory tape. There, in the amazing creation of your mind or soul, is some process, some electric arm that, when you need this in a story you are writing—whether you are plotting it in your head or putting it down on paper—reaches in and pulls it out and comes up with it for your use.

Patience and gestation

Ninety-two per cent of the time, the elapsed time, on a short story is, with a few rare exceptions, spent before you put pencil or typewriter to paper. This is the period of time between the idea and the time you start to write it down.

Edna Ferber, unquestionably one of the all-time greats, said that the longer you have a story around the easier it is to write, like picking a peach that is ripe instead of tearing it off the tree green. This is usually true and is important to know, and to know also how to ripen a story to the best advantage.

Don't expect all ideas to come whole. Very, very, very few do. Once in a while one springs full-orbed from the head of Jove and you say thank you to the Source of all creative processes.

So there are the stories that you put away and add to inside, for weeks or years. There are the ones on which you work at once and pretty definitely to arrange the plot. Once you get a flash, don't let it leave you. Install somewhere inside yourself a repository for ideas for short stories. Always write them down at once in a notebook, but that's just a small part of it—I use the notebook to jog my memory, to start the wheels going on something that appeals to me from it that perhaps I haven't thought of in a long time.

But put your ideas inside and this becomes the gestation period.

They grow.

More than that, if you train whatever it is inside you, these ideas magnetize to themselves whatever comes along that fits them. They reach out and pull in, sometimes without your own awareness, a word of dialogue, a certain gesture, some bit of business or minor character.

Lovely things can come to pass. Lines of dialogue you hear, Bits of business you stored away years ago and that have ripened. A laugh you needed. Smooth progression and clear, clean scenes.

If you start at the right place.

If you don't, the whole story gets out of gear and stays that way. You keep trying to get it in the groove and it won't go.

So, if after a month of trying, thinking, outlining, you can't or haven't been able to jell it, put it away and keep going to symphony concerts. I mean that. Nothing starts the creative flow in many writers like music.

Patience is just as essential to a good short story writer. You have to learn to wait and not let anybody push you into making a move until you and your story are ready.

How to recognize a story

Stories are things that happen to people.

Or to you and people.

Sometimes of course they are hurricanes and earthquakes and wars, but let me reiterate that they are better stories if they happen to people.

Mostly they are not hurricanes and earthquakes and wars.

If you look, you are apt to find one right beside you. Or hear one tonight when you go over to watch the ball game on television with your neighbors. Or on the counter at the corner drugstore at lunch time.

Most stories begin with people.

Some with what I suppose should be called a theme, though I don't like the word, but it seems the one best understood in this connection.

Some with a strange incident or happening, or offbeat or unusual circumstance or situation in which people do or could find themselves.

An idea rings a bell inside you.

At first you will have to do this for yourself, do your own watching, listening, recognizing. But *do* it. Start where you are, with the people around you.

You must be prepared to spend your life looking for stories.

Above all things, start where you are.

It may be years before you can go traveling around the world, as Maugham and Gallico did.

Damon Runyon never traveled more than a couple of blocks each way on Broadway and maybe up to Boston once in a while.

Kipling always had a story to tell.

But it was hardly ever a very new story. He didn't strive for the unusual in plot or approach or even background.

He had a story he wanted to tell and it became a story because of that great desire, that passionate urge. He wanted to tell it, and it poured out of him with fervor and excitement, with a completely unegotistical conviction that this was a great story and therefore must be told and he was the channel, the vessel, the mouthpiece, the amanuensis.

He found stories everywhere. Nothing escaped him. Nobody escaped him, he was undoubtedly a born storyteller, and there must be some of that or it is hardly worthwhile for anyone to try this profession. Kipling was never afraid of a story because it was too big or too little, too old or too new, he picked ideas up any time, anyhow, from anybody. He was, I can testify, a listener, not a talker, and that is true of most good short story writers. They listen. It is amazing what stories about and on themselves people will tell, in beauty parlors, in cocktail lounges, on trains, in cars or hotel lobbies or department stores or over coffee cups. Kipling, as his stories prove, listened on street corners, aboard tramp steamers, in barracks, at dinner parties, in hot city rooms. He remembered from his childhood, his school days, his young manhood. His hero worship led him to watch bridges being built and railroad engines being run and doctors and civil servants living their own lives all around him. He had as many eyes as a peacock and ears as long as a donkey's and a memory like a tape recorder.

He knew what a story was.

It was something that happened to people.

Something moving or dangerous or exciting or terrible or heartbreaking or unusual or usual or glorious or triumphant.

Everything was a potential story to Kipling.

That must be implanted deep and firm in the mind of the man or woman, girl or boy who wants to write short stories. Look for stories everywhere. Somerset Maugham said that if he spent an hour with any person he would be able to write some kind of story about that person, and I would guarantee to do the same. We couldn't have done it of course in the beginning, but we learned by always looking, watching, expecting, listening for stories.

I doubt if there ever was a moment when that deep important layer of sensitive sponge just under the surface of social chat wasn't actively absorbing, sorting, selecting, rejecting, retaining impressions. Putting them away sometimes in bits and pieces, sometimes laying one out all but an end or beginning, once in a while getting one whole.

Maybe someday that good-looking young man rolling dice with such an expert hand, and quite, quite silently, will come in handy. Maybe the pretty waitress in a lunchroom down near the railroad tracks in Needles who looked as though she belonged in 21 instead will play a part. Maybe the teenage girl who looked at Gallico's Rolls-Bentley with bright dark eyes and said to the redheaded boy, "It don't look much fun to me, I'd rather have ours," will put a topper on something.

I am trying to find a way to tell you how to recognize a story.

How to know what a story is.

For I believe that is the thing most people who want to write short stories need to know and don't know.

Why?

On the whole I think it is because they are always looking for something outside themselves, something distant, something stupendous and dramatic, taking place if possible in Paris, where they have never been, or the South Seas, ditto, or having to do with something of vast significance which they know nothing about at all.

I am inclined to say here that anyone who has no story sense, who hasn't at least a few ideas and responses and reactions ought to find some other profession. When I run into a writer who isn't working because he hasn't any ideas, or is waiting for a story, I know that he isn't a real storyteller.

Plain tales are all around you. Always.

Miscellany

The vital quality to be cultivated by anyone who wants to know how to write short stories is reaction. Constant and never failing interest.

A short story is so many words of prose that deal with something happening to real people passed through the writer's imagination and viewpoint. Chekhov, probably most artistic critics' favorite short story writer, says, "Why write about a man getting into a submarine and going to the North Pole to reconcile himself to the world, while his beloved at that moment throws herself with a hysterical shriek from the belfry? All that is untrue and does not happen in real life. One must write about simple things: how Peter Semionovitch married Maria Ivanovna. That is all."

The short story is more sculpture than painting. Always chip-chip-chipping away. I will tell you one of my few trade secrets. Of course it is always better to write long and then cut and tighten, it gives you a richer product, but you must learn to cut. It hurts, too. I always cut when I am as tired as it is possible for me to get. When my eyes burn and my back aches and my typewriter chair is the rack, I find that anything I just plain can't bear to cut so it will shorten the time before I can go to bed ought to stay in. You don't need to worry about cutting too close. That never happens. Something won't let you, that's the point. But by the time you finish this last cut under those circumstances, all your fancy writing and your unnecessary (favorite) words are under the desk, in the wastebasket! Which in short story writing is where they belong.

Which brings us to instinct or invention or intuition, of which Mr. Saroyan obviously had so much.

Nobody can teach you that, or even tell you what it is or much about it. Except this:

Goethe said once that we build character in the stream of the world but talent in solitude.

After the bustle of reporting and observation and living, it is well to go into solitude. To withdraw. Into an attic, a place beside the sea, an alp, anywhere you can be alone. Where all these things that you have observed, all the people you have loved or despised or wished to drive from the temple, all you have heard, all the songs you have sung and the dances you have danced may have time to become your own. Where your mind and your soul may, in seclusion, have time to function.

If they do, then you may be a very good or even a great storyteller.

If they don't, you may still be a successful storyteller but you will always be in the second or third class.

For invention, inspiration, intuition come from the Source, which every writer knows exists. All any of us can do is be still sometimes and see if we can hear what it says to us.

I have always believed that what you say is more important than how you say it. Certainly it is better to write well than to write badly, but too often I find people worrying desperately about how to say something that isn't worth saying anyhow. I have wished more time was spent on thinking, feeling, knowing people, and less on the thought of style and construction, which has to be second at least. No amount of technique can repair an engine that isn't under the hood, and no glory of style, knack with words, or fancy writing can conceal the horrid barrenness and vacuum where sincerity, passion, and a great need and desire to tell a story that will make people laugh or cry or fight ought to be.

Anything that helps to get a short story written is permissible. Anyplace that the writer finds opens the floodgates, I don't care whether it's a tree house or a bomb shelter. Gallico thought he wrote best on top of an alp. I prefer the sound of the sea. Katharine Brush had an octagonal desk built for her by the great Joseph Urban and used to shut herself inside it and close the gate so she couldn't get out. *Write*.

Sir Gilbert Parker, Canadian author, once said to me, "As you go ahead with creative fiction, be very careful of your awakening moments in the morning. Train yourself to this. When you go to sleep at night, open your consciousness to the Source of imagination, and ask specifically for whatever you need or want in any story you are composing, or for a story itself in connection with something that has intrigued. Then, when you awaken, *do not open your eyes*. Lie quiet, with your eyes closed so that reality cannot impinge you, and very often you will find the full exposition of your story quite clear and definite in your mind."

There is about as much ham in most skillful writers as in most skillful actors. If a young or new writer doesn't have editorial help and interest as yet, he ought to try to get it someplace. A wife, husband, friends, mother, father, teacher, somebody to exchange ideas with, someone who wants to listen and cheer a bit, someone who is waiting to read a story when you finish it, someone who cares whether you ever write it or not.

Find someone who cares—who will listen—to explore an idea with if you can and maybe to read your second—or third—or whatever draft comes up that you feel anybody could read.

If there is someone to whom you can talk, it's a great help. Bounce it around. Hear yourself saying it. Try telling it instead of writing it, because you are primarily a story-teller, as the minstrels were, and while the written word is different and I have never known a good writer who dictated anything printable, the story line can be the same.

If you want to be a storyteller, start telling stories. To anybody who will listen. Or if nobody will or you are the kind who cannot talk them, go off and tell them to yourself. Tell them constantly in your head. Put them together in your own mind. Live with your characters until you can actually hold conversations with them. Your family will soon get used to it. They become part of it. Look what James Thurber did with his family. His grandfather is almost my favorite character in the whole world, and don't tell me anybody but Thurber was Grandpa just that way, either. You have to be utterly ruthless with your family.

When you start the idea of a short story, there is always a tempo to it. A feel. You have to read. Every writer reads as he breathes or eats—from necessity. Like Somerset Maugham, he carried a book bag. Or located the public library. When the short story starts and the tempo is apparent, I decide who would have written this short story best. Mrs. Wharton? Steinbeck? Ben Hecht? Sally Benson? Maugham? Runyon? Henry James? The world is wide. Once I get it figured out, I try to get that style and tempo into my ear. My insides. Try to get it to permeate that from which the story comes when I begin to write it.

If you will study great short stories, you will see that each one begins at the precise moment that gives it the best leverage, as it were. Naturally, no one even contemplates beginning a short story until the end is clear as crystal. The one sure way to crack up anything is not to know where you're going to land. I often write the last paragraph and pin it on the curtain, where I can see it. This is simple, for it has to happen in your head to make a plausible, believable story—that is part of the plotting. Nearly always, with me, part of the spontaneity.

But where to begin?

This is the superlative of technique. It is the whole matter of timing—of time and space and distance. For between that first line and the ending you must tell your story. There must be no tag ends. There must be no unanswered questions about anything that happens or any of the people it happens to. You will have no room for long, wordy explanations. No space to repair errors. The furniture has to fit in *this* room.

I do not think that more than six times in 200 stories and 50 years I have known what was going to happen between those two points—not all of it anyhow. You draw on the reservoir of your memory and your experience and your urge and desire, and often unexpected things come forth. Nobody knows better than most writers that you don't do it all. Ever. But you must tune in to the right station, you must dial the right number or what comes forth at the call won't fit. The response won't be clear and definite.

A professional writer must write often when the urge isn't hot. He will sometimes have the urge and the desire and yet they will run head on into lethargy, inertia, opposition, rebellion, and despair. This must be faced by anyone who thinks of selling enough short stories to make a living, of becoming a pro.

The most helpful words I have ever heard on this subject were said to me many years ago by Charlie Chaplin and must carry weight because of his own supreme artistry.

"You start," he said, "with spontaneity, pure spontaneity. It bubbles, it's glorious, and of course it captures people. You haven't the faintest idea how you do it. That lasts a little while. Then you begin to develop technique. You have to, for there are times when the spontaneity betrays and deserts you. You develop the technique—and the first thing you know it's all you have, the spontaneity is gone, it seems, for good. Then you must learn to combine the two. Those who can do this with both at their peak are geniuses. And on down the scale in the quality they produce. But if you intend to make a life's work of your art, your talent, you must, through self-discipline and control and balance, learn to combine spontaneity and technique."

Spontaneity is the gift of God.

Technique can be learned.

The most crucial technical approach to a short story is where you start it.

This I know.

It seems to me that laziness, inertia prevent writers from doing the proper reporting on fiction stories rather than the excuses of high-brow artistry which some of them give me. Unless you are writing *Alice in Wonderland*, or *The Wizard of Oz*, also a grown-up classic if you read it right, or *Gulliver's Travels*, you are working from life as definitely as does a painter. It's silly to pretend anything else, and if that is what is meant by the use of the word "creative," it's phony. Each writer will give a new, a more humorous, a more tragic or fantastic, a lighter or some serious interpretation of the thing seen, he will select the character of whom he wishes to paint a portrait, and obviously the grandfather of Thurber will be different from the grandfather of Chekhov, but there was a grandfather in life to begin with.

About names. Sinclair Lewis couldn't write about characters unless the names fitted them in his consciousness. He told me it took him months to find Babbitt—which became part of our language, and Arrowsmith, and Dodsworth. He told me that he got halfway through a book one time and knew it was all wrong, nothing worked, the man was of straw, not flesh and blood, and then he discovered he had the wrong name for him. This is true, I think, of every writer. I search the telephone book, Burke's Peerage, the society sections of the Sunday papers, I keep a notebook and put down names I like—not unusual ones, necessarily. The ones I find in there at the moment are Shannon, Les, Valdez, Adrienne, Chess, Miss Billings, Thea, Rance, Alix, Coralie, and Hap. They don't seem to amount to much, but they may fit somebody. I believe Red Lewis was right and that you cannot create a character properly if the name isn't right in your own mind.

A reader picks his writers as he does his friends, because he likes and is interested in them, in what they say, stand for, convey, as well as for the entertainment of the story itself. The writer does come through. Therefore it is well for the writer to learn to be himself, to be honest in his viewpoint of his story and characters.

Face the fact immediately that writing means long, hard, backbreaking hours at the typewriter or desk. Some of them hours of joy beyond description, of course. But also some of them pure unadulterated grind.

Writers stop producing in their later years only because they have lost active touch with the life it has been their occupation to report fictionally, after having passed it through the spectrum of their imagination.

I never said to write to sell. Never. I did say that is was no disgrace to use a little of the wisdom of the serpent, as Fulton Oursler used to tell me many years ago. If you are writing to put over a Cause, you will have to wrap it up and let the reader get it for himself. You will have to entertain your reader—or listener—as Jesus did when he told the parables, and the moral can't be rammed down their throats. But it is always fatal to write for the purpose of selling.

Plotting is working out what happens to your characters as you unfold the story you have to tell about them.
Plotting, we have discovered, is mostly character.
To plot is to determine how characters would react to situations and each other. Or, since we need certain reactions from them, to determine or invent or dream up the occurrences or business or sights or sounds which would produce the anger or tenderness or humor or niggardliness or jealousy that is necessary to unfold your story.

Three things go into plotting the character.
Let's call them present observation, memory, and invention or intuition. A lot of plotting takes place inside as you brood. It goes round and round and comes out *there*.

One way to make old plots new is to lay them in a new, exciting locality or industrial or professional setting. Maupassant, O. Henry, and Sherwood Anderson used many of the same situations, but they looked very, very different laid in Paris, New York, and Winesburg, Ohio, and told about the people who lived in these places.

The thing the reader gets from a short story must, in part, be what the writer sees, his own way of looking at people, his own reactions to the world. The picture he sets down in character, action, and plot is his view of life as it has passed through his mind, his imagination, and it must bear his imprint.

All the characters a short story writer draws come from living people. Anyone who is interested in short stories should get this firmly fixed in his own consciousness, remind himself of it night and morning, so that he will never fail in observing everybody he meets all the time.

Never try to get too close to the truth. Never allow yourself to tell a story exactly as it happened. It won't come off if you do. A painter makes a portrait a third larger than life to make it come out life-size. When he makes a sketch, he puts in everything. From that he eliminates, rearranges, highlights, adds or subtracts what he needs. There must always be room as you move from facts to fiction for the creative glory to do its work.

The truer to life you get the less likely people are to recognize themselves. So few of them have any idea of what they look like to others or what they actually are.

The short story writer must always be believed, what he writes must be entirely possible and probable to the reader, his characters must live so that the reader recognizes them as human beings whether he has ever happened to meet them or not.

Writing is a lonely business, in the end it has to be done alone, but the interest someone else has is a magnetic force that helps to pull the story out—it is like the light at the end of a tunnel which assures you that there is an end and that there is light.

Now this is told here to demonstrate beyond any possible doubt that there is little chance of any professional writer possessed of any honor, humor, or honesty ever getting a swelled head or falling into any trap of egotism or self-satisfaction. Humility has to pervade the very air you breathe. I remember once Marie Dressler said to me, "Life is always knocking me to my knees, but after all that's the best position in which to pray." Writing short stories is always knocking you to your knees until at last you find yourself all plowed up and broken up and humility can come in and light the prayer candle inside as well as outside.

I have said you will never, as long as you live, sell anything that isn't the best you can do. Never.
And this I believe.
To write to sell is absolute and utter defeat before you have put a word on paper.
To accept prostitution of all that is the light that makes writing is death.
Writers may write mediocre stories and sell them, but they don't do it on purpose. There are just some people who write stories like that, and editors buy them because they need them and they have some degree of sincerity shining through the thin veneer.
No story has ever failed to find a market because it was too good.
Never.
Somebody find me one!

Tips from a master

All good short stories get published.
Writing is not writing until it is read any more than an airplane is an airplane until it takes off and flies.
The heaps of yellow paper are among the things I can tell you about how to.

There are others I have learned, some of them the hard way.

1. What you have to say is always more important than how you say it.
2. Anybody can learn to write, but there are very few writers and always have been.
3. Ninety-two per cent of the elapsed time on a short story takes place before you ever put a word on paper.
4. The short story equivalent of a nose for news, the ability to know a story when you see it, is the one thing with which a writer of short stories must be born.
5. An absolute Must is the training and development of the writer's memory, which is different from any other, and unless the aspiring writer can recognize it he would be better advised to go looking for uranium direct.
6. The majority—I should say 85%—of short stories are in some degree reportorial, they are sparked by something the writer saw, heard, felt, or read.
7. Therefore it is necessary to have a nose like an anteater for everybody's business, a rubber ear that hears what people say, a spyglass that sees what's going on, a keen faculty of observation for little things, all motivated by a burning, unquenchable curiosity about people.
8. All successful short story writers are utterly ruthless about where and how they get material. Nothing can be inviolate to them. Change it around so it won't be recognized, use it to benefit mankind, but the story comes first always. Get it.
9. Read, read, read, read. Read all the short stories ever published.
10. Right now, check your own story reactions to these ideas . . . A boy's blue suit with two pairs of pants . . . A borrowed diamond necklace . . . A mechanic's afternoon off . . . An old lady whose most treasured possession is a moth-eaten fur tippet . . . A young man and woman who, as children, had the same dreams . . . A son who took his inheritance and skipped . . . A girl whose step-father kept snakes . . . The longest walk in the world . . . *If you do not within a couple of days react with some kind of a yarn about at least one of them, give up the whole idea. All of these made very, very popular and well-known short stories. Good ones, too, if one of 'em is mine.*
11. There are no new plots. There are only new people, new treatment, new reactions, new locations, new times. But it is necessary to invent a good story to tell, because a short story writer must be a storyteller.
12. A professional writer will starve if he waits for inspiration, he must learn to combine spontaneity of emotion with sound technique to make the result read like inspiration.

Summing up

I would like to sum up here the few things I have found it possible to say honestly about the technique of writing a short story. There are not many, but I believe those I do know are sound.

Spend most of your time before you start to write, in the sense of putting anything except notes down on paper.

Know your characters well. *Know* them. In the same way that Kipling made me as sure as I was at nine and still am that Mowgli was real, as sure as Mary Roberts Rinehart made Tish part of my acquaintance, or Steinbeck made me know Jody, you must know your characters before you start. Live with them. Pay no attention to what other people think of you as you blithely or gloomily inhabit a world where you converse with and watch these people you are painting from life—putting together. Live with them until one day you hear yourself laugh out loud at something one of them said to you or find you have to wipe away a real tear because one of them said to you, "It's—all over. So *quick.*" Then you can begin to plot.

Plotting, then, is working out those things which could and would happen to a particular character or characters. This is a combination of reporting, memory, and invention. But you have to do it.

Always have your ending clear from the beginning.

This most vital technical point in any short story is where you start it. Spend any amount of time needed to measure this one. In the end it will be time saved.

Stick to the point.

One minor story maybe, interwoven to prove a point. No more.

Art grows. It is a living thing. Writing must be a living thing, growing from the heart and soul of the writer. Many will never achieve it. But to produce any honest, real writing is a great career, a fine profession, a service to mankind, and a magnificent life.

So let's take up the one about your best being too good.

And then my conviction that there never is a time, never has been, never will be, when good short stories will not find publication. The only thing that could shadow this would be failure to get enough good stories.

There is one last word. Always, always, always give it everything you've got. Otherwise, it's not worth doing. Reach, and every time reach for the moon. Try with all your heart to write a great story.

66 *The short story is an 'exposition'; the novel is often and perhaps at its best an inquisition into the unknown depths of the novelist's mind.*
                                                                    Malcolm Cowley **99**

Plots and plans

by Maxine Rock

Organizing a work of fiction is one of the writer's most serious and difficult tasks. When you are seized by the joyful and urgent desire to write, it's hard to temporarily dam the gush of words until you've carved out the proper channels through which the tide must flow. But unless you discipline talent with organization, the result is a flood of thought that only confuses and irritates readers. Good fiction takes planning.

Planning also makes it easier to get words on paper; you'll be more creative if you don't have to stop every few sentences to grumble, "What comes next?" You'll already know, because your plot—call it a blueprint, map, outline, plan, or guide—will tell you.

Characters "misbehave"

Good writers are well-organized. Many of them nurse both their first and last sentences in their heads for some time before they write them down. In the meantime, they outline the great middle portion of their novels or short stories. The outline can be a general ten-page wrap-up of what the characters do, the problems they confront, and how things all work out at the end. Or it can span 50 pages or more, and include charts of action, lists of characters' traits, and detailed descriptions of environment. Usually, the more detailed the better. Unless you're a very experienced writer, you're bound to start sweating when things don't turn out as you pictured them in your mind. Ficticious characters and events have a way of twisting themselves out of your grasp, like children who

---

Maxine Rock has published more than 600 articles and stories in The New York Times, Smithsonian, Travel and Leisure *and many other publications. A longtime freelancer, she has taught writing at Georgia State University, her classes structured around her personal experiences and shared knowledge from other writers. Rock has written* Fiction Writer's Help Book *and co-authored* Gut Reactions. *She is currently working on two books.*

misbehave. Seasoned writers can accept that misbehavior with good humor, and even welcome it as Truman Capote does when he calls such misbehavior "the unexpected dividend." Capote says his novels are usually completely organized in his mind before he puts down a single word, but surprises do come along.

"I invariably have the illusion that the whole play of a story, its start, middle and finish, occurs in my mind simultaneously—that I'm seeing it in one flash. But in the working-out, the writing-out, infinite surprises happen. Thank God, because the surprise, the twist, the phrase that comes at the right moment out of nowhere, is the unexpected dividend, that joyful little push that keeps a writer going."

But you can't count on surprises to produce a well-rounded story. For that, you need organization. And organization means the careful, conscious construction of a plot. It means creating biographies for your major characters, boiling your theme down to a few succinct words, fixing your story's ambience firmly in your mind, and writing down key descriptions of place and atmosphere. Careful writers also know, well in advance, how their characters will resolve the major conflicts in the story. Very little is left to chance.

Are outlines contrived?

Some writers scoff at outlining, believing it's too contrived. Fletcher Knebel, author of *Vanished*, *Seven Days in May*, and *Crossing in Berlin*, says he often has no idea where a book is going, and likes the sudden self-surprise that comes when the story switches. "I don't know how those guys write who have everything charted out like an engineer's blueprint," he says. "What's the fun of that? It's like filling in a crossword puzzle."

Other writers claim fiction *is* a puzzle, to be pieced together bit by bit until the whole picture emerges. John Irving, author of *The World According to Garp*, says his book took four years to write, and that most of it was like pasting together "the pieces of a filmcutter's work." Historian and author Charles L. Mee, Jr., looks upon writing "as a painter works on a painting . . . You can come to the work as if it's on a canvas, start at the upper corner, or sketch some other subjects in, or rework it 10 or 15 times." Thomas Wolfe once told his agent that his novels were done in bits and pieces and resembled "the bones of some great prehistoric animal." But Wolfe was careful to assemble those bones in final form before he let an editor see his work. He organized chunks of scenes, crafted elaborate outlines, and polished and revised many times.

Subconscious planning

I suspect that authors who sneer at written outlines have a powerful subconscious. They're probably plotting and planning without even knowing it. Then, when it's time to write, the words just seem to pour out. But those words are really the end result of a deep-seated inner process of selection. If they're fussy about what they select, these subconscious planners will have less rewriting to do when they finally put things down on paper.

Careful organization and intricate written outlines usually do cut down on the task of rewriting. Some writers who say they don't outline are merely planning at the end of the first writing period, rather than at the beginning. They apparently prefer to spill the story in one or several creative bursts, then go back and rewrite until it flows smoothly. Most writers eventually wind up working both ways: planning at the start, and rewriting when the first draft is on paper. Planning provides a path to follow. Rewriting sharpens both plot and prose, and helps eliminate obvious faults in the story, such as a weak ending. You might not spot those misconstructions the first time around.

Think before you write

There might be more disagreement about how to plan and organize fiction than about any other aspect of writing. Methods vary greatly, and writers change those methods as they mature. There is no set way to think before the words go down on paper; there's just a vague, general agreement among professional writers that it must be done. A novelist who starts with carefully planned written plots may eventually decide he's better at subconscious organization. Or, a "head planner" might tire of so much cranial exercise in advance of each book and take to writing out the plot and characterization of every scene.

Beginners usually do best if they think out and write down the skeleton of stories before they put flesh on fiction. Eventually, each writer comes up with a method of outlining and organizing that best fits his own particular needs. The methods can be borrowed from other writers or invented after personal trial and error. The most important task is to develop the discipline it takes to devise *some* method of thinking before you write.

Outline characters first, says Tom Cook. Cook, who writes both literary and popular novels, says the difference between them is that literary novels embrace ideas, while popular novels run on what happens next. To do either, he says, a writer must start with a thorough outline of his main character.

"In most cases, any type of novel relies on good characterization. So I really concentrate on knowing my characters very well. While I don't normally need a written outline, the characters and settings in my fiction are very firmly set down in my mind before I start the first sentence. I know the ending of the book about halfway through. If it's what I call a literary novel, the idea goes far beyond the character. The character either embodies the idea or creates the atmosphere in which the idea develops. All this takes a lot of pre-thought. Sometimes plot changes slightly; sometimes I have to change what happens if I think the events I've planned will force my characters to do something unnatural. If I have a good mental road map, however, changes remain slight. My characters all do what I'd intended. They understand each other and are capable of drawing out the idea that each embodies."

Planning starts early, stresses Stuart Woods, who planned his second book while he was finishing his first. As he wrote the first book, Woods was on the lookout for characters or subplots he could use in the construction of a new novel.

"One reason I could even think about a second book is that my first was pretty tightly organized. To even begin, I had to hand my publisher an outline and 200 completed pages which followed that outline. I didn't always know the exact words I was going to use, but I did have quite specific ideas about what would happen in each chapter. I also wanted to let the publisher see I knew how my book would begin and end.

"My first novel is complex. A lot of things happen to a lot of different people. In one scene, a policeman is called in to stop a quarrel between a man and his wife. The man is beating his wife, and there's a new baby in the house. Later, I realized that a main character in my book number two would be that new baby.

"There it was: my first step in planning a new book. I immediately started outlining a scene in the second book which tied in with the situation in the first book. I wanted the beating to be a key factor in shaping the baby's personality—the personality of my new character. So you can see that I really do plan ahead, and very early. I've already written the last sentence of my next book. It's been in my head for years."

Pre-plan in your head, advises novelist Robert Newton Peck. He is the author of *A Day No Pigs Would Die*, *Fawn*, and *Kirk's Lane*, among others and usually turns out three or four books a year.

"I never do an outline on paper. It's all skull work beforehand. Besides, fiction is based on characters, and on what characters do. They sometimes do things you can't plan out. In fiction you have strong people who want to act. They act out of greed, mostly. It's the character, not your pre-digested plot, who determines the book.

"If your character is weak, that will sometimes give you a different ending. Often I don't know how things are going to end until I'm on the last chapter.

"The things you do think out in advance are your time frame—is it taking place in 1920, say, or 1982?—your locale, and the issues at stake. This last thing is your plot. Plot is two dogs and a bone: The bone is at stake. That's the dramatic situation. Once I've thought out my dramatic situation, I'm ready to start writing.

"Fiction needs a conflict. Somebody wants something, tries to get it, and is opposed by somebody else. If Fido has a bone and Rover wants it but Fido won't give it to him, you've got a story if Rover really goes after that bone with all he's got. You need two contestants and a prize. You need two armies and one fort, two men and one woman, two grabby corporate vice presidents and one presidential vacancy. Who will win the tussle?

"Fiction is musical chairs. The most important thing for you to plan is how to set up 19 chairs and 20 asses. Because if there are 20 chairs, nobody hustles."

Characters move; the plot follows, according to *Sharky's Machine* author Bill Diehl. He claims that if his characters are meticulously outlined in advance, it's easier to plan out the novel's plot.

"On the wall of my office is a huge white bulletin board. On that board I have headings like 'Prologue,' 'Book I,' 'Book II,' 'Subplots,' and 'Characters.' Tacked on to the head of 'Characters' is a thick sheaf of papers with each character's name, and brief paragraphs of description. I also put down who they are and what functions they perform in the book.

"First I create the character. Then I go back and fill in a biography for that character. I know how he grew up, what motivates him, if his father was an alcoholic, all the background stuff. I think readers like to know about a character's childhood and early experiences.

"I don't outline plots. I can wrap things up if my characters all stay in line. In the end it will all come together as long as I've outlined the characters in advance.

"I know what characters to use to provide drama, and which ones will provide comic relief. In *Sharky's Machine*, for example, I needed a lovable guy to help break the tension. Somebody funny. So I used my friend Larry to create a character called The Nosh. Larry, like The Nosh, knows how to do bugging and electronic stuff. I used him pretty straight, but I didn't tell him what I was going to do. I told his wife. I also told her what I didn't tell Larry: that The Nosh gets killed. So when Larry finally read the book and realized that The Nosh was him, he called me at three in the morning and he was crying! He was crying because he just came to the part where he dies! I wouldn't pick just anybody to model my characters after. I pick wonderful people: my friends. Otherwise if I picked a jerk, he might get mad and sue me.

"Oh, one more reason why I outline characters, but not plots: I want to know my characters very well, and really don't want them pulling tricks on me. But sometimes I do think of tricks, silly things to stick in the plot. I might have a crazy idea, like a bear drinking a beer in a bar, or a team of midgets playing basketball. If the idea amuses me, I put it in one of my chapters. I find a place where it will fit, and make the plot curve around and embrace the idea. I couldn't do that if everything was rigidly outlined up front.''

Outlines impress publishers, according to longtime novelist Dean R. Koontz. Koontz, the author of 50 novels, has written comedy, suspense, and science fiction.

''I write from outlines. Most of the time the outline has already been sold to a publisher. He or she wants to read a clear picture of what you have in mind. It's rare that someone sells a book idea without an outline to back it up. Your careful outline is like a pact with the publisher, a way of telling him or her that you are serious about what you're doing, and capable of carrying it through.

''My outlines are done scene by scene or chapter by chapter. First, I choose the major scenes. Then, I set them up like flagstones in a wet garden; I'm concerned with how the reader will make his way through that garden. Later I can fill in the flowers (the details) between scenes.

''I never start a book unless I know the fate of the characters: Who will die, who will marry whom. The characters remain true, even if the plot wanders. If I have a large outline I may not even use it, except the end. I *always* keep the end intact. Knowing the ending of the book reinforces the point I'm trying to make. No matter what happens, the structure is steady if I know the end.

''You might hand your publisher a 30-page outline. From that, he'll expect a manuscript of about 450 pages. Sometimes in my case only seven or eight of the original outline pages come out of the book. And about three quarters of that concerns the end.

''I also find that research is a tremendous help in organizing and outlining the book. If you get the bits and pieces of research organized before you start writing, if the background is accurate and the events chronologically correct, it will carry you right along.

Experience comes later, observes 79-year-old mystery writer Lawrence Treat. The author of 300 short stories and 20 novels, Treat started his career during the Depression, selling ''mystery puzzles,'' which were brief tales of imagined crimes. Treat supplied clues to help readers solve the mystery. It was hard to sell books in the money-tight 1930s, but Treat's puzzles did well and he went on to novels.

At first, he says, he made up elaborate charts for his books. ''That was when I didn't have too much confidence. I had vertical columns for the chapters and then across I had squares to write in what what was going on with plot, character, clues. I don't consciously do plotting any longer. I work mostly from character . . . if you do have a gimmick that's something you have to work up to.''

Work up to complicated plots, suggests Lawrence Block. His monthly columns of advice on fiction have recently been gathered into a new book, *Telling Lies for Fun and Profit*, Block's term for working up to plot events is ''foreshadowing.''

''Through skillful foreshadowing the writer prepares the reader for a sharp turn in the plot without tipping his hand altogether. The reader knows the turn is coming but doesn't know what sort of beast is lurking around the bend . . . Toward the end of *The Dead Zone*, Stephen King's novel that pits a clairvoyant against a potential despot, the plot is literally advanced by a bolt out of the blue. Johnny Smith, the prescient hero, is given the foreknowledge that a roadhouse where a graduation party is to be held will be struck by lightning. He tries to get the party canceled . . . Lightning strikes, as we know it will . . . How admirable of Stephen King to have laid the groundwork so carefully. How meticulously he must have plotted his book in advance in order to set up that business with the lightning rods (which figure greatly in the disaster) . . . ''

Be firm but flexible, advises Damon Knight. Knight believes in clear outlining and tight organization, but remains flexible enough to anticipate—and even welcome—changes in parts of the plot.

''I do outline, but the outline modifies itself as I go along. For a short story, I outline five or six scenes. For a novel, I try to have a very clear idea of structure, which is where I'm going and how I'll get there. It's also important to know the beginning and ending. The material in between does change as I write.

''I advise other writers to be flexible and leave room in your outline for such changes. Do have a clear idea of place; know the area where your action is happening. That way your descriptions will come alive and you won't have to strain for the sounds and smells and textures of the environment around the characters. And, even if parts of the plot stray from your outline, other vital elements will remain constant. It will eliminate confusion if and when changes do occur to you.''

Outlining spurs creativity, Anne Rivers Siddons believes. The writing in her novels conjures up a constant parade of sparkling images; she says that outlining a book frees her to concentrate on the creativity of words.

''I make simple charts, putting down when my characters were born, married and died. I always put in the year. The plot comes with the outline, which is a 15- or 20-page synopsis of the novel. When I have those things down, I can write more freely and feel that my energies are more creatively spent.

''Things do change as I go along. But the characters usually mature as I had orginally intended. I knew Maggie, one of my characters in *Heartbreak Hotel*, like the back of my hand.

''It's hard on a writer when things change so much that you have to revamp your outline and do a lot of revising. That happened to me when I wrote *Fox's Earth*. It took me three years to write. Then it was rewritten and cut over a five-month period. I got it down to 965 pages, then redid a pivotal character. When the character was redone, a change had to be made in every page thereafter. And when I realized that, I sat down in the middle of my room and cried for three hours! I couldn't stand the idea of all that extra work. But it was like being three quarters of the way through labor. It hurts a lot, but you can't stop.''

Organization keeps characters in line, declares Robert Stone. His novels include *A Hall of Mirrors*, which won the Faulkner Award for best first novel in 1968, and *Dog Soldiers*, which in 1974 won the National Book Award for fiction. Stone's new novel, *A Flag for Sunrise*, focuses on angry Americans participating in Central America's revolutions. Stone keeps a firm hold on his characters by sticking to an outline.

''I didn't develop early as a writer. It took me a long time to learn the trade—organization and all that—and I write very, very slowly now. My most important thing in constructing a novel is to outline my characters. I want my characters to speak for themselves. They all have a voice, a way of talking, a theme, and a way of looking at the world. As you go on, characters may surprise you. Sometimes, out of their own strength, they change the plot. But you have to stay in control, and you do it with much organization. If your characters run away with things, you lose your sense of organization. If that happens, it's probably time to take a break of about a month from writing.''

Questions help organize a novel, says Sol Stein, author and president of Stein & Day Publishing. Stein has written *The Magician*, among other novels, and subjects other authors to intensive questioning before he will accept their book proposals. He says those questions help novelists find the really important elements of their work and organize around those elements.

"On any Monday morning, some writer will have a proposal for me. It will say 'I want to write a story about a janitor who is going to explode a plastic bomb in the men's urinal in the Department of Defense . . .'

"Then I ask, 'Who is the janitor? Is he a Polish resistance fighter? Where does he live?' And the more I ask, the further away we get from the plot.

"We hone in on *character*. That's where the story is: in the character. Yet most proposals center on plot. That's the big mistake.

"Your book has to create an emotional effect on the audience. Your leading character has to want something very badly. The more important that thing is, and the more your character wants it, the better your novel will be. Unless you have this conflict—this drama—you'd don't have a novel.

"You can find the essential elements in your novel by asking yourself questions about character and drama. Don't wait for the editor to do it; it may never happen. When the answers to the questions come clear, you'll be in a better position to organize plot around character. Questions of an exploring nature should be part of any writer's planning process.''

" " *The good novelist is distinguished from the bad one chiefly by gift of choice. Choice, itself a talent, is not, however, enough. Only extreme sanity and balance of selection can give to prose fiction the dignity and excitement inherent in more rigid forms of writing: drama, poetry, and the exposition of ideas.*

—Colette " "

Rules for storytelling

by Mark Twain

The following is an abridged version of the succinct set of rules for writing by Mark Twain. In the art of storytelling, these rules are as appropriate and effective today as they were years ago when set down by the master.

The Mark Twain Rules require:

1. That a tale shall accomplish something and arrive somewhere.

2. That the episodes of a tale shall be necessary parts of the tale, and shall help develop it.

3. That the personages in a tale shall be alive, except in the case of corpses, and that always the reader shall be able to tell the corpses from the others.

4. That the personages in a tale, both dead and alive, shall exhibit a sufficient excuse for being there.

5. That when the personages of a tale deal in conversation, the talk shall sound like human talk, and be talk such as human beings would be likely to talk in the given circumstances, and have a discoverable meaning, also a discoverable purpose, and a show of relevancy, and remain in the neighborhood of the subject in hand, and be interesting to the reader, and help out the tale, and stop when the people cannot think of anything more to say.

6. That when the author describes the character of a personage in his tale, the conduct and conversation of that personage shall justify said description.

Mark Twain (Samuel Clemens) was a humorist, satirist, lecturer, critic and one of America's most beloved writers. From his childhood and riverboat experiences in Missouri and travel experiences abroad, he captured the mood and spirit of his time in such classics as Roughing It, Tom Sawyer, Life on the Mississippi, The Adventures of Huckleberry Finn, Puddn' head Wilson *and* A Connecticut Yankee in King Arthur's Court. *Many consider Mark Twain the father of American literature.*

7. That when a personage talks like an illustrated, gilt-edged, tree-calf, hand-tooled, seven-dollar Friendship's Offering in the beginning of a paragraph, he shall not talk like a Negro minstrel at the end of it.

8. That crass stupidities shall not be played upon the reader by either the author or the people in the tale.

9. That the personages of a tale shall confine themselves to possibilities and let miracles alone; or, if they venture a miracle, the author must so plausibly set it forth as to make it look possible and reasonable.

10. That the author shall make the reader feel a deep interest in the personages of his tale and in their fate; and that he shall make the reader love the good people in the tale and hate the bad ones.

11. That the characters in a tale be so clearly defined that the reader can tell beforehand what each will do in a given emergency.

In addition, the author should:

12. *Say* what he is proposing to say, not merely come near it.

13. Use the right word, not its second cousin.

14. Eschew surplusage.

15. Not omit necessary details.

16. Avoid slovenliness of form.

17. Use good grammar.

18. Employ a simple, straightforward style.

---

66   *I never quite know when I'm not writing. Sometimes my wife comes up to me at a dinner party and says, 'Dammit, Thurber. Stop writing.' She usually catches me in the middle of a paragraph.*
—*James Thurber* 99

My first novel: good news for unpublished novelists

by Candy Schulman

For the last year (or two or three), you have retreated into a room at every opportunity to stare lovingly at your typewriter. You have turned down dinner invitations and play-off tickets: You've neglected your children and forgotten to eat, until finally you have written the last scene, the very last line. You suddenly panic: *What now? Should I try to get an agent? Do I submit the book unsolicited, over the transom? And with printing costs up and conglomerates taking over publishing houses, is anybody even buying first novels these days?*

"The first novel is quite healthy today," says Bette-Lee Fox, who, as an associate editor, produces a tri-annual feature for *Library Journal* called "First Novelists." After checking with 50 major publishing houses and a few small presses, Fox concludes that at least 80 hardcover first novels were published between February and May 1982. "As far as we're able to ascertain, about 200 to 220 first novels are published a year." This estimate doesn't include paperback originals or novels published by most university and small presses.

"Publishing houses were taking a bigger chance with first novels in the last few years," says Fox. "There seemed to suddenly be a lot more first novels coming out—and they're *good*."

Yet, the number of novels published yearly continues to decline. *Publishers Weekly* estimates that 2,455 original hardcover fiction titles were published in 1978. In 1980, the number fell to 1,918, and to 1,697 in 1981. Nonetheless, publishers remain interested in new talent.

And why not? Many recent first novels have excelled—both critically and commer-

---

Candy Schulman is a Writer's Digest *correspondent in New York. She has freelanced for* The New York Times, Newsday *and other periodicals and is working on a novel of her own.*

cially. *A Separate Peace*, by John Knowles, has become a modern classic with more than five million copies in print. Other first novels of note: *The Sun Also Rises*; *Catch-22*; *Goodbye, Columbus*; *Gone With the Wind*; *Peyton Place*; *The Heart Is a Lonely Hunter*; *Valley of the Dolls*; *The Women's Room*; *The Catcher in the Rye*; *Carrie*; *Final Payments*.

Two first novels appeared on *Publishers Weekly*'s 1981 bestseller list. *The Cardinal Sins*, by Andrew M. Greeley, was # 13 on the annual list with sales of 143,000 copies. Clocking in at # 17, Bette Bao Lord's *Spring Moon* sold 121,907 copies, and continued to be a bestseller in 1982.

A 1980 first novel, *The Clan of the Cave Bear*, by Jean Auel, not only was a bestseller, but also dispels the myth that first novelists can't get agents to represent them. "I met Jean Auel at a writers conference in Oregon," says agent Jean Naggar. "I gave her my card and invited her to write me when her book was finished."

Like most agents, Naggar doesn't accept completed manuscripts; she reads queries only. And after reading the outline for *The Clan of the Cave Bear*, she asked to see the book.

"There was hardly a typo in the manuscript," says Naggar. "It required very little editing. She'd been through several drafts on her own, and it was really fine—not just in content, but also in presentation. I feel that's really important. Other than talent, Jean Auel's professionalism, hard work and research helped sell her first novel.

"I'm continuing to place first novels in both hardcover and paperback. My list ranges from literary to romances. I hear very often that you can't place first novels, but I don't find it to be true."

Robert D. Loomis, executive editor of Random House Adult Books, says: "The first novel that's good is the heart of this business. I think everybody in it has a soft, sentimental spot for those books."

Unfortunately, claims Loomis, bookstores don't feel the same way. Yet, despite the difficulty of getting first novels into bookstores, and despite declining paperback reprint sales that once provided necessary income for both writer and publisher, Random House published six first novels on their 1982 spring list—out of a total of 15.

"Any of these people could be a future Updike; that's the way one thinks," says Loomis. "I *live* for reading something that's new and exciting. *Everybody* does. First novels will always be special. We tend to treat first novels as something of a plus because it's new talent; it's exciting; it's a discovery.

"It's just out in the marketplace that it's tough," Loomis adds. "There's less of an inclination to take on a second novel at the publishing house if the first book has failed."

Says Michael V. Korda, editor-in-chief of Trade Books (and author of *Worldly Goods*): "I'm perfectly receptive to first novels coming in to Simon & Schuster, provided they're salable and readable." But whereas Random House publishes books from its "slush pile"—the stacks of unsolicited submissions—the opposite is true of Simon & Schuster. "We don't accept stuff over the transom," says Korda. "We send it back unopened."

Because of publishing policies such as Simon & Schuster's, and for other reasons, many writers claim that an agent is not only an asset, but also sometimes a necessity. *Publishers Weekly* conducted a survey of first novels that were published between September 1980 and January 1981. Out of 115 first novels, 82 had been sold by agents—a total of 71%.

"An agent can't make me *like* a novel," says Robert Loomis, "but he can put me in a frame of mind to read it receptively and positively."

There's no doubt about it: Selling a first novel can be a struggle. Persistence and patience seem to be two key elements of success. Irving Stone, who has published 27 books, couldn't sell his first book, *Lust for Life*. After 17 rejections, he began writing another book. It wasn't until after his second manuscript was published that he sold his first.

How do you sell a first novel in today's competitive market? Let's take a look at some of last year's first novelists to find out how they did it, and listen to their advice.

Moses in the published land: the selling of Edwin Moses' *One Smart Kid*

One Smart Kid, a story of growing up, takes place in the fictional town of Fox Creek, Kansas. Author Edwin Moses, an English professor at the University of Kansas, has just published his first novel—but he has written three previous ones.

"I submitted them over the transom in a frenzy of enthusiasm at having finished something," says 39-year-old Moses. "I didn't work hard at selling them. The first two are simply apprentice books; I was just out of grad school and pretty naive—I didn't know enough about writing fiction. The third novel, a mystery, has some possibilities."

Moses' mystery was submitted to three publishers and three agents. "The agents said, 'No, it doesn't work for me.' Two publishers sent apologetic notes, which I took to be relatively encouraging for over the transom."

Finally, Moses queried agent Ann Elmo, briefly describing his third novel. "I didn't hear from her for months, and I'd written her off. By the time she got back to me and asked to see it, I'd written *One Smart Kid*. I sent her a chapter of that and she agreed to take it on."

One Smart Kid was submitted to five publishers before Macmillan bought it. "The rejection letters were brief," says Moses. "They didn't make a lot of sense to me. One said it bogged down toward the end. Later, *Publishers Weekly* said it *builds up* pace.

"I think the rejection letters were mostly polite put-offs. Nothing implied there was one specific thing I should do to revise it. You're not likely to get helpful criticism until the editor is *your* editor."

An acceptance came after a year. "I'd almost given up hope of its getting published. When my agent told me, it was a total shock. When you live as far from New York as Kansas, and all you read is that first novels are essentially unmarketable, you tend, after a while, to feel pessimistic.

"It's good to get an agent who believes in your work and will persistently try to sell it. I asked my editor if I'd submitted *One Smart Kid* without an agent, would Macmillan have taken it? He assured me they would have. He personally might never have seen it, however."

Moses believes that his fourth/first novel sold because of the narrator's voice. "People tell me they like the character; they're sympathetic with him. My editor said that *appealing* characters are the most important thing in a novel. Put people in your book who are likable and identifiable."

What kept Moses going through three unpublished novels? "Every time I wrote a book, I felt: This one is definitely better; I'm learning. Writing is simply an obsession. A book demands to be written. If your main objective were money, then discouragement would be inevitable because if you don't succeed, you've done a lot of work for nothing. If you write a novel from your *heart* and it doesn't get published, at least you've created something that's of value to you."

Moses received a $6,000 advance ("modest by big-book terms, but above-average for a first novel," he says), and paperback rights have been sold to Ace Books. He has been autographing books in local Kansas bookstores. "I did better than Saul Bellow in Lawrence," he says.

Although Moses hopes to keep selling his novels, he would continue writing even if the books didn't sell. "Ultimately, the achievement itself has to be more important for you than the recognition. That's true even if you get published. Writers are ruined by taking too seriously what flattering people say about them. Inner resources are vital to whether you succeed or not. You have to say: *Appreciated or not, I did it!* It's an accomplishment. Few people could have sat down and written a whole novel."

Blair Facts: The Story of Leona Blair's *A Woman's Place*

Leona Blair's historical saga, *A Woman's Place*, spans four decades of a Jewish family's life in New York and Israel. It was sold on the basis of an outline "which left nothing to the imagination," she says.

After conducting 18 months of research, Blair wrote the outline and began telephoning agents. "They wanted to know what kind of book it was. Some said they didn't handle that kind of book. Certain agents know better where to place certain kinds of books."

For the next four months, Blair submitted her manuscript to three different agents. They agreed to represent her if she made some changes, but she found their suggestions too general. Says Blair: "Finally I found somebody who was able to tell me what was wrong." Agent Jane Berkey helped Blair get the outline ready for submission.

Blair's detailed synopsis of plot movement contained sample scenes from the book to indicate character development and drama. Berkey submitted the 75-page outline to four publishers. All wanted to buy it, and an auction ensued. Delacorte bid the highest and bought both hardcover and paperback rights.

Is an auction unusual for a first novelist? "Not one as good as Leona," says Berkey, who doesn't judge books on whether they are first novels; she looks at the *content* to decide whether she wants to market it.

"If you're writing a literary, serious social commentary novel, you'd better write *all of it*, and you'd better be good," Berkey adds. "If you're writing a big story with major mass appeal, and you're good—there's room."

An advance from Delacorte enabled Blair to quit a secretarial job and write fulltime. In the year that it took to write *A Woman's Place*, she didn't feel bound to the outline. "There were changes that took place as the writing went on. When the characters took on lives of their own, they began to do things that I hadn't foreseen in the outline."

She submitted the book in parts and waited for editorial comments before continuing. "It's easier to sew it right the first time than to rip seams."

Her editor advised: "Use events to move the story along." Says Blair: "If I was going to use world events, they had to relate to my story. You can't include history just because it's interesting."

She believes she sold her first novel because "those sample chapters made people cry. It made *me* cry when I wrote them. Whatever you're writing, as long as you *really mean it*, you're on your way to something that will move people. Get right down to the bottom of what you're writing. Don't skim the surface. You already know it in your head, and the one thing you have to remember all the time is that your reader doesn't. You have to be careful that what is absolutely essential gets on the page."

She encourages first novelists to get an agent. "There's no harm in submitting to an agent. What if the agent says, 'This isn't the sort of book we can place'? Go on to another agent, and another.'' Having an agent gave Blair one less problem to worry about. "You have to worry about so many other things—if your facts are right, doing research, getting the quiet time to know how you're going to get from A to B in a novel."

A Woman's Place was chosen as alternate selections for The Literary Guild and Doubleday book clubs. Blair went on a national tour to promote the book. The publication of her first novel, says Blair, "has just confirmed that I'm *probably* a writer"—she giggles—"and that's how I want to spend the rest of my life. I don't want to do anything else but write books."

Small business administration: the selling of David Small's *Almost Famous*

"Writing a novel is like holding down two jobs," says 45-year-old David Small, associate executive vice-president of Pennsylvania Medical Society in Camp Hill, Pennsylvania. "I got into the habit of writing from 9 to 11 in the evenings because my son went to bed. The house was quiet, and I had time to myself."

Five years of work went into *Almost Famous* ("I've written a lot of this book on airplanes and in motel rooms while away on business"), followed by a year of submissions and a year of rewriting *on speculation* before Norton offered a contract.

When Small mailed the manuscript to publishing houses, he would wait six to eight weeks for a response. "I reminded one editor of a nice letter he'd written on an earlier novel's submission. The editor said that they had limited resources, and that this book didn't fit in—but that didn't mean it wasn't publishable.

"When I was in Boston on business, I went to publishing houses with my manuscript. I talked to a few people on the telephone in reception rooms. They said, 'Leave the book and we'll get back to you.' Once a security guard took the manuscript from me.

"I went to a writers conference in Maine and met John Cole [author of nonfiction books, including *Striper*]. I had my manuscript with me. Cole took it to his editor. I got my book read seriously. It didn't result in the book's being published, but I've kept up a line of correspondence with that editor. It's a name in my file. It's part of my business to know the people in my business.

"Make yourself available. Show up at writers conferences. I used to haunt a local bookstore here in town. The owner gave my book to one of the book representatives. He liked it and gave it to the people in his editorial department. They rejected it, but I got a couple of names out of it. Try to establish contacts, as in any line of business.

"It's amazing how many contacts you can rake up if you just quiz the people around you. I think you have to exploit whatever points of entry you can—whether it's a book representative that sells to your local bookstores, or a secretary in a publisher's office. It's necessary to get somebody on the inside to run a little interference for you because of this tremendous, mountainous blur of manuscripts that descends on these people. Somebody has to say, 'Hey, this one over here looks pretty good.'

"Use whatever informal method possible. If you went to college, you might uncover a professor you had a good rapport with who's a published writer." After six rejections, Small showed his novel to a Franklin-and-Marshall professor Small had never lost touch with. The professor showed it to a friend at Norton. Two months later, they "expressed cautious interest."

"They said it was good, but it had problems. I had a double narrator—one voice was a modified stream of consciousness—and they said it made too great a demand on the reader. An editor offered to work with me without any guarantees. I had the difficult decision to go along with their advice or peddle my papers elsewhere. The fact that *any-one* was willing to work with me represented progress. What did I have before? Rejection slips. So I took my chances.

"I spent a year trying to convince them that using the two narratives was correct. The editor said, 'No soap.' I was a year older and no further ahead. I decided to rewrite again, using one voice. At that time, they bought it.

"Compulsiveness kept me going. I didn't have any choice; I *have* to write. People who succeed can take a hell of a lot of punishment; they can absorb repeated failure. 'Sorry, we didn't like the book; it's no good.' . . . You get 10, 15, 20, maybe 25 rejections and you hang in there. People who fail take that two, three, maybe four times and quit; they've had enough.

"If you've been hungry for years to achieve something in the field of writing, during that time of no recognition or publication, *you're the only one* who believes in yourself. You must keep that belief of yourself."

The only one: the story of John Katzenbach's *In the Heat of the Summer*

"I knew a few pivotal scenes and how the book would begin and end," says John Katzenbach of the time when he began writing his thriller, *In the Heat of the Summer*. Finishing the book was difficult. "All your fears get opened at the end. You have to worry about other people reading it and wonder whether it's worthwhile, well written, well conceived."

After nine months of writing (an average of 15 to 20 pages a week), and his wife yelling, "Finish already!", Katzenbach, a 31-year-old criminal-court reporter for the *Miami Herald*, produced a completed manuscript—and left it sitting on his desk for two more weeks, "to let it age like wine, I guess."

Before Atheneum bought the book for "less than a $10,000 advance," Katzenbach experienced the usual series of rejections. "It's the most intense experience. People in New York are reviewing this *thing* that is of absolutely cataclysmic importance to your life—in which you've invested not only your time and money, but also so much of your sense of who you are. Faceless people *up there* are cavalierly deciding whether to publish it or not. It's agonizing.

"Only one or two houses said, 'Why are you sending us this piece of junk?' One house said, 'It was a terrific read, but we're not going to publish it.' Another said, 'We wish the house that accepts it all the luck in the world.' How do you figure out the logic in all that?

"Many publishers fudge over reasons why the book is turned down. It's subjective—not specific, like, 'Your punctuation is bad.' When you get what doesn't sound like a form letter, take it as reasonable encouragement.

"You simply have to persist. If one house turns it down . . . 10 houses . . . 20 . . . that doesn't mean the 21st won't take it and turn it into a bestseller. Don't ever despair! Keep trying. Selling a book is getting the *right* editor at the *right* mood at the *right* house and handing him the *right* manuscript. An agent knows which editor to send the manuscript to. Without an agent, there's no coordination; you have no idea who's reading your book. It's hard for a first novelist nowadays—not impossible—and if you try to do it without an agent, you're increasing the difficulty."

William Reiss, Katzenbach's agent, didn't find any negative reactions from publishers to first novelists. "In some ways, a first novel has more possibilities than an author who has published before without an impressive track record—which can have a negative effect on publishers. With a first novel, publishers think, 'Anything can happen.' "

Although this is the first novel that Katzenbach has submitted, he worked on two previous ones, including a coming-of-age novel written in college. "It's terrible," he says. He claims the book is locked up, but he might pull a few scenes out of it for future use.

One of his creative writing teachers was Mary Lee Settle. He recalls her advice: "Any book is a collection of important moments. You have to make the mass of writing *between* the important moments as good as possible." Katzenbach adds, "You know the nature of the conflict, but creating the atmosphere where that scene works is what makes or breaks a book." Katzenbach believes that writing teachers "pounded a few lessons into my head," not the least of which was learning to spell correctly.

His goal was to write an exciting book that was also serious. "You can inspire readers intellectually, but it's important for a writer to remember that you have to *entertain* the reader." He didn't deliberately study other thrillers in preparation for writing *In the Heat of the Summer*. "I read a lot. If you want to become a successful writer, it helps to read widely—from the most elegant books to basic page-turners."

When it comes to selling a first novel, "The only way to succeed is through persistence. It's the faint of heart who fall by the wayside in publishing. You have to be prepared to take a lot of body slams because it's hard to be rejected. Even when you get a rejection telling you 'This is wonderful, but . . .', it makes you feel crummy."

Katzenbach's determination and persistence has led to a $250,000 paperback sale, as well as a movie offer. He now must struggle to remember how frustrated he had felt during his novel's submissions. Still, he says, "I wouldn't trade it for anything."

Tiersten on the telephone: the selling of Irene Tiersten's *One Big Happy Family*

"I've been writing since I was ten; I've grown very patient," says 42-year-old Irene Tiersten of Maplewood, New Jersey. And patient she was—through six unpublished novels.

"I was learning—not only to write novels, but also how to get them out in the world. I have an enormous collection of positive rejection slips; they said, 'very talented . . . perceptive . . . good ear for dialogue . . . we like it, but we can't put this on our list because it won't sell.' "

Many of these novels, Tiersten believes, were experimental. Dell called one "skeletal," saying that it was more an outline than a novel. "I was playing in an esoteric fashion in terms of style," says Tiersten. "They might have sold 23 copies; no one would publish it—except *maybe* a small press."

Meanwhile, Tiersten published short stories in literary magazines and small press anthologies. After The Women's Press included her story, "Nina," in their anthology, *Love Stories By New Women*, Tiersten sent her short story collection, *Among Friends*, to the editor. The editor rejected it, but gave Tiersten a list of other editors to send it to, along with permission to use her name.

Tiersten sent the collection to Atlantic Monthly Press. "It was rejected because short stories weren't selling." Next she sent it to Hope Dellon at St. Martin's Press. After two months, Tiersten courageously telephoned Dellon.

"Her assistant said she was going to read it. I waited another month and called again. I said, 'I hope I'm not being a pest, but has she read my manuscript?' Her assistant said, 'Please have patience.' So I hung in a little more."

The next time Tiersten called, Dellon answered the phone, "which astonished me. She said, 'I'll read it and get back to you.' She called three days later."

Dellon wanted to buy the short story collection, but she thought it would make commercial sense to publish a novel first. When she asked Tiersten if she had a novel, Tiersten replied, "I've got seven or eight of them."

She showed Dellon a first draft of *One Big Happy Family*, a contemporary novel about divorce and remarriage. St. Martin's offered a two-book contract: the novel to be published first, the stories second. Attorney Neal Gantcher, who often represents writers, negotiated the contract and obtained an advance of $7,000 total for both books.

Had she called Dellon earlier, Tiersten thinks, a decision would have come sooner. "Every editor's room is filled with manuscripts. If you're pleasant, calling won't make them *not* read your book. Don't be afraid to call. You're a writer, and editors are looking for books to publish."

Tiersten speculates that *One Big Happy Family* sold because "it was timely in a sense that it deals with families that have split up and been recombined. And it's more commercial than my other ones were."

Tiersten showed Dellon a previous novel that she had never submitted. Dellon thought it was "too slight." Rather than reshaping old novels, Tiersten is going forward. A new novel has been submitted to Dellon, and Tiersten is working on another.

Before she had an editor to work with, Tiersten found attending writing courses and joining writing groups helpful. "The best forum for learning is to sit down with others who are writing."

She has submitted novels herself, and has submitted others through a literary agent or lawyer. She believes that her manuscripts got read just as seriously with or without an agent. "My editor told me she read my manuscript because another editor had recommended it. Put a reference in with your submission, if you have one. Then the book goes into a different pile. I learned from working in a law office that the squeaky wheels get the grease.

"Separate yourself when sending out manuscripts. Be your own secretary. When a manuscript comes back, get used to it. Just consider that your job. Take another envelope and address it to another publishing house, write another cover letter, and send it out again. If an editor rejects your book but recommends you send it somewhere else, put that in a cover letter. Develop some kind of résumé and list your previous publications, if you've won any prizes or awards, if you've gone to writers conferences. Include this with your submission. Then telephone and follow through after a month."

Line by line: the story of Alice McDermott's *A Bigamist's Daughter*

The very first publisher that a novel is submitted to buys it within a month. Sound like a fantasy? It happened to Alice McDermott's first novel.

"A writer I studied with at the University of New Hampshire said I'd need an agent," says McDermott. "He gave me an agent's name. I sent her some short stories—one published, two new ones—and 50 pages of my novel. She said: 'I love your writing. Bring me everything you've got.' "

McDermott, a 29-year-old New Yorker, gave Harriet Wasserman, her new agent, another 50 pages of the novel. Wasserman suggested submitting the first 100 pages of *A Bigamist's Daughter*. "I'd never heard of a first novel being sold without being completed," says McDermott. "I thought Harriet would get some nice letters that said, 'Keep going; when it's finished we'll look at it.' "

Wasserman submitted the first 100 pages to Jonathan Galassi, a Houghton Mifflin editor that she thought worked well with first novelists. Galassi asked McDermott to meet him. "He asked what the book was going to be about. I put it in a letter so he could present it to the editorial board."

A week later, Houghton Mifflin bought the book for $12,500—which would be paid in three installments. McDermott continued writing. In the interim, her editor left Houghton Mifflin for Random House. McDermott went with him, since the book wasn't yet in production. Random House repaid the advance to Houghton Mifflin.

McDermott submitted another 100 pages. Her editor simply said, "You're doing fine." She recalls: "When I had a beginning and an end, and I wasn't happy with parts of it, *then* we talked. I knew something was wrong toward the end, but I couldn't put my finger on it."

Her editor asked questions like: Do you like this character? Do you dislike this scene? What is the book doing that you don't want it to do? "He didn't say, 'Put a scene in here,' or 'Kill somebody off.' It was subtle. He helped me to realize what *I* wanted the book to be about—which is an art.

"Later, when I was happy with the book as a whole, he went over it line by line. He'd mark a sentence and say, 'Is this as good as it can be?' I didn't feel there were bigger and better authors who needed his time if I wanted advice or explanations."

Although success came quickly for McDermott's first novel, she understands the nature of rejection from marketing her short stories. Now she advises other writers to keep the writing and publishing processes separate.

"It's dangerous for writers to be concerned with what's selling, or what publishers want. Publishers want *good books*. They need new writers because sooner or later they'll run out of *old* writers.

"You can't write your first novel with the idea: 'Can I sell this? Is it a good topic?' Give your energy and concern to the work; make it the best you can do. When the writing is finished, *then* think about marketing and getting an agent. If the book is as good as it can be, you'll be a good salesperson.

"A lot of it is being in the right place at the right time. It's not as impossible as it seems. A good book can eventually find a publisher. You can't say, 'If this book is rejected, I'm throwing it out.' If I get a bad review, that doesn't mean I'm a bad writer."

Submitting a partial manuscript made it harder for McDermott to give up during those "bleak days when it wasn't going well. It was helpful to know somebody liked the first 100 pages; it kept me going." Both her editor and agent were receptive to seeing a partial manuscript. McDermott thinks she was able to submit the book that way because she wrote chronologically.

"The best thing to do when you're discouraged is to read something really fine and say, 'Quality wins out.' Or read something really bad and say, 'I can write better than that.'"

The butler did it: the selling of Robert Olen Butler's *The Alleys of Eden*

Robert Olen Butler submitted his first novel in 1974. No one bought it—or his second or third. Seven years later, *The Alleys of Eden*—his fourth of six unpublished novels—went to press.

The first three novels were "well traveled," says Butler, age 36, "drawing absolutely glorious rejection letters." One editor compared him to Hemingway and wrote: "I shan't be surprised if a distinguished and successful career lies ahead of Butler."

In the three and a half years it took to sell *Alleys*, editors "spoke in glowing terms about the writing, characters and drama." Publishers seemed concerned, however, about the "marketability" of a novel about an American Army deserter and a Saigon prostitute.

An agent submitted *Alleys* to 12 publishers, but did not continue because "she was fundamentally a dramatic agent and she decided to concentrate more on plays than novels." Butler then sold the book himself to Methuen. "The book went into galleys and was two months from publication date. On Halloween 1980, Methuen gave me a call and said they were canceling their spring list and getting out of trade book publishing. The book was orphaned again."

A new agent submitted *Alleys* to eight more publishers before he and Butler parted company "because of artistic differences and the kind of relationship we'd have over my future work. I didn't want to have to try to write for my agent." Afterwards, Butler submitted the book to Horizon Press—which bought it.

"Ultimately I found the right man at the right publishing house. Ben Raeburn is a brilliant editor. He's willing to support my career while I'm establishing myself. I'm a serious, yet prolific, writer. Horizon Press is ideal; they're in there for the long haul with me. They'll publish my books as fast as I can turn them out. I'll be back every year with one. They'll get progressively better and develop a following. Many major houses aren't prepared to do that anymore."

John Irving, Butler points out, published three novels before his bestseller, *Garp*. Joyce Carol Oates developed a wide readership by publishing with Vanguard, a small house. "Once she found her audience, it didn't make any difference. The publishing house is just a stamp on the binding. The *editor* is crucial."

Was Horizon Press different from a larger house? "I'm sure I got a lot more personal attention there." And it took only 14 weeks to publish *Alleys*. Butler's second published novel (his seventh book) was released in September.

"Since *Alleys* came out and got such glorious reviews, a number of publishers and agents have sought me out. I've gently deflected the publishers. As soon as I tell the agents I'm going to let Raeburn continue to publish my books, they say, 'If you change your mind, let me know.' The agents won't touch me because I'm with a small house. They say, 'If you're staying with Horizon, you're tying my hands; I can't do anything for you.'

"The agent's prime negotiating function is to find a hardcover publisher. He wants to take you someplace with more prestige. He wants a bigger advance and would make the argument that a larger house could get me into more bookstores. I think Horizon's done a good job in getting my books out. The rest of those publishers were either blind or gutless for years, and I'm not interested in leaving Raeburn—who had courage and insight—because I suddenly have some clout."

Butler believes that faith kept him going through years of rejection, "both a faith in my ability to express my vision of things, and a religious faith."

He advises others to "keep writing. Keep your focus on the thing you're writing *now*, rather than the one out there getting rejected. Every rejection letter suggests there is something *wrong* with the book; that's what hurts an unpublished writer. I had 21 such letters. Once a publisher published it, however, I had 20 rave reviews. We've sold the paperback rights to Ballantine. We have serious movie interest. Twenty professional reviewers loved the book, whereas 20 professional editors *didn't*. Wonderful things can be totally overlooked.

"You should be objective: see flaws and fix them. But don't overlook the fact that rejection doesn't necessarily mean there's anything wrong with what you've written. There are many reasons for rejection that don't have anything to do with the quality of your work.''

Butler divides his time between a wife and son in Sea Cliff, New York, and a full-time job as editor-in-chief of a weekly business newspaper, *Energy User News*. He does most of his novel writing on the Long Island Railroad. "It's not easy. The psychologists call it 'functional fixedness.' If you have a certain place, desk or object that you associate with a specific task, then automatically it aids you in getting your concentration going." He estimates that the writing of *The Alleys of Eden* took 180 train rides.

Goldman in them thar hills: the story of Laurel Goldman's *Sounding the Territory*

After graduating from Indiana University, Laurel Goldman wanted to work in the radio and television industry. "I went around with some scripts and thought I'd waltz into a writing job. I was handed forms: 'Can you type?' So I learned typing and speedwriting. Then I got my first job, as a Gal Friday.''

Several nonwriting jobs later, Goldman moved to Durham, North Carolina, and started a novel. That was ten years ago. Now Alfred A. Knopf has published *Sounding the Territory*.

"If I compressed the time, the book was four years of work. My editor said it was fairly typical for a first novel. I'm a slow writer. But I wrote faster in the second and third parts of the book; I knew what I was doing then.

"I don't have the temperament to work 9-to-5 and come home to work on a book. I saved money and quit my job when I really *had* something. Living here is not terribly expensive. I ran out of money after a year and borrowed from family and friends. It was tense knowing you owe people money and living so marginally. Most of my advance [$7,500] went to pay back people who'd loaned me money. I don't recommend my path, but I can't say I regret it.''

Goldman traveled to New York expressly to find an agent. "It wasn't necessary, but it may have speeded things up because I could bring a copy of the manuscript over right after I talked to an agent; I didn't have to put it in the mail. It helps to be on the spot. It indicated how earnest I was, how much I wanted this to happen. I can remember sitting in front of the phone for ten minutes and breaking into a sweat before *calling* an agent.

"The first agent turned me down and said it wasn't commercial. The second said it wasn't his kind of book—but that I really had something and shouldn't be discouraged." Then Goldman submitted her book simultaneously to three agents, one of whom, Melanie Jackson, got in touch with Goldman to express interest in representing her.

"I can't imagine how much more difficult it would have been without an agent. A good agent knows what house is likely to be interested in your kind of manuscript. She can zero in on who's going to like your manuscript *within* a house. *I* don't know what house publishes what kind of material, and I certainly don't know what *editors* would like my material. With an agent, you have the emotional feeling that somebody out in that big world you really don't know is working for you. There's somebody to say, 'We sent the book to this house and they're not interested—but don't feel bad; that always happens.' ''

If Goldman hadn't found an agent, she would have submitted over the transom. "It's not a totally discouraging picture. The feeling I got everywhere, from agents and publishers, is that manuscripts really get read. An agent makes it a much faster process.''

She urges other writers not to take rejections personally. "I had people who loved my book—and others who thought it was *nothing*. You can't go into a decline every time somebody says he doesn't want your book. You may go through 10, 20 publishers; it may be a long process. It's important to have support people . . . an agent, family, friends . . . somebody out there to say, 'Hey, don't take it so hard,' because selling a novel is *tough*. You feel like you're out on a limb. Publishers can say, 'Yuk! This is terrible!', and that's hard to take.

"I hear people talk about the publishing industry—it's crass, commercial, nobody cares—and my experience has been how interested people are in getting out a good book; how much they care about supporting writers. I don't feel that you get lost in the shuffle. My experience hasn't been cold and heartless at all."

Goldman and her editor worked together on the book—mostly through the mail, once in New York. "I tend to overwrite," she says. Her advice for others with the same affliction: "Keep going over and over it. When you think there's absolutely nothing more you can take out, there almost certainly is. Cutting makes the good parts stand out.

"My story is an encouraging one. I didn't have a mentor or a well-known writer backing me. I just sat down and *did* it—which, of course, is what any writer does. But people do sell books. Everybody tells you how tough the odds are—and they *are*—but it doesn't mean you won't be one of them. Publishers care about finding new writers, new talent. Who's to say you're not going to be one of them?"

John Cheever, author of *Oh What A Paradise It Seems*, published by Knopf.

John Cheever

Interview by Annette Grant

Note: The following interview was conducted on two separate occasions several years prior to John Cheever's death in 1982.

The first meeting with John Cheever took place in the spring of 1969, just after his novel Bullet Park *was published. Normally, Cheever leaves the country when a new book is released, but this time he had not, and as a result many interviewers on the East Coast were making their way to Ossining, New York, where the master storyteller offered them the pleasures of a day in the country—but very little conversation about his book or the art of writing.*

Cheever has a reputation for being a difficult interviewee. He does not pay attention to reviews, never rereads his books or stories once published, and is often vague about their details. He dislikes talking about his work (especially into ''one of those machines'') because he prefers not to look where he has been, but where he's going.

For the interview Cheever was wearing a faded blue shirt and khakis. Everything about him was casual and easy, as though we were already old friends. The Cheevers live in a house built in 1799, so a tour of buildings and grounds was obligatory. Soon we were settled in a sunny second floor study where we discussed his dislike of window curtains, a highway construction near Ossining that he was trying to stop, traveling in Italy, a story he was drafting about a man who lost his car keys at a nude theater performance, Hollywood, gardeners and cooks, cocktail parties, Greenwich Village in the '30s, television reception, and a number of other writers named John (especially John Updike, who is a friend).

Although Cheever talked freely about himself, he changed the subject when the con-

---

Annette Grant has worked for The New York Times *as the editor of the Living section, the deputy style editor and editor of the Weekend section, her current title. Her former positions included magazine staff work on* Mademoiselle, Newsweek *and* Seventeen.

*versation turned to his work. Aren't you bored with all this talk? Would you like a drink?
Perhaps lunch is ready, I'll just go downstairs and check. A walk in the woods, and maybe a swim afterwards? Or would you rather drive to town and see my office? Do you play
backgammon? Do you watch much television?*

*During the course of several visits we did in fact mostly eat, drink, walk, swim, play
backgammon, or watch television. Cheever did not invite me to cut any wood with his
chain saw, an activity to which he is rumored to be addicted. On the day of the last tap-
ing, we spent an afternoon watching the New York Mets win the World Series from the
Baltimore Orioles, at the end of which the fans at Shea Stadium tore up plots of turf for
souvenirs. "Isn't that amazing," he said repeatedly, referring both to the Mets and their
fans.*

*Afterward we walked in the woods, and as we circled back to the house, Cheever
said, "Go ahead and pack your gear, I'll be along in a minute to drive you to the station" . . . upon which he stepped out of his clothes and jumped with a loud splash into a
pond, doubtless cleansing himself with his skinny-dip from one more interview.*

Grant: I was reading the confessions of a novelist on writing novels: "If you want to be
true to reality, start lying about it." What do you think?

Cheever: Rubbish. For one thing the words "truth" and "reality" have no meaning at
all unless they are fixed in a comprehensible frame of reference. There are no stubborn
truths. As for lying, it seems to me that falsehood is a critical element in fiction. Part of
the thrill of being told a story is the chance of being hoodwinked or taken. Nabokov is a
master at this. The telling of lies is a sort of sleight of hand that displays our deepest feelings about life.

Grant: Can you give an example of a preposterous lie that tells a great deal about life?

Cheever: Indeed. The vows of holy matrimony.

Grant: What about verisimilitude and reality?

Cheever: Verisimilitude is, by my lights, a technique one exploits in order to assure the
reader of the truthfulness of what he's being told. If he truly believes he is standing on a
rug, you can pull it out from under him. Of course, verisimilitude is also a lie. What I've
always wanted of verisimilitude is probability, which is very much the way I live. This
table seems real, the fruit basket belonged to my grandmother, but a madwoman could
come in the door any moment.

Grant: How do you feel about parting with books when you finish them?

Cheever: I usually have a sense of clinical fatigue after finishing a book. When my first
novel, *The Wapshot Chronicle*, was finished, I was very happy about it. We left for Europe and remained there, so I didn't see the reviews and wouldn't know of Maxwell
Geismar's disapproval for nearly ten years. *The Wapshot Scandal* was very different. I
never much liked the book, and when it was done I was in a bad way. I wanted to burn the
book. I'd wake up in the night and I would hear Hemingway's voice—I've never actually
heard Hemingway's voice, but it was conspicuously his—saying, "This is the small agony. The great agony comes later." I'd get up and sit on the edge of the bathtub and
chain-smoke until three or four in the morning. I once swore to the dark powers outside
the window that I would never, *never* again try to be better than Irving Wallace. It wasn't
so bad after *Bullet Park*, where I'd done precisely what I wanted: a cast of three characters, a simple and resonant prose style, and a scene where a man saves his beloved son
from death by fire. The manuscript was received enthusiastically everywhere, but when
Benjamin DeMott dumped on it in the *Times*, everybody picked up their marbles and ran
home. I ruined my left leg in a skiing accident and ended up so broke that I took out working papers for my youngest son. It was simply a question of journalistic bad luck and an

overestimation of my powers. However, when you finish a book, whatever its reception, there is some dislodgement of the imagination. I wouldn't say derangement. But finishing a novel, assuming it's something you want to do and that you take very seriously, is invariably something of a psychological shock.

Grant: How long does it take the psychological shock to wear off? Is there any treatment?

Cheever: I don't quite know what you mean by treatment. To diminish shock I throw high dice, get sauced, go to Egypt, scythe a field, screw. Dive into a cold pool.

Grant: Do characters take on identities of their own? Do they ever become so unmanageable that you have to drop them from the work?

Cheever: The legend that characters run away from their authors—taking up drugs, having sex operations, and becoming president—implies that the writer is a fool with no knowledge or mastery of his craft. This is absurd. Of course, any estimable exercise of the imagination draws upon such a complex richness of memory that it truly enjoys the expansiveness—the surprising turns, the response to light and darkness—of any living thing. But the idea of authors running around helplessly behind their cretinous inventions is contemptible.

Grant: Must the novelist remain the critic as well?

Cheever: I don't have any critical vocabulary and very little critical acumen, and this is, I think, one of the reasons I'm always evasive with interviewers. My critical grasp of literature is largely at a practical level. I use what I love, and this can be anything. Cavalcanti, Dante, Frost, anybody. My library is terribly disordered and disorganized; I tear out what I want. I don't think that a writer has any responsibility to view literature as a continuous process. I believe that very little of literature is immortal. I've known books in my lifetime to serve beautifully, and then to lose their usefulness, perhaps briefly.

Grant: How do you "use" these books . . . and what is it that makes them lose their "usefulness"?

Cheever: My sense of "using" a book is the excitement of finding myself at the receiving end of our most intimate and acute means of communication. These infatuations are sometimes passing.

Grant: Assuming a lack of critical vocabulary, how, then, without a long formal education, do you explain your considerable learning?

Cheever: I am not erudite. I do not regret this lack of discipline, but I do admire erudition in my colleagues. Of course, I am not uninformed. That can be accounted for by the fact that I was raised in the tag end of cultural New England. Everybody in the family was painting and writing and singing and especially reading, which was a fairly common and accepted means of communication in New England at the turn of the decade. My mother claimed to have read *Middlemarch* 13 times; I daresay she didn't. It would take a lifetime.

Grant: Isn't there someone in *The Wapshot Chronicle* who has done it?

Cheever: Yes, Honora . . . or I don't remember who it is . . . claims to have read it 13 times. My mother used to leave *Middlemarch* out in the garden and it got rained on. Most of it is in the novel; it's true.

Grant: One almost has a feeling of eavesdropping on your family in that book.

Cheever: The *Chronicle* was not published (and this was a consideration) until after my mother's death. An aunt (who does not appear in the book) said, "I would never speak to him again if I didn't know him to be a split personality."

Grant: Do friends or family often think they appear in your books?

Cheever: Only (and I think everyone feels this way) in a discreditable sense. If you put anyone in with a hearing aid, then they assume that you have described them . . . although the character may be from another country and in an altogether different role. If you put people in as infirm or clumsy or in some way imperfect, then they readily associate. But if you put them in as beauties, they never associate. People are always ready to accuse rather than to celebrate themselves, especially people who read fiction. I don't know what the association is. I've had instances when a woman will cross a large social floor and say, "Why did you write that story about me?" And I try to figure out what story I've written. Well, ten stories back apparently I mentioned someone with red eyes; she noticed that she had bloodshot eyes that day and so she assumed that I'd nailed her.

Grant: They feel indignant, that you have no right to live their lives?

Cheever: It would be nicer if they thought of the creative aspect of writing. I don't like to see people who feel that they've been maligned when this was not anyone's intention. Of course, some young writers try to be libelous. And some old writers, too. Libel is, of course, a vast source of energy. But these are not the pure energies of fiction, but simply the libelousness of a child. The sort of thing one gets in freshman themes. Libel is not one of my energies.

Grant: Do you think narcissism is a necessary quality of fiction?

Cheever: That's an interesting question. By narcissism we mean, of course, clinical self-love, an embittered girl, the wrath of Nemesis, and the rest of eternity as a leggy plant. Who wants that? We do love ourselves from time to time; no more, I think than most men.

Grant: What about megalomania?

Cheever: I think writers are inclined to be intensely egocentric. Good writers are often excellent at a hundred other things, but writing promises a greater latitude for the ego. My dear friend Yevtushenko has, I claim, an ego that can crack crystal at a distance of 20 feet; but I know a crooked investment banker who can do better.

Grant: Do you think that your inner screen of imagination, the way you project characters, is in any way influenced by film?

Cheever: Writers of my generation and those who were raised with films have become sophisticated about these vastly different mediums and know what is best for the camera and best for the writer. One learns to skip the crowd scene, the portentous door, the banal irony of zooming into the beauty's crow's-feet. The difference in these crafts is, I think, clearly understood, and as a result no good film comes from an adaptation of a good novel. I would love to write an original screenplay if I found a sympathetic director. Years ago René Clair was going to film some of my stories, but as soon as the front office heard about this, they took away all the money.

Grant: What do you think of working in Hollywood?

Cheever: Southern California always smells very much like a summer night . . . which to me means the end of sailing, the end of games, but it isn't that at all. It simply doesn't correspond to my experience. I'm very much concerned with trees . . . with the nativity of trees, and when you find yourself in a place where all trees are transplanted and have no history, I find it disconcerting.

I went to Hollywood to make money. It's very simple. The people are friendly and the food is good, but I've never been happy there, perhaps because I only went there to pick up a check. I do have the deepest respect for a dozen or so directors whose affairs are centered there and who, in spite of the overwhelming problems of financing films, continue to turn out brilliant and original films. But my principal feeling about Hollywood is suicide. If I could get out of bed and into the shower, I was all right. Since I never paid the bills, I'd reach for the phone and order the most elaborate breakfast I could think of, and then I'd try to make it to the shower before I hanged myself. This is no reflection on Hollywood, but it's just that I seemed to have a suicide complex there. I don't like the freeways, for one thing. Also, the pools are too hot . . . 85 degrees, and when I was last there, in late January, in the stores they were selling yarmulkes for dogs—my God! I went to a dinner and across the room a woman lost her balance and fell down. Her husband shouted over to her, "When I told you to bring your crutches, you wouldn't listen to me." That line couldn't be better!

Grant: What about another community—the academic? It provides so much of the critical work . . . with such an excessive necessity to categorize and label.

Cheever: The vast academic world exists like everything else, on what it can produce that will secure an income. So we have papers on fiction, but they come out of what is largely an industry. In no way does it help those who write fiction or those who love to read fiction. The whole business is a subsidiary undertaking, like extracting useful chemicals from smoke. Did I tell you about the review of *Bullet Park* in *Ramparts*? It said I missed greatness by having left St. Boltophs. Had I stayed, as Faulkner did in Oxford, I would have probably been as great as Faulkner. But I made the mistake of leaving this place, which, of course, never existed at all. It was so odd to be told to go back to a place that was a complete fiction.

Grant: I suppose they meant Quincy.

Cheever: Yes, which it wasn't. But I was very sad when I read it. I understood what they were trying to say. It's like being told to go back to a tree that one spent 14 years living in.

Grant: Who are the people that you imagine or hope read your books?

Cheever: All sorts of pleasant and intelligent people read the books and write thoughtful letters about them. I don't know who they are, but they are marvelous and seem to live quite independently of the prejudices of advertising, journalism, and the cranky academic world. Think of the books that have enjoyed independent lives. *Let Us Now Praise Famous Men. Under the Volcano. Henderson the Rain King.* A splendid book like *Humboldt's Gift* was received with confusion and dismay, but hundreds of thousands of people went out and bought hardcover copies. The room where I work has a window looking into a wood, and I like to think that these earnest, lovable, and mysterious readers are in there.

Grant: Do you think contemporary writing is becoming more specialized, more autobiographical?

Cheever: It may be. Autobiography and letters may be more interesting than fiction, but still, I'll stick with the novel. The novel is an acute means of communication from which all kinds of people get responses that you don't get from letters or journals.

Grant: Did you start writing as a child?

Cheever: I used to tell stories. I went to a permissive school called Thayerland. I loved to tell stories, and if everybody did their arithmetic—it was a very small school, probably not more than 18 or 19 students—then the teacher would promise that I would tell a story. I told serials. This was very shrewd of me, because I knew that if I didn't finish the story by the end of the period, which was an hour, then everyone would ask to hear the end during the next period.

Grant: How old were you?

Cheever: Well, I'm inclined to lie about my age, but I suppose it was when I was eight or nine.

Grant: You could think of a story to spin out for an hour at that age?

Cheever: Oh, yes. I could then. And I still do.

Grant: What comes first, the plot?

Cheever: I don't work with plots. I work with intuition, apprehension, dreams, concepts. Characters and events come simultaneously to me. Plot implies narrative and a lot of crap. It is a calculated attempt to hold the reader's interest at the sacrifice of moral conviction. Of course, one doesn't want to be boring . . . one needs an element of suspense. But a good narrative is a rudimentary structure, rather like a kidney.

Grant: Have you always been a writer, or have you had other jobs?

Cheever: I drove a newspaper truck once. I liked it very much, especially during the World Series, when the Quincy paper would carry the box scores and full accounts. No one had radios, or television—which is not to say that the town was lit with candles, but they used to wait for the news; it made me feel good to be the one delivering the good news. Also, I spent four years in the Army. I was 17 when I sold my first story, "Expelled," to *The New Republic*. *The New Yorker* started taking my stuff when I was 22. I was supported by the *The New Yorker* for years and years. It has been a very pleasant association. I sent in 12 or 14 stories a year. At the start I lived in a squalid slum room on Hudson Street with a broken windowpane. I had a job at MGM with Paul Goodman, doing synopses. Jim Farrell, too. We had to boil down just about every book published into either a three-, five-, or twelve-page précis for which you got something like five dollars. You did your own typing. And, oh, carbons.

Grant: What was it like writing stories for *The New Yorker* in those days? Who was the fiction editor?

Cheever: Wolcott Gibbs was the fiction editor very briefly, and then Gus Lobrano. I knew him very well; he was a fishing companion. And, of course, Harold Ross, who was difficult but I loved him. He asked preposterous queries on a manuscript—everyone's written about that—something like 36 queries on a story. The author always thought it outrageous, a violation of taste, but Ross really didn't care. He liked to show his hand, to shake the writer up. Occasionally he was brilliant. In "The Enormous Radio" he made two changes. A diamond is found on the bathroom floor after a party. The man says, "Sell it, we can use a few dollars." Ross had changed "dollars" to "bucks," which was absolutely perfect. Brilliant. Then I had "the radio came softly" and Ross penciled in another "softly." "The radio came softly, softly." He was absolutely right. But then there were 29 other suggestions like, "This story has gone on for 24 hours and no one has eaten anything. There's no mention of a meal." A typical example of this sort of thing was Shirley Jackson's "The Lottery," about the stoning ritual. He hated the story; he started turning vicious. He said there was town in Vermont where there were rocks of that sort. He nagged and nagged and nagged. It was not surprising. Ross used to scare the hell out of me. I would go in for lunch. I never knew Ross was coming until he'd bring in an egg cup. I'd sit with my back pressed against my chair. I was really afraid. He was a scratcher and a nose picker, and the sort of man who could get his underwear up so there was a strip of it showing between his trousers and his shirt. He used to hop at me, sort of jump about in his chair. It was a creative, destructive relationship from which I learned a great deal, and I miss him.

Grant: You met a lot of writers during that time, didn't you?

Cheever: It was all terribly important to me, since I had been brought up in a small town. I was in doubt that I could make something of myself as a writer until I met two people who were very important to me: One was Gaston Lachaise and the other was E. E. Cummings. Cummings I loved, and I love his memory. He did a wonderful imitation of a woodburning locomotive going from Tiflis to Minsk. He could hear a pin falling in soft dirt at the distance of three miles. Do you remember the story of Cummings' death? It was September, hot, and Cummings was cutting kindling in the back of his house in New Hampshire. He was 66 or 67 or something like that. Marion, his wife, leaned out the window and asked, "Cummings, isn't it frightfully hot to be chopping wood?" He said, "I'm going to stop now, but I'm going to sharpen the ax before I put it up, dear." Those were the last words he spoke. At his funeral Marianne Moore gave the eulogy. Marion Cummings had enormous eyes. You could make a place in a book with them. She smoked cigarettes as though they were heavy, and she wore a dark dress with a cigarette hole in it.

Grant: And Lachaise?

Cheever: I'm not sure what to say about him. I thought him an outstanding artist and I found him a contented man. He used to go to the Metropolitan—where he was not represented—and embrace the statues he loved.

Grant: Did Cummings have any advice for you as a writer?

Cheever: Cummings was never paternal. But the cant of his head, his wind-in-the-chimney voice, his courtesy to boobs, and the vastness of his love for Marion were all advisory.

Grant: Have you ever written poetry?

Cheever: No. It seems to me that the discipline is very different . . . another language, another continent from that of fiction. In some cases short stories are more highly disciplined than a lot of poetry that we have. Yet the disciplines are as different as shooting a 12-gauge shotgun and swimming.

Grant: Have magazines asked you to write journalism for them?

Cheever: I was asked to do an interview with Sophia Loren by the *Saturday Evening Post*. I did. I got to kiss her. I've had other offers but nothing good.

Grant: Do you think there's a trend for novelists to write journalism, as Norman Mailer does?

Cheever: I don't like your question. Fiction must compete with first-rate reporting. If you cannot write a story that is equal to a factual account of battle in the streets or demonstrations, then you can't write a story. You might as well give up. In many cases, fiction hasn't competed successfully. These days the field of fiction is littered with tales about the sensibilities of a child coming of age on a chicken farm, or a whore who strips her profession of its glamour. The *Times* has never been so full of rubbish in its recent book ads. Still, the use of the word "death" or "invalidism" about fiction diminishes as it does with anything else.

Grant: Do you feel drawn to experiment in fiction, to move toward bizarre things?

Cheever: Fiction *is* experimentation; when it ceases to be that, it ceases to be fiction. One never puts down a sentence without the feeling that it has never been put down before in such a way, and that perhaps even the substance of the sentence has never been felt. Every sentence is an innovation.

Grant: Do you feel that you belong to any particular tradition in American letters?

Cheever: No. As a matter of fact, I can't think of any American writers who could be classified as part of a tradition. You certainly can't put Updike, Mailer, Ellison, or Styron in a tradition. The individuality of the writer has never been as intense as it is in the United States.

Grant: Well, would you think of yourself as a realistic writer?

Cheever: We have to agree on what we mean before we can talk about such definitions. Documentary novels, such as those of Dreiser, Zola, Dos Passos—even though I don't like them—can, I think, be classified as realistic. Jim Farrell was another documentary novelist; in a way, Scott Fitzgerald was, though to think of him that way diminishes what he could do best . . . which was to try to give a sense of what a very particular world was like.

Grant: Do you think Fitzgerald was conscious of documenting?

Cheever: I've written something on Fitzgerald, and I've read all the biographies and critical works, and wept freely at the end of each one—cried like a baby—it is such a sad story. All the estimates of him bring in his descriptions of the '29 crash, the excessive prosperity, the clothes, the music, and by doing so, his work is described as being heavily dated . . . sort of period pieces. This all greatly diminishes Fitzgerald at his best. One always knows reading Fitzgerald what time it is, precisely where you are, the kind of country. No writer has ever been so true in placing the scene. But I feel that this isn't pseudohistory, but his sense of being alive. All great men are scrupulously true to their times.

Grant: Do you think your works will be similarly dated?

Cheever: Oh, I don't anticipate that my work will be read. That isn't the sort of thing that concerns me. I might be forgotten tomorrow; it wouldn't disconcert me in the least.

Grant: But a great number of your stories defy dating; they could take place anytime and almost anyplace.

Cheever: That, of course, has been my intention. The ones that you can pinpoint in an era are apt to be the worst. The bomb-shelter story (''The Brigadier and the Golf Widow'') is about a level of basic anxiety, and the bomb shelter, which places the story at a very particular time, is just a metaphor . . . that's what I intended anyhow.

Grant: It was a sad story.

Cheever: Everyone keeps saying that about my stories, ''Oh, they're so sad.'' My agent, Candida Donadio, called me about a new story and said, ''Oh, what a beautiful story, it's so sad.'' I said, ''All right, so I'm a sad man.'' The sad thing about ''The Brigadier and the Golf Widow'' is the woman standing looking at the bomb shelter in the end of the story and then being sent away by a maid. Did you know that *The New Yorker* tried to take that out? They thought the story was much more effective without my ending. When I went in to look at page proofs, I thought there was a page missing. I asked where the end of the story was. Some girl said, ''Mr. Shawn thinks it's better this way.'' I went into a very deep slow burn, took the train home, drank a lot of gin, and got one of the editors on the telephone. I was by then loud, abusive, and obscene. He was entertaining Elizabeth Bowen and Eudora Welty. He kept asking if he couldn't take this call in another place. Anyhow, I returned to New York in the morning. They had reset the whole magazine—poems, newsbreaks, cartoons—and replaced the scene.

Grant: It's the classic story about what *The New Yorker* is rumored to do—''remove the last paragraph and you've got a typical *New Yorker* ending.'' What is your definition of a good editor?

Cheever: My definition of a good editor is a man I think charming, who sends me large checks, praises my work, my physical beauty, and my sexual prowess, and who has a stranglehold on the publisher and the bank.

Grant: What about the beginning of stories? Yours start off very quickly. It's striking.

Cheever: Well, if you're trying as storyteller to establish some rapport with your reader, you don't open by telling him that you have a headache and indigestion and that you picked up a gravelly rash at Jones Beach. One of the reasons is that advertising in magazines is much more common today than it was 20 to 30 years ago. In publishing in a magazine you are competing against girdle advertisements, travel advertisements, nakedness, cartoons, even poetry. The competition almost makes it hopeless. There's a stock beginning that I've always had in mind. Someone is coming back from a year in Italy on a Fulbright Scholarship. His trunk is opened in customs, and instead of his clothing and souvenirs, they find the mutilated body of an Italian seaman, everything there but the head. Another opening sentence I often think of is, ''The first day I robbed Tiffany's it was raining." Of course, you can open a short story that way, but that's not how one should function with fiction. One is tempted because there has been a genuine loss of serenity, not only in the reading public, but in all our lives. Patience, perhaps, or even the ability to concentrate. At one point when television first came in no one was publishing an article that couldn't be read during a commercial. But fiction is durable enough to survive all this. I don't like the short story that starts out "I'm about to shoot myself" or "I'm about to shoot you. Or the Pirandello thing of "I'm going to shoot you or you are going to shoot me, or we are going to shoot someone, maybe each other." Or the erotic thing, either: "He started to undo his pants, but the zipper stuck . . . he got the can of three-in-one oil . . ." and on and on we go.

Grant: Certainly your stories have a fast pace, they move along.

Cheever: The first principle of aesthetics is either interest or suspense. You can't expect to communicate with anyone if you're a bore.

Grant: William Golding wrote tht there are two kinds of novelists. One lets meaning develop with the characters or situations, and the other has an idea and looks for a myth to embody it. He's an example of the second kind. He thinks of Dickens as belonging to the first. Do you think you fit into either category?

Cheever: I don't know what Golding is talking about. Cocteau said that writing is a force of memory that is not understood. I agree with this. Raymond Chandler described it as a direct line to the subconscious. The books that you really love give the sense, when you first open them, of having been there. It is a creation, almost like a chamber in the memory. Places that one has never been to, things that one has never seen or heard, but their fitness is so sound that you've been there somehow.

Grant: But certainly you use a lot of resonances from myths . . . for example, references to the Bible and Greek mythology.

Cheever: It's explained by the fact that I was brought up in southern Massachusetts, where it was thought that mythology was a subject that we should all grasp. It was very much part of my education. The easiest way to parse the world is through mythology. There have been thousands of papers written along those lines—Leander is Poseidon and somebody is Ceres, and so forth. It seems to be a superficial parsing. But it makes a passable paper.

Grant: Still, you want the resonance.

Cheever: The resonance, of course.

Grant: How do you work? Do you put ideas down immediately, or do you walk around with them for a while, letting them incubate?

Cheever: I do both. What I love is when totally disparate facts come together. For example, I was sitting in a café reading a letter from home with the news that a neighboring housewife had taken the lead in a nude show. As I read I could hear an Englishwoman scolding her children. "If you don't do thus and so before Mummy counts to three" was her line. A leaf fell through the air, reminding me of winter and of the fact that my wife had left me and was in Rome. There was my story. I had an equivalently great time with the close of "Goodbye My Brother" and "The Country Husband." Hemingway and Nabokov liked these. I had everything in there: a cat wearing a hat, some naked women coming out of the sea, a dog with a shoe in his mouth, and a king in golden mail riding an elephant over some mountains.

Grant: Or Ping-Pong in the rain?

Cheever: I don't remember what story that was.

Grant: Sometimes you played Ping-Pong in the rain.

Cheever: I probably did.

Grant: Do you save up such things?

Cheever: It isn't a question of saving up. It's a question of some sort of galvanic energy. It's also, of course, a question of making sense of one's experiences.

Grant: Do you think that fiction should give lessons?

Cheever: No. Fiction is meant to illuminate, to explode, to refresh. I don't think there's any consecutive moral philosophy in fiction beyond excellence. Acuteness of feeling and velocity have always seemed to me terribly important. People look for morals in fiction because there has always been a confusion between fiction and philosophy.

Grant: How do you know when a story is right? Does it hit you right the first time, or are you critical as you go along?

Cheever: I think there is a certain heft in fiction. For example, my latest story isn't right. I have to do the ending over again. It's a question, I guess, of trying to get it to correspond to a vision. There is a shape, a proportion, and one knows when something that happens is wrong.

Grant: By instinct?

Cheever: I suppose that anyone who has written for as long as I have, it's probably what you'd call instinct. When a line falls wrong, it simply isn't right.

Grant: You told me once you were interested in thinking up names for characters.

Cheever: That seems to me very important. I've written a story about men with a lot of names, all abstract, names with the fewest possible allusions: Pell, Weed, Hammer, and Nailles, of course, which was thought to be arch, but it wasn't meant to be at all . . .

Grant: Hammer's house appears in "The Swimmer."

Cheever: That's true, it's quite a good story. It was a terribly difficult story to write.

Grant: Why?

Cheever: Because I couldn't ever show my hand. Night was falling, the year was dying. It wasn't a question of technical problems, but one of imponderables. When he finds it's dark and cold, it has to have happened. And, by God, it did happen. I felt dark and cold for some time after I finished that story. As a matter of fact, it's one of the last stories I wrote for a long time, because I started on *Bullet Park*. Sometimes the easiest-seeming stories to a reader are the hardest kind to write.

Grant: How long does it take you to write such a story?

Cheever: Three days, three weeks, three months. I seldom read my own work. It seems to be a particularly offensive form of narcissism. It's like playing back tapes of your own conversation. It's like looking over your shoulder to see where you've run. That's why I've often used the image of the swimmer, the runner, the jumper. The point is to finish and go on to the next thing. I also feel, not as strongly as I used to, that if I looked over my shoulder I would die. I think frequently of Satchel Paige and his warning that you might see something gaining on you.

Grant: Are there stories that you feel particularly good about when you are finished?

Cheever: Yes, there were about 15 of them that were absolutely BANG! I loved them, I loved everybody—the buildings, the houses, wherever I was. It was a great sensation. Most of these were stories written in the space of three days and which run to about 35 pages. I love them, but I can't read them; in many cases, I wouldn't love them any longer if I did.

Grant: Recently you have talked bluntly about having a writer's block, which had never happened to you before. How do you feel about it now?

Cheever: Any memory of pain is deeply buried, and there is nothing more painful for a writer than an inability to work.

Grant: Four years is a rather long haul on a novel, isn't it?

Cheever: It's about what it usually takes. There's a certain monotony in this way of life, which I can very easily change.

Grant: Why?

Cheever: Because it doesn't seem to me the proper function of writing. If possible, it is to enlarge people. To give them their risk, if possible to give them their divinity, not to cut them down.

Grant: Do you feel that you had diminished them too far in *Bullet Park*?

Cheever: No, I didn't feel that. But I believe that it was understood in those terms. I believe that Hammer and Nailles were thought to be social casualties, which isn't what I intended at all. And I thought I made my intentions quite clear. But if you don't communicate, it's not anybody else's fault. Neither Hammer nor Nailles was meant to be either psychiatric or social metaphors; they were meant to be two men with their own risks. I think the book was misunderstood on those terms. But then I don't read reviews, so I don't really know what goes on.

Grant: How do you know when the literary work is finished to your satisfaction?

Cheever: I have never completed anything in my life to my absolute and lasting satisfaction.

Grant: Do you feel that you're putting a lot of yourself on the line when you are writing?

Cheever: Oh yes, oh yes! When I speak as a writer I speak with my own voice—quite as unique as my fingerprints—and I take the maximum risk at seeming profound or foolish.

Grant: Does one get the feeling while sitting at the typewriter that one is godlike, or creating the whole show at once?

Cheever: No, I've never felt godlike. No, the sense is of one's total usefulness. We all have a power of control, it's part of our lives: We have it in love, in work that we love doing. It's a sense of ecstasy, as simple as that. The sense is that "this is my usefulness, and I can do it all the way through." It always leaves you feeling great. In short, you've made sense of your life.

Grant: Do you feel that way during or after the event? Isn't work, well, work?

Cheever: I've had very little drudgery in my life. When I write a story that I really like, it's . . . why, wonderful. That is what I can do, and I love it while I'm doing it. I can feel that it's good. I'll say to Mary and the children, "All right, I'm off, leave me alone. I'll be through in three days."

> " Fiction is often in trouble, but people respond to imagination, talent, genius for language. They're born knowing what life is about and ultimately this is what fiction tells you. You learn from the imaginative what the real world is.
>
> —*Bernard Malamud* "

Some notes on time in fiction

by Eudora Welty

Time and place, the two bases of reference upon which the novel, in seeking to come to grips with human experience, must depend for its validity, operate together, of course. They might be taken for granted as ordinary factors, until the novelist at his work comes to scrutinize them apart.

Place, the accessible one, the inhabited one, has blessed identity—a proper name, a human history, a visible character. Time is anonymous; when we give it a face, it's the same face the world over. While place is in itself as informing as an old gossip, time tells us nothing about itself except by the signals that it is passing. It has never given anything away.

Unlike time, place has surface, which will take the imprint of man—his hand, his foot, his mind; it can be tamed, domesticated. It has shape, size, boundaries, man can measure himself against them. It has atmosphere and temperature, change of light and show of season, qualities to which man spontaneously responds. Place has always nursed, nourished and instructed man; he in turn can rule it and ruin it, take it and lose it, suffer if he is exiled from it, and after living on it he goes to it in his grave. It is the stuff of fiction, as close to our living lives as the earth we can pick up and rub between our fingers, something we can feel and smell. But time is like the wind of the abstract. Beyond its all-pervasiveness, it has no quality that we apprehend but rate of speed, and our own acts and thoughts are said to give it that. Man can feel love for place; he is prone to regard time as something of an enemy.

Eudora Welty is a major novelist, critic, and chronicler of life in the South. She received the Pulitzer Prize in 1973 for The Optimist's Daughter *and has written many novels, short stories and essays for magazines and literaries which have earned her numerous awards.* The Collected Stories of Eudora Welty *was published in 1980.*

Time's child

Yet the novelist lives on closer terms with time than he does with place. The reasons for this are much older than any novel; they reach back into our oldest lore. How many of our proverbs are little nutshells to pack the meat of time in! ("He that diggeth a pit shall fall into it." "Pride goeth before destruction, and a haughty spirit before a fall.") The allwithstanding devices of myth and legend (the riddle of the Sphinx, Penelope's web, the Thousand and One Nights) are constructed of time. And time goes to make that most central device of all, the plot itself—as Scheherazade showed us in her own telling.

Indeed, these little ingots of time are ingots of plot too. Not only do they contain stories, they convey the stories—they speak of life-in-the-movement, with a beginning and an end. All that needed to be added was the middle; then the novel came along and saw to that.

Only the nursery fairy tale is not answerable to time, and time has no effect upon it; time winds up like a toy, and toy it is: When set to "Once upon a time" it spins till it runs down at "Happy ever after." Fairy tales don't come from old wisdom, they come from old foolishness—just as potent. They follow rules of their own that are quite as strict as time's (the magic of number and repetition, the governing of the spell); their fairy perfection forbids the existence of choices, and the telling always has to be the same. Their listener is the child, whose gratification comes of the fairy tale's having no suspense. The tale is about wishes, and thus grants a wish itself.

Real life is not wished, it is lived; stories and novels, whose subject is human beings in relationship with experience to undergo, make their own difficult way, struggle toward their own resolutions. Instead of fairy immunity to change, there is the vulnerability of human imperfection caught up in human emotion, and so there is growth, there is crisis, there is fulfillment, there is decay. Life moves toward death. The novel's progress is one of causality, and with that comes suspense. Suspense is a necessity in a novel because it is a main condition of our existence. Suspense is known only to mortals, and its agent and messenger is time.

The novel is time's child—"I could a tale *unfold*"—and bears all the earmarks, and all the consequences.

Plot's right arm

The novelist can never do otherwise than work with time, and nothing in his novel can escape it. The novel cannot begin without his starting of the clock; the characters then, and not until then, are seen to be alive, in motion; their situation can declare itself only by its unfolding. While place lies passive, time moves and is a mover. Time is the bringer-on of action, the instrument of change. If time should break down, the novel itself would lie in collapse, its meaning gone. For time has the closest possible connection with the novel's meaning, in being the chief conductor of the plot.

Thus time is not a simple length, on which to string beadlike the novel's episodes. Though it does join acts and events in a row, it's truer to say that it leads them in a direction, it induces each one out of the one before and into the one next. It is not only the story's "then—and then," it may also be a "but" or a "nevertheless"; and it is always a "thus" and a "therefore."

Why does a man do a certain thing now, what in the past has brought him to it, what in the future will come of it, and into what sequence will he set things moving now? Time, in which the characters behave and perform, alone and with others, through the changes rung by their situation, uncovers motive and develops the consequences. Time carries out a role of resolver. ("As a man soweth, so shall he reap.")

Clock time has an arbitrary, bullying power over daily affairs that of course can't be got around (the Mad Hatter's tea party). But it has not the same power in fiction that it has in life. Time is plot's right arm, indeed, but is always answerable to it. It can act only in accordance with the plot, lead only toward the plot's development and fulfillment.

Fiction does not hesitate to accelerate time, slow it down, project it forward or run it backward, cause it to skip over itself or repeat itself. It may require time to travel in a circle, to meet itself in coincidence. It can freeze an action in the middle of its performance. It can expand a single moment like the skin of a balloon or bite off a life like a thread. It can put time through the hoop of a dream, trap it inside an obsession. It can see a fragment of the past within a frame of the present and cause them to exist simultaneously. In Katherine Anne Porter's perfect short story "The Grave," a forgotten incident from her country-Texas childhood abruptly projects itself upon a woman's present; its meaning—too deep for the child's understanding—travels 20 years through time and strikes her full force on a city street in another country. In this story, time moves by metamorphosis, and in the flash it discloses another, earlier metamorphosis—the real one, which had lain there all the while in the past that the young woman had left behind her.

Move toward resolution

In going in the direction of meaning, time has to move through a mind. What it will bring about is an awakening there. Through whatever motions it goes through, it will call forth, in a mind or heart, some crucial recognition. ("I imagined that I bore my chalice safely through a throng of foes.")

What can a character come to know, of himself and others, by working through a given situation? This is what fiction asks, with an emotional urgency driving it all the way; and can he know it in time? Thus time becomes, as sharply as needed, an instrument of pressure. Any novel's situation must constitute some version of a matter of life or death. In the face of time, life is always at stake. This may or may not be the case in a literal sense; but it does need to be always the case as a matter of spiritual or moral survival. It may lie not so much in being rescued as in having learned what constitutes one's own danger, and one's own salvation. With the refinements of the danger involved, suspense is increased. Suspense has exactly the value of its own meaning.

In fiction, then, time can throb like a pulse, tick like a bomb, beat like the waves of a rising tide against the shore; it can be made out as the whisper of attrition, or come to an end with the explosion of a gun. For time is of course subjective, too. ("It tolls for thee.")

Time appears to do all these things in novels, but they are *effects*, necessary illusions performed by the novelist; and they make no alteration in the pace of the novel, which is one of a uniform steadiness and imperturbability. The novel might be told episodically, hovering over one section of time and skipping over the next; or by some eccentric method—Henry Green spoke of his as going crabwise; but however its style of moving, its own advance must remain smooth and unbroken, its own time all of a piece. The plot goes forward at the pace of its own necessity, its own heartbeat. It provides the order for the dramatic unfolding of the plot: Revelation is not revelation until it is dramatically conceived and carried out.

The close three-way alliance of time, plot and significance can be seen clearly demonstrated in the well-written detective novel. We can learn from it that plot, by the very strength, spareness and boldness of its construction-in-motion, forms a kind of metaphor. I believe every well-made plot does, and needs to do so. But a living metaphor. From the simplest to the most awesomely complicated, a plot is a device organic to human struggle designed for the searching out of human truth. It is fron inception highly sensitive to time, it acts within time, and it is in its time that we ourselves see it and follow it.

Indelible images of time

As readers, we accept more or less without blinking the novel's playing-free with time. Don't we by familiar practice accept discrepancies much like them in daily living? Fictional time bears a not too curious resemblance to our own interior clock; it is so by design. Fiction penetrates chronological time to reach our deeper version of time that's given to us by the way we think and feel. This is one of the reasons why even the first "stream-of-consciousness" novels, difficult as they must have been for their authors breaking new ground, were rather contrarily easy for the reader to follow.

Fictional time may be more congenial to us than clock time, precisely for human reasons. An awareness of time goes with us all our lives. Watch or no watch, we carry the awareness with us. It lies so deep, in the very grain of our characters, that who knows if it isn't as singular to each of us as our thumbprints. In the sense of our own transience may lie the one irreducible urgency telling us to do, to understand, to love.

We are mortal: This is time's deepest meaning in the novel as it is to us alive. Fiction shows us the past as well as the present moment in mortal light; it is an art served by the indelibility of our memory, and one empowered by a sharp and prophetic awareness of what is ephemeral. It is by the ephemeral that our feeling is so strongly aroused for what endures, or strives to endure. One time compellingly calls up the other. Thus the ephemeral, being alive only in the present moment, must be made to live in the novel as *now*, while it transpires, in the transpiring.

Fiction's concern is with the ephemeral—that is, the human—effects of time, these alone. In action, scene and metaphor, these are set how unforgettably before our eyes! I believe the images of time may be the most indelible that fiction's art can produce. Miss Havisham's table in its spiderwebs still laid for her wedding feast; the "certain airs" in *To the Lighthouse* that "fumbled the petals of roses"—they come instantaneously to mind. And do you not see the movement of Gusev's body in the sea, after his burial from the hospital ship: See it go below the surface of the sea, moving on down and swaying rhythmically with the current, and then being met by the shark: "After playing a little with the body the shark nonchalantly puts its jaws under it, cautiously touches it with its teeth, and the sailcoth is rent its full length from head to foot." "Was it possible that such a thing might happen to anyone?" is the question Chekhov has asked as Gusev was slid into the sea, and in this chilling moment we look upon the story's answer, and we see not simply an act taking place in time; we are made, as witnesses, to see time happen. We look upon its answer as it occurs in time. This moment, this *rending*, is what might happen to anyone.

Visible and audible memory

When passion comes into the telling, with a quickening of human meaning, changes take place in fictional time. Some of them are formidable.

I was recently lent a book by a student which had set itself to clear up *The Sound and the Fury* by means of a timetable; the characters' arrival and departures, including births and deaths, were listed in schedule, with connections to and from the main points of action in the novel. What has defeated the compiler is that *The Sound and the Fury* remains, after his work as before it, approachable only as a novel. He was right, of course, in seeing time to be at the bottom of it. Time, though—not chronology.

Think of the timepieces alone. Think of only one timepiece: Dilsey has to use the Compson clock; it has only one hand. "The clock tick-tocked, solemn and profound. It might have been the dry pulse of the decaying house itself; after a while it whirred and cleared its throat and struck." It strikes five times. "Eight o'clock," says Dilsey. Even while the clock is striking, chronology is in the act of yielding to another sort of time.

Through the telling of the story three times in succession by three different Compsons in the first-person and then once again in the third-person, we are exposed to three different worlds of memory, each moving in its own orbit. "He thirty-three," Luster says of Benjy, "thirty-three this morning," and the reply comes, "You mean he been three years old thirty years." Benjy's memory is involuntary and not conscious of sequence or connections: a stick run along the palings of a fence. But time of whatever nature leaves a residue in passing, and out of Benjy comes a wail "hopeless and prolonged. It was nothing." Just sound. It might have been all time and injustice and sorrow become vocal for an instant by a conjunction of planets."

Time to Quentin is visible—his shadow; is audible—his grandfather's watch; and it is the heavy load that has to be carried inside him—his memory. Excruciatingly conscious, possessing him in torture, that memory works in spite of him and of all he can do, anywhere he can go, this last day of his life. The particular moment in time that links him forever to the past—his world—conditions *all* time. The future may be an extension of the past *where possible*; the future can include memory *if bearable*. But time will repeatedly assault what has been intact; which may be as frail as the virginity of Caddy. If experience is now, at every stage, a tragedy of association in the memory, how is the rememberer to survive? Quentin spends his last day, as he's spent his life, answering that he is already dead. He has willed the past some quality, some power, by which it can arrest the present, try to stop it from happening; can stop it.

Who, in the swirling time of this novel, knows the actual time, and can tell the story by it? Jason, of course. He keeps track of time to the second as he keeps track of money to the penny. Time is money, says Jason. And he cheats on both and is in turn cheated by both; we see him at the end a man "sitting quietly behind the wheel of a small car, with his invisible life ravelled out about him like a worn-out sock."

Distortion for drama

By all the interior evidence, we will come nearest to an understanding of this novel through the way it speaks to us out of its total saturation with time. We read not in spite of the eccentric handling of time, but as well as we can by the aid of it. If a point is reached in fiction where chronology has to be torn down, it must be in order to admit and make room for what matters overwhelmingly more to the human beings who are its characters.

Faulkner has crowded chronology out of the way many times to make way for memory and the life of the past, as we know, and we know for what reason. "Memory believes before knowing remembers," he says (in *Light in August*). Remembering is so basic and vital a part of staying alive that it takes on the strength of an instinct of survival, and acquires the power of an art. Remembering is done through the blood, it is a bequeathment, it takes account of what happens before a man is born as if he were there taking part. It is a physical absorption through the living body, it is a spiritual heritage. It is also a life's work.

"There is no such thing as was," Falkner remarked in answer to a student's question as to why he wrote long sentences. "To me, no man is himself, he is the sum of his past. There is no such thing really as was, because the past is. It is a part of every man, every woman, and every moment. All of his and her ancestry, background, is all a part of himself and herself at any moment. And so a man, a character in a story at any moment in action, is not just himself as he is then, he is all that made him; and the long sentence," he adds, "is an attempt to get his past and possibly his future into the instant in which he does something . . ."

Distortion of time is a deeply conscious part of any novel's conception, is an organic part of its dramatic procedure, and throughout the novel's course it matters continuously and increasingly, and exactly as the author gives it to us. The dilations, the freezing of moment, the persistent recurrences and proliferations, all the extraordinary tamperings with time in *The Sound and the Fury*, are answers to the meaning's questions, evolving on demand. For all Faulkner does to chronological time here—he explodes it—he does nothing that does not increase the dramatic power of his story. The distortions to time give the novel its deepest seriousness of meaning, and charge it with an intense emotional power that could come from nowhere else. Time, in the result, is the living essence of *The Sound and the Fury*. It appears to stand so extremely close to the plot that, in a most extraordinary way, it almost becomes the plot itself. It *is* the portentous part; it is the plot's long reverberation. Time has taken us through every degree of the long down-spiral to the novel's meaning—into the meaning; it has penetrated its way. It has searched out every convolution of a human predicament and brought us to the findings of tragedy.

Duration of emotional exploration

Faulkner's work is, we know, magnetized to a core of time, to his conception of it as the continuing and continuousness of man. Faulknerian time is in the most profound and irrefutable sense *human* time. (*Corruption* is that which time brings to the Compsons' lives. *Progress* is the notion of those who are going to make something out of it: "What's in it for me?" ask the Snopeses.) His deepest felt and most often repeated convictions— "They endured." "Man will prevail"—are the long-reached and never-to-be-relinquished resolutions of his passionate idea of human time. And they contain, burned into them, all the plots of Faulkner's novels and stories.

Time, in a novel, may become the subject itself. Mann, attacking the subjectivity of man's knowledge of time, and Proust, discovering a way to make time give back all it has taken, through turning life by way of the memory into art, left masterpieces that are like clocks themselves, giant clocks stationed for always out in the world, sounding for us the high hours of our literature. But from greatest to least, don't most novels reflect that personal subjective time that lived for their writers throughout the writing?

There is the constant evidence of it in a writer's tempo, harmony, the inflections of his work, the symmetry and proportions of the parts in the whole; in the felt rhythms of his prose, his emotion is given its truest and most spontaneous voice; the cadence which is his alone tells us—it would almost do so in spite of him—his belief or disbelief in the story he intends us to hear. But I have in mind something more than this governing of a writer's style.

Faulkner has spoken for the record of his difficulties in writing *The Sound and the Fury*, the novel he loved best and considered his most imperfect; he spoke of its four parts as four attempts, and four failures, to tell his story. In their own degree, many other novels give evidence in themselves of what this difficulty suggests: The novel's duration is in part the measurable amount of time the novelist needs to apprehend and harness what is before him; time is part of the writing too. The novel finished and standing free of him is not the mirror-reflection of that writing-time, but is its equivalent. A novel's duration is, in some respect, exactly how long it takes the particular author of a particular novel to explore its emotional resources, and to give his full powers to learning their scope and meeting their demands, and finding out their truest procedure.

In the very imperfections of *The Sound and the Fury*, which come of a giant effort pushed to its limit and still trying, lies a strength we may set above perfection. They are the human quotient, and honorable as the marks left by the hand-held chisel in bringing the figure out of recalcitrant stone—which is another way of looking at time.

> *Through the study of technique—not canoeing or logging or slinging hash—one learns the best, most efficient ways of making characters come alive, learns to know the difference between emotion and sentimentality, learns to discern, in the planning stages, the difference between the better dramatic action and the worse. It is this kind of knowledge . . . that leads to mastery. . . . Mastery is not something that strikes in an instant, like a thunderbolt, but a gathering power that moves through time, like weather.*
>
> *—John Gardner*

Creating imaginary characters

by Dianne Doubtfire

"We are not interested in the sort of objectivity that turns out machine-made collections of types and characters, but in the purely poetic capacity to represent one's own hopes, one's own fears, one's own resentments, one's own loves, in human form: to define oneself by subdividing oneself and multiplying oneself in one or a hundred creatures."

Alberto Moravia

How does one create believable characters? Whip them up out of nothing, or copy real people? The answer is neither of these alone, but a mixture of both. We must base our imaginative creations on what we know of ourselves and of the people we have met. Writers of fiction are people of many facets, and some of their characters are developments of themselves, the good and the bad magnified or tempered by a sensitive imagination.

"The novelist's job is to see and say clearly what people are." In this simple statement I think John Masters has summed up the whole art of characterization. But *how* are we to see clearly and to say clearly? The first depends on our understanding of human nature, the second on the writing technique we acquire through study and experience.

Characters in a novel should never be taken straight from life. Apart from the risk of libel, it is artistically unsatisfactory, in that one must know one's characters completely, as one can never know a real person. No one reveals every secret experience, every hope, fear and passion to another person, however close, and it is impossible to understand a

---

Dianne Doubtfire writes both adult and teenage novels, including Lust for Innocence, The Flesh Is Still Strong, Behind the Screen *and* Escape on Monday. *Her book,* The Craft of Novel-Writing *was reissued in 1981.*

person's behaviour completely unless one knows his whole history from earliest child-hood. Therefore, to put an actual person into a novel, and invent imaginary actions for him, would be to build without a sound foundation. The best way to create character is to invent the whole person in his entirety, so that all is known to you and every action is based on a temperament and background which you yourself have devised. You will then be in a position to invent behaviour for him which is not only convincing but inevitable. If you work this way, your characters grow from within themselves. If you take someone from real life you impose on him activities for which you do not understand the root causes. Established writers, of course, have sometimes done this very thing, but I would certainly not advise it. Some authors add a note to the effect that all their characters are entirely fictitious and bear no resemblance to any actual persons, living or dead, but this statement carries no legal weight whatsoever.

Regeneration, not degeneration.

One of your main objectives as a novelist is to make your readers care what happens to your characters; this is the secret of readability. If the reader is to care, you yourself must care, so don't be tempted to continue with a novel unless you feel an intense in-volvement with all your key characters. To make them true to life you must understand their motives, good and bad. If we are honest we can usually understand our own mo-tives, so we must use ourselves as models. We know all about those subtle stabs of re-venge we deal out when we've been hurt. We know the love and gratitude that wells up in response to kindness and sympathy. We know how cruelty engenders more cruelty. The novelist should be continually interrogating himself. "Why did I say that?" "Why did I do that?" "Why am I so touchy about certain things?" A study of psychology is valu-able, but the best thing is to study yourself objectively and other people compassionate-ly, so that you can see the principles of human nature at work and compose your novel accordingly. Every person alive is different, and you, as a novelist, must create more people—quite new. You can't expect it to be easy!

Why do some characters seem "cardboard"? Stilted dialogue has a lot to do with it, but I think you will also find that the cardboard character is either too good, too bad, or too predictable. Up to a point, most of us are "true to type" but there are always devia-tions. We often hear someone say: "I'd never have expected that of So-and-So!" A con-ventional person may suddenly behave wildly for no apparent reason. But if you have created the character yourself with deep involvement, you *know* the reason; you know, for example, that he had been forced into conventional channels against his will and that the time had come for him to revert to his true nature. A mean person may be extravagant in certain little ways, perhaps in an effort to compensate for secret guilt. If he is your cre-ation you will understand, and his behaviour will carry conviction.

Another symptom of the cardboard character is that he remains the same throughout the book. In reality people change, however slightly, as a result of their experiences. There must be some sort of conversion brought about by the events you devise; the cen-tral character must develop along with the novel and acquire new attitudes—preferably wiser ones; I believe in regeneration not degeneration.

A great deal of "thinking time"—and possibly some note-taking—is required be-fore a character can develop fully in the mind. If you feel that one of your characters is lacking in depth it is probably because you are unsure of his true nature. Unless you know your people so well that you feel you are in their presence as you write, they are unlikely to come over as flesh-and-blood creations.

Highlighting special qualities

How much visual description should you give? This is for you to decide but I think the modern reader prefers to picture the characters for himself, basing his impression on a few well-chosen details. E.g. In Graham Green's *A Burnt-Out Case*, ''Father Thomas' long narrow nose was oddly twisted at the end; it gave him the effect of smelling sideways at some elusive odor.'' And in Nina Bawden's *George Beneath a Paper Moon*, of George's grandmother: ''Her face was old now, a used crumpled envelope, but a child still looked out from her eyes.''

The following extracts will further illustrate the art of sketching a character in a few words:

She always kissed him when he got home, not a conventional peck on the cheek but a light kiss full on the mouth: She had moist, wide lips and usually forgot to wear lipstick. There was always a smell that he liked at this time of day, faded perfume not yet renewed, so that it had the aura of powder or soap rather than a scent. Blindfolded, he would have said, ''That's Cassie.''

(*A Bouquet of Barbed Wire* by Andrea Newman)

''Hey, miss,'' said a soft voice. ''You like a cup of tea?''

I looked up. Beside the bed stood a huge bulky figure in a plaid shirt, surmounted by a broad black head split like a ripe chestnut on a crescent of snowy teeth. Dwarfed by the enormous black paw which held it was a steaming cup.

(*The L-Shaped Room* by Lynne Reid Banks)

Sometimes when she wasn't reading her part she looked plain, in fact downright ugly: Her chin had a heavy shapelessness and the lines on her forehead and neck were as if scored with a knife. When she was acting her face came to life: It wasn't so much that you forgot its blemishes as that they became endearing and exciting.

(*Room at the Top* by John Braine)

When Bretherton woke, beer-flushed, with belches of discomfort, at the sound of the caddy spoon on the side of the teapot, he looked like one of those model porkers, fat and pinkish, squatting on its hind-legs with an advertisement for sausages in its lap, that you see in butchers' windows. The sausages were his fingers. They glistened, a pink-grey colour, as they grasped tremulously at each other and then at his tobacco-yellow moustache.

(*Love for Lydia* by H.E. Bates)

An experienced writer can sustain a lengthy description without becoming tedious:

Now she sat there, tired and comfortable, in a deep arm chair, with her feet curled up under her, looking at the pictures. She wore a long wool skirt, and expensive shoes. She was tall, slight and bony, her face was lined and hard and sweet. She had the gallant air of a woman fighting a losing battle, but nobody could guess the terms of her defeat, for she was discreet and silent about herself. She had a well-shaped mouth, curiously curved, with thin and conscious delicate lips, a careful and precise and gentle way of speech. Her hair was dyed. It had turned, in the course of nature, from brown to a miserable, mustardy yellowy fuzzy grey, and so she dyed it, back to its original brown. It was her one weak gesture, and·it was a realistic one, for she did, as she had said to Frances one day some years ago, look like the Witch of Endor with it undyed. And who wants to look like *that*? she had said. It isn't fair to other people, she had said. Who could tell what vanity lay concealed in her? Certainly she always wore extremely expensive shoes. Now they were tucked under her, out of sight. . . .

(*The Realms of Gold* by Margaret Drabble)

I was particularly impressed by the second reference to the expensive shoes. Such repetitions can serve to highlight some special quality of a person or a place, but obviously they must be introduced with great care.

Animals, too, demand characterization. Study this beautiful example from Iris Murdoch's *Under the Net*:

Another peculiarity of Mrs. Tinckham's shop is that it is full of cats. An ever-increasing family of tabbies, sprung from one enormous matriarch, sit about upon the counter and on empty shelves, somnolent and contemplative, their amber eyes narrowed and winking in the sun, a reluctant slit of liquid in an expanse of hot fur.

You might practice characterization by describing someone you know, choosing one thing only to clarify the personality. For instance: an old woman who wears men's shoes; a man who always taps his pipe out on the dot of 10 pm; a girl with no ear for music who is constantly humming popular songs off-key; a small schoolboy with thin legs whose socks are always round his ankles.

Larger than life

Let your characters reveal themselves gradually, as people do: appearance first, voice, mannerisms, followed by subtleties of behaviour and attitude. Let the deeper aspects emerge later, although some of them will perhaps be implied from the start; an unkind remark in the first chapter can be a pointer towards an act of brutality in the last. Keep reminding your readers (very unobtrusively) of the facts you have imparted. If you describe a woman with trembling hands, later she might have difficulty in fitting a key into a lock, and the reader will remember about the trembling hands, even though it was six chapters ago. If you portray a girl who longs for a leather jacket, you have only to press her nose against a shop window and we know what she is gazing at. As a rule it is best not to describe a person until he is actually there in the narrative; a previous build-up can sometimes be effective, but this is the exception.

When you create an evil character, know *why* he or she is evil. Reveal his confusion and unhappiness as well as his malice. To carry conviction, your characters will be a mixture of good and bad, as we all are. You will probably dislike your most beloved character from time to time, just as we dislike our friends when they display their worst selves to us.

If you analyze the people in your favorite novels you will discover that many of them are portrayed as "larger than life." The exaggeration may not be great enough for them to be described as caricatures but they are often more eccentric or impressive than most of the folk we meet every day. Take this into account when you are creating your characters; don't be afraid of that extra helping of personality.

> When some new thought gripped his heart he went to the kitchen, his headquarters, to write it down. The white paint was scaling from the brick walls and Herzog sometimes wiped mouse droppings from the table with his sleeve, calmly wondering why field mice should have such a passion for wax and paraffin. They made holes in paraffin-sealed preserves; they gnawed birthday candles down to the wicks. A rat chewed into a package of bread, leaving the shape of its body in the layer of slices. Herzog ate the other half of the loaf spread with jam. He could share with rats, too.
>
> (*Herzog* by Saul Bellow)

Sometimes a character becomes so real that he refuses to do what you have planned for him. When this happens, don't coerce him; it means you have created a real person with a will of his own and this is a marvellous moment in any novelist's life. Hold him on a light rein, as it were, giving him his head to a certain degree but ensuring that he does not stampede you out of your story. You must remain in command whilst allowing your creations to behave in accordance with the qualities you have given them. Write your scene with all the skill you have and let your instinct tell you whether or not it carries conviction. Creating imaginary characters is the core of novel-writing—and the possibilities are endless.

> 66 *The man on paper is always a more admirable character than his creator who is a miserable creature of nose colds, minor compromises, and sudden flights to nobility.*
>
> —*E.B. White* 99

Just a bunch of words: how to develop believable characters

by Colleen Reece

My earliest childhood memories are of our entire family gathered under the yellow glow of kerosene lamps, each with head bent over a book. We shivered with George Washington at Valley Forge, traveled with Columbus to the New World, and cowered with Dorothy of Kansas as she faced the Wicked Witch in the Land of Oz.

Yet, how many times did Mom turn to Dad and ask, "How's your book?"

And how many times did Dad sigh, "Just a bunch of words." We learned early that this was the highest insult that could be paid to a book—to call it, "Just a bunch of words."

Now, 20 published novels later, I often seek the hidden meaning in Dad's indictment, "Just a bunch of words." What magic formula changes that conglomeration of words trailing one another from being as interesting as a statement of ownership to a novel that can't be put down no matter what television offers? My Dad's voice echoes from the past: "Words, just words. Folks don't act like that! The heroine's a ninny. No hero would act like that." Dad was right. The magic formula in one word is: *characters*. Persons. Folks. Yet, so often it is overlooked. If readers cannot love, hate, or despair with those people who walk the pages of your novel, all the twists, plots, quirks and clever writing in the world will not redeem that manuscript.

Cry for help

That's why I developed my 38-point "character chart" that helps me create whole,

---

Colleen Reece has published 20 different types of novels (inspirational career, teenage, and high-interest, low-reading level types) and close to 100 articles, short stories, poems and children stories. A Writer's Digest School instructor, she also teaches creative writing at a local college.

fully realized characters. The character chart is a list of characteristics, special qualities, opinions, etc. that each major character in the story possesses. Using the chart can help you create believable characters that even my discerning Dad would have enjoyed.

I developed the chart through my work with the Writer's Digest School and my creative writing classes for Green River Community College in Auburn, Washington. It would have been impossible to count the anguished wails: "But how? How can I make my characters come alive?"

How could I, as an instructor, best answer that question? I never had trouble with characterization in my own work. Now I needed to communicate not only the importance of characterization, but also a concrete method my students could follow. Over the next few weeks my mind churned until one thought stood out: *What is the most important thing to know about a specific character?* I immediately rejected the physical. Anyone could describe a tall, willowy blonde with long-lashed, gorgeous blue eyes. So what? Why did this particular blonde qualify to become a heroine, or a villain?

Close behind the first thought was: *Do I like or dislike her? If I had to describe her in one sentence, what would I say? Why is she the way she is? Who were her parents?* I jotted down all the questions I would usually ask in making a new friend; I felt I was on the trail of something important. Within a short time I had put together a 38-point character chart for my college students. Every student gets one, with the advice to fill it out for every major character and every minor one who will play an important part in the story—*before* starting the manuscript. I also advise completing the character charts before outlining the plot.

As I say, not as I do

I have always known my characters well. They swim around in my head for months while I am completing a project whose characters are "ripe" from living in my brain six months or a year before starting the book they appear in. Yet, several books ago I decided to fill in one of the character charts as a lesson in self-discipline—even though I was convinced I already knew everything there was to know about my next set of characters.

What a shock! I was red-faced with apology to my readers. After I filled out the chart, that particular book took a giant stride forward. I solved problems with "prewriting" instead of "rewriting." At each turning point in the plot, I could see my characters clearly. I knew how each would react and why. For example, my hero was sure of himself, almost to the point of arrogance—his strongest and weakest character traits. Scenes would be easier to write because I already knew how the characters would react to an incident—which was better than "discovering" their reactions when a crisis arose in my manuscript.

I could allow my characters to move freely, and I could refrain from shoving them around like so many pawns in a game of chess. They did not control the story; they simply lived, moved and breathed like "real folks" in their natural habitat, because they had become my friends and enemies, neighbors and strangers.

Since that time, the first work I do on a book is complete my character charts. I don't know anything more exciting than sitting down with a blank chart, a head full of ideas and trembling fingers that list, cross out and relist characteristics about new acquaintances who will grow into part of my own life. Charts are not done at one sitting. A few items may be charted one day; nothing else for a week or longer. Just as friendships take time to form and mature, so should relationships with characters be given time to grow. And the results of this process are characters who are "more." More appealing, more despicable, more understanding, more understandable. Characters who would satisfy even my Dad by "acting as they ought to act."

Following is the chart I now use religiously:

Character Chart

1. Name
2. Age
3. Height
4. Weight
5. Birthdate
6. Birthplace
7. Color hair
8. Color eyes
9. Scars or handicaps (physical, mental or emotional)
10. Educational background
11. Work experience
12. Best friend
13. Men/women friends
14. Enemies and why
15. Parents
16. Present problem
17. How it will get worse
18. Strongest and weakest character traits
19. Sees self as—
20. Is seen by others as—
21. Sense of humor and kind
22. Basic nature
23. Ambitions
24. Philosophy of life
25. Hobbies
26. Kinds of music, art, reading material preferred
27. Dress
28. Favorite colors
29. Pastimes
30. Description of home (physical, mental, emotional atmosphere)
31. Most important thing to know about character
32. One-line characterization
33. What trait will make character come alive, and why
34. Why character is worth writing about
35. Why he/she is different from other similar characters
36. Do I like/dislike this character, and why
37. Will readers like/dislike character for same reasons
38. Characters who are remembered are those who are strong in some way, saints, sinners, or combination of both. Why will this character be remembered?

One of the most interesting things about my character chart is the reaction I get from students. Inevitably, there is a look of panic when students receive the blank form. Inevitably it is followed by comments such as:

"Who cares about all this stuff?" Indignant stares.

"You expect us to fill in this entire chart?"

''I thought you said to write crisply, not to waste words. What's all this? We can't put it in our manuscripts!'' Disdainful fingers pointing, ''Favorite colors? How do I know? Why should I care? Never in a million years will it be in my manuscript!''

''I certainly hope not,'' I say.

When gasps subside, I point out, ''When you see a ship at anchor, you don't see the bottom two thirds. Yet it is that powerful, unseen portion that keeps what you *do* see riding smoothly. It is the same with novels and short stories. What doesn't show about the characters is what supports the part you want readers to see. What you don't know about them also can hurt you. It can cause you to stop short in the middle of your story, stuck because you don't know how that character will react.''

Getting to know a hero

My last nurse/romance, *Alpine Meadows Nurse*, called for a strong hero. Not macho, just strong. It was through my character chart this hero was developed. The first 15 points were easy:

1. *Name*—Kirk Long
2. *Age*—30 +
3. *Height*—6'0''
4. *Weight*—180
5. *Birthdate*—Sept. 15
6. *Birthplace*—Seattle, Washington
7. *Color hair*—sandy
8. *Color eyes*—blue
9. *Scars or handicaps*—walks with slight limp, result of polio as child
10. *Educational background*—University of Washington graduate in forestry
11. *Work experience*—several years with Forest Service
12. *Best friend*—Bob Campbell, engineer from Boeing
13. *Men/women friends*—generally liked but too busy for many friends
14. *Enemies and why*—closest thing to an enemy is Lydia Jackson, former fiancée, now married to Tom Jackson, another Boeing engineer and good friend of Kirk's. Lydia is a green-eyed siren, determined to prove to everyone how desirable she is.
15. *Parents*—travelers, insignificant to plot. However, grandparents are important. In will, Alpine Meadows has been left to Kirk.

With question # 16 came the heart of what made Kirk Long different from all the other six-foot, sandy-haired, blue-eyed men in my repertoire. It took much thought and time before I could go on with my chart. When I did, it shaped up like this:

16. *Present problem*—finding medical help to get started with a camp for children who needed a place to exercise, rest, and most of all, have self-confidence restored.

17. *How will it get worse*—no one local is interested or available. In desperation writes to doctor who helped him overcome his own weaknesses years before.

18. *Strongest and weakest character traits*—Kirk is sure of himself, almost to point of arrogance. He is also bullheaded, unwilling at times to listen to others' viewpoints.

19. *Sees self as*—never takes time for self-examination.

20. *Is seen by others as*—strong, self-assured, in control.

21. *Sense of humor and kind*—good sense of humor, rather dry wit

22. *Basic nature*—outdoorsy

23. *Ambitions*—to help others the way Dr. Lawrence once helped him, by be-lieving he could *overcome* handicap when others doubted.

24. *Philosophy of life*—finds quiet enjoyment of God in nature and recogni-tion of creation as part of his creed.

25. *Hobbies*—too busy for "hobby" type activities

26. *Kinds of music, art, reading material preferred*—does little reading, likes quiet music, prefers the artwork in nature to what people produce

27. *Dress*—casual, hiking boots and khaki

28. *Favorite colors*—browns, blues

29. *Pastimes*—anything outdoors. Natural athlete. Swimming, hiking.

30. *Description of home*—log lodge, originally belonged to grandparents who knew he would cherish it. Set with Mount Rainier for a background, is sur-rounded by woods, flowers, wildlife and peace. It is this peace that reaches out to all those who become part of Kirk's Alpine Meadows camp.

The last eight points were the most difficult. In these questions lie the key to memo-rable characters. It took a lot of time to honestly answer:

31. *Most important thing to know about character*—What did I want to bring out? Finally it came out in two words: He cares. Kirk Long cares enough to do something about the things he believes.

32. *One-line characterization*—Again, how to capture the essence of this strong man in a few words? The only way I knew to do it was to liken him to the acres and acres he had inherited: A man as big as his Alpine Meadows property. The novel itself never said this—it showed in the way Kirk lived.

33. *What trait will make character come alive and why*—his fresh and appeal-ing approach in helping kids.

34. *Why character is worth writing about*—*Note*: Not every character who grabs your imagination deserves to be part of your work. This is the question that can separate professionals from amateurs. This is also the question that has caused me to toss out some of my most appealing applicants for positions in my manu-scripts. No matter how much they appeal to me, if I cannot answer this question to my own satisfaction, out they go.

Answer: Kirk Long made it—he is the type man the world needs more of

35. *Why character is different from other similar characters*—his determina-tion to accomplish what he sets out to do also sets him apart.

36. *Do I like/dislike this character and why?*—I like him. I wish he lived next door. He represents a type of person who could be depended on, called on, and would respond to any need.

37. *Will readers like/dislike character for same reasons*—Yes.

38. *Why will Kirk Long be remembered?*—This was perhaps the hardest question of all. There were many things, but my answer was: Because he's a man who never gave up even in the face of insurmountable obstacles. Like the fellow in the old poem, he "tackled the job that couldn't be done—and he did it."

Kirk Long cared more about setting up a place for crippled children than anything in life. Item # 23 told me how much he wanted that. So when I wrote the following pas-sages, I could visualize the determination that dominated this man:

"Kirk, why are you so insistent that they not be called patients?"

"For the same reason I'm asking you not to wear a white uniform or anything that looks like a hospital. I don't want these kids to see themselves as patients. They will all have been discharged. They need to see themselves as alive, healthy, strong. They need to see themselves as achievers."

and

He brought his big fist down on top of the well-stocked medicine cabinet. "They have to keep on trying and trying! It's the only way some of them will be able to keep from becoming hopeless cripples, or from seeing themselves as such."

I didn't have to stop and think how much he cared, how important it was to him to succeed—I already knew and it was natural to simply record those feelings.

I also knew from items # 18 and # 35 that Kirk would accomplish exactly what he planned. I could see him riding the trail to the camp-out, watching the kids ahead but thinking, and I wrote . . .

Kirk's heart lurched. What about Kelly? He would definitely want a nurse, especially that nurse. Would she stay? Her agreement was for the summer. Would she be able to stand the cold winters so close to Mt. Rainier?

"She'll stay," he told an inquisitive chipmunk. "I'm going to marry her." His decision was in the air, spoken aloud. Now all he had to do was carry it out. He laughed at his own brashness.

There was a long way between now and winter . . .

She already loved it [Alpine Meadows]; he knew that. His blood raced at the thought of her running through the snow, tumbling into his arms after a snowball fight, curled up on the hearth of the big log house. Why not? If a person worked hard enough at anything, there was no reason he couldn't achieve it.

A little smile started. He would marry Kelly Lee Lawrence, spend the rest of his life here helping kids, and someday have some of his own. She might as well get used to the idea.

Kirk Long had passed the character test with banners flying and went on to become what I wanted him to be—a strong but human character, one to whom readers could relate. If he had not passed the test, I would have left him on the "cutting room floor," no matter how much I personally agonized over that decision.

Wrap-up

I challenge each of you who is having trouble with characters or who thinks you know your characters well to put them to this test. If you want to have some fun, do a chart on your spouse or a close friend. You may be amazed. I threw out this challenge in my college class a few weeks ago. One woman came back and told us, "I started one on my husband and haven't been able to complete it yet!"

"How long have you been married?" I asked.

"More than 40 years!"

Enough said.

When that magnificent moment comes and your creation is wrapped for mailing to that special editor who has indicated a desire to meet those characters, before dropping in the mailbox, give yourself one more acid test:

1. Is there a sore, empty feeling inside you, just knowing those new friends are leaving, or tremendous relief when the villain has been defeated?

2. Are you glad the suspense is over, and your characters have resolved their problems—win, lose, or draw?

3. Do you wish you had said just one more thing to one of them?

4. Do you feel the way you did on your daughter's wedding day or the day your last child left for kindergarten in a cold, uncaring world?

There was only one Scarlett O'Hara, one Rhett Butler. Carbon copies will not stand. Yet, lurking in the dim recesses of writers' brains are the qualities and ideas that can create equally powerful "persons on paper." At a recent writers conference, someone said: "Never say, 'I can write a story just as good as' something else. Always say 'I intend to write a better one.' "

I would paraphrase. Never say you can create a character "just as good as" Scrooge, Paul Bunyan or Dr. Jekyll. Invite your parade of characters into your home. Sit across from them at your dinner table. Wait during their endless showers in your one bathroom. Observe their pettiness in daily life and nobility in crises. And when you finally fill in your chart and write about those characters, you will have far more than "just a bunch of words."

> 66 . . . the real, if unavowed, purpose of fiction is to give pleasure by gratifying the love of the uncommon in human experience.
> —*Thomas Hardy* 99

Speaking of dialogue

by John Braine

Dialogue must always be speakable. I apologize for being so obvious, but if I am not obvious, it will be useless. The working rule is this: If you can't speak it aloud, it's no good. Unless you're willing to expend the time to apply this test, you shouldn't attempt to write a novel. It goes without saying that you should do no more than indicate the repetitiousness and incoherences and unfinished sentences of actual speech.

You must of course learn how to listen. As far as is consistent with your temperament, apply the techniques of the professional interviewer in daily life. What this boils down to is learning to ask questions which cannot be answered by a simple yes or no, and learning how to convey the impression of all-consuming interest in the speaker. It's also necessary to learn how to merge into the background, how sometimes to appear as if you're not listening at all.

If you don't do this, then there's no way of learning how to write good dialogue. All books on idiom are out of date as soon as they're written. This is inescapable. Usage and idiom change all the time. But this is only the general pattern. Everyone doesn't change simultaneously. And there are some people who are always out-of-date in their idiom or who use it incorrectly. A novel in which all the characters used idiom which was exactly right for the period would be absolutely unreal.

To complicate matters still further, it's not always necessary that your idiom and usage be correct. You can write superb dialogue which will have very little relation to the way in which people actually speak. (The rule about it being speakable still holds good.) It might well be that this is how you hear people, what you translate unconsciously into

---

John Braine once said of his writing, "I'm a novelist and only a novelist." Known for his critically acclaimed novel Room at the Top, *Braine has also been a British journalist and writer of nonfiction. His other works include* The Queen of a Distant Country, The Crying Game *and* The View From Tower Hill.

an English of your own. If it sounds right to the reader, then it is right. The writing of a novel is an art, not a science, and the novel is an infinitely flexible medium. A novel is a work of fiction, not a sociological report. Listen, but not too much; in the end it's the voices inside your head which are the most authentic.

Mulligan stews

But don't carry this business of writing for the ear too far. When a speaker has a regional or foreign accent, or uses broad dialect, or has some marked peculiarity of pronunciation, it is fatal to attempt to produce it phonetically. Another rule comes into force here: If it doesn't look right, if it is more difficult to read than it would be to listen to in real life, then put it in Standard English. The English alphabet isn't suited for phonetics. It is enough to indicate, outside the dialogue, the special way of speaking; what most accurately conveys the essence of a region, for instance, are the expressions and constructions which are peculiar to the region.

Generally speaking, if you wish to convey that someone has, for instance, a broad Northumbrian accent, then simply say so. If it's very broad, then you can make a brief approximation of what it sounds like phonetically, then say that whoever is listening translates it into plain English, and continue in plain English. In point of fact, this is the most realistic way of doing it; faced with an unfamiliar accent, we're slightly puzzled at first, then rapidly become used to it. And even when faced with unfamiliar expressions or familiar expressions used in an unfamiliar way, we understand by the context. In fact, regardless of how the words are delivered, we manage to get their message—or as much as we want to get.

As an example of how it ought to be done, here is a passage from James Joyce's *Ulysses*:

—The blessings of God on you, Buck Mulligan cried, jumping from his chair. Sit down. Pour out the tea there. The sugar is in the bag. Here, I can't go fumbling at the damned eggs. He hacked through the fry on the dish and slapped it out on three plates, saying:

—*In nomine Patris et Filii et Spiritus Sancti.*

Haines sat down to pour out the tea.

—I'm giving you two lumps each, he said. But, I say, Mulligan, you do make strong tea, don't you?

Buck Mulligan, hewing thick slices from the loaf, said in an old woman's wheedling voice:

—When I makes tea I makes tea, as old mother Grogan said. And when I makes water I makes water.

—By Jove, it is tea, Haines said.

Buck Mulligan went on hewing and wheedling:

—So I do, Mrs. Cahill, says she. Begob, ma'am, says Mrs. Cahill, God send you don't make them in the one pot . . .

The doorway was darkened by an entering form.

—The milk, sir.

—Come in, ma'am, Mulligan said. Kinch, get the jug.

An old woman came forward and stood by Stephen's elbow.

—That's a lovely morning, sir, she said. Glory be to God.

—To whom? Mulligan said, glancing at her. Ah, to be sure.

Stephen reached back and took the milkjug from the locker.

—The islanders, Mulligan said to Haines casually, speak frequently of the collector of prepuces.

—How much sir? asked the old woman.

—A quart, Stephen said . . .

—It is indeed, ma'am, Buck Mulligan said, pouring milk into their cups.

—Taste it, sir, she said.

He drank at her bidding.

—If we could only live on good food like that, he said to her somewhat loudly, we wouldn't have the country full of rotten teeth and rotten guts. Living in a bogswamp, eating cheap food and the streets paved with dust, horsedung and consumptives' spits.

—Are you a medical student, sir? the old woman asked.

—I am, ma'am, Buck Mulligan answered . . .

—Do you understand what he says? Stephen asked her.

—Is it French you are talking, sir? the old woman said to Haines.

Haines spoke to her again a longer speech, confidently.

—Irish, Buck Mulligan said. Is there Gaelic on you?

—I thought it was Irish, she said, by the sound of it. Are you from the west, sir?

—I am an Englishman, Haines answered.

—He's English, Buck Mulligan said, and he thinks we ought to speak Irish in Ireland.

—Sure we ought to, the old woman said, and I'm ashamed I don't speak the language myself. I'm told it's a grand language by them that knows.

—Grand is no name for it, said Buck Mulligan. Wonderful entirely. Fill us out some more tea, Kinch. Would you like a cup, ma'am? (James Joyce, Ulysses [The Bodley Head, 1980], pp. 13-16.)

There are four different voices here. We're told at the beginning that Haines is English; even if we hadn't been, it would have been obvious from his way of speaking—"I say, Mulligan, you do make strong tea . . ." Buck Mulligan and Stephen have the clear enunciation of the educated Dubliner; we can hear Mulligan thicken his accent when he says "in an old woman's wheedling voice" what old mother Grogan says about making tea. The old woman who brings in the milk speaks differently again. She has what neo-Irish call the brogue; this is instantly established without any *shures* or *begorrahs* or *bejabers* or even a dropped consonant.

Character test

You don't have to be a philologist, much less a sociologist, in order to write good dialogue. You need only have a good ear. It's possible to know too much, to become more interested in the words themselves than in what they add up to. The basic purpose of dialogue is to show character. There is no law which decrees that dialogue must always reveal region and class. It's perfectly possible to select what your characters say so as to make these considerations irrelevant.

The American novelist is, because of the far greater variety and richness of US idiom and accent, in a far stronger position than the British novelist. It's always seemed to me that it should be virtually impossible for an American novelist to write bad dialogue. And I should expect a wide assortment of regional accents.

What would seem a great waste if I were an American novelist would be to limit the speech of my characters to one kind. It would be inaccurate, because within most American communities there is a wider variety of accents than in Britain. The reason is that Americans move around more. I don't mean that isolated communities with a few immigrants don't exist, or that the novelist may not for his own purposes elect to have his characters use the same accent and idioms. A novelist isn't a philologist or sociologist except incidentally. But he must always bear in mind just what resources of speech he has to draw from, and if he does limit himself, he should do so only because it makes his novel more effective.

And he should never be in the least influenced by literary fashion as by the consideration of what he considers to be salable. If he writes about any group from poor whites in the South to poor blacks in Harlem it should be only because he is besottedly and drawingly compelled to write about them: He wants to put down on paper the way they talk because he never tires of hearing it.

Another working rule for dialogue is that it should be possible to discover from the dialogue alone what sort of person is speaking.

I apply this test to a passage from Anthony Powell's *A Buyer's Market*:

"As a matter of fact, I have been about very little this summer," he said, frowning. "I found I had been working a shade too hard and had to—well—give myself a bit of rest . . . . Then, the year before, I got jaundice in the middle of the season."

"Are you fit again now?"

"I am better . . . . But I intend to take care of myself . . . . My mother often tells me I go at things too hard. Besides, I don't really get enough air and exercise—without which one can never be truly robust."

"Do you still go down to Barnes and drive golfballs into a net?"

"Whenever feasible . . . ."

"Actually, one can spend too much time on sport if one is really going to get on . . . . And then I have my Territorials."

"You were going to be a solicitor when we last met."

"That would hardly preclude me from holding a Territorial officer's commission . . . ."

"Of course it wouldn't."

"I am with a firm of solicitors—Turnbull, Welford and Puckering, to be exact," he said. "But you may be sure that I have other interests too. Some of them not unimportant, I might add." (Anthony Powell, *A Buyer's Market* [Penguin, 1962], pp. 34-35)

The speaker here has a huge ego. He hasn't any sense of humor. He's obviously very pleased about his status as a professional man and speaks in the way he considers befitting to a professional man. To triumph over others, even though in a small way, gives him great pleasure. If there is any human warmth in his character, it isn't discernible.

Half and half

And what my statement amounts to is no more than a collection of facts, and not even concrete facts. Even if they were expressed with more grace and precision or even wit, we wouldn't be shown a human being. Making statements isn't characterization, no matter how forcefully we make the statements. It's only when people speak that we know them.

But it isn't only by what they say and how they say it that we know them. Along with their speech we must detail their mannerisms, facial expressions or lack of facial expressions, their gestures, their physical state if relevant. Narrative and dialogue cannot be considered in separation. A novel isn't a play with detailed stage directions. Line by line your dialogue should be as speakable as stage dialogue, but it has to flow out of the narrative.

Nothing should be added to the dialogue unless it's necessary in order to make its meaning clear. For the way in which something is said may entirely alter its meaning. For example, ''I'm sorry your dog is dead'' means just that if the speaker has tears in his eyes. If he's smiling broadly, it means the exact opposite. And if a dog is to die in your novel, it's much more interesting if we know that the statement is accompanied by a smile.

Apart from this, too much straight dialogue can rapidly become tedious. Even if it's very good, there's always the problem of not being quite sure who's speaking. Whenever I as a reader come across a run of straight dialogue of much longer than a page, what I suspect as being the reason for it isn't artistic necessity but plain laziness. It's easier to write dialogue than narrative because narrative can be judged by set standards, even if only as prose. The only intention of dialogue is credibility, and this is a matter of opinion.

But, strangely enough, those who can't write credible dialogue can't write good prose either, and there is an inextricable relationship between the fact that Scott Fitzgerald writes superb narrative and superb dialogue. It isn't that the dialogue is merely an extension of his narrative. It could never be so, for its function is to give us words that we can accept as having been spoken in real life. But the same standards of craftsmanship apply to both.

I suspect that the reason that the ability to write good prose and good dialogue go hand-in-hand is simply that a good writer knows how to listen and is prepared to take infinite trouble.

But as a working rule, not more than one half of any novel should be dialogue. It isn't only that dialogue is easier to write—or seems easier to write—it's that the quotation marks have the effect of an authentic professionalism. They are, as it were, a guarantee that what's contained between them is actual speech. Once the quotation marks begin, the action appears to begin.

Shock value

In fact, nothing at all has begun unless we remember from the outset two words of Henry James: Dramatize, dramatize. Every line of dialogue must advance the story, have conflict within it. Even when dialogue must be used to convey essential information, the information must have within it some element of surprise; it must be conveyed through the dialogue because this is the only possible way. And if information is to be conveyed through dialogue, it must be briefly.

"The bastard," said Tom. "I'll kill him, I swear to God I'll kill him." He looked as if he were going to vomit; his face was flushed and there were beads of sweat round his mouth and on his forehead. I put my hand on his arm. He was trembling violently. "Calm down. Who are you going to kill?"

The way you don't do it is to have Tom charge in, describe him, and then have him say: "I'll kill that bastard Travers. He's run off with Hilda. When I came home at six she'd gone and taken the kids. She left this note . . . ."

For once great dollops of information are ladled out, there is no drama, there is nothing to make us read on. Equally to be avoided is fake drama and the use of monosyllables.

> Calm down. Who are you going to kill?''
> "You know.''
> "I don't.''
> "Travers.''
> "Not Travers!''
> "Yes.''

This sort of dialogue can extend a situation to two or three pages, or rather fill out two or three pages with the same effort that it would cost to fill half a page if the job were being done properly. There are, of course, times when a monosyllable can have shocking power, can reverberate through the whole book, can come between the reader and his sleep; but only on condition that the ground is prepared before hand, so that the monosyllable has crammed into it everything that has gone before.

It won't, incidentally, make this sort of dialogue any better if you attempt to build it up with descriptions of the way in which it's spoken:

> "Yes.'' His voice had a dreadful finality.

For you really can't put very much expression into a monosyllable; expression depends upon timing, speed, rhythm, and emphasis, and no one can put these into a three-letter word. So make sure that all your stage directions work.

Selective summaries

There is no need to put down everything which your characters would say in real life. Only put it down if it's essential to the story. Once you've established the speaker, once we've heard his authentic voice, then that's enough. Move to another speaker, or adapt the Raymond Chandler technique of having a man come into the room with a gun in his hand, or summarize. But the new voice has to be worth listening to, the new incident just as surprising as a man coming into the room with a gun in his hand, and the summary smooth and efficient. It should be far more than an abstract statement.

I will quote an example from my own novel, *Room at the Top*. Joe, the ex-sergeant, the working-class boy with a job at the Town Hall, is being put in his place by Brown, the rich industrialist, and his wife, and by Jack, the rich boyfriend of Brown's daughter. The problem was that to detail all that would be said would have taken about 2,000 words. To put someone in his place, to impress upon him his inferior status, has to be done with some degree of finesse. If it's too blatant, it doesn't have the desired effect. But to have had 2,000 words of dialogue at this point would have slowed up the pace which I wanted for this chapter. And a passage of dialogue of that kind, of that length, wouldn't have belonged to the novel.

So I began with Jack speaking:

> "By the way, weren't you at Compton Basset?'' he asked.
> "The Fifty-first,'' I said.
> "A *very* great friend of mine was with that squadron. Darrow, Chick Darrow. Thoroughly decent chap, went to school with him. Went for a Burton over the Ruhr.''

We noncoms used to say *got the chopper*. Going for a Burton was journalist's talk. It sickened me a bit, though I suppose that he was merely making an attempt to talk what he thought was my language. "I don't remember him."

"Oh, you must have met him. You couldn't miss old Chick. Bright red hair and a terrific baritone. Could've been professional."

"I never met him," I said, and kept saying for the next 15 minutes during which he, assisted from time to time by Brown and his wife, played the Do You Know So and So game hard and fast from all angles, social, political, and even religious—they were *astounded* that I didn't know Canon Jones at Leddersford, he was very High of course but he was the only clergyman of any intellectual distinction whatever in the North of England . . . . It's a well-known game, its object being the humiliation of those with less money than yourself; I wouldn't exactly say that they were successful in this, but I certainly paid dearly for Brown's whisky and the whisky which Jack also bought me. The extra refinement, the grace-note, was Jack's waving away of my offer to buy the drinks. ("No, no old boy, frightfully dear stuff this.")

I've never in all my life felt so completely friendless; I was at bay among the glasses of sherry and whisky, with the vicious little darts laden with the pride-paralyzing curare of Do you know—? and Surely you've met—? and You must have come across—? thrown at me unceasingly. Susan said very little but I could see that she knew what was going on. She would have helped me if she could but didn't possess the necessary experience or strength of character to do so.

I'd had two pints of old at the St. Clair before I went into the dance; combined with four whiskies and my increasing irritation they made me forget my usual caution. I wasn't drunk; but I wasn't fully in control of myself. Jack asked me if I knew the Smiling Zombie's son.

"Amazing chap," he said. "Mind you, he'll kill himself in that old Alfa. Drives like a maniac. You must know him, he's always around Dufton."

"I don't know any tallymen," I said.

There was silence.

"I don't follow you, old man."

"A tallyman sells clothes on credit," I said. "In effect it's moneylending. You buy direct from the manufacturer and sell at a retail price about 50 per cent above what I, or any other person with eyes in his head, would pay. Then you charge interest—"

"It's business," Jack cut in. "You wouldn't refuse the profits, would you?"

"It's a dirty business," I said. (John Braine, *Room at the Top* [Eyre & Spottiswoode, 1957])

The summary is, I hope, interesting because it's specific and because of the use of the metaphor of the Do You Know So and So game. I'm specific about time, too; what Joe is also saying is that there was an actual conversation and he's summarizing it. He remembers exactly how long it lasted because every minute lasted the full 60 seconds.

I don't, of course, say that this is the only way to do it. There are times when the summary need only be brief. But the reader should always be left with the feeling that you've been selective, that the words which are summarized have all actually been spoken, but you haven't put them down because they'd be boring.

Uncontrived humor

How to portray a boring person is a different matter. This must necessarily be done mainly through his conversation, since there is a limit to what you can write about his effect upon other people. You certainly can't do it through being strictly realistic: Apart from their habit of repetition, what makes bores boring is the simple fact that they talk too much. Your bores in that case would actually be boring, and to be boring is the one offense of which you must never be guilty. What you must do is to convey the essence of the bore's character—which is an overweening sense of his own importance and an almost complete lack of humor. (There are bores who imagine that they possess a sense of humor, and they're the worst bores of all.)

"As you probably know," he said, "my opinions have moved steadily to the left of late years. I quite see that there are aspects of Hitler's program to which objection may most legitimately be taken. For example, I myself possess a number of Jewish friends, some of them very able men—Jimmy Klein, for example—and I should therefore much prefer that item of the National Socialist policy to be dropped. I am, in fact, not at all sure that it will *not* be dropped when matters get straightened out a bit. After all, it is sometimes forgotten that the National Socialists are not only 'national,' they are also 'socialist.' So far as that goes, I am with them. They believe in planning. Everyone will agree that there was a great deal of the old Germany that it was right to sweep away—the Kaisers and Krupps, Hindenburgs and mediatized princes, stuff of that sort—we want to hear no more about them." (Anthony Powell, *At Lady Molly's* [Penguin, 1963], p. 59.)

Widmerpool isn't, of course, at all concerned whether his audience is interested in his opinions about Nazi Germany. He doesn't know anything about the realities of Nazi rule—he can't, because he has no imagination, another essential quality of the bore. He doesn't expect to be disagreed with, even when he finally makes a most fantastic suggestion:

"Take a man like Goering. Now, it seems pretty plain to me from looking at photographs of him in the papers that he only likes swaggering about in uniforms and decorations. I expect he is a bit of a snob—most of us are at heart—well, ask him to Buckingham Palace. Show him round. What is there against giving him the Garter? After all, it is what such things are for, isn't it?" (Anthony Powell, *At Lady Molly's* [Penguin, 1963], p.59)

And this is the heart of the matter. The bore is essentially comic; he is always unaware that he's lost his trousers and someone's painted his nose red.

A general note here about humor: No formula exists for the proportion of humor in your dialogue. But dialogue that is entirely serious, which doesn't contain at least some atttempts at humor, is not only ultimately depressing, but also false. Not very many people are genuinely funny all the time, but the majority try to be funny some of the time. You don't have to introduce comic characters deliberately, you don't have to contrive comic incidents, but merely remember that most people say or hear at least one funny thing every day.

Start with clashing goals

by F.A. Rockwell

A successful plot, like an admirable life, is one in which a character does not achieve his purpose too easily. There must be several seemingly insurmountable obstacles to be hurdled. These are assured in a story when the antagonistic force is working constantly to achieve a goal that clashes with that of the protagonist. Right in or near the beginning you should set up the opposing entities—each with clearly stated goals that clash with those of the other.

Many lawyers like Erle Stanley Gardner, Robert Traver, Balzac, and Michael Gilbert became successful fiction writers because they were trained to think in terms of clashing goals—prosecution versus defense, with all the accompanying conflict and suspense that make good plots. Their experience in legal cases taught them the importance of thoroughly developed arguments for *both* sides in a contest.

The tragic truth about many rejected stories that are near-misses is *incompleteness*. The author may do a good job of dramatizing the struggle of a protagonist hurdling obstacles in his attempts to achieve a goal, but it may be a one-man show, lacking the counter-plot of one or more characters who work as hard as the hero to block him.

Be sure to develop the counter-plot with goals that clash with the hero's desire, so that oppositional forces are clearly antipodal. If the hero's goal is escape, the villain's is to trap him; if his goal is to catch a criminal, the latter's purpose is to elude or even kill him. Preplan your clashing goals, emphasizing the counter-plot action so that it is as strong as the main story line.

You can develop marvelous stories by starting with contrasting characters who have clashing goals. For instance, a man is a meat-lover (perhaps even a butcher) and his wife,

F.A. Rockwell, *author of* How to Write Plots That Sell *and* How to Write Nonfiction That Sells, *has written more than 600 articles on writing. She also wrote and produced the television series* Writing for Profit. *Rockwell is a former* Writer's Digest *editor.*

an antivivisectionist and vegetarian. One spouse loves culture, the other, wrestling matches and rough sports; one character favors formal education, the other life-living; one is a devout churchgoer, the other anti-dogmatic religion or perhaps even atheistic. In a relationship in which harmony is necessary, the clashing goals can result from contrasting character traits or rivalry that must be worked out for mutual benefit. In a hero-villain conflict story, one tries to destroy the other.

In either case, if your story is to attain its goal of publication, it must start with your protagonist wanting *desperately* to achieve a specific goal. If possible, introduce a time limit for additional pressure and suspense, as the scientists in the Wildfire Project must solve the riddle of the microorganism called Andromeda Strain that has killed all but two citizens of Piedmont, Arizona, and thereby prevent a worldwide epidemic.

Opposing and antagonistic

Perhaps a protagonist *must* rescue himself or a loved one from nuclear or germ warfare, earthquake, fire, flood, human villain, or some other catastrophe. He *must* win the girl, game, contest, election, job, fight, or the confidence of a group. Or he *must* kick a bad habit: drugs, drink, gambling, kleptomania, gossip, lying, or some other compulsion that's causing tragedy. The condemned man or his lawyer, friend, or relative *must* prove his innocence before his sentence is carried out; or the parolee *must* prove the guilt of the real culprit who framed him before he is returned to prison. These are just a few ideas to which you should add others that coincide with your interests and ideas.

Choose a character and goal you care about so that you can intensify the emotional power of the goal desire. Your protagonist must want his goal as deeply as Abel wants Rima (William Henry Hudson's *Green Mansions*), as Murray Burns wants to be a nonconformist and rebel against society's rat-race (Herb Gardner's *A Thousand Clowns*); as Yakov Bok wants to maintain his integrity (Bernard Malamud's *The Fixer*); as Maria wants to serve the Lord (*Sound of Music* by Howard Lindsay and Russel Crouse); as Eliza Doolittle wants to become a lady and Henry Higgins wants to prove his speech theories (*My Fair Lady*); and as Mattie Ross *must* avenge her father's murder (Charles Portis' *True Grit*).

When you preplan your story, try to open with a situation in which the hero's desire to *gain the goal* is thwarted by the *impossibility of achieving it*. Such a confrontation will probably snatch reader interest immediately so that you will not lose it forever. Watch customers in a bookstore. How many read a first page, then either put the book down and pick up another, or decide to buy it?

One of Hollywood's top story editors always warns writers: "*A story begins when the conflict begins. A story ends when the conflict ends. All else is wasted.*"

Conflict means *clashing goals*, which must be quickly established between the opposing entities who or which will keep defying each other actively throughout the whole plot. They must teeter-totter dynamically up and down, with one triumphing over the other in one place, and then being defeated in another—up, down, up, down, constantly alternating until the ultimate victory or defeat of the main character.

The private eye, law enforcement officer, or private citizen-hero wants to solve a crime and/or catch a criminal, whereas the latter wants to "get away with it." The prisoner or slave wants freedom, whereas the authorities or master wants to keep him or her confined. (*Papillon*, *The Great Escape* or the BBC-TV series *Colditz*, which dramatizes the many escape attempts of Allied officers from the notorious "escape-proof" German castle-prison 22 miles southeast of Leipzig.) The kidnaper wants money or acquiescence to certain terms whereas the law wants to catch the criminal(s) and recover the victim unharmed.

Police Chief Martin Brody wants to close the beaches to protect swimmers from the great white killer-shark, whereas Mayor Larry Vaughan and news editor Harry Meadows want them "open for business" (Peter Benchley's *Jaws*).

Harvard law student Hart and his classmates want to graduate and become attorneys but tough Professor Kingsfield makes it extremely difficult, doing everything to over-power, overwork, insult, and discourage them (Jim Bridges' *The Paper Chase*).

Strong obstacles, strong plot

The more clashing goals you have, the stronger and more suspenseful your plot will be, especially if your hero must battle many different opposing entities. Serpico must fight not only crime and criminals but corruption in his own police department as well. In John McGreevey's telefilm *A Man Whose Name Was John*, Archbishop Angelo Roncalli (later Pope John XXIII) wants to save 647 German Jewish children stranded aboard a steamer in Istanbul harbor. He locks horns with Turkish, German, and Portuguese authorities, whose goal is to send the children back to Germany and death. His own sister opposes him, begging him to forget the kids and go to their dying father in Italy instead. He keeps on course to his goal, which seems impossible to attain. As in all good plots, the crisis contains the seed of the solution. His last hope, the Portuguese ambassador, whose baby he has previously baptized, says he isn't interested in saving anyone who isn't Roman Catholic. This inspires the hero to issue the children baptismal papers, which will enable them to enter Portugal and survive.

Study the multiple opposition each protagonist is up against in professional plots. Be sure to have at least that many in your own—even more, if feasible.

In Pat Conroy's novel, *The Water is Wide* which became the movie, *Conrack* (scripted by Irving Ravetch and Harriet Frank, Jr.), the white Southerner goes to teach at an all-black school on a remote island off the coast of South Carolina. The natives are im-poverished fisherfolk with no hope, knowledge, or ambition. He wants to enlighten the illiterate kids and, of course, there must be clashing goals to transform a so-what situa-tion into an engrossing plot. He has three strong obstacles:

1. The abysmal ignorance of the traditionally illiterate black children.
2. The black woman principal who feels that knowledge would be a danger-ous thing, arousing unrealizable hopes. Her dogma of despair is as much an oppo-nent to the hero as she is.
3. The racist superintendent who upholds the biased black-inferiority tradi-tion and who hates the hero for making school a place to discover what could be in-stead of what is.

After you have decided upon a protagonist with a strong goal (against which there are stronger opposing goals), consider carefully the six ways you can work out the plot action:

1. Protagonist wins goal
2. Protagonist loses goal
3. Both characters win
4. Both lose
5. Compromise ending
6. Pyrrhic victory (winning the original goal but at an incredible price—named for King Pyrrhus of Epirus who defeated the Romans but suffered such heavy casualties that he said: "One more such victory and I am lost.")

Study professional plots that end in each of the six ways, keeping a file that may start with fairy story classics and go on through the newest publications and productions.

1. Protagonist wins goal

This is the most frequent formula, exemplified by such Bible stories as little David slaying Goliath, Daniel surviving the lions, and Moses leading his people into the Promised Land; fairy tales like Cinderella, Jack the Giant-Killer, and the Ugly Duckling; and the usual Western and whodunit in which Good conquers Evil. In this hurray-for-the-good-guy happy-ending story you must create strong obstacles for the hero to conquer, but triumph he does! As the Santa Vittorians outwit the Germans and save their 1,320,000 bottles of vermouth from the Germans in *The Secret of Santa Vittoria*, as Sam Varner saves Sarah Carver from murderous Salvaje in *Stalking Moon* and as Dr. Mark Hall and Project Wildfire avoid world destruction from *The Andromeda Strain*.

2. Protagonist loses goal

Here, the "good guy" loses out and there is a tragic ending, all the way from Hans Christian Andersen's "The Little Mermaid" and Little Red Riding Hood to Anne Frank's lost goal of survival in *The Diary of a Young Girl* and the slice-of-life stories of frustration in many quality magazines. In Frederick Pohl's *Playboy* yarn "Speed Trap," Dr. Chesley Grew's goal is to work uninterrupted and to perfect his theory of the Quantum of Debate, the irreducible minimum of argument that each participant in a discussion can use to make a point understood, accomplishing his goal in one-fourth of the usual time and having the remaining three-fourths of the time for doing other work. His goal is totally defeated by pleasant and unpleasant interruptions, by friends, enemies, his own weaknesses, and by supernatural as well as natural influences, all of which conspire to prevent human accomplishment. Likewise in Evan Hunter's "The Sharers," successful Negro accountant Howard's goal is to maintain his high position in white society. A psychologically sadistic white co-commuter, Harry Pryor, carries on an insidious campaign by quizzing him daily in a shared taxi-ride to work. Howard's pride, self-confidence, and goal are eventually lost, and even his desperate efforts to avoid his inquisitor make him feel like a runaway slave.

3. Characters with different or opposing goals both win

In George Kelly's play *The Show Off*, braggart Aubrey Piper's goal is to impress everyone with his back-slapping personality and his overinflated delusions of grandeur. His girl's mother, Mrs. Fisher, wants her daughter Amy to marry a worthwhile husband instead of a windbag like Piper. Although he's a poorly paid shipping clerk when he marries Amy and moves into the Fisher home, he proves he's not all brag and braggage by helping her brother get twice as much money for an invention.

Both ex-GI buddies win contrasting goals in Garson Kanin's "Buddy." Ambitious, self-motivated Rod wants success, whereas Pete Rossi wants love. Rod seems on his way to fortune by courting the boss' daughter Jennie, but upon learning that a man should marry the boss' daughter but not *his own* boss' daughter, he ditches Jennie for a richer, more brilliant redhead whom he marries. Later, to keep her ignorant of his affair with an English model, Rod enlists Pete to cover up for his weekends with the model. Pete pities the wife, takes her flowers, and they develop true rapport and love, which culminates in a happy marriage after Rod divorces her and marries still-rich Jennie (who by now is twice-divorced with two bratty kids). Pete gains the love he has been seeking and

Rod is able to conceal any disappointment behind a facade of wealth.

In Robert Louis Stevenson's *The Sire de Maletroit's Door*, everybody wins: The hero vindicates his honor, the old gentleman puts an end to scandal and restores his self-esteem, and the girl, who has suffered rejection, finds true requited love.

4. Both lose

This method of plot resolution is most frequently found in stories of unfulfilled love. In "The Prison" by Harry Mark Petrakis, Alexandra, lonely 40 year-old librarian, finds companionship, rapport, and love with 45 year-old bachelor, Harry Kladis, whose father has died, leaving his mother to smother him. "They were delighted to find they both enjoyed concerts and chop suey with black pekoe tea and almond cookies." Their planned marriage is postponed by Harry's devotion to his grieving, widowed mother and her hold on him. When his mother finally dies, he tries futilely to regain Alexandra's love, but gets a furious rebuff and slapped face in the "Hell hath no fury like a woman scorned" ending.

A classic example of lost goals for all characters appears in Edith Wharton's *Ethan Frome*. Ethan, unhappily married to hypochondriacal invalid Zenobia, loves Mattie Silver, Zenobia's lovely young cousin who is persecuted by the jealous, irascible wife, whose goal is to have both Ethan and Mattie wait on her as her slaves. When it is clear that Ethan and Mattie cannot live and love together, their goal is double suicide by sledding into an elm tree. But they lose even their suicide goal as both are hopelessly crippled so that Zenobia must hereafter take care of them.

5. Compromise ending

In John Hersey's *A Bell for Adano*, Major Victor Jappolo's goal is to bring American democracy and friendship to the formerly German-occupied Sicilian town. The military's goal is to rule by might, regimentation, and red tape. The Major brings to the people American good will and the bell they want, but in bucking military brass, he is transferred to North Africa and forced to leave Adano and its people whom he loves.

Alexander Frater's *New Yorker* story "The Practitioner" opens with a tight stalemate of clashing goals between a Tonkinese husband and his wife. Matua is an ardent pearl-diver who wants to spend all his time pearl diving, whereas his wife wants more of his time and companionship. She precipitates a crisis by taking a B.O.A.C. flight bag full of her husband's most precious pearls to the crest of a steep cliff from which the men think she'll jump or throw the pearls. She increases their fears by talking about feeding imaginary dragons in the seas. "These Tonk ladies have very weak heads, you know," says the Ravu, the Medical Practitioner. He gives his diagnosis and prognosis: "She is perfectly well . . . But you, Matua, if you don't mind my saying so, could help by spending a little more of your time on dry land. I mean here at home with your-. . . spouse." A happy, compromise ending is achieved when Matua rescues the flight bag of pearls and promises: "Listen, Mister. Tomorrow I'll take this woman and her kite up Mount Koro, and we'll fly it in the trade winds."

Compromise endings are popular because of their usual valuable premise: "You have to give in a little to gain a lot." Most relationships benefit from each member compromising to the other person's goals rather than insisting upon gaining his own. In Sophie Kerr's "Madame Learns about Americans," Madame Flanier, "French as the Eiffel Tower," dislikes her daughter's new country, America, and her inlaws, whom she considers uncouth. They, in turn, hate her hostility and snobbishness, and the two mothers-in-law, Madame Flanier and Mrs. Jenkins, continue a battle royal until young Arthur

Jenkins tells a story about two bears who keep fighting to see which can put the highest scratch on the tree. All they accomplish is killing the tree and proving what destructive claws they have. This makes each woman call off hostilities and compliment each other's cooking. Complete family happiness results from compromise.

6. Pyrrhic victory

By refusing to compromise, characters in certain works stubbornly strive to achieve a specific goal (usually a selfish one), do actually win it, but lose something greater. In short, they win the battle but lose the war. In George Kelly's *Craig's Wife*, Harriet wants a meticulously beautiful house, which she gets at the cost of losing her husband and any hope for marital happiness. In Guy de Maupassant's "The Necklace," Madame Loisel succeeds in winning her social-climbing goal of borrowing a rich woman's necklace to become "the belle of the ball," and eventually in earning money to repay her when the necklace is lost, but only after years of exhausting work that costs her youth, looks, and energy. The bitter irony is that the necklace was only paste!

In the movie *The Way We Were*, the radical, idealistic wife wants to combat the Establishment, whereas her conventional, materialistic husband wants to become successful within its framework. Each achieves the immediate goal but loses their marriage and family togetherness with their little girl (similar to the *Craig's Wife* structure). In Uris' *QB VII*, Dr. Kelno wins his lawsuit for libel against Abe Cady but loses his self-respect, son, and reputation.

An excellent way to preplan your story is to begin with opposing goals and tentatively work out the action to each of the six different types of endings. How many professional examples can you think of in which a sharp generation gap is caused by an adult's wanting to discipline a child or children whose goal is to be rebellious and untamed? The following illustrations demonstrate how each method of resolution has been used.

1. Adult protagonist wants to tame child (or children) and wins this goal. In Enid Bagnold's *Chalk Garden*, Miss Maitland civilizes wildly destructive Laurel; Annie Sullivan tames savage blind-deaf-and-dumb Helen Keller in William Gibson's *The Miracle Worker*; Maria wins over the hostile von Trapp children in the *Sound of Music*; Mary Poppins enchants her wild youngsters; and each teacher tames, disciplines, and teaches antagonistic pupils in James Clavell's *To Sir, With Love*, Bel Kaufman's *Up the Down Staircase*, and Evan Hunter's *The Blackboard Jungle*.

2. Adult protagonist loses goal of reforming a revolting child. *Bad Seed* (by William March) dramatizes the futile efforts of a mother to civilize her hopelessly delinquent daughter. She loses not only her goal but also her life. Less gruesome but as unsuccessful are Aunt Sally's and the Widow Douglas' goal to tame and educate the untamable Huckleberry Finn in Mark Twain's classics. Adults also are conquered by the will of youth in Alan Sillitoe's *The Loneliness of the Long Distance Runner*, when the teenager deliberately loses the race that his schoolmasters want him to win.

3. Both win. Study happy-ending generation-conflict stories like Jean Webster's *Daddy Long Legs*, or any drama in which a creative child wants to be or expresses himself or herself; the adult tries to modify the child's exuberance and win respect and the youngster's successful expression of ingenuity brings rewards to both of them. Other successful uses of this ending can be found in the motion pictures *Popi* and *Me, Natalie*.

4. Both lose. In Lillian Hellman's *The Children's Hour*, the teachers, Karen Wright and Martha Dobie, want to run a successful girls' school. A neurotic troublemaker, Mary Tilford, defies their authority and seeks to destroy them by spreading a rumor that they

are lesbians. The teachers lose all their goals: Their desire to educate the girls and discipline Mary; their school, which is ruined by the scandal and ensuing lawsuit; also Karen loses her fiancé and Martha, her life through suicide. Although Mary appears to win her goal of defying and destroying her teachers, she loses her greater goal: power over her grandmother and her schoolmates who will never completely trust her again.

5. Compromise ending. In Lesley Conger's *Good Housekeeping* story "When You Give Your Heart," the mother wants her six-year-old son Ted to break off his friendship with a mentally retarded boy, Perry, whereas Ted wants to keep playing with Perry. A crisis scene in which Ted battles other boys in defense of the retarded child proves to the mother her son's maturity that cannot be held back, since he has true kindness, understanding, and compassion. She compromises by not breaking up the friendship; he, by going to school and making new friends but not giving up Perry completely.

6. Pyrrhic victory. Adult Riccardo Ghione wanted to capture childhood from one to three in a film. He succeeded with his unrehearsed, revealing movie, *Il Limbo*, but in capturing the spontaneous actions and expressions of the toddlers he lost his illusions about childish innocence. He learned that: "Every authentic child is a rebel and an anarchist; if one allowed him to develop following his instincts there would be such a radical transformation of society, any adult who allowed him to develop following his revolution would be put to shame."

Common, basic, identifiable goals

By now you probably realize how vital clashing goals and the correct resolution of them are to your story. *Conflict* is achieved when the goals of people who love each other clash, or when rivals fight for the same goal, which only one of them can attain. *Suspense* is achieved when the reader cannot guess who will win out and when there is an exciting teeter-tottering of triumphs and defeats. *Surprise* is achieved when unexpected events explode to generate unexpected (but credible) drama. *Satisfaction* is achieved by the ways in which the goals are won by deserving characters and lost by villains in a commercial story. In a quality yarn, however, the hero may not win and the villain may not lose, but *Insight* is achieved as the tragedy illuminates a great moral truth and adds significance in the form of a revealing premise. *Salability* is assured when your plot action dramatizes the attainment of goals that are emotionally valid, identifiable, and timely.

Before writing a story, novel, or play, list the goals of each character, why each wants what, the steps he will take in his goal-direction, and what obstacles he will meet. Remember that:

1. The plus or minus nature of the goal usually determines the type of character. A person who wants to destroy, expose, or harm an innocent victim for his own selfish advantage is a villain. A person who endangers himself to help others is a hero.

In Noah Gordon's *A World Apart* all the medical personnel share a general goal: to cure illness. Nurse Beth Sommers altruistically dedicates her life to helping humanity, which makes her a radiant heroine. Older Dr. Weintraub shares her love of people but has an added specific goal of wanting to make better doctors and is especially interested in softening the character of young Dr. Michael Cooper, whose original goal was to become rich through medicine. All the while he is calloused to human suffering and uses patients for selfish means, he is unsympathetic. But after his affirmative-goaled coworkers kindle his finer instincts and he becomes considerate, he regenerates into a hero. In all scripts, whether the character has a good or evil goal determines whether the reader likes or dislikes him.

2. All characters must have goals, even the minor actors. Usually the goals are revealed when each person steps into the story or shortly thereafter. But in certain cases the

goal may take shape after a specific action, for instance a revenge or reward goal resulting from motivating incidents. In novels like *The $300 Man*, the boy's search for his replacement begins *after* he learns how his own father cheated to get him out of the draft. Changed goals often appear in stories like *Ben Hur*, whose original goal was peaceful coexistence with the Roman conquerors of his country, particularly Messala. Later, after his mother and his sister disappear, his goal is to find them. Throughout the rest of the plot action as Messala's sadistic villainies increase, Ben Hur's original plus goals of peace and love reverse to revenge and destruction. *The Guns of Navarone* travels in the opposite direction. The original revenge goal of the Greek colonel was to kill the English officer whom he blames for his wife's death. Later, when the two men are assigned to the same mission of destroying a huge German cannon to save 2,500 British soldiers, his goal switches to cooperation to the point of risking his life to save the Briton. Then, after they've shared hardships and dangers and the Colonel has found love, he abandons his original hate-revenge goal for a new goal of building a new loving life.

    3. The goal must be in line with basic human values that concern all people of all time and with which the reader can idenifity: life, liberty, happiness, approbation, security, retribution, fame, etc.

    4. The goal must never be too easy to attain nor the means of attaining it transparent and guessable by the reader.

    5. The goal must have emotional significance so that the reader shares the character's involvement.

    6. Before starting to write be sure to ask: What does each character want? Why? Why can't he have it? Who or what opposes him? What steps will he take to overcome each obstacle? Who or what will help him? Are there enough obstacles for a long script? Too many for a short one?

Individual goals, overall success

Don't be satisfied with a single-goaled situation, rather, plan an opening that presents an exciting stalemate caused by a clash of antipodal goals, something along the lines of the irresistible force meeting the immovable object. In *Wild River*, Chuck Glover's goal is to clear the land for flooding for the TVA project, which means removing Ella Garth from her home; her goal is to remain. In Roger O. Hirson's "The First Day," Nora's goal after release from the mental institution is to build a brand new self; her family's goal is to make her the same old Nora.

For variety, try reversing the ordinary goal-clashing situations. It is usual for a girl to want marriage, a man just an affair. In Max Shulman's *How Now, Dow Jones?*, the heroine consents to the affair but refuses to marry the boy. Your hero could want home and kiddies and the domestic life, while the girl is a Women's Libber and wants to stay single and unfettered. Since most people want success, fame, or fortune, your protagonist could go to great lengths to be poor and unknown. Or, like Mr. Deeks in John Hess' *The Wicked Scheme of Jebel Deeks*, your character could sneak money into the bank instead of robbing it.

All the time you are working out the individual goals of your actors, you'll be speeding toward your overall goal of writing success. Christopher Isherwood is right when he says that if this is your goal and you work hard enough, you can't miss! He insists that "If a person wants to become a writer, he'll become one . . . *The desire is the vocation.*" He adds that no discouragement will stop the real writer, whereas no one has to discourage the others. They'll do it themselves.

What is your writing goal: success or failure? Being goal-conscious will make the difference.

The right viewpoint: how to choose and use point of view effectively

by Les Boston

Some people (Are you one of them?) write grammatically but cannot explain grammar. They may even become annoyed at the mention of grammar.

It is the same with point of view in fiction: Some writers who get it right—instinctively or otherwise—do not like the subject. One highly successful novelist, when asked about his handling of point of view, showed much annoyance and said he never bothered with point of view, that all he did was "keep in mind whose story it is." Another novelist, a Pulitzer Prize winner speaking at another gathering of writers, spent many minutes detailing violations by the great writers of all the "rules" governing point of view, then dismissed the subject.

Unfortunately, such commentary is not very helpful to the writer who hasn't mastered point of view, and, also unfortunately, point of view is very often a problem or the cause of a problem in a piece of fiction. Fortunately, there is a certain basic knowledge that the writer can master and with which the writer can make good decisions about point of view. What follows is that basic writer's information.

Getting a point of view on point of view

In principle

Physical point of view is easy: It is the *point* from which something is *viewed*. If you are standing at the flag pole on the east side of a building, you can, from that point, describe the east side of the building but not the west. In fiction, point of view (let's use the screenwriter's abbreviation, POV) is not that simple. It has to do with

---

Les Boston, a professor of English, teaches short story writing at Los Angeles Valley College and classes at the UCLA Extension Writer's Program. A freelance writer and editor when time permits, Boston is also the author of one of Approaches to Professional Writing, *one of the college texts he uses for his classes.*

—whose story it is;
—who tells or perceives—or can tell or perceive—the story;
—how much of the story any character is to know—and when;
—how the reader is to receive and perceive the story.

Those four concerns may fall into place or may have to be edited into place. The second is what is usually treated as POV and will get most attention here, but the others are not to be ignored.

In practice

There are no absolute rules governing POV. Almost everything has been tried, and published writers break the ''rules'' and get away with violations because of their skill, their technique, their reputation, superior stories, sleepy editors, or some other reason. If, however, your story does not work because of unclear, uncontrolled, or inconsistent POV, naming 20 famous writers who did the same thing will not make your story work. Keeping in mind the practical points below will enable you to make POV work:

1. A character is or becomes a POV character whenever the reader gets information (observations, thoughts, feelings) from or through—or inside information about—that character. For example:

—It was a cool spring afternoon when I joined an angry crowd at City Hall.
—Sarah saw the car pull away from the curb.
—Wilbur wondered where he had gone wrong.

An adverb included carelessly in a sentence can take the reader into the wrong character's mind; watch for them when revising:

—Sarah looked *cautiously* around the corner.
—Wilbur sang *happily* as he walked.

The characters may appear *cautious* or *happy* to an observer, but strictly speaking that is inside information.

2. Stories may have no POV character, but usually have one or more; and generally the fewer, the better.

3. When readers get stories through POV characters, at least one character must be present for all action.

4. Readers may or may not be aware of the person of the storysteller.

5. Readers must know whatever a POV character knows—and at the same time; that includes decisions reached as well as outside information.

6. Problems occur when it is not clear who the POV character is, when there are too many POV characters, when there are uncontrolled shifts of POV, when information is withheld, and when information is given too early or too late or by the wrong character.

7. Stories that seem not to work for other reasons sometimes work when written from a different POV.

Whose story is it?

Knowing whose story you are writing is critical; it might take care of POV entirely.

The possibilities are many: You may write the story of one character, of two, three, ten; of one spouse or both; of the child, the parents, or all three; of the coal miners, the mine owners, or all of them; of the captain, the crew, or both. But you *must* make choices.

One writer used the first two pages of a short story to establish sympathy for a good son's efforts to find a retirement home for his father. Then the father's POV—and his wish to live and die in the house he had built—took over, and the story never recovered. It could have been the story of either or both, but the writer resisted the choice and lost the story.

In another family story, a young woman learned that her parents were divorcing just as she was ready to announce her engagement. The writer wanted to like all three, wanted the reader to like all three, and tried to make the story about all three. An unfocused and uninteresting first draft led to the realization that it was the daughter's story; the parents could still be presented sympathetically, but it was not their story.

Decisions may be made in the planning or writing stage. Obviously, the earlier the decision—if it's a good one—the more efficient the writing.

You must know your characters to decide which are major and which are minor, which will have their stories told and which will only assist. The fewer characters in the story and the fewer POV characters, the easier the story will be to keep in focus.

Who will—or can—tell the story?

As noted earlier, discussions of POV usually center on who tells the story. Possibilities, treated below, are several; in the simplest sense, a story may be told by the author, by a narrator, or seemingly by no one, that is, a storyteller without a presence.

The author as storyteller

The story told by the author in editorial omniscience has largely disappeared. Decades ago, the author addressed the reader, and said: "I'm going to tell you a story," and told everything. The author not only told the story, but commented on it, judged it, and departed from it in authorial intrusions short and long: "And, now, dear reader, we must leave Wilbur to nurse his wounds while we . . . ."

It is not easy to keep all real-world opinions out of fiction, but for most stories you are well advised to avoid editorial comments and let the characters and the actions tell the story.

A narrator as storyteller

A narrator is a person who tells the reader what happened. The narrator may or may not be a part of the story, and the narrator's position relative to the story can be variable and complex. (As a reader, you may be unable to tell whether some stories are being told by the author or by the narrator, but as a writer, you should know what you are doing.)

The narrator can be the main character, the protagonist. That is your best choice for a personal, intimate story in which the character's thoughts, feelings, perceptions, personality changes, and responses to other people and events are vital and interesting. We all like to share another's experience, to hear another person's story. and we are prepared to be sympathetic when we read: "It was a silly mistake to make—getting off the subway at the wrong stop—but I made it, and there I was in a strange part of town, no change in my purse, and already half an hour late for . . . ." That approach works equally well for short stories and novels; the question is whether the narrator can carry all that needs carrying.

Using the main character as a narrator is not a good choice if the reader needs information that the character could not know or if the reader must not learn until later what the character must know earlier. It is not a good choice for showing complex action. It is not a good choice for autobiographical stories if the writer cannot avoid being rigid, self-indulgent, or evasive; we do not like narrators who brag about their achievements or who will not admit flaws and failures.

The narrator can be a secondary character, someone who knows the main character, who can see that character in a perspective that the main character cannot, who can give the reader information at times more critical for plot development, and who need not give unwanted or unnecessary information.

Fitzgerald, in *The Great Gatsby*, for example, made Nick Carraway a person in whom others confide. Nick gets Gatsby's story and the stories of other people and gives them to the reader along with his own insights. Note how smoothly Fitzgerald lets the reader know that Nick got information from Gatsby's butler and how Nick's reflections reveal Gatsby's character:

> At two o'clock Gatsby . . . left word with the butler that if any one phoned word was to be brought to him . . . .
> No telephone message arrived, but the butler went without his sleep and waited for it until four o'clock . . . . I have an idea that Gatsby himself didn't believe it would come, and perhaps he no longer cared. If that was true he must have felt that he had lost the old warm world, paid a high price for living too long with a single dream . . . .

In the Sherlock Holmes stories, Holmes' slower witted partner, Dr. Watson, is the narrator, and he and the reader figure out how it happened at the same time. The brilliant Holmes has, of course, already solved the crime, and if he were the narrator, the POV character, the reader would have to know as soon as Holmes knows, and suspense would be lost. Near the end of *The Hound of the Baskervilles*, for example, Watson gets a five-page response when he asks Holmes for "a sketch of the course of events." Watson (and the reader) must call for more: ". . . there is one point which you have left unexplained. What became of the hound when its master was in London?" After Holmes answer, for Watson: "There only remains one difficulty," which Holmes resolves in the last paragraph.

The narrator may be a marginal character, barely a part of the action of the story. "Haircut," by Ring Lardner, is a monologue that begins:

> I got another barber that comes over from Carterville and helps me out Saturdays . . . .
> You're a newcomer, ain't you? I thought I hadn't seen you round before. I hope you like it good enough to stay. As I say, we ain't no New York City or Chicago, but we have pretty good times. Not as good, though, since Jim Kendall got killed. When he was alive, him and Hod Myers used to keep this town in an uproar. I bet they was more laughin' done here than any town its size in America.

The monologue ends:

> It probably served Jim right, what he got. But still we miss him round here. He certainly was a card!
> Comb it wet or dry?

Although the barber is not a participant in the events that lead to Jim's death, his admiration for Jim makes him an unwitting accomplice to cruelty, and that POV puts the story in a sharper perspective than could the use of the third person—or another narrator.

In "The Celebrated Jumping Frog of Calaveras County," by Mark Twain, and "Youth," by Joseph Conrad, narrators are completely outside, repeating stories told to them by others. Each writer sets the scene and lets the storyteller start. Twain writes: "I let him go . . . and never interrupted him once:" Conrad writes: "Marlow . . . told the story, or rather the chronicle, of a voyage:—" After each storyteller is finished, each narrator has a final comment to conclude the piece.

A narrator who tells a story from outside provides a "frame" for the story. Use of a frame narrator—a barber, lawyer, doctor, any observer—to tell a series of stories is a good device, working much like the host on a television series. Two cautions should be noted: First, the narrator should help the story, not get in the way; and, second, the opening of the frame should be so constructed that the return to the narrator is not unexpected by the reader.

In addition to the monologue addressed to a particular listener, a monologue may be addressed to anybody. An interior monologue is a character's talking or thinking to himself. Diaries and memoirs are a narrator's written record or monologue. Letters are addressed to someone (the letter form—the epistolary novel—could carry the correspondence of one, two, or more persons). Such specialized forms work for certain stories but are strained for others. The question always is whether they can carry the action of the story.

The identity of a narrator may remain vague (if a vague narrator serves any purpose), but the presence of a narrator must be established early; otherwise, the reader adjusts to a third-person narrative and is jarred when the narrator appears. There should be an "I" or a "me" in the first or second paragraph and enough others for the reader to become accustomed to the reference. If the presence of the narrator is so little in evidence that there are only a few scattered "I's" or "me's," the story should perhaps be in third person.

Whatever the role of the narrator, the chief limitations are the giving of information the narrator does not have and the showing of events for which the narrator is not present. Actually, the writer can give much information—places, dates, details—that the narrator might not *have* but that the narrator could *get*. ("The leaves turned early that year, and the tourists went scurrying for their cameras while out in the wood the squirrels went scurrying for acorns.") The reader balks, however, and the story is weakened when information is given that the narrator could not know or learn. (A narrator trapped in a cave-in could not know that a single ten-ton rock is blocking his escape.) Events for which the narrator cannot be present can be related to the narrator either directly or indirectly (as the butler gives information to Nick in *The Great Gatsby*). If witnessing the event is critical to the plot, the story may have to be told another way.

In spite of such limitations, the narrator can give the reader more knowledge and insight than the narrator has. It happens in "Haircut," and it happens in "I'm a Fool," by Sherwood Anderson, which is now part of a television series on The American Short Story. And, yes, stories have been written in which the narrator dies, but the great advantage of first person narration is that it gives the tightest possible control over the material. Therefore it is a wise choice for the beginning writer who is learning the craft.

No one as storyteller

If you are going to stay out of your story as the author, and if you are not going to employ a narrator, you use the third method: giving the story straight to the reader without the presence of a storyteller. The story will be in third person; the POV will be *objec-*

tive, omniscient, or *limited omniscient*. Which is used depends on the mental and emotional processes given the characters. You choose by deciding—consciously or unconsciously—how many characters you will go inside. You may go:

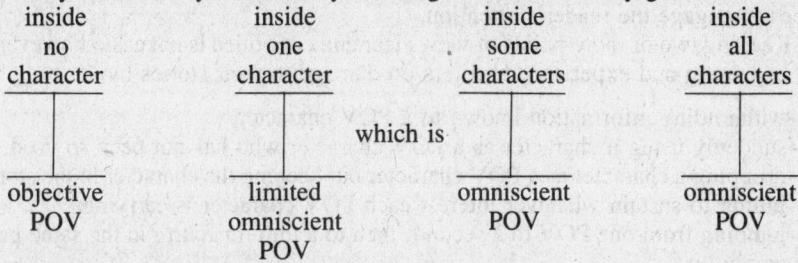

inside	inside	inside	inside
no	one	some	all
character	character	characters	characters

which is

objective	limited	omniscient	omniscient
POV	omniscient	POV	POV
	POV		

Each of these possibilities requires some discussion.

Objective point of view

The POV that goes inside no character is termed *objective*, *dramatic*, or *camera*. It sets down actions and statements as a camera or microphone would record them without any indication of thoughts or feelings. It consists of action and dialogue with perhaps a little description.

Hemingway's short story "Hills Like White Elephants" is usually given as an example of this POV (and as a study in dialogue). A man and woman waiting for a train drink and talk. The sparseness of the dialogue and narration makes the characters clear and the conflict strong.

"Should we have another drink?"
"All right."
The warm wind blew the bead curtain against the table.
"The beer's nice and cool," the man said.
"It's lovely," the girl said.
"It's really an awfully simple operation, Jig," the man said. "It's not really an operation at all."
The girl looked at the ground the table legs rested on.

The passage would not be objective if the last line continued: "and wished that he would drop the subject," or even if the word "sadly" were added to "looked." It might be charged that the word "warm" (and two or three other references in the story) cannot be called objective, but the over-all effect is objective.

For the right kind of story, staying outside the characters and telling the story with action and dialogue can generate great power and suspense. For many stories, however, the objective POV is restrictive, difficult to sustain, and, sometimes, quite impracticable.

Stage, screen, and television plays, of course, are in this POV, but use of soliloquies, voice-over, and other techniques can get inside characters.

Omniscient point of view

At the other end of the continuum is the POV that goes inside any character the author wishes. The author is omniscient, or all-knowing, in the sense that the author provides whatever information is needed for the telling of the story, but the author is neutral; the writer's presence is not felt. There may be much outside information, but the story is seen and heard and felt through the eyes and ears and emotions of the POV characters.

Using more than one POV can give great advantage. Showing the inner struggles and tensions of several characters can heighten conflict. Movement in time and space is more flexible, and the reader can be kept with the action. There are more people and themes to engage the reader's attention.

Keeping two or more points of view clear and controlled is not easy, however, and both beginning and experienced writers do damage to their stories by:

—withholding information known to a POV character;
—suddenly using a character as a POV character who has not been so used;
—dropping a character as a POV character but keeping the character in the story;
—failing to sustain whatever interest each POV character is carrying;
—jumping from one POV to a second, then to a third or fourth in the same paragraph;
—cluttering the story by going into the minds and feelings of the mother, father, sister, brother, cousin, neighbor, nurse, mail carrier, cashier, or piano player;
—shifting from single to multiple POV or from first to third person without thought or purpose;
—tacking on an additional POV for effect.

Avoiding such problems makes for more efficient and satisfying writing than eliminating them in revision. The best way to do that and to take advantage of multiple POV is to master progressively more complex forms of writing while studying techniques used in the best of published fiction.

Limited omniscient point of view

Going inside only one character in third person is called *limited* or *selective omniscience*. Everything the reader learns, sees, hears, and feels goes through the mind, eyes, ears, and emotions of that one character.

Limited omniscience is like full omniscience in every respect except that it goes inside only that one character. In that sense, it is a third person parallel of first person narration: The POV character may be the major or a minor character; the choice works well or poorly in the same kinds of stories; there are the same limitations concerning giving information and having the POV character present for all action; and there is the same strong advantage of focus and control.

Sustaining limited omniscience requires more attention, however, for it is easy to slip into use of a second POV. Sometimes the slip does no damage. Sometimes it destroys the story. In a baseball story, for example, when the POV character was knocked out, two sentences went inside the coach who recalled a similar injury that was fatal. The story immediately went back to the POV character who was trying to understand why his coach's face looked so strange; the shift was largely unnoticed, and the complication of possible death added to the suspense.

Damage was done, however, to the story of a young woman who wanted to marry to please her parents but who knew her parents would not accept the man she wanted because he was handicapped. For 20 or more pages, she was the sole POV, was dropped for a three-page scene in which the fiancé proved himself to the parents, and was then restored as the POV character for the remainder of the story. Reader involvement was interrupted, and a strong story became weak. The writer wanted that scene and could not have the young woman present because her presence would take away the man's fateful opportunity. The story could have been omniscient, but limited omniscience was a better choice because of its focus on the woman's being pulled between her parents' wishes and her own. Having the parents report the man's heroic action lost the immediacy of the scene but gave the story unity and gained a more dramatic acceptance from the parents.

Use omniscience or limited omniscience when either affords you some definite advantage; when you cannot decide between the two, prefer the limited omniscience.

Second person point of view

For the curious, and for comprehensive coverage: Yes, stories can be written in second person, "Moon Deluxe" by Frederick Barthelme, which appeared in the February 15, 1982 issue of *The New Yorker*, is so written. It begins:

> You're stuck in traffic on the way home from work, counting blue cars, and when a blue metallic Jetta pulls alongside, you count it—twenty eight. You've seen the driver on other evenings. . . .

Second person narration is interesting as an exercise, but it is not a natural story telling method. You might want to play with it, but you will likely never use it.

How much do characters know?

What—and when—characters know is tied up in points already covered. You look at your characters and your plot (in outline or draft) to be certain that POV characters and the reader have information when needed and that no POV character has critical plot information that is withheld—even briefly—from the reader.

If you have taken the reader into the mind of the wife, the reader is justified in calling "foul" if you withhold information she has about her husband's infidelity. If it is critical to the plot that she not know whether he has been unfaithful until the end of the story and that the reader know early, then she cannot be a POV character—although it may still be her story.

It may often be necessary to change a POV character to a non-POV character—or vice versa—to make a plot work. It may be possible to keep a POV character from knowing something too soon, but it may be easier to re-plot than to convince the reader the character could remain ignorant. Whenever things must be revealed that the main character cannot or would not reveal, a secondary character should be a first person narrator or a limited omniscient POV character.

How does the reader receive and perceive the story?

This topic is also tied up in the earlier considerations. In addition to plot and character requirements, it is worthwhile to ask about each story what would be the best medium for getting that story to the potential reader. The directness or intimacy of a first person narrator will be best for one; the detachment of the objective will be best for another; the added revelations of omniscience will be best for still another.

Choices and possibilities

When you are ready to write a piece of fiction, if the POV seems obvious, start writing; if it works, continue.

If you cannot settle on a POV or have tired one that did not work, set down in writing whose story you want to tell. Simply because certain characters are needed to make a story work, that does not mean it is their story, and—just as many of us choose the wrong marriage partners—writers do choose characters to whom stories do not belong. Next, list who could see, hear, and feel the story as plotted. Then, consider the effect on the reader, select what seems to be the best choice, and start writing. It may be necessary to write part or all of a story from more than one POV before knowing which is best. (Do not be surprised if it seems to be a different story when told from a different POV.)

With control, many variations and combinations are possible:

Some portions of a story might be from one POV and other parts from other POV's, with a patterned alternation or a sequential development.

Half the story might belong to one character and half to another—in effect, a double limited omniscience.

An opening might be from one character's POV and the remainder from another's POV, the first preparing the way for the second.

A story can begin as omniscient and then narrow its focus to limited omniscient.

The POV of a single character can change from one age to another; a combined or split child/adult POV can continue throughout.

A story could alternately be in first and third persons.

Other such techniques can and do work, but the advantage to the story may be questionable. Often the purpose seems to be to dazzle the reader with technique rather than to strengthen the story. Just as often, the writer focuses on some other matter, forgets POV, and loses both.

As you are developing your craft, you can do two things to be sure of your own technique. First, when you find fiction that is especially satisfying, study it to see how POV was handled. Second, you should get others to read your stories before you submit them; there is no point in taking an editor's time with stories that are not ready.

Checklist for revision

You (and others) can check POV with these three questions:

Is the POV clear?
Is the POV controlled?
Is the POV consistent?

A very little thoughtful rewriting can solve problems that arise from momentary lapses; extensive overhaul may be required in some cases.

When you can produce fiction that works against that checklist, the *consistent* requirement might be dropped. The question then becomes whether there is a cogent reason for any shift of POV and whether that shift is clear and controlled (Does it work?).

Perhaps the *clear* requirement can at some time be dropped. The mixed points of view in *The Sound and the Fury* may not readily be clear to many of us; yet the story works.

The *controlled* requirement should remain. It may be dropped for some experimental fiction, but such pieces appeal to a limited audience.

For *most* writers, for *most* stories, for *most* readers, and for *most* markets, POV should remain clear, controlled, and consistent—with exceptions being made only for very good reasons.

❝ *The most important ingredient in writing fiction is that choice is always available:* Who *will?* What *will?*

—*Joseph Heller* ❞

Using symbols as a shortcut to meaning

by Rega Kramer McCarty

Our culture is full of symbols: The barber pole, the turkey at Thanksgiving, the wedding ring, the wedding veil, the christening . . . in each, the object or the ceremony takes the place of hundreds, thousands, of descriptive words.

If you would like to give added dimension to your story, consider using a symbol as a shortcut to meaning.

A symbol may be an image standing for a small moment in the story, or it may be a substitute for action—a literary figure used throughout the work, pervading it, carrying the deeper meaning.

I once wrote a play titled *The White Fences of China*, based on a story told me by a missionary. The mission orphanage built a white fence around its grounds, not to keep the orphans in but to keep others out, because the mission was already over-crowded and was without funds. Day after day, Chinese children, homeless and hungry, came to stand outside the fence, peering longingly in. One small girl wouldn't leave. Every day she came and remained far into the night . . . until at last the missionary could stand it no longer and invited her inside.

The fence became symbolic of the limits put upon missionary help by the lack of funds, and the little orphan symbolized all the orphans of China who looked longingly for help. Thus, the symbol also helped to carry the story's theme, or meaning.

Fences have been used as symbols in fiction many times, but in different ways. I recall a story of a ''spite fence'' built to shut out a neighbor's view of the ocean. Other objects frequently used are bridges, vases, birds, the seasons, to name a few. The writer must strive to find fresh uses for familiar symbols. Or to find new symbols.

Rega Kramer McCarty is an instructor in short story writing for Writer's Digest School. She has published career-romance novels, more than 100 confession stories and religious and juvenile fiction.

Resolving device

A symbol must be carefully selected as the one best able to bring subtle inference to the meaning to be drawn from it. *The symbol should come naturally from the environment and the characters, and should fit easily into the action and movement of the story.* One of my students wrote a story of people in a coal-mining community. The main character, a young woman, longs to escape the environment. As the story opens, she is planning her escape. In the background she hears the train whistle, a symbol of her means of escape. One feels an urgency in her actions, but it is not until the end of the story that one discovers a part of the urgency is due to a murder she has committed in order to have the money for escape. At the end of the story the town marshal comes for her. The train whistle she hears then, growing fainter and fainter, symbolizes her receding hope of escape. Other images used in the story were in keeping with the grime and hopelessness of the girl's environment.

A symbol must have universality—be an object familiar to all. It must have an emotional quality. The train whistle spoke for the emotions of all miners, perhaps of all people who feel trapped in the hopelessness of their environment.

The symbol must have purpose. The writer must know when and how to bring it into the story. It might, for instance, have a parallel in nature. I recall the story of a mother whose son wants to go to camp. His father feels he should be allowed to go, but the mother fears for him. One day she goes outside to feed the cat and sees the mother cat push her nursing kitten from her toward the saucer. The kitten cries and clings to the mother, but she pushes him forward and walks away. Thus the mother realizes that she, too, must push her child toward maturity. This symbol has been used many times in various ways. A fresher way to use it might be to have a mother and son loading a truck when they are moving, and as they lift a heavy carton over the tail-gate, the mother realizes that, for the first time, the son is lifting more than half the load. Thus she realizes that he can shoulder his share of responsibility.

In these stories, the symbol is used as the resolving device. It causes the main character to achieve new insight which changes her attitude and thus resolves her problem by bringing her to a decision. *When the symbol is used as a resolving device, it must be planted early in the story*, so that it is present when the time comes to use it. It should be planted in such a way that its purpose is not obvious. For instance, when the cat and kitten appear early in the story, they seem to be only part of the background. The boy is playing with them; this serves to underscore his immaturity and to support the mother's feeling that he is too young to go to camp. It isn't until later that their real purpose becomes evident. In the story of the mining camp, the reader is led to think of the train as a means of escape rather than, as he later discovers, of typifying her abandonment.

The idea is to lead away from the real purpose of the symbol, actually to divert the reader from seeing its real purpose until the time comes to use it in resolving the problem.

Parallel story action

A symbol must never be too abstract to be understood. If too abstract, its inference is lost upon the reader. The purpose of a symbol is to emblematise, to imply, rather than to obtrude.

In some stories a symbol parallels the story action. For instance, suppose a man has withdrawn to his cabin on the Bay to struggle with a depression which threatens to bring him to a suicidal act. His wife has died, his business is failing, life seems to be falling apart. About to take his life, he sees a boat fighting the rising storm on the Bay, and he identifies with its struggle for life, seeing it as akin to his own struggle. As he watches, sometimes thinking back to his past which throws light upon the present condition, the reader knows that the boat's success in riding out the storm will determine the man's decision as well. The story could take one of several different turns. The man could get caught up in the boat's struggle and liken it to his own (with the help of the flashbacks of his own struggle). When he sees that the boat can come through what seems like insurmountable odds, he feels that he, too, can overcome if he continues to fight.

Perhaps if a writer wished to shape the story differently—the boat could be battered and sink but the man could come to the conclusion that while the boat is defeated because it can't win out over the storm, *he* can call upon his strength of will and determine to win his struggle. If the story were shaped in this way, the boat and the storm would still serve as a symbol, acting as a resolving factor. Thus the man's conflict is paralleled and made more dramatic by the struggle of the boat. Such a parallel is often used when otherwise the conflict would take place only in the mind of the main character, offering little drama or suspense.

Worsening plight, personal fight

Symbolism was at its best in the movie *The Defiant Ones*, in which Tony Curtis played the role of the white prisoner, and Sidney Poitier the role of the black prisoner. The surface, or visible story, was of the two convicts chained together, returning in the prison truck from a day's labor. They escape, but cannot escape each other because of their chains. During the days following they come to despise each other, hurling at each other all their buried resentments and hatreds. The surface story is filled with action and suspense, but it is at its deeper level of meaning that it becomes great. The entire story stands as a comment upon the relationship of the two races. The theme is that neither white nor black race can save itself alone, for the two are irrevocably chained together, the fate of the one hanging on the fate of the other. The chains are the symbol of their bondage. Even when they are finally able to sever them and the black man goes on, while the white man remains in the lonely cabin to rape the woman living there, he is not free, for he sees the captors heading toward the cabin and knows he must return to warn the white man. If he is captured he realizes, he, too, will be overtaken.

Sometimes a symbol is used to create mood, such as a bleak moor to create somberness, or a raging storm to create violence. The symbol both implies and intensifies action. The recurring wail of a wolf in a wilderness background can symbolize loneliness, or can foreshadow and intensify danger.

Sometimes writers have more than one symbol at work in the same story. Take, for example, a story by Esther Wagner titled "The Slip" which appeared several years ago in *Atlantic Monthly*.

The main character has an alcoholic problem and has gone to the oceanside to visit her sister-in-law, who is away from home as the story takes place. One knows early in the story that she has gone with the secret purpose of "slipping." She sees a car on the beach, mired in the sand, and three young men trying frantically to free the wheels as the tide comes in. As she imbibes quite freely from her sister-in-law's liquor supply, she watches the frantic effort of the boys, and though she knows that the tide will overwhelm the car, she goes down the long flight of steps from the cottage to the beach, to offer them at one time the suggestion that there is a gas station where they might seek help (well knowing the man couldn't leave his station to come); at another time, when that has failed, she goes down to offer them a drink from her bottle. Each time the trip up and down the long flight of steps grows increasingly difficult, and the plight of the boys worsens.

Here you have two symbols—the steps and the worsening plight of the car, though the parallelism is stronger with the car's plight and therefore the frantic plight of the boys, since the father of one of them owns the car. The steps are directly related to her own physical condition. Throughout her watching of the car and her trips down to the beach, there are flashbacks giving clues as to what may have caused her problem (mother, husband, particularly the older husband's role) as well as incidents showing how her condition has worsened through the years, until she has been told that one more time will be the final time for her. As the story ends, she manages the uphill climb of the long steps, but falls as she reaches the top. The boys have had to abandon the car to the tide.

I am often amazed to find an object in a story that would make a perfect symbol, yet the writer has failed to make use of it. Perhaps instinctively we reach for symbols, yet do not always recognize them or find their use.

Symbols are everywhere. They will enhance your writing. It will take practice to use them effectively, but the enrichment they bring to your work is well worth the effort.

For me, a page of good prose is where one hears the rain. A page of good prose is when one hears the noise of battle. A page of good prose has the power to give grief or universality that lends it a youthful beauty. A page of good prose has the power to make us laugh. A page of good prose seems to me the most serious dialogue that well-informed and intelligent men and women carry on today in their endeavor to make sure that the fires of this planet burn peaceably.
John Cheever

The manner of the telling

by Hallie and Whit Burnett

Writing, to be effective, must follow closely the thoughts of the writer, but not necessarily in the order in which these thoughts occur.

—E.B. White, *The Elements of Style*

"Mrs. Hatton believed that thought came first and one developed a writing style through much practice putting his thoughts on paper," wrote Jesse Stuart about his teacher in the Greenup (Kentucky) High School, who first stimulated his desire to write. "When I stop long enough to look back over the past, I think she was one of the greatest English teachers that ever lived." And he added conclusively that above all she warned, "One shouldn't just try to do a style for style's sake."

He could never explain, Jesse said, how "gray-haired Mrs. Hatton, who never wrote a short story, essay, poem, or novel, who never made a speech in public, who just taught school all her life and kept a home for her husband and son, knew all these things about creative writing." But with all of Jesse's achievements, his style, which Samuel Butler might have been describing when he advocated just "common, simple straightforwardness," has remained purely and singularly his own.

Many writers have had their say on style, and most of these statements have some value. There is a truism that the best style is the least noticeable, "the manner of which least stands in the way of the matter presented." No one denies the strong influence that

Hallie and Whit Burnett, *well-known fiction experts, drew on their long experience as co-editors of* Story *Magazine in their varied careers. Whit Burnett was a reporter, city editor, instructor in advanced short story writing at Columbia University, and writer and editor of more than 35 books. Hallie Burnett is the author of seven books and co-editor of 12 anthologies. She has taught creative writing at Sarah Lawrence College and Hunter College.*

Hemingway's simple, direct style has had on American writers living today.

Faulkner, on the other hand, whose Sartoris and Compson families of Jefferson, Mississippi, are known equally well in the literature of the world, seemed to favor a more complex, evocative prose. Faulkner was of the old South; Hemingway was of the North and the Middle West. Faulkner wrote in the tradition of Joyce, erecting Gothic cathedrals beside the simplicity of Hemingway's identifiable modern structures, in the manner of Anderson and Flaubert. Each went through a war, and while it was to some extent the same war, each wrote differently of his experiences. Both were Americans of the same generation; each was foremost in his fictional authority and perceptions, and each finally was appreciated by the great world beyond our shores, considered equally representative of the American culture. And yet consider their styles.

Individually authoritative and representative

Consider William Faulkner in "A Rose for Emily," which has, as Ray B. West described it, "a general tone of mystery, foreboding, and decay."

Miss Emily Grierson, who has been a concern of the town for many years, living alone with only a Negro manservant and discouraging all others from entering her house, has died. During her lifetime these things have happened (told almost in conversational flashbacks):

Her father died and she refused to have him buried for three days, saying he was not dead. "Just as they were about to resort to law and force, she broke down, and they buried her father quickly."

That was when people had begun to feel really sorry for her. People in our town, remembering how old Lady Wyatt, her great-aunt, had gone completely crazy at last, believed that the Griersons held themselves a little too high for what they really were. None of the young men were quite good enough for Miss Emily and such. We had long thought of them as a tableau: Miss Emily a slender figure in white in the background, her father a spraddled silhouette in the foreground, his back to her and clutching a horsewhip, the two of them framed by the back-flung front door. So when she got to be 30 and was still single, we were not pleased exactly, but vindicated; even with insanity in the family she wouldn't have turned down all of her chances if they had really materialized.

But then, after she was ill for a time, she took in a man to live with her, Homer Barron, a Yankee—"a big, dark, ready man, with a big voice and eyes lighter than his face."

Eventually he disappeared, and the people thought he had left her. But when she died, and the townsmen pounded down a door that seemed never to have been opened, they found the body of Homer Barron "apparently once lain in an embrace" on the bed.

Ernest Hemingway in giving Whit [Burnett] permission to reprint "The Short Happy Life of Francis Macomber" in *This Is My Best*, told him to say that "Mr. Hemingway thought that was as reprintable as any other of his stories." There is the Hemingway style, even in a routine permission.

This story is so well known that it is only necessary to remind a reader that it is about Francis Macomber and his wife, Margaret, on safari with Robert Wilson, a white hunter and guide. As the story opens Macomber has been carried into his tent in triumph, having killed his first lion. But it soon develops from the scornful attitude of his wife, and Macomber's own embarrassment, that he has actually bolted and that even the native gunbearers are aware of it, that it is Wilson who has shot the lion.

There seems only one way for Macomber to redeem his cowardice, and that is to kill an animal for himself. He knows his wife will probably leave him anyway, and that the night of his cowardice she has gone to Wilson's bed; but he makes a decision to hunt the buffalo.

They set out on the hunt and suddenly come across three old bull elephants, "three huge, black animals looking almost cylindrical in their long heaviness, like big black tank cars, moving at a gallop across the far edge of the open prairie. They moved at a stiff-necked, stiff-bodied gallop and he could see the up-swept wide black horns on their heads as they galloped heads out; the heads not moving."

Both men shoot; Macomber kills the first bull, Wilson the second; the third has gone into the bush. But Macomber has a great feeling of elation. "I feel absolutely different," he says.

They go in the bush after the third elephant, when suddenly they see him "coming out of the bush sideways, fast as a crab, and the bull coming, nose out, mouth tight closed, blood dripping, massive head straight out, coming in a charge, his little pig eyes bloodshot as he looked at them."

Wilson shot for the nose, "shooting too high each time and hitting the heavy horns, splintering and chipping them like hitting a slate roof," and then Mrs. Macomber in the car shot at the buffalo "with the 6.5 Mannlicher as it seemed about to gore Macomber and had hit her husband about two inches up and a little to one side of the base of his skull."

The dialogue at the end is in a style characteristically Hemingway's.

"That was a pretty thing to do," he [Wilson] said in a toneless voice. 'He *would* have left you, too."

"Stop it," she said.

"Of course it's an accident," he said. "I know that."

"Stop it," she said.

"Don't worry," he said. "There will be a certain amount of unpleasantness but I will have some photographs taken that will be very useful at the inquest. There's the testimony of the gunbearers and the driver too. You're perfectly all right."

"Stop it," she said.

"There's a hell of a lot to be done," he said. "And I'll have to send a truck off to the lake to wireless for a plane to take the three of us into Nairobi. Why didn't you poison him? That's the way they do in England."

"Stop it. Stop it. Stop it," the woman cried.

Wilson looked at her with his flat blue eyes.

"I'm through now," he said. "I was a little angry. I'd begun to like you husband."

"Oh, please stop it," she said. "Please, please stop it."

"That's better," Wilson said. "Please is much better. Now I'll stop."

Serving the narrative

When fiction stresses less what is happening than to whom, or why, more subtleties may be brought into play. Samuel Butler was a straightforward fellow; Marcel Proust was not. Young Pontifex walks as straight a line as Butler's time and explantory style allowed. Hemingway and Faulkner try to use it all, the facts, the characters, the subtleties, in a style peculiarly of their generation.

Sherwood Anderson's style was described by Waldo Frank. In spite of "occasional superficial carelessnesses of language," he wrote, "on the whole the prose is perfect in its selective economy and in its melodious flow; the choice of details is stripped, strong, sure; the movement is an unswerving musical fulfillment of the already stated theme. Like Schubert, and like the Old Testament story tellers, the author of *Winesburg* comes at the end of a psychological process; is a man with an inherited culture and a deeply assimilated skill."

In "I Want to Know Why" Anderson writes about a boy at the Saratoga races, a boy who loves horses and idealizes the trainer, Jerry Tilford.

"I liked him that afternoon even more than I ever liked my own father. I almost forgot the horses, thinking that way about him. It was because of what I had seen in his eyes as he stood in the paddocks beside Sunstreak before the race started. . . ."

The race is won, and the boy follows Jerry with some other men who are celebrating the race in a farmhouse "for bad women to stay in." He watches Jerry through the window, hears him bragging "like a fool. I never heard such silly talk." And then he sees him kiss a woman, "the one that was lean and hard-mouthed and looked a little like the gelding Middlestride, but not clean like him, and his eyes began to shine just as they did when he looked at me and at Sunstreak in the paddocks at the track in the afternoon."

The boy runs home and doesn't tell anyone what he's seen. But "I been thinking about it ever since. I can't make it out. Spring has come again and I'm nearly 16 and go to the tracks mornings same as always, and I see Sunstreak and Middlestride and a new colt named Strident I'll bet will lay them all out, but no one thinks so but me and two or three niggers.

"But things are different. . . . What did he do it for? I want to know why."

Philip Roth, one of today's best writers but an erratically challenging stylist not only in his prose but also in his subject matter, writes appreciatively of his friend Saul Bellow's style. It "combines a literary complexity with a conversational ease, a language that joins the idiom of the academy with the idiom of the streets (not all streets—certain streets); the style is special, private, and energetic, and though occasionally unwieldy and indulgent, it generally, I believe, serves the narrative and serves it brilliantly."

Take this passage from *Herzog*, with Herzog remembering his second wife, who has left him. One day, in a Catholic church:

She pushed the swinging door open with her shoulder. She put her hands in the front and crossed herself, as if she'd been doing it all her life. She'd learned that in the movies, probably. But the look of terrible eagerness and twisted perplexity and appeal on her face—where did that come from? Madeleine in her gray suit with the squirrel collar, her large hat, hurried forward on high heels. He followed slowly, holding his salt-and-pepper topcoat at the neck as he took off his hat. Madeleine's body seemed gathered upward in the breast and shoulders, and her face was red with excitement. Her hair was pulled back severely under the hat but escaped in wisps to form sidelocks. The church was a new building—small, cold, dark, the varnish shining hard on the oak pews, and balots of flame standing motionless near the altar. Madeleine genuflected in the aisle. Only it was more than genuflection. She sank, she cast herself down, she wanted to spread herself on the floor and press her heart to the boards—he recognized that. Shading his face on both sides, like a horse in blinkers, he sat in the pew. What was he doing here? He was a husband, a father. He was married, he was a Jew. Why was he in a church?

Unique combinations

The London *Times* once stated that Hemingway's style succeeded because of his artful way of using American vernacular, which they believed most characteristic of our writing. Robert Frost has written that there are really two kinds of language: "The spoken language and the written language—our everyday speech which we call the vernacular; and a more literary, sophisticated, artificial, elegant language that belongs to books. I myself could get along very well without the bookish language altogether."

"Writing, to be effective, must follow closely the thoughts of the writer, but not necessarily in the order in which these thoughts occur," wrote E.B. White in *The Elements of Style*. In other words, the arrangment of thoughts becomes the writer's vernacular.

A note by Whit Burnett: "Style has always been in my mind the author's Self, the creative expression of that Self." But, "If a writer becomes too vague, even though one enjoys the style of writing and manages to grasp the meaning somehow, intellectually I usually am left empty. Yet if you kill style for the sake of the story, on the other hand, you kill the 'I' of the author. Do we read the author or the story? I, for one, demand that each enhance the other. To be successful, the author's intentions must be both clear and implicit."

There are other styles in which greater subtlety prevails. Eudora Welty wrote of Willa Cather that the uniqueness of her style resulted from her skill in not giving us "the landscape but her vision of it; we are looking at a work of art." It is the angle of that vision which distinguishes one writer's style from another's, that angle which is the writer's exclusive property.

For the developing writer who is not yet certain how his own style may develop, such examples may not explain much. For all writers, however, there is one starting point which cannot be passed over: the use of language and its suitability. To be a master of language is to be a master chef: In the preparation of gourmet dishes no ingredient is rare in itself. The seasonings and flavor may come from many sources, but the results are dependent on the skill and imagination of the chef, if he is to produce a unique dish. Caviar and corned beef would never be combined to make a pudding.

A writer like Erskine Caldwell did not use the elegant language of a Proust to write his *Tobacco Road*; nor would Proust have written in the ribald manner of Balzac's *Droll Tales*. And it is hard to imagine J.D. Salinger creating *Franny and Zooey* in the style of Thomas Mann's *Mario the Magician*. Style is the product of a writer's culture, the imprint of his temperament, and his feeling for the requirements of the subject matter.

We also include here an example of a style which is having an influence on writers today. Donald Barthelme is described on the jacket of his book *City Life* as a "master of the languages used to conceal truth." Years after Eugene Jolas's *transition* magazine in Paris, far beyond Joyce or Kafka or Gertrude Stein, we read:

Laughing aristocrats moved up and down the corridors of the city.
Else, Jacques, Romona and Charles drove out to the combined race track and art gallery. Ramona had a Heineken and everyone else had one too. The tables were crowded with laughing aristocrats. More laughing aristocrats arrived in their carriages drawn by dancing matched pairs. Some drifted in from Flushing and São Paulo. Management of the funded indebtedness was discussed; the Queen's behavior was discussed. All of the horses ran very well, and the pictures ran well too.

The laughing aristocrats sucked on the heads of their gold-headed canes some more.

Style is, someone has wisely said, a matter of knowing when one has said enough.

We have metaphor and simile which may be used for visual and imaginative effect. These, however, must also be un-self-conscious, acting as instinctive amplification of our thought or imagery, and not used as an end in themselves. A writer of the stature of Elizabeth Bowen sometimes created metaphors that illumined whole passages; at other times she seemed to manufacture them as embellishments she felt obliged to insert.

A metaphor, to Virginia Woolf, was a means of ''digging caves behind'' her characters.

Use punctuation as it comes naturally, as an aid to breathing, or for emphasis in style, or rhythm, or emotion.

Paragraph also by instinct: one introduces a thought; one develops it; and one concludes its meaning. That's all there is to it.

Use shorter sentences for action; longer sentences for reflection or, sometimes, the development of an emotion with sensuous undertones. Anger is usually in staccato style.

Avoid colorless, tame, hestitant speech, and use active verbs when possible without strain.

66 *When we encounter a natural style, we are astonished and delighted; for we expected to see an author, and we find a man.*
—*Mark Twain* 99

All's well that ends well

by James McKimmey

Once, early in my career, I spent a day driving along the coast south of San Francisco, trying to conjure up a new idea for a novel. By the time I got home I had an idea not for a novel, but for a short story. I felt so inspired that, after my wife had retired, I stayed up and started writing.

I wrote the entire story before the night was over, then left it on a table for my wife. When I awoke late the next morning, I read her written appraisal.

Of the three basic parts a short story must comprise—a beginning, a middle, an end—she liked the first two. But she thought the ending needed fixing and suggested how.

I made the change. The suggestion proved to be right.

Cosmopolitan bought it within five days after I'd put it in the mail, my first short-story sale there. They paid four figures. Shortly after it was published, it was purchased for television adaptation, again at a four-figure price. The presentation starred Lee Marvin, and was introduced by a host who is now President of the United States.

If the ending hadn't been corrected, however, none of it would have happened. I still accept spousal help, of course. But I now try to be more careful from the start to make sure the ending will match the rest of the short story.

To learn to do that, I studied the work of my favorite short story writers. I found that the balanced endings they achieved invariably contained four essential ingredients: *satisfaction, a definite conclusion, inevitability, surprise.*

James McKimmey has written about 300 short manuscripts, most of them short fiction, for magazines including Good Housekeeping, Cosmopolitan, Alfred Hitchcock's Mystery Magazine *and many others. He is also the author of 16 novels; the latest is a juvenile entitled* The Martindales' Nightmare, *published under the pseudonym of Dewey Daniels.*

Keys to success

I then studied to find out how each ingredient came about and discovered the following:

Satisfaction results when the other three ingredients are contained in an ending.

A *definite conclusion* is realized when the sympathetic hero or heroine overcomes the problem, or, if the hero is unsympathetic, when the problem overcomes him.

Inevitability is achieved when everything about the ending seems to be the logical result of all that has previously transpired. Nothing in it can be alien to what has preceded. For example: A hero is trapped in a room. The doors are locked and he has no key. He removes a wire from a pocket, skillfully picks a lock, and sets himself free. But if the wire in the hero's pocket and his ability to pick locks have not been mentioned previously, they are alien to what has preceded. Such an ending, therefore, is unacceptable in the rules of the short story game. It's cheating.

Consequently, some earlier mention must be made that the hero is carrying a piece of wire and that he is capable of picking locks. Carefully planted, these necessary foreshadowings might appear in the thoughts of the main character, in physical description, or in dialogue:

He thought of his first job as an apprentice to a locksmith and of how his slim fingers, which matched the rest of his spare figure, had become so skilled in that work. Then that was forgotten as he remembered his wife, who had become proficient at making artificial flowers out of paper and wire, saying as he'd been about to leave the house, "This is the exact diameter wire I need—please don't forget to pick some more up." She'd handed him the sample, and it was now in a pocket.

The foreshadowings might be used to characterize, to make a scene more vivid, or to set a mood:

He'd always been interested in small, intricate problems, which was why he'd been good at his first job as an apprentice to a locksmith. He'd always enjoyed being alone as well, which was perhaps why his marriage was falling apart. And then he was remembering how his wife, livid with rage, working at her stupid hobby of making ugly flowers out of paper and wire, had suddenly thrown a piece of wire at him, demanding that he get a new supply for her. Well, the piece of wire was in his pocket now, and he would buy more of it, but with gloomy reluctance.

These are not subtle examples. But they make clear how foreshadowings must be planted so that the reader, when that ending arrives, will say: "Of course! The story could have ended no other way!"

Surprise party

And then we come to *surprise*.

How, if everything about an ending has been foreshadowed, can the writer possibly surprise the reader?

By carefully manipulating the *way* in which a foreshadowing is presented.

To see how this is most expertly done, let's examine a story written by Irwin Shaw. "Tip on a Dead Jockey" was published in *The New Yorker* in the decade following World War II, but it holds up over the years as a classic, and has been reprinted many times, most recently in Shaw's Delacorte Press anthology, *Short Stories, Five Decades*.

Lloyd Barber, a pilot during the war, now an unemployed expatriate living in Paris, is offered a large sum by a mysterious man named Smith to fly a small plane in an illegal, dangerous, month-long scheme to make a huge profit exchanging money on the black market. Before making his decision, Barber introduces Smith to a man named Richardson who once flew in his squadron. Barber, after much nervous contemplation, turns down Smith's offer. Over a month later, Richardson's wife, Maureen, looks up Barber and tells him that Richardson has been gone for just over a month, she has no idea where or why. She is terribly worried and asks if Barber knows where Richardson might be. Barber promises to ask around.

As the story nears the end, Barber has found no trace of Richardson. But he is now certain that Richardson took the offer that he, Barber, turned down. And by this time the reader has developed the impression that Barber, despite his unemployment, is a rather handsome, heroic, glamorous, sensible individual. Richardson, on the other hand, round and fat and somewhat sloppy in appearance as Barber views him, appears to be one of the all-time stupid, incompetent losers. There seems to be no doubt about the ending of the story: Barber will be required to inform Maureen, Richardson's wife, that Richardson obviously got foolishly involved in a dangerous scheme and is now undoubtedly dead. Although this ending is a definite enough conclusion, there is no surprise in it. But it does seem inevitable, if lacking in satisfaction.

The foreshadow does . . .

Now let's examine how Shaw deliberately took the reader to that conclusion by the clever and often subtle use of foreshadowings along the way.

A photograph in Barber's room pictures Barber and Richardson together. Examining it, Barber sees that he appears tall and handsome next to Richardson, who seems like a pudgy, incapable baby.

There is a letter from a woman asking Barber to come stay with her in her villa near Eze where it is beautiful and warm. Surely Barber must have his attractions to have received such an invitation.

Barber worked a few months as a technical expert for an American movie production in Paris. In the course of the story he is casually asked about the female star, which gives the impression that he had known her intimately.

Barber also owns a letter from a former member of his flight crew who keeps insisting that Barber saved his life during the war, surely an act that is associated with heroism.

These and other foreshadowings strengthen the notion that Barber is indeed handsome, glamorous and heroic. That he is also sensible is best illustrated by the fact that he had the wisdom to turn down the offer that would have gotten him involved in the dangerous scheme. Richardson, on the other hand, obviously took that offer, proving his incompetence and stupidity.

A few other impressions of Richardson, as Barber surveys him from a distance, are that he owns a face that is empty and a voice that is vacant and that he is no man for a dangerous mission such as the one that obviously did him in.

Even Richardson's wife, Maureen, seems to reflect Richardson's inability to do well. When she comes to Barber to find out if he knows where her husband has gone, she is wearing a worn cloth coat that is soaked. In the green-tinted light of the lobby of Barber's cheap hotel, her face is no longer pretty, as it once was. Her hands are red. Her fingernails are irregular. Even though he can't afford it, Barber feels it necessary to insist that she take money. Maureen's taking it proves to Barber that she is broke, which also proves to him that Richardson hadn't even had the sense to have asked the mysterious Smith for an advance before leaving on the dangerous mission.

When Barber meets Maureen at a bar near the finish of the story, he is annoyed to see that she is drinking champagne—obviously she used his money to buy it. He notices she is wearing an enormous ring that he has never before seen. He asks himself, almost frightened: What has she gotten into to have a ring like that (making the reader feel almost certain that it is prostitution).

But then the true ending arrives as Richardson appears on scene, grinning widely. He has lost weight and is tanned. *He* bought the champagne. *He* gave the huge ring to his wife. Obviously he has completed the mission successfully. The effort has made him rich. He and Maureen are celebrating.

Barber shop

Barber bitterly decides to leave Paris. He is, in fact, done with the entire continent.

There is *surprise* in this ending. But did Shaw also provide the other necessary elements, *inevitability*, *a definite conclusion* and *satisfaction*?

By going back and consciously re-examining examples of those deliberately planted foreshadowings, we can see what he did.

In the photograph that Barber has in his room, he appears tall and handsome next to Richardson, who seems like a pudgy, incapable baby. But the author did not state this as a fact. The estimation is *Barber's*.

A woman did invite Barber to come stay with her in her villa near Eze where it is beautiful and warm. But Shaw did not write that the *woman* was beautiful and warm. She might very well have been ugly and cold, a hundred years old.

It was never actually stated that Barber had a solitary thing, personally, to do with the female movie star.

The former member of Barber's flight crew who writes letters to him and insists that Barber had saved his life during the war is also described as strange, emotional, embarrassing, preoccupied with himself, and tending toward being overly dramatic, all of which diminishes the validity of the man's personal belief that Barber is a hero.

Not only was it Barber's estimation that Richardson seemed to be a pudgy, incapable baby in the photograph, but it was also Barber's subjective judgment that Richardson owned a face that was empty and a voice that was vacant and that Richardson was no man for such a dangerous mission. There is nothing in the story that really indicates that Richardson was a bad pilot. Even Barber, with a shrug, admits to the mysterious Smith that better ones got killed and worse ones won medals.

As far as Richardson's wife, Maureen, reflecting his failure: Shaw's putting her in a worn, soaked cloth coat seems to emphasize her aura of looking rundown. But the coat is soaked simply because she just came out of the rain. Her face would hardly look pretty in the green light of a cheap hotel lobby. Her hands are red, befitting any housewife in an age of harsh soap. Her fingernails are irregular because she has obviously been nibbling them out of worry.

Maureen didn't ask for money. She simply accepted it when Barber insisted she take it, not proving at all that she was broke or that Richardson hadn't had the sense to have asked the mysterious Smith for an advance before leaving on the mission, as Barber chose to believe.

Final facts

Shaw's unexpected ending proves that Barber's assumptions that Maureen used Barber's money to buy the champagne and that she is into something the reader feels almost certain is prostitution to have gotten the huge ring are both absolutely wrong.

Yet, Shaw in no way cheated us, because there is nothing in the ending that is alien to what preceded it in the story. It is just that Shaw used a collection of foreshadowings that can be read two different ways. That the reader reads them the wrong way is due to the story being written from *Barber's* viewpoint. When the final facts of the ending have been revealed, the reader's mind consciously or unconsciously can search back over those foreshadowings and realize it.

The ending is successful because it contains *surprise* and yet seems *inevitable* as the logical result of all that previously transpired. There is a *definite conclusion* when Barber, at last revealed as an unsympathetic hero, is overcome by the problem. All of which creates *satisfaction*.

End game

As you work to improve your technique in developing endings that contain ingredients of success you will find that there are only two ways to approach those endings: A) knowing them in advance, or B) not knowing them in advance. Each has its advantages.

If you get an idea that would make a terrific ending for a short story, creating an A situation, you surely don't want to throw it away—it's terrific and there's the advantage. But you must construct that story backward. You must invent situations, characters and actions that will instill the manuscript with the four ingredients necessary to keep that ending terrific in the final draft.

Because you know exactly where you're headed when you write the A-type story, however, you must insert more misdirecting foreshadowings than might be necessary in the B type, in order to prevent telegraphing that ending to the reader long before he gets there.

For example, if what you are writing gives you sadness (you feel an ache in the throat, possibly a sting of tears, because you are so into the creating), there is almost no doubt that the reader will feel that same kind of sadness. If it's joy, the reader will feel joy.

As a result of that same phenomenon, there is an unconscious tendency to give away your ending to the eventual reader, *if* you have been certain of it right from the beginning.

But in the B situation, the phenomenon works for you. If you don't know your ending in advance, and it surprises you even in the planning, it will be more likely to surprise the reader as well.

As easy as ab

My short story, "A Proper Environment" (*Alfred Hitchcock's Mystery Magazine*, Nov. 11, 1981), was an A-type story that began with the idea of the ending only: ink that gradually disappears after being penned on paper. From that idea, I worked backward to create a story about a man, Ambleton, through whose viewpoint the story is told, living with his young son Kevin on a large inheritance gotten years before when his wife was presumed to have been murdered by a prowler. The truth is that Ambleton, in a fit of temper, killed his wife, using an Old World candle holder from his desk. Kevin doesn't know this at the start of the story, because he was a child asleep in his room at the time.

But the murder was witnessed by a servant, Edward Harms, a monstrous giant, who suggested that Ambleton retire to the room where his infant son was sleeping, after which the servant lied to the authorities that he'd seen the wife killed by an escaped prowler.

The servant left his job after that. But there was method in his failure to name Ambleton as a murderer: Ever since, once a year, Harms telephones and demands that

Ambleton mail $50,000 to him. If Harms does not receive the money within a declared deadline, he will return and kill Ambleton.

Near the end, the reader learns that Kevin, an avid collector of magic tricks, accidentally heard the last phone call from Harms on an extension phone, to find out at last that his father murdered his mother, whose memory he cherishes.

The boy then puts the disappearing ink into the old-fashioned well on his father's desk knowing that his father will address the latest package of money to Harms with a quill pen, using the ink.

The story finishes with Ambleton and Kevin in Ambleton's study. Ambleton is defending his murder of the boy's mother condemning her as being evil and worthless. But Kevin is unresponsive, and the ending reads:

> "Killer," Kevin said.
> "If you'd only been old enough to know what she really was!"
> "You didn't give me the chance," Kevin said coolly.
> Behind Kevin as he spoke, Edward Harms appeared in the doorway, looking much as he had the day seven years ago when the boy had been asleep in his room.
> "No!" Ambleton told him. "No no no no no!"

There should be no doubt that Harms has arrived as the result of not receiving the latest money package because the address disappeared along the way. Since I had carefully placed in the story clues to the above ending, including describing how the ex-servant had killed and torn apart wild animals with his bare hands, the reader can imagine what will happen after the last line.

A special problem here was to plant misdirecting foreshadowings that would divert the reader from thinking about why the father used an old-fashioned quill pen and a brass inkwell that would eventually hold the disappearing ink. I wrote that he owned a variety of items that were both brass and old-fashioned, including what turned out to be the murder weapon.

By giving the boy a foreshadowing hobby of magic, there is a sense of inevitability in the fact that, at the end, he used magic ink to revenge his mother's murder. But the misdirecting factor used in the foreshadowing was having him earlier demonstrate a magic trick accomplished with mathematics, something far removed from magic-ink tricks.

A definite conclusion came about because the main character was unsympathetic and the problem overcame him.

To b, or not to b

In the case of my story, "The Lie Detector" (*Alfred Hitchcock's Mystery Magazine*, April 29, 1981), I started with a B situation, not having a hint of what the ending would be, just an idea: An excellent actor guilty of a crime deceives a lie detector by playing an innocent person.

In this instance I planned from front to back, finally developing a story told from the viewpoint of a sympathetic hero, a young lawyer who is an assistant to a famous San Francisco attorney, Blackmore, who is defending the wife of a movie director. The woman has been accused of having shot her husband to death.

Blackmore is losing his first murder trial because a handsome young carpenter with a Texas accent, who could have done it, has asked for and has taken a lie detector test with the agreement that the results could be used in court. The results indicate that the carpenter is innocent. No such test has been taken by the accused wife.

The hero, who wishes to emulate Blackmore, investigates the carpenter between court sessions. He presents the typed results to his employer the next morning. Blackmore then uses his great courtroom skills and the material given him by his assistant to unmask the carpenter as a highly skilled English actor. The actor's English preferences for warm beer and gin and tonic without ice, as well as habits such as referring to French-fried potatoes as chips, give him away.

The actor confesses to killing the director for not giving him an important movie role and admits to fooling the lie detector. He vows that no jail can hold him (a deliberately placed foreshadowing). He is then jailed.

Blackmore, selfish and egotistical, takes complete credit in front of the media for what was mostly accomplished by his young assistant.

In the last scene, Blackmore is being driven in his limousine back to San Francisco not by his young assistant, who usually drives him about, but by a just-hired chauffeur, white-haired with a neat white mustache and goatee. The assistant has explained to Blackmore that he'd fallen down in his room and broken a wrist, which is now bandaged, and had then hired the professional driver.

The glory of the victory claimed in full by Blackmore has now been tarnished by the fact that, after being jailed, the actor escaped as the result of an unknown person smuggling a small pistol into his cell. The story ends:

"Bugs," said the driver, pointing to where an insect had just smashed into the glass in front of us. "Gettin' all over da windscreen."

"What did he say?" Blackmore said angrily from the back seat.

"He said bugs are getting all over the *windshield*!" I replied, looking back and smiling.

I then relaxed. I might not enjoy it, but I could use several more months as F. Berton Blackmore's assistant in order to study his courtroom manners at greater length. I had the intelligence and inventiveness—all I needed was the style. And, with the help of another expert drama coach, I was going to get it. Success would ensue, and beautiful women would follow.

Contentedly, I turned my attention to the driver, hoping that he'd have the sense to keep quiet when not required to speak and that the bloke wasn't absentminded enough to suddenly start driving down the left side of the road instead of the right.

Everything that had previously transpired, strengthened by deliberately placed foreshadowings, made this ending seem inevitable. But surprise is there, in this case primarily because the ending surprised *me* when it developed during the planning.

Although these stories end with someone getting away with a crime (allowed by the sophistication of *The New Yorker* and the familiar stamp of *Alfred Hitchcock's* wry style), they still satisfy readers.

End so on . . .

So—read the stories *you* admire. Study the foreshadowings. See how they lead to endings that contain definite conclusions, inevitability, surprise and over-all satisfaction.

Then write your own stories, making sure that they have those same ingredients in the endings. You will see the improvement in your finished manuscripts.

So will the editors.

Is your children's story really marketable?

by Jane Fitz-Randolph

"Any story that is salable will eventually find a market." Years ago I heard a teacher say that to a writing class. And the longer I'm in the business of writing and teaching writing, the surer I am that it's true. It may be harder to *write* a salable story today. Magazines are fewer, and those that remain are slimmer. But whether you're writing for young people or adults, the opportunities are there. It's just a matter of learning to recognize a marketable idea, plotting and writing it professionally, and marketing it intelligently.

The first step is really *knowing* the market. Too many hopeful writers for children look to dim recollections of stories and magazines *they* enjoyed as children—or those they read to their own now-grown children—for material. No one would think of consulting style catalogs of a generation ago for clothing models, and yesterday's stories are just as out of date.

The only way to know today's market is to read recent issues of the magazines themselves. If you were a fashion designer, you'd expect to read the fashion magazines, get out to fashion shows, attend functions patronized by fashion pace-setters, learn who your competition is and what other designers are doing. The same is true of designing successful stories. Articles in *Writer's Digest* and *The Writer* are helpful, and market lists in *Writer's Market* and *Fiction Writer's Market* are basic tools. They tell you what publications exist and something about editorial policies and needs. But market lists alone are not enough.

Jane Fitz-Randolph is the author of How to Write for Children and Young Adults *and the co-author of two science books with James Jespersen, the latest being* Mercury's Web: the Story of Telecommunications, *which won an Honorable Mention Award for the New York Academy of Sciences. Her other credits include children's films, filmstrips and short stories. A former teacher of adult and juvenile writing in university and adult education classes, she frequently participates in writers' workshops and seminars.*

Books for children are not much help either in writing magazine stories. The style is different in subtle ways, and some subjects suitable for books are unacceptable for magazine fiction. A book is unique, written for a selective audience, whereas magazines are planned for a continuing mass audience; stories must fit the personality of the magazine.

Research highlights

Building a collection of magazines and stories for young people is the first solid step in writing salable stories. Where can you find them? Newsstands have very few—or none at all in some communities. And even such well-established magazines as *Boys' Life* or *Highlights for Children* and many religious publications cannot be found there either. *Cricket* is more likely to be found in a bookstore than at a newsstand. It's also likely to be in the children's department of your public library, as are several other youth publications.

Beyond these common public sources, you have to develop your own. Churches and Sunday schools nearly always have leftover copies of their denominational papers. Most doctors, dentists, optometrists, and similar professionals subscribe to one or more youth publications for young patients in their waiting rooms; usually they're willing to give you back issues. Salvation Army, Goodwill, and other thrift stores often have stacks of fairly recent youth magazines for 5¢ to 10¢ each. School libraries and teachers are possible sources. Ask neighborhood children and children of your friends if they subscribe to publications they'll share with you. One source leads to others, and before long you'll have a good collection.

Of course you can—and should—subscribe to one or more magazines yourself, shifting frequently. And you can also write directly to any magazine for a sample copy. Publishers used to send these free, and a few still do. But most can't afford this anymore. So enclose a dollar bill with your request; if that's too generous, the extra will go for a good cause, and surely you're willing to invest a little in your research. The favorable impression you make with the editor could be a plus when you send her a story—if you don't wait so long she's forgotten your name. If you say you're interested in writing for the magazine, you'll probably receive a helpful "tips for writers" leaflet, too.

How well you learn to use your collection will have a lot to do with your writing success. Analysis is much more than just reading the stories. Read everything else in the magazine also—plays, poems, puzzles, jokes and riddles. If there's a section of contributions from readers, give it special attention. Look at pictures and graphics, the advertisements, if any. This will help you understand the personality of the magazine, the audience it expects to reach.

Skillful analysis

Some publications you'll find appealing; others you'll know at once are not for you. Go back over stories in the magazines you like, and ask yourself important questions: How many are "here and now" stories about ordinary boys and girls in ordinary American urban or suburban settings? Are there any with a foreign setting? Historicals or period stories? Animal stories? Fantasies or science fiction?

What percentage of the main characters are girls? Boys? Are they shown in traditional roles, or do you find girls repairing bicycles and mowing lawns, boys babysitting and entering cake-decorating contests?

How old is the main character? What makes him or her likable? What makes the *story* likable? Are there any facts or information in the content that might add to the reader's general knowledge? Why do you think the editor bought the story? As you develop skill in analysis, you'll look for other details that will help *you* plan and write successful stories.

Probably you'll feel more interest in one age group than others. Teens, perhaps, or 8-12s, where the largest market is. Or maybe you have a rare aptitude for simple stories for the very young—children under 8. It's all right to zero in on one group, but don't reject the others. Someday you'll bump into a story idea that's just right for one of them.

In a few publications, you'll find some incredibly poor stories. Give these special attention. See if you can discover why the editor bought them. The poor story, really, should be an encouragement. Editors buy the best of what they receive. If they sometimes publish a dud, it must be because they had nothing better. So here's your opportunity.

The more you know about the market, the better prepared you are to select appropriate story material and tailor it to fit editors' needs. *Your* first need, of course, is for fresh, salable ideas. Where can you find them?

Ideas are all around you, as you've doubtless heard a hundred times, just waiting to be recognized. Trite as it sounds, it's true. And once you cultivate skill in recognizing them, you'll find them pouring in faster than you can use them. Since the greatest demand by far is for here-and-now stories—and since this is the easiest to write well—let's concentrate on them for discussion.

Idea treasure troves

Some ideas have been so overworked that editors and writing teachers know from the first paragraph how the story will unfold. The old lady whom the neighborhood kids believe to be a witch, but who proves to be an interesting and likable person who loves children. The boy who is too small to make the team but finds a niche as bat boy or sports reporter for the school paper. The kids who set out to solve the mystery of what's going on in a supposedly deserted house. The treasure or document hidden away in the newly acquired house.

But even these and other oldies can be given a fresh angle. Suppose the old "witch" who keeps weird blue lights burning all night is developing a new strain of tomatoes or snapdragons through selective pollination. The boy who is too small to make the team is an expert at video games, and he develops a system that helps team members analyze plays. What's going on in the empty house is a sophisticated computer operation that helps criminals fence stolen goods. The hidden treasure in the newly-acquired house comes to light when the main character is helping his or her father install insulation or a solar heating system.

Kids themselves are a primary source for ideas. One of my own stories came from the ingenious way my son recovered a jacket he'd left at a playground and that had been appropriated by the neighborhood bully. Another dealt with a boy—whom I changed to a girl—who won a trip to Disneyland by cleverly estimating the number of beans in a bucket.

A teacher in one of my classes shared her homework assignment with her ninth grade English class. I had asked my students to bring in ten problems that today's young people might face, and to be as specific as possible. The teacher asked each of her pupils to write at least one such problem that they themselves had had to deal with, either recently or when they were younger. And she came up with six whole pages of situations that would keep any writer busy for years. Most of these responses presented a dilemma in which neither option offered a satisfactory answer. Here's a sample:

"When I learned to ride really well, my mom said I could buy a horse. We went to look at some and I tried one out, and because he was so pretty my mom went ahead and bought him. But he was the worst horse I ever rode. But if I complain, my mom will say I'm not grateful and maybe not let me have a horse.''

You can find ideas even if you have no contact with kids at all. Your newspaper is a treasure trove. I have a very fat file of clippings like this gem: "INSURANCE OFFERED: A 4-H club in Bend, Oregon is selling trick-or-treat insurance at $1 per policy. If a policy holder awakens the morning after Halloween and finds his windows soaped, his garbage can knocked over, the air let out of his tires, or evidence of a similar prank, the 4-Hers will fix things up.''

Others deal with simulated marriages in high school family living classes; a butterfly sent from Maryland to California via United Air Lines by a second-grade class who thought Maryland too cold for the butterfly to survive the winter there; and one headlined "Boy's Ad for a Grandfather Brings Flood of Responses.'' Other headlines are "Third Graders to Study Computer Literacy,'' and "Manners Are In Again.''

The best test

Transforming the idea into a story takes know-how and practice. It's not our purpose here to teach plotting skills, but rather to test the idea and plot and writing for salability. A few questions serve as guidelines:

1. Is the main character likable, someone readers will want to see succeed? People want to read about winners, not losers. There's nothing very interesting about a pimply boy who lives in a slum with an alcoholic mother. Or a girl who turns off all potential friends because of her bad temper or because she lies—unless she has the humility and spirit to overcome her shortcomings and does so.

2. Is the main character about the age of the oldest reader who would enjoy the story? Kids like to read about someone their own age, possibly a year or so older; they won't read about someone younger than they are. So a nine-year-old main character is less marketable to a magazine for 8-12s than one who is 11-12. Rarely is the main character for teen stories older than 16-17. These stories are mostly for *young* teens. High school sophomores and juniors, and even younger students, sometimes are into *adult* fiction.

3. Has the character a specific problem or goal that will interest readers of the publications to which you expect to send it? Does he or she make a real struggle, against challenging obstacles, to solve the problem and reach the goal? Does he solve the problem himself after a real "black moment"—the hardest battle of all—just before the ending? The main character must *do* things throughout the story, not just talk or think the problem away. A plot that editors—but never readers!—see again and again, for instance, involves the child who is miserable about his or her strange name that others make ugly remarks about. But mother sits down with the child and explains in a tender story why they chose the name and all is well. Nothing *happens* in such a story; it lacks drama. And besides, it's the mother who solves the problem, not the child.

4. Does the story open with a main character facing the problem and close promptly when the problem is solved? Openings are vitally important. They must capture reader interest in the first 75 words or the reader won't go on. Once the reader is hooked, he must be kept hoping that one thing will happen but fearing equally or more that something else will happen. This is the secret of suspense. Nearly all stories for children have a "happy" ending, though stories for teens often have an "open" ending that doesn't tie everything up neatly but leaves the main character on solid ground and with good *prospects* for success.

5. Does the main character *grow*? Although stories do get published in which the main character is essentially the same person at the end of the story as he or she was at the

beginning, the story in which the character—and therefore the reader—learns something from the experience is far more marketable. Editors of the religious publications, especially, even though most don't insist on or even want stories with a strictly religious message, do want character growth. The character should be wiser, kinder, less critical, more self-confident—in some way more *mature* because of what he or she learned from what happened.

Professional and systematic

A few basic principles of good fiction writing also need checking before your story is ready to leave home:

1. Show, don't tell. Think of your story as a play unfolding on a stage, where you, the author, can tell nothing; the characters themselves must tell their own story through action and dialogue. Use as much dialogue as possible; it makes for interesting reading, more interesting looking pages. Paint word pictures. Build images in the reader's mind. Keep the reader *seeing* the action, people, places. Keep even the exposition and narration in the vernacular of the main character; if you do this, you won't have to worry about vocabulary level.

2. Be sure you handle the technique of the single viewpoint professionally. Some stories go better told from the first-person viewpoint, others from third. If you use third-person, and you're ever in doubt about whether you're doing it correctly, just transpose momentarily into first person and you'll see your error at once. Suppose, for example, you've written, "Her large blue eyes filled with tears." You'd never say, "*My* large blue eyes filled with tears." It sounds silly. And if it's silly in first person, it's just as silly in third—to anyone who understands the *principle*.

3. It seems almost unnecessary to mention this, but it involves a major complaint of editors: Be sure your manuscript looks professional. It is *you* going in to meet a person on whom you wish to make a good impression. If you think of it that way—and you've done your homework on proper manuscript preparation—you'll do it right.

Marketing takes time, systematic planning, and perseverance. Your market knowledge may have guided you in planning your story; you may have written it with specific possiblities in mind. That's an intelligent start. Using all the information you've acquired, list all the possibilities for the particular story. Then rearrange them in the order you'll follow in your try for a sale.

What should determine this order? Several things. Begin by being *sure* your story really fits the editorial requirements. Editors' one loudest and constant complaint is the large amount of material they get that's not appropriate for their publication. *Trails* and *Touch* are girls' magazines; they can't use a boy main character. *Ranger Rick's Nature Magazine* is just that; it doesn't buy stories about "people" animals like Peter Rabbit or the Little Red Hen. And when editors say they buy stories up to 1,200 words long, they don't mean 1,500, or even 1,300.

Rightfully yours

When you're sure your story meets editorial needs, think about your own interests. You'll look at how much different magazines pay, of course; but this is not necessarily the most important consideration. Some magazines pay "on acceptance," others "on publication." As a rule, choose those that pay on acceptance; there's no guarantee that the others will *ever* publish your story—although most do, eventually, sometimes after 2-3 years or even more. But some of the most prestigious and best paying do pay on publication. *Cricket*, for example.

And this brings up another very important point: What "rights" does the magazine buy? There's no legitimate reason for it to own any rights except those it's prepared to use. Most magazines have accepted the intent of the new Copyright Act that became effective in 1978; they buy only "first serial rights" or sometimes magazine reprint rights. Since *Cricket* uses reprints, you could be free to offer the story elsewhere before it appeared there. Other magazines continue to buy "all rights." Of these, a good many will either return unused rights to the author on request or share with the author any proceeds from resales. But a few simply insist on buying all rights and cut the author out of all future consideration. Since they may resell a story for which they paid you only $35 or $40 to one or several publishers of school readers for $100 or more for each sale, this is a matter not to be taken lightly.

You'll also find some magazines—practically all in the religious field—that accept "multiple submissions." This means you can send the same story to two or more such markets at the same time, and both may buy it at their regular price; just be sure you *never* attempt this with any publication that does not buy on this basis—and that you tell both editors where else you're sending the story.

Since so many factors enter into decisions on marketing, you just have to weigh the advantages and disadvantages and choose the best combinations. Obviously, any magazine that offers very low payment in the first place, pays on publication, and insists on buying all rights should be at the very bottom of your prospect list.

But even if you have to accept these terms, a poor sale is better than no sale; and if you've tried all the better markets first, you'll be better satisfied with the poor sale. Keep your stories out, making the rounds until you've exhausted every possibility. No story can sell while "resting" in your files. Most writers give up much too easily. Various surveys made among writers show that the average number of submissions per sale is about 12; so if you quit after three or four submissions, you really haven't tried at all.

Most important—*keep writing*. It's the only way to stay in practice, and to keep your inventory strong. No writer is ever made or broken on the basis of a single story—or half a dozen stories. Any story that's salable will eventually find a market, and you certainly don't want to be caught short of new material to send out when that happens.

> ❝ *Everything I ever wrote in the way of fiction is based very securely on something in real life.*
> —*Katherine Anne Porter* ❞

Background and atmosphere

by Dorothy Salisbury Davis

No doubt some writers are good talkers, but, to my mind, good writers are necessarily even better listeners. They are receptive not merely to the ideas which sputter out of talk, but to the sputtering itself, the instinctive selection of words, images, illustrations plucked out of the environment in which the talk occurs, be it the corner bar, the intensive care unit of a hospital, a logging camp, or a police lock-up. They are receptive, too, to the ambience of place, its felicitousness, its hostility—its vibrations, if you will. The writer absorbs background as naturally as he breathes air. It becomes the reservoir from which his work continually draws its vitality.

Very often the idea for a story comes out of background, a setting which gets to a writer. What a place for a murder! Which of us has not said that? But wherever the idea comes from, it is imperative that it *seem* to come out of its background, that the crime could only have happened where it did.

Background, in the structural sense, is where the action occurs. It is the scene in which diverse characters are interrupted in their normal pursuits by the occurrence of something abnormal. A sentence like ''A stranger came to our villge,'' can set off a reader's imagination without a descriptive adjective because the word ''village'' suggests a small community of people who know one another and the word ''stranger'' suggests a new, disruptive element. The contrast creates almost instant suspense. But for the suspense to hold, the background must become as solid as the action is fluid. We must know the people, their houses, church, clubs, traditions—in a word, the lore of the place. Background is the credible scene which makes the incredible event, when it happens, the

---

Dorothy Salisbury Davis began a successful writing career at her husband's encouragement. Now, over 30 years later she is the author of four mainstream novels and 14 highly acclaimed mysteries, including her most recent spine-chiller, Scarlet Night. *Davis is a past president of Mystery Writers of America.*

more deliciously bizarre and, paradoxically, the more believable. The ring of authenticity in background establishes faith between reader and writer.

It may seem that I am suggesting long swatches of descriptive prose. I'm not. Adjectives, by and large, are dead words. Like it or not, we are living in the age of the verb. It is imperative to the modern mystery that background and action be strongly integrated. And this, I suggest, is best accomplished by the lively use of character.

Poke and ponder

Background is actually composed of two elements, place and people. The people— secondary characters, in craft parlance—integrate place and plot; they must, then, be a part of the action. In the mystery story, they function as witnesses. Character is dealt with elsewhere in this book, so I shall concern myself here only with its function in projecting background, but it is an arbitrary line which must not be drawn in practice.

Select people with personal color as well as vital functions in the community. By community I mean village, city, laboratory, university, international compound, whatever. Try to give their speech freshness by creating allusions which sound like the language of their trades or their mother-lore. I have a personal antipathy toward written dialect. It is obstructive to the reader, and since it is basically an unfamiliar sound given to an otherwise familiar word, the spelling of the sound is open to any number of choices. The pattern of speech and the choice of images quite adequately convey the character's origins. ("He's the beggar at the pump with his cup running over, but he can't see the water for the tears in his eyes." what would I have added to that characterization by spelling water, *watther* or *watjer* or *waather*?)

The use of foreign words or phrases to bolster a sense of locale is more generally felicitous. I have used them myself, combining them with the rest of the speech in English, but I think they are a crutch that sticks out.

I know of no other way to achieve verisimilitude of place than, to the extent of one's ability, to become a part of that place oneself. It involves that particular kind of listening I spoke of in the beginning. It involves seeing, touching, smelling, tasting. But since words are the mode of our communication, listening is our prime obligation to ourselves as writers.

Curiosity never killed a mystery writer. Poke in dark corners, explore abandoned structures. I don't mean merely the structures of buildings, but of businesses, and dreams; look into the sites and circumstances of sealed up cyclotrons, coal mines, theaters, churches where nobody prays any more. In every defeated dream there is a story, and one susceptible of violence, and the place where it began is the background. Don't be afraid to ask questions. Wait for the answers; and oh, dear writer, have the patience to understand the answers. Think of Sherlock Holmes and his pipe.

Adding color, suggesting tension

A veteran mystery writer used to say you could get away with a smattering of background knowledge by making your protagonist an outsider coming on that particular scene for the first time. This still holds, of course, but not as firmly as it once did. So much is known in our times about so many things. Patently, it is not possible to become a physicist in order to write about murder in a high-energy installation. But it is both possible and desirable to know a physicist. I once interviewed a physicist and asked questions that provoked her to thrust a book in my hands. "Before we talk," she said, "read this. Any 15 year-old could understand it." Under that challenge I learned more about physics in one night than I could have in a year of self-motivation. An invaluable shortcut to creating believable background is the use of words indigenous to the occupation of the characters. I think of a policeman "taking a squeal." My friend, the physicist, corrected my reference to "the experiment," which, in the trade, is simply referred to as "experiment." A handy writer's gadget is a file box in which to note the patois of various professions, adding to it a colorful phrase or anecdote when one comes your way. File under actor, burglar, cabdriver, doctor, and so on.

Study the motion picture for the effective use of background to suggest atmosphere. What is called the Establishing Shot tells the viewer where he is. Someone making a call from an outdoor phone booth against the interfering noise of traffic, the impatience of others waiting to use the phone, the graffiti on a dirty brick wall, swiftly combine to establish "city." The protagonist's selection of a record on a juke box identifies immediately: an interior scene, the protagonist's taste in music, his concern—or lack of it—for the other patrons, and the reaction of the patrons themselves.

A street vendor always adds color and can add much more. In the mystery he should have at least a small part in the action: He may get in the way of the protagonist, who is in a hurry; the protagonist may upset his wares producing some colorful language; he may button into the protagonist with a vaguely menacing hard sell, and he is always a potential witness. And if you have picked up the patter of his trade, the background is richer, the story stronger, because when he comes in again he will immediately recall that first vivid picture of him.

Any mode of travel in which the writer uses a detail of place that suggests tension—the protagonist's concern for an attaché case among overhead luggage and the people aware of this concern—starts action simultaneously with the showing of background. The involvement of the protagonist in some "Power" operation is good. Excavation machinery comes to mind, high power tools, a police dispatch room. The stronger the link between action and background at the opening, the less necessity for detail in background.

Distortion for effect

The beginning writer—indeed, the veteran as well—often gets hung up on getting a character into a room, or the scene where the action is to start. Why not start in the room, the action already under way? Then move back from the particular to encompass as much of the general as is needed. Given striking particulars, readers are marvelously adept at filling in background for themselves.

A rule of my own that I try not to violate: Have at least a line or two of dialogue on the first page. Its very visibility is a kind of come-on to the reader, telling him that action is imminent, that people are coming into the story at once, and people are the principal ingredient of story.

And every time I sit down to work I say to myself: Show, don't tell. Showing is action, involvement. Telling is preparation for or explanation of action, and should be unnecessary.

If I were to advise you to study one writer for believable and economical background, it would be Georges Simenon.

Atmosphere in the mystery is like *rubato* in music: Used judiciously, it heightens the experience; over-used, it blows up into sentimental mush. Atmosphere is distortion for effect. It plays upon the emotions of the characters, and therefore of the reader. The protagonist is particularly susceptible to it. Atmosphere contributes to suspense, roughly, in the way background strengthens action. And here again credibility is crucial. Atmosphere for its own sake is as unacceptable as a character who has no function in the plot.

Once again I am going to film for an example: In that old classic, *The Informer*, Gyppo is looking in a store window. He is cold and the night is wet. He is looking at an advertisement for a Bermuda cruise. The wind picks up flotsam from the street and wraps a paper around his legs. As he peels it off, he sees that it is the "wanted" flyer on Frankie McPhillips, ten pounds reward. The tapping of the blind singer's cane is the only sound. Here is a perfect orchestration of atmosphere, background, and action.

Atmospheric gambit

We must all choose our images. Contrast is the key: light and shadow, the grotesque which becomes familiar or the familiar which reveals itself to be grotesque; the cloaked figure in the moonlight that turns out to be a tree stump; or the tree stump which suddenly assaults the victim. The sound like machine-gun fire breaking out on a quiet street may turn out to be a cop drawing his nightstick across a window grate. To me, storm is a willow tree flailing in the wind, downed wires hissing with sparks, the blackened chimney of a hurricane lamp; fear is the smell of one's own sweat, a dry tongue. The deeper and more varied the exploitation of the sense, the better. There is a kind of reverse imagery I like: the building flooded with light when not a soul is moving through it; the dark deed in daylight.

It goes without saying that the kind of mystery story you are writing determines the degree and kind of atmosphere you want. So-called straight suspense is generally heavy with atmosphere. I think it is fair to say that books aimed at a woman's audience are richer in atmosphere than others, with the lush, eerie feeling of lurking horror.

There are shortcuts, of course, and fancying myself an economical writer, I particularly like them, the single strokes that set the mood: "I could hear the clack of my heels on the bare floors as I went from room to room to see that nothing was left." The meowing of a cat behind a locked door, the ringing of the telephone at four in the morning.

A very good atmospheric gambit is the dream. Remember in *Wild Strawberries*, the coffin sliding from the carriage and bursting open to reveal that the corpse was the dreamer? Or, "Last night I dreamt I went to Manderley again." Who would not take that for an opening?

Finally, I go to a poet for the epitome of atmospheric menace. Surely there is no more chilling opening to any fiction, prose or poetry, than Robert Browning's:

"That's my last Duchess painted on the wall,
Looking as if she were alive. . . ."

> **❝** *The mystery will never die. You may have to murder the victim but you can't kill the mystery.*
> —*Joan Kahn* **❞**

The last waltz—horror and morality, horror and magic

by Stephen King

1

"Yes, BUT HOW do you justify earning a living by feeding off people's worst fears?"

2

The police have been summoned by a neighbor who has heard a commotion of some kind. What they find is a bloodbath—and something worse. The young man admits, quite calmly, that he has murdered his grandmother with a pipe, and then cut her throat.

"I needed her blood," the young man tells the police calmly. "I'm a vampire. Without her blood, I would have died."

In his room the police find magazine articles about vampires, vampire comic books, stories, novels.

3

We'd been having a pretty nice lunch, this reporter from the *Washington Post* and I, something I was grateful for. I'd just started a 12-city tour for my novel *The Dead Zone* the day before in New York with a kick-off party thrown by the Viking Press at Tavern on the Green, a huge, rococo eating and drinking establishment on the edge of Central Park. I had tried to take it easy at the party, but I still managed to put away about eight beers there, and another six or so at a smaller, more relaxed party with some friends from Maine later on. Nevertheless I was up the next morning at quarter of five to make the six

---

Stephen King has parlayed America's love/hate conflict with horror stories into a successful enterprise. His books Carrie *and* The Shining *were both adapted for movies, and* Firestarter, Danse Macabre, Cujo *and his most recent book of four novellas* Different Seasons *have all been on the bestseller lists. King has also written many short stories with a horror theme.*

o'clock Eastern shuttle to Washington so I could, in turn, make a seven o'clock TV appearance to plug my novel. Welcome to touring, friends and neighbors.

I made the shuttle handily, telling invisible beads as it took off in a pouring rainstorm (sitting next to an overweight businessman who read the *Wall Street Journal* through the entire flight and ate Tums one after another, deliberately and reflectively, as if enjoying them) and made *A.M. Washington* with at least ten minutes to spare. The television lights intensified the mild hangover I'd gotten up with, and I was grateful for what had been a fairly laid-back lunch with the *Post* reporter, whose questions had been interesting and relatively unthreatening. Then this spitball about feeding off people's fears comes out of nowhere. The reporter, a young, lanky guy, was looking at me over his sandwich, eyes bright.

4

It's 1960, and a lonely Ohio youth has left the movie theater where he has just seen Psycho *for the fifth time. This young man goes home and stabs his grandmother to death. The pathologist would later count over 40 separate stab wounds.*

Why? the police asked.

Voices, the young man replies. Voices told me to do it.

5

"Look," I said, putting my own sandwich down. "You take any big-city psychiatrist. He's got a marvelous home in the suburbs, a hundred thousand dollars' worth of house at the very least. He drives a Mercedes-Benz, either tobacco-brown or silver-gray. His wife has got a Country Squire wagon. His kids go to private schools during the academic year and to good summer camps in New England or in the northwest every summer. Sonny has got Harvard if he can make the grades—money is certainly no problem—and his daughter can go to some reet and compleet girls' school where the sorority motto is 'We don't conjugate, we decline.' And how is he making the money that produces all of these wonders? He is listening to women weep over their frigidity, he is listening to men with suicidal impulses, he is dealing with paranoia both high and low, he's maybe striking on the occasional true schizophrenic. He's dealing with people who most of all are scared shitless that their lives have somehow gotten out of control and that things are falling apart . . . and if that isn't earning a living by feeding off people's fears, I don't know what is."

I picked up my sandwich again and bit into it, convinced that if I hadn't hit the spitter he had thrown me, I'd at least managed to foul it back and stay alive at the plate. When I looked up from my Reuben, the little half-smile on the reporter's face was gone.

"I," he said softly, "happen to be in analysis."

6

January of 1980. The woman and her mother are having a worried conference over the woman's three-month-old baby. The baby won't stop crying. It always cries. They agree on the source of the problem: The baby has been possessed by a demon, like that little girl in The Exorcist. *They pour gasoline on the baby as it lies crying in its crib and then light the child on fire to drive the demon out. The baby lingers in a burn ward for three days. Then it dies.*

7

The reporter's article was clean and fair for all of that; he was unkind about my physical appearance and I suppose he had some cause—I was in the slobbiest shape I've been in for ten years during that late summer of 1979—but other than that, I felt I got a pretty square shake. But even in the piece he wrote, you can feel the place where his path and mine diverged; there is that quiet snap which is the sound of ideas suddenly going off in two completely different directions.

"You get the impression that King likes this sort of sparring," he wrote.

8

Boston, 1977. A woman is killed by a young man who uses a number of kitchen implements to effect the murder. Police speculate that he might have gotten the idea from a movie—Brian De Palma's Carrie, *from the novel by Stephen King. In the film version, Carrie kills her mother by causing all sorts of kitchen implements—including a corkscrew and a potato-peeler—to fly across the room and literally nail the woman to the wall.*

9

Prime-time television survived the call by pressure groups to end the excessive, graphic depiction of violence on the tube for over ten years and House and Senate subcommittees almost without number which were convened to discuss the subject. Private eyes went on shooting bad guys and getting clopped over the head after the assassinations of John F. Kennedy, Robert F. Kennedy, Martin Luther King; you could order up a dose of carnage at the twist of the channel selector on any night of the week, including Sundays. The undeclared war in Vietnam was heating up quite nicely, thank you; body counts were spiralling into the stratosphere. Child pscyhologists testified that after watching two hours of violent prime-time TV, groups of children in the test group showed a marked increase in play aggressiveness—beating the toy truck against the floor rather than rolling it back and forth, for instance.

10

Los Angeles, 1969. Janis Joplin, who will later die of a drug overdose, is belting out "Ball and Chain." Jim Morrison, who will die of a heart attack in a bathtub, is chanting "Kill, kill, kill, kill" at the end of a song titled "The End"—Francis Ford Coppola will use the song ten years later to fade in the prologue of Apocalypse Now. Newsweek *publishes a picture of a shyly-smiling U.S. soldier holding up a severed human ear. And in a Los Angeles suburb, a young boy puts out his brother's eyes with his fingers. He was, he explained, only trying to imitate the old Three Stooges two-fingered* boinnng! *When they do it on TV, the weeping child explains, no one gets hurt.*

11

Television's make-believe violence rolled on nevertheless, through the '60s, past Charles Whitman up on the Texas Tower ("There was a rumor/about a tumor," Kinky Friedman and the Texas Jewboys sang gleefully, "nestled at the base of his braiyyyyn . . ."), and what finally killed it and ushered in the Sitcom Seventies was a seemingly unimportant event when compared to the deaths of a President, a Senator, a great civil rights leader. Television execs were finally forced to rethink their position because a young girl ran out of gas in Roxbury.

She had a gas can in her trunk, unfortunately. She got it filled at a gas station, and while walking back to her beached car, she was set upon by a gang of black youths who took her gas can away from her, doused her with the gas, and then—like the woman and her mother trying to drive the demon out of the baby—lit her on fire. Days later she died. The youths were caught, and someone finally asked them the sixty-four-dollar question: Where did you get such a horrible idea?

From TV, came the response. From *The ABC Movie of the Week*.

Near the end of the '60s, Ed McBain (in reality novelist Evan Hunter) wrote one of his finest 87th Precinct novels of the policeman's lot. It was called *Fuzz*, and dealt in part with a gang of teenagers who went around dousing winos with gasoline and lighting them up. The film version, which is described by Steven Scheuer in his invaluable tubeside companion *Movies on TV* as a "scatterbrained comedy," starring Burt Reynolds and Raquel Welch. The biggest yucks in the movie come when several cops on stakeout dress up as nuns and then chase after a suspect, holding their habits up to reveal big, clunky workshoes. Pretty funny, right, gang? A real gut-buster.

McBain's novel isn't a gut-buster. It's grim and almost beautiful. Certainly he has never come any closer to defining exactly what the policeman's lot may be than near the end of the novel when Steve Carella, masquerading as a wino, is lit on fire himself. The producers of the movie apparently saw something between *M*A*S*H* and *Naked City* in this, and the misbegotten result is in most respects as forgettable as a Tracy Stallard fastball . . . except that one of Stallard's fastballs went out of Fenway Park to become Roger Maris' record-breaking 61st home run. And *Fuzz*, a poorly executed comedy-drama, effectively ended TV violence.

The message? You are responsible. And network TV accepted the message.

12

"How do you justify the violence of the shower scene in Psycho?*"* a critic once asked Sir Alfred Hitchcock.

"How do you justify the opening scene in Hiroshima, Mon Amour?*" Hitchcock is reputed to have replied. In that opening scene, which was certainly scandalous by American standards in 1959, we see Emmanuele Riva and Eliji Okada in a naked embrace.*

"The opening scene was necessary to the integrity of the film," the critic answered.

"So was the shower scene in Psycho,*" Hitchcock said.*

13

What sort of burden does the writer—particularly the writer of horror fiction—have to bear in all of this? Certainly there has never been a writer in the field (with the possible exception of Shirley Jackson) who has not been regarded with more than a degree of critical caution. The morality of horror fiction has been called into question for a hundred years. One of the blood-spattered forerunners of *Dracula*, *Varney the Vampyre*, was referred to as a "penny dreadful." Later on, inflation turned the penny dreadfuls into dime dreadfuls. In the 1930s there were cries that pulps such as *Weird Tales* and *Spicy Stories* (which regularly served up lip-smacking S&M covers on which lovely ladies were tied down, always in their "small clothes," and menaced by some beastly—but identifiably male—creature of the night) were ruining the morals of the youth of America. Similarly in the '50s, the comics industry choked off such outlaw growths as E.C.'s *Tales from the Crypt* and instituted a Comics Code when it became clear that Congress intended to clean their house for them if they would not clean it for themselves. There would be no more tales of dismemberment, corpses come back from the dead, and premature burials—or at least not for the next ten years. The return was signalled by the unpretentious birth of *Creepy*, a Warren Group magazine which was a complete throwback to the salad days of Bill Gaines's E.C. horror comics. Uncle Creepy, and his buddy Cousin Eerie, who came along two years or so later, were really interchangeable with the Old Witch and the Crypt-Keeper. Even some of the old artists were back—Joe Orlando, who made his debut as an E.C. artist, was also represented in the premiere issue of *Creepy*, if memory serves.

I would suggest that there has always been a great tendency, particularly when it comes to such popular forms as movies, television, and mainstream fiction, to kill the messenger for the message. I do not now and never have doubted that the youths who burned the lady in Roxbury got the idea from the telecast of *Fuzz* one Sunday night on ABC; if it had not been shown, stupidity and lack of imagination might well have reduced them to murdering her in some more mundane way. The same holds true with many of the other cases mentioned here.

The danse macabre is a waltz with death. This is a truth we cannot afford to shy away from. Like the rides in the amusement park which mimic violent death, the tale of horror is a chance to examine what's going on behind doors which we usually keep double-locked. Yet the human imagination is not content with locked doors. Somewhere there is another dancing partner, the imagination whispers in the night—a partner in a rotting ball gown, a partner with empty eyesockets, green mold growing on her elbow-length gloves, maggots squirming in the thin remains of her hair. To hold such a creature in our arms? Who, you ask me, would be so mad? Well . . . ?

"You will not want to open this door," Bluebeard tells his wife in that most horrible of all horror stories, "because your husband has forbidden it." But this, of course, only makes her all the more curious. . . .and at last, her curiosity is satisfied.

"You may go anywhere you wish in the castle," Count Dracula tells Jonathan Harker, "except where the doors are locked, where of course you will not wish to go." But Harker goes soon enough.

And so do we all. Perhaps we go to the forbidden door or window willingly because we understand that a time comes when we must go whether we want to or not . . . and not just to look, but to be pushed through. Forever.

14

Baltimore, 1980. The woman is reading a book and waiting for her bus to arrive. The demobbed soldier who approaches her is a Vietnam vet, a sometime dope addict. He has a history of mental problems which seem to date from his period of service. The woman has noticed him on the bus before, sometimes weaving, sometimes staggering, sometimes calling loudly and wildly to people who are not there. "That's right, Captain!" she has heard him say. "That's right, that's right!"

He attacks the woman as she waits for her bus; later, the police will theorize he was after drug money. No matter. He will be just as dead, no matter what he was after. The neighborhood is a tough one. The woman has a knife secreted upon her person. In the struggle, she uses it. When the bus comes, the black ex-soldier lies dying in the gutter.

What were you reading? a reporter asks her later; she shows him The Stand, *by Stephen King.*

15

With its disguise of semantics carefully removed and laid aside, what those who criticize the tale of horror (or who simply feel uneasy about it and their liking for it) seem to be saying is this: You are selling death and disfigurement and monstrosity; you are trading upon hate and violence, morbidity and loathing; you are just another representative of those forces of chaos which so endanger the world today.

You are, in short, immoral.

A critic asked George Romero, following the release of *Dawn of the Dead*, if he felt such a movie, with its scenes of gore, cannibalism, and gaudy pop violence, was a sign of a healthy society. Romero's reply, worthy of the Hitchcock anecdote related earlier, was to ask the critic if he felt the DC-10 engine-mount assembly was a healthy thing for society. His response was dismissed as a quibble ("You get the impression Romero likes this kind of sparring," I can almost hear the critic thinking).

Well, let's see if the quibble really is a quibble—and let's go one layer deeper than we have yet gone. The hour has grown late, the last waltz is playing, and if we don't say certain things now, I suppose we never will.

I've tried to suggest that the horror story, beneath its fangs and fright wig, is really as conservative as an Illinois Republican in a three-piece pinstriped suit; that its main purpose is to reaffirm the virtues of the norm by showing us what awful things happen to people who venture into taboo lands. Within the framework of most horror tales we find a moral code so strong it would make a Puritan smile. In the old E.C. comics, adulterers inevitably came to bad ends and murderers suffered fates that would make the rack and the boot look like kiddy rides at the carnival. My all-time favorite (he said affectionately): A crazed husband stuffs the hose of an air compressor down his skinny wife's throat and blows her up like a balloon until she bursts. "Fat at last," he tells her happily just moments before the pop. But later on the husband, who is roughly the size of Jackie Gleason, trips a booby-trap she has set for him and is squashed to a shadow when a huge safe falls on him. This ingenious reworking of the old story of Jack Sprat and his wife is not only gruesomely funny; it offers us a delicious example of the Old Testament eye-for-an-eye theory. Or, as the Spanish say, revenge is a dish best eaten cold.

Modern horror stories are not much different from the morality plays of the 15th, 16th, and 17th centuries, when we get right down to it. The horror story most generally not only stands foursquare for the Ten Commandments, it blows them up to tabloid size. We have the comforting knowledge when the lights go down in the theater or when we open the book that the evildoers will almost certainly be punished, and measure will be returned for measure.

Further, I've used one pompously academic metaphor, suggesting that the horror tale generally details the outbreak of some Dionysian madness in an Apollonian existence, and that the horror will continue until the Dionysian forces have been repelled and the Apollonian norm restored again. Excluding a powerful if puzzling prologue set in Iraq, William Friedkin's film *The Exorcist* actually begins in Georgetown, an Apollonian suburb if ever there was one. In the first scene, Ellen Burstyn is awakened by a crashing, roaring sound in the attic—it sounds like maybe someone let a lion loose up there. It is the first crack in the Apollonian world; soon everything else will pour through in a nightmare torrent. But this disturbing crack between our normal world and a chaos where demons are allowed to prey on innocent children is finally closed again at the end of the film. When Burstyn leads the pallid but obviously okay Linda Blair to the car in the film's final scene, we understand that the nightmare is over. Steady state has been restored. We have watched for the mutant and repulsed it. Equilibrium never felt so good.

Suppose all of that is only a sham and a false front? I don't say that it is, but perhaps (since this *is* the last dance) we ought to discuss the possibility, at least.

In our discussion of archetypes, there's the Werewolf, that fellow who is sometimes hairy and who is sometimes deceptively smooth. Suppose there was a double werewolf? Suppose that the creator of the horror story was, under his/her fright wig and plastic fangs, a Republican in a three-button suit, as we have said . . . ah, but suppose below *that* there is a *real* monster, with real fangs and a squirming Medusa-tangle of snakes for hair? Suppose it's all a self-serving lie and that when the creator of horror is finally stripped all the way to his or her core of being we find not an agent of the norm but a friend—a capering, gleeful, red-eyed agent of chaos?

What about *that* possibility, friends and neighbors?

16

About five years ago I finished *The Shining*, took a month off, and then set about writing a new novel, the working title of which was *The House on Value Street*. It was going to be a *roman à clef* about the kidnapping of Patty Hearst, her brainwashing (or her sociopolitical awakening, depending on your point of view, I guess), her participation in the bank robbery, the shootout at the SLA hideout in Los Angeles—in my book, the hideout was on Value Street, natch—the fugitive run across the country, the whole ball of wax. It seemed to me to be a highly potent subject, and while I was aware that lots of nonfiction books were sure to be written on the subject, it seemed to me that only a novel might really succeed in explaining all the contradictions. The novelist is, after all, God's liar, and if he does his job well, keeps his head and his courage, he can sometimes find the truth that lives at the center of the lie.

Well, I never wrote that book. I gathered my research materials, such as they were, to hand (Patty was still at large then, which was another attraction the idea had for me; I could make up my own ending), and then I attacked the novel. I attacked it from one side and nothing happened. I tried it from another side and felt it was going pretty well until I discovered all my characters sounded as if they had just stepped whole and sweaty from the dance marathon in Horace McCoy's *They Shoot Horses, Don't They?* I tried it *in medias res*. I tried to imagine it as a stage play, a trick that sometimes works for me when I'm badly stuck. It didn't work this time.

In his marvelous novel *The Hair of Harold Roux*, Thomas Williams tells us that writing a long work of fiction is like gathering characters together on a great black plain. They stand around the small fire of the writer's invention, warming their hands at the blaze, hoping the fire will grow into a blaze which will provide light as well as heat. But often it goes out, all light is extinguished, and the characters are smothered in black. It's a lovely metaphor for the fiction-making process, but it's not mine . . . maybe it's too gentle to be mine. I've always seen the novel as a large black castle to be attacked, a bastion to be taken by force or by trick. The thing about this castle is, it appears to be open. It doesn't look buttoned up for siege at all. The drawbridge is down. The gates are open. There are no bowmen on the turrets. Trouble is, there's really only one safe way in; every other attempt at entry results in sudden annihilation from some hidden source.

With my Patty Hearst book, I never found the right way in . . . and during that entire six-week period, something else was nagging very quietly at the back of my mind. It was a news story I had read about an accidental CBW spill in Utah. All the bad nasty bugs got out of their cannister and killed a bunch of sheep. But, the news article stated, if the wind had been blowing the other way, the good people of Salt Lake City might have gotten a very nasty surprise. This article called up memories of a novel called *Earth Abides*, by George R. Stewart. In Stewart's book, a plague wipes out most of mankind, and the protagonist, who has been made immune by virtue of a well-timed snakebite, witnesses the ecological changes which the passing of man causes. The first half of Stewart's long book is riveting; the second half is more of an uphill push—too much ecology, not enough story.

We were living in Boulder, Colorado, at the time, and I used to listen to the Bible-thumping station which broadcast out of Arvada quite regularly. One day I heard a preacher dilating upon the text ''Once in every generation the plague will fall among them.'' I liked the sound of the phrase—which sounds like a Biblical quotation but is not—so well that I wrote it down and tacked it over my typewriter: *Once in every generation the plague will fall among them*.

The phrase and the story about the CBW spill in Utah and my memories of Stewart's fine book all became entwined in my thoughts about Patty Hearst and the SLA, and one day while sitting at my typewriter, my eyes traveling back and forth between that creepy homily on the wall to the maddeningly blank sheet of paper in the machine, I wrote—just to write something: *The world comes to an end but everybody in the SLA is somehow immune. Snake bit them.* I looked at that for a while and then typed: *No more gas shortages*. That was sort of cheerful, in a horrible sort of way. No more people, no more gas lines. Below *No more gas shortages* I wrote in rapid order: *No more cold war. No more pollution. No more alligator handbags. No more crime. A season of rest.* I liked that last; it sounded like something that should be written down. I underlined it. I sat there for another 15 minutes or so, listening to the Eagles on my little cassette player, and then I wrote: *Donald DeFreeze is a dark man.* I did not mean that DeFreeze was black; it had suddenly occurred to me that, in the photos taken during the bank robbery in which Patty Hearst participated, you could barely see DeFreeze's face. He was wearing a big badass hat, and what he looked like was mostly guesswork. I wrote *A dark man with no face* and then glanced up and saw that grisly little motto again: *Once in every generation the plague will fall among them.* And that was that. I spend the next two years writing an apparently endless book called *The Stand*. It got to the point where I began describing it to friends as my own little Vietnam, because I kept telling myself that in another hundred pages or so I would begin to see light at the end of the tunnel. The finished manuscript was over 1,200 pages long and weighed 12 pounds, the same weight as the sort of bowling ball I favor. I carried it 30 blocks from the U.N. Plaza Hotel to my editor's apartment one warm night in July. My wife had wrapped the entire block of pages in Saran Wrap for some reason known only to her, and after I'd switched it from one arm to the other for the third or fourth time, I had a sudden premonition: I was going to die, right there on Third Avenue. The Rescue Unit would find me sprawled in the gutter, dead of a heart attack, my monster manuscript, triumphantly encased in Saran Wrap, resting by my outstretched hands, the victor.

There were times when I actively hated *The Stand*, but there was never a time when I did not feel compelled to go on with it. Even when things were going bad with my guys in Boulder, there was a crazy, joyful feeling about the book. I couldn't wait to sit down in front of the typewriter every morning and slip back into that world where Randy Flagg could sometimes become a crow, sometimes a wolf, and where the big battle was not for gasoline allocations but for human souls. There was a feeling—I must admit it—that I was doing a fast, happy tapdance on the grave of the whole world. Its writing came during a troubled period for the world in general and America in particular; we were suffering from our first gas pains in history, we had just witnessed the sorry end of the Nixon administration and the first presidential resignation in history, we had been resoundingly defeated in Southeast Asia, and we were grappling with a host of domestic problems, from the troubling question of abortion-on-demand to an inflation rate that was beginning to spiral upward in a positively scary way.

Me? I was suffering from a really good case of career jet lag. Four years before, I had been running sheets in an industrial laundry for $1.60 an hour and writing *Carrie* in the furnace-room of a trailer. My daughter, who was then almost a year old, was dressed mostly in scrounged clothes. The year before that, I had married my wife Tabitha in a borrowed suit that was too big for me. I left the laundry when a teaching position opened up at a nearby school, Hampden Academy, and my wife Tabby and I were dismayed to learn that my first-year salary of $6,400 was not going to take us much further than my laundry salary—and pretty soon I'd secured my laundry job back for the following summer.

Then *Carrie* sold to Doubleday, and Doubleday sold the reprint rights for a staggering sum of money which was, in those days, nearly a record-breaker. Life began to move at Concorde speed. *Carrie* was bought for films; *'Salem's Lot* was bought for a huge sum of money and then also bought for films; *The Shining* likewise. Suddenly all of my friends thought I was rich. That was bad enough, scary enough; what was worse was the fact that maybe I was. People began to talk to me about investments, about tax shelters, about moving to California. These were changes enough to try and cope with, but on top of them, the America I had grown up in seemed to be crumbling beneath my feet . . . it began to seem like an elaborate castle of sand unfortunately built well below the high-tide line.

The first wave to touch that castle (or the first one that I perceived) was that long-ago announcement that the Russians had beaten us into space . . . but now the tide was coming in for fair.

And so here, I think, is the face of the double werewolf, revealed at last. On the surface, *The Stand* pretty much conforms to those conventions we have already discussed: An Apollonian society is disrupted by a Dionysian force (in this case a deadly strain of superflu that kills almost everybody). Further, the survivors of this plague discover themselves in two camps: One, located in Boulder, Colorado, mimics the Apollonian society just destroyed (with a few significant changes); the other, located in Las Vegas, Nevada, is violently Dionysian.

The first Dionysian incursion in *The Exorcist* comes when Chris MacNeil (Ellen Burstyn) hears that lionlike roar in the attic. In *The Stand*, Dionysus announces himself with the crash of an old Chevy into the pumps of an out-of-the-way gas station in Texas. In *The Exorcist*, the Apollonian steady state is restored when we see a pallid Regan MacNeil being led to her mother's Mercedes-Benz; in *The Stand* I believe that this moment comes when the book's two main characters, Stu Redman and Frannie Goldsmith, look through a plate-glass window in the Boulder hospital at Frannie's obviously normal baby. As with *The Exorcist*, the return of equilibrium never felt so good.

But below all of this, hidden by the moral conventions of the horror tale (but perhaps not all that hidden), the face of the *real* Werewolf can be dimly seen. Much of the compulsion I felt while writing *The Stand* obviously came from envisioning an entire entrenched societal process destroyed at a stroke. I felt a bit like Alexander, lifting his sword over the Gordian knot and growling, "*Fuck* untying it; I've got a better way." And I felt a bit the way Johnny Rotten sounds at the beginning of that classic and electrifying Sex Pistols song, "Anarchy for the U.K." He utters a low, throaty chuckle that might have come from Randall Flagg's own throat and then intones, "Right . . . *NOW!*" We hear that voice, and our reaction is one of intense relief. The worst is now known; we are in the hands of an authentic madman.

In this frame of mind, the destruction of THE WORLD AS WE KNOW IT became an actual relief. No more Ronald McDonald! No more *Gong Show* or *Soap* on TV—just soothing snow! No more terrorists! *No more bullshit!* Only the Gordian knot unwinding there in the dust. I am suggesting that below the writer of the moral horror tale (whose feet, like those of Henry Jekyll, are "always treading the upward path") there lies another creature altogether. He lives, let us say, down there on Jack Finney's third level, and he is a capering nihilist who, to extend the Jekyll-Hyde metaphor, is not content to tread over the tender bones of one screaming little girl but in this case feels it necessary to do the funky chicken over the whole world. Yes, folks, in *The Stand* I got a chance to scrub the whole human race, and *it was fun!*

So where is morality now?

Well, I'll give you my idea. I think it lies where it has always lain: in the hearts and minds of men and women of good will. In the case of the writer, this may mean beginning with a nihilistic premise and gradually relearning old lessons of human values and human conduct. In the case of *The Stand*, this meant beginning with the glum premise that the human race carries a kind of germ with it—I began by seeing this germ symbolically visualized in the SLA, and ended by seeing it visualized in the superflu germ—which grows more and more virulent as technology grows in power. The superflu is unleashed by a single technological misstep (not such a far-fetched presumption, either, when you consider what happened at Three Mile Island last year or the fact that Loring AFB in my own state scrambled bombers and fighters ready to head over the pole toward Russia as the result of an amusing little computer foulup which suggested that the Russians had launched their missiles and the Big Hot One was on). By simple agreement with myself to allow a few survivors—no survivors, no story, am I right?—I was able to envision a world in which all the nuclear stockpiles would simply rust away and some kind of normal moral, political, and ecological balance would return to the mad universe we call home.

But I don't think anyone knows what they really think—or perhaps even what they really know—until it's written down, and I came to realize that the survivors would be very likely to first take up all the old quarrels and then all the old weapons. Worse, all those deadly toys would be available to them, and things might well become a sprint to see which group of loonies could figure out how to launch them first. My own lesson in writing *The Stand* was that cutting the Gordian knot simply destroys the riddle instead of solving it, and the book's last line is an admission that the riddle still remains.

The book also tries to celebrate brighter aspects of our lives: simple human courage, friendship, and love in a world which so often seems mostly loveless. In spite of its apocalyptic theme, *The Stand* is mostly a hopeful book that echoes Albert Camus' remark that "happiness, too, is inevitable."

More prosaically, my mother used to tell my brother David and me to "hope for the best and expect the worst," and that expresses the book I remember writing as well as anything.

So, in short, we hope for a fourth level (a triple Werewolf?), one that will bring us full circle again to the horror writer not just as writer but as human being, mortal man or woman, just another passenger in the boat, another pilgrim on the way to whatever there is. And we hope that if he sees another pilgrim fall down that he will write about it—but not before he or she has helped the fallen one to his or her feet, brushed off his or her clothes, and seen if he or she is all right, and able to go on. If such behavior is to be, it cannot be as a result of an intellectual moral stance; it is because there is such a thing as love, merely a practical fact, a practical force in human affairs.

Morality is, after all, a codification of those things which the heart understands to be true and those things which the heart understands to be the demands of a life lived among others . . . civilization, in a word. And if we remove the label "horror story" or "fantasy genre" or whatever, and replace it with "literature" or more simply still, "fiction," we may realize more easily that no such blanket accusations of immorality can be made. If we say that morality proceeds simply from a good heart—which has little to do with ridiculous posturings and happily-ever-afterings—and immorality proceeds from a lack of care, from shoddy observation, and from the prostitution of drama or melodrama for some sort of gain, monetary or otherwise, then we may realize that we have arrived at a critical stance which is both workable and humane. Fiction is the truth inside the lie, and in the tale of horror as in any other tale, the same rule applies now as when Aristophanes told his horror tale of the frogs: Morality is telling the truth as your heart knows it. When asked if he was not ashamed of the rawness and sordidness of his turn-of-the-century novel *McTeague*, Frank Norris replied: "Why should I be? I did not lie. I did not truckle. I told them the truth."

Seen in that light, I think the horror tale may more often be adjudged innocent than guilty.

17

My, look at this . . . I do believe the sun is coming up. We have danced the night away, like lovers in some old MGM musical. But now the band has packed their melodies back inside their cases and has quitted the stage. The dancers have left, all but you and I, and I suppose we must go, as well. I cannot tell you how much I've enjoyed the evening, and if you sometimes found me a clumsy partner (or if I occasionally stepped on your toes), I do apologize, I feel as I suppose all lovers feel when the dance has finally ended, tired . . . but still gay.

As I walk you to the door, may I tell you one more thing? We'll stand here in the vestibule as they unroll the rug again and douse the lights. Let me help you with your coat; I'll not keep you long.

Questions of morality in the pursuit of horror may be begging the actual question. The Russians have a phrase, "the scream of the woodcock." The phrase is derisory because the woodcock is nature's ventriloquist, and if you fire your shotgun at the place where the sound came from, you'll go hungry. Shoot the woodcock, not the scream, the Russians say.

So let's see if we can't find a woodcock—just one—in all these screaming thickets. It might just be hiding in this item, truth rather than fiction, from *The Book of Lists*, the Wallace/Wallechinsky clan's attic full of fascinating rickrack and useful junk. As you get ready to leave, think about this . . . or brood upon it:

THE MYSTERY OF LITTLE MISS NOBODY
On July 6, 1944, the Ringling Brothers and Barnum & Bailey circus was giving a performance in Hartford, Connecticut, before 7,000 paid customers. A fire broke out; 168 persons died in the blaze and 487 were injured. One of the dead, a small girl thought to be six years old, was unidentified. Since no one came to claim her, and since her face was unmarred, a photograph was taken of her and distributed locally and then throughout the US. Days passed, weeks and months passed, but no relative, no playmate, no one in the nation came forward to identify her. She remains unknown to this day.

My idea of growing up is that the process consists mainly of developing a good case of mental tunnel vision and a gradual ossification of the imaginative faculty (what about Little Miss Nobody, you ask me—well, hang on; we'll get there). Children see everything, consider everything; the typical expression of the baby which is full, dry, and awake is a wide-eyed goggle at everything. Hello, pleased to meet you, freaked to be here. A child has not yet developed the obsessional behavior patterns which we approvingly call "good work habits." He or she has not yet internalized the idea that a straight line is the shortest distance between two points.

All of that comes later. Children believe in Santa Claus. It's no big deal; just a piece of stored information. They likewise believe in the boogeyman, the Trix Rabbit, McDonaldland (where hamburgers grow on trees and moderate thievery is approved behavior—witness the lovable Hamburglar), the Tooth Fairy who takes ivory and leaves silver . . . all of these things are taken as a matter of course. These are some of the popular myths; there are others which, while more specialized, seem just as *outré*. Grampa has gone to live with the angels. The stuff in the middle of the golf ball is the worst poison in the world. Step on a crack, break your mother's back. If you walk through holly bushes, your shadow can get caught and it will be left there forever, flapping on the sharp leaves.

The changes come gradually, as logic and rationalism assert themselves. The child begins to wonder how Santa can be at the Value House, on a downtown corner ringing a bell over a Salvation Army pot, and up at the North Pole generaling his troop of elves all at the same time. The child maybe realizes that although he's stepped on a hell of a lot of cracks, his or her mother's back is yet all right. Age begins to settle into that child's face. "Don't be a baby!" he or she is told impatiently. "Your head is always in the clouds!" And the kicker, of course: "Aren't you ever going to *grow up*?"

After awhile, the song says, Puff the magic dragon stopped trundling his way up the Cherry Lane to see his old goodbuddy Jackie Paper. Wendy and her brothers finally left Peter Pan and the Wild Boys to their fate. No more Magic Dust and only an occasional Happy Thought . . . but there was always something a little dangerous about Peter Pan, wasn't there? Something just a little too woodsy-wild? Something in his eyes that was . . . well, downright Dionysian.

Oh, the gods of childhood are immortal; the big kids don't really sacrifice them; they just pass them on to their bratty kid brothers and kid sisters. It's childhood itself that's mortal: Man is in love, and loves what passes. And it's not just Puff and Tink and Peter Pan that are left behind in that rush for the driver's license, the high school and college diploma, in that mostly eager training to achieve "good work habits." We have each exiled the Tooth Fairy (or perhaps he exiles us when we are no longer able to provide the product he requires), murdered Santa Claus (only to reanimate the corpse for our own children), killed the giant that chased Jack down the beanstalk. And the poor old boogeyman! Laughed to death again and again, like Mr. Dark at the conclusion of *Something Wicked This Way Comes*.

Listen to me now: At 18 or 20 or 21, whatever the legal drinking age may be in your state, "getting carded" is something of an embarrassment. You have to fumble around for a driver's license or your State Liquor Card or maybe even a photostat of your birth certificate so you can get a simple fa' Chrissakes glass of beer. But you let ten years go past, get so you are looking the big three-o right in the eye, and there is something absurdly flattering about getting carded. It means you still look like you might not be old enough to buy a drink over the bar. You still look a little wet behind the ears. You still look *young*.

This got into my head a few years ago when I was in a bar called Benjamin's in Bangor, getting pleasantly loaded. I began to study the faces of entering patrons. The guy standing unobtrusively by the door let this one pass . . . and that one . . . and the next one. Then, bang! He stopped a guy in a U of M jacket and carded him. And I'll be damned if that guy didn't do a quick fade. The drinking age in Maine was then 18 (booze-related accidents on the highways have since caused the lawmakers to move the age up to

20), and all of those people had looked about 18 to me. So I got up and asked the bouncer how he knew that last guy was underage. He shrugged. "You just know," he said. "It's mostly in their eyes."

For weeks after, my hobby was looking at the faces of adults and trying to decide exactly what it was that made them "adult faces." The face of a 30-year-old is healthy, unwrinkled, and no bigger than the face of a 17-year-old. Yet you know that's no kid; you *know*. There seems to be some hidden yet overriding characteristic that makes what we all agree is the Adult Face. It isn't just the clothes or the stance, it isn't the fact that the 30-year-old is toting a briefcase and the 17-year-old is toting a knapsack; if you put the head of each in one of those carnival cut-outs which show the body of a capering sailor or a prize-fighter, you could still pick out the adult ten tries out of ten.

I came to believe that the bouncer was right. It's in the eyes.

Not something that's there; something, rather, that has left.

Kids are bent. They think around corners. But starting at roughly age eight, when childhood's second great era begins, the kinks begin to straighten out, one by one. The boundaries of thought and vision begin to close down to a tunnel as we gear up to get along. At last, unable to grapple to any profit with Never-Never Land anymore, we may settle for the minor league version available at the local disco . . . or for a trip to Disney World one February or March.

The imagination is an eye, a marvelous third eye that floats free. As children, that eye sees with 20/20 clarity. As we grow older, its vision begins to dim . . . and one day the guy at the door lets you into the bar without asking to see any ID and that's it for you, Cholly; your hat is over the windmill. It's in your eyes. Something in your eyes. Check them out in the mirror and tell me if I'm wrong.

The job of the fantasy writer, or the horror writer, is to bust the walls of that tunnel vision wide for a little while; to provide a single powerful spectacle for that third eye. The job of the fantasy-horror writer is to make you, for a little while, a child again.

And the horror writer himself/herself? Someone else looks at that item about Little Miss Nobody (toldja we'd get back to her, and here she is, still unidentified, as mysterious as the Wolf Boy of Paris) and says, "Jeez, you never can tell, can you?" and goes on to something else. But the fantasist begins to play with it as a child would, speculating about children from other dimensions, about doppelgangers, about God knows what. It's a child's toy, something bright and shiny and strange. Let us pull a lever and see what it does, let us push it across the floor and see if it goes *Rum-Rum-Rum* or *wacka-wacka-wacka*. Let us turn it over and see if it will magically right itself again. In short, let us have our Fortian rains of frogs and people who have mysteriously burned to death while sitting at home in their easy chairs; let us have our vampires and our werewolves. Let us have Little Nobody, who perhaps slipped sideways through a crack in reality, only to be trampled to death in the rush from a burning circus tent.

And something of this is reflected in the eyes of those who write horror stories. Ray Bradbury has the dreamy eyes of a child. So, behind his thick glasses, does Jack Finney. The same look is in Lovecraft's eyes—they startle with their simple dark directness, especially in that narrow, pinched and somehow eternal New England face. Harlan Ellison, in spite of his rapid, jive talking shoot-from-the-hip Nervous-Norvus mode of conversation (talking with Harlan can sometimes be like talking with an apocalyptic Saladmaster salesman who has just taken three large bennies), has those eyes. Every now and then he'll pause, looking away, looking at something else, and you know that it's true: Harlan is bent and he just thought his way around a corner. Peter Straub, who dresses impeccably and who always seems to project the aura of some big company success, also has that look in his eyes. It is an indefinable look, but it's there.

"It's the best set of electric trains a boy ever had," Orson Welles once said of making movies; the same can be said of making books and stories. Here is a chance to bust that tunnel vision wide open, bricks flying everywhere so that, for a moment at least, a dreamscape of wonders and horrors stands forth as clearly and with all the magic reality of the first Ferris wheel you ever saw as a kid, turning and turning against the sky. Someone's dead son is on the late movie. Somewhere a foul man—boogeyman!—is slouching through the snowy night with shining yellow eyes. Boys are thundering through autumn leaves on their way home past the library at four in the morning, and somewhere else, in some other world, even as I write this, Frodo and Sam are making their way toward Mordor, where the shadows lie. I am quite sure of it.

Ready to go? Fine. I'll just grab my coat.

It's not a dance of death at all, not really. There is a third level here, as well. It is, at bottom, a dance of dreams. It's a way of awakening the child inside, who never dies but only sleeps ever more deeply. If the horror story is our rehearsal for death, then its strict moralities make it also a reaffirmation of life and good will and simple imagination—just one more pipeline to the infinite.

In his epic poem of a stewardess falling to her death from high above the fields of Kansas, James Dickey suggests a metaphor for the life of the rational being, who must grapple as best he/she can with the fact of his/her own mortality. We fall from womb to tomb, from one blackness and toward another, remembering little of the one and knowing nothing of the other . . . except through faith. That we retain our sanity in the face of these simple yet blinding mysteries is nearly divine. That we may turn the powerful intuition of our imaginations upon them and regard them in this glass of dreams—that we may, however timidly, place our hands within the hole which opens at the center of the column of truth—that is . . .

. . . well, it's magic, isn't it?

Yeah. I think maybe that's what I want to leave you with, in lieu of a goodnight kiss, that word which children respect instinctively, that word whose truth we only rediscover as adults in our stories . . . and in our dreams:

Magic.

> *We writers are lucky: Nothing truly bad can happen to us. It's all material.*
>
> **—Philip Roth**

The science of writing science fiction

by Stanley Schmidt

The last time we polled readers of *Analog*, the two most popular stories of 1981 turned out to be "Emergence," by David R. Palmer (January), and "Petals of Rose," by Marc Stiegler (November). As editor of *Analog*, I wasn't surprised, because those were two of my favorites, too. What may surprise you is that "Emergence" was a first story by an author whose manuscript turned up in my slush pile one day, and "Petals of Rose" was from an author with only one previous sale. Editors do buy, and successfully publish, stories from new writers.

Yet, a magazine like *Analog* receives so many submissions that it has room for only one or two percent of them. Many stories are rejected not because of anything conspicuously *wrong* with them, but simply because nothing sufficiently *special* about them makes them stand out from 98% of the competition.

What makes stories like "Emergence" and "Petals of Rose" stand out? How can you make *your* stories do the same? The key words are *imagination*, *discipline*—and the first word in "science fiction."

What about writing? It's important, but *good writing is not enough*. Oh, it *can* be. If your writing is truly extraordinary, you may breathe enough new life into an old idea to make something fresh and commanding of it. "Emergence" brings some novel twists to the global holocaust and superman themes—such as minimal use of nuclear weapons to trigger biological ones, and a plausible way for a natural epidemic to produce a new "species"—but the basic ideas behind the story are among the oldest in science fiction. The story draws most of its impact from a remarkably vivid portrayal of an exceptionally memorable character. Author David Palmer dared to tell his story through the journal of

Stanley Schmidt is the editor of Analog Science Fiction/Science Fact *Magazine and the author of three novels. His short stories have appeared in* The Magazine of Fantasy and Science Fiction, Isaac Asimov's Science Fiction Magazine, *and other publications.*

an 11-year-old girl, trapped alone in an underground shelter after the war, who doesn't yet realize just how special she is. Her personality is so unusual, engaging and wide-ranging, and every word is so carefully chosen, that when Palmer complained that a routine copy-editing change of a single word was "out of character," there was no question that he was right.

Few stories can pull that off. What I see more often are stories that are competently written—but little more—and don't *say* very much. They lack content—*ideas*. Science fiction requires two sets of skills: writing, and imagining in that special way that makes speculations both plausible and integral to the story. I want to concentrate on that second set of skills. Too many writers try to get by on good writing alone, without developing the *other* tools of their trade.

Adam and Eve, revisited

To write science fiction, you must first understand what it is. Watching movies is not enough; most "science fiction" in movies and television is not science fiction at all, by the standards of *written* science fiction. If you haven't read many science fiction books and magazines, you should—both to get a feel for what it takes to write them, and to avoid rehashing worn-out ideas. (Ben Bova, my predecessor at *Analog*, warned me that I'd get several stories a month involving a man and woman who find themselves alone on an unnamed planet and turn out to be Adam and Eve. I quickly learned to recognize these stories on the first page.)

Science fiction is fiction in which:

- At least one speculative idea is *integral* to the story.
- Whatever science the story uses is *plausible* in the light of known science.

What do these criteria mean? In "Emergence," the speculative ideas on which the story depends are a war that wipes out most of humanity and a new kind of human being that supersedes *Homo sapiens*. In "Petals of Rose," humans must cooperate on a long-range project with beings whose adult lives are one-day frenzies of intensely concentrated activity.

As demonstrated in these examples, an idea being "integral" to a story means that you can't remove the speculation without destroying the whole story. This does *not* mean that stories must contain a lot of talk about science or technology—or that the presence of such talk automatically makes the stories science fiction. The movie *Star Wars* is full of "science fictional" hardware and trappings, but at heart it's a western. Replace the spaceships and light sabers with horses and six-guns, and you can tell essentially the same story in the Old West. In contrast, Daniel Keyes' *Flowers for Algernon* (or the movie *Charly*) contains almost *no* science fictional gimmickry or jargon, yet it is quite clearly science fiction. It is a story first and foremost of what goes on in a particular human being's mind; the speculative element—the one that makes *Flowers* a science fiction story in its comfortably contemporary setting—is the operation that increases Charlie Gordon's intelligence. The book does not go into much detail about the operation—but *everything that happens to Charlie grows directly out of it*. Remove the operation and nothing remains of the story. You might still tell a story about Charlie Gordon, but it would not be even remotely *this* story. And it certainly wouldn't be science fiction.

The plausibility of that speculation is also important. What can and can't happen in a particular setting is determined by scientific laws, primarily those of physics, chemistry and astronomy; there is strong evidence that these laws apply everywhere in the universe. Others, such as the principles of earthly biology, are special applications of the more general laws of physics and chemistry. You must reckon with them if you're writing about life on Earth, but physics and chemistry may lead to quite different biologies elsewhere (such as the silicon-based organisms in Stanley G. Weinbaum's classic short story, "A Martian Odyssey").

To tell a plausible story about a situation covered by known scientific laws, you must know what those laws say and how they apply to your imagined situation. You will not, for example, write about enormous spiders running around eating people: a spider of such a size could not support its own weight.

Original sins

For another example, my two novels, *The Sins of the Fathers* and *Lifeboat Earth*, form a single large story in which humans must escape an explosion of our galaxy's core by accepting the aid of mysterious aliens who offer to move Earth bodily to another galaxy. The *story* is about *people* and what happens to their lives—but the changes in their lives are all consequences of the core explosion and planet-moving. In writing *Lifeboat Earth*, I had to make such calculations as the apparent position and brightness of the sun at various stages of the Earth's journey and how much the ground appeared to tilt as a result of acceleration. It got so involved that I bought a programmable calculator and developed some fairly exotic programs that will probably never be used again.

"But I can't do that," you say. "You're talking about *calculation*, and I'm a writer, not a mathematician." Sorry; you *must* do that, to the extent that you can, and get help when you need it. You don't have to be a professional scientist or engineer; few stories need as much background calculation as *Lifeboat Earth*. But if you want to write real science fiction, and not fantasy or westerns with spaceships, you must check the consequences of your assumptions and see whether they work and what side effects they have.

How can you develop solid scientific backgrounds if you're not a scientist? Learn all you can about everything. Take courses—but don't depend on them. Learn to teach yourself. Read widely. Basic physics, chemistry, astronomy and biology are essential. Virtually anything else will sooner or later prove useful: geology, psychology, anthropology, history, linguistics—the more the merrier. Use *recent* books, and don't stop there. These fields change rapidly (astronomy has changed more in the last 20 years than in the preceding 400). Watch the tip of the iceberg, at least, in magazines like *Scientific American*. All this reading serves not only as a safeguard against unworkable story ideas, but also as a source of good ones. Knowing where the present limits of knowledge are will suggest what lies beyond.

No matter how thorough your basic education, you'll run into questions for which it has no ready answers. Things like, "How long does a radio message take to get from Earth to Titan?" or "How high can a Piper Cherokee fly on a planet with 90% the gravity and 80% the atmospheric pressure of Earth?" Sometimes you can evade such questions by setting up your story in such a way that the exact numbers aren't critical. But if you do give (or imply) numbers, make sure they're consistent, because readers *love* to catch authors in mistakes. Learning about all kinds of things is part of the fun of writing science fiction; but since you also want to make money at it, you can't afford to spend too much time answering simple questions. So it pays to develop good library skills, covering not only encyclopedias and card files but also the semipopular scientific journals and the scientific abstract indices. The more you can do for yourself, the better; but don't hesitate to ask the reference librarian for needed help. The same applies to calculations: It's nice to do them yourself, but some will probably be beyond you. For those cases, cultivate experts you can ask for help. Universities have them on all kinds of subjects, and many of them are surprisingly willing to help writers who approach them politely and professionally (which means *first* having done all you can on your own).

Fundamentals

Does all this mean that you must prove rigorously that everything you write about is possible, and that you must avoid things not covered by present-day science? Not at all. Science has changed radically just in this century; it would be arrogant and unrealistic to assume we're not due for more big surprises. A fundamental breakthrough, by definition, cannot be deduced from existing theories. I use a "negative impossibility" criterion: anything that nobody can currently prove impossible is fair game for science fiction. For example, faster-than-light travel (FTL) is OK *if* you postulate it in a form that doesn't contradict existing theory in any region of experience that has been thoroughly tested experimentally—even though it would surely require radical changes in theory outside the tested range. Several of my own stories, including *Lifeboat Earth*, have used a form of FTL in which objects can "tunnel" to superlight speeds without an increase in energy, while objects traveling below the speed of light act just as Einstein said they do. (The resulting consternation among theoretical physicists becomes part of the story background.) Other writers have used scientific rationales ranging from "hyperspace" (a shortcut through a dimension not normally perceived by humans, as in John W. Campbell's *The Mightiest Machine* and Robert A. Heinlein's *Starman Jones*) to a new kind of force that increases with the mass it is accelerating (as in Norman Spinrad's "Outward Bound").

Most speculative ideas are either "extrapolations" (based solidly on known science) or "innovations" (radically new concepts, subject only to the negative impossibility test). With either type of idea, work out as much detail as you can—and include no more in the story than the reader needs in order to understand what's going on. After doing all that work, it's tempting to show it off—but resist the temptation. You don't want to scare off readers who aren't specialists—and even they will sense that you did the work, in a feeling of solidity that the story would otherwise lack. If explanation is *necessary*, slip it in subtly. Readers won't accept large blocks of lecture, even if they're disguised by having characters ask questions they wouldn't really need to ask. A good rule of thumb: *Know as much as you can about your background—and tell no more than you have to.*

From idea to story

In its early days, much science fiction was written by scientists or engineers, such as Isaac Asimov, E.E. "Doc" Smith, and George O. Smith, who picked up storytelling as a sideline (and perhaps as an outlet for speculations too far out for the "respectable" journals of their professions). Many early writers, primarily concerned with exploring challenging ideas, did not shape words into stories with the finesse of today's best writers. The "New Wave" of the '60s, associated with such writers as Harlan Ellison, Thomas M. Disch, and Samuel R. Delany, stressed experimentation with literary forms and techniques, sometimes giving these aspects greater emphasis than they did to idea content. There is less avant-gardism now; many editors are leaning toward clear, straightforward, vivid storytelling—and if it happens also to be especially evocative or subtle, so much the better. The lasting heritage of the "New Wave" is a set of standards for *writing* which are higher than ever before.

Yet, trying to make a story stand out with *writing* alone, without fresh and interesting ideas, requires *awfully* impressive writing. Trying to make it on *ideas* alone requires awfully impressive ideas. Most stories must be good on *both* counts. "Petals of Rose," for example, is a story based on an idea so striking that it would have stood out even with mediocre writing. The Rosans, the aliens with whom humans must cooperate, live so fast and intensely that contact with them is dazzling and exhausting. The number of characters in the story is enormous and each exists for a very short time, yet the reader must come to know and care about each one during his brief appearance. That requires vivid, concentrated characterization (for example, the life of Sor Lai Don Shee lasts less than three pages, and Dor Laff To Lin lives and dies on a single page). Long-term cooperation between humans and Rosans is possible only because part of the memory of each Rosan generation is transmitted chemically to the next—but only a small part. One human, Cal, is driven over the edge by the inevitable death of one special Rosan student. He tells a psychologist:

> "I can't stand it. Every day I teach the same thing, again and again, and the faces are *different*." The last ended in a howl of horror. "Every day different, never the same person twice." He whimpered. "Please, let me have just one student twice."

Since a story can almost always be analyzed as one or more people (or reasonable facsimiles) struggling to solve a problem, start plotting by trying to imagine the problems that would arise should your speculation become reality. Don't try to plunge right into the story; play with the implications of the idea. Use "Petals of Rose" as an example. The Rosans live and die in a single day. How does that affect their concept of life? What do they think about humans, who the Rosans consider immortal? What frustrations and other problems do the humans suffer because of the short lives of their allies? Because of the short individual life spans, generations flash by, and the entire structure of the society can change within a week—how will this "instability" affect the humans?

Think of all the problems that will result from your idea that you can; don't stop with the first one that comes to mind. Thinking of problems will inevitably suggest people who have them—and they will become your characters. When you know them well enough, you will begin to understand how they will react to their problems, and how those reactions create other problems, including conflicts with other characters. At each key point in the story, ask yourself what is the best thing *each* character can do—*from his own point of view*. Then let him do it. All you have to do is write it down.

Perhaps the most important fact a science fiction writer must grasp is that all the changes that make a future or a new world are interdependent. In *Lifeboat Earth*, for example, I started with an almost contemporary Earth, let the aliens make certain changes in it, and then figured out everything I could about what effects those changes had on life. Both individuals and political-economic systems had to react to the physical changes, and some of their actions in turn produced still more changes. And so on.

Building worlds—and moving them

Oddly enough, the first step in the creation of *Lifeboat* focused on an idea that is barely visible in the finished story. I wrote a minor short story based on the realization that a FTL ship could be used to get a second look at an astronomical event seen years ago on Earth. Ben Bova, then editor at *Analog*, quite rightly bounced the story, but added: "The basic idea is good. What can you build on it?"

That kind of question is one of the few things editors are good for. It got me thinking, and when I realized that that idea could combine with a couple of others I had in my "What-do-I-do-with-it?" file, the story ignited and took off. The other two ideas were:

● A galactic core explosion, like those seen in other galaxies, could have occurred in ours any time in the last 30,000 years—and we wouldn't know it until the light reached us.

● Suppose the Earth were about to become uninhabitable and aliens offered to rescue us, but refused to discuss the reasons for their offer. Should we accept their help?

That last question is the basis of *The Sins of the Fathers*. Before you can start telling such a story, you must recognize and answer key questions. The questions, at this point, are more important than the answers, because knowing the problems that must be solved will lead to your story. In the case of *Sins*, the questions were: *Is such an explosion possible and how would it affect Earth?* That took library research. *How could the aliens move planets, how did they get the ability, and why didn't they want to talk about it?* That required me to invent their civilization in quite a bit of depth, including tracing their history back far enough to provide consistent origins for all their characteristics. I had to invent their methods of travel in enough detail to provide a consistent chronology for the trip and, once the trip was underway, to understand how it would affect the planet being moved.

The central question of *Lifeboat Earth* became: *What happens to human life during the trip?* First I had to know the purely physical effects; that required the calculations I described earlier, which, given the assumed properties of the aliens' innovative technology, was mostly extrapolation. Finally, I had to get to know some of the people affected and watch how they coped with such problems as surviving the loss of the sun, changing apparent gravity, radical changes in political systems to cope with the practical problems of survival, and the psychological problems of underground life and the wholesale extinction of other species.

Then—and only then—I could write the story.

Writer Poul Anderson once remarked that the best science fiction requires a "unitary" approach, in which "philosophy, love, technology, poetry, and the minutiae of daily living would all play parts concomitant with their roles in real life, but heightened by the imagination of the writer."

To which fellow science fiction writer James Blish added, "You will note, I think, that this is more than just a prescription for good science fiction. It is a prescription for good fiction of any kind."

Sourcebooks

The first group of books listed here deal primarily with *writing* science fiction, though they also touch on the skills of *scientific imagining* to varying extents. This is not an exhaustive list, but merely a selection that I know to have value. The magazine *Empire* (by and for science fiction writers; 1596 Chapel St. # 4C, New Haven, Connecticut 06511) is also helpful.

● Barry B. Longyear, *Science Fiction Writer's Workshop I*, Owlswick Press, 1980.

● The [former] editors of Isaac Asimov's SF Magazine (George H. Scithers, *et al*), *On Writing Science Fiction*, Owlswick Press, 1981.

● L. Sprague & Catherine C. de Camp, *Science Fiction Handbook, Revised*, Owlswick Press, 1975.

● Reginald Bretnor (ed.), *The Craft of Science Fiction*, Harper & Row, 1976.

● Science Fiction Writers of America, *Writing and Selling Science Fiction*, Writer's Digest Books, Second Edition, 1982.

The following books and articles deal specifically with aspects of science especially important to SF writers, in some cases with specific suggestions on how to apply the science to developing SF backgrounds. The books have the added virtue of being rich sources of story ideas (though some of the science is already a bit dated).

● Poul Anderson, ''The Creation of Imaginary Worlds,'' in *Science Fiction, Today and Tomorrow* (Reginald Bretnor, ed.), Harper & Row, 1974.

● Hal Clement, ''The Creation of Imaginary Beings,'' also in *Science Fiction, Today and Tomorrow*.

● I.S. Shklovskii & Carl Sagan, *Intelligent Life in the Universe*, Holden-Day, 1966.

● Poul Anderson, *Is There Life on Other Worlds?*, Crowell-Collier, 1963.

● Stephen H. Dole, *Habitable Planets for Man (Second Edition)*, American Elsevier, 1970.

Two of my *Analog* editorials may be of interest in connection with the concepts of extrapolation and innovation: ''Extrapolation'' (Feb. 1979) and ''Nonlogical Processes in Science and Elsewhere'' (Feb. 1981). The background development for *Lifeboat Earth* is described in considerably more detail in an article, ''How to Move the Earth,'' *Analog*, May 1976.

66   *Science fiction is virtually the only kind of writing that's dealing with real problems and possibilities.*
—*Arthur C. Clarke* 99

Formulas for writing the romantic novel

by Anne Gisonny

"Make them laugh, make them cry, make them work."
—Charles Dickens

The quote cited above was Dickens' secret formula for success—a formula to which he attributed his tremendous popularity with an audience that cut across all segments of Victorian society. I like to interpret his words in this way: The power of a story is in the telling of it, in the ability of the author to engage a reader's emotions and to convincingly portray a full spectrum of the human experience.

Doesn't sound very easy, does it?

When speaking of romance fiction, particularly category, or "formula" romance, the novelist faces an even greater challenge. A writer of formula romance must first contend with the limitations of plot, length and charactertizations intrinsic to the genre. Unfortunately, the limitations sometimes win out and the resulting text is simply an exercise in convention—a book peopled with bloodless characters, mouthing dialogue that we have not only heard before, but have already committed to heart. The author has failed to interpret the formula and make a conventional plot one's own by telling it in one's own personal voice.

However, to see a novelist wrestle down the strictures of formula and *win* is a delightful and often startling sight—something like watching an acrobat attired in a straight jacket perform a very fluid, graceful handspring. A reader wants to stand up and cheer.

Anne Gisonny began her publishing career as an editor with MacFadden Romances and later became director of the line. In 1981 she was an editor for Simon & Schuster's Silhouette Books. Shortly thereafter she joined Dell Publishing where she is presently editor and director of the Candleight Romance line. A former newspaper reporter and photographer, Gisonny has also published poetry in numerous literary journals.

Sights, sounds, sensations

"There's nothing wrong with formula," the very popular Ecstasy author Anne Reisser points out, "as long as you allow the characters to behave in a way that is consistent with their individual personalities." When the internal or psychological design of a characterization is forced to conform with some external convention or set pattern of behavior, the illusion of reality an author has worked so hard to achieve begins to unravel and a story may lose credibility. Anne speaks of her method of using "decision points" in a novel, points where a character must make some choice. Take five different heroines, each placed at the same decision point in the same plot and, according to their separate and distinct personalities, they will all make different choices. And, each of these characters would move the storyline in a different direction.

In essence, formula or plot convention should mean the barest of outlines, a thin tracing that the author must fill in with one's own broad brush strokes of vibrant color. With the present boom in the popularity of romance fiction, publishing houses are flooded with submissions. The field has traditionally been accessible to new writers, and probably will continue to remain so. However, a writer must be sure that a manuscript stands out and offers something more than a simple paraphrase of thousands of other novels. How many times have we read about "a man too rugged to ever be called handsome"? Or, "luminous violet-blue eyes, a vise-like grip, the perfection of her heart-shaped face," and so on and so on and so on . . . . Such pat phrases may keep a work afloat for a time, but if the author offers nothing more, the reader's interest will certainly be overwhelmed by the burden of such tedium. Yes, the romance audience wants—is *addicted* to—all the sights and sounds and sensations that are the hardware of any good love affair. But they want to experience it as if they were reading it all for the first time. Here freshness, originality and an energy that will push your imagination to reach for something are called into play.

Of course, the next question is how far can an author depart from the formula and yet produce a salable manuscript. One can only say that editorial standards differ from publisher to publisher. Very often the question of publishing a book which departs greatly from the "standard" depends upon the author's ability to create convincing, appealing characters who act in a believable way, even when placed in unbelievable circumstances. Another consideration is the quality of the story. A strong, moving love story that literally sweeps the reader away will usually win out every time—no matter what the editorial guidelines dictate. After all, editors want what the readers want.

Carefully plotted

Who was it that said there are only seven basic plots in all of literature? Or is it five? Well, be that as it may, at the heart of every romantic novel there's only one: the story of two people who fall in love. Distilled to the bare essentials we find 1) the initial meeting and attraction, 2) some obstacle to the complete realization of their love and finally, 3) a resolution to the problem and a pledge of total commitment. As a rule, complications or subplots should be kept to a minimum and the same general rule applies to populating your book with extra characters. Steer clear of plots that allow a mystery or adventure subplot to overpower the love story. Presenting scenes of the heroine's life prior to her meeting with the hero is nonessential as well.

Novels of a larger scope may focus on a single character, and depict the various stages of her maturing process or "search for identity." But it's important to keep in mind that even though the heroine's maturing process may be *implied* in the narrative of a romantic novel, the novel is not the story of her personal growth. Any background information about her past should be presented indirectly, through memory and flashback, or through dialogue. Yes, she's a ''young woman on her own who must make decisions for herself,'' but it's a good idea not to kill off her entire family in one paragraph—a string of tragic car accidents and cardiac arrests that would rival the finale of any opera! By all means be inventive. Maybe her parents are marine biologists, and because they've always had to travel she has had her lessons in independence.

Whether the novel is set in St. Tropez or a ranch in west Texas, the author's unflinching focus must be on the unfolding relationship of the hero and heroine. One could almost say that the story line is merely a subplot of this type of novel, since its primary function is to support and illuminate the central action—the romance. The developing love affair is the very framework of your novel and any story line must be carefully and completely interwoven with the various stages of this relationship.

But how shall these two people meet and come to know each other? What event or situation will intertwine their lives and make a chemical reaction between them unavoidable? In answering that question, you should hit upon the single, directing idea of your novel. This guiding idea will supply both a backdrop for romance, and a special kind of energy that will move events along. A successful plot must be comprised of a carefully planned series of events—events which flow logically and organically from each other and always contribute in some way to the romance.

Initial tension

The lack of a directing idea can be identified as a common failing in many manuscripts. The book as a whole seems a collection of chance meetings, a sequence of illogical or petty misunderstandings, arguments and embraces. As one editor remarked, ''If they bumped fenders on page one and in every scene after that she's falling over her own feet (only to be resolved by Mr. Right), the book is *still* missing a plot.'' Though characterization and certain dramatic scenes may be well written, when the hero and heroine finally decide to marry we're not at all sure how this all came about. The haphazard series of events has been unconvincing and unless the novel possesses some other saving grace, we probably don't care much about the outcome.

Lack of focus can plague a novel in many ways. The first and worst offense, which I've just pointed out above, is the lack of any controlling idea. The remedy is obvious— *total* revision. But many times a novel seems to follow along convincingly enough until the author presents the relationship's major obstacle, or the reason why these two lovestruck individuals must wait until Chapter 12 to declare themselves.

Let's look at one classic scene as an example. The heroine overhears the hero's conversation with another woman, probably some tall, dark temptress who wears a lot of nail polish. (We've seen *her* before.) Naturally, our heroine ''misunderstands'' the whole situation and, after reflecting on the fact that she's been used and abused by the hero, she makes a decision to have nothing more to do with him. Nine times out of ten she will make this crucial decision while ''soaking in a steaming hot bath.''

Typical, but a weak hinge on which to fix the turning point of an entire novel. Especially if the author has done a good job of creating a warm and realistic understanding between the hero and heroine. Too often this type of plot obstacle, i.e. overheard conversations, or a villainess lying about her relationship to the hero, seems contrived and unconvincing. Most editors seem to feel that the major conflict between the hero and heroine should not be dependent on a third party, or on some bizarre misunderstanding. This all important tension between the main characters should be generated from the very start of the book. If you're staking everything on the heroine's misapprehension of the hero, the reason behind her blindness to his true worth has to be convincing. For example, she has certain proof that he's trying to swindle her father, but finds that she has fallen in love with him in spite of family loyalty.

Constant interaction

One possible way to generate this kind of tension is to formulate a plot that gives one character the upper hand from the start and consequently allows him or her to manipulate events.

Whatever the source of tension between them, the seeds of this obstacle should be sown early. Plan your story line in a single paragraph that capsulizes the book's directing idea, an idea that in some way contains this dramatic tension. Then, in a chapter-by-chapter outline, work out each major event: the first meeting, romantic evening out, love scenes or some danger/rescue scene, and the event that brings the plot full circle. Above all the causal links between these events should be thought out to your satisfaction. The scheme of your novel should finally be a tightly integrated series of scenes set in motion by some directing idea. Something like a line of dominoes, falling one into the next.

Is it necessary to present every single bit of information that links one event to the next? No, not at all. We're not asking for tedium, just logic. Incomplete knowledge is a fact of life, and in a novel motivation or certain bits of information may be intentionally withheld from the reader. In a romantic novel this effect is sometimes unavoidable, especially with respect to the hero, since so much of his motivation remains unknown to us. However, whether explicit or implicit, the logical links of cause and effect must be there.

When formulating a plot idea, one major consideration should be the proximity of the hero and heroine. Will the story line force them to live under one roof, or to meet daily in a side by side work setting? Great! You're half-way there. The best plots seem to throw the hero and heroine into a situation where almost *constant* interaction is unavoidable. A second important consideration is time span. Sure, this is love at first sight—whether they realize it or not. But if you're out to depict a convincing and realistic relationship, give your characters a little time to get to know each other. In the lucid and succinct words of the Dell Candlelight guideline, "Two days is *not* long enough."

The "real" romance heroine

I've sometimes wondered what the outcome would be if a vote were taken to establish romance literature's top ten best loved heroines. Frankly, I would have to split my vote two ways (between Hardy's Bathsheba Everdine and Hester Prynne of *The Scarlet Letter*). No, maybe three ways—how could I be heartless enough to forget Jane Eyre? Or Elizabeth Bennet? And I haven't even gotten to anything written in the twentieth century. In fact, I don't think I would be able to vote at all. I would have to abstain. How could I choose between such dear old friends?

The point here is, of course, when creating a character the author hopes that the presentation will be as lively, vivid and appealing as, well . . . a real person. Creating a strong, fully developed heroine is perhaps doubly important for the author of a romance novel. The heroine's personality and outlook are literally the foundation of the love story. Since most romance novels (and nearly all category length) are told through the heroine's point of view, she is not only at the center of the action, but is a filter for the reader, in terms of her impressions of other characters and events. She must possess a kind of flesh and blood presence. As readers, we seem to admire traits in fictitious personalities which we admire in real personalities: humor, intelligence, insight and compassion into the feelings of others. We admire a woman who can keep herself together in a tight situation, or can hold her own in a relationship.

One fault of the novice romance novelist is the temptation to make the heroine an image of perfection, so perfect in fact that it is impossible for the average reader to identify with her. For example, the story opens—as far too many do—with our heroine getting ready for a work day. In all of three pages we learn that she is a cross between Farrah Fawcett and Catherine Deneuve in looks, has an IQ which would rival Einstein's, eats only the most nutritious of foods, rises at 5 o'clock each morning for a 3 mile run. Oh yes, I nearly forgot, she also plays the piano and would have undoubtedly been a concert pianist of world renown by now (she's all of 24) if she hadn't been forced to quit music school and support her younger sister after the "tragic death" of their parents. This is *not* a woman I could identify with. In fact, she sounds suspiciously like that certain someone we all knew and despised in high school, you know, the girl who got straight A's, never had a blemish or frizzled out hair and had a locker that was neater than an operating room.

Acquaint with action

When you are setting a scene that will introduce your audience to your heroine, draw upon your own experiences and feelings. Most people's mornings begin with gulping down coffee, putting a run in their last pair of panty hose and burning the toast, which of course, invariably sets off the smoke alarm and causes them to miss their train. Granted, most women are reading these books to escape from such mundane details of everyday life. But what if, among the coffee mugs and jam pot, our hero (a devastatingly handsome neighbor) comes charging through a smoke-filled kitchen ready to save her from a charred English muffin or worse? She, of course, is discovered in a semi-ravishing, absolutely charming state of dishabille.

Ah, now we're talking. That is where fantasy enters the realm of believability. Here's a woman anyone can sympathize with and look what just happened, the most gorgeous man burst into her apartment by mistake while she was dressing for work. Sure beats listening to the traffic report on all news radio.

Of course, there is more to humanizing a character than showing her at the mercy of everyday life. Before you can even begin to tell the story of how this woman meets the love of her life, you should feel as if you know her completely, as well as you know yourself. She should be conceptualized as a distinct personality, one with bad habits as well as good, favorite foods, and special fantasies. Her secret ambition has always been to travel in a hot air balloon. You know that she has a terrible singing voice and is a disaster in the kitchen. You also know that she enjoys puttering around the house with minor repairs and is a whiz at plumbing. Since your story is told through her perspective, through her thoughts and sensations, the narrative is filtered through her personality, and for better or worse, her outlook and sensitivities will establish the tone of your book.

The best way to acquaint your heroine and your reader is of course through scenes of action and dialogue, not through lengthy pages of internal monologues. The presentation of the heroine's character should be simultaneous with the developing story line which should be set in motion from page one. Your reader should not have to wade through a chapter or two reading about your heroine's past before the love story begins. After all, your aim is not to show her personal growth, though that may in fact be part of your story. Your object is to show how this woman falls in love.

Attractive, appealing and human

Memory is another important dimension of your heroine's personality. She is the person she is because of influences in her past life. The *selective* use of memory can be highly effective in fleshing out a character and can serve to clarify motivation, to make her actions and reactions more convincing, more real. The danger of course, is in bogging your narrative down with her reminiscences and neglecting your storyline. Since your storyline is your first concern you will want to be sure that any lengthy flashbacks serve an integral function in your plot, either to further the action or explain a situation or motivation.

Naturally, as your story progresses, your heroine will be pressed to expose a great deal of her inner self and should be shown demonstrating a wide range of emotions and responses. Don't rob your heroine of her full potential or dimension. Remember, she thinks and feels and acts on a variety of levels, just as you do. She may say one thing, and be feeling and thinking another. When you make your reader aware of this disparity, it is as if your heroine has taken the reader into her confidence.

Above all, your heroine should be an attractive, warm, appealing person. The reader should be able to understand why the hero has fallen madly in love with her. Though this may sound like a terribly obvious point, it's amazing to see how many characters are presented as unattractive, either because they are so depressed, weak and timid, or simply so bland—boring actually. As the professional woman begins to emerge on the romance scene (Bravo!) characterizations are in danger of another serious flaw. The new breed of female vice-presidents, lawyers and brain surgeons are often portrayed as overly serious, solemn and pompous individuals. This kind of dehumanized, or one dimensional, characterization, is just as unappealing as the classic female of romance fiction—mindless, naive and always in need of a rescuer. She has to sparkle and her personality should be strong and fully developed.

> 66 *I have a notion that people's personalities are their own particular works of art; the way they have relationships, their tastes, their thoughts, their dreams, the way they are themselves is an artistic process. Obviously I'm interested in romantic love—how people conduct the journeys of their lives which seems to me a very artistic process. . . . People interested in the goodness of their lives are usually more unpredictable than those who are interested in the destruction of their lives. Happiness is an interesting topic.*
> —*Laurie Colwin* 99

Beyond the rebuff

by John White

Rejection is as old as literature itself:

    More than a dozen publishers rejected a book by the poet e e cummings. So when it was finally published it had this dedication: "No Thanks to: Farrar & Rinehart, Simon & Schuster, Coward-McCann, Limited Editions, Harcourt Brace, Random House, Equinox Press, Smith & Haas, Viking Press, Knopf, Dutton, Harper's, Scribners, Covici, Friede." (cummings must have been upset to put all of those capitals in.) Finally published . . . by whom? By e e's mother.

    Roger Tory Peterson's *Field Guide to the Birds*, now a birder's bible, was rejected by five publishers before Houghton Mifflin took it.

    What ultimately became one of the favorite children's books of all time, *The Tale of Peter Rabbit*, was prenatally "courteously rejected" by the English publisher Frederick Warne and then "returned with or without thanks by at least six [other] firms," author-illustrator Beatrix Potter noted. (According to an almost certainly apocryphal story one rejecter commented that the tale "smelled like rotting carrots.") Finally she took her savings and paid for publication herself. The little book sold so well that Warne changed his mind, took over publication, and voila! That was more than 80 years ago, and Peter Rabbit and his friends are still selling briskly.

    Peyton Place, that ersatz *Desire Under the Elms*, a mish-mash of small-town sex steamy enough to tempt, you would think, all profit-minded publishers (and what other kind, you might ask, is there?), was turned down by 14 of them. A work as different from *Peyton Place* as can be imagined, William Appleman Williams' *The Tragedy of American Diplomacy*, was rejected by more than 20 publishers before it was finally accepted.

John White is a former newspaper reporter for the Boston Herald Traveler and the Washington Times Herald during which time he collected stories for Rejection to prove that rejection can be the best thing that ever happens to a person.

It has now been reprinted several times and is recognized as an outstanding revisionist work. *Jonathan Livingston Seagull* also flew through some 20 rejections.

Irving Stone's first book was about Van Gogh. He took it to Alfred Knopf, and "they never opened it—the package with the manuscript got home before I did." He took it to Doubleday. Everybody liked it except the sales department—they said, "There is no way to sell a book about an unknown Dutch painter." After 15 more rejections the book, *Lust for Life*, was finally accepted and published in 1934. It has now sold about twenty-five million copies.

As might be expected, James Joyce's writings excited some splendidly grandiose rejections. His *Dubliners* was refused by 22 publishers and then shot down in flames by an irate citizen. As Joyce reported it, "When at last it was printed some very kind person bought out the entire edition and had it burnt in Dublin—a new and private *auto-da-fé*." The odyssey of his *Ulysses* was even more spectacular—it was rejected, in fire, by two governments. Parts of the novel were serialized in the New York *Little Review* in 1918-20, and after rejection by a US publisher the whole book was published in France in 1922 by Sylvia Beach's Shakespeare Press. Copies were sent to America and England. They were, reported Joyce, "Seized and burnt by the Custom authorities of New York and Folkestone." Not until 1933 was the US ban on *Ulysses* lifted; the book was published by Random House the following year.

Dr. Seuss, the creator of a whole menagerie of lovable floppy monsters, many of which have strayed into radio and TV, survived initial rejection by some two dozen publishers, and according to legend *Gone With The Wind* survived 38. (Very much "according to legend"—according to Burke Wilkinson [an author of 11 successful books who had his latest, *Zeal of the Convert*, now optioned by Hollywood, rejected 14 times], "Harold Latham, the conscientious editor at Macmillan, learned about *GWTW* early, commuted to Atlanta to keep Margaret Mitchell tracking, and truly no other firm ever saw the manuscript.")

James M. Cain's novel *The Postman Always Rings Twice* stirred up something of a sensation when it was first published in 1934. It wasn't about the postal service, it was about sex. Cain explained that he had given his book its odd title because before it was accepted for publication it was rejected many times, and each day that the postman brought a letter of rejection he rang twice.

Sorry . . .

Sometimes it seems—to writers—that the number of possible rejections of a would-be book is limited only by the number of publishers. Says the 1978 *Guinness Book of World Records*, "The greatest number of publishers' rejections for a manuscript is 106 for *World Government Crusade* by Gilbert Young . . . . His public meeting in Bath, England, in support of his parliamentary candidacy as a World Government candidate, however, drew a crowd of one."

Lee Pennington has been published in more than 300 magazines—and rejected so many thousand times that in one six-month period he papered all four walls of a room with rejection slips. ("I loved getting the 8½x11 rejections more than the 3x5 ones because they covered more space.") He has also filled scrapbooks with rejection slips, used them for coasters, and given rejection parties—invitations written on the backs of rejection slips.

Other suggested uses for those slips: Make lampshades of them, laminate coffee tables with them, make (as does Muriel Rukeyser) wastebaskets of them. Put them on the refrigerator so you won't eat so much.

Pennington once wrote a poem about William Faulkner, sent it off, and got back a two-page single-spaced rejection, the first two sentences of which read, "This is the worst poem in the English language. You are the worst poet in the English language." He burned that rejection letter (an act he has since repented—it would have graced his scrapbook) and sent the poem to another magazine, which accepted it "with glowing praise," and chose it as its year's best poem.

Before William Saroyan (who became one of this country's most published authors) got his first acceptance he had a pile of rejection slips 30 inches high—maybe 7,000 in all.

Publishers say, somewhat defensively, that their rejections are different from those of other rejecters, not necessarily based on value judgments. They may like a manuscript, they say, but be unable to publish it because of prior commitments or scheduling jams or lack of money or other such operational obstacles. Still and all, they have let some amazingly big fish slip through their nets, ultimate blockbusters of all varieties: *War and Peace*, *The Good Earth*, *The Sun Is My Undoing*, *The Fountainhead*, *To Kill a Mockingbird*, *Rubàiyàt*, *Watership Down* . . . . The list goes on and on.

There is a story in the trade that a publisher once accepted a book and sent it to an artist for illustrations. When he had finished the artist sent the manuscript back—and it was returned to him with a rejection slip.

So many books rejected by so many publishers so many times—how do those murdering bastards *feel* when they strangle yet another unborn child? William Styron's 1979 novel, *Sophie's Choice*, tells it like it was in 1947 when the hero was a forty-dollar-a-week reader for McGraw-Hill. The "lusterless drudgery" of trudging through the "club-footed syntax" and "unrelenting mediocrity" of manuscripts like *Tall Grows the Eelgrass*, by Edmonia Biersticker ("fiction . . . may be the worst novel ever penned by woman or beast. Decline with all possible speed."), and *The Plumber's Wrench*, by Audrey Smillie (". . . absolutely imperative that this book never be published"), so stupefied the poor wretch that when a manuscript about a "long, solemn, and tedious Pacific voyage" made by "men adrift on a raft" fell into his hands he recommended rejection—"maybe a university press would buy it, but it's definitely not for us"—and the book was *Kon-Tiki*.

Small, cosmetic changes can open doors. Longmans, Green rejected a manuscript titled *The Problems of the Single Woman* only to see it become a bestseller after publication by another house as *Live Alone and Like It*. The same thing happened to a reject called *The Birds and the Bees*. It went on to prosper as *Everything You Always Wanted to Know About Sex but Were Afraid To Ask*.

Unhappy endings

There is a half-baked belief among non-kitchen-minded folk that the culinary bible *Mastering the Art of French Cooking* was a much-wanted child, called into existence to satisfy a demand created by the popular TV series, *The French Chef*. Not so. *Mastering* started life as a twice-rejected orphan.

In 1953 Houghton Mifflin signed a contract with Julia Child, Simone Beck, and Louisette Bertholle for a book with the working title *French Cooking for the American Kitchen*. Five years later the three cook-writers submitted their manuscript, an 850-page compendium called *French Sauces and French Poultry*. Houghton Mifflin rejected it. The next year they brought back a drastically revised 684-page version titled *French Recipes for American Cooks*. Houghton Mifflin rejected that too.

Knopf accepted it and published it in 1961 with the *Mastering* title. Though large and expensive, it sold fairly well right from the start. Impressed by the book's success, public television dreamed up the series *The French Chef*, starring Julia Child, which made its debut on February 11, 1963. That series was a smash hit (pardon the expression) from the cavalier flipping of that first famous potato pancake onto the stove; *Mastering* mastered the air. That same year it was a Book of the Month Club selection, and on November 25, 1966, Julia Child made the cover of *Time* magazine.

If the book (augmented by a second volume in 1970) were a record it would have gone platinum by now—it has sold more than a million copies.

Verily, verily the stone which certain builders rejected is become a head of the corner.

Another head of that corner, Irma Rombauer's inimitable *Joy of Cooking*, is also, apparently, a salvaged reject. According to a memoir written by her daughter, the late Marion Rombauer Beck, a small *Joy* was first privately printed in 1931. "Mother's friends made sales lively, but not brisk enough to suit her," so she added some recipes and tried the marketplace. Only after "making the rounds," meaning, presumably, being rejected by various publishers, was the fattened *Joy* accepted, by Bobbs-Merrill, in 1936. When Irma Rombauer died in 1962 her book had sold six million copies.

In the case of *Mastering the Art of French Cooking*, Knopf seems to have outguessed Houghton Mifflin, but Knopf has not always been so prescient. In 1955 Laurence Wylie, Harvard's esteemed professor of French civilization, sent the manuscript of a sensitive chronicle of French country life, *A Village in the Vaucluse*, to Knopf. Back it came with a letter of rejection which said, "It is so far from being a book for the general reader that nothing can be done about it." Wylie did nothing "about" it—he sent it on to the Harvard University Press, which published it the next year. It became and has remained an extremely popular book for the general reader and the scholar alike. And Houghton Mifflin, as we shall see, was very prescient in publishing two books that brought their authors more fame than they could digest.

Ross Lockridge's first novel, *Raintree County*, was never rejected. Houghton Mifflin published it in January 1948 and on February 27 Lockridge got word that it had become the country's number one bestseller; on March 6 he asphyxiated himself. Tom Heggen's first novel, *Mister Roberts*, was not rejected. It was published, also by Houghton Mifflin, in 1946, and became a bestseller at once; in 1948 it was turned into the smash hit play. In May 1949 Heggen took an overdose of pills and drowned himself.

Query: If those two quick-bloomers had been forced to climb the ladder of success in the usual way, gradually, step by step—been slow-fired in the furnace of rejection— would they be alive today?

In his definitive book about them, *Ross and Tom*, John Leggett doesn't answer that question. How could he? How could anybody separate and measure the impacts of success, failure, challenge, and the responses—hope, fear, joy, motion, emptiness?

W. Somerset Maugham had surmounted many rejections when he rang the big bell with *Of Human Bondage* in 1915. He weathered that storm of success gracefully enough and went on to other triumphs.

A southern writer named John Kennedy Toole wrote a comic novel about life in New Orleans called *A Confederacy of Dunces*. It was so relentlessly rejected by publishers that he killed himself. That was in 1969. His mother refused to give up on the book. She sent it out and got it back, rejected, over and over again. At last she won the patronage of Walker Percy, who got it accepted by the Louisiana State University Press, and in 1980 it won the Pulitzer Prize for fiction.

After it had won that prize critics fell all over themselves praising it, as if to soothe

the dull cold ear of death—but when the dust had settled it seemed that the book wasn't really all that good; the Pulitzer judges were not immune to feelings of displaced guilt.

Classic answers

A classic example of authorial rejection-of-rejection, positive response to negative challenge, is Samuel Johnson's celebrated letter to the Earl of Chesterfield. English teachers love to quote that, and it is indeed a masterful display of articulate, muscular rage—even if it might have been uncalled for.

As told by most of those teachers, the story is as simple as it is infuriating. Johnson, overworked and poor in health and in pocket, labored alone for years to put together his monumental *Dictionary of the English Language*, a Herculean task that would have daunted a whole library full of ordinary scholars; many times he appealed to the eminent Lord Chesterfield for patronage that would have been vastly helpful, but his desperate pleas were not answered; then, when the *Dictionary* was completed, about to be published and stirring up favorable comment, the Earl graciously allowed his countenance to shine upon it, and Johnson fired off the famous letter:

> Seven years, my Lord, have now past since I waited in your outward rooms, or was repulsed from your door, during which time I have been pushing on my work through difficulties, of which it is useless to complain, and have brought it, at last, to the verge of publication, without one act of assistance, one word of encouragement, or one smile of favour. Such treatment I did not expect, for I never had a Patron before . . . .
> Is not a Patron, my Lord, one who looks with unconcern on a man struggling for life in the water, and, when he has reached ground, encumbers him with help? The notice which you have been pleased to take of my labours, had it been early, had been kind; but it has been delayed till I am indifferent, and cannot enjoy it; till I am solitary, and cannot impart it; till I am known and do not want it. I hope it is no very cynical asperity not to confess obligations where no benefit has been received, or to be unwilling that the Publick should consider me as owing that to a Patron, which Providence has enabled me to do for myself.

A well-deserved demolition of a would-be bandwagoner? Not necessarily so.

In his authoritative biography, *Samuel Johnson*, W. Jackson Bate says that in 1747, when the *Dictionary* was a'borning, a "Plan" of the huge project, dedicated to Chesterfield, was published. The Earl "expressed his interest . . . and sent a gift of 10 pounds," enough money in those days to rent a room for two years. Johnson called on his benefactor and found him "exquisitely elegant," with "more knowledge than I expected." (Bate says that Chesterfield was noted for his "good sense," "integrity," and knowledge of languages.) During the next seven years the "aging and weary" Earl was caught up in his work as Secretary of State and had many worries, including crippling arthritis, and forgot about the *Dictionary*. When a friend told him that it was finished he publicly praised it, "more from courtesy and a belated stirring of conscience than any thought of the honor of beng associated with the work"—and was hit by Johnson's letter.

"Chesterfield accepted the rebuke with good nature," Bate says, "and was also quite impressed by the letter." He left it on a table where any visitor could see it, "and, reading it aloud to Dodsley, he said, 'This man has great powers,' and 'pointed out the severest passages, and observed how well they were expressed.' "

He also said, according to Bate, that he "would have turned off the best servant he ever had, if he had known that he denied him to a man who would have always been more than welcome.''

The reporter of that revealing episode was Robert Dodsley, a publisher noted for the un-Johnsonian gentleness of his own rejections. Sample:

> Mr. Dodsley presents his compliments to the gentleman who favoured him with the enclosed poem, which he has returned, as he apprehends the sale of it would probably not enable him to give any consideration. He does not mean by this to insinuate a want of merit in the poem, but rather a want of attention in the public.

The kindly spirit that had animated Mr. Dodsley was still alive in the next century. In 1847 Charlotte Brontë (using the name Currer Bell) sent the manuscript of *The Professor* to a publishing house named Smith, Elder. That firm's letter of rejection actually encouraged the author: It discussed the book's merits and demerits so courteously, so considerately, in a spirit so rational, with a discrimination so enlightened, that this very refusal cheered the author better than a vulgarly expressed acceptance would have done.'' (Later that same year Smith, Elder published *Jane Eyre*.)

Steps Leading Nowhere could be the title of a real-life story written in the blood (if you could call it that) of our literary Solomons not so long ago.

In 1969 *Steps*, a novel by the well-known author Jerzy Kosinski, won the National Book Award. Six years later a freelance writer named Chuck Ross, to test the old theory that a novel by an unknown writer doesn't have a chance, typed the first 21 pages of *Steps* and sent them out to four publishers as the work of ''Erik Demos.'' All four rejected the manuscript. Two years after that he typed out the whole book and sent it, again credited to Erik Demos, to more publishers, including the original publisher of the Kosinski book, Random House. Again, all rejected it with unhelpful comments—Random House used a form letter. Altogether, 14 publishers (and 13 literary agents) failed to recognize a book that had already been published and had won an important prize.

"Kippled," not stifled

In 1911 Marcel Proust had 800 pages of what was ultimately to become the huge complex of novels called *Remembrance of Things Past* ready for publication. Where? Who would accept such an actionless, plotless sprawl of innerness revisited? He approached the house of Fasquelle and was rejected. He went to the *Nouvelle Revue Française* and was rejected again, by a very special rejecter—the celebrated writer André Gide. After a third publisher, Ollendorf, had refused his manuscript (with the comment that it took him 30 pages to tell how he turned over in bed), Proust decided to pay for publication himself.

Eugène Grasset published *Du Côté de chez Swann* (*Swann's Way*) in November 1913. Gide read it, and the following January wrote to Proust apologizing for the rejection, which he called the ''gravest error of the N.R.F. . . . one of the most burning regrets, remorses, of my life.'' He explained that he had considered Proust a ''snob'' and a ''social butterfly,'' had only glanced at his manuscript, and has been unimpressed by what he had glimpsed: ''My attention fell into the cup of camomile tea . . . then wandered . . . to the phrase [about] a forehead through which vertebrae could be seen.'' He asked pardon. Proust forgave him and the two became good friends.

Proust went on to become more famous than his rejecter, but he was never awarded the Nobel Prize for Literature, as Gide was in 1947.

Emily (''You cannot fold a flood'') Dickinson had only seven of her poems published in her lifetime (now her collected words actually fill a fat volume) but her rejecter became her friend. In 1858 Thomas Wentworth Higginson of the *Atlantic Monthly* issued an appeal for fresh talent and the Belle of Amherst sent him some of her poems. He thought her a ''half-cracked poetess'' and advised her not to try to get anything published. But he did offer friendship and they corresponded for several years.

Oddly enough Thoreau's *Walden*, an unprecedented work so offbeat that one would suppose that no publisher would have dreamed of giving it house room, was not rejected. Ticknor and Fields published it at their own risk in 1854, and while by no means a success it was not a total failure: By 1859 the first printing of 2000 copies was sold out. Perhaps this author's well known defiant attitude helped launch his unusual book without the usual multi-publisher refusal. As he said in *Walden*, ''I do not propose to write an ode to dejection, but to brag as lustily as a chanticleer in the morning, standing on his roost, if only to wake my neighbors up.''

Lewis Carroll rejected rather than was rejected, pictures rather than words. He paid for initial publication of *Alice's Adventures in Wonderland* (then titled *Alice's Adventures Under Ground*) by Macmillan in 1865 but he and his illustrator, John Tenniel, were dissatisfied with the quality of the reproductions in the first printing and rejected it. (Subsequent printings pleased author, illustrator, publisher and public.) Carroll got another artist, Henry Holiday, to illustrate *The Hunting of the Snark*, published by Macmillan in 1876, but he rejected one of Holiday's pictures, a very important one. It will be remembered that the *Hunting* ends when the Baker meets the Snark, shrieks, and disappears—because the Snark is a Boojum and as everybody knows it is the fate of whoever meets a Boojum to ''softly and suddenly vanish away.'' Holiday drew a picture of the Boojum as a great squat indistinct figure radiating mindless power, oddly reminiscent of phase two of the explosion of an atom bomb, and very frightening indeed, and Carroll rejected it because it was too good. The unimaginable had been imagined, and that shouldn't be.

In 1889 Macmillan published a juvenile version of *Alice* (which psychologists never tire of saying is not really a children's book) with 20 of the Tenniel pictures enlarged and colored, and Carroll rejected the first printing because, he said, the colors were too gaudy. The rejected books were sent to a New York publisher who re-rejected them because, he said, the colors were too dull. (More whimsical Carrolliana may be found in Martin Gardner's books about Alice and the Snark.)

William Saroyan rejected the 1940 Pulitzer Prize for his play *The Time of Your Life* because, he said, business had no business judging art.

Rudyard Kipling was rejected three times for his country's highest literary honor. He was a world famous writer when Tennyson's death left the post of Great Britain's Poet Laureate vacant in 1892. Kipling was passed over and the honor was given to a relatively unknown author, Alfred Austin. When Austin died in 1913 Kipling was even more famous—in 1907 he had won the Nobel Prize for literature; again he was rejected for a less eminent writer, Robert Bridges. In 1930 the title was given to John Masefield.

It has been said that one reason for Kipling's rejections was his poem ''The Widow at Windsor,'' which cast Victoria as a Queen whose dominions cost the lives of her soldiers.

In any case, the reject's name became familiar to more people than those of all the lofty Laureates together. The most popular picture post card ever devised (six million sold) showed a young couple. He: "Do you like Kipling?" She: "I don't know, you naughty boy, I've never kippled."

(A man once rejected a vendor's offer to sell him some "pornographic post cards" because "I haven't got a pornograph.")

Sometimes even the best of our writers nod. Here, mainly from that lovely book, *The Stuffed Owl* (D.B. Wyndham Lewis and Charles Lee), are some outstandingly bad lines from good writers (bad writers don't matter because they get rejected before they hit print.):

"Her smile was silent as the smile on corpses three hours old."—Earl of
Lyton

"He fell upon his hands in warm wet slop."—Alfred Austin

"Thou little bounder, rest."—John Ruskin (speaking to his heart)

"A fly that up and down himself doth shove."—William Wordsworth

Kipling said that authors should do their best to reject their own work, on the grounds that no matter how good a piece of writing might seem to the writer it could always be improved by reworking, and especially improved by shortening. (His own corpus could certainly have benefited by extensive rewriting and massive excisions.)

What, any author might add, could be more conducive to rewriting than the goad of rejection?

> **❝** Sometimes a piece of paper doesn't want to be written on. I throw it away and look for another one that is more congenial.
> —*Russell Baker* **❞**

Revising the first draft

by Paul R. Reynolds

The author has done his research, has prepared an idea outline. He is raring to go. He starts his actual writing. Some authors write at high speed, never stopping for revision. Perhaps 5000 words a day are written and a first draft completed in three or four weeks. Other authors will outline a chapter, then write the chapter, then revise the chapter and continue this process over perhaps a 12-month period. Some authors will prepare a 100-page outline before starting the writing. There is no best method. It is a matter of individual preference, with no two authors working alike. Whatever method is used (there are dozens of possibilities) ultimately a draft must result. Whether this draft has had much or little or no revision, it is going to need more revision and can be considered a first draft. Now comes the great test of whether the novel will ultimately be good. Can the author revise and improve? Can he cut his work, expand his work, rewrite his work, invent new scenes to replace old and have a better resulting novel? How often can he do this? And how often will he improve his draft? In connection with the revising of the first draft the author should ask himself the following questions:

1. Is the opening really good?

Professional writers sometimes claim that the first page of a manuscript is the hardest to write. Part of the reason is the difficulty the author has in getting the feel of his book, getting into his stride. But the first paragraph (the only one that follows nothing) presents its own difficulties. Many professional writers will try half a dozen or more different openings and select the one that seems best. An opening should catch the reader's attention, seem true to life, and yet be an opening that will easily move into the further sequences of the first chapter.

Paul R. Reynolds was a literary agent for 50 years, during which time 32 books by his clients were dedicated to him in appreciation for his efforts. Now retired and living in Connecticut, he is the author of several books including The Nonfiction Book, The Middleman *and* The Writing and Selling of Fiction.

2. Does the novel open at the beginning of the story the author wants to tell?

This question refers to the first chapter rather than to the first paragraph of the first chapter. Many authors start their stories too early. They have thought so much about the background that they have lost their perspective. Some start too late and then have to resort to the flashback. Morris West opens with one of his two themes, Meredith dying of cancer, and how he shall spend the final weeks of his life. Likewise Howard Fast's *April Morning* opens with one of the themes. *Treasure Island* opens with the appearance of a pirate without whom there would have been no story. The first chapter of an author's novel should be essential to the story. In general an author should open his story at the same place that he would begin it if telling the story orally.

3. Does the story end at the right place?

There are several dangers here. An author may hurry his end leaving inadequate explanations. Explanations can be dull, and perhaps many of them should have been introduced earlier. Sometimes an author fails to settle the problem of a major character, or make it clear that the problem is going to continue. Sometimes the author ties up everything so neatly that the end lacks reality. This is especially a danger with the happy-ending romance. In life it is rare for everyone to have a happy ending. Sometimes an author may fail to stop when his story is over. This is like a public speaker going on and on after he has said what he has to say.

West, two pages before the end of his book, has the following:

"Blaise Meredith is dead," said Aldo Meyer.
"He is with God," said Aurelio, the Bishop.

Then follows a long letter which sums up the accomplishments of Blaise Meredith, the souls he has saved. Then to keep the story true to life West shows us the Cardinal writing in his notebook "Remembrance in Mass . . . Meredith" and then we see the Cardinal ringing for his car to be taken to one of the many meetings of the rulers of the Catholic Church.

April Morning ends with Adam going to sleep, his thoughts repeating the major theme of the book.

The page before the last of *Treasure Island* tells of the escape of the arch-villain Silver, the one-legged man. Then a capsule account of what the characters did with the treasure. Then Stevenson ends the book with an echo. Jim Hawkins in his dreams hears Silver's parrot saying "Pieces of Eight, Pieces of Eight." This echo refers to a dramatic scene of movement in the middle of the book.

4. Is the plot satisfactorily organized?

The author should compare the organization of his draft with his idea outline. This does not mean that his outline should have been followed blindly. An author does not follow a pattern the way a person knits a sweater. But when the organization of a novel varies from the outline, is the result still well organized? Is there a chapter or large section which has little relation to the main plot or theme? Perhaps Aunt Mary took a trip and the author has written delightful, amusing description, some of the best writing he has done; but does this trip add to the total effect of the novel? The author is not writing a collection of short stories or essays on charming trips. He is writing a novel, and charm, humor, what you will, do not belong if they are not part of the unity of the novel. Perhaps the outline called for one or more chapters dealing with events which are now omitted or condensed to a page. What were the reasons for suggesting in the outline much space for these events? Are the reasons valid? Perhaps the present versions is just as well organized and no expansion is called for.

5. Are the major plots plausible?

The major plots were suggested in the idea outline and seemed at that time basically plausible. But plausibility is a matter of degree. Do the characters act plausibly? Many an author has a character do something because his plot requires it. If in real life the character, faced with the situation which the author has contrived, would not have done what he does, a drastic change is required. Either a different character must be devised or the plot altered, usually the latter. Authors should be wary of acts of God. They occur in real life, but only rarely and often in fiction they seem to have been used only for the author's convenience.

6. Do the plots contain elements of the unexpected?

The ability to create the plausibly unexpected in major and minor plots is one of the skills of the born storyteller. It is difficult to make constructive suggestions to the novelist-in-training. Part of the author's skill is to have a character do something unexpected but which the reader recognizes as being in accord with the traits of the character. When Howard Fast has his character, the father, require an extra chair and place set on the table each night his family dines, there is something unexpected. The father has the ostensible motive of wanting to seem a genial host always welcoming the uninvited guest. His real motive is to encourage company with whom he can argue. Without the ostensible motive the father's action would not be plausible. Without the real motive, which was in accordance with the father's character, the action would probably not be completely plausible.

7. Are the minor plots plausible?

Most plots can be made plausible but taking the space to do so may be dull. An author may convince the reader that a particular dog might find a rope trailing from a particular plane, grab the rope in his mouth, and be carried into the air, but the reader may be bored reading about this particular dog, plane, and situation. The necessary build-up will probably just be dull. Plots must be plausible and never dull.

8. Are the characters consistent?

Is Dorothy the same person at the end of the book that she was in the beginning? If the color of Dorothy's hair has changed, that can be easily fixed, but such an error suggests something more serious. It suggests that the author never had a clear picture of Dorothy, and hence she may not be consistent. If Dorothy had been the author's mother, the author would never have made the mistake about the color of her hair. He would have had a clear picture of his mother. It is true that a character may change as a book progresses, but the changes are growths or retardations of the same character. Blaise Meredith is a man of greater compassion, less narrowmindedness, and more a servant of God at the end of The Devil's Advocate than he was in the beginning. But he is still the same person. The grandmother at the end of April Morning recognizes Adam as a man but she is still the same crotchety, peppery, forthright old lady. An author's characters must be consistent.

9. Are the major characters characterized simply?

An author gets his characterization from exemplifying a few character traits, rarely more than four or five, often only one or two or three. In real life a person is a complex assortment of characteristics. Most of these characteristics we do not know of. When we meet Mr. X for the first or the fifth time, we are rarely conscious of more than one or two or three character traits. A man appears effeminate or masculine, verbose or reticent, polite, unctuous, rude, or egotistical. The novelist-in-training is in danger of trying to unfold too many character traits in the case of any one character. As a result no one trait makes a strong impression upon the reader. The professional tends to emphasize one or two dominant traits. As a result the reader can remember them so that the character has an identity other than that of his name. In every scene of movement that a major character plays a part in, one or more of these traits come out. A writer develops a character by listing certain traits in his mind such as bravery, selfishness, listlessness, etc. and then applying them in scenes of movement. He does this by visualizing a character with perhaps two to five dominant character traits, and ignoring or forgetting about his other traits. Perhaps the great geniuses can develop a character with a greater number of traits but West, Fast, and Stevenson do not, and the novelist-in-training had better first master simple characterization. Too many character traits usually give a blurred picture to the reader and result in little characterization. Often the same character trait is brought out by the character doing different things. For instance, West shows us the Contessa smoking too much when she is alone, having her chief interest in her toilette, and being discontented with each new day just like the last. These three activities give us a picture of a woman bored with life, namely a woman with one character trait, one character trait expressed in different ways.

10. Have adjectives been used to describe a character's traits?

If so in most cases they had better be eliminated. We do not get a picture of a brave man by being told the man is brave.

11. Are the motives of the characters clear?

The author knows the motives but has he conveyed them clearly to the reader? In real life we often are not sure of a person's motives, but the person has done the thing, and we cannot question it. In fiction if the motives are not clear, the reader may not believe that the character would have done the thing, and the novel becomes unconvincing.

12. Are there minor characters who are characterized when they should not be?

Amateur writers often overcharacterize minor characters. In many a manuscript by a writer who has not learned his trade, the bellboy in a hotel who takes the hero's bag is "sullen" or has a "chubby face" or is a "tall, thin man with frayed cuffs and unpolished shoes." This description or characterization may be unnecessary and may hurt the book. Stevenson in *Treasure Island* does not describe or characterize in any way the man who carries the pirate captain's chest to the inn even though this man gives Jim Hawkins, a major character, some important information. This porter is a most unimportant minor character; he never again appears in the novel. To characterize him would distract the reader from the major characters. In real life we meet a few people we know well (major characters if they plan an important part in the novel) and many we know slightly or not at all (minor characters). If the minor character is characterized, there may be an unreal note in the story. Of course this is all a matter of degree. There are cases where characterization of a minor character helps. Likewise, a novel may have major characters, semi-major, important minor and unimportant minor ones. The author has to hunt for what seems to him the right proportions of description or characterization.

13. How effective are the scenes of movement?

Every scene of movement should be contemplated. In some cases they can be rewritten and improved. More often a new scene can be devised that is superior to the one in the first draft. This does not mean a struggle for the highly dramatic. Most scenes of movement in real life are not especially dramatic, and being true to life is essential. What the author is after is a scene of movement which is true to life and best accomplishes the author's purpose whether the purpose be to exhibit character or advance the plot or what not.

14. Does each scene of movement serve a purpose?

The reasons for having a scene of movement have already been mentioned. A scene of movement that serves no purpose should be eliminated. Often a slight purpose warrants the inclusion of a scene of movement.

15. Is a scene of movement dull?

Cutting may help. Often improvement means inventing a new scene to replace the old. If a dull scene of movement serves a purpose, the author should be wary of taking the easy way out by changing it to narration. But dullness must be eliminated.

16. Are there stretches of narrative which should be told on stage as scenes of movement?

Here the author should devise scenes of movement to replace the narrative and see if they seem preferable. It is probably better for the novelist-in-training to have an excess of scenes of movement than the reverse.

17. Is the scene of movement plausible?

Being true to life is essential. Better no scene than an unconvincing one.

18. Is the dialogue true to life?

Think about your characters, live with them, do research with people similar to your characters, make the dialogue true to life.

19. Should a scene told in dialogue be changed to narrative?

Usually the answer to this question depends upon the importance of the dialogue. Trivia should rarely be told as conversation. The purpose of the dialogue is all-important. Maybe what the characters say is trivia, but the emotional overtones warrant its inclusion as dialogue.

20. Should a narrative scene be put into dialogue?

Often here the author should experiment. He should try a narrative scene in dialogue and see how it reads.

21. Are parts of the novel underwritten?

Authors either underwrite or overwrite; some do both in the same manuscript. Underwriting may mean skeletonized action. Often it means an insufficient number of scenes of movement. Sometimes it means hurrying too fast in the narrative. The result of underwriting may be a lack of clarity. The following suggestions may help:

A. *Is there a feeling of abruptness?*
Usually it is better for one scene to seem to glide into the next.

B. *When a time period is skipped is it clear?*
An author must continually skip time periods. He may skip weeks or months or just hours or minutes. For example, most people eat three meals a day but few novels describe every meal their leading character must have eaten during the period of the novel. Because of slight underwriting, the skipping, the transitions, may not be clear.

C. *Is an important scene told in too few sentences?*
If so, it may lose a sense of importance. The solution may be to expand the scene, it may be to lead into it more slowly or leave it more slowly. Or maybe echoes of such an important scene, echoes before and after, may help the scene stand out in the reader's mind, and seem important.

22. Are parts of the novel overwritten?

This is a major problem for most writers whether novelists-in-training or professionals. A large number of novels in manuscript form can be cut to advantage. Cutting may be the elimination of spurious material, incidents that add little to plot theme or characterization or emotion. Most cutting resolves itself into saying what has been said as effectively in fewer words.

Most authors do not know until they try. Often it is wise to jump in, cut, slash a chapter, and see what happens. Retype the cut chapter and see if it doesn't read better than before. If it does, then look for anything essential which was eliminated and must be reinstated. Follow the same procedure with succeeding chapters.

Much of cutting resolves itself into whether the author can write in fewer words what he has written. This involves improving one's English, which will be discussed in the next chapter.

23. Are there places where the author has become lyrical or original or profound? Are there favorite passages which the author himself admires and hopes readers will admire?

Any paragraph which has an especially lyrical tone to it, or a philosophical bent to it, or is profound in itself, any paragraph which is one of the author's favorites, should be reexamined with a critical eye. The author is not writing poetry or philosophy, he is not trying to encourage the reader to praise his writing; the author is writing a novel. Often the favorite paragraph can be eliminated with no loss. Samuel Johnson made the following comment to Boswell:

> An old tutor of a college said to one of his pupils: Read over your compositions, and whenever you meet with a passage which you think is particularly fine, strike it out.

The answers to these questions often involve decisions as to matters of degree. Here it is hard for the critic to help the novelist-in-training. Nearly every author experiments continually. The author tries a paragraph or a page one way, then tries a completely different way. Then if still dissatisfied, he goes back to a rewriting of the first way. The only thing the critic can say is, Experiment, and use good judgment as to the final copy.

The problem in connection with these 23 questions is that they pertain not just to one part of the book, but to every chapter, every page. Theoretically one revision should be all that is necessary. Because of the length of the average novel and the number of the problems, most authors find they cannot do everything in one revision. Perhaps two or three revisions are common. The late Conrad Richter, Pulitzer prize winner, would revise some of his novels as many as ten times.

In these questions, mood, theme, tone, having something to say, have been ignored. Perhaps the word "inspiration" is as good as any to express these qualities. Inspiration is of paramount importance.

Writing an effective novel requires a nice balance between inspiration and logical sequence building. The danger inherent in any book on the writing craft is that it may be too concerned with technique, that it may treat writing as something constructed of specific ingredients, the way a stonemason constructs a wall with stones. It has been suggested that the novelist-in-training write his first draft under an emotional drive without stopping to think and weigh various different writing possibilities. Then the preparation of succeeding drafts wll involve struggling over the aforementioned questions, acting more like a stonemason than a creative artist. If some such procedure is followed, there is the further step after much revision, the step of worrying about tone, mood, atmosphere, theme, what the novel says. If in reading over the revised manuscript, any false note is found, something must be done. Regardless of how logical the scene may seem, out it must go, and the author must attempt to recapture the first, fine, careless rapture and let inspiration take over. Of the authors of the novels discussed, Stevenson was probably the greatest craftsman and the one with the least inspiration or soul or with the least fragments of greatness. But Stevenson claimed that little people helped him write his books, that the unconscious inspiration was a major factor. One of the greatest writing craftsmen of all times had to have more than just craftsmanship. There is no way of telling a writer how to obtain the requisite inspiration; we cannot even satisfactorily define what inspiration is. The novelist-in-training can only be reminded that technique in itself never made a fine novel, that the stonemasonry of writing can be only an addendum to inspiration.

> *You know when the book is finished; you begin to sense it. Clouds begin to lift. There's a terrifically exhilarating time when you know you're on that final run and everything behind you is just the way you want it to be. It's like skiing down a slope and you feel really good, with enormous energy.*
>
> —*E.L. Doctorow*

Presenting the perfect proposal

by Ellis Booker

Today's novelist must be more than a creative artist dedicated to his work; he must also recognize his book as a product in a brutally competitive market. Writers who can manage this dual role of artist and seller certainly are not guaranteed success or the elusive publisher's contract, but they will be in a better position to see the publishing industry as an industry—full of its own standards, rules of conduct and procedures. An awareness of these procedures, coupled with the knowledge of how to present a book effectively to an editor, distinguishes the professional writer from the amateur.

The basics

Imagine 200-300 pages of text, arriving unannounced one morning with only a brief letter asking for "consideration" and a "prompt" reply. Multiplied, this scenario represents the formidable workload of many editors. In view of the sheer volume of submissions, it is essential that the writer make his work *accessible* to the editor by supplying a package of materials that describe and condense the book's many pages. This is the primary function of the proposal. The basic proposal includes: a cover letter, a plot synopsis, and sample chapters (or sometimes the entire manuscript).

In effect, the proposal provides the vital statistics about a book: the genre and setting, the characters and plot, and any special features. Alerting the reader to what follows, the proposal allows the editor to make a number of basic evaluations, even before seeing the first manuscript page. "Is this the kind of book we'd be interested in publishing? Do we have any similar novels already under contract? How is the competition in this genre? Has this kind of book been a success for us in the past?" Equally important,

---

Ellis Booker graduated from Oberlin College with a degree in English and philosophy. He has since worked for Vantage Press and written for trade journals and college publications. Presently Booker is an editorial assistant for St. Martin's Press.

by looking at a proposal the editor can ask the simple question: "Is this the kind of book *I* would enjoy reading, and, if not, who would be the best person to direct it to?"

The manuscript accompanied by a proposal is likely to fare better, or at least receive a better preliminary evaluation, than the novel that arrives proclaiming "the words speak for themselves." Some fledgling novelists include a page listing previously published works—short stories, magazine articles, even published nonfiction books. It is clear, however, that the value of a vitae is more to affirm that one is a professional writer, familiar with the editorial process, than to give any relevant insights into the novel under consideration. Ultimately, it will be the quality of the work itself, not the author's track record, which the editor will judge.

Take aim

Effectively targeting the manuscript to a publishing house and then to editors on the inside is a major stumbling block to many uninformed writers.

Addressing a proposal to a specific editor is crucially important. With most of the major houses receiving dozens of unsolicited manuscripts each week, mail addressed to anonymous titles like "Fiction Editor" or "Trade Editor" are placed at the very lowest priority.

Some publishers have ceased to consider such submissions altogether; others delegate these arrivals to back-room piles which are perfunctorily examined by editorial assistants or "readers" when the stacks become too high. A manuscript that lands there is unlikely to get a fair reading because of lack of time. A submission marked "Attention: Fiction Editor" is also considered a sign of an unprofessional author. Of course, there are cases where a talented writer has been "uncovered" in this way, but it would be foolish to regard such rare, happy endings as the norm. A far more intelligent strategy is always to direct a manuscript to an individual. This also facilitates inquiries about the status of the book, with a note or a phone call, after the reporting period has elapsed.

Names of editors, along with a statement of the fiction needs of various publishing houses, can be culled from source books such as *Writer's Market*, *Fiction Writer's Market* or *Literary Marketplace (LMP)*. A quick phone call asking the name of the editor who handles a particular genre, such as, romance or science fiction, is another tactic, although it is best to treat this call as only a method of obtaining a name. Attempting to sell a book over the phone is not a good idea; publishers will always be more interested in seeing the written final product.

The cover letter

Composing the cover letter is sometimes the most agonizing part of constructing a proposal. It is the first "writing sample" an editor sees; if something there offends him he'll never read on. To get over this fear it is helpful to understand that there are really just three objectives to the cover letter: 1) Announce the book's title and genre (". . . for consideration of my gothic horror novel *The Beast of Wiloshire*"); 2) Tell why you have chosen this publishing house over others (". . . reading your catalog I've noticed that Fulton Press has done a number of suspense/horror books"), and 3) Refer the editor to the materials the proposal includes ("Enclosed is a two-page synopsis and three sample chapters"). Remember the principle that although one author has one book, one editor has many. Thus, the cover letter should be informative and concise—two or three paragraphs are generally sufficient.

In tone the letter should be straightforward, even formal. Stylistic language is fine for the manuscript text, and the interested editor will encounter this soon enough, but it's safest to keep the cover simple. Cute introductions such as ''Boy, have I got a western y'all gonna love!'' or other eye-catching phrases are not recommended. *Professionalism is the key word.*

Placing the book in one of the broad genre classifications—romance, thriller, science fiction, etc.—is especially appreciated from the editorial standpoint and can assist in directing the manuscript to the appropriate editor. A sentence that locates the book's setting—where and when the action takes place—is also helpful. One way of accomplishing this is to compare the book with another novel with a similar subject and/or style. Of course, a fair comparison is always best; not every love story can be set up against *Gone With the Wind*.

One thing a cover letter should never do is prognosticate the future market sales of the book. Trying to convince an editor the book will be a blockbuster that will sell X number of copies is like telling a banker where he can find the best investments. It is a presumption and a universal turn-off among editors especially in commercial publishing houses. Guessing about a book's probable success or profit is the *editor's job*, and should be left to him.

Still, the cover letter can note things about the market that the editor might find interesting. For example, the physician who writes a book about a young surgeon's decision whether or not to maintain the life of a coma victim, might allude to recent magazine articles on the topic, or mention that the issue of euthanasia was a focus at the last three conventions of the AMA, and so on. While not making specific marketing suggestions or sales predictions, such additional insights, where appropriate, can enter into the editor's evaluation of a book's potential, along with helping to entice him into reading the synopsis.

The synopsis

''I want a synopsis that shows the action,'' advises one seasoned editor. An exercise in restraint, the synopsis must outline what happens in the story, introduce the major characters, and in essence give the flavor of the entire novel, all in under two pages. Beware of the impulse to give long, chapter-by-chapter descriptions. These read like screen plays and are inevitably too long. Also avoid making critical analyses of the characters or their motivations. The editor doesn't need to know that Benny, the hard-boiled detective, is operating through a classic quest for self knowledge or that Jungian archetypes figure prominently in the protagonist's dreams. Remember that the synopsis, like the genre classification, is a device to give an editor a handle on the book.

The following is a portion of a good synopsis. Notice how it concentrates on the action in the story, giving a bit of dialogue to further aid the editor in visualizing the characters.

The death of her husband, Evan, leaves 45 year-old Victoria McLeod alone for the first time in her life. Her daughter, Melissa, a sophomore at Wellesley, and son Peter, in his last year at St. Alban's, are shaken as well, but with the resilience of youth are soon drawn back into their busy routines. Victoria, too, resumes her tennis matches at the Chevy Chase Club, shopping sprees at Neiman Marcus, and quiet dinners wth the circle of friends which Evan's architectural practice had provided them.

But, months later, even the most sympathetic friends have wearied of Victoria's persistent melancholy. In fact, as she confesses to her oldest friend, wise-cracking Carey, she can see why. ''I know I have to get over Evan, but those boring bachelors they dredge up for me are harder to stomach than a TV dinner,'' she moans.

"If I didn't have to show up at the real estate office every morning, I'd go bananas,'' says Carey, and with her knees firmly in Victoria's back, she succeeds in finding Victoria an administrative position at the Georgetown University Alumni Office. A month later, Carey can't believe the change. She's sure it must be the job, but Victoria blurts out, "Wait till you meet him!" Samuel is a 39 year-old Senatorial hopeful, charming, articulate and sophisticated. But Victoria's isn't always the first number he calls, as she discovers when she spots a lovely young redhead on his arm at a black-tie benefit for the new wing at the National Gallery.

Crushed and bewildered, she withdraws once again, vowing that she's past this stage in her life. "Hell, ma,'' says Peter, home after lacrosse practice, "You're not exactly over the hill.''

Taking her son's comment to heart, Victoria soon finds herself seeking out younger and younger partners for a few transient affairs. Carey confronts her angrily. "The next gossip I hear will be that you've asked Peter to bring home his roommate for your personal lottery!''

Impressed by a well-written synopsis, the editor is finally ready to read the manuscript itself. Acting together, the cover letter and synopsis have familiarized him with the book. Now, of course, the novel must live up to the promises made in the preliminary materials. Professionalism demonstrated in the first two parts of the proposal will point the way to the sample chapters.

Sample chapters

There is no established rule for how much text to enclose with the proposal. At the minimum, though, there should be two or three chapters, amounting to about 50 pages of the manuscript. These chapters should be *consecutive*, however, so that the editor can see the author's ability to evolve plot and characterizations over time.

Many editors prefer to see the completed manuscript. Proposals for nonfiction works, such as travel guides, how-to books, or even biographies, require less of the final product to give an editor a sense of the project.

Novels, on the other hand, are more organic in structure, and depend more on the author's skill at holding the reader's attention. An editor may have lingering doubts about an author's capacity to sustain his novel over the long haul, when only two or three introductory chapters are provided and he may feel inadequate in his assessment of a manuscript not in its entirety.

A second rationale for submitting the entire manuscript at once is that a respective editor will not then be forced to request the outstanding chapters and have to wait for them to be delivered (an interim when even an enthusiastic reader's interest might wane).

Generally contracts are not discussed on the basis of a partial manuscript; the entire work usually has to be seen first, especially in the case of first novelists. It is important to realize also that the reading/reviewing/decision process may take several months.

Submitting a work of book-length fiction to a publishing house is often a tremendously intimidating experience for the unpublished, unagented novelist. But the anxieties about one's unsolicited submission can be lessened by remembering that publishers are in business to find books that fit the requirements of their markets. And the writer can improve his chances of getting published considerably by an intelligent presentation of his novel.

The Markets

Find your market

When looking for a specific publication or publisher for your manuscript, check the index of listings. Of if you are unsure of a market, but have an idea for a story or a manuscript already prepared, first refer to the category index immediately preceding the market index. Fiction subjects are listed alphabetically by category or genre and contain those markets requesting short stories or novels in that field.

After finding a market to pursue, *read the entire listing carefully*, before submitting a manuscript.

Unlisted markets

On occasion we receive letters asking why a certain magazine, publisher, contest, award or agent is not listed in *Fiction Writer's Market*. Chances are we have already contacted the party in question, but the editors have elected *not* to list with us for several reasons:

- The magazine or publisher may use very little fiction or be over-inventoried with manuscripts for the year; and as the editor of *Rolling Stone* said, "it would be misleading to the readership to list us as a possible vehicle" for freelancers.

- The magazine or press may be in financial difficulty or in a state of flux with their staffs or policies at our press time, and is therefore unable to state their needs for the coming year.

- A listing in *Fiction Writer's Market* means additional manuscripts. Some magazines or publishers are grateful for the choice of material and exposure to new talent; others may not be adequately staffed or have the time or money to respond to additional submissions or those that may be inappropriate because the writer has not read the listing.

- The decision is an arbitrary one with no reason given.

The decision not to list a market may also be ours—to protect you, the writer. If we receive complaints about unfair treatment to writers, misrepresentation of the information in the listing or unethical or unprofessional action in their dealings with writers, and if after thorough investigation we find these reports to be true, we will delete the listing. Or sometimes if the information is not complete because the publication is too new to formulate specific requirements or we feel the needs are too limited to encourage submissions, we will not add this market to our list.

Let us hear

The listings in *Fiction Writer's Market* are based on correspondence, questionnaires, phone conversations with editors, publishers, agents, and the information is updated annually and is as current as possible. The publishing industry is a volatile one, however, and changes in addresses, policy, editorial staffs, needs and submission requirements occur frequently, and sometimes after we have gone to press.

To keep abreast of these changes, we ask your help. If in your writing and publishing endeavors, you are aware of differences, changes, or problems with a particular market, or know of a new magazine or press publishing fiction—or have suggestions on how we can publish a better book, we encourage you to let us hear from you.

Important

Listings are not paid advertisements; although the information therein is as accurate as possible, the listings are not endorsed or guaranteed by the editor of *Fiction Writer's Market*.

Manuscript mechanics

It's a grand thing to dream of seeing a story with your byline in one of the major national or literary magazines, or to envision your novel in a publisher's catalog. The actual *writing* of it may be a bit difficult, but once you have it down in good shape in a rough draft, the rest is a snap . . . you *think*. There is still one very important—though often irksome—chore to do: preparing the final manuscript for submission to an editor.

It's irritating. It's bothersome. But it's a necessary evil and the quicker you start using the right way, the easier it is to live with.

Type of paper. One of the things to consider is the paper. It must measure 8½x11 inches. That's a standard size and editors are adamant; they don't want offbeat sizes—or colors. White is right.

There's a wide range of white, 8½x11 papers. The cheaper ones are all wood content. They will suffice but they are not recommended. Your best bet is a good 25 percent cotton fiber content paper. It has quality feel, smoothness, shows type neatly and holds up under white-outs and erasing. Editors almost unanimously discourage the use of erasable bond for manuscripts, as it tends to smear when handled. Where weight of the paper is concerned, never use onionskin or anything less than a 16-pound bond; 20-pound is preferred.

File copies. Always make a carbon or photocopy of your manuscript before you send it off to a publisher. You might even want to make several photocopies while the original manuscript is still fresh and crisp looking—as insurance against losing a submission in the mails, and as a means of circulating the same manuscript to other editors for reprint sales after the original has been accepted for publication. (Inform editors that the manuscript offered for reprint should not be used before it has first appeared in the original publication buying it, of course.) Some writers keep their original manuscript as a file copy, and submit a good-quality photocopy of the manuscript to an editor, with a personal note explaining that it is *not* a simultaneous or multiple submission. They tell the editor that he may toss the manuscript if it is of no interest to him, and reply with a self-addressed postcard (also enclosed). This costs a writer some photocopy expense, but saves on the postage bill—and may speed the manuscript review process in some editorial offices.

Type characters. Another firm rule: For manuscripts, always type double space, using either elite or pica type. The slightly larger pica type is easier to read and many editors prefer it, but they don't object to elite. They *do* dislike (and often will refuse) hard-to-read or unusual typewritten characters, such as script, italics, Old English, all capitals, unusual letter styles, etc.

Page format. Do not use a cover sheet; nor should you use a binder—unless you are submittng a play or television or movie script. Instead, in the upper left corner of page one list your name, address and phone number on four single-spaced lines. In the upper right corner, on three single-spaced lines, indicate the aproximate word count for the manuscript, the rights you are offering for sale, and your copyright notice (© 1983 Joe Jones). It is *not* necessary to indicate that this is page one. Its format is self-evident.

On every page after the first, type your last name, a dash, and the page number in the upper right corner (page two, for example, would be: Jones--2). If you are typing a novel, indicate the chapter sequence as well as page number on each page in the top right location, beginning each chapter halfway down on a new page one. Chapter three, page five would have the following "slugline": Jones--III/5. Then drop down two double-spaces and begin copy.

How to estimate wordage. To estimate wordage, count the exact number of words on three interior pages of your manuscript (in manuscripts up to 25 pages), divide the total by three and multiply the result by the number of pages (your first and last pages are likely to be less than full). Carry the total to the nearest 100 words. For example, say you have a 12-page manuscript with totals of 265, 316 and 289 words on the three inside pages. Divide your total of 870 by three to get 290. Now multiply 290 x 12 pages and you get 3,480. Your approximate wordage, therefore, will be 3,500 words. On manuscripts over 25 pages, count five pages instead of three, then follow the same process, dividing by five.

Now, flip the lever to double-space and center the title in capital letters halfway down the page. To center, set the tabulator to stop in the exact left-right center of the page. Count the letters in the title (including spaces and punctuation) and back-space half that number. Centered one double-space under that, type "by" and centered one double-space under that, your name or pseudonym.

Margins should be 1¼ inches on all sides of each full page of typewritten manuscript. Paragraph indentation is five or six letter spaces, consistently.

Now after the title and byline block, drop down three double-spaces, paragraph indent and start your story; or if you are typing a novel, center the words Chapter One on this line, then double space twice, indent and begin your novel.

Concluding page. Carry on just as you have on the other pages after page one. After your last word and period on this page, however, skip three double-spaces and then center the words "The End" or, more commonly, the old telegrapher's symbol of — 30— meaning the same thing. **- 30 -**

Special points to keep in mind. Always use a good dark black (*not* colored) typewriter ribbon and clean your keys frequently. If the enclosures in the letters a,b,d,e,g, etc. get inked-in, your keys need cleaning. Keep your manuscript neat *always*. Occasional retyping over erasures is acceptable, but strikeovers are bad and give a manuscript a sloppy, careless appearance. Sloppy typing is viewed by many editors as an index to sloppy work habits—and the likelihood of careless research and writing. Strive for a

Jones--2

Begin the second page, and all following pages, in this manner--with a page-number line (as above) that includes your name, in case loose manuscript pages get shuffled by mistake.

Joe Jones
1234 My Street
Anytown, U. S. A.
Tel 123/456-7890

About 3,000 words
First Serial Rights
© 1983 Joe Jones

YOUR STORY OR NOVEL TITLE HERE

by

Joe Jones

The manuscript begins here--about halfway down the first page. It should be cleanly type, double-spaced, using either elite or pica type. Use one side of the paper only, and leave a margin of about 1-1/2 inches on all four sides.

NEATNESS COUNTS. Here are sample pages of a manuscript ready for submission to an editor. If the author uses a pseudonym, it should be placed on the title page only in the byline position; the author's real name must always appear in the top left corner of the title page—for manuscript mailing and payment purpose.

clean, professional-looking manuscript that reflects pride in your work.

Mailing your manuscript. Except when working on assignment from a magazine, or when under contract to do a novel for a publisher, always enclose a self-addressed return envelope (SASE) and the correct amount of postage with your manuscript. Manuscript pages should be held together with a paper clip only—never stapled together.

For foreign publications and publishers, including the Canadian markets, always enclose an international reply coupon (IRC), determined by the weight of the manuscript at the post office. Small presses and little magazines are on low budgets, so to be safe, send a SASE or IRC with all correspondence.

Most editors won't object too much if manuscripts under five pages are folded in thirds and letter-mailed. However, there is a market *preference* for flat mailing (in large envelopes) of manuscripts over four pages. You will need two sizes of large gummed or clasped mailing envelopes—9x12 for the return envelope, and 9½x12½ or 10x13 for the one used to send out the manuscript and return envelope. Or you may buy two 9x12 envelopes, fold the return one and use the other for the outgoing manuscript, a less expensive method in the long run.

Mark your envelope, as desired with FIRST CLASS MAIL, or SPECIAL FOURTH CLASS RATE: MANUSCRIPT. First Class mail costs more but assures better handling and faster delivery. Special Fourth Class mail is handled the same as Parcel Post, so wrap it well. Also, the Special Fourth Class rate only applies in the US, and to manuscripts that weigh one pound or more; otherwise there is no price difference. Third class is the alternative for anything over five ounces, but it is very slow.

For lighter weight manuscripts, First Class mail is recommended because of the better speed and handling. First Class mail is handled the same as Air Mail.

Insurance is available, but payable only on the tangible value of what is in the package, i.e., writing paper, so your best insurance is to keep a copy at home of what you send. Moreover, publishers do not appreciate receiving (and signing for) unsolicited manuscripts marked Certified or Registered or Insured.

First Class mail is forwarded or returned automatically; however, Special Fourth Rate mail is not. To make sure you get your submission back if undeliverable, print "Return Postage Guaranteed" under your return address.

Cover letters. You may enclose a personal letter with your manuscript sent at the Special Fourth Class Rate but you must also add enough First Class postage to cover the letter and mark *FIRST CLASS LETTER ENCLOSED* on the outside.

In most cases, a brief cover letter is helpful in personalizing the submission. Nothing you say will make the editor decide in your favor (the story must stand by itself in that regard), so don't use the letter to make a sales pitch. But you may want to tell an editor something about yourself, your publishing history, or any particular qualifications you have for writing the enclosed manuscript. If you have written to the editor earlier, he probably already has the background information—so the note should be a brief reminder: "Here is the story we discussed earlier. I look forward to hearing from you at your earliest convenience."

If the manuscript is a photocopy, be sure to indicate whether or not it is a multiple submission. An editor is likely to assume it is, unless you tell him otherwise—and many are offended by writers using this marketing tactic (though when agents use it, that seems to be OK).

Mailing book manuscripts. Do not bind your book manuscript pages in any way. They should be mailed loose in a box (a ream-size stationery box is perfect) without binding. To ensure a safe return, enclose a self-addressed label and suitable postage in stamps clipped to the label. If your manuscript is returned, it will either come back in your original box, or—increasingly likely today—in an insulated bag-like mailer, with your label and postage used thereon. Many publishing houses open the box a manuscript is mailed in, and toss the box (if it has not been damaged in the mails, or in the opening already); they then read and circulate the manuscript as necessary for editorial consideration, and finally route it through the mail room back to you with a letter or rejection slip. This kind of handling makes it likely that a freshly typed manuscript will be in rough shape even after one or two submissions. So it is wise to have several photocopies made of a novel-length manuscript while it is still fresh—and to circulate those to publishers, rather than risk an expensive retyping job in the midst of your marketing effort. As mentioned above, indicate in a cover note that the submission is not a multiple submission if such is the case.

Book manuscripts can be mailed Special Fourth Class Book Rate, but that can be slow and have an additional mauling effect on the package in the mails. When doing so, if you include a letter, state this on the outer wrapping and add appropriate postage to your manuscript postal rate. Most writers use First Class, secure in the feeling that their manuscript is in an editorial office within a few days. Some send book manuscripts using the United Parcel Service, which can be less expensive than First Class mail when you drop the package off at UPS yourself. The drawback here is that UPS cannot legally carry First Class mail, so you will have to send your cover letter a few days before giving UPS the manuscript, and both will arrive at about the same time. Check with UPS in your area to see if it has benefits for you. The cost depends on the weight of your manuscript and the delivery distance.

The tips and recommendations made here are based upon what editors prefer. Give editors what they prefer and you won't be beginning with a strike or two against you before the manuscript is even read.

The waiting game. The writer who sends off a story or book manuscript to an editor should turn immediately to other ideas and try to forget about the submission. Unless you are on assignment, or under contract to do a book—in which case a phone call to your editor saying the manuscript is in the mail is quite appropriate—it's best to use your time productively on other writing projects, and let the submission take care of itself. But one day you realize it's been too long. According to the *Fiction Writer's Market* listing, your editor responds to submissions in a maximum of four weeks—and it's been six already, and you haven't heard a word. Will inquiring about it jeopardize a possible sale? Are they really considering it, or has the editor had an accident and your manuscript is at the bottom of a huge stack of unread mail?

If you have had no report from a publisher by the maximum reporting time given in a *FWM* listing, allow a few weeks' grace period and then write a brief letter to the editor asking if your manuscript (give the title, a brief description, and the date you mailed it) has in fact reached his office. If so, is it still under consideration? Your concern at this point is the mails: Is the manuscript safely delivered? Don't act impatient with an editor—who may be swamped, or short-handed, or about to give your manuscript a second reading. The wrong word or attitude from you at this point could be hazardous to your manuscript's health. Be polite, be professional. Enclose another SASE to expedite a reply. This is usually enough to stir a decision, if matters are lagging in an editorial office, even during rush season (which is year 'round).

If you still hear nothing from a publisher one month after your follow-up, send the editor a short note asking if he received your previous follow-up, and include a photocopy of that second letter. If, after another month, you are still without word, send a polite letter saying that you are withdrawing the manuscript without consideration (include the title, date of submission, and dates of follow-up correspondence), and ask that the manuscript be returned immediately in the SASE your original correspondence included. You are now free to market the manuscript elsewhere.

Even though matters have not worked out, and you have lost months of precious marketing time—never write in anger. Be cool, professional, and set about the business of finding another publisher for your work. The advantage of having a clean photocopy of the manuscript in your files at this point cannot be overstated. Move on to another editor or publisher with it, using a personal cover letter and the same methods outlined above. In the meantime, continue working on your own writing projects.

At times like these, the advantage of having an agent who can insulate you from such marketing discouragement is considerable. See our section on Agents for guidelines on getting and working with a literary agent, especially if you are working on book-length projects.

Literary/little magazines

The general philosophy of literary/little magazines is the freedom to create and experiment. Each year there are hundreds of idealistic and devoted writers and editors who start their own magazines while already established literaries persist in their publishing endeavors—often with financial difficulties that threaten their existence. Despite the hardships, literaries continue to increase in number and remain the natural habitat of the young, innovative writer. Often they are the only forum open to new forms of literary expressions—or as Cyril Connolly of *The Evening Colonnade* says, "the pollinators of works of art." Literary movements and eventually literature itself would not exist without them.

There is an unlimited range in not only the number of new publications each year but great individuality in size, theme, format and even management. Little magazines may be associated with colleges or universities (*Missouri Review*, *Iowa Review*); they may be devoted to a special genre (*Erotic Fiction Quarterly*, *Fantasy Macabre*) or interest/hobby (*California Horse*, *High Performance*); they may be directed to an audience or ethnic group (*Black Scholar*, *Revista/Review Interamericana*); they may be centered around a city or region (*Another Chicago Magazine*, *Berkeley Monthly*); or they may be Canadian or foreign publications in English and have a very general theme for lovers of good literature. What these magazines do have in common, however, is that they all accept short fiction. The diversity offers a haven for readers *and* writers of all types of fiction, but it also demands that the writer have subject expertise, too.

Resourceful and determined

Even in the free-spirited literaries there were discernible trends in 1982. The year brought more new special interest magazines, especially in fantasy, science fiction, erotica and humor—escapist subjects that often surface in times of economic need or distress. There are now publications even more narrowly focused; for example, there are science fiction and fantasy comic books, and feminist magazines for each of the different age groups of women. There are also little magazines just for the handicapped, visually impaired or the deaf.

Editors in general seem to be stressing less poetry and more fiction. Magazines like *Ploughshares* are publishing all fiction issues, and literaries like *Triquarterly*, *Fiction International*, *Fiction Energy* and *Story Quarterly* are consistently devoted to an almost all fiction format.

In short story subjects there has been a gradual move away from the social issues of the '60s and '70s and back to more traditional story lines, such as nostalgia, recollection and going-home. The tendency in form is for a more structured story with deeper plots and strong characterization; short fiction is now somewhat less innovative or avant garde in form. The traditional or less experimental fiction does not mean lack of originality, however. Writers are still encouraged to risk new methods and ideas. Or as one literary editor says, "variation supplies the surprises that make fiction worthwhile and imaginative."

The free-of-restraints spirit and idealism are evident in the little magazines themselves. Editors' dreams are daunted, however, by the economic realities of keeping their magazines alive. "Each new issue carries with it a bare-knuckled, back to the wall funding battle," says Marvin Diogenes, editor of *Sonora Review*. The postal rates have been "devastating," as have the government agencies' unwillingness to continue support; loans as private businesses are usually not affordable.

As a result editors have had to tighten their belts in the production process. Magazines are paying less, paying late or not at all, and they are publishing fewer or shorter short stories. Initially most little magazines are low budget ventures anyway, and the staffs are "more adept at stretching it," as the editor of *Nostoc* says after ten years of publishing.

Personal attention

There have been, however, changes that affect the reader and writer. Magazine editors are curtailing free copies, raising subscription prices, changing to cheaper stock or format, becoming more selective in their choices of stories, trimming future projects or using more staff written material. They also do much of the work themselves and have developed resourceful strategies with effective fund raising sales and advertising/promotional projects. And to allay complete economic disaster, many magazines have had to resort to reading fees in 1982. "But if I worry about it [the economy]," says Fred Soltysik, editor of *Pacific Rim Review* philosophically, "then I, too, am caught."

Two nonprofit organizations—the Coordinating Council of Literary Magazines (CCLM) and the Committee of Small Magazine Editors and Publishers (COSMEP)—and regional groups continue to support literary/little magazines. They provide grants; set up educational conferences and bookfairs; assist in promotion, distribution and new publishing techniques. The struggle is a constant one—but not insurmountable. The spirit to grow is unflagging, and more often than not, editors are willing to make sacrifices to keep their publications going.

The literary/little market offers the fiction writer many advantages. Editorial staffs are invariably small; thus communication is often directly with the editor who, as a writer himself, might send along constructive advice or a few encouraging words, sometimes even with a rejection. Little magazines have finally begun to come into their own, and have greater credibility in the publishing industry. Stories are regularly chosen for national awards; contributions are reprinted in high school texts, developed into novels or scouted by commercial magazines and publishers, editors and agents who contact the literaries for authors' addresses.

It should be remembered, however, that the little magazines are not necessarily for every writer, nor are they an alternative market for a previously rejected manuscript or a good bet for a commercial short story.

Editors' needs

Although the magazines are diverse, the editors' requirements for short fiction are similar. They all want *vitality*, *variety*, *originality*, and they demand good professional work and manuscript preparation. Editors also agree in their reasons for rejection: The story line or theme is unexceptional or stereotypical; the style is imitative or amateurish; the language is forced and not written from sentiment or feeling; the research is insufficent; or more basically, the story simply doesn't fit the publication's format.

To meet their magazines' needs, editors recommend that you:

● Ask for sample copies of many magazines; study the short stories and format to be knowledgeable of the entire contents in the magazine. Know the publishing history of the publication and be aware that the publishing life of a small magazine is often short.

● Read the market listings in *Fiction Writer's Market* very carefully for exact needs and requirements and follow the individual requests of each magazine. Do not send out manuscripts blindly; target your submissions to avoid wasting your time and the editor's.

● Know what to expect in payments and rights. Magazines vary greatly in business and ethics.

● Query only if requested. The majority of editors prefer to see the entire manuscript. A short cover letter with a few words about your background may accompany the submission. But let your story make the impression, not your credits.

● Write only what you want to read.

● Avoid pathos. Strive for intensity of feeling without sentimentality. Concentrate on clarity; learn to control language and style will follow. Don't let enthusiasm obscure truth.

● Be original, be natural. Write for a long lasting effect on the reader.

● Rewrite and rewrite; polish and tighten; eliminate excess verbiage.

● Prepare your work carefully before sending it off; a clear and neatly-typed manuscript is your sales tool for publication.

● *Always* include a self-addressed stamped envelope (SASE), or international reply coupon (IRC) if writing for a foreign market.

● Be persistent as a way of life. Remember what one literary editor says and believes: "All visions are possible."

● Finally, support the literary/little magazines as much as you can. A willingness to pay the cover price for copies of several magazines will help maintain these publications and ensure a literary tradition.

ABBEY, White Urp Press, 5011-2 Green Mountain Circle, Columbia MD 20144. Editor: David Greisman. "Unassumed intelligence in a publication of finite production for the type of person who knows the pure poetry of Molson Ale." Quarterly. Estab. 1970. Circ. 200.
Needs: Literary, contemporary, science fiction and regional (appreciation of Maryland). "Nothing political! Nothing espousing a cause. Nothing explicit." Accepts 3-6 mss/year. Receives approximately 10 unsolicited fiction mss each month. Length: 1,000-2,000 words. Sometimes recommends markets.
How to Contact: Query with SASE. Reports in 1 month. Sample copy 50¢.
Payment: 1-2 free author's copies.
Terms: Acquires one-time rights.

Tips: "Plug in the typewriter. Buy stamps. Don't imitate Thomas Hardy. Drink less than Behan or Thomas. Tell stories like Frederic Raphael." Most mss are rejected because "the stories themselves aren't interesting. Also, too many writers tend to lose their narrative strengths by introducing gimmicks and tricks where they are least needed. I'll accept nothing more than 6-7 pages."

AFTA/The Alternative Magazine, AFTA Press, Inc., 153 George St., Suite #2, New Brunswick NJ 08901. (201)846-0226. Editor: Bill-Dale Marcinko. "We are basically a review magazine of books and media—TV, films, science fiction, rock music. Our audience is primarily young adults who are very interested in pop culture and social issues. Most of our readers are attending college or are college graduates." Quarterly. Estab. February 1978. Circ. 25,000.
Needs: Contemporary, psychic/supernatural, science fiction, fantasy, horror, women's, feminist, gay/lesbian, mystery and humor. "Fiction should be of a rather emotional, honest tone, rather than 'light' or 'literary.' We like stories with irony, satire, and a humorous, perhaps even morbid, character. No religious, erotic, pornographic or romantic work will be considered." Buys 5-6 mss/issue. Receives approximately 30 unsolicited fiction mss each month. Length: 1,000-3,000 words. Critiques rejected mss "when there is time." Sends mss on to editors of other publications. Sometimes recommends markets.
How to Contact: Query with SASE. Reports in 1 week on queries, 2 weeks on mss. Sample copy $3.50.
Payment: Free author's copies.
Terms: Acquires one-time rights. Publication copyrighted.
Tips: "Be honest, simple, direct, and don't write about what you haven't experienced in some way. Have a particular feeling, tone, and thrust to your work that is clear as the work progresses." Mss are rejected because they are "generally totally dissimilar to tone of AFTA. Potential contributors should buy a sample issue first."

THE AGNI REVIEW, The Agni Review Inc., Box 229, Cambridge MA 02138. Contact: Editor-in-Chief. "Eclectic literary magazine publishing first-rate poems and stories." Published semiannually. Estab. 1972.
Needs: Excerpted novel and translations. Receives 150 unsolicited fiction mss/month. Accepts 4-7 mss/issue, 8-12 mss/year. Rarely critiques rejected mss.
How to Contact: Send complete ms wth SASE. Simultaneous and photocopied submissions OK. Reports in 4 weeks. Sample copy $3.50.
Payment: 3 contributor's copies 60% of retail price.
Terms: Pays on publication for first North American serial rights. Publication copyrighted.
Tips: "Read *Agni* carefully to understand the kinds of stories we publish. Our fiction might be described as highly literate (but not literary). At times experimental, always crafted with great attention to language and to telling a story."

AHNENE PUBLICATIONS, Poetry 'N Prose, Ahnene Publications, Box 456, Maxville, Ontario, Canada K0C 1T0. Editor-in-Chief: M. Williams. Magazine of poetry, prose and mood pieces for the general public, poetry lovers. Bimonthly. Estab. 1982.
Needs: Contemporary, experimental, fantasy, horror, humor/satire, literary, mainstream, prose poem, religious/inspirational, romance (contemporary) and women's. "No science fiction, cops 'n robbers or who-dun-its." Receives "too many" unsolicited fiction mss of poor quality. Length: 2,000 words maximum. Occasionally critiques rejected mss.
How to Contact: Send complete ms with SASE or IRCs. Photocopied submissions and previously published work OK (where rights have reverted to authors). Reports in 2 months on mss. Sample copy $2 with business-size SASE and 2 first class Canadian stamps.
Payment: $1-$10. Payment varies; see magazine for details. 2 contributor's copies. Charges $1 for extras.
Terms: Pays on publication for first rights, second serial rights. Publication copyrighted.
Tips: "Submit stories that make their point succinctly—nothing vague and day-dreamy."

THE AKROS REVIEW, English Department, University of Akron, Akron OH 44325. Editor: Victoria Quaint. Magazine for a small literary journal public. "We are searching for the highest level of artistic creativity in poetry, fiction, essays. We only ask for something new, something that will last." Published semiannually. Estab. 1978. Circ. 1,000.
Needs: Contemporary, experimental, fantasy, humor/satire, literary, prose poem, translations. "Theme and style are at the discretion of author. We are searching for the highest possible literary merit in contemporary fiction." Receives 50 unsolicited fiction mss/month. Accepts 5 mss/issue, 10 mss/year. Occasionally critiques rejected mss if requested.
How to Contact: Send complete ms with SASE. Reports in 4-6 weeks. Sample copy $3.50.
Payment: 2 free contributor's copies. Charges $3.50 for extra copies.
Terms: Pays on publication for all rights. Publication copyrighted.

ALASKA QUARTERLY REVIEW, University of Alaska, 3221 Providence Dr., Anchorage AK 99508. (907)263-1750. Contact: Fiction Editor. Magazine of "contemporary literary art and criticism for a general literary audience." Published semiannually. Estab. 1982.
Needs: Contemporary, experimental, literary, prose poem, translations. Receives 50 unsolicited fiction mss/month. Accepts 3-4 mss/issue, 6-8 mss/year. Occasionally critiques rejected mss.
How to Contact: Send complete ms with SASE. Photocopied submissions OK. Reports in 2 months. Sample copy $4.50.
Payment: 2 free contributor's copies.
Terms: Pays on publication for first rights. Publication copyrighted.

THE ALCHEMIST, Box 123, Lasalle, Quebec, Canada H8R 3T7. Editor: Marco Fraticelli. Fiction Editor: Guy LaFlamme. "We publish prose in every issue with no prejudices in regard to style, but we tend to favor the experimental rather than the traditional." Published irregularly. Estab. 1974. Circ. 500.
Needs: Literary. Buys 1 ms/issue.
How to Contact: Send complete ms with SASE. Reports in 1 month. Free sample copy.
Payment: Free author's copies.
Terms: Pays on publication. Rights remain with author. Publication copyrighted.

ALDEBARAN, Roger Williams College, Ferry Rd., Bristol RI 02809. (401)255-1000. Co-Editors: Mary Lou Blockett, Jim Griggs. Literary publication of prose and poetry for a general audience. Published annually or twice a year. Estab. 1970.
Needs: Will consider all fiction. Short stories preferred. Receives approximately 10 unsolicited fiction mss each month. Critiques rejected mss "when there is time."
How to Contact: Send complete ms with SASE. Reports in 1 month. Sample copy $1 with SASE.
Payment: 2 free author's copies.
Terms: Pays on publication. Publication copyrighted. Copyright reverts to author on publication.
Tips: Mss are rejected because of "incomplete stories, no live character, basic grammatical errors; usually returned with suggestions for revision and character change."

AMAZON, Milwaukee's Feminist Press, Amazon, 2211 E. Kenwood Blvd., Milwaukee WI 53211. (414)964-6118. Editor-in-Chief: Miki Doxtater. Fiction Editor: Betty Edwards. Magazine. "We are a feminist publication and limit our material to work *by* women and of interest *to* women. Our audience is predominantly feminist women." Bimonthly. Estab. 1972. Circ. 2,000.
Needs; Adventure, comics, contemporary, ethnic, feminist, gay, historical (general), humor/satire, juvenile, psychic/supernatural, science fiction, suspense/mystery, women's, young adult. "Fiction should be oriented to women and/or feminist audiences." No "fiction where men are the main characters; where women are heavily 'put down'." Receives 6-8 unsolicited fiction mss/month. Accepts 1-2 mss/issue, 6-12 mss/year. Occasionally critiques rejected mss.
How to Contact: Query first or send complete mss with SASE. Simultaneous submission, pho-

tocopied submissions and previously published work OK. Reports in 3 weeks on queries, 2 months on mss. Sample copy $1.
Payment: Pays in complimentary copies only. Publication copyrighted.
Tips: "No longhand manuscripts accepted."

AMERICAN WHEELMAN, League of American Wheelmen, Box 988, Baltimore MD 21203. (301)727-2022. Editor-in-Chief: Walter K. Ezell. "A magazine that informs and entertains bicycle enthusiasts: recreational, touring, utilitarian and commuting, who are members of the L.A.W. or buy the magazine in bicycle shops. We publish very little fiction, and it must be in keeping with the literacy and high quality of the entire magazine." Published monthly.
Needs: "Bicycling topics only." Receives 1 unsolicited fiction ms/month. Accepts 2 mss/year. Length: 2,000 words average.
How to Contact: Send complete ms with SASE. Photocopied submissions and previously published work OK. Reports in 3 months on mss. Sample copy $1.50.
Payment: 5 free contributor's copies.
Terms: Acquires one-time rights. Publication copyrighted.

ANOTHER CHICAGO MAGAZINE (ACM), Thunder's Mouth Press, Box 11223, Chicago IL 60611. (312)524-1289. Editor: Lee Webster. Fiction Editor: Dawn Webber. Estab. 1977.
Needs: Contemporary, literary, experimental, feminist, gay/lesbian, ethnic, humor/satire, translations and political/socio-historical. Receives 30-50 unsolicited fiction mss each month. Sometimes recommends markets.
How to Contact: Unsolicited mss. acceptable with SASE. Sample copies are available for $2.50 ppd. Reports in 6 weeks.
Payment: Contributor's copies.
Terms: Publication copyrighted.
Tips: "Write and submit, constantly and continuously. Get used to rejection slips, and don't get discouraged. Keep query and introductory letters short. Make sure ms has name and address on it, and that it is clean, neat and proofread. We are looking for full length fiction mss."

ANTAEUS, The Ecco Press, 18 W. 30th St., New York NY 10001. (212)685-8240. Editor-in-Chief: Daniel Halpern. Literary magazine of fiction and poetry, literary documents and occasional essays for those seriously interested in contemporary writing. Published quarterly. Estab. 1970. Circ. 5,000.
Needs: Contemporary, literary, prose poem, excerpted novel, translations. No gothic romance, romance, science fiction. Receives 200 unsolicited fiction mss/month. Rarely critiques rejected mss.
How to Contact: Send complete ms with SASE. Photocopied submissions OK. Reports in 6-8 weeks. Sample copy $5.25. Fiction guidelines free with SASE.
Payment: Pays $5/page minimum and 2 free contributor's copies. Discount of 40% for extras.
Terms: Pays on publication for First North American serial rights and right to reprint in any anthology consisting of 75% or more of material from *Antaeus*. Publication copyrighted.
Tips: "Read the magazine before submitting. Unless stories are extremely short (2-3 pages), send only one. Do not be mad if you get only a printed rejection note; we *have* read the manuscript. Always include an SASE. Keep cover letters short, cordial and to the point."

THE ANTIGONISH REVIEW, St. F.X. University, Antigonish, Nova Scotia, Canada B2G 1C0. 867-2221. Editor: George Sanderson. Literary magazine for the educated and creative. Quarterly. Estab. 1970. Circ. 800.
Needs: Literary, contemporary and translations. No erotic or political material. Buys 6 mss/issue. Receives 25 unsolicited fiction mss each month. Length: 3,000-5,000 words. Sometimes comments briefly on rejected mss.
How to Contact: Send complete ms with SASE. Reports in 8 weeks.
Payment: 2 free author's copies.

Terms: Acquires first rights. Publication copyrighted
Tips: "Learn the fundamentals and do not deluge an editor." Rejects mss because of "poor style—usually foggy, dour or unclear."

ANTIGRUPPO, (formerly *Two Worlds*), Coop. Antigruppo Siciliano, via Argenteria Km4, Trapani, Sicily. Editor: Nat Scammacca. Fiction Editor: Gianni Diecidue. "We publish books of poetry (Italian and English), novels, 2 reviews, essays, art, a newspaper, anthologies, short stories, etc." Audience: "Local and national lovers of poetry, politics, prose, language." Quarterly. Estab. 1973. Circ. 2,000.
Needs: Literary, contemporary, humor, translations, history (local, Sicilian, Scots, Greek, English, Hungarian and French). Buys 100 mss/year. Receives approximately 150 unsolicited fiction mss each month. Length: No requirement. Send mss "to other literary reviews in northern Italy."
How to Contact: "Send previously published material so we can then ask for the material we want." Reports in 2 weeks. Free sample copy.
Payment: $50 minimum for short stories. Free author's copies at author's request.
Terms: "No rights."
Tips: "Ask for our 21 points of the Antigruppo which is a pluralistic guide and encouragement to write as one speaks. Don't copy anyone but oneself and write the way the language is spoken at home in your own region, not imitating others. Material must interest the Sicilian reader."

ANTIOCH REVIEW, Antioch Review, Inc., Box 148, Yellow Springs OH 45387. (513)767-7386. Editor: Robert S. Fogarty. Fiction Editor: Nolan Miller. "Literary and cultural review of contemporary issues in politics, American and international studies, literature for general readership. Quarterly. Estab. January 1941. Circ. 4,000.
Needs: Literary, contemporary, translations and experimental. No children's, science fiction or popular market. Buys 3-4 mss/issue, 10-12 mss/year. Receives approximately 175 unsolicited fiction mss each month. Length: any length the story justifies.
How to Contact: Send complete ms with SASE preferably mailed flat. Reports in 2 months. Sample copy $2; free guidelines with SASE.
Payment: $10/page. 2 free author's copies. $2.10 charge for extras.
Terms: Pays on publication for first and one-time rights (rights returned to author on request). Publication copyrighted.
Tips: "Our best advice, always, is to *read* the *Antioch Review* to see what type of material we publish. Quality fiction requires an engagement of the reader's intellectual interest supported by mature emotional relevance, written in a style that is rich and rewarding without being freaky."

ANTITHESIS, Triad Publications, 687 E. Market St., Marietta PA 17547. (717)426-2723. Executive Editor: Patricia M. Spath. Fiction Editor: Cathie Whitehead. Magazine of "experimental science fiction with an eye to material that would not be found in pro publications. New authors that are willing to tread fresh ground, no safe plots in which the reader receives nothing for the effort he/she has put forth. We have readership of all ages, but with a taste for the innovative. Those interested in science fiction/fantasy/horror." Published quarterly. Estab. 1978. Circ. 1,000.
Needs: Comics, fantasy, horror, humor/satire, prose poem, psychic/supernatural, science fiction, serialized/excerpted novel. No erotica with an X rating, gay, lesbian, gothic/romance. Receives 15-20 unsolicited fiction mss/month. Accepts 4-5 mss/issue, 25 mss/year. Occasionally recommends markets.
How to Contact: Send complete ms with SASE. Photocopied submissions OK. Reports in 3 weeks. Sample story $2. Free fiction guidelines with business size SASE.
Payment: Free contributor's copies (number depends on length of piece).
Terms: Pays on publication for one-time rights. Publication copyrighted.
Tips: "Freshness, please! We aren't looking for a rehash of Asimov, we want your thoughts and feelings. Pay attention to plot and character, we want creatures/people that exist for the length of time that the reader is involved with the story. Submit clean material, no coffee stains or leftover sandwiches. Nothing screams amateur like a messy manuscript or art piece. We welcome writers

of all ages and have a special section for the young writer, but we would like to know if you are between 10-16.''

APALACHEE QUARTERLY, D.D.B. Press, Inc., Box 20106, Tallahassee FL 32304. (904)878-1591. Editors: P.V. LeForge, D.M. Morrill, Monica Faeth, Len Schweitzer, Rick Johnson. Contemporary journal of fiction poetry and drama for educated readers from 20-75. Quarterly. Estab. 1972. Circ. 400.
Needs: Literary and contemporary. ''All categories of fiction are considered as long as the works aspire toward the very pinnacles of art. Dostoevsky wrote a mystery; the Brontes wrote gothic romances; I.B. Singer writes ethnic stories; Rechy gay stories; Lessing and Pynchon have delved into science fiction. Yet these writers have transcended these 'sub-genres.' We encourage writing in all areas, but if the writing is thin, send it to a magazine that will appreciate it more than we will.'' Buys 5 mss/issue, 20 mss/year. Receives 200 unsolicited fiction mss each month. Length: 700-6,000 words. Critiques rejected mss ''when there is time.''
How to Contact: Send complete ms with SASE. Reports in 1 month. Sample copy $2, includes postage.
Payment: 2 free author's copies. $1.50 charge for extras.
Terms: Acquires first rights. Publication copyrighted.
Tips: ''Write 4 hours every day. Read 100 pages every day. Work diligently, but learn the fundamentals of fiction (point of view, motivation) as soon as possible. Show your work to as many people as possible. If you're rejected more than five times, it may be time to consider revising. We sometimes sponsor regional or statewide contests, depending on grant money.''

AQUARIUS, Aquarium Ltd., 114 Sutherland Ave., London W9 England. 01-286-3317. Editor-in-Chief: Eddie S. Linden. Magazine for a literary audience. Annual. Estab. 1968. Circ. 2,000.
Needs: Humor/satire, literary, prose poem, serialized/excerpted novel. Receives 10 unsolicited fiction mss/month. Accepts 1-2 mss/issue. Length: 2,000 words maximum.
How to Contact: Send complete ms. Send query with SASE or IRCs. Simultaneous submissions, photocopied submissions and previously published work OK. Sample copy £2.50 plus £2 in postage.
Terms: Acquires first rights. Publication copyrighted.

ARBA SICULA, ARBA Sicula, Inc., Box D, Brooklyn NY 11204. (212)331-0613. Editor: Alissandru Caldiero. Bilingual ethnic literary review (Sicilian-English) dedicated to the dissemination of Sicilian culture. Published 2-4 times a year. Estab. 1979. Circ. 1,000.
Needs: Accepts ethnic literary material consisting of various forms of folklore; stories both contemporary and classical. Material submitted must be in the Sicilian language with English translation desirable. Critiques rejected mss ''when there is time.''
How to Contact: Send complete ms with SASE. Reports in 2 months. Sample copy $5 with 8½x11 SASE and 90¢ postage.
Payment: 1-2 free author's copies. $4 charge for extra copies.
Terms: Acquires all rights. Publication copyrighted.
Tips: ''This review is a must for those who nurture a love of the Sicilian language.'' Mss are rejected because of ''poor Sicilian language.''

AREITO, Ediciones Vitral, Box 1913, New York NY 10116. (2121)594-6664. Editor-in-Chief: Albor Ruiz. Magazine of ''cultural and political topics related to minorities in US and Latin America; in Spanish for persons in the field of Latin American studies and a general audience interested in these topics.'' Quarterly. Estab. 1974.
Needs: Contemporary, ethnic, historical (general). Receives 5 unsolicited fiction mss/month. Accepts 2 mss/issue; 8-10 mss/year. Prefers 3 double-spaced typewritten pages.
How to Contact: Send complete ms. Simultaneous submissions, photocopied submissions and previously published work OK. Reports in 2 months. Free sample copy.
Payment: 5 free contributor's copies.
Terms: Publication copyrighted.

THE ARGONAUT, Box 7985, Austin TX 78712. (512)478-2396. Editor: Michael Ambrose. *"The Argonaut* is a fantasy magazine, by which we mean stories in the genres of science fiction, mystery, occult, adventure; the word 'fantasy' carries few restrictions here. Our readership is primarily college-educated and mature. Many are themselves writers of fantasy. *Argonaut* readers want original, literate, unusual stories.'' Semiannually. Estab. March 1972. Circ. 300.
Needs: Science fiction, fantasy, horror, mystery, occult, adventure. "As indicated above, such categories do not constrain the writer to remain rigidly within traditional forms. Well-written stories in the detective, mystery, and adventure fields are also welcome. No heroic fantasy in rank imitation of the Robert E. Howard school, or wide-eyed Tolkienesque fantasies. In general, I want nothing that has been said before and better.'' Buys 8-10 mss/issue, 20-25 mss/year. Receives 40-50 unsolicited fiction mss each month. Length: 1,500-6,000 words. Critiques rejected mss "when there is time.'' Sometimes recommends other markets.
How to Contact: Send complete ms with SASE. Reports in 1-2 months. Sample copy $2
Payment: .005¢/word. Free author's copy. $2 charge for extras or 5 copies or more at 40% discount.
Terms: Pays on acceptance for first North American serial rights. Publication copyrighted.
Tips: "Know the fields of fantasy and science fiction thoroughly, and remember, most of it has already been done in one form or another. Read the professional magazines, sample *The Argonaut* and other small press magazines before submitting anything. Be professional—lightly-photocopied mss and faded ribbons are a waste of the editor's eyes and time. Don't submit more than one ms at a time, and keep trying when rejected. *The Argonaut*'s infrequent publishing schedule lets me be very selective of the stories I receive. It takes more than a polished style with no originality of idea, or all idea with no style on the other hand, to get me interested.''

ARIZONA QUARTERLY, The University of Arizona, Tucson AZ 85721. (602)626-1029. Editor: Albert F. Gegenheimer. Quarterly. Estab. March 1945.
Needs: Literary, contemporary and translations. Receives approximately 25 unsolicited fiction mss each month. Length: 3,000-4,000 words. Critiques rejected mss "when there is time.'' Sometimes recommends other markets.
How to Contact: Send complete ms with SASE. Reports in 1 month. Free sample copy.
Payment: Subscription and 20 author's copies.
Terms: Acquires all rights. Publication copyrighted.
Tips: Mss are rejected because they are "badly written; formula stories; stories that say nothing and get nowhere.'' Annual award for best short story published in AQ.

THE ARK RIVER REVIEW, The Ark River Review, Inc., Box 14, Wichita State University, Wichita KS 67208. (316)689-3130. Editors: Anthony Sobin and Jonathan Katz. "We are a literary magazine publishing only three-writer issues in poetry and fiction. We present large selections of an individual's work, usually by writers who have yet to publish a book with a major house. Our audience tends to be made up of well-educated people over 21, especially in the university community. The review is well-known as a magazine of sophisticated and leading-edge fiction and poetry." Publishes 2 double issues/year. Estab. 1971. Circ. 1,000 + .
Needs: Literary and contemporary. Chapbook-sized collections of short fiction (or novellas if self-contained). Total of 130 typewritten pages up to one-third of which may have been previously published in magazine form. "We are not as particular about the content as the way it is written and the general quality and sophistication of the piece. No *ordinary* fiction of any genre, science fiction or satire." Buys 3 mss/issue. Length: 75-130 pages.
How to Contact: Order sample fiction issues and then submit full ms with SASE. Reports in 1 week to several weeks and months if a finalist on mss. Sample copy $2.50 (specify fiction). Free guidelines with legal-sized SASE.
Payment: $250. 10 free author's copies.
Terms: Pays on publication for all rights (we will grant any reprint request made by the author, free).
Tips: "Our criteria are that you demonstrate an understanding of the literary tradition and advance upon what's already been done. We prefer to take a chance with something really new rather

than print what is highly competent but ordinary. See back issues for best indication. We tend to be very receptive to writers who are underpublished because their material has been too unusual for the audiences of widely distributed magazines. Be warned, however, that our standards are high and the competition for these three spots is very tough.''

ARTFUL DODGE, Artful Dodge Publications, Box 1473, Bloomington IN 47402. (812)332-0324. Editor-in-Chief: Daniel Bourne. ''There is no theme in this magazine, though we publish primarily first appearances in English of original works and translated works. Readers are interested in both American literature and foreign literature in translation.'' Published quarterly. Estab. 1979. Circ. 500.
Needs: Contemporary, erotica, ethnic, experimental, fantasy, feminist/lesbian, gay, literary, mainstream, prose poem, science fiction, serialized/excerpted novel, translations. Not interested in literature-coated propaganda in any of the above categories, no ''museum pieces'' in imitation of someone else, no empty cleverness. Receives 20 unsolicited fiction mss/month. Accepts 2-3 mss/issue, 10 mss/year. Length: 10,000 or so words maximum; 2,500 words average. Usually critiques rejected mss.
How to Contact: Send complete ms with SASE. Photocopied submissions OK. Reports in 2-3 months. Sample copy $2.75. Free fiction guidelines for legal size SAE and 1 first class stamp.
Payment: 1 free contributor's copy (subject to change for the better).
Terms: Pays on publication for first North American serial rights. Publication copyrighted.
Tips: ''If we take time to offer criticism, do not subsequently flood us with other stories no better than the first. If we say story would be better revised, take us at our word. We do work on revisions. If starting out, get as many readers, good ones, as possible. The voice of your story is as important as the plot; learn when you are disclosing your story effectively. And above all, read!''

AURA Literary/Arts Review, University of Alabama in Birmingham, 117 Campbell, University Station, Birmingham AL 35294. (205)934-3216. Editor: Laurie Youngers. ''We publish various types of fiction with an emphasis on short stories. Our audience is college students, the university community and literary-minded adults, the arts community.'' Published semiannually. Estab. 1974. Circ. 1,000.
Needs: Literary, contemporary, science fiction, men's, women's, feminist and ethnic (black). No mss longer than 5,000-6,000 words or pornographic material. Buys 2-3 mss/issue. Receives 8-10 unsolicited fiction mss each month. Length: 2,000-6,000 words. Critiques rejected mss ''when there is time.''
How to Contact: Send complete ms with SASE. Reports in 2 months. Free sample copy with 9x12 SASE and 90¢ postage.
Payment: Free author's copies.
Terms: Pays on publication for first North American serial rights.
Tips: ''If it's fiction and shows evidence of craft, we will consider it. No simultaneous submissions; please include biographical information.'' Mss are rejected because ''the storylines are unclear. Many writers try 'experimental' fiction before they have mastered the basics of telling a story.''

AURORA, Speculative Feminism, SF3, Society for the Furtherance & Study of Fantasy & Science Fiction, Box 1624, Madison WI 53701-1624. (608)267-7483 (days). Head: Jeanne Gomoll. Fiction Editor: Lucy Nash. Magazine of ''feminist-oriented science fiction and fantasy; fiction, poetry, articles, reviews, drawings, photographs for science fiction and fantasy fans and feminists.'' Published 3 times/year. Estab. 1976. Circ. 500.
Needs: Comics, fantasy, feminist/lesbian, gay, humor/satire, literary, science fiction, serialized/excerpted novel, translations, women's. ''Send for a list of upcoming themes and guidelines for submissions before sending mss. Nothing over 5,000 words, and/or those mss having nothing to do with science fiction or fantasy.'' Receives 10 unsolicited fiction mss/month. Accepts 1-2 mss/issue, 3-6 mss/year. Length: no minimum, 5,000 words maximum, 3,000 words average. Occasionally critiques rejected mss.
How to Contact: Query first. Send complete ms with SASE. Simultaneous and photocopied

submissions OK. Reports in 2 weeks on queries; 6-8 weeks on mss. Sample copy $3. Free guidelines.
Payment: 1 free contributor's copy.
Terms: Pays on publication for first North American serial rights. Publication copyrighted.
Tips: "Read a sample copy first. Make sure you know what kind of market you are sending to. Always enclose return postage. Feel free to send a follow-up if you haven't heard from us in two months."

BACKSPACE, 431 Schenley Hall, University of Pittsburgh, Pittsburgh PA 15260. (412)624-5801. Editor-in-Chief: Walter Ray Watson. Magazine "for a literary audience, for readers who enjoy new, fresh and serious work in poetry, fiction and art. Size of *Backspace* fluctuates between 68 and 96 pages per issue." Annually. Estab. 1973. Circ. 500.
Needs: Experimental, humor/satire, literary, mainstream, translations. "We want new writers; although we primarily publish submissions for students, we accept outside contributions. No science fiction, inspirational, juvenile, or psychic fiction considered. We want serious fiction; can be humorous, but work should be of high literary quality." Receives 10-20 unsolicited fiction mss/month. Accepts 4-8 mss/issue, 8-15 mss/year. Length: 300 words minimum, 5,000 words maximum, 3,500 words average. Critiques rejected mss "on request."
How to Contact: "Send up to 5 mss with SASE." Send query with SASE. Simultaneous and photocopied submissions OK. Sample copy $3.50 with 12x16 envelope with 5 first class stamps.
Payment: 3 contributor's copies. Charges $2 for extra copies.
Terms: Pays on publication for one-time rights. Publication copyrighted. "We may sponsor contest beginning in Fall '82. Send letter to inquire."
Tips: "The magazine thrives on diversity."

BALL STATE UNIVERSITY FORUM, Ball State University, Muncie IN 47306. (317)285-5188. Editors: Frances M. Rippy, Dick A. Renner. Magazine for "educated non-specialists." One issue a year devoted to fiction of all types. Quarterly. Estab. 1960. Circ. 600.
Needs: Adventure, condensed novel (30 pages or less), confession, contemporary, ethnic, experimental, fantasy, feminist, gothic/historical romance, historical/general, humor/satire, literary, mainstream, men's, prose poem, psychic/supernatural, religious/inspirational, romance (contemporary), science fiction, excerpted novel, suspense/mystery, translations, western, women's. Receives 20 unsolicited fiction mss/month. Accepts 15 mss/year. Length: 200 words minimum, 6,000 words maximum, 4,000 words average. "Only occasionally" critiques rejected mss.
How to Contact: Send complete ms with SASE. Simultaneous and photocopied submissions OK. Reports in 2 weeks on queries, 4 months on mss. Sample copy $2.50.
Payment: 3 free contributor's copies.
Terms: Pays on publication for all rights. Publication copyrighted.
Tips: "Send an original, polished story in a clean copy. If it is rejected, we tell you if the vote was close and suggest sending another. Read broadly, write carefully, revise painstakingly, submit mss persistently." Short stories from the *Forum* gave been listed in the Houghton Mifflin edition of *Best American Short Stories*."

BARE WIRES, A Harmless Flirtation with Wealth, 2343 Burgener Blvd., San Diego CA 92110. (714)276-6120. Editor: Helen McKenna.
Needs: Literary, women's, feminist, gay/lesbian, humor/satire, short, clever puzzles and cartoons. "We want very short pieces. No war, gore, porn or religious mss." Receives approximately 4 unsolicited fiction mss each month. Critiques rejected mss "when there is time."
How to Contact: Query with SASE. Simultaneous and photocopied submissions OK. Reports in 2 weeks.
Payment: 6 author's copies.
Tips: "Read a lot and learn to appreciate quality. Query first."

BARNWOOD, The Barnwood Press Cooperative, RR #2, Box 11C, Daleville IN 47334. (312)378-0921. Editors: Tom Koontz, Thom Tammaro. Magazine of "letters, poetry, and prose poems for writers and readers of poetry and prose." Quarterly. Estab. 1980. Circ. 700.

Needs: Prose poem. Receives 3-5 unsolicited fiction mss/month. Buys 1 fiction ms/issue, 2-3 mss/year. Length: 500 words maximum. Occasionally critiques rejected mss.
How to Contact: Query first with SASE. Photocopied submissions OK. Reports in 2 months on queries and mss. Sample copy for business size SAE and 1 first class stamp.
Payments: $5. 5 free contributor's copies.
Terms: Acquires first North American serial rights. Publication copyrighted.
Tips: "Most readers have noted the high quality of material published in *Barnwood*. We read each piece on its own merits. Quality of thought most important."

(LE) BEACON REVIEW, Le Beacon Presse, 2921 E. Madison St., Suite 7 FWM, Seattle WA 98122. Editor-in-Chief: K.S. Gormezano. Fiction Editor: Michael Boer. Publishes the work of new and unknown writers and artists in poetry, fiction and graphics for a college educated audience up to age 35. Quarterly. Estab. January 1980. Circ. 200.
Needs: Literary, contemporary, science fiction, fantasy, horror, men's, women's, erotica, western, mystery, adventure, humor, translations and short shorts. Buys 10-20 mss/year. Receives approximately 20 unsolicited fiction mss each month. Length: 25-1,000 words. Comments occasionally on rejected mss for 25¢/page.
How to Contact: Query or send complete ms with SASE. Varied reporting time. Sample copy $2 with size # 10 SASE.
Terms: Acquires one-time rights.
Tips: "Send us your shortest works with name and address on all sheets. We will not consider ANY unsolicited mss *unless* author is familiar or has obtained a sample copy ($2)." Mss are rejected because they are too long.

THE BELLINGHAM REVIEW, 412 N. State St., Bellingham WA 98225. Fiction Editor: Richard Dills. "A literary magazine featuring original short stories, novel excerpts and poetry of palpable quality." Semiannual. Estab. 1977. Circ. 500.
Needs: Literary, contemporary, psychic/supernatural, science fiction, fantasy, horror, feminist, gay/lesbian, erotica, gothic, mystery, humor, ethnic, serialized novels, condensed novels and translations. Buys 1-2 mss/issue. Length: 5,000 words. Critiques rejected mss "when there is time."
How to Contact: Send complete ms. Reports in 2 months. Sample copy $2.
Payment: 2 free author's copies plus 2-issue subscription. $1.50 charge for extras.
Terms: Acquires first North American serial and one-time rights. Publication copyrighted.
Tips: Mss are rejected for various reasons, "but the most common problem is too much *telling* and not enough *showing* of crucial details and situations."

THE BERKELEY MONTHLY MAGAZINE, 910 Parker St., Berkeley CA 94710. (415)848-7900. Editor: Adele Framer. Estab. 1970.
Needs: Contemporary, literary, experimental, adventure, historical, western, anti-war, women's and humor/satire. Receives approximately 50 unsolicited fiction mss each month. Critiques rejected mss "when there is time."
How to Contact: Send complete ms with SASE. Photocopied submissions OK. Reports in 6-10 weeks on ms.
Payment: Pays $50-150. Offers 25% kill fee for assigned ms not published.
Terms: Acquires first serial rights. Publication copyrighted.
Tips: Mss are rejected because of "poor style, over-concentration on plot. Most are maudlin, uninteresting, and immature. We have a very good reputation for fiction."

BERKELEY POETS CO-OPERATIVE, Berkeley Poets Workshop And Press, Box 459, Berkeley CA 94701. (415)527-1039. Editor-in-Chief: Charles Entrekin. Fiction Editor: Bruce Boston. Literary magazine—contemporary, speculative fiction. Published semiannually. Estab. 1969. Circ. 1,800.
Needs: Contemporary, experimental, fantasy, humor/satire, prose poem. Receives 5-10 unso-

licited fiction mss/month. Accepts 2-4 mss/issue, 4-8 mss/year. Length: 1,500 words minimum; 5,000 words maximum; 2,500 words average. Occasionally critiques rejected mss.

How to Contact: Send complete ms with SASE. Photocopied submissions OK. Reports in 1 month on queries; 1 month on mss. Sample copy $4.

Payment: Varies (prize money available if merited). 2 free contributor's copies.

Terms: Pays on publication for first rights. Publication copyrighted.

Tips: "Read past issue to gauge our preferences." Offers Berkeley Poets Cooperative Fiction Awards." No fiction submissions until fall 1983.

BEYOND FICTION, From Beyond Fiction to Fact, Aladoree Press, Box 61521, Vancouver WA 98666. (206)694-3466. Editor-in-Chief: Della Williamson. "Our magazine prints science fiction stories, puzzles and poetry for a general audience. An occasional fact article is done if interest shown. Our work force is made up of students. So we are *amateur*." Published quarterly. Estab. 1981. Circ. 250.

Needs: Science fiction. "We do not want to see homosexual or supernatural types; no outright foul language (an occasional damn or hell okay)." Receives 3 unsolicited fiction mss/month. Accepts 4 mss/issue, 16 mss/year. No restrictions on length. Occasionally critiques rejected mss.

How to Contact: Send complete ms with SASE. Simultanous submissions and previously published work OK. Reports in 2 months. Sample copy $3.50. Free fiction guidelines with SASE.

Payment: 1 contributor's copy. $3.50 charge for extras.

Terms: Pays on publication for first rights. Publication copyrighted.

Tips: "Mail in. Our primary concern is for the beginner. In both the writing and publishing aspects of magazines."

BIBLIOPHILOS, A Journal for Literati, Savants, Those Who Love Animals, Etc., Bibliophile Publishing Co., 48 N. Main St., Union City PA 16438. (814)438-7417. Editor-in-Chief: Gerald J. Bobango. Magazine which aims for "fiction (and nonfiction) by new, largely unpublished writers, especially short stories and nonrhyming poetry for educated, post high school, acedemically-oriented reading public." Quarterly. Estab. 1981. Circ. 400.

Needs: Ethnic, experimental, fantasy, gothic/historical romance, historical (general), horror, humor/satire, literary, mainstream, prose poem, psychic/supernatural, science fiction, serialized/excerpted novel, suspense/mystery, translations, young adult, avant-garde genre pieces. "Mss must be typed and double spaced." No "boy meets girl; accepting Jesus changed my life; Erma Bombeck material." Accepts 2 fiction mss/issue, 8 mss/year. Charges $2.65 reading fee. Length: 1,500 words minimum, 3,000 words maximum, 2,500 words average. Critiques rejected mss for "same $2.65 required with submission."

How to Contact: Query, query with clips of published work with SASE, or "telephone (not collect)." Simultaneous submissions, photocopied submissions and previously published work OK. Reports in 2 weeks on queries, 4 weeks on mss. Sample copy $2.65; guidelines for # 10 SAE and 1 first class stamp.

Payment: Subscription to magazine (1 issue) and 5 free contributor's offprints.

Terms: Pays on publication, retains first North American serial rights. Publication copyrighted. "Contest details will appear in Fall 1982 issue."

Tips: "Send us a compact well-constructed short story showing non-determined people (or beings) ignoring mass conventions/institutions successfully. Negative protagonists are best. Send perfect copy—no misspellings, typos, etc., double spaced typed mss only."

BILINGUAL REVIEW, Bilingual Review Press, Department of Foreign Language, Eastern Michigan University, Ypsilanti MI 48197. (313)487-0042. Editor-in-Chief: Gary D. Keller. Magazine of US Hispanic life: Poetry, short stories, other prose, theater. Published 3 times/year. Estab. 1974. Circ. 4,000.

Needs: US Hispanic creative literature, literary criticism. "We accept material in English or Spanish." US/Hispanic themes only. Receives 50 unsolicited fiction mss/month. Accepts 4 mss/issue, 12 mss/year. Often critiques rejected mss.

How to Contact: Send complete ms with SAE and loose stamps. Simultaneous and photocopied submissions OK. Reports in 4 weeks on mss. Sample copy $5.
Payment: 2 contributor's copies. Discount of 30% for extras.
Terms: Pays on publication for all rights or second serial rights (50% given to author as matter of policy). Publication copyrighted.
Tips: "Write about events reinforced by deep personal experience or knowledge."

BLACK CAT MYSTERY MAGAZINE, March Chase Publishing, Box 279, Toronto, Ontario, Canada M6S 4T3. Editor-in-Chief: F. Clare-Joynt. Magazine of "mystery stories (fiction)—detective and occult for mystery fans. Features writers from Canada, USA and British Commonwealth." Published quarterly. Estab. 1981. Circ. 2,000.
Needs: Horror, supernatural, suspense/mystery. "Must be in good taste—crime must not pay. No sex or excessive violence or bad language or profanity." Receives 100 unsolicited fiction mss/month. Accepts 8 mss/issue, 40 mss/year. Length: 1,000 words minimum; 3,000 words maximum; 2,000 words average. Critiques mss for $25 minimum. Occasionally recommends markets.
How to Contact: Query first with International Reply Coupons. Photocopied submissions OK. Reports in 2 weeks on queries, 2-3 months on mss. Sample copy $2.50. Fiction guidelines free with SAE and 1 IRC.
Payment: Pays 2¢/word and 1 contributor's copy. $2.50 charge for extras.
Terms: Pays on publication for all rights, first rights, second serial rights or one-time rights. Publication copyrighted.
Tips: "Get story moving right away, build suspense. Don't have a predictable ending. Make clear distinction between characters—don't keep switching from first names to last names."

BLACK JACK, Seven Buffaloes Press, Box 249, Big Timber MT 59011. Editor: Art Cuelho. "Main theme: Rural. Publishes material on the American Indian, farm and ranch, American hobo, the common working man, folklore, the Southwest, Okies, Montana, humor, Central California, etc. for people who make their living off the land. The writers write about their roots, experiences and values they receive from the American soil." Annual. Estab. 1973. Circ. 600.
Needs: Literary, contemporary, western, adventure, humor, American Indian, American hobo and parts of novels and long short stories. "Anything that strikes me as being amateurish, without depth, without craft, I refuse. Actually I'm not opposed to any kind of writing, if the author is genuine and has spent his lifetime dedicated to the written word." Buys 5-10 mss/year. Receives approximately 10-15 unsolicited fiction mss each month. Length: 3,500-5,000 words (there can be exceptions). If requested, critiques rejected mss "when there is time."
How to Contact: Query for current theme with SASE. Reports in 1 week on queries, 2 weeks on mss. Sample copy $3.
Payment: Pays 1-2 author's copies.
Terms: Acquires first North American serial rights and reserves the right to reprint material in an anthology or future *Black Jack* publications. Publication copyrighted. Rights revert to author after publication.
Tips: "Enthusiasm should be matched with skill as a craftsman. That's not saying that we don't continue to learn, but every writer must have enough command of the language to compete with other proven writers. Save postage by writing first to the editor to find out his needs. A small press magazine always has specific needs at any given time. I sometimes accept material from country writers that aren't all that good at punctuation and grammar, but make up for it with life's experience. This is not a highbrow publication; it belongs to the salt of the earth."

BLACK MARIA, Black Maria Collective, Box 25187, Chicago IL 60625. "Women's creative writing that is women identified. Poetry, fiction, articles, essays. For feminists for enjoyment, enlightenment, consciousness raising, living in a liberated way in the midst of oppression and finding sources of power." Annually. Estab. 1971. Circ. approximately 800.
Needs: Literary, feminist, and lesbian. "Images of women should be strong and creative. We do not consider material written by men or with male viewpoints, book-length material, or subjects

Close-up

Dev Hathaway
Black Warrior Review

Nine lively years old, going on ten. *Black Warrior Review*, the literary magazine of the University of Alabama, is excited about the upcoming tenth anniversary issue. Editor Dev Hathaway anticipates a landmark year for '83-'84. Circulation has just doubled (from 1,000 to 2,000), some especially fine writing has been submitted, and he hopes to begin paying contributors per page.

"In these times of budget cuts, a small magazine had better promote itself and find friends," Hathaway says. *BWR* did just that. Though they'd hit their stride as an established literary magazine, circulation had not kept pace. A national subscription drive, funded by grant money, really paid off. And Hathaway gives equal credit for their success to the university's sponsorship and the patronage of the Tuscaloosa community, including faculty, area businesses, professionals and public figures like Coach "Bear" Bryant. "We'd be a middling or defunct publication without our patrons," he concludes. In order to flourish, a literary magazine "must have charity at home."

Financing is one of the important differences between *BWR* and commercial publications. "A good literary magazine doesn't . . . make concessions in its work to advertising interests," Hathaway says. Another difference, closely related, is censorship. Where the commercials necessarily have some restrictive bias toward what pleases, what entertains, the literary magazine doesn't censor.

True, not all *Black Warrior* readers are pleased all the time—"not everyone is willing to give art the license to go where it pleases"—but generally their response has been excellent. Hathaway looks for "passion and vision *contained in language and style*" in fiction submitted to him. No particular style—he likes diversity. The acid test? "If any piece of fiction picks me up and lets me out in a new place, and

I can still feel the road humming under me, that's good writing," he says. Dev Hathaway also has more pragmatic advice to offer the fiction writer: "Don't take rejections on the chin. Keep sending your best work to different magazines. Don't multiple submit, either. Give a magazine a couple months; if you haven't heard from them, let them know you've decided to try elsewhere."

Spoken like a writer. And editor Hathaway has written lots. He has published fiction, poetry, and reviews in *Missouri Review*, *Quarterly West*, *Shenandoah*, *BWR*, and others. He is completing a book of short stories, *The Life of Howard and Other Stories*, and is about to receive a M.F.A. in creative writing from Alabama. (He already holds a M.A. in the same field from Hollins College.)

Serving first as poetry editor, Hathaway as editor is now responsible for content, design, production, promotion, and distribution—with the help of a staff of 20, mostly dedicated volunteers. Although his position, funded by the university, is half-time, *BWR* headquarters is busy all the time: "Our office is small and tight, bristling with ordered clutter, like most small magazines. We do our layout right here."

Ten years ago there was no literary magazine whatsoever at Alabama; *Black Warrior Review* has come a long way.

—Catherine Cooper

that are violent or denigrate women." Receives approximately 80 unsolicited fiction mss each month. Critiques rejected mss "when there is time."
How to Contact: Send complete ms with SASE. Reports in 2-6 months. Sample copy $3 with 8½x11 SAE and 60¢ postage. Subscription for 4 issues is $12.
Payment: 2 free author's copies.
Terms: Acquires first rights. Publication copyrighted.
Tips: "The motivation should be communicating with other women. We prefer giving exposure to heretofore unpublished women. *Black Maria* has a political philosophy that is apparent in issues so it helps to be familiar with our publication. Mss are rejected because the viewpoint is often lacking in terms of reinforcing the image of woman as capable of choice, action and fully-realized personhood. Study our back issues. Writers should submit work with the understanding that we are a volunteer collective and cannot respond and evaluate submissions within the time frames of commercial, mainstream publications."

THE BLACK SCHOLAR, The Black World Foundation, Box 7106, San Francisco CA 94120. (415)541-0311. Editor: Robert Allen. Fiction Editor: Conyus Calhoun. Magazine on black culture, research and black studies for Afro-Americans, college graduates and students. "We are also widely read by teachers, professionals, and intellectuals, and are required reading for many black and Third World Studies." Bimonthly. Estab. 1969. Circ. 15,000.
Needs: Literary, contemporary, men's, women's, juvenile, young adult and ethnic. No religious/inspirational, psychic, etc. Receives approximately 75 unsolicited fiction mss each month. Sometimes recommends markets. Length: 2,000-5,000 words.
How to Contact: Query with clips of published work with SASE. Reports in 3 weeks on queries, 1 month on mss. Free sample copy with SASE.
Payment: 12 author's copies and 1 year's free subscription to *TBS*.
Terms: Pays on publication for all rights. Publication copyrighted.

BLACK WARRIOR REVIEW, Box 2936, University AL 35486. (205)348-5526. Editor-in-Chief: Dev Hathaway. Fiction Editor: Rick Shelton. "We publish contemporary fiction, poetry, reviews, essays, interviews for a literary audience." Published semiannually. Estab. 1974. Circ. 1,000.
Needs: Contemporary, experimental, literary, mainstream, prose poem. No types that are clearly "types." Receives 75 unsolicited fiction mss/month. Accepts 5 mss/issue, 10 mss/year. Length: 7,500 words maximum; 3,000-5,000 words average. Occasionally critiques rejected mss.
How to Contact: Send complete ms with SASE. Photocopied submissions OK. Reports in 6 weeks. Sample copy $3. Free fiction guidelines for SAE and 1 first class stamp.
Payment: 2 contributor's copies.
Terms: Pays on publication. Publication copyrighted.
Tips: "Send only best work, after reviewing past issue(s). We are not a good bet for 'commercial' fiction. In 1983 the *Black Warrior Review* will award $500 to a fiction writer whose work has been published in either the fall 1982 or spring 1983 issue of the *BWR* to be announced in the fall 1983 issue. Regular submission deadlines are Oct. 1 for fall issue, Feb. 1 for spring issue.

BLOODRAKE, 1330 Bainbridge, La Crosse WI 54601. (608)784-1896. Editor-in-Chief: Philip Schuth. Fiction Editor: Julia Springsteen. "Anti-establishment, left-wing magazine of fiction and poetry relating to science fiction, fantasy, and horror for anti-fascists of all stripes." Semiannually. Estab. 1981. Circ. 1,000.
Needs: Experimental, fantasy, horror, science fiction. "No right-wing drivel; no hard technology science fiction stories." Receives 50 unsolicited science fiction mss/month. Buys 4 mss/issue, 8 mss/year. Length: 500 words minimum, 10,000 words maximum, 5,000 words average. Occasionally critiques rejected mss.
How to Contact: Send query, complete mss with SASE. Photocopied submissions OK. Reports in 1 week on queries, 2 weeks on mss. Sample copy $1.50 with 9¼x4 SAE and 1 first class stamps.
Payment: 2¢/word.

Terms: Pays on publication for first North American serial rights. Publication copyrighted.

BLOODROOT, Bloodroot, Inc., Box 891, Grand Forks ND 58201. Editor-in-Chief: Joan Eades. "We publish contemporary fiction and poetry of quality by women writers. *Bloodroot* is a showcase for women writers; our ideal audience is women who write and all those interested in good writing." Published irregularly (2 or 3 issues/year). Estab. 1976. Circ. 800.
Needs: Contemporary, experimental, feminist/lesbian, literary. No undistilled autobiography. Receives 50-75 unsolicited fiction mss/month. Accepts 3-10 mss/issue, 10-20 mss/year. Length: 1,000 words minimum; 10,000 words maximum; 3,000-5,000 words average. Occasionally critiques rejected mss.
How to Contact: Send complete mss with SASE. Photocopied submissions OK. Reports in 1 week to 6 months. Sample copy $2.50.
Payment: $5/page, grants permitting, and 2-6 contributor's copies. $2 charge for extras.
Terms: Pays on publication for first North American serial rights. Publication copyrighted.
Tips: "Buy a sample copy and study it."

THE BLOOMSBURY REVIEW, Owaissa Publishing Co., Box 8928. Denver CO 80201. (303)455-0593. Editor-in-Chief: Tom Auer. "*The Bloomsbury Review* is a book magazine. We publish book reviews, essays, short fiction, poetry and interviews with book-related persons." Bimonthly. Estab. 1980. Circ. 8,000.
Needs: Contemporary, literary, mainstream. Receives 80 unsolicited fiction mss/month. Buys 1 mss/issue. Length: 800 words minimum, 2,000 words maximum, 1,500 words average. Occasionally critiques rejected mss.
How to Contact: Query with clips of published work with SASE. Simultaneous and photocopied submissions OK. Reports in 2 months on queries and mss. Sample copy $2 with 8x10 SAE and 70¢ postage. Guidelines for legal size envelope and 1 first class stamp.
Payment: $5-25; $6/year subscription to magazine. 10 free contributor's copies.
Terms: Pays on publication for first rights. Rights revert back to writer. Publication copyrighted.
Tips: "Send well-written, well-thought-out, and well-documented work."

BLUELINE, Blue Mountain Lake, New York NY 12812. (518)352-7365. Editor-in-Chief: Alice Gilborn. "*Blueline* is interested in quality writing about the Adirondacks or other places similar in geography and spirit. We publish fiction, poetry, personal essays, book reviews, and oral history for those interested in the Adirondacks, nature in general, and well-crafted writing." Published semiannually. Estab. 1979. Circ. 550.
Needs: Adventure, contemporary, humor/satire, literary, prose poem, reminiscences, oral history, nature, outdoors. Receives 3-4 unsolicited fiction mss/month. Accepts 2-3 mss/issue, 4-6 mss/year. Length: 500 words minimum; 2,500 words maximum; 2,200 words average. Occasionally critiques rejected mss. Sometimes recommends other markets.
How to Contact: Send complete ms with SASE. Photocopied submissions OK. Submit mss Feb. 15-Apr.15; Aug. 15-Oct. 15. Reports in 6-8 weeks. Sample copy $2.25. Free fiction guidelines for 3½x6½ SAE and 1 first class stamp.
Payment: 1 contributor's copy plus 1 year subscription. $1.50 each for 3 or more extra copies; $1.75 each for less than 3.
Terms: Pays on publication for first rights. Publication copyrighted.
Tips: "We look for concise, clear, concrete prose that tells a story and touches upon a universal theme or situation. We prefer realism to romanticism but will consider nostalgia if well done. Pay attention to grammar and syntax. Avoid murky language, sentimentality, cuteness or folksiness. Read Strunk and White's *The Elements of Style*. Please include short bio and word count. Always enclose SASE." Mss are rejected because of "inappropriate subject matter; lack of conciseness; juvenile; trite. If ms has potential, we work with author to improve and reconsider for publication."

BOGG, A Magazine of British & North American Writing, Bogg Publications, 422 N. Cleveland St., Arlington VA 22201. (703)243-6019. US Editor: John Elsberg. Magazine—"½

American, ½ British, poetry, short fiction, reviews, essays on small press." Published 3 times a year. Estab. 1968. Circ. 400.
Needs: Comics, contemporary, erotica, experimental, humor/satire, literary, prose poem, science fiction. Nothing over 15 typewritten pages. Receives 25 unsolicited fiction mss/month. Accepts 2-3 mss/issue; 6-8 mss/year. Length: 4,000 words maximum; 1,500 words average. Occasionally critiques rejected mss.
How to Contact: Query first or send complete mss with SASE. Photocopied submissions and previously published work OK. Reports in 1 week on queries; 2 weeks on mss. Sample copy $2.
Payment: 2 contributor's copies. Reduced charge for extras.
Terms: Acquires one-time rights. Publication copyrighted.
Tips: "Read magazine first."

BOSTON REVIEW, Boston Critic Inc., 10B Mt. Auburn St., Cambridge MA 02138. (617)492-5478. Editor: Nicholas Bromell. "A bimonthly magazine of the arts and culture since 1975 for graduate school age and older readers." Bimonthly. Estab. 1975. Circ. 10,000.
Needs: Contemporary, ethnic, experimental, humor/satire, literary, mainstream, serialized/excerpted novel, translations. Receives 40-70 unsolicited fiction mss/month. Buys 4-6 mss/year. Length: 3,000 words maximum; 2,000 words average. Ocassionally critiques rejected ms.
How to Contact: Send complete ms with SASE. Simultaneous and photocopied mss OK. Reports in 2-3 months on mss. Sample copy $2.50.
Payment: $50-200; and 4 contributor's copies.
Terms: Pays on publication for first rights, second serial (reprint) rights, one-time rights and assignments on work-for-hire basis. Publication copyrighted.

BOTH SIDES NOW, An Alternative Journal of New Age/Aquarian Transformations, Free People Press, Rt. 6, Box 28, Tyler TX 75704. (214)592-4263. Editor-in-Chief: Elihu Edelson. Magazine. Estab. 1969. Circ. 2,000.
Needs: Fantasy, feminist, lesbian/gay ("acceptable if conducive to open attitudes in others"), humor/satire ("including political"), psychic/supernatural, religious inspirational ("much preferred"). "No violence (including S/M), prurience (pornography), fascistic views." Receives various number unsolicited fiction mss/month. Accepts various number mss/issue. Length: "about 4 magazine pages at most." Occasionally critiques rejected mss with "brief note."
How to Contact: Send complete ms with SASE. Simultaneous submissions, photocopied submissions and previously published work OK. Reports in 3 months on mss. Sample copy 50¢.
Payment: 6 free contributor's copies. Charges 3 for $1 for extra copies.
Terms: Pays on publication. "Authors retain rights." Publication copyrighted.
Tips: "Heed our editorial interests."

BOTTOMFISH MAGAZINE, Bottomfish Press, Language Arts Division, De Anza College, 21250 Steven Creek Blvd., Cupertino CA 95014. (408)996-4550. Editor-in-Chief: Frank Berry. Magazine of "contemporary poetry, fiction (under 5,000 words), excerpts of novels, black and white graphics and photos for literary and writing community." Annual. Estab. 1976. Circ. 500.
Needs: Experimental, literary, prose poem. "Literary excellence is our only criteria. We will consider all subjects except pornography." Receives 3-5 unsolicited fiction mss/month. Accepts 2-3 mss/issue. Length: 2,500-3,000 words minimum, 5,000 words maximum, 2,500 words average.
How to Contact: Send complete ms. SASE with ms. Photocopied submissions OK. Reports in 6 weeks on queries and mss. Sample copy for 8x10 envelope and 2 first class stamps.
Payment: 2 free contributor's copies. Charges $1.50 for extra copies.
Terms: Pays on publication for one-time rights.
Tips: "Strive for orginality and high level of craft; avoid clichéd or stereotyped characters and plots. We don't print slick, commercial fiction, regardless of quality."

BOX 749, The Printable Arts Society, Inc., Box 749, Old Chelsea Station, New York NY 10113. Editor: David Ferguson. "We publish fiction and poetry of every length and any theme; satire, belles-lettres, plays, music and any artwork reproducible by photo-offset. We have no particular stylistic or ideological bias. *Box 749* is directed to people of diverse backgrounds, education, income and age—an audience not necessarily above or underground. Such an audience is consistent with our belief that literature (plus art and music) is accessible to and even desired by a larger and more varied portion of society than has generally been acknowledged." Annually. Estab. 1972. Circ. 5,000.

Needs: Literary, contemporary, fantasy, humor and translations. "Fiction in any of the categories here could be art. If so, we would consider it for publication. We ask that all translations be accompanied by 'translation history' of the work: Has this work ever been translated into English? If so, when? By whom? Where did the translation appear?" Receives approximately 15 unsolicited fiction mss each month. Buys 10-15 mss/issue, 10-15 mss/year. Critiques rejected mss "when there is time." Occasionally suggests other markets.

How to Contact: Send complete ms with SASE. Reports in up to 3 months or longer on mss depending on length. Sample copy $3.25 for mail orders.

Payment: Author's copies. Charge for extras: regular $2.50 cover price unless buying in bulk.

Terms: Acquires all rights, but we reassign rights to author after publication. Publication copyrighted.

Tips: Mss are rejected because of "lack of imagination for character, not well written or not about anything that is worth sharing with the general public."

BREAD & ROSES, A Women's Journal of Issues and the Arts ,Box 1230, Madison WI 53711. Editor-in-Chief: Brenda Murphree. "Women's journal of issues and the arts, feminist in theme for women and men concerned about women's issues. Articles range from the scholarly to the personal; journal entries, dreams, experimental fiction welcome." Quarterly. Estab. 1977. Circ. 2,000

Needs: Contemporary, erotica, ethnic, experimental, fantasy, feminist/lesbian, gay, prose poem, psychic/supernatural, translations, women's. "Fiction need not be, should not be, self-consciously feminist, yet neither should it be anti-woman." Receives 2 unsolicited fiction mss/month. Accepts 1 mss/issue, 4-8 mss/year. Any length. Occasionally critiques rejected mss.

How to Contact: Send complete ms with SASE. Simultaneous, photocopied and previously published submissions OK. Reports in 2 months on mss. Sample copy $2.50 and 8 ½x11 envelope with 3 first class stamps. Fiction guidelines for business size envelope and 1 first class stamp.

Payment: 3 free contributor's copies; $2.50 charge for extras.

Terms: Pays on publication for first rights. Publication copyrighted.

Tips: *Bread & Roses* is carefully and thoughtfully read by an intelligent, well-educated audience. Keep sending us material. Ask for comments. Think before you write and edit after you write. Don't be trite. Don't write love stories. Write what you know. *Bread & Roses* is not difficult to break into. We welcome new writers who have never published before. We are particularly interested in experimental writings: prose poems, journal entries, dreams, etc. We use such material in our Arts section, as well as in Woman to Woman, a section of personal writing. Though we are feminist publication, all articles need not concern 'the movement.' Whatever thoughtful, intelligent women are interested in today, we're interested in."

THE BREATH OF THE PEOPLE, The Garlic Press, 1631 Grant St., Berkeley CA 94703. (415)548-2208. Editor-in-Chief: Susan Moon. Tabloid of "humorous material—drawings, articles, poems, stories, by both children and adults." Published quarterly. Estab. 1977. Circ. 500.

Needs: Comics, humor/satire, juvenile. "Anything by adults should be humorous (in the broadest sense of the word)." Receives 3 unsolicited fiction mss/month. Accepts 1 ms/issue; 4 mss/year. Length: 25 words minimum; 2,500 words maximum; 750 words average.

How to Contact: Send complete ms with SASE. Simultaneous, photocopied and previously published submissions OK. Reports in 3 weeks. Free sample copy.

Payment: None.

Terms: Publication copyrighted.

BRIDGE: Asian American Perspectives, Asian Cine Vision, 32 E. Broadway, New York NY 10002. (212)925-8685. Fiction Editor: Shanlon Wu. Magazine intended "to serve as a vehicle for Asian American writers, poets. *Bridge* seeks to express the views of Asian Americans via fiction, poetry, feature articles, community news and reviews on the arts." Published quarterly. Estab. 1971. Circ. 5,000.

Needs: Writing by or concerning Asia Americans. Receives 3 or more unsolicited fiction mss/month. Accepts varied number of mss. Length: 15 typed double-spaced pages maximum. Occasionally critiques rejected mss.

How to Contact: Query first or send complete ms with SASE. Reports in 2 months on queries; 3-6 months on mss.

Payment: Complimentary copies.

Terms: Publication copyrighted.

Tips: "Most of our rejects fall into 2 categories: 1) the subject matter is entirely inappropriate for us. This always makes me think that many people/writers do *not* research the magazines they submit to!! 2) The quality of the fiction doesn't meet our standards."

BRILLIANT STAR/CHILD'S WAY, National Spiritual Assembly of the Baha'is of the US, 5010 Austin Rd., Chattanooga TN 37343. (615)875-5443. Editor-in-Chief: M.K. Radpour. Fiction Editor: M.K. Editor. "Children's magazine which promotes such principles of the Baha'i Faith as harmony of races, religions and nationalities, equality of sexes." For children, aged 5-12. Bimonthly. Estab. 1968. Circ. 2,000.

Needs: "Especially value material emphasizing values, though non-didactic in tone." No "preachy or superstitious stories; or too great emphasis on unpleasant truths." Receives 30 unsolicited fiction mss/month. Accepts 1 ms/issue; 6 mss/year. Length: 100 words minimum; 1,200 words maximum; 800 words average.

How to Contact: Send complete ms with SASE. Simultaneous and photocopied submissions OK. Reports in 2 weeks on mss. Sample copy for 10x9 SAE and 80¢ postage. Fiction guidelines for # 10 envelope and 20¢ postage.

Payment: "We make no payments; all manuscripts are considered donations."

Terms: Acquires all rights. Publication copyrighted.

Tips: "Keep trying."

BROADSHEET MAGAZINE, Broadsheet Magazine, Ltd., Box 5799, Auckland, New Zealand. 794-751AUCK. Editor: Sanda Coney. Feminist magazine of news, reviews, interviews, fiction and poetry for people interested in feminism. Monthly. Estab. June 1972. Circ. 10,000.

Needs: Women's, feminist and gay/lesbian. Receives 5 unsolicited fiction mss each month. Length: 2,500 words. Critiques rejected mss "when there is time."

How to Contact: Send complete ms with SASE. Reports in 1 month on mss. Sample copy $2.

Payment: No payment.

Terms: Publication copyrighted.

BROOMSTICK, A Periodical by, for, and About Women Over Forty, 3543 18th St., San Francisco CA 94110. (415)552-7460. Editors: Mickey Spencer and Polly Taylor. "Our first priority in selecting and editing material is that it convey clear images of older women that are positive, that it take a stand against the denigration of older women which our culture purveys, and that it offer us alternatives which will make our lives better." For "women over forty interested in being part of a network which will help us all develop understanding of our life situations and to acquire the skills to improve them." Bimonthly. Estab. 1978. Circ. 3,000.

Needs: Adventure, comics, ethnic, feminist/lesbian, gay (not male-lesbian only), women's. No mss of "romantic love, saccharine acceptance, about men or young women." Receives 10 unsolicited fiction mss/month. Accepts 2-3 mss/issue; 20 mss/year. Occasionally critiques rejected mss.

How to Contact: Send complete mss with SASE. Simultaneous, photocopied and previously published submissions OK. Reports in 3 months on queries and mss. Sample copy for $2.50. Fiction guidelines for $2.50.

Payment: 2 free contributor's copies; $3 charge for extras.

Tips: "Read our writers' packet."

THE BROWN REVIEW, Brown University, Box 1852, English Dept., Providence RI 02912. (401)863-3265. Fiction Editor: Jessica Brilliant. Magazine of "poetry, short stories, interviews with working writers for college educated lovers of good literature." Semiannually. Estab. 1981. Circ. 500.
Needs: Contemporary, experimental, fantasy, humor/satire, literary, mainstream, prose poem. Receives "several" unsolicited fiction mss/month. Accepts various number mss/issue "when funding available." Length: 1,000 words minimum, 4,000 words maximum, 2,000 words average. Occasionally critiques rejected mss.
How to Contact: Send complete ms with SASE. Simultaneous and photocopied submissions OK. Reports in 6 weeks on queries and mss. Sample copy $2.50 and SAE. Fiction guidelines with 7½x10½ envelope.
Payment: 2 free contributor's copies; $2.50 charge for extras.
Tips: "Send short, short fiction that elicits some form of satisfaction from reader; no tricks."

BUFF, S.U.N.Y. at Buffalo, Dept. of English, 306 Clemens Hall, Buffalo NY 14260. (716)636-2570. Fiction Co-Editors: Edmund Cardoni, Dennis Cullinan. Magazine of "artful and entertaining fiction and poetry inclined towards the avant garde for literate readers, other writers, and the university community." Semiannually. Estab. 1981. Circ. 500.
Needs: Contemporary, experimental, excerpted novel. No "formula ficton of any kind." Receives "a large number of fiction mss but it varies each month." Accepts 10 mss/issue. Length: no minimum, 3,600 words maximum, 1,250-1,500 words average. Occasionally critiques rejected mss.
How to Contact: Send complete ms with cover letter and "short bio" with SASE. Photocopied submissions OK. Reports in 3 months on mss. Sample copy for SAE and 4 first class stamps.
Payment: 2 free contributor's copies; postage charge for more than 2 copies.
Terms: Acquires first rights, one-time rights. Publication copyrighted.
Tips: "Readers are excited, enthusiastic, critical of short stories. Expect a critical reading by graduate student editors at a university English department renowned for its celebrated (and predominantly avant garde) faculty of writers and critics."

BUG TAR, Bug Tar Press, Box 1534, San Jose, CA 95109. (408)279-2517. Editor: Scott Mace. Fiction Editor: M.A. Olds. "*Bug Tar* explores the question: Is mankind becoming a large insect colony? Not literally, of course, but intellectually and spirtually. Anything that touches upon the loss of individuality, society's increasing regimentation, and other, larger human themes is welcome. But our fiction is also personal and human, not expository or experimental. All approaches—humorous, grotesque, what have you—are explored. *Bug Tar* is for all who wish to think, question and not be merely entertained." Quarterly. Estab. August 1977. Circ. 50.
Needs: Literary, contemporary and humor. No experimental fiction. Buys 4 mss/issue. Length: 5,000 words, maximum of 20,000.
How to Contact: Send for sample issue first with SASE. Reports in 2 months on queries, 2 months on mss. Sample copy $2.
Payment: Contributor's copies. 75¢ charge for extra copies.

BUSY BEES' NEWS, People's Dispensary for Sick Animals, PDSA House, South St. Dorking, Surrey, England RH4 2LB, 888219. Editor-in-Chief: R.I. Cookson. "Magazine for children up to 11 years old interested in animals; stories, puzzles, things to do, cartoons, jokes, features, etc. on animals—mostly *pet* animals, but not essential." Bimonthly. Estab. 1934. Circ. 10,000.
Needs: Juvenile. "Anything considered, fact or fiction for children." Receives 20-30 unsolicited fiction mss/month. Accepts 6 mss/issue, 36 mss/year. Length: 600-800 words maximum. Occasionally critiques rejected mss.
How to Contact: Send complete ms.

BYLINE, McCarville Publications, 5805-C N. Grand Blvd., Oklahoma City OK 73118. (405)843-9534. Editor-in-Chief: Mike McCarville. Magazine for the "encouragement of writers and poets, with emphasis on inspiring beginners." Monthly. Estab. 1981. Circ. 2,800.

Needs: Literary, suspense/mystery, "short stories with a writing or literary twist or setting." No science fiction. Receives 100 unsolicited fiction mss/month. Accepts 2-3 mss/issue, 40-50 mss/year. Length: 2,000 words maximum, 1,750 words average. Occasionally critiques rejected mss.
How to Contact: Send complete ms with SASE. Photocopied submissions OK. "All fiction must be original and unpublished previously." Reports in 6-8 weeks on mss. Sample copy $2. Fiction guidelines for # 10 envelope and 1 first class stamp.
Payment: $60-200. 1 free contributor's copies; $1 charge for extras if subscriber, $2 if not. Offers 50% kill fee on articles only.
Terms: Pays on acceptance for first rights. Publication copyrighted.
Tips: "Try us, work with us, don't get discouraged and never quit. Submit a professional manuscript with SASE; story line must be strong, include a writing or literary twist and have an ending (surprise preferred)." Sponsors short story and poetry contests several times a year.

CACHE REVIEW, Cache Press, 131 Fishback, Ft. Collins CO 80521. (303)221-0846. Editor: Steven Brady. Magazine which publishes "quality writing of all styles and modes for anyone interested in good writing." Semiannually. Estab. 1982. Circ. 200-500.
Needs: Experimental, fantasy, historical (general), horror, humor/satire, mainstream, prose poem, science fiction, serialized/excerpted novel, suspense/mystery, translations. "We will look at anything. The only criterion is excellence." Receives 10-20 unsolicited fiction mss/month. Accepts 3-6 mss/issue, 6-12 mss/year. Length: 10,000 words maximum. "Nearly every manuscript will receive some critical comment."
How to Contact: Send complete ms with SASE. Photocopied submissions OK, "but we prefer the original." Reports in 2 weeks on mss. Sample copy $1 with 9x12 envelope and 3 first class stamps. Fiction guidelines free with legal size envelope and 1 first class stamp.
Payment: 2 free contributor's copies; $1.50 charge for extras.
Terms: Pays on publication for all rights. Publication copyrighted. "Cash awards may be presented for the best pieces of fiction and/or poetry in each issue."
Tips: "Send your best. We are looking for excellence and authenticity of voice. Give us an honest story, not one manipulated for a specific market."

CALIFORNIA HORSE REVIEW, The Largest All-Breeds Horse Magazine in the Nation, Related Industries Corp., Box 646, North Highlands CA 95660. (916)485-4301. Editor: Bill Shepard. Magazine which "provides entertaining and useful information to professional horsemen and to serious amateurs for horse owners, breeders, trainers, competitors and pleasure riders." Monthly. Estab. 1964. Circ. 8,000.
Needs: Adventure, condensed novel, western. "Horse angle must be predominant." Receives approximately 16 unsolicited fiction mss/month. Accepts 1 mss/issue, 12 mss/year. Length: 1,500 words minimum, 5,000 words maximum, 2,500 words average. "Rarely" critiques rejected mss.
How to Contact: Query first. Photocopied and previously published submissions OK "if published in non-competitive magazine." Reports in 3-4 weeks on queries. Sample copy $1.25 and # 10 envelope with one first class stamp. Fiction guidelines for # 10 envelope and one first class stamp.
Payment: Pays $50-125. 2 free contributor's copies.
Terms: Pays on acceptance for first rights, first North American serial rights. Publication copyrighted.
Tips: "Read the magazine. If you have a story to tell that has a good horse angle, describe the story in a query. Don't oversell. Produce what you say you have. If you are convinced that it is a good story, send it without a query."

CALIFORNIA PELICAN, California Pelican & Berkeleyan Assoc., 515 Eshlemon Hall, U.C. Berkeley, Berkeley CA 99720. Editor: John P. Farley. Magazine of "humor, cartoons, parodies, clever sayings, trenchant observations upon the human condition, witty epigrams and sex jokes for U.C. Berkeley students, alumni and staff—well educated, bright, middle-class, somewhat cynical at times." Published 3 times/school year. Estab. 1903. Circ. 5,000.

Needs: Comics, humor/satire. "Best to be a local writer, affiliated with U.C." No "*National Lampoon* or *Mad Magazine* ripoffs." Receives 3-5 unsolicited fiction mss/month. Accepts 1-3 mss/issue, 3-9 mss/year. Length: varies. Occasionally critiques rejected mss.

How to Contact: Send query with SASE. Photocopied submissions OK. Reports in 1-4 weeks on queries. Sample copy $1.

Payment: 1-3 free contributor's copies.

CALIFORNIA QUARTERLY, 100 Sproul Hall, University of California, Davis CA 95616. 9916)752-2257. Editor-in-Chief: Elliot Gilbert. Fiction Editors: Diane Johnson and Charles Rosenthal. Managing Editor: Katrina V. Ringrose. Literary magazine of poetry, fiction, graphics for readers of literary material. Published quarterly. Estab. 1971. Circ 600.

Needs: Adventure, condensed novel, confession, contemporary, erotica, ethnic, experimental, fantasy, feminist/lesbian, gay, humor/satire, mainstream, men's, prose poem, psychic/supernatural, religious/inspirational, romance (contemporary), science fiction, serialized/excerpted novel, suspense/mystery, translations, western and women's. "We consider all types of writing, if it's done well; good writing and a story line are a must. We don't want to see a writer's first attempts, or stories that happened to the writer and aren't fictionalized." Receives 40-50 unsolicited fiction mss/month. Accepts 8 mss/issue, 18 mss/year. Length: 5,000 words maximum ("exceptions made"). Occasionally critiques rejected mss.

How to Contact: Send complete ms with SASE. Photocopied submissions OK (if good copy). Reports in 1-2 months on ms.

Payment: $2 per published page and 2 contributor's copies.

Terms: Pays on publication for first rights. Publication copyrighted. "Announcements appear in magazine about occasional fiction contests."

CALLALOO, A Black South Journal of Arts and Letters, University of Kentucky, English Department, Lexington KY 40506. (606)257-3114 and 257-3605. Editor-in-Chief: Charles H. Rowell. Magazine of "fiction, drama, photography, poetry, criticism and book reviews for a professional, general audience." Published triannually. Estab. 1976. Circ. 700.

Needs: Adventure, contemporary, ethnic, literary. "Works are primarily by Afro-American, Caribbean, and African writers." Receives 15 unsolicited fiction mss/month. Accepts 3 mss/issue, 6 mss/year. Length: 1,000 words minimum, 5,000 words maximum, 2,500 words average.

How to Contact: Send complete ms with SASE. Simultaneous and clear photocopied submissions OK. Reports in 6 months. Sample copy $5.

Payment: 2 free contributor's copies.

Terms: Pays on publication for simultaneous rights. Publication copyrighted.

CALLIOPE, Creative Writing Program, Roger Williams College, Bristol, RI 02809. (401)255-2185. Advisory Editor: Martha Christina. "We are an eclectic little magazine publishing contemporary poetry, fiction, interviews, and reviews of other little magazines for those who appreciate fine contemporary writing." Published semiannually. Estab. December 1977. Circ. 300.

Needs: Literary, contemporary, men's, women's, feminist, humor and experimental/innovative. "We are receptive to a wide variety of subject matter but insist on high quality work in the above categories. We try to include 3 pieces of fiction in each issue." Receives approximately 10-20 unsolicited fiction mss each month. Length: 2,500 words. Critiques rejected mss "when there is time."

How to Contact: Send complete ms with SASE. Reports immediately to 3 months on mss. Sample copy $1.

Payment: 2 free author's copies. $1 charge for extras.

Terms: Rights revert to author on publication. Publication copyrighted.

Tips: "We are not interested in reading anyone's very first story. If the piece is good it will be given careful consideration. Reading a sample copy of *Calliope* is recommended." Mss are rejected because of "poor characterization, too much summary narration, not enough dialogue."

CALYX, A Journal of Art & Literature by Women, Calyx, Inc., Box B, Corvallis OR 97339. (503)753-9384. Managing Editor: M. Donnelly. Associate Editors: Eva Bowman, Meredith Jenkins, Rebecca Gordon, Eleanor Wilner and Joyce Thompson. Publishes prose, poetry, art and critical and review articles. *Calyx* editors are seeking innovative and literary fiction works. Published triannually. Estab. June 1976. Circ. 2,000.

Needs: Accepts 2-3 mss/issue, 9 mss/year. Receives approximately 100 unsolicited fiction mss each month. Length: 5,000 words maximum. Critiques rejected mss "when there is time."

How to Contact: Send ms with SASE and biographical notes. Reports in up to 6 months on mss. Sample copy $4.75.

Payment: "In copies."

Terms: Pays on publication for one-time rights and copyright by *Calyx*. Publication copyrighted.

Tips: Most mss are rejected because "the writers are not familiar with *Calyx*—writers should read *Calyx* and be familiar with the publication."

CANADIAN AUTHOR & BOOKMAN, Canadian Authors Association, Suite 412, 131 Bloor St. W, Toronto, Ontario, Canada M5S 1R1. Fiction Editor: Geoff Hancock. "We are mainly a craft magazine for Canadian writers, publishing articles that tell how to write and where to sell. We publish half-a-dozen poems and one short story per issue as well as the craft articles. We aim at the beginning or newly emerging writer who reads us to find out how to create the salable article (story or poem) and reap the benefits of his seminal imagination and feverish activity." Quarterly. Estab. 1921. Circ. 4,000.

Needs: Literary, contemporary, science fiction, fantasy, horror, men's, women's, feminist, gothic, romance, western, mystery, adventure and humor. "No porn, near-miss inspirational, personal essays masquerading as short stories, formula writing with tired blood or whatever else is trite, banal, or just dull." Buys 1 ms/issue, 4 mss/year. Length: 2,000-3,500 words. Sometimes recommends other markets.

How to Contact: Send complete ms with SASE. Reports in 1 month on mss. Sample copy $3.

Payment: $125. Free author's copy.

Terms: Pays on publication for first rights.

Tips: "Send Geoff Hancock a story that will dominate memory and you are in business. He reads with an eye for originality, flair, and imaginative work. He asks, whatever the form or procedure of the story, that it succeed in the author's intention. To write good stories, you must read great stories, and read them from the inside out. The writer's strategy must be examined, from the overall structure, to the rise and fall of the sentences, to the placement of the punctuation. For more specific information send $1 to Canadian Authors' Assoc. with your request for a reprint of "The Green Glad Bag Review" by Geoff Hancock (*CAB, November 1979*)."

CANADIAN FICTION MAGAZINE, Box 946, Station F, Toronto, Ontario, Canada M4Y 2N9. Editor: Geoffrey Hancock. "This magazine is a quarterly anthology devoted exclusively to the contemporary creative writing of writers and artists in Canada and Canadians living abroad. Fiction only, no poetry. The ideal reader of *CFM* is a writer or somebody interested in all the modes, manners, voices, and conventions of contemporary fiction." Quarterly. Estab. 1971. Circ. 1,800.

Needs: Literary. "Theme, style, length, and subject matter are at the discretion of the author. The only requirement is that the work be of the highest possible literary standard. Each issue is approximately 148 pages. Buys 10 mss/issue, 35 mss/year. No restriction on length.

How to Contact: Send complete ms with SASE or IRC. Reports in 6 weeks on mss.

Payment: $10/page plus one year subscription.

Terms: Pays on publication for first North American serial rights.

Tips: "It is absolutely crucial that three or four issues be read. We sell back issues up to 1976 for $3; current issue $5.50 (postage included). Some double issues are $7.85. *CFM* publishes Canada's leading writers as well as those in early stages of their careers. This is a professional literary magazine. A wide knowledge of contemporary literature (in English, and in translation) plus expertise in creative writing, modern fiction theories, current Canadian literature, and the innovative short story would be of great help to a potential contributor. *CFM* is an independent journal not associated with any academic institution. Each issue includes French Canadian fiction in translation, interviews with well known Canadian writers on the techniques of their fiction, forums and manifestoes on the future of fiction, as well as art work and reviews. $250 annual prize for the best story submitted in either French or English. Previous winners include John Metcalf, Mavis Gallant, Leon Rooke, W.P. Kinsella, Anne Copeland, Keath Fraser, and Guy Vanderhaege.''

THE CAPILANO REVIEW, Purcell, 2055 Purcell Way, North Vancouver, British Columbia, Canada V7J 3H5. Editor-in-Chief: Ann Rosenberg. Fiction Editor: Robert G. Sherrin. High quality literary and art magazine for broad literary and artistic community. Published quarterly. Estab. 1972. Circ. 1,000.
Needs: Experimental. "We look for freshness." No derivative or traditional fiction. Receives 100 unsolicited fiction mss/month. Accepts 3 mss/issue; 12 mss/year. Sometimes recommends markets.
How to Contact: Send complete ms. Simultaneous and photocopied submissions OK. Reports in several months on queries. Sample copy $3. Free fiction guidelines with SAE.
Payment: $10-40 and 2 contributor's copies. 40% discount for extras.
Terms: Pays on publication for first North American serial rights. Publication copyrighted.
Tips: "Read several issues before submitting. We notify our subscribers of our annual competition which in the past has been for play scripts or fiction." Rejections occur because "it is difficult to find fresh, non-derivative fiction."

CAPRICE, 2 Bucks Ave., Watford, Herts England UK WD1 4AS. Telephone number: (Watford)29784. Editors: Keith Seddon and Jocelyn Almond. Magazine. "We want to fight establishment boredom—be that in fiction, nonfiction, politics, literature, art. Basically we're looking for innovative material of all sorts. Readers are artistic and semi-artistic thinking young people, students, the unemployed, the bored—strictly non-establishment." Published annually. Estab. 1980. Circ. 200.
Needs: Erotica, ethnic, experimental, fantasy, gay, humor/satire, literary, mainstream, absurdist. No "junk which other (establishment mostly) mags publish." Receives about 6 unsolicited fiction mss/month. Accepts about 6 mss/issue. Length: 50 words minimum; 3,000 words maximum, 1,200 words average. Occasionally critiques rejected mss. Sometimes recommends markets.
How to Contact: Send complete ms with SASE. Simultaneous, photocopied, and previously published submissions OK. Reports in 2 months. Sample copy for .65 pound, size A4 SAE and 1.70 pound (airmail), .70 pound (surface). Fiction guidelines for size A5 SAE and .40 pound (airmail).
Payment: 1 free contributor's copy.
Terms: "Whatever it takes to make us legal, and not to infringe existing copyright agreements." Publication copyrighted.
Tips: "Be natural. Be original. Say something you believe in. Knock the establishment. Be shocking. Be a genius. Type it properly. Study the magazine you are going to submit to. Don't copy it. Figure out the aim of its editor. Further that aim with your offering. Don't anger him with shoddy mss, or lack of SAE, or cocky self-appraisals, like 'I've got a BA in creative writing' coz we know what that really means."

CAROLINA QUARTERLY, Greenlaw Hall 066A, University of North Carolina, Chapel Hill NC 27514. (919)962-0244. Editor-in-Chief: Marc Manganaro. Fiction Editor: Mary Titus. "Literary journal: fiction; poetry; graphics and some reviews, for that audience—whether academic or not—with an interest in the best in poetry and short fiction." Published tri-quarterly. Estab. 1948. Circ. 1,000.
Needs: No pornography. Receives 150-200 unsolicited fiction mss/month. Buys 3-6 mss/issue, 12-18 mss/year. Length: 7,000 words maximum; no minimum; no preferred length. One story at a time. Occasionally critiques rejected mss.

How to Contact: Send complete ms with SASE to Fiction Editor. Photocopied submissions OK. Reports in 2-4 months. Sample copy $4; SASE for writer's guidelines.
Payment: $3/printed page; 2 free contributor's copies. Regular copy price for extras.
Terms: Pays on publication for first North American serial rights. Publication copyrighted.
Tips: "We publish a good many unsolicited stories; *CQ* is a market for newcomer and professional alike."

CEDAR ROCK, Cedar Rock Press, 1121 Madeline, New Braunfels TX 78130. (512)625-6002. Editor: David C. Yates. Fiction Editor: John O'Keefe. "We publish quality fiction and poetry, as well as essays pertaining to literature. We direct our publication to intelligent and sensitive persons, not necessarily college-educated." Quarterly. Estab. January 1976. Circ. 2,000.
Needs: Contemporary, psychic/supernatural, science fiction, fantasy and adventure. "Fiction should be readable and meaningful. We prefer stories with a strong plot, with effective characterization, and with something significant to say." Buys 1-2 mss/issue, 4-8 mss/year. Receives approximately 60 unsolicited fiction mss each month. Length: 1,000-3,500 words.
How to Contact: Send complete ms with SASE to John O'Keefe, 732 W. Coll, New Braunfels TX 78130. Reports in 1 month on mss. Sample copy $2.50. Free guidelines with legal-sized SASE.
Payment: $20-200. Free author's copy. $2 charge for extras.
Terms: Pays on acceptance for first North American serial rights. Publication copyrighted.
Tips: "Look at back issues. Write stories with strong characterization. Keep submitting. Important: Send fiction to our fiction editor, John O'Keefe. Do not send it to our central office." Rejects mss because "we publish serious fiction. Most mss coming in unsolicited are slick in nature. Those writers are not familiar with our magazine."

CELERY, Dept. of English, Western Michigan Univ., Kalamazoo MI 49008. (616)383-0972. Editor: John Cooley. "*Celery* is a magazine of poetry, fiction, feature articles and interviews, affiliated with the writing programs at Western Michigan University. Our readership seems to be well read and reasonably discriminating; the majority of our readers are also writers." Published semiannually. Estab. 1977. Circ. 400-500.
Needs: Contemporary, ethnic, experimental, humor/satire, literary, prose poem. *No* comics, gothic/historical romance, confessions, condensed novels, or inspirational works. Receives 5 unsolicited fiction mss/month. Accepts 3-4 mss/issue, 6-7 mss/year. Length: 6,000 words maximum; 2,500 words average. Critiques rejected mss "if we like the work but are unable to use it."
How to Contact: Send complete ms with SASE. Photocopied submissions OK. Reports in 4 months. Sample copy $1.50.
Payment: 2 contributor's copies; $1 charge for extras.
Terms: Pays on publication for first North American serial rights. Publication copyrighted.
Tips: "Although we are university affiliated, we are independent enough to accept mss from around the country. Buy a few back copies and you will get a sense of what we are looking for."

CHANDRABHAGA, A Magazine of New Writing, The Chandrabhaga Society, Tinkonia Bagicha, Cuttack, Orissa, India 753 001. 20-566. Editor: Jayanta Mahapatra. Magazine of "poetry mainly, fiction, essays on poetry/fiction, with a bias on Indian poetry for University English departments, poets, writers and discriminating readers. Semiannually. Estab. 1979. Circ. 500.
Needs: Contemporary, prose poem, translations. Receives 10 unsolicited fiction mss/month. Accepts 1-2 mss/issue, 2-3 mss/year. Length: 1,000 words minimum, 4,000 words maximum, 3,000 words average.
How to Contact: Send complete ms with SASE. Photocopied submissions OK. Reports in 3 months on ms. Sample copy $5 with $3 postage.
Payment: 2 free contributor's copies; $2.50 charge for extras.
Terms: Pays on publication for first rights.

CHANGIN', Changin' Magazine, 833 Koman Dr., Paramus NJ 07652. Fiction Editor: Carol Weissbein. "A magazine for Bob Dylan fans which publishes articles related to Bob Dylan in some way—reviews, interpretations, listings, interviews; fiction relating to Bob Dylan (rock music, related topics). For his fans to keep up with his career and to keep in touch with other fans. Semiannual. Estab. 1976. Circ. 1,000 + .

Needs: Contemporary. Does not want "anything that could not be construed as somehow, at least remotely, related to Bob Dylan or of special interest to his fans." Length: 700-2,800 words.

How to Contact: Query. Reports in 1 month on query and 2 months on mss. Sample copy $2.

Payment: 2 free author's copies. $2 charge for extras.

Terms: Acquires all rights.

Tips: "Be a clear-writing, clear-thinking Bob Dylan fan."

CHANNEL X, Padre Productions, Box 1275, San Luis Obispo CA 93406. (805)543-5404. Editor: Lachlan P. MacDonald. Fiction Editor: Mack Sullivan. "*Channel X* is a paperback fiction anthology featuring vignettes, short shorts and brief experimental forms of fiction. All stories have a twist, a bizarre note, or break taboos of one kind or other. It is for the viewer of TV who wants quick fiction that engages his attention briefly and stays in the mind and for the short-attention-span yet sophisticated reader." Annually. First volume, Spring, 1983.

Needs: Literary, contemporary, fantasy, adventure, and humor. "We are also publishers of novels in the categories checked above. No long stories." Buys 40-60 mss/year. Receives approximately 40-60 unsolicited fiction mss each month. Length: 100-1,200 words. Critiques rejected mss "when there is time."

How to Contact: Send complete ms with SASE. Reports in 2 months on mss.

Payment: Pro-rated royalties on each edition. Free author's copies. Full rate for extras.

Terms: Pays on publication for first North American serial rights, book rights and radio-TV rights. Publication copyrighted.

Tips: "Make every word count. Rewrite, polish. Type clearly. Innovate. Think of the reader. Avoid photocopies, unclean typewriter keys, spelling errors (they kill it right there). *Channel X* is dedicated to reviving and vitalizing the short short form of fiction that will be remembered by readers of the American vignettes, Mark Hellinger, etc. Welcomes new writers. First edition features 85% of first-time authors."

THE CHARITON REVIEW, Northeast Missouri State University, Kirksville MO 63501. (816)785-4499. Editor: Jim Barnes. "We demand only excellence in fiction and fiction translation for a general and college readership." Semiannually. Estab. 1975. Circ. 700 + .

Needs: Literary, contemporary and translation. Buys 3-5 mss/issue, 6-10 mss/year. Length: 3,000-6,000 words. Critiques rejected mss "when there is time." Sometimes recommends markets.

How to Contact: Send complete ms with SASE. Reports in less than 1 month on mss. Sample copy $2 with SASE.

Payment: $5/page. Free author's copy. $2 charge for extras.

Terms: Pays on publication for all rights; rights returned on request. Publication copyrighted.

Tips: "Write well and study the publication you are submitting to. We are interested only in the very best fiction and fiction translation. We are not interested in slick material. We do not read photocopies or carbon copies. You send the original; you keep the copy."

CHELSEA, Chelsea Associates, Inc. Box 5880, Grand Central Station, New York NY 10163. (212)988-2276. Editor: Sonia Raiziss. "We have no consistent theme except for single special issues. Otherwise, we use general material of an eclectic nature: poetry, prose, artwork, etc. for a sophisticated, literate audience interested in avant-garde literature and current writing both national and international." Annual. Estab. 1958. Circ. 1,000 + .

Needs: Literary, contemporary and translations. No humorous, scatological, purely confessional, child/young-adult experiences. Receives approximately 8-12 unsolicited fiction mss each month. Length: not over 25 printed pages. Critiques rejected mss "when there is time."

How to Contact: Query with SASE. Reports in 3 weeks on queries, 2 months on mss. Sample copy $3 plus postage.

Payment: 2 free author's copies.
Terms: Pays on publication for one-time rights. Publication copyrighted.
Tips: "Familiarize yourself with issues of the magazine for character of contributions. Mss should be legible, clearly typed, with minimal number of typographical errors and cross-outs, sufficient return postage, and if a covering letter is included it should be short, to the point, with a few major credits and publications." Most mss are rejected because they are "conventional in theme and/or style, uninspired, contrived, etc."

CHICAGO REVIEW, Chicago Review, Box C, University of Chicago, 5700 S. Ingleside, Chicago IL 60637. (312)753-3571. Editor: Keith Toma. Fiction Editors: Janet Deckenbach and Anne Orens. Magazine for a highly literate general audience. Quarterly. Estab. 1946. Circ. 2,000.
Needs: Literary, contemporary, science fiction, fantasy, and especially experimental. Accepts 5 mss/issue, 20 mss/year. Receives 50-100 unsolicited fiction mss each month. No preferred length. Critiques rejected mss "when there is time."
How to Contact: Send complete ms with SASE. Simultaneous submissions. Reports in 4 months on mss. Sample copy $3.75. Free guidelines with SASE.
Payment: 3 free author's copies and subscription. 40% discount for extras. "We have an annual award and prize for our best fiction."
Terms: Publication copyrighted.
Tips: Mss are rejected because they are "predictable and boring. Authors give too much 'background' explanation."

CHIRICÚ, Ballantine Hall 849, Indiana University, Bloomington IN 47405. (812)337-8577. Editor-in-Chief: Omar S. Castañeda. "We publish essays, translations, poetry, fiction, reviews, interviews, and artwork (illustrations and photos) that are either by or about Hispanics. Recent issue had an interview with Jorge Luis Borges and a translation from Virgilio Pinero. We have no barriers on style, content or ideology, but would like to see well-written material." Published annually. Estab. 1976. Circ. 500.
Needs: Contemporary, erotica, ethnic, experimental, fantasy, feminist/lesbian, gay, humor/satire, literary, mainstream, prose poem, science fiction, serialized/excerpted novel, translations, women's. No fiction that has nothing to do with Hispanics (when not written by one). Buys up to 6 mss/issue. Length: 7,000 words maximum; 4,000 words average. Occasionally critiques rejected mss. Sends mss to editors of other publications. Sometimes recommends markets.
How to Contact: Send complete ms with SASE. Photocopied submissions OK. Reports in 5 weeks on mss. Sample copy $1.50.
Payment: $25 maximum and 2-3 contributor's copies. $1 charge for extras.
Terms: Pays on publication for first rights. Publication copyrighted.
Tips: "Realize that we are an Hispanic literary review so that if you are not Hispanic, then your work must reflect an interest in Hispanic issues or have an Hispanic bent to it in literature. We try to have $25 prizes given to the best pieces submitted in the following categories: fiction, poetry, essay, art, translation." Mss rejected "quite simply because beginning writers force their language instead of writing from genuine sentiment and natural language."

CIMARRON REVIEW, Oklahoma State University, 208 LSE, Stillwater OK 74078. (405)624-6573. Editor: Neil John Hackett. Managing Editor: Jeanne Adams Wray. "Poetry and fiction on contemporary themes; personal essay on contemporary issues that cope with life in the 20th century for educated literary cognoscenti. We work hard to reflect quality." Quarterly. Estab. 1967. Circ. 500.
Needs: Literary and contemporary. No collegiate reminiscences or "juvenilia". Accepts 5-6 mss/issue, 20-24 mss/year.
How to Contact: Send complete ms with SASE. Reports in 1 month on mss. Free sample copy with 6½x9½ SASE and 65¢ postage.
Payment: 2 free author's copies. $1.50 charge for extras.
Terms: Acquires all rights on publication.

CLIFTON MAGAZINE, Communications Board, 204 Tangeman University Center, Cincinnati OH 45221. Editor: Greg May. Fiction Editor: Randy Rupp. "*Clifton* is the magazine of the University of Cincinnati, presenting fiction, poetry, and feature articles of interest to the university community. It is read by a highly literate audience of students, academics and professionals looking for original and exciting ideas presented in our award winning format." Quarterly. Estab. 1972. Circ. 10,000.

Needs: Literary, contemporary, science fiction, fantasy, feminist, gay/lesbian, erotica, humor and ethnic. "Will consider anything we haven't read a thousand times before. We try to have no preconceptions when approaching fiction. No semi-autobiographies of sensitive young people finding themselves." Accepts 1-2 mss/issue, 5 mss/year. Receives approximately 25 unsolicited fiction mss each month. Length: 30,000 words.

How to Contact: Send complete ms with SASE. Reports in 1 month on mss. Sample copy $1. Free guidelines with legal-sized SASE.

Payment: 5 free author's copies.

Terms: Acquires first rights. Publication copyrighted.

Tips: "*Clifton* often publishes work by unpublished authors, and is quite open to any fiction just as long as it doesn't bore us. We have previously published Allen Ginsberg, Richard Price, Jonathan Valin and James Wright, as well as unpublished writers who now are professionals. We look forward to continuing the publication with both young and established writers. Most rejected fiction manuscripts are turned down because they're trite or clichéd. *Clifton* tries to find mechanically sound, intricate, original work for publication."

THE COE REVIEW, Student Senate of Coe College, 1220 1st St., Cedar Rapids IA 52402. Contact: Editor-in-Chief. Annual anthology of "quality experimental writing in both poetry and fiction. Especially directed to an academic or experimental literary audience that is concerned with current literature." Annual. Estab. 1972. Circ. 500.

Needs: Literary, contemporary, psychic/supernatural, science fiction, fantasy, men's, women's, feminist, gay/lesbian, erotica, quality ethnic, serialized and condensed novels, translations. "We publish students, unsolicited professional, and solicited professional mss. *The Coe Review* is growing and it is our goal to become nationally acknowledged in literary circles as a forerunner in the publication of experimental writing. We support writing workshops and invite both writing professors and student writers to submit." No "religious propaganda, gothic, romance, western, mystery or adventure. We avoid 'sap' and predictability." Buys 8-10 mss/issue. Length: 500-4,000 words.

How to Contact: Send complete ms with SASE. "Mss sent in summer will possibly not be returned until fall depending on availability of a fiction editor in summer." Sample copy $3 with SASE plus $2.75 postage.

Payment: $25-$100 for solicitations. 1-2 free author's copies. $5 charge for extras.

Terms: Pays on publication for all rights "but possibly sooner with solicited mss. Upon request we will reassign rights to the author."

Tips: "We desire material that seeks to explore the vast imaginative landscape and expand the boundaries thereof. We use the I CHING symbol or 'breakthrough' to exemplify this intention. Study experimental writers such as Borges, Vonnegut, Brautigan, J. Baumbach and E. Gorman. Avoid sentimentalism. Do not be afraid to experiment or to write intelligent fiction."

COFFEE BREAK, Coffee Break Press, Box 103, Burley WA 98322. (206)857-4329. Editor/Publisher: D.M. Nicolai. Fiction Editor: C. Parkhurst. "Our slogan is: A magazine to brighten commuting time, coffee breaks and other hum-drum lulls." It contains short fiction, articles, how-to's, cartoons and poetry for adults. Adult readership. Annually. Estab. 1977. Circ. 5,000.

Needs: Literary, contemporary, psychic/supernatural, science fiction, fantasy, horror, men's, women's, romance, western, mystery, adventure, and especially humor. "Our editors are looking for quality and freshness, new ideas, excellent fiction, new forms, fillers and humor. We need mss in good taste but not sugar coated. Our editorial policy is flexible. A sparkling style will help. We will accept any manuscript that is skillfully constructed by a writer who has bothered to apply knowledge and craftsmanship, especially if it is coupled with fresh ideas. No religion, erotica, politics or pornography." Receives approximately 400 unsolicited fiction mss/month. Length: 1,500 words maximum. Critiques rejected mss "when there is time."

How to Contact: Send complete ms with SASE. "No queries for fiction." Reports in 6 weeks. Sample copy $1. Free guidelines with legal-sized SASE.

Payment: $5-$25 or 10 free author's copies.

Terms: Pays on publication for one-time rights. Publication copyrighted.

Tips: "Ask for editorial comments. You will be pleasantly surprised to find that our editors take the time to write personal replies and comments to anyone who wants them. Read at least one copy of *Coffee Break* before submitting a ms. We try not to be subjective in our selections but a clever writer will soon learn what we prefer. Do not submit a ms with the same plot that you found in our last issue. Many new writers start with *Coffee Break*. Many professionals stay with us."

THE COFFEEHOUSE, Wire Press, 3448 19th St., San Francisco CA 94110. Contact: Editor. "Theme is contemporary Greek Arts and Letters. Mostly we publish Greek short stories, fiction and poetry in English translation. Our audience is comprised of people who are interested in what's happening in Greece today concerning arts and letters." Semiannual. Estab. October 1975. Circ. 1,000.

Needs: Greek ethnic, literary, translations. "We publish only works by Greeks, Greek-Americans and Americans if the subject of their writing has to do with the theme of the magazine." Accepts 2 mss/issue, 4 mss/year. Length: 1,000-1,500 words.

How to Contact: Query with SASE. Reports in 1 month. Sample copy $2.

Payment: Pays in contributor's copies.

COLONNADES, The Literary Magazine of Elon College, Box 5246, Elon College NC 27244. (919)578-2258. Faculty Advisor: Dr. Andrew J. Angyal. "Undergraduate college literary magazine with North Carolina regional focus for Elon College students, faculty, and alumni." Published annually. Estab. 1934. Circ. 2,500.

Needs: Ethnic, humor/satire, literary, mainstream. "Nothing except traditional short stories and sketches." Receives 1-2 unsolicited fiction mss/month. Accepts 3-5 mss/issue; 3-5 mss/year. Length: 500 words minimum; 5,000 words maximum; 1,000 words average.

How to Contact: Send complete ms with SASE. Reports in 1 year. Sample copy $1 with 5x8 SAE and 5 first class stamps.

Payment: 1 contributor's copy; $1 (plus postage) charge for extras.

Tips: "Keep the story brief. We are primarily interested in North Carolina material written by new talent within the state. Submit triple copies. Occassionally, when time permits, I have tried to help encourage writers in their future ventures."

COLORADO-NORTH REVIEW, Journal Publishing Company, University of Northern Colorado, Greeley CO 80639. (303)351-4347. Editor-in-Chief: Laurel J. Kallenbach. Magazine of poetry, short fiction, photography and graphic arts for writers or those interested in contemporary creativity. Published in fall, winter and spring. Estab. 1975. Circ. 3,000.

Needs: Contemporary, literary. Receives 350 unsolicited fiction mss/month. Accepts 70 mss/issue, 210 mss/year. Length: 2,000 words maximum. Occasionally critiques rejected mss.

How to Contact: Send complete ms with SASE. Photocopied submissions OK. Reports in 3 months. Sample copy $2; free guidelines with SASE.

Terms: Makes assignments on work-for-hire-basis. Publication copyrighted.

Tips: "We are glad to read anything you feel worthy of submission. We take seriously the writer's efforts and support the creative process. We reject stories because space is limited. Many stories are predictable, too abstract, distasteful and lack character and plot development."

COLORADO STATE REVIEW, English Department, Colorado State University, Fort Collins CO 80525. (303)491-6428. Managing Editor: Wayne Ude. Literary magazine. Fiction issue published annually. Estab. 1977. Circ. 300-500.

Needs: Contemporary, ethnic, experimental, literary, mainstream, translations, western, women's. "Especially interested in magical realism, as in the work of Gabriel Garcia Marquez." Receives 100 unsolicited fiction mss/month. Accepts 8 mss/issue, 8 mss/year. No preferred length. Occasionally critiques rejected mss.
How to Contact: Send complete ms with SASE. "Fiction read Aug. 1-Dec. 31 each year only." Reports in 3 months. Sample copy $2.
Payment: 1 subscription to magazine; 2 free contributor's copies; $1.50 charge for extras.
Terms: Pays on publication for first North American serial rights. "We assign copyright to author on request." Publication copyrighted.
Tips: Rejects mss because "(1) we receive 10-20 manuscripts for each one we have room to print, and (2) we're not very interested in anything which isn't magical realism."

COLUMBIA: A MAGAZINE OF POETRY & PROSE, 404 Dodge Hall, Columbia University, New York NY 10027. Editor: Kristen Debner. Fiction Editor: Trudy Ditmar. "We are not looking for a set formula—just good writing. Short stories, parts of novels, translations, interviews, and poetry are all welcome." Annual.
Needs: Literary and translations but "although we only mention 2 categories, we will consider anything of literary merit." Accepts 3-6 mss/issue, 3-6 mss/year. Receives approximately 10-20 unsolicited fiction mss each month.
How to Contact: Send complete ms with SASE. Reports in 2 months.
Payment: 2 free author's copies. $3 charge for extras.
Terms: Publication copyrighted.
Tips: "We will consider all mss. Mss are rejected because of "limited, rambling story lines; inability to zero in and concentrate on why it's being written." $100 Carlos Fuentes Award for Best Fiction chosen for publication."

COMPASS POETRY & PROSE, Compass, Box 51, Burwood, NSW, Australia 2134. (02)799-6626. Editor:: C. Mansell. Quarterly. Estab. 1978. Circ. 1,000.
Needs: Literary, contemporary, poetry, short stories. Length: 2,000-5,000 prose words. Critiques rejected mss "when requested."
How to Contact: Send complete ms with SASE or IRC. Reports in 2 months on mss. Sample copy $3 (Australian).
Payment: $10/page and 1 free author's copy. $3 charge for extras.
Terms: Buys first rights (Australian). Publication copyrighted.
Tips: "Subscribe first." Mss rejected because of "lack of originality in style and content."

CONDITIONS: A Feminist Magazine with an Emphasis on Writings by Lesbians, Box 592, Van Brunt Station, Brooklyn NY 11215. "Collective of editors." A magazine of work "by published and unpublished writers of many different backgrounds for women of all ages and backgrounds who feel that a commitment to other women is an integral part of their lives." Semiannually. Estab. 1977.
Needs: Ethnic, feminist/lesbian, literary, prose poem, translations, women's. Wants to see mss "which reflect the experiences and viewpoints of Third World, working-class, and older women." Receives 10 unsolicited fiction mss/month. Accepts 5 mss/issue, 10 mss/year. Length: 500 words minimum, 10,000 words maximum, 5,000 words average. Occasionally critiques rejected mss.
How to Contact: Send complete ms with SASE. Photocopied submissions OK. Reports in 2 months. Sample copy $4.50.
Payment: 1 free contributor's copy.
Terms: Pays on publication. Publication copyrighted.
Tips: "Buy a magazine first to understand purpose of magazine."

CONFRONTATION, Long Island University, English Dept., 1 University Plaza, Brooklyn NY 11201. (212)834-6170. Editor: Martin Tucker. Fiction Editor: Ken Bernard. "We like to have a 'range' of subjects, form and style in each issue and are open to all forms. Quality is our major concern. Our audience is literate, thinking college students, educated and self-educated lay persons.'' Semiannual. Estab. 1968. Circ. 2,000.

Needs: Literary, contemporary, science fiction, confession, gothic, humor, translations. No "proseletyzing" literature. Buys 10 mss/issue, 20 mss/year. Receives 250 unsolicited fiction mss each month. Length: 500-2,000 words. Critiques rejected mss "when there is time." Sometimes recommends other markets.

How to Contact: Send complete ms with SASE. Reports in 6 weeks on mss. Sample copy $1.50.

Payment: $15-$100. 1 free author's copy. Half price charge for extras.

Terms: Pays on publication for all rights "with transfer on request to author." Publication copyrighted.

CONFRONTATION/CHANGE REVIEW, 1107 Lexington Ave., Dayton OH 45407. Editor: F.M. Finney. "A journal of political economy and Americana (including Caribbean) fiction and poetry. Readership is college level, literary and just 'plain readers.' Style is designed to allow readers to enjoy material." Published 3 times/year. Estab. 1976. Circ. 1,910.

Needs: Literary, contemporary, fantasy, black ethnic. No gay/lesbian, women's liberation or alternative life style pieces at this time. Buys 2 mss/issue, 6 mss/year. Length: 1,500-3,000 words.

How to Contact: Send complete ms with SASE. Reports in 1 month. Sample copy $1.25 with SASE.

Payment: $50 maximum, usual or 3 free author's copies.

Terms: Pays on publication for first North American serial rights.

CONJUNCTIONS, 33 W. 9th St., New York NY 10011. Editor: Bradford Morrow. "*Conjunctions*: a conjoining of texts by many diverse writers: a forum of work-in-progress by both well-known and new writers. We represent no clique but are highly concerned solely with publishing works of high artistic and technical calibre. Recent issues have included new work by Sorrentino, Busch, Purdy, Rexroth, Davenport, Dorn, Creeley, Levertov, Gass, Hawkes, Abish, Tarn, Paz, many others." Semiannually. Estab. 1982. Circ. 2,500.

Needs: Experimental, literary, translations. Receives 40 unsolicited fiction mss/month. Accepts 3-4 mss/issue, 6-8 mss/year. No preferred length.

How to Contact: Send complete ms with SASE. Reports in 8-12 weeks on mss.

Payment: 3 free contributor's copies; extra copies available at 40% discunt to contributors.

Terms: Pays on publication for one-time rights. Publication copyrighted.

THE CONNECTICUT WRITER, Connecticut Writers League, Inc., Box 78, Farmington CT 06032. Publication Director: Maryland Lincoln. Magazine "interested in providing a forum for the new writer in the fields of fiction." Annually. Estab. 1974. Circ. 650.

Needs: "We consider everything. Submissions must be typed and adhere to the guidelines furnished upon request. We receive about 400 mss/year through the contest." Occasionally critiques rejected mss.

How to Contact: "Write for contest guidelines with SASE. Contest begins in January." Sample copy $3.95. Fiction guidelines free for # 10 envelope.

Payment: 1 contributor's copy.

Terms: One-time rights. Publication copyrighted.

Tips: "We are a non-profit organization and the longest, continuous forum for new writers in Connecticut. We expanded our contest nationally to provide more encouragement. Our publication offers a new writer opportunities to be published. We also hold a publication party which editors, writers and other attend. The contacts are good."

CONSTELLATIONS, New Traditions, Box 4378, Santa Rosa CA 95402. (707)526-6020. Editor: Harold Brown. Magazine of short fiction and other narratives for writers, teachers, secretaries, college students, corporate personnel, housewives and tradespeople. Semiannually. Estab. 1981.

Needs: Adventure, contemporary, ethnic, experimental, fantasy, gothic/historical romance, historical (general), humor/satire, literary, mainstream, romance (contemporary), science fiction, suspense/mystery, translations, western, women's, young adult, autobiographical, biographical. Nothing bizarre, erotic, didactic. Accepts 15-20 mss/issue, 30-40 mss/year. "Rarely" critiques rejected mss.
How to Contact: Send complete ms with SASE. Simultaneous and photocopied submissions OK. Reports in 2 weeks on queries, up to 4 months on mss. Sample copy $6.
Payment: 2 free contributor's copies.
Terms: Pays on publication. Rights revert to the author upon request. Publication copyrighted.
Tips: "Submit, clean, well-typed copy. Frequent out mailings; for more rapid return of material include SASE. Read editions of the publications before submitting."

CONTRABAND PRESS & MAGAZINE, Box 4073, Station A, Portland ME 04101. Contact: Editor-in-Chief. Magazine of serious literature for those interested in same. Published irregularly. Estab. 1971. Circ. 1,000.
Needs: Contemporary, experimental, literary, prose poem, translations. No commercial mss. Receives 4-5 unsolicited fiction mss/month. Accepts 2 mss/issue. No preferred length. Occasionally critiques rejected mss.
How to Contact: Send complete ms with SASE. Photocopied submissions OK. Reports in 2 weeks on mss. Sample copy 61¢ postage.
Payment: 2-5 free contributor's copies; 40% discount for extras.
Terms: Pays on publication for one-time rights. Publication copyrighted.
Tips: "Know your art. Don't waste people's time unnecessarily."

CORONA, Marking the Edges of Many Circles, Department of History and Philosophy, Montana State University, Bozeman MT 59717. (406)994-4395. "Interdisciplinary magazine—essays, poetry, fiction, imagery, science, history, recipes, humor, etc., for those educated, curious, with a profound interest in the arts and contemporary thought." Published annually. Estab. 1980. Circ. 2,000.
Needs: Comics, contemporary, experimental, fantasy, feminist, humor/satire, literary, prose poem. "Our fiction ranges from the traditional Talmudic tale to fiction engendered by speculative science, from the extended joke to regional reflection—if it isn't accessible and original, please don't send it." Receives varying number of unsolicited fiction mss/month. Accepts 6 mss/issue. Occasionally critiques rejected mss.
How to Contact: Send complete ms with SASE. Reports in 4 months on mss. Sample copy $6.
Payment: Minimal honorarium; 2 free contributor's copies; discounted charge for extras.
Terms: Pays on publication for first rights. Publication copyrighted.
Tips: "Be knowledgeable of contents other than fiction in *Corona*; one must know the journal." Recent contributors include Frederick Turner, William Irwin Thompson, Donald Hall, Richard Hugo (Pulitzer Prize for Poetry), Richard Brautigan.

CORRIDORS MAGAZINE, Detroit Writers' Guild, Box 15296, Detroit MI 48215. (313)824-1817. Editor: Jane Dobija. "A literary magazine featuring poetry, fiction, and drama by Detroit-area writers." Biannually. Estab. 1979. Circ. 300.
Needs: "We are especially interested in pieces which deal with the experience of the work place, i.e., stories and poems about factory or office jobs. We are not interested in work that presents women *or* men in stereotypical characterizations." Receives 60 unsolicited fiction mss/month. Accepts 3-5 mss/issue, 6-10 mss/year. Length: 3,000 words maximum, 2,000 words average. Occasionally critiques rejected mss.
How to Contact: Send complete ms with SASE. Photocopied submissions OK. Reports in 4-8 weeks on mss. Sample copy $2.
Payment: 3 free contributor's copies.
Terms: Pays on publication for one-time rights. Publication copyrighted.

COSMIC CIRCUS, Cosmic Brain Trust, 414 S. 41st St., Richmond CA 94804. Editor: Rey King. Cosmic magazine for heavy metal magazine readers. Annual. Estab. 1972. Circ. 1,000.

Needs: Comics, erotica, experimental, fantasy, gay, horror, humor/satire, psychic/supernatural, science fiction. "No long manuscripts." Receives 5 unsolicited fiction mss/month. Accepts 1 ms/issue, 3 mss/year. Length: 50 words minimum, 2,000-4,000 words maximum. Occasionally critiques rejected mss.
How to Contact: Send complete ms with SASE. Photocopied submissions OK. Reports in 2 months on mss. Sample copy $2.
Payment: $5 and 5 free contributor's copies.
Terms: Pays on publication for first rights. Publication copyrighted.
Tips: "Many stories are adapted to illustrated format. Cartoonists are given special attention. Don't send originals—send copies."

COTTONWOOD REVIEW, Cottonwood Review Press, Box J, Student Union, Kansas University, Lawrence KS 66045. Editor: Erleen J. Christensen. Fiction Editor: Sharon Oard Warner. "*Cottonwood Review* is a literary magazine that publishes new and well known writers. We have no theme aside from quality. For readers of fine literature, poetry and fiction in the Midwest and the nation." Semiannual. Estab. 1965. Circ. 800.
Needs: Literary, contemporary, men's and women's. "We are not interested in contrived, slick material. Accepts 3-4 mss/issue, 9 mss/year. Receives 12-15 unsolicited fiction mss each month. Length: 500-3,000 words. Critiques rejected mss "when there is time."
How to Contact: Query, send complete ms. SASE for query, ms. Reports in 1 month on queries, 2 months on ms. Sample copy $2 (back issues only).
Payment: 2 free author's copies. $2.80 charge for extras.
Terms: Acquires one-time rights. Publication copyrighted.
Tips: "Read sample issues. *Rewrite*. Many of the mss we reject are not polished. Be certain your story is as 'finished' as you can make it before you sumbit."

CREAM CITY REVIEW, University of Wisconsin-Milwaukee, Box 413, Milwaukee WI 53201. Editor: Jessie Glass. "We publish traditional and innovative poetry, fiction and nonfiction. Themes vary with editorial staff changes each year." National as well as regional audience. Semiannual. Estab. 1975. Circ. 1,000.
Needs: Contemporary, fantasy, avant-garde. Accepts 6-8 mss/issue. Receives approximately 20-40 unsolicited fiction mss each month. Length: 1,000-10,000 words. Critiques rejected mss "when there is time."
How to Contact: Send complete ms with SASE. Photocopies OK. Reports in 2 months. Sample copy $2.50. Free guidelines with SASE.
Payment: 1 free author's copy.
Terms: Acquires first rights. Publication copyrighted.
Tips: Mss are rejected because of "poor subject matter, lack of depth/insight, poor grammar/mechanics, etc."

CRITIQUE, Exploring Conspiracy Theories, Metaphysics & the American Culture, Critique Foundation, 2364 Valley West Dr., Santa Rosa CA 95401. (707)526-5990. Editor: Bob Banner. Magazine of occult, conspiracy, metaphysics, politics, fiction, book reviews, news analyses, global psyche for students and intelligent readers. Quarterly. Estab. 1980. Circ. 600.
Needs: Confession, contemporary, historical (general), literary, psychic/supernatural, religious/inspirational, science fiction, translations. Receives 2 unsolicited fiction mss/month. Accepts 3 mss/year. Length: 3,000 words maximum. Occasionally critiques rejected mss.
How to Contact: Send complete ms with SASE. Photocopied and previously published submissions OK. Reports in 3 weeks on mss. Sample copy free. Fiction guidelines free.
Payment: $10 maximum and 3 free contributor's copies.
Terms: Pays on publication. Publication copyrighted.
Tips: "Send for sample issue to understand what we're publishing."

CROP DUST, Crop Dust Press, Rt. 2, Box 389-1, Bealeton VA 22712. (703)439-2140. Contact: Editor. Rural and city landscapes for the university and general writing community. Semiannual. Estab. Spring 1979. Circ. 500.
Needs: Literary and contemporary, all types of fiction. Accepts 5 mss/issue, 10 mss/year. Receives approximately 15 unsolicited fiction mss each month. Length: 500-5,000 words. Critiques rejected mss "when there is time."
How to Contact: Send complete ms. Reports in 3 months. Sample copy $1.50. Free guidelines with legal-sized SASE.
Payment: 1 free author's copy.
Terms: Acquires first North American serial rights, which revert to author on publication. Publication copyrighted.
Tips: "Read a copy of the magazine before submitting. Send only one story. Short stories fare better with editors in our publishing space." Mss are rejected because "short stories seem incomplete—too much experimental and vignettes." Future contests planned.

CROSS-CANADA WRITERS' QUARTERLY, Box 277, Station F, Toronto, Ontario, Canada M4Y 2L7. Editor-in-Chief: Ted Plantos. "A complete and distinctive literary package." Published quarterly. Estab. 1978. Circ. 2,000.
Needs: "*Cross-Canada Writers' Quarterly* welcomes submissions of fiction from American authors. We offer American as well as Canadian writers the most comprehensive, current literary market listings published in Canada. We keep our readers in touch with the Canadian literary scene and available markets for their work." Receives 25-30 unsolicited fiction mss/month. Accepts 2-4- mss/issue, 10-12 mss/year. No preferred length. Occasionally critiques rejected mss.
How to Contact: Send complete ms with SASE. Photocopied submissions OK. Reports in 2 weeks on queries; 5 weeks on mss. Sample copy $2.
Payment: 3 free contributor's copies.
Terms: Pays on publication for first rights and one-time rights. Publication copyrighted.
Tips: Recommends studying an issue before submitting. Subscriptions: $10 (individuals); $12 (institutions). Rejects mss because of "lack of manuscript quality."

CROSSCURRENTS, 2200 Glastonbury Rd., Westlake Village CA 91361. Editor: Linda Brown Michelson. "*Crosscurrents* is a magazine of the West which offers another corner for today's artistry. This is not a limitation but a slant. We publish short fiction, poetry, graphic arts, and nonfiction. We direct our publication toward an educated audience which appreciates good writing, good art and enjoys a periodic sampling of current trends in these fields." Quarterly. Estab. March 1980. Circ. 1,800.
Needs: Most all categories except heavy erotica, juvenile and young adult. "We try to remain open to as many types of fiction as possible. Good writing is what we look for and consider first. Limitations as to type are few." Buys 6-10 mss/issue, 45 mss/year. Length: 6,000 words maximum. Critiques rejected mss "when there is time."
How to Contact: Send complete ms with SASE. Reports in 6 weeks on mss. Sample copy $3.
Payment: $35 minimum. Offers 50% kill fee for assigned ms not published.
Terms: Pays on acceptance for first North American serial rights. Publication copyrighted.
Tips: "Look at a sample issue to see what we publish. Include a short letter with your ms to let us know who you are. Good quality photocopies fine, but no simultaneous submissions. Many rejected manuscripts are well done but do not fit our coming issues. Many others, however, are simply not professional." Sponsors fiction contest.

THE CROSSTOWN RAG, Bimonthly Newsletter for Advanced & Challenge Dancers, 1405 Kahler Ct., San Jose CA 95132. (408)262-6863. Editor-in-Chief: Andrea L. Fuller. "Newsletter for high-level square dancers using articles, humor, occasional fiction, poetry, cartoons, jokes." Published annually. Estab. 1979. Circ. 500.
Needs: Contemporary, experimental, fantasy, humor/satire, romance (contemporary), science fiction, suspense/mystery. "All mss must involve square dancing or dancers." Receives "very

few" unsolicited fiction mss/month. Accepts 2-6 mss/year. Length: 500 words preferred; longer mss considered but not over 1,000. Occasionally critiques rejected mss.
How to Contact: Send complete ms with SASE. Simultaneous, photocopied, and previously published submissions OK. Reports in 2 weeks on mss. Sample copy 50¢ with legal size SAE and 1 first class stamp.
Payment: 1 free contributor's copy.
Terms: Pays on publication for one-time rights.
Tips: "We're very easy; a good place to learn fiction techniques for the short-short story. Material should be short, concise, loaded with imagery and action. No preach material. Readers want to be entertained and informed."

CROTON REVIEW, Croton Council on the Arts, Inc. (non-profit organization), Box 277, Croton on Hudson NY 10520. Editor: Ruth Lisa Schechter. An award-winning publication (supported by National Endowment on the Arts grant and CAW) based on quality of literary content. Publishes contemporary, diverse short prose, poetry, literary essays and translations, as well as art. Annual. Estab. 1978. Circ. 2,000.
Needs: Literary, contemporary. "No trite or hackneyed themes. Avoid clichés." Approximate length: 8-16 double spaced pages.
How to Contact: Send complete ms with brief biography. SASE. Reports in 8-12 weeks. Sample copy $2 (add 70¢ postage) or subscription $6 (postpaid—3 annual issues).
Payment: 2 free author's copies; author's payments for Issue #6 (published spring 1983).
Terms: Publication copyrighted.
Tips: "Subscribe to and read the *Croton Review*. Originality and craft desirable. Our contributors submit from throughout the US. Known and well known writers are invited. All submissions are read carefully. The editorial board consists of writers and editors."

C.S.P. WORLD NEWS, Edition Stencil, Box 2608, Station D, Ottawa, Ontario, Canada K1P 5W7. Editor: Guy F. Claude Hamel. Publishes poetry and fiction for a general readership. Monthly. Estab. 1962.
Needs: Literary. "I'll look at anything." Buys 2 mss/year. Length: 1,000-1,200 words.
How to Contact: Query first or query with clips of published work. SASE for query, ms. Reports in 3 weeks. Sample copy $2 with legal-sized SASE.
Payment: Negotiates pay for fiction.
Terms: Pays on acceptance on a work-for-hire basis. Publication copyrighted.
Tips: "Be yourself and research well."

CUMBERLAND JOURNAL, Box 2648, Harrisburg PA 17105. Contact: Editor. Publishes literary biography and innovative cultural criticism for serious fiction readers, artists and critics. Quarterly. Estab. 976. Circ. 400.
Needs: Literary, men's, women's, adventure, translations. Charges $5 for reading fee. Length: 1,000-18,000 words. Critiques rejected mss "when there is time."
How to Contact: Query or send complete ms. SASE for query, ms. Reports in 2 weeks. Sample copy $3.
Payment: Free author's copies.
Terms: Acquires first rights or first North American serial rights. Publication copyrighted.
Tips: "Purchase sample copy to see what we publish." Mss are rejected because writers are "unfamiliar with market."

CUMBERLANDS, Pikeville College, College Box 2, Pikeville KY 41501. (606)432-9227. Editor: Leonard Roberts. A "little magazine, light, somewhat experimental, with articles, fiction, art, Appalachian settings, etc. for not only the young and college age readers but practicing writers and poets who read it to find new and challenging material, humor and magic (in our folktales)." Published 2 times/year. Estab. 1979 (*Twigs*-1965). Circ. 500.
Needs: Literary, contemporary, psychic/supernatural, fantasy, men's, women's, mystery, ad-

venture, humor. "No explicit sex, horror, pulp western or romance, gay, freakish." Accepts 3-4 mss/issue. Receives 20-30 unsolicited fiction mss each month. Length: 1,500-2,500 words. Critiques rejected mss "when there is time."

How to Contact: Send complete ms with SASE. Reports in 1 month. Sample copy $1 with 9x12 SAE plus 80¢ postage. Free guidelines.

Payment: 1-2 free author's copies plus $25 award/volume for best contribution. Half price charge for extras.

Terms: Acquires first rights. Publication copyrighted.

Tips: "Send photocopy draft of short piece which you feel good about. We will read and do minor editing; we like to see corrections made by author. Avoid humorless long, creeping, awkward discourses with poor or no dialogue or with no defined point of view." Mss are rejected because they are "vague, poorly paced, plotted practice pieces, often not proofread."

CUT BANK, Smoke Root Press, English Department, University of Montana, Missoula MT 59812. Editors: Robert Ross and Carole DeMarinis. "Magazine of fine writing—poetry, fiction, articles, art, photos, interviews, criticism, reviews, parts of novels, long poems—for anyone interested in the best prose and poetry being written today." Semiannually. Estab. 1973. Circ. 600.

Needs: Adventure, contemporary, erotica, ethnic, experimental, fantasy, historical, humor/satire, literary, men's, prose poem, translation, western, women's. "Only the highest quality will be considered." Receives 30 unsolicited fiction mss/month. Accepts 2 mss/issue, 4 mss/year. Length: 10,000 words maximum; 4,000 words average. Occasionally critiques rejected mss.

How to Contact: Send complete ms with SASE. Simultaneous, photocopied, and previously published submissions OK. Reports in 3 weeks on mss. Sample copy $2.50.

Payment: 2 free contributor's copies; regular newsstand price for extras.

Terms: Pays on publication for all rights. Publication copyrighted.

THE CYGNUS CHRONICLER, The Eperex Press, Box 770, Canberra City, ACT 2601, Australia. 062-806588. Editor: Neville J. Angove. Fiction Editor: Michael Hailstone. Quarterly magazine.

Needs: Comics, science fiction, fantasy. Length: 5,000 words maximum.

How to Contact: Query first with SASE or IRCs. "Prefer non-returnable photocopies." Reports in 2 weeks on queries.

Payment: $10-250 and 5 free contributor's copies.

Terms: Pays on publication. Annual contest—$250/$100 prizes.

Tips: "We see a greater demand for fiction (in Australia). If you have something to say, there is someone who will pay to read it; just make it attractive enough so he/she *will* make the attempt."

DARK HORIZONS, British Fantasy Society, 194 Station Rd., Kings Heath, Birmingham, England. Editor: Dave Sutton. Magazine of fantasy-oriented fact and fiction for fantasy fans. Semiannually. Estab. 1971. Circ. 350.

Needs: Fantasy, horror, psychic/supernatural. Receives 2 unsolicited fiction mss/month. Length: 1,000 words minimum; 5,000 words maximum. Occasionally critiques rejected mss.

How to Contact: Query first with SASE. Photocopied submissions OK. Reports in various number of weeks on queries. Sample copy $1.50. Fiction guidelines for SAE and $1 postage.

Terms: Publication copyrighted. Sponsors the British Fantasy Awards based on publication during year in question.

DARK HORSE, Box 9, Somerville MA 02143. Editor: Seth Steinzor. Estab. 1974.

Needs: "Literate, contemporary, very high quality fiction. No science fiction, mystery, juvenile.

How to Contact: Submit complete ms with SASE and bio note. Reports in 3 months on ms. Simultaneous submissions OK.

Payment: 2 copies. Sample copy $2.

Tips: "Stories should be no longer than 15 double-spaced typewritten pages."

DAY TONIGHT/NIGHT TODAY, Box 353, Hull MA 02045. (617)925-2860. Editor: S.R. Jade. Magazine of "poetry, fiction, graphics (including cartoons), essays with a feminist/humanist slant with a sense of humor for a varied readership—probably 75% women because that's who we publish." Seven to nine issues yearly. Estab. 1981. Circ. 250.

Needs: Comics, erotica, ethnic, experimental, feminist/lesbian, gay, humor/satire, literary, prose poem, science fiction, serialized/excerpted novel, women's. "We only publish women. Especially interested in stream-of-consciousness, prose and free style. No sexism, racism, or pornography." Receives 12-15 unsolicited fiction mss/month. Accepts 0-5 mss/issue; 12-15 mss/year. Length: 4,000 words maximum; 2,500 words average. Occasionally critiques rejected mss.

How to Contact: Send complete ms with SASE. Simultaneous, photocopied and previously published submission OK. Reports in 6 weeks on mss. Sample copy for $2.50 with 6x9 SAE and 71¢ postage. Fiction guidelines free for standard SAE and 20¢ postage.

Payment: 1 free contibutor's copy; $2.50 charge for extras.

Terms: Rights revert to author/artist on publication. Publication copyrighted.

Tips: "Send several short strong pieces revolving around being a woman or circumstance special to women—health relationships, economics. Request critique if wanted. No *Reader's Digest* type (no slant intended) stuff—more 'un-cut', gutsy, real-life published here."

DE COLORES JOURNAL, Pajarito Publications, Box 7264, Albuquerque NM 87194. Publisher: Jose Armas. "Chicano literature for college audiences." Quarterly. Estab. 1972. Circ. 10,000.

Needs: Chicano ethnic, literary, contemporary, psychic/supernatural, science fiction, fantasy, men's, women's, feminist, romance, western, mystery, adventure, humor, juvenile, young adult, serialized and condensed novels and translations. No religion or confession. Buys 15 mss/issue. Length: 1,000-10,000 words.

How to Contact: Query with SASE. Reports in 2 weeks on queries, 2 months on mss. Sample copy for $5 with 6x9 SASE.

Payment: Free author's copies.

Terms: Payment is on publication for first rights.

Tips: "Write, write, write. Then rewrite, rewrite, rewrite."

DEADSPAWN, c/o Joe Treacy, 303 Conway Ave., Narberth PA 19072. Editor-in-Chief: Joe Treacy. "Magazine/portfolio. A high quality, highly experimental package publishing short stories of fantasy, mystery, horror, and humor; also comic strips and illustrations, primarily for serious comics/fantasy collectors." Published annually. Estab. 1976. Circ. 10,000.

Needs: Adventure, comics, experimental, fantasy, horror, humor/satire, science fiction, suspense/mystery. "Absolutely will not consider explicit sexual or explicit violent material. However, not too somber or boring either." Receives 15-20 unsolicited fiction mss/month. Buys 2-3 mss/issue; 2-3 mss/year. Length: 2,000 words minimum; 10,000 words maximum; 5,000 words average. Critiques rejected mss.

How to Contact: Query first (or send complete ms) with SASE. Photocopied submissions OK. Reports in 5 weeks on queries; 5 weeks on mss. Sample copy # 3 $5.50 and $1.95 postage; # 4 $7.95 and $1.50 postage; free guidelines for SAE and 1 first class stamp.

Payment: 0.005¢/word-0.015¢/word; 3 free contributor's copies.

Terms: Pays on acceptance for first rights. Publication copyrighted.

Tips: "Be as different as you can. (There's enough out there already that's bland and colorless enough to make one cry.) Complete originality is all-important. And don't be sensationalistic. Be creative. It's really much better."

DENVER QUARTERLY, University of Denver, Denver CO 80208. (303)753-2869. Editor: Leland H. Chambers. "We publish fiction, articles and poetry for a generally well-educated audience primarily interested in literature and the literary experience. They read *DQ* to find something a little different from a strictly academic quarterly or a creative writing outlet." Quarterly. Estab. 1966. Circ. 450.

Needs: Literary, contemporary and translations. "No superficial, sleazy, cute, tricky or incompetently crafted fiction." Buys 1-2 mss/issue, 5-8 mss/year. Sometimes recommends markets.
How to Contact: Send complete ms with SASE. Reports in 2 months on mss. Sample copy $2 with SASE.
Payment: Pays $5/page. 2 free author's copies plus 5 tear sheets.
Terms: Acquires first North American serial rights.
Tips: "Write intelligently and sensitively. Photocopy OK. The majority of rejected mss are simply not done competently—too much reliance on plot or 'clever' sentences, too little on character or thought."

DESCANT, Department of English, Texas Christian University, Fort Worth TX 76129. (817)921-7240. Editor: Betsy Colquitt. "*Descant* uses fiction, poetry, essays. No restriction on style, content or theme. It is a little literary magazine, and its readers are those who have interest in such publications." Quarterly. Estab. 1955. Circ. 500.
Needs: Literary and contemporary. No genre or category fiction. Receives approximately 50 unsolicited fiction mss each month. Length: 1,500-5,000 words. Sometimes recommends markets.
How to Contact: Send complete ms with SASE. Reports usually within 6 weeks on ms. Sample copy $2.50.
Payment: 4 free author's copies. $2.50 charge/extra copy.
Terms: Acquires first North American serial rights. Publication copyrighted.
Tips: "Submit good material. Even though a small publication, *Descant* receives many submissions, and acceptances are few compared to the total number of mss received." Mss are rejected because they "are badly written, careless in style and development, shallow in characterization, trite in handling and in conception." We offer a $100 annual prize for fiction—the Frank O'Connor Prize. Award is made to the story considered (by a judge not connected to the magazine) to be the best published in a given volume of the journal."

DESCANT, Box 314, Station P, Toronto, Ontario, Canada M5S 2S8. (416)766-9241. Editor: Karen Mulhallen. High quality poetry and prose for an intelligent audience who wants to see good, new poetry and prose. Triannual. Estab. 1970. Circ. 1,000.
Needs: Literary, contemporary, and translations. "Although most themes are acceptable, all works must have literary merit." Receives 50-100 unsolicited mss/month. Critiques rejected mss "when there is time."
How to Contact: Send complete ms with SASE. Reports in 4 months on mss. Sample copy $5 with 9x11 SASE and IRC (32¢ Canadian postage.)
Payment: Pays in free author's copies. Extra author's copies at discount.
Terms: Acquires one-time rights. Publication copyrighted.
Tips: "Edit yourself first. Send your best work. Rewrite your material until you are convinced it is the best that can be done on that theme. Know the journal you submit to; each one has a personality. Rejects manuscripts because writer is unfamiliar with type of magazine or has not mastered his craft."

DIANA'S ALMANAC, Diana's Bimonthly Press, 71 Elmgrove Ave., Providence RI 02906. (401)274-5417. Editor: Tom Ahern. Anthology of contemporary American literature, literature in translation, and illustrated artists' narratives. "*Diana's* is read by people interested in innovative design and is directed to those well-informed about contemporary concerns in literature." Annual. Estab. 1972. Circ. 1,100.
Needs: "No mass-market, popular or derivative fiction." Buys 2-3 mss/issue. Receives approximately 30 unsolicited fiction mss each month. Length: 5,000-30,000 words. Critiques rejected mss "when there is time."
How to Contact: Query with clips of published work with SASE. Reports in 1 week on queries and mss. Sample copy $5.
Payment: Pays $150 minimum and 10 free author's copies. Offers kill fee for assigned ms not published.
Terms: Pays on publication for one-time rights. Publication copyrighted.

Tips: Most mss are rejected because "they mimic mainstream fiction."

DIMENSION, Contemporary German Arts & Letters, Box 26673, Austin TX 78755. (512)471-4314. Editor-in-Chief: A. Leslie Willson. Magazine of contemporary (post-1945) German literature *in translation* for scholars, students of literature, general readers. Published 3 times/year. Estab. 1968. Circ. 1,200.
Needs: Translations of German fiction since 1945. Receives 5 unsolicited fiction mss/month. Accepts 3-5 mss/issue, 12-15 mss/year. Length: 2,000 words minimum; 10,000 words maximum; 4,000 words average. Occasionally critiques rejected mss. Sometimes recommends markets.
How to Contact: Send ms of translation with copy of original and SASE. Reports in 2 months on mss. Sample copy $6.
Payment: 1 contributor's copy; $4 charge for extra copies of magazine.
Terms: Publication retains all rights. Publication copyrighted.

DISABLED WRITERS' QUARTERLY, The International Literary Magazine of Physically Disabled Writers, 2495 Major St., St. Laurent, Quebec, Canada H4M 1E5. (514)747-0773. Editor-in-Chief: Samuel Miller. "Magazine of contemporary creative writing of physically disabled writers for disabled writers, rehabilitation professionals, and the able-bodied reader." Published quarterly. Estab. 1981. Circ. 1,000.
Needs: Adventure, comics, condensed novel, contemporary, experimental, fantasy, feminist/lesbian, gay, horror, humor/satire, literary, mainstream, prose poem, psychic/supernatural, religious/inspirational, science fiction, serialized/excerpted novel, suspense/mystery, translations, personal fiction. "Contributors must be physically disabled and are requested to enclose biographical notes with ms and b&w glossy photo of self if possible." No juvenile pieces. Receives 5 unsolicited fiction mss/month. Buys 5 mss/issue, 20 mss/year. Length: 2,000 words minimum; 20,000 words maximum; 3,000 words average. Occasionally critiques rejected mss. Sends mss to editors of other publications. Sometimes recommends markets.
How to Contact: Send complete ms with ample IRC's. Simultaneous submissions and previously published work OK. Reports in 1 month. Sample copy $1.75; free guidelines for legal-size SAE.
Payment: $5-100; 2 free contributor's copies; $1.75 charge for extras.
Terms: Pays on publication for one-time rights.
Tips: "We recommend that writers read *Writer's Digest* and purchase writing manuals. All submissions should be typed (double-spaced) on 8 1/2x11 paper and should be free of grammatical errors. Enclose return postage, please! We periodically sponsor contests, but contributors must be subscribers in order to participate or apply. Rule sheet published within magazine."

DOG RIVER REVIEW, Trout Creek Press, Box 125, Parkdale OR 97041-0125. (503)352-6494. Editor: Laurence F. Hawkins Jr. Literary magazine for the educated and poetic. Semiannually. Estab. 1982. Circ. 250.
Needs: Experimental, fantasy, humor/satire, literary, mainstream, prose poem, translations. Receives 4-6 unsolicited fiction mss/month. Accepts 3-4 mss/issue; 6-8 mss/year. Length: 3,000 words maximum; 2,500 words average.
How to Contact: Send complete ms with SASE. Photocopied submissions OK. Reports in 2 months on mss. Sample copy for $3.50. Fiction guidelines for #10 envelope and 1 first class stamp.
Payment: Varied number of contributor's copies.
Terms: Acquires first North American serial rights. Publication copyrighted.
Tips: "Piece should be unique, well-constructed. Avoid trite, commonplace subjects."

DOUBLE HARNESS MAGAZINE, DH/AVED, 66 Millfield Road, York, England Y02 1NQ. Editor: Andrew Cozens. Literary magazine with socio-political side interests for a literary audience. Annual. Estab. August 1979. Circ. 750.
Needs: Literary, contemporary, men's, women's, feminist, gay/lesbian, erotica, confession,

gothic, humor, serialized novels and translations. No romance. Receives approximately 10 unsolicited fiction mss each month. Length: 500-8,000 words. Critiques rejected mss "when there is time."

How to Contact: Query with clips of published work. Reports in 1 month on both queries and mss. Free sample copy.

Payment: Unlimited amount of free author's copies.

Tips: Mss are rejected because they are "derivative or ill-wrought."

DREAMS UNLIMITED, Box 247, Middleton WI 53562. (608)238-6575. Editor: Elizabeth Lowe. "In addition to self-help materials on dreams and dream interpretation, we recognize dreams as a major source of creativity in the arts and therefore publish dream-based or dream-related fiction (short stories). Prefer utilization of actual dream(s) or dream-related experience in the plot. We publish in a booklet format (12-22 + pages), and fiction is in a series: *Dream Stories* followed by Roman numeral. Directed to people interested in dreams from a psychological, humanistic, psychic or new age perspective." Estab. 1979.

Needs: Contemporary, religious, psychic/supernatural, science fiction, fantasy, feminist, gothic, romance, western, mystery, adventure, humor, ethnic (author's choice) and experimental psychological. "No subject matter which seems unlikely to yield dream-based fiction, hard-core or anarchist." Buys 4-10 mss/year. Length: 1,000-10,000 words. Critiques rejected mss "when there is time."

How to Contact: Query with a discursive letter telling about your dream and the story you have in mind with SASE. Reports as soon as possible but no longer than 1 month on queries, 2 months on mss. Publication list enclosed with response to queries.

Payment: Pays $25 and up, plus 10 copies.

Terms: Negotiates rights. Publication copyrighted.

Tips: "Have a dream. Record it. Plan how that dream could be used in or as a basis of a story. Share your dream and ideas with me. If it's appealing, we can take it from there. New writers are especially welcome." Most rejected mss come from writers "who fail to query and their manuscript does not conform to dream requirements."

DREAMWEAVER MAGAZINE, Dreamweaver, 6 Charles St. E, Toronto, Ontario, Canada M4Y 1T2. (416)654-5617 or 651-4966. Editors: Harry Posner and Nick Trusolino. Associate Editor: Steve Solomon. "We explore the world of sleep, dreams and imagination, including articles focusing upon current sleep and dream research, the world of children, symbols, dream interpretations, film, poetry and fiction. Aimed at professionals in mental health fields, university educated individuals (18-39),creative artists and any who take an interest in dreaming, sleep, and the inner life. Our magazine is informative, entertaining, and challenging." Quarterly. Estab. April 1980. Circ. 15,000.

Needs: Literary, contemporary, psychic/supernatural, science fiction, fantasy, horror, feminist, gay/lesbian, erotica, gothic, western, mystery, adventure, humor and translations. "Almost any genre is acceptable, as long as the theme of the story relates *directly* to *any* aspect of the world of sleep, dreams or the inner life of imagination." Buys 2 mss/issue, 8 mss/year. Receives approximately 10-15 unsolicited fiction mss each month. Length: 2,000-2,500 words.

How to Contact: Send complete ms with SASE or IRC. Reports in 3 weeks on mss. Free sample copy.

Payment: Pays $50-70 or 3¢/word.

Terms: Pays on publication for all rights. Publication copyrighted.

Tips: "Keep writing and keep submitting. Eventually you will hit us where it counts. Always make copies of the story—never send an original. Most rejected manuscripts are: too confused in plot development, hackneyed in terms of expressive language, not daring enough (not challenging to the reader's sensibilities), or too long or too short in length."

EARTH'S DAUGHTERS, A Feminist Arts Periodical, Box 41, Central Park Station, Buffalo NY 14215. (716)837-7778. Editor: Ryki Zuckerman. Magazine. "We publish poetry and short fiction; topics of interest to women; also graphics, art work, photos.'' For a general/women/feminist audience. Quarterly. Estab. 1971. Circ. 500.

Needs: Adventure, contemporary, erotica, ethnic, experimental, fantasy, feminist/lesbian, humor/satire, literary, prose poem, religious/inspirational, women's. ''Keep the fiction short.'' Receives 25-50 unsolicited fiction mss/month. Accepts 2-4 mss/issue; 8-12 mss/year. Length: 400 words minimum; 1,000 words maximum; 800 words average. Occasionally critiques rejected mss.

How to Contact: Query first or send complete ms. SASE for query. Simultaneous and photocopied submissions OK. Reports in 3 weeks on queries; 3 weeks to 3 months on mss. Sample copy for $2.

Payment: 4 free contributor's copy.

Terms: Acquires first rights. Publication copyrighted.

Tips: Submit ''*good* writing supportive of women.''

EARTHWISE QUARTERLY, Earthwise Publications, Inc., Box 680536, Miami FL 33168. (305)688-8558. Editor: Barbara Holley. Fiction Editor: Kaye Carter. ''A quarterly journal mainly of poetry and interviews. We are aiming for larger issues with more space for fiction, articles, etc. We have various quarterly themes, usually announced at start of year. We have an eclectic audience of mainly poets, some artists, authors. We aim for quality literature and are attaining a fine reputation. We also publish a quarterly newsletter announcing contests, markets, etc.'' Quarterly. Estab. 1978. Circ. 350.

Needs: Literary, contemporary, psychic/supernatural, science fiction, fantasy, gothic, romance, western, mystery, adventure, humor and any ethnic. Very interested in translations. Nothing morally or ethically pornographic. Buys 1-2 mss/issue, 4-6 mss/year. Length: 900-1,200 words.

How to Contact: Query with clips of published work with SASE. Reports in 1 month on queries and mss. Sample copy $3.50.

Payment: Pays $25 + .

Terms: Pays on publication for first North American serial rights.

Tips: ''We like light, amusing or warm stories for *Earthwise*. We much prefer the well done story even if a bit longer. Cameos or vignettes are also acceptable. No submissions are read from June 30 through September 5th each year.''

EERIE COUNTRY, Weirdbook Press, Box 149, Amherst Branch, Buffalo NY 14226. Editor: W. Paul Ganley. ''Latter day pulp magazine of supernatural horror and fantasy of lesser known writers for literate fans of horror/supernatural.'' Published irregularly. Estab. 1976. Circ. 150.

Needs: Psychic/supernatural, fantasy, horror and gothic (not modern). No psychological mystery or physical horror (blood), traditional stories, science fiction, or reincarnation stories or swords and sorcery without a supernatural element. Overstocked until Jan. 1, 1983.

How to Contact: Send complete ms with SASE. Reports in 2 months on mss. Sample copy $2. Free guidelines with legal-sized SASE.

Payment: Pays ¼¢/word and free author's copy.

Terms: Acquires first North American serial rights plus rights to reprint entire issues.

ELDRITCH TALES, Yith Press, 1051 Wellington Rd., Lawrence KS 66044. (913)843-4341. Editor-in-Chief: Crispin Burnham. ''The magazine concerns horror fiction in the tradition of the old *Weird Tales* magazine. We publish fiction in the tradition of H.P. Lovecraft, Robert Bloch and Stephen King, among others, for fans of this particular genre.'' Published semiannually. Estab. 1975. Circ. 500.

Needs: Horror. No mad slasher stories or similar non-supernatural horror stories. Receives about 8 unsolicited fiction mss/month. Accepts 12 mss/issue, 24 mss/year. Length: 50-100 words minimum; 20,000 words maximum; 10,000 words average. Occasionally critiques rejected mss. Sometimes recommends markets.

How to Contact: Send complete ms with SASE. Photocopied and previously published submis-

sions OK. Reports in 4 months. Sample copy $6; free guidelines with SASE.
Payment: 3 free contributor's copies; $6 charge for extras.
Terms: Pays on publication for first rights. Publication copyrighted.
Tips: "Buy a sample copy and read it thoroughly. Most rejects with my magazine are because people have not checked out what an issue is like or what type of stories I accept. Most rejected stories fall into one of two categories: non-horror fantasy (sword & sorcery, high fantasy) or nonsupernatural horror (mad slasher stories. 'Halloween Clones' I call them). When I say that they should read my publication, I'm not whistling Dixie."

EMPIRE, The Magazine for Science Fiction Writers, 35 Sherman Ct., New Haven CT 06511. (203)865-4373. Editor-in-Chief: Mary Kittredge. "A writers' magazine—we publish articles that assist, inform, and entertain science fiction writers from tyro to professional." Published quarterly. Estab. 1974. Circ. 1,100.
Needs: Fantasy (occasionally), science fiction. "Every issue contains a story written by a subscriber, and three critiques of the story by professional SF writers. Nothing but SF. Only subscribers to *Empire* are eligible." Receives 8-10 unsolicited fiction ms/month. Accepts 1 mss/issue, 4 mss/year. Length: 2,000 words minimum; 3,500 words maximum; 3,000 words average. Occasionally critiques rejected mss.
How to Contact: Send complete ms with SASE. Photocopied submissions OK. Reports in 2 weeks. Sample copy $2 with 9x12 SAE and 3 first class stamps.
Payment: 2 free contributor's copies and 1 year subscription. Extra copies by arrangement.
Terms: Pays on publication for first English language serial rights. Publication copyrighted.
Tips: "Read *Empire* and other books on writing, especially Reginald Bretnor's *Craft of Science Fiction*. We like a solid conflict with a solid resolution, in a well-thought-out plot, with believable characters. Correct spelling, grammar, carefully! We do not change *anything* in fiction mss. Type double-spaced, one side of 8½x11 white bond (no corrasable). Enclose SASE!"

ENCOUNTER, Encounter, Ltd., 59 St. Martin's Lane, London, England WC2N 4JS. Tel. 01-836-4194. Editor: M.J. Lasky. Fiction Editor: Anthony Thwaite. A monthly review of current affairs, literature and the arts for a mainly professional and academic audience. Monthly. Estab. 1953. Circ. 17,000.
Needs: Contemporary, literary. Buys 1 ms/issue; 12 mss/issue. Length: 2,500 words minimum; 5,000 words maximum.
How to Contact: Send complete ms with SASE. Photocopied submissions OK. Reports in 6 weeks on mss. Sample copy for $3.50.
Payment: Approximately £10 per 1,000 words.
Terms: Pays on publication for first rights. Publication copyrighted.
Tips: "Study the magazine first."

EPOCH MAGAZINE, 245 Goldwin Smith Hall, Cornell University, Ithaca NY 14853. (607)256-3385. Editors: Jas McConkey, Walter Slatoff and C.S. Giscombe. "Top level fiction and poetry for people who are interested in and capable of being entertained by good literature." Published 3 times a year. Estab. 1947. Circ. 1,000.
Needs: Literary, contemporary and ethnic. "So many categories seem insufficient to describe the kind of fiction we're looking for. We have not, for example, specified the category of western because I'm afraid of being inundated with a lot of the pale and mindless action/adventure/horse-opera stuff I see in the popular western magazines at the newsstands. We would be thrilled, though, to publish the work of a young Walter Van Tilberg Clark." Buys 4-5 mss/issue. Receives approximately 100 unsolicited fiction mss each month. Length: 10-30 typed, double-spaced pages. Critiques rejected mss "when there is time."
How to Contact: Send complete ms with SASE. Reports in 2 weeks-2 months on mss. Sample copy $2.50.
Terms: Pays on publication for first North American serial rights. Publication copyrighted.
Tips: "We *strongly suggest* that potential contributors either examine a copy of *Epoch* at the library or purchase one from us before submitting work."

EROTIC FICTION QUARTERLY, EFQ Publications, Box 4958, San Francisco CA 94101. Editor: Richard Hiller. Magazine of erotic or other sexual fiction for imaginative, thoughtful adults. Quarterly. Publication planned for mid-1983.
Needs: Erotica, ethnic, experimental, fantasy, feminist, gay, humor/satire, literary, men's and women's, romance, science fiction. "We will consider any category with sexual *theme* (not slant). Innovative, high quality writing, free of cliché or pretension." No standard pornography; no "men's" stories; no contrived plots. Length: 500 words minimum; 5,000 words maximum; 1,500 words average. Occasionally critiques rejected ms. "Willing to work with beginners on very exceptional mss."
How to Contact: Send complete ms only with SASE. Photocopied submissions OK; non-returnable copy also OK with 20¢ SASE for reply. Fiction guidelines free with SAE.
Payment: Pays $35 minimum.
Terms: Pay on acceptance for all rights. Publication copyrighted.
Tips: "I specifically encourage beginners who have something to say regarding sexual attitudes, emotions, roles, etc. Story ideas should come from real life, not media; characters should be real people. There are essentially no restrictions regarding content, style, explicitness, etc.; *originality*, *clarity*, an *integrity* are most important."

EUREKA REVIEW, Orion Press, 90 Harrison Ave., New Canaan CT 06840. Editor: Roger Memmott. A journal of fiction, poetry and art; eclectic in subject matter for a literary audience. Annual. Estab. 1975. Circ. 600.
Needs: Literary, contemporary, science fiction and humor. No sentimental or pseudo-academic material. Buys 8-12 mss/issue. Length: 1,000-7,500 words.
How to Contact: Send complete ms with SASE. Reports in 2 months on mss. Sample copy $1.50.
Payment: Pays with 2 free author's copies. $1.50 charge for extras.
Terms: Pays on publication for first North American serial rights.

EVENT, Kwantlen College, Box 9030, Surrey, British Columbia, Canada V3T 5H8. Editor: Leona Gom. Fiction Editor: Maureen Shaw. Managing Editor: Vye Flindall. Primarily a literary magazine, publishing poetry, fiction, reviews, plays and graphics for creative writers, artists, anyone interested in contemporary literature. Semiannual. Estab. 1970. Circ. 1,000.
Needs: Literary, contemporary, science fiction, fantasy, feminist, gay/lesbian, adventure and humor. No technically poor or unoriginal pieces. Buys 4-6 mss/issue. Receives approximately 50 unsolicited fiction mss each month. Length: 4,000 words. Critiques rejected mss "when there is time."
How to Contact: Send complete ms with SASE (*must* be Canadian postage or IRC). Reports in 4 months on mss. Sample copy $2.50.
Payment: Pays $20 minimum plus free subscription and 2 author's copies.
Terms: Pays on publication for first North American serial rights. Publication copyrighted.
Tips: "*Read* our magazine first; and read a lot of contemporary literature." Mss are rejected because of "level of maturity."

EXIT, A Journal of the Arts, Rochester Routes/Creative Arts Projects, 50 Inglewood Dr., Rochester NY 14619. (716)436-0178. Publishers: Frank Judge and Gregory FitzGerald. Fiction Editor: Gregory FitzGerald. "Our magazine has no theme and no particular bias but *quality*; there are some restrictions on length and content, as detailed below. We assume our readership is the 'little magazine' audience; we've had nothing to disprove this assumption so far." Published 3 times/year. Estab. 1976. Circ. 1,000.
Needs: Literary, contemporary, science fiction, fantasy, erotica, mystery and translations. "Science fiction, fantasy, erotica and mystery submissions should have a 'literary' slant giving a broader appeal than that of the respective forms; query preferred for these categories." No religious/inspirational, psychic/supernatural, men's, women's, feminist, gay/lesbian, confession, gothic, romance, western, adventure, juvenile, young adult, ethnic, or serialized or condensed

novels. Accepts 1-2 mss/issue. Receives 2-3 unsolicited fiction mss each month. Length: 2,000 words maximum. Critiques rejected mss "when there is time."
How to Contact: Send query or complete ms with SASE. Reports in 3 weeks on queries, 1 month on mss. Sample copy $3.
Payment: 2 free author's copies. $2 charge for extras.
Terms: Pays on publication for first North American serial rights and second serial rights. Publication copyrighted.
Tips: Mss are rejected because they are "loaded with adolescent clichés and trite concepts; have no sense of plot, liveliness."

FAMILY PASTIMES, R.R. 4, Perth, Ontario, Canada K7H 3C6. (613)267-4819. Editor: Jim Deacove. Tabloid by a game company.
Needs: Mystery. "We need a writer(s) of cases for our mystery game, 'Eagle Eye Agency.' "
How to Contact: Query first with IRC. Photocopied submissions OK. Reports in 3 weeks on queries.
Terms: Acquires all rights. Publication copyrighted.

FANTASY BOOK, Fantasy Book Enterprises, Box 4193, Pasadena CA 91106. (213)428-4124 (after 12 Noon). Executive Editor: Dennis Mallonee. Editor/Art Director: Nick Smith. Magazine of fantasy fiction of all sorts: high fantasy, light fantasy, heroic fantasy, dark fantasy, fairy stories, fables, poems . . . for an older audience, college and up, "though we are not averse to using an occasional piece aimed at the younger reader." Published quarterly. Estab. 1981. Circ. 4,500.
Needs: Adventure, fantasy, horror, psychic/supernatural, science fiction, excerpted novel. Receives 45 unsolicited fiction mss/month. Buys 10 mss/issue, 60 mss/year. Length: 2,000 words minimum; 10,000 words maximum; 5,000 words average. Occasionally critiques rejected mss.
How to Contact: Send complete ms with SASE. Photocopied and previously published submissions OK. Reports in 6 weeks. Sample copy $3; free guidelines with SASE.
Payment: 2-4¢/word; 2 free contributor's copies; charge for extras: 50% of cover price.
Terms: Pays on "approval of galleys" for first North American serial rights. Copyright notification printed in author's name.
Tips: "The only advice we can give to an author attempting to write for *Fantasy Book* is to tell his story well. We look for strong characterization and a coherent and cohesive plot. We frown upon carelessness and sloppy workmanship. We do want to encourage new writers."

FANTASY MACABRE, A Little Magazine of Spectral Pandemonium, c/o Richard Fawcett, 61 Teecomwas Dr., Uncasville CT 06382. (203)848-0636. Editor-in-Chief: Dave Reeder. US Editor: Richard Fawcett. Magazine of "stories of the supernatural in the *Weird Tales* tradition for lovers of the weird and the uncanny story. See the writings of Stephen King, Peter Straub, Robert Bloch, et. al. for examples of what we like." Published 3 times/year. Estab. 1980. Circ. 500.
Needs: Fantasy, horror, psychic/supernatural, suspense/mystery. Receives 10-12 unsolicited fiction mss/month. Accepts 5-6 mss/issue, 6-12 mss/year. Length: 2,000 words minimum; 5,000 words maximum; 3,000 words average. Occasionally critiques rejected mss.
How to Contact: Send complete ms with SASE. Photocopied and previously published submissions OK. Reports in 3 weeks. Sample copy $2; free guidelines for SASE.
Payment: 5 free contributor's copies; $2 charge for extras.
Terms: Pays on publication for one-time rights. Publication copyrighted.

FANTASY TALES, A Magazine of the Weird and Unusual, 194 Station Rd., Kings Heath, Birmingham, England B14 7TE. Editor-in-Chief: Stephen Jones. Fiction Editor: David Sutton. "A magazine of entertaining stories and verse which visually is a tribute to the pulps. We publish a wide range of themes in the fantasy genre for both devotees of fantasy and more general readers." Published 3 times/year. Estab. 1977. Circ. 1,000.
Needs: Fantasy, "sword and sorcery," horror, psychic/supernatural. No hard science fiction. Receives about 20 unsolicited fiction mss/month. Buys 5-6 mss/issue. Length: 1,500 words mini-

mum; 7,000 words maximum. Occasionally critiques rejected mss. Sometimes recommends markets.

How to Contact: Send complete ms with SASE. Simultaneous, photocopied, and previously published submissions OK. Reports in 1 month. Sample copy $3.50.

Payment: 1/2¢/word.

Terms: Pays on publication for first rights, second serial rights. Publication copyrighted.

Tips: "Study magazine, submit and keep fingers crossed!"

FAT TUESDAY, 853 N. Citrus, Los Angeles CA 90038. Editor-in-Chief: F.M. Cotolo. Fiction Editors: B. Lyle Tabor and Thom Savion. "Generally, we are an eclectic journal of fiction, poetry and visual treats. Our debut issue featured fiction by FM Cotolo, B. Lyle Tabor, and Dom Cimei, all of which focused on an individualistic nature with fiery elements. We are a literary mardi gras—as the title indicates—and irreverancy is as acceptable to us as profundity as long as there is fire! Our audience is anyone who can praise literature and condemn it at the same time. Anyone too serious about it on either level will not like *Fat Tuesday*." Published semiannually. Estab. 1981. Circ. 500.

Needs: Comics, erotica, experimental, humor/satire, literary, prose poem, serialized/excerpted novel, dada. "Although we list categories, we are open to feeling out various fields if they are delivered with the mark of an individual and not just in the format of the particular field. In fiction, we do not appreciate the polished piece which has lost all flair due to the author's concern with form." Receives 10 unsolicited fiction mss/month. Accepts 4-5 mss/issue, 10-20 mss/year. Length: 1,000 words maximum. Occasionally critiques rejected mss. Sometimes recommends markets.

How to Contact: Send complete ms with SASE. Photocopied submissions OK. Reports in 4 weeks. Sample copy $3.50.

Payment: 2 free contributor's copies.

Terms: Pays on publication for one-time rights. Publication copyrighted.

Tips: "Retain your enthusiasm. Never write and submit anything without it. Buy an issue and eat it up, page by page. Suffer through it if you have to, give in to enjoying it as much as you like. Take it to bed with you, whatever. Then, go into your guts and write something. You'll be amazed at what comes out and what could be accepted by a publication with our outlook. Never be afraid. If you're not on fire, we'll tell you so and encourage you to try again. One flop ms doesn't mean a thing to us. Neither do ten from the same author. Bug us if you must. Don't get discouraged. Curse at us if you disagree with what we suggest; write us a scathing letter if you feel we don't know what we're doing. Just stay alive, stay awake, and chances are your writing will, too. We feel it is essential that a potential submitter buy a sample issue and experience the 'zine. The results are twofold: 1) He or she will understand what would work and get a better idea of what we're talking about in this blurb and 2) He or she will help support the continuation of this free form of expression that *FT* calls 'litteraire verité and help us exist for it."

FELLOWSHIP IN PRAYER, Fellowship in Prayer, Inc., 20 Nassau St., Suite 250 E., Princeton NJ 08540. (609)924-0880. Editor: Paul Griffith. Magazine with prayer and meditation theme. Monthly. Estab. 1949. Circ. 4,000.

Needs: Religious/inspirational. Buys 1-2 mss/issue. Length: 1,500 words.

How to Contact: Send complete ms with SASE. Reports in 2-3 weeks on mss. Free sample copy.

Payment: Pays 1/2¢/word and up for quality work. 6 free author's copies.

Terms: Pays on publication for first rights. Publication copyrighted.

FEMINIST STUDIES, Feminist Studies, Inc., c/o Women's Studies Program, University of Maryland, College Park MD 20742. (301)454-2363. Editor: Claire G. Moses. Fiction Editor: Rachel Blau Duplessis. Editorial Assistant: D. Johnson-Clagett. Journal of feminist issues. A forum for analysis, debate and exchange. Audience consists of Women's Studies faculty, students, anyone interested in feminist issues and research. Published 3 times/year. Estab. 1972. Circ. 5,000.

Needs: Women's, feminist, gay/lesbian and Third World women's writing. Receives very few unsolicited fiction mss. Critiques rejected mss "when there is time."
How to Contact: Send complete ms with SASE. Reports in 1-3 months on mss. Free guidelines with SASE.
Terms: Publication copyrighted.

FICTION ENERGY, Box 57, Bronx NY 10470. Co-Editors: Michael Santora, John Deacy and Brian McGlynn. Magazine of fiction, articles, poetry for general audience. Semiannually. Estab. 1983. Circ. "expect 500."
Needs: Adventure, contemporary, erotica, experimental, fantasy, horror, humor/satire, literary, mainstream, prose poem, psychic/supernatural, science fiction, suspense/mystery. No stories of gratuitous violence. Accepts 10-15 mss/issue; 20-30 mss/year. Length: 500 words minimum; 1,500 words maximum; 1,000 words average. Prefers *shorter* fiction, 7 pages or less. Occasionally critiques rejected mss.
How to Contact: Send complete ms with SASE. Simultaneous, photocopied and previously published submissions OK. Reports in 3-4 weeks on mss. Sample copy $3.
Payment: Pays in 1 contributor's copy; $3 charge for extras.
Terms: Acquires one-time rights. Publication copyrighted.
Tips: "Proofread copy carefully. If you believe in your talent and couldn't place ms elsewhere send it to us. Write what is true to you and not for any literary market; we prefer originality."

FICTION INTERNATIONAL, St. Lawrence University, Canton NY 13617. (315)379-5961. Editor: Joe David Bellamy. "For writers interested in fiction in all its forms; readers interested in contemporary literary developments and possibilities. Previous contributors include Jayne Anne Phillips, Russell Banks, T. Coraghessan Boyle, Rosellen Brown, Jerry Bumpus, David Madden, Joyce Carol Oates, Ronald Sukenick, Gordon Weaver, and Robley Wilson, Jr." Annual. Estab. 1973. Circ. 2,500.
Needs: Literary and contemporary. Buys 12-16 mss/issue. Receives approximately 300 unsolicited fiction mss each month. No length limitations but rarely uses short shorts or manuscripts over 30 pages. Portions of novels acceptable if self-contained enough for independent publication. Unsolicited mss will be considered only from Sept. through Dec. of each year.
How to Contact: Send complete ms with SASE. Reports in 1-3 months on mss. Sample copy $8.
Payment: Varies.
Terms: Pays on publication for first and first North American serial rights. Publication copyrighted.
Tips: "Study the magazine. Highly selective. Not an easy market for unsophisticated writers."

THE FIDDLEHEAD, University of New Brunswick, Box 4400, Fredericton, New Brunswick, Canada E3B 5A3. (506)454-3591. Editor: Peter Thomas. Fiction Editors: Ted Colson, William Bauer. Literary magazine with poetry, short stories, book reviews and sketches. Quarterly. Estab. March 1945. Circ. 1,100.
Needs: Literary. Buys 4-5 mss/issue, 20-25 mss/year. Critiques rejected mss "when there is time." Sometimes recommends markets.
How to Contact: Send complete ms with IRC and SAE. Reports in 1-2 months on mss. Sample copy $4.25.
Payment: Pays $10. Free author's copy; $4.25 charge for extras.
Terms: Pays on publication for first North American serial rights.

FIFTH SUN, Quincunx Press, 1134-B Chelsea Ave., Santa Monica CA 90403. (213)828-2918. Contact: Editor. "Revelations into the cultural crossroads of the North American continent. Stories and excerpts which confront hypocrisy and intolerance in interpersonal, intergroup and international relationships. Also interested in fiction which deals with identity crisis. Audience is mostly artists, writers, academics with a sprinkling of general readership. It is read by those who desire a perspective often lacking in most outlets." Annual. Estab. 1978. Circ. 450-500.

Needs: Literary, contemporary, science fiction, fantasy, horror, men's, women's, feminist, gay/lesbian, erotica, humor, condensed novels and experimental. "We will also consider any worthwhile fiction regardless of category. No male-oriented sex fantasy or pornography lacking any social worth." Accepts 4-5 mss/issue. Length: 750-3,000 words.

How to Contact: Query with clips of published work with SASE. Reports in 1 month on queries, 2 months on mss. Sample copy $2 with 8½x11 SASE and $1 postage.

Payment: 5 free author's copies. $1 charge per extra copy.

Terms: Pays on publication for all rights (sometimes), first rights and one-time rights.

FIGHTING WOMAN NEWS, Fighting Woman News, Box 1459, Grand Central Station, New York NY 10163. Editor: Valerie Eads. Fiction Editor: Muskat Buckby. "Women's martial arts, self-defense, combative sports. Articles, reviews, etc., related to these subjects. Well-educated adult women who are actually involved with martial arts read us because we're there and we're good." Quarterly. Estab. 1975. Circ. 5,600.

Needs: Science fiction, fantasy, feminist, adventure and translations. "No material that shows women as victims, incompetents, stereotypes or 'fight scenes' written by people who don't know anything about fighting skills." Receives very few unsolicited fiction mss. Length: 2,500 words. Critiques rejected mss "when there is time."

How to Contact: Query with clips of published work with SASE. Reports as soon as possible on queries and mss. Sample copy $2.50. Free guidelines with legal-sized SASE.

Payment: Pays in 5 free author's copies. Cover price plus postage charged for extras.

Terms: Pays on publication for one-time rights. Publication copyrighted.

Tips: "It never hu gts to read the magazine you want to write for." Mss are rejected because they are "not suitable for our magazine, i.e., submitted to the wrong market by writers who've never read our magazine."

FIREWEED, A Feminist Quarterly, Fireweed, Inc., Box 279, Station B, Toronto, Ontario, Canada M5T 2W2. Editors: The Fireweed Collective. Magazine of non-sexist fiction, poetry, nonfiction, scholarly articles for "feminists." Quarterly. Estab. 1978. Circ. 2,000.

Needs: Novel, excerpts, journals, ethnic, experimental, fantasy, lesbian/feminist, women's/feminist studies, humor/satire, feminist literary criticism, translations. No "women's formula style." Receives 100 unsolicited fiction mss/month. Accepts 4 mss/issue; 16 mss/year. Length: 1,200 words minimum; 18,000 words maximum; 6,000 words average; poetry (maximum 6). Occasionally critiques rejected ms.

How to Contact: Query with SASE. Photocopied submissions OK. Reports in 3 months on queries.

Payment: 2 free contributor's copies.

Terms: Publication copyrighted.

Tips: "Submit and hope for the best! We're very enthusiastic, too. We nominate writers who have been published in *Fireweed* for grants and awards. Please do not send visual art through the mail."

FLOATING ISLAND, Floating Island Publications, Box 516, Point Reyes Station CA 94956. Editor: Michael Sykes. Anthology with poetry, prose, photography and graphic arts. Short fiction, journals, essays and explorations. For artists and writers, libraries, small press bookstores, poetry centers, colleges and institutions. The emphasis is literary, artistic and non-commercial. Published once every 2-3 years. Circ. 2,000.

Needs: Literary, contemporary, psychic/supernatural, science fiction and fantasy. Receives 2-3 unsolicited fiction mss each month. Length: short. Critiques rejected mss "when there is time."

How to Contact: Query with SASE. Reports in 2 weeks on queries, 2 months on mss. Sample copy $6.95 with $1.30 postage.

Payment: 2 free author's copies. $5 charge for extras.

Terms: Acquires simultaneous rights. Publication copyrighted.

Tips: Also publishes books by individual authors: short novels, stories and essays.

FOCUS: A JOURNAL FOR LESBIANS, Daughters of Bilitis Boston, O.C.B.C., 1151 Massachusetts Ave., Cambridge MA 02138. Editor: Paula Bennett, Collective Liaison. Magazine with literature and art relevant to and for lesbians. Bimonthly. Estab. 1970. Circ. 300.
Needs: Lesbian. "All categories are 'acceptable' to us as long as they are oriented toward a lesbian audience. No pornography, anything by, for or about men." Accepts 4-5 mss/issue, 24 mss/year. Receives approximately 15 unsolicited fiction mss each month. Length: 2,000-4,000 words. Critiques rejected mss "when there is time."
How to Contact: Send complete ms with SASE or SAE and IRC. Reports in 2 months on mss. Sample copy with SASE and 30¢ postage.
Payment: Free author's copy. $1.35 charge for extras.
Terms: Pays on publication for first rights. Publication copyrighted.
Tips: "Our concern is quality writing—not politics. Try us. Be neat and professional. Proofread. Type double-spaced, have something to say and say it well. We have a prose contest each summer with a $35 award." Mss are rejected because "they are not well-written: formless, negligible story line, poor style, clichéd, etc."

FOREIGN ARTISTS, POETS AND AUTHORS REVIEW (FAPAR!), Le Beacon Presse, 2921 E. Madison St., Suite 7, Seattle WA 98112. (206)322-1431. Editor-in-Chief: Keith S. Gormezano. Fiction Editor: Mirium Vargas. Magazine "only for artists, poets and authors not born in U.S. and Canada. *FAPAR* strives to inform its North American readership what non-North American writers, artists and poets are creating." Publishes one short fiction story, book reviews, poetry (10 pages), graphics (2 pages) each issue. Published quarterly. Estab. Fall. 1981. Circ. 200.
Needs: Condensed novel, contemporary, erotica, ethnic, humor/satire, literary, science fiction, suspense/mystery, young adult. Receives 20 unsolicited fiction mss/month. Accepts 1 mss/issue, 10 mss/year. Charges 50¢/page reading fee. Length: 25 words minimum; 1,000 words maximum. Critiques mss for 25¢/page.
How to Contact: Query first with SASE. Simultaneous, photocopied and previously published submissions OK. Reports in 1 month on queries; 4 months on mss. Sample copy $2.
Payment: 1 free contributor's copy; $2 charge for extras.
Terms: Pays on publication for one-time rights.
Tips: "Buy a copy or be familiar with works of other foreign fiction writers. Have your work critiqued by at least two other published writers." Presents *FAPAR* Awards in poetry, fiction, graphics, book reviews.

FORESIGHT, Foresight, 29 Beaufort Ave., Hodge Hill, Birmingham, England B34 6AD. (021)783-0587. Editor: John Barklam. Fiction Editor: Judy Barklam. Magazine with "new age material, world peace, psychic phenomena, research, occultism, spirtualism, mysticism, U.F.O's, philosophy, etc. For psychic enthusiasts, people with an open mind who take pleasure in their search for truth." Published every 3 months. Estab. August 1970. Circ. 800.
Needs: Psychic/supernatural. Length: 300-1,500 words. Critiques rejected mss "when there is time."
How to Contact: Query with clips of published work with SASE. Reports in 2 weeks on queries, 1 month on mss. Sample copy $1.
Payment: Free author's copy. 75¢ charge for extras.
Tips: "Send original, exciting material with a good strong, topical theme, relating to the present times." Mss are rejected because of "lengthy, complicated plots and story-lines."

FORMAT: ART & THE WORLD, Seven Oaks Press, 405 S. 7th St., St. Charles IL 60174. (312)584-0187. Editor: Ms. C.L. Morrison. "Magazine of art, survival information for contemporary artists, essays, interviews, poetry, articles and short fiction with useful information for artists." Monthly. Estab. September 1978. Circ. 1,000.
Needs: Survival-oriented; stories related to art, artists, economics or current events. Receives

approximately two unsolicited fiction mss each month. Length: 1,500 words maximum.
How to Contact: Send complete ms with SASE. Reports in 3 weeks on ms. Sample copy $2.50.
Payment: Pays $5-15. 6 free author's copies. $1 charge for extras.
Terms: Pays on publication for simultaneous rights. Publication copyrighted.
Tips: "Write honestly about something you know with insight and understanding." Mss are rejected because they are "not original."

FOUR QUARTERS, LaSalle College, 20th and Olney Ave., Philadelphia PA 19141. (215)951-1171. Editor: John C. Kleis. Magazine of poetry, fiction, nonfiction for mainly academic audience. Quarterly. Estab. November 1951. Circ. 750.
Needs: Literary and contemporary. Buys 5 mss/issue, 20 mss/year. Receives approximately 40 unsolicited fiction mss each month. Length: 2,000-5,000 words. Critiques rejected mss "when there is time."
How to Contact: Send complete ms with SASE. Reports in 4-6 weeks on mss. Sample copy $1 and free guidelines with SASE.
Payment: Pays $25 and 3 free author's copies. $1 charge for extras.
Terms: Pays on publication for all rights. Publication copyrighted.
Tips: "Technical mastery gets our attention and respect immediately. We admire writers who use the language with precision, economy, and imagination. But fine writing for its own sake is unsatisfying unless it can lead the reader to some insight into the complexity of the human condition without falling into heavy-handed didacticism. We reject most of the mss we receive, mostly because their ideas and expression are clichés."

FOUR WINDS, International Forum for Native American Art, Literature & History, Hundred Arrows Press, Box 156, Austin TX 78767. (512) 472-7701. Editor: Charles J. Lohrmann. Magazine of American Indian and Western art and history, contemporary issues for art collectors, historians, museum personnel. "Generally well-educated and affluent audience with a strong interest in American Indian and Western art." Quarterly. Estab. 1980. Circ. 10,000.
Needs: Historical (general), western, American Indian. "Please include illustration possibilities." Receives 2-5 unsolicited fiction mss/month. Buys 1-3 mss/year. Length: 750 words minimum; 2,500 words maximum; 1,500 words average. Will critique rejected mss.
How to Contact: Query with clips of published work and SASE. Simultaneous, photocopied and previously published submissions OK. Reports in 1 month on queries. Sample copy $5.50.
Payment: $75-300. 4 free contributor's copies. Offers kill fee.
Terms: Pays on publication for first rights. Publication copyrighted.

FREEDOM'S HEART, The Philosophy and Science of Freedom, Quantum Universe Productions, Box 6821, Silver Spring MD 20906. Editor: Carl R. Dietrich. Magazine of "the libertine ethic/free market economics." Quarterly. Estab 1983.
Needs: Adventure, contemporary, fantasy, historical (general), humor/satire, science fiction. Receives "not enough" unsolicited fiction mss/month. Accepts 1-2 mss/issue; 4-8 mss/year. Length: 500 words minimum; 5,000 words maximum; 4,000 words average. Occasionally critiques rejected ms.
How to Contact: Send complete ms with SASE. "No phone calls, please."Simultaneous and photocopied submissions OK. Reports in 2-3 weeks on mss. Sample copy $2. Fiction guidelines for business size envelope and 2 first class stamps.
Payment: Small percentage per word and 2 free contributor's copies; $2 charge for extras.
Terms: Pays on publication for first rights. Publication copyrighted.
Tips: "Read *Alongside Night* by J. Neil Schulman, and *The Survival of Freedom*, edited by Jerry Pournelle and J.F. Carr."

FRONT STREET TROLLEY, Trolley, Inc., 2125 Acklen Ave., Nashville TN 37212. (615)741-3816. Editor-in-Chief: Molly McIntosh. Fiction Editor: R. A. Brannon. "Small magazine: prose, specializing in satire; short stories, any subject, for young to mature adults."

Published semiannually. Estab. 1974. Circ. 500.

Needs: "We are interested in anything which is well-written." Receives 5-10 unsolicited fiction mss/month. Accepts 2 mss/issue, 4 mss/year. Length: 2,500 words average. Occasionally critiques rejected mss.

How to Contact: Send complete ms with SASE. Simultaneous and photocopied submissions OK. Reports in 3 months. Free sample copy for 9x12 SAE and 70¢ postage; free guidelines for SAE and 1 first class stamp.

Payment: 2 free contributor's copies; $1 charge for extras.

Terms: Acquires one-time rights. Publication copyrighted.

Tips: "We are very interested in our stories having a definite beginning, middle and end with congruity and creative language throughout the manuscript."

FRUITION, The Plan, Box 872, Santa Cruz CA 95061. (408)429-3020. Editor: C. Olson. Newsletter promoting "public access to fruit and nut trees and establishing community food tree nurseries in which to grow them. We also publish stories, poetry, photos." Semiannually. Estab. 1979. Circ. 250.

Needs: Contemporary, fantasy, historical (general), juvenile, prose poem. "Send it in if you believe in it and/or see it in a vision or dream-like state." Receives 1 unsolicited fiction ms/month. Buys 1 ms/issue; 2 mss/year. Reading fee of $1 "requested but not necessary." Length: 1,500 words maximum; 750-1,000 words average. Usually critiques rejected ms.

How to Contact: Send complete ms with SASE. Simultaneous, photocopied and previously published submissions OK. Reports in 2-4 weeks on mss. Sample copy $2.

Payment: "All payments negotiable."

Terms: Pays on publication for first rights. Publication copyrighted.

GALACTIC DISCOURSE, Satori Press, 208 W. Crow, Eureka IL 61530. (309)467-3117. Editor-in-Chief: Laurie Huff. Magazine of "*Star Trek* fiction (characterization and character interaction is emphasized), poetry, artwork; some visionary/science fiction poetry and art for *Star Trek* fans. *Note*: "This is a 'when there's time' venture!" Published irregularly—annually or once every two years. Estab. 1977. Circ. 1,000.

Needs: Adventure, fantasy, feminist/lesbian, gay, humor/satire, prose poem, psychic/supernatural, science fiction, suspense/mystery, women's. No pure adventure, x-rated (explicit erotica), "Mary-Sue." Receives less than 5 unsolicited fiction mss/month. Accepts 8-12 mss/issue. Length: 12,000 words maximum; 5,000 words average. "We would consider publishing novellas/novels as a special issue apart from other work." Occasionally critiques rejected mss. Occasionally recommends markets.

How to Contact: Query first with SASE. Photocopied submissions OK. Reports in 6 weeks on queries; 2 months on mss. Sample copy "not offered, sorry; send SASE for purchasing info." Fiction guidelines for business size SAE and 2 first class stamps.

Terms: Pays on publication for second serial rights. Publication copyrighted.

Tips: "Type double-space; put your name on your material (and address); enclose return postage (if you want your ms returned) and SASE (for notification); *proofread* your ms." Mss are rejected because they are poorly written, have inappropriate content, and lack (personal) appeal.

GALLERY WORKS, Poets' Communue Publications, 1465 Hammersley Ave., Bronx NY 10469. (212)379-1519. Editor: Peter Holland. Literary magazine of poetry, short prose and artwork for mainly poets." Annually. Estab. 1973. Circ. 350.

Needs: Experimental, literary, prose poem, only. "We don't want unsolicited mss." Accepts 1 short story/year. Length: 1,000 words maximum. Short work only.

How to Contact: "Buy an issue of the magazine from the address above. Make check payable to Jeanne Lance." Sample copy $3.50.

Payment: 2 free contributor's copies.

Terms: Publication copyrighted.

Tips: "Good response to short stories. Buy a copy before submitting query."

GARGOYLE MAGAZINE, Paycock Press. Box 57206, Washington DC 20037. (202)333-1544. Editor: Richard Peabody. Estab. 1976. Published 3 times/year.
Needs: Contemporary, literary, experimental, humor/satire and translations. "We like fiction in the 2-10 typed page range, with an emphasis on the short short story. We generally print 3-6 stories an issue." Receives approximately 20 unsolicited fiction mss each month. Critiques rejected mss "when there is time." Sometimes recommends markets.
How to Contact: Submit complete ms with SASE. Photocopied submissions OK. Reports in 1-2 months on mss.
Payment: Free author's copy. Half the cover price for extras.
Terms: Publication copyrighted.
Tips: "Small magazines are deluged with mss these days. Writers should keep in mind that rejection doesn't mean a story is bad, only that the magazine editor doesn't want to, or can't, use it. You have to learn to endure. Most submitters have never seen our magazine and don't have the slightest idea what we're publishing. Writers should always be familiar with the market. This means reading all the short stories/fiction you can get your hands on. It is also important to keep up with movements in contemporary fiction. Recent fiction issue contained 460 pages. We're interested in printing excerpts from unpublished novels. We're consciously seeking out the new young writers (20 to 30 years old and younger). The new music, new films (*Diva* is a prime example), and new writing are welcome. We're tired of the current MFA vogue. I think the trend is away from poetry and toward fiction once again. I know an awful lot of poets who are writing novels all of a sudden."

GAY CHICAGO MAGAZINE, Ultra Ink, Inc. 1437 N. Wells, Chicago IL 60610. (312)751-0130. Editor: Dan Dileo. Entertainment guide, information for the gay community.
Needs: erotica, feminist/lesbian, gay. Receives "just a few" unsolicited fiction mss/month. Accepts 1-3 mss/year. Length: 600-800 words maximum.
How to Contact: Send complete ms with SASE. Photocopied submissions OK. Reports in 4-6 weeks on mss. Free sample copy for 6x9 envelope and 54¢ postage.
Payment: "None or minimal." 5-10 free contributor's copies; no charge for extras "if within reason."
Terms: Acquires one-time rights.

GAY SUNSHINE JOURNAL, Gay Sunshine Press, Box 40397, San Francisco CA 94140. (415)824-3184. Editor: Winston Leyland. "An intellectual gay cultural/literary journal, published irregularly in paperback book format (6x9"). We publish short fiction, poetry, interviews, essays and articles directed at a highly literate readership nationwide, mainly gay." Estab. 1970. Circ. 5,000.
Needs: Literary, contemporary, men's, gay, erotica, ethnic (Latin American) and translations. Fiction must have a bearing on a gay theme/consciousness. Length: Maximum of 20 typed double-spaced pages. Novellas also considered.
How to Contact: Query with clips of published work. Reports in 2 weeks on queries, 1 month on mss. Sample paperback copy: $8.
Payment: Free author's copies (amount of copies negotiable) plus nominal cash payment or books.
Terms: Pays on publication for first North American serial rights.

THE GEORGIA REVIEW, The University of Georgia, Athens GA 30602. (404)542-3481. Editor-in-Chief: Stanley W. Lindberg. Managing Editor: Sarah S. East. "*The Georgia Review* is a journal of arts and letters, featuring a blend of the best in contemporary thought and literature—essays, fiction, poetry, graphics, and book reviews—for the intelligent nonspecialist as well as the specialist reader. We seek material that appeals across disciplinary lines by drawing from a wide range of interests." Published quarterly. Estab. 1947. Circ. 4,300.
Needs: Experimental, literary. "We're looking for the highest quality fiction—work that is capable of sustaining subsequent readings, not throw-away pulp-magazine entertainment. Nothing

that fits too easily into a 'category,' e.g., adventure, confession, erotica, ethnic, lesbian, gay, gothic, horror, juvenile, men's, psychic, religious, romance, suspense, women's, etc.'' Receives about 100 unsolicited fiction mss/month. Buys 2-3 mss/issue, 8-10 mss/year. Length: open. Occasionally critiques rejected mss.

How to Contact: Send complete ms with SASE. ''Unsolicited mss are not considered during the months of June-August.'' Photocopied submissions OK; no multiple submissions. Reports in 2 months. Sample copy $2; free guidelines for ‰10 SAE and 1 first class stamp.

Payment: $10/printed page; 1-year complimentary subscription; 1 contributor's copy, reduced charge for extras.

Terms: Pays on publication for first North American serial rights.Publication copyrighted.

Tips: ''Obviously the best way to become acquainted with any journal is to look at its recent issues.''

GLOBAL TAPESTRY JOURNAL, BB Books, 1 Spring Bank, Longsight Rd, Salesbury, Blackburn, Lancs, England BB1 9EU. 0254-49218. Editor: Dave Cunliffe. ''Post-underground with avant-garde, experimental, alternative, counterculture, psychedelic, mystical, anarchist, etc., fiction used for a bohemian and counter culture. Magazine has readership ranging from academics to New Wave punks. Only present United Kingdom literary magazine of its kind.'' Quarterly. Circ. 1,000.

Needs: Literary, contemporary, science fiction, fantasy, erotica, confession, translations and novel extracts. ''The mystical material we do use is largely Buddhist, Taoist, Tantric, occult. We do use creative prose which blurs the distinction between fiction and reportage.'' No romance, western, mystery and detective. Uses 2 mss/issue. Receives 25 unsolicited fiction mss each month. Length: 500-2,000 words.

How to Contact: Send complete ms with SAE, IRC. Reports as soon as possible. Sample copy $1.20.

Payment: Free author's copy. Half the cover price for extras charge.

Terms: Pays on publication for one-time rights.

Tips: ''This specialized publication needs to be studied. We are interested in honest, uncontrived writing. Don't copy established authors. We don't require reflected Kerouac, Burroughs, Miller. Prefer the genuine article. This is a little magazine (edited, typeset, printed, distributed, etc., by one person) published by a small press with no outside funding. Therefore, its quarterly frequency often breaks down, due to available time and finance being limited.'' Mss are rejected because they are ''too contrived and lack originality. Develop a personal style and believe in it.''

GORHAM, Axios Newsletter, Inc., 1365 Edgecliffe Dr., Los Angeles Ca 90026. (213)663-1888. Editor: Daniel J. Gorham. Magazine covering material for geneologists and those interested in the Gorham family. Monthly.

Needs: Historical (general). Buys 1 ms/issue; 12 mss/year.

How to Contact: Query first with SASE. Simultaneous submissions OK. Reports in 4 weeks on queries. Sample copy for 12x18 envelope and 37¢ postage.

Payment: $50-500; 5 free contributor's copies. Offers kill fee of 50%.

Terms: Pays on publication for first rights. Publication copyrighted.

GRAIN, Saskatchewan Writers' Guild, Box 1885, Saskatchewan, Canada S7K 3S2. Editor: Ed Dyck. Fiction Editor: Brenda Riches. Literary magazine of ''fiction, poetry, songs, drama and essays of the highest quality for people who enjoy high quality writing. Many of our subscribers are writers.'' No theme. Quarterly. Estab. 1973. Circ. 800.

Needs: Contemporary, experimental, literary, mainstream, prose poem. ''No propaganda—only artistic/literary writing.'' No mss ''that stay *within* the limits of conventions such as women's magazines, science fiction, or that push a message.'' Receives 25-30 unsolicited fiction mss/month. Buys 4-5 mss/issue; 16-20 mss/year. Occasionally critiques rejected ms.

How to Contact: Send complete ms with SASE or IRCs. Photocopied submissions OK. Reports in 3 months on mss. Sample copy $2.

Payment: $35-100; 1 free contributor's copy.
Terms: Pays on publication for one-time rights. "We expect acknowledgement if the article is republished elsewhere."
Tips: "Attend reputable workshops conducted by practicing writers. Don't submit until a practicing writer of long experience and good judgment feels the work is ready. Keep the cover letter brief and not too clever. Don't describe your work in the letter. Don't tell the editor what a good writer you are. Don't tell the editor your work is just what the magazine needs. *Grain* publishes writing that challenges the traditions of reading and of writing. Our audience responds strongly!"

GRANTA, Granta, The Hobson Gallery, 44a Hobson St., Cambridge, England, CB1 1NL. Editor: Bill Buford. "Paperback magazine (250-400 pp.) publishing contemporary, imaginative writing: fiction (including novellas and works-in progress), essays, biography, journalism, etc." Quarterly. Estab. 1977. Circ. 16,000.
Needs: Contemporary, experimental, fantasy, feminist/lesbian, gay, literary, mainstream, serialized/excerpted novel, translations. "*Granta* has the space to accommodate pieces of exceptional length provided they are of exceptional quality." No genre fiction. Receives "hundreds of" unsolicited fiction mss/month. Buys 10-20 mss/issue; 40-100 mss/year. Occasionally critiques rejected ms.
How to Contact: "A query is always best, although we accept manuscripts sent with SASE or IRCs." Reports in 4-6 weeks on mss. Sample copy $6 surface mail; $13 airmail.
Payment: 50-500£, "depending on work and its length." 2 free contributor's copies (plus 10 off-prints). Offers kill fee for non-fiction.
Terms: Pays on publication for all rights. Publication copyrighted. "Competition provisonally planned for 1982-83. Details available at a later date."

GREAT RIVER REVIEW, Box 14805, Minneapolis MN 55414. Editor: Jean Ervin. Literary publication of fiction, poetry, art and book reviews. Semiannual. Estab. 1977.
Needs: Contemporary and experimental. No mass-circulation style fiction. Buys 6-7 mss/issue. Receives approximately 50 unsolicited fiction mss each month. Length: 2,000-10,000 words. Critiques rejected mss "when there is time."
How to Contact: Send complete ms with SASE. Sample copy $3.
Terms: Photocopied submissions OK. Publication copyrighted.
Tips: Priority to midwestern writers.

GREEN FEATHER, Quality Publications, Inc., Box 2633, Lakewood OH 44107. Editor-in-Chief: Gary S. Skeens. Fiction Editors: Robin Moser and Gary S. Skeens. "A magazine featuring poetry, fiction (short stories and novels), essays, nonfiction coverage of current events and people. This magazine is one dedicated and devoted to the people; to informing, entertaining, perhaps bringing some laughter to the lives that it may touch as well as some thought and quite possibly a few tears, but in the end it is a magazine that wishes to build a family. A group of people, whether they be artists, writers, poets, or bookkeepers, secretaries, teachers, people regardless of their walks of life who know what they want to read." Published annually. Estab. 1979. Circ. 100-150.
Needs: Adventure, contemporary, literary, western. "No mss of poor taste, thin or no plot, weak characterizations or dialogue." Receives 3-4 unsolicited fiction mss/month. Accepts 2 mss/issue. Length: 1,500 words minimum; 5,000 words maximum; 2,500 words average. Occasionally critiques rejected mss.
How to Contact: Send complete ms with SASE. Photocopied and previously published submissions OK. Reports in 2 months. Sample copy $1.50; free guidelines with SASE.
Payment: 1-3 free contributor's copies; $1 charge for extras.
Terms: Pays on publication for first rights, first North American serial rights. Publication copyrighted.
Tips: "I look for characterization, plot and dialogue; the writer should be honest, write from the 'gut' and must move me (as editor). Of course, read the magazine."

THE GREENFIELD REVIEW, RD 1, Box 80, Greenfield Center NY 12833. (518)584-1728. Editor-in-Chief: Joseph Bruchac. "Primarily a magazine of poetry but also interested in very short fiction. Special interest in work by Third World writers." For the general literate reader. Published twice yearly. Estab. 1970. Circ. 1,000.
Needs: Literary. Receives 20-30 unsolicited fiction mss/month. Accepts 2-4 mss/issue, 4-8 mss/ year. Length: 500 words minimum; 2,000 words maximum; 1,500 words average. Somtimes recommends other markets.
How to Contact: Send complete ms with SASE. Reports in 1 week on queries; 4 weeks on mss. Sample copy $3.
Payment: 1 contributor's copy. 50% discount for extras.
Terms: Pays on publication for first North American serial rights. Publication copyrighted.
Tips: "We look for prose as finely crafted as a poem, strongly imagistic and clearly written. Avoid overblown accompanying letters. Let the work speak for itself." Rejects mss for "two reasons: one is that the work may not fit our needs or our interests, which is why it pays people to READ PREVIOUS ISSUES before submitting to any magazine; second reason is that we're often overstocked with material and have no space for even excellent work."

GREEN'S MAGAZINE, Green's Educational Publications, Box 3236, Regina, Saskatchewan, Canada S4P 3H1. Editor: David Green. "A family magazine with a carefully balanced array of short fiction and poetry, intended to be exemplary in a variety of high-standard styles for a general audience." Quarterly. Estab. 1972. Circ. 500.
Needs: Literary. Buys 12 mss/issue. Receives approximately 350 unsolicited fiction mss each month. Length: 1,000-2,500 words. Critiques rejected mss "when there is time." Sometimes recommends markets.
How to Contact: Send complete ms with SAE and IRC. Reports in 2 months on mss. Sample copy $3 and free guidelines with legal-sized SAE and IRC.
Payment: Pays $10-25. 2 free author's copies. $3 charge for extras.
Terms: Pays on publication for first North American serial rights. Publication copyrighted.
Tips: "Study the magazine. We will not read photostats or other copies."

GREENSBORO REVIEW, University of North Carolina, Dept. of English, Greensboro NC 27412. (919)379-5459. Editor: Lee Zacharias. Fiction Editor: Stan Jenkins. Poetry Editor: Sarah Lindsay. Literary magazine featuring fiction and poetry for readers interested in contemporary literature. Semiannual. Circ. 500.
Needs: Contemporary and experimental. Accepts 8-10 mss/issue, 16-20 mss/year. Length: 6,000 words maximum.
How to Contact: Send complete ms with SASE.
Payment: Pays in contributor's copies.
Terms: Acquires first North American serial rights. Byline given. Photocopied submissions OK. Acceptances in September and January only. Publication copyrighted.

GRIMOIRE, c/o Thomas Wloch, 8181 Wayne Rd., Apt. H2084, Westland MI 48185. Editor: Thomas Wiloch. Magazine. "The theme is the realm of dreams—the surreal, macabre, and fantastic—presented in a sardonic manner and a lush graphic style. Humor that is unsettling; horror that is slyly jovial." For "literate readers, somewhat jaded, who appreciate the absurd and demonic." Quarterly. Estab. 1982.
Needs: Experimental, fantasy, horror, literary, prose poem, supernatural, surrealist. "The ideal submission would combine elements from Poe, Lewis Carroll, and the surrealists without getting bogged down in any single tradition." No "realism, character, surprise endings, new twists on old themes, messages." Accepts 10 mss/issue, 40 + mss/year. Length: 150 words minimum; 3,000 words maximum, 1,500 words average.
How to Contact: Send complete ms with SASE. Photocopied and previously published submissions OK. Reports in 2 weeks on mss. Sample copy for $2.50. Fiction guidelines free with business SAE and 20¢ postage.

Payment: 1-2 free contributor's copies.
Terms: Acquires one-time rights. Publication copyrighted.

THE GUERNICA REVIEW, Guernica Editions, Box 633, Station N.D.G., Montreal, Quebec, Canada H4A 3R1. Editor: Antonio D'Alfonso. Fiction Editor: Umberto Claudio. A new publication for prose, criticism and interviews that deals with current issues on literature, film, politics for poets and artists and interested non-elitist people. Quarterly. Circ. 500-1,000.
Needs: No "concrete, experimental for experimental sake" type material. Length: 500-2,000 words.
How to Contact: Query first with SASE. Reports in 2 weeks on queries, 1 month on mss. Free sample copy with SASE.
Payment: 2 free author's copies.
Terms: Acquires one-time rights.
Tips: "Perseverance, intelligent hard work pay off. Try to base yourself on tradition, instead of contemporary art. Let modernism come from the past. Avoid arrogance, anything that smells too stiff or is not open-minded enough." The *Review* is due out in 1983.

THE HAGUE REVIEW, A Literary Journal, The Hague Press, Box 385, Norfolk VA 23501. (804)853-4661. Editor: Roger Hunt Carroll. Semiannually. Estab. 1983.
Needs: Experimental, literary, translations. Occasionally critiques rejected mss.
How to Contact: Send complete ms with SASE. Photocopied submissions OK. Reports in 6 weeks on mss.
Payments: Pays in 3 contributor's copies.
Terms: Publication copyrighted.
Tips: "Write with excellence."

HAPPINESS HOLDING TANK, Stone Press, 1790 Grand River, Okemos MI 48864. Editor: Albert Drake. Primarily a magazine of poetry, articles, reviews, and literary information for poets, students, teachers, other editors and lay people. "I think a good many people read it for the literary information, much of which isn't available elsewhere." Published irregularly. Estab. Oct. 1970. Circ. 300-500.
Needs: Literary. "We publish a limited amount of fiction: very short stories, parables, prose poems, fragments, episodes. Not a good market for traditional fiction." Accepts 4-5 mss/year. Receives very few unsolicited fiction mss each month. Critiques rejected mss "when there is time."
How to Contact: Query. SASE for query, ms. Reports in 1 week on queries, 3 weeks on mss (except during summer). Sample copy $1 plus 68¢ postage.
Payment: 2 free author's copies.
Terms: Acquires one-time rights with automatic return of all rights to author.
Tips: "Be more careful about what you send out. Rewrite. Tighten. Compress. Read it aloud."

HARVARD ADVOCATE, Harvard Advocate Trustees, Inc., 21 South St., Cambridge MA 02138. (617)495-7820. Editor: Lynne H. Murphy. Fiction Editor: Barbara Epler. "We publish only work of Harvard affiliates—i.e., alumni, faculty, undergraduates, and staff. We generally focus on fiction, poetry, photographs, drawings, and criticism. Readership is primarily students and readers who live in and around Boston and New York. Limited national circulation." Quarterly. Estab. 1866. Circ. 15,000-20,000.
Needs: Literary, feminist, gay/lesbian, translations, art criticism, fiction fragments. Length: 7,000 words maximum.
How to Contact: Send complete ms with SASE. Reports within 3 months on mss. Free sample copy.
Payment: 10 free author's copies. $2 charge for extras.
Tips: Harvard affiliation required. "There are no specific sorts of fiction we favor except as the staff's taste might dictate year by year."

HECATE, A Women's Interdisciplinary Journal, Hecate Press, Box 99, St. Lucia, Queensland 4067, Australia. Editor: Carole Ferrier. Magazine of "material relating to women, particularly that which employs a feminist, marxist or other radical methodology to focus on the position of women in relation to patriarchy and capitalism in any given area." Two issues/year. Estab. 1975. Circ. 2,000.

Needs: Contemporary, experimental, feminist/lesbian, gay, literary, prose poem. Receives several unsolicited fiction mss/month. Occasionally critiques rejected ms.

How to Contact: Send completed ms with SASE or IRCs. Photocopied submissions OK. Reports as soon as possible on mss. Sample copy $3.

Payment: Rates vary.

Terms: Pays on publication for all rights. Publication copyrighted.

HELICON NINE, The Journal of Women's Arts & Letters, Box 22412, Kansas City MO 64113. (913)381-6383. Editor: Gloria Vando Hickok. Fiction Editor: Pinky Kase. Magazine publishing "a celebration of women in the arts, past, present and future for women and men interested in women in the arts." Published 3 times/year. Estab. 1979. Circ. 5,000.

Needs: Condensed novel, contemporary, ethnic, experimental, fantasy, historical (general), humor/satire, literary, prose poem, translations, women's, young adult. No "militant feminist tracts." Receives 50-100 unsolicited fiction mss/month. "No set limit" on mss/year.

How to Contact: Send complete ms with SASE. Simultaneous and photocopied submissions OK. Reports in 6 weeks on mss. Sample copy $5.50.

Payment: 2 free contributor's copies.

Terms: Acquires one-time rights. Publication copyrighted.

HERESIES: A Feminist Publication on Art & Politics, Heresies, Box 766, Canal St. Station, New York NY 10013. "We are a feminist collective. Each issue is put together by a separate group of women which forms the editorial collective." Nationwide readership gathered from alternative bookshops and women's spaces. Quarterly. Estab. January 1977. Circ. 8,000.

Needs: Women's, feminist and lesbian.

How to Contact: Query. Reports in 1 month on queries. Free guidelines with SASE.

Payment: Small payment post publication and free author's copies.

Terms: Publication copyrighted.

Tips: "Check back issues for special themes and content. Since each issue has its own guidelines, be specific. We only accept mss directed to special issues which are noted in the back of each publication."

HIGH PERFORMANCE, Astro Artz Publisher, 240 S. Broadway, 5th floor, Los Angeles CA 90012. (213)687-7362. Editor: Linda Frye Burnham. "A documentary magazine about performance art (live works by visual artists or happenings) including fiction and poetry by visual and performance artists. Avant-garde art audience and general public interested in esoteric activity." Quarterly. Estab. Feb. 1978. Circ. 15,000.

Needs: "We are only interested in fiction by those who work primarily in visual and performance art. This is not to say that the story/poem must be visual or illustrated. No very long works." Buys 1 ms/issue, 4 mss/year. Length: 1,000-20,000.

How to Contact: Send complete ms and resumé with SASE for ms. Reports in 3 months on mss. Sample copy $4.50.

Payment: $100. 2 free author's copies. Extras available at half price.

Terms: Pays on publication for one-time rights.

Tips: "Get MFA in art. Type. Double-space. Learn to spell. It is truly essential for anyone interested in submitting work to get a look at our publication and have an understanding of contemporary art, especially performance art."

HIGH ROCK REVIEW, An Upstate Journal of the Verbal and Visual Arts, 4th Floor Productions, Box 614, Saratoga Springs NY 12866. (518)584-6189. Editor: Dave Scavone. Fiction Editor: Wayne Perras. "We emphasize Native American lore and outlooks, jazz-sensibilities, and other such evocations of both mountain and urban culture. Our classiness of production attempts to bring 'underground' sentiments to a respectable marketplace. Mostly sold in NE region—but a broad-ranged audience is sought as we integrate fine photography and graphics with the best fiction and poetry we receive." Semiannually. Estab. 1980. Circ. 2,000.

Needs: Contemporary, erotica, ethnic, experimental, prose poem, psychic/supernatural, serialized/excerpted novel, translations. "Pieces under 12 pages probably have the best chance, unless phenomenal." Receives an average of 12 unsolicited fiction mss/month. Accepts 6-10 mss/issue; 12-20 mss/year. Length: 50 words minimum; 3,000 words maximum; 1,500-2,000 words average. Critiques rejected ms "when warranted."

How to Contact: Send complete ms with SASE. "We prefer intro letters of some sort—cordial, interested correspondents get the kindest 'read' in return." "Good quality" photocopied and previously published submissions OK. Reports in 1-3 months on mss. Sample copy $4/ppd. first class return.

Payment: 1 free contributor's copy; charges half-price for extras.

Terms: Pays on publication for one-time rights. Publication copyrighted.

Tips: "Read magazine first—this endears you to any editor. However, don't come across as too ardent/eager/amateurish. Must be ready for high quality company. Know your market—an investment of a few dollars will result in stimulation, idea exchange, and a real knowledge of any magazine's preferences and tendencies."

HOB-NOB ANNUAL, 715 Dorsea Rd., Lancaster PA 17601. Editor/Publisher: Mildred K. Henderson. "*Hob-Nob* is a small amateur publication currently with a literary emphasis in original prose and poetry. This publication is directed toward amateur writers and poets, but many of them would like to be professional. For some, appearance in *Hob-Nob* is simply an opportunity to be published somewhere, while others possibly see it as a springboard to bigger and better things." Annual. Estab. Fall 1969. Circ. 100-200.

Needs: Literary, contemporary, religious/inspirational, psychic/supernatural, science fiction, fantasy, romance, mystery, adventure, humor, young adult, very brief condensed novels, excerpts from novels, short stories in installments. "No erotica, works with excessive swearing or blatantly sexual words, gross violence, etc." Accepts 4-10 mss/issue. Receives 2-3 unsolicited fiction mss each month. Length: preferably 500-1,000 (longer if serialized). Critiques rejected mss "when there is time." Sometimes recommends other markets.

How to Contact: Send complete ms with SASE. Rejections in 2 weeks. Sample copy for 71¢ postage. "No submissions between May 1 and November 1, please. Annual usually appears in the summer."

Payment: 1 free author's copy. $1 plus 71¢ postage for extras.

Terms: Acquires first rights. Publication copyrighted.

Tips: "Read over your work before handing it in and see whether it makes sense. Get someone else to read it, if possible. Number pages. Include name and address on at least the first page, and name on others. State 'original and unpublished.' " My biggest reason for outright rejection is OFFENSIVE SUBJECT MATTER or language, or else generally poor writing. I do sometimes send a story back for a rewrite when it has possibilities but 'problems'." Occasional contests, announced as they develop. There may be an extra issue occasionally.

HOME PLANET NEWS, Box 415, Stuyvesant Station, New York NY. Co-editorial Directors: Donald Lev and Enid Dame. Fiction Editor: Robin Lamiere, 3000 Brighton 12th Street, Brooklyn NY 11235. Quarterly. Estab. 1978.

Needs: Literary, contemporary, regional, feminist, gay/lesbian, ethnic, science fiction, humor, translations. No "dreams, journals or anything racist, sexist, 'age-ist', or anti-semitic. No plotless stories or those in which the author looks down on or 'hates' the characters." Receives 0-10 unsolicited fiction mss each month. Length: "The shorter the better (1,200 words or less)." Critiques rejected mss "when there is time." Sometimes recommends markets: "Keep the faith."

How to Contact: Send complete ms. Reports in 6 weeks.
Payment: Pays in author's copies.
Terms: Publication copyrighted.
Tips: "Don't use footnotes. A short cover letter is better than an essay explaining the work submitted. Be objective about your work and ask 'Has anything happened?', 'To whom?', 'Has any change occurred? or any insight been granted, if not at least to the character, to the reader?' And don't tell—in the cover letter—what's wrong with the story." Many mss are rejected because the writer "seems to unconsciously want to 'satirize something'—a friend, a boss, an enemy—creating as a result characters poorly delineated and communicated."

HOR-TASY, Ansuda Publications, Box 158-J, Harris IA 51345. Editor/Publisher: Daniel R. Betz. "*Hor-Tasy* is bringing back actual *horror* to horror lovers tired of seeing so much science fiction and SF passed off as horror. We're also very much interested in true, poetic pure fantasy. Directed toward horror fans sick of SF."
Needs: Fantasy and horror. "Pure fantasy: Examples are trolls, fairies, mythology. The horror we're looking for comes from the human mind—the ultimate form of horror. It must sound real—so real that in fact it could very possibly happen at any time and place. We must be able to feel the diseased mind behind the personality. No science fiction in any way, shape, or form. We don't want stories in which the main character spends half his time talking to a shrink. We don't want stories that start out with: 'You're crazy,' said so and so." Accepts 6 mss/issue. Receives approximately 0-2 unsolicited fiction mss each month. Critiques rejected mss "unless it's way off from what we're looking for."
How to Contact: Query or send complete ms with SASE. Reports in 1 day for queries. "If not interested (in ms), we return immediately. If interested, we may keep it as long as 6 months." Sample copy $2.95. Guidelines for legal-sized SASE.
Payment: 2 free author's copies. Charge for extras: Cover price less regular discount rates.
Terms: Acquires first North American serial rights. Publication copyrighted.
Tips: "*Hor-Tasy* is a unique publication. Most stories rejected are about spooks, monsters, haunted houses, spacemen, etc—because *Hor-Tasy* is a unique publication, I suggest the potential writer get a sample copy (price: $2.95). Only unpublished work will be considered."

THE HOT SPRINGS GAZETTE, The Doodly-Squat Press, Box 480740, Los Angeles CA 90048. Editor: Eric Irving. "A small press magazine specializing in material about hot springs. Kind of a cross between *The Sierra Club Bulletin* and *High Times*." Published irregularly. Estab. 1977. Circ. 1,000.
Needs: "We will accept quality prose or poetry that concerns wilderness experience, especially hot springs." Length: 50-2,000 words.
How to Contact: Send complete manuscript with SASE. Reports in 3 weeks. Sample copy $2.
Payment: Free lifetime subscription.
Terms: Acquires all rights.
Tips: "Find some hot springs. Send for a copy."

HYSTERIA, A Feminist Magazine, Little Red Media Foundation, Box 2481, Station B, Kitchener, Ontario, Canada N2H 6M3. (519)884-9035. Editor: Catherine Edwards. "A feminist magazine which provides a blend of news, information and analysis to a feminist readership. We publish articles, fiction, poetry, reviews and original graphic work by women only." Quarterly. Estab. 1980. Circ. 1,200.
Needs: Comics, erotica, ethnic, experimental, fantasy, feminist/lesbian, gay, science fiction. "We are interested in most types of fiction but they must be under 4,500 words, written by women and be of interest to a feminist audience. We are not interested in condensed novels or novellas. We are not interested in work by men. Traditional romance is out too." Receives 5 unsolicited fiction mss/month. Accepts 1 ms/issue; 4 mss/year. Length: 2,000 words minimum; 4,500 words maximum; 3,000 words average. When requested to, critiques rejected ms.
How to Contact: Send complete ms with SASE. "For fiction send mss; for other types of writ-

ing query with clips (if possible)." Reports in 1 month on queries; 2-3 months on mss. Sample copy free. Fiction guidelines free.

Payment: $5 honorarium; 1 free contributor's copy. Charges $2.50 for extras; 40% discount on order of five or more copies.

Terms: Pays on publication for first rights. Publication copyrighted.

Tips: "Our audience tends to like stories which portray women with positive qualities and outlooks. For submissions to a feminist magazine it is important to write from a feminist perspective; it is equally important to avoid turning your story into a political tract. The most common problem we encounter in the short fiction we get is that the writer is trying to cram the complex plotting of a novel into a few pages. Rule of thumb: in short stories, one thing happens."

THE ICELANDIC CANADIAN, The Icelandic Canadian Club, 1-67C Gertrude Ave., Winnipeg, Manitoba, Canada R3G 1J0. Editor-in-Chief: Axel Vopnfjord. Editor: Paul A. Sigurdson. Literary promoting knowledge of Icelandic culture, activities and accomplishments of American and Canadian people of Icelandic lineage. For people interested in Iceland and Icelandic culture. Quarterly. Estab. 1944. Circ. 1,300.

Needs: Literary, contemporary, adventure, humor, ethnic (Icelandic) and translations. No erotic or avant-garde. Accepts 1 ms/issue, 4-6 mss/year. Length: 1,000-2,000 words.

How to Contact: Send complete ms with International Reply Coupons. Reports in 2 months on mss. Sample copy $2 with 7x10 SAE, IRC.

Payment: Free author's copy with $2 (Canadian) charge for extras.

Terms: Acquires one-time rights.

Tips: "Write an authentic story or article about Icelandic people.

IMAGE MAGAZINE, Cornerstone Press, Box 28048, St. Louis MO 63119. (314)752-3703. Editor: Anthony J. Summers. Assistant Editor: James J. Finnegan. "*Image* uses only the best material it receives from all over the world. There is no definite theme, but we prefer material to be well-written with no sloppy attempts at creativity. It must be a bit different, off the wall. Directed toward college students, free thinkers, writers, poets, editors, teachers. They read it to be educated, amused, entertained, to cause them to think and see life in a different perspective." Published 3 times/year. Estab. 1970. Circ. 600.

Needs: "We are willing to take a chance with anybody, anything. No murder mysteries or anything sloppy." Buys variable amount of mss/issue. Receives approximately 20-35 unsolicited fiction mss each month. Critiques rejected mss "when there is time."

How to Contact: Query. SASE for ms. Reports in 4 weeks on queries, 6 weeks on mss. Sample copy $2 with SASE plus 75¢ postage.

Payment: $10-$100 and 1 free author's copy. $2 charge for extras.

Terms: Pays on publication. Negotiates rights with author. Publication copyrighted.

Tips: "Buy a sample copy and see what we use. I look for the well-written ms free from the errors of illiteracy. Too many manuscripts have a romance or religious moral; they are rejected as are those that lack that certain spark of creativity that we look for. Most mss lack that essence that causes emotional response."

IMPEGNO, Casella Postale, n. 30. Mazara Del Vallo, Sicily, Italy 91026. (0923)945492. Editor: Rolando Certa. Emphasizes "poetry, prose, essays, theater, narrative, book reviews, art criticism, sociology for intellectuals, poets, students, etc. who want to know what is going on in cultural quarters in Sicily and the southern countries of Europe." Quarterly. Estab. 1971. Circ. 1,500.

Needs: Literary, contemporary, humor, translations, narrative, book reviews. "No pseudo-cultural literature efforts." Receives 50 unsolicited fiction mss/month. Length: 500-1,500 words. Critiques rejected mss "when there is time."

How to Contact: Send complete ms. Reports "as soon as possible." Free sample copy.

Payment: Up to 5 free author's copies.

Terms: "We leave publishing rights to the author."

Tips: "Study others, literature, and contemporary writers. Do not be in a hurry to see yourself in print. Before publication, reflect. We are interested in an international cultural exchange between ourselves and others in the world."

IMPULSE MAGAZINE, Impulse Publishing Co., Box 901, Station Q, Toronto, Ontario, Canada M4T 2P1. (416)368-7511. Editors: Eldon Garnet, Judith Doyle and Joan Brouwer. "Theme is art and culture with an emphasis on technology of the future and its relation to the artist. We publish experimental/innovative fiction, interviews for an audience of 18 to 35 years old. They read *Impulse* to keep informed of the changes now happening in the art and science field." Quarterly. Estab. summer 1971. Circ. 10,000.
Needs: "Experimental, innovative writing. We are also a visual publication and would appreciate any accompanying photos, illustrations, etc. No plays." Accepts 4-5 mss/issue, 15-20 mss/year. Receives approximately 30 unsolicited fiction mss/month. Length: 250-2,000 words. Critiques rejected mss "when there is time."
How to Contact: Send complete ms with SASE. Reports in 1 month on mss. Sample copy $3.
Terms: Acquires first rights. Publication copyrighted.
Tips: "Keep trying. Avoid too lengthy a ms. Most manuscripts are either poorly conceived or simply too conventional in style and content and do not exhibit suitable awareness of the idiosyncracies of *IMPULSE*. We are interested in more experimental pieces of fiction." Writer's grants available for writers whose work is accepted for publication.

INDIAN LITERATURE, National Academy of Letters, Rabrindra Bhavan, New Delhi, Delhi, India 110001. Tel. 388667. Editor: Keshav Malik. Magazine of fiction, poetry, novelettes, critical literary essays for a select audience. Bimonthly. Estab. 1956. Circ. 2,000.
Needs: Experimental, humor/satire, literary, prose poem. No commercial fiction. Receives 10 unsolicited fiction mss/month. Accepts 10 mss/issue; 60 mss/year. Length: 1,000 words minimum; 4,000 words maximum; 2,000 words average. Occasionally critiques rejected ms.
How to Contact: Send complete ms. Simultaneous, photocopied and previously published submissions OK. Fiction guidelines free.
Payment: 100 rupees; 1 free contributor's copy, plus 12 offprints.
Terms: Pays on publication.
Tips: "Good response to short stories. Only serious work accepted."

INDIANA REVIEW, (formerly *Indiana Writes*), 316 N. Jordan Ave., Bloomington IN 47405. (812)337-3439. Editor: Clint McCown. Associate Editor: Jane Hillenberg. "Magazine of contemporary fiction and poetry in which there is a zest for language, some relationship between form and conent, and some awareness of the world. For fiction writers/readers, followers of lively contemporary poetry. Triannually. Estab. 1975. Circ. 500 + .
Needs: Literary, contemporary, experimental, mainstream, prose poetry. "We are interested in innovation, logic, unity, a social context, formal experimentation. All genres that meet some of these criteria are welcome." Accepts 6-8 mss/issue.
How to Contact: Send complete ms with SASE. Reports in 1 month. Sample copy $3.
Payment: 2-3 free author's copies.
Terms: Acquires North American serial rights. Publication copyrighted.
Tips: "Be daring, love the language. Don't imitate anyone."

INKY TRAILS PUBLICATIONS, Box 345, Middleton, ID 83644. Editor/Publisher: Pearl Kirk. Magazine consisting of poetry, art, fillers, quotes, fiction and TV or radio scripts. Published 3 times/year. Estab. 1967. Circ. 300.
Needs: Literary, contemporary, religious/inspirational, psychic/supernatural, fantasy, romance, western, mystery, adventure, humor, juvenile, young adult. "Would like to have some art with mss for illustrations and novels to run in several issues. No filth or four letter words." Length: 3,500 words maximum. Sometimes recommends markets.
How to Contact: Send complete ms with SASE. Reports in 2 months. Sample copy $4 with

10x13 SASE plus 70¢ postage. Free guidelines for legal-sized SASE.
Payment: "Due to postal and material increase we will not be able to give any more free copies. A copy with author's material will be $5, when his/her material is published—or if sending for a sample copy, $4". Occasional cash ($15/first, $10/second place) awards.
Terms: "All rights stay with the writers as long as *Inky Trails* is given credit for first printing." Publication copyrighted.
Tips: "Have a title, start with characters and conflict. Let the characters come alive with emotion, and write about something familiar. Solve the problem or conflict. Surprise endings are good. I use all types of good clean material. Awards given at end of year but recipient must be a subscriber."

INLET, Virginia Wesleyan College, Norfolk VA 23502. Editor: Joseph Harkey. "A little magazine publishing poetry and short fiction for people of all ages." Annual. Estab. 1970. Circ. 700.
Needs: Literary, contemporary, science fiction, fantasy, humor. "Our main interest is well-written fiction." Accepts 2-5 mss/issue. Receives 10-20 unsolicited fiction mss each month. Length: 500-1,500 words but "will consider up to 3,000." Sometimes recommends markets.
How to Contact: "Mss are read September through March only." Send complete ms to fiction editor with SASE. Reports in 2 months. Sample copy 75¢. Addressed labels welcomed.
Payment: 2 free author's copies. Negotiates charge for extras.
Terms: Publication copyrighted.
Tips: "Write carefully and present a neatly typed ms with SASE. Send an example of your best work; short shorts preferred. Some rejected mss are poorly written. Some are polished and professional, but lack imaginative treatments of the problems they raise."

INS & OUTS, A Magazine of Awareness, Ins & Outs Press, Box 3759, Amsterdam, Holland. Tel. (020)27-6868. Editor: Eddie Woods. "An eclectic magazine. Only criterion is quality. All subjects and styles considered. Erotica especially welcome. For lovers of language in its most meaningful form as well as incorrigible word addicts who can't resist a good read." Published irregularly. Estab. 1978. Circ. 2,500.
Needs: Will consider all categories. "Be so certain that your story is *good*, that if for any reason we reject it, your urge to write will in no way be diminished. We like Somerset Maugham, Apuleius and Charles Bukowski (etc.)." Length: "no more than necessary." Occasionally critiques rejected mss "but don't expect it." Sends mss to editors of other publications. Sometimes recommends markets.
How to Contact: "Play it by ear. Prefer previously unpublished work, but *will* consider simultaneous and photocopied submissions upon query." Reports as soon as possible on queries. Sample copy $5 postpaid.
Payment: Subscription to magazine. Charge for extras: 50% of retail price (varies with each issue); postpaid surface.
Terms: Pays on publication for first rights. Publication copyrighted; but reverts to writer/artists, preference upon request.
Tips: "We dare you to submit to us . . . Please be neat as possible (well typed, double-spaced mss preferred). Also take a deep breath and reread before mailing."

INSIDE/OUT, Prose and Poetry from America's Prisons, Time Capsule, Inc., Box 1185, New York NY 10116. (212)675-7197. Editor-in-Chief: Marc Crawford. Fiction Editor: Matthew Hejna. "*Inside/Out* publishes fiction and poetry written by prisoners dealing with real human problems and concerns in social situations for inmates, people involved with corrections, the literary community, educators, students and the general public." Published quarterly. Estab. 1980. Circ. 3,000.
Needs: Comics, contemporary, ethnic, experimental, feminist/lesbian, gay, humor/satire, literary, mainstream, men's, prose poem, serialized/excerpted novel, suspense/mystery, translations, women's, young adult. "Any well-written story with relevance to the human condition. Themes need not be prison related; work should reflect common experience; fantasy and science fiction as

escapism not encouraged.'' Receives 30 unsolicited fiction mss/month. Buys 5 mss/issue, 20 mss/ year. Length: 1,000 words minimum; 5,000 words maximum; 2,500 words average. Occasionally critiques rejected mss.

How to Contact: Send complete ms. SASE preferred. Simultaneous and photocopied submissions OK. Reports in 2 months. Free sample copy for 4 first class stamps; free guidelines with SASE.

Payment: 10 free contributor's copies.

Terms: Pays on publication for one-time rights. Publication copyrighted.

Tips: ''Create out of personal experience; picture each sentence as a photograph; keep story active; sustain strong conflict. Keep the narrator out of story and let characters give information through thoughts, action and dialogue; write simple sentences using strong active verbs.''

INTERSTATE, Noumenon Foundation, Box 7068, Austin TX 78712. (512) 928-2911. Editor-in-Chief: Loris Essary. Magazine of ''avant-garde and experimental fiction; psychologically-centered prose.'' Published annually. Estab. 1974. Circ. 600.

Needs: All categories. Receives 100 unsolicited fiction mss/month. Length: open. Occasionally critiques rejected mss.

How to Contact: Send complete ms with SASE. Photocopied submissions and previously published work OK. Reports as soon as possible on mss. Sample copy $6 postpaid.

Payment: 2 contributor's copies.

Terms: Pays on publication for one-time rights. Publication copyrighted.

Tips: ''Read a sample copy and see the styles and contents representative of accepted manuscripts.''

INTRO, Associated Writing Programs, Old Dominion University, Norfolk VA 23508. (804)440-3840. Annual journal of literary fiction, poetry and drama by university writing students. Annually. Estab. 1968. Circ. 2,000.

Needs: ''Will consider any genre.'' Mss read only October through November. Accepts 15 mss/ issue. Charges reading fee of $1.

How to Contact: Query first for entry requirements with SASE. Simultaneous and photocopied submissions OK. Reports within 2 weeks on queries. Sample copy $4. Fiction guidelines for SASE.

Payment: 2 free contributor's copies. 40% discount on extras.

Terms: Pays on publication; assignments on work-for-hire-basis. Publication copyrighted.

THE IOWA REVIEW, University of Iowa, 308 EPB, Iowa City IA 52242. (319)353-6048. Editor: David Hamilton. Magazine of ''stories, essays, poems for a general readership interested in contemporary literature.'' Published quarterly. Estab. 1970. Circ. 1,000.

Needs: Receives 150-200 unsolicited fiction mss/month. Buys 3-5 mss/issue, 12-16 mss/year.

How to Contact: Send complete ms with SASE. ''Don't bother with queries.'' Simultaneous submissions accepted ''reluctantly.'' Photocopied submissions OK. Reports in 3 months on mss. Sample copy $3.

Payment: $10/page; 3 free contributor's copies; charge for extras: 30% off cover price.

Terms: Pays on publication for first North American serial rights. Publication copyrighted.

IRON MAGAZINE, Iron Press, 5 Marden Ter., Cullercoats, North Shields, Tyne & Wear NE30 4PD, UK. (0632)531901. Editor: Peter Mortimer. ''Literary magazine which publishes contemporary fiction, poetry, articles and graphics. We seek an audience sympathetic to new literature or, in some small way, hope to create one.'' Quarterly. Estab. April 1973. Circ. 700.

Needs: Literary, science fiction, humor, translations. ''Generally we are open to all styles of fiction if we feel the author is serious about intentions (though he or she may, of course, be humorous in application). We are not interested in the 'mechanical' type of story specifically written with an automatic market in mind, such as teenage romance stories or others which seem to fit a well-worn framework and offer the reader little which is new.'' Accepts 4 mss/issue, 14 mss/year. Receives approximately 20 unsolicited fiction mss each month. Length: 7,000 words maximum. Critiques rejected mss "when there is time."

How to Contact: Send complete ms with SASE. Reports in 3 weeks. Sample copy $2 with SAE plus 2 op (UK) or 2 IRC coupons (USA).

Payment: 1 free author's copy. $2 charge for extras.

Terms: "Copyright remains with author."

Tips: "We advise authors to see the magazine initially and make themselves familiar with our approach to publishing fiction. No lengthy letters of why the story is so good (we'll make up our own minds). No more than two pieces of fiction to be submitted at the same time."

JAM TO-DAY, Jam To-day, Box 249, Northfield VT 05663. Fiction Editor: Judith Stanford. Co-editors: Don Stanford and Floyd Stuart. Forum for serious nonacademic poetry and fiction by unknown and little-known contemporary writers. Annually. Estab. 1973. Circ. 400.

Needs: Literary, contemporary, science fiction and feminist. No light fiction, word-play fiction, highly allusive or allegorical fiction. Buys 1 ms/year. Receives approximately 25 unsolicited fiction mss each month. Length: 1,500-7,500. Critiques rejected mss "when there is time." Sometimes recommends other markets.

How to Contact: Send complete ms with SASE. Reports in 2 months on mss. Sample copy $2.50.

Payment: $5/printed page.

Terms: Pays on publication for first rights. Publication copyrighted.

Tips: Reasons for rejections: "(1) Poorly conceived: trite, uninteresting, poorly written, too academic; (2) better suited to another market: well written and holds interest but better suited to mass-market magazine, or extraordinarily obscure but not obviously foolish and ought to go to experimental literary magazine."

JAPANOPHILE, Box 223, Okemos MI 48864. (517)349-1795. Editor-in-Chief: Earl Snodgrass. Magazine of "articles, photos, poetry, humor, short stories about Japanese culture, not necessarily in Japan, for an adult audience, most with college background; travelers." Published quarterly. Estab. 1974. Circ. 600.

Needs: Adventure, historical (general), humor/satire, literary, mainstream, suspense/mystery. Receives 40-100 unsolicited fiction mss/month. Buys 1 ms/issue, 4 mss/year. Length: 2,000 words minimum; 9,000 words maximum; 4,000 words average.

How to Contact: Send complete ms with SASE. Photocopied and previously published submissions OK. Reports in 2 months on mss. Sample copy $3; free guidelines for large SAE and 1 first class stamp.

Payment: $15-50.

Terms: Pays on publication for all rights, first North American serial rights or one-time rights (depends on situation). Publication copyrighted.

Tips: Short stories usually involve Japanese and 'foreign' (non-Japanese) characters in a way that contributes to understanding of Japanese culture and the Japanese people. However, a *good* story dealing with Japan or Japanese cultural aspects anywhere in the world will be considered even if it does not involve this encounter or meeting of Japanese and foreign characters. Accepted short stories receive $20 on publication plus $100 for the story judged the best. Some stories may also be published in an anthology."

JAZZ, Jazz Press, 17930 Highway 9, Boulder Creek CA 95006. (408)423-6275. Contact: Editor-in-Chief. Magazine of prose, poetry, photography, graphics. Published semiannually. Estab. 1977. Circ. 750.

Needs: Experimental, literary, prose poem, serialized/excerpted novel, translations, women's. "If selection from novel, please do *not* send entire novel. Author to select." Receives 3-4 unsolicited fiction mss/month. Accepts 6 mss/issue, 12 mss/year. Length: 10,000 words maximum. Occasionally comments on rejected mss.

How to Contact: Send complete ms with SASE. Photocopied submissions OK. Reports in 1 month on mss. Sample copy $3; free guidelines with SASE.

Payment: 2 free contributor's copies; charge for extras: 60% of retail price.

Terms: Pays on publication. Publication copyrighted.

JEWISH CURRENTS MAGAZINE, 22 E. 17th St., New York NY 11201. (212)924-5740. Editor-in-Chief: Morris U. Schappes. "We are a progressive monthly, broad in our interests, printing feature articles on political and cultural aspects of Jewish life in the US and elsewhere, reviews of books and film, poetry and fiction, Yiddish translation; regular columns on Israel, US Jewish community, current events, secular Jewish life; monthly themes include Women, Holocaust and Resistance, Black-Jewish relations, etc. National audience, many 50-80 years old; many younger; literate and politically left, well educated." Published monthly. Estab. 1946. Circ. 4,000.

Needs: Contemporary, ethnic, historical (general), humor/satire, literary, prose poem, translations, women's. "We are interested in *authentic* experience and readable prose; Jewish themes; humanistic orientation. No religious, political sectarian; no porn or hard sex, no escapist stuff. Go easy on experimentation, but we're interested." Receives 6-10 unsolicited fiction mss/month. Accepts 0-1 mss/issue, 8-10 mss/year. Length: 100 words minimum; 3,000 words maximum; 1,800 words average. Occasionally critiques rejected mss.

How to Contact: Send complete ms with SASE. Reports in 1 month on mss. Sample copy $1 with SAE and 3 first class stamps.

Payment: 1 complimentary subscription; 6 free contributor's copies.

Terms: Pays on publication for all rights. "We readily give reprint permission at no charge." Publication copyrighted.

Tips: "Family themes are good, but avoid sentimentality; keep the prose tight, not sprawling; matters of character and moral dilemma, maturing into pain and joy, dealing with Jewish conflicts OK."

JOINT ENDEAVOR, The Endeavor News, Box 32, Huntsville TX 77340. Editor-in-Chief: William D. Walker, Jr. Fiction Editor: Carl Robins. "*Joint Endeavor* is a criminal justice, offender, correctional, and crime news mag. We publish news, articles, satire, poetry, fiction, and interviews for the overall criminal justice and offender audience. We also have subscribers that are non-professional: many of them are average citizens." Published bimonthly. Estab. 1973. Circ. 2,500.

Needs: Mainstream, prose poem, suspense/mystery, crime. Receives about 50 unsolicited fiction mss/month. Length: 2,500 words minimum; 5,000 words maximum; 3,000 words average. Occasionally critiques rejected mss.

How to Contact: Send complete ms with SASE. Simultaneous submissions OK. Reports in 3 weeks on mss. Free guidelines with SASE.

Payment: 1 year subscription; 25 free contributor's copies.

Terms: Pays on publication for all rights. Publication copyrighted.

Tips: "Be as accurate as possible, and go into the actual life of the story, as things are. This is a crime and offender publication; the fiction must be relative or it won't suit the readers."

JOURNAL FANTOME, Fantome Press, 720 N. Park Ave., Warren OH 44483. Editor/Publisher: C.M. James. "A review of the macabre in the arts and letters for people interested in macabre aspects of literature, film, and graphics arts." Annual. Estab. 1979. Circ. 500.

Needs: Fantasy, horror, and short prose poems of that nature. "While we are primarily interested in reviews, we will consider very short works of prose. No material without macabre aspect." Accepts 10-20 mss/year. Receives approximately 2-6 unsolicited fiction mss each month. Length 10-1,000 words.

How to Contact: Query. SASE for query, ms. Reports in 6 months. Free sample copy for legal-sized SASE.

Payment: 5 free author's copies. 50% discount on extras.

Terms: Acquires first North American serial rights. Publication copyrighted.

Tips: "Be brief and succinct. Study the market carefully." Mss are rejected because they are of the "wrong genre and too long."

THE JOURNAL OF THE NORTH AMERICAN WOLF SOCIETY, North American Wolf Society, 6461 Troy Pike, Versailles KY 40383. (606)873-6450. Editor: Sandra Gray Thacker. "Our emphasis is wildlife education with specific priority on wild canids, their necessity and value to natural ecosystems, etc. We publish articles under our 'Post Scripts' section which are devoted to creative ecological fiction. The *Journal*'s view is that our readers are intelligent activists who need to receive valid information." Readership: "Professional biologists/zoologists/ethologists, lay conservationists, federal and state wildlife personnel, universities, etc. Informed, active participants in the area of wildlife conservation. They read it because it maintains high standards of credibility and rationality." Published 3 times/year. Estab. 1974. Circ. 400 + .
Needs: "Predator conservation with specific themes relative to wild canids: wolf, coyote, or their prey. We are especially interested in historical approaches. All submissions should be based on sound ecological/biological fact. No overly emotional, fantasy articles which do not reflect the true character or existence of wild canids or their prey." Accepts 1 ms/issue, 3-4 mss/year. Receives approximately 3 unsolicited fiction mss each month. Length 2,000-4,000 words (prefers 2,000). Critiques rejected mss "when there is time." Sometimes recommends other markets.
How to Contact: Send complete ms with SASE. Reports in 1 month. Sample copy $3. Free guidelines with SASE.
Payment: 5 free author's copies. $3 charge for extras.
Tips: "We are interested in well-researched folkloric scenarios, factual bases, etc., all with a strong ecologic message. We are not interested in personal philosophizing or overly emotional dissertations. The *Journal* has enjoyed, and worked very hard for, a reputation of objectivism and high credibility, which is very important to the continuation of our work, and our effectiveness in wildlife conservation. We welcome new writers who also place a high priority on the credibility of their work." Rejects mss because of "unrealistic, anthropocentric approach to the subject. Too many writers attempt to utilize the publication's space to air personal philosophies. Such articles, whether true-life or fictional, would be better placed in editorial sections."

JUMP RIVER REVIEW, Jump River Press, Inc., 810 Vernon Ave., # 4, Madison WI 53714. (608)221-9402. Editor: Mark Bruner. "We are a nonprofit literary quarterly with an interest in any form of written art. Specific interests: myth, folklife, enchantment." Readership: "Directed to writers and anyone interested in contemporary literature of quality." Quarterly. Estab. August 1979. Circ. 400.
Needs: Literary, contemporary, psychic/supernatural, fantasy, horror, erotica, ethnic, translations, myth, folklore. "No religiosity, purple sentiment, confessionals or cute bunny rabbit stories. No self-centered streams of consciousness." Accepts 2 mss/issue, 8-10 mss/year. Receives 20-30 unsolicited fiction mss each month. No preferred length.
How to Contact: Query or send complete ms with SASE. Reports in 1-3 weeks usually. Sample copy $2.50.
Payment: Copies.
Terms: Acquires one-time rights. Publication copyrighted.
Tips: "Do not send a pretentious cover letter. If you're a young writer, mention that—it might help and get you feedback. Remember that the sensory image is all important—show your fiction instead of telling it." Mss rejected usually because of "lack of imagery, dialogue and inventiveness." Occasional award and cash incentives.

KADATH, Weird and Fantasy Fiction, Kadath Press, Corso Aurelio Saffi 5/9, 16128 Genova, Italy. Editor: Francesco Cova. Magazine of "original stories in English—weird and fantasy fiction—for fans and collectors of weird and fantasy fiction." Semiannually. Estab. 1979. Circ. 600.
Needs: Fantasy, horror, psychic/supernatural. No science fiction. Receives 10 unsolicited fiction mss/month. Accepts 6 + mss/issue; 12 + mss/year. Length: 3,000 words minimum; 10,000 words maximum; 6,000 words average.
How to Contact: Query first with SASE. Photocopied submissions OK. Reports in 3 weeks on mss. Sample copy $4. Fiction guidelines free.

Payment: $25-150; 3 free contributor's copies; $4 charge for extras.
Terms: Pays on acceptance or publication for first rights. Publication copyrighted.

KALEIDOSCOPE, Literary/Art Magazine, Kaleidoscope Pres-United Cerebral Palsy and Services for the Handicapped, 318 Water St., Akron OH 44308. (216)376-6041. Editor-in-Chief: Carson Heiner, Jr. Magazine for disabled people. Published semiannually. Estab. 1979. Circ. 3,000+.
Needs: Adventure, contemporary, experimental, fantasy, gothic/historical romance, humor/satire, literary, prose poem, psychic/supernatural, religious/inspirational, science fiction, serialized/excerpted novel, suspense/mystery, young adult. "Writers need not limit themselves to writing about being disabled. Any quality fiction is acceptable." Receives 10 unsolicited fiction mss/month. Accepts 20+ mss/issue, 40+ mss/year. Length: no preferred minimum; 10,000 words maximum; 1,000-2,000 words average.
How to Contact: Query first or send complete ms. SASE with query, mss. Reports in 2 months on queries; 2 months on mss. Sample copy $2 with 8½x11 SAE and 75¢ postage; free guidelines for 8½x3 SAE and 1 first class stamp.
Payment: 1 free contributor's copy; charge for extras: $2 plus 75¢ postage.
Terms: Pays on publication for first rights. Publication copyrighted.
Tips: "Read the magazine, and get fiction guidelines. Query or send complete ms with SASE. If writer is disabled he may write about that, but need not limit himself to it. Broad range of topics wanted. Stay away from triteness. Avoid stereotyping. Portray characters and situations realistically. Show characters in a wide range of situations, circumstances." Mss are rejected because of "unclear plots and characterizations. Also, many writers tend to write about disability in the same tired ways."

KALLIOPE, A JOURNAL OF WOMEN'S ART, Florida Junior College at Jacksonville, 3939 Roosevelt Blvd., Jacksonville FL 32205. Project Director: Peggy Friedmann. Business Manager: Sharon Wilson. A literary and visual arts journal for women, *Kalliope* celebrates women in the arts by publishing their work and by providing a medium of communication through which they may share ideas and opinions. Short stories, poems, plays, essays, criticism, reviews, drawings, photos. For people interested in visual and verbal art by women. Published 3 times/year. Estab. fall 1979. Circ. 1,000.
Needs: "Literary, contemporary, science fiction, fantasy, women's work with a historical perspective, past, present and future. Accepts 2-4 mss/issue. Receives approximately 10 unsolicited fiction mss each month. No preferred length-"just short fiction." Critiques rejected mss "when there is time and if requested."
How to Contact: Send complete ms with SASE. Reports in 1-2 months on ms. Sample copy $3.50 with 6x9 SASE.
Payment: 3 free author's copies. $3.50 charge for extras.
Terms: Acquires first rights. "We accept only unpublished work. Copyright remains with author." Publication copyrighted.
Tips: "Read our magazine. The work we consider for publication will be well written and the characters and dialogue will be convincing and have strength and movement. We like a fresh approach and are interested in new or unusual forms. Create characters capable of living, characters we can care about." Ms is rejected because "1) nothing *happens*! 2) it is thinly disguised autobiography. (Richly disguised autobiography is OK.); 3) Ending is either too pat or else just trails off. We seem to be getting a good many mss that are well written but should go to *LHJ* or *Redbook*, not a feminist journal. (Vol. 4, # 2 has four very different prose pieces so it's a good one for writers to study.)"

KANSAS QUARTERLY, Kansas Quarterly Association, Denison Hall, Kansas State University, Manhattan KS 66506. (913)532-6716. Editors: Harold Schneider, Ben Nyberg, W.R. Moses, John O. Rees. "A literary and cultural arts magazine publishing fiction and poetry. Special material on selected, announced topics in literary criticism, art history, folklore, and regional history.

For well-read, general and academic audiences." Quarterly. Estab. 1968. Circ. 1,300.
Needs: "We consider most categories as long as the fiction is of sufficient literary quality to merit inclusion, though we have no interest in children's literature. We resist translations and parts of novels, but do not absolutely refuse them." Accepts 25-30 mss/year. Length: 350-12,000 words. Sometimes recommends markets.
How to Contact: Send complete ms with SASE. Reports in 3 months on mss. Sample copy $3.
Payment: 2 free author's copies and annual awards to the best of the stories published.
Terms: Acquires all rights. "We reassign rights on request at time of republication."
Tips: "Send story after examining magazine." Sponsors awards: *KQ*/KAC (national); Seaton awards (for Kansas natives or residents).

KARAMU, English Dept., Eastern Illinois University, Charleston IL 61920. (217)581-5614. Editor: John Guzlowski. Fiction Editors: Victor Bobb, Peggy Brayfield, and Curt White. "We have no theme as such; our wish is simply to publish the best poetry and fiction submitted to the magazine." For a literate, college-educated audience. Annual. Estab. 1967. Circ. 600.
Needs: Literary, contemporary, gothic, humor. Accepts 4-5 mss/issue. Receives approximately 10-20 unsolicited fiction mss each month. Length: 3,000-10,000 words. Critiques rejected mss "when there is time." Sends mss onto editors of other publications. Sometimes recommends markets.
How to Contact: Send complete ms with SASE. Reports in 2 months on mss. Sample copy $1.50.
Payment: 2 free author's copies. Half price charge for extras.
Tips: "Send for a sample copy, read it, and send a complete ms if your stories seem to match our taste. Please be patient—we sometimes get behind in our reading. Mss submitted between January and June have the best chance."

KAYAK, Kayak Books, Inc., 325 Ocean View Ave., Santa Cruz CA 95062. Editor: George Hitchcock. Theme: primarily poetry; some off-beat fiction. Readership: poets, writers. Quarterly. Estab. 1964. Circ. 1,300.
Needs: Literary, fantasy. "We are interested only in short parables, tales or fantasies of high literary quality. No straightaway realism." Accepts 2-3 mss/issue.
How to Contact: Send complete ms with SASE. Sample copy $2.
Payment: 2 free author's copies.
Terms: Acquires first rights.
Tips: "Read the magazine first."

THE KINDRED SPIRIT, Pandora's Box Publications (c/o Michael Hathaway), 808 Maple, Great Bend KS 67530. (316)792-6795. Editor: Michael Hathaway. Tabloid for "open-minded people who enjoy poetry and short stories." Semiannually. Estab. 1982. Circ. 1,000.
Needs: Contemporary, erotica, experimental, fantasy, feminist/lesbian, gay, humor/satire, literary, mainstream, men's, prose poem, psychic/supernatural, science fiction, translations. No "history, war, derogatory stories." Receives several unsolicited fiction mss/month. Accepts several mss/issue; 30 mss/year. Length: 10,000 words maximum; 2,000-5,000 words average. Occasionally critiques rejected ms.
How to Contact: Send complete ms with SASE, introductory letter and photo if possible. Photocopied and previously published submissions OK. Reports in 3 weeks on mss. Sample copy $1.40. Fiction guidelines for SAE and 1 first class stamp.
Payment: 3 free contributor's copies; 50% discount for extras.
Terms: Pays on publication for one-time rights.
Tips: "Advice only with SASE."

KONGLOMERATI, Konglomerati Florida Foundation for Literature and the Book Arts, Inc., Box 5001, Gulfport FL 33737. (813)323-0386. Editors: Richard Mathews and Barbara Russ. "A finely printed letterpress showcase for contemporary literature. We publish intelligent and beautiful writing, including experimental and avant-garde as well as traditional forms." Readership: general, college educated, "persons with an interest in fine typography and printing, collectors of contemporary literature and fine printing."

Needs: Literary, contemporary, science fiction, fantasy. "Literary quality is more important than category. We want the best fiction we can find regardless of form or subject." Buys 1-2 mss/issue, 2-6 mss/year. Receives approximately 10-15 unsolicited fiction mss each month.

How to Contact: Query or send complete ms with SASE. Reports in 6 weeks on queries, 2 months on mss. Sample copy $7.50 plus $1.30 for postage and packing.

Payment: $5-$10/printed page and 3 free author's copies.

Terms: Buys first rights. Publication copyrighted.

Tips: "Send us your best story. Be courteous to and patient with overworked editors. Wait a little while after a rejection slip before submitting again to the same place unless the editor asks to see another story."

KUDOS, 7 Belle Vue Drive, Farsley, W. Yorks, England LS28 5HG. Editor-in-Chief: Graham Sykes. "*Kudos* is a literary and general arts magazine using poetry, fiction, articles, reviews, translations, artwork for people interested in literature and the arts in general." Estab. 1979, Circ. 1,000.

Needs: Contemporary, experimental, literary, prose poem, serialized/excerpted novel, translations. "Must be written to a high literary standard." Accepts 3-4 mss/issue, 10-12 mss/year. Length: 10,000 words maximum; 2,000-3,000 words average. Occasionally critiques rejected mss. Occasionally recommends markets.

How to Contact: Query or send complete ms. SASE for queries, ms. Reports in 1 week on queries; 3 weeks on mss. Sample copy $3; free guidelines for A5 size SAE.

Payment: Contributor's copies, number of copies "depending on number of pages." Charge for extras: $3 each.

Terms: Pays on publication for first rights. Publication copyrighted.

Tips: "First study the magazine. Remember to enclose sufficient postage for return of mss if a reply is wanted. We publish little fiction in proportion to poetry, and the fiction we use must have more going for it than just a good story line."

KUNAPIPI, Dangaroo Press, English Dept., University of Aarhus, 8000 Aarhus C., Denmark. Tel. (06) 13 67 11. Editor: Anna Rutherford. Magazine "essentially concerned with new literatures written in English, e.g., Australain, Canadian, Caribbean, African, but will consider others. Poetry, short stories, criticism, graphics, photographs. Amongst others we have published Nadine Gordimer, Bob Marley, Robert Kroetsch, David Williamson, Nirad Chaudhuri, Buchi Emecheta, Ngugi wa Thiong'o, Les Murray, Frank Moorhouse, Jack Mapanje, Wilson Harris, Mark O'Connor, Randolph Stow. We aim to fulfill the requirements T.S. Eliot believed a journal should have: to introduce the works of new or little known writers of talent, to provide critical evaluation of the work of living authors both famous and unknown, and to be truly international." Readers in Sydney, Samoa, Stockholm, and Sophiatown. Semiannually. Estab. 1979.

Needs: "The only criterion is quality." Receives 10 unsolicited fiction mss/month. Accepts 2-3 mss/issue. Length: 3,500 words maximum, but flexible. No preferred minimum. Occasionally critiques rejected ms.

How to Contact: Send complete ms with SASE. Photocopied submissions OK. Reports in 2 months on mss. Sample copy $3 and 21x26 cm envelope.

Payment: $30, 1 subscription and 1 free contributor's copy; $3 charge for extras.

Terms: Pays on publication. Publication copyrighted. "The editor in her capacity of chairperson of the European Association of Commonwealth Literature sponsors a short story competiton for previously unpublished stories. Entry fee of $4, prize of $4,000. Enquire to editor for more details."

LAKE STREET REVIEW, Lake Street Review Press, Box 7188, Powderhorn Station, Minneapolis MN 55407. Editor: Kevin FitzPatrick. "A Minneapolis-St. Paul literary magazine which focuses on the work of writers and artists that live or have lived in this area. Readers are interested in contemporary writing by writers who have some connection with the Minneapolis-St. Paul area.'' Biannual. Estab. 1976. Circ. 600.

Needs: Literary, contemporary. Accepts 5 mss/issue. Receives approximately 5 unsolicited fiction mss each month. Length 500-4,000 words. Critiques rejected mss ''when there is time.''

How to Contact: Send complete ms with SASE. Reports in 1 month on mss. Sample copy $1.50.

Payment: 2 free author's copies.

Terms: Acquires first rights. Publication copyrighted.

Tips: ''Buy a sample copy and read what we have recently printed.''

LAPIS, LAPIS Educational Association, Inc., 18420 Klimm Ave., Homewood IL 60430. (312)957-5856. Editor-in-Chief: Karen Degenhart. ''A professional journal which publishes informative, scholarly, articles about Jungian Psychology, with related literary criticism, and psycho/spiritual ideas'' for an audience of psychologists and educators. Published annually. Estab. 1977. Circ. 200.

Needs: ''We publish little fiction''—only with Jungian slant, nothing over 15 pages. Accepts 0-4 mss/issue. Occasionally critiques rejected mss.

How to Contact: Query first or send complete ms with SASE. Simultaneous and photocopied submissions and previously published work OK. Reports in 3 weeks on queries; 3 weeks on mss. Sample copy $2. Free guidelines with 1 regular SAE.

Payment: 3 contributor's copies if person joins for a year for $10.

Terms: Acquires one-time rights. Publication copyrighted.

Tips: ''Query first for articles over 10 pages—be sure to send enough return postage.''

LATIN AMERICAN LITERARY REVIEW, Latin American Literary Review, Department of Hispanic Languages and Literatures, 1309 Cathedral of Learning, University of Pittsburgh, Pittsburgh PA 15260. (412)578-2896. ''A journal in English devoted to the literature of Latin America and Latin American minorities in the US. Our publication is directed primarily to an audience of young adults and adults with an interest in Latin American literature.'' Biannual. Estab. 1972. Circ. 1,000.

Needs: Literary, contemporary, ethnic (Hispanic, Latin American, chicano). No ''themes not pertaining to the focus of our journal.'' Accepts 3-5 mss/issue. Charges $100 reading fee for books. No preferred length. Critiques rejected mss ''when there is time.''

How to Contact: Send complete ms with SASE. Reports in 2 months. Sample copy if requested.

Terms: ''Rights are relinquished by author upon publication of ms.'' Publication copyrighted.

Tips: ''The fiction which appears in the *LALR* is usually translations of works originally written in Spanish by established authors.'' *LALR* is associated with the Latin American Literary Review Press (Box 8385, Pittsburgh PA 15218) which publishes novels in Spanish and Portuguese and English translations.''

LAUREL REVIEW, West Virginia Wesleyan College, Dept. of English, Buckhannon WV 26201. (304)473-8006. Editor: Mark DeFoe. Fiction Editor: Martha Keating. ''We publish poetry and fiction of high quality, from the traditional to the avant-garde. We are eclectic, open, and flexible. Good writing is all we seek. We try to encourage writers from Appalachian America, although we publish material from across the country, Canada, and the world.'' Biannual. Estab. 1960. Circ. 500.

Needs: Literary, contemporary, humor, ethnic (Appalachian). Accepts 2-3 mss/issue, 4-6 mss/year. Receives approximately 7 unsolicited fiction mss each month. Length: 2,000-10,000 words. Critiques rejected mss ''when there is time.''

How to Contact: Send complete ms with SASE. Reports in 3 months on mss. ''Sometimes slow!'' Sample copy $2.

Payment: $10 maximum. 2 free author's copies.

Terms: Pays on publication for first rights. Publication copyrighted.

Tips: Send $2.50 for a back copy of the magazine.

LESBIAN VOICES, Jonnik Enterprises, Box 2066, San Jose CA 95109. (408)289-1088. Editor: Rosalie Nichols. Magazine. "Theme: Lesbianism (and indeed life itself) can and should be good, wholesome, fulfilling and joyful." Quarterly (irregularly). Estab. 1974. Circ. 1,200.
Needs: Feminist or lesbian. "Material should be of interest to our audience. We welcome differing points of view and controversial material but request that views expressed be clearly and rationally presented and in keeping with our philosophy. We reject the view of lesbianism as material for psychiatric study, religious censure or pornography, all of which treat lesbianism as sick, sinful or salacious." Receives various number of unsolicited fiction mss/month. Accepts 2-3 mss/issue; 8-12 mss/year. Length: open. Occasionally critiques rejected ms.
How to Contact: Send complete ms with SASE. Simultaneous and photocopied submissions OK. Report in 3 weeks on mss. Sample copy $3.
Payment: 5 free contributor's copies for fiction; 2 free contributor's copies for poetry.
Terms: Pays on publication for one-time rights.

LETTERS MAGAZINE, Maine Writers Workshop, Mainespring Press, Box 82, Stonington MA 04681. (207)367-2484. Editor: Helen Nash. "Accepts only high quality material in all ethical fields of literature." Readership: General public. Quarterly. Estab. 1975. Circ. 4,500.
Needs: Literary, science fiction, mystery. "No porno, confessions, etc." Buys 5-10 mss/year. Receives 40-60 unsolicited fiction mss each month. Length: 500-1,000. Critiques rejected mss "when there is time."
How to Contact: Query with SASE or send complete ms with SASE. Reports in 1 month on queries. Free sample copy with SASE.
Payment: Varies.
Terms: Pays on publication for all rights. Publication copyrighted.

LETTERS MAGAZINE, Box 786, New York NY 10008. (212)732-0475. Editors: Carole Bovoso. Estab. 1974. Circ. 6,500.
Needs: Letters, literary, women's, men's, feminist, gay/lesbian, humor/satire, translations. No pornography, confessions, religious, or western. Receives approximately 20 unsolicited fiction mss each month. Critiques rejected mss "when there is time."
How to Contact: Send inquiries or complete ms with SASE.
Payment: 2 free author's copies.
Terms: Publication copyrighted.
Tips: Most rejected mss are "not right for our magazine. Include a cover letter."

LINQ, Literature in North Queensland, English Language and Literature Association, P.O. James Cook University, Townsville, Queensland, Australia 4811. Editor: Elizabeth Perkins. Editorial Panel: Kay Ferres, Elizabeth Perkins, Graham Barwell, Cheryl Frost. Magazine of articles, stories, poems, reveries on literature, history for academic and general audience. Published 3/year. Estab. 1971. Circ. 250.
Needs: Contemporary, ethnic, experimental, feminist/lesbian, gay, historical (general), humor/satire, juvenile, literary, mainstream, prose poem, science fiction. Receives about 8 unsolicited fiction mss/month. Buys 6 mss/issue; 18 mss/year. Length: 500 words minimum; 5,000 words maximum; 2,000 words average. Sometimes critiques rejected ms.
How to Contact: Send complete ms with SASE or IRCs. Simultaneous and photocopied submissions OK. Reports in 3 months on ms. Sample copy $3 and $2 postage.
Payment: $10 and 1 free contributor's copy.
Terms: Pays on publication for first rights. Publication copyrighted.

LIONHEAD PUBLISHING, Lionhead Publishing/ROAR Recording Publications, 2521 E. Stratford Ct., Shorewood WI 53211. (414) 332-7474. Editor: Dr. M.J. Rosenblum. "Experimental fiction magazine for literary audience. Title varies with each issue." Estab. 1972.
Needs: Experimental (only). Receives 2-3 unsolicited fiction mss/month. Number of fiction mss varies with each issue. No preferred word length. Occasionally critiques rejected ms.

How to Contact: Query first with SASE. Photocopied submissons OK. Reports in 2 weeks on queries. Fiction guidelines for SAE.
Payment: Free contributor's copies.
Terms: Publication copyrighted.

THE LITERARY REVIEW, An International Journal of Contemporary Writing, Fairleigh Dickinson University, 285 Madison Ave., Madison NJ 07940. (201)377-4050. Editor-in-Chief: Martin Green. "Academic literary magazine specializing in fiction, poetry, criticism, reviews for general readers, professional writers, developing writers, academic and other libraries." Published quarterly. Estab. 1957. Circ. 1,000.
Needs: Literary works only. Receives 30-40 unsolicited fiction mss/month. Accepts 10-12 mss/year. Occasionally critiques rejected mss. Sometimes recommends other markets.
How to Contact: Send complete ms with SASE. Photocopied submissions OK. Reports in 10 weeks on mss. Sample copy $3.50; free guidelines with SASE.
Payment: 2 free contributor's copies; 25% discount for extras.
Terms: Pays on publication for first rights. Publication copyrighted.
Tips: "Send us a ms, we're open to all submissions; we read everything we get. Read our magazine and others. Know the market. Writers we publish are eligible for small annual award." Rejects mss because "first, there are more mss submitted than we can possibly print! Second, many that come our way are very amateurish in craft: naive stories, thinly disguised autobiography, over-done themes and situations, awkward language and dialogue."

LITTLE APPLE, Little Apple, Inc. Box 429, Federal Station, Worcester MA 01608. (617)752-8947. Editors: Alan Levine, Dan Belanger. Fiction Editors: John Dufresne, Mary Bonime. Magazine for the arts providing "a place for new as well as established writers to experiment and grow with a literary and general audience." Quarterly. Estab. 1974. Circ. 3,000.
Needs: Adventure, comics, condensed novel, ethnic, experimental, fantasy, horror, humor/satire, literary, mainstream, prose poem, psychic/supernatural, science fiction, suspense/mystery, translations, western, women's. Receives 20-30 unsolicited fiction mss/month. Accepts 2-5 mss/issue; 20-30 mss/year. Length: 2,000 words minimum; 20,000 words maximum; 5,000 words average. Occasionally critiques rejected ms.
How to Contact: Send complete ms with SASE. Simultaneous and photocopied submissions OK. Reports in 2 months on mss. Sample copy $2 and 8½x11 envelope and 3 first class stamps. Fiction guidelines free for business size envelope and 2 first class stamps.
Payment: 2 free contributor's copies; no charge for up to 5 extra copies.
Terms: All rights reassigned to authors. Publication copyrighted.
Tips: "We have an established New England readership—many who have become friends over the years. The readers send letters, call or stop by the office to express their opinions on the magazine. Write and rewrite. Keep sending us your work."

LIVE WRITERS!, La Reina Press, Box 8182, Cincinnati OH 45208. Editor/Publisher: Lupe A. Gonzalez. Fiction Editor: Karen Feinberg. We have expanded from Southern Ohio to across the country in publishing mss. We publish short fiction and poetry ranging from humorous to serious, as well as foreign work with English translations. For small press aficionados and those looking to discover upcoming American authors. Publication months: June and December. Established March 1980. Circ. 500 "and increasing."
Needs: Literary, science fiction, feminist, mystery, humor, ethnic (Native and Latin American and others). No religious, inspirational, romance, or westerns. Accepts 1-2 mss/issue, 5 mss/year. Receives 10-12 unsolicited fiction mss each month. "But we want more." Length: 1,000-3,000 words. Sometimes recommends markets.
How to Contact: Send complete ms with SASE and brief biography, or query if you wish. Reports in 6-8 weeks on mss. Sample copy $3 (current issue) and 60¢ postage.
Payment: Free 3 author's copies plus 10% discount of cover price for extra copies.
Terms: Makes assignments on a work-for-hire basis. Publication copyrighted.

Tips: "Read the classics and the contemporary works that appeal to you. Try to write what you observe, experience and know about as if you're writing to a best friend who doesn't know the details. Remember the five senses. Hone the basic writing tools, use the dictionary and please check your spelling. We give suggestions and comments we feel are helpful to the writers whose work we reject. We point out where they miss the mark with us, what we think are their strong and weak points. We want writers to know why their fiction is being rejected. It takes more of our time and energy, but it seems to have improved the quality of the mss we receive. Mss are rejected because of "poorly worked out plots and ideas; inferior sentence structure, word usage, vocabulary; pompous, overblown style; gratuitous violence. The remedies: read good writing; think, plan, polish. La Reina Press Creative Writing Awards and La Reina Press Escritores Latino Awards both open June 15 and close November 15 as an annual event. Rule sheets available."

THE LIVING COLOR, The Magazine of Film and Fiction, Living Color Productions, 417 Euclid Ave., Elmira NY 14905. (607)732-7509. Editor: Jack Stevenson. "We print a variety of fiction styles, also: articles and interviews concerning underground writers and filmmakers. As such, we have no specific theme. Recently published contributions by poet Charles Bukowski, filmmaker John Waters. Read by literates and semi-literates who like things that are free (us). Folks wo like a cheap laugh without being beat over the head with a message. People who like to look at pictures." Bimontly. Estab. 1982. Circ. 2,000.
Needs: Comics, horror, humor/satire, prose poem; "modern parable and fairy tales. If you consider yourself foremost a 'writer' of the Hemingway school, you're probably wasting our time. We like Celine, Kafka, Gogol, Burroughs—writers with some sense of humor. No New Yorker or Paris Review clone stories, no political or feminist material. Absolutely nothing set in Vermont. No 'relationship-awareness' type stuff." Receves 50-100 unsolicited fiction mss/month. Accepts 3-6 mss/issue; 40 mss/year. Occasionally critiques rejected mss.
How to Contact: Send complete ms with SASE. Simultaneous, photocopied and previously published submissions OK. Reports in 1 month on mss. Sample copy free with 9x12 envelope and 70¢ postage. Fiction guidelines free.
Payment: Pays in magazine subscription and free contributor's copies.
Terms: Acquires all rights. Publication copyrighted.
Tips: "Fiction is such an individual appreciation—much more so then interviews, say, or articles—that overwhelming mass approval is rarely to be expected. Naturally, a reader has to find 'his' magazine and a magazine has to find its audience. Don't waste your tme just writing to get printed somewhere—you've got to amuse yourself first, that's most important. Also, don't take an editor's rejection too seriously: other people's advice is only applicable to a point. You'll never make it following their instructions."

LOONFEATHER/Minnesota North Country Art, Box 48, Hagg-Sauer Hall, Bemidji State University, Bemidji MN 56601. (218)755-2813. Editor: William D. Elliott. A literary journal of fiction, poetry and photography. Mostly a market for North Central Minnesota, Minnesota, and Midwest writers. Published 3 times/year. Estab. Fall 1979. Circ. 2,000.
Needs: Literary, contemporary, serialized novels. Accepts 2 mss/issue, 6 mss/year. Length: 600-1,500 words (prefers 1,500).
How to Contact: Send complete ms with SASE. Reports in 1 month. Sample copy $2.
Payment: Free author's copies.
Terms: Acquires one-time rights.
Tips: "Send carefully crafted but experimental and literary fiction. No long mss."

LOST AND FOUND TIMES, Luna Bisonte Prods, 137 Leland Ave., Columbus OH 43214. (614)846-4126. Editor: John M. Bennett. Theme: Experimental, avant-garde and folk literature, art. Published irregularly. Estab. 1975. Circ. 300.
Needs: Literary, contemporary. Prefers short pieces. Accepts approximately 2 mss/issue. Sometimes recommends markets.

How to Contact: Query with clips of published work. SASE for query, ms. Reports in 1 week on queries, 2 weeks on mss. Sample copy $2.
Payment: 2 free author's copies.
Terms: Rights revert to authors.

LUDDS MILL, Eight Miles High Products, 44 Spa Croft Rd., Teall St., Ossett, W. Yorkshire WF5 0HE, UK. Wakefield 275814. Editor: Andrew Darlington. "Alternative culture in the Bohemian tradition, experimental but accessible, direct, exciting, 'beat,' 'hipster,' 'punk,' etc. Aimed at late-teens, twenties, plus anyone with a mental orientation open to 'alternative' culture. Dada, surrealism, anarchist-left, pre-raphaelite, 60s underground, beat generation, etc." Biannual. Estab. 1971. Circ. 1,500.
Needs: Literary, contemporary, science fiction, feminist, gay/lesbian, erotica, condensed novels, experimental fiction. "Emphasis is not on commercial quality, but on originality, ability to excite, experiment with artistic integrity." Receives approximately 20 unsolicited fiction mss each month. Length: 10,000 words maximum. Critiques rejected mss "when there is time." Occasionally sends mss on to editors of other publications. Routinely recommends markets.
How to Contact: Send complete ms with SASE, IRC. Reports in 1 month. Sample copy $2.
Payment: Free author's copies.
Terms: All rights remain with contributor.
Tips: "Get in contact. Send selection of work with brief biographical note/friendly letter. If work is not suitable we will supply address list of alternatives. Check requirements of magazine before submitting material. Keep mss circulating." Mss are rejected because of "lack of integration of ideas. Writer should have clear idea of concept he/she's attempting to put over, even if the idea is abstract/experimental/symbolist."

LUNA, A Literary Magazine, Luna Collective, 101, Edgevale Rd. Kew, Melbourne, Victoria, Australia 3101. Editor: Barbara Giles. "We publish poetry, short stories on any theme, and articles mainly on Australian writing, or interviews with literary figures for appreciative readers of good poetry and fiction, both men and women." Semiannually. Estab. 1975. Circ. 500.
Needs: Contemporary, ethnic, experimental, fantasy, feminist, historical, humor/satire, literary, prose poem, psychic/supernatural, science fiction. "In each of these categories we require good writing." Receives 40-50 unsolicited fiction mss/month. Buys 3 mss/issue; 6 mss/year. Length: 1,000 words minimum; 4,500 words maximum; 2,500 words average. Occasionally critiques rejected mss.
How to Contact: Send complete ms with SASE. Photocopied submissions OK. Reports in 3 months on mss.
Payment: Pays $25-50 and 1 free contributor's copy.
Terms: Pays on publication for one-time rights.

LYNN VOICES, BLT Press, 72 Lowell St., Peabody MA 01960. (617)531-7348. Contact: Editors. "A community tabloid supplement publishing satire, poetry, fiction, photos, and drawings. Survival in the city for the dispossessed, down-and-out, fixed-income, industrial worker, trade unionist, feminist, social radical." Annual. Estab. June 1980. Circ. 15,000.
Needs: Literary, contemporary, science fiction, humor, ethnic (black, Latino), satire. "Please no tripped-out, God-and-doom-dwellers, reactionaries, or racists." Accepts 1 ms/issue, 1 ms/year. Receives very few unsolicited fiction mss. Length: 1-500 (prefers 500) words.
How to Contact: Query. SAE for ms. Reports in 1 month on queries, 2 months on mss. Sample copy 25¢ with large manilla SAE plus 40¢ postage.
Payment: Free author's copies.
Terms: Acquires simultaneous rights.
Tips: "Please, be at least 40% satirist; deal with social issues (jobs, government, sexism, racism). Move away from the lyrical and toward the dramatic. Stop thinking about yourself. . . . distance yourself and reader." Mss are rejected because "subject matter is far off the mark . . . as though what we specified wasn't read."

THE MADISON REVIEW, Department of English, White Hall, University of Wisconsin, Madison WI 53706. Editor-in-Chief: Jay Clayton. Magazine of "fiction and poetry, with special emphasis on literary stories and some emphasis on Midwestern writers." Published semiannually. Estab. 1978. Circ. 750.
Needs: Experimental, literary, prose poem. Receives 20 unsolicited fiction mss/month. Accepts 7-10 mss/issue. Length: 500 words minimum; 7,000 words maximum. Occasionally critiques rejected mss. Sometimes recommends markets.
How to Contact: Send complete ms with SASE. Reports in 6 weeks on mss. "We do not report on mss during the summer." Sample copy $2.
Payment: 2 free contributor's copies; $2 charge for extras.
Terms: Pays on publication for first North American serial rights. Publication copyrighted.

MAELSTROM REVIEW, 34 Winter St., Portland ME 04102. Editor/Publisher: Leo Mailman. "Poetry, fiction and reviews with contemporary fiction format, but not too experimental, for literary, college-educated, or student readership." Semiannual. Estab. 1972. Circ. 400-700.
Needs: Literary, contemporary. "No highly romantic, gothic, religious, political, or highly experimental material." Accepts 2-3 mss/issue, 5-6 mss/year. Receives approximately 5-10 unsolicited fiction mss each month. Length: 2,000 words, 10-20 ms pages. Critiques rejected mss "when there is time." Occasionally sends mss on to editors of other publications.
How to Contact: Send complete ms with SASE. Reports in 2 months on mss. Sample copy $2.
Payment: 3-5 free author's copies "with eligibility for annual award and payment." Half price charge for extra copies.
Terms: Rights revert to author upon publication. Publication copyrighted.
Tips: "Buy a sample issue and read the fiction before submitting. Mss accepted are eligible for best short story award of year in *Maelstrom Review*."

MAENAD, LTD., A Women's Literary Journal, Box 738, 84 Main St., Gloucester MA 01930. (617)283-7401. Editor: Paula Estey. "*Maenad* is a high-quality literary and visual arts thematic quarterly which publishes controversial and radical feminist ideas and theories." Quarterly. Estab. 1980. Circ. 2,000.
Needs: Adventure, comics, condensed novel, contemporary, ethnic, experimental, fantasy, feminist/lesbian, gay, gothic/historical romance, horror, humor/satire, literary, prose poem, psychic/supernatural, religious/inspirational, science fiction, serialized/excerpted novel, suspense/mystery, translations, women's. Receives 23 unsolicited fiction mss/month. Accepts 4 mss/issue; 16 mss/year. Length: 15-page maximum. Occasionally critiques rejected mss.
How to Contact: Send complete ms, cover letter and short bio with SASE. Photocopied and previously published submissions OK. Reports in 8 weeks on mss. Sample copy free. Fiction guidelines free.
Payment: 2 free contributor's copies.
Terms: Acquires one-time rights. Publication copyrighted.
Tips: "Good writing, feminist perspective, no journalism."

MAGAZINE, (formerly *Beyond Baroque*), Beyond Baroque Foundation, 681 Venice Blvd., Venice CA 90291. (213)822-3006. Co-Editors: Jocelyn Fisher and Alexandra Garrett. Magazine of contemporary poetry, fiction, reviews. Published quarterly. Estab. 1969. Circ. 6,000.
Needs: Literary. "No genre fiction unless very good. We sometimes publish an issue totally devoted to one author's work—poetry, short stories or novel." Receives 12-20 unsolicited fiction mss/month. Accepts varying number of mss/issue. Occasionally critiques rejected mss.
How to Contact: Send complete ms with SASE. Photocopied submissions OK. Reports in 2 months on mss. Sample copy $1 with 9x10 SAE and 56¢ postage.
Payment: 10 free contributor's copies.
Terms: Acquires first North American serial rights, (revert to author after 90 days). Publication copyrighted.

MAGIC CHANGES, Celestial Otter Press, 553 W. Oakdale, #317, Chicago IL 60657. (312)327-5606. Editors: John Sennett and Don Bullen. "Theme: arts renaissance. Material: poetry, songs, fiction, stories, reviews, art, essays, etc. For the entertainment and enlightenment of all ages." Quarterly. Estab. December 1979. Circ. 1,000.
Needs: Literary, psychic/supernatural, science fiction, fantasy, erotica. "Fiction should have an artistic slant." Accepts 2-3 mss/issue, 8-12 mss/year. Receives approximately 10 unsolicited fiction mss each month. Length: 3,000 words maximum.
How to Contact: Send complete ms with SASE. Reports in 1 month. Sample copy $4.
Payment: 1-2 free author's copies. $3.50 charge for extras.
Terms: Acquires first North American serial rights. Publication copyrighted.
Tips: "Write well. Rewrite. Read poetry. Read good fiction. Most rejected mss are poorly written and offer dull stories or not at all. Just write a good story." Sponsors contest. Offers critiquing service.

MAGICAL BLEND, A Magazine of Synergy, Box 11303, San Francisco CA 94101. (415) 282-9338. Editor: Michael P. Langevin. Fiction Editor: Lisa Shulman. "We believe that people's thoughts create their realities. We publish positive, uplifting material—often visionary—on a variety of themes ranging from mystical/magical/spiritual to the practical for those interested in taking control of their lives, expanding their consciousness, focusing on the positive." Quarterly. Estab. Spring 1980. Circ. 5,000.
Needs: Psychic/supernatural, fantasy, adventure. "We also feature specialized issues, for example: sea mammals, health. No dark or dismal portrayal of life." Accepts 5-7 mss/issue, 20-28 mss/year. Receives approximately 20 unsolicited fiction mss each month. Length: 500-3,000 words. Critiques rejected mss "when there is time."
How to Contact: Send complete ms with SASE. Reports in 3 months on mss. Sample copy $3. Guidelines for legal-sized SASE.
Payment: 5 free author's copies. $1.50 plus postage and handling for extras.
Terms: Acquires first North American serial rights and second serial rights. Publication copyrighted.
Tips: "We like fiction that takes our readers to beautiful worlds and ends happily. Share your fantasies, dreams and stories of magic with us. *Proofread* your ms, send a neat, polished copy. Cover letters are nice, SASEs are essential. Your story should be interesting to others besides you. *Believe in yourself*!" Mss are rejected because they are "not well-written, not positive or spiritual—too much violence or sex."

MAIZE, NOTEBOOKS OF XICANO ART AND LITERATURE, Maize, Box 8251, San Diego CA 92102. (714)455-1128. Editors: Xelina and Alurista. "Works of Third World social consciousness: fiction, poetry, drama, graphics, art, line drawing, photos, literary criticism. Readers: Third World and chicano. *Maize* provides a long overdue outlet for abundant material." Biannual. Estab. 1977. Circ. 1,000.
Needs: Literary, contemporary, men's, women's, erotica, humor, ethnic. Wants to see "that literature which relates to the social concerns of Third World people—their culture and lives." No scientific material. Accepts 2 mss/issue. Sometimes recommends markets. Length: 1,500-4,000 (prefers 3,000) words.
How to Contact: Send complete ms with SASE. Reports in 2 months on mss. $5/sample copy.
Payment: 3 free author's copies. $5 charge for extras.
Terms: Acquires first rights. Publication copyrighted.
Tips: "Aim toward the consciousness of Third World people. Remain honest and simple." Mss are rejected because "themes are not complimentary to our editorial policy."

THE MALAHAT REVIEW, University of Victoria, Box 1700, Victoria, B.C., Canada V8W 2Y2. Contact: Editor. "An international literary quarterly of life and letters. Publishing first in English, fiction, poetry, criticism, essays, and art for public and university libraries, colleges and senior high schools, and individuals with literary interests." Quarterly. Estab. 1967. Circ. 800.

Needs: Literary, contemporary, science fiction, men's, women's, humor, translations. No horror, romance or juvenile. Buys 4 mss/issue, 50 mss/year. Receives approximately 30 unsolicited fiction mss/month. Length: 4,000-5,000 words. Critiques rejected mss "when there is time."
How to Contact: Query or send complete ms. SASE for query, ms. "Work not returned without Canadian stamps or International Reply Coupons." Reports in 1 week on queries, 2 months on mss. Free sample copy with 10½x7½ SASE plus $1 postage.
Payment: $25 per thousand words and 2 free author's copies. $3 less 33⅓% discount for extras. Offers kill fee of full amount for commissioned ms not published.
Terms: Acquires first world serial rights. All rights revert to author after publication. Publication copyrighted.
Tips: "Be sure to keep your own duplicate of ms." Mss are rejected because of "commonplace subject matter, clumsy prose style, mere reportage."

MALINI, Pan-Asian Journal for the Literati, 1425 Paseo de Peralta, No. 5, Santa Fe NM 87501. Editor: Ms. Chitra Chakraborty. Magazine "to promote the essence of Pan-Asian cultures (i.e., from India to Japan including some Pacific Islands)." Bimonthly. Estab. 1981. "Libraries are among our subscribers. Therefore, we have a very large readership."
Needs: Ethnic, literary, prose poem, translations. Receives few ("fortunately") mss/month. Accepts 1 ms/issue; 6-12 (approximately)/year. Length: 900 words minimum; 1,200 words maximum. Occasionally critiques rejected mss.
How to Contact: Query first with SASE. Reports in 3-4 weeks on queries. Sample copy $1.37.
Payment: Pays in 3 contributor's copies.
Terms: Acquires all rights. Publication copyrighted.
Tips: "Write about nothing other than Asian/immigrant experience."

THE MASSACHUSETTS REVIEW, Memorial Hall, University of Massachusetts, Amherst MA 01003. Editors: John Hicks and Robert Tucker. Quarterly.
Needs: Short stories. Critiques rejected mss "when there is time." .
How to Contact: Send complete ms. No ms returned without SASE. Reports promptly. Sample copy $3.
Payment: Pays $50 maximum.
Terms: Pays on publication for first North American serial rights. Publication copyrighted.
Tips: "Shorter rather than longer stories preferred (20-25 pp.) Avoid submitting material during summer months."

MATI, Ommation Press, 5548 N. Sawyer, Chicago IL 60625. Editor: Effie Mihopoulos. "Primarily a poetry magazine but we do occasional special fiction and science fiction issues." Quarterly. Estab. 1975. Circ. 1,000.
Needs: Literary, contemporary, science fiction, feminist, translations. No mystery, gothic, western, religious. Receives approximately 10 unsolicited fiction mss each month. Length: 1-2 pages. Occasionally sends mss on to editors of other publications. Sometimes recommends markets.
How to Contact: Send complete ms with SASE. Reports in 1 week. Sample copy $1.50 with 9x12 SASE (preferred) plus 80¢ postage.
Payment: 1 free author's copy. Special contributor's rates available for extras.
Terms: Acquires first North American serial rights. "Rights revert to author but *Mati* retains reprint rights." Publication copyrighted.
Tips: "We want to see good quality writing and a neat ms with sufficient return postage; same size return as outside envelope and intelligent cover letter. Editor to be addressed as 'Dear Sir/Ms' instead of 'Dear Sir' when it's a woman editor."

MATRIX, Champlain College, Box 510, Lennoxville, Quebec, Canada J1M 1Z6. Editor: Philip Lanthier. Fiction Editor: Marjorie Retzleff. "A literary magazine with Canadian and American content. We invite both experimental and traditional story forms and are especially interested in

English translations from Quebec writing in French.'' Biannual. Estab. 1975. Circ. 800.
Needs: Literary. Buys 3-4 mss/issue. Length: 1,000-5,000 words.
How to Contact: Send complete manuscript with SASE. Reports in 6 weeks on mss. Free sample copy.
Payment: $15-$125. Contributors copies $1 each.
Terms: Pays on publication for first North American serial rights.
Tips: ''Use strong dialogue, good endings. Avoid hackneyed themes.''

MEMPHIS STATE REVIEW, Memphis State University, Dept. of English, Memphis State, Memphis TN 38152. (901)454-2668. Editor: William Page. Magazine. National review of poetry and fiction for university audience and readers of serious poetry and fiction. Semiannually. Estab. 1980. Circ. 2,500.
Needs: Contemporary, fantasy, literary, science fiction, short stories, excerpted novel. Accepts 3-4 mss/issue; 6-8 mss/year.
How to Contact: Send complete ms with SASE. Reports in 3 weeks to 3 months (except in the summer) on mss. Sample copy for $2.
Payment: Annual $100 prize for best poem or short story and 2 free contributor's copies.
Terms: Acquires first North American serial rights. Publication copyrighted.

MENDOCINO REVIEW, Box 888, Mendocino CA 95460. (707)964-3831. Editor-in-Chief: Camille Ranker. ''Journal for art, literature and music, also photography, poetry and short stories.'' Published annually. Estab. 1972. Circ. 5,000.
Needs: Comics, contemporary, fantasy, historical (general), humor/satire, juvenile, literary, prose poem, science fiction, serialized/excerpted novel, suspense/mystery. No political mss. Receives 10-15 unsolicited fiction mss/month. Accepts varying number of mss/issue. Length: no preferred minimum; 5,000 words maximum.
How to Contact: Send complete ms with SASE. Simultaneous and photocopied submissions OK. Reports in 3 months on mss. Free sample copy and fiction guidelines ''with submission of ms if requested.''
Payment: ''Payment in copies and dealt with on individual basis.''
Terms: Pays on publication for one-time rights. Publication copyrighted.
Tips: ''Submit ms and keep on writing and submitting. Be professional—type, double spaced, and package your submission as though you value it. The folks that receive it will respect it if you do.''

THE MENOMONIE REVIEW, English Dept., University of Wisconsin-Stout, Menomonie WI 54751. Editor: William O'Neill. Magazine of stories and poems for a highly literate audience. Annually. Estab. 1982. Circ. 300.
Needs: Adventure, contemporary, ethnic, experimental, fantasy, feminist/lesbian, gay, humor/satire, literary, mainstream, men's, prose poem, science fiction, women's. No sentimental stories. Receives 5 unsolicited fiction mss/month. Accepts 2-3 mss/issue; 2-3 mss/year. Length: 6,000 words maximum; 2,500 words average. Occasionally critiques rejected mss.
How to Contact: Send complete ms with SASE. Reports in 6-10 weeks (if submitted during school year) on mss. Sample copy for $2.
Payment: 2 free contributor's copies.
Terms: Acquires one-time rights. Publication copyrighted.

METAMORFOSIS, Center for Chicano Studies GN-09, University of Washington, Seattle WA 98195. (206)543-9080. Magazine of ''chicano literature and culture, Spanish/English bilingual format for a general audience. Published semiannually. Estab. 1977. Circ. 500.
Needs: Condensed novel, ethnic, humor/satire, literary, prose poem. Receives 5 unsolicited fiction mss/month. Sends mss on to editors of publications. Sometimes recommends markets.
How to Contact: Send complete ms with SASE. Simultaneous and photocopied submissions OK. Reports in 6 months on mss.

Payment: 5 free contributor's copies.
Terms: Pays on publication. Publication copyrighted.
Tips: "We encourage beginning writers to submit."

THE METRO, Reflections on Life and Culture, 610 Mulberry St., Scranton PA 18510.
(717)348-1010. Publisher: Richard Powell. "A monthly arts and news magazine dedicated to the
arts and humanities. *The Metro* is distributed free of charge to students at all colleges in northeast-
ern Pennsylvania. Published monthly. Estab. 1977. Circ. 15,000.
Needs: Experimental, historical (general), literary, prose poem, avant-garde. No science fiction, serialized novels or women's. Receives 30 unsolicited fiction mss/month. Accepts 2 mss/is-
sue, 20 mss/year. Length: 1,000 words minimum; 3,500 words maximum; 2,200 words average.
Occasionally critiques rejected mss.
How to Contact: Query first with SASE. "Will not read unsolicited mss." Simultaneous and
photocopied submissions OK. Reports in 6 weeks on queries. Sample copy $1.
Payment: Pays in free contributor's copies.
Terms: Acquires first rights. Publication copyrighted.
Tips: "Undergo disciplined study at a good university for at least 4 years."

M 'GODOLIM, LeBeacon Presse, 2921 E. Madison St., Suite 7 FWM, Seattle WA 98122. Editor: Shabatai Gormezano. Publishes the works of Jewish writers and artists for a Jewish-oriented
audience. Quarterly. Estab. June 1980. Circ. 200.
Needs: Literary, contemporary, religious/inspirational, science fiction, fantasy, horror, feminist, mystery, adventure, humor, ethnic (Jewish) and translations. Buys 10 mss/year. Receives
approximately 25 unsolicited fiction mss each month. Length: 25-1,000 words. Comments occasionally on rejected mss for 25¢/page.
How to Contact: Query or send complete ms with SASE. Reporting time varies on both queries
and mss. Sample copy $2 with size # 10 SASE.
Terms: Acquires one-time rights.
Payment: Free author's copies.
Tips: Mss are rejected because they are "too long, wordy; writers haven't read magazine!"

MICHIGAN QUARTERLY REVIEW, University of Michigan, 3032 Rackham, Ann Arbor MI
48109. (213)764-9265. Editor: Laurence Goldstein. "An interdisciplinary journal which
publishes mainly essays and reviews, with some high-quality fiction and poetry, for an intellectual, widely-read audience." Quarterly. Estab. 1962. Circ. 1,500.
Needs: Literary. No "genre" fiction written for a "market." Receives 200 unsolicited fiction
mss/month. Buys 2 mss/issue; 8 mss/year. Length: 1,500 words minimum; 7,000 words maximum; 5,000 words average.
How to Contact: Send complete ms with SASE. Photocopied submissions OK. Sample copy for
$2 and 2 first class stamps.
Payment: Pays $70-170.
Terms: Pays on acceptance for first rights. Publication copyrighted. Awards the Laurence Foun-
dation Prize of $500 for best story in *MQR* previous year.
Tips: "Read back issues to get a sense of tone; level of writing. *MQR* is very selective; only send
the very finest, best-plotted, most-revised fiction."

MICRON, 1424 N. Poinsettia Pl. # 104, Los Angeles CA 90046. (213)851-3407. Editor-in-
Chief: Stefan Munteanu. Magazine for students, writers, artists. Published quarterly.
Needs: Receives 203 unsolicited fiction mss month. Publishes also in Romanian, Spanish, and
French.
Payment: *Micron* is a non-profit organization.
Terms: Acquires all rights. Publication copyrighted.
Tips: Stories are well received (70-100 letters a year from readers).

THE MICROPSYCHOLOGY NEWSLETTER, "Little Things That Mean A Lot," Microsphere Enterprises, 234 Fifth Ave., New York NY 10001. (212)462-8573. Editor: Joan Virzera. Newsletter with the theme: Little things can be important—such as minor, seemingly insignificant, daily frustrations that affect people on a level beyond awareness; minor problems that snowball into major ones; resulting stress; humor as therapy. The Micropsychology Newsletter is a forum for both professional and layman. Publishes research in the area of micropsychology and literary material. Bimonthly. Estab. 1982. Circ. 2,500.
Needs: Contemporary, humor/satire, literary, mainstream, prose poem, didactic material. "Most important is that material conform to the theme of the importance of little things and it be interesting and convincing. Mature writing stressed." No mss too lengthy—short-short stories preferred. Receives 100 unsolicited fiction mss/month. Accepts 10-15 mss/issue; 60-90 mss/year. Length: 2,000 words maximum. Occasionally critiques rejected mss.
How to Contact: Send complete ms with SASE. Simultaneous, photocopied and previously published submissions OK. Fiction guidelines free with SASE.
Payment: 3 free contributor's copies.
Terms: Acquires simultaneous, second serial or first North American serial rights.
Tips: "Convincingly demonstrate how a seemingly unimportant detail has important psychological implications. We will not hesitate to publish never-published writers whose material is of high quality and applicable. Our audience identifies with the situations in the stories; there is an enthusiastic response."

MID-AMERICAN REVIEW, Popular Press, Department of English, Bowling Green State University, Bowling Green OH 43403. (419)372-2725. Contact: Editor-in-Chief. Magazine. "We publish serious fiction and poetry, as well as critical studies in modern literature and book reviews." Published biannually. Estab. Spring 1981.
Needs: Experimental, literary, prose poem, excerpted novel, translations. Receives about 50 unsolicited fiction mss/month. Buys 5-6 mss/issue. Occasionally critiques rejected mss.
How to Contact: Send complete ms with SASE. Reports in 2 months on mss. Sample copy $4.50.
Payment: $5/page; 2 free contributor's copies; $2 charge for extras.
Terms: Pays on publication for one-time rights. Publication copyrighted.
Tips: "One fiction award yearly, The Sherwood Anderson Short Fiction Prize ($200) for material that has appeared in the magazine."

MIDSTREAM-A MONTHLY JEWISH REVIEW, The Theodor Herzl Foundation, 515 Park Ave., New York NY 10022. (212)752-0600. Editor: Joel Carmichael. Fiction Editor: Debra Berman. Theme: articles, essays, poetry, reviews dealing with world and cultural subjects of Jewish interest. "We are aimed at those who wish to keep abreast of developments in world and cultural Jewish affairs." Monthly. Estab. 1955. Circ. 15,000.
Needs: Literary, religious and Jewish ethnic. Buys 1 ms/issue. Receives approximately 50 unsolicited fiction mss each month. Length: 1,000-3,000 words.
How to Contact: Send complete ms with SASE. Reports in 1 month. Free sample copy.
Payment: 5¢ per word and 3 free author's copies.
Terms: Pays on publication for first rights. Publication copyrighted.

MIDWEST ARTS & LITERATURE, (formerly *Sheba Review—The Literary Magazine for the Arts*), Sheba Review, Inc., Box 1623, Jefferson City MO 65102. Editor: S.D. Hansom. Theme: to promote the arts and artists in the Midwest; poetry; literary and journalistic prose. For those interested in cultural (artistic) concerns. Biannual. Estab. 1978.
Needs: Literary, contemporary, religious/inspirational, psychic/supernatural, science fiction, fantasy, humor, ethnic, translations. No pornographic material. Receives approximately 10 unsolicited fiction mss each month. Critiques rejected mss "when there is time." Recommends markets.
How to Contact: Send complete ms with SASE. Reports in 5 months on mss.

Payment: Free authors copies and discount subscription to publications.
Terms: Acquires one-time rights. Publication copyrighted.
Tips: "Review a sample copy prior to submissions." Sponsors contests, poetry readings, work-shops.

MINOTAUR, Minotaur Press, Box 4094, Burlingame CA 94010. Editor/Publisher: Jim Gove. "Contemporary poetry, short fiction, articles on the literary scene, reviews. We tend to favor experimental work but we are not exclusive about it. Readers are those who probably write or study contemporary literature." Quarterly. Estab. 1976. Circ. 500.
Needs: Literary, contemporary. "No genre fiction." Accepts 1 ms/issue. Receives approximately 4-8 unsolicited fiction mss each month. Length: 2,000 maximum. Critiques rejected mss "when there is time."
How to Contact: Send complete manuscript with SASE. Reports in 3 weeks. Free sample copy with 6½x9½ SASE with 33¢ postage.
Payment: Free author's copies.
Terms: Acquires first rights. Publication copyrighted.
Tips: "For us, fiction, to be considered, must be literate and probably have enough of an experimental element to be difficult to publish elsewhere."

MISSISSIPPI REVIEW, University of Southern Mississippi, Southern Station, Box 5144, Hattiesburg MS 39406. (601)266-4321. Editor: Frederick Barthelme. Associate Editor: Elizabeth Inness-Brown. Literary publication for those interested in contemporary literature—writers, editors who read to be in touch with current modes. Semiannual. Estab. 1972. Circ. 1,500.
Needs: Literary, contemporary, fantasy, humor, translations, experimental, avant-garde and "art" fiction. No juvenile. Buys varied amount of mss/issue. Length: 100 pages maximum.
How to Contact: Send complete ms with SASE including a short cover letter. Sample copy $4.50.
Payment: Pays with 6 free author's copies. Charges cover price for extras.
Terms: Pays on publication for first North American serial rights.

MISSISSIPPI VALLEY REVIEW, Western Illinois University. Dept. of English, Simpkins Hall, Macomb IL 61455. Editor: Forrest Robinson. Fiction Editor: Loren Logsdon. "A small magazine, *MVR* has won eleven Illinois Arts Council awards in poetry and fiction. We publish stories, poems, and reviews." Biannual. Estab. 1971. Circ. 400.
Needs: Literary, contemporary.
How to Contact: Send complete ms with SASE. Reports in 3 months.
Payment: 2 free author's copies, plus one copy of the following two numbers.
Terms: Individual author retains rights.
Tips: "We prefer to receive one story at a time."

THE MISSOURI REVIEW, 231 Arts & Science, English Dept., University of Missouri, Columbia MO 65211. (314)882-6421. Editor: Speer Morgan. Theme: fiction, poetry, criticism, essays, reviews, interviews. "All with a distinctly contemporary orientation. For writers, academics, others. We present non-established as well as established writers of excellence and offer a forum for modern critical theory." Published 3 times/academic year. Estab. 1977. Circ. 1,250.
Needs: Literary, contemporary; open to all categories except juvenile, young adult. Buys 4-5 mss/issue, 12-15 mss/year. Receives approximately 200 unsolicited fiction mss each month. No preferred length. Critiques rejected mss "when there is time."
How to Contact: Send complete ms with SASE. Reports in 6 weeks. Sample copy $1.
Payment: $5-10/page.
Terms: Pays on publication for all rights. Publication copyrighted.
Tips: "Practice writing and wait three years to try to break into a publication." Mss are rejected because they are "sloppy, unpolished, too academic." Awards William Peden Prize in fiction; $500 to best story published in *Missouri Review* in a given year.

THE MONTANA REVIEW, Owl Creek Press, 2220 Quail, Missoula MT 59802. Editor-in-Chief: Rich Ives. Magazine for readers of contemporary literature. "We publish only work of literary merit. Any subject, style or approach is acceptable if the result is of lasting literary quality." Published annually. Estab. 1979. Circ. 500.
Needs: Adventure, contemporary, erotica, ethnic, experimental, historical (general), literary, mainstream, men's, prose poem, serialized/excerpted novel, translations, women's. "Genre is irrelevant. Quality of the writing is our only consideration." Receives 20-30 unsolicited fiction mss/month. Accepts 6-10 mss/year. Length: no preferred length. Occasionally critiques rejected mss. Sometimes recommends other markets.
How to Contact: Send complete ms with SASE. Simultaneous and photocopied submissions OK. "Work published in magazines may be considered in book form." Reports in 1 month. Sample copy $3.
Payment: 2 year subscription; 3 free contributor's copies; $3 charge for extras.
Terms: Pays on publication for all rights (books) and first North American serial rights (for magazine stories). Publication copyrighted.
Tips: "Seek the advice and assistance of established writers through workshops, conferences and college creative writing programs."

MOOSE MAGAZINE, Moose Magazine, Inc., 1807 S.E. Stark St., Portland OR 97206. (503)775-4582. Editor: Kathleen M. Reyes. Fiction Editors: Kathleen Reyes and Doug Spangle. "We are a little magazine publishing poetry, fiction, reviews (literary), and graphic arts including calligraphy." For "persons with interest in things literary and in fine magazine production, meaning the use of good papers and high-quality illustration." Semiannually. Estab. 1980. Circ. 350.
Needs: "Surprise us." Receives 3-4 unsolicited fiction mss/month. Acquires 2 mss/issue; 6 mss/year. Work should not exceed 10 pages typed, double-spaced. Critiques rejected ms "particularly if ms shows promise."
How to Contact: Send complete ms with SASE. "*Always* enclose SASE even with query if reply desired." Reports in 2 months on mss. Sample copy $3 for 8½x11 SAE and 85¢ postage. Fiction guidelines free for 8½x3½ SAE and 20¢ postage.
Payment: "If/when we receive grant support, we may pay contributors." 2 free contributor's copies; $3 charge for each extra mailed.
Terms: Acquires first rights. All rights rever to author following publication. Publication copyrighted.
Tips: "Do not be trivial (boring) or cute. Use appropriate language consistently. Care in packaging *is* important; photocopies on limp papers will not help with an overall impression. Beware, beware of padding! Be well armed with a dictionary. Make sure your story starts at the beginning of the text. We have been hoping a long time for fiction worth publishing, and have yet to be satisfied!"

MOOSEHEAD REVIEW, Moosehead Press, Box 169, Ayer's Cliff, Quebec, Canada J0B 1C0. (819)838-5921 (4801). Editors: Robert Allen, Hugh Dow, Steve Luxton, Jan Draper. "A small literary and political periodical." Semiannual. Estab. 1978. Circ. 500.
Needs: Literary, science fiction, translations, literary theory (especially Marxist). Accepts 2-3 mss/issue, 4-6 mss/year. No preferred length.
How to Contact: Send complete ms with SASE. Reports in 6 weeks. Sample copy $3.
Payment: 3 free author's copies.
Terms: Acquires one-time rights.
Tips: "We are a very competitive market. We accept roughly one of every 30 stories submitted. Only top quality fiction is considered, but we do not judge by reputation. A first story has as much chance as a story by a well-known writer."

MOVING OUT, Feminist Literary & Arts Journal, Box 21879, Detroit MI 48221. Editors: Joan W. Gartland, Margaret Kaminski, Paula Rabinowitz, and Amy Cherry. Magazine of "material which captures the experience of women for feminists and other humane human beings."

Published semiannually. Estab. 1971. Circ. 1,000 + .

Needs: No male chauvinist creations. Accepts about 4-8 mss/issue. Occasionally critiques rejected mss.

How to Contact: Send complete ms with SASE. Reports in 4 months or longer. Sample copy $2.50; free guidelines for SASE.

Payment: 1 free contributor's copy.

Terms: Acquires first rights. Publication copyrighted.

MSS, State University of New York at Binghamton, S.U.N.Y. at Binghamton, Binghamton NY 13901. Co-editors: L.M. Rosenberg and Joanna Higgins. Literary of poetry, essays and fiction. Triquarterly. Estab. 1960s by John Gardner.

Needs: Receives about 100 unsolicited fiction mss/month. Buys 5-10 mss/issue; 15-30 mss/year. Occasionally critiques rejected mss.

How to Contact: Send complete ms with SASE. Photocopied submissions OK. Reports in 1-2 months on mss. Sample copy $4. Fiction guidelines free with SASE.

Payment: Pays $50-500 fiction; 2 free contributor's copies; $4 charge for extras.

Terms: Pays on publication; varied rights purchased. Publication copyrighted.

Tips: Read a copy before submitting.

MUNDUS ARTIUM, A Journal of International Literature and Arts, University of Texas at Dallas, Box 688, Richardson TX 75080. Contact: Editor. Literary review of nonfiction, poetry, fiction with bilingual format for all levels, "except the scholarly, footnote-starved type." Semiannual. Estab. 1967. Circ. 2,000.

Needs: Stories must be experimental and fantasy or translations. Length is open. Critiques rejected mss "when there is time."

How to Contact: Send complete ms with SASE. Reports in 3 months. Sample copy $3.50.

Payment: Pays $5 minimum.

Terms: Pays on publication for all rights. Photocopied submissions OK. Publication copyrighted.

MUSCADINE, 1111 Lincoln Pl., Boulder CO 80302. (303)443-9748. Editor: Lucille Cyphers. "Writers must be over 60 years of age. Everyone enjoys *Muscadine* as a glimpse of oldsters' rich experiences and creativity." Bimonthly. Estab. 1977. Circ. 400.

Needs: Literary, contemporary, psychic/supernatural, science fiction, fantasy, men's, women's, western, mystery, adventure, humor, juvenile, ethnic (all). No horror, erotica, novels. Receives 1 unsolicited fiction ms each month. Length: 350-1,500 words. Critiques rejected mss "when there is time."

How to Contact: Send complete ms with SASE. Reports in 1 month on mss. Sample copy $1.

Payment: 1 free author's copy. $1 charge for extras.

Terms: Acquires first rights.

Tips: "We give priority to beginners. Try to stay off trite themes. Express it your way. It might have the freshness we value—the common touch. The more skilled writers have to compete for space. Brevity is a priority. Mss don't have to be typewritten."

MYSTERY TIME, An Anthology of Short Stories, Rhyme Time/Story Time, Box 2377, Coeur d'Alene ID 83814. (208)667-7511. Editor: Linda Hutton. "Annual collection of short stories to 2,000 words with a suspense or mystery theme for mystery buffs." Estab. 1983.

Needs: Suspense/mystery only. Receives 10-15 unsolicited fiction mss/month. Acquires 10-12 mss/year. Length: 2,000 words maximum. Occasionally critiques rejected mss.

How to Contact: Send complete ms with SASE. Simultaneous, photocopied and previously published submissions OK. Reports in 1 month on mss. Sample copy for $5. Fiction guidelines free for + 10 SAE and 20¢ postage.

Payment: 1 free contributor's copy; $5 charge for extras.

Terms: Acquires one-time rights. Publication copyrighted.

Tips: "Concentrate on plot! A neatly typed manuscript is always welcome." Sponsors annual short story, essay and play contests.

MYTHELLANY, The Fiction Journal of The Mythopoeic Society, Box 4671, Whittier CA 90607. Editor-in-Chief: Veida Wissler. Magazine for fantasy readers, high school and up. Published annually. Estab. Summer 1981. Circ. 300.
Needs: Fantasy, humor/satire, juvenile fantasy, young adult fantasy. "Tolkien themes OK, but no re-writes of *Lord of The Rings*. No hard-core science fiction, *Star Wars*, D&D stuff or erotica. Receives about 6 unsolicited fiction mss/month. Accepts 10-15 mss/issue, 10-15 mss/year. Length: 50 words minimum; 10,000 words maximum; 4-5,000 words average. Occasionally critiques rejected mss.
How to Contact: Query or send complete ms. with SASE. Photocopied and previously published submissions OK. Reports in 3 weeks on queries; 6 weeks on mss. Sample copy $2; free guidelines with SASE.
Payment: 1 free contributor's copy/submission; $2 charge for extras.
Terms: Pays on publication for one-time rights. Publication copyrighted.
Tips: "We are a beginning fiction magazine so new writers are welcome! Please be sure your fantasy story *is* fantasy of the type we like i.e., 'fairy-tale-like.' Mythical, wonderous."

NAKED MAN, 1718 Vermont, Apt. A, Lawrence KS 66044. Editor: Mike Smetzer. Magazine. "I have eclectic tastes but generally dislike work that is only clever and spontaneous without discipline. Since *Naked Man* reflects my personal interests and tastes, writers should examine a copy before submitting." Published irregularly. Estab. 1982.
Needs: Comics, contemporary, experimental, humor/satire, literary, mainstream, prose poem. Length: no minimum; 15,000 words maximum. Occasionally critiques rejected ms "as time permits."
How to Contact: Send complete ms with SASE. Photocopied submissions OK. Sample copy $1.50.
Payment: Pays in 2 contributor's copies.
Terms: Acquires first rights. Publication copyrighted.

NAKED SINGULARITY, Speculative and Fantasy Fiction, Quantum Universe Productions, Box 6821, Silver Spring MD 20906. Editor: Carl R. Dietrich. Fiction Editor: K.G. Herbster. Magazine for an audience from 18 to 80. Bimonthly. Estab. 1983.
Needs: Fantasy, horror, psychic/supernatural, science fiction, serialized/excerpted novel. Receives "not nearly enough" unsolicited fiction mss each month. Buys 8 mss/issue; 48 mss/year. Length: 1,000 words minimum; 75,000 words maximum. Occasionally critiques rejected mss.
How to Contact: Send complete ms with SASE. "No phone calls, please." Simultaneous and photocopied submissions OK. Reports in 2 weeks on mss. Sample copy for $2.50. Fiction guidelines free with SAE and 40¢ postage.
Payment: Pays small percentage per word; 2 free contributor's copies; $2.50 charge for extras.
Terms: Pays on publication for first rights. Publication copyrighted.
Tips: "Read the genre widely. Join Bo McScience for scientific backgrounds; they offer the best works."

THE NANTUCKET REVIEW, Box 1234, Nantucket MA 02554. Co-Editors: Richard Cumbie and Richard Burns. "We are a general literary magazine ascribing to no specific school(s) of literature. We publish primarily fiction (60%) and poetry (40%), but also satire, essays, cultural articles for those interested in new writing, students, writers. They read us to see work by new writers side-by-side with work by established writers." Published 3 times/year. Estab. 1974. Circ. 600.
Needs: Literary, feminist, translations. "It's difficult for us to rule out some types of fiction. *The Man From Laramie* and *The Ox-Bow Incident* are both 'western' stories, for example, but stories like the former wouldn't be of much interest to us, while those like the latter would be. We are interested in serious (that is not to say, humorless) fiction." Receives approximately 75 unsolicited

fiction mss each month. Length: 1,500-6,000 words. Critiques rejected mss "when there is time."

How to Contact: Send complete ms with SASE. Reports in 2 months. Sample copy with 6x9 SASE plus 56¢ postage.

Payment: $5-$25 ("occasional payment becomes more frequent") and 2 free author's copies. $1.50 charge for extras.

Terms: Pays on publication for first North American serial rights. Publication copyrighted.

Tips: "Read an issue of the magazine before submitting fiction to us. It's a constant complaint among editors that they receive many mss totally unsuited to their publications. Any writer serious about his craft and eager to publish can, for $15-$20 (or less, depending on library availability), examine a dozen magazines he wishes to try with stories. Be neat. Always, if you feel compelled to do multiple submissions, inform the editor when you submit. Please don't submit stories of more than 6,000 words." Mss are rejected because they are "poorly written and are not entertaining." Sponsors annual fiction contest.

NEBO, A Literary Journal, Arkansas Tech University, Dept. of English, Russellville AR 72801. Fiction Editor: B.C. Hall. Literary, fiction and poetry magazine for a general, academic audience. Semiannually. Estab. 1983. Circ. 500.

Needs: Experimental, literary, mainstream, prose poem, science fiction. Receives 20-30 unsolicited fiction mss/month. Acquires 3-4 mss/issue; 6-10 mss/year. Length: 3,000 words maximum. Occasionally critiques rejected mss.

How to Contact: Send complete ms with SASE. Simultaneous and photocopied submissions OK. Reports in 12 weeks on mss. Sample copy for $1.

Payment: 2-3 free contributor's copies.

Terms: Acquires one-time rights. Publication copyrighted.

NEBULA MAGAZINE, Nebula Press, 970 Copeland, North Bay, Ontario, Canada P1B 3E4. Editor: Ken Stange. Fiction Editor: Gil McElroy. Theme: literary. Readership: well-read. Quarterly. Estab. 1975. Circ. 750.

Needs: Literary—"but open to all genres if treated maturely. No poorly written mss." Accepts about 6 mss/year. Receives approximately 15 unsolicited fiction mss each month. No preferred length.

How to Contact: Send complete ms with SASE or IRC. Reports in 1 month. Sample copy $2.

Payment: 2 free author's copies.

Terms: Acquires first rights. Publication copyrighted.

Tips: "Read us first. We sometimes sponsor grants (Ontario Arts Council) to writers we publish."

NEGATIVE CAPABILITY, A Literary Quarterly, Negative Capability Press, 6116 Timberly Rd. N, Mobile AL 36609. (205)661-9114. Editor-in-Chief: Sue Walker. Fiction Editor: Righter North. Magazine of short fiction, prose poems, poetry, criticism, commentaries, journals and translations for those interested in contemporary trends, innovations in literature. Published quarterly. Estab. July 1981. Circ. 600.

Needs: Adventure, contemporary, ethnic, experimental, fantasy, gothic/historical romance, historical (general), literary, prose poem, psychic/supernatural, romance (contemporary), science fiction, suspense/mystery, translations, women's, young adult. Accepts 2-3 mss/issue, 6-10 mss/year. Length: 1,000 words minimum. Sometimes recommends markets.

How to Contact: Query or send complete ms. SASE for query, ms. Reports in 2 weeks on queries; 1 month on mss. Sample copy $3; free guidelines for legal size SAE and 1 first class stamp.

Payment: 1 free contributor's copy; 40% reduction on all subsequent orders.

Terms: Acquires first rights; first North American serial rights and one-time rights. Publication copyrighted.

Tips: "We consider all mss and often offer suggestions for revisions and work with new authors to encourage and support."

NEPGAN REVIEW, An Australian Magazine of the Arts, Nepgan Review, Box 10, Kingsword, Sydney, Australia 2750. Tel. (047)360-344. Editor: Phillip Kay. Fiction Editor: Sally Carthew. Magazine of the arts for literary groups, artists, academics, students. Quarterly. Estab. 1975. Circ. 500.
Needs: Experimental, fantasy, horror, literary, psychic/supernatural, science fiction, excerpted novel, suspense/mystery, translations. No unrevised, unedited or confessional material. Receives 40-50 unsolicited fiction mss/month. Accepts 3-4 mss/issue; 12 mss/year. Length: 5,000-6,000 words average. Occasionally critiques rejected mss.
How to Contact: Send complete ms with SASE. Simultaneous and photocopied submissions OK. Reports in 5-6 weeks on mss. Sample copy for $3. Fiction guidelines free.
Payment: 1 free contributor's copy.
Terms: Acquires first rights. Publication copyrighted.

NEW AMERICA, c/o Dept. of American Studies, University of New Mexico, Albuquerque NM 87131. (505)277-4557. Editors are rotating. "A journal of American and Southwestern culture. Our material includes fiction, poetry, photography, and graphic art exploring American and Southwestern culture. Our audience is very diverse. Past themes have been geared toward those interested in SW culture, American studies, chicano literature, Native American literature, photographers, energy buffs, etc. Our aim is to reach a larger audience by having different themes." Semiannual. Estab. 1974. Circ. 700.
Needs: Literary, contemporary, men's, women's, ethnic (Chicano, Native American), and Southwestern American studies. "We solicit different material for each specific issue." No preferred length.
How to Contact: Query. SASE for query, ms. Reports in 1 week on queries, 3 months on mss. Sample copy $4.
Payment: 1 free author's copy. 40% discount for 10 or more extras.
Terms: Buys all rights. Publication copyrighted.
Tips: Mss are rejected because "they don't apply to specific theme."

NEW ARTS REVIEW, Athens Avant-Garde Society, Inc., Box 887, Athens GA 30603. (904)543-7444. Editor: Carol L. Kefalas. Fiction Editor: Robert Cooperman. Tabloid of fiction, poetry, reviews (film, book, performance), interviews, arts-related articles for arts/literary enthusiasts. Bimonthly. Estab. 1978. Circ. 2,000.
Needs: Adventure, contemporary, ethnic, historical, humor/satire, literary, mainstream, psychic/supernatural, science fiction, excerpted novel, suspense/mystery, translations, western. No self-indulgent, confessional, "cute" manuscripts. Receives 3 unsolicited fiction mss/month. Buys 1-2 mss/issue; 7-10 mss/year. Length: 1,000 words minimum; 25,000 words maximum; 10,000-12,000 words average. Occasionally critiques rejected mss.
How to Contact: Send complete ms with SASE. Simultaneous and photocopied submissions OK. Reports in 2 weeks on mss. Sample copy for $2 with 8½x11 SAE and 3 first class stamps.
Payment: Pays $25; 10 free contributor's copies.
Terms: Pays on publication for all or first North American serial rights. Publication copyrighted.
Tips: Prefers "lively writing with real characters in real situations."

NEW EDINBURGH REVIEW, EUSPB, 1 Buccleuch Pl., Edinburgh 8 Scotland. (031)667-5718. Editor: James Campbell. Features, fiction, poetry, reviews for a general readership. Quarterly. Estab. 1969.
Needs: Literary, contemporary, ethnic, translations only. Buys 2 mss/issue, 8 mss/year. Receives approximately 40 unsolicited fiction mss each month. Length: 1,000-4,000 words. Critiques rejected mss "when there is time."
How to Contact: Send complete ms. SASE or IRC for ms. Reports in 3 weeks. Sample copy available for fee.
Payment: Negotiates pay for fiction. 1 free author's copy. Offers kill fee for assigned ms not published.

Terms: Pays on publication for first rights. Publication copyrighted.
Tips: "Read our magazine before submitting."

NEW ENGLAND SAMPLER, Seacoast Press, Rt. 1, Box 2280, Brooks ME 04921. (207)525-3575. Editor/Publisher: Virginia M. Rimm. "An upbeat family magazine featuring old-time New England values and heritage. We use historic and humorous material, nature articles, interviews, poetry, book reviews, ESP experiences, fiction, off-beat places to visit, etc. Audience consists of well-educated rural families, senior citizens, middle-aged adults. We reflect the values with which these segments were raised, and we try to provide a feeling of hope and encouragement. They read us because we give them a 'lift.' " Monthly. Estab. August 1980. Circ. 2,000.
Needs: Inspirational, psychic, science fiction, fantasy, gothic, mystery, adventure, humor, juvenile, nature and outdoor. "We use only wholesome material suited to a family audience. No angry, anti-establishment articles; no erotic, gay/lesbian, feminist, ethnic or confession themes. We want general inspirational material, not denominational work. New England slant required." Accepts 8-12 mss/year. Receives approximately 8-10 unsolicited fiction mss each month. Length: 2,500-3,500 words. Critiques rejected mss "when there is time."
How to Contact: Query on fiction. SASE for query, ms. Reports in 2 weeks on queries, 3 months on mss. Sample copy $1. Free general writer's guideline for SASE.
Payment: 1-4 free author's copies. $1 charge for extras.
Terms: Acquires first rights. Publication copyrighted.
Tips: "Send for sample copy and free guidelines. Remember, we're a New England regional with an upbeat format aimed at the family audience. Pick a subject with strong New England flavor, write in lively, fast-paced fashion with good plot and characterization. Be fresh and original. Don't use subject matter incompatible with our format and purpose. We judge our material only by the quality of the workmanship; new and established writers have an equal opportunity with us. We're a young magazine and our entire staff works without pay. To build and grow, we need professional calibre writing. We hope in time to be able to pay. Since we're new, we're a good place for would-be professionals to break into print."

NEW HEAT, A Black Literary Publication, Box 22A22A, 762 Union St., Suite 4, Brooklyn NY 11202. (212)636-8673. Editors: Akua Lezli Hope. Magazine of "black literature: all that produced by literary writers of African descent including Afro-Americans, Afro-Caribbeans, etc." Published quarterly. Estab. Fall 1982.
Needs: Contemporary, erotica, ethnic (black), experimental, fantasy, horror, humor/satire, literary, men's, prose poem, psychic/supernatural, romance (contemporary), science fiction, suspense/mystery, translations, women's, young adult. Receives 3 unsolicited fiction mss/month. Accepts 2 mss/issue. Length: 1,000 words minimum; 7,500 words maximum; 5,000 words average. Occasionally critiques rejected mss.
How to Contact: Send complete ms with SASE. Simultaneous, photocopied and previously published submissions OK. Sample copy $3 and 6 first class stamps; free guidelines for SAE and 1 first class stamp.
Payment: 1 year subscription; 5 free contributor's copies; $2.40 charge for extras.
Terms: Pays on publication for one-time rights. Publication copyrighted.

THE NEW KENT QUARTERLY, Campus Printing, 239 Student Center, Kent State University, Kent OH 44240. Contact: Editor. "The magazine is a creative arts outlet for the university community and other interested artists. We publish poems, prose, and photography for the general public." Biannual. Circ. 300.
Needs: Literary. Receives 1-2 unsolicited fiction mss each month. Length: 1,600 words maximum.
How to Contact: Send complete ms with SASE. Reports in 1 month. Sample copy $1 with SASE.
Payment: Pays in contributor's copies.
Terms: Acquires all rights, revert to author 60 days after issue publication. Publication copyrighted.

NEW LAUREL REVIEW, 828 Lesseps St., New Orleans LA 70117. (504)271-4209. Editor: Lee M. Grue. Journal of poetry, fiction, critical articles and reviews. "We have published such nationally known writers as Guy Owen, Jesse Stuart, H.E. Francis, Tonita Gardner, Dorothy Stanfill, and Jim Barnes (translations)." Readership: "Literate, adult audiences as well as anyone interested in writing with significance, human interest, vitality, subtlety, etc." Biannual. Estab. 1970. Circ. 500.

Needs: Literary, contemporary, fantasy, translations. No "dogmatic, excessively inspirational or political" material. Accepts 1-2 mss/issue. Receives approximately 5 unsolicited fiction mss each month. Length: about 10 printed pages. Critiques rejected mss "when there is time."

How to Contact: Send complete ms. with SASE. Reports in 1 month. Sample copy $2.

Payment: 2 free author's copies.

Terms: Acquires first rights. Publication copyrighted.

Tips: "Write fresh, alive 'moving' work. Not interested in egocentric work without any importance to others. Be sure to watch simple details such as putting one's name and address on ms and clipping all pages together. Caution: Don't use overfancy or trite language."

NEW MEXICO HUMANITIES REVIEW, New Mexico Tech, Box A, NMT, Socorro NM 87801. (505)835-5445. Editor: Jerry Bradley. Review of poetry, essays and prose of Southwest. Readership: academic but not specialized. Published 3 times/year. Estab. 1978. Circ. 700.

Needs: Literary. "No formula." Buys 40-50 mss/year. Receives approximately 20 unsolicited fiction mss each month. Length: 6,000 words maximum. Critiques rejected mss "when there is time." Sometimes recommends markets.

How to Contact: Send complete ms with SASE. Reports in 2 months. Sample copy $3.

Payment: 1 year subscription.

Terms: Pays on publication. Publication copyrighted.

Tips: Mss are rejected because they are "unimaginative, predictable, technically flawed."

NEW OREGON REVIEW, NOR Publications, 537 NE Lincoln St., Hillsboro OR 97123. (503)640-1375. Editor-in-Chief: Steven Dimeo, Ph.D. Magazine. "We seek to publish fiction of lasting literary merit from both unacknowledged and well-established artists who recognize the time-honored values of literary excellence, for the literate and learned who shun the dry self-indulgence of consciously academic fiction in favor of strong, interesting narratives of substance." Published semiannually. Estab. 1981 (*NOR*); 1977 (*Transition*). Circ. 300.

Needs: Adventure, contemporary, erotica, fantasy, historical (general), horror, humor/satire, literary, mainstream, men's, psychic/supernatural, science fiction, suspense/mystery. "We're always looking for the well-integrated tale with thematic depth, skillful characterization, wit, dramatic change, imaginative symbolism, and a strong sense of structure, including an effective narrative hook at the beginning. No self-consciously experimental, moralistic or superficially 'cute' mss." Receives 100 unsolicited fiction mss/month. Buys 3 mss/issue, 6 mss/year. Length: 3,000 words minimum; 5,000 words maximum. Occasionally critiques rejected mss.

How to Contact: Send complete ms with SASE. "Mss should also be accompanied by a short bio/bibliographical statement." Simultaneous, photocopied, and previously published submissions OK. Reports in 2 months on mss. Sample copy $2 for 5½x8 SAE and 2 first class stamps; free guidelines for 3½x8½ SAE and 1 first class stamp.

Payment: $25 flat fee. Charge for extra copies: 1 for $2, 2 for $3.75, 3 for $5, 4 for $6.

Terms: Pays on publication for first rights. Publication copyrighted.

Tips: "Purchase a sample copy of the publication. We're always in the market for realistic narratives laced with horror or the fantastic in the manner of Faulkner's 'A Rose for Emily' or Cheever's 'The Enormous Radio.' Remember the Jamesian tenet that a work of art must above all be *interesting*. Overstocked through 1983."

NEW ORLEANS REVIEW, Box 195, Loyola University, New Orleans LA 70118. (504)865-2294. Editor: John Mosier. Publishes poetry, fiction, translations, photographs, nonfiction on literature and film. Readership: those interested in current culture, literature. Published 3 times/year. Estab. 1968. Circ. 2,500.

Needs: Literary, contemporary, translations. No special categories designated. Buys 9-12 mss/year. Length: Under 40 pages. Recommends markets.
How to Contact: Send complete ms with SASE. Reports in 1 month. Sample copy $5.
Payment: "Rates are changing."
Terms: Pays on publication for first North American serial rights.

THE NEW RENAISSANCE, 9 Heath Rd., Arlington MA 02174. Fiction Editors: Louise T. Reynolds and Harry Jackel. "An international magazine of ideas and opinions, with a classicist position in literature and the arts. Publishes a variety of quality fiction, always well crafted, sometimes experimental. For the literate reader. *tnr* is unique among literary magazines for its marriage of the literary and visual arts with articles and essays on current events. We publish the beginning as well as the established writer." Biannual. Estab. 1968. Circ. 1,500.
Needs: Literary, humor, translations, off-beat, quality fiction and, occasionally, experimental fiction. "We don't want to see heavily plotted stories with one-dimensional characters or academic fiction, or writing that is self-indulgent. *tnr* is interested in fiction that has something to say, that says it with style or grace and that speaks in a highly personalized voice." Buys 3-5 mss/issue, 6-8 mss/year. Receives approximately 30 unsolicited fiction mss each month. Charges $2.10 for reading fee (sample copy). Length: 3-38 pages. Critiques rejected mss "when there is time."
How to Contact: Send complete ms with SASE, of sufficient size for return. Reports in 6-7 months. Sample copy $2.10 (specify fiction issue). "We do no readings from July 1 through September 10 and none from December 10 to January 14."
Payment: $23-$65. 1 free author's copy. $4 each for 1-2 copies, $3.50 for additional copies, $3 for 12 or more copies.
Terms: Pays on publication for all rights. Publication copyrighted.
Tips: "Read an issue or two very carefully and send us the (i.e., one only) very best story you have. We are not interested in imitative or derivative fiction. Beginning and new writers should, first of all, be readers of fiction and, ideally, not merely readers of contemporary or *just*modern work. Writers should study the markets, and submit ONLY to magazines they respect. At *tnr*, we have a philosophy and it is not 'anything goes.' " Mss are rejected because "usually writers send to wrong markets—markets they haven't examined thoroughly or markets they do not fully understand. No mss accepted from April 1, 1983 to Nov. 1, 1983 (overstocked).

THE NEW SOUTHERN LITERARY MESSENGER, The Airplane Press, 302 S. Laurel St., Richmond VA 23220. (804)780-1244. Magazine. "We are not regional in viewpoint, but prefer local material. Emphasis on short stories and poems dealing with contemporary themes." Issues have different themes. Quarterly. Estab. 1981. Circ. 400 + .
Needs: Adventure, comics, contemporary, erotica, ethnic, experimental, humor/satire, literary, prose poem, psychic/supernatural, serialized/excerpted novel, stories set in the outdoors, away from civilization. Wants to see "political satire dealing with specific people or groups—left viewpoint. Good craftsmanship, well-made stories on any subject. No formula stories unless the formula is twisted out of shape." Receives 5-10 unsolicited fiction mss/month. Buys "at least 1 or more" mss/issue. Length: 500 words minimum; 10,000 words maximum; 5,250 words average. Occasionally critiques rejected mss.
How to Contact: Send complete ms with SASE. Previously published work OK. Reports in varied amount of weeks on mss. Sample copy $1 with 6x9 SAE and 37¢ postage. Fiction guidelines for business size SASE.
Payment: Pays $5; subscription to magazine; 2 free contributor's copies.
Terms: Pays on publication for one-time rights. Publication copyrighted.
Tips: "Send the ms with cover letter and sufficient postage on the SASE, making sure the ms is neatly typed. I will read it ASAP. Keep extra copies. Find a local small magazine and talk to the editor face to face. Deal first with small magazines and publishers. Learn to love writing if you don't already."

NEWCOMERS LITERARY MAGAZINE, The Magazine for Unpublished Writers, Newcomers Publishing Co., Box 6102, Chicago IL 60680. (312)871-2986. Editor: Eric A. Newcomer. "*Newcomers* provides a medium for unpublished writers whose work deserves publication, and through that publication to encourage those writers to continue and improve their work." Bimonthly. Estab. 1980. Circ. 500.

Needs: Adventure, comics, condensed novel, contemporary, erotica, ethnic, historical, horror, humor/satire, literary, mainstream, prose poem, serialized/excerpted novel, suspense/mystery. "Naturalistic, realistic fiction given preference. Content over form. Unpublished writers only." Receives 2-6 unsolicited fiction mss/month. Accepts 1-2 mss/issue; 12-24 mss/year. Length: 250 words minimum; 10,000 words maximum. Occasionally critiques rejected mss.

How to Contact: Send complete ms with SASE. Simultaneous and photocopied submissions OK. Reports in 4 weeks on mss. Sample copy for $1.

Payment: Free subscription; up to 5 free contributor's copies.

Terms: Acquires first rights or one-time rights. Publication copyrighted.

Tips: "Send in realistic, well-crafted stories. Short ones are better than long ones for now. Please type all submissions and watch spelling. Writers are urged to apply for our 'Newcomer of the Month' feature."

THE NEWSCRIBES INC., c/o P. Scarpa, 140 Bay Ridge Pkwy., Brooklyn NY 11209. Editor: Roger Cappozi. Poetry, short stories, novel excerpts, and some essays. Readership: all types. Quarterly or biannual. Estab. 1976. Circ. 500.

Needs: Literary, contemporary, science fiction, serialized novels. 10,000 words maximum.

How to Contact: Send complete ms with SASE. Reports in 3 weeks.

Payment: Free author's copies.

Terms: "All rights to the author."

NEXUS, Wright State University, 006 U.C. Wright State University, Dayton OH 45431. (513)873-2505. Editor: Kimberly Willardson. Magazine. "We publish short fiction, poetry and graphic art for mostly students, young writers—basically, anyone interested in new writers and new techniques." Quarterly. Estab. 1966. Circ. 4,000.

Needs: Contemporary, experimental, fantasy, feminist, humor/satire, literary, mainstream, prose poem, science fiction. No erotica, translations or strong political statements. Receives 20 unsolicited fiction mss/month. Accepts 2-3 mss/issue; 6-9 mss/year. Length: 300 words minimum; 3,000 words maximum; 1,500 words average. Short stories should be limited to 20 pages. Occasionally critiques rejected mss.

How to Contact: Send complete ms with SASE. Simultaneous and photocopied submissions OK. Reports in 2 weeks on queries, 1 month on mss. Sample copy free with 10x15 SAE and 3 first class stamps. Fiction guidelines free with 10x15 SAE and 3 first class stamps.

Payment: 2 free contributor's copies; $1 plus postage charged for extras.

Terms: All rights revert to author upon publication. Publication copyrighted.

Tips: "Query first, then send sample of work. Send neat copy. Concise, clear writing. No twisting, confusing plots. Be sure to include SASE with sufficient postage. Always include a *brief* cover letter."

NIGHTSUN, Department of Philosphy, Frostburg State College, Frostburg MD 21532. Editor-in-Chief: Jorn K. Bramann. Magazine of "all literary forms and philosophical and literary essays for a literary and/or academic audience." Published annually. Estab. Feb. 1981. Circ. 1,000.

Needs: Comics, contemporary, experimental, feminist, prose poem. "We are not dogmatic, but have little interest in science fiction, supernatural, etc." Receives 5 unsolicited fiction mss/month. Accepts 2-7 mss/issue. Charges reading fee for literary contest. Length: 5,000 words minimum (if reading fee charged). Occasionally critiques rejected mss.

How to Contact: Send complete ms with SASE. Reporting time "varies." Sample copy $6.80.

Payment: Pays in free contributor's copies.

Terms: Pays on publication for one-time rights (rights revert to author after publication). Publication copyrighted.

Tips: "Try to *say* something. There is too much entertainment writing." Annual literary contest.

NIMROD, International Literary Journal, Arts & Humanities Council of Tulsa, 2210 S. Main, Tulsa OK 74114. Editor-in-Chief: Francine Ringold. Fiction Editor: Gerry McLoud. Magazine for good readers and writers. "We publish 1 thematic issue and 1 open issue (which includes prize winners) each year. Thematic issues, e.g., 'Frontiers' and 'Latin American Voices' are announced. Otherwise, we seek vigorous, imaginative, quality writing." Published semiannually. Estab. 1956. Circ. 1,000.
Needs: Adventure, contemporary, ethnic, experimental, literary, prose poem, science fiction, translations. Receives 60 unsolicited fiction mss/month. Accepts 3 mss/issue, 6 mss/year. Length: no minimum; 6,000 words average. Occasionally critiques rejected mss.
How to Contact: Send complete ms with SASE. Photocopied submissions OK. Reports in 3 months. Sample copy $3.50 and $1.50 postage.
Payment: $5/page "when available"; 3 free contributor's copies.
Terms: Buys one-time rights. Publication copyrighted.
Tips: "Read the magazine. Write well. Be neat. Don't copy. Be courageous."

NIR/NEW INFINITY REVIEW, Infinity Publications, Box 804, Ironton OH 45638. (614)533-9276. Editor: James R. Pack. Manuscript Editor: Ron Houchin. Theme: "Material by new and unknown writers—fiction; experimental, avant-garde, visual poetry; creative photography; surrealistic and visionary art." Readership: Famous people awarded lifetime merit subscriptions for contributions made in the arts, literature, science, etc., that advance new perspectives and challenge the mysterious and unknown. Quarterly. Estab. 1974. Circ. 500.
Needs: Contemporary, psychic/supernatural, science fiction, fantasy, mystery, humor. No religious, romance, gothic, feminist, gay/lesbian, erotica. Accepts 2-4 mss/issue. Length: 500-2,000 words.
How to Contact: Send complete ms with SASE. Reports in 10 weeks. Sample copy $1. Free guidelines, but provide SASE.
Payment: 2 free author's copies. 75¢ charge for extras.
Terms: Acquires first North American serial rights.
Tips: "We are looking for writers with 'pizazz and verve' (creative energy and personal integrity), so the clearer and more direct the ms the better. Good English usage is a must. Avoid excessive use of profanities. Be original. Strive for a new perspective."

NIT&WIT, A Cultural Arts Magazine, Box 14685, Chicago IL 60614. (312)248-1183. Senior Editor: Leonard J. Dominguez. Fiction Editor: Sheila Golub. Publisher: Kathleen J. Cummings. A literary arts magazine of dance, theater, music, film, fiction, humor, poetry, photography and art. Bimonthly. Estab. 1977. Circ. 5,000.
Needs: Fiction, humor, and translations. Accepts 7 mss/issue, 42 mss/year. Receives approximately 50 unsolicited fiction mss each month. Maximum length: 1,500 words. Critiques rejected mss "when there is time." Frequently recommends markets.
How to Contact: Send complete ms with SASE. Reports in 2 months on mss. Sample copy and guidelines $1.50.
Payment: Contributor's copy for now.
Terms: Acquires first rights. Publication copyrighted.
Tips: Mss are rejected because "most are either too long and/or lack interest. Please include name and address on each piece of work submitted."

NORTH AMERICAN MENTOR MAGAZINE, John Westburg, 1745 Madison St., Fennimore WI 53809. (608)822-6237. Editor/Publisher: John Westburg. "We publish short fiction, poetry, essays, including criticism, philosophy, social sciences, humanities in general. We are eclectic, cosmopolitan, and international. Mature readers, most with college education or equivalent. Many are professional writers, professional persons in other fields, including education, law, medicine, religion, engineering, government, military." Quarterly. Estab. 1974. Circ. 500 + .
Needs: Literary, contemporary, science fiction, fantasy. "Undesirable fiction would be that which is from the viewpoint of a religious true believer, a political ideologue or person with a loud

message or sales pitch. We frown upon raw sex, sensationalism, minority causes, abuse of any race or nation, use of obscenity and vulgarity.'' Accepts 1-3 mss/issue, 6-8 + mss/year. Receives 250 + unsolicited fiction mss/month. Length: 3,500 words (prefers 1,500).

How to Contact: Send complete ms with SASE. Reports in 6 months. Sample copy $3.

Payment: Free author's copies.

Terms: Acquires all rights. ''We reject mss offering only first North American rights or one-time rights. We must acquire all rights, but we do, upon request, grant permission without charge for publication elsewhere.'' Publication copyrighted.

Tips: ''We would consider any kind of fiction that is well-written, well-organized, with a beginning, middle, and ending, good characterization, good description, and reasonable action. We are still looking for a modern Charles Dickens who can combine all those qualities with a keen wit and insight to character. We have yet to find the ideal story, and we are still looking for it, one with clarity, good characterization, description, action, wit, unity, plot, and a good point to it. Modern writers would do well to study the 19th century English short story writers to emulate them in modern or contemporary scenarios.''

THE NORTH AMERICAN REVIEW, University of Northern Iowa, Cedar Falls IA 50614. Editor: Robley Wilson, Jr. Theme: quality fiction. Quarterly. Estab. 1815. Circ. 4,100.

Needs: ''We print quality fiction of any length and/or subject matter. Excellence is the only criterion.'' Buys 30-40 mss/year. No preferred length.

How to Contact: Send complete ms with SASE. Reports in 2-3 months. Sample copy $1.50.

Payment: $10/printed page. 2 free author's copies. $1.75 charge for extras.

Terms: Pays on publication for first North American serial rights.

Tips: ''We stress literary excellence and read 5,000 mss a year to find an average of 35 stories that we publish. The fiction department is closed from April 1 to October 1 annually, during which period we do not read mss. Please *read* the magazine first.''

NORTH COUNTRY ANVIL, North Country Anvil, Inc. Box 402, Winona MN 55987. Managing Editor: Evelyn Roehl. ''We publish a variety of material, including articles on lifestyles, social issues, the arts, the environment and fiction. Our audience is made up of people concerned with our themes. Though we include articles from all over the country our readers are mostly in the upper Midwest.'' Published five times/year. Estab. 1972. Circ. 2,000.

Needs: Literary, contemporary, fantasy, horror, humor. ''No stories taking place in Los Angeles or New York City.'' Accepts 1 ms/issue, 6 mss/year. Receives approximately 10 unsolicited fiction mss each month. Length: 1,000-3,000 words. Critiques rejected mss ''when there is time.'' Sometimes recommends markets.

How to Contact: Send complete ms with SASE. Reports in 2 months. Sample copy $2.

Payment: 3 free author's copies plus 1 year subscription. $2 charge for extras.

Terms: Acquires one-time rights. Publication copyrighted.

Tips: ''Give the reader some new insights and food for thought concerning society or human nature. Address yourself to an intelligent audience, but keep it simple.'' Mss are rejected because of ''too many stereotypical ('man in bar' or 'woman in heartbreak') pieces. The *ANVIL* likes stories with some social significance or message rather than pure entertainment.''

NORTHEAST JOURNAL, Box 235, Annex Station, Providence RI 02901. Editor: Miles D. Parker III. ''A journal concerned with publishing a diverse selection of contemporary literature. The primary focus is on poetry, prose and reviews. The average reader is probably a writer or teacher.'' Annual. Estab. 1969 (under name of *Harbinger*). Circ. 600.

Needs: ''We will consider any work of quality which can stand on its own outside a specialized format.'' Length: 4,000-10,000 words.

How to Contact: Send complete ms with SASE. Reports in 6 months. Sample copy with 10x12 SASE plus $1 postage.

Payment: 2 free author's copies.

Terms: Acquires all rights (negotiable).

Tips: ''Just send work—clean, proofed copy.'' Rejects mss because of frequent special issues.

NORTHWARD JOURNAL, Penumbra Press, Box 340, Moonbeam, Ontario, Canada P0L 1V0. Editor: John Flood. "A magazine of northern arts which publishes northern (thematically) artwork, poetry, fiction, drama." Quarterly. Estab. 1974. Circ. 2,000.
Needs: Literary, ethnic (native peoples). "Note that work must be of the North (Far North)." Buys 6-10 mss/year. Length: 1,500-2,500 words.
How to Contact: Send complete ms with biography and SASE (Canadian stamps) or IRC. Reports in 2 months on mss. Sample copies available.
Payment: $50 and 1 free author's copy. $5 less 40% discount for extras.
Terms: Pays on publication for first North American serial rights.
Tips: "Read and know the magazine. Read as much as you write."

NORTHWEST REVIEW, 369 PLC, University of Oregon, Eugene OR 97403. (503)686-3957. Editor: John Witte. Fiction Editor: Deb Casey. "A general literary review, featuring poems, stories, essays and reviews, circulated nationally and internationally. For a literate audience in avant-garde as well as traditional literary forms; interested in the important younger writers who have not yet achieved their readership." Published 3 times/year. Estab. 1957. Circ. 2,000.
Needs: Literary, contemporary, translations, experimental. Accepts 5-7 mss/issue, 20-30 mss/year. Receives approximately 80-100 unsolicited fiction mss each month. Length: "Ms of longer than 25-30 pages is at a disadvantage." Critiques rejected mss "when there is time."
How to Contact: Send complete ms with SASE. Reports in 2 months. Sample copy $2.50.
Payment: 3 free author's copies. $2.50 charge for extras.
Terms: Acquires first rights. Publication copyrighted.
Tips: "Persist. Copy should be clean, double-spaced, with generous margins. Careful proofing for spelling and grammar errors will reduce irksome slowing of editorial process." Mss are rejected because of "weak characters, lack of plot, poor execution."

NOSTOC MAGAZINE, Arts End Books, Box 162, Waban MA 02168. (617)965-2478. Editor: Marshall Brooks. "We publish the best of what we receive." Biannual. Estab. 1973. Circ. 500.
Needs: "We are open-minded." Receives approximately 15 unsolicited fiction mss each month. Prefers brief word length. Critiques rejected mss "when there is time." Frequently recommends other markets.
How to Contact: Query. SASE for ms. Reports in 1 week on queries, 1 month on mss. Sample copy $1.50.
Payment: Free author's copies.
Terms: "Copyright; rights revert to author."
Tips: "We tend to publish *short* short stories that are precise and lyrical. Many people who submit do not read the stories we do publish. Request a sample copy before submitting."

NOVALIS, Fantasy & Fable, Headplay Press, Box 13945, Arlington TX 76013. Editor: Walter Gammons. Fiction Editor: Marshall Bonfire. Magazine of illustrated fantasy and fable fiction for a well educated audience between 18-80. Bimonthly. Estab. 1982. Circ. 5,000.
Needs: Adventure, erotica, experimental, fantasy, horror, psychic/supernatural (all fantasy and fable). Must be well written, plotted, with resolution. Nothing political or religious; no pure sex. Receives 100 unsolicited fiction mss/month. Buys 12 mss/issue; 72 mss/year. Length: 3,000 words minimum, 8,000 words maximum, 5,000 words average. Occasionally critiques rejected mss.
How to Contact: Send complete ms with SASE and cover letter with credits, if any. Photocopied (clean) submissions OK. Reports in 6-8 weeks on mss. Sample copy for $3 with 9x12 SAE and 5 first class stamps. Fiction guidelines for $1 with 9x12 SAE and 2 first class stamps.
Payment: Pays 1-5¢/word; 2 free contributor's copies; $3 charge for extras.
Terms: Pays on publication for first North American serial rights. Publication copyrighted.
Tips: "Send in a good, fast moving fantasy yarn that's entertaining, well-written with good characterization. No vignettes, lectures, surprise endings, clichés."

OBSIDIAN: BLACK LITERATURE IN REVIEW, English Dept., Wayne State University, Detroit MI 48202. (313)577-3213. Editor: Alvin Aubert. Works in English by and about black writers worldwide. Readership: "General ethnic/small press who read *Obsidian* to keep in touch with contemporary black writing." Published 3 times/year. Estab. 1975. Circ. 750.
Needs: Ethnic (black). Accepts 7-9 mss/year. Length: 1,500-10,000 words. Sometimes recommends other markets.
How to Contact: Send complete ms with SASE. Reports in 2 months. Sample copy $3.
Terms: Acquires one-time rights.
Tips: Rejects mss because "fiction is harder to write than poetry (stories than poems, to be more precise); the latter mode seems to accommodate itself to the individual writer, being more interior. Plots are scarce. We don't get that many fiction manuscripts."

OCCASIONAL REVIEW, Realities Library, 1976 Waverly Ave., San Jose CA 95122. Editor: R. Soos. Reviews and interviews. Readership: "Directed toward persons looking to buy small press material." Published irregularly. Estab. 1979. Circ. 600.
Needs: Literary, science fiction. "I am specifically looking for fictional interviews with historic poets; however, I will consider other fiction." Accepts 1 ms/issue. Receives approximately 10-12 unsolicited fiction mss each month. Length: 5,000 words maximum.
How to Contact: Query with proposal. SASE for query, ms. Reports in 2 weeks. Sample copy $1.
Payment: 5 free author's copies. 50¢ charge for extras.
Terms: Acquires first rights. Publication copyrighted.
Tips: "Read. Read—Richard Grayson, Franz Kafka, Mark Twain, etc. Be prepared by knowing what is going on and then write. Fiction is not reality." Mss are rejected because of "too much preaching. Get the ego out of writing."

OCCIDENT, 103 Sproul Hall, University of California, Berkeley CA 94720. Fiction Editor: John Talbot Hawkes. Literary. Quarterly. Estab. 1881. Circ. 1,500.
Needs: Literary, men's, women's, feminist, gay/lesbian, translations. Length: 10,000 words maximum.
How to Contact: Send complete ms with SASE. Reports in 2 months on mss. Sample copy $2.
Payment: 5 free author's copies. $2 charge for extras.
Terms: Acquires first rights.

THE OHIO JOURNAL, Department of English, Ohio State University, 164 W. 17th St., Columbus OH 43210. Editor: William Allen. Theme: "general interest: fiction, poetry, interviews, book reviews, nonfiction, and photo essays. For an educated audience, knowledgeable in literature and the arts, but not of an academic nature." Biannual. Estab. 1973. Circ. 1,000.
Needs: "Any subject." Accepts 1-5 mss/issue. Receives approximately 25 unsolicited fiction mss each month. Length: 4,000 words maximum. Critiques rejected mss "when there is time." Sometimes recommends markets.
How to Contact: Send complete ms with SASE. Reports in 2 months. Sample copy $2.
Payment: Free author's copies. $2 charge for extras.
Terms: "Will reassign rights in exchange for mentioning material first published in *O.J.*"
Tips: Mss are rejected because of "lack of understanding of the short story form, shallow plots, undeveloped characters. Cure: Read as much well-written fiction as possible. Each contribution is automatically entered into competition for the annual President's Awards: $100 for fiction and $100 for poetry. No manuscripts accepted during the summer months."

OKIKE, An African Journal of New Writing, Box 53, Nsukka, Anambra, Nigeria. Editor-in-Chief: Chinua Achebe. Magazine. "Literature of contemporary commitment by Africans and others for an academic/literary/general audience." Published biannually. Estab. 1971. Circ. 6000.

Needs: Ethnic, experimental, literary, prose poem, serialized/excerpted novel, translations, women's. Receives 3-4 unsolicited fiction mss/month. Accepts 3-4 mss/issue, 9-12 mss/year. Length: "flexible."
How to Contact: Send complete ms with SASE. Simultaneous submissions OK. Reports in 3 months on mss. Sample copy $5.
Payment: 3 free contributor's copies.
Terms: Publication copyrighted.

THE OLD RED KIMONO, Box 1864, Rome GA 30161. (404)295-6312. Editor: Ken Anderson. Magazine of short fiction and poetry. Annually. Estab. 1972. Circ. 1,000.
Needs: Accepts varied amount of mss "depending on quality."
gay, historical, horror, humor/satire, literary, mainstream, men's, prose poem, psychic/supernatural science fiction, suspense/mystery, western, women's, young adult. Accepts varied amount of mss "depending on quality."
How to Contact: Send complete ms with SASE. Reports in 3 months on mss. Sample copy free.
Payment: 2 free contributor's copies.
Terms: Acquires first rights. Publication copyrighted.

ORIGINS, Box 168, Norval, Ontario, Canada L0P 1K0. Editor-in-Chief: Herb Barrett. Fiction Editor: R. Filter. Magazine for people interested in poetry, prose—teachers, students and writers. "We support quality poetry and prose. Our aim is to provide access to the public for writers who are both established and starting out." Published 3 times/year. Estab. 1967. Circ. 500.
Needs: Adventure, contemporary, ethnic, experimental, fantasy, humor/satire, literary, prose poem, science fiction, serialized/excerpted novel, suspense/mystery, translations. Receives 30-50 unsolicited fiction mss/month. Buys 5-7 mss/issue, 20-30 mss/year. Length: 2,500 words minimum; 10,000 words maximum; 5,000 words average. Occasionally critiques rejected mss.
How to Contact: Send complete ms with SASE. Photocopied and previously published submissions OK.
Payment: $20 maximum; subscription to magazine; 3 free contributor's copies.
Terms: Pays on publication for first rights. Publication copyrighted.

OSIRIS, Box 297, Deerfield MA 01324. Editor: Andrea Moorhead. Fiction Editor: Robert Moorhead. "An apolitical, international journal which prints original texts in English, French, Spanish, and Italian. Material tends to be non-narrative. For an urban intellectual audience. Cuts across cultural boundaries." Semiannual. Estab. 1972. Circ. 1,000.
Needs: Literary, contemporary, experimental fiction in English, Spanish or French. No science fiction material. Receives approximately 3 unsolicited fiction mss each month. Length: 1,100-3,000 words. Critiques rejected mss "when there is time."
How to Contact: Query with SASE. Reports in 1 week. Sample copy $1.
Payment: 3 free author's copies. $2 charge for extras.
Terms: "Inquire." Publication copyrighted.
Tips: "Send piece after piece. Do not be offended by rejection slips."

THE OTHER SIDE OF PARADISE, 323 Higdon Ave. # 3, Mountain View CA 94041. (415)961-9109. Editor-in-Chief: Amy Falkowitz. Magazine for "fans of *Star Trek*, *Star Wars*, also of other fantasy and science fiction—all ages, though reaches college age and older mostly. Emphasis on strong plot and characterization. Science fiction and fantasy based on or derived from media shows, especially *Star Trek* and *Star Wars*, also original fantasy, science fiction; also articles and art on the above media shows." Published irregularly, usually between 1 year and 18 months. Estab. 1975. Circ. 400.
Needs: Adventure, comics, fantasy, feminist, horror, humor/satire, literary, prose poem, science fiction, young adult. "No explicit graphic sex or violence. Preference for straight plot—short story to novella length. No novel excerpts, please." Receives 1-2 unsolicited fiction mss/month. Accepts 1-10 mss/issue. Occasionally critiques rejected mss. Sometimes recommends markets.

How to Contact: Query or send complete ms. SASE for query, ms. Photocopied and previously published submissions OK "only if properly notified." Reports in 6 weeks on queries; 3 months on mss. Sample copy $8.25; guidelines for # 10 SAE and 1 first class stamp. "This is merely a note written in response to any questions from the writer. I do not have a standard set of guidelines."

Payment: 1 free contributor's copy; cover cost (plus postage) charge for extras.

Terms: Pays on publication for one-time rights. Publication "only under general copyright-individual copyrights must be handled by contributors."

Tips: "If you write in an established media universe, I need strong, *consistent* characterization. I am interested in *new* plots and *new* characters; original 'alien' peoples are definite plus. Clear photocopies, double spaced mss preferred. Also permission to write on the ms copy. Please do not send previously published ms without appropriate notification. I cannot emphasize *enough* that I am looking both for strong plot and characterization."

OUTERBRIDGE, The College of Staten Island (CUNY), (A323), 715 Ocean Terr., Staten Island NY 10301. (212)390-7654. Editor: Charlotte Alexander. "We are a national literary magazine publishing mostly fiction and poetry. To date, we have had three special focus issues (the 'urban' and the 'rural' experience; 'Southern' in 1981). For anyone with enough interest in literature to look for writing of quality and writers on the contemporary scene who deserve attention. There probably is a growing circuit of writers, some academics, reading us by recommendations." Biannual. Estab. 1975. Circ. 500-700.

Needs: Literary. "No *Reader's Digest* style; that is, very popularly oriented." Accepts 4-5 mss/issue, 8-10 mss/year. Length: 10-25 pages.

How to Contact: Query. Send complete ms. SASE for query, ms. Reports in 2 weeks on queries, 2 months on mss. Sample copy $2 for single and $4 for double issues.

Payment: 2 free author's copies. Charges ½ price of current issues for extras to its authors.

Terms: Acquires one-time rights. Requests credits for further publication of material used by *OB*.

Tips: "Read our publication first. Don't send out blindly; get some idea of what the magazine might want. A *short* personal note with biography is appreciated. Competition is keen."

OUTERMOST, Science Fiction and Fantasy Poetry, Prose and Other Things, 4038 Sunset Blvd., Youngstown OH 44514. Editor: Dr. Jean McClure Kelty. Fiction Editor: Timothy Stanley. Magazine. "We wish to give new writers and anyone else working in fantasy and science fiction poetry and prose a medium for experimentation and development." Readers are college age and adult science fiction and fantasy enthusiasts. Annually. Estab. 1983.

Needs: Comics, experimental, fantasy, horror, humor/satire, prose poem, psychic/supernatural, science fiction. Occasionally critiques rejected mss.

How to Contact: Send complete ms with SASE. Reports in 2 weeks on mss. Sample copy for 8x10 SAE and 2 first class stamps.

Payment: 2 free contributor's copies.

Terms: Acquires first rights. Publication copyrighted.

Tips: "Get together your best stuff, and for goodness sake send it to us!"

OVERTONE SERIES, Quarterly, Overtone Press, 4421 Chestnut St., # 3, Philadelphia PA. (215)386-4279. Editor: Beth Brown. Fiction/Poetry Editor: Otis Brown. Magazine. Quarterly.

Needs: Contemporary, erotica, ethnic, experimental, feminist/lesbian, gay, historical, literary, mainstream, prose poem, serialized/excerpted novel, translations, women's. Receives 5 unsolicited fiction mss/month. Accepts 5 mss/issue; 20 mss/year. Charges $5 for a reading fee. Length: 5,000 word minimum; 20,000 words maximum; 15,000 words average. Occasionally critiques rejected mss.

How to Contact: Query or send complete ms with SASE. Simultaneous, photocopied and previously published work OK. Reports in 4 weeks on queries; 6 weeks on mss. Sample copy for $2 with 8½x11 SAE and 75¢ postage. Fiction guidelines free for business SAE and 20¢ postage.

Payment: 5 free contributor's copies; $1.50 charge for extras.
Terms: Rights revert to author. Publication copyrighted.

OWLFLIGHT, Alternative Magazine of Science Fiction & Fantasy, Unique Graphics, 1025 55th St., Oakland CA 94608. (415)655-3024. Editor-in-Chief: (Ms) Millea Kenin. Magazine of "science fiction and fantasy of professional quality which has been rejected by the major commercial markets, for people who already read science fiction and fantasy, are familiar with it, discriminating about it, and looking for more of it." Published twice a year, not necessarily at even intervals. Estab. Jan. 1981. Circ. 1,500.
Needs: Adventure, comics, erotica, ethnic, experimental, fantasy, feminist/lesbian, gay, historical fantasy, horror, humor/satire, prose poem, psychic/supernatural, science fiction, suspense/mystery, translations (query first), western. "I use these types of material only if they are *also* science fiction or fantasy. No fiction that is sexist or pro-war or racist." Receives 50-100 unsolicited fiction mss/month. Buys 10-15 mss/issue, 30 mss/year. Length: no preferred minimum; 10,000 words maximum. (Query first with longer work.) Usually critiques rejected mss.
How to Contact: "Query first as to whether we're open; send complete ms if informed that we are." SASE for query, ms. Query first on simultaneous submissions; photocopied and previously published submissions OK. Reports in 1 week on queries, 3 weeks on mss. Sample copy $3. Guidelines free with magazine order; otherwise send business size SAE and 1 first class stamp.
Payment: $1 total minimum; 1¢/word—no maximum; 1-3 free contributor's copies; half retail price for extras. Offers $10 or purchase price (whichever is less) kill fee for assigned ms not published.
Terms: Pays on publication or before (when firm date is set) for first North American serial rights or one-time rights as applicable. Publication copyrighted; copyright in author's name if requested.
Tips: "Send for guidelines—they are very detailed. Then send a story. Never submit without querying first; we're often overstocked. All first submissions rejected are critiqued in enough detail so you'll know what to send next time. I buy a high proportion of repeat submissions, and frequently recommend other markets. I appreciate cover letters telling me a little about yourself, but not lengthy credit sheets."

PACIFIC QUARTERLY MOANA, A Multi-Cultural and Multi-lingual Review, Outrigger Publishers, Box 13-049, Hamilton, New Zealand. Editor-in-Chief: Norman Simms. Magazine. "We alternate general and special issues; mostly concerned with interaction of multi-cultural and multi-lingual societies for intelligent, imaginative readers with cosmopolitan tastes." Quarterly. Estab. 1972. Circ. 600-900.
Needs: Contemporary, ethnic, humor/satire, literary, translations. "Translations acceptable; also short pieces in other languages than English, if it fits with topic of special issues. No frothy, self-indulgent nonsense." Receives 2-3 unsolicited fiction mss/month. Accepts 3-6 mss/issue; 12-25 mss/year. Charges $20 reading fee (i.e., subscription for year). Length: 2,000 words maximum; 1,000 words average. Occasionally critiques rejected mss. Charges $20 for critique (i.e., subscription). Sometimes recommends markets.
How to Contact: Query with SASE. Reports in 2 weeks on queries. Sample copy $8.
Payment: 1-3 free contributor's copies.
Terms: Acquires one-time rights. Publication copyrighted.

PACIFIC REVIEW, (formerly *Pacific Poetry and Fiction Review*), Dept. of English and Comparative Lit., San Diego State University, San Diego CA 92182. Editors: Marc DeBaca, Doug Zoffel. "There is no designated theme. We publish high-quality fiction and poetry: academic work meant for, but not restricted to, an academic audience." Annual. Estab. 1974. Circ. 500.
Needs: "We do not restrict or limit our fiction in any way other than quality. We are interested in all fiction, from the very traditional to the highly experimental. Acceptance is determined by the quality of submissions." No preferred length.
How to Contact: Send original ms with SASE. Reports in 2-4 months on mss. Sample copy $4.
Payment: 1 author's copy.

Terms: "Rights revert to author."
Tips: "Send us mss that will trigger paroxysms of glee, fascination, terror, revulsion, transcendence: the point being, we want fiction which produces striking effects. Rattle our sensibilities. Give us language that glows and bleeds and explodes."

PACIFIC RIM REVIEW, Sky Hi Productions, 7203 Del Norte, Goleta CA 93117. (805)968-5671. Editor-in-Chief: Fred Soltysik. Magazine for "those who've ever wondered about 'history' prior to language. To anyone who has felt an inkling of primitiveness and been awed by its presence in contemporary time." Plans to publish quarterly. Estab. 1982.
Needs: Adventure, condensed novel, contemporary, experimental, literary, Vietnam pieces, men's, women's, fishing stories. "Nothing hip, cute, hyped, whatever." Receives 10 unsolicited fiction mss/month. Accepts 4-6 mss/issue, 8-12 mss/year. Length: 500 words minimum; 5,000 words maximum; 3,000 words average. Occasionally critiques rejected mss.
How to Contact: Send complete ms with SASE. Simultaneous, photocopied and previously published submissions OK. Reports in 2 weeks. Sample copy $4 with 9x12 SAE and 3 first class stamps. Free fiction guidelines with SAE and 1 first class stamp.
Payment: 2 free contributor's copies. $2 charge for extras.
Terms: Pays on publication for all rights. Publication copyrighted.
Tips: "Tell a story with a real voice. Editor likes oceanic material." Mss rejected because "too many characters are caught in the grip of stasis. Characters seemed paralyzed."

THE PALE FIRE REVIEW, Arrant Press (formerly SC Press), 162 Academy Ave., Providence RI 02908. Editors: Steven Strang and Catherine Reed. Magazine of fiction, poetry, satire, parts-of-novels, novellas, plays, non-fiction. Any subject matter, any form, drawings and cartoons for anyone interested in good writing. Semiannually. Estab. 1980. Circ. 500.
Needs: Contemporary, ethnic, experimental, fantasy, feminist/lesbian, humor/satire, literary, mainstream, prose poem, psychic/supernatural, science fiction, serialized/excerpted novel, suspense/mystery, women's. "As far as genre fiction is concerned, we're only interested in mss which use the conventions for literary purposes." Receives 50 unsolicited fiction mss/month. Accepts 7-10 mss/issue; 20 mss/year. Length: 3,000-6,000 words average. Occasionally critiques rejected mss.
How to Contact: Send complete ms with SASE. Simultaneous and photocopied submissions OK. Reports in 2-3 weeks on mss. Sample copy for $4.
Payment: 1 free contributor's copy; $4 charge for extras.
Terms: Acquires first North American serial rights. Publication copyrighted.
Tips: "Have a concern for quality (style and form as well as content) and send us a ms. Avoid careless/indiscriminate obscenity that's meant to be merely attention-getting rather than integral to the story. Avoid polemics."

PANDORA, Sproing, 3721 Barcelona St., Tampa FL 33609. (813)837-5500. Fiction Editors: Lois Wickstrom and Jean Lorrah. Magazine for feminists and science fiction and fantasy readers. Published 3 times/year. Estab. 1978. Circ. 1,000.
Needs: Fantasy, science fiction, sword and sorcery. "Nothing X-rated. Unless the author created the universe, she/he should not send us stories in that universe." Receives 80 unsolicited fiction mss/month. Buys 5-6 mss/issue, 15-18 mss/year. Length: 200 words minimum; 5,000 words maximum (except controversial stories may go double); 3,000 words average. Occasionally critiques rejected mss.
How to Contact: Send complete ms with SASE. Photocopied and previously published submissions, if substantially revised, OK. Reports in 1 week on mss. Sample copy $2.50. Free fiction guidelines with SASE.
Payment: 1¢/word and 1 contributor's copy.
Terms: Pays on publication (within 5 months) for first North American serial rights or one-time rights on rewritten previously published mss. Publication copyrighted.
Tips: "Feel free to argue with me if you believe I have misunderstood the intent of your story. I

try not to use form letters and I'm willing to help a writer do rewriting if an idea intrigues me. I'm interested in characters and ideas. I like clear images and I particularly appreciate problem-solving stories.''

PANDORA, A Literary Magazine, Pandora, Inc., Box 271, Caldwell NJ 07006. (201)227-2324. Editor: Pat Renga-Connors. Magazine designed to provide a showcase for 25-32 women artists per issue. Quarterly. Estab. 1982. Circ. 500.

Needs: Condensed novel, contemporary, feminist/lesbian, humor/satire, literary, women's. Highly professional writing required. Nothing amateur or grammatically incorrect, etc. Receives 40-60 unsolicited fiction mss/month. Accepts 40-60 mss/year. Length: 500 words minimum; 3,000 words maximum; 1,500 words average. Occasionally critiques rejected mss. Personally replies to all submissions.

How to Contact: Send complete ms with SASE. Simultaneous, photocopied and previously published submissions OK. Reports in 2 weeks on mss. Sample copy $3 for 5 1/2x8 1/2 SAE and 75¢ postage.

Payment: Pays in copies.

Terms: Pays on publication for one-time rights. Publication copyrighted.

Tips: ''Adhere to poem, proper grammar, spelling—good story line is key! Material that other women can relate to. Experimental material within reason.''

PARABOLA, The Society for the Study of Myth and Tradition, 150 5th Ave., New York NY 10011. (212)924-0004. Editor: Lorraine Kisly. Fiction Editor: Alice Van Buren. ''Mythology, folklore, comparative religion—stories, parables, fairytales retold, original fiction, poetry, translations. We have an open cross-cultured, intelligent but not scholarly approach. Audience is educated, professional, informed book readers interested in stories, myths, folklore, psychology, comparative religion and the arts.'' Quarterly. Estab. 1976. Circ. 15,000.

Needs: Literary, contemporary, men's, women's, translations. No humor, romance, erotica, western, inspirational, gothic, horror. Buys 5 mss/issue. Receives approximately 50 unsolicited fiction mss each month. Length: 1,000-5,000 words.

How to Contact: Send complete ms with SASE. Reports in 2 months. Sample copy $6.50. Free guidelines.

Payment: $25-$100.

Terms: Pays on publication for first rights, second serial rights, one-time rights. Publication copyrighted.

Tips: ''Read previous issues to understand our flavor and direction. Most rejected mss are not related to subject matter set forth in guidelines.''

PARADOX, The Magazine of Science Fiction and Fantasy Adventures, (Monthly supplement to *Rising Star*, the science fiction/fantasy/horror writer's newsletter), 143 Whitemarsh Way, Delran NJ 08075. Editor: John Betancourt. Magazine. ''We publish only science fiction, fantasy and horror adventure stories; we prefer action-based fiction in traditional forms. Nothing experimental.'' Monthly. Estab. 1981. Circ. 1,000 + .

Needs: Adventure, fantasy, horror, science fiction. No *Star Trek*, *Star Wars*, or Tolkein clones or other copyrighted worlds/characters. Receives 40-50 unsolicited fiction mss/month. Buys 2-3mss/issue; 30 mss/year. Length: 150 words minimum; 5,000 words maximum; 5,000 words average. Occasionally critiques rejected mss.

How to Contact: Send complete ms with SASE. Photocopied submissions OK. Reports in 2-3 weeks on mss. Sample copy for $1.50.

Payment: Pays $1-25; 1 free contributor's copy; $1.50 charge for extras.

Terms: Pays on acceptance for first rights.

Tips: ''Read a copy first. Avoid purple prose/experimental stories. No sex, bad language, graphic violence.''

THE PARIS REVIEW, 45-39 171st Place, Flushing NY 11358. (212)539-7085. Editor: George A. Plimpton. Fiction Editor: David Evanier. ''Fiction and poetry of superlative quality, whatever the genre, style or mode. Our contributors include the most prominent, as well as little-known and previously unpublished writers. Recent issues have included the work of Thomas Disch, Ray Russell, Joseph Brodsky, Sena Jeter Naslund, Bart Midwood, Helen Chasin, Peter Handke, C.W. Gusewelle, Thom Gunn, Jerome Charyn, Phyllis Janowitz and Andre Dubus. 'The Art of Fiction' interview series includes the most important contemporary writers discussing their own work and the craft of writing in general.''

Needs: Serious, intense, committed work of boldness and originality, combining excellence of form and content. Buys 2-3 mss/issue. Receives several hundred unsolicited fiction mss each month. No preferred length. Critiques rejected mss "when there is time."

How to Contact: Send complete ms with SASE. Reports in 2 months on ms. Sample copy $5.75.

Payment: $75-$200. 2 free author's copies. Regular charge for extras.

Terms: Pays on publication for first North American serial rights. Publication copyrighted.

Tips: "Electricity, intensity, the unmistakable roundedness of a fully-realized work of art are what we are seeking. *The Paris Review* has the widest circulation of all the small presses. We are devoted to helping talented, original writers find larger audiences. The Aga Khan Fiction Prize is awarded annually to the best piece of previously unpublished fiction by a relatively unknown writer.''

PARSEC FANZINE OF SF/FANTASY, SLB Communications, 48466 Jasper Dr., Oakridge OR 97463. (503)782-3029. Editor: S.L. Blumenthal. Magazine. "We publish unproduced screenplays, original or adapted, from sf/fantasy short stories." Annually. Estab. 1978.

Needs: Fantasy, science fiction only. Receives 5-6 unsolicited fiction mss/month. Accepts 4 mss/issue; 4 mss/year. Length: 20 pages minimum; 30 pages maximum.

How to Contact: Writer must send for free submission requirements. SASE for query and ms. Photocopied submissions OK. Reports in 4 weeks on mss.

Payment: 2 free contributor's copies; charges one-half the cover price for extras. A standard rate payment established early 1983.

Terms: Acquires all rights. Rights revert to author after publication. Publication copyrighted.

Tips: "Keep writing! Keep sending it off! Make sure you send SF or fantasy: no westerns, etc.''

PARTISAN REVIEW, Partisan Review, Inc., 121 Bay State Rd., Boston MA 02215. (617)353-4260. Editor: William Phillips. Executive Editor: Edith Kurzweil. Magazine. Theme is of world literature and contemporary culture: fiction, essays and poetry with emphasis on the arts and political and social commentary, for the general intellectual public; scholars. Quarterly. Estab. 1934. Circ. 8,000.

Needs: Contemporary, experimental, literary, prose poem, translations. Receives 30 unsolicited fiction mss/month. Buys 2 mss/issue; 8 mss/year. Length: 800 words miminum; 4,000 words maximum. Occasionally critiques rejected mss.

How to Contact: Send complete ms with SASE. Photocopied submissions OK. Reports in 4 months on mss. Sample copy for $3.50.

Payment: Pays $25-$200; 1 free contributor's copy.

Terms: Pays on publication for first rights. Publication copyrighted.

PASSAGES NORTH, Wm. Bonifas Fine Arts Center, Escanaba MI 49829. (906)786-3833. Editor: Elinor Benedict. "The purpose of *Passages North* is two-fold: To stimulate and recognize writing of high quality in the Northern Michigan region and to bring to the same region writing of high quality from other parts of the nation and beyond." Readership: general and literary. Semiannual. Estab. October 1979. Circ. 500.

Needs: Short fiction, sketches. "High quality is our aim. Subjects and genre are open. No excerpts of novels, unless they stand alone in a coherent way. No 'pop' or formula stories." Accepts 6-8 mss/year. Length: 300-2,000 words. Critiques rejected mss "when there is time." Occasionally recommends markets.

How to Contact: Send complete ms with SASE. Reports in 1 week to several months on mss.

Sample copy $1.50. Guidelines for legal-sized SASE.
Payment: 3 free author's copies. $1 charge for extras.
Terms: Copyrighted; rights revert to author on publication.
Tips: "Be aware of what is happening in contemporary poetry and fiction. Strive for writing that makes readers see, feel, imagine, and experience. The first page must inspire interest and confidence in what the writer is saying."

THE PAWN REVIEW, The Pawn Review, Inc., 4122 Cove Lane # E, Glenview IL 60025. Editors: Michael Anderson and Thomas Zigal. "No theme in particular; we publish quality short stories, poetry, photos and articles and reviews by authors from every region, but we have a preference for young Texas writers." Readership: "libraries (which maintain literary magazine collections); individuals and writers (who are interested in contemporary Southwest literature); college English teachers (who read our reviews and articles)." Biannual. Estab. 1976. Circ. 700.
Needs: Literary, contemporary, science fiction, erotica, humor, translations. No religious or juvenile. Accepts 10-12 mss/year. Receives approximately 25-30 unsolicited fiction mss each month. Length: 1,000-25,000 words. Critiques rejected mss "when there is time."
How to Contact: Query or query with clips of published work. SASE for query, ms. Reports in 2 weeks on queries, 2 months on mss. Sample copy $3.
Payment: 1 free author's copy. 25% discount for extras.
Terms: Acquires first rights. Copyright reverts to author upon publication. Publication copyrighted.
Tips: "We require traditional stories—in the sense that plot and characters interweave to create a unified narrative; otherwise, subject matter and form run from traditional to avant-garde. Read a copy of the magazine. Avoid overly dramatic or overworked plots and obtuse, trite or arcane images. Strive for clean narrative line and revealing (but not obvious or overstated) characterization. Read the contemporary *and* early masters of short fiction."

PDSA CLUB NEWS, PDSA (People's Dispensary for Sick Animals), South Street, Dorking, Surrey, England RH4 2LP. Tel. 888219. Editor: R.I. Cookson. "Magazine for PDSA supporters to promote responsible pet ownership." Bimonthly. Estab. 1980. Circ. 4,500.
Needs: Adventure, comics, fantasy, historical, humor/satire, juvenile, romance, serialized/excerpted novel, suspense/mystery, women's, young adult. "All submissions must be about animals. Puzzles, anecdotes, drawings also accepted." Receives approximately 10 unsolicited fiction mss/month. Accepts 3-4 mss/issue; 24 mss/year. Length: 300 words minimum; 1,000 words maximum. Occasionally critiques rejected mss.
How to Contact: Send complete ms with SASE. Simultaneous, photocopied and previously published submissions OK. Reports in 2 weeks on mss. Sample copy free.
Terms: Publication copyrighted.

PENNSYLVANIA REVIEW, 532 North 25th St., Pennside, PA 19606. (215)779-5269. Editor: David M. Hinrichs. "*Pennsylvania Review* is devoted to short fiction, poetry, criticism, articles and reviews. Open to work from new as well as established writers. Our principle interest is in serious literary achievement by writers with integrity to their craft. We have no university affiliation and we are not committed to any narrow academic aim, nor to any particular political perspective. Editorial policy is based solely on literary merit. We have as our goal the publication of superlative writing for a discriminating and appreciative audience." Quarterly. Estab. 1983.
Needs: Contemporary, experimental, humor/satire, literary, mainstream, prose poem. "We seek finely-honed, honest fiction aimed at an intelligent audience. The best fiction achieves a balance between form and content. We object to the sentimental, the didactic, the artificially structured, the fashionable. In general, we object to all ill-conceived and dishonest writing." Buys 4-6 mss/issue; 16-24 mss/year. Length: 1,000 words minimum; 4,000 words maximum; 2,500 words average. Occasionally critiques rejected mss.
How to Contact: Send complete ms with SASE. Simultaneous and photocopied submissions OK. Reports in 4-6 weeks on mss. Sample copy for $1.75.

Payment: Pays $2-30. $50 cash prizes awarded annually for best short story, poem and article published.
Terms: Pays on acceptance for one-time rights.
Tips: "Our sole bias is toward excellent writing, no other predisposition. We want fiction that comes from a writer's deep and broad interaction with and commitment to his or her work. We want honest, original well-conceived work. No genre fiction, please. No fiction aimed at a narrow academic quarterly market."

PERSONS, The Magazine for Hattiesburg and South Mississippi, Persons, 805 Short Katie, Hattiesburg MS 39401. (601)545-2949. Editor: Gabi Clayton. City magazine, upbeat with emphasis on people more than events—lots of local area history/nostalgia/legends—for a 25-40 year old, college-educated audience. Monthly. Estab. 1982. Circ. 7,000.
Needs: Adventure, contemporary, fantasy, feminist, humor/satire, literary, mainstream, science fiction, young adult. No mushy romance. Accepts 1 ms/issue; 12 mss/year. Length: 800 words minimum; 10,000 words maximum; 5,000 words average. Occasionally critiques rejected mss.
How to Contact: Send complete ms with SASE. Simultaneous, photocopied and previously published submissions OK. Reports in 2 months on mss. Sample copy free with 9x12 SAE and 4 first class stamps. Fiction guidelines free with SAE and 1 first class stamp.
Payment: 10 free contributor's copies; 25¢ charge for extras. "We hope to be able to start paying soon."
Tips: Acquires first rights or second serial rights. Publication copyrighted.
Tips: "Good humor gets to us quicker than anything—and/or anything that gets a good emotional response without being mushy. Neatness counts—verbosity doesn't."

THE PET-LOVER'S NEWSLETTER, Lee Miller Publications, 190 E. 21 St., Suite 6D, Brooklyn NY 11226. (212)IN2-6328. Fiction Editor: Lee Miller. Newsletter about pets (domestic/household) for adults and young people (general family). Bimonthly. Estab. 1983.
Needs: Adventure, experimental, fantasy, historical, humor/satire, juvenile, psychic/supernatural, science fiction, suspense/mystery. "All subjects must be pet related." No smut/porno. Charges reading fee of $10. Length: 800 words minimum; 1,600 words maximum. Occasionally critiques rejected mss.
How to Contact: Send complete ms with SASE. Simultaneous and previously published submissions OK. Reports in 3-4 weeks on mss. Sample copy $5 for 9x12 SAE and 2 first class stamps.
Payment: 1 contributor's copy; $3.50 charge for extras.

PHANTASM, Heidelberg Graphics, Box 3606W, Chico CA 95927. Editor: Larry S. Jackson. "A multi-cultural eclectic magazine publishing current literary events, fiction, poetry, translations, literary features, guest columns, interviews, contemporary art, national literary announcements, photos, book reviews and editorials. The publication is directed toward a literate audience which is primarily comprised of educators, poets, writers, libraries, and small press editors. Subscribers read *Phantasm* for its exclusive articles, creative writing and literary news." Estab. 1976. Circ. 1,100.
Needs: Literary, contemporary, men's, women's, feminist, gay/lesbian, erotica, western, mystery, adventure, humor, ethnic (all), translations. Buys 2 mss/issue. Length: 800-5,000 words.
How to Contact: Send complete ms with SASE. Reports in 4 months. Sample copy $3.
Payment: $2 plus 1 free author's copy. Cover price charge for extras.
Terms: Pays on publication for first rights.
Tips: "We do not publish reprints nor do we consider mss simultaneously submitted to other publishers."

PHOEBE, THE GEORGE MASON REVIEW, 4400 University Dr., Fairfax VA 22030. Editor: J.W. Harchick. "*Phoebe* publishes stories that contain well delineated characters, balanced plots, and interesting subject matters." Quarterly. Estab. 1970. Circ. 5,000.

Needs: Literary, contemporary, historical, humor. "No action/adventure, murder/mystery/detective/spy stories." Receives approximately 35-40 unsolicited fiction mss each month. Length: 5,000 words maximum. Critiques rejected mss "when there is time." Sometimes recommends other markets.
How to Contact: Send complete ms with SASE. Reports in 6 weeks. Sample copy $3.
Payment: 2 free author's copies. $3 charge for extras.
Terms: Acquires one-time rights. Publication copyrighted.
Tips: Avoid using clichés; search for fresh and exciting ways to present your material. "Manuscripts are rejected because they are poorly written, story lines lack substance, and the subject matter is boring. They usually contain clichés and dialogue is unrealistic."

THE PHOENIX, Morning Star Press, RFD Haydenville MA 01039. Editor: James Cooney. Theme: "A literary magazine actively engaged in spreading mutiny against the ancient crime of war." Subscriptions come from public libraries, universities, colleges, and individuals. Quarterly. Estab. 1938. Letterpress printing; sewn binding; issues of 352 to 384 pages. Sample issue, $3. Special rates for those who cannot afford regular rates. Free subscriptions to prison libraries, state hospitals and mental institutions.
Needs: Stories, diaries, serialized novels. No length limitations. Complete contents of each issue covered by the *Arts & Humanities Citation Index.*
How to Contact: Send SASE with ms. Reports within 1 to 4 weeks.
Terms: Acquires copyright for protection of published materials but arranges permission for author to reprint in collections, anthologies, etc. Publication copyrighted.
Tips: "Write truthfully."

PIEDMONT LITERARY REVIEW, Piedmont Literary Society, Box 3656, Danville VA 24543. (804)793-0956. Editor: David Craig. "The theme of our publication is human expression through the written word. We publish short stories, essays, and articles. Our publication is directed toward all lovers of literature regardless of their stature in life." Quarterly. Estab. 1976. Circ. 400.
Needs: Literary, contemporary, science fiction, fantasy, humor. Accepts 8-12 mss/year. Receives approximately 50-100 unsolicited fiction mss each month. Length: 2,000 words maximum. Will exceed maximum if story is of highest quality. I have 4,000 word short story for Winter issue." Critiques rejected mss "when there is time." Recommends markets.
How to Contact: Send complete ms with SASE. Reports in 3 months on mss. Sample copy $2. Guidelines for legal-sized SASE.
Payment: 1 free author's copy. $2.50 charge for extras.
Terms: Acquires one-time rights.
Tips: "I have none that would guarantee publication. 'Write the truest sentence you know' as Hemingway said. Be honest. Use the tools of fiction. An experience is not a story. To me, characters are what makes a story. If I believe the characters, the plot will naturally follow."

PIERIAN SPRING, Pierian Press, Box 5, Brandon University, Brandon, Manitoba, Canada R7A 6A9. Editor: Dr. Robert W. Brockway. Fiction Editor: Linda West. "We publish short fiction and poetry, mostly mainstream rather than avant-garde, and try to assist new writers as well as established. Directed toward those who like comprehensible verse and stories with plot and characterization. Most of our readers are writers themselves, but we are attracting others." Quarterly. Estab. 1968. Circ. 350.
Needs: Literary. "The theme of the story could be almost anything, as long as the story has literary quality. We don't like plotless or aimless fiction, stream-of-consciousness, or incomprehensible material. No translations, juveniles." Length: 1,500-3,500 words. Critiques rejected mss "when there is time."
How to Contact: Send complete ms with SASE. Reports in 3 months on mss. Sample copy $1. Free guidelines with SASE.
Payment: 3 free author's copies. $1 charge for extras.

Terms: Acquires one-time rights.
Tips: "Get a sample copy and try us. We have a $25 first prize every issue for best short story and poem, and a book prize for second best."

PIG IRON, Pig Iron Press, Box 237, Youngstown OH 44501. (216)744-2258. Editor: Jim Villani. Fiction Editor: Rose Sayre. "Contemporary literature by new writers, especially concerned with surreal, experimental, fantasy, psychological, science fiction, and political material. For college-educated young adults—upwardly mobile." Semiannual. Estab. 1975. Circ. 1,000.
Needs: Literary, fantasy. No mainstream. Buys 1-15 mss/issue; 2-30 mss/year. Receives approximately 50 unsolicited fiction mss each month. Length: 15,000 maximum.
How to Contact: Send complete ms with SASE. Reports in 3 months. Sample copy $2.50.
Payment: $2/printed page. 2 free author's copies. $2 charge for extras.
Terms: Pays on publication for first North American serial rights.
Tips: "Looking for experimental works that do not ignore characterization and plot-action." Mss are rejected because of "lack of new ideas. Writers need to work out interesting plot-action and setting/set."

THE PIKESTAFF FORUM, Box 127, Normal IL 61761. (309)452-4831. Editors: Robert D. Sutherland and James Scrimgeour. "*The Pikestaff Forum* is a general literary magazine publishing poetry, prose fiction, drama. Readership: "General literary with a wide circulation in the small press world. Readers are educated (but not academic) and have a taste for excellent serious fiction." Published irregularly—"whenever we have sufficient quality material to warrant an issue." Estab. 1977. Circ. 1,000.
Needs: Literary, contemporary with a continuing need for good short stories or novel excerpts. We welcome traditional and experimental works from established and non-established writers. We look for writing that is clear, concise, and to the point; contains vivid imagery and sufficient concrete detail; is grounded in lived human experience; contains memorable characters and situations; and lifts us right out of our chairs. No confessional self-pity or puffery; self-indulgent first or second drafts; sterile intellectual word games or five-finger exercises or slick formula writing, genre-pieces that do not go beyond their form (westerns, mysteries, gothic, horror, science fiction, swords-and-sorcery fantasy), commercially-oriented mass-market stuff, violence for its own sake, or pornography (sexploitation)." Accepts 1-4 mss/issue. Receives approximately 15-20 unsolicited fiction mss each month. Length: From 1 paragraph to 4,000 or 5,000 words. Critiques rejected mss "when there is time."
How to Contact: Query. Send complete ms. SASE for query, ms. Reports in 3 weeks on queries, 3 months on mss. Sample copy $2.
Payment: 3 free author's copies. Cover price less 50% discount for extras.
Terms: Acquires first rights. Copyright remains with author. Publication copyrighted.
Tips: "Read other authors with an appreciative and critical eye; don't send out work prematurely; develop keen powers of observation and a good visual memory; get to know your characters thoroughly; don't let others (editors, friends, etc.) define or 'determine' your sense of self-worth; stick to your guns. Don't be easily discouraged; if you have an eggshell ego you're in for trouble; be willing to learn; outgrow self-indulgence. Develop discipline. Show, don't tell; and leave some work for the reader to do." Mss are rejected because "they are boring—dealing with characters and situations we cannot, or are not made to, care about. Frequently of too private a significance to the author. Often characterization is thin, storyline implausible (even within the fictional frame)."

THE PILGRIM WAY, 012 Oak Ave. NE, Box 277, Cass Lake MN 56633. (218)335-6190. Editor: James E. Johnston. Magazine "for ethnic Mayflower Pilgrims and those who confess that there are strangers an Pilgrims on earth. Estab. 1957. Circ. 500.
Needs: Historical (general), juvenile, religious/inspirational. "Separatist, against religious monopoly, land monopoly, wealth monopoly, abortions, euthanasia, liquor." Length: 500 words minimum; 1,000 words maximum.
How to Contact: Query first. Reports in 3 weeks on queries. Sample copy $1.

Payment: 25 contributor's copies. $1 charge for extras.
Terms: Pays on publication for one-time rights.
Tips: "Write about the Pilgrims, past or present with geneological tracings, especially of the Browns. (Editor's mother was a Brown). Also write against stereotyping, discriminating against, and segregating seniors. *The Pilgrim Way* will be $1 per copy in 1983."

PLAINSWOMAN, INC., Plainswoman, Inc., Box 8027, Grand Forks ND 58202. (701)781-4234. Editor: Elizabeth Hampsten. Fiction Editor: Joan Eades. Managing Editor: Jeanne Anderegg. "A feminist, informational publication which publishes some fiction and poetry." Readership: "Mainly women and girls of the Plains area who want information concerning national and regional women's issues." 10 times/year (February and August excluded). Estab. 1977. Circ. 540.
Needs: Receives approximately 10 unsolicited fiction mss each month.
How to Contact: Send complete ms with SASE. Reports in 2 weeks-3 months. Sample copy $2.
Terms: Acquires all rights. Publication copyrighted.
Tips: "Rejected mss are sometimes too long, sometimes inappropriate, occasionally not well-crafted."

PLOUGHSHARES, Ploughshares, Inc., Dept. M, Box 529, Cambridge MA 02139. Editor: DeWitt Henry. "Our theme is new writing (poetry, fiction, criticism) that addresses contemporary adult readers who look to fiction and poetry for help in making sense of themselves and of each other." Quarterly. Estab. 1971. Circ. 3,400.
Needs: Literary. "No genre (science fiction, detective, gothic, adventure, etc.), popular formula or commercial fiction whose purpose is to entertain rather than to illuminate." Buys 20 + mss/year. Receives approximately 300-400 unsolicited fiction mss each month. Length: 2,000-6,000 words. Sometimes recommends markets.
How to Contact: "Query for best time to submit and examine a sample issue." SASE for query, ms. Reports in 3 weeks on queries, 3 months on mss. Sample copy $4.
Payment: $5/page to $50 maximum, plus copies. Offers 50% kill fee for assigned ms not published.
Terms: Pays on publication for first North American serial rights. Publication copyrighted.
Tips: "Be familiar with our fiction issues, fiction by our writers and by our various editors (e.g. Rosellen Brown, Tim O'Brien, Jay Neugeboren, Jayne Anne Phillips) and more generally acquaint yourself with the best short fiction currently appearing in the literary quarterlies, and the annual prize anthologies (*Pushcart Prize, O'Henry Awards, Best American Short Stories*). Don't, in submitting, look for help in writing. The professional question is: Can you use this, yes or no? Also realistically consider whether the work you are submitting is as good as or better than—in your own opinion—the work appearing in the magazine you're sending to. What is the level of competition? And what is its volume (in our case, we accept about 1 ms in 200). Never send 'blindly' to a magazine, or without carefully weighing your prospect there against those elsewhere. Always keep a copy of work you submit, and if you don't hear back in reasonable time, withdraw your submission and keep it circulating."

PORTLAND REVIEW, Portland State University, Box 751, Portland; OR 97207. (503)229-4468. Editor: Jhan Hochman. Magazine with an eye towards the new and fresh. *PR* is a literary/arts magazine for people who are interested in contemporary writing. Semiannually. Estab. 1955. Circ. 500.
Needs: Contemporary, experimental fantasy, feminist/lesbian, gay, historical, humor/satire, literary, prose poem, psychic/supernatural, science fiction, translations, women's, young adult. Receives 6-10 unsolicited fiction mss/month. Accepts 5 mss/issue; 10 mss/year. Length: 2,000 words average. Occasionally critiques rejected ms.
How to Contact: Query first or submit through agent. SASE for query. Photocopied submissions OK. Reports in 3-4 weeks on queries. Sample copy for $2. Fiction guidelines free.
Payment: 1 free contributor's copy; 50% discount for extras.
Terms: Acquires one-time rights. Publication copyrighted.

POTBOILER, Lari Davidson Books, Richards Rd., Roberts Creek, British Columbia, Canada V0N 2W0. (604)885-3985. Editor-in-Chief: L.R. Davidson. Magazine for science fiction/fantasy and comics fans of all ages. ''I publish science fiction, fantasy, horror and unusual mainstream material in prose and graphic form. All mss are illustrated by the best artists I can find. The magazine is intended to be both a literary and visual delight.'' Published semiannually. Estab. 1980. Circ. 600.

Needs: Adventure, comics, erotica, experimental, fantasy, horror, humor/satire, mainstream (unusual), science fiction, suspense/mystery. ''Unusually good juvenile material might be considered. No pretentious material of any sort.'' Receives 12 unsolicited fiction mss/month. Accepts 6-8 mss/issue; 12-16 mss/year. Length: 600 words minimum; 20,000 words maximum; 4,000-5,000 words average. Occasionally critiques rejected mss.

How to Contact: Send complete ms with SASE. Previously published work OK. Reports in 6 weeks on mss. Sample copy $2. Free fiction guidelines with SAE and International Reply Coupons. ''Absolutely *NO* photocopied mss without a cover letter stating that it is *not* a simultaneous submission . . . if there is no statement then I do not read the ms and return it promptly. Further, it would be nice if the author would include a cover letter, no matter how brief.''

Payment: 2 free contributor's copies.

Terms: Pays on publication for second serial rights and first North American serial rights. Publication copyrighted.

Tips: ''Be entertaining and concise. Most fiction manuscripts are not very well written . . . a large majority are not even stories. I strongly suggest would-be writers see Harlan Elison's article in *Fantasy Newsletter* # 47, April/May '82.''

POULTRY, A Magazine of Voice, Poultry, Inc., Box 727, Truro MA 02666. Editors: Brendan Galvin and George Garrett. Tabloid of fiction and poetry that parodies contemporary poems, styles, lit-biz, contribution notes, contests, prizes, etc; for writers and readers of contemporary literature. Semiannually. Estab. 1979. Circ. 1,000.

Needs: Humor/satire. ''We want fiction that satirizes contemporary writing's foibles, pretensions, politics, etc. No serious fiction.'' Receives 10-20 unsolicited fiction mss/month. Accepts 3-4 mss/issue; 10 mss/year. Occasionally critiques rejected ms.

How to Contact: Send complete ms with SASE. Reports in 1 month on mss. Sample copy for $1.

Payment: 10 free contributor's copies.

Terms: Acquires one-time rights.

Tips: ''Read us; send us parodies of the things in contemporary writing and its scene that bug you the most!''

PRAIRIE SCHOONER, University of Nebraska, English Department, 201 Andrews Hall, Lincoln NE 68588. (402)472-1800. A general literary quarterly of stories, poems, essays and reviews for a general educated audience who reads for pleasure. Quarterly. Estab. 1927. Circ. 1,500.

Needs: Good fiction. Accepts 4-5 mss/issue. Receives approximately 200-500 unsolicited fiction mss each month. Length: varies. Critiques rejected mss ''when there is time.''

How to Contact: Send complete ms with SASE. Reports in 2 months on mss.

Payment: 2 free author's copies, 10 offprints.

Terms: Acquires all rights. Publication copyrighted.

Tips: ''Read *Prairie Schooner*.'' Annual prize of $500 for best fiction, $100 for best new writer (poetry or fiction).

PRIMAVERA, University of Chicago, 1212 E. 59th St., Chicago IL 60637. (312)524-1561. Editorial Board. Literature and graphics by women: poetry, short stories, essays, photos, drawings. Readership: ''an audience interested in women's ideas and experiences.'' Annual. Estab. 1975. Circ. 1,000.

Needs: Literary, contemporary, science fiction, fantasy, feminist, gay/lesbian, humor. ''We dislike slick stories packaged for more traditional women's magazines.'' Note: ''We publish only women writers and artists." Accepts 6-10 mss/issue. Receives approximately 40 unsolicited fiction mss each month. Length: 25 pages maximum. Critiques rejected mss "when there is time. Often gives suggestions for revisions and invites re-submission of revised manuscript. Occasionally recommends markets to writers."

How to Contact: Send complete ms with SASE. Reports in 5 months on mss. Sample copy $5. Guidelines for legal-sized SASE.

Payment: 2 free author's copies. $3 charge for extras.

Terms: Acquires first rights. Publication copyrighted.

Tips: "Read the magazine. We publish a wide variety of stories. We like stories with well developed characters, interesting plots, and convincing dialogue. We like new ideas and techniques."

PRISM INTERNATIONAL, 1874 E. Mall # 204, University of British Columbia, Vancouver, B.C., Canada V6T 1W5. (604)228-2514. Editor: Brian Burke. "A journal of contemporary writing—fiction, poetry, drama and translation. *Prism*'s audience is world-wide, as are our contributors." Readership: "Public and university libraries, individual subscriptions, bookstores—an audience concerned with the contemporary in literature." Published 4 times/year. Estab. 1959. Circ. 1,000.

Needs: Literary, contemporary or translations. "Most any category as long as it is *fresh*. No overtly religious, overtly theme-heavy material or anything more message or category-oriented than self-contained." Buys approximately 50 mss/year. Receives 40 unsolicited fiction mss each month. Length: 5,000 words maximum "though flexible for outstanding work." Critiques rejected mss "when there is time." Recommends occasionally other markets.

How to Contact: Send complete ms with SAE and International Reply Coupons. Reports in 2 months. Sample copy $4.

Payment: $10/printed page, 1 free year's subscription.

Terms: Pays on publication for first North American serial rights. Publication copyrighted.

Tips: "Too many derivative, self-indulgent pieces; sloppy construction and imprecise word usage. There's not enough attention to voice and a beginning and not enough invention."

PROOF ROCK, Literary Arts Journal, Proof Rock Press, Box 607, Halifax VA 24558. Editor: Don R. Conner. Magazine. "We publish the best of what is submitted in a given period. No taboos if well done." For all segments of the literary readership. Semiannually. Estab. 1982. Circ. 300.

Needs: Adventure, contemporary, erotica, experimental, fantasy, humor/satire, literary, mainstream, men's, prose poem, psychic/supernatural, romance, translations, women's. "Excessive sentimentality is frowned upon." Receives 8-10 unsolitied fiction mss/month. Accepts 2-4 mss/issue; 4-8 mss/year. Length: 2,500 words maximum; 2,000 words average. Occasionally critiques rejected ms.

How to Contact: Send complete ms with SASE. Simultaneous, photocopied and previously published submissions OK. Reports in 3 months on mss. Sample copy $2.50. Fiction guidelines free with # 10 SAE and 1 first class stamp.

Payment: 1 free contributor's copy; $2.50 charge for extras.

Terms: Acquires one-time rights.

Tips: "Our audience is passive. We need something to stir them up. Try to find something new under the sun."

PROP, Workspace Loft, Inc., 845 Park Ave., Albany NY 12208. (518)474-7002. Rotating editors. "A journal devoted to the informal exchange of ideas that take visual or literary form, or that can only be expressed by a combination of both." Readership: "art and free form literature-oriented." Quarterly. Estab. March 1979. Circ. 1,000.

Needs: Literary, contemporary, fantasy. Receives approximately 10 unsolicited fiction mss each month. Length: 1,200 words maximum. Critiques rejected mss "when there is time."

How to Contact: Send complete ms with SASE. Reports in 3 months on mss. Sample copy $1.50.

Payment: 1 free author's copy. 50¢ charge for extras.
Terms: Rights remain with author.
Tips: "We cannot publish more than a few mss per issue, and have only 4 issues per year. Our selection is therefore very scrupulous." Mss are rejected because of "abundance of adjectivès, too much dwelling on a few ideas, lack of grace in using language. Be patient if mss are returned. We have a rotating editorship with different tastes. Mss over the maximum length have no chance; the shorter the better."

PRORODEO SPORTS NEWS, Professional Rodeo Cowboys Association Properties, Inc., 101 Prorodeo Dr., Colorado Springs CO 80919. (303)593-8840. Editor-in-Chief: Bill Crawford. Tabloid of professional rodeo news, information, features, photos, columns, book reviews, letters to editor, etc., for professional rodeo contestants, contract people, stock contractors, fans and committeemen. Published biweekly. Estab. 1952. Circ. 30,000.
Needs: Adventure, humor, men's, suspense/mystery, western. "Must have a clearly defined connection with professional rodeo." No unprofessional work, "switches" plagiarized from other writers. "*PSN* has been willing to look at professional crafted fiction dealing with the sport of professional rodeo for almost five years. So far, however, we've received only two story manuscripts and both were unsuitable. If we could get quality rodeo fiction, we would publish 12 to 15 stories a year, possibly as many as 20 a year." Length: 500-1,500 words.
How to Contact: Send complete ms with SASE. Previously published work OK. Reports in 3 weeks on mss. Sample copy $1. Free fiction guidelines with # 10 SAE and 2 first class stamps.
Payment: $60 minimum and 5 contributor's copies. 75¢ charge for extras plus postage.
Terms: Pays on acceptance for all rights. Publication copyrighted.
Tips: "Have or acquire a thorough knowledge and understanding of professional rodeo and its people." Mss are rejected because "they indicate lack of any knowledge whatever about professional rodeo, what it is and what it means. We have seen some stories that were plagiarized and switched to a rodeo setting."

PROSPICE, Aquila Publishing/Johnston Green and Co. (Publishers) Ltd., Box 1, Portree, Isle of Skye, Scotland IV51 9BT. Editor/Managing Director: J.C.R. Green. Theme: Literary. Biannual. Estab. 1974. Circ. 5,000.
Needs: Literary, contemporary, translations. Short stories or prose pieces. No "popular" type material. Accepts 10 mss/year. Receives 200 unsolicited fiction mss each month. Charges variable reading fee. Variable length. Sends mss on to editors of other publications. Sometimes recommends markets.
How to Contact: SASE or IRC for query, ms. Reports in 1 month on queries, 2 months on mss. Sample copy $4.
Payment: Free author's copies. Amount "depends on length of submission."
Terms: Makes assignments on a work-for-hire basis.

PTERANODON MAGAZINE, Lieb/Schott Publication, Box 229, Bourbonnais IL 60914. Editors: Patricia Lieb and Carol Schott. A literary magazine containing short stories and poetry. Aimed toward poets and writers. Published 3 times/year. Estab. January 1979. Circ. 500.
Needs: Literary, contemporary, science fiction, fantasy, gothic, romance, western, mystery, adventure, humor. Accepts 1-3 mss/issue. Receives 10 unsolicited fiction mss each month. Length: 1,200 words preferred. Critiques rejected mss "when there is time."
How to Contact: Send complete ms with SASE. Reports in 3 weeks. Sample copy $2.50. Free guidelines with SASE.
Payment: 1-3 free author's copies. $2.50 charge for extras.
Terms: Acquires one-time rights. Publication copyrighted.
Tips: "Most stories are trite or have been said before. Read more."

PTOLEMY/THE BROWNS MILLS REVIEW, Press Inc., Box 908, Browns Mills NJ 08015. (216)893-7594. Editor-in-Chief: David C. Vajda. Magazine. Published annually. Estab. 1980. Circ. 250.

Needs: Contemporary, erotica, experimental, historical, humor/satire, mainstream, translations. No "plagiarized material, racist—racism—sexist—per se." Length: 50 words minimum; 10,000 words maximum; 400-2,400 words average. Occasionally critiques rejected mss. Sends mss on to editors of other publications. Recommends markets.
How to Contact: Query first with unpublished samples with SASE. Reports in 1 month on queries; 1 month on mss.
Payment: 5 contributor's copies per page.
Terms: Pays on publication for all rights. Publication copyrighted.
Tips: "No previously published material submitted as 'samples' considered."

THE PUB, Ansuda Publication, Box 158J, Harris IA 51345. Editor/Publisher: Daniel R. Betz. "We prefer stories to have some sort of social impact within them, no matter how slight, so our fiction is different from what's published in most magazines. We aren't afraid to be different or publish something that might be objectionable to current thought. *Pub* is directed toward those people, from all walks of life, who are themselves "different" and unique, who are interested in new ideas & forms of reasoning. Our readers enjoy *Pub* and believe in what we are doing." Published 3 times/year. Estab. January 1979. Circ. 200.
Needs: Literary, psychic/supernatural, fantasy, horror, mystery, adventure, serialized and condensed novels. "We are looking for honest, straightforward stories. No love stories or stories that ramble on for pages about nothing in particular. Accepts 1-4 mss/issue. Receives approximately 25-30 unsolicited fiction mss each month. Length: 8,000 words maximum. Sometimes recommends other markets.
How to Contact: Send complete ms with SASE. Reports in 1-4 weeks on mss. Sample copy $1.50. Guidelines for legal-sized SASE.
Payment: 2 free author's copies. Cover price less regular bulk discount for extras.
Terms: Acquires first North American serial rights and second serial rights on reprints. Publication copyrighted.
Tips: "Read the magazine—that is *very* important. If you send a story close to what we're looking for, we'll try to help guide you to exactly what we want." Mss are rejected "mainly because the work doesn't fit our magazine."

PUERTO DEL SOL, Puerto Del Sol Press, New Mexico State University, Box 3E, Las Cruces NM 88003. (505)646-3931. Editor-in-Chief: Kevin McIlvoy. Poetry Editor: Joe Somoza. Magazine. "Though emphasis has been on Chicano, Native American and Latin American writers, we publish quality material from anyone. Poetry, fiction, art, photos, interviews, reviews, parts-of-novels, long-poems, plays." Published semiannually. Estab. 1961. Circ. 1,000.
Needs: Contemporary, ethnic, experimental, literary, mainstream, prose poem, excerpted novel, translations. Receives varied amount of unsolicited fiction mss/month. Accepts 4-6 mss/issue; 12-15 mss/year. Occasionally critiques rejected ms.
How to Contact: Send complete ms with SASE. Simultaneous and photocopied submissions OK. Reports in 3 weeks on mss. Sample copy $3.
Payment: 3 contributor's copies.
Terms: Pays on publication for one-time rights (reverts to author). Publication copyrighted.
Tips: "We are open to all forms of fiction, from the conventional to the wildly experimental, as long as they have integrity and are well-written. Too often we receive very impressively 'polished' manuscripts that will dazzle readers with their sheen but offer no character/reader experience of lasting value."

PULP, 720 Greenwich St., New York NY 10014. Editor/Publisher: Howard Sage. Theme: fiction, poetry, international and intercultural relations for writers/readers interested in various styles of fine writing on all subjects. Biannual. Estab. 1975. Circ. 2,000.
Needs: Literary, ethnic (all), serialized novels, translations (send original; camera ready if non-English alphabet). Accepts 8 mss/year. Length: 2,500-7,500 words.
How to Contact: Send complete ms with SASE. Reports in 1 month. Sample copy $1 cash.
Payment: 2 free author's copies. 50¢ charge for extras.

Terms: Acquires first North American serial rights.
Tips: "Brief biography should accompany all submissions. See sample before submitting."

PULPSMITH, Anything Goes as Long as It's Good, The Smith, 5 Beekman St., New York NY 10038. Editors: Harry Smith and Tom Tolnay. Fiction Editor: Nancy Hallinan. "A modern pocket-sized version of pulp-styled pop magazines with a literary bent for people who like to read for entertainment, and with a sense of quality." Published quarterly. Estab. 1981. Circ. 10,000.
Needs: Adventure, contemporary, fantasy, horror, humor/satire, literary, mainstream, science fiction, suspense/mystery, western. No women's/men's mass mag-oriented stories. Receives 200-300 unsolicited fiction mss/month. Buys 15 mss/issue; 60 mss/year. Length: 15,000 words maximum; 3,000 words average.
How to Contact: Send complete ms with SASE. Simultaneous and photocopied submissions OK. Reports in 6 weeks on mss. Sample copy $1.50; writer's subscription: $5/4 issues.
Payment: $25-100 and 2 contributor's copies. $1 charge for extras.
Terms: Pays on acceptance for first North American serial rights. Publication copyrighted.
Tips: "Read several issues of *Pulpsmith* to get a handle on it. Submit strong writing that avoids clichews—both in language and situation, and which goes beyond merely the genre in which it functions."

PURPLE COW "Atlanta's Newspaper for Teens", Purple Cow, Inc., Suite 315, 110 E. Andrews Drive, Atlanta GA 39327. (404)233-7618. Editor: Marilyn Staats. Tabloid for teens aged 12-18. Monthly. Feburary 1976. Circ. 41,000.
Needs: Young adult. Length: 1,500 words minimum; 5,000 words maximum. Occasionally critiques rejected ms.
How to Contact: Send complete ms with SASE. Simultaneous, photocopied and previously published work OK. Reports in 3-6 weeks on mss. Sample copy for $1 with 10x11 SAE and 42¢ postage.
Payment: 5 free contributor's copies; 50¢ charge for extras.
Terms: Acquires one-time rights. Publication copyrighted.
Tips: "Don't write down to teens. No vulgar language or explicit sex."

QUANTUM UNIVERSE MAGAZINE, The QUP Showcase, Quantum Universe Productions, Box 6821, Silver Spring MD 20906. Editor: Carl R. Dietrich. Magazine of science fiction and fantasy, some special fiction. Monthly. Estab. 1983.
Needs: Aventure, fantasy, historical, horror, humor/satire, psychic/supernatural science fiction, serialized/excerpted novel. Buys 1-2 mss/issue; 12-24 mss/year. Length: 500 words minimum; 100,000 words maximum; 5,000 words average. Occasionally critiques rejected ms.
How to Contact: Send complete ms with SASE. No phone calls, please. Simultaneous and photocopied submissions OK. Reports in 2-3 weeks on ms. Sample copy for $2. Fiction guidelines free with business SAE and 40¢ postage.
Payment: Pays small percentage per word; 2 free contributor's copies; $2 charge for extras.
Terms: Acquires first rights. Publication copyrighted.

QUARRY, Quarry Press, Box 1061, Kingston, Ontario, Canada K7L 4Y5. (613)544-5400, ext. 165. Editor-in-Chief: David J. Schleich. "Quarterly anthology of new Canadian poetry, prose. Also includes graphics, photographs and book reviews. We seek readers interested in vigorous, disciplined, new Canadian writing." Published quarterly. Estab. 1952. Circ. 1,100.
Needs: Experimental, fantasy, literary, science fiction, serialized/excerpted novel, translations. "We do not want highly derivative or clichéd style." Receives 30-40 unsolicited fiction mss/month. Buys 4-5 mss/issue; 20 mss/year. Length: 3,000 words average. Occasionally critiques rejected ms.
How to Contact: Send complete ms with SASE. Photocopied submissions OK. Sample copy $2.50 with 4x7 SAE and 31¢ postage or IRC.

Payment: $10/page; 1 year subscription to magazine and 1 contributor's copy.
Terms: Pays on publication for first North American serial rights.
Tips: "Read previous *Quarry* and *Canadian Fiction Magazine* to see standard we seek. We seek aggressive experimentation which is coupled with competence (form, style) and stimulating subject matter. We also like traditional forms."

QUARRY WEST, Porter College, ULSC, Santa Cruze CA 95064. (408)429-4645 or 429-2951. Editor: Peter Radetsky. Magazine of fiction, poetry, general nonfiction, art, graphics for a general audience. Semiannually. Estab. 1971. Circ. 450.
Needs: Accepts 2-5 mss/issue; 4-10 mss/year. Occasionally critiques rejected ms.
How to Contact: Send complete ms with SASE. Photocopied submissions OK. Reports in 6 weeks on mss. Sample copy for $2.50.
Payment: 2 free contributor's copies.
Terms: Acquires first North American serial rights. Publication copyrighted.
Tips: "We're interested in good writing—we've published first time writers and experienced professionals—the only criterion is good writing. Don't submit material you are unsure of or perhaps don't like just for the sake of publication—only show your *best* work—read the magazine for a feeling of the kind of fiction we've published."

QUARTERLY WEST, University of Utah, 317 Olpin Union, Salt Lake City UT 84112. (801)581-3839. Editors: David Baker, Robert Shapard. Fiction Editor: Pete Hager. "We try to publish a variety of fiction by writers from all over the country. Our publication is aimed primarily at an educated audience which is interested in contemporary literature and criticism." Semiannual. Estab. 1976. Circ. 800.
Needs: Literary, contemporary, translations. Buys 4-6 mss/issue, 10-12 mss/year. Receives approximately 50 unsolicited fiction mss each month. No preferred length. Critiques rejected mss "when there is time."
How to Contact: Send complete ms. Cover letters welcome. SASE for ms. Reports in 2 months; "sooner, if possible."
Payment: $25-100.
Terms: Pays on publication for first North American serial rights. Publication copyrighted.
Tips: "Write a clear and unified story which does not rely on tricks or gimmicks for its effects. Mss are rejected because of "poor style, formula writing, clichés, weak characterization." Don't send more than 2 stories at a time." Contest for novellas planned for Spring, 1983.

QUEEN'S QUARTERLY: A Canadian Review, Queen's Quarterly Committee, John Watson Hall, Queen's University, Kingston, Ontario, Canada K7L 3N6. (613)547-6968. Editor: Dr. Michael Fox. "A general interest intellectual review, featuring articles on science, politics, humanities, arts and letters. Extensive book reviews, some poetry and fiction." Published quarterly. Estab. 1893. Circ. 2,000.
Needs: Adventure, contemporary, experimental, fantasy, historical (general), humor/satire, literary, mainstream, science fiction, women's. Buys 1 ms/issue; 4 mss/year. Length: 5,000 words maximum.
How to Contact: "Send complete ms—only one at a time—plus one paragraph résumé and a brief description of piece submitted with SASE." Photocopied submissions OK if not part of multiple submission. Reports in 8 weeks on mss. Sample copy $4.
Payment: $25-100 and 2 contributor's copies. $3 charge for extras.
Terms: Pays on publication for first North American serial rights. Publication copyrighted.

QUIXOTE, Quixote Press, Box 70013, Houston TX 77007. Editor: Morris Edelson. Fiction Editor: Melissa Bondy. Theme: "anti-capitalist satire, humor, fiction." Readership: "the disaffected, the discontented. Misery loves company." Monthly. Estab. 1965. Circ. 500.
Needs: "Unconventional material." Accepts 10 mss/year. Receives 20-50 unsolicited fiction mss/month. Length: "shortish." Critiques rejected mss "briefly, when there is time."

How to Contact: Query. Reports in 2 weeks. Sample copy $1.50.

Payment: 5 free author's copies.

Terms: Acquires one-time rights. Publication copyrighted.

Tips: "Read our publication. Talk to working class and disenfranchised people. Write about something you care about. We are eclectic but exclude usually the merely clever. We do, however, print the best of what we get, so we often relax from our puritanical leftism." Rejected mss "need integration of action and subjective impression; need point of view consistent with editorial policy of magazine."

THE RAMPANT GUINEA PIG, A Magazine of Fantasy & Subcreative Fiction, 10639 Deveron Dr., Whittier CA 90601. Editor-in-Chief: Mary Ann Hodge. Magazine. "Though we emphasize fantasy fiction, we also publish some poetry, occasional book reviews, and material relating to the life and works of Donald K. Grundy. Our readers are literate, and well read in fantasy. Many have an interest in children's literature." Published semiannually. Estab. 1978. Circ. 100.

Needs: Fantasy, science fantasy, religious fantasy. "Humorous, satire parody, and pastiche okay. All stories should be PG rated. No sword and sorcery/barbarian fiction, no *Star Trek* or *Star Wars* stories." Receives 1-3 unsolicited fiction mss/month. Accepts 2-4 mss/issue; 4-8 mss/year. Length: 8,000 words maximum; 5,000 words average (serials may be longer). Occasionally critiques rejected ms. Sometimes recommends markets.

How to Contact: Send complete ms with SASE. Photocopied submissions OK. Reports in 4 weeks on mss. Sample copy $2.25. Fiction guidelines with # 10 SAE and 1 first class stamp.

Payment: 2 contributor's copies. $2.25 charge for extras.

Terms: Pays on publication for first North American serial rights. Publication copyrighted.

Tips: "Read as much fantasy as you can. Don't write it unless you love it. And read one or more issues of *The Rampant Guinea Pig* before submitting so you'll know the niche we occupy in the genre. At least send for the fiction guidelines."

RAPSCALLION'S DREAM, Box 183, Bronx NY 10470. Editor-in-Chief: Stephen DiPresso. "Magazine of poetry and fiction that is intriguing, mysterious, and hopefully street-wise for bright persons tired of the usual banality polluting contemporary 'literature.' " Published semiannually. Estab. 1981. Circ. 500.

Needs: Contemporary, erotica, ethnic, experimental, fantasy, horror, humor/satire, literary, mainstream, men's, prose poem, psychic/supernatural, science fiction. "Serious artists only." Receives 6-10 unsolicited fiction mss/month. Accepts 5-7 mss/issue; 10-18 mss/year. Length: 100 words minimum; 2,000 words maximum; 1,200 words average. Occasionally critiques rejected ms.

How to Contact: Send complete ms and brief biography with SASE. Simultaneous, photocopied and previously published submissions OK. Reports in 8 weeks on mss. Sample copy $3 with 8½x11 SAE and 3 first class stamps.

Payment: 1-2 contributor's copies.

Terms: Pays on publication for first rights. Publication copyrighted.

Tips: "Ask for a critique. Be well-read in contemporary fiction since 1945, especially Bukowski, Brautigan, Pynchon, et al."

RED CEDAR REVIEW, Red Cedar Press, Dept. of English, Morrill Hall, Michigan State University, East Lansing MI 48824. (517)355-9656. Editor: Deirdre Pense. Theme: "literary—poetry, fiction, book reviews, one-act plays, interviews, graphics." Biannual. Estab. 1961. Circ. 500.

Needs: Literary, science fiction. Accepts 3-4 mss/issue, 6-10 mss/year. Length: 500-7,000 words.

How to Contact: Send complete ms with SASE. Reports in 2 months on mss. Sample copy $1.

Payment: 1 free author's copy. $2.50 charge for extras.

Terms: Acquires all rights.

Tips: "Read the magazine and good literary fiction. Annual creative writing contest for MSU students only."

REFLECT, 3306 Argonne Ave., Norfolk VA 23509. (804)857-1097. Editor: W.S. Kennedy. "A magazine of thought-inspiring fiction, articles, poetry, *Reflect*'s editorial policy and direction might be described by saying that it suggests the question: 'Did you ever think of that, or look at it that way?' Following the truth where it may lead takes us into diverse fields including science, philosophy, the occult. In addition, we use cartoons, regular columns on antiques/collectibles and on organic gardening. So audience is literate but diverse." Published quarterly. Estab. 1979.

Needs: Adventure, comics, contemporary, ethnic, experimental, fantasy, historical (general), humor/satire, literary, men's, psychic/supernatural, science fiction, women's. Accepts 3 mss/issue; 12 mss/year. Length: 500 words minimum; 2,500 words maximum; 2,000 words average. Occasionally critiques rejected mss. Sometimes recommends markets.

How to Contact: Send complete ms with SASE. Reports in 4 weeks on mss. Sample copy $1. Free fiction guidelines with SAE and 1 first class stamp.

Payment: 1 contributor's copy. $1 charge for extras.

Terms: Pays on publication for first rights.

Tips: "Ideally, writers should study several issues of the magazine before submitting. Many don't, and get accepted anyway, but a study of the publication is needed to learn our needs; guidelines are offered on request, of course with SASE."

REVIEW OF BOOKS AND RELIGION, Forward-Movement, Box 1460, Lexington KY 40502. (606)255-0990. Editor: Kendig Brubaker Cully. Tabloid of "primarily book reviews in religion and related humanities fields plus reviews of fiction that has a bearing on religion broadly conceived for intelligent, well-educated readership. Publishes 10 issues/year. Estab. 1971. Circ. 3,000+.

Needs: "Fiction only in one form, very brief stories, and only a few could be used annually." Experimental, fantasy, historical (general), literary, psychic/supernatural, religious/inspirational. "We publish very little fictional material, but would welcome very short stories with a sophisticated slant. Nothing sentimental ever—or weird." Receives "very few" unsolicited fiction mss/month. Length: 600 words minimum, 900 words maximum.

How to Contact: Query first with SASE. Reports in 3 weeks on queries. Request sample copy from *Review* business office, Forward Movement Publications, 412 Sycamore St., Cincinnati OH 45202.

Payment: "We do not pay."

Terms: Publication copyrighted by publisher.

REVISTA/REVIEW INTERAMERICANA, Interamerican University Press, Box 3255, San Juan PR 00936. (809)754-8415 or 754-8370. Acting Director-Editor: Gerard P. Marin. "A scholarly journal oriented to Puerto Rican, Caribbean and Hispanic subjects. Poetry, short stories, reviews. For educated laymen and professionals, including academics and scholars who read us because we're the foremost such journal in this field." Quarterly. Estab. 1971. Circ. 1,200.

Needs: Literary, contemporary, ethnic (Puerto Rican, Hispanic, Caribbean), translations, scholarly, experimental. "We are bilingual and seek mss in either English or Spanish." Accepts 1-2 mss/issue, 4-8 mss/year. Length: 4,000-5,000 (prefers 1,500-2,000) words. Sometimes recommends other markets.

How to Contact: Query. Send complete ms with SASE. Reports in 1 week on queries, 3 months on mss. Free sample copy.

Payment: 15 free author's copies.

Terms: Acquires all rights. "We will revert copyright and pay 50% of reprint rights."

Tips: "Originality, good writing, clean copy are important. We are always short of good fiction and poetry and are always looking for new writers in either Spanish or English." Rejects mss "only when stylistically poor and/or pedestrian, uncouth language, gross sexual subject and depiction of violence. There is a tendency of 'stream of consciousness technique' without restraint in the above-mentioned."

RFD, Box 127 E, Bakersville NC 28705. Contact: Fiction Editor. "Published by and for gay men who share a country or rural consciousness. We seek fiction, poetry and articles dealing with gay men living in a non-urban environment. Gay men read the magazine mainly for contact with other gay men in the country and relief from a feeling of isolation." Quarterly. Estab. 1974. Circ. 1,600.

Needs: Gay, adventure. "No sexist or racist material or anything not dealing with gay men or a non-urban consciousness." Receives 1 unsolicited fiction mss each month. Critiques rejected mss "when there is time."

How to Contact: Send complete ms with SASE. Reports in 2 months on mss. Sample copy $2 with 9x12 SASE. Free guidelines.

Payment: 2 free author's copies. $2 charge for extras.

Terms: Acquires simultaneous rights.

Tips: "Write for guidelines or read some back issues." Most mss are rejected because of "inappropriate subject matter."

RHINO, The Poetry Forum, 77 Lakewood Pl., Highland Park IL 60035. Editors: Liz Peterson, Lee Berkson, and Helen Degen Cohen. "Exists for writers of short prose and poetry—for new writers whose eyes and ears for language are becoming practiced, and whose approaches to it are individualistic. Aimed toward the poetically inclined." Annual. Estab. 1976. Circ. 600.

Needs: "Short prose (sometimes referred to as prose poems—approx. 200 to 500 words). We aim for artistic writing; we also accept the well-written piece of wide or general appeal." Receives approximately 4 unsolicited fiction mss each month. Length: 200-750 words. Critiques rejected mss "when there is time." Sometimes recommends other markets.

How to Contact: Send complete ms with SASE. Reports in 1 month on mss. Sample copy $2.

Payment: 1 free author's copy.

Terms: Acquires one-time rights. Publication copyrighted.

Tips: "We recommend you know how to construct a variety of idiomatic English sentences; take as fresh an approach as possible toward the chosen subject; and take time to polish the ms for its keenest effect." Mss are rejected because they are "either too grim or too sentimental. We like strong writing—human warmth, humor, originality, beauty! We 'read' mss between March 1-May 31. Our publication appears the first week in October of each year."

RIVER STYX MAGAZINE, Big River Association, 7420 Cornell, St. Louis MO 63130. (314)725-0602. Editor: Jan Garden Castro. Address to Fiction Editor. Journal of "mixed media with multicultural, contemporary, mythic focus for active, alive, sensitive people." Semiannually. Estab. 1975. Circ. 3,000.

Needs: "We publish primarily poetry, interviews, art, and photography. We will consider any fiction category if the work is alive, rich in metaphor, well-crafted and unique." Receives 100 unsolicited fiction mss/month. Buys 3-5 mss/issue, 6-8 mss/year. Length: any number of words minimum, 1,500 words maximum. Occasionally critiques rejected mss.

How to Contact: Send query with unpublished sample under 10 pages (in September and October only). Photocopied submissions OK. Acceptances ONLY in November and December. Sample copy $3.60. Fiction guidelines for legal size envelope and 20¢ postage.

Payment: $7/page minimum; 4 free contributor's copies; $3 charge for extras. Offers kill fee of 2 copies.

Terms: Pays on publication for one-time rights. Publication copyrighted.

Tips: "Send a short, sparkling work. Read the publication to which you submit work; avoid long letters and biographical material."

RIVERSIDE QUARTERLY, Box 1763, Hartsville SC 29550. (803)332-1381. Editor: Leland Sapiro. Fiction Editor: Redd Boggs. Magazine which "performs the same office for the subfields of science fiction and fantasy that a magazine like *Partisan Review* does for literature in general. Our emphasis, then, is literary criticism—but we like to print at least once story per issue. Our readers are literate in both science and literature." Quarterly. Estab. 1964. Circ. 1,200.

Needs: Fantasy, science fiction. "Especially to be avoided are space-war stories, media-derived science fiction or allegories set in science fictional form (e.g., a future society in which Caucasians are the victims of racial prejudice).'' Accepts 1 ms/issue, 4 mss/year. Length: 3,500 words maximum. Occasionally critiques rejected mss.

How to Contact: Send complete ms with SASE. Photocopied submissions OK. Reports in 1 week on queries. Sample copy $1.25 and 8½x5½ envelope and 2 first class stamps. ''No fiction guidelines are offered, since we think a contributor can best determine the *type* of material we print by examining a few copies of the magazine.''

Payment: 3 free contributor's copies.

Terms: All copyrights released to contributors. Publication copyrighted.

Tips: ''Ours is the most critical audience anywhere, which means that our editors are the most critical anywhere. Would-be contributors are urged to read a copy of the magazine before sending in any ms.''

ROOM OF ONE'S OWN, Growing Room Collective, Box 46160, Station G, Vancouver, B.C., Canada V6R 4G5. Editors: Gayla Reid, Joanna Dean, Victoria Freeman, Jeannie Wexler, Eleanor Wachtel. Feminist literary: fiction, poetry, criticism, reviews. Readership: general, non-scholarly. Quarterly. Estab. 1975. Circ. 1,200.

Needs: Literary, women's feminist, lesbian. No ''sexist or macho material.'' Buys 3 mss/issue. Receives approximately 20 unsolicited fiction mss each month. Length: 3,000 words preferred. Critiques rejected mss ''when there is time.''

How to Contact: Send complete ms with SASE or International Reply Coupon. Reports in 3 months. Sample copy $2.75 with SASE, IRC.

Payment: $10 plus 2 free author's copies and subscription. $2 charge for extras.

Terms: Pays on publication for first rights. Publication copyrighted.

Tips: ''Write well and unpretentiously.'' Mss are rejected because they are ''unimaginative.''

ST. MAWR, St. Mawr of Vermont, Box 356, Randolph VT 05060. Editor: J.H. Kennedy. ''A tape cassette periodical with emphasis upon experience in jazz sub-culture for persons interested in oral literature and/or jazz music.'' Quarterly. Estab. 1977.

Needs: Literary, music. ''Submissions must be on tape cassettes.'' Accepts 3 cassettes/issue, 12/year. Length: 500-3,000 words.

How to Contact: Submit tape cassette of reading with SAE. Reports in 2 weeks on mss. Sample copy for 6x9 SAE, tape cassette and 30¢ postage.

Payment: 2 free author's copies. Half price charge for extras.

Terms: Acquires first rights.

SALOME: A LITERARY DANCE MAGAZINE, Ommation Press, 5548 N. Sawyer, Chicago IL 60625. Editor: Effie Mihopoulos. ''*Salome* tries to bring together all the arts with a prime focus on literature and dance for all those interested in the arts.'' Quarterly. Estab. 1976. Circ. 1,000.

Needs: Literary, contemporary, science fiction, fantasy, women's, feminist, gothic, romance, mystery, adventure, humor, serialized novels, prose poems, translations. ''We seek mss relating to the dance. The theme doesn't have to be specifically about dance (one of the characters can be a dancer or choreographer; one of the characters might have a friend who is, etc.) but there must be some sort of dance relation. We seek dance-related fiction of all kinds and lengths, including prose poems.'' Accepts 40 mss/year. Receives approximately 25 unsolicited fiction mss each month. No preferred length. Sends mss on to editors of other publications. Recommends markets.

How to Contact: Send complete ms with SASE. Reports in 1 month. Sample copy $4. 9x12 SASE with 80¢ postage preferred.

Payment: 1 free author's copy. Contributor's rates for extras upon request.

Terms: Acquires first North American serial rights. ''Rights revert to author but we retain reprint rights.'' Publication copyrighted.

Tips: ''Write a well-written story or prose poem relating to dance.'' Rejected mss are ''usually badly written—improve style, grammar, etc.—too often writers send out mss before they're ready. See a sample copy. Specify fiction interest.''

SALT LICK, Box 1064, Quincy IL 62301. Editor: James Haining. A journal of new literature and art. "We publish the best material received regardless of form, style, or content." Published irregularly. Estab. 1969. Circ. 1,500.
Needs: Literary, contemporary, religious/inspirational, psychic/supernatural, science fiction, fantasy, horror, men's, women's, feminist, gay/lesbian, erotica, gothic, adventure, humor, juvenile, young adult, ethnic (open), serialized and condensed novels, translations. Accepts varying number of mss/issue. Receives approximately 20 unsolicited fiction mss each month. No preferred length. Critiques rejected mss "when there is time."
How to Contact: Send complete ms with SASE. Reports in 3 weeks. Sample copy $3.
Payment: Free author's copies.
Terms: Acquires first rights, second serial rights. Publication copyrighted.
Tips: "Think. Write what you want to read."

SAMISDAT, Box 129, Richford VT 05476. Editor: Merritt Clifton. "*Samisdat* creates the culture of the future. Our stories, poems, and essays discuss the gradual but inevitable and necessary trend toward self-reliance, conservation, live-and-let-live politics, and Transcendentalist philosophy. We're outlaws and activists who direct our publication to reading eco-freaks, war-resisters, back-to-the-earthers, unschoolers, atheists, anarchists, libertarians—individualists who extend a willing hand from choice, not because Big Brother says so. They read us because we live out the beliefs we espouse and set a good, honest example of the possibilities." Published irregularly. Estab. 1973. Circ. 300-500.
Needs: Literary, contemporary, psychic/supernatural, science fiction, feminist, gay/lesbian, erotica, gothic, western, humor. "We don't use anything belonging to narrow genre confines. Our most frequent fiction contributors write war-stories, gothics, outdoor stories, contemporary, psychic, and religious/inspirational—but the common denominator is that we all write about life, for the living, for those of us daring to choose our own destinies. No material modeled after anything seen in slicks or on bestseller lists. We'll consider anything genuine." Accepts 3-10 mss/issue, 15-50 mss/year. Receives approximately 100-300 unsolicited fiction mss each month. Length: 1,500-5,000 words. Critiques rejected mss "when there is time."
How to Contact: Send complete ms with SASE. Reports in 3 weeks. Sample copy $2.50.
Payment: 2 free author's copies. Cover price less discount for extras.
Terms: Acquires first rights, one-time rights. Publication copyrighted.
Tips: "Read *Samisdat* first. If you belong here, you'll know it instinctively. Be willing to rewrite and rethink. We prefer short mss. Anything over 3,000 words is usually padded and verbose. We will reprint submissions if so designated. We work hard to help writers and expect writers to work equally hard toward helping themselves. Have a particular reason for submitting to us. We tend to introduce half a dozen new writers per issue. In addition to the magazine we also publish occasional novels and a great many single-author chapbooks presenting longer selections from regular magazine contributors. NO PHOTOCOPIES." Mss are rejected because "they're ill-conceived, trite, insults to a thinking reader's intelligence; or, as often, simply misdirected—things that never should have come here in the first place. Solution: read *Samisdat* before submitting."

SAN JOSE STUDIES, San Jose State University Foundation, 125 S. 7th St., San Jose CA 95152. Editor: Selma Burkom. "A journal for the general, educated reader. Covers a wide variety of materials: fiction, poetry, interviews, interdisciplinary essays. Aimed toward the college-educated common reader with an interest in the broad scope of materials." Tri-annual. Estab. 1975. Circ. 500.
Needs: Literary, contemporary, men's, women's, humor, ethnic (black/Jewish, etc.). Accepts 1-2 mss/issue, 3-6 mss/year. Receives approximately 25-40 unsolicited fiction mss each month. Length: 2,500-5,000 + words. Critiques rejected mss "when there is time." Sometimes recommends markets.
How to Contact: Send complete ms with SASE. Reports in 2 months.
Payment: 2 free author's copies.
Terms: Acquires first rights. Publication copyrighted.

Tips: "Mss read 'blind.' Name should appear *only* on cover sheet. We seldom print beginning writers of fiction." Annual $100 award for best story, essay or poem.

SAN JUAN HORSESHOE ,Box 662, Montrose CO 81402. (303) 249-7821. Editor: Kevin J. Haley. Tabloid of "western fiction/humor, political satire, rural-oriented dry humor for local college educated to agricultural community." Monthly. Estab. 1977. Circ. 10,000.
Needs: Comics, humor/satire, western. No urban-oriented, erotic or gay material. Receives 10 unsolicited fiction mss/month. Buys 5 mss/year. Length: 1,000 words minimum, 3,000 words maximum, 1,000 words average.
How to Contact: Send complete ms with SASE. Simultaneous, photocopied and previously published submissions OK. Sample copy free. Fiction guidelines for SAE.
Payment: $10-30; $7.50 subscription to magazine.
Terms: Pays on publication for one-time rights. Publication copyrighted.

SANDS, A Literary Review, 17302 Club Hill Dr., Dallas TX 75248. (214)931-0190. Editor: Joyce Meier. Magazine of short fiction, poetry, reviews, essays, art work, cartoons. Published annually. Estab. 1979. Circ. 300.
Needs: Contemporary, fantasy, literary, mainstream, prose poem, translations. "We have no restrictions, really, but the writing must be of fine quality with emphasis on excellent use of the English language. No porno, lesbian or gay. Receives 15-20 unsolicited fiction mss/month. Accepts 6-10 mss/issue. Length: 4,000 words maximum. Occasionally critiques rejected ms.
How to Contact: Send complete ms with SASE. Simultaneous and photocopied submissions OK. Reports in 8 weeks on mss. Sample copy $4.
Payment: 2 contributor's copies.
Terms: Acquires first rights. Publication copyrighted.
Tips: "Send us a ms with a clear story, specific details, fine language and interesting narrative and we will seriously consider it."

SCREE, Duck Down, Box 1047, Fallon NV 89406. (702)423-6643. Editor-in-Chief: Kirk Robertson. Magazine of contemporary literature and art. Published semiannually. Estab. 1973. Circ. 500.
Needs: Confession, erotica, ethnic, experimental, prose poem, western. Receives 10-15 unsolicited fiction mss/month. Accepts 3-4 mss/issue; 6-8 mss/year. Length: 500 words minimum, 2,500 words maximum, 1,500 words average. Prefer *short*—almost prose poem length. Occasionally critiques rejected ms.
How to Contact: Query first with SASE. Reports in 2-3 days on queries; 2-3 weeks on mss. Sample copy $5 with $1 postage.
Payment: 3-6 contributor's copies.
Terms: Pays on publication for first rights. Publication copyrighted.
Tips: Mss rejected because they are "inappropriate—potential contributors have never read an issue."

SCHOLIA SATYRICA, University of South Florida, English Dept., Tampa FL 33620. (813)974-2421. Editor: R.D. Wyly. Fiction Editor: John Iorio. Theme: satirical fiction and poetry for writers and readers interested in modern and critical satire. Biannual. Estab. 1975. Circ. 250.
Needs: Humor, satirical fiction only. Preference given to shorter mss. Critiques rejected mss about 50% of the time. Recommends markets.
How to Contact: Send complete ms with SASE. Reports in 2 months.
Payment: 2 free author's copies. $1 charge for extras.
Terms: Acquires first rights. Publication copyrighted.
Tips: "We stress wit and stylistic excellence. Verbose, drawnout mss immediately returned. Most writers waste words (and space). We are not interested in writing that is not succinct. Also, poor grammar and spelling are simply inexcusable. We are interested *only* in satire. Much of what we receive is *not* satire and we must reject it even though it may be fiction."

SECOND COMING, Second Coming, Inc., Box 31249, San Francisco CA 94131. Editor/Publisher: A.D. Winans. "An international literary journal. Publishes only first class prose and fiction from professional writers for a literary audience." Biannual. Estab. 1971. Circ. 1,000.
Needs: Literary, science fiction, humor. "We do not buy the common or trite story outlines and first person confessional stories seen elsewhere." Accepts 2-6 mss/issue. Receives approximately 50-100 unsolicited fiction mss each month. Length: 1,500-3,500 (prefers 3,000) words. Not accepting new material until after Summer, 1983.
How to Contact: Query. Send complete ms. SASE for query, ms. Reports in 1 month. Sample copy $3.
Payment: Free author's copies. Occasionally pays $25 on publication.
Terms: Acquires first rights. Publication copyrighted.
Tips: "See a sample copy of magazine. Be previously published in other literary journals before contacting us. We are a small publishing house, but our reputation is world-wide and we have published some of the best writers practicing their trade today."

SECOND GROWTH: APPALACHIAN NATURE & CULTURE, East Tennessee State University, Box 24,292, ETSU, Johnson City, TN 37614. (615)929-4339. Editor: Frederick O. Waage. Theme: "Environmental and cultural writings of all kinds related to Appalachian area of US for a regional audience seeking information and enjoyment." Semiannually. Estab. 1979.
Needs: Literary, contemporary, adventure, humor, ethnic (regional). "No real limitation on genre but must be of high literary quality." Accepts 1-2 mss/issue. Length: 4,000 words maximum.
How to Contact: Send complete ms with SASE. Reports as soon as possible. Free sample copy for 8½x11 SASE with 60¢ postage.
Payment: 2 free author's copies.
Terms: Acquires first rights.

SEEMS, Lakeland College, Sheboygan WI 53081. (414)565-3871. Editor: Karl Elder. "We publish fiction and poetry for an audience which tends to be highly literate. People read the publication, I suspect, for the sake of reading it." Published irregularly. Estab. 1971. Circ. 250.
Needs: Literary. Accepts 6-8 mss/issue. Receives approximately 10 unsolicited fiction mss each month. Length: 5,000 words maximum. Critiques rejected mss "when there is time."
How to Contact: Send complete ms with SASE. Reports in 2 months on mss. Sample copy $2.50.
Payment: 2 free author's copies. $2.50 charge for extras.
Terms: "Rights revert to author." Publication copyrighted.
Tips: "Read the magazine in order to help determine the taste of the editor." Mss are rejected because of "lack of economical expression, or saying with many words what could be said in only a few. Good fiction contains all of the essential elements of poetry; study poetry and apply those elements to fiction."

SEPIA, Poetry & Prose Magazine, Kawabata Press, Knill Cross House, HR Anderton Rd., Millbrook, NR Torpoint, Cornwall, England. Editor-in-Chief: Colin David Webb. Magazine for those interested in modern un-clichéd work. Published quarterly. Estab. 1977. Circ. 120.
Needs: Contemporary, experimental, humor/satire, literary, prose poem, translations. No fantasy, adventure, romance, science fiction, etc. Receives 1-3 unsolicited fiction mss/month. Accepts 2 mss/issue; 8-10 mss/year. Length: 20,000 words maximum; 5,000 words average. Occasionally critiques rejected ms.
How to Contact: Send complete ms with SASE. Simultaneous, photocopied and previously published submissions OK. Reports in 4 weeks on mss. Sample copy 50¢ with 8x6 SAE.
Payment: 1 contributor's copy. 50¢ charge for extras.
Terms: Pays on publication for one-time rights. Publication copyrighted.

SEQUOIA MAGAZINE, Storke Publications Bldg., Stanford CA 94305. "Publishes poetry, prose, fiction, interviews with selected authors, b&w photography and artwork; 90% freelance; student writing welcome. *Sequoia* prints fiction and poetry to be read by those outside as well as within the Stanford community. Many of our readers are authors themselves; others are interested in our magazine because of the well-known writers and interviewees featured in past issues." Published 3 times/year. Estab. 1956. Circ. 100.

Needs: "Literary excellence is the primary criterion. We'll consider anything but prefer literary, contemporary, men's, women's, ethnic, translations, and satire." Length: 8,000 words or 20 pp. maximum.

How to Contact: Send complete ms with SASE. Reports in 3 months "during academic year." Sample copy $1.

Payment: 1-2 free author's copies. Contributor's rates on request.

Terms: Acquires all rights.

Tips: "Be persistent. Don't allow your fiction to rely on shock value. Don't submit to a student-run publication during the summer; we generally close down then. In the past, we've had theme issues (translation, student writing) which naturally affect what's selected for a given issue."

THE SEWANEE REVIEW, University of the South, Sewanee TN 37375. (615)598-5931, Ext. 245. Editor: George Core. "A literary quarterly, publishing original fiction, poetry, essays on literary and related subjects, book reviews and book notices for well-educated readers who appreciate good American and English literature." Quarterly. Estab. 1892. Circ. 3,200.

Needs: "Literary, contemporary. No translations, juvenile, gay/lesbian, erotica." Buys 4-10 mss/year. Receives approximately 90 unsolicited fiction mss each month. Length: 6,000-7,500 words. Critiques rejected mss "when there is time." Sometimes recommends markets.

How to Contact: Send complete ms with SASE. Reports in 1 month on mss. Sample copy $4.75.

Payment: $10-$12/printed page. 2 free author's copies. $4.75 charge for extras.

Terms: Pays on publication for first North American serial rights and second serial rights by agreement. Publication copyrighted.

Tips: "Send only one story at a time, with a serious and sensible cover letter."

SEZ/A MULTI-RACIAL JOURNAL OF POETRY & PEOPLE'S CULTURE, Shadow Press, USA, Box 8803, Minneapolis MN 55408. (612)823-1319. Editor/Publisher: Jim Dochniak. "Minnesota's only multi-cultural literary magazine. It places special emphasis on supporting writing which is class-conscious, deals with current social concerns, and, in some way, helps readers focus on building a new human culture. Publishes poetry, journal/diary excerpts, reportage, interviews, articles dealing with current social/cultural concerns and reviews, in addition to fiction. *Sez* is geared toward readers who may not necessarily read or appreciate academic, obscure, or self-indulgent art for art's sake journals. Our audience, therefore, is one which believes that art is for humanity's sake, an audience which reads clear, understandable writing that is meaningful to their lives." Published irregularly. Estab. 1978. Circ. 1,500.

Needs: Literary, contemporary, men's, women's, feminist, gay/lesbian, ethnic (all), folklore, reportage, political. "We favor first-person, subjective narrative in any form. No material that is self-indulgent, cynical, racist, elitist, sexist or degrading." Accepts 2-10 mss/issue. Receives approximately 10 unsolicited fiction mss each month. Mss must be accompanied by a check for a sample copy or a subscription. Length: 250-2,500 words. Critiques rejected mss "on request." Sometimes recommends markets.

How to Contact: "Request sample copy with query." Manuscripts unaccompanied with a check for a sample copy or a subscription will not be read. Sample copy $3.50, subscription $6. SASE for query, ms. Reports in 1 month on queries, up to 6 months on mss.

Payment: Free author's copies. Cover price less 50% discount for extras.

Terms: Acquires one-time rights. Publication copyrighted.

Tips: "Study sample issues; query with list of possible writing ideas or projects. We try to support younger and unknown writers. Quality is very important. We favor writers and writing from and about the upper Midwest region and writing from Third World writers. Each issue is often focused on a particular theme and, therefore, writers should inquire before sending. Writers east of the Hudson are discouraged from sending.'' Mss are rejected because ''they are self-righteous, self-indulgent, cynical, too removed from the direct experience of the author and too geared toward an elite readership; others are not developed enough, not thought out enough, not studied and re-worked enough. To correct: Study what you're trying to say, why you're trying to say it, who you're trying to say it to, and what you want to leave your reader with after the story is finished.''

SHADOWS OF . . . Science Fiction and Fantasy Magazine, Dawn Press, Box 1696, Norman OK 73070. (405)794-9616. Editor-in-Chief: Dawn Atkins. ''We are a science fiction and fantasy, art and literary magazine. We publish short stories, poetry, illustrations, and art portfolios.'' Published semiannually. Estab. 1979. Circ. 5,000.

Needs: Adventure, contemporary, experimental, fantasy, horror, humor/satire, literary, prose poem, psychic/supernatural, romance (contemporary), science fiction, suspense/mystery. ''All must be science fiction and/or fantasy regardless of any sub-category. No material in which the characters, setting, etc., are taken from a TV show, movie or any other published work not by the author.'' Receives 50-100 unsolicited fiction mss/month. Buys 7 mss/issue; 14 mss/year. Occasionally critiques rejected ms. Sometimes recommends other markets.

How to Contact: Query first with SASE. Simultaneous submissions OK. Reports in 4 weeks on queries; 2 months on mss. Sample copy $4 with 75¢ postage. Free fiction guidelines with legal size SAE and 1 first class stamp.

Payment: $.005/word.

Terms: Pays on publication for first North American serial rights. Publication copyrighted.

Tips: ''I would say the major fault in the mss we get is that they are story fragments and not the entire story. Writers need to learn those basics!''

SHEBA REVIEW-THE LITERARY MAGAZINE FOR THE ARTS, Sheba Review, Inc., 2631 Sue Dr., Jefferson City MO 65101. Editor: S.D. Hanson. Theme: to promote the arts and artists in the Midwest; poetry; literary and journalistic prose. For those interested in cultural (artistic) concerns. Biannual. Estab. 1978.

Needs: Literary, contemporary, religious/inspirational, psychic/supernatural, science fiction, fantasy, humor, ethnic, translations. No pornographic material. Receives approximately 5 unsolicited fiction mss each month. Critiques rejected mss ''when there is time.''

How to Contact: Send complete ms with SASE. Reports in 8 months on mss.

Payment: Free author's copies.

Terms: Acquires one-time rights. Publication copyrighted.

Tips: ''Review a sample copy prior to submissions.'' Sponsors contests.

SHENANDOAH: THE WASHINGTON AND LEE UNIVERSITY REVIEW, Box 722, Lexington VA 24450. (703)463-9111, Ext. 283. Editor: James Boatwright. Poetry Editor: Richard Howard. ''We are a quarterly literary review publishing fiction, poetry, essays, and reviews.'' Estab. 1950. Circ. 1,000.

Needs: Quality fiction.

How to Contact: Send complete ms with SASE.

Payment: ''By arrangement.'' 2 free author's copies. $1.25 charge for extras.

SIBYL-CHILD: A Woman's Arts and Culture Journal, Sibyl-Child Press, Box 1773, Hyattsville MD 20788. (301)423-2113. Editors: Doris Mozer, Saundra Maley. Fiction Editor: Nancy Prothro. Magazine for ''mostly women, but anyone who is interested in good literature for and about women.'' Semiannually. Estab. 1974. Circ. 200.

Needs: ''Open to all categories.'' Receives 10 unsolicited fiction mss/month. Length: 500 words minimum, 2,500 words maximum, 2,000 words average. Occasionally critiques rejected mss.

How to Contact: Send complete ms with SASE. Send query with SASE. Photocopied submissions OK. Reports in 2 months on mss. Sample copy $2 and 5 first class stamps. Fiction guidelines for SAE.
Payment: 3 free contributor's copies; $2 charge for extras.
Terms: Acquires one-time rights. Publication copyrighted.
Tips: "Proficiency in the use of the English language is obligatory. We are often republished."

SIGNALS, Alpha Epsilon Rho, The National Broadcasting Society, USC College of Journalism, U of South Carolina, Columbia SC 29208. (803)777-6783. Executive Secretary: Dr. Richard Uray. "Geared to articles, mainly nonfiction, about the radio-TV film business, industry, personalities; for university students majoring in broadcasting and professionals employed in radio-TV-film." Monthly (Sept.-May). Estab. 1977. Circ. 2,000.
Needs: Men's women's; humor. "We are not really seeking fiction pieces as much as in-depth nonfiction related to the communications industry." Receives approximately 4-5 unsolicited fiction mss each month. Critiques rejected mss "when there is time."
How to Contact: Query. SASE for query, ms. Reports in 3 weeks on queries, 2 weeks on mss. Sample copy with 9x14 SAE plus 50¢ postage.
Payment: 2 free author's copies. $2 charge for extras.
Terms: Acquires first rights.

SILVERFISH REVIEW, Silverfish Press, Box 3541, Eugene OR 97403. (503)344-3535. Editor: Rodger Moody. High quality literary material for a general audience. Published 3 times/year. Estab. 1979. Circ. 500.
Needs: Literary. Accepts 1-2 mss/issue.
How to Contact: Send complete ms with SASE. Reports in 1 month on mss. Sample copy $2 with SAE and 80¢ for postage.
Payment: 3 free author's copies.
Terms: Pays on publication; rights revert to author.

SING HEAVENLY MUSE!, Sing Heavenly Muse, Box 14059, Minneapolis MN 55414. (612)822-8713. Editor: Sue Ann Martinson. Women's poetry, prose and artwork. Semiannual. Estab. 1977.
Needs: Literary, contemporary, fantasy, women's, feminist, mystery, humor, and ethnic minority. Receives approximately 10 unsolicited fiction mss each month.
How to Contact: Reports in 1-3 months on queries and mss. Sample copy $3.
Payment: 2 free copies.
Terms: Pays on publication for first rights. Publication copyrighted.

SLICK ,Box 11142, San Francisco CA 94101. Editor: Mr. Jaen Anderson. "*Slick* is a mini-magazine dedicated to the avantgarde scene for young adults interested in the latest developments in art, fashion, music, and other forms of creative expression." Quarterly. Estab. 1979. Circ. 20,000.
Needs: Experimental, fantasy, humor/satire, psychic/supernatural, science fiction, translations. Accepts 4 mss/year. Length: 5,000 words maximum. Occasionally critiques rejected mss.
How to Contact: Send complete ms with SASE. Simultaneous, photocopied and previously published submissions OK. Reports in 4-6 weeks on mss. Sample copy $1.
Payment: $25 subscription to magazine; 3 free contributor's copies; 50¢ charge for extras.
Terms: "All rights, preferably; however we are open to other negotiations depending on circumstances." Publication copyrighted.
Tips: "Send clippings or copies of previously published work if any are available . . . always reveal any other publisher or media you wish to contact."

SMACKWARM, A Literary Review ,University of Nebraska at Omaha, Annex 21, Omaha NE 68182. (402)554-2771. Editor: Richard Duggin. Fiction Editor: Joe Goecke. "*Smackwarm* attempts to publish the finest available contemporary fiction and poetry for college and literary types.'' Publishes 2 issues/year. Estab. 1973. Circ. 300.

Needs: Contemporary, experimental, fantasy, humor/satire, literary, mainstream. Receives 20 unsolicited fiction mss/month. Accepts 3 mss/issue, 6 mss/year. Length: 5,000-6,000 words average. Occasionally critiques rejected mss.

How to Contact: Send complete ms with SASE. Simultaneous and photocopied submissions OK. Reports in 4 weeks on mss. Sample copy $2.50. Fiction guidelines for SAE. No mss accepted between May 15 and Sept. 1.

Payment: 2 free contributor's copies; $2 charge for extras.

Terms: Acquires first North American serial rights. Publication copyrighted.

THE SMALL POND MAGAZINE, Box 664, Stratford, CT 06497. (203)378-4066. Editor: Napoleon St. Cyr. ''Features contemporary poetry, the salt of the earth, peppered with short prose pieces of various kinds. The college educated and erudite read it for good poetry, prose and pleasure.'' Triannual. Estab. 1964. Circ. 300.

Needs: ''Rarely use science fiction or formula stories you'd find in *Cosmo*, *Redbook*, *Ladies Home Journal*, etc.'' Buys 10-12 mss/year. Receives approximately 50 unsolicited fiction mss each month. Length: 200-2,500 words. Critiques rejected mss ''when there is time.''

How to Contact: Send complete ms with SASE. Reports in 2 weeks-1 month on mss. Sample copy $2.25

Payment: 2 free author's copies. $2/copy charge for extras.

Terms: Pays on publication for all rights. Publication copyrighted.

Tips: ''Send for a sample copy first. All mss must be typed. Name and address and story title on front page, name of story on succeeding pages.'' Mss are rejected because of ''tired plots and poor grammar.''

SMOKE, Windows Project, 23A Brent Way, Halewood, Liverpool, England L26 9XH. Tel. (051)486-0828. Editor: Dave Ward. Magazine of poetry, graphics, and short fiction for the general public. Publishes 3 issues/year. Estab. 1974. Circ. 1,500.

Needs: Contemporary, literary, prose poem. Receives 5 unsolicited fiction mss/month. Buys 2-3 mss/issue, 6-9 mss/year. Length: 200 words minimum, 2,000 words maximum, 400-800 words average. Occasionally critiques rejected mss.

How to Contact: Send complete ms with SASE. Simultaneous, photocopied and previously published submissions OK. Reports in 1 month on mss. Sample copy $1.

Payment: £5.

Terms: Pays on publication for one-time rights. Publication copyrighted.

SNAPDRAGON, English Dept., University of Idaho, Moscow ID 83843. (208)885-6937. Editors: Ron McFarland, Margaret Snyder and Tina Foriyes. ''Poems, artwork, photos and stories are the types of material published for a largely local, Northwest audience of mostly college students or graduates.'' Biannual. Estab. 1977. Circ. 200.

Needs: Literary, contemporary. ''We will consider whatever we see. We don't invite special types of work. No gay, feminist, erotica, science fiction (except literary) or juvenile.'' Accepts 2 or 3 mss/issue, 5 mss/year. Receives approximately 1-2 unsolicited fiction mss each month. Length: 200-5,000 words.

How to Contact: Send complete ms with SASE. Reporting time varies on mss; if sent in September or early March there is a rapid response. Sample copy $1.50 and 80¢ for postage.

Payment: Free author's copy, occasionally small cash payments.

Terms: Pays on publication for one-time rights. Publication copyrighted.

Tips: ''Be honest, proofread your work, don't overwrite. Write a sound conventional story (without clichés) before you try experimental modes.'' Mss are rejected because ''they lack sophistication in the development of character and of a recognizable style. In general, the writer simply hasn't the maturity of style.''

SNOWY EGRET, 205 S. Ninth St., Williamsburg KY 40269. (606)549-0850. Editor: Humphrey A. Olsen. Fiction Editor: Dr. William T. Hamilton. Natural history and material related to natural history. Semipopular. Semiannual. Estab. February 1922. Circ. 400.
Needs: Literary and translations, stories that are natural history related. Buys 1-2 mss/issue, 3-4 mss/year. Length: 0-10,000 words. Critiques rejected mss "when there is time." Sometimes recommends markets.
How to Contact: Query with SASE. Reports in 2 weeks on queries, 2 months on mss. Sample copy $2.
Payment: Pays $2/magazine page. Free author's copy. $1.50 per copy up to 5 extra. Offers 100% kill fee for assigned ms not published.
Terms: Pays on publication for first North American serial rights. Publication copyrighted.
Tips: "Write the kind of fiction we are looking for. Be sure material is related to natural history and has the element of surprise."

SOJOURNER, The New England Women's Journal of News, Opinions & The Arts, 143 Albany St., Cambridge MA 02139. (617)661-3567. Editor-in-Chief: Martha J. Thurber. "Feminist journal publishing interviews, nonfiction features, news, viewpoints, poetry, reviews (music, theater, dance, cinema, books) and fiction for women." Published monthly. Estab. 1975. Circ. 20,000.
Needs: Adventure, contemporary, ethnic, experimental, fantasy, feminist, gay, lesbian, gothic, romance, historical (general), humor/satire, juvenile, literary, mainstream, prose poem, science fiction, suspense/mystery, translations, western, women's, young adult. Receives 5 unsolicited fiction mss/month. Accepts 5 mss/year. Length: 1,000 words minimum; 1,600 words maximum; 1,250 words average.
How to Contact: Send complete ms with SASE. Photocopied submissions OK. Sample copy $1.50 with 10x13 SAE and 86¢ postage. Free fiction guidelines with SASE.
Payment: 1 contributor's copy. No extra charge up to 5; $1 charge each thereafter.
Terms: Publication copyrighted.
Tips: "We publish an annual issue featuring poetry, fiction and photography in August (deadline July 1). That's the issue in which most of our fiction is published."

SOME OTHER MAGAZINE, Robert Richman, 47 Hazen Ct., Wayne NJ 07470. Editors: Robert Richman and Barry Schwabsky. Fiction, confession and poetry magazine for literary types. Biannual. Estab. December 1978. Circ. 200.
Needs: Literary, contemporary, erotica, confession and translations. Buys 1 ms/issue, 2 mss/year. Length: 500-1,000 words. Critiques rejected mss "when there is time."
How to Contact: Send complete ms with SASE. Reports in 1 month on mss.
Payment: Pays in contributor's copies.
Terms: Pays on publication; rights revert to author. Publication copyrighted.
Tips: "Be bold, funny, parodic. Don't be shocking or avant-garde just for the sake of being so." Mss are rejected because of abysmal quality. It seems that most 'writers' have no regard for the demands of art and are interested only in seeing their names in print; also, a surprising number of submissions are totally out of character with the kind of material we publish, and therefore we can assume they have never seen our publication."

SONORA REVIEW, University of Arizona, Department of English, Tucson AZ 85721. Editors: Marvin Diogenes, David Rivard. Fiction Editors: Susan Sample, Greg Kayko, Leslie Johnson. *The Sonora Review* publishes short fiction and poetry of high literary quality. Semiannual. Estab. August 1980. Circ. 500-700.
Needs: Literary. "We are open to a wide range of stories with accessibility and vitality being important in any case. We're not interested in genre fiction, formula work." Buys 4-6 mss/issue. Length: open, though prefers work under 25 pages.
How to Contact: Send complete ms with SASE. Reports in 1 month on mss. Sample copy $3.

Payment: 3 free author's copies. $2 charge for extras. Annual cash prizes.
Terms: Acquires first North American serial rights.
Tips: "We ask that writers send us mss they have confidence in. All mss are read carefully and we try to make brief comments if time permits. Our hope is that an author will keep us interested in his or her treatment of a subject by using fresh details and writing with an authority that is absorbing." Mss are rejected because "1) we only have space for 6-8 manuscripts out of several hundred submissions annually, and 2) most of the manuscripts we receive have some merit, but are not of publishable quality."

SOUNDINGS EAST, English Dept., Salem State College, Salem MA 01970. (617)745-0556, Ext. 2333. Advisory Editor: Claire Keyes. "No theme necessarily. Mainly a college audience, but we also distribute to libraries throughout the country." Biannual. Estab. 1973. Circ. 2,000.
Needs: Literary and contemporary. No juvenile. Publishes 2 mss/issue. Receives 5-7 unsolicited fiction mss each month. Length: 2,500-10,000 words. "We are open to short pieces as well as to long works." Critiques rejected mss "when there is time."
How to Contact: Send complete ms with SASE only between September and March. Reports in 2 months on mss. Sample copy $2.
Payment: 2 free author's copies.
Terms: All publication rights revert to authors.
Tips: "The writer should read a few of our issues to get a sense of the range of fiction we publish. The mss should be clean-that is, clearly typed with no hand-written revisions."

SOURCE, Queens Council on the Arts, 161-04 Jamaica Ave., Jamaica NY 11432. (212)291-1100. Editor: Marie Ponsot. Coordinator: Lucy Angeleri. A literary magazine of fiction, poetry, criticism, essays, book reviews, interviews, etc., for college educated, those interested in quality writing. Annual. Estab. 1976. Circ. 600.
Needs: Literary, contemporary, feminist, gay/lesbian and translations. "We will take horror, fantasy, science fiction, if they are done in a literary vein. We are not interested in slickly done magazine style fiction. No gothic or romance." Length: 2,500 words maximum.
How to Contact: Send complete ms with SASE. Reports in 4-6 months on mss. Sample copy $1.50.
Payment: Free author's copy. $1 charge for extras.
Terms: Acquires one-time rights.

SOUTH CAROLINA REVIEW, Clemson University, Clemson SC 29631. (803)656-3229. Editors: R.J. Calhoun and R.W. Hill. Managing Editor: Carol Johnston. Semiannual. Estab. 1967. Circ. 700.
Needs: Literary, contemporary, humor and ethnic. Receives approximately 50-60 unsolicited fiction mss each month. Critiques rejected mss "when there is time."
How to Contact: Send complete ms with SASE. Reports in 2 months on mss. Sample copy $2.
Payment: Pays in contributor's copies.
Terms: Publication copyrighted.
Tips: Mss are rejected because of "poorly structured stories, or stories without vividness or intensity. Get away from realism."

SOUTH DAKOTA REVIEW, University of South Dakota, Box 111, University Exchange, Vermillion SD 57069. (605)677-5229. Editor: John R. Milton. Literary magazine for university and college audiences and their equivalent. Emphasis is on the West and its writers, but will accept mss from anywhere. Issues are generally fiction and poetry with some literary essays. Specific needs vary according to budget and other conditions. Quarterly. Estab. 1963. Circ. 600.
Needs: Literary, contemporary, ethnic, experimental, excerpted novel, translations. "We like very well-written stories. Western American setting appeals, but not necessary. No formula stories, sports, or adolescent 'I' narrator." Receives 30 unsolicited fiction mss/month. Accepts about 8-12 mss/year. Length: 3,000 words minimum; 6,000 words maximum. Send mss on to editors of

other publications. Sometimes recommends markets.
How to Contact: Send complete ms with SASE. Photocopied submissions OK. Reports in 1 month. Sample copy $3.
Payment: 2-4 free author's copies depending on length of ms. $2 charge for extras.
Terms: Acquires first rights and second serial rights. Publication copyrighted.
Tips: $100 to best story published in the magazine every year or every other year. Rejects mss because of "careless writing; often careless typing; stories too personal ('I' confessional); adolescent; working-manuscript, not polished; subject matter that editor finds trivial."

SOUTHERN HUMANITIES REVIEW, Auburn University, 9090 Haley Center, Auburn University AL 36849. Co-Editors: D.K. Jeffrey and Barbara A. Mowat. "We publish essays, poetry, fiction, and reviews. Our fiction has ranged from very traditional in form and content to very experimental. Literate, college-educated audience. We hope they read it for enlightenment and pleasure both." Quarterly. Estab. 1968. Circ. 750.
Needs: Serious fiction, fantasy, humor. Receives approximately 8-10 unsolicited fiction mss each month. Accepts and prints 1-2 mss/issue, 6-8 mss/year. Length: 500-5,000 words. Critiques rejected mss "when there is time."
How to Contact: Send complete ms with SASE. Reports in 90 days on mss. Sample copy $2.
Payment: 5-10 free author's copies. $2.50 charge for each extra.
Terms: Pays on publication for first rights. Publication copyrighted.
Tips: "Send us the ms with SASE. If we like it, we'll take it or we'll recommend changes. If we don't like it, we'll send it back as promptly as possible. Read the journal. Send a typewritten, clean copy carefully proofread. We also award annually the Hoepfner Prize of $100 for the best essay or short story of the year."

THE SOUTHERN REVIEW, Louisiana State University, Drawer D, University Station, Baton Rouge LA 70893. (504)388-5108. Editors: Donald E. Stanford and Lewis P. Simpson. A literary publishing critical essays, poetry and fiction for the highly intellectual audience. Quarterly. Estab. 1935. Circ. 3,000.
Needs: Literary and contemporary. "We emphasize style and substantial content. No mystery, fantasy or religious mss." Buys 3-4 mss/issue. Receives approximately 100 unsolicited fiction mss each month. Length: 2,000-10,000 words. Sends mss on to editors of other publications. Sometimes recommends markets.
How to Contact: Send complete ms with SASE. Reports in 2 months on mss. Sample copy $2.00.
Payment: Pays $12-20/printed page. 2 free author's copies.
Terms: Pays on publication for first North American serial rights. "We transfer copyright to author on request." Publication copyrighted.
Tips: "Develop a careful style with characters in depth." Sponsors annual contest for best collection of short stories published during the calendar year.

SOUTHWEST REVIEW, SMU Press, Southern Methodist University, Dallas TX 75275. (214)692-2263. Editor: Charlotte T. Whaley. Fiction Editor: Charlotte T. Whaley. "*Southwest Review* embraces almost every area of adult interest, with emphasis on short fiction, poetry, literary criticism, essays on contemporary affairs, and book reviews. The majority of our readers are college-educated adults, who wish to stay abreast of the latest and best in contemporary fiction, poetry, literary criticism, and books in all but the most specialized disciplines." Quarterly. Estab. 1915. Circ. 1,250.
Needs: Literary and contemporary. "No sentimental, religious, western, poor science fiction, pornographic, true confessions, mysteries, juvenile, serialized novels or condensed novels." Receives approximately 60 unsolicited fiction mss each month. Length: 3,000-5,000 words. Critiques rejected mss "when there is time." Sometimes recommends markets.
How to Contact: Send complete ms with SASE. Reports in 3 months on mss. Sample copy $1. Free guidelines with SASE.

Payment: Pays ½¢/word, plus 4 free author's copies.
Terms: Pays on publication for one-time rights. Publication copyrighted.

SOUTHWESTERN REVIEW, University of Southwestern Louisiana, Box 44691, Lafayette LA 70504. (318)231-6808. Editor: J. Naid Sharif. "Fiction of all sorts but restricted to local authors." Semiannual. Estab. 1975. Circ. 4,000.
Needs: Literary. Buys 10-20 mss/year. Receives approximately 5-25 unsolicited fiction mss each month. Length: 1,500-3,500 words.
How to Contact: "Query first. God only knows when we can report." Free sample copy with 9x11 SASE.
Payment: 2 free author's copies.
Terms: Acquires first rights. Publication copyrighted.
Tips: "It is unlikely we will take your ms unless you are from our region. But who knows? You might have something we think our readers will find interesting. That something will have to be a local theme, topic, etc."

SOU'WESTER, English Dept., Southern Illinois University-Edwardsville, Edwardsville IL 62026. (618)692-2289. Editor-in-Chief: Dickie A. Spurgeon. General magazine of poetry and fiction (to 10,000 words). Published 3 times/year. Estab. 1960. Circ. 300.
Needs: Contemporary, erotica, ethnic, experimental, fantasy, feminist/lesbian, gay, literary, mainstream, translations. Receives 40-50 unsolicited fiction mss/month. Accepts 3 mss/issue, 9 mss/year. Length: 500 words minimum; 10,000 words maximum. Occasionally critiques rejected mss.
How to Contact: Send complete ms with SASE. Simultaneous and photocopied submissions OK. Reports in 4 weeks on mss. Sample copy $1.50.
Payment: 2 contributor's copies. $1.50 charge for extras.
Terms: Acquires all rights. Publication copyrighted.
Tips: "Keep sending us new mss, even though we have rejected earlier work."

SPACE AND TIME, 138 W. 70th St., New York NY 10023. Editor-in-Chief: Gordon Linzner. Magazine of "fantasy fiction of all types and sub-genres (including science fiction)—the less categorizable, the better. *S&T* tends to feature new writers and odd pieces for which there are few if any other markets. Some poetry. *S&T* attracts readers who cannot get enough of this material or who want something new and different. Because it is small, *S&T* can take chances on stories that are either too traditional or too experimental, and prides itself on its variety of styles and story types. Also well illustrated." Published semiannually. Estab. 1966. Circ. 400.
Needs: Adventure, fantasy, horror, humor/satire, supernatural, science fiction. "Actually, will consider almost any type of fiction as long as it has a fantastic slant. No media clones—no tales involving characters/situations that are not your creation (*Star Trek*, et al) except for certain types of satire. No stories based on Von Daniken, etc., type cults." Receives 75-100 unsolicited fiction mss/month. Accepts 12 mss/issue, 24 mss/year. Length: 15,000 words maximum. Occasionally critiques rejected mss. Sometimes recommends markets.
How to Contact: Send complete ms with SASE. Photocopied submissions OK. Reports in 8 weeks on mss. Sample copy $4.
Payment: ¼¢/word and 2 contributor's copies. Charges cover price less 40% contributor discount for extras.
Terms: Pays on acceptance for first North American serial rights. Publication copyrighted.
Tips: "Keep writing and learning your craft."

SPECTRUM MAGAZINE, University of California at Santa Barbara Literary Magazine, Spectrum, Box 14800, University of California, Santa Barbara CA 93107. "We are looking for good fresh poetry and fiction. Our goal is to come up with a good magazine; theme is not important." Directed "mainly to a university and university library audience, and anyone else who will read us." Published annually. Estab. 1957. Circ. 1,000.

Close-up

Morty Sklar
The Spirit That Moves Us Magazine and Press

The Spirit That Moves Us Press and the literary magazine (of the same name) are strictly cottage industries. So closely tied are editor-publisher Morty Sklar's business and personal concerns that survival is a matter of "living as cheaply as possible." He admits his own expenses come second to printing, mailing and author payments. In fact, to keep his publishing interests alive: "I do typesetting for other literary magazines and presses. . . . I have also driven a bus, worked as a drug counselor, and have done many other things."

Sklar does all his press work—reading, selecting and developing manuscripts with the authors; typesetting on a 12-year-old IBM table-top composer; and the layout—at home in a small apartment plus basement storage area. The staff consists of his wife Shelley Sterling-Sklar, who tends to subscriber lists, handles manuscript submissions and processes orders; and volunteers, who help with promotional mailings in return for books or copies of his literary periodical, *The Spirit That Moves Us*.

The magazine evolved from Sklar's "desire to pack between its covers the most excellent poetry and fiction I could find and a desire to define my own aesthetics and possibly influence the way others think of poetry and fiction." The first issue in 1975 was all poetry, but an all-fiction issue is planned for fall 1983, and Sklar is currently reading stories and parts of novels for this publication.

TSTMU Press published *Editor's Choice: Literature & Graphics From the U.S. Small Press, 1966-1977*, consisting of nominated selections from editors of other little magazines and small presses. In November 1982 they did *TSTMU Reader: Seventh Anniversary Anthology*, comprising 104 stories, poems and visuals from the 1975-1982 issues of the magazine, including reproductions of all covers. Occasionally special theme issues are planned, such as "Nuke Rebuke: Writers & Artists Against Nu-

Photo by John Riley

clear Energy & Weapons," in the making for spring 1983.

"Write what you feel most and is closest to your experience and concerns," Sklar urges the fiction writer. "I look for concern for and expression of life and living in the short story, as well as in other forms of writing and other arts. I'm open to any style. . . . I hope people will write closer to their lives and not follow fashions." He adds a practical postscript: "Don't depend on writing for your income."

In spite of the difficult economic times, Morty Sklar is confident the serious literary/little magazines will survive. In the case of *TSTMU*, government funding through the National Endowment for the Arts and underwriting from the Iowa Arts Council and the Coordinating Council of Literary Magazines help pay about half the expenses, which are tax-exempt. Money is also solicited from local businesses and foundations. And of course, there is constant promotion: a complete catalog out in November 1982, direct-mail advertising, paid and exchange ads. Sklar notes the two basic differences between *TSTMU* and commercial magazines: "We publish only what we love best, and we just don't get the exposure (mainly distribution) the commercials do. The first we don't want to change. The second we do."
—*Catherine Cooper*

Needs: "We would prefer relaxed literature that isn't trying to *do* anything; stories about people." Receives 25-30 unsolicited fiction mss/month. Accepts 100 mss/issue; 100 mss/year. Occasionally critiques rejected mss.

How to Contact: Send complete ms with SASE. Photocopied submissions OK. Reports in 1 year on mss ("we are once a year only."). Sample copy $3.

Payment: 2 contributor's copies. $3 charge for extras.

Terms: Pays on publication for one-time rights and possible anthology reprint. Publication copyrighted.

Tips: "Relax and write. Avoid politics, suicide, murder and sensationalist subjects."

SPIDERWEB, (formerly *Skullduggery*), Corsair Press, Box F, MIT Branch Station, Cambridge MA 02139. (617)267-0051. Editor: Ron Rouse. Magazine. "We publish a wide range of mystery fiction: detective, crime, suspense, horror, humor, even science fiction. We look for stories with strong plots and well-defined characters. We are open to unusual sorts of stories." Published quarterly. Estab. 1980. Circ. 1,000.

Needs: Horror, suspense/mystery. "Avoid sketches or mood pieces; avoid stories where the ending is obvious, implausible, or comes out of left field. Avoid stories based on gimmicks. Avoid stories where the characters are left untouched by the actions they perform." Receives approximately 300 unsolicited fiction mss/month. Buys 7 mss/issue, 28-30 mss/year. Length: 6,000 words maximum; 5,000 words average. Occasionally critiques rejected mss. Sometimes recommends other markets.

How to Contact: Send complete ms with SASE. Reports in 1 month ("if longer, we're considering it for publication"). Sample copy $2.50. Free fiction guidelines for SAE and 1 first class stamp.

Payment: Up to 1½¢/word and 2 contributor's copies.

Terms: Pays on publication for first world serial rights. Publication copyrighted.

Tips: "We are looking for a type of story that differs sufficiently from what others have been and still are publishing as 'mystery stories'. Consequently, stories written with the larger market in mind rarely click with us."

THE SPIRIT THAT MOVES US, The Spirit That Moves Us Press, Inc., Box 1585, Iowa City IA 52244. (319)338-5569. Editor: Morty Sklar. Publishes fiction, poetry, essays and artwork. "We want feeling and imagination for lovers of real, not academic writing, those who care for work coming from the human experience." Semiannual. Estab. 1975. Circ. 800.

Needs: Literary and contemporary, men's, women's, feminist, gay/lesbian, humor, ethnic and translations. No sensational. Buys 1-2 mss/issue and 25 mss for special fiction issue. Receives approximately 30 unsolicited fiction mss each month. Length: 7,000 words maximum. Critiques rejected mss "when there is time. We're publishing a special fiction issue in 1983. Deadline is January 1, 1983."

How to Contact: Send ms and SASE. Reports in 1 week to 1 month on mss. Sample copy $2.

Payment: 2 free author's copies and $10-20 for special fiction issue (see deadline above). 40% discount on extras.

Terms: Pays on publication for first rights. Publication copyrighted.

Tips: "We're small but good and well-reviewed. Send the work you love best. Write from yourself and not from what you feel is the fashion or what the editor wants. This editor wants what you want if it has heart, guts, imagination and skill. Aside from the obvious reason for rejection, poor writing, the main reason for rejection is lack of human concerns or moral conviction . . . that is, the writer seems to be concerned with style more than content. Read a copy of the magazine you'll be submitting work to. Don't rely on your writing for money unless you're in it for the money. Have time to write, as much time as you can get (be anti-social if necessary). We have published a 504 page volume of fiction, poetry, essays and graphics entitled *Editor's Choice: Literature & Graphics From The US Small Press, 1965-1977*. If anything can succinctly express our taste and needs, it will."

SPITBALL ,231 E. 7th St., Covington KY 41011. Editor: Mike Shannon. Magazine publishing "fiction and poetry about *baseball* exclusively for an educated, literary segment of the baseball fan population." Quarterly. Estab. 1981. Circ. 500.

Needs: Confession, contemporary, experimental, historical, literary, mainstream, suspense. "Our only requirement concerning the type of fiction written is that the story be *primarily* about baseball." Receives "10 or so" unsolicited fiction mss/year. Accepts 1-2 mss/year, "7-8 if we would receive that many publishable manuscripts." Length: 2,500 words maximum. "Almost always critiques" rejected mss; "sometimes at length."

How to Contact: Send complete ms with SASE. Simultaneous, photocopied and previously published submissions OK. Reports in 1 month on mss. Sample copy $2 and business size envelope and 1 first class stamp.

Payment: "No monetary payment at present. We may offer nominal payment in the future." 1 free contributor's copy per issue in which work appears.

Terms: Acquires first North American serial rights. Publication copyrighted. "We sponsor an annual fiction contest. We award baseball-related merchandise prizes to winners."

Tips: "Our audience is mostly college educated and knowledgable about baseball. The stories we have published so far have been very well written and displayed a firm grasp of the baseball world and its people. In short, audience response has been great because the stories are simply good as stories. Thus, mere use of baseball as subject is no guarantee of acceptance. We need many submissions. Unlike many literary magazines, we have no backlog of accepted material. Thus, we can publish good stories almost immediately. Submit, get our feed-back and keep trying. We take pains to encourage and direct writers of promise. Remember, however, that we must have stories about baseball. If one doesn't know how to go about writing readable baseball *fiction*, he should read other writers' work. Consult Charles Einsteins' *Fireside Books of Baseball* as a start. Also read sample *Spitballs*."

STAND, US address: 45 Old Peterborough Rd., Jaffrey NH 03452 and 179 Windgrove Rd., Newcastle upon Tyne, Newcastle, England NE49DA. Editors: Jon Silkin, David McDuff, Lorna Tracy (England) and Jim Kates (US). "Our audience is the common reader, in the sense that Virginia Woolf and Samuel Johnson used the term. Presumably readers' minds and sensibilities are stimulated and that is why they read the magazine." Quarterly. Estab. 1952. Circ. 6,000.

Needs: Literary, contemporary and translations. "We're all for humor if it provokes *thoughtful* laughter. We are just as interested in work by women as by men and work that makes a subtle argument for a case. Don't want propaganda, mindless violence or any 'throw-away' stories, any tricky endings, or dreary 'social realism,' or dreary 'art-about-art,' for that matter. No formula fiction; what we want is good writing, with a high degree of internal organization. Plots and 'themes' don't interest us." Buys 15-20 mss/year. Receives 10-20 unsolicited fiction mss each month. Length: 10,000 words. Critiques rejected mss "when there is time."

How to Contact: Send complete ms with SASE. Reports in 2 months on mss. Sample copy $2.50

Payment: Pays $25/1,000 words. Free author's copy. $2.50 less 1/3 charge for extras.

Terms: Pays on publication for first North American serial and first British serial rights. Publication copyrighted.

Tips: "Write well and honestly. Study this magazine before sending work; don't send us work that's been taken by some other publication, or that is under consideration elsewhere. We want live, energetic fiction, with its own strong vision. We report promptly. Use the American address."

STARDATE, Stardate Press, c/o Randall Landers, Box 21224, Emory University, Atlanta GA 30322. (404)633-9251. Editor-in-Chief: Randall Landers. Co-Editor: Rick Endres. Magazine of *Star Trek* fiction and nonfiction articles for *Star Trek* fans. Currently published annually. Estab. 1979. Circ. 350+.

Needs: Adventure, comics, condensed novel, experimental, fantasy, horror, humor/satire, novels, psychic/supernatural, romance (contemporary), science fiction, serialized/excerpted novel, suspense/mystery. "No non-*Star Trek* material considered or printed. No hard core pornography, monologues, homosexual, Kraith, Nu Ormenel, Kershu." Receives 2 unsolicited fiction mss/ month. Accepts 3-4 mss/issue, 10-15 mss/year. Length: no preference. Occasionally critiques rejected mss "upon request." Sometimes recommends markets.

How to Contact: Query first with SASE. Simultaneous, photocopied and previously published (after 18 months) submissions OK. Reports in 2 weeks on queries, 3 weeks on mss. Cost of sample copy depends on the issue. Free fiction guidelines with legal SAE and 1 first class stamp.

Payment: 1 contributor's copy.

Terms: Pays on publication for one-time rights (not to be reprinted for 18 months after publication in *Stardate*. Author owns all other rights, including sale of story to other publications).

Tips: "Be willing to listen to criticism, open-minded to changes, patient for responses. Editors do not enjoy snide comments regarding editing, so don't ever make them and don't think your work cannot be imperfect, either."

STARDUST, The Canadian SF Magazine ,Stardust Publications, 1170 Davenport Rd., Toronto, Ontario, Canada (416)653-9189. Editor: Forrest Fusco, Jr. Magazine of science fiction and fantasy for a general young adult audieince. Quarterly. Estab. 1976. Circ. 5,000.

Needs: Adventure, erotica, experimental, fantasy, feminist/lesbian, humor/satire, psychic/supernatural, science fiction. "All must be SF or fantasy-oriented. No juvenile stuff." Receives 50-75 unsolicited fiction mss/month. Buys 5-6 mss/issue, 20-24 mss/year. Length: 1,000 words minimum, 10,000 words maximum, 4,000 words average. Occasionally critiques rejected mss.

How to Contact: Send complete ms with SASE. Simultaneous, photocopied and previously published submissions OK. Reports in 2 weeks on mss. Sample copy $2.

Payment: $15 minimum; 1¢/word maximum.

Terms: Pays on publication for first North American serial rights. Publication copyrighted.

Tips: "Start with the shorter lengths. Use narrative hook."

STAR-WEB PAPER, All This & Less Publishers, General Delivery, Mesilla NM 88046. (505)523-7923. Editor: Thomas Michael Fisher. Magazine of "20th-century consciousness, all types of material" for "enlightened doers of the literate world." Annually. Estab. 1974.

Needs: Comics, condensed novel, contemporary, erotica, ethnic, experimental, fantasy, humor/satire, literary, prose poem, psychic/supernatural, serialized/excerpted novel, translations, women's. Receives 10 unsolicited mss/month. Accepts 5 mss/issue; 5 mss/year. Occasionally critiques rejected mss.

How to Contact: Query first with SASE. Reports in 1 month on queries. Sample copy $4. Fiction guidelines free with SAE.

Payment: Pays in 2 contributor's copies.

Terms: Publication copyrighted.

Tips: "Try us. Go for it."

START MAGAZINE, Start Press, Burslem Leisure Centre, Market Place, Burslem, Stoke on Trent, Staffs, England. ST6 3DS. Tel. 813363. Editor-in-Chief: Paul Smith. "*Start* is a regional arts review for writers, artists and the general populace of North Staffordshire and the surrounding area. We publish only previously unpublished material and also invite submissions from freelance arts critics." Published bimonthly. Estab. 1978. Circ. 1,800.

Needs: Condensed novel, contemporary, ethnic, experimental, literary, prose poem, science fiction, serialized/excerpted novel, translations, narrative. Receives 10-20 unsolicited fiction mss/month. Accepts 1-6 mss/issue, 6-36 mss/year. Length: 250 words minimum; 3,000 words maximum; 1,500 words average. Occasionally critiques rejected mss.

How to Contact: Send complete ms with IRC. Photocopied submissions OK. Reports in 6 weeks on mss. Free sample copy with SAE and 4 first class stamps (IRC).

Payment: 1 contributor's copy.

Terms: Acquires first rights.

Tips: "Read the magazine—be innovative—if the writer does not live locally he or she must be outstanding in the mss. Nothing longer than 3,000 words. *Start* is a proving ground for new writing; we are looking for crafted innovation."

STONE SOUP, THE MAGAZINE BY CHILDREN, Children's Art Foundation, Box 83, Santa Cruz CA 95063. (408)426-5557. Editor: Gerry Mandel. Theme: Stories, poems, book reviews, and art by children up to age 12. Readership: children, librarians, educators. Published 5 times/year. Estab. 1973. Circ. 10,000.
Needs: Serious writing by children on themes based on their own experiences. No clichés, no formulas, no writing exercises; original work only. Accepts approx. 15 mss/issue. Receives approximately 200 unsolicited fiction mss each month. Length: 150-2,500 words. Critiques rejected mss upon request."
How to Contact: Send complete ms with SASE. Reports in 2 months on mss. Sample copy $3. Free guidelines with SASE.
Payment: 2 free author's copies. $1.50 charge for extras.
Terms: Acquires all rights. Publication copyrighted.
Tips: Mss are rejected because they are "derivatives of movies, TV, comic books; or classroom assignments or other formulas."

THE STONY THURSDAY BOOK, 128 Sycamore Ave., Rathbane, Limerick, Ireland. Editor-in-Chief: John Liddy. "Literary magazine: prose, story, poetry, review, illustration." Published semiannually. Estab. 1975. Circ. 1,500.
Needs: Contemporary, humor/satire, serialized/excerpted novel, translations. No sloppy work. Length: 2,000 words minimum; 3,000 words maximum. Occasionally critiques rejected mss.
How to Contact: Send complete ms with IRC. Simultaneous and photocopied submissions OK. Reports in 3 months on mss. Sample copy $4. Free fiction guidelines with SAE and 1 first class stamp (IRC).
Payment: 2 contributor's copies.
Terms: Publication copyrighted.
Tips: "The writer should believe in what is written." Issue No.8 (9/82) is a special feature on American writing.

STORY QUARTERLY, Story Quarterly, Inc., Box 1416, Northbrook IL 60062. (312)831-4684. Co-Editors: F.R. Katz, Janine Warsaw, Dolores Weinberg. A magazine devoted to the short story and committed to a full range of styles and forms. Also features interviews with writers. Readership: "literate readers and writers of short fiction who read us for our quality and variety." Published irregularly. Estab. 1975. Circ. 3,000.
Needs: Literary, contemporary, women's, humor, self-contained novel excerpts. "No slick women's magazine material with contrived endings. No science fiction, religious, psychic, horror, romantic, juvenile, or young adult material." Accepts 12-15 mss/issue, 20-30 mss/year. Receives 100-125 unsolicited fiction mss each month. Length: 5,000 words maximum. Critiques rejected mss "when there is time." Sometimes recommends markets.
How to Contact: Send complete ms with SASE. Reports in 3 months on mss. Sample copy $3.00.
Payment: 3 free author's copies.
Terms: Acquires one-time rights. Copyright reverts to author after publication. Publication copyrighted.
Tips: "Have sensibility, a mastery of language and technique, relationships, and a non-imitative, fresh voice." Mss are rejected because of "clumsy prose; lack of story."

STREET BAGEL, Street Bagel Press, 90 Atlantic Dr., Parsippany, N.J. 07054. Editor-in-Chief: Charlie Lebeda. Fiction editor: Charlotte Kinskey. Magazine. "We publish fiction, poetry and experimental writing by new and established writers and poets." Published annually. Estab. 1979. Circ. 200.

Needs: Contemporary, experimental, humor/satire, literary, men's, prose poem, women's. Accepts 1-2 mss/issue, 7-10 mss/year. Length: 8,000 words maximum. Occasionally critiques rejected mss.

How to Contact: Send complete ms with SASE. Photocopied submissions OK. Reports in 8 weeks. Sample copy $1.50.

Payment: 2 contributor's copies.

Terms: Acquires all rights. Publication copyrighted.

Tips: "It is essential that a beginning writer have a theme to power her/his story through the use of time, place, point-of-view, characterization, dialogue or plot."

STREET MAGAZINE ,Street Press, Box 555, Port Jefferson NY 11777. (516)584-5545. Editor: Graham Everett. Thematic. Quarterly (pending). Estab. 1973. Circ 750.

Needs: Adventure, condensed novel, confession, contemporary, ethnic, experimental, fantasy, historical (general), horror, psychic/supernatural, religious/inspirational, romance (contemporary), serialized/excerpted novel, suspense/mystery. "Stories should be short, tight, precise—as much as needed." Receives "not enough" unsolicited fiction mss/month. Buys various number mss/year. Length: 10 pp. double spaced average. Occasionally critiques rejected mss.

How to Contact: Query first with sample and SASE. Photocopied submissions OK, especially if they're readable." Reports in 2 months on queries. Sample copy $3.

Payment: $0-100; contributor's copies; 60% of list price charge for extras.

Terms: Publication copyrighted.

Tips: "Often positive/often downright hostile" response to stories. "No schools-of-thought stylists unless it's strong satire. Don't expect a thing."

STROKER MAGAZINE, 129 2nd Ave., # 3, New York NY 10003. Editor: Irving Stettner. Un-literary literary review interested in sincerity, verve, anger, humor and beauty. For an intelligent audience—non-academic, non-media dazed in the US and throughout the world." Published 3-4 times/year. Estab. 1974, 23 issues to date. Circ. 500.

Needs: Literary, contemporary. No academic material. Length: "3-5 pages preferred but not essential." Sometimes recommends markets.

How to Contact: Send complete ms with SASE. Reports in 6 weeks. Sample copy $2.

Payment: 2 free author's copies. $1 charge for extras.

Terms: Acquires one-time rights.

STUDIA MYSTICA, The Foundation, California State University, 6000 J St., Sacramento CA 95819. (916)454-6444. Editor: Mary E. Giles. Magazine featuring "mystical experience for an artistic, scholarly, religious audience." Quarterly. Estab. 1978. Circ. 400.

Needs: Literary, religious/inspirational. No occult stories. Receives 4 unsolicited fiction mss/month. Accepts 2 mss/year. Length: 3,500 words minimum. Occasionally critiques rejected mss.

How to Contact: Send complete ms with SASE. Simultaneous submissions OK. Reports in 4 weeks on mss. Sample copy $4.

Terms: Acquires first rights. Publication copyrighted.

THE SUN, The Sun Publishing Company, Inc., 412 W. Rosemary St., Chapel Hill NC 27514. (919)942-5282. Editor: Sy Safransky. "*The Sun* is a magazine of ideas. We publish all kinds of writing—fiction, articles, poetry. Our only criteria are that the writing make sense and enrich our common space. We direct *The Sun* toward interests which move us, and we trust our readers will respond." Monthly. Estab. 1974. Circ. 10,000.

Needs: Open to all fiction. Accepts 1 ms/issue. Receives approximately 10 unsolicited fiction mss each month. Length: 5,000 words maximum. Critiques rejected mss "when there is time."

How to Contact: Send complete ms with SASE. Reports in 1 month. Free sample copy.

Payment: 5 free author's copies and a complimentary subscription.

Terms: Acquires one-time rights. Publication copyrighted.

Tips: "Nothing's necessarily 'wrong' with most rejected mss—just not what we're looking for. Helpful to read magazine first."

SUN DOG, English Department, 4th Floor Williams, Florida State University, Tallahassee FL 32306. (904)644-4230. Editors: Joe Taylor, Jesse Kercheval, and Allen Woodman. Published biannually. Estab. 1979. Circ. 2,000.
Needs: "We want stories which are well-written, beautifully written, with striking images, incidents, and characters. We are interested more in quality than in style or genre." Accepts 10-20 mss/year. Receives approximately 100 unsolicited fiction mss each month. Critiques rejected mss "when there is time."
How to Contact: Send complete ms with SASE. Typed, double-spaced, on good bond.
Payment: 3 free author's copies. $2 charge for extras. Each issue of *Sun Dog* awards $100 to the outstanding story as picked by an independent judge.
Terms: Acquires one-time rights which then revert to author. Publication copyrighted.
Tips: Mss rejected because of "poor plots; not enough characterization."

SUN TRACKS: AN AMERICAN INDIAN LITERARY SERIES, Sun Tracks, Department of English, University of Arizona, Tucson AZ 85721. Editor: Larry Evers. "We publish material that comes from or draws on native American literary traditions. For a literary audience interested in American Indian affairs." Published irregularly. Estab. 1971. Circ. 1,500.
Needs: Ethnic (American Indian) only. Monograph length preferred.
How to Contact: Query or send complete ms with SASE. Reports in 2 weeks on queries, 1 month on mss. Send SASE for book prices.
Payment: 2 free author's copies. Charge for extras: at "our cost."
Terms: Acquires first rights.

SYRACUSE SCHOLAR, An Interdisciplinary Journal of Ideas, Syracuse University, 220 Sims 3, Syracuse NY 13210. (315)423-3501. Editor-in-Chief: Peter B. Goldman. "We are an interdisciplinary journal interested in nonfiction (commentaries on matters of general scholarly or public interest, discussions of controversial issues, review essays, scientific articles appropriate to a general readership), as well as creative literary works such as short stories or poetry." Published semiannually. Estab. 1979. Circ. 10,000.
Needs: Condensed novel, contemporary, ethnic, experimental, fantasy, historical (general), humor/satire, literary, mainstream, prose poem, science fiction. "We will consider almost any category if the material is directed to an educated readership and is handled with literary excellence, taste and style. Contributors must have some past or present affiliation with Syracuse University. No poor writing or pornography." Receives approximately 5 unsolicited fiction mss/month. Length: 4,000 words miminum. Occasionally critiques rejected mss.
How to Contact: Send complete ms with SASE. Simultaneous and photocopied submissions OK. Reports in several months on mss. Sample copy free with 9½x12½ SAE and 63¢ postage. Free guidelines with SASE.
Payment: "Competitive" for short stories; 50 contributor's copies.
Terms: Pays on publication for one-time rights. Publication copyrighted.
Tips: "Send us your work, bearing in mind that we have a serious, well-educated readership."

TAMARISK, 319 S. Juniper St., Philadelphia PA 19107. (201)327-7469. Editors: Dennis Barone and Deborah Ducoff-Barone. "A literary magazine of fiction, poetry, photography, reviews for an educated literary audience." Biannual. Estab. 1975. Circ. 300.
Needs: Literary. Accepts 1-2 mss/issue, 2-4 mss/year.
How to Contact: Query only. Reports immediately. Sample copy $1 with 8x11 SAE plus 63¢ postage.
Payment: 3 free author's copies. $1 charge for extras. "We usually pay small amounts."
Terms: Acquires one-time rights.
Tips: Looks for clarity and innovation in mss.

TAYLOR ONE-SHOTS, Taylor Publications, Box 19, SharWinn Estates, Redfield SD 57469. (605)472-2641. Editor-in-Chief: Kathleen Taylor. "*TOS* issues will be small press publications, irregularly published, each pertaining to a single subject explored in various ways in the fields of science fiction/fantasy etc., for science fiction/fantasy, horror, sword and sorcery buffs—fans of small press publications.'' Published irregularly. Estab. 1981. Circ. approximately 200.

Needs: Comics, experimental, fantasy, horror, humor/satire, prose poem, science fiction, suspense/mystery. ''No thinly disguised religious dogma.'' Receives 5-15 unsolicited fiction mss/month. Buys 15-20 mss/issue. Length: 500 words minimum; 10,000 words maximum; 3,000 words average. Occasionally critiques rejected mss.

How to Contact: Query first with SASE. Simultaneous, photocopied and previously published submissions OK. Reports in 3 weeks on queries, 3 weeks on mss. Sample copy $2.50. Free guidelines with # 10 SAE and 1 first class stamp.

Payment: $3.50-$10 and 1 contributor's copy. Charges publisher's cost up to 5 copies for extras.

Terms: Pays on publication for first rights, second serial rights and first North American serial rights. Publication copyrighted.

Tips: ''Be open to rewrite suggestions. Query as to which subject is to be featured in the issue accepting submissions at that time. Please, please enclose return postage—study the guideline sheet. Make sure your story pertains to the issue subject.''

TELESCOPE, The Galileo Press, Box 2117, Iowa City IA 52244. Contact: Editor-in-Chief. ''*Telescope* is a review of literature. Poetry, criticism, fiction, drama, interviews, and more can be found within. For the literate, sensitive, interested in what's new and progressive in literature.'' Published 3 times/year. Estab. 1981. Circ. 750.

Needs: Contemporary, ethnic, experimental, literary, prose poem, translations. ''By 'literary' we mean anything well written, with a meshing of content *and* form, style, etc.'' Receives very few unsolicited fiction mss/month. Buys 1-4 mss/issue. Length: no preference. Occasionally critiques rejected mss.

How to Contact: Send complete ms with SASE. Reports in 1-2 months on mss. Sample copy $1 or 6½x9½ SAE and 5 first class stamps.

Payment: $3-5 and 2 contributor's copies.

Terms: Pays on acceptance for first North American serial rights. Publication copyrighted.

Tips: ''Check a sample copy first.''

TEMPEST, Earthwise Publications, Inc., Box 680536, Miami FL 33168. Editor: Barbara Holley. Fiction Editor: Kaye Carter. A journal with avant-garde theme. Biannual. Estab. 1979. Circ. 200.

Needs: Human interest. No pornography or religious submissions.

How to Contact: Query with clips of published work. SASE for query, ms. Reports in 1 month. Sample copy $3.

Payment: $5-$25.

Terms: Pays on publication for first North American serial rights.

Tips: ''No mss from June 30-Sept. 5, please.''

THE TEXAS REVIEW, Sam Houston State University Press, Huntsville, TX 77341. (713)294-1423. Editor: Paul Ruffin. Fiction Editor: Phillip Parotti. ''We publish top quality poetry, fiction, articles, interviews, and reviews for a general audience.'' Semiannual. Estab. 1976 (as *Sam Houston Literary Review*). Circ. 500.

Needs: Literary, contemporary. ''We are eager enough to consider fiction of quality, no matter what its theme or subject matter. No juvenile fiction.'' Accepts 4 mss/issue. Receives approximately 10-20 unsolicited fiction mss each month. Length: 500-10,000 words. Critiques rejected mss ''when there is time.''

How to Contact: Send complete ms with SASE. Reports in 2 months on mss. Sample copy $2.00.

Payment: Free author's copies plus one year subscription.

Terms: Acquires all rights. Publication copyrighted.

Tips: ''We publish many new writers.''

13TH MOON, 13th Moon, Inc., Drawer F, Inwood Station, New York NY 10034. (212)569-7614. Editors: Marilyn Nacker, Ellen Marie Bissert. "*13th Moon* is a literary magazine publishing quality fiction by women with a feminist perspective. The audience is intelligent, sophisticated, and interested in women's issues and culture." Biannual. Estab. 1973. Circ. 4,000.
Needs: Working-class feminist, lesbian, Third World. "No traditional, commercial women's fiction." Accepts 2-4 mss/issue; 4-10 mss/year. Receives approximately 150 unsolicited fiction mss each month. Length: 4,000-15,000 words. Critiques rejected mss "when there is time."
How to Contact: Send complete ms with SASE. Reports "between 1 week and 6 months depending on mss." Sample copy $5.95 plus 75¢ postage.
Payment: Free author's copies.
Terms: Acquires first rights. Publication copyrighted.
Tips: "Read the magazine before submitting work. We're interested in receiving more material about women's working-class experience and also experimental fiction for our special fiction issue."

THE THREEPENNY REVIEW, Box 9131, Berkeley CA 94709. (415)849-4545. Editor: Wendy Lesser. Publishes "literature and performing arts reviews, essays, fiction, poetry, and other reviews for a wide-ranging audience including anyone interested in the arts." Quarterly. Estab. winter/spring 1980. Circ. 10,000.
Needs: Short fiction. Accepts 1 ms/issue; 4 mss/year. Receives approximately 20-30 unsolicited fiction mss each month. Length: 3,000-5,000 words.
How to Contact: Query. SASE for query, ms. Reports in 2 weeks on queries, 2 months on mss. Sample copy $2 with 9x12 SAE plus 70¢ postage. Guidelines for legal-sized SASE.
Payment: Six free subscriptions for author and 5 friends. No cash payment at present.
Terms: Acquires first rights. Publication copyrighted.
Tips: "We receive approximately 100 times as many stories as we can publish in a given quarter. Also, most of the stories we receive are either stylistically experimental without having any interesting plot or characters, or naively sentimental."

THRESHOLD OF FANTASY, A Magazine of Fantastic Literature, Fandom Unlimited Enterprises, Box 70868, Sunnyvale CA 94086. (415)960-1151. Editor: Randall D. Larson. Magazine of original short fiction (fantasy, science fiction and horror) for active SF and fantasy fans. Semiannually. Estab. 1982. Circ. 600.
Needs: Fantasy, horror, humor/satire, psychic/supernatural, science fiction. No "rehashes of familiar plots or themes (unless featuring a twist)." Receives 5 unsolicited fiction mss/month. Accepts 7-10 mss/issue. Length: 8,000 words maximum; 4,000 words average. Occasionally critiques rejected mss.
How to Contact: Send complete ms with SASE. Photocopied submissions OK. Reports in 4 weeks on mss. Sample copy $2. Fiction guidelines free with letter size SASE.
Payment: 1-10 free contributor's copies; 40% discount for additional copies.
Terms: Acquires first North American serial or one-time rights. Publication copyrighted.
Tips: Readers are "enthusiastic, with constructive criticism. Submit ms in clean, professional format with cover letter."

THUNDER MOUNTAIN REVIEW, Thunder City Press, Box 11126, Birmingham AL 35202. Editor/Publisher: Steven Ford Brown. "A magazine of poetry, translations and reviews; will concentrate on special kinds of fiction, especially experimental and the prose poem form, etc. For the college level, university, literary type audience, the general public in the future." Biannual. Estab. 1979. Circ. 500.
Needs: Literary, contemporary, translations. "No junk or beginner pieces." Accepts 1 ms/issue, 1-2 mss/year. Receives approximately 5 unsolicited fiction mss each month. Length: 10,000 words maximum.
How to Contact: Query. SASE for query, ms. Reports in 2 weeks. Sample copy $5.
Payment: Free author's copies.

Terms: Acquires first North American serial rights. Publication copyrighted.
Tips: "Read the magazine and be an accomplished writer. It is hard to break in the first time. There really is a need for good fiction these days and many editors are unable to find it." Sometimes sponsors awards.

TIME CAPSULE, Prose and Poetry from America's Prisons, Time Capsule, Inc., Box 1185, New York NY 10116. (212)675-7197. Editor-in-Chief: Marc Crawford. Fiction Editor: Matthew Hejna. "*Time Capsule* publishes fiction and poetry written by prisoners dealing with real human problems and concerns in social situations for inmates, people involved with corrections, the literary community, educators, students and the general public." Published quarterly. Estab. 1980. Circ. 3,000.
Needs: Comics, contemporary, ethnic, experimental, feminist/lesbian, gay, historical (general), humor/satire, juvenile, literary, mainstream, men's, prose poem, science fiction, serialized/ excerpted novel, suspense/mystery, translations, women's, young adult. "Any well-written story with relevance to the human condition. Themes need not be prison related; work should reflect common experience; fantasy and science fiction as escapism not encouraged." Receives 30 unsolicited fiction mss/month. Buys 5 mss/issue, 20 mss/year. Length: 1,000 words minimum; 5,000 words maximum; 2,500 words average. Occasionally critiques rejected mss.
How to Contact: Send complete ms. SASE preferred. Simultaneous and photocopied submissions OK. Reports in 2 months. Free sample copy for 9x12 SAE and 4 first class stamps; free guidelines with SASE.
Payment: 10 free contributor's copies.
Terms: Pays on publication for one-time rights. Publication copyrighted.
Tips: "Create out of personal experience; picture each sentence as a photograph; keep story active; sustain strong conflict. Keep the narrator out of story and let characters give information through thoughts, action and dialogue; write simple sentences using strong active verbs."

TIME TO PAUSE, Inky Trails, Box 345, Middleton ID 83644. Editor: Pearl Kirk. A review of prose and poetry. Biannual. Estab. 1970. Circ. 150.
Needs: Literary, contemporary, religious/inspirational, psychic/supernatural, fantasy, romance, western, mystery, adventure, humor, juvenile, young adult, novels. No horror, gay/lesbian, erotica, profanity. Accepts 5-8 mss/year in *Time to Pause* and *Inky Trails*. Receives approximately 10 unsolicited fiction mss each month. Length: 5,500 words maximum. Sometimes recommends manuscripts.
How to Contact: Send complete ms with SASE. Reports in 6 weeks. Sample copy $3 with 9x12 or 10x13 SAE plus 70¢ postage. Guidelines for legal-sized SASE.
Payment: Author's copy $4. Occasional cash awards.
Terms: All rights stay with the writer as long as *Time to Pause* is given credit for 1st printing. Fiction contest each year; cash awards.

TOGETHER, For All Concerned with Christian Education, General Synod Board of Education, Church House, Dean's Yard, London, England SW1P 3NZ. Tel. 222-9011. Editor-in-Chief: Mrs. P. Egan. Magazine of forward-looking Christian education for children under 12. Short stories, plays, services, projects, etc. Also songs, cards, occasional poems. Readers are primary school and Sunday school teachers, clergy. Ecumenical readership. Published 9 times/year. Estab. 1956. Circ. 5,000.
Needs: Juvenile, religious. "Stories with religious implications which children can appreciate. Humor an advantage. No pious, old-fashioned moral tales or rewrites of Bible stories." Receives 20 unsolicited fiction mss/month. Buys 2-3 mss/issue, 20 mss/year. Length: 500 words minimum; 1,200 words maximum; 750 words average. Occasionally critiques rejected mss. Frequently recommends other markets.
How to Contact: Send complete ms with SAE and IRC. Previously published work OK. Reports in 3 weeks on mss.
Payment: $10 maximum and 1 contributor's copy.

Terms: Pays on publication for first rights. Publication copyrighted.

Tips: "Look for unusual angles, child's-eye view of relationships, stories that convey a message about caring for other people without needing a moral drafted out in words. Writing for children is often old-fashioned—authors write for the child that they were rather than the child of today. Stories may be cozy and sentimental or have too explicit a moral—children today are very quick to perceive implications without being hit over the head. Send clean, tidy, *typed* mss—and send one sample, rather than a batch."

TOTAL ABANDON MODERN ARTS MAGAZINE, Total Abandon Publishers, Box 40502, Portland OR 97240. (503)771-9346. Editor/Publisher: Rick Stanck. Theme: "Avant-garde, experimental, progressive, political, erotic, conceptual, abstract, surreal, dada, constructivist, occult, unusual; "non-pretentious, cathartic, and honest transcendentalism." Readership: "Young artists; non-commercial artists; open-minded; non-righteous; artists; and people who will give credence and space to this kind of work." Semiannual to annual. Estab. 1977. Circ. 1,000.

Needs: Literary, contemporary, erotica, translations, occult, experimental prose, satiric, anthropological. No "western, religious, any fiction that is not stretching the limits of all we have seen so far in the literary tradition. Let us be modern and transcend patterns." Accepts 3 mss/issue, 8 mss/year. Receives approximately 5 unsolicited fiction mss/month. Length: 500-4,000 words. Critiques rejected mss "when there is time."

How to Contact: Send complete ms with SASE. Reports in 3 months on mss. Free sample copy with legal size SASE (new format is legal-size paper).

Payment: 5 free author's copies. $1 charge for extras.

Terms: Rights revert to author. Publication copyrighted.

Tips: "Send several different works in the above mentioned modes. Don't bother to submit if your work is not pushing the norms for creative writing. You may include a cover letter which talks about yourself on a personal level, your artistic philosophy. Soliciting criticism, open to harsh reality of change, causes fruition." Mss are rejected because they are "self-indulgent or self-absorbed; writers are not aware of readership, many times are personally or therapeutically involved."

TOUCHSTONE, New Age Journal ,Houston Writers Guild, Box 42331, Houston Tx 77042. Editor: Eugenia Riley. Magazine seeking "constructive material with an affirmative view of life. We publish poetry, short stories, articles, reviews letters and quotations on cause and effect. We reach a liberal, well-educated, upper-middle-class audience." Quarterly. Estab. 1976. Circ. 1,000.

Needs: Contemporary, ethnic, experimental, fantasy, historical (general), humor/satire, literary, mainstream, prose poem, suspense/mystery, translations. "No moralizing; nothing obscene or obscure." Receives 24 unsolicited fiction mss/month. Accepts 2 mss/issue, 8 mss/year. Length: 750 words minimum, 2,000 words maximum, 1,500 words average. Occasionally critiques rejected mss. Charges $7.50 (one-year subscription) for critique.

How to Contact: Send complete ms with SASE. Photocopied submissions OK. Reports in 6 weeks on mss. Sample copy $1.95 and 6x9 SAE and 2 first class stamps. Fiction guidelines for legal size SAE and 1 first class stamp.

Payment: 1 free contributor's copy; charges $1.95, 6x9 envelope and 1 first class stamps for extras.

Terms: Acquires first rights. Publication copyrighted.

Tips: "*Study our publication*, and send us your best work. We enjoy cover letters. Neatness and professionalism *counts*, as does clarity and skill."

TRANSLATION, The Translation Center, Columbia University, 307A Mathematics Bldg., New York NY 10027. (212)280-2305. Executive Director: Diane G.H. Cook. Semiannual. Estab. 1973. Circ. 1,500.

Needs: Literary translations only. Accepts varying number of mss/year. Receives approximately 20-30 unsolicited fiction mss each month. Length: very short or excerpts; not in excess of 15 mss pages. Critiques rejected mss "rarely because of time involved."

How to Contact: Send complete translation ms accompanied by original language text with SASE. Reports in 3-6 months on mss. Sample copy $8. Subscription $15.

Payment: 2 complimentary translator copies. Annual award of $500 for outstanding translation of a substantial part of a book-length literary work. Applicants must be US citizens.

Terms: Acquires first North American serial rights. Publication copyrighted.

Tips: "We are particularly interested in translations from the lesser-known languages."

TRIQUARTERLY, Northwestern University, 1735 Benson Ave., Evanston IL 60201. (312)492-3490. Fiction Editor: Reginald Gibbons. "A general literary quarterly of fiction. We publish short stories, novellas, or excerpts from novels, usually by American writers. Genre or style is not a primary consideration. We aim for the general reader, someone looking for good stories, told well. Many of our readers are also writers." Published 3 times/year. Estab. 1964. Circ. 5,000.

Needs: Literary, contemporary, translations. Buys 15 mss/issue, 45 mss/year. Receives approximately 200 unsolicited fiction mss each month. Length: No requirement.

How to Contact: Send complete ms with SASE. Reports in 6 weeks on mss. Sample copy $2.

Payment: $100-$500. 4 free author's copies. Cover price less 30% discount for extras.

Terms: Pays on publication for first North American serial rights. Publication copyrighted.

Tips: "Read a few recent copies of the magazine to become familiar with the kinds of fiction we publish."

TULE RIVER TIMES, Box 692, Springville, CA 93265. (209) 539-3166. "The *Times* is a local weekly newspaper. Aside from the usual local news, we print entertainment features, short stories and serials for a family market—middle class education and background." Weekly. Estab. 1979. Circ. 1,700.

Needs: Adventure, historical (general), humor/satire, serialized/excerpted novel, suspense/mystery, western. "The fiction we buy is of the Romantic School only. 'Romantic' is not 'love stories' but a type of fiction that shows man in control of himself, with values and morals that guide him. No naturalist or existentialist works need be sent to us." Buys 1-2 mss/issue, 50 mss/year. Length: 2,000 words minimum, 7,000 words maximum, 5,000 words average. Occasionally critiques rejected mss.

How to Contact: Query with clips of published work "if any" and SASE. Photocopied and previously published submissions OK. Reports in 2 weeks on queries. Sample copy $1. Fiction guidelines free.

Payment: $90-350; 10 free contributor's copies.

Terms: Pays on acceptance for all rights. Publication copyrighted.

Tips: "Our audience wants entertainment as well as the local news. They wait for each issue and many of them have every issue since we began publishing. Read Ayn Rand's *The Romantic Manifesto*. Read O. Henry, Victor Hugo, and Mickey Spillane. You'll know what type of fiction we want. We publish for the family. An occasional 'damn' or 'Hell' is all right, but it had better belong in the story."

UNCLE MAGAZINE, Heart's Desire Press, Rt. 1, Box 1134, Springfield MO 65803. Editor: Ed DeBriese. Fiction Editor: John Mort. "Our magazine is for those who have given up. Humor, satire, whimsy, parody—we seek to be contrary and ornery. We hope to have more than a literary audience, but realize that *Uncle* will appeal mainly to those interested in little magazines. We believe we will appeal to those eager for a brash approach to contemporary sacred cows." Quarterly. Estab. November 1980.

Needs: "We will consider fiction from any category as long as its emphasis is humorous. We are not interested in heavily confessional material or giddy new celebrations of the Universe." Accepts 2-4 mss/issue. Receives approximately 15-20 unsolicited fiction mss each month. Length: around 2,000 words. Critiques rejected mss "when there is time."

Close-up

Reginald Gibbons
TriQuarterly Magazine

TriQuarterly's editor, Reginald Gibbons, has a "tremendous, consuming amount of work" to do, but he says that editors of literary magazines often have final responsibility for everything—content, budget, production, schedule. Despite the help of a small staff, Gibbons does not have as much time as he would like for reading manuscripts. Two bags of mail leaning against a wall in the magazine's office emphasize his point. "I set days aside when I say, 'I don't care what happens, I'm just going to read manuscripts today.' "

Gibbons says he finds "enormous pleasure in reading good new work. And *TriQuarterly* will always have the door open to new writers." The last three issues have included the first published stories of five authors.

Gibbons, a poet, is familiar with the other side of the editorial desk as well, having published two books of poems, and fiction and essays in magazines. He has also published numerous translations of Spanish poetry. Gibbons taught writing at Princeton and Columbia before assuming his position at *TriQuarterly* in September, 1981.

TriQuarterly has been supported by Northwestern University since it was founded there in 1964. Gibbons is continuing the magazine's tradition of short fiction, while adding poetry and some reviews. "*TriQuarterly* has a special place among American literary magazines because of its devotion to short fiction," Gibbons says.

In fiction, Gibbons looks for "work that comes out of a special sort of engagement with life, with feeling and thought. I like what Lorca calls *duende*. Fiction that comes primarily out of ingenuity doesn't always interest me," he says. "We reject a lot of fiction that is mostly creative writing. It is written in a fairly interesting, clever way, but it is not about anything," he explains.

Gibbons feels something needs to be at issue or at stake in a good piece of fiction. "It could be very subtle or very small," he says, "but something needs to be hanging in the balance, so that it affects our understanding of some human situation or action or attitude."

Gibbons' advice to young writers is "to read and study; to be hungry for understanding, but not eager to impress; to be serious artists but not humorless people. You have to find those affinities—in life and literature—that will be important to you as an artist.

"And write. Henry James said, 'Be one of those people on whom nothing is lost.' That is probably the best advice ever given."

On getting published, Gibbons says that a young writer may feel that literary magazines reflect groups of friends, and that breaking in is not possible. "But that is not true of all magazines."

It is, of course, discouraging to get work back, but that is really not the issue, according to Gibbons. Producing good work should be the writer's primary concern.

"This magazine and any serious magazine will always be interested in powerful, sensitive, intelligent work. A good piece of work can find a home," he adds, "but it may take a while.

"Nobody's work suits everyone. That's why there are so many literary magazines."

—Joan Filan

How to Contact: Send complete ms with SASE. Reports in 1 month on mss. Sample copy $1.
Payment: Free author's copies.
Terms: Acquires one-time rights. Publication copyrighted.
Tips: "Keep it short and be outrageously funny. Humor mixed with line drawings would be well-received. Very short surrealistic pieces would be welcome. For our purposes, writers aren't irreverent enough. They satirize things from a liberal, political perspective, rather than opening up on everything (feminism, let's say, as well as the Moral Majority) without blinders."

UNDINAL SONGS, A Magazine of Macabre Fantasy ,Undinal Songs Press, Box 70, Oakdale, Long Island NY 11769. (516)589-8715. Editor: Leilah Wendell. Associate Editor: Kiel Stuart. "We are a macabre fantasy journal publishing poetry, art, articles and fiction in the weird tales fashion. We are the only international magazine focusing on necrophilia and vampirism in modern literature." Directed to "those interested in forms of obscure dark fantasy with an antiquated edge. We are somewhat Victorian in our writing preferences." Quarterly. Estab. 1980. Circ. 1,200.
Needs: Experimental, fantasy, gothic, horror, prose poem, psychic/supernatural, weird tales. "We are especially fond of material that portrays a personified Death entity, specifically material that portrays Death as a lover. We wish *not* to see science fiction, pornography, or media topics." Receives 80 unsolicited fiction mss/month. Buys 5 mss/issue, 20 mss/year. Length: 3,000 words average. Occasionally critiques rejected mss.
How to Contact: Send complete ms with SASE. Simultaneous and photocopied submissions OK. Reports in 1 week on queries; 3 weeks on mss. Sample copy $2.50. Fiction guidelines for SAE and 20¢ postage.
Payment: $1-3, 2 free contributor's copies; charges $2 for extras.
Terms: Pays on publication for first North American serial rights, one time reprint rights by request. Publication copyrighted. "We sponsor three different contests. Rules free for SASE."
Tips: "Keep in mind our theme at all times as we very rarely diverge from it. Give us a story where the reader can feel intensely what the characters are feeling. Keep in mind a somewhat Edgar A. Poe style. Please type double spaced, with your name and address on the front page, upper left hand corner. Sloppy mss and an extraordinary amount of typos will lead an editor to the conclusion that you don't care about your work."

UNICORN, Loyola College, 4501 N. Charles St., Baltimore MD 21210. (301)323-1010. Editor: David Zeiler. Fiction Editor: Susan McIntyre. Magazine of poetry and short fiction for the college community. Semiannually. Estab. 1972. Circ. 1,500.
Needs: Contemporary, ethnic, fantasy, humor/satire, prose poem, romance (contemporary), science fiction. Receives 50 unsolicited fiction mss/month. Accepts 4 mss/issue, 10 mss/year. Length: 500 words minimum, 1,200 words maximum, 700 words average.
How to Contact: Send complete ms with SASE. Simultaneous submissions OK. Reports in 1 month on mss. Sample copy $1 and SAE.
Payment: 1 free contributor's copy, $1 charge for extras.
Terms: Acquires all rights.

U.S. 1 WORKSHEETS, U.S. 1 Poets Cooperative, 21 Lake Dr., Roosevelt NJ 08555. Rotating Editors. "We publish poetry and prose of many styles for anyone interested in contemporary fiction and poetry." Biannual. Estab. 1971. Circ. 1,000.
Needs: Literary, contemporary. "We have published a broad range of fiction, including pieces that *might* be labelled confessional, gay/lesbian, feminist, or western. We're interested in good, traditional, plotted fiction as well as experimental work." Receives approximately 5 unsolicited fiction mss each month. More would be welcome. Length: Approximately 2,500-6,000 words. Critiques rejected mss "when there is time."
How to Contact: Send complete ms with SASE. Reports in up to 6 months on mss. Sample copy $1.50 with 8x11 SAE plus 71¢ postage.
Payment: 2 free author's copies. 75¢ charge for extras. Publication copyrighted.

Tips: "I think we might best be described as a publication that wants to avoid labels and stereotypes; we seek instead good writing. Write carefully, rather than in over-enthusiastic haste. Tell a good story. Most of the manuscripts we reject have craft flaws including grammatical and spelling errors. We desire style and sophistication in craft beyond what we find in many mss."

THE UNIVERSAL BLACK WRITER MAGAZINE, Box 5, Radio City Station, New York NY 10101. Editor-in-Chief: Linda Cousins. Magazine for black writers and readers of black literature. Published quarterly. Estab. 1979.
Needs: Ethnic, experimental, fantasy, humor/satire, literary, women's. "We are interested in works which educate, uplift, inspire, entertain black writers and black reading audiences in general." No gory, violent, or sexually explicit pieces. Receives 2-3 unsolicited fiction mss/month. Accepts 1 ms/issue, 4-8 mss/year. Length: 1,500 words minimum; 2,000 words maximum; 1,500 words average.
How to Contact: Send complete ms with SASE. Simultaneous and photocopied submissions OK. Sample copy $2 with 9x13 SAE and 4 first class stamps. Free fiction guidelines with SASE.
Payment: 2 contributor's copies.
Terms: Acquires first rights. Publication copyrighted.

UNIVERSITY OF PORTLAND REVIEW, University of Portland, 5000 N. Willamette Blvd., Portland OR 97203. (503)283-7144. Editor-in-Chief: Thompson M. Faller. Magazine for the college-educated layman of liberal arts background. "Its purpose is to comment on the human condition and to present information in different fields with relevance to the contemporary scene." Published semiannually. Established 1948. Circ. 1,000.
Needs: "Only fiction that makes a significant statement about the contemporary scene will be employed." Receives 4 unsolicited mss/month. Accepts 2-3 mss/issue, 4-6 mss/year. Length: 1,500 words minimum; 3,500 words maximum; 2,000 words average.
How to Contact: Send complete ms with SASE. Reports in 3 weeks on queries; 6 months on mss. Sample copy 50¢.
Payment: 5 contributor's copies. 50¢ charge for extras.
Terms: Pays on publication for all rights. Publication copyrighted.
Tips: "Send manuscript in line with guidelines."

UNIVERSITY OF WINDSOR REVIEW, University of Windsor, Windsor, Ontario, Canada N9B 3P4. Editor: E. McNamara. Fiction Editor: Alistair MacLeod. Estab. 1965.
Needs: Literary, contemporary. We wish to see lots of experimental fiction. Buys 4 mss/year. Receives 2-3 unsolicited fiction mss each month. Length: No requirement.
How to Contact: Send complete ms with SASE. Reports in 6 weeks.
Payment: $25.
Terms: Publication copyrighted.

UNKNOWNS, An Atlanta Creative Alliance, 1900 Century Blvd., Suite 1, Atlanta GA 30345. (404)636-3145. Publisher: Julia B. Davidson. Editor: Denver Stull, Magazine. "*Unknowns* is dedicated to the development of talent that might never have the opportunity for recognition or publication. We will look at fiction on any subject but accept no smut." Published quarterly. Estab. 1973. Circ. 100 + .
Needs: Adventure, condensed novel, fantasy, historical (general), humor/satire, literary, mainstream, prose poem, science fiction, serialized/excerpted novel, suspense/mystery, western, young adult. "We publish several stories in series, or continued form. No sex oriented subjects please." Receives 40-50 unsolicited fiction mss/month. Accepts 25-30 mss/issue, 100 mss/year. Length: 5,000 words average. Occasionally critiques rejected mss. Sometimes recommends markets.
How to Contact: Send complete ms with SASE. Simultaneous submissions OK. Reports in 3 weeks on mss. Sample copy $2.
Payment: 1 contributor's copy. $2 charge for extras.

Terms: Pays on publication for first rights (all rights returned to author). Publication copyrighted.
Tips: "Just send us your story. We *will* read it. No manuscript gathers dust or coffee stains at *Unknowns*. We read them all."

UROBOROS, Allegany Mountain Press, 111 N. 10th Street, Olean NY 14760. (716)372-0935. Fiction Editor: Ford F. Ruggieri. "Fiction dealing with current mythological motifs, dreams, folklore, psychological insights, history of consciousness, etc. for those interested in these topics." Published irregularly. Estab. 1973. Circ. 500.
Needs: Literary, erotica, humor, experimental. "No formula hackwork." Accepts 4-6 mss/year. Receives approximately 30 unsolicited fiction mss each month. Length: No requirement. Critiques rejected mss "when there is time."
How to Contact: Send complete ms with SASE. Reports in 2 months on mss. Sample copy $2.
Payment: Free author's copies. Cover price less 50% discount for extras.
Terms: Acquires first rights and one-time rights. Rights revert to author. Publication copyrighted.
Tips: "Be familiar with a magazine before sending mss (saves time and money in the long run)."

VALLEY GRAPEVINE, Seven Buffaloes Press, Box 249, Big Timber MT 59011. Editor/Publisher: Art Cuelho. Theme: "Poems, stories, history, folklore, photographs, ink drawings, or anything native to the Great Central Valley of California which includes the San Joaquin and Sacramento Valleys. Focus is on land and people and the oilfields, farms, orchards, Okies, small town life, hobos." Readership: "Rural and small town audience, the common man with a rural background, salt-of-the-earth. The working man reads *Valley Grapevine* because it's his personal history recorded." Annual. Estab. 1978. Circ. 500.
Needs: Literary, contemporary, western, ethnic (Okie, Arkie). No academic, religious (unless natural to theme), gay/lesbian, supernatural material. Receives approximately 10-15 unsolicited fiction mss each month. Length: 2,500-10,000 (prefers 5,000) words.
How to Contact: Query. SASE for query, ms. Reports in 1 week. Sample copy available to writers for $3.
Payment: 1-2 author's copies.
Terms: Acquires first North American serial rights. Returns rights to author after publication, but reserves the right to reprint in an anthology or any future special collection of Seven Buffaloes Press. Publication copyrighted.
Tips: "Buy a copy to get a feel of the professional quality of the writing. Know the theme of a particular issue. Some contributors have 30 years experience as writers; most 15 years. Age does not matter; quality does."

THE VILLAGER, The Bronxville Women's Club, 135 Midland Ave., Bronxville NY 10708. (914)337-5252. Editor: Amy Murphy. "Literary magazine—fiction, nonfiction, poetry, articles on current affairs—for families in area." Published monthly (October through June only). Estab. 1928. Circ. 750.
Needs: Adventure, historical (general), humor/satire, literary, suspense/mystery. Length: 800 words minimum; 2,000 words maximum.
How to Contact: Send complete ms with SASE. Sample copy $1.
Payment: 1 contributor's copy.
Terms: Acquires first rights. Publication copyrighted.

VIRGINIA QUARTERLY REVIEW, 1 W. Range, Charlottesville VA 22903. (804)924-3124. Editor: Staige Blackford. "A national magazine of literature and discussion. A lay, intellectual audience, people who are not out-and-out scholars but who are interested in ideas and literature." Quarterly. Estab. 1925. Circ. 4,500.
Needs: Literary, contemporary, fantasy, men's, women's, feminist, romance, adventure, humor, ethnic, serialized novels (excerpts), translations. "No gay/lesbian or pornography." Buys 3

mss/issue, 20 mss/year. Length: 3,000-7,000 words.
How to Contact: Query or send complete ms. SASE for query, ms. Reports in 2 weeks on queries, 2 months on mss. Sample copy $3.
Payment: $10/printed page.
Terms: Pays on publication for all rights. "Will transfer upon request."
Tips: "Because of the competition it's difficult for a non-published writer to break in." Emily Clark Balch Award for best published short story of the year.

WASCANA REVIEW, University of Regina, Regina, Saskatchewan, Canada. Editor: John S. Chamberlain. Theme: "literary criticism, fiction, poetry for readers of serious fiction." Semiannual. Estab. 1966. Circ. 500.
Needs: Literary, humor. Buys 6 mss/year. Receives approximately 20 unsolicited fiction mss/month. Length: No requirement. Occasionally recommends other markets.
How to Contact: Send complete ms with SASE. Reports in 2 months on mss. Sample copy $2.50. Free guidelines with SASE and IRC.
Payment: $3/page for prose; $10/page for poetry. 2 free author's copies.
Terms: Pays on publication for all rights. Publication copyrighted.
Tips: "Stories are usually rejected because they are technically incompetent or because they deal with trite subjects."

WASHINGTON REVIEW, Friends of the Washington Review of the Arts, Box 50132, Washington DC 20004. (202)638-0515. Fiction Editor: Patricia Griffith. "We publish fiction, poetry, articles and reviews on all areas of the arts. We have a particular interest in the interrelationships of the arts and emphasize the cultural life of the DC area." Readership: "Artists, writers and those interested in cultural life in this area." Bimonthly. Estab. 1975. Circ. 10,000.
Needs: Literary. Buys 1-2 mss/issue. Receives approximately 10 unsolicited fiction mss each month. Length: Prefers 2,000 words. Critiques rejected mss "when there is time."
How to Contact: Send complete ms with SASE. Reports in 2 months. Sample copy for tabloid-sized SASE.
Payment: Author's copies plus small payment whenever possible.
Terms: Pays on publication for first North American serial rights. Publication copyrighted.
Tips: "Read our publication. Occasionally we have an all fiction issue." Mss are rejected because of "incorrect length, insufficient quality. Most manuscripts we receive are not of the literary quality we seek."

WAVES, 79 Denham Dr., Thornhill, Ontario, Canada L4J 1P2. (416)889-6703. Contact: Editor. "A college literary journal, printing poems, short stories, reviews with graphics by international artists and writers." Readership: English teachers, writers and fans of quality literature. Published 3 times/year. Estab. 1972. Circ. 1,000.
Needs: Literary, contemporary, inspirational, supernatural, science fiction, fantasy, horror, erotica, gothic, romance, western, mystery, adventure, humor, young adult, ethnic, translations. Also interested in "sample chapters of novels. Type of submission is not important—style and quality are. No dull plots, careless writing, cardboard characters, lecturing dialogues, stupid themes, boring clichés, etc." Accepts 3-6 mss/issue, 15 mss/year. Receives approximately 20 unsolicited fiction mss each month. Length: 1,000-5,000 words. Critiques rejected mss "if requested and time permits."
How to Contact: Send complete ms with SAE and IRC. Reports in 1 month on mss. Sample back issue copy $1.
Payment: 2 free author's copies. $1 charge for extras.
Terms: Acquires first North American serial rights. Publication copyrighted.
Tips: "Read *Waves* in a library or buy a sample. Look at several literary magazines. Spend time being creative with the writing and inventive with language. Know contemporary writing. Develop your own voice."

WEBSTER REVIEW, Webster College, Webster Groves MO 63119. Editor/Publisher: Nancy Schapiro. "We have no specific theme. We're interested in quality contemporary fiction and in translations of international fiction." Readership: Writers, students, teachers and anyone interested in contemporary international fiction. Semiannual. Estab. 1974. Circ. 1,500.

Needs: Literary, contemporary, translations, prose poems, excerpted novels. "Not interested in popular (i.e., non-serious) work." No pornographic, sentimental, or *Star Wars*-type science fiction. Accepts 4 mss/issue, 8 mss/year. Receives approximately 40 unsolicited fiction mss each month. No preferred length. Critiques rejected mss "when there is time."

How to Contact: Send complete ms with SASE. Simultaneous and photocopied submissions OK. Reports in 1 month. Free sample copy.

Payment: 2 free author's copies. No charge for extras.

Terms: Acquires first rights. Publication copyrighted.

Tips: "The competition is stiff so a writer should master his craft before attempting to publish."

WEE GIANT, Wee Giant Press, 178 Bond St. N., Hamilton, Ontario, Canada L8S 3W6. Editor: Margaret Saunders. "A little literary magazine of poetry, book reviews, fiction. Audience reads *Wee Giant* to keep up with what is going on in the wee magazine field." Published 3 times/year. Estab. 1977. Circ. 600.

Needs: Literary. Accepts 5 mss/year. Receives approximately 10 unsolicited fiction mss each month. Length: 2,500 words maximum. Critiques rejected mss "when there is time."

How to Contact: Send complete ms with SASE. Reports in 3 weeks. Sample copy $1 with 9½x6⅓ SAE plus 48¢ postage.

Payment: 1 free author's copy. $1.35 charge for extras.

Terms: Acquires first North American serial rights. Publication copyrighted.

Tips: "Send for a sample copy of our magazine and study it. Submit to the right market. We publish the work of unknown writers along with established writers such as John Robert Columbo."

WEIRDBOOK, Weirdbook Press, Box 149, Amherst Branch, Buffalo NY 14226. Editor: W. Paul Ganley. "Latter day 'pulp magazine' along the lines of the old pulp magazine *Weird Tales*. We tend to use established writers. We look for an audience of fairly literate people who like good writing and good characterization in their fantasy and horror fiction, but are tired of the clichés in the field." Annual. Estab. 1968. Circ. 900.

Needs: Psychic/supernatural, fantasy, horror, gothic (not modern). No psychological horror; mystery fiction; physical horror (blood); traditional ghost stories (unless original theme); science fiction; swords and sorcery without a supernatural element; reincarnation stories that conclude with 'And the doctor patted him on . . . THE END!' " Buys 8-12 mss/issue. Length: 15,000 + words maximum. Overstocked with fiction until Jan. 1, 1983. Sometimes recommends markets.

How to Contact: Send complete ms with SASE. Reports in 2 months on mss. Sample copy $4.50. Guidelines for legal-sized SASE.

Payment: ½¢/word minimum, and 1 free author's copy.

Terms: Pays on publication ("part acceptance only for solicited mss") for first North American serial rights plus right to reprint the entire issue.

Tips: "Read a copy and then some of the best anthologies in the field (such as Daw's 'Best Horror of the Year,' Arkham House anthologies, etc.) Occasionally we keep mss longer than planned. When sending a SASE marked 'book rate' (or anything not first class) the writer should add 'Forwarding Postage Guaranteed.' "

WEST BRANCH, Dept. of English, Bucknell University, Lewisburg PA 17837. Editors: K. Patten and R. Taylor. Theme: Fiction and poetry. Readership: "Readers of contemporary literature." Biannual. Estab. 1977. Circ. 600.

Needs: Literary, contemporary, translations. No science fiction. Accepts 3-4 mss/issue. No preferred length.

How to Contact: Send complete ms with SASE. Reports in 6 weeks on mss. Sample copy $2.

Payment: 2 free author's copies. Cover price less 20% discount for extras.

Terms: Acquires first rights. Publication copyrighted.

Tips: Mss are rejected because of "lack of depth, shallow conception, no vision, flat style, dull characters."

WEST COAST REVIEW, A Quarterly Magazine of the Arts ,West Coast Review Publishing Society, c/o English Dept., Simon Fraser University, Burnaby, British Columbia, Canada V5A 1S6. (604)291-4287. Magazine focusing on "contemporary poetry, short fiction, drama, music, graphics, photography and reviews of books for persons interested in the contemporary arts." Quarterly. Estab 1966. Circ. 500.

Needs: Contemporary, experimental, literary, prose poem, serialized/excerpted novel (possibly), translations (possible if translator arranges for all necessary permissions). Receives 10-20 unsolicited fiction mss/month. Accepts 1 ms/issue, 3-4 mss/year. Length: 250 words minimum, 3,000 words maximum.

How to Contact: Send complete ms with SASE. "Photocopies acceptable with assurances that they are not under consideration elsewhere." Reports in "generally" 2 weeks-4 months on mss. Sample copy $3.50 and 8x11 envelope and 50¢ postage.

Payment: $50 maximum; 2 free contributor's copies; $3 charge for extras.

Terms: Pays on acceptance for first rights. Publication copyrighted.

Tips: "Read several issues of th *Review* before submitting. Send standard, professional submissions. Have patience, patience and more patience."

WESTERFIELD'S REVIEW, Ashford Press, RFD. 1, Box 182A, Willimantic CT 06226. Editor-in-Chief: M.J. Westerfield. "We publish a literary magazine using prose and poetry in any style or genre that strikes our fancy, for a college educated audience interested in contemporary literature." Published semiannually. Estab. 1976. Circ. 850.

Needs: Contemporary, erotica, ethnic, experimental, fantasy, horror, humor/satire, literary, mainstream, prose poem, science fiction, serialized/excerpted novel. Receives 20 unsolicited fiction mss/month. Buys 3-5 mss/issue; 6-10 mss/year. Length: 100 words minimum; 5,000 words maximum; 2,500 words average.

How to Contact: Send complete ms with SASE; query on novels or send excerpt. Photocopied submissions and previously published work OK. Reports in 3 weeks on queries; 6 weeks on mss. Sample copy $1.50.

Payment: 2 contributor's copies.

Terms: Pays on publication for one-time rights. Publication copyrighted.

Tips: "Submit your best work. If we think you have talent and the right slant, we will request to see more of your work. Read the magazine. Editors' tastes vary so much it is almost impossible to hit it right without knowledge of the publication."

WESTERN HUMANITIES REVIEW, University of Utah, Salt Lake City UT 84112. (801)581-7438. Editor: Jack Garlington. "Articles on various aspects of the humanities: Fiction, poetry, book and film reviews." Readership: Highly educated. Quarterly. Estab. 1947. Circ. about 1,200.

Needs: Literary, contemporary, humor, ethnic (all), serialized and condensed novels, translations. Buys 2-3 mss/issue; 8-12 mss/year. Receives approximately 60 unsolicited fiction mss each month. Length: No requirement. Sometimes critiques rejected ms.

How to Contact: Send complete ms with SASE. Reports in 1 month on mss. Sample copy $4.

Payment: $150 maximum.

Terms: Pays on acceptance for all rights. Publication copyrighted.

Tips: "Read an issue and see what we like." Mss rejected because of "poor style, overworked themes."

WHETSTONE ,University of Lethbridge, English Dept., Lethbridge, Alberta, Canada T1K 3M4. (403)329-2365. Editor: Ildiko Szujka. Magazine publishing "poetry, prose, drama, prints, photographs, and occasional music compostions for a university audience." Publishes 3 issues/year. Estab. 1971. Circ. 100.

Needs: Experimental, literary, mainstream. Receives 1 unsolicited fiction ms/month. Accepts 1

ms/issue, 3 mss/year. Length: 12 double-spaced pages maximum.
How to Contact: Send complete ms with SASE. Simultaneous and photocopied submissions OK. Reports in 3 months on mss. Sample copy $50¢ and 10½x7½ or larger envelope and 2 Canadian first class stamps or IRCs.
Payment: 1 free contributor's copies.
Terms: Acquires no rights. Publication copyrighted.
Tips: "We seek good writing. Avoid moralizing."

WHISKEY ISLAND MAGAZINE, Cleveland State University, University Center 7, Cleveland OH 44115. (216)687-2056. Contact: Attention: Fiction Editor. Magazine with no specific theme of fiction, poetry, photography. For college/liberal/humanist/literary audience. Published 3 times/year. Estab. 1978. Circ. 2,500.
Needs: Confession, contemporary, erotica, ethnic, experimental, fantasy, feminist/lesbian, gay, humor/satire, literary, mainstream, prose poem, science fiction, suspense/mystery, translations. "Nothing by a member of any right-wing group." Receives 5-10 unsolicited fiction mss/month. Acquires 4-8 mss/issue. Length: 5,000 words maximum; 2,000-3,000 words average. Occasionally critiques rejected mss.
How to Contact: Send complete ms with SASE. Simultaneous, photocopied and previously published submissions OK. Reports in 2 months on mss. Sample copy free.
Payment: 2 free contributor's copies.
Terms: Acquires one-time rights. Publication copyrighted.
Tips: Recommends a "professional presentation of ms with a *brief* bio."

THE WILLIAM AND MARY REVIEW, College of William and Mary, Williamsburg VA 23185. (804)253-4862. Editors change annually. "We publish quality fiction, poetry, and essays. Our audience is primarily undergraduate and professional." Semiannual. Estab. 1943. Circ. 2,800.
Needs: Literary, contemporary, humor. Accepts 7 mss/issue, 14 mss/year. Receives approximately 50 unsolicited fiction mss each month. Length: 5,000 words maximum. Critiques rejected mss "when there is time."
How to Contact: Send complete ms with SASE. Reports in 2 months. Do not submit in June, July or August.
Payment: 5 free author's copies.
Terms: Acquires first rights. Publication copyrighted.
Tips: "We want original, well-written stories."

WILLOW SPRINGS, Pub Box 1063, Eastern Washington University, Cheney WA 99004. Editor: Bill O'Daly. Fiction Editor: Cindy Call. Semiannually. Estab. 1977. Circ. 800.
Needs: Erotica, feminist or lesbian, gay, literary, prose poem, translations. Receives 50 unsolicited fiction mss/month. Accepts 2 mss/issue; 4 mss/year. Length: 5,000 words average. Occasionally critiques rejected mss.
How to Contact: Send complete ms with SASE. Photocopied submissions OK. Reports in 1-2 months on mss. Sample copy for $4.

WIND/LITERARY JOURNAL, The Wind Press, Rt. 1, Box 809K, Pikeville KY 41501. (606)631-1129. Editor: Quentin R. Howard. "Literary journal with stories, poems, book reviews from the small presses and some university presses. Readership is students, literary people, professors, housewives and others." Triannually. Estab. 1971. Circ. 500.
Needs: Literary. "No restriction on form, content or subject." Accepts 4 mss/issue. Receives approximately 450 unsolicited fiction mss each month. Length: No requirement. Critiques rejected mss "when there is time."
How to Contact: Send complete ms with SASE. Photocopied submissions OK. Reports in 1 month. Sample copy $1.50. Fiction guidelines $1.50.
Payment: Free author's copies. $1.25 charge for extras.

Terms: Acquires first rights. Publication copyrighted.

Tips: "We're constantly looking for beginning fiction writers. Diversity is one of our major editorial goals. We have published since 1971 approximately 80 beginners in fiction; 45 are publishing regularly today in many magazines. No multiple submissions please. We have no taboos, but set our own standards on reading each ms."

WISCONSIN ACADEMY REVIEW, Wisconsin Academy of Sciences, Arts & Letters, 1922 University Ave., Madison WI 53705. (608)263-1692. Editor-in-Chief: Patricia Powell. "The *Review* reflects the focus of the sponsoring institution with its editorial emphasis on Wisconsin's intellectual, cultural, social, and physical environment. It features short fiction, poetry, essays, and Wisconsin-related book reviews for well-educated, well-traveled people interested in furthering regional arts and literature and disseminating information about sciences." Published quarterly. Estab. 1954. Circ. 2,000.

Needs: Experimental, historical (general), humor/satire, literary, mainstream, prose poem, science fiction, suspense/mystery, women's. "Author must have lived or be living in Wisconsin or fiction must be set in Wisconsin." Receives 5-6 unsolicited fiction mss/month. Buys 1-2 mss/issue; 8-10 mss/year. Length: 1,000 words minimum; 4,000 words maximum; 3,000 words average.

How to Contact: Send complete ms with SASE. Photocopied submissions OK. Sample copy $1. Free fiction guidelines with SAE and 1 first class stamp.

Payment: 5 contributor's copies. $1.75 charge for extras.

Terms: Pays on publication for first rights. Publication copyrighted.

WISCONSIN REVIEW, Box 276, Dempsey Hall, University of Wisconsin, Oshkosh WI 54901. (414)424-2267. Editor: T. Scott Plutchak. Literary magazine of prose and poetry. Triquarterly. Estab. 1966. Circ. 2,000.

Needs: Literary and experimental. "Imaginative materials that are experimental should include explanation of writer's intent." Receives 30 unsolicited fiction mss each month. Length: up to 4,000 words. Critiques rejected mss "when there is time." Sometimes recommends markets.

How to Contact: Send complete ms with SASE. Reports in 0-5 months. Sample copy $1.50.

Payment: Pays in contributor's copies.

Terms: Acquires first rights. Publication copyrighted.

Tips: "Length is the major problem with rejected mss. Due to space limitations, shorter pieces are best."

WOLFSONG, Wolfsong Publications, 3123 S. Kennedy, Sturtevant WI 53177. Editor: Gary C. Busha. "Chapbooks of quality poetry and prose." Published irregularly. Estab. 1978.

Needs: Experimental, fantasy, humor/satire, literary, prose poems. Receives approximately 12 unsolicited fiction mss/year. Accepts 1 mss/issue. Length: 5,000-10,000 words. Occasionally critiques rejected ms. Sends mss on to editors of other publications. Sometimes recommends markets.

How to Contact: Send complete ms or query with SASE. Photocopied submissions OK. Reports in 1 week on queries; 3 weeks on mss.

Payment: 2-5 contributor's copies.

Terms: Pays on publication for one-time rights (rights returned to author).

WOMEN: A JOURNAL OF LIBERATION, 3028 Greenmount Ave., Baltimore MD 21218. Contact: M. Campbell. "Issues related to women; non-sexist, feminist, non-classist." Readership: "Women, generally feminist." Published by volume. Estab. 1969. Circ. 10,000.

Needs: Contemporary, fantasy, women's, feminist, gay/lesbian, mystery, adventure, humor. Accepts 4 mss/issue. Length: 3,000 words maximum.

How to Contact: Send complete ms with SASE. Reports in 6-10 months on mss. Sample copy $2.

Payment: 1 free author's copy. 50¢ charge for extras.

Terms: Acquires all rights.

Tips: "We are a thematic publication. Therefore, there's a better chance if the ms is related to the issue."

WORD LOOM, An International Magazine of Socially Committed Literature, Box 21, 242 Montrose, Winnipeg, Manitoba, Canada R3M 3M7. (204)452-1487 and 944-4225. Editor: Michael Rennie. Magazine of "work, daily life, and social conflict with an international emphasis. Want rich and subtle material with an implicit social critique, not simplistic 'message.' Work with vision of Third World, labour, native and immigrant communities, the North, etc. For anyone with literary interests, a progressive bent, and/or an international perspective—teachers, students, workers, prisoners, political organizers, social workers, clergy, as well as usual academic literary audeince." Semiannually. Estab. 1981.
Needs: Contemporary, ethnic, experimental, feminist, historical, humor/satire, literary, prose poem, excerpted novel, translations. "Be sure to note our thematic bias. We favor submissions with accompanying b&w art or photos." Receives 10 unsolicited fiction mss/month. Accepts 2-5 mss/issue; 4-10 mss/year. Length: 150 words minimum; 6,000 words maximum; 2,500 words average. Critiques rejected mss if requested, "but allow time."
How to Contact: Send complete ms with SASE. Photocopied submissions OK. Reports in 6 weeks on mss confirming receipt or immediate rejection; up to 6 months on mss reporting final decision on the item. Sample copy for $5 ($2 for writers who submit). Fiction guidelines free with # 10 and 30¢ postage or IRC.
Payment: Modest cash award (less that $50) for best item(s) in each issue; up to 4 free contributor's copies; $2 charge for extras.
Terms: Acquires first North American serial rights. Rights revert to writer on publication.
Tips: "Looking for complexity, maturity, interest, in handling of subject matter, as well as good form."

WORLDS LOST . . . , The Lupreci Press, Box 51, Alhambra IL 62001. (901)488-7969. Fiction Editor: John W. Smith. Illustrated magazine of science fiction, fantasy and horror. No *Star Trek*, *Star Wars*, etc. or pornographic material of any kind. Semiannually. Estab. 1981. Circ. 700.
Needs: Fantasy, horror, science fiction. Receives 8 unsolicited fiction mss/month. Accepts a varied number of mss/issue. Length: 7,000 words maximum. Occasionally critiques rejected mss.
How to Contact: Query first or send complete ms with SASE. Simultaneous and photocopied submissions OK. Reports in 3 months on mss. Sample copy for $3 and 70¢ postage. Fiction guidelines free for SAE.
Payment: Pays $5; 1 free contributor's copy; $3 charge for extras plus 70¢ postage.
Terms: Pays on publication for first North American serial rights. Publication copyrighted.
Tips: "Send original story lines. They should have plenty of action and adventure. We would like more than rocket riding, ray gun blasting stories. Put thought into material submitted. Neatness counts. We don't have time to wade through excessive typing and grammar errors."

WOT, WOT Publications, 657 Andmore Dr., RR 2, Sidney, British Columbia, Canada V8L 3S1. Editor-in-Chief: Dennis Reid. Publishes poems, short stories excerpts of novels, photographs, artwork. "For a fairly literate audience; writers, university libraries, selected bookstores." Published semiannually. Estab. 1979. Circ. 200.
Needs: Subject matter is author's choice. We judge works on basis of merit. No science fiction. Receives "not enough" fiction mss each month. Accepts 1-2 mss/issue; 3-4 mss/year. Length: 1,500 words minimum; 5,000 words maximum. Occasionally critiques rejected mss.
How to Contact: Send complete ms with SASE. No simultaneous, photocopied submissions or previously pulished work "under any circumstances." Send 4-6 poems per submission. Reports in 2 months on mss. Sample copy $1.50
Payment: $3 subscription to the magazine (institutional subscriptions $6) and 1 contributor's copy. $1.50 charge for extras.
Terms: Rights revert to author on publication. Publication copyrighted.

Tips: "Read a copy before submitting. Accepts manuscripts primarily from Canadians, but does publish material originating from other countries."

WRIT MAGAZINE, 2 Sussex Ave., Toronto, Canada M5S 1J5. Editor: Roger Greenwald. "Literary magazine for literate readers interested in the work of new writers." Annual. Estab. 1970. Circ. 600.
Needs: Literary, translations, parts of novels. No other categories. Accepts 4-5 mss/year. Length: 300-20,000 words. Critiques rejected mss "when there is time."
How to Contact: Send complete ms with SASE. Reports in 6 weeks—"longer May-August." Sample copy $2.50.
Payment: 2 free author's copies. Negotiates charge for extras.
Terms: Acquires first North American serial rights. Copyright reverts to author.

WRITERS FORUM, University of Colorado at Colorado Springs, Colorado Springs CO 80933-7150. Editor: Dr. Alex Blackburn. "Eight to ten short stories or self-contained novel excerpts published once a year along with 25-35 poems. Highest literary quality only: mainstream, avantgarde, with preference to western themes. For small press enthusiasts, teachers and students of creative writing, commercial agents/publishers, university libraries and departments interested in contemporary American literature." Annual. Estab. 1974. Circ. 800.
Needs: Literary, contemporary, ethnic (Native American, chicano, not excluding others). No "sentimental, over-plotted, pornographic, anecdotal, polemical, trendy, disguised autobiographical, fantasy (sexual, extra-terrestrial), pseudo-philosophical, passionless, placeless, undramatized, etc. material." Accepts 8-10 mss/issue. Receives approximately 40 unsolicited fiction mss each month. Length: 1,500-10,000. Critiques rejected mss "when there is time and perceived merit."
How to Contact: Send complete ms (two copies) and letter with brief bio and relevant career information with SASE. Reports in 3-5 weeks on mss. Sample copy $8.95.
Payment: 1 free author's copy. Cover price less 20% discount for extras.
Terms: Acquires one-time rights. Rights revert to author. Publication copyrighted.
Tips: "Read our publication. Have an experienced author recommend your ms. Be prepared for constructive criticism. Persist. Send best work only. Have a serious intention about fiction as an art. Most accepted mss tend to come from established writers or new writers who have studied in writing classes. We're open, but that's the tendency because excellence is our primary criterion. We especially seek submissions that show immersion in place (trans-Mississippi West) and development of credible characters. Probably the TV-influenced fiction is the most quickly rejected. Every volume is introduced by a distinguished American author whose critical commentary can be of enormous help in encouraging writers in their careers. Furthermore our format—a 5 1/2x8 1/2 professionally edited and printed paperback book—lends credibility to authors published in our imprint." Funded by grants from National Endowment for the Arts and from Coordinating Council for Literary Magazines.

WRITER'S GAZETTE NEWSLETTER, Trouvere Company, Rt. 2, Box 290, Eclectic AL 36024. (205)541-2331. Editor: Brenda Williamson. Newsletter for writers, by writers, about writing. Estab. 1983.
Needs: Adventure, contemporary, fantasy, gothic/historical romance, horror, humor/satire, literary, mainstream, prose poem, psychic/supernatural, religious/inspirational, contemporary romance, science fiction, suspense/mystery, western. Wants to see a "definite story—ficticious." Buys 6 mss/year. Length: 300 words minimum; 2,000 words maximum; 800 words average. Occasionally critiques rejected mss. Charges 1¢/word for critique.
How to Contact: Send complete ms with SASE. Simultaneous and photocopied submissions OK. Reports in 1 month on ms. Sample copy $2 with #10 SAE and 1 first class stamp. Fiction guidelines for 50¢ with #10 SAE and 1 first class stamp.
Payment: Pays $6-40 plus magazine subscription for one year; 1 free contributor's copy.
Terms: Pays on publication for first rights. Publication copyrighted.
Tips: Be "creative and unique."

WRITER'S LIFELINE, Highway Book Shop, Cobalt, Ontario, Canada P0J 1C0. (705)679-8375. Contact: Editor. "A market newsletter for freelance writers and poets." Bimonthly. Estab. 1974. Circ. 1,000.
Needs: Short fiction articles on writers and poets. Receives approximately 1-2 unsolicited fiction mss each month. Length: 500-1,000 words. Critiques rejected mss "when there is time."
How to Contact: Send complete ms with SASE. Reports in 1 month. Free sample copy.
Payment: One year free subscription.
Terms: Acquires one-time rights. Publication copyrighted.
Tips: "Short stories and humorous scenarios should concern writing and publishing."

WRITERS NEWS MANITOBA, MWN Publications, 304 Parkview St., Winnipeg, Manitoba, Canada R3J 1S3. (204)885-2652. Editor: Andris Taskans. Fiction Editor: Kate Bitney. "Information, critical reviews, short fiction, poetry by and for Manitoba/Canadian writers and readers. For writers and readers interested in Canadian/Manitoba literature and literary activities." Published 5 times/year. Estab. 1978. Circ. 500.
Needs: Literary, contemporary, fantasy, feminist, ethnic (French Canadian, possibly others). "We will consider work on any topic (except juvenile) of artistic merit, including short chapters from novels-in-progress. We wish to avoid gothic, confession, romance and pornography." Buys 1 ms/issue, 5 mss/year. Receives 1-2 unsolicited fiction mss each month. Length: 500-3,000 words. Critiques rejected mss "if requested and when there is time."
How to Contact: Send complete ms with SASE. Reports in 1 month.
Payment: $15 for the first page, $5 for each additional page. 1 free author's copy. $1 charge for extras.
Terms: Buys one-time rights. Rights revert to author on publication. Publication copyrighted.
Tips: "Read our publication before submitting. Send a ms and expect possible rejection."

WYRD, The Magazine of Illustrated Scientifiction & Phantasie, Box 3226, Berkeley CA 94703. Editor: Robert N. Abercrombie. Magazine of weird phantasie, scientifiction, poetry, illustrations; the unusual and the bizarre for anyone willing to suspend disbelief. Published very irregularly. Estab. 1971. Circ. 400 + .
Needs: Adventure, comics, contemporary, experimental, fantasy, horror, humor/satire, prose poem, psychic/supernatural, science fiction. Receives several unsolicited fiction mss/month. Buys several mss/issue. Length: 10,000 words maximum; 5,000 words average. Occasionally critiques rejected mss.
How to Contact: Send complete ms (typewritten, double-spaced, 8½x11) with SASE. Photocopied and previously published submissions OK. Reports in 2 months on mss. Sample copy $3.25 with 8½x11 SAE. Fiction guidelines free for legal SAE and 1 first class stamp.
Payment: Pays ¼¢/word; 2 free contributor's copies.
Terms: Pays on acceptance for first North American serial rights. Publication copyrighted.
Tips: "Read extensively in the field of phantasie/horror/SF. Don't be afraid to try anything. We accept quality, not quantity. Be patient. We are a very irregular publication, and we are generally at work on several other projects."

XAVIER REVIEW, Xavier University, Box 110C, New Orleans LA 70125. (504)486-7411, ext. 481. Editor: Thomas Bonner Jr.. Magazine of "poetry/fiction/nonfiction/reviews (contemporary literature) for professional writers/libraries/colleges/universities." Published semiannually. Estab. 1981. Circ. 500.
Needs: Contemporary, ethnic, experimental, fantasy, historical (general), literary, Latin-American, prose poem, Southern, religious, serialized/excerpted novel, translations, women's. Receives 50 unsolicited fiction mss/month. Buys 4 mss/issue; 10 mss/year. Length: 10-15 pages. Occasionally critiques rejected mss.
How to Contact: Send complete ms or query with clips of published work. SASE with ms, query. Sample copy $3. Free fiction guidelines with SASE.
Payment: 2 contributor's copies.
Terms: Pays on publication. Publication copyrighted.

Close-up

Andrei Navrozov
Yale Literary Magazine

Andrei Navrozov and the staff of the *Yale Literary Magazine* exemplify the true independent spirit of publishing a literary magazine—exercising the right to experiment and develop an individual style to promote excellence in literature.

The Yale Literary Magazine is the oldest review in America with an exceptional literary heritage. Its financial history is checkered, however; it faltered in the tumultous '60s and sagged into decline in the mid-'70s. During that time as an undergraduate, Navrozov contributed to *The Lit*. After graduation in 1978, with the financial backing of a non-profit organization, he bought the magazine and resolved to reshape it into the highly respectable publication it once was.

Navrozov and his young four-member team of Yale alumni invested long hours of hard work with little or no pay, and in two years the magazine was completely revamped. The formerly modest and unassuming campus forum for students was transformed into an elegant glossy journal with national circulation, prestigious advertising, and a neo-conservative voice.

Reception to this drastic reversal in tone and format ranged from outrage from the university to acclaim and support from the outside. Despite the controversy, however, the *Yale Literary* staff has remained steadfast and confident in its convictions and has withstood the criticism, the university's threat to close down the magazine, and even a lawsuit involvement.

According to Navrozov, the *Yale Literary* today is "one of the few magazines published that attempts serious encounters with literature, thought and ideas." Their vision is perfection and publishing only the finest work, thus attempting to create a sort of cultural evolution similar to the pre-revolutionary period in Russia.

Understandably there is difficulty in finding submissions to meet the criteria of excellence. Navrozov and his editors continually search for talent in books and magazines in English as well as in other languages for translations. They are "completely open-minded" about receiving unsolicited manuscripts, which presently comprise only about five percent of the magazine's content. Their goal is to discover "genius writers" to fill the magazine with work of their own choosing, like the poetry of an unknown American who recently submitted several poems. Navrozov recognized the unusual quality, asked to see more, and later devoted the entire poetry section of one issue to the young poet's work.

For fiction a "name" means very little; it's talent they seek at *The Lit*, unknowns whom they can develop from unsolicited material. Again the problem is finding the quality—a level of writers like Mark Twain, Saul Bellow or Ionesco, masters the magazine staff acknowledges. As a result very little fiction has been published in the last three years, and the magazine's primary focus has been social and cultural criticism.

If there were time apart from his magazine work, Navrozov would devote himself more to his personal writing and translating work from Russian, like his father Lev Navrozov, the writer and scholar who defected from Russia in 1972 with his family. For now Navrozov's energies and interests are channeled into his objectives and beliefs: creating "a magazine that is the literary equivalent of the Metropolitan Opera," a publication that someday might "touch history."

THE YALE LITERARY MAGAZINE, American Literary Society, Inc., Box 243A, Yale Station, New Haven CT 06520. (203)436-4946. Editor-in-Chief: Andrei Navrozov. Magazine. ''The paper we print on is guaranteed to endure for centuries and we seek to publish and reproduce what will last at least as long. The content of America's oldest review, enhanced and augmented by its appearance, attracted an exceptional audience, comprised of some of the most influential men in the United States, in the very first year of national publication.'' Published quarterly. Estab. 1821. Circ. 10,000.

Needs: Translations, memoirs. ''*No* Barth, Doctorow, (John) Irving, Styron, Kosinski, Talese, Roth, Capote, Updike, Mailer, Gardner, Oates—and certainly not those who sound like them. We are sure you will understand.'' Receives 50 unsolicited fiction mss/month. Buys 1-3 mss/issue; 3-10 mss/year. Length: 600 words minimum; 3,000 words maximum. Occasionally critiques rejected ms.

How to Contact: Send complete ms with SASE. Simultaneous, photocopied and previously published submissions OK. Reports in 3 months on mss. Sample copy $6 with 9x12 SAE. Free fiction guidelines with SASE.

Payment: $25-1,000.

Terms: Pays on publication for all rights, first rights, or first North American serial rights; makes assignments on work-for-hire basis. Publication copyrighted.

Tips: ''Discover a new truth about man. Do not sound 'almost like Tolstoy.' Every line must be honestly new—a genuine Tolstoy, great or small to be judged by history, but genuine and one of a kind.''

THE YALE REVIEW, Yale University Press, 1902A Yale Station, New Haven CT 06520. (203)436-8307. Editor: Kai T. Erikson. Associate Editor: Penelope Laurans. ''A general interest quarterly; publishes literary criticism, original fiction and poetry, cultural commentary, book reviews for an educated, informed, general audience.'' Quarterly. Estab. 1911. Circ. 5,000.

Needs: Literary, contemporary. Buys 1-4 mss/year. Length: 3,000-5,000 words.

How to Contact: Send complete ms with SASE. Reports in 2 months. Sample copy $4.50.

Payment: Approximately $100. 1 free author's copy. $2 charge for extras.

Terms: Makes assignments on a work-for-hire basis. Pays on publication for first North American serial rights.

YELLOW SILK: Journal of Erotic Arts, Verygraphics, Box 6374, Albany CA 94706. Editor/Publisher: Lily Pond. Magazine. ''We are interested in non-pornographic erotica: joyous, mad; musical, elegant, passionate and beautiful. 'All persuasions; no brutality' is our simplest editorial policy. Literary excellence is a priority; innovative forms are welcomed, as well as traditional ones.'' Published quarterly. Estab. 1981. Circ. 5,000.

Needs: Comics, erotica, ethnic, experimental, fantasy, feminist/lesbian, gay, humor/satire, literary, prose poem, science fiction, translations. No ''blow-by-blow'' descriptions; no hackneyed writing except when used for satirical purposes. Nothing containing brutality. Buys 4-5 mss/issue; 16-20 mss/year. Length: no preference. Occasionally critiques rejected ms.

How to Contact: Send complete ms with SASE and include short, *personal* bio notes; copies acceptable. No pre-published material. Photocopied submissions OK. Reports in 6 weeks on mss. Sample copy $3.

Payment: 3 contributor's copies.

Terms: Pays on publication for all rights for one year following publication at which time they revert back to author unless used for anthology. Publication copyrighted.

Tips: ''Read, read, read! Including our magazine. Read Nabokov and Nin, and Rimbaud, Virginia Woolf, William Kotzwinkle, James Joyce. Then send in your story! Trust that the magazine/editor will not rip you off—they don't. As they say, 'find your own voice,' then trust it. Read the magazine to be sure your manuscript is appropriate. Proof and prepare typed submission carefully. Most manuscripts I see appear to be written by people without great amounts of writing experience. It takes years (frequently) to develop your work to publishable quality; it can take many rewrites on each individual piece. I also see many approaches to sexuality (for my magazine) that are trite and not fresh. The use of language is not original and the people do not seem real.''

Commercial periodicals

Editors of most commercial periodicals accepting fiction agree that their magazines are a good place for a beginning writer. Every magazine seeks *quality* fiction and is generally more interested in a good story than a well-known byline. So if publications are only printing the established short story writers, it is primarily because of the *excellence* in writing.

There is definite room for new blood, new talent. Editors are eager for it and generally read everything that comes in with an equal eye toward publication. Some of the better-known publications actively acknowledge the role that fiction plays in selling their magazines, and they are willing to assist new writers. *Ellery Queen's Mystery Magazine* has a Department of First Stories most issues; *Woman's World's* fiction editor scouts romance writers conferences for new writers; and for years *Redbook* has been one of the greatest proponents of fiction. This year in addition to its annual contest, *Redbook* surveyed its readers about their interests in subjects and their reactions to the short stories.

Again this year opportunities continue to grow for writers of short fiction, especially in the new specialty magazines that accept fiction. These publications are based on a hobby, interest, activity or sport (running, computers, animals, square dancing); genres or category fiction (romance, science fiction, mystery); locations (cities, regions); and religious, minority and ethnic groups (Jewish, Catholic, Italian, Greek). Editors of these publications all want short stories set in the appropriate thematic background or with the particular interest an intricate part of the story, thus demanding at least basic subject expertise from the writer.

Individually, special interest magazines are not large fiction markets; they generally publish one story (occasionally more) per issue. But their appearance does broaden the scope of fiction in subject and theme. They may mean a more limited audience and perhaps a smaller paycheck, but there are more publications to choose from.

Back to basics

Writing for a genre/specialty magazine is not as limiting as it might seem despite the specific requirements you must adhere to. A children's magazine may want juvenile fantasy, a feminist magazine may look for children's stories, and a black magazine might seek a science fiction story. There might also be needs for teen mysteries, young adult romances or religious adventure stories. Changes in our mores and social structure have opened up more possibilities for candid themes and the use of formerly controversial subjects in short fiction within these special subjects and genres, particularly in feminist, working women's, men's, confession and romance magazines.

In general, today's short story subjects reflect modern day trends and the effects of the recession. Stories are now more hearth and home-oriented and with a contemporary perspective. Prominent themes are family life, working mothers, single parent families and back to nature. Editors report that children are portrayed in a better moral perspective with less of a real slice of life thrust; and life on campus is not just the *Animal House* setting of a few years ago. Scientific themes (computers, video games) appear frequently, in concurrence with America's love affair with machines and high technology. Within short fiction, characters are clever, up-to-date and enjoy good positive relationships; stories are more conversational; and settings are in a less formal atmosphere. In style, black and Jewish short fiction tends to be more experimental, freer in form, while stories involving other ethnic groups are more traditional in structure.

Although the number of publishing opportunities increases, the individual magazine becomes more cautious. In publishing a magazine, "so much depends on the economy," says Eleanor Sullivan, editor of *Ellery Queen's Mystery Magazine*. Circulation drops, because more often than not the first thing the consumer cuts back on is the magazine subscription. That means less money for production. Small budgeted magazines are affected the most, but as one editors asks, "Isn't everyone?" Short fiction is often the first area to be pruned. Editors are asking for shorter stories, and even deleting fiction from some issues, using more reprints (children's magazines particularly), or they may now pay on publication instead of acceptance. Combining issues and raising subscription rates are also thrift measures. As a result editors can buy only what they are sure to use; they are demanding even more *excellence* and *professionalism* and are more selective. And in Canada the shrinking Canadian dollar precludes more sales by American authors.

Developing your ideas

To sell a short story to a commerical periodical, it is important to understand the responsibilities and demands of an editor. Staffs are small to skeletal; often one person is *the* fiction department. As many as 5,000 manuscripts might pass through an editorial office annually for which he/she is personally responsible. Editors are conscientious (or they wouldn't keep their jobs) and read each manuscript as there is time, in addition to their myriad other editorial duties involved in the magazine production. Most editors have been (or are) writers themselves and are familiar with and empathetic about rejection. They do have heart; *what they lack is time*. "The days of Maxwell Perkins [the famous editor] are long gone," says Rhoda Katerinsky of *MS* Magazine. A writer can't expect personal feedback on his/her work.

In your submission process, the editors implore: Have someone evaluate your story before sending it off; don't practice on busy editors. Gear your fiction to the tastes of the magazine; don't send scattershot to a lot of publications. Read many magazines and familiarize yourself with the contents and feel of each. *Study* the guidelines. Have an awareness of what has been published. Read *all* the magazines in your field to discern the differences and personalities in each publication. Knowing what pleases the readers (and not necessarily yourself) will please the editor. And above all, have patience and tolerance. If your manuscript is properly identified and addressed (with SASE), the editor will get back to you.

Editors also say: Let your story make the impression, not a fancy cover letter with credits. Learn the courtesies of the market. A professionally prepared manuscript is your entrée into the publishing world. *Some* editors can overlook bad typing, even poor grammar, *if* the material is outstanding. But a light typewriter ribbon, a single-spaced or hand-written story promotes immediate rejection.

In regard to general story structure and development editors agree by saying:

• Get off to a fast start and be sure of the direction of your story.

• Involve your characters in action and keep the story moving.

• Avoid stilted dialogue; *listen* to people talk; study expressions and slang, especially in teens and children.

• Make your subject universally compelling, broad in interest—without self pitying or banal personal reflections on life.

• Don't be afraid of the ordinary, but treat the subject with credibility and originality.

• Look for that inner voice for richness, depth and reality, regardless of the level of the audience. And hold the pathos.

ACTION, (formerly Discovery), Dept. of Christian Education, Free Methodist Headquarters, 901 College Ave., Winona Lake IN 46590. (219)267-7161. Editor: Vera Bethel. Sunday School take-home paper for children in grades 4-5-6. Weekly. Estab. 1970. Circ. 35,000.
Needs: Juvenile. "We buy fiction involving kids 9-12 in school and play situations wherein some conflict must be solved in a manner suggesting positive attitudes and growth." No talking animals, Biblical background, informational articles parading as fiction. Buys 1 ms/issue, 52 mss/year. Receives approximately 100 unsolicited fiction mss each month. Length: 1,000-1,200 words. Critiques rejected mss "when there is time." Sometimes recommends other markets.
How to Contact: Send complete ms with SASE. Reports in 1 month on mss. Free sample copy. Free fiction guidelines with SASE.
Payment: $25; 2 free author's copies. 10¢ charge for extra.
Terms: Pays on publication for simultaneous, first, second serial (reprint) and one-time rights.
Tips: Rejects mss because of "predictable, yet unbelievable (unreal) characters."

AFFAIRE DE COEUR, Leading Publication for Romance Readers and Writers, Affaire de Coeur, Inc., 5660 Roosevelt Place, Fremont CA 94538. (415)656-4804. Editor: Barbara N. Keenan. Magazine. Theme: The Romance Genre—book reviews, author/agent profiles; publishing tips and trends; articles geared to the romance writer and reader. Monthly. Estab. 1981. Circ. 3,000.
Needs: Gothic/historical romance, contemporary romance. Romantic fiction only. Receives variable number of unsolicited fiction mss/month. Buys 1 ms/issue; 12 mss/year. Charges reading fee of $35/ms—novel length. Length: variable. Occasionally critiques rejected mss. Charges $35/novel-length ms.
How to Contact: Query first with SASE. Simultaneous, photocopied and previously published submissions (with appropriate permissions) OK. Reports in 1 month on queries, 3 months on mss. Sample copy $2. Fiction guidelines free with SAE.
Payment: Pays $25.
Terms: Pays on publication for all rights. Publication copyrighted.

Tips: "Think of creative ways of dealing with the romantic fiction genre. Avoid the blatantly graphic—our publication is dedicated to building a credibility of respect and professionalism in the romantic genre."

AHOY, A Children's Magazine, Two Fathoms Publishing, 2021 Brunswick, Suite 209B, Halifax, Nova Scotia, Canada B3K 2Y5. (902)422-8230. Editor: Holly Book. Fiction Editor: Sue Cradduck. "*Ahoy* is an educational children's magazine with a strong Canadian bias. We publish fiction and nonfiction articles, puzzles, poetry and crafts for children aged 7-13." Quarterly. Estab. 1976. Circ. 5,000.
Needs: Adventure, juvenile, suspense/mystery. No "condescending, racist or sexist material; no adventures which encourage bad behavior." Receives 40 unsolicited fiction mss/month. Buys 2-5 mss/issue; 10-20 mss/year. Length: 750-1,500. 1,000 words average.
How to Contact: Send complete ms with SASE or IRCs. Photocopied submissions OK. Reports in 6 weeks on mss. Sample copy for $1 postage and 8x10 envelope. Fiction guidelines free.
Payment: Payment varies. Query.
Terms: Pays on publication for first North American serial rights. Publication copyrighted.
Tips: "Stick with contemporary issues and situations."

ALASKA OUTDOORS, Swensen's Publishing Co., Box 6324, Anchorage AL 99502. (907)276-2672. Contact: Editor-in-Chief. "The only magazine dealing exclusively in outdoor recreation in Alaska," directed to "the avid outdoorsman interested in Alaska." Published bimonthly. Estab. 1978. Circ. 60,000.
Needs: Adventure, humor/satire. "Setting must be Alaska; no Canada or Northwestern material." Buys 2 mss/issue, 15 mss/year. Length: 600 words minimum; 2,000 words maximum; 1,400 words average. Occasionally critiques rejected mss.
How to Contact: Query first with SASE. Reports in 2 weeks on queries, 3 weeks on mss. Sample copy $2.25. Free fiction guidelines for SAE and 1 first class stamp.
Payment: $50-200. Offers 20% kill fee for assigned ms not published.
Terms: Pays on acceptance for first North American serial rights. Publication copyrighted.
Tips: "Read the publication first. Keep to humor/satire. 90% of the manuscripts we purchase fall in this category. Experience in the outdoor sports is helpful."

ALFRED HITCHCOCK'S MYSTERY MAGAZINE, Davis Publications, Inc., 380 Lexington Ave., New York NY 10017. (212)557-9100. Editor: Cathleen Jordan. Mystery fiction magazine for mystery lovers. Published 13 times/year. Estab. December 1956. Circ. 200,000.
Needs: Mystery. No horror or sensationalism. Number of mss/issue varies with length of ms. Length: up to 15,000 words.
How to Contact: Send complete ms and SASE. Reports in 2 months. Free guideline sheet for SASE.
Payment: 3¢/word and up on acceptance. Manuscripts submitted to *AHMM* receive an alternate reading for *Ellery Queen's Mystery Magazines*, also published by Davis.
Tips: Also buying nonfiction articles on unsolved historical mysteries.

ALIVE! for Young, Christian Board of Publication, Box 179, St. Louis MO 63166. (314)371-6900. Editor: Michael Dixon. *Alive!* is a leisure reading magazine for junior high youth (12-15) in several major protestant denominations. Monthly. Estab. September 1969. Circ. 20,000. "We are one of the few magazines to slant toward the specific needs and interests of this age group, and we encourage youth participation in its creation."
Needs: Religious/inspirational, adventure, humor, young adult and ethnic. "Please deal with concerns and situations peculiar to the age group of *Alive!* readers (12-15). Stories about children or older youth have little chance of acceptance. Religious stories shouldn't be 'preachy' or with obvious moral." Buys 1-2 mss/issue. Receives approximately 50 unsolicited fiction mss each month. Length: 500-1,200 words.
How to Contact: Send complete ms with SASE. Reports in 3 weeks on ms. Sample copy 50¢. Free guidelines for legal-sized SASE.

Payment: 2¢/word. Free author's copy. 50¢ charge for extras.
Terms: Pays on publication for simultaneous and one-time rights. Publication copyrighted.
Tips: "Keep your audience in mind—know what would interest junior high youth. We return many well—written manuscripts that are too 'childish' or oriented around older teen interests. We are very strict on maximum length of stories."

ALIVE NOW!, The Upper Room, Box 189, Nashville TN 37202. (615)327-2700. Editor: Mary R. Coffman. Magazine of devotional writing and visuals for young adults. Bimonthly. Estab. 1971. Circ. 75,000.
Needs: Religious/inspirational. Buys 2 mss/issue; 12 mss/year. Length: 10 words minimum; 300 words maximum.
How to Contact: Send complete mss with SASE. Photocopied and previously published submissions OK. Reports in 4 weeks on mss. Sample copy free. Fiction guidelines free.
Payment: Pays $5-25; 12 contributor's copies.
Terms: Pays on publication for first rights, one-time rights, newspaper and periodical rights. Publication copyrighted.

AMAZING SCIENCE FICTION STORIES, Fantastic, TSR Hobbies, Inc., Box 110, Lake Geneva WI 53147. (414)248-8044. Editor: George H. Scithers. Magazine of science fiction and fantasy fiction stories for adults and young adults. Bimonthly. Estab. 1926. Circ. 14,000.
Needs: Adventure, fantasy, humor/satire, science fiction, serialized/excerpted novel. No "stories that are boring and do not hold interest or manuscripts typed with worn-out ribbons." Receives 500 unsolicited fiction mss/month. Buys 8 mss/issue; 48 mss/year. Length: 300 words minimum; 30,000 words maximum. Occasionally critiques rejected ms.
How to Contact: Send complete ms with SASE. Photocopied submissions OK. Reports in 2 weeks on mss. Sample copy $2. Fiction guidelines $1.
Payment: Pays 4-6¢/word.
Terms: Pays on acceptance for first North American serial rights. Publication copyrighted.
Tips: "*Read* this or other science fiction magazines. Read our book *On Writing Science Fiction*—it is a Writers Digest Book Club selection. *Know* proper ms format—it is hard to take seriously a really sloppy ms."

THE AMERICAN MIZRACHI WOMAN, American Mizrachi Women, 817 Broadway, New York NY 10003. (212)477-4720. Editor: Micheline Ratzersdorfer "*The American Mizrachi Woman* is the national magazine for the major religious women's Zionist organization in the United States. Our readers are concerned with Jews the world over, Israel, aspects of Judaism and current world events affecting all three." Monthly. Estab. 1925. Circ. 55,000.
Needs: Jewish/Israeli ethnic and Jewish holiday stories. Buys 1 ms/issue, 6 mss/year. Length: 750-2,000 words.
How to Contact: Query and send complete ms. SASE always. Reports in 1 month on both query and ms. Free sample copy with 10x13 SASE. Free guidelines with SASE.
Payment: Pays $25-50 for fiction. Free author's copy.
Terms: Pays on publication for first rights.
Tips: Mss rejected because "material unsuitable for our public, generally."

AMERICAN SQUAREDANCE, Burdick Enterprises, Box 488, Huron OH 44839. (419)433-2188. Editors: Stan and Cathie Burdick. Magazine about square dancing. Bimonthly. Estab. 1945. Circ. 13,000.
Needs: Adventure, fantasy, historical, humor/satire, romance, science fiction, western. "Haven't received any unsolicited mss for some time." Buys 2 + mss/year. Length: 2,500 words average.
How to Contact: Send complete ms with SASE. Reports in 2 weeks on queries. Sample copy free. Fiction guidelines free.
Payment: Pays 50¢/column inch minimum; free magazine subscription or free contributor's copies.
Terms: Pays on publication for all rights. Publication copyrighted.

ANALOG SCIENCE FICTION/SCIENCE FACT, Davis Publications, Inc., 380 Lexington Ave., New York NY 10017: (212)557-9100. Editor: Stanley Schmidt. "Well-written science fiction based on speculative ideas and fact articles on topics on the present and future frontiers of research. Our readership includes intelligent laymen and/or those professionally active in science and technology." Thirteen times yearly. Estab. 1930. Circ. 100,000.
Needs: Science fiction and serialized novels. "No stories which are not truly science fiction in the sense of having a plausible speculative idea *integral to the story*." Buys 4-8 mss/issue. Receives 300-400 unsolicited fiction mss each month. Length: 2,000-80,000 words. Critiques rejected mss "when there is time." Sometimes recommends other markets.
How to Contact: Send complete ms with SASE. Query with SASE only on serials. Reports in 3 weeks on both query and ms. Free guidelines with SASE.
Payment: 5.7¢-6.9¢/word.
Terms: Pays on acceptance for First North American serial rights and non-exclusive foreign rights. Publication copyrighted.
Tips: Mss are rejected because of "inaccurate science; poor plotting, characterization, or writing in general. We literally only have room for 1-2% of what we get. Many stories are rejected not because of anything conspicuously *wrong*, but because they lack anything sufficiently *special*. What we buy must stand out from the crowd."

ARARAT, Armenian General Benevolent Union of America, 585 Saddle River Rd., Saddle Brook NJ 07682. (201)797-7600. Editor: Leo Hamalian. Readership consists of people interested in Armenian background, culture and history. Quarterly. Estab. 1960. Circ. 2,000.
Needs: Armenian ethnic. Prefers to be Armenian written. Buys 1-2 mss/issue.
How to Contact: Query with SASE. Reports in 1 month on query, 3 months on ms. Free guidelines with SASE.
Payment: $10-75 plus 2 free author's copies.
Terms: Pays on publication.

ARES MAGAZINE, TSR Hobbies Inc., Box 110, Lake Geneva, WI 53147. Editor: Michael Moore. "*Ares* is the magazine of science fiction. Readers enjoy playing games, reading science fiction, solving problems and dealing with complex, fully detailed world constructs." Bimonthly. Estab. Feb. 1980. Circ. 14,500.
Needs: Science fiction. "We seek action-oriented stories with strong central conflicts and interesting characters. 'Hard' science fiction, exciting science fantasy, sword & sorcery, and quest/adventure stories are needed. No scientifically inaccurate stories or serials." Buys 12-15/year. Receives approximately 150 unsolicited fiction mss each month. Length: 3,000-8,000 words. Critiques rejected mss "when there is time."
How to Contact: Send complete ms with SASE. Reports in 45 days on ms. Sample copy $6. Free guidelines and future game schedule upon request with SASE.
Payment: 3-6¢/word. Offers $50 kill fee for assigned ms not published.
Terms: Pays on acceptance for first English language serial rights. Publication copyrighted.
Tips: "Stories should have a beginning, middle and end; the central conflict should be resolved using elements of the world constructed. The story should have a feeling of 'strangeness.' Try to think of fresh plots, not the tired old space opera themes. Keep in touch with current trends of science to find where the future is heading. The fiction editor will attempt to point out strengths and failures of submissions." Mss are rejected for "three main reasons: The plot is trite or a rehash of someone else's ideas; the writing style is dull and the characters are not realistically drawn; there is no central conflict that is resolved by the end of the story."

ATLANTIC MONTHLY, 8 Arlington St., Boston MA 02116. (617)536-9500. Senior Editor: Michael Curtis. Editor: William Whitworth. General magazine for the college educated with broad cultural interests. Monthly. Estab. 1857. Circ. 365,000.
Needs: Literary and contemporary. "Seeks fiction that is clear, tightly written with strong sense of 'story' and well-defined characters." Buys 2 mss/issue. Receives approximately 1,000 unso-

Close-up

Elizabeth Mitchell
Analog Science Fiction/Science Fact

"Here at *Analog* we consider it a privilege to find new capable authors and work with them from their first stories on," says Elizabeth Mitchell, managing editor and one-half of the main editorial team. Editor Stanley Schmidt is the other half. "As long as there are authors who can keep imagining what can happen—and write it up in enjoyable ways," she continues, "we're going to have a nice healthy field."

The *Analog* policy to encourage new writers—plus the *Star Wars*, *E.T.* mania—has helped science fiction remain a strong market for short fiction and generally a better area than mainstream fiction. "We're interested in stories with a strong scientific footing," Mitchell says. "Of course, we also look for good plots and strong believable characters (not necessarily human)." The science must be accurate and can be physical, sociological and/or psychological. The technology is unlimited in range.

Schmidt and Mitchell hesitate to impose "Thou Shalt Nots" for fear of inhibiting creative story topics. Science fiction today is "a much broader field than it used to be and much more than monsters and pretty ladies in distress," or crazy video games, a current overworked theme.

Mitchell herself was always interested in science and journalism, a combination which brought her to New York from the University of Nebraska and landed her the *Analog* position. Editor Stan Schmidt is a SF writer with a Ph.D. in physics. Thus it is only very occasionally that an attentive reader finds even the slightest scientific inaccuracy which got beyond the two editors.

Many submissions are returned because of scientific mistakes. Some stories just have "microwriting"—or good quality sentences and paragraph structure; and some have "macrowriting" or "good construction of a story as a unified whole." The latter is sometimes acceptable if the grammar and spelling can be "cleaned up." The preference, of course, is a combination of the two skills. Every manuscript gets an equal chance, however, Mitchell insists, and stories are read entirely.

Twenty percent of the manuscripts *Analog* buys are found in the slush pile of stories from new authors. Most others go back to the authors with the standard rejection slips, and a small percentage will get a note from the editor. "A personal comment of any kind is always a good sign," says Mitchell. The usual reply period is about two weeks, which means the small staff must stay on top of the 75 submissions they receive a week. If there is no response within that time, it is generally because of no return envelope or postage or no address on the first page of the manuscript (all outside envelopes are thrown away). Thus there is, "alas," a "dead" pile of unknowns due to poor manuscript preparation and handling.

For potential publication in *Analog*, Mitchell offers this advice to the short story writer of science fiction: Enjoy science and be willing to do research. Read the classics and the current reputable writers or at least know what has been done. And before starting your story, get a sense of the entire science fiction magazine field. Each SF publication today has an individual personality and a distinct thrust of its own.

licited fiction mss each month. Length: 4,000-6,000 words.
How to Contact: Send complete ms with SASE. Reports in 2 months on mss.
Payment: Pays $1,500 to $2,000 and beyond.
Terms: Pays on acceptance for first and first North American serial rights. Publication copyrighted.
Tips: "Read magazine with great care and write well."

ATTENZIONE, Paulucci Publications, Inc., 55 E. 34th St., New York NY 10016. Editor: Lois Spritzer. Senior Editor: Tony Shugaar. General interest magazine with emphasis on Italian and Italian-American political and social endeavors. Monthly. Estab. 1979. Circ. 160,000.
Needs: All mss must have some Italian-related theme. Buys 6 mss/year. Length: 3,000 words.
How to Contact: Send complete ms with SASE.
Payment: Pays $350.
Terms: Pays 3 months after acceptance for first North American serial rights.

THE AUGUSTA SPECTATOR, FKB Enterprises., Box 3168, Augusta GA 30904. (404)733-1476. Publisher/Editor: Faith B. Bertsche. Regional publication, modern in outlook; short stories, poems, articles for upper income marrieds; average age 45. Published every 4 months. Estab. April 1980. Circ. 5,000.
Needs: Literary, contemporary, romance, mystery, adventure and humor. No explicit sex or violence. Buys 1-2 mss/issue. Receives approximately 12 unsolicited fiction mss each month. Critiques rejected mss "when there is time."
How to Contact: Query with SASE. Reports in 2 months. Free guidelines with SASE.
Payment: $25-50/copy.
Terms: Pays on publication for first rights. Publication copyrighted.
Tips: Mss are rejected because they "ramble—no story."

AUTOBUFF MAGAZINE, The Magazine for the Adult Automotive Enthusiast, Carnaby Communications Corp., Box 88690, Atlanta GA 30338. (404)394-0010. Editor. D. Beckstead Naef. Magazine of "automotive related material in a fun, light-hearted style for 18-34 year old men with an interest in cars and beautiful women." Bimonthly. Estab. 1982. Circ. 200,000.
Needs: Adventure, fantasy, humor/satire, men's, automotive street racing. "No gay stories or stories written in heavy, cumbersome style." Receives 3-5 unsolicited fiction mss/month. Buys 2-3 mss/issue. Length: 2,000 words minimum; 3,000 words maximum; 2,500 words average. Occasionally critiques rejected mss.
How to Contact: Send complete ms with SASE. Photocopied submissions OK. Sample copy for $1.28 postage and 9x12 envelope. Fiction guidelines free.
Payment: Pays $100-250.
Terms: Pays on acceptance for all rights. Publication copyrighted.
Tips: "Fiction should be in a lighthearted style with a high-performance street machine involved in the plot. Also ladies in the story are helpful. Write story in macho style."

BALTIMORE JEWISH TIMES, 2104 N. Charles St., Baltimore MD 21218. (301)752-3504. Magazine with subjects of interest to Jewish readers. Weekly. Estab. 1918. Circ. 19,000.
Needs: Contemporary Jewish themes only. Receives 7-10 unsolicited fiction mss/month. Buys 5-6 mss/year. Length: 1,500 words minimum; 5,000 words maximum (or 6-20 typed pages). Occasionally critiques rejected mss.
How to Contact: Send complete ms. Simultaneous, photocopies and previously published submissions OK "on occasion." Reports in 4-6 weeks on mss. Sample copy $1 and legal size envelope.
Payment: Pays $35-100.
Terms: Pays on publication. Publication copyrighted.

BEAVER, QMG, Magazines Corp., 235 Park Ave., South, New York NY 10003. Editor: Biff Norganski. Magazine with sex themes and general interest subjects related to men for men of all ages. Monthly. Estab. 1975. Circ. 200,000.
Needs: "We want to see erotic mystery, erotic scientific fiction, erotic fantasy. No 'graffiti' (erotica by itself). Buys 2 mss/issue, 24 mss/year. Length: 2,500-3,000 words.
How to Contact: Send complete ms with SASE. Reports in 2 weeks on mss. Sample copy $2.95 with free guidelines.
Payment: Pays $400.
Terms: Pays on acceptance for all rights.

BIBLE IN LIFE FRIENDS, David C. Cook Publishing Co., 850 North Grove, Elgin IL 60120. (312)741-2400. Editor: Judy Couchman. Editor, Primary Curriculum: Betty Free. Take home Sunday School paper for 6 and 7 year-olds, first and second grades, and family. Weekly.
Needs: "Stories with beginning second grade reading level; Bible stories rewritten or stories relating to Bible stories dealing with present day situations." No "short story with moral tacked on end." Length: 300-500 words maximum.
How to Contact: Send query with attached sample of writing style and SASE. Reports in 1-2 months on queries.
Payment: Pays $25-40/story.
Terms: Pays on acceptance for all rights.
Tips: "Get to know today's kids in real situations. Don't moralize. Write story with a realistic situation that will make a child want to read."

BIBLE IN LIFE STORIES, David C. Cook Publishing Co., 850 North Grove, Elgin IL 60120. (312)741-2400. Administrative Editor: Elspeth Murphy. Sunday School take-home paper for Sunday School age children 4 and 5 years of age. Quarterly, "handed out weekly."
Needs: Religious/inspirational. "We want stories that reflect a specific weekly theme. Well developed with beginning, middle and end. No poorly written stories with a moral tacked on at the end." Receives "very few" unsolicited fiction mss/month, "most are assigned." Length: 300-500 words maximum.
How to Contact: Query first "with letter describing your experience with education, church and children in general terms. Clippings or sample story would be useful for making future assignments." Reports in 1-2 months on queries.
Payment: Pays $25/story.
Terms: Pays on acceptance for all rights.
Tips: "Understand the present day child. Observe children; study good writing. Best if child solves the problem. Moral must be integral part of the story. Be on the same wave length as the Sunday School."

BIRD TALK, A Magazine for Every Bird Lover, Bell Publishing, Box 1029, Angels Camp CA 95222. (209)736-0505. Managing Editor: Rod Ruthel. Fiction Editor: Nancy Bigelow. Magazine "to promote knowledge and understanding in the areas of birdwatching, breeding, raising and caring for all types of birds for anyone with an interest in birds: bird breeders, cage bird owners, bird watchers and bird fanciers." Bimonthly. Estab. 1982. Circ. 10,000.
Needs: Adventure, comics, contemporary, fantasy, humor/satire, juvenile, mainstream, prose poem, religious/inspirational. "Must contain some relationship to birds (any kind). No shooting articles or stories." Receives 1-3 unsolicited fiction mss/month. Buys 1 ms/issue; 6-8 mss/year. Length: 600 minimum; 2,000 maximum.
How to Contact: Send complete ms. Simultaneous and photocopied submissions OK. Reports in 4 weeks on mss. Sample copy $2.50. Fiction guidelines for business size envelope and 1 first class stamp.
Payment: Payment negotiable ($10-$25) and 1 contributor's copy.
Terms: Pays on publication for first rights, one-time rights. Publication copyrighted.
Tips: "Neatness, accuracy and credibility count. Typed (double-spaced) manuscripts are best of

course, but we will consider anything that is easy to read." Send photos and/or illustrations if available.

THE BIRMINGHAM SETTLEMENT MAGAZINES, Marooned, Future Studies Newsletter, Meridian, NALK (National Association for the Childless), 318 Summer Lane, Birmingham, England B19 ZRL. (21)359-3562. Director: Peter Houghton. *Marooned* is a quarterly magazine of the Islands Adventures Club. *Future Studies Newsletter* is published every two months. Occasional science fiction stories welcome. *Meridian, Journal of Mid-Life Opportunity* is for the 35-55 age group. Good short stories welcome. *NALK, Journal of the National Association for the Childless* includes personal stories. Bimonthly and quarterly.
Needs: Adventure, contemporary, experimental, science ficton, women's (childless and mid-life). Length: 1,000 words minimum; 3,000 words maximum.
How to Contact: Query first with SASE. Simultaneous and photocopied submissions OK. Reports in 3 weeks on queries.
Payment: Pay depends on length of story.

THE B'NAI B'RITH INTERNATIONAL JEWISH MONTHLY, B'nai B'rith International, 1640 Rhode Island Ave. NW, Washington DC 20036. (202)857-6645. Editor-in-Chief: Marc Silver. "Magazine publishing primarily articles of general Jewish interest, occasionally fiction, for a Jewish family audience." Published monthly. Estab. 1890. Circ. 200,000.
Needs: Ethnic, humor/satire, literary, serialized/excerpted novel. "All stories must have a Jewish theme." Receives approximately 5 unsolicited fiction mss/month. Accepts 2 mss/year. Length: 2,500 words minimum; 3,000 words maximum; 2,500 words average. Occasionally critiques rejected mss.
How to Contact: Send complete ms or query with clips of published work. SASE always. Reports in 3 weeks on queries, 4 weeks on mss. Free sample copy.
Payment: 5-10¢/word.
Terms: Pays on publication for first rights. Publication copyrighted.

BOYS' LIFE, For All Boys, Boy Scouts of America, Magazine Division, 1325 Walnut Hill Lane, Irving TX 75062. (214)659-2000. Editor: Robert E. Hood. Fiction Editor: Kris Imherr. "*Boys' Life* covers Boy Scout activities and general interest subjects for ages 8 to 18, Boy Scouts, Cub Scouts and others of that age group." Monthly. Estab. 1911. Circ. 1,500,000.
Needs: Adventure, contemporary, humor/satire, science fiction, suspense/mystery, western, young adult, sports. "We publish short stories aimed at a young adult audience and usually written from the viewpoint of a 10- to 16-year-old boy protagonist." Receives approximately 100 unsolicited mss/month. Buys 12-18 mss/year. Length: 1,000 words minimum; 3,000 words maximum; 2,500 words average. "Very rarely" critiques rejected ms.
How to Contact: Send complete ms with SASE. "We'd much rather see manuscripts than queries." Simultaneous and photocopied submissions OK. Reports in 2 weeks on mss. Sample copy "check your local library."
Payment: Pays $350 and up, "depending on an author's reputation." Offers 50% kill fee.
Terms: Pays on acceptance for one-time rights. Publication copyrighted.
Tips: "We tend to use many of the same authors repeatedly because their characters, themes, etc., develop a following among our readers. We do not encourage beginning writers or unsolicited manuscripts."

BREAD, Church of the Nazarene, 6401 The Paseo, Kansas City MO 64131. Editor: Gary Sivewright. Christian leisure reading magazine for junior and senior high students. Monthly.
Needs: Adventure. Themes should be school and church oriented. Adventure stories wanted, but without sermonizing. Buys 1,500 mss/year.
How to Contact: Send complete ms with SASE. Reports in 6 weeks on mss. Free sample copy and guidelines.

Payment: Pays 3¢/word for first rights and 2¢/word for second rights.
Terms: Pays on acceptance for first rights and sometimes second serial rights. Accepts simultaneous submissions. Byline given.

BRIGADE LEADER, For Men Guiding Boys, Christian Service Brigade, 380 Schmale Rd., Carol Stream IL 60187. (312)665-0630. Editor-in-Chief: Michael J. Chiapperino. Managing Editor: Mark L. Carpenter. "We seek to provide practical material for men committed to helping boys." Readers are "Christian men seeking to guide and direct boys 6-18." Published quarterly. Circ. 15,500.
Needs: Religious/inspirational. Receives 3-4 unsolicited fiction mss/month. Accepts 2 mss/year. Length: 800 words minimum; 1,500 words maximum; 1,200 words average.
How to Contact: Query first or send complete ms. SASE always. Simultaneous and photocopied submissions and previously published work OK, if labeled as such. Reports in 2 weeks on queries, 3 weeks on mss. Sample copy $1. Free fiction guidelines for business-size SAE and 1 first class stamp.
Payment: $35-100.
Terms: Pays on publication for first rights, second serial rights, one-time rights or assignments on work-for-hire-basis. Publication copyrighted.

BRONZE THRILLS, Lexington Library, Inc., 3131 N. Stemmons, Suite A, Dallas TX 75427. (214) 630-2167. Editor: Karen Thompson. "Romance magazine with romantic, heart-throbbing fiction stories for women between the ages of 18-35 (black)." Published monthly. Estab. 1952. Circ. nationwide.
Needs: Adventure, confession, ethnic, fantasy, feminist/lesbian, gay, psychic/supernatural, romance (contemporary), serialized/excerpted novel. "No unrealistic, untimely stories or manuscripts that do not have some type of romantic content." Receives 10-20 unsolicited fiction mss/month. Accepts 7 mss/issue, 84 mss/year. Length: 3,000 words minimum; 5,000 words maximum. Occasionally critiques rejected mss.
How to Contact: Send complete ms with SASE. Simultaneous and photocopied submissions and previously published work OK. Reports in 2 weeks on mss. Free sample copy. Free fiction guidelines with SASE.
Payment: $40-75 with 1 contributor's copy and $15 magazine subscription. $1.50 charge for extra contributor's copies.
Terms: Pays on publication for one-time rights and assignment on work-for-hire-basis. Publication copyrighted.
Tips: "Be enthusiastic, creative, and send material that is relevant to today."

BUF, G & S Publications, Inc. 1472 Broadway, New York NY 10036. (212)840-7224. Editor: Will Martin. Men's sophisticate magazine. Bimonthly (alternating with *GEM*—see listing for that title). Estab. 1961, Circ. 100,000.
Needs: Erotica ("but not pornography"), humor/satire, men's. Receives 25-50 unsolicited fiction mss/month. Buys 4-5 mss/issue; 48-60 mss/year (for *GEM* and *Buf*). Length: 1,000 words minimum; 3,000 words maximum; 2,500 words average. Occasionally critiques rejected mss.
How to Contact: Send complete ms with SASE. Simultaneous and photocopied submissions OK. Sample copy $3.
Payment: Pays $40 for short shorts to 500 words; $100 maximum.
Terms: "Payment is usually on assignment to a specific issue;" for all rights. Publication copyrighted.

BUFFALO SPREE MAGAZINE, Spree Publishing Co., Inc., 4511 Harlem Rd., Buffalo NY 14226. (716)839-3405. Editor: Johanna V. Shotell. Fiction Editor: Gary L. Goss. "City magazine for professional, educated and above-average income people." Quarterly. Estab. 1967. Circ. 20,000.
Needs: Literary, contemporary, men's, women's, feminist, mystery, adventure, humor and eth-

nic. No pornographic or religious. Buys 1 ms/issue, 4 mss/year. Length: 1,000-2,000 words.
How to Contact: Send complete ms with SASE. Reports within 1 week to 2 months on ms. Sample copy for $1 with 9x12 SASE and $1.00 postage.
Payment: $50-125. 2 free author's copies. $1 charge for extra.
Terms: Pays on publication for first rights.

BUTTERFAT MAGAZINE, Fraser Valley Milk Producers Cooperative Association, Box 9100, Vancouver, British Columbia, Canada V6B 4G4. (604)420-6611. Editor-in-Chief: C.A. Paulson. Publishes material on "dairy farming and industry in British Columbia—mostly factual, technical, informative—for dairy farmers, staff and agribusiness." Published bimonthly. Estab. 1922. Circ. 3,700.
Needs: Adventure, ethnic, historical (general), prose poem, farm family. Do not use "non traditional grammar." Receives approximately 10 unsolicited fiction mss/month. Buys 1 mss/year. Length: 500 words minimum; 1,500 words maximum. Sometimes recommends other markets.
How to Contact: Send complete ms. Simultaneous and photocopied submissions OK. Reports in 4 weeks. Free sample copy and fiction guidelines.
Payment: $35-85.
Terms: Pays on acceptance for one-time rights.
Tips: We use "Christmas/winter stories, poetry, quips, preferably written by British Columbians." Rejects mss because "not absolutely on target."

CAMPUS LIFE MAGAZINE, Christianity Today, Inc., 465 Gundersen Drive, Carol Stream IL 60187. (312)260-6200. Editor: Gregg Lewis. "General interest magazine with a religious twist. Not limited to strictly Christian content. Articles on mopeds and forgiveness, videogames and divorce, Frisbees and self-worth, etc., for high school and college age readers." Monthly. Estab. 1942. Circ. 200,000.
Needs: Condensed novel, fantasy, humor/satire, prose poem, science fiction, serialized/excerpted novel, young adult. Prefers "realistic situations. We are a Christian magazine but are *not* interested in sappy, formulaic, sentimentally religious stores. We *are* interested in well-crafted stories that portray life realistically, stories high school and college youth relate to. Nothing contradictory of Christian values. If you don't understand our market and style, don't submit." Receives 30 unsolicited fiction mss/month. Buys 1-2 mss/year. Length: 1,000-3,000 average, "possibly longer."
How to Contact: Query with clips of published work and SASE. Simultaneous, photocopied and previously published submissions OK. Reports in 4-6 weeks on queries. Sample copy $2 and 9½x11 envelope.
Payment: Pays $175-250, "generally"; 2 contributor's copies.
Terms: Pays on acceptance for one-time rights.
Tips: "A good realistic story generally captures high readership in *Campus Life*. Read the magazine—understand our purpose, style, and stance. Perfect your craft. Ask us for sample copy with fiction story. Query first. Send published samples. Avoid shallow, formulaic writing or simplistic inspirational fiction. Do not submit anything contradictory to Christian principles or values."

CANADIAN SKATER, Canadian Figure Skating Assoc., 333 River Rd., Ottawa, Ontario K1L 8B9. (613)746-5953. Editor: Teresa Moore. Bimonthly. Estab. 1974. Circ. 10,000.
Needs: Adventure, young adult and skating. Buys 1 ms/issue. Length: 1,200-2,000 words.
How to Contact: Send complete ms with SAE, IRC. Reports in 1 month on ms. Free sample copy.
Payment: $50-80.
Terms: Pays on acceptance for first rights and one-time rights.
Tips: Rejects mss because "most are not very good. We need more children's stories."

CANINE CHRONICLE, Routledge Publications, Inc., Box 115, Montpelier IN 47359. (317)728-2464. Editor: Ric Routledge. Tabloid about purebred dogs for devoted dog show exhibitors. Weekly. Estab. 1975. Circ. 7,000.

Needs: "Anything regarding dogs." No "boy meets dog" stories. Receives 10 unsolicited mss/ month. Buys 12 mss/year.
How to Contact: Send complete ms with SASE. Photocopied and previously published submissions OK. Reports in 2 months on mss. Sample copy free.
Payment: Pays $25-100.
Terms: Pays on acceptance for all rights. Publication copyrighted.
Tips: "Understand the theory of special interest publications."

CAPPER'S WEEKLY, Stauffer Communications, Inc., 616 Jefferson, Topeka KS 66607. (913)295-1108. Editor: Dorothy Harvey. A "clean, uplifting and nonsensational newspaper for families from children to grandparents." Biweekly. Estab. July 1879. Circ. 416,000.
Needs: Serialized Novels. "We only accept novel-length stories for serialization. No fiction containing violence or obscenity." Buys 2-3 stories/year. Receives 2-3 unsolicited fiction mss each month.
How to Contact: Send complete ms with SASE. Reports in 5-6 months on ms. Sample copy 45¢.
Payment: $150-200 for one-time serialization. Free author's copies (1-2 copies as needed for copyright).
Terms: Pays on acceptance for second serial (reprint) rights and one-time rights.
Tips: "Most rejections are because we try to avoid obscenity in language, explicit sex, bloody violence, or lack of morality. And sometimes the stories are poorly written."

CAT FANCY, Fancy Publications, Box 4030, San Clemente CA 92672. (714)498-1600. Editor-in-Chief: Linda W. Lewis. General cat and kitten magazine, consumer oriented for "cat and kitten lovers." Published monthly. Circ. 80,000.
Needs: Cat-related themes only. Receives approximately 40 unsolicited fiction mss/month. Accepts 12 mss/year. Length: 3,000 words maximum. Sometimes recommends other markets.
How to Contact: Send complete ms with SASE. Simultaneous and photocopied submissions OK. Reports in 6 weeks. Sample copy $2.50. Free fiction guidelines with SASE.
Payment: 3¢/word and 2 contributor's copies. $2.50 charge for extras.
Terms: Publication copyrighted.
Tips: "Stories should focus on a cat or cats, not just be about people who happen to have a cat."

CAVALIER MAGAZINE, Dugent Publishing Corp., 2355 Salzedo St., Coral Gables FL 33134. (305)443-2378. Editor: Douglas Allen. Fiction Editor: M. DeWalt. Sexually-oriented, sophisticated magazine for single men aged 18-35. Monthly. Estab. 1952. Circ. 250,000.
Needs: Adventure, horror, men's and erotica. No material on children, religious subjects or anything that might be libelous. Buys 3 mss/issue. Receives approximately 200 unsolicited fiction mss each month. Length: 1,500-3,000 words. Critiques rejected mss "when there is time." Sometimes recommends other markets.
How to Contact: Send complete ms with SASE. Reports in 3 weeks on mss. Sample copy for $3. Free fiction guidelines with SASE.
Payment: $200-300 per ms. Offers 50% kill fee for assigned mss not published.
Terms: Pays on publication for first North American serial rights. Publication copyrighted.
Tips: Mss are rejected because writers "either don't know our market or the mss are too long or too short. Length and erotic content are crucial (erotica in *every* story). In many cases it is selecting the most outstanding story from a multitude of submissions, otherwise, rejections a result of unrelated subject matter, sloppy manuscripts, carbon copies or trite, tired subjects. All writers should ask for our guidelines first before submitting. They are detailed and helpful." Occasionally sponsors contests . . . watch publication.

CHARISMA, Communications Ministries, Inc., 174 W. Comstock Ave., Winter Park FL 32789. (305)645-2022. Editor: Stephen Strang. Fiction Editor: Howard Earl. Magazine for Christians. Published 12 times/year.
Needs: Religious/inspirational, testimonial. Fiction is built around Christian living. Receives

comm. periodicals

20-30 unsolicited fiction mss/month. Buys 1-2 mss/issue usually by assignment or established writers. Length: 2,000-3,000 words average. Occasionally critiques rejected mss.

How to Contact: Query first with SASE. Sample copy free for SAE.

Payment: Pays $150-300; varied amount of free contributor's copies. Offers kill fee.

Terms: Pays on publication for first, second, first North American serial or one-time rights. Publication copyrighted.

Tips: Read the magazine. Writer's guidelines on request.

CHATELAINE, Maclean-Hunter Publishing Co., 481 University Ave., Toronto, Canada M5W 1A7. 596-5000. Editor: Mildred Istona. Fiction Editor: Barbara West. "This is a magazine for Canadian women. We present articles, fiction, service material, news and reviews relevant to their lives. Because Canada's population is relatively small we do not concentrate on a specific part of the market but address ourselves to all Canadian women, including housewives, career women, feminists, mothers, singles, etc." Monthly. Estab. March 1928. Circ. 1 million w.

Needs: Literary, contemporary, romance, mystery, adventure, humor. Buys 1-2 ms/issue, approximately 25/year. Receives approximately 70 unsolicited fiction mss each month. Length: 3,000-4,500 words. Sometimes recommends other markets.

How to Contact: Send complete ms with SAE and IRC. Reports in 4 weeks on ms. Free fiction guidelines with SAE, IRC.

Payment: $1,500 in Canadian currency. 2 free author's copies. $1.25 (Canadian) per extra copy.

Terms: Pays on acceptance for first North American serial rights in English and French. Publication copyrighted.

Tips: "We're looking for good, human interest stories in which women play the leading parts, or at least share center stage with men. We are primarily interested in Canadian stories, particularly those about contemporary relationships. Stories that are too explicit sexually don't work for us, nor do avant-garde pieces, nor nostalgic reminiscences. Drug taking, four-letter words, not for us, nor do old-fashioned-type 'women's stories' appeal." Mss are rejected because they are the "wrong type of stories for this magazine; also because of poor writing, poor structure, hackneyed subject. Not many writers can produce the kind of story—fast-moving, involving, readable—that we are looking for. We are eager to discover new talent, and to this end sponsor an annual fiction contest for Canadian writers only."

CHESAPEAKE BAY MAGAZINE, Chesapeake Bay Communications, Inc., 1819 Bay Ridge Ave., Annapolis MD 21403. (301)263-2662. Editor: Betty Rigoli. "*Chesapeake Bay Magazine* is a regional publication for those who enjoy reading about the Bay and its tributaries. Most of our articles are boating-related. Our readers are yachtsmen, boating families, fishermen, ecologists, anyone who is part of Chesapeake Bay life." Monthly. Estab. 1971. Circ. 15,000.

Needs: Fantasy, mystery, adventure, humor and historical. "Any fiction piece *must* concern the Chesapeake Bay. Only stories done by authors who are familiar with the area are accepted. No general type stories with the Chesapeake Bay superimposed in an attempt to make a sale." Buys 1 ms/issue, 8 mss/year. Receives approximately 3 unsolicited fiction mss each month. Length: 1,250-3,000 words. Critiques rejected mss "when there is time." Recommends other markets.

How to Contact: Query or send ms. SASE always. Reports in 1 month on queries, 2 months on mss. Sample copy $1.50. Free fiction guidelines with SASE.

Payment: $50-85. 2 free author's copies.

Terms: Pays on publication for all rights or first North American serial rights. Publication copyrighted.

Tips: "Always query first. Make sure you have knowledge of the area. Send only material that is related to our market. All mss must be typed, double-spaced, in duplicate." Mss are rejected because "writers lack knowledge of Chesapeake Bay area or material is not marine oriented, or it is too obviously novice work—poor grammatical construction—which makes re-writing here too time consuming."

CHIC MAGAZINE, Larry Flynt Publications, 2029 Century Park East, Suite 3800, Los Angeles CA 90067. (213)556-9200. Executive Editor: Donald R. Evans. Fiction Editor: Jim Gregory.

"*Chic* is a major slick men's magazine for ages 18-40. It publishes adventure fiction which has a fully developed plot and characterization. Sexual activities should grow out of the plot rather than being the main theme of the story. Include a one-and-a-half-page erotic scene and a twist ending." Monthly. Estab. November 1976. Circ. 300,000.

Needs: Adventure fiction. No incomplete mss. Buys 1 ms/issue. Receives 70-80 unsolicited fiction mss each month. Length: 4,500 words.

How to Contact: Send complete ms with SASE. Reports in 1 month on ms.

Payment: $300. Offers 20% kill fee for assigned mss not published.

Terms: Pays on acceptance for first and second worldwide publication rights. Publication copyrighted.

Tips: "*Chic* recommends that the writer read the magazine to get an idea of publishable fiction. We must have twist endings. We would like to point out once again that a series of sexual events strung together does not produce a short story to qualify for *Chic*. This is a common mistake made by many writers. Get off to a fast start in your story. Let the story itself make the impression."

CHICAGO MAGAZINE, WFMT Inc., 303 East Wacker Drive, Chicago IL 60601. (312)565-5000. Editor: John Fink. Fiction Editor: Christine Newman. City magazine for well-educated professional people who are interested in the arts. Monthly. Estab. October 1969. Circ. 215,000.

Needs: Literary, contemporary, men's, women's, humor, ethnic and book excerpts. No juvenile, young adult or erotic. Buys 9 mss/year. Receives approximately 150 unsolicited fiction mss each month. Length: 5-20 double spaced pages. Critiques rejected mss "when there is time."

How to Contact: Send complete ms with SASE. Reports in 1 month on mss. Sample copy $3.

Payment: Pays $500-850 with free author's copies. Offers 25% kill fee for assigned ms not published.

Terms: Pays on acceptance for first time North American rights. Publication copyrighted.

Tips: "Submit caring mss."

CHICKADEE, The Magazine for Young Children, Young Naturalist Foundation, 59 Front St. E, Toronto, Ontario, Canada M5E 1B3. (416)364-3333. Editor: Janis Nostbakken. "*Chickadee* is created to give children under eight a lively, fun-filled look at the world around them. Each issue has a mix of activities, puzzles, games and read-aloud stories." Monthly except July and August. Estab. 1979. Circ. 85,000.

Needs: Juvenile. No fantasy, religious or anthropomorphic material. Receives a varied amount of unsolicited fiction mss/month. Buys 1 ms/issue; 10 mss/year. Length: 500 words minimum; 1,200 words maximum; 1,000 words average.

How to Contact: Query with outline of story and sample paragraphs with SASE. Reports in 8 weeks on queries. Sample copy for $1.25 for 8x11 SAE and IRC's. Fiction guidelines free for SAE, IRC.

Payment: Pays $25-350; 1 free contributor's copy; $1.25 charge for extras.

Payment: Pays on publication for all rights. Publication copyrighted.

Tips: "Read back issues and review editorial guidelines. Avoid writing 'down' to children. Know the interests of your readers. Thoroughly research subject matter."

CHILD LIFE, The Benjamin Franklin Literary & Medical Society, Inc., 1100 Waterway Blvd., Box 567, Indianapolis IN 46206. (317)636-8881. Editor: William Wagner. Juvenile magazine for youngsters ages 7-9. Material should be health-related, i.e. good nutrition, safety, exercise.

Needs: Juvenile. No adult or adolescent fiction. Length: 1,600 words maximum.

How to Contact: Send complete ms with SASE. Reports in 8-10 weeks. Sample copy 75¢. Free writer's guidelines with SASE.

Payment: Approximately 4¢/word for all rights. Publication copyrighted.

Terms: Pays on publication.

CHILDREN'S DIGEST, Children's Better Health Institute, 1100 Waterway Blvd., Box 567, Indianapolis IN 46206. Magazine with special emphasis on health, nutrition, exercise, and safety for 8-10 year olds.

Needs: Health-related material. "Realistic stories, adventure and mysteries. Humorous stories are highly desirable. If possible, the material should *subtly* encourage readers to develop better health or safety habits. Stories should not exceed 1,800 words." Receives 40-50 unsolicited fiction mss each month.

How to Contact: Send complete ms with SASE. Sample copy 75¢. Queries not needed. Reports in 10 weeks. Free guidelines with SASE.

Payment: Pays approximately 4¢/word with 2 free author's copies.

Terms: Pays on publication for all rights. Publication copyrighted.

Tips: "We try to present our health-related material in a postive—not a negative—light and we try to incorporate humor and a light approach wherever possible without minimizing the seriousness of what we are saying. Fiction stories that deal with a health theme need not have health as the primary subject but should include it in some way in the course of events. Most rejected health-related manuscripts are too preachy or they lack substance. Although we emphasize the development of better health habits, we want our stories to be exciting and interesting as well as educational. Simultaneous submissions are not accepted."

CHILDREN'S PLAYMATE, The Benjamin Franklin Literary & Medical Society, Inc., 1100 Waterway Blvd., Box 567, Indianapolis IN 46206. (317)636-8881. Editor: Kathleen B. Mosher. Juvenile magazine for children ages 5-7 years.

Needs: Juvenile with special emphasis on health, nutrition, safety, exercise. No adult or adolescent fiction. Receives approximately 150 unsolicited fiction mss each month. Length: 600 words or less. Indicate word count on material. Sometimes send mss to editors of other pulications.

How to Contact: Send complete ms with SASE. Reports in 8-10 weeks.

Payment: Approximately 4¢/word.

Terms: Pays on publication for all rights. Publication copyrighted.

Tips: "Stories should be kept simple and entertaining. Study past issues of the magazines—be aware of vocabulary limitations of the readers. Avoid errors in spelling, grammar, punctuation. Stories or articles must be interesting for the target age of the readers." Rejects mss because "we receive thousands of manuscripts every year and have space to publish only about 40 stories a year."

CHRISTIAN ADVENTURER, Messenger Publishing House, Box 850, Joplin MO 64802. (417)624-7050. Editor-in-Chief: Dr. Roy M. Chappell. Fiction Editor: Rosmarie Foreman. "Religious-oriented teen magazine." Published weekly. Circ. 2,500.

Needs: Adventure, historical (general), religious/inspirational, suspense/mystery, young adult. *All* material must be religious oriented. Receives approximately 100 unsolicited fiction mss/month. Buys 13 mss/issue, 52 mss/year. Length: 1,500 words minimum; 1,750 words maximum; 1,600 words average. Occasionally critiques rejected mss.

How to Contact: Send complete ms with SASE. Simultaneous and photocopied submissions and previously published work OK. Reports in 2 weeks on mss. Sample copy 50¢ or standard size SAE and 1 first class stamp. Fiction guidelines for 50¢ or standard size SAE and 1 first class stamp.

Payment: 1¢/word and 2 contributor's copies

Terms: Pays on publication for simultaneous rights. Publication copyrighted.

CHRISTIAN LIFE, Christian Life Missions, 396 E. St. Charles, Wheaton IL 60187. (312)653-4200. Editor-in-Chief: Robert Walker. Fiction Editor: Jan Franzen. *Christian Life* magazine is read by the leadership group in religious circles. Surveys show that 40.3 percent have attended college; 14.3 percent have gone on to graduate school. Therefore, copy for *Christian Life* should be bright, contemporary and significant. It also should be highly readable to attract the prospective buyer who sees it on a newsstand." Published monthly. Estab. 1945. Circ. approximately 100,000.

Needs: Adventure, religious/inspirational, women's. "All fiction must have a strong spiritual emphasis." Occasionally critiques rejected mss.

How to Contact: Send complete ms with SASE. Free sample copy.
Payment: $50-125.
Terms: Pays on publication for all rights, "but usually are happy to let second rights revert to author upon request." Publication copyrighted.
Tips: "Fiction must be top quality. Obvious solutions, pat endings, stilted dialogue, unreal characters too often make stories unacceptable. We are looking for tightly written short-stories of approximately 1000 words, and also longer stories (up to 2800 words) with a strong interwoven spiritual emphasis—not preachy. We especially need seasonal stories—Easter, Thanksgiving, Christmas, etc."

CHRISTIAN LIVING FOR SENIOR HIGHS, David C. Cook Publishing Co., 850 N. Grove, Elgin IL 60120. (312)741-2400. Editor: John Conaway. A take-home Sunday School paper used for senior high classes. Weekly. Estab. 1895.
Needs: "Each piece must present some aspect of the Christian life without being preachy. No closing sermons and no pat answers. Any topic appropriate to senior high is acceptable." Buys 16-20 mss/year. Length: 900-1,200 words.
How to Contact: Send complete ms with SASE. Reports in 2 months on mss. Phone queries OK. Free guidelines with SASE.
Payment: Pays $75-80.
Terms: Pays on acceptance for all rights.
Tips: "Get to know as much as possible about today's senior high age student. Write from a firm evangelical conviction. We encourage teens to write to us." Reject mss because "many are contrived and shallow; they are written to make a moralistic or spiritual point. Writer should write a good story, and let publisher decide what it might illustrate rather than writing toward a moral."

THE CHURCH HERALD, The Church Herald, 1324 Lake Dr. S.E., Grand Rapids MI 49506. (616)458-5156. Editor: Dr. John Stapert. "Our publication is directed toward Reformed Protestants who are interested in issues arising in the church, ethics and theology, society and 'culture' from the audience's point of view." Semimonthly; monthly in July and August. Estab. 1826. Circ. 65,000.
Needs: Literary, religious/inspirational, juvenile and young adult. Buys 24 mss/year. Receives 50 unsolicited fiction mss each month. Length: 750-1,500 words. Sometimes recommends other markets.
How to Contact: Send completed mss with SASE. Reports in 4 weeks on mss. Free sample copy with SASE.
Payment: Based on word and volume of ms. Offers 50% kill fee for assigned mss not published.
Terms: Pays on acceptance or publication on all rights, first rights, second serial (reprint) rights and one-time rights. Publication copyrighted.

THE CHURCH MUSICIAN, The Sunday School Board of the Southern Baptist Convention, 127 9th Ave. N., Nashville TN 37234. (615)251-2964. Editor: William M. Anderson Jr. "*The Church Musician* is for church music leaders in local churches—music directors, pastors, organists, pianists, choir coordinators, and members of music councils and/or other planning committees or groups. Music leaders read the magazine for spiritual enrichment, testimonials, human interest stories and other materials related to music programs in local churches." Monthly. Estab. October 1950. Circ. 20,000
Needs: Categories related toward church music. Receives 1-2 unsolicited fiction mss each month. Length: 750-2,000 words.
How to Contact: Send complete ms with SAE. Reports in 2 months on ms. Free sample copy with SAE and 30¢ postage.
Payment: Maximum 3½¢ per word.
Terms: Pays on acceptance for all rights. Publication copyrighted.
Tips: "Avoid mushy sentiment when writing. It must be believable and, of course, practical." Many mss are rejected because they are "too long, too general, too sweet and sentimental, shallow."

CLUBHOUSE, (formerly The Good Deeder), Your Story Hour, Box 15, Berrien Springs MI 49103. (616)471-3701. Editor-in-Chief: Elaine Meseraull. "A Christian magazine designed to help young people feel good about themselves. Our primary goal is to let them know there is a God, and that He loves kids. Stories are non-moralistic in tone, full of adventure and high principles." Readers are "children between the ages of 9-13. Primary audience—kids without church affiliation." Published 10 times/year. Estab. 1982. Circ. 11,000.
Needs: Adventure, contemporary, ethnic, historical (general), juvenile, religious/inspirational, suspense/mystery, western. No science fiction, fantasy or anything which does not uphold high morals. Receives 100-150 unsolicited fiction mss/month. Buys 3 mss/issue, 30 mss/year. Length: 650-750 words and 1,000-1,200 words (2 different stories in magazine). Occasionally critiques rejected mss.
How to Contact: Query first or send complete ms. SASE always. Simultaneous and photocopied submissions and previously published work OK. Reports in 2 weeks on queries, 2 weeks on mss. Free sample copy with 6½x9½ SAE and 3 first class stamps. Free fiction guidelines with business SAE and 1 first class stamp.
Payment: 2-3¢/word and 2 contributor's copies.
Terms: Pays on acceptance for simultaneous rights, first rights and second serial rights. Publication copyrighted.
Tips: "Especially interested in stories in which children are responsible, heroic, kind, etc., not stories in which children are humiliated into admitting that a parent, sibling, friend, etc., was right all along. I want up-beat, fun, exciting stories. Do not mention church, Sunday-school, etc., just because this is a Christian magazine. Sometimes this a turn-off for our non-churched audience. General tone of the magazine is warmth, not criticism. Most stories I reject involve kids who have regrettable turns of behavior which they finally change, appeal to a too-young age group, are preachy, are the wrong length or lack sparkle."

THE COASTAL JOURNALS: Gloucester, Salem, Newburyport, New Bedford, Fall River, New Bedford Magazine Inc., 5 S. 6th St., New Bedford MA 02740. (617)992-6682. Editor: Deirdre G. Forsythe. Magazines serving the coastal communities of Massachusetts (and New England in general) and those interested in coastal living and history. Bimonthly.
Needs: Adventure, historical. "All fiction must be seacoast related—nautical or historical fiction, humor (if good)." Buys 1 ms/issue; 6-8 mss/year. Length: 8-10 typewritten double spaced pages. Occasionally critiques rejected mss.
How to Contact: Send complete ms with SASE. Simultaneous, photocopied and previously published submissions OK. Reports in 2-4 weeks on mss. Sample copy $2.
Payment: Pays $50-100; 2 free contributor's copies; cover price charged for extras.
Terms: Pays on publication for one-time rights. Publication copyrighted.

COBBLESTONE, Cobblestone Publishing, Inc., 28 Main St., Peterborough NH 03458. Editor: Mark Corsey. History magazine for children (8-13 years old). Monthly with a national distribution.
Needs: Young adult, adventures, historical and biographical fiction, reminiscences, plays and retold folk tales. Must relate to month's theme. Length: 800-1,200 words.
How to Contact: Sample copy $2.75. Free guidelines with SASE
Payment: Pays up to 15¢/word.
Terms: Pays on publication. Buys all rights.
Tips: "We make some assignments on a work-for-hire basis. Request an editorial guideline sheet that explains the upcoming issue themes and gives query deadlines. Prefer queries to unsolicited manuscripts. Submit material 3-4 months in advance. Simultaneous and previously published submissions OK." Rejects mss because "it appears that many writers do not obtain our guidelines before submitting fiction. In addition, we receive much fiction that is predictable and *too* juvenile for our readers."

CO-ED, Scholastic Inc., 50 W. 44th St., New York NY 10036. Publication for girls and boys, ages 13-18 Monthly.

Needs: "We prefer stories of older (16, 17, 18 year old) teenagers which deal with contemporary problems. Characters should show growth as they confront problems with relationships with friends, family, dating. Suggested themes are finding identity, reconciling, reality and fantasy, making correct life decisions. Non-preachy themes should help initiate class discussions, since the magazine is used as a teaching tool in home economics classes. Charactacters should be well-rounded, strong, non-stereotyped and plots must be logical. No clichéd fluffy romances. Girls with conventional 'feminine' interests must be interesting, active and realistic people."
How to Contact: Free sample copy and writer's guidelines with SASE.

THE COLOR COMPUTER MAGAZINE, For TRS-80 Color Computer and TDP-100 Users, New England Publications, Inc., Highland Mill, Camden ME 04843. (207)236-9621. Editor: Kerry Leichtman. "Machine specific computer magazine. Material published: computer programs and how-to's. Also fiction" for "owners of the mentioned computer, mostly home hobbyists." Monthly. Estab. 1983. Circ. 30,000.
Needs: Adventure, comics, contemporary, fantasy, humor/satire, mainstream, psychic/supernatural, science fiction. "Fiction in computer magazines is a new concept. Although in the future any genre will be acceptable, SF is better for now." Length: 1,500 minimum; 3,000 words maximum. Occasionally critiques rejected ms.
How to Contact: Send complete ms with SASE. Previously published submissions OK. Reports in 3 weeks on mss. Sample copy for $2.50 with 9x12 SAE and $1.05 postage.
Payment: Pays $75-200; 2 free contributor's copies; $2.50 charge for extras. Offers 25% kill fee.
Terms: Pays on acceptance for all rights. Publication copyrighted.
Tips: Plans on using fiction sporadically. "The right stories, presented correctly, should draw a favorable reader response. If it does I will publish fiction monthly. If the response stays favorable I'm sure other magazines will follow suit."

COLUMBIA, Largest Catholic Family Magazine In North America, Knights of Columbus, 1 Columbus Plaza, New Haven CT 06507. (203)772-2130, ext. 263. Editor-in-Chief: Elmer Von Feldt. Catholic/fraternal magazine. Published monthly. Estab. 1920. Circ. 1.3 million.
Needs: "We look for a good story with a Judeo-Christian viewpoint." Receives 200 unsolicited fiction mss/month. Accepts 1 ms/issue, 12 mss/year. Length: 2,000 words minimum; 3,000 words maximum; 2,500 words average. Occasionally critiques rejected.
How to Contact: Send complete ms with SASE. Reports in 4-6 weeks. Free sample copy and fiction guidelines.
Payment: $300-500 and 2 contributor's copies.
Terms: Pays on acceptance for all rights. Publication copyrighted.
Tips: "Have an interesting story with a dramatic point."

COMMONWEALTH, 121 College Place, Norfolk VA 23510. (804)625-4800. Editor: Susan Harb. General interest and regional magazine of lifestyles and important issues on Virginia for urban adults. Monthly. Estab. 1932. Circ. 20,000.
Needs: Uses occasiona fiction if exceptional by local author or about the local region. Receives very few unsolicited fiction mss. Critiques rejected mss "when there is time."
How to Contact: Query or send complete ms. SASE always. Reports in 6 weeks on both queries and mss. Sample copy $1.79; free guidelines with SASE.
Payment: Pays negotiable kill fee; byline given. Submit seasonal stories 6 months in advance.
Terms: Pays on publication for all rights. Publication copyrighted.

CONTACT HIGH, THE Magazine for Independent Singles, Landsend Publishing Co., Box 504, Mendocino CA 95460. Editor-in-Chief: John Fremont. Publishes short stories, poetry and articles about single life and relationships, living alone, independence, consciousness-raising for an audience of non-sexist unmarried men and women. Published bimonthly. Estab. 1979. Circ. 10,000.
Needs: Contemporary, feminist, humor/satire, men's (no erotica), inspirational, women's (non-

traditional). Prefer short works (1,000-2,000 words). ''We are always interested in seeing short fiction on the subject of relating, relationships, and human growth and potential. We especially are interested in work that offers alternatives to the traditional roles and stereotypes that mark contemporary culture. Nothing unrealistic, experimental, or sexist.'' Receives approximately 50 unsolicited fiction mss/month. Accepts 1 mss/issue, 6 mss/year. Length: 500 words minimum; 5,000 words maximum; 1,000-2,000 words average. Occasionally critiques rejected mss.
How to Contact: Send complete ms with SASE. Simultaneous and photocopied submissions and previously published work OK. Reports in 2 months on mss. Free sample copy for 9x12 SAE and 71¢ postage.
Payment: $0-100 or magazine subscription and 10 contributor's copies.
Terms: Pays on acceptance for first rights or one-time rights. Publication copyrighted.
Tips: ''Write simple, straight-forward prose based on personal experience. Read authors like Herb Gold, Anais Nin, Tillie Olson, Nancy Friday, etc.'' Most rejections occur because mss ''do not relate to our subject: relationships.''

CORVETTE FEVER MAGAZINE, Prospect Publishing Co., Inc., Box 55532, Ft. Washington MD 20744. (301)839-2221. Editor-in-Chief: Patricia E. Stivers. ''General magazine about Corvettes covering history of the car, restorations, stock and customizing, how-to articles on maintenance and repair, and coverage of the Corvette culture that surrounds the car. Corvette owners mainly are 25 to 45 years in age with incomes ranging $15,000 to $35,000 average. Majority are male. All have a keen loyalty in the Corvette.'' Published bimonthly. Estab. 1978. Circ. 35,000.
Needs: Adventure, fantasy, humor/satire. ''Must deal with Corvettes.'' Receives 2-3 unsolicited fiction mss/month. Accepts 1-2 mss/issue, 6-8 mss/year. Length: 800-1,500 words. Occasionally critiques rejected mss, ''but not extensively.''
How to Contact: Send complete ms with SASE. Photocopied submissions OK. Reports in 8 weeks. Sample copy $2. Free fiction guidelines with SASE.
Payment: 10¢/word.
Terms: Pays on publication (within 60 days) for first rights and second serial rights (second rights can be non-exclusive). Publication copyrighted.
Tips: Likes to see ''good humor or satire that laughs with the Corvette owner but not at him.''

COSMOPOLITAN MAGAZINE, The Hearst Corp., 224 W. 57th St., New York NY 10019. (212)262-5700. Editor: Helen Gurley Brown. Fiction Editor: Betty Kelly. Associate Fiction Editor: Mary Lou Mullen. Most stories include male-female relationships, traditional plots, characterizations. Single career women (18-34). Monthly. Circ. just under 3 million.
Needs: Contemporary, women's, romance, mystery, adventure. ''Stories should include a romantic relationship or women in jobs with the woman being the protagonist. The characters should be in their 20s or 30s. (i.e., same ages as our readers). No highly experimental pieces. Upbeat endings.'' Buys 2 short stories plus a novel or book excerpt/issue. Length: short shorts (1,500-3,000 words); longer (4,000-6,000 words). Occasionally recommends other markets.
How to Contact: Send complete ms with SASE. Reports in 2-6 weeks on mss. Free guidelines with legal-sized SASE.
Payment: Pays $750-1,000. Short shorts $500-$750.
Terms: Pays on acceptance for first North American serial rights.
Tips: ''It is rare that unsolicited mss are accepted. We tend to use agented, professional writers. The majority of unsolicited short stories we receive are inappropriate for *Cosmo* in terms of characters used and situations presented, or they just are not well written. Research the magazine you are submitting to.''

CRICKET MAGAZINE, Open Court Publishing Co., Box 100, La Salle IL 61301. (815)224-6666. Editor: Marianne Carus. Magazine for children, ages 6-12. Monthly. Estab. September 1973. Circ. 150,000.
Needs: Juvenile including literary, contemporary, science fiction, fantasy, western, mystery, adventure, humor, juvenile, ethnic and translations. No adult articles. Buys 10-12 mss/year. Re-

ceives approximately 500 unsolicited fiction mss each month. Length: 500-1,500 words.
How to Contact: Do not query first. Send complete ms with SASE. Reports in 2 months on mss. Sample copy for $2.00. Free guidelines with SASE.
Payment: Up to 25¢ per word. 2 free author's copies. $1 charge for extras.
Terms: Pays on publication for first North American serial rights and one-time rights. Publication copyrighted.
Tips: "Do not write *down* to children. Write about subjects you are familiar with which have been well-researched." Sponsors contests for children, ages 6-12.

CRUSADER MAGAZINE, Calvinist Cadet Corps, Box 7244, Grand Rapids MI 49510. (616)241-5616. Editor: David J. Koetje. Magazine to help boys 10-14 discover how God is at work in their lives and in the world around them. Monthly. Estab. 1957. Circ. 14,000.
Needs: Adventure, comics, confession, ethnic, juvenile, religious/inspirational, science fiction. Receives 80 unsolicited fiction mss/month. Buys 3 mss/issue; 30 mss/year. Length: 800 words minimum; 1,500 words maximum; 1,200 words average.
How to Contact: Send complete ms with SASE. Simultaneous, photocopied and previously published submissions OK. Reports in 3 weeks on mss. Sample copy free. Fiction guidelins free with # 10 SAE and 1 first class stamp.
Payment: Pays 2-5¢/word; 1 free contributor's copy.
Terms: Pays on acceptance for one-time rights.

CURRENTS, Voice of the National Organization for River Sports, National Organization for River Sports, 314 N. 20th St., Colorado Springs CO 80904. (303)473-2466. Editor: Mary McCurdy. Magazine of kayaking and rafting—news, events, techniques, features—for kayakers and rafters. Monthly. Estab. 1979. Circ. 5,000.
Needs: Adventure, historical, literary, prose poem, psychic/supernatural, science fiction. No cliché accounts of "killer rivers" and "violent rapids." Buys 2 mss/year. Length: 1,500 words minimum; 5,000 words maximum; 2,500 words average. Occasionally critiques rejected mss.
How to Contact: Query first. Simultaneous, photocopied and previously published submissions OK; "just tell us who else is getting it." Reports in 2 weeks on queries. Sample copy for $1 including postage. Fiction guidelines free for # 10 SAE and 1 first class stamp.
Payment: Pays $25-250; subscription to the magazine; 3 free contributor's copies; postage charged for extras. Offers kill fee of 25%.
Terms: Pays on acceptance for first North American serial rights. Publication copyrighted.
Tips: "Don't make grammatical or typographical errors. Send us a sample page to see if we're even on the same wave length."

DARLING, Republican Press, Box 32083, Mobeni, Durban, South Africa 4060. Tel. 422041. Editor-in-Chief: Margaret Wasserfall. Fiction Editor: Ingrid Staude. Magazine featuring fashion and beauty, career advancement, personal self-improvement, people who are making it, contemporary fiction, for 18-36-year-olds, single/marrieds, predominantly women but considerable male readership. High black readership. Published fortnightly. Estab. 1972. Circ. 83,000.
Needs: Condensed novel, contemporary, humor/satire, romance (contemporary). "No pedestrian mss with predictable endings." Receives 60-70 unsolicited fiction mss/month. Buys 3-4 mss/issue, 75w mss/year. Length: 6,000 words minimum; 8,000 words maximum. Sometimes recommends other markets.
How to Contact: Send complete ms with SAE, IRC. Simultaneous, photocopied and previously published submissions (provided not previously published in South Africa) OK. Free sample copy with SAE.
Payment: $150-200 and 1 free contributor's copy (by request). Supply SAE and International Reply Coupons.
Terms: Pays on publication for first South African rights. Publication copyrighted.
Tips: "It is essential to read our magazine to familiarize yourself with contents and feel. Characters should be credible and should come through strong. Story line should be strong and should re-

late to modern day living.'' Contests usually restricted to South Africa residents; announcement of competition and rules in magazine. ''Rejections result from poor writing technique or wrong story for editorial climate.''

DASH, Christian Service Brigade, Box 150, Wheaton IL 60187. (312)665-0630. Editor: Michael J. Chiapperino. Managing Editor: Mark Carpenter. ''Our magazine aims to provide entertaining wholesome reading while challenging our constituency to love and serve Jesus Christ. Readers are boys, ages 8-11 years, registered in Christian Service Brigade. Published 8 times/year. Circ. 30,000.
Needs: Religious/inspirational, adventure, humor, juvenile. No stories that contain boring, pat answers. Buys 2 mss/issue, 15-20 mss/year. Receives 30-50 unsolicited fiction mss each month. Length: 800-1,200 words.
How to Contact: Query with or without clips of published work with SASE. Reports in 1 week on queries, 2 weeks on mss. Free fiction guidelines with SASE.
Payment: $35-75. 2 free author's copies. $1 charge for extras. Offers 20% kill fee for assigned mss not published.
Terms: Buys first or reprint rights. Publication copyrighted.
Tips: ''Make dialogue up to date and realistic; aim for conflict or suspense. Teach something worthwhile with taste and subtlety. Use a gripping lead.'' Mss are rejected because ''they are not slanted for our magazine, are poorly written or lack organization.''

DAUGHTERS OF SARAH, 2716 W. Cortland, Chicago IL 60647. (312)252-3344. Editor: Reta Finger. Magazine. ''Religious, feminist publication, relating to history of Christian church, women and social issues with feminist point of view.'' Bimonthly. Estab. 1974. Circ. 2,800.
Needs: Historical, religious/inspirational, women's. ''No subjects unrelated to feminism from Christian viewpoint.'' Receives 2 unsolicited fiction mss/month. Buys 2-3 mss/year. Length: 1,500 words maximum. Occasionally critiques rejected mss ''if related and close to acceptance.''
How to Contact: Query first with description of ms with SASE. Simultaneous, photocopied and previously published submissions OK ''but won't pay.'' Reports in 2 weeks on queries. Sample copy for $1.25.
Payment: Pays a minimum $10/printed page; 5 free contributor's copies. Offers kill fee of one-half stated fee.
Terms: Pays on publication for first North American serial or one-time rights.

THE DEAF CANADIAN MAGAZINE, Deaf Canadian Readers' Association, Box 1291, Edmonton, Alberta, Canada T5J 2M8. (403)466-6707. Executive Editor: David Burnett. ''Magazine published for deaf persons, families, and also for teachers, physicians, psychologists, rehabilitation counselors, audiologists, speech pathologists, nurses, social workers, occupational therapists, linguists, sociologists, clergymen, and students in these disciplines. The magazine is a very valuable source of information on deafness.'' Monthly. Estab. September 1972. Circ. 172,000.
Needs: Fiction on deafness. ''We do not want anything not related to deafness but will accept any kind of fiction provided it is written by a deaf person.'' Accepts 12 mss/year. Receives approximately 20 unsolicited fiction mss each month. Length: 2,000 words. Critiques rejected mss ''when there is time.''
How to Contact: Query or send complete ms. SASE always (must be Canadian postage or IRC minimum $1). Contributions cannot be acknowledged or returned. Sample copy $2.50.
Payment: Free author's copy.
Terms: Pays on publication for assignments on a work-for-hire basis, first rights and first North American serial rights. Publication copyrighted.
Tips: ''We recommend that a potential writer subscribe to the magazine to be oriented with our materialistic use ($20 regular subscription . . . a special price of $15 for any fiction writer or nonfiction writer). To writers unversed in deafness and the deaf world, our suggestion is that you try to become acquainted with its ways before trying to write anything.'' Mss are rejected because they are ''not related to deafness.'' Sponsors contests.

comm. periodicals

DELTA SCENE MAGAZINE, Delta State University, Box B3, Delta State University, Cleveland MS 38733. (601)846-1976. Editor-in-Chief: Curt Lamar. Magazine for college graduates. Published quarterly. Estab. 1973. Circ. 1,000.
Needs: Adventure, gothic/historical romance, historical (general), humor/satire, literary, suspense/mystery. "Stories are about or set in the Mississippi Delta. We accept manuscripts of quality material." Receives approximately 4 unsolicited fiction mss/month. Buys 1-2 mss/issue, 4-8 mss/year. Length: 1,000 words minimum; 2,000 words maximum; 1,500 words average.
How to Contact: Send complete ms with SASE. Simultaneous submissions OK. Reports in 3 months. Sample copy $1. Free fiction guidelines with SASE.
Payment: $15-20 and 3 contributor's copies.
Terms: Pays on publication for one-time rights. Publication copyrighted.

DIALOGUE, The Magazine for the Visually Impaired, Dialogue Publications, Inc., 3100 Oak Park Ave., Berwyn IL 60402. (312)749-1908. Editor-in-Chief: Louise Kimbrough. Fiction editor: Annette Victorin. Recorded, Braille, and large print magazine, general interest, for visually impaired adults." Published quarterly. Estab. 1962. Circ. 40,000.
Needs: Adventure, contemporary, humor/satire, men's, psychic/supernatural, suspense/mystery, western, women's. "*Dialogue*'s contributors are themselves visually handicapped. Graphic sex or violence is out, as is religious material, or portrayals of blind characters as helpless or pathetic." Receives approximately 20 unsolicited fiction mss/month. Buys 3-4 mss/issue, 10-12 mss/year. No fixed length requirements but short pieces (2-5 typed pages) strongly preferred. Occasionally critiques rejected mss. Sometimes recommends other markets.
How to Contact: Send complete ms with SASE. Simultaneous and photocopied submissions OK. Reports in 4-6 weeks. Sample copy free to visually -impaired prospective contributors. Free fiction guidelines with SASE.
Payment: $50 maximum and 1 contributor's copy.
Terms: Pays on acceptance for first North American serial rights. Publication copyrighted.
Tips: "Study back issues; write a believable story with a beginning, a middle and an end. Use dialogue to keep the action moving." Rejections occur because of "failure to study magazine for slant and subject matter; weak plots, vague character delineation, and stilted dialogue." All published short stories from *Dialogue* are eligible for $100 James Victorin award, granted annually.

DISCOVERIES, Nazarene Publishing House, 6401 The Paseo, Kansas City MO 64131. (816)333-7000. Editor: Mark A. York. *Discoveries* is a Sunday School story paper for children ages 8-11. Stories should be character building and teach Christian truths. The audience is composed of children who attend Sunday School in the church of the Nazarene. The paper is for leisure reading. Weekly. Estab. January 1976. Circ. 75,000.
Needs: Religious/inspirational, mystery, adventure and juvenile. Fiction must appeal to children ages 8-11. In a survey of our readership they listed mystery as the favorite type of fiction. No erotica, horror, gay/lesbian, fantasy, confession, gothic, etc. Buys 1-2 mss/issue, 75-104 mss/year. Receives 400 unsolicited fiction mss each month. Length: 500-1,000 words.
How to Contact: Send complete ms with SASE. Reports in 3-6 weeks. Free sample copy with SAE plus postage. Free fiction guidelines with SASE.
Payment: 3¢ per word up to $30; 2¢ per word for second rights. Offers 100% kill fee for assigned mss not published.
Terms: Pays on acceptance for first rights or whatever is offered. Publication copyrighted.
Tips: "Writers should contact our office for the brochure describing our publication's needs. Stories which fit our requirements should then be submitted for consideration. Fiction should be action-oriented with a strong beginning and ending. Christian teaching should be implicit and not added on at the end of the manuscript. It must correlate with the purposes of one of our Sunday School lessons for it to be purchased and used. Most of the stories published in *Discoveries* are fiction; we are always looking for talented authors of short stories for children that teach Christian principles. Manuscripts submitted to *Discoveries* that show merit may be purchased and edited as much as necessary to adjust them to fit the purposes of the story paper."

DOG FANCY, Fancy Publications, Box 4030, San Clemente CA 92672. (714)498-1600. Editor-in-Chief: Linda W. Lewis. General dog and puppy magazine, consumer oriented, "for dog and puppy lovers." Published monthly. Circ. 75,000.
Needs: Dog-centered theme. Receives approximately 40 unsolicited fiction mss/month. Buys 12 mss/year. Length: 3,000 words maximum.
How to Contact: Query first or send complete ms. SASE always. Simultaneous and photocopied submissions OK. Reports in 1 week on queries, 2 months on mss. Sample copy $2.50. Free fiction guidelines with SASE.
Payment: 3¢/word and 2 contributor's copies. $2.50 charge for extras.
Terms: Publication copyrighted.

DOLLY MAGAZINE, Magazine Promotions, 57 Regent St., Chippendale, NSW, Australia 2008. (02)699-3622. Editor-in-Chief: Lisa Wilkinson. Magazine of fashion, beauty, music, personalities, relationships general interest for teenage girls. Published month. Estab. 1970. Circ. 165,000.
Needs: Adventure (with a touch of romance), condensed novel (very condensed), confession, fantasy (not kinky fantasy), historical romance, humor/satire, juvenile, mainstream, romance (contemporary), suspense/mystery, women's, young adult. "Characters to between 17 and 20 and unmarried. We like element of romance." Receives 15-20 unsolicited fiction mss/month. Accepts 2 mss/issue, 24 mss/year. Length: 1,000 words minimum; 25,000 words maximum; 2,500 words average. Occasionally critiques rejected mss.
How to Contact: Send complete ms with any examples of previously published work with International Reply Coupons. Simultaneous submissions and previously published work OK. Reports in 2 weeks on queries; 4-6 weeks on mss. Sample copy $1.50 with 32x27 SAE and 60¢ postage. Free fiction guidelines with standard SAE and 30¢ postage.
Payment: "Depends upon story content and size." $1.50 each for extras.
Terms: Pays on acceptance for first rights and second serial (reprint) rights. "If so we must be informed of previous publications." Publication copyrighted.
Tips: "Write interesting stories. A sense of humor never goes astray."

DRAGON MAGAZINE, The Monthly Adventure Role-Playing Aid, Dragon Publishing, Box 110, Lake Geneva WI 53147. (414)248-8044. Editor: Kim Mohan. Magazine. "*Dragon* contains primarily non-fiction—articles and essays on various aspects of the hobby of gaming, particularly fantasy role-playing. Fiction is used occasionally as a counterpoint, or if the story has relevance to fantasy or fantasy gaming. Readers are mature teens and young adults; over half our readers are under 18." Monthly. Estab. 1976. Circ. 70,000.
Needs: "It's not essential for a fiction writer to be involved or familiar with role-playing games, but it helps. The gaming approach to fantasy is somewhat different than the so-called 'traditional' fantasy genre." Receives 10-20 unsolicited fiction mss/month. Buys 4-6 mss/year. Length: 1,500 words minimum; 10,000 words maximum; 3,000-4,000 words average. Occasionally critiques rejected mss.
How to Contact: Query with clips of published work with SASE. Photocopied submissions OK. Reports in 2-3 weeks on queries. Sample copy for $4.50. Fiction guidelines free for 9" wide SAE and 1 first class stamp.
Payment: Pays 3-5¢/word; 1 free contributor's copy; $2 charge for extras. Offers kill fee of 25%.
Terms: Pays on publication (or by prior arrangement, in advance) for all or first rights. Publication copyrighted.
Tips: "Know the basic principles of fantasy role-playing games, to develop a feel for the specific sort of fantasy fiction we're interested in."

EASYRIDERS MAGAZINE, Entertainment for Adult Riders, Box 52, Malibu CA 90265. (213)889-8701. Editor: Lou Kimzey. Men's magazine with bike-related material: how-to's, travel, new equipment information, fiction for adult men who own or desire to own expensive custom motorcycles, rugged individualists who own and enjoy their choppers and the good times derived from them. Monthly. Circ. 488,000.

Needs: Men's and adventure. Only interested in hard-hitting rugged fiction. Should be bike oriented, but doesn't have to dwell on the fact. Length: 3,000-5,000 words.

How to Contact: Send complete ms with SASE. Reports in 3 weeks on mss. Sample copy $2.

Payment: Pays 10-15¢/word; payment depends on quality, length and use in magazine.

Terms: Pays on acceptance for first rights.

Tips: "Gut level language accepted; dope or sex scenes OK but are not to be graphically described. As long as the material is directly aimed at our macho intelligent male audience, there should be no great problem breaking into our magazine. Before submitting material, however, we strongly recommend that the writer observe our requirements and study a sample copy."

EBONY JR!, Johnson Publishing Co., Inc., 820 S. Michigan Ave., Chicago IL 60605. (312)322-9272. Editor: Marcia V. Roebuck-Hoard. "A magazine designed to highlight the outstanding experiences of blacks, both past and present, as well as to improve children's learning skills, particularly in language arts. Directed to children ages 6-12, with special attention to black children of those ages. Due to the content emphasis on black history and current events as they relate to blacks, *Ebony Jr!* provides a good learning tool." Monthly; bimonthly June/July and August/September. Estab. May 1973. Circ. 100,000.

Needs: Contemporary, science fiction, fantasy, western, mystery, adventure, humor, juvenile, ethnic (black) and condensed novels. "All categories must be geared with our audience in mind. No articles using characters with stereotypical images of blacks or women, violence and/or death unnecessarily; or stories poking fun at culture's traditions." Buys 5-8 mss/issue, 35-50 mss/year. Receives approximately 100 unsolicited fiction mss each month. Length: 400-1,500 words. Critiques rejected mss "when there is time."

How to Contact: Query or send complete ms. SASE always. Reports in 3 weeks to 3 months on queries and mss. Sample copy $1. Free guidelines with legal-sized SASE.

Payment: $75-150. Free author's copy. 75¢ charge per extra copy.

Terms: Pays on acceptance for all rights and second serial (reprint) rights. Publication copyrighted.

Tips: "Purchase at least one sample copy and peruse fiction therein carefully for style, content, characterizations; query first giving specific idea as well as indication of deadline for submission. Request writer's guidelines; if rejected, continue to submit ideas/queries. Follow up on your submissions (don't be discouraged by any initial rejections) with further ideas. Don't send in a manuscript without doing research on the publication first." *Ebony Jr!* sponsors an annual writing contest for children ages 6-12. This contest involves short story entries; contest is announced in the April and May issues (1st and 2nd prize winners' stories are published in the October issue).

ELECTRICITY, National News Bureau, 262 S. 12th St., Philadelphia PA 19107. (215)985-1990. Editor-in-Chief: Harry Jay Katz. Fiction Editor: Bruce Klauber. Tabloid, "upbeat/entertainment oriented" for audience 18-45 years. Published weekly. Estab. 1980. Circ. 80,000.

Needs: Comics, contemporary, erotica, fantasy, humor/satire, women's, young adult. Receives 100 or more unsolicited fiction mss/month. Length: 500 words minimum; 1,500 words maximum; 750 words average.

How to Contact: Send complete ms or query with clips of published work. SASE always. Photocopied submissions OK. Reports in 1 week on queries. Sample copy $1 with 9x12 SAE and 35¢ postage.

Payment: $5-50

Terms: Pays on publication for all rights. Publication copyrighted.

Tips: "Keep on trying." Also publishes weekly tabloids: *The Drummer*, (Penn State Campus); *The Drummer*, (University of Tennessee Campus); *Philadelphia Style*, (Philadelphia Convention and Visitor's Bureau); *Univercity*, (33 Philadelphia area college campuses).

ELITE, Stamford Hills Communications, 234 Eglinton Ave. E., Suite 401, Toronto, Ontario, Canada M4P 1K5. (416)487-7183. Editor: D.S. Wells. Fiction Editor: Andrew Dowler. Men's magazine with general and erotic material, ages 18-40. Monthly. Estab. February 1974. Circ. 200,000.

Needs: Contemporary, fantasy, men's, erotica and humor. Buys 2 mss/issue, 24 mss/year. Length: 3,000-3,500 words.

How to Contact: Send complete ms with SAE, IRC. Reports in 3 months on mss. Sample copy $3 with 9x12 SAE plus IRC (63¢ postage). Free fiction guidelines with SAE, IRC. Recommends other markets.

Payment: $75-250.

Terms: Pays on publication for one-time rights.

Tips: Mss are rejected because they are "unrelated to the theme of the publication, the subject is all wrong, or they are too long or too short."

ELLERY QUEEN'S MYSTERY MAGAZINE, Davis Publications, Inc., 380 Lexington Ave., New York NY 10017. (212)557-9100. Editor: Eleanor Sullivan. Magazine for lovers of mystery fiction. Published 13 times/year. Estab. 1941. Circ. 350,000.

Needs: "We accept only mystery, crime, and detective fiction." Buys 10-15 mss/issue. Receives approximately 300 unsolicited fiction mss each month. Length: up to 9,000 words. Critiques rejected mss "only when a story might be a possibility for us if revised." Sometimes recommends other markets.

How to Contact: Send complete ms with SASE. Reports in 1 month or sooner on mss. Free fiction guidelines with SASE.

Payment: 3¢ per word and up.

Terms: Pays on acceptance for first North American serial rights. Publication copyrighted.

Tips: "Read the magazine; know what we publish. Originality of a writer's work and an awareness of what has been published helps. We have Department of First Stories and usually publish at least one first story an issue—i.e., the author's first published fiction. No magazine can begin to publish the huge number of manuscripts submitted to them. We select stories that are fresh and of the kind our readers have expressed a liking for."

ESQUIRE, 13-30 Corp., 2 Park Ave., New York City NY 10016. (212)561-8100. Editor: Phillip Moffitt. Fiction Editor: Rust Hills. Male-oriented magazine with good modern American writing for young professional men 25-40. Estab. 1933.

Needs: Literary, contemporary, short stories. No erotica, horror, religious or inspirational. Buys 1 ms/issue. Length: 5,000-7,000 words.

How to Contact: Send complete ms with SASE. Reports in 1 month on mss.

Payment: Varies.

Terms: Pays on acceptance for varied rights.

Tips: "Send a clearly typed proofread story with plain straightforward cover letter. Never send a query for fiction mss."

ESSENCE, 1500 Broadway, New York NY 10036. (212)730-4260. Editor: Susan L. Taylor. Fiction Editor: Alice Jones-Miller, Cheryl Everette. General interest magazine with historical, how-to, humor, fashion, career, food, interior design, financial, health, education, beauty, travel subjects for black women. Monthly. Estab. May 1970. Circ. 700,000.

Needs: Romance, adventure, humor, fantasy, experimental and condensed and serialized novels. Buys 12 mss/year. Length: 1,500-3,000 words.

How to Contact: Send complete ms with SASE. Reports in 2 months on mss. Sample copy $1.25. Free guidelines with SASE.

Payment: Pay varies.

Terms: Pays on acceptance. 25% kill fee and byline given. Buys second serial rights for serialized novels.

Tips: "We're looking for fiction that teaches and inspires. Stories about contemporary black people, the challenges they face, their joys and sorrows."

Close-up

Eleanor Sullivan
Ellery Queen's Mystery Magazine

It's no mystery how *Ellery Queen's Mystery Magazine* is published 13 times a year. Eleanor Sullivan is there to edit the magazine and run the small, tidy and efficient editorial office at Davis Publications in New York.

As editor, Sullivan reads the manuscripts that come in and selects the stories for each issue. Before the death in mid-1982 of Frederic Dannay, one-half of the original Ellery Queen writing team, Sullivan would send stories along to Dannay for approval. But now the primary responsibilities are hers. She also edits the writing, oversees the contracts, writes the story introductions, lays out the issues, and sends them to press.

With the help of Karen Prince, associate editor, Sullivan goes through the ever-growing slush pile with a practiced eye from her 22 years publishing experience. She manages to get back to the writers quickly, "sometimes too quickly. . . . Some writers complain; they reject rejection," the editor says, but at times she writes personal notes, and all manuscripts are read.

"It's the correspondence that is hardest to keep up with," Sullivan says about her 50-60 hour work week, much of which has to be done at home. "But the extra time put into correspondence pays off," she maintains. Writers respond to her notes, "and they keep coming back."

What kind of mystery is popular today? The psychological thriller has developed into its own sub-genre; and *EQMM* is constantly looking for good detective fiction. "We rarely find a good 'locked-room mystery anymore,' one that is believable and/or hasn't been done. "The interest in good classical detective stories isn't waning, but finding original ones is a problem," Sullivan says.

Common reasons for rejection at *EQMM* are amateurish writing or a predictable plot or story ending. A poorly constructed cover letter can be an editor "turn-off" that might not do justice to the accompanying story. It is also not professional of the writer to ask for criticism. "Editors are not teachers," but Sullivan *will* suggest revision or offer recommendations where she thinks there is promise.

When possible at least one new mystery writer is featured each issue in The First Story Department, and from the best selections over the years, Sullivan and Dannay compiled *Ellery Queen's Book of First Appearances*. "Many of the people who send us their first fiction, however, either don't know the field well enough," she says, "or they know it too well and tend to imitate what has been successful."

Eleanor Sullivan, a 12-year veteran with *EQMM* and also *Alfred Hitchcock's Mystery Magazine* from 1976-1981, seeks originality and unusual concepts. The writer's own style should emerge. An agented manuscript receives no more attention than an unsolicited story. "We read everything with an equal eye toward publication, no matter who sends it in," she states. Once a story is published, however, agents may scout the magazine for clients and encourage writers to pursue a novel or a series about the detective figure.

Working with mystery writers is an obvious pleasure for Eleanor Sullivan, who writes occasional mystery stories herself and has just finished a novel. She says, "We're as eager to start new careers for beginning writers as they are themselves."

EVANGEL, Dept. of Christian Education, Free Methodist Headquarters, 901 College Ave., Winona Lake IN 46590. (219)267-7161. Editor: Vera Bethel. Sunday School take-home paper for distribution to young adults who attend church. Fiction involves young couples and singles coping with everyday crises, making decisions that show growth; ages 25-35. Weekly. Estab. 1896. Circ. 35,000.
Needs: Religious/inspirational. "No fiction without any semblance of Christian message or where the message clobbers the reader." Buys 1 ms/issue, 52 mss/year. Receives approximately 75 unsolicited fiction mss each month. Length: 1,000-1,500. Critiques rejected mss "when there is time." Sometimes recommends other markets.
How to Contact: Send complete ms with SASE. Reports in 1 month on ms. Free sample copy. Free fiction guidelines with SASE.
Payment: $35. 2 free author's copies. 10¢ charge for each extra.
Terms: Pays on publication for simultaneous, first, second serial (reprint), first North American serial rights and one-time rights.
Tips: "Choose a contemporary situation or conflict, create a good mix for the characters (not all-good or all-bad heroes and villains). Don't spell out everything in detail; let the reader fill in some blanks in the story. Too much detail is boring. Keep him guessing." Rejects mss because "unbelievable characters and predictable events in story."

FACE-TO-FACE, United Methodist Publishing House, Box 801, Nashville TN 37202. (615)749-6224. Editor: Barbara A. Summey. Religious-oriented magazine for teens, ages 15-18. Quarterly. Estab. 1968. Circ. 12,000.
Needs: Literary, contemporary and religious/inspirational. Fiction should deal with major problems and concerns of older teens, such as finding one's own identity, dealing with family and peer group pressures, and so forth. No straight moral fiction or stories with pat answers or easy solutions used. No serials. Buys 8-10 mss/year. Length: 1,800-2,500 words. Occasionally recommends other markets.
How to Contact: Send complete ms with SASE. Reports in 2 months on mss. Free sample copy with 9x12 SAE and 55¢ postage. Free fiction guidelines with SASE.
Payment: 4¢ per word. 1 free author's copy.
Terms: Pays on acceptance for all periodical rights.
Tips: Rejects mss because "some are too long; we prefer that the fiction manuscripts not exceed 2,500 words, and some are too moralistic in tone; we get too many dealing with drug use."

FAIR LADY, National Magazine, Box 1802, Cape Town 8000, South Africa. Tel. (021)25-48-78. Editor: Jane Raphaely. Fiction Editor: Stephanie von Hirschberg. "Women's glossy magazine with regular fashion features, beauty, cooking, teen and young world section, competitions, fiction, book reviews, interviews (especially celebrity), serious articles in general on self-help, health, current affairs, for a very broad spectrum of population, including men. Highest percentage of readers in the women 16-35 category." Biweekly. Estab. 1965. Circ. 230,000.
Needs: Condensed novel, contemporary, feminist/lesbian, gothic/historical romance, literary, mainstream, romance, science fiction, serialized/excerpted novel, suspense/mystery, women's. "We always have a serialized novel run in 4-6 parts over 4-6 issues." Receives 90 unsolicited fiction mss/month. Buys 3 mss/issue; 80 mss/year. Length: 2,000 words minimum; 6,000 words maximum; 4,000 words average.
How to Contact: Send complete ms. Photocopied and previously published submissions OK (provided not previously published in South Africa). Reports in 4 weeks on mss plus time for surface return mail. Fiction guidelines free.
Payment: Pays around $150.
Terms: Pays on acceptance for first or second serial rights. Publication copyrighted.
Tips: "Use real, believable characters; avoid strong American orientation/setting."

THE FAMILY, Daughters of St. Paul, 50 St. Paul's Ave., Boston MA 02130. (617)522-8911. Editor: Sister Mary Helen Wallace. "Family magazine of religious truths and ideals in a format that is interesting, informative and appealing. Contents include feature articles on topics of current interest and inspiration, talks of Pope John Paul II, short stories, poems, questions and answers on religious questions, etc.'' Monthly. Estab. 1952. Circ. 36,000.

Needs: Juvenile, prose poem, religious/inspirational. Receives 3-4 unsolicited fiction mss/year. Accepts 1 mss/month; 10-12 mss/year. Length: 1,000 words minimum; 3,000 words maximum; 2,000 words average.

How to Contact: Send complete ms with SASE. Simultaneous, photocopied and previously published submissions OK. Reports in 3-4 weeks on mss. Sample copy free for 9x12 SAE and 71¢ postage.

Payment: Pays 6-12 free contributor's copies; subscription to magazine possible for regular contributors.

Terms: Acquires one-time rights.

Tips: ''Often a fiction writer can 'punch home harder' than a writer that must stick to a 'facts only' story. Write a fiction story with a message—a story that will bring inspiration or a 'religious thought' into someone's life.''

FAMILY CIRCLE, Family Circle, 488 Madison Ave., New York NY 10022. Editor: Arthur Hettich. Books and Features Editor: Diane Hynd. Service magazine, mostly how-to articles on food, crafts, work, money saving, health and beauty for women, ages 20-70 + who read it for information, advice and to find out how to do everything better. Published every 3 weeks. Estab. 1932. Circ. 8 million.

Needs: Short stories should be family-oriented, contemporary, inspirational, women's, confession, romance, mystery, humor, and nostalgia. ''We also serialize and condense novels.'' Buys 10 mss/issue. Receives approximately 250 unsolicited short story mss each month. Length: 700-5,000 words. Sometimes critiques rejected mss.

How to Contact: Send complete ms with SASE. Reports in 2 months on mss. Free guidelines with SASE.

Payment: Pay varies. 10 free author's copies. Offers 20% kill fee for assigned ms not published.

Terms: Pays on acceptance generally for all rights. Publication copyrighted.

Tips: ''Read the magazine and be familiar with material of interest to our readers.''

FAMILY RADIO & TV MAGAZINE, Republican Press (PTY) Ltd., Box 32083 Mobeni, Durban, South Africa 4060. (031)422041. Editor: Mike Fisher. Family magazine concentrating on TV and film stars for a middle income group with a bias towards married women.'' Weekly. Estab. 1976. Circ. 140,000.

Needs: Adventure, romance, women's. Receives 20 unsolicited fiction mss/month. Buys 1 mss/month; 52 mss/year. Length: 2,000 words minimum; 5,000 words maximum; 4,000 words average.

How to Contact: Send complete ms. Photocopied submissions OK. Reports in 2 weeks on mss. Sample copy 75¢ with A4 SAE.

Payment: Pays Rand 80-Rand 200.

Terms: Buys on acceptance first South African rights. Publication copyrighted.

FARM & FOREST, Henley Publishing Ltd., Box 130, Woodstock, New Brunswick, Canada E0J 2B0. (506)328-8863. Editor: Gordon F. Catt. Tabloid of news and features of interest to farmers, woodlot owners in Atlantic Canada region. Bimonthly. Estab. 1980. Circ. 7,000.

Needs: Juvenile, young adult. ''We use very little fiction other than children's stories.'' Receives 6 unsolicited fiction mss/month. Buys 1-2 fiction mss/month. Length: 600 words minimum. Occasionally critiques rejected mss.

How to Contact: Query first with SASE. Reports in 4 weeks on queries. Sample copy for $1.

Payment: Pays 5¢/word minimum.

Terms: Pays on publication for first rights; assignments on work-for-hire basis.

FARM WIFE NEWS, Box 643, Milwaukee WI 53201. (414)423-0100. Managing Editor: Ruth Benedict. General interest publication with focus on subjects of daily interest to the farm and ranch woman; for national farm and ranch women of all ages. Estab. 1970. Circ. 328,000.

Needs: Contemporary, humor, or serious. Themes should relate to country living. Buys 20-30 mss/year. Receives approximately 20 unsolicited fiction mss each month. Length: 1,000 words.

How to Contact: Written query or send complete ms. SASE always. Submit seasonal material at least 6 months in advance. No photocopied submissions. Reports in 6 weeks on queries and mss. Sample copy $2.00 with free guidelines.

Payment: Pays $55-$150. Offers kill fee (approximately ⅓ rate of purchase) for assigned mss not published.

Terms: Pays on publication. Byline given. Publication copyrighted.

Tips: "We are always looking for good freelance material. Topic, subject should be approached from a rural woman's point of view or appeal to the farm wife or single farm woman." Mss are rejected because "they are not unique or well written—or have the same old themes." Sponsors contests occasionally; entrants must be subscribers. "Study back issues for further insight on what is needed."

FINE LINE PRODUCTIONS, Box 5341, Grand Central Station, New York NY 10017. Editor-in-Chief: Nick Giordano. Fiction Editor: Bob Steel. Magazine of "humor only—witty, clever—photos, cartoons, but mostly funny articles, prose, poems, clean jokes." Wide age-range audience. Published monthly. Estab. 1982. Circ. 200,000 (anticipated).

Needs: Adventure, comics, contemporary, ethnic (clean), experimental, fantasy, historical, humor, juvenile, literary, mainstream, men's, prose poem, psychic/supernatural, science fiction, western, women's, young adult. "All must be funny, witty and well written; no dirty, profane, sacrilegious, cynical material." Receives approximately 100 unsolicited fiction mss/month. Accepts 100-200 mss/year. Occasionally critiques rejected mss.

How to Contact: "Writer should request our guidelines and send SASE. Both are a must first." Simultaneous and photocopied submissions and previously published work OK.

Payment: Variable. Negotiates kill fee for assigned ms not published.

Terms: Pays on publication for all rights or all remaining rights. Publication copyrighted.

Tips: "Study the guidelines very carefully and keep rewriting material to polish it. We look for a humorous jolt within the first three paragraphs and periodic reinforcement thereafter."

FIRST CLASS, Box 220074, Dallas TX 75222. Manager of Public Relations: Janna Aynes. General interest magazine of Airline Passengers Association for first class passengers all over the world. Bimonthly.

Needs: Contemporary, romance and humor. Light, positive, upbeat stories relating to travel anywhere. No plane crash stories. Length: 2,000 words. May recommend other markets.

How to Contact: Query with SASE. Photocopied submissions OK. Submit seasonal stories one year in advance of issue date. Reports in 3 months on mss.

Payment: Pays 10¢/word. Offers 50% kill fee for assigned ms not published.

Terms: Pays on publication for all rights. Byline given.

Tips: "Due to lack of good fiction, we seldom print short stories. We're looking for material with an international perspective." Rejections occur because "most manuscripts received do not relate to travel, international lifestyles or major destinations—not affluent enough in style for our market."

FLARE, 481 University Ave., Toronto, Ontario, Canada M5W 1A7. (416)596-5453. Editor: Keitha McLean. Associate Editor: Julie Beddoes. Magazine of fashion, beauty and lifestyle for Canadian working women from 18-34. Published 10 times/year. Estab. 1979. Circ. 190,000.

How to Contact: Send complete ms with SAE and International Reply Coupons. Sample copy 60¢ with free guidelines.

Terms: Pays on acceptance for first North American serial rights. Byline given. Seasonal material 3 months in advance. Simultaneous, photocopied and previously published submissions OK.

Tips: "Canadian writers only. We promote new Canadian literary talent, which we find through an annual competition announced in each September issue." Rejects mss because "poor quality, shortage of space."

THE FLYFISHER, Federation of Flyfishers, 390 Bella Vista, San Francisco CA 94127. (415)586-8332. Editor-in-Chief: Michael Fong. Magazine for fly fishermen. "We only publish material directly related to fly fishing." Published quarterly. Estab. 1967. Circ. 10,000.
Needs: Fiction related to fly fishing only. Accepts 1 ms/issue, 4 mss/year. Length: 1,500 words minimum; 3,500 words maximum; 3,000 words average (preferred).
How to Contact: Query first with SASE. Reports in 4 weeks on queries, 4 weeks on mss. Sample copy $1.50 with 9x12 SAE and 10 first class stamps. Free fiction guidelines with legal size SAE and 1 first class stamp.
Payment: $50-175.
Terms: Pays on publication for first North American serial rights and one-time rights. Publication copyrighted.
Tips: "See a current issue of the magazine."

FRIDAY OF THE JEWISH EXPONENT, A Forum of Literature and Opinion, Federation of Jewish Agencies, 226 S. 16th St., Philadelphia PA 19102. (215)893-5745. Editor-in-Chief: Jane Biberman. Newspaper for Jewish community of Philadelphia. "We publish short fiction and articles on Jewish themes." Published monthly. Circ. 100,000.
Needs: Condensed novel, confession, contemporary, ethnic, historical (general), humor/satire, literary, prose poem, religious/inspirational, translations. Receives approximately 20 unsolicited fiction mss/month. Accepts 1-2 mss/issue, 12-16 mss/year. Length: 1,000-2,000 words preferred; 5,000 words maximum. Occasionally critiques rejected mss. Sometimes recommends other markets.
How to Contact: Send complete ms with SASE. Photocopied submissions OK. Reports in 3 weeks. Free sample copy; fiction guidelines with SASE.
Payment: $50-150 and 2 contributor's copies. Offers 25% kill fee for assigned ms not published.
Terms: Pays on publication for first rights. Publication copyrighted. Rejects mss because "poorly written, cliché-ridden."

THE FRIEND, Church of Jesus Christ of Latter-day Saints, 50 E. North Temple, Salt Lake City UT 84150. (801)531-2210. Managing Editor: Vivian Paulsen. Children's magazine directed toward ages 12 and under. Monthly except for a combined August/September issue. Estab. January 1971. Circ. 210,000.
Needs: Literary, contemporary, inspirational, adventure, humor, and juvenile. Buys 8-10 mss/issue. Length: 1,000-2,000 words.
How to Contact: Send complete ms with SASE. Reports in 1 month on ms. Free sample copy and guidelines.
Payment: 7¢ and up per word.
Terms: Pays on acceptance for all rights unless otherwise specified. Publication copyrighted.
Tips: Mss are rejected because of "poor writing, wrong market."

GALLERY MAGAZINE, Montcalm Publishing Corp., 800 2nd Ave., New York NY 10017. Editorial Director: Eric Protter. Senior Editor: John Bensink. Sophisticated men's magazine similar to *Playboy*; general interest, how-to's, humor, interviews, investigative reports and fiction for men between 18 and 35 years old. Monthly. Estab. November 1972. Circ. 650,000.
Needs: Literary, science fiction, fantasy, horror, erotica and humor. No romance. Buys 1-2 mss/issue, 20-24 mss/year. Length: 3,500-6,000 words.
How to Contact: For fiction send complete ms with SASE. Prefers short fiction. Reading time 8-10 weeks. Sample copy $3.25.
Payment: Pays $250-$750 (special arrangements with established name writers).
Terms: Pays half on acceptance and half on publication for first North American serial rights. Byline given.
Tips: "Submit seasonal/holiday stories six months in advance. Photocopied mss accepted."

THE GAMBLING SCENE WEST, (formerly The Gambling Scene), Box 4483, Stanford CA 94305. Editor: Michael Wiesenberg. Monthly tabloid for readers interested in gambling and gam-

ing, particularly that of cardrooms and casinos of the West. Monthly. Estab. 1978. Circ. 10,000.
Needs: Gambling-related subjects. Fiction, poetry, satire, humor. Nothing derogatory to gambling, overly sexual, sexist or discriminatory. Buys 2-3 fiction mss/year. Receives approximately 5 unsolicited fiction mss each month. Length: 300-1,800 words. Critiques rejected mss if specifically requested.
How to Contact: Send complete ms with SASE. Reports on mss in 1 month. Sample copy $1.
Payment: 2-5¢/word, $25-50.
Terms: Pays on publication for first North American serial rights and second serial (reprint) rights. Publication copyrighted.
Tips: "We might publish more fiction, but 99% of what we receive is unsuitable—obviously sent by people who have not read *GSW* and usually have not even read more of this listing than our name. Unless your story is of exceptional quality and eminently suitable, consider us not a good fiction market."

GEM, G&S Publications Inc., 1472 Broadway, New York NY 10036. (212)840-7224. Editor: Will Martin. Men's sophisticate magazine. Bimonthly. Estab. 1961. Circ. 100,000.
Needs: Erotica (but not pornography), humor/satire, men's. Receives 25-50 unsolicited fiction mss/month. Buys 4-5 mss/month; 48-60 mss/year. Length: 1,000 words minimum; 3,000 words maximum; 2,500 words average. Occasionally critiques rejected mss.
How to Contact: Send complete ms with SASE. Simultaneous and photocopied submissions OK. Sample copy for $3.
Payment: Pays $40 (for short-shorts, 400-500 words)-$100; 1 free contributor's copy if requested.
Terms: Payment is usually on assignment to a specific issue for all rights. Publication copyrighted.

GENT, Dugent Publishing Corp., 2355 Salzedo St. Suite 204, Coral Gables FL 33134. (305)443-2378. Editor: John C. Fox. "Men's magazine designed to have erotic appeal for the reader. Our publications are directed to a male audience, but we do have a certain percentage of female readers. For the most part, our audience is interested in erotically stimulating material, but not exclusively." Monthly. Estab. 1959. Circ. 175,000.
Needs: Contemporary, psychic/supernatural, science fiction, horror, men's, erotica, mystery, adventure and humor. *Gent* specializes in D-Cup cheesecake, and fiction should be slanted accordingly. "Most of the fiction published includes several sex scenes, although on occasion we do use stories without prurient interest. No fiction that concerns children, religious subjects, or anything that might be libelous." Buys 3 mss/issue, 36 mss/year. Receives approximately 30-50 unsolicited fiction mss each month. Length: 2,000-3,500 words. Critiques rejected mss "when there is time."
How to Contact: Send complete ms with SASE. Reports in 1 month on mss. Sample copy $3. Fiction guidelines free with legal-sized SASE.
Payment: $125-175. Free author's copy.
Terms: Pays on publication for first North American serial rights. Publication copyrighted.
Tips: "Since *Gent* magazine is the 'Home of the D-Cups,' stories and articles containing either characters or themes with a major emphasis on large breasts will have the best chance for consideration. We advise would-be contributors to obtain and study a sample copy first." Mss are rejected because "there are not enough or ineffective erotic sequences, plot is not plausible, wrong length, not slanted specifically for us."

GENTLEMAN'S COMPANION, Larry Flynt Publications, 2029 Century Park, East Suite 3800, Los Angeles CA 90067. (213)556-9200, ext. 250. Managing Editor: Ted Newsom. "A men's magazine looking for material that is sexually stimulating, informative and entertaining. Readers are males, 18-34, high school graduates. Some columns geared for both men and women." Published monthly. Estab. 1980. Circ. 250,000.
Needs: Adventure, contemporary, erotica, fantasy, historical (general),horror, men's, psychic/

supernatural, romance (contemporary), western. "All fiction must include an erotic scene. No erotic fiction dealing with male homosexuality, beastiality or sedophillia." Receives 25-30 unsolicited fiction mss/month. Buys 2 mss/issue, 24 mss/year. Length: 2,500 words minimum; 4,000 words maximum; 3,250 words average. Monthly column "Private Affairs," erotic story in first person, from woman's point of view; 2,000 words, $50. Occasionally critiques rejected mss.
How to Contact: Send complete ms with SASE. Photocopied submissions OK. Reports in 6-8 weeks on mss. Free fiction guidelines with SASE.
Payment: $300 and 1 contributor's copy.
Terms: Pays on acceptance for first North American serial rights. Publication copyrighted.
Tips: "Purchase a copy of *Gentleman's Companion* or send for a manuscript specification packet to get a precise understanding of our needs. Allow 6-8 weeks for a response. Make sure you send an SASE. Make sure the length and subject matters are appropriate."

GOLF JOURNAL, United States Golf Assoc., Golf House, Far Hills NJ 07931. (201)234-2300. Editor: Robert Sommers. Managing Editor: George Eberl. "The magazine's subject is golf—its history, lore, rules, equipment, and general information. The focus is on amateur golf and those things applying to the millions of American golfers. Our audience is generally professional, highly literate, and knowledgeable; presumably they read *Golf Journal* because of an interest in the game, its traditions, and its noncommercial aspects." Published 8 times a year. Estab. 1949. Circ. 140,000.
Needs: Humor. "Fiction is very limited. *Golf Journal* has had an occasional humorous story, topical in nature. Generally speaking, short stories are not used. Golf jokes will not be used." Buys 10-12 mss/year. Length: 1,000-2,000 words. Critiques rejected mss "when there is time."
How to Contact: Send complete ms with SASE. Reports in 2 months on mss. Free sample copy with SASE.
Payment: $150-300. 1-10 free author's copies.
Terms: Pays on acceptance. Publication copyrighted.
Tips: "Know your subject (golf); edit your copy thoroughly; familiarize yourself first with the publication." Rejects mss because "fiction does not serve the function of *Golf Journal*, which, as the official magazine of the United States Golf Association, deals chiefly with nonfiction subjects. Fiction just doesn't fit."

GOOD HOUSEKEEPING, 959 Eighth Ave., New York NY 10019. Editor: John Mack Carter. Fiction Editor: Naome Lewis. Homemaking magazine of informational articles, how-to's for homemakers of all ages. Monthly. Circ. 5 million.
Needs: Contemporary, women's, gothic, romance, and mother-child stories. Buys 2 short stories/issue. Length: 1,000-4,000 words.
How to Contact: Query or send complete ms. SASE always. Reports in 1 month on both queries and mss.
Payment: Pays standard magazine rates.
Terms: Pays on acceptance for periodical publishing rights, second serial and first North American serial rights.

GOSPEL CARRIER, Messenger Publishing House, Box 50, Joplin MO 64802. (417)624-7050. Editor-in-Chief: Dr. Roy M. Chappell. Fiction Editor: Rosmarie Foreman. Magazine for adults— all material religious oriented. Published weekly. Circ. 2,500.
Needs: Adventure, historical (general), religious/inspirational, suspense/mystery, young adult. "All material must be religious oriented." Receives approximately 100 unsolicited fiction mss/month. Length: 1,500 words minimum; 1,750 words maximum; 1,600 words average. Occasionally critiques rejected mss.
How to Contact: Send complete ms with SASE. Simultaneous, photocopied and previously published submissions OK. Reports in 2 weeks on mss. Sample copy 50¢ or free with standard-size SAE and 1 first class stamp. Fiction guidelines 50¢ or free with standard-size SASE.
Payment: 1¢/word and 2 contributor's copies.
Terms: Pays on publication for simultaneous rights. Publication copyrighted.

GREEK ACCENT, Greek Accent Publishing Corp., 41-17 Crescent St., Long Island City, NY 11101.(212)784-5255. Executive Editor: Orania Papazoglou. Fiction Editor: George Kalogera-kis. Magazine "by, for, and about Greeks and Greek Americans for Greek, Greek-Americans and philhellenes (people who love Greece)." Published 11 times a year, combined July and August. Estab. 1980. Circ. 20,000.
Needs: Adventure, contemporary, ethnic, humor/satire, mainstream, suspense/mystery, trans-lations (from Greek). "No mss with Greek *names* but no real Greek or Greek American theme." Receives 18-28 unsolicited fiction mss/month. Length: 1,500 words minimum; 3,000 words max-imum; 2,000 words average. Occasionally critiques rejected mss.
How to Contact: Send complete ms with SASE. Photocopied submissions OK. Reports in 4 months on mss. Sample copy $2.50.
Payment: $50-100 and 1 contributor's copy. Offers 20% kill fee for assigned ms not published.
Terms: Pays on publication for first North American serial rights. Publication copyrighted.
Tips: "Grow up in the Greek American community and write about what you know."

GULFSHORE LIFE, Gulfshore Publishing Co., Inc., 3620 Tamiami Trail N., Naples FL 33940. (813)262-6425. Editor: Molly J. Burns. Lifestyle magazine about people, sports, homes, boats, features of interest to winter residents, and year-round residents of and visitors to Southwest Florida. Published October through June. Estab. 1970. Circ. 18,000.
Needs: Stories must have Florida setting. Buys mss for annual fiction writer's contest; deadline is March 1; 3,000 word limit.
How to Contact: Send complete ms with SASE beginning January 1. Reports after contest judg-ing.
Terms: Pays on publication for first-time rights. Byline given. Photocopied and simultaneous submissions OK. Publication copyrighted.
Tips: Mss are rejected because of "inappropriate subject matter."

HADASSAH MAGAZINE, 50 W. 58th St., New York NY 10019. Executive Editor: Alan M. Tigay. General interest magazine primarily concerned with Israel, the American Jewish commu-nity and American current affairs for members of Hadassah. Monthly except combined June/July and August/September issues. Circ. 375,000.
Needs: Ethnic (Jewish). Receives 20-25 unsolicited fiction mss each month. Length: 3,000 words maximum.
How to Contact: Send complete ms with SASE. Reports in 6 weeks on mss.
Payment: Pays $300 minimum. Offers $100 kill fee for assigned mss not published.
Terms: Pays on publication for US publication rights. Publication copyrighted.
Tips: "We get too many 'I Remember Mama' stories. Write a good short story with strong plot showing positive Jewish values." Mss are rejected because they are "too long, not an appropriate theme for magazine, not well written, not written for a 'family' audience." Occasionally sponsors contests.

HANG GLIDING MAGAZINE, US Hang Gliding Association, Box 66306, Los Angeles CA 90066. (213)390-3065. Editor-in-Chief: Gil Dodgen. Magazine for hang glider pilots. Publishes stories, technical articles, competition reports and features about hang gliding. Published month-ly. Estab. 1971. Circ. approximately 10,000.
Needs: Adventure, comics, experimental, fantasy, historical (general), horror, humor/satire, science fiction, suspense/mystery. "Fiction must relate strongly to the sport of hang gliding." Oc-casionally critiques rejected mss.
How to Contact: Query, query with clips of published work or send complete ms. SASE al-ways. Reports in 1 month on queries, 1 month on mss. Free sample copy for 8½x11 SAE and $1.03 postage.
Payment: "Negotiable—varies with the quality of the work and our needs at the time." Up to 4 free contributor's copies.
Terms: Pays on publication for all rights (usually). Publication copyrighted.
Tips: "Learn to hang glide, read the magazine. No erotica."

HARPER'S MAGAZINE, 2 Park Ave., Room 1809, New York NY 10016. Editor: Michael E. Kinsley. Magazine for well-educated, widely read and socially concerned college-aged and older, those active in political and community affairs. Monthly. Circ. 140,000.
Needs: Contemporary and humor. Stories on contemporary life and its problems. Receives approximately 300 unsolicited fiction mss each month. Length: 1,000-5,000 words.
How to Contact: Query through agent. Reports in 6 weeks on queries.
Payment: Pays $500-1,000. Negotiable kill fee and byline given.
Terms: Pays on publication for rights though they vary on each author and material. Publication copyrighted.
Tips: Mss are rejected because of "poor writing and petty concerns—often they are too long (over 25 pages)." Buys very little fiction.

HARVEY FOR LOVING PEOPLE, Harvey Shapiro Inc., 450 7th Ave., Suite 2305, New York NY 10001. (212)564-0112. Editor: Harvey Shapiro. Managing Editor: Harold James. Magazine dedicated to the enrichment of loving relationships between couples, offering sexually informative material in graphically erotic manner. "Our readership consists of people interested in highly informative sex-related information." Monthly. Estab. December 1979. Circ. 300,000.
Needs: Lesbian and heterosexual-erotica. No material accepted that is not sexually oriented. Buys 2-3 mss/issue. Length: 1,000-2,000 words.
How to Contact: Query with SASE. Reports in 1 month.
Payment: $75-250
Terms: Pays on publication for all rights.

HEALTH EXPLORER, Children's Better Health Institute, Benjamin Franklin Literary and Medical Society, 1100 Waterway Blvd., Box 567, Indianapolis IN 46206. (317)636-8881. Editor: Beth Wood Thomas. Fiction Editor: Ray A. Randolph. Magazine. "*Health Explorer* contains stories and articles dealing with health, specifically nutrition, exercise, disease, the environment, anatomy and physiology, and mental health, for children ages 9 to 11." Quarterly. Estab. 1981.
Needs: Health-related. "To make a subject more interesting and more informative, the writer can put the factual material into a fictional setting. Make sure that the setting does not distort or overpower the facts." Receives 12-15 unsolicited fiction mss/month. Buys 4-6 mss/month; 16-24 mss/year. Length: 500 words minimum; 1,500 words maximum; 1,000 words average. Occasionally critiques rejected mss.
How to Contact: Send complete ms with SASE. Photocopied submissions OK. Reports in 6-10 weeks (usually sooner) on mss. Sample copy for 75¢. Fiction guidelines free for # 10 SAE and 1 first class stamp.
Payment: Pays 4¢/word minimum; 2 free contributor's copies.
Terms: Pays on publication for all rights. Publication copyrighted.
Tips: "Send for the editorial requirements and copy(ies) of the magazine. Write on a subject you can handle. Don't forget who your audience is. Last, but not least, pay attention to ms mechanics."

HERS, I.P.C. Magazines, Ltd., King's Reach Tower, Stamford St., London, England SE1 9LS. Editor H. Dawson. Fiction Editor: Ms. J. Meek. Fictionalized true-life magazine with stories dramatic, romantic and slightly sexual in content and written in the first person style. For young women (19-26) either married with young children or dating. Low to middle socio/economic background. Monthly. Estab. 1968. Circ. 140,000.
Needs: Psychic/supernatural, men's, women's, confession, escapist, young adult and ethnic. No romantic, third person stories or overtly pornographic material. Buys 11 mss/issue. Receives approximately 150 unsolicited fiction mss each month. Length: 1,000-5,000 words. Critiques rejected mss "when there is time."
How to Contact: Query or send complete ms. SAE and International Reply Coupons always. Reports on queries in 3 weeks, 2 months on mss. Free fiction guidelines with SAE and IRC.
Payment: Offers 10% kill fee for assigned ms not published.
Terms: Pays on acceptance for first British serial rights. Publication copyrighted.

Tips: "Know your characters and have the story outline clear in your mind from beginning to end before you start. Keep stories dramatic and/or emotional and the principal female characters young; avoid characters with teenage children. The material must relate to the reader's lifestyle." Mss are rejected because "they are submitted without reference to requirements or target market."

HI-CALL, Gospel Publishing House, 1445 Boonville Ave., Springfield MO 65802. (417)862-2781. Editor: William P. Campbell. Ass't. Editor: Tom Young. Take-home Sunday School paper for teenagers (12-17). Weekly. Estab. 1954. Circ. 160,000.
Needs: Religious/inspirational, romance, western, mystery/suspense, adventure, humor, young adult with a strong but not preachy Biblical emphasis. Receives approximately 100 unsolicited fiction mss each month. Length: up to 1,800 words. Critiques rejected mss "when there is time."
How to Contact: Send complete ms with SASE. Reports in 3 weeks on mss. Free sample copy and guidelines.
Payment: Pays 2-3¢/word. Offers 100% kill fee for assigned mss not published.
Terms: Pays on acceptance for one-time rights. Simultaneous and previously published submissions OK.
Tips: "Most manuscripts are rejected because of shallow characters, shallow or predictable plots, and/or a lack of spiritual emphasis."

HIGH ADVENTURE, General Council Assemblies of God (Gospel Publishing Co.), 1445 Boonville, Springfield MO 65802. (417)862-2781, ext. 1497. Editor-in-Chief: Johnnie Barnes. Magazine for adolescent age boys. "Designed to provide boys with worthwhile, enjoyable, leisure reading; to challenge them in narrative form to higher ideals and greater spiritual dedication; and to perpetuate the spirit of the Royal Rangers program through stories, ideas and illustrations." Published quarterly. Estab. 1971. Circ. 55,000.
Needs: Adventure, historical (general), religious/inspirational, suspense/mystery, western. Length: 1,200 words minimum. Occasionally critiques rejected mss.
How to Contact: Send ms with SASE. Simultaneous, photocopied and previously published submissions OK. Reports in 6 weeks on mss. Free sample copy; fiction guidelines free for 9x12 SASE.
Payment: 2¢/word (base) and 3 contributor's copies.
Terms: Pays on acceptance for first rights and one-time rights. Publication copyrighted.
Tips: "Read the magazine; know the readership; give attention to writing style; be accurate."

HIGHLIGHTS FOR CHILDREN, 803 Church St., Honesdale PA 18431. (717)253-1080. Editor-in-Chief: Walter Barbe. Editor: Kent L. Brown Jr. Address fiction to: Constance McAllister, Associate Editor. Published 11 times/year. Circ. 1.6 million.
Needs: Juvenile (2-12). "We are eager for easy stories for very young readers but realize that this is the most difficult kind of writing. No war, crime or violence." Buys 6-7 mss/issue. Receives 400-500 unsolicited fiction mss each month. Maximum length: 900 words. Critiques rejected mss "when there is time."
How to Contact: Send complete ms with SASE. Reports in 2 months on mss. Free guidelines with SASE.
Payment: Pays 6¢ and up per word.
Terms: Pays on acceptance for all rights. Publication copyrighted.
Tips: "It is not our policy to consider fiction on the strength of the reputation of the author. We judge each submission on its own merits. We like stories with real-life children, unusual fiction, vivid and full of action for boys and girls. Moral teaching should be subtle." Mss are rejected because of "poor characterization, trite or worn-out plot." Sponsors occasional contests. Write for information.

HIGHWIRE MAGAZINE, The National Student Magazine, Highwire Associates, 217 Jackson St., Box 948, Lowell MA 01853. (617)458-6416. Editor: Ed Miller. Fiction Editor:

Kathleen Cushman. "*Highwire* is a general interest, news and humor magazine, for and by literate high school students." Quarterly. Estab. 1981. Circ. 100,000.

Needs: Adventure, contemporary, ethnic, experimental, feminist/lesbian, gay, horror, humor/satire, literary, mainstream, men's, psychic/supernatural, suspense/mystery, women's, young adult. "*Highwire* is most interested in fiction written by high school and college students and will usually not accept fiction by other freelancers. No poetry, inspirational pieces, moralistic tales or erotica." Receives approximately 40 unsolicited fiction mss/month. Buys 0-1 ms/month; 4 mss/year. Length: 1,000 words minimum; 2,000 words maximum; 1,500 words average. Occasionally critiques rejected mss written by a student.

How to Contact: Send complete ms with SASE. Photocopied submissions OK. Reports in 6 weeks on ms. Sample copy for $1. Fiction guidelines free.

Payment: Pays 10¢/word to $250. Offers kill fee of 25%.

Terms: Pays on acceptance for first rights. Publication copyrighted.

HIS MAGAZINE, Inter-Varsity Christian Fellowship, 5206 Main St., Downers Grove IL 60515. (312)964-5700. "Magazine of Christian discipleship; helping students integrate their faith with daily life on campus. First-person; stories with biblical teachings in them; allegories." Published monthly during the school year. Estab. 1941. Circ. 30,000.

Needs: Religious/inspirational, young adult. "No general fiction—we need stories with a biblical Christian viewpoint." Receives 20 unsolicited fiction mss/month. Buys 6 mss/year. Length: 200 words minimum; 2,000 words maximum; 1,500 words average.

How to Contact: Send complete ms with SASE. Previously published submissions (if identified as such) OK. Reports in 3 months. Sample copy free for 9x12 SAE and 1 first class stamp.

Payment: Pays $20-75; 2 free contributor's copies.

Terms: Pays on acceptance for first rights. Publication copyrighted.

HOCKEY MAGAZINE, The Quality Hockey Magazine, Hockey Magazine, Inc., 6 South Edgewood Rd., Niantic CT 06357. Editor-in-Chief: Keith A. Bellows. Slick, 4-color magazine that stresses good writing and photography for a well educated audience, 21-50, plus young hockey players. Published 8 times/year. Estab. 1975. Circ. 45,000.

Needs: Hockey. "No rah-rah sports heroism." Receives about 2 unsolicited fiction mss/month. Buys 2 mss/year. Length: 2,200 words maximum; 2,200 words average. Occasionally critiques rejected mss.

How to Contact: Send complete ms with SASE. Photocopied submissions and previously published work OK. Reports in 2 weeks on mss. Free sample copy with 11x8½ SAE and 5 first class stamps.

Payment: 10¢/word. Offers 25% kill fee for assigned ms not published.

Terms: Pays on publication (sometimes on acceptance) for first North American serial rights. Publication copyrighted.

Tips: "We look for imagination, flair and a grasp of hockey. Steer away from the clichéd and toward the offbeat."

HOME LIFE, The Sunday School Board of the Southern Baptist Convention, 127 9th Ave., N., Nashville TN 37234. (615)251-2271. Editor: Reuben Herring. A Christian family magazine. "Top priorities are strengthening and enriching marriage; parenthood; family concerns and problems; and spiritual and personal growth. Most of our readers are parents between the age of 25-50. They read it out of denominational loyalty and desire for Christian growth and discipleship." Monthly. Estab. January 1947. Circ. 800,000.

Needs: Contemporary, religious/inspirational, humor and young adult. "We do not want distasteful, risque or raunchy fiction. Nor should it be too fanciful or far-fetched." Buys 1-2 mss/issue, 12-24 mss/year. Receives approximately 800 unsolicited fiction mss each month. Critiques rejected mss "when there is time." Length: 750-2500 words.

How to Contact: Query or send complete ms. SASE always. Reports in 2 weeks on queries, 4 weeks on mss. Free sample copy with 9x11½ SAE and 70¢ postage. Free fiction guidelines with SASE.

Payment 4¢/word for unsolicited manuscripts. 3 free author's copies.
Terms: Pays on acceptance for all rights, first rights and first North American serial rights. Publication copyrighted.

HUDSON VALLEY MAGAZINE, Box 425, Woodstock NY 12498, (914)679-5100. Editor-in-Chief: Joanne Michaels. "General interest magazine with an editorial thrust toward leisure activities and folklore of this historical, beautiful town and country region of New York, West Connecticut and Western Massachusetts. Appeals to people of all ages and both sexes. Readership is upscale in education and income." Monthly. Estab. 1971. Circ. 27,000.
Needs: "We seek short stories by Hudson Valley residents of interest to Hudson Valley residents." Receives 5-10 unsolicited fiction mss each month. Length: 1,000-2,000 words.
How to Contact: Send complete ms with SASE. Reports in 1 month on mss.
Payment: Pays $20/story.
Terms: Acquires all rights. Simultaneous and photocopied submissions OK. Publication copyrighted.
Tips: Rejects mss because "inappropriate submissions—writers don't even *read* the publiction before sending material."

HUMPTY DUMPTY'S MAGAZINE, Children's Better Health Institute, Benjamin Franklin Literary & Medical Society, Inc., 1100 Waterway Blvd., Box 567, Indianapolis, IN 46206. Editor: Christine French Clark. Children's magazine stressing health, nutrition, hygiene, exercise, and safety for children ages 4-6. Monthly, except bimonthly February-March, April-May, June-July and August-September. Circ. 500,000.
Needs: Juvenile health-related material. No inanimate talking objects. Rhyming stories should flow easily with no contrived rhymes. Buys 1-3 mss/issue. Receives 250-300 unsolicited fiction mss each month. 600 words maximum.
How to Contact: Send complete ms with SASE. Reports in 8-10 weeks. Sample copy 75¢. Editorial guidelines with SASE.
Payment: Pays 4¢/word for stories plus 2 author's copies.
Terms: Buys all rights. Publication copyrighted.
Tips: In contemporary stories, characters should be up-to-date, with realistic dialogue. We're looking for health-related stories with unusual twists or surprise endings. We want to avoid stories and poems that 'preach.' We try to present the health material in a positive way, utilizing a light humorous approach wherever possible." Most rejected mss "are unsuitable for the 4-6 age range, using too difficult vocabulary and situations unfamiliar to young children. Many stories are too long; they should not exceed 600 words." Also, "authors do not study *current* issues of our magazine. They don't know their market."

HUSTLER MAGAZINE, Larry Flynt Publications, 2029 Century Park East, Los Angeles CA 90067. (213)556-9200. Executive Editor: Donald R. Evans. Fiction Editor: James Gregory. Adult men's magazine. Monthly. Estab. 1974. Circ. 1.9 million.
Needs: Adventure stories with one erotica scene and twist ending. Buys 1 ms/issue. Receives approximately 75-100 unsolicited fiction mss each month. Length: 4,500 words. Critiques rejected mss "when there is time."
How to Contact: Send complete ms with SASE. Reports on mss in 2 months. Free fiction guidelines with SASE.
Payment: $1,000 minimum.
Terms: Pays on acceptance for exclusive first and second magazine rights.
Tips: "Double-space typewritten mss, with 1 inch margins; start half-way down first page. Be familiar with magazine!!"

IDEALS MAGAZINE, Ideals Publishing Corp., 11315 Watertown Plank Rd., Milwaukee WI 53226. (414)771-2700. V.P. Publishing: James A. Kuse. *Ideals* is a family-oriented magazine with issues corresponding to seasons and based on traditional values. Published 8 times a year. Estab. 1944. Circ. 700,000.

Needs: Religious/inspirational, men's, women's, humor, juvenile, seasonal/holidays, nostalgia and travel. No lewd or risque fiction. Buys 4-5 mss/issue, 40 mss/year. Length: 500-2,500 words.
How to Contact: Send complete ms with SASE. Reports in 2 months on mss. Free sample copy with 8½x11 SASE and $1.35 postage.
Payment: Varies.
Terms: Pays on publication for one-time rights.

IN TOUCH, Wesleyan Publishing House, Box 2000, Marion IN 46952. (317)674-3301. Editor: Jim Watkins. Publication for teens, ages 13-18. Weekly.
Needs: Realistic stories by authors who are working with teens on a regular basis. Should reinforce Biblical values and principles, but not "preachy". First person fiction discouraged. Receives 200-300 unsolicited fiction mss each month. Length: 1,200-1,600 words."
How to Contact: Send complete ms with SASE. "Queries are not encouraged." Reports in 1-3 weeks on mss. Sample copy, with SASE.
Payment: Pays 2.5¢/word.
Terms: Pays on acceptance. Byline given and brief auto-biographical sketch.
Tips: Rejects mss because "unrealistic."

INSIDE, The Magazine of the Jewish Exponent, Jewish Federation, 226 S. 16th St., Philadelphia PA 19102. (215)893-5700. Editor-in-Chief: Jane Biberman. Magazine aimed at middle- and upper-middle class audience, Jewish-oriented articles and fiction. Published quarterly. Estab. 1980. Circ. 85,000.
Needs: Contemporary, ethnic, humor/satire, literary, translations. No erotica. Receives approximately 10 unsolicited fiction mss/month. Buys 1-2 mss/issue, 4-8 mss/year. Length: 1,500 words minimum; 4,000 words maximum; 3,000 words average. Occasionally critiques rejected mss.
How to Contact: Send complete ms with SASE. Simultaneous and photocopied submissions OK. Sample copy $1.50 with 8x10 SAE. Free fiction guidelines with SASE.
Payment: $100-300.
Terms: Pays on publication for first rights. Publication copyrighted.
Tips: "Fiction is a new department. We have no sampling. Slant with a Jewish eye and ear. Keep it neat and clear and easy to read."

INSIDE KUNG FU, The Ultimate in Martial Arts Coverage, Unique Publications, 7011 Sunset Blvd., Hollywood CA 90028. (213)467-1300. Editor-in-Chief: John Stewart. Magazine of martial arts—history, technique, philosophy, theory, training methods, self defense. (Especially Chinese arts.) Audience: most men, sports-oriented, 18-35 years of age. Published monthly. Estab. 1975. Circ. 85,000.
Needs: "Want Chinese-flavored fiction, rather than Japanese (as in *Shogun*, etc.). No movie-plots, please. We do not accept mundane, personal, diary-type writing." Receives 2 unsolicited fiction mss/month. Buys 1 ms/issue, 10 mss/year. Length: 1,000 words minimum; 2,200 words maximum; 1,500 words average. Occasionally critiques rejected mss.
How to Contact: Send complete ms with SASE. Reports in 4 weeks on mss. Sample copy free with 9x12 SAE and 3 first class stamps.
Payment: $75-250 and 2 contributor's copies.
Terms: Pays on publication for first North American serial rights. Publication copyrighted.
Tips: "We need very compelling material to use it at all."

INSIDE RUNNING, The Tabloid Magazine That Runs Texas, 8100 Bellaire, Suite 1318, Houston TX 77036. (713)777-9084. Publisher/Editor: Joanne Schmidt. Specialized tabloid for Texas joggers/runners—novice to marathoner. Published monthly. Estab. 1977. Circ. 10,000.
Needs: Adventure, condensed novel, contemporary, fantasy, historical (general), horror, humor/satire, literary, science fiction, serialized/excerpted novel, suspense/mystery. "Nothing sexually explicit—we're family-oriented." Buys 1 ms/issue. Length: 1,000 words minimum; 2,000 words maximum. Occasionally critiques rejected mss.
How to Contact: Send complete ms with SASE. Simultaneous, photocopied and previously

comm. periodicals

published submissions OK. Reports in 4 weeks on mss. Sample copy $1. Free fiction guidelines with SASE.

Payment: $25-75.

Terms: Pays on acceptance for one-time rights. Publication copyrighted.

Tips: "Know running basics and keep story clean. Avoid typical race experience (first marathon, etc.)."

INSIGHT, Young Calvinist Federation, Box 7244, Grand Rapids MI 49510. (616)241-5616. Editor: John Knight. Fiction Editor: Martha Kalk. *"Insight* magazine is designed to help young people recognize Christ as Lord, and to prepare them to serve Him always and everywhere. Our readership is made up of young people 15 to 21 years of age in American and Canadian urban and rural areas." Published 10 times per year. Estab. 1919. Circ. 22,000.

Needs: Literary, contemporary, religious/inspirational and young adult and teen. Buys 3 mss/issue, 30 mss/year. Length: 900-2,000 words.

How to Contact: Send complete ms with SAE. Reports in 1 month on mss. Free sample copy with 9x12 SAE and 50¢ postage. Free fiction guidelines with legal-sized SASE.

Payment: $35-100.

Terms: Pays on publication for simultaneous, first, second serial (reprint) and one-time rights. Publication copyrighted.

Tips: "Short stories should lead our readers into a better understanding of how their Christian beliefs apply to their daily lives. The events and the characters must be lively, and so must the dialogue. Anything unrealistic or overly sentimental cannot be used. Quality is a high priority; the pieces must be well-written and professional." Mss are rejected because they are "preachy, simplistic."

ISAAC ASIMOV'S SCIENCE FICTION MAGAZINE, Davis Publications, Inc., 380 Lexington Ave., New York NY 10017. Editor: Shawna McCarthy. Magazine consists of science fiction stories for adults and young adults. 13 issues a year. Estab. 1977. Circ. 100,000.

Needs: Science fiction, fantasy. No horror or psychic/supernatural. Buys 10 mss/issue. Receives approximately 800 unsolicited fiction mss each month. Length: up to 20,000 words. Critiques rejected mss "when there is time."

How to Contact: Send complete ms with SASE. Photocopied submissions OK. Reports in 1 week on mss. Free fiction guidelines with legal-sized SASE. Sample copy $1.75.

Payment: 5.75¢/word for stories up to 7,500 words long, 3.5¢ a word for stories over 12,500 long, $375 for stories between those limits.

Terms: Pays on acceptance for first North American serial rights plus specified foreign rights, as explained in contract. Publication copyrighted.

Tips: We are "looking for character stories, rather than those emphasizing technology or science."

ISLAND MAGAZINE, Box 207, Sandy Bay, Tasmania, Australia. Tel. (002)202325. Editors: Michael Denholm and Andrew Sant. Magazine of articles on politics, social issues, literature and the arts both within Australia and overseas plus a substantial range of poetry and fiction. For academics, writers, general readers. Quarterly. Estab. 1979.

Needs: Contemporary, experimental, literary, prose poem, translations. Receives varied amount of unsolicited fiction mss/month. Buys 2-3 mss/issue; 8-12 mss/year. Length: 5,000 words maximum. Occasionally critiques rejected mss.

How to Contact: Send complete ms with SASE. Reports in 2 months on mss. Sample copy $2.95 (Australian currency).

Payment: Pays $20 (Australian) minimum; 1 free contributor's copy; $2.95 (Australian) charge for extras.

Terms: Pays on publication for first rights. Publication copyrighted.

Tips: "Send a clearly typed, clean manuscript with return postage."

IT MAGAZINE, Irish Tatler Publications, Ltd., Marino Grove, Marino Ave., West, Killiney, Dublin, Ireland. Tel. 823743/853641. Editor-in-Chief: Noelle Campbell-Sharp. "Fashion and social magazine primarily for women age 18-40." Published monthly. Estab. 1890. Circ. 35,000.
Needs: Humor/satire, psychic/supernatural, romance (contemporary), suspense/mystery. No feminist/lesbian or religious/inspirational mss. Receives 6-10 unsolicited fiction mss/month. Length: 2,000 words minimum. Occasionally critiques rejected mss.
How to Contact: Query first or send complete ms with SAE and IRC. Free sample copy.
Payment: $45-72.
Terms: Pays on publication for all rights. Publication copyrighted.
Tips: "Submit ideas—we're always open to new ideas. Make them topical to our publication and readership."

JACK AND JILL, The Benjamin Franklin Literary & Medical Society, Inc., 1100 Waterway Blvd., Box 567, Indianapolis IN 46206. (317)636-8881. Editor: William Wagner. Children's magazine of articles, stories and activities with a health, safety, exercise or nutritionally-oriented theme, ages 6-8 years. Monthly except April/May, June/July, August/September. Estab. 1938.
Needs: Science fiction, mystery, adventure, humor and juvenile. No religious subjects. Length: 500-1,500 words.
How to Contact: Send complete ms with SASE. Reports in 10 weeks on mss. Sample copy 75¢. Free fiction guidelines with SASE.
Payment: 4¢/word.
Terms: Pays on publication for all rights.
Tips: Try to present health material in a positive—not a negative—light. Use humor and a light approach wherever possible without minimizing the seriousness of the subject.

JIVE, Lexington Library, 313 N. Stemmons, Suite A, Dallas TX 75427. (214)630-2167. Senior Editor: Karen Thompson. Fiction Editor: Jeannette M. Barrett. Confession magazine with "romantic, heart-throbbing fiction stories" for women between the ages of 18-35 (black). Buys 7 mss/issue.
Needs: Confession. "No unrealistic, untimely stories." Length: 3,000 words minimum; 5,000 words maximum. Occasionally critiques rejected mss.
How to Contact: Send complete ms with SASE. Reports in 2 weeks on mss. Free sample copy; fiction guidelines with SASE.
Payment: $40-75; subscription to magazine and 1 contributor's copy. $1.50 charge for extras.
Terms: Pays on publication for one-time rights and assignments on work-for-hire basis. Publication copyrighted.
Tips: "Be enthusiastic, creative, and send material that is relevant to today."

JR. MEDICAL DETECTIVE, Children's Better Health Institute, Benjamin Franklin Literary and Medical Society, 1100 Waterway Blvd., Box 567, Indianapolis IN 46206. (317)636-8881. Editor: Beth Wood Thomas. Fiction Editor: Ray A. Randolph. "*Jr. Medical Detective* contains stories and articles dealing with the 'whys' and 'hows' of the human body, and introduces children 10 to 12 years of age to the 'mysterious' aspects of health and illness." Quarterly. Estab. 1981.
Needs: Health-related. "To make a subject more interesting and more informative, the writer can put factual material into a fictional setting. Make sure that that setting does not distort the facts." Receives 12-15 unsolicited fiction mss/month. Buys 4-6 mss/month; 16-24 mss/year. Length: 500 words minimum; 1,500 words maximum; 1,000 words average. Occasionally critiques rejected mss.
How to Contact: Send complete ms with SASE. Photocopied submissions OK. Reports in 6-10 weeks (usually sooner) on ms. Sample copy for 75¢.
Payment: Pays 4¢/word minimum; 2 free contributor's copies.
Terms: Pays on publication for all rights. Publication copyrighted.
Tips: "Send for the editorial requirements and copy(ies) of the magazine. Write on a subject you can handle. Don't forget who your audience is. Last, but not least, pay attention to ms mechanics."

JUNIOR TRAILS, Gospel Publishing House, 1445 Boonville Ave., Springfield MO 65802. (417)862-2781. Editor: Charles Ford. Elementary Editor: John Maempa. A Sunday School take-home paper of nature articles and fictional stories that apply Christian principles to everyday living for 9-12 year old children. Weekly. Estab. 1920. Circ. 85,000.
Needs: Contemporary, religious/inspirational and juvenile. Adventure stories are welcome. No Biblical fiction or science fiction. Buys 2 mss/issue. Length: 1,000-1,200 words.
How to Contact: Send complete ms with SASE. Reports in 1 month on mss. Free sample copy and guidelines.
Payment: 2½-3¢/word. 3 free author's copies.
Terms: Pays on acceptance for first rights.
Tips: "Know the age level and direct stories relevant to that age group." Mss are rejected because of "weak or worn plots, triteness, irrelevancy to the age level, lack of spiritual/moral emphasis."

LADIES' HOME JOURNAL, Publishing Co. (Family Media Inc.), 641 Lexington Ave., New York NY 10022. Editor: Myrna Blyth. Fiction/Books Editor: Constance Leisure.
Needs: Book mss and short stories are accepted only through an agent. Return of unsolicited material cannot be guaranteed. "We do not have the facilities that permit proper handling."

LADY'S CIRCLE, Lopez Publications, 23 West 26 St., New York NY 10010. (212)689-3933. Editor-in-Chief: Mary Terzella. Homemakers' magazine with articles on homemaking, crafts, child care, time and money management, etc. and short emotional fiction. Published monthly.
Needs: Women's. Accepts 1 mss/issue. Length: 2,000 words minimum; 2,500 words maximum; 2,000 words average. Occasionally critiques rejected mss. Recommends other markets.
How to Contact: Send complete ms with SASE. Photocopied submissions OK. Reports in 3 months on mss. Sample copy $1.50. Free fiction guidelines with SASE.
Payment: $75-125. All submissions must be on speculation.
Terms: Pays on publication for all rights. Publication copyrighted.
Tips: "Read several issues of the magazine. We usually feature one fiction piece per issue. Almost 100% of those mss published were unsolicited."

LIGHTED PATHWAY, Church of God Publishing House (Pathway Press), 922 Montgomery Ave., Cleveland TN 37311. (615)476-4512. Editor-in-Chief: Hoyt E. Stone. Christian, evangelical, youth inspiration magazine (ages 15-25) with at least two fiction short stories per issue. Published monthly. Estab. 1929. Circ. 26,000.
Needs: Adventure, contemporary, historical (general), humor/satire, juvenile, religious/inspirational, young adult. "Real life problems, no profanity." Receives 1-24 unsolicited fiction mss/month. Buys 2 (minimum) mss/issue, 24 (minimum) mss/year. Length: 800-1,600 preferred; 2,000 words maximum. Occasionally critiques rejected mss.
How to Contact: Query first or send complete ms. SASE always. Simultaneous and previously published submissions OK sometimes. Reports in 3 weeks on queries, 3 weeks on mss. Free sample copy with SAE and free fiction guidelines with SASE.
Payment: 2-4¢/word; 3 contributor's copies. 30¢ charge for extras.
Terms: Pays on acceptance for first North American serial rights and one-time rights. Publication copyrighted.
Tips: "Study a sample. Make story exciting."

LIGUORIAN, "A Leading Catholic Magazine", Liguori Publications, 1 Liguori Dr., Liguori MO 63057. (314)464-2500. Editor-in-Chief: Norman J. Muckerman, CSS.R. Managing Editor: Francine M. O'Connor. "*Liguorian* is a Catholic magazine aimed at helping our readers to live a full Christian life. We publish articles for families, young people, children, religious and singles—all with the same aim." Published monthly. Estab. 1918. Circ. 570,000.
Needs: Religious/inspirational, young adult (with moral Christian thrust). "Stories submitted to *Liguorian* must have as their goal the lifting up of the reader to a higher Christian view of values and goals. We are not interested in contemporary works that lack purpose or are of questionable

moral value." Receives approximately 12 unsolicited fiction mss/month. Buys 4-5 mss/year. Length: 1,500-2,000 words preferred. Occasionally critiques rejected mss "if we feel the author is capable of giving us something we need even though this story did not suit us." Occasionally recommends other markets.

How to Contact: Send complete ms with SASE. Reports in 6 weeks on mss. Free sample copy and fiction guidelines.

Payment: 7-10¢/word and 6 contributor's copies. Offers 50% kill fee for assigned ms not published.

Terms: Pays on acceptance for all rights. Publication copyrighted.

Tips: "First read several issues of our magazine containing short stories. Our usual fiction material should be used as a goal for beginning writers but we look for originality and creative input in each story we read. Since most editors must wade through mounds of manuscripts each month, consideration for the editor requires that the market be studied, the manuscript be carefully presented, and polished before submitting. Our publication uses only one fiction a month. Compare this with the 12 or more we receive over the transom each month, and you can see the problem our editors face. Also, many fiction mss are written without a specific goal or thrust, i.e. an interesting incident that goes nowhere is *not a story*."

LIVE, The Gospel Publishing House, 1445 Boonville, Springfield MO 65802. Editor: Kenneth D. Barney. A Sunday School take-home paper for adults (30 years on up)containing articles and stories of believable characters working out their problems according to Bible principles. Weekly. Circ. 224,000.

Needs: Religious/inspirational. No controversial stories about such subjects as race, feminism, war or capital punishment. Buys 2 mss/issue. Length: 1,200-2,000 words.

How to Contact: Send complete ms with SASE. Reports in 6 weeks on mss. Free sample copy with SASE. Free fiction guidelines with SASE.

Payment: 3¢/word (first rights); 2¢/word (second rights).

Terms: Pays on acceptance for one-time rights. Mss are rejected because "many are just not of acceptable quality."

LIVING & LOVING, The Magazine That Cares, Republican Press (PTY) Ltd., Box 32083 Mobeni, Durban, South Africa 4060. Tel. 422041. Editor: John Ireland. Magazine for mothers, pregnant mothers, families, dealing mainly with pregnancy, children, etc. Semi-specialized medical magazine. Monthly. Estab. 1970. Circ. 186,000.

Needs: Romance. Receives 15-20 unsolicited fiction mss/month. Buys 3 mss/issue; 24 mss/year. Length: 1,500 words minimum; 2,000 words average. Occasionally critiques rejected mss.

How to Contact: Send complete ms.

Payment: Pays R and 30-R and 200 and 1 free contributor's copy.

Terms: Pays on publication for first South African rights.

Tips: "Study the fiction in our magazine before submitting any ms, as we cater for a certain audience."

LIVING MESSAGE, The Anglican Church of Canada, Box 820, Petrolia, Ontario, Canada N0N 1R0. (519)882-2497. Editor: Rita Baker. "*Living Message* calls forth from its readers a Christian response to family and social concerns. Encourages and aids the ministry of clergy and lay people. Especially interested in human rights. Our readers are committed Christians, especially of the Anglican Church (Episcopal). Readers want to know about Anglican work in all areas of the world. They want to know how they can minister to people in local communities." Monthly except July and August. Estab. 1889. Circ. 14,000.

Needs: Literary, contemporary and humor. "We do not require religious/inspirational stories. No sentimental writing; no moralizing please!" Buys 1 ms/issue. Receives approximately 10 unsolicited fiction mss each month. Length: 1,000-1,500 words. Critiques rejected mss "when there is time."

How to Contact: Send complete ms with SAE and International Reply Coupons (Not U.S.

stamps). Reports in 1 month on ms. Free sample copy.
Payment: $15-25. 2 free author's copies. Extras are free on request.
Terms: Pays on acceptance for second serial (reprint) and first North American serial rights. Publication copyrighted.
Tips: "Don't write long letters to the editor. Make sure you study the market; read the whole magazine, not just the fiction. We receive very few good stories. If you can write simply, with insight and sensitivity, let us see your work." Mss are rejected because they are "too long or there is too much moralising. We want to publish stories of high quality, but we are unable to pay adequate rates for these, therefore we probably do not attract highly skilled writers. However, we sometimes 'discover' a beginning writer who has potential."

LIVING WITH TEENAGERS, Baptist Sunday School Board, 127 9th Ave. North, Nashville TN 37234. (615)251-2273. Editor: E. Lee Sizemore. Magazine especially designed "to enrich the parent-teen relationship with reading material from a Christian perspective" for Southern Baptist parents of teenagers. Quarterly. Estab. October 1978. Circ. 35,000.
Needs: Religious/inspirational and parent-teen relationships. Nothing not related to parent-teen relationships or from a Christian perspective. Buys 2 mss/issue. Receives approximately 50 unsolicited fiction mss each month. Length: 600-2,400 words.
How to Contact: Query with clips of published work or send complete ms. SASE always. Reports in 1 month on both queries and mss. Free sample copy with 9x12 SAE and 30¢ postage.
Payment: 4¢/published word. 3 free author's copies
Terms: Pays on acceptance for all and first rights. Publication copyrighted.
Tips: Mss are rejected most often because "denouement is unrealistic, the events and characters are unrealistic."

THE LOOKOUT, Standard Publishing, 8121 Hamilton Ave., Cincinnati OH 45231. (513)931-4050. Editor: Mark A. Taylor. Inspirational/motivational publication "for Christian adults who need to be informed, to get tips for building Christian marriages and families, to find help in living a Christian life in a secular world." Weekly. Estab. 1894. Circ. 160,000 + .
Needs: Religious/inspirational, men's, women's and young adults. No predictable, preachy material. Taboos are blatant sex, swear words, drinking alcohol. Buys 1 ms/issue. Length: 1,200-2,000 words.
How to Contact: Send complete ms with SASE. Reports in 2 months on ms. Sample copy 50¢. Free guidelines with legal-sized SASE.
Payment: 4¢/word for first rights. Free author's copies.
Terms: Pays on acceptance for simultaneous, first, second serial (reprint), first North American serial and one-time rights.
Tips: "No queries please. Send us a believable story which is inspirational and helpful but down to earth."

LOS ANGELES READER, 5225 Wilshire Blvd., # 324, Los Angeles CA 90036. (213)930-1214. Editor: James Vowell. Fiction Editor: Randy Michael Signor. Newspaper of features and reviews with emphasis on Los Angeles themes/subjects. "We publish little fiction (3-4 per year); may be experimental but not off-the-wall. Readers are young (20-40), well educated, affluent, sophisticated." Weekly. Estab. 1978. Circ. 65,000.
Needs: Receives less that 12 unsolicited fiction mss/month. Buys 3-4 mss/year. Length: 1,000 words minimum; 4,000 words maximum; 1,500 words average. Occasionally critiques rejected ms.
How to Contact: Send complete ms with SASE. Photocopied submissions OK. Reports in 2 months on mss. Sample copy free for 9x12 SAE and $1.25 postage. Fiction guidelines free to business SAE and 20¢ postage.
Payment: Pays $50-200; 2 free contributor's copies; $1 charge for extras.
Terms: Pays on publication for first North American serial rights. Publication copyrighted.
Tips: "Stories should have L.A. setting or theme (with rare exceptions). Resist the urge to submit satires/parodies/jokes/dream stories."

THE LUTHERAN JOURNAL, Outlook Publications, Inc., 7317 Cahill Rd., Minneapolis MN 55435. (612)941-6830. Editor: Rev. A.U. Deye. A family magazine to provide wholesome and inspirational reading material for the enjoyment and enrichment of Lutherans. Quarterly. Estab. 1936. Circ. 112,000.
Needs: Literary, contemporary, religious/inspirationl, men's, women's and young adult. Must be appropriate for distribution in the churches. Buys 2-4 mss/issue. Length: 1,000-2,500 words.
How to Contact: Send complete ms with SASE. Free sample copy with SASE (52¢ postage).
Payment: $10-20. 6 free author's copies.
Terms: Pays on publication for all and first rights.

LUTHERAN WOMEN, Lutheran Church Women, 2900 Queen Ln., Philadelphia PA 19129. (215)438-2200. Editor-in-Chief: Ms. Terry Schutz. Magazine of articles and fiction addressing issues and concerns of Christian women today "who are more interested in insightful formulations of questions than in pat answers." Published 10 times/year. Estab. 1962. Circ. 40,000.
Needs: "We look for stories showing growth of character and understanding. Explicitly Christian or religious themes are not essential. We do not want to see anything sentimental, what is usually thought of as 'inspirational.' " Receives approximately 50 unsolicited fiction mss/month. Buys 1 ms/issue, 10 mss/year. Length: 500 words minimum; 2,000 words maximum. Occasionally critiques rejected mss.
How to Contact: Send complete ms with SASE. Simultaneous, photocopied and previously published submissions OK. Reports in 8 weeks on mss. Sample copy free with 9x12 SAE and 69¢ postage. Free fiction guidelines with SASE.
Payment: $20-50 and 2 contributor's copies. 75¢ charge for extras.
Terms: Pays on publication for simultaneous and one-time rights. Publication copyrighted.
Tips: "Become familiar with our magazine and with basic rules of fiction; be credible, don't be solemn, don't be afraid of the ordinary, write well. Rejects mss because not appropriate for our audience or purpose. Best come from writers who are familiar with what we do."

MADEMOISELLE MAGAZINE, Condé Nast Publications, Inc., 350 Madison Ave., New York NY 10017. (212)880-8591. Editor: Amy Levin. Fiction Editor: Susan Schneider. Fashion magazine for women from 18 to 25 with articles of interest to women; beauty and health tips, features, home and food, fiction. Audience interested in self-improvement, curious about trends, interested in updating lifestyle and pursuing a career. Monthly. Estab. 1935. Circ. 1 million.
Needs: Literary, contemporary, men's, women's, feminist, gay/lesbian, ethnic and excerpts from novels. Buys 1 ms/issue, 12/year. Length: 2,000-4,600 words.
How to Contact: Send complete ms with SASE. Reports in 6 weeks. Free fiction guidelines with SASE.
Payment: $1,000 minimum.
Terms: Pays on acceptance for first North American serial rights.
Tips: "We want stories that have an obvious appeal for young single women and we continue in the tradition of demanding very high literary quality. Be sure to see the listing in Contest and Awards section for guidelines for *Mademoiselle's* all new fiction writer's contest."

MAINE LIFE, Maine Life Press, Inc., Sedgwick ME 04676. (207)359-2280. Editor: George Frangoulis. "Theme is found in the title of our magazine—'*Maine Life*, past, present and future. The people and places of Maine.' Our readers are people who love Maine and its remote environment, what it was like and is like now." Published 6 times a year. Estab. 1945. Circ. 25,000.
Needs: "Rather free, innovative or traditional material welcomed, but nothing risque, please. No erotic, too romantic love stories or personal crises." Buys 2-3 mss/year. Receives 2-3 unsolicited fiction mss each month. Length: 1,000-4,000 words. Critiques rejected mss "when there is time." Sometimes recommends other markets.
How to Contact: Send complete ms with SASE. Reports ASAP. Free sample copy with SASE, from Farmstead Press, Inc., Box 111, Freedom ME 04941.
Payment: 5¢/word. 2 free author's copies.

Terms: Pays on publication for first rights.
Tips: "Hold out very little hope of acceptance. Submit only when convinced the fiction might be appropriate for our mostly nonfiction magazine." Mss are rejected because they are "dull, poorly written, irrelevant, untimely, self-indulgent."

MATURE LIVING, Sunday School Board of the Southern Baptist Conv., MSN 140, 127 Ninth Ave. N., Nashville TN 37234. (615)251-2191. Editor: Jack Gulledge. Fiction Editor: Zada Malugen. "Our magazine is Christian in content and the material required is what would appeal to 60*f* age group (mainly Southern Baptists): inspirational, instructional, nostalgic, humorous. Our magazine is distributed mainly through churches (especially Southern Baptists churches) that buy the magazine in bulk and distribute it to members in this age group." Monthly. Estab. April 1977. Circ. 241,000.
Needs: Contemporary, religious/inspirational, humor and senior adults. Avoid all types of pornography, drugs, liquor, horror, science fiction, stories demeaning to the elderly. Buys 1 ms/issue. Length: 400-1,400 words (prefers 875).
How to Contact: Send complete ms with SASE. Reports in 6 weeks on mss. Free sample copy. Free guidelines with SASE.
Payment: $16-52. 3 free author's copies. 75¢ charge for extras.
Terms: Pays on acceptance for all and first rights. Publication copyrighted.
Tips: Mss are rejected because they are too long.

MATURE YEARS, United Methodist Publishing House, 201 Eight Ave. S., Nashville TN 37202. (615)749-6438. Editor: Dr. Ewart Watts. Fiction Editor: Daisy D. Warren. Magazine helps persons in and nearing retirement to appropriate the resources of the Christian faith as they seek to face the problems and opportunities related to aging. Quarterly. Estab. January 1953.
Needs: Religious/inspirational. "We don't want anything poking fun at old age, saccharine stories or anything not for older adults." Buys 1-2 mss/issue, 4-8 mss/year. Receives very few unsolicited fiction mss each month. Length: 1,000-2,000 words.
How to Contact: Send complete ms with SASE. Reports in 2 months on mss. Free sample copy with 10½x11 SAE and 67¢ postage.
Payment: 4¢/word.
Terms: Pays on acceptance for all and first rights. Publication copyrighted.

McCALL'S, The McCall's Publishing Co., 230 Park Ave., New York NY 10169. (212)551-9500. Editor: Robert Stein. Fiction Editor: Helen DelMonte. General women's magazine for "adult women of considerable literary sensibility who are interested in every facet of family life as well as the world around them." Monthly. Estab. April 1876. Circ. 6,200,000.
Needs: Literary, contemporary, humor, love, family stories. "No vague mood pieces; character sketches that aren't real stories; slick, formula stories; stories that are heavily contrived; depressing stories that offer no redeeming catharsis; stories that have no discernible point." Buys approximately 15 mss/year. Receives approximately 1,000 unsolicited fiction mss each month. Length: 1,500-5,000 words. Critiques rejected mss "if story is a strong possibility for purchase but in need of revision."
How to Contact: Send complete ms with SASE. Reports in 1 month on ms. Free guidelines with SASE.
Payment: $1,250-3,000.
Terms: Pays on acceptance for first North American serial rights. Publication copyrighted.

MEN MAGAZINE, Rolat Publishing Corp., 667 Madison Ave., New York NY 10021. Editor: Hasey Munson. Men's sophisticated magazine. Monthly. Estab. 1951.
Needs: Erotica, fantasy, humor/satire, men's, science fiction with erotic overtones, suspense/mystery. Receives 20-30 unsolicited fiction mss/month. Buys 1 mss/month; 12 mss/year. Length: 2,000-2,500 words average. Occasionally critiques rejected mss.
How to Contact: Send complete ms with SASE. Photocopied submissions OK. Reports as soon

as possible on mss. Sample copy for $3.50 with 8½x11 SAE.
Payment: Pays $200-275. Offers kill fee of 25%.
Terms: Pays on publication for first North American serial rights. Publication copyrighted.
Tips: "Study the market, forget art, write like a pro. Write spare—editors hate taking out purple prose which shouldn't have been there in the first place."

MESSENGER OF THE SACRED HEART, Apostleship of Prayer, 661 Greenwood Ave., Toronto, Ontario, Canada M4J 4B3. (416)466-1195. Editor: Rev. F.J. Power, S.J. Fiction Editor: Mary Pujolas. Magazine for Canadian and US Catholics who are interested in the Apostleship of Prayer as a way to lead a Christian life. Monthly. Estab. 1891. Circ. 23,000.
Needs: Religious/inspirational, psychic/supernatural, science fiction, romance, western, mystery, adventure and humor. No gay/lesbian, erotica, confession or feminist stories. Buys 1 ms/issue. Length: 1,800-2,200 words.
How to Contact: Send complete ms with SASE or International Reply Coupons. Reports in 1 month on mss. Free sample guide with SASE or IRC.
Payment: 2¢/word. 3 free author's copies.
Terms: Pays on acceptance for first North American serial rights.
Tips: "Use a dictionary to ensure words are used correctly. Develop a plot that does not peter out but reaches a climax. Do not preach but get the message across through plot and characters. A light touch and a sense of humor help."

MIKE SHAYNE MYSTERY MAGAZINE, Renown Publications, Inc., Box 178, Reseda CA 91335. (213)708-2157. Editor: Charles E. Fritch. A mystery/suspense magazine for mystery lovers of all ages. Monthly. Estab. 1956. Circ. 80,000.
Needs: Offbeat crime fiction. "Elements of psychic/supernatural, science fiction, fantasy, horror, gothic, mystery, adventure and humor might be acceptable, but the major classification of mystery/suspense should not be overpowered by these other elements. No standard situations such as would-be spouse killers; routine cop investigations; cliché private eye yarns; hitpersons; little old ladies being threatened; nice guys clobbered just for plot purposes." Buys 5-8 mss/issue. Length: up to 3,500 words.
How to Contact: Send complete ms with SASE. Reports in 3 months or less on mss. Sample copy $1.50.
Payment: 1½¢/word.
Terms: Pays after publication for non-exclusive world magazine serial rights.
Tips: "Make it short and unusual; avoid standard situations. Learn the craft first, then submit mss."

MODERN LITURGY, Resource Publications, Inc., 7291 Coronado Dr., #5, San Jose CA 95129. Editor-in-Chief: Rev. James L. Empereur, S.J. Fiction Editor: Mary Hicks. Magazine for religious leaders, artists, teachers, and worship leaders, using "themes from the field of liturgy, the seasons, scripture—especially contemporary parables, and imaginative pieces which express contemporary theology well." Published monthly. Estab. 1973. Circ. 15,000.
Needs: Religious. Receives 4-6 unsolicited fiction mss/month. Buys 1 ms/issue, 9 mss/year. Length: 500 words minimum; 2,000 words maximum; 1,000 words average. Occasionally critiques rejected mss. Sometimes recomends other markets.
How to Contact: Query first with SASE. Reports in 6 weeks on queries, 6 weeks on mss. Sample copy $3.
Payment: 3¢/word-$50 and 2 contributor's copies.
Terms: Pays on publication for all rights. Publication copyrighted.
Tips: "Read several copies of published issues, and try to prepare something that the readers will find practical use for in worship or in religious education." Mss are rejected because most "are not appropriate to the readership or to the thematic content plan of our issues. Submit a schedule of personal appearances, lectures, workshops, talks, conferences, that you plan to give in coming months."

THE MODERN WOODMEN MAGAZINE, Modern Woodmen of America, 1701 First Avenue, Rock Island IL 61201. (309)786-6481. Editor-in-Chief: Gloria Bergh. Magazine for various age groups, adult and juvenile, secular, family. Published quarterly. Circ. 328,000.
Needs: Adventure, historical (general), juvenile, young adult, adult. "Original, entertaining, holiday themes or educational." Receives approximately 50 unsolicited fiction mss/month. Buys 2 mss/issue, 20 mss/year. Length: 1,200 words minimum; 2,000 words maximum. Occasionally critiques rejected mss.
How to Contact: Send complete ms with SASE. Simultaneous, photocopied and previously published submissions OK. Reports in 2 weeks on mss. Free sample copy and fiction guidelines for SAE and 2 first class stamps.
Payment: $40 minimum and 3 contributor's copies.
Terms: Pays on acceptance for one-time rights.
Tips: "*Modern Woodmen* is a nonsectarian organization encompassing all faiths; therefore, secular material is preferred. We stress plot and characterization in fiction; a moral is a pleasant addition but not required."

MOMENT MAGAZINE, Jewish Educational Ventures, 462 Boylston St., Boston MA 02116. (617)536-6252. Editor-in-Chief: Leonard Fein. Assistant Editor: Nechama Katz. Magazine—modern, historical—publishing material on intellectual, cultural, political issues of interest to the Jewish community. Audience is college-educated, liberal. Published monthly. Estab. 1975. Circ. 25,000.
Needs: Contemporary, ethnic, historical, religious, excerpted novel, translations. "All fiction should have Jewish content. No sentimental stories about 'Grandma' etc. Do not encourage Holocaust themes." Receives 40-50 unsolicited fiction mss/month. Buys 1 ms/issue or less, 6 mss/year. Length: 1,500 words minimum; 6,000 words maximum; 3,000 words average.
How to Contact: Query first or send complete ms. SASE always. Photocopied submissions OK. Reports in 3 weeks on queries, 1-2 months on mss. Sample copy $2.50. Free fiction guidelines for business SAE and 1 first class stamp.
Payment: Varies.
Terms: Pays on publication for first rights. Publication copyrighted.
Tips: "We caution against over sentimentalized writing, which we get way too much of all the time. Query first is helpful, reading stories we've published a must."

MOTHER, IPC Magazines, King's Reach Tower, Stamford St., London, England SE1. Editor-in-Chief: Margaret Carter. Fiction Editor: Rob Lowthian. Magazine for mothers with young children. Published monthly. Estab. 1930. Circ. 80,000.
Needs: Romance (contemporary), suspense/mystery, women's. Receives approximately 100 unsolicited fiction mss/month. Buys 1 ms/issue, 12 mss/year. Length: 2,500 words minimum; 4,000 words maximum; 3,000 words average.
How to Contact: Send complete ms with SAE or IRC. Photocopied and previously published submissions OK. Reports in 6 weeks on mss.
Payment: 65-100 pounds and 2 contributor's copies.
Terms: Pays on acceptance for first rights, first British serial rights and one-time rights. Publication copyrighted.

MS MAGAZINE, 119 W. 40th St., New York NY 10018. (212)719-9800. Managing Editor: Suzanne Levine. Consciousness-raising magazine for "feminists of all ages," those committed to exploring new lifestyles and changing roles in society. Monthly. Estab. 1972. Circ. 400,000.
Needs: Literary, contemporary, science fiction, fantasy, women's, feminist, gay/lesbian, mystery, adventure, humor, juvenile, and ethnic. Needs stories about women from all backgrounds or of progressive child rearing. No pornography or derogatory attitudes toward women or children or any ethnic group, or right wing political stories. Buys 1 ms/issue. Receives approximately 500 unsolicited fiction mss each month. Length: 2,500-3,000 words.
How to Contact: Send complete ms with SASE. Reports in 4 to 6 weeks on mss.

Close-up

Rhoda Katerinsky
MS Magazine

At *MS* Magazine when there's an important research question, a phone call for help, or something's missing, the standard solution is: "Ask Rhoda."

Rhoda Katerinsky is first reader, the editorial resource/research guide, and the general office troubleshooter, or "the Hot Potato Department" as she calls herself. Katerinsky and a shifting group of editors and interns handle some 150-200 pieces of unsolicited fiction and nonfiction manuscripts received a week.

"Our main job is to find something *MS* wants to buy. I read a manuscript, recommend it or return it." If an unsolicited manuscript gets by Katerinsky's discerning eye, it is sent on to others for more editorial scrutiny.

"I look for something in the story that will make me want to read it through to the end," says Katerinsky. "If *I* can't read it all, no one else will be able to either." Regrettably she finds the quality of short stories is disappointing and amateurish. Katerinsky advises finding a teacher, writer friend, kindred spirit, someone to evaluate the writer's work and to be a sounding board for ideas and stories before submitting it to editors who have no time to critique it. She also stresses the importance of a professionally prepared manuscript. A sloppy single-spaced or hand-scrawled submission shows that the author is someone who has not taken the time to learn his/her craft or the courtesies of the profession. "And there's no harm in using a dictionary"—for simple spelling.

The *MS* fiction market is wide open with one original fiction piece per issue (3,000 words maximum) plus Stories for Free Children, short pieces for children of all ages. The magazine's fiction subjects frequently reflect changing feminist concerns and consequently at times various themes are overdone: getting out of a stifling marriage or piling the kids in the van and heading for the Rockies. Story topics also, Katerinsky adds, may be of personal value to the author, but often *not* to a broad audience.

The entire range is greater today, however, because fiction has broken barriers. Taboos (words, themes, concepts) are fewer than before. A fine-tuned, well-told and developed short story can temper the shock value of a controversial subject.

MS strives hard for a manuscript turnaround of eight weeks. Katerinsky requests: "Be reasonable. Be patient. We read everything that comes in."

> 66 *Write as often as possible, not with the idea at once of getting into print, but as if you were learning an instrument.*
> —*J.B. Priestly* 99

Payment: Offers kill fee for assigned mss not published.
Terms: Pays on acceptance for first North American serial rights. Publication copyrighted.
Tips: "We seek good writing." Mss are rejected because they are "badly written or contain old information." Sponsors college fiction contest.

MUSIC & SOUND OUTPUT, Testa Communications, 220 Westbury Ave., Carle Place NY 11514. (516)334-7880. Editor: Bill Stephen. "*MSO* is a music-related magazine featuring articles, profiles, self-help pieces, reviews and fiction with a popular music theme." For "primarily professional and semi-professional musicians as well as serious music fans." Bimonthly. Estab. 1980.
Needs: Anything related to music. "Will refuse with initial perusal only if it's not music oriented." Receives 5 unsolicited fiction mss/month. Buys 1-2 mss/month; 6-12 mss/year. Length: 2,500 words minimum; 3,500 words maximum.
How to Contact: Send complete ms or query with clips of published work with SASE. Photocopied submissions OK. Reports in 3 weeks on queries and mss. Sample copy free only with query or ms. Fiction guidelines free.
Payment: Pays $200-350. Offers kill fee of 25%.
Terms: Pays on publication for first North American serial rights. Publication copyrighted.
Tips: "Know the world of music; it must be authentic."

MY FRIEND, A Magazine for Children, Daughters of St. Paul, 50 St. Paul's Ave., Boston MA 02130. (617)522-8911. Editor: Sister Mary Anne. Magazine of "religious truths and ideals for children in a format which is enjoyable and attractive. Each issue contains Bible stories, lives of saints and famous people, short stories, science corner, contests, projects, etc." Monthly during school year (Sept.-June). Estab. 1979. Circ. 14,000.
Needs: Juvenile, prose poem, religious/inspirational. Receives 4-5 unsolicited fiction mss/month. Accepts 2-3 mss/issue; 15-20 mss/year. Length: 700 words minimum; 2,000 words maximum; 1,500 words average.
How to Contact: Send complete ms with SASE. Simultaneous, photocopied and previously published submissions OK. Reports in 4-8 weeks on mss. Sample copy free for 8x10 SAE and 71¢ postage.
Payment: Free subscription possible to magazine for regular contributor; 6 free contributor's copies.

MY WEEKLY, The Magazine for Women Everywhere, D.C. Thomson & Co., Ltd., 80 Kingsway East, Dundee, Scotland. Editor: Stewart D. Brown. Magazine whose theme is to entertain women of all ages. Weekly. Estab. 1906. Circ. 823,603.
Needs: Humor/feminist interest, romance, serialized/excerpted novel, women's. Nothing dealing with explicit sex and violence. Receives "many" unsolicited fiction mss/month. Accepts 3 mss/issue; 150 mss/year. Length: 1,500 words minimum; 5,000 words maximum; 3,750 words average. Occasionally critiques rejected mss.
How to Contact: Send complete ms with SASE. Simultaneous, photocopied and previously published submissions OK. Reports in 4 weeks on mss. Sample copy free on request.
Payment: "Offer upon acceptance."
Terms: Acquires first rights (British only). Publication copyrighted.
Tips: "There is a very positive response to short stories. Tell stories about real, feet-on-the-ground characters, dealing with real problems. Happy endings are not essential but ending must be positive, hopeful. A fresh approach is welcome but don't try to be clever. A strongly emotional, humorous and romantic theme is more important than flowery prose."

NATIONAL DOLL WORLD, House of White Birches, Box 1952, Brooksville FL 33512. Editor: Barbara Hall Pedersen. Magazine for doll hobbyists and collectors. "We use articles about doll makers, antique dolls, modern dolls, miniatures, etc., which doll collectors, doll makers, doll artists read for instruction, information and entertainment." Bimonthly. Estab. April 1976. Circ. 50,000.

Needs: Inspirational, psychic/supernatural, fantasy and humor. Only doll-related fiction considered. No sex, horror or drug-related subjects. Buys 3-4 mss/year. Receives approximately 6 unsolicited fiction mss each month. Length: 800-1,500 words. Critiques rejected mss "when there is time." Sometimes recommends other markets.
How to Contact: Send complete ms with SASE. Reports in 2 months on mss. Free sample copy with 9x12 SAE and $1 postage.
Payment: $50-100.
Terms: Pays on acceptance for all rights. Publication copyrighted.
Tips: "Write a seasonal story about dolls, about 1000 words. Illustrate it with pen and ink drawings. Remember to submit 10 months early for holidays." Mss are rejected because they are "not suitable for our magazine. Read the magazine." Many mss are rejected because "we only use one fiction ms per issue."

NATIONAL FORUM: THE PHI KAPPA PHI JOURNAL, The Honor Society of Phi Kappa Phi, Box 19420A, East Tennessee State University, Johnson City TN 37614. (615)929-5347. Editor-in-Chief: Stephen W. White. Scholarly, general interest journal. The Honor Society of Phi Kappa Phi has chapters at 229 universities. Its journal is located on the campus of East Tennessee State University. "Each issue of *National Forum* deals with a specific theme of social concern, such as 'Perspectives on the Future,' 'World Hunger,' etc. Each issue features 10-12 scholarly essays, 3-5 poems, and several book reviews." Published quarterly. Estab. 1924. Circ. 90,000.
Needs: Humor/satire, literary, prose poem, science fiction, serialized/excerpted novel, suspense/mystery, short stories. No confession, juvenile, etc. Buys 60 mss/year. Length: 1,500 words minimum; 3,500 words maximum; 2,200 words average.
How to Contact: Send complete ms or query with clips of published work. SASE always. Simultaneous and photocopied submissions OK. Reports in 6 weeks on queries, 2 months on mss. Fiction guidelines, sample copy: 65¢.
Payment: $50-150; 10-20 contributor's copy.
Terms: Pays on publication for all rights. Publication copyrighted.
Tips: "Authors should query the Editor and be aware of length requirements. Attention to these details can prevent inappropriate submissions."

THE NATIONAL SUPERMARKET SHOPPER, The American Coupon Club, Inc., Box 1149, Great Neck NY 11023. (516)328-6222. Editor: Lee Shore. Magazine informing shoppers on how to save money on their grocery bills through coupons, refunds, and smart shopping. Monthly, Estab. July 1978. Circ. 50,000.
Needs: Fantasy, women's, confession, romance, mystery and humor. But the action must take place in the supermarket, at the dinner table, etc. Buys 6-8 mss/year. Length: 1,000-2,500 words.
How to Contact: Send complete ms with SASE. Reports in 1 month on ms. Free sample copy.
Payment: 5¢/published word.
Terms: Pays on publication for all rights.

NEW AGE MAGAZINE, New Age Communications, Box 1200, Boston MA 02134. (617)254-5400. Editor: Peggy Taylor. Fiction Editor: Sandy MacDonald. Magazine. "Our focus is on empowerment: what individuals can do to help solve the many problems facing the world. Readers are people with an interest in self development and awareness." Monthly. Estab. 1974. Circ. 55,000.
Needs: Adventure, contemporary, experimental, feminist/lesbian, gay, humor/satire, literary, psychic/supernatural, religious/inspirational, serialized/excerpted novel, translations. Receives 12 unsolicited fiction mss/month. Buys 1 ms/issue, usually less; 12 mss/year maximum. Length: 1,200 words minimum; 4,000 words maximum. Occasionally critiques rejected mss.
How to Contact: Query; send complete ms or query with clips of published work with SASE. Previously published submissions OK. Reports in 4 weeks on queries; 6 weeks on mss. Sample copy for $1.50.
Payment: Pays 5¢/word; 2 free contributor's copies.
Terms: Pays on publication for first North American serial rights. Publication copyrighted.

Tips: "Become familiar with *New Age*'s theme. Start small; send very little material to start; keep trying."

NEW ALASKAN, R.W. Pickrell Agency, Rt. 1 Box 677, Ketchikan, AK 99901. (907)247-2490. Magazine with both fiction and nonfiction dealing with the history and lifestyle of Southeast Alaska. Monthly. Estab. 1964. Circ. 6,000.
Needs: Adventure and humor. "We accept only stories dealing with Southeast Alaska." Buys 12 mss/year. Length: 1,000-5,000 words.
How to Contact: Send complete ms with SASE. Reports in 4 months on mss. Sample copy $1.50 with 8x13 or larger SAE with 66¢ postage.
Payment: 2¢/word.
Terms: Pays on publication for first, second serial (reprint) and one-time rights.

NEW ENGLAND SENIOR CITIZEN/SENIOR AMERICAN NEWS, Prime National Publishing Co., 470 Boston Post Rd., Weston MA 02193. (617)899-2702. Editor-in-Chief: Ira Alterman. Fiction Editor: Karen Rafeld. Tabloid newspaper for senior citizens. "We publish articles of particular interest to seniors." Published monthly. Estab. 1970.
Needs: Adventure, comics, contemporary, ethnic, historical (general), humor/satire, mainstream, suspense/mystery, western. Receives about 15-20 unsolicited fiction mss/month. Buys 1 ms/issue, 12 mss/year. Length: 1,500 words minimum; 2,000 words maximum.
How to Contact: Send complete ms with SASE. Simultaneous, photocopied and previously published submissions OK. Reports in 6 months on mss. Sample copy 50¢.
Payment: $25-100.
Terms: Pays on publication for all rights. Publication copyrighted.
Tips: Mss rejected because "we have limited space for fiction."

THE NEW SATIRIST, Box 341, New Canaan CT 06840. (203)966-6349. Editor: Randy McAusland. Magazine of satire, humor, parody, etc., for men and women, 20-60, bright, well-educated, sense of humor. Bimonthly. Estab. 1981. Circ. 100,000.
Needs: Contemporary, experimental, fantasy, humor/satire, serialized/excerpted novel. "No sophomoric, scatological, right wing, left wing politics." Receives 25 unsolicited fiction mss/month. Buys 20 mss/issue; 180 mss/year. Length: 500 words minimum; 3,000 words maximum; 1,500 words average. Occasionally critiques rejected mss.
How to Contact: Send complete ms with SASE. Photocopied submissions OK. Reports in 4-6 weeks on mss. Sample copy for $2.50.
Payment: Pays $75-300; free subscription to magazine; 2 free contributor's copies. Offers kill fee of 50%.
Terms: Pays on publication for first rights. Publication copyrighted.

THE NEW YORKER, The New Yorker, Inc., 25 W. 43rd St., New York NY 10036. (212)840-3800. Editor: William Shawn. A quality magazine of interesting, well-written stories, articles, essays, and poems for a literate audience. Weekly. Estab. 1925.
Needs: No fables or short anecdotal fillers. Buys 1-2 mss/issue.
How to Contact: Send complete ms with SASE. Reports in 6-8 weeks on mss.
Payment: Varies.
Terms: Pays on acceptance.
Tips: "Be lively, original, not overly literary. Write what you want to write, not what you think the editor would like."

NORTHERN LIGHT, Courier Publishing Co., Box 2206, Jarvis Ave., Rochester NH 03867. (603)332-1182. Editor: Tim Sandler. Tabloid. "We are a publication which publishes both fiction and nonfiction with a focus on events of Maine, NH and Northern NH. Fiction requirements are more general." For "a general audience ranging from older natives to younger transients." Weekly. Estab. 1980. Circ. 15,000.

Needs: Adventure, contemporary, experimental, horror, humor/satire, literary, mainstream, science fiction, serailized/excerpted novel, suspense/mystery. "No fiction too racy or controversial." Buys 1 ms/month; 12 mss/year. Length: 1,000-2,000 words. Occasionally critiques rejected mss.
How to Contact: Query first; send complete ms; query with clips of published work. SASE. Simultaneous, photocopied and previously published work OK. Reports in 2 months on queries; 2 months on ms. Sample copy free for 9x12 SAE.
Payment: Pays $20-75.
Terms: Pays on publication for one-time rights. Publication copyrighted.
Tips: Looking for "polished, tight writing with substance."

NUGGET, Dugent Publishing Corp., 2355 Salzedo St., Suite 204, Coral Gables FL 33134. (305)443-2378. Editor: John C. Fox. A newsstand magazine designed to have erotic appeal for a fetish-oriented audience. Bimonthly. Estab. 1956. Circ. 100,000.
Needs: Contemporary, psychic/supernatural, science fiction, horror, men's, erotica, mystery, adventure and humor. Offbeat, fetish-oriented material should encompass a variety of subjects. Most of fiction includes several sex scenes. No fiction that concerns children or religious subjects, or material that is unnecessarily abstract or in an overly mannered style. Buys 3 mss/issue. Length: 2,000-3,500 words.
How to Contact: Send complete ms with SASE. Reports in 1 month on ms. Sample copy $3. Free guidelines with legal-sized SASE.
Payment: $125-150. Free author's copy.
Terms: Pays on publication for first rights.
Tips: "Keep in mind the nature of the publication which is erotically-oriented. Subject matter can vary, but prefer fetish themes."

OMNI, Penthouse International, 909 3rd Ave., New York NY 10022. Executive Editor: Dick Teresi. Fiction Editor: Ellen Datlow. Magazine of science and science fiction with an interest in near future; stories and articles of what science holds, what life and lifestyles will be like in areas affected by science for a young, bright and well-educated audience between 18-30. Monthly. Estab. October 1978. Circ. 1,000,000.
Needs: Science fiction and fantasy. No sword and sorcery or other genres. Buys 3 mss/issue, 36 mss/year. Receives approximately 400 unsolicited fiction mss each month. Length: 9,000 words maximum. Critiques rejected mss "when there is time." Sometimes recommends other markets.
How to Contact: Send complete ms with SASE. Reports within 1 month on mss. Free guidelines with legal-sized SASE.
Payment: Pays $1,250-2,000; 1 free author's copy.
Terms: Pays on acceptance for first North American serial rights with exclusive worldwide English language periodical rights and nonexclusive anthology rights. Publication copyrighted.
Tips: "Buy a copy and study our magazine. We are not the same as other science fiction magazines. Young authors should read a lot of the best science fiction and short stories today. Don't rewrite *Star Wars*. We are looking for strongly written stories dealing with the next 100 years." Mss are rejected because "they rehash old ideas, are poorly written or are trite."

ONE MAGAZINE, A Life-style Magazine for College/Career Youth, Beacon Hill Press of Kansas City, 6401 The Paseo, Kansas City MO 64131. (816)333-7000. Editor: Mike Estep. Managing Editor: David Best. Magazine. "*One* seeks to shape an authentic Christian life-style for its readers and their community. We are interested in material that will enhance spiritual growth or present spiritual challenge. *One* will consider poetry, short fiction, humor in good taste, especially articles compatible with Weslyan-Arminean tradition. Directed to the 18 to 23 year old. We look for writers who treat their audience as intelligent young adults—not teens." Monthly except Dec/Jan, May/June, July/Aug when bimonthly. Estab. 1980. Circ. 20,000.
Needs: Humor/satire, literary, prose poem, religious/inspirational, young adult. "We do *not* want cute, preacy, or easily pedictable manuscripts." Receives 15-20 unsolicited fiction mss/

month. Buys 1-2 mss/issue; 9 mss/year. Length: 2,500 words maximum; 1,500 words average.
How to Contact: Query first or send complete ms with SASE. Simultaneous and previously published submissions OK. Reports in 1 month on queries; 1-2 months on mss. Sample copy free for 8x11 SAE and 1 first class stamp. Fiction guidelines free for 4x8 ½ SAE and 1 first class stamp.
Payment: Pays 3¢/word.
Terms: Pays on acceptance for simultaneous, first, second, first North American serial or one-time rights; assignment on work-for-hire-basis. Publication copyrighted.
Tips: "Study our writers guidelines and sample copy—know you audience and the purpose of our magazine."

ORACLE Science-Fiction & Fantasy Anthology Magazine, S.F.&F. Productions, Incorporated, Box 19222-FWM, Detroit MI 48219. Editor-in-Chief: Dave Lillard. Publishes "action, adventure and/or humorous stories in the science fiction and fantasy genre." Published quarterly. Estab. 1981. Print run: 10,000.
Needs: Fantasy, psychic, science fiction, sword and sorcery; also adventure, comics, humor/satire, and serialized/excerpted novels if within science fiction and fantasy genre. "No pornographic stories or stories that *depend* on explicit sex or violence. Receives about 4 unsolicited fiction mss/month. Buys 8-15 mss/issue, 40 mss/year. Occasionally critiques rejected mss. Sometimes recommends other markets.
How to Contact: Send complete ms with SASE. Photocopied (if clear) and previously published submissions (if not in print for at least 3 years) OK. Reports in 4 weeks on mss. Sample copy $3. Free fiction guidelines for # 10 SASE.
Payment: 1-3¢/word and 1 contributor's copy.
Terms: Pays one-half on acceptance and one-half on publication for one-time rights. Publication copyrighted.
Tips: "Write an entertaining, imaginative story (within science fiction or fantasy, of course) and send it in. Make certain grammar is correct; and that the ms is free of excessive corrections." Rejects because "most mss have been horror stories or stories that *depend* on violence."

THE OTHER SIDE, Jubilee, Inc., Box 3948, Fredericksburg VA 22402. (703)371-7416. Editor: Mark Olson. Fiction Editor: Eunice Amarantides Smith. Magazine of justice rooted in discipleship for Christians with a strong interest in peace and social and economic justice. Monthly. Estab. 1965. Circ. 15,000.
Needs: Contemporary, ethnic, experimental, fantasy, feminist, humor/satire, literary, mainstream, suspense/mystery. Receives 10 unsolicited fiction mss/month. Buys 1 mss/year. Length: 1,000 words minimum; 4,000 words maximum; 2,500 words average.
How to Contact: Send complete ms with SASE. Photocopied submissions OK. Reports in 6 weeks on mss. Sample copy for $1.50.
Payment: Pays $40-150; free subscription to magazine; 5 free contributor's copies.
Terms: Pays on acceptance for all or first rights; assignments on work-for-hire-basis. Publication copyrighted.

OUI MAGAZINE, 300 W. 43rd St., 6th floor, New York NY 10036. Editor: Peter Wolff. Magazine for college age males and older. Monthly. Estab. 1972. Circ. 1 million.
Needs: Contemporary, fantasy, men's, mystery, humor. Buys 1 ms/issue, 12 mss/year. Receives 200-300 unsolicited fiction mss each month. Length: 1,500 words.
How to Contact: Send complete ms with SASE. Reports in 6 weeks on mss.
Payment: Pays $750-1,000. Offers kill fee for assigned mss not published.
Terms: Pays on acceptance for first rights. Publication copyrighted.
Tips: "We prefer extremely exotic, artistic material. Many mss rejected because of massive amounts of submissions in stock."

OUR FAMILY, Oblate Fathers of St. Mary's Province, Box 249, Battleford, SK, Canada S0M 0E0. (306)937-7344. Editor: Albert Lalonde, O.M.I. Magazine primarily for Catholic families who want information, inspiration and encouragement in Christian living. Monthly. Estab. 1949. Circ. 13,521.

Needs: Religious/inspirational. "The material we use must have Christian content and values. No science fiction or adult sex stories." Buys 3 mss/month. Length: 1,000-3,000 words.

How to Contact: Send complete ms with SAE and IRC or personal check. Reports in 2-3 weeks on ms. Sample copy $1.50. Free Fiction Requirement Guide with SAE and IRC.

Payment: 3-5¢/word. 2-4 free author's copies. $1 charge for extras.

Terms: Pays on acceptance for simultaneous, second serial (reprint) and first North American serial rights.

Tips: "Base your story on an actual Christian experience, a personal experience or one you have come to know. Obtain our guide and study it to understand the policy we follow consistently."

PENTHOUSE, Penthouse International, Ltd., 909 Third Ave., New York NY 10022. (212)593-3301. Fiction Editor: Kathryn Green. A men's entertainment magazine featuring high quality sophisticated articles of interest to men between the ages of 18-34. Exposés, humor, interviews, fashion and fiction. Monthly. Estab. 1965. Circ. 5,350,000.

Needs: Contemporary, psychic/supernatural, science fiction, horror, men's, erotica, western, adventure and first serial excerpts from novels. No stories with women's point of view, plotless sexual encounters or extreme avant-garde fiction. Buys 12 mss/year. Receives approximately 100 unsolicited fiction mss each month. Length: 3,000-6,000 words.

How to Contact: Send ms with SASE. Reports in 1 month on mss.

Terms: Pays on acceptance for first English language rights and sometimes world rights. Publication copyrighted.

Tips: "Send us well-written stories, neatly typed and of interest to our audience. We are always looking for new fiction talent." Many mss are rejected because they are "not right for our audience; characters are not fully developed; they are too short."

PENTHOUSE (UK), International Magazine for Men, Penthouse Publicatons, Ltd., 2 Bramber Rd., London, England W14 9PB. Tel. 385-6181. Editor: David Jones. General men's interest magazine—political leads, service reports (drink/hi-fi/cars/cameras), profiles, interviews, fiction. Monthly. Estab. 1964. Circ. 200,000.

Needs: Erotica, humor/satire, men's. Receives approximately 50 unsolicited fiction mss/month. Buys 2 mss/issue; 24 mss/year. Length: 3,000 words minimum; 4,000 words maximum. Occasionally critiques rejected mss.

How to Contact: Send complete ms with SASE, IRC. Simultaneous and photocopied submissions OK. Reports in 4 weeks on mss.

Payment: Pays £350 maximum. Offers kill fee of 50%.

Terms: Pays on publication for first rights. Publication copyrighted.

Tips: Demonstrate "high literary standard and originality."

PILLOW TALK, Carla Publishing, 215 Lexington Ave., New York NY 10016. Editor: I. Catherine Duff. Magazine offering self-help and advice to the lovelorn, etc. Articles on meeting people, improving relationships, expanding sexualtiy for male/female, ages 18-35. Readers are looking for ways to improve their lives. Monthly. Estab. 1975. Circ. 200,000.

Needs: Erotica only. Buys 1 ms/issue. Length: 1,500-2,000 words.

How to Contact: Send complete ms with SASE. Reports in 1 week. Sample copy $1.75. Free guidelines with SASE.

Payment: $50-150. Free author's copy.

Terms: Pays on publication for all rights.

Tips: "Read us, slant erotica to our format, send complete ms. *No other fiction except* titillating erotica."

PIONEER WOMAN, Magazine of Pioneer Women/Na'amat, The Women's Labor Zionist Organization of America, Pioneer Women/Na'amat, 200 Madison Ave., New York

NY 10016. (212)725-8010. Editor: Judith A. Sokoloff. Magazine covering a wide variety of subjects of interest to the Jewish community—including political and social issues, arts, profiles; many articles about Israel; women's issues. Fiction must have a Jewish theme. Readers are the American Jewish community. Published 5 times/year. Estab. 1926. Circ. 30,000.
Needs: Contemporary, literary, women's. Receives 10 unsolicited fiction mss/month. Buys 3-5 mss/year. Length: 1,500 words minimum; 3,000 words maximum. Occasionally critiques rejected mss.
How to Contact: Query first or send complete ms with SASE. Photocopied submissions OK. Reports in 2 months on mss. Sample copy free for 9x11½ SAE and 71¢ postage.
Payment: Pays 5¢/word; 2 free contributor's copies. Offers kill fee of 25%.
Terms: Pays on publication for first, second, first North American serial or one-time rights; assignments on work-for-hire-basis.
Tips: Submit "good writing—no maudlin nostalgia or romance; no hackneyed Jewish humor."

PLAYBOY MAGAZINE, Playboy Enterprises, Inc., 919 N. Michigan Ave., Chicago IL 60611. (312)751-8000. Editorial Director: Arthur Kretchmer. Fiction Editor: Alice K. Turner. Entertainment magazine for a male audience. Monthly. Estab. December 1953. Circ. 5,700,000.
Needs: Literary, contemporary, science fiction, fantasy, horror, men's, western, mystery, adventure and humor. No pornography or fiction geared to a female audience. Buys 1-3 mss/issue, 22 mss/year. Receives approximately 400 unsolicited fiction mss each month. Length: 1,000-10,000 (average 6,000) words. Critiques rejected mss "when there is time."
How to Contact: Send complete ms with SASE. Reports in 1 month on mss. Free guidelines with SASE.
Payment: $2,000 minimum; $1,000 minimum for short-shorts.
Terms: Pays on acceptance for all rights. Publication copyrighted.
Tips: "Writers should take a close look at *Playboy* fiction to see the kind and quality of fiction we publish."

PLAYERS MAGAZINE, Players International Publications, 8060 Melrose Ave., Los Angeles CA 90046. (213)653-8060. Editor: Emory Holmes II. Associate Editor: Leslie Gersicoff. The "basic black" *Playboy* magazine with profiles, reviews, sports, travel, and general interest for the black male. Monthly. Estab. 1973. Circ. 202,000.
Needs: Science fiction, fantasy, erotica, adventure, historical, humor and experimental. "No crime or prison-type stories. We get 'tons' of those." Receives approximately 50 unsolicited fiction mss/month. Length: 1,000-4,000 words. Critiques rejected mss "when there is time." Sometimes sends mss to editors of other publicatins.
How to Contact: Send complete ms with SASE. Reports in 3-4 weeks.
Payment: Pays 10¢/word maximum.
Terms: Pays on publication for one-time use. Publication copyrighted.
Tips: "We want to see stories that are light-hearted and positive." Many mss are rejected because "they are poorly written, not for our market. Our market is select. Our readers are interested in fiction composed of Black characters and situations—reality-based."

PLAYGIRL MAGAZINE, Ritter/Geller Communications, Inc., 3420 Ocean Park Blvd., Santa Monica CA 90405. (213)450-0900. Editor-in-Chief: Dianne Grosskopf. Fiction Editor: Mary Ellen Strote. Magazine for today's young women 18-40, average age 26, featuring entertainment, fiction, beauty and fashion, current events, sex and health. Published monthly. Estab. 1973. Circ. 800,000.
Needs: Feminist, romance (contemporary), excerpted novel, women's. "No gay, juvenile, murder, mystery, graphic sex." Receives approximately 200 unsolicited fiction mss/month. Buys 1-2 mss/issue. Length: 1,000 words minimum; 5,000 words maximum; 3,500 words average. Occasionally critiques rejected mss.
How to Contact: Send complete ms with SASE. Simultaneous, photocopied and previously published submissions OK. Reports in 4-6 weeks on mss. Sample copy from Customer Service

Department; $5 includes postage and handling. Free fiction guidelines with SASE.
Payment: $300 minimum and 1-2 contributor's copies.
Terms: Pays on acceptance for one-time magazine rights in the English language. Publication copyrighted.

POCKETS, Devotional Magazine for Children, The Upper Room, 1908 Grand Ave., Box 189, Nashville TN 37202. (615)327-2700. Editor-in-Chief: Judith E. Smith. Magazine for children 6-12, with articles specifically geared for ages 8 to 11. "The magazine offers stories, activities, prayers, poems—all geared to giving children a better understanding of themselves as children of God. Much of the material will not be overtly religious but will deal with situations, special seasons and holidays, ecological concerns from a Christian perspective. The overall goal is to build into a child's daily life a need for a devotional aspect." Published monthly except for January. Estab. 1981. Estimated Circ.70,000.
Needs: Adventure, contemporary, ethnic, fantasy, historical (general), juvenile, religious/inspirational, suspense/mystery. "All submissions, whatever the genre should address the broad theme of the magazine. Each issue will be built around several themes with material which can be used by children in a variety of ways. Scripture stories, fiction, poetry, prayers, art, graphics, puzzles, and activities will all be included. Submissions do not need to be overtly religious. They should help children experience a Christian lifestyle that is not always a neatly wrapped moral package, but is open to the continuing revelation of God's will. Seasonal material, both secular and liturgical, is desired. No violence, horror, sexual, and racial stereotyping or fiction containing heavy moralizing." Receives approximately 40 unsolicited fiction mss/month. Buys 1-2 mss/issue, 11-22 mss/year. Length: 600 words minimum; 1,500 words maximum; 1,200 words average.
How to Contact: Send complete ms with SASE. Photocopied and previously published submissions OK. Reports in 2 months on mss. Sample copy $1.25. Free fiction guidelines and themes with SASE.
Payment: 5¢/word and up and 2-5 contributor's copies. $1.25 charge for extras; 65¢ each for 10 or more.
Terms: Pays on acceptance for first North American serial rights.
Tips: "Do not write *down* to children." Rejects mss because "we receive far more submissions than we can use. If all were of high quality, we still would purchase only a few. The most common problems are overworked story line and flat, unrealistic characters. Most stories simply do not 'ring true' and children know that."

PONY RIDE MAGAZINE, The Magazine for Southern California Parents, Pony Publications, Box 65795, Los Angeles CA 90065. (213)240-7669. Editor: Jack Bierman. Fiction Editor: Ginger Collins. "A city magazine for LA parents, calendar of events, local features on southland parenting; plans for short fiction." Monthly. Estab. 1980. Circ. 50 million.
Needs: Juvenile, young adult. "We would like age-targeted material for youngsters. No religious, sci-fi, or romance material." Receives 6 unsolicited fiction mss/month. Length: 700 words minimum; 1,200 words maximum; 1,000 words average. Occasionally critiques rejected mss.
How to Contact: Query first. Reports in 3 weeks on mss. Sample copy for $1.
Payment: Pays $25 minimum; 2 free contributor's copies.
Terms: Pays on publication for first rights. Publication copyrighted.
Tips: "Provide us with ms that a parent/teacher can read out loud to young audiences."

PORT SOUTH MAGAZINE, The Magazine of Coastal South Carolina & Georgia, SeaCoast Publishing Co., 10 Gillon St., Charleston SC 29401. (803)577-6013. Editor: Anne Reeves. Magazine of general interest, travel, sports, fiction, photofeatures, economy, tourism and interior decorating for educated, upper-income, over 35 readers. Bimonthly. Estab. 1981. Circ. 20,000.
Needs: Adventure, comic, contemporary, historical, humor/satire, mainstream, serialized/excerpted novel. No erotic or young adult material. Receives 3 unsolicited fiction mss/month. Buys 1 ms/issue; 10 mss/year. Length: 800 words minimum; 1,600 words maximum; 1,500 words average. Occasionally critiques rejected mss.

How to Contact: Send complete ms with SASE. Simultaneous, photocopied and previously published submissions OK. Reports in 1 month on ms. Sample copy for $1.50. Fiction guidelines free with 20¢ postage.
Payment: Pays $50.
Terms: Pays on publication for one-time rights. Publication copyrighted.

PRESTIGE MAGAZINE—Afro Colonial Magazine, Prestige Publications, Box 22557, Denver CO 80222. (303)296-9938. General interest magazine of travel, fiction, sports, history, gourmet, for a black audience. Quarterly. Circ. 250,000.
Needs: Adventure, comics, condensed novel, confession, contemporary, ethnic, fantasy, historical, humor/satire, mainstream, prose poem, religious/inspirational, romance, science fiction, serialized/excerpted novel, suspense/mystery, women's, young adult. Length: 1,000 words minimum; 1,500 words average.
How to Contact: Send complete ms with SASE. Reports in 3 months on mss. Sample copy for $2.
Payment: Pays $100-500.
Terms: Pays on publication for all rights. Publication copyrighted.

PRIME TIMES, National Association for Retired Credit Union People, Inc., (NARCUP), Editorial Offices: Suite 120, 2802 International Ln., Madison WI 53704. Managing Editor: Glenn Deutsch. Magazine for people 50 and older who once belonged or currently belong to a credit union, who care to "redefine retirement and aging." Each edition based around a general theme: health, energy, retirement communities, money management, etc. Readers share the common bond of CU membershp and the CU philosophy: "Self reliance and cooperative credit: People of even meager means can pool their resources to pull themselves up." Quarterly. Estab. 1979. Circ. 50,000.
Needs: Literary, contemporary, men's, women's, feminist, erotica, romance, mystery, adventure, humor and ethnic (US Hispanic and black). "*Protagonist* must be 50 or older." Buys 1 ms/issue, 4 mss/year. Length: 1,500-2,500 words.
How to Contact: Send complete ms or query with clips of published work.SASE always. Reports in 2 weeks on queries, 1 month on mss. Free sample copy with 9x12 SASE (five 1st class stamps). Free guidelines with SASE.
Payment: $150-500. 3 free author's copies. $1 charge for each extra.
Terms: Pays on publication for first, second serial (reprint) and first North American serial rights.
Tips: "We are very happy to feature second serial work as long as it hasn't appeared in another *national* 'maturity market' publication." Rejects mss because "the endings are suspect even before you get to the third page. Due to the economic situation of the nation in general people want to laugh. They don't want to be preached to or told that there are others in as bad, if not worse, situations than they are."

QUEEN OF ALL HEARTS, Queen Magazine, Montfort Missionaries, 26 S. Saxon Ave., Bay Shore NY 11706. (516)665-0726. Editor-in-Chief: James McMillan, S.M.M. Fiction Editor: Roger M. Charest, S.M.M. Magazine of "stories, articles and features on the Mother of God by explaining the Scriptural basis and traditional teaching of Catholic Church concerning the Mother of Jesus, her influence in fields of history, literature, art, music, poetry, etc." Published bimonthly. Estab. 1950. Circ. 7,000.
Needs: Religious/inspirational. "No mss not about Our Lady, the Mother of God, the Mother of Jesus." Receives 3 unsolicited fiction mss/month. Buys 3-4 mss/issue, 24 mss/year. Length: 1,500-2,000 words.
How to Contact: Send complete ms with SASE. Photocopied submissions OK. Reports in 1 month on mss. Sample copy $1.25 with 9x12 SAE.
Payment: Varies. 6 free contributor's copies.
Terms: Pays on acceptance. Publication copyrighted.

RACQUETBALL ILLUSTRATED, CFW Enterprises, 7011 Sunset Blvd., Hollywood CA 90028. (213)467-1300. Editor: Ben Kalb. "General feature magazine on instruction, interviews, medical advice all related to racquetball and racquetball players of all levels; mostly for the 21-45 age group. Monthly. Estab. June 1978. Circ. 100,000.

Needs: Literary, contemporary and satire. "Must have racquetball theme to it." Buys 6 mss/year. Receives 1-2 unsolicited fiction mss each month. Length: 2,000-3,000 words. Critiques rejected mss "when there is time."

How to Contact: Send complete ms with SASE. Sample copy $1.50.

Payment: $100-300.

Terms: Pays on publication for first rights. Publication copyrighted.

Tips: Many mss are rejected because "humor is not humorous (satire will sell me better); writing is poor, story line has holes in it, not exciting enough."

R-A-D-A-R, Standard Publishing, 8121 Hamilton Ave., Cincinnati OH 45231. (513)931-4050. Editor: Margaret Williams. "*R-A-D-A-R* is a take-home paper, distributed in Sunday School classes for children aged 8-11. The stories and other features reinforce the Bible lesson taught in class. Boys and girls who attend Sunday School make up the audience. The fiction stories, Bible picture stories, and other special features appeal to their interests." Weekly. Estab. 1877.

Needs: "No talking animal stories, science fiction, Halloween or first-person stories from an adult's viewpoint. Stories should contain Christian teaching or moral values." Receives approximately 150 unsolicited fiction mss each month. Length: 900-1,100 words.

How to Contact: Send complete ms with SASE. Reports in 1 month. Free sample copy and guidelines.

Payment: 1½-2¢/word. Free author's copy.

Terms: Pays on acceptance for first and second serial (reprint) rights. Publication copyrighted.

Tips: "Send for sample copy, guidesheet, and theme list. Study them carefully and follow instructions." Mss are rejected because "they are too lengthy, have fuzzy plots, poorly-constructed sentences."

RANGER RICK'S NATURE MAGAZINE, National Wildlife Federation, 1412 16th St. NW, Washington DC 20036. (703)790-4217. Editor: Trudy Farrand. Fiction Editor: Lee Stowell Cullen. "*Ranger Rick* emphasizes conservation and the enjoyment of nature through full-color photos and art, fiction and nonfiction articles, games and puzzles and special columns. Our audience ranges in ages from 4-12, with the greatest number in the 7 to 10 group. We aim for a fourth grade reading level. They read for fun and information." Monthly. Estab. January 1967. Circ. 700,000.

Needs: Science fiction, fantasy, mystery, adventure, humor and juvenile. "Any kind of interesting stories for kids about nature. Science fiction which carries a conservation message is always needed, as are adventure stories involving kids with nature or the outdoors. Moralistic 'lessons' taught children by parents or teachers are not accepted. Human qualities are attributed to animals only in our regular feature, 'Ranger Rick and His Friends.' " Buys 1 ms/issue, 12 mss/year. Receives 6-8 unsolicited fiction mss each month. Length: 900 words maximum. Critiques rejected mss "when there is time."

How to Contact: Query with clips of published work with SASE. Reports in 2 weeks on queries, 2 months on mss. Free sample copy. Free guidelines with legal-sized SASE.

Payment: $300 maximum/full-length ms.

Terms: Pays on acceptance for all rights. Publication copyrighted.

Tips: "Read past issues to learn preferred style and approach; write naturally with no affectation; keep reader in mind at all times without being condescending. Think of your own childhood and include the best from it." Mss are rejected because they are "contrived and/or condescending—often overwritten. Some mss are anthropomorphic, others are above our readers' level."

RAPPORT, 12 Imbrie Place, Sea Bright NJ 07760. (607)272-6484. Editor: Michael S. Turback. Magazine with "issues of concern to couples/couples lifestyles." For relationship-oriented men and women, ages 21-50. Bimonthly.

Needs: Erotica, humor/satire, romance. "Nothing sexist, please." Receives 15-20 unsolicited fiction mss/month. Buys 1 ms/issue; 6 mss/year. Length: 1,500 words minimum; 3,500 words maximum; 3,000 words average. Occasionally critiques rejected mss.
How to Contact: Send complete ms with SASE. Simultaneous, photocopied and previously published submissions OK. Reports in 1 month on mss.
Payment: Pays $40-250.
Terms: Pays on publication for one-time rights. Publication copyrighted.

READ, Weekly Reader Publications, 245 Long Hill Rd., Middletown CT 06457. (203)347-7521. Senior Editor: Edwin A. Hoey. "*Read* is a bimonthly magazine for young people in junior high schools. Each issue includes a play and a short story." For junior high/middle school students. Bimonthly. Estab. 1951.
Needs: Adventure, fantasy, science fiction, suspense/mystery, young adult. No historical, religious or animal fiction. Receives 45-50 unsolicited fiction mss/month. Accepts 5 mss/year. Length: 1,000 words minimum; 4,000 words maximum.
How to Contact: Send complete ms with SASE. Simultaneous, photocopied and previously published submissions OK. Reports in 8 weeks on mss. Sample copy free for 7x9 SAE. Fiction guidelines free for 8½x4 SAE.
Terms: Acquires all or one-time rights. Publication copyrighted.

READER'S CHOICE, Canada's Short Story Magazine, The Cheritan Company, Box 205 (FWM), Station S, Toronto, Ontario, Canada M5M 4L7. (416)783-7028. Editor: Amalia Lindal. Magazine of "stories of sympathetically identifiable people who experience character growth and insight as a result of coping with the kind of real crisis most of us face or will face, for a 'middle brow' adult mass audience. Quarterly. Estab. 1982. Circ. 1,000.
Needs: Contemporary, humor, mainstream, inspirational. "We think English language is beautiful. *We like* grammar, punctuation, and a minimum of slang as we don't wish to 'date' our material. No arty stories which are all style and no content; explicit sex, vulgarity." Receives about 50 unsolicited fiction mss/month. Buys 10-12 mss/issue; 40+ mss/year. Length: 700 words minimum; 5,000 words maximum; 3,500 words average. Occasionally critiques rejected mss.
How to Contact: Send complete ms with SAE and IRC. Photocopied submissions OK. Reports in 6 weeks on mss. Sample copy for $4.28 US currency.
Payment: Pays $10-120 (Canadian currency); 1 free contributor's copy; $4 (US currency) plus 7% sales tax charge for extras.
Terms: Pays on publication for first North American serial rights. Publication copyrighted.
Tips: Writers should "know what 'character growth' means and what 'universal crisis' means. Take a creative writing workshop or study books on plot, characterization and dramatic action. No philosophical or sentimental musings, diary-type outpourings; no 'once upon a time' or 'a funny thing happened' story types."

REALITY, Christian Living Magazine, Redemptorist Publications, 75 Orwell Rd., Dublin 6, Ireland. Tel. (01)961488/961688. Editor-in-Chief: K.H. Donlon. Magazine for "the broad center of the educated public." Published monthly. Estab. 1937. Circ. 35,000.
Needs: Humor/satire, religious/inspirational, women's, young adult. "No erotica, fantasy." Receives approximately 10 unsolicited fiction mss/month. Buys 11 mss/issue, 100 mss/year. Length: 900 words minimum; 1,200 words maximum; 1,000 words average. Sometimes recommends other markets.
How to Contact: Send complete ms with SAE and IRC. Reports in 6 months on mss.
Payment: 25 pounds per 1,000 words.
Tips: Rejects mss because "most fiction material is unreal—it is out of touch with what life is really like or about."

REDBOOK, The Redbook Publishing Co., 230 Park Ave., New York NY 10169. Editor: Anne Mollegen Smith. Fiction Editor: Jacqueline Johnson. *Redbook*'s readership consists primarily of young American women 18-34 years of age, most married, some single, many mothers of young children, many working outside the home. *Redbook* readers are well-educated, progressive in their attitudes toward the roles and opportunities open to them as women and concerned with larger social issues as well as with their homes, their personal relationships and their health and appearance." Monthly. Estab. 1903. Circ. 4,500,000.

Needs: "*Redbook* takes fiction very seriously, which may be why *Redbook* was the first magazine to win the National Magazine Award for fiction *twice*. We publish three short stories in every issue (except in August, when our special fiction issue features eight or nine stories), as well as a condensed complete-in-the-issue novel. We are looking for fiction that will appeal to vital, thinking, contemporary young women. Stories need not be about young women exclusively; we also look for fiction reflecting the broad range of human experience. We are interested in new voices and buy around a quarter of what we publish each year from our unsolicited submissions. But standards are high; stories must be fresh, felt and intelligent; no straight formula fiction, surprise endings, highly oblique or symbolic stories without conclusions, please." Receives approximately 3,000 unsolicited fiction mss each month. Length: 15-20 manuscript pages for short stories, 5-10 pages for short shorts.

How to Contact: Send complete ms with large SASE. Reports in 6-8 weeks. Free guidelines with legal-sized SASE.

Terms: Pays on acceptance. Buys first North American serial rights. Publication copyrighted.

Tips: "Short short stories are always in demand. We wish we saw more of the following: intelligently humorous stories (not anecdotes); stories about women in situations other than the home, in jobs other than the traditionally female ones, in relationships with persons other than family, mates or lovers; stories from a sensitive, enlightened male point of view. Submit seasonal material at least three months before the appropriate issue." Sponsors Young Writers Contests for unpublished writers 18 to 28 years old. "We announce contests and publish rules in the magazine. Information available by request (send SASE) to Redbook's Young Writers Contest."

ROAD KING MAGAZINE, William A. Coop, Inc., 23060 S. Cicero, Richton Park IL 60471. (312)481-9240. "Quarterly leisure-reading magazine for long-haul, over-the-road professional truckers. Contains short articles, short fiction, some product news, games, puzzles and industry news. Truck drivers read it while eating, fueling, during layovers and at other similar times while they are enroute."

Needs: Science fiction, fantasy, men's, western, mystery, adventure, humor. "No erotica or violence." Buys 1 ms/issue, 4 mss/year. Receives 10-20 unsolicited fiction mss each month. Length: 1,200 words. Critiques rejected mss "when there is time."

How to Contact: Send complete ms with SASE. Reports in 3 months on mss. Sample copy with 6x9 SAE with 68¢ postage.

Payment: $150 maximum.

Terms: Pays on acceptance for all rights. Publication copyrighted.

Tips: "Remember that our magazine gets into the home and that truckers tend to be Bible belt types. Don't phone. Don't send mss by registered or insured mail or they will be returned unopened by post office. Don't try to get us involved in lengthy correspondence. Be patient. We have a small staff and we are slow." Mss are rejected because "most don't fit our format. . . . they are too long; they do not have enough knowledge of trucking; there is too much violence; they are not really short stories, nothing happens."

ROAD RIDER, Road Rider Magazine, Box 678, South Laguna CA 92677. Editor: Roger Hull. Managing Editor: Clement Salvadori. "Our magazine is a source of information and entertainment 'for the touring motorcyclist since 1969' and relates in one way or another to road and street motorcycling." Monthly. Estab. August 1969. Circ. 35,000.

Needs: Road/street cycling only. "We do not accept the same old stuff, stuff written by non-cyclists, stories with no credibility or pretentious in any way." Buys 2-3 mss/year. Receives 2-3 unsolicited fiction mss each month. Length: 2,000 words maximum. Critiques rejected mss "when there is time."

How to Contact: Send complete ms with SASE. Reports in 1 month on mss. Sample copy $1.50.

Payment: $100 (first timers).

Terms: Pays on acceptance for all rights. Publication copyrighted.

Tips: "Reading a copy won't be all that much help since we rarely print fiction. It is essential that road motorcyclists/motorcycles be a prominent part of the story—not just window dressing—so non-cyclists are discouraged from submitting. Never submit in duplicate; humorous material (within our specifications) stands the best chance here. Cannot emphasize too strongly—don't try to fool us on cycle knowledge; we're experts. We print very little fiction because there is very little new and fresh which meets our requirements. We like good humor; always looking for it. But too many writers—again, particularly non-cyclists—seem to think crashing a cycle is funny. Usually we disagree. We are a difficult market to crash with fiction." Mss are rejected because "they are the 'same ol' thing' or a clumsy attempt to convert an unsold story to a cycle background . . . and they show lack of knowledge/experience on part of the author."

ROMANTIC TIMES, Romantic Times, Inc., 163 Joralemon St., Suite 1234. Brooklyn Heights NY 11201. (212)875-5019. Publisher/Editor: Kathryn Falk. A newspaper for readers of romantic fiction. "We are looking for short stories, novels, serials for the historical, contemporary, regency and romantic suspense genres. For readers of romantic fiction, primarily women, interested in the latest book reviews, profiles of the authors, articles about romantic fiction, gossip, publishers' trade talk and a how-to section." Bimonthly. Estab. 1981. Circ. 50,000.

Needs: Gothic, romance, suspense, serialized and condensed novels, Regency and historical sagas and series. No erotica or soft-core pornography. Receives approximately 20 unsolicited fiction mss/month. Length: 1,000-2,000 words.

How to Contact: Query letter with outline and SASE. Reports in 1 month on queries. Sample copy $2.

Payment: $50.

Terms: Pays on acceptance for second serial rights. Publication copyrighted.

Tips: "We are looking for intelligent stories for intelligent women. Mss should include the following elements: 1) strong character development, 2) accurate and detailed historical description, 3) realistic plots, 4) vicarious female reader identification, 5) romantic sex. Women who read romantic fiction are looking for romantic and adventurous escape for a few hours."

THE RUNNER, Ziff-Davis Publishing Company, One Park Ave., New York NY 10016. (212)725-4248. Editor: Marc Bloom. Fiction Editor: Frederika Randall. Magazine of running—profiles, reporting, science (health and fitness), science (training advice), humor, fiction—for runners and readers interested in the sport and in fitness. Monthly. Estab. 1978. Circ. 225,000.

Needs: Experimental, feminist, humor/satire, literary, excerpted novel, translations, sports. "Must treat running in some fashion." Receives 50-100 unsolicited fiction mss/month. Buys 4-6 mss/year. Length: 2,000 words minimum; 4,000 words maximum.

How to contact: Send complete ms with SASE or submit through agent. Reports in 4 weeks on mss. Sample copy for $1.95.

Payment: Pays $150 minimum.

Terms: Pays on acceptance for all, first, second serial or first North American serial rights. Publication copyrighted.

RUNNING TIMES MAGAZINE, Running Times, Inc., 14416 Jefferson Davis Hwy., Woodbridge VA 22191. (703)491-2044. Editor: Ed Ayres. Magazine of running and jogging for "serious" recreational and competitive runners. Monthly. Estab. 1977. Circ. 41,000.

Needs: Adventure, comics, erotica, fantasy, historical, humor/satire, literary, mainstream, science fiction. No crude erotica, cute "surprise" endings, and stories about magic running shoes. Receives 3-5 unsolicited fiction mss/month. Buys 3 mss/year. Length: 1,500 words minimum; 5,000 words maximum; 3,000 words average. Rarely critiques rejected mss.

How to Contact: Query first if widely published; query with clips of published work or send

comm. periodicals

complete ms with SASE. Simultaneous and photocopied submissions OK. Reports in 2 months on queries and mss. Sample copy free for $2 with 9x12 SAE.
Payment: Pays $40-200.
Terms: Pays on publication for first, second or first North American serial rights. Publication copyrighted.
Tips: "Beginners are advised to try elsewhere first. Ninety-nine percent of the manuscripts we have received lack freshness or originality, or lean on plot gimmicks and pretentious language rather than on real storytelling skill."

RV'N ON, 10417 Chandler Blvd., N. Hollywood CA 91601. Editor: Kim Ouimet. "We publish an entertaining but informative mini-newspaper for recreational vehicle owners. Adding fiction in '81 will be a new feature. Our audience is made up of people who own RVs or are just interested in camping and travel. They are involved in all walks of life." Monthly. Estab. June 1979. Circ. 4,000.
Needs: Contemporary, science fiction, fantasy, horror, gothic, western, mystery, adventure, humor, preferably travel oriented in USA. "We plan to run a fiction piece in several parts unless the story is told in only a few paragraphs. No handwritten material." Buys 3 mss/year, then serializes into parts. Receives approximately 2 unsolicited fiction mss each month. Length: 300-1,000 words.
How to Contact: Query with SASE. Reports in 2 months on queries. Sample copy $1.
Payment: 3¢/word-$15.
Terms: Pays 60 days after publication for first North American serial rights; may later make a reprint deal on a percentage basis. Publication copyrighted.

ST. ANTHONY MESSENGER, St. Anthony Messenger, 1615 Republic St., Cincinnati OH 45210. Editor: Norman Perry, O.F.M. "*St. Anthony Messenger* is a Catholic family magazine which aims to help its readers lead more fully human and Christian lives. We publish articles which report on a changing church and world, opinion pieces written from the perspective of Christian faith and values, personality profiles, and fiction which entertains and informs." Monthly. Estab. 1893. Circ. 320,000.
Needs: Contemporary and religious/inspirational. "We do not want mawkishly sentimental or preachy fiction. Stories are most often rejected for poor plotting and characterization; bad dialog—listen to how people talk; inadequate motivation. Many stories say nothing, are 'happenings' rather than stories." No fetal journals, no rewritten Bible stories. Buys 1 ms/issue, 12 mss/year. Receives 50-60 unsolicited fiction mss each month. Length: 2,500-3,000 words. Critiques rejected mss "when there is time." Sometimes recommends other markets.
How to Contact: Send complete ms with SASE. Reports in 1 month on mss. Free sample copy and guideline with legal-sized SASE.
Payment: 10¢/word maximum. 2 free author's copies. $1 charge for extras.
Terms: Pays on acceptance for first North American serial rights. Publication copyrighted.
Tips: Rejects mss because "we publish one story a month and we get 500 or 600 a year. Many are inappropriate and don't fit magazine or audience or are poorly written."

ST. JOSEPH'S MESSENGER AND ADVOCATE OF THE BLIND, Sisters of St. Joseph of Peace, 541 Pavonia Ave., Jersey City NJ 07306. (201)798-4141. Magazine for Catholics generally but not exclusively. Theme is "religious—relevant—real." Published quarterly. Estab. 1903. Circ. 52,500.
Needs: Contemporary, humor/satire, mainstream, religious/inspirational, romance (contemporary). Receives 30-40 unsolicited fiction mss/month. Buys 3 mss/issue; 20 mss/year. Length: 800 words minimum; 1,800 words maximum; 1,500 words average. Occasionally critiques rejected ms.
How to Contact: Send complete ms with SASE. Simultaneous, photocopied and previously published submissions OK. Free sample copy with legal size SAE and 1 first class stamp. Free fiction guidelines with SASE.

Payment: $10-25 and 2 contributor's copies.
Terms: Pays on acceptance for one-time rights.
Tips: Rejects mss because "vague focus or theme."

SAN GABRIEL VALLEY MAGAZINE, Miller Books, 2908 W. Valley Blvd., Alhambra CA 91803. (213)284-7607. Editor: Joseph Miller. "Regional magazine for the valley featuring local entertainment, dining, sports and events. We also carry articles about successful people from the area. For upper middle class people who enjoy going out a lot." Bimonthly. Estab. 1976. Circ. 3,000.
Needs: Contemporary, inspirational, western, adventure and humor. No articles on sex or ERA. Buys 2 mss/issue, 20 mss/year. Receives approximately 10 unsolicited fiction mss each month. Length: 500-2,500 words.
How to Contact: Send complete ms with SASE. Reports in 2 weeks on mss. Sample copy $1 with 9x12 SASE.
Payment: 5¢/word. 2 free author's copies.
Terms: Payment on acceptance for one-time rights. Publication copyrighted.
Tips: "Write a good story with positive attitudes." Mss are rejected because "they do not relate to our region or readers."

SATURDAY EVENING POST, Benjamin Franklin Literary and Medical Society, 1100 Waterway Blvd., Indianapolis IN 46202. (317)634-1100 Editor: Dr. Cory Servaas, M.D. Senior Editor: Ted Kreiter. Magazine with articles on general interest, health care, personalities, book reviews and games for conservative middle age, middle income, college-educated audience. Published 9 times/year. Estab. 1728. Circ. 700,000.
Needs: Religious/inspirational, science fiction, gothic, romance, western, mystery, adventure and humor. No explicit sex, profanity, perversion, ethnic humor or anti-traditional family life. Buys 1 ms/issue. Length: average of 2,500 words.
How to Contact: Send complete ms with SASE. Reports in 1-8 weeks.
Payment: Pays average of $250.
Terms: Pays on publication for all rights.
Tips: "We want positive stories about romance, family and love, people winning out in the end. Humor has a better chance. Keep it simple."

SCANDINAVIAN REVIEW, American-Scandinavian Foundation, 127 E. 73 St., New York NY 10021. (212)879-0418. Editors: Kate Daniels and Richard Jones. "Contemporary Scandinavian articles, illustrative graphics, fiction and poetry in translation, reviews of books, films, music for well-educated general public with interest in Scandinavian life and culture." Quarterly; 3 issues general interest, 1 issue all literary. Estab. 1910. Circ. 6,500.
Needs: Ethnic (Scandinavian) and translations in English. Nothing without a Scandinavian connection. Length: 2,500 words.
How to Contact: Send complete ms with SASE. Reports in 1 month on mss.
Payment: $40-80 plus 2 contributor's copies.
Terms: Pays on publication for all, first and second serial (reprint) rights.
Tips: ASF/Pen Translation Prizes sponsored by American-Scandinavian Foundation and Pen American Center.

SCHOLASTIC SCOPE, Scholastic, Inc., 50 W. 44th St., New York NY 10036. Editor: Katherine Robinson. National publication on subjects of general and human interest; profiles of teenagers who have overcome obstacles or done something unusual; short stories and plays for teens. Weekly. Circ. 1,100,000.
Needs: Stories about the problems of teens (drugs, prejudice, runaways, failure in school, family problems, etc.); relationships between people in family; job, and school situations. Looking for material about American Indian, chicano, Mexican-American, Puerto Rican and black experiences and other ethnic groups. No crime stories. Length: 400-1,200 words.

How to Contact: Send complete ms with SASE.
Payment: Pays $125 minimum.
Terms: Acquires all rights; byline given.
Tips: "Strive for directness, realism and action in dialogue rather than narrative. Characters should have depth. Avoid too many coincidences and random happenings."

SECRETS, Gospel Light Publications, 2300 Knoll Dr., Ventura CA 93003. (805)644-9721. Special Products Editor: Kristen Fellman. Sunday School take-home paper for first and second graders (6 to 8 years of age). Weekly. Estab. 1983.
Needs: Juvenile: adventure, contemporary, religious, suspense/mystery. Buys 1 ms/issue; 12/year. Length: 500 words maximum. Occasionally critiques rejected mss.
How to Contact: Query first; query with outline and/or ms with SASE. Simultaneous and photocopied submissions OK. Reports in 2 weeks on queries.
Payment: Pays $15/story.
Terms: Pays on acceptance for all rights. Publication copyrighted.

SECRETS, Macfadden Women's Group, 215 Lexington Ave., New York NY 10016. (212)340-7500. Editor: Jean Press Silberg. Confession magazine for blue-collar women with families; ages 18-35. Monthly. Estab. 1936.
Needs: Women's interest pieces, based on true incidents or situations. Themes involving family, marriage, work; should be relevant to readers' lives. First person narrator may be male or female. Buys 150 mss/year, 10-12 mss an issue. Occasionally critiques rejected mss when they "may be usable, if reworked." Length: 1,500-10,000 words. Some 10,000-word "novelettes."
How to Contact: Send complete ms with SASE. Reports in 2 months on mss. No photocopied or simultaneous submissions. Seasonal stories should be submitted 4-5 months in advance.
Payment: Pays 3¢/word.
Terms: Pays on publication for all rights. Publication copyrighted.
Tips: Mss are rejected because of "lack of familiarity with our needs and our style. Suggest close examination of magazine, and understanding of our readers. Stories must be written in first person."

SEEK, Standard Publishing, 8121 Hamilton Ave., Cincinnati OH 45231. Editor: Leah Ann Cook. "Inspirational stories of faith-in-action for Christian young adults; a Sunday School take-home paper." Weekly. Estab. January 1970. Circ. 75,000.
Needs: Religious/inspirational. Buys 100 mss/year. Length: 500-1,500 words.
How to Contact: Send complete ms with SASE. Reports in 2 weeks on mss. Free sample copy and guidelines.
Payment: 2½-3¢/word.
Terms: Pays on acceptance.
Tips: "Write a credible story with Christian slant—no preachments; avoid overworked themes such as joy in suffering, generation gaps, etc. Most mss are rejected by us because of irrelevant topic or message; unrealistic story; or poor character and/or plot development."

ROD SERLING'S THE TWILIGHT ZONE MAGAZINE, TZ Publications, Inc., 800 Second Ave., New York NY 10017. (212)986-9600. Editor: T.E.D. Klein. "A monthly magazine devoted to imaginative and speculative fiction. We're always on the lookout for originality, strong writing, and a fresh viewpoint." Monthly. Estab. 1981. Circ. 200,000.
Needs: Experimental, fantasy, horror, psychic/supernatural, science fiction, suspense/mystery. "Characterizations are important. No hard-core science fiction, sword-and-sorcery, or imaginary world fantasy." Receives 1,500 unsolicited fiction mss/month. Buys 8-10 mss/month. Length: 2,000 words minimum; 5,000 words maximum. Occasionally critiques rejected mss.
How to Contact: Send complete ms with SASE. Simultaneous, photocopied and previously published submissions OK. Reports in 4 months on mss. Sample copy for $3. Fiction guidelines free for legal SAE and 20¢ postage.

Payment: Pays $150-800; 2 free contributor's copies.
Terms: Pays one-half on acceptance and one-half on publication. Publication copyrighted.

SEVENTEEN, Triangle Communications, 850 3rd Ave., New York NY 10022. (212)759-8100. Editor: Midge Richardson. Ray Robinson, Executive Editor. Fiction Editor: Dawn Raffel. A service magazine with fashion, beauty care, pertinent topics such as trends in dating, attitudes, experiences and concerns during the teenage years. Monthly. Estab. 1944. Circ. 1½ million.
Needs: High quality fiction, any style, which is of interest to teen-age girls. We look for fresh themes and well-paced plots; no vulgar language. Buys 1 ms/issue. Receives 600-800 unsolicited fiction mss each month. Length: appoximately 3,000 words. Critiques rejected mss "when there is time."
How to Contact: Send complete ms with SASE. Reports in 2 months on mss. Free guidelines with SASE.
Payment: Pays average of $500. Offers kill fee for assigned mss not published.
Terms: Pays on acceptance for one-time rights. Publication copyrighted.
Tips: "Read back issues of the magazine; pay attention to grammar, spelling, character and plot development." Mss are rejected because "adult writers underestimate the intelligence and sophistication of today's teen-age reader and are out of touch with teenagers; plots are either worn out or sloppily constructed, with too little character development." Sponsors annual fiction contest. Rules are announced each year in April issue.

THE SINGLE PARENT, Journal of Parents Without Partners, Parents Without Partners, Inc., 7910 Woodmont Ave., Suite 1000, Bethesda MD 20814. (301)654-8850. Editor: Kate Gerwig. Managing Editor: Virginia Rhodes Nuta. Publication for divorced, separated, widowed or never-married parents and their children. Published 10 times/year; Jan/Feb.; July/Aug. combined. Estab. 1965. Circ. 215,000.
Needs: Short stories for *children only*, not adults. Stories should deal with issues that children from one-parent families might face. Buys 1 ms/issue. Length: 1,000 words maximum.
How to Contact: Send complete ms with SASE. Reports within 6 weeks.
Payment: Pays $50; 2 free contributor's copies.
Terms: Pays on publication.
Tips: "A children's page is a new addition to the magazine. Would prefer stories short enough to fit on one page. Upbeat, problem-solving themes preferred."

SPRINT for Junior Highs, David C. Cook Publishing Co., 850 N. Grove, Elgin IL 60120. Editor-in-Chief: David C. Cook III. Administrative Editor: Kristine Tomasik. "*Sprint* provides a Christian perspective on life for junior high Sunday School students. We are looking for high-quality fiction with believable, real characters and dialogue. The Christian viewpoint should be integrated into the story, not a moral tacked onto the end of it." Weekly. Estab. for over 100 years.
Needs: Religious/inspirational, adventure, humor and young adult. Preachy, patronizing or implausible fiction is not acceptable. Buys 20-30 mss/year. Length: 1,000-1,200 words.
How to Contact: Send complete ms with SASE. Reports in 3 months on mss. Free sample copy with business SASE and 20¢ postage.
Payment: $75-90.
Terms: Pays on acceptance for all rights.
Tips: "Please read us first and be sure you understand our market. Be your own toughest judge of a story. Ask yourself, 'Would a teen be simply unable to put this story down?' "

STAG MAGAZINE, 888 7th Ave., New York NY 10106. (212)541-7100. Editor-in-Chief: Colette Connor. Slick men's sex magazine, mostly photos, also humor, interviews. Readers are blue collar men 20-45. Published monthly. Estab. 1951. Circ. 125,000.
Needs: Adventure, contemporary, erotica, humor/satire, men's. Do not send "boring ms; has to have more than just sex." Receives approximately 15 unsolicited fiction mss/month. Buys 1 mss/issue; 12 mss/year. Length: 2,000 words minimum; 3,000 words maximum; 2,500 words average.

How to Contact: Query with clips of published work with SASE. Photocopied submissions OK. Reports in 4 weeks on queries; 4 weeks on mss. Free sample copy with SAE.
Payment: $250-400.
Tips: Rejects mss because "the stories are unimaginative or not geared to reader interests."

STORIES, 14 Beacon St., Boston MA 02108. (617)742-3345. Editor-in-Chief: Amy R. Kaufman. "This bimonthly national magazine is designed to provide wide circulation of literature that caters to no commercial standard. By 'commercial standard' we mean a standard other than the author's. Even as a periodical, we value literature that will endure changes in fashion and language, whose meaning is not rooted in a particular setting but in the universal mysteries of human nature. We prefer literature that is 'traditional,' as T.S. Eliot defines it: written 'with a feeling that the whole of literature has a simultaneous existence' and with a sense of the 'timeless and of the temporal together.' " Published bimonthly. Estab. 1982.
Needs: Contemporary, ethnic, historical (general), humor/satire, literary, serialized/excerpted novel, translations. "We wish to promote literature that is capable of eliciting emotional response, not the type whose exclusive purpose is to entertain, inform, horrify, or impress. We appreciate humor that is sharply perceptive, not merely amusing; political or moral pieces that make a point, not merely hint at one, and that do not proselytize. Ordinarily, romance, mystery, fantasy, and science fiction do not suit our purposes, but we will not exclude any story on the basis of genre; we wish only that the piece be the best of its genre." Buys 6-8 mss/issue; 36-48 mss/year. Length: 750 words minimum; 15,000 words maximum; 4,000-7,000 words average. Occasionally critiques rejected mss. Sometimes recommends other markets.
How to Contact: Send complete ms with SASE. Photocopied and simultaneous submissions OK. Reports in 2 months on mss. Free fiction guidelines with SASE.
Payment: $150 minimum.
Terms: Pays $100 on acceptance and balance within 7 days of publication for first North American serial rights.
Tips: "We look for characters identifiable not by name, age, profession, or appearance, but by symbolic qualities; themes that are timeless, or, if timely, told with artistic intensity, a sense of urgency that enables us to feel its significance; styles that are sophisiticated but not affected, straightforward but not artless, descriptive but not nearsighted. The chances that a story will conform to an editor's highly individual taste are very slim. I feel most writers submit half-finished work—they haven't taken themselves seriously enough to perfect their stories. Study Strunk & White's *Elements of Style*."

STORY FRIENDS, Mennonite Publishing House, 616 Walnut Ave., Scottdale PA 15683. (412)887-8500. Editor: Marjorie Waybill. Sunday School publication which portrays Jesus as a friend and helper. Nonfiction and fiction for children 4-9 years of age. Weekly.
Needs: Juvenile. Stories of everyday experiences at home, in church, in school or at play, which provide models of Christian values. "It is important to include relationships, patterns of forgiveness, respect, honesty, trust and caring. Prefer exciting yet plausible short stories which offer different settings, introduce children to wide ranges of friends and demonstrate joys, fears, temptations and successes of the readers." Length: 300-800 words.
How to Contact: Send complete ms with SASE. Seasonal or holiday material should be submitted six months in advance. Free sample copy.
Payment: Pays 2½-3¢/word.
Terms: Pays on acceptance for rights. Not copyrighted. Byline given.

STRAIGHT, Standard Publishing Co., 8121 Hamilton Ave., Cincinnati OH 45231. (513)931-4050. Editor: Dawn Brettschneider. Publication helping and encouraging teens to cope with problems by using Christian principles. Distributed through churches and some private subscriptions. Quarterly in weekly parts. Estab. October 1951. Circ. 140,000.
Needs: Contemporary, religious/inspirational, romance, mystery, adventure, and humor all with Christian emphasis. "Stories must have character building elements and interesting, well-constructed plots. Problems should be dealt with positively, showing a Christian teen's response.

Nothing preachy or in poor taste, no suggestive stories, moral situations dealt with distastefully or language used abusively." Buys 1-2 mss/issue, 75-100 mss/year. Receives approximately 75 unsolicited fiction mss each month. Length: 1,000-2,000 words.

How to Contact: Send complete ms with SASE. Reports in 6 weeks on mss. Free sample copy and guidelines with SASE.

Payment: 2¢/word.

Terms: Pays on acceptance for first and one-time rights. Publication copyrighted.

Tips: "Don't try to be a writer that you are not—write naturally, not stylistically." Many mss are rejected because of "unrealistic situations that involve *unbelievable* teen characters! A writer must know about his characters to make them true-to-life, and have at least a vague idea of what real-life conflicts are."

THE STUDENT, A Christian Collegiate Magazine, National Student Ministries of the Baptist Sunday School Board, 127 Ninth Ave., North, Nashville TN 37234. (615)251-2783. Editor: W. Howard Bramlette. Magazine for Christians and non-Christians about work with Christian students on campus—campus-related articles on living in dorm setting, missions activities, Bible study. Published monthly. Estab. 1929. Circ. 22,000.

Needs: Adventure, comics, confession, contemporary, ethnic, religious/inspirational. Do not want to see mss "without purpose or without moral closure." Receives approximately 25 unsolicited fiction mss/month. Buys 1-2 mss/issue; 12-24 mss/year. Length: 250 words minimum (or less, depending on treatment); 1,000 words maximum; 750 words average. Occasionally critiques rejected mss.

How to Contact: Query first with SASE. Simultaneous, photocopied and previously published submissions OK. Reports in 3 weeks on queries; 1 month on mss. Sample copy 61¢. Free fiction guidelines with SASE.

Payment: 3½¢/word and 3 contributor's copies.

Terms: Pays on publication for all rights, first rights, one-time rights and assignments for work-for-hire basis. Publication copyrighted.

Tips: "Fit writing to format and concept of the piece. View many issues of the magazine before you write."

STUDENT LAWYER, American Bar Assoc., 1155 E. 60th St., Chicago IL 60637. (312)947-4087. Editor: Catherine Cahan. "Magazine for law students as part of their Law Student Division/ABA membership. Features legal aspects, trends in the law, social/legal issues and lawyer profiles. Monthly (September-May). Circ. 45,000.

Needs: "All stories have to have a legal/law/lawyer/law school element to them. No science fiction." Buys 2 full length or 2-3 short humorous pieces/year. Length: 1,000-3,000 words. Sometimes recommends other markets.

How to Contact: Send complete ms with SASE. Reports in 1 month on mss. Sample copy $1.

Payment: $75-300.

Terms: Pays on acceptance for all rights.

Tips: Rejects mss because "usually, the stories are of mediocre quality. Because we usually favor nonfiction pieces, the fiction we do publish has to be outstanding or at least very original."

SUNDAY DIGEST, David C. Cook Publishing Co., 850 N. Grove Ave., Elgin IL 60120. (312)741-2400. Editor: Gregory D. Cook. A take-home paper distributed weekly to adults in Sunday Schools. "We are a nondenominational, Christian magazine. We tell stories that inspire by showing how faith relates to everyday living." Published quarterly.

Needs: Religious/inspirational. Only accepts Christian themes. Receives approximately 50 unsolicited fiction mss each month. Length: 300-2,000 words.

How to Contact: Send complete ms with SASE. Reports in 1 month on mss. Free sample copy with 6x9 SAE and 40¢ postage.

Payment: $25-200.

Terms: Pays on acceptance for First North American serial rights. Publication copyrighted.

Tips: "Write believable fiction with an implicit—not tacked-on or phony-Christian emphasis. Much fiction we see is simplistic, overly sentimental, with undefined characters or poorly developed plot."

SUNSHINE MAGAZINE, Henrichs Publications, Box 40, Litchfield IL 62056. "Family publication with inspirational short stories generally based on true life experiences. Humorous at times and uplifting. *Sunshine* is also produced in large print format. Audience ranges in age from preschool through the 90s. Stories are brief and inspiring and can be read quickly." Monthly. Estab. 1924. Circ. 100,000.
Needs: Literary, inspirational, men's, women's, humor and juvenile. No religious subjects dealing with heavily depressing material, sex or violence. Buys 8-11 mss/issue. Receives 375-425 unsolicited fiction mss each month. Length: 500-1,000 words.
How to Contact: Send complete ms with SASE. Reports in 2 months on mss. Sample copy 50¢. Free guidelines with legal-sized SASE.
Payment: $10-100. Free author's copy. 40¢ charge for extra copy.
Terms: Pays on acceptance for first North American serial rights. Publication copyrighted.
Tips: Many mss are rejected because "they are sloppily prepared, too long, about unsuitable subjects. Writers should send for our guidelines and a sample copy. Mss are rejected because "only a dozen or so stories can appear each month, and over 350 are received. Other major reasons are excess length, sloppily written, or subjects not suitable for our magazine."

THE SURGICAL TECHNOLOGIST, Association of Surgical Technologists, Inc., Caller E, Littleton CO 80120. (303)978-9010. Editor: William Teutsch. Magazine of surgery, operating room and hospital environment for surgical technologists—20-50, predominantly female. Bimonthly. Estab. 1969. Circ. 12,000.
Needs: Contemporary, humor/satire, mainstream, religious/inspirational, science fiction, suspense/mystery, women's. Length: 3,000 words minimum; 5,000 words maximum. Occasionally critiques rejected mss.
How to Contact: Send complete ms with SASE. Simultaneous submissions OK. Reports in 1 month on mss.
Payment: Pays $100-500.
Terms: Pays on acceptance for all rights. Publication copyrighted.

SURPRISES, Gospel Light Publications, 2300 Knoll Dr., Ventura CA 93003. (805)644-9721. Special Products Editor: Kristen Fellman. Sunday School take-home paper for 2, 3, 4 or 5 year olds. Studies to be read for pre-schooler by parents. Weekly. Estab. 1983.
Needs: Juvenile: adventure, contemporary, mystery, religious. Buys 1 ms/issue; 12 mss/year. Length: 500 words maximum. Occasionally critiques rejected ms.
How to Contact: Query with outline for ms with SASE. Simultaneous and photocopied submissions OK. Reports in 2 weeks on queries.
Payment: Pays $15/story.
Terms: Pays on acceptance for all rights. Publication copyrighted.

SUSQUEHANNA MAGAZINE, Susquehanna Times & Magazine, Inc., Box 75A, R.D.1, Marietta PA 17547. (717)426-2212. Editor: Richard S. Bromer. Publisher: Nancy H. Bromer. "Regional, general interest for Lancaster County, Pennsylvania, and Southeastern Pennsylvania. Emphasis on local history, culture, ecology, etc., for upper middle, better educated, family/community-oriented, intellectual audience." Monthly. Estab. 1976. Circ. 6,000.
Needs: Regional. "We print very little fiction. When we do, it has a very definite tie to our regional distribution." Length: 1,200-3,000 words. Sometimes recommends other markets.
How to Contact: Query with clips of published work with SASE. Reports in 1 month on both queries and mss. Sample copy $2.
Payment: $25-75. Pays on acceptance; negotiable rights.
Tips: "Become familiar with our publication for style, topics, format, etc., to submit appropriate

material.'' Rejects mss because ''material not appropriate for our publication or not well organized—sometimes 'juvenile.' ''

SWANK MAGAZINE, Swank Corp., 888 Seventh Ave., New York NY 10106. Editor: David Harrison.''Men's sophisticate format. Sexually-oriented material as well as investigative reporting, humor, fiction, interviews, etc. Presumably our reader is after a mix of erotic material and lifestyle information.'' Monthly. Estab. 1952. Circ. 350,000.
Needs: High-caliber erotica and medium-length humor pieces. Fiction always has an erotic theme; writers should try to avoid the clichés of the genre. Buys 1 ms/issue, 12/year. Receives approximately 80 unsolicited fiction mss each month. Length: 3,000-4,000 words.
How to Contact: Send complete ms with SASE. Reports in 1 month on mss. Sample copy $3 with SASE.
Payment: $250-400. Offers 25% kill fee for assigned ms not published.
Terms: Pays on publication for second serial (reprint) and first North American serial rights. Publication copyrighted.
Tips: ''Research the men's magazine market. Try to write lucid, intelligent material which will sell us on the project.'' Mss are rejected because of ''lame storylines, poor execution. Stories are usually either all plot and no sex or all sex and no plot. We need a mixture of tight plot and hot sex. Also, I often find writers submit fiction without even looking at our magazine. That is extremely foolish.''

TAMPA MAGAZINE, City Magazines, Inc., 4100 W. Kennedy Blvd., Tampa FL 33609. (813)872-7449. Editor: Frank Bentayou. Articles Editor: Bob Casterline. ''We're a city magazine concentrating on the Tampa Bay area. Our editorial range is from hard investigative stories to soft life-style features on food and fashion. Up-scale, professional class readers interested in the development of the fast-growing Bay Area.'' Monthly. Estab. 1980. Circ. 21,000.
Needs: ''Serious short fiction that focuses on the greater Tampa Bay area.'' Length: 2,500 words minimum, 10,000 words maximum, 4,000 words average.
How to Contact: ''We conduct an annual short story fiction contest starting in October. The winning story runs in March.'' SASE. Sample copy for $2.25.
Payment: $300 ''for winner of our fiction contest.''
Terms: Pays on publication for first North American serial rights.
Tips: ''Submit an entry to our annual fiction contest before Nov. 30. We're looking for high-quality, stylish fiction that is set in our area and, moreover, tells the reader something about the character of Tampa and its environs.''

'TEEN MAGAZINE, Petersen Publishing, Co., 8490 Sunset Blvd., Los Angeles CA 90069. Editor: Roxanne Camron. Managing Editor: Lori Shaw-Cohen. ''The magazine contains fashion, beauty, and features for the young teenage girl. The median age of our readers is 16. Our success stems from our dealing with relevant issues teens face, printing recent entertainment news and showing the latest fashions and beauty looks.'' Monthly. Estab. 1957. Circ. 1 million.
Needs: Romance, mystery, humor and young adult. Every story, whether romance, mystery, humor, etc., must be aimed for teenage girls. The protagonist should be a teenager, preferably female. No experimental, science fiction, fantasy or horror. Buys 1 mss/issue, 12 mss/year. Length: 2,500-4,000 words.
How to Contact: Send complete ms with SASE. Reports in 2 months on mss. Free guidelines with SASE.
Payment: Pays $100.
Terms: Pays on acceptance for all rights.
Tips: ''Try to find themes that suit the modern teen. We need innovative ways of looking at the age-old problems of young love, parental pressures, making friends, being left out, etc. Mss must be typed neatly and double spaced. Handwritten mss will not be read. Send ms to Fiction Editor.''

TEENS TODAY, Church of the Nazarene, 6401 The Paseo, Kansas City MO 64131. (816)333-7000. Editor: Gary Sivewright. Sunday School take home paper for junior and senior high students involved with the Church of the Nazarene who find it interesting and helpful to their areas of life. Weekly. Circ. 50,000.

Needs: Contemporary, religious/inspirational, romance, humor, juvenile, young adult and ethnic. "Nothing that puts teens down or condemns lifestyle not in keeping with denomination's beliefs and standards." Buys 1-2 mss/issue. Length: 1,500-2,500 words.

How to Contact: Send complete ms with SASE. Reports in 6 weeks on mss. Free sample copy and guidelines.

Payment: Pays 3¢/word and 2¢/word on second reprint.

Terms: Pays on acceptance for first and second serial rights.

Tips: "Study sample copies. Don't be too juvenile. Target on a higher quality of writing than what we are presently receiving and publishing."

TODAY'S CHRISTIAN WOMAN, Fleming H. Revell, 2029 P St. NW, Washington DC 20036. (202)296-3760. Editor-in-Chief: Dale Hanson Bourke. "*TCW* is a magazine for Christian women of all ages, single and married, homemakers and career women. It includes a variety of articles on topics ranging from self-help to fiction, cooking to careers." Published quarterly. Estab. 1978. Circ. 75,000.

Needs: Contemporary, literary, religious/inspirational, women's. "No mss not women-oriented with a distinctly moral or Christian message." Receives 5 unsolicited fiction mss/month. Buys 1 ms/issue; 4 mss/year. Length: 1,000 words minimum; 3,500 words maximum.

How to Contact: Send query letter first. Simultaneous and photocopied submissions OK.

Payment: 10¢/word and 1 contributor's copy. Offers 50% kill fee for assigned ms not published.

Terms: Pays on acceptance for first rights. Publication copyrighted.

TOUCH, Calvinettes, Box 7244, Grand Rapids MI 49510. (616)241-5616. Editor: Joanne Ilbrink. Magazine. "Our purpose is to lead girls into a living relationship with Jesus Christ. Puzzles, poetry, crafts, stories, articles, club input for girls age 9-14." Monthly.

Needs: Adventure, ethnic, juvenile, religious/inspirational. "Articles must help girls discover how God is at work in their world and the world around them." Receives 50 unsolicited fiction mss/month. Buys 3 mss/issue; 30 mss/year. Length: 900 words minimum; 1,200 words maximum; 1,000 words average. Occasionally critiques rejected mss.

How to Contact: Send complete ms with SASE. Simultaneous, photocopied and previously published submissions OK. Reports in 4 weeks on mss. Sample copy free for SASE. Fiction guidelines free.

Payment: Pays 2¢/word-$35.

Terms: Pays on acceptance for simultaneous, first or second serial rights.

Tips: "Write for guidelines and theme update and submit manuscripts in advance of deadline. Our magazine fills early because of limited use of manuscripts so it is best to submit early and indicate for which theme the article has been written."

TRAILER BOATS MAGAZINE, Poole Publications Inc., Box 2307, 16427 S. Avalon, Gardena, CA 90248. Editor-in-Chief: Jim Youngs. "Our magazine covers boats of 26 feet and shorter, (trailerable size limits), and related activities; skiing, fishing, cruising, travel, racing, etc. We publish how-to articles on boat and trailer maintenance, travel, skiing, boat tests, and evaluations of new products." Audience: owners and prospective owners of trailerable size boats. Published monthly. Estab. 1971. Circ. 80,000.

Needs: Adventure, contemporary, fantasy, humor/satire, science fiction, suspense/mystery. "Must meet general guidelines of the magazine regarding boats and related activities." Receives very few unsolicited fiction mss/month. Buys 1-3 mss/year. Length: 200 words minimum; 1000 words maximum. Occasionally critiques rejected mss. Sometimes recommends other markets.

How to Contact: Query first with SASE. Reports in 4 weeks on queries; 4-6 weeks on mss. Free sample copy and general guidelines.

Payment: 7-10¢/word.

Terms: Pays on publication for all rights. Publication copyrighted.

Tips: "In our case, knowing the audience is of prime importance. Our readership and experience with fiction is limited. We are a consumer magazine with an audience of dedicated boaters. My suggestion is to know the audience and write for it specifically."

TRAILS, Pioneer Ministries, Inc., Box 788, Wheaton IL 60187. (312)293-1600. Editor: Lora-Beth Norton. Associate Editor: Lorraine G. Mulligan. *Trails'* purpose is to present Christ in every phase of life through story, biography and personal experience for children in grades 1-6. 5 times/year. Estab. 1961. Circ. 50,000.
Needs: Literary, contemporary, religious/inspirational, science fiction, fantasy, romance, mystery, adventure, humor, juvenile and young adult. "No stories with a tacked-on moral. Christian principles should be inherent in the stories." Buys 2-3 mss/issue. Receives 40-50 unsolicited fiction mss each month. Length: 500-1,500 words. Sometimes recommends other markets.
How to Contact: Send complete ms with SASE. Reports in 2 months on mss. Writer's packet $2 (sample copy and guidelines).
Payment: $25-55.
Terms: Pays on acceptance for assignments on a work-for-hire basis, first and second serial (reprint) rights.
Tips: "Large portion of our magazine is done on assignment. Rejected manuscripts are often entirely inappropriate for our readers in subject matter or are worn-out themes."

TURTLE MAGAZINE, The Benjamin Franklin Literary & Medical Society, Inc., 1100 Waterway Blvd., Box 567, Indianapolis IN 46206. Editorial Director: Beth Wood Thomas. Magazine of picture stories and articles for preschool children, 2-5 years old.
Needs: Juvenile (preschool). Receives approximately 25 unsolicited fiction mss each month. Length: 8-12 lines for picture stories; 500 words for bedtime or naptime stories. Special emphasis on health, nutrition, exercise, safety.
How to Contact: Send complete ms with SASE. Reports in 8-10 weeks on mss. No queries.
Payment: 4¢/word (approximate).
Terms: Pays on publication for all rights. Publication copyrighted.
Tips: "Keep it simple and easy to read. Vocabulary must be below first grade level. Be familiar with past issues of the magazine. Mss should be checked thoroughly before submission for misspelled words, errors in grammar, and suitability of subject matter and vocabularly for the preschooler."

VENTURE, Christian Service Brigade, Box 150, Wheaton IL 60187. Editor: Michael J. Chiapperino. Managing Editor: Mark Carpenter. "Our magazines aim to provide entertaining, wholesome reading, while challenging our constituency to love and serve Jesus Christ. CSB is a boys' organization that operates through evangelical churches across North America. When a boy registers in CSB, he automatically receives a subscription to one of our magazines." Published 8 times/year. Circ. 23,000.
Needs: Religious/inspirational, adventure, humor, juvenile and young adult. "No stories that contain boring, pat answers." Buys 1 ms/issue, 12-15 mss/year. Receives 30-50 unsolicited fiction mss each month. Length: 800-1,200 words.
How to Contact: Query or query with clips of published work. SASE always. Reports in 1 week on queries, 2 weeks on mss. Sample copy $1. Free guidelines with legal-sized SASE.
Payment: $35-75. 2 free author's copies. $1 charge for extra copies. Offers 10% kill fee for assigned mss not published.
Terms: Pays on publication for first or reprint rights. Publication copyrighted.
Tips: "Query first, make dialogue up-to-date and realistic; aim for a conflict or suspense. Teach worthwhile lessons with taste and subtlety." Mss are rejected because they are "unrealistic, trite, have little appeal for our audience, or lack suspense and action."

VIRTUE, The Magazine for Christian Women, Virtue Ministries, Inc., Box 850, Sisters OR 97759. (503)549-8261. Editor: Clare Forward. Managing Editor: Lee Ann Zanon. Christian

women's magazine featuring food, fashion, family, etc., aimed primarily at homemakers—"real women with everyday problems, etc." Published 6 times/year. Estab. 1978. Circ. 60,000.
Needs: Condensed novel, contemporary, humor/satire, religious/inspirational, serialized/excerpted novel, women's. "Must have Christian slant." Receives approximately 40 unsolicited fiction mss/month. Buys 1-2 mss/issue; 10 mss/year (maximum). Length: 1,500 words minimum; 2,500 words maximum; 2,000 words average. Sometimes recommends other markets.
How to Contact: Send complete ms with SASE. Simultaneous, photocopied and previously published submissions OK. Reports in 6 weeks on mss. Sample copy $2 with 9x13 SAE and 90¢ postage. Free fiction guidelines with SASE and 1 first class stamp.
Payment: 5¢/word published.
Terms: Pays on publication for first rights or reprint rights. Publication copyrighted.
Tips: "Send us descriptive, colorful writing with good style. *Please*—no simplistic, unrealistic pat endings. There are three main reasons *Virtue* rejects fiction: 1.) The stories are not believable, 2.) and writing is dull, and 3.) the story does not convey a Christian message."

VISTA, Wesleyan Publishing House, Box 2000, Marion IN 46952. Managing Editor: Cindy Holloway. Publication of the Wesleyan Church for adults. Weekly. Circ. 56,000.
Needs: First-person fiction (1,500-1,800 words) humor: "Humor is an excellent way to convey spiritual instruction in palatable form (500-800 words). True stories (first-person or "as told to")—1,000-1,500 wds. "Receives 200-300 unsolicited fiction mss each month."
How to Contact: Send complete mss with SASE. Reports in 6-8 weeks.
Payment: Pays 2½¢/word. Offers kill fee for assigned mss not published.
Terms: "Not copyrighted. Along with mss for first use, we also accept simultaneous submissions, second rights and reprint rights. It is the writer's obligation to secure clearance from original publisher."
Tips: "Stories should have definite Christian emphasis and character-building values without being preachy. Setting, plot and action should be *realistic*." Mss are rejected because of "poor sentence structure" or because fiction resembles "soap operas."

THE WASHINGTONIAN, Washington Magazine Co., Suite 200, 1828 L St. NW, Washington DC 20036. (202)296-3600. Editor-in-Chief: John A. Limpert. General interest, regional magazine. Published monthly. Estab. 1965. Circ. 130,000.
Needs: Short pieces, must be set in Washington. Receives 8-10 unsolicited fiction mss/month. Buys 3 fiction mss/year. Length: 1,000 words minimum; 3,000 words maximum. Occasionally critiques rejected mss.
How to Contact: Send complete ms with SASE. Simultaneous and photocopied submissions OK. Reports in 1½ months on mss.
Payment: $100-350. Negotiates kill fee for assigned mss not published.
Terms: Pays on publication for all rights. Publication copyrighted.

WESTCHESTER ILLUSTRATED, 16 School St., Yonkers NY 10701. (914)423-4722. Attn: Bill Holiber. Regional and general interest magazine with emphasis on life in Westchester County, New York for active, sophisticated, college-educated readers, 25-49 years of age. Monthly. Estab. 1976. Circ. 30,000.
Needs: Good objective fiction; all categories open. Length: 800-1,500 words.
How to Contact: Send complete ms with SASE. Reports in 5 weeks on mss. Sample copy $1.50; free guidelines with SASE.
Payment: Varies.
Terms: Acquires all rights.

WESTERN PEOPLE, Western Producer Publications, Box 2500, Saskatoon, Saskatchewan, Canada S7K 2C4. (306)665-3500. Editor/Publisher: R.H.D. Phillips. Managing Editor: Mary Gilchrist. "*Western People* is for and about Western Canadians, a supplement of the region's foremost weekly agricultural newspaper. Includes fiction, nonfiction (contemporary and history) and poetry. Readership is mainly rural and Western Canadian.'' Weekly. Estab. August 1978. Circ. 142,097.

Needs: Contemporary, adventure, humor and serialized novels. Buys 50 mss/year. Length: 750-2500 words (unless for serialization).

How to Contact: Send complete ms with SAE, IRC. Reports in 3 weeks on mss. Free sample copy with 9x12 SAE, IRC. Free general guidelines with legal-sized SAE, IRC.

Payment: $150 maximum (more for serials).

Terms: Pays on acceptance for first and first North American serial rights.

Tips: ''The story should be lively, not long, related in some way to the experience of rural Western Canadians.''

THE WESTERN PRODUCER, The Western Producer, Box 2500, Saskatoon, Saskatchewan, Canada S7K 2C4. (306)665-3500. Editor/Publisher: R.H.D. Phillips. Managing Editor: Clarence Fairbairn. ''Material of interest to rural residents of Western Canada. Farm families read *The Western Producer* because it's a complete package of information.'' Weekly. Estab. 1922. Circ. 137,392.

Needs: Men's, women's, western, mystery, adventure, humor, juvenile and serialized novels. ''Stories should be of interest to farm families of all ages.'' Buys 50 + mss/year. Length: 750-1,500 words.

How to Contact: Send complete ms with SAE, IRC. Reports in 2 weeks on mss. Free sample copy with 8x12 SAE, IRC. Free guidelines with SAE, IRC.

Terms: Pays on acceptance for first rights.

Tips: ''Read the story twice more before sending it; don't underestimate a rural audience.''

THE WISCONSIN RESTAURATEUR, Published: Wisconsin Restaurant Association, 122 W. Washington, Madison WI 53703. (608)251-3663. Editor: Jan LaRue. Published for foodservice operators in the state of Wisconsin and for suppliers of those operations. Theme is the promotion, protection and improvement of the foodservice industry for foodservice students, operators and suppliers. Monthly except November/December combined. Estab. 1933. Circ. 3,600.

Needs: Literary, contemporary, science fiction, men's, women's, western, mystery, adventure, humor, juvenile and young adult. ''Only exceptional fiction material used. No stories accepted that put down persons in the foodservice business or poke fun at any group of people. No off-color material. No religious. No political.'' Buys 1-2 mss/issue, 12-24 mss/year. Receives 15-20 unsolicited fiction mss each month. Length: 500-2,500 words. Critiques rejected mss ''when there is time.''

How to Contact: Send complete ms with SASE. Reports in 4 weeks on mss. Free sample copy with 8½x11 SASE. Free guidelines with SASE.

Payment: $2.50-20. Free author's copy. 50¢ charge for extra copy.

Terms: Pays on acceptance for first and first North American serial rights. Publication copyrighted.

Tips: ''Make sure there is some kind of lesson to be learned, a humorous aspect, or some kind of moral to your story.'' Mss are rejected because they are not written for the restaurateur/reader.

WOMAN'S DAY, CBS Publications, 1515 Broadway, New York NY 10036. (212)719-6250. Editor-in-Chief: Ellen R. Levine. Editorial Director: Geraldine Rhoads. Fiction Editor: Eileen Herbert Jordan. A strong service magazine, geared to women, with a wide variety of well-written subjects (foods, crafts, beauty, medical, etc.). Publishes 15 issues/year. Estab. 1939. Circ. 7½ million; readership 17 million.

Needs: Literary, contemporary, religious/inspirational, fantasy, women's, feminist, humor and juvenile of high quality. No violence, crime, totally male-oriented or period stories.

How to Contact: Send complete ms with SASE. Reports in 4 weeks. Free guidelines with SASE.

Payment: Pays top rates.

Terms: Pays on acceptance.

Tips: ''Read the magazine and keep trying.''

Close-up

Nancy McCarthy
Woman's World

On a weekly basis *Woman's World* publishes one mini-mystery and one long romantic short story. That means 104 opportunities a year for writers—a bonanza in today's fiction market.

Many first-timers have successfully placed their short fiction with *Woman's World*, the two-year old New Jersey based magazine, and Nancy McCarthy, fiction editor, is eager to receive more manuscripts from talented writers. But first, she urges, "Get the guidelines and read them—*really read them*. It's obvious that some writers do not follow our rules after requesting them. A short story doesn't fit just *anywhere*."

Romantic fiction, extensive market research has demonstrated, is the most popular with *W.W.* readers, especially those stories with mature, modern protagonists in realistic and contemporary settings and situations. That doesn't include characters who are demeaned or helpless victims waiting to be rescued. It does, however, mean women who are working out their own lives and problems. In the story man and woman do have to get together, but "getting to that traditional ending is very open-ended," says McCarthy.

New writers, warns McCarthy, have an overwhelming urge to write about the most mundane of life's events as though they were unique. Any of life's situations can be made into art, but it's rare to deal with what is *very* ordinary and make it good. And please, she requests, no dying or dead animals as the story's focal points.

McCarthy cautions beginners to avoid the common pitfalls. Keep the story immediate with direct character involvement rather than reflection or looking back on a situation. And use action for impact. An author's age is sometimes telltale from the narrative. Women who grew up in the '40s and '50s were not as physically active as young women today, and their writing lacks character activity and physical mobility. Also, McCarthy advises, strive for real rather than contrived emotion.

Nancy McCarthy, *the* fiction department at *W.W.*, insists on a higher caliber of writing quality than she thinks is generally found in romantic novels, thus competition for publication in the magazine is competitive. Each manuscript is individually judged, and neither the writer's background nor the cover letter is very important.

The 90-200 unsolicited manuscripts received weekly are placed in one of three large slush piles after being read: the rejects, those that are returned immediately; the maybes, ones that receive individual personal notes and suggestions for revisions; and the read-agains, a very small percentage of which may see print after a month or so of decision making by McCarthy and ultimately the editor.

"The real joy in this job is giving writers money. They need to eat—and this is one way for them to do it," says the empathetic fiction editor, a former writer of films, TV news, documentaries and presently a novelist. "There's always hope. I know some days the mail will bring lovely stories—and that's a real delight."

WOMAN'S WORLD, The Woman's Weekly, Heinrich Bauer, N.A., 177 N. Dean St., Englewood NJ 07631. (201)569-0006. Editor-in-Chief: Dennis Neeld. Fiction editor: Nancy McCarthy. Service magazine for women, lower to middle income, ages 18-80. Includes both career and family oriented stories. Published weekly. Estab. 1981.
Needs: Mainstream romance (contemporary), suspense/mystery, women's. "No science-fiction, explicit sex, gruesome or grotesque stories." Receives 450-700 unsolicited fiction mss/month. Buys 2 mss/issue; 104 mss/year. Length: 6,000 words for short stories, 1,500 words for mini-mysteries. Occasionally critiques rejected mss.
How to Contact: Send complete ms with SASE. Simultaneous and photocopied submissions OK. Reports in 1 month on mss. Free fiction guidelines with SASE.
Payment: $500-1,200 and 2 contributor's copies.
Terms: Pays on acceptance for first North American serial rights. Publication copyrighted.
Tips: "Read several issues first before submitting stories. Our prime interest is stories with a romance theme and positive resolution." Most rejected mss "are from beginning writers."

WONDER TIME, Beacon Hill, Press of Kansas City, 6401 Paseo, Kansas City MO 64131. (816)333-7000. Editor: Evelyn Beals. Hand-out story paper published through the Church of the Nazarene Sunday School; stories should follow outline of Sunday School lesson for 6-7 year olds. Weekly. Circ. 60,000.
Needs: Religious/inspirational and juvenile. Stories must have controlled vocabulary and be easy to read. No fairy tales or science fiction. Buys 1 ms/issue. Receives 50-75 unsolicited fiction mss each month. Length: 600 words.
How to Contact: Send complete ms with SASE. Reports in 6 weeks on mss. Free sample copy and curriculum outline with SASE.
Payment: Pays 3¢/word.
Terms: Pays on acceptance for first rights and will buy reprints. Publication copyrighted.
Tips: "Control vocabulary. Study children to know what children are interested in; stories should deal with children's problems of today and must be tastefully handled." Mss are rejected because they "do not correlate with the Sunday School lessons."

WORKING FOR BOYS, Xaverian Brothers, Box A, Danvers MA 01923. (617)774-2664. Editor: Bro. Alphonsus Dwyer. "We publish articles of human interest, nature, biography, travel, religion, how-to, sports, etc., for elementary school children and their parents." Published 3 times/year. Estab. 1884. Circ. 16,000.
Needs: Literary, religious/inspirational, adventure, humor and juvenile. Buys 25 mss/year. Receives approximately 10 unsolicited fiction mss each month. Length: 800-1,200 words.
How to Contact: Query or send complete ms. SASE always. Reports in 2 weeks on queries and mss. Free sample copy. Free guidelines with SASE.
Payment: 4¢/word.
Terms: Pays on acceptance.

WORKING MOTHER, McCall's Publishing, Co., 230 Park Ave., New York NY 10169. (212)551-9412. Editor: Vivian Cadden. Magazine for working mothers. Monthly. Estab. October 1978. Circ. 400,000.
Needs: Contemporary, women's and juvenile. Length: 2,500-3,000 words. Critiques rejected mss "when there is time." Sometimes recommends other markets.
How to Contact: Send complete ms with SASE. Reports in 1 month. Sample copy $1.50.
Payment: Average $500. Offers 20% kill fee for assigned mss not published.
Terms: Pays on acceptance for all rights. Publication copyrighted.
Tips: "The stories we like most feature a working mother as the central character." Many mss are rejected because of poor writing, the subject doesn't interest us, or the story is not well developed."

WORLD OVER, Board of Jewish Education, 426 W 58th St., New York NY 10019. (212)245-8200. Editor: Stephen Schaffzin. Fiction Editor: Linda Schaffzin. Administrative Assistant: Bar-

bara Salomon. Children's magazine for Jewish children between 8-13 years. Monthly. Estab. 1939. Circ. 50,000.
Needs: Religious/inspirational, ethnic (Jewish), translations. Buys 1-2 mss/issue. Receives approximately 10 unsolicited fiction mss each month. Length: 500-750 words.
How to Contact: Send complete ms with SASE. Reports in 2 months on mss. Free sample copy with SASE. Free guidelines with legal-sized SASE.
Payment: $50-125. 3 free author's copies. 25¢ charge for each extra copy.
Terms: Pays on acceptance for first rights. Publication copyrighted.
Tips: Mss are rejected because they are "too long, too sentimental or didactic."

WYOMING RURAL ELECTRIC NEWS (WREN), Wyoming Rural Electric Association, 340 W. B St., Suite 101, Casper WY 82601. (307)234-6152. Editor-in-Chief: Gale Eisenhauer. Magazine for rural Wyoming people, people who use rural electric power. Publishes a variety of material: features on western people, places, historicals, short fiction and some poetry; energy and conservation material pertinent to readers. Published monthly. Circ. 27,000.
Needs: Adventure, ethnic, historical (general), humor/satire, literary, men's, western, women's, energy. "Fiction must appeal in one form or another to our audience of rural Wyomingites." Receives approximately 6 unsolicited fiction mss/month. Buys 1 ms/issue (maximum); approximately 8 mss/year. Length: 750 words minimum; 2,000 words maximum; 1,600 words average. Occasionally critiques rejected mss.
How to Contact: Send complete ms with SASE. Simultaneous and photocopied submissions OK. "We prefer not to use previously published work, but will if it is exactly something we are looking for." Reports in 4 weeks on mss. Free sample copy with 8½x11 SASE and 35¢ postage. Free fiction guidelines with SASE.
Payment: $25 minimum; 4 contributor's copies.
Terms: Pays on acceptance for first rights or one-time rights.

YANKEE MAGAZINE, Yankee, Inc., Dublin NH 03444. Editor: Judson D. Hale. Fiction Editor: Deborah Navas Karr. Entertaining and informative New England regional of current issues, people, history, antiques, crafts for general reading audience. Monthly. Estab. 1935. Circ. 850,000.
Needs: Literary. Fiction is to be set in New England or compatible with the area. No religious/inspirational, formula fiction or stereotypical dialect, novels or novellas. Buys 1 ms/issue, 12 mss/year. Length: 2,000-4,500 words.
How to Contact: Send complete ms with SASE. Reports in 3 weeks on mss. Free sample copy and guidelines.
Payment: $500-750.
Terms: Pays on acceptance for first rights.
Tips: "Read previous 10 stories in *Yankee* and keep writing until you write well. Emphasis should be on character development rather than plot. Fiction must be realisitc and reflect life as it is—complexities and ambiguities inherent." Fiction prize awarded to best story published each year.

YOUNG AMBASSADOR, Good News Broadcasting Co., Box 82808, Lincoln NE 68501. (402)474-4567. Editor: Melvin A. Jones. Managing Editor: David Lambert. "It's designed to aid the spiritual growth of young teen Christian readers by presenting Biblical principles." 11 issues/year. Estab. 1946. Circ. 80,000.
Needs: Religious/inspirational. "Stories must be grounded in Biblical Christianity. We will not buy anything that doesn't have more than a merely moral perspective. Also, stories should feature teens in the 14-17 year range." Buys 3-4 mss/issue, 35-40 mss/year. Receives 50-60 unsolicited fiction mss each month. Length: up to 2,000 words. Critiques rejected mss "when there is time."
How to Contact: Send complete ms with SASE. Reports in 2 months. Free sample copy and guidelines.
Payment: 4-7¢/word for unassigned fiction. More for assignments.

Terms: Pays on acceptance for first and second serial (reprint) rights. Publication copyrighted.
Tips: Mss are rejected because "plots are not original, craftsmanship is poor, there is no spiritual emphasis, writing doesn't appeal to teens." Teen fiction writers under 18 may enter annual contest.

YOUNG AND ALIVE, Christian Record Braille Foundation, Inc., 4444 S. 52nd St., Lincoln NE 68506. Editor: Richard Kaiser. Magazine for blind and visually impaired young adults; published in braille and large print for an interdenominational Christian audience. Monthly.
Needs: "Need all forms of stories, including serials, parables, satires; stories usually based on tension or conflict provoked by the clash of Christian principles and people, situations, or ideas which are in opposition. We seek interesting, credible stories of an interesting manner with themes familiar to Christian youngsters." Receives approximately 75 unsolicited fiction mss each month. Length: 1,400 words maximum. Critiques rejected mss "when there is time."
How to Contact: Query with SASE. Free guidelines with SASE.
Payment: Pays 3-5¢/word.
Terms: Pays on acceptance. Publication copyrighted.
Tips: Mss are rejected because they are "poorly written, with little or no plot."

THE YOUNG CRUSADER, National Woman's Christian Temperance Union, 1730 Chicago Ave., Evanston IL 60201. (312)864-1396. Editor-in-Chief: Mrs. Kermit S. Edgar. Managing Editor: Michael C. Vitucci. Character building material showing high morals and sound values; inspirational, informational nature articles and stories for the 6-12 year olds. Monthly. Estab. 1887. Circ. 10,000.
Needs: Juvenile. Stories should be naturally written pieces not saccharine or preachy. Buys 3-4 mss/issue, 60 mss/year. Length: 600-800 words.
How to Contact: Send complete ms with SASE. Reports in 6 months or longer on mss. Free sample copy with SASE
Payment: Pays 1¢/word and free author's copy.
Terms: Pays on publication. "If I like the story and use it, I'm very lenient and allow the author to use it elsewhere."

YOUNG JUDAEAN, Hadassah Zionist Youth Commission, 50 W. 58th St., New York NY 10019. (212)355-7900, ext. 452. Editor: Mordecai Newman. Magazine. "*Young Judaean* is for members of the Young Judaea Zionist youth movement, ages 9-12." Published 7 times/year. Circ. 4,000.
Needs: Adventure, ethnic, fantasy, historical, humor/satire, juvenile, prose poem, religious/inspirational, science fiction, suspense/mystery, translations. "All stories must have Jewish relevance." Receives 3-4 unsolicited fiction mss/month. Buys 1 ms/issue; 7 mss/year. Length: 500 words minimum; 1,500 words maximum; 1,000 words average.
How to Contact: Send complete ms with SASE. Simultaneous, photocopied and previously published submissions OK. Reports in 4 weeks on mss. Sample copy for 75¢. Fiction guidelines free.
Payment: Pays $20-40; 4 free contributor's copies; 75¢ charge for extras.
Terms: Pays on publication. Publication copyrighted.
Tips: "Stories must be of Jewish interest—lively and accessible to children without being condescending."

YOUNG MISS, Griner and Jahr USA, Inc., 685 Third Ave., New York NY 10017. Editor: Phyllis Schneider. Magazine for teenage girls (ages 12-17). Published 10 times/year.
Needs: Contemporary, young adult (particularly romance). No explicit sex. Buys 1-2 mss/issue. Receives hundreds of unsolicited fiction mss each month. Length: 2,000-2,500 words. Sometimes recommends other markets.
How to Contact: Send complete ms with SASE to Deborah Purcell, Features/Fiction Editor. Reports in 6 weeks on mss. Sample copy $1.25 with free writer's guidelines.

Close-up

Deborah Purcell
Young Miss

High atop the Third Avenue office building in a bright office with a commanding view of New York, Deborah Purcell spends at least half of her work week as fiction editor of *Young Miss* Magazine. Purcell, whose full title is features/fiction editor, is part of the staff that revamped the teen magazine in 1981. *Young Miss* now has a new look, format and a broader audience—12-17 year-old girls.

"We plan to grow," says Purcell, the one-person fiction department who tackles the mounting slush piles daily and selects the one story for each monthly issue. "And we're looking for more fiction," she says, despite the average 35-50 unsolicited manuscripts she receives a week.

Y.M. readers respond especially well to romances, which are "of paramount concern to a teenage girl." Purcell would also like to see stories concerning adolescent's personal struggles—to define their values and goals; to adjust to life's changes; to establish their identities at home and at school. (Either young women or young men may be the protagonists.) Animal stories are popular with *YM*'s younger readers, as are adventure, mystery and science fiction stories, but those are harder to pull off with a good clear story line in the short shorts of 1,000 to 1,500 words or even the longer stories of 3,000 words (maximum length), especially by beginning writers. Subjects to avoid are drug and alcohol abuse, explicit sex and teen pregnancy.

"Remember," says Purcell, "a portion of our audience is on the youngish side and still has a kind of rosy glowing view of the world. Stories should have a basic positivism rather than a worldly gloomy view," but they should also reflect reality. Young women's lives and problems are more complex than just not having a date for the prom. Short fiction should demonstrate the real ups and downs of life.

Adult writers—men and women—write the majority of the published fiction in *Young Miss*; teen writers may show potential, but generally are not ready for publication. Purcell is quick to acknowledge talent that she sees, however, and if a manuscript has an intriguing style, but is not right for the magazine, she will write an encouraging note to the author with a market suggestion. If there is a story with obvious potential, Purcell will suggest specific revisions and ask for a rewrite on speculation.

Deborah Purcell, a former editor at *Weight Watchers* and CBS Inc., is conscientious, thorough and enthusiastic about her work, but her job—like most editors'—is very demanding; she also selects and edits nonfiction features for each issue. And although one of her greatest joys is accepting a short story by a beginning writer and nurturing a new career, she says justifiably: "It's not realistic to expect a lot of personal feedback from an editor. He/she simply doesn't have the time to critique or always give encouragement."

Young Miss readers particularly enjoy the fiction—and they want more. Therefore plans for the future may include a fiction bonus issue and occasionally two stories a month. Purcell is receptive to beginners to fill the demands, but she reminds interested short story writers: "Fiction is a craft. It's not just a set of innate talents and the 'givens' of writing. You have to do so much work in addition to that. . . . It's a lifetime effort." Practice, rework and then submit.

Payment: $250-500. 2 free author's copies.

Terms: Pays on acceptance for first rights. Publication copyrighted.

Tips: Mss are rejected because of "awkward style, trite themes, undeveloped plots, and weak characterizations. Poor understanding of teen behavior and concerns—resulting in outdated dialogue and themes."

YOUR FAMILY, Republican Press, Box 32083, Mobeni-4060, South Africa. Tel. Durban 422041. Editor: Angela Waller-Paton. Magazine for informed housewives: cooking, crafts, homemaking. Monthly. Estab. 1973. Circ. 280,000.

Needs: Humor/satire (family situation), romance, women's. "Short punchy stories: unpredictable; twist ending; historical romance themes; family themes. No unhappy endings." Receives 20-30 unsolicited fiction mss/month. Buys 1 ms/issue; 14 mss plus 1 serial for special issue/year.

How to Contact: Send complete ms to *YF* c/o George Snor, 150 E. 35th St., Suite 210, New York NY 10016, U.S.A. (American representative) with SASE. Photocopied and previously published submissions OK. Reports within a varied amount of weeks on mss.

Payment: Pays $100 maximum.

Terms: Pays on acceptance for first South African English speaking rights. Publication copyrighted.

> ❝ *Why do I go on writing? Because I enjoy it as my life, and in the hope that if I try again I will choose the right words or a tone, a gesture that will open the door of a closed room, connect to the world, give another some small revelation or unexpected delight.*
>
> *—Maureen Howard* ❞

Small press

Small presses continue to enjoy dynamic growth each year. Bowker's International Standard Book Number division assigns more than 110 ISBN's (numbers issued to new books) a month to *new* houses. More than 1,300 independent presses demonstrate annually the small press credo of publishing freedom as expressed by Overlook Press' motto: "What you can do, or dream you can, begin it."

Because small press representation is spread over all the states, their literary power is fragmented and decentralized. The heaviest concentration is in New York, Massachusetts and especially in the San Francisco and Santa Barbara sections of California—a fact that prompted Patricia Holt, book editor of the *San Francisco Chronicle* and *Examiner* to say that the most adventurous and innovative publishing today comes from an area west of the Sierras.

Individually, small presses tend to publish just a few books each year. Their subjects, however, are diverse, inclusive and specialized. What they do have in common is their strength of purpose and sense of real commitment, a particular care for the writing and publishing processes, and direction in addressing the real needs of the reader. "We see a lot of good books going to smaller houses because their authors get disgusted with the big houses," says Robert Sheldon, marketing director of Bookpeople, a distributing company for small presses. The smaller operations "fill the niches the big houses leave empty."

Full steam ahead

The literary successes of the small presses offer great competition to the commercial presses. However, that fact receives little publicity because news of commercial blockbusters and the industry's self-promotion eclipse word about serious literary works from the independent houses with their limited promotional budgets. The result is an information gap. While many of the major publishers are publicly ailing, the small presses are actually enjoying relative good health. Sales were up in the last year, and about 25%

of the total number of exhibitors at the American Book Association conference last year were independent publishers.

The growth rate, or freedom to expand, evokes the general mood of optimism. Editors' excitement and enthusiasm, and the byproduct of great pleasure in their work, fuel their interests to continue and expand. In the last few years—especially with the assistance of groups and events like COSMEP (Committee of Small Magazine Editors and Publishers), national and regional conferences and bookfairs—editors have become more professional and resourceful in business and accounting. They are more realistic today about government funding, or the lack thereof, and are not devastated by cutbacks.

The small presses are, of course, affected by the economic downturn, but running a business on a shoestring is a way of life. "We're always short of money," says one editor. "It's nothing new." It's often a matter of learning to market and promote books more strategically. The general feeling is, as Carol Marron of Carnival Press says: "Damn the economic torpedoes, full steam ahead." The failure rate of small presses, according to Richard Morris of COSMEP, is no higher than that of other businesses. Several small press editors report that they foresaw the crunch and planned ahead; others even plan for expansion in the coming year.

Expansion

Because the small presses are singularly dedicated to producing high quality books, work published out of love and initiative, they are for the most part beyond the whims and dictates of the current trends that govern the commercial publishing world. They are trend-setters themselves, innovators in literature. Nevertheless even the independent houses notice certain themes and recurring subjects in the manuscripts that come in and in ones they choose to publish.

In general, editors say they are seeing better quality manuscripts, and many regret having to return material simply because of lack of space, time or money. In specialty books feminist, utopian, lesbian, and young adult feminist novels are "growing apace." Small independent bookstores report increased sales in gay fiction. Fantasy, science fiction, the occult phenomena, and erotica—popular escapist subjects in tight times—continue to sell. And strong regional markets in Hispanic fiction are developing in the US.

In structure editors see a return to traditional values, a rejection of gore, violence, mayhem, too much realism. In style they notice more clarity of narration and acknowledge that much of the experimental work, especially by unknowns, does not sell well. With tighter budgets, editors find they have less freedom to experiment, and will publish only the highest quality they can find.

In the last year more university presses began to publish fiction. Encouraged by the success of Louisiana State University Press' find in 1980 of John Kennedy Toole's award-winning *A Confederacy of Dunces*, more university presses are now seeking novels defined as serious, non-genre, non-commercial fiction, novels and short story collections. To start, they plan to publish one to four titles a year and expand slowly.

Study and research

Small press editors offer their reasons for rejection: The writing is plain, boring, sophomoric; there is poor thought, inappropriate material, or lack of involvement with the reader; the plot is unorganized and not carried through; there is repetition in theme, especially in children's books; or the manuscript is an "unoriginal clonish copy of pre-marketed garbage rampant in the publishing world today." *Originality* and *quality* they seek.

To avoid rejection, the editors suggest that you:

- *Study* the individual specifications in the *Fiction Writer's Market* listings to know exactly what a certain press needs. If available, ask for a book catalog and review the titles and subjects; or visit small press/independent bookstores and familiarize yourself with material and subjects published by small presses.
- Have something of value to say in your manuscript, and not just a need to say it.
- Avoid too much subjectivity; it limits the style.
- Know the language, how it is used; strive for beauty of phraseology without pretension.
- Practice and master skills and techniques; but *don't* imitate or copy. "Be, in a word, yourself."
- Be patient—and don't expect a quick reply. Most independent presses are small and understaffed. Editors may hold down other jobs to keep their businesses going, and are very busy.
- Observe requests for a professionally prepared manuscript and a SASE (or IRC for foreign presses) for all correspondence. Small presses are simply not financially equipped to handle return postage.
- Be realistic in your financial expectations. Small presses offer opportunities for publishing serious fiction, but payment may be only in contributor's copies.
- Be sure to research the markets before signing a contract or reaching an agreement. Get the specifics in writing; have the royalty agreement spelled out. Be aware of the broad publishing terms and expressions: "By arrangement and mutual agreement"; "We'll work things out with the author"; or "Honorarium awarded if grant money available." Thoroughly understanding the exact terms for a book manuscript will help make your publishing experience a favorable one.
- Study the sample small press book contract that follows.

small press

> *It takes genius to make an end—to give the touch of inevitableness to the conclusion of any work of art.*
> —*Neitzsche*

Sample book publishing agreement; guidelines for publishers and authors

by Richard Balkin

The number of small presses, depending upon which sources you quote, ranges from 1,500 to 3,000. Their publishing philosophies, areas of interest, and methods of operation are almost as diverse. Equally varied are the contracts they issue to authors, which can range from a brief letter to a six-page document, though some presses are still content with a handshake or a phone call.

A need exists for a model contract that can be modified or negotiated to suit the individual small press publisher or author or one that can merely be used as a guideline. The ground rules in commercial trade book publishing are somewhat different from those of small presses, and this contract was drawn up—after being reviewed by over a dozen representative small press publishers—with three principles in mind:

a) to be flexible enough to suit virtually any small press or author, whether the subject is fiction, nonfiction, or poetry;

b) to translate and simplify the "legalese" and small print that make most trade contracts incomprehensible to anyone who is not a lawyer;

c) to provide for any contingency.

This last principle accounts, in part, for the length of this contract. Misunderstandings and problems are more likely to occur when the parties to an agreement have not clearly spelled out their mutual obligations. Furthermore, unexpected developments or successes can complicate or sour the friendliest of author/publisher relations unless these contingencies have already been provided for in the contract.

Richard Balkin has had his own literary agency for ten years; he represents more than 50 writers. Previously, he was a book sales representative and executive editor for Bobbs-Merrill. Balkin, a frequent lecturer at writers' conferences, has also taught publishing courses at colleges and written A Writer's Guide to Book Publishing *plus articles for national magazines.*

In addition, it is especially important to remember that compromise is the essential ingredient in any negotiation between an author and a publisher, for the straightforward, businesslike and ethical agreement that you seek.

BOOK PUBLISHING AGREEMENT

This agreement is made on _____

between (Author) _____

residing at _____

and (Publisher) _____

doing business at _____

for a Work tentatively titled _____

This Form © 1982 by Richard Balkin
Published by Dustbooks, Box 100, Paradise, CA 95969
Additional Forms Available at 60¢ each.

Publisher and Author agree as follows:

1. GRANT OF RIGHTS

The Author hereby grants and assigns to the Publisher the sole and exclusive right to print, publish, distribute, sell or license the Work, in book form, under its own name or imprints, throughout the world, in the following territories:
A. U.S.A., its territories and possessions, the Philippine Republic and Canada
B. The British Commonwealth of Nations
C. Nonexclusively in English throughout the rest of the world
D. Non-English-speaking countries for foreign-language editions

2. PUBLICATION

Publisher agrees to publish the Work, at its own expense, within _____ months after acceptance of the final copy, in a style and manner, and at such price, as it deems best suited to the sale thereof.

3. MANUSCRIPT AND DELIVERY

The Author agrees to submit/has already submitted a manuscript suitable for publication, in form and content satisfactory to the Publisher, consisting of approximately _____ words/pages on or by _____. The Author agrees to furnish the following camera-ready artwork (unless otherwise agreed upon): line drawings, photos, charts, graphs or tables, and to furnish any consent forms, permissions, or copyright assignment necessary or required by the Publisher. If payment is necessary for artwork, permissions, or other similar documents, the costs shall be:

A) assumed by the Author

B) shared equally between Author and Publisher

C) paid by the Publisher and deducted from future royalties

4. COPYRIGHT

The Publisher agrees to copyright the Work in the name of _____ and to secure its rights and the Author's rights under the U.S. Copyright Act. Both Author and Publisher agree to execute all papers and documents as may be necessary in order to protect or assign the rights therein.

5. ALTERATIONS AND INDEX

The Author agrees to read, correct, and return galley proofs of the Work within _____ weeks of receipt. All changes requested or made by the Author in galleys (except those resulting from the Publisher's or typesetter's errors), in excess of 10% of the cost of composition, shall be charged to the Author's royalty account. The cost of all changes requested or made by the Author at any subsequent stage of book production shall be assumed by the Author and paid within thirty days of receipt of an itemized invoice. The Author agrees to prepare an index, if suitable and requested by the Publisher, at the Author's own expense, or may ask the Publisher to have one prepared, in which case the cost will be deducted from future royalties.

6. EDITING

The Publisher has the right to edit the work so that it conforms to proper English usage, grammar and punctuation, but shall make no substantive changes in the text or artwork without the consent of the Author.

7. COMPETING WORK

The Author agrees, during the term of this agreement, not to print or publish, or cause to be printed or published, any portion of this Work (whether revised, enlarged, abridged, or corrected), or any other Work that might compete with or reduce the sales of the Work covered by this agreement.

8. AUTHOR'S REPRESENTATIONS

The Author represents and warrants to be the sole Author and proprietor of this Work, and to have full power to make this agreement and grant of rights, and that—to the best of the Author's knowledge—it in no way infringes upon any copyright or proprietary right of others, or contains anything libelous or in violation of any right of privacy. The Author agrees to exempt the Publisher from penalties and hold the Publisher harmless against all liabilities, losses, damages, and expense of any kind whatsoever resulting from any claim, action, or proceeding asserted or instituted and sustained on the ground that the said Work violates any copyright or proprietary right, or contains anything libelous or in violation of any right of privacy. The Author further agrees to cooperate fully in the defense thereof.

In case of any infringement of the copyright of this Work by others, the Author shall have the right to bring action based on such infringement. In such event the legal costs and the net proceeds of any recovery shall be divided equally between the Author and Publisher. If the Author does not take action within fifteen days of being notified of the infringement, the Publisher may at its discretion, sue or employ such remedies as deemed expedient; all such suits or proceedings shall be at joint expense, and the net proceeds shall be divided equally. However, the Author shall not be liable for any expenditure in excess of $500 undertaken by the Publisher for such purposes without his previous written consent.

9. ROYALTIES

The Publisher agrees to pay the following royalties on all copies sold minus returns:

A. Hardcover edition:

i _____% of the retail price on the first _____ copies sold

ii _____% of the retail price on the next _____ copies sold

iii _____% of the retail price thereafter

B. Paperback edition:

i _____% of the retail price on the first _____ copies sold

ii _____% of the retail price thereafter

C. Copies only:

i 10% of the number of copies on the first print run, and 10% of each subsequent reprinting

D. With the following exceptions:

i on copies sold at a discount of _____or more of the retail price, _____% of the amount the Publisher receives

ii on copies sold for export to Canada or overseas, _____% of the amount the Publisher receives

iii sale of overstock or remainders: _____% of the amount the Publisher receives, but no royalty shall be paid on copies sold at or below cost

iv gratis copies: no royalty shall be paid on the free copies given to the Author, or the copies given away for promotional purposes (such as review and publicity copies)

v direct sales to individual retail customers by mail or by advertisements in newspapers or magazines or on radio and television: _____ of the amount the Publisher receives

vi no royalty shall be paid when the Publisher, at its discretion, permits reproduction of the Work, without charge, in braille or other forms for use by the physically handicapped.

10. ADVANCE AGAINST ROYALTIES

The Publisher agrees to pay the Author the sum of _____ as an advance against future royalties, as follows:

_____ within 30 days of receipt of signed contract

_____ within 30 days of acceptance of a final manuscript

_____ within 30 days of book publication

small press

11. SUBSIDIARY RIGHTS

Proceeds from the sale or licensing of the following rights shall be divided as follows:

	Author	Publisher
A. Publication of parts of the Work in magazines, newspapers, or journals before publication in book form	_____%	_____%
B. Publication in English by British or other foreign publishers	_____%	_____%
C. Publication in foreign languages by other publishers	_____%	_____%
D. Reprints in hardcover, trade paperback, or mass-market editions	_____%	_____%
E. Motion picture, dramatic, radio, and television rights	_____%	_____%
F. Publication of parts of the Work after book publication in anthologies, newspapers, magazines, journals, etc.	_____%	_____%
G. Book-club rights	_____%	_____%
H. Commercial rights	_____%	_____%
I. Storage and retrieval systems, including microfilm or other electronic means	_____%	_____%

The Publisher agrees to secure the Author's approval for the sale or licensing of any subsidiary rights, such approval not to be unreasonably withheld. All rights not herein granted are reserved for the Author.

The Publisher agrees to pay the Author's share of the sale or licensing of any of the heretofore mentioned rights when the Author's share exceeds _____, within _____ days receipt thereof, after deducting any unearned advance, and to furnish the Author, upon written request, with copies of any contract from such sale or license.

12. STATEMENT OF ACCOUNTS

After publication, the Publisher agrees to render semiannual/annual statements for sales made during the preceding six-month/twelve-month periods ending _____ and _____, and within 90 days thereof to furnish such statement with payments of all sums due thereon, unless the amount due shall be less than $10, in which case it shall be paid on the following statement. The Author or his representative may, at a time mutually convenient, inspect the Publisher's records relating to his account, but no more than once a year.

13. FREE COPIES AND PURCHASES

Upon publication, the Publisher shall give _____ free hardcover and _____ free paperback copies to the Author. The Author may purchase additional copies of the Work at a discount of _____%, for resale or personal use; no royalties shall be paid on these copies. Shipping costs are to be paid by the _____. Payments for Author's purchases are to be subtracted from the royalties of the same accounting period or paid within ninety days of date of invoice, whichever comes first.

14. TERMINATION AND REVERSION OF RIGHTS

If the Publisher fails to publish the Work within _____ months of the time period of Clause # 2, and does not inform the Author of the reasons for the delay and show reasonable progress in the production of the Work, and if such delays are not the result of conditions beyond the control of the Publisher (such as strikes, shortage of materials, fire, or flood), then the Author, upon written notice to the Publisher, will have the option to inform the Publisher that if the Work is not published within _____ months after such notice, all rights herein granted will terminate and revert to the Author.

If the published Work shall be out of stock for a period exceeding _____ months, or out of print, or not listed for sale in the Publisher's catalog, and not available for sale in volume form as the result of any license or subsidiary right, then the Author may so inform the Publisher in writing who shall declare within _____ days in writing whether it intends to reprint the Work. Failure to give such notice or to reprint the Work within _____ months shall cause all rights herein granted to revert to the Author at the expiration of said periods, without further procedure. Upon termination, the Author may, within 30 days of notification, purchase the plates, negatives, tapes, or remaining copies at cost; otherwise, the Publisher may dispose of these materials at its discretion, but subject to the royalty rates in provision # 9Diii.

15. BANKRUPTCY AND DEFAULT OF PAYMENT

If the Publisher fails to pay all or part of the Author's advance as designated in Clause # 10, or the Publisher fails to render semiannual/annual statements or defaults in the payment of royalties due with such statements, then the Author has the option, upon written request, to demand such payment. If the Publisher fails to deliver such payment within _____ days of request, or declares bankruptcy or liquidates its business for any reason whatsoever, all rights herein granted shall terminate and revert to the Author without further procedure and without prejudice to the Author's claim for monies due.

16. ASSIGNMENT AND SUCCESSORS

No assignment of this contract shall be binding upon either party without the written consent of both the Author and the Publisher, except that the Author may assign any monies due under this agreement to any person or persons.

The provisions of this agreement shall be binding upon the Author and the Author's legal representatives, heirs, and assigns, as well as upon the successors and assigns of the Publisher.

17. LAWS GOVERNING AGREEMENT AND ARBITRATION

This agreement will be governed by and interpreted in accordance with the laws of the State of _____. In the event of disputes or disagreements arising from the agreement, both Author and Publisher consent to settle such disputes under the auspices of the American Arbitration Association, and to abide by its judgment.

18. COMPLETE AGREEMENT

This agreement represents the complete understanding of both parties, and no modification, deletion, addition, or change will be valid except in writing and signed by both parties or herewith inserted as a rider(s) to this agreement:

RIDER(S)

In witness hereof, the parties affix their signatures.

_____   _____
Author/Date   Publisher/Date

_____
Author's Social Security #

Small press contract guidelines for publishers and authors

The "boilerplate," as a printed but not completed contract is generally called, is a flexible and negotiable document. Since the number of small presses is legion, and the needs of the individual Publishers and Authors so varied, this contract was designed to accommodate virtually any book, from a chapbook to an encyclopedia. Therefore, though its length and number of clauses and provisions may be too skimpy for one publisher, or too detailed for another, it should be a simple matter to delete those provisions not applicable (all such deletions or changes made in the boilerplate, except for filling in blanks, are generally initialed in the margin by both Author and Publisher). Conversely, riders, when necessary, may simply be added to the contract. Furthermore, some individual clauses or provisions are constructed so that the Author or Publisher can choose the appropriate phrase and merely delete the superfluous one; for example, "semiannual/annual" (referring to the rendering of royalty statements).

As with any contract, a number of clauses or provisions contain blanks to be filled in either with percentages (such as the Author's and Publisher's share of subsidiary rights), or with numbers or dates (such as when royalty statements will be issues), or with information appropriate to the particular project (such as in whose name the copyright will be taken out).

Many of these blanks require no discussion here, but for the benefit of Authors who are unfamiliar with conventional contracts and for those Publshers who wish to know what many of their colleagues generally do, it may help to discuss here some common features.

1. Grant of rights—Unless the Author has reason to believe that he or she can more effectively license rights overseas, it is common to grant the Publisher World Rights (A, B, C, and D), and to share any income derived from licensing or selling the Work.

9. Royalties—Many small presses pay a flat 10%-of-list-price royalty (some few pay on "net receipts"; i.e., the amount remaining after the discount given to the bookseller or consumer) on both the hardcover and the paperback, regardless of whether the sale is to bookstores, to individuals by mail, or even to Canada. However, it is not uncommon to see:

A. An escalating royalty for the hardcover (such as 10% of the first 5,000 copies sold, 12½% of the next 5,000, and 15% thereafter).

B. An escalating royalty for the paperback, beginning at 6%, 7½%, or 8%, escalating by 2% or 2½% after the sale of anywhere from 5,000 to 10,000 copies.

C. Royalties paid only in the form of free copies to the Author, usually amounting to 10% of the first and subsequent print runs.

D. Exceptions; that is, reduced royalties where discounts exceed 50%, when sales are made outside of the U.S.A., when books are remaindered, or when individual copies are sold by mail to consumers.

Share of profits. A percentage of profits in lieu of royalties; that is, after the sale of X number of copies, when the publishing house has recouped its costs (composition, paper, printing, binding, etc.), it pays the Author from 20% to 50% of the net income derived from additional sales (this provision can be added to the contract as a rider).

10. Advances—An advance against royalties is not conventional at many small presses, but when given, may range from $250 to $2,000. One rule of thumb for calculating a fair advance is to figure out the amount of royalties the book will earn from its first printing or first year's sales (which the publisher guesstimates), and then deduct 20% to 25% from that amount, to account for returns from booksellers.

11. Subsidiary rights—A & E (First Serial Rights and Performance Rights): These are sometimes retained by the Author (i.e., 100% Author, 0% Publisher). When the Publisher controls these rights, the split rnges from 90/10 to 80/20, although some houses are less generous.

B, C, & H (Publication in the U.K., in a Foreign Language, or Commercial Rights, such as the cornucopia of products engendered by the Peanuts books and cartoons): The Author/Publisher split usually ranges from 80/20 to 75/25.

D, F, G, & I (Reprint rights, Second Serial rights, Book-club rights, and Electronic rights) are generally shared 50/50.

Filling in the remainder of the blanks is a question of common sense, what is conventional practice for a particular Publisher, what seems fair and is negotiated by both parties, and what is suitable for the particular book involved.

Three common riders are:

A. **Revision**—If, in the opinion of the Publisher, the Work needs revision during the term of this agreement, the Author agrees to revise the Work or supply the new matter required. If, for any reason, the Author does not do so within a reasonable amount of time, the Publisher may cause such revision to be made, and may deduct the expense thereof from the first royalties accruing from the sales of such revised edition.

B. **Option**—The Author agrees to give the Publisher an option to publish the Author's next work at terms to be mutually agreed upon. Such option shall be exercised within 45 days of receipt of an extended outline (for a work of nonfiction) or on receipt of a completed manuscript (for a work of fiction or poetry).

C. **Reserve against returns**—The Publisher may set up a reserve which, in its opinion, will allow for returns during the three royalty accounting periods following the first publication of the Work. The reserve shall not exceed _____ percent of the earnings due the Author in the respective royalty period.

small press

ACHERON PRESS, Bear Creek at the Kettle, Friendsville MD 21531. (301)689-3774. Fiction Editor: J. Bramann. Estab. 1981. Publishes paperpack originals. Plans 1 first novel this year. Averages 5 total titles, 1 fiction title each year. Occasionally critiques mss for $60, except for short pieces.
Needs: Adventure, comics, contemporary, experimental, juvenile (historical), literary, suspense/mystery, young adult (problem novels). Recently published: *Gainful Unemployment*, by J. Bramann and James Ralston.
How to Contact: Query first or submit outline/synopsis and sample chapters or complete ms. SASE always. Photocopied submissions OK. Reports "as promptly as possible, but sometimes at irregular intervals because of frequent traveling."
Terms: Negotiable. Free book catalog.
Tips: "Form: Have a story (plot) and/or wit. Content: a serious problem, not just 'a good story.' "

AGAPÉ, Subsidiary includes Cypress Books, 921 3rd St., Franklin LA 70538. (318)828-4170. Fiction Editors: Bernard Broussard and Ray Broussard. Estab. 1980. Publishes hardcover and paperback originals. Plans 2 first novels this year. Averages 8-10 total titles, 3-4 fiction titles each year. Sometimes critiques rejected mss.
Needs: Adventure, contemporary, juvenile (historical), religious/inspirational, women's. No erotica, fantasy.
How to Contact: Submit complete ms with SASE. Simultaneous submissions OK. Reports in 2 weeks on mss.
Terms: Pays in royalties. Subsidy publishes "3-4 books/year."
Tips: "We publish books dealing with (1) love of neighbor as the touchstone of morality, (2)

works showing how there is mystery present in all our human relationships, (3) works promoting international peace, interracial and social justice, human liberation, creative love, and the celebration of life.''

AKIBA PRESS, Box 13086, Oakland CA 94661. (415)339-1283. Fiction Editor: Sheila Baker. Estab. 1978. Publishes hardcover and paperback originals and paperback reprints. Plans 2 first novels this year. Averages 2-3 total titles, 1 fiction title each year. Sometimes critiques rejected mss.
Needs: Ethnic (Jewish), historical (general), psychic/supernatural, short story collections, young adult (historical). No erotic or gothic romances.
How to Contact: Query first with SASE, then submit outline/synopsis and 3 sample chapters with SASE. Simultaneous and photocopied submissions OK. Reports in 2 weeks on queries; 6 weeks on mss.
Terms: Pays in royalties of 10% minimum, 12% maximum. Free book catalog on request.
Tips: ''We like good fiction and feel people are becoming more responsive.''

ALLEGANY MOUNTAIN PRESS, 111 N. 10th St., Olean NY 14760. (716)372-0935. Imprints include Uroboros Books. Editorial Director: Ford F. Ruggieri. Estab. 1972. Publishes hardcover and paperback originals. Number of titles: 2 in 1981; 3 in 1982. Encourages new writers. Sometimes comments on rejected mss.
Needs: Literary, experimental, erotica, humor/satire. ''We want to see fiction with a serious literary intent. Though we are interested in books that will sell, we are not interested in 'bestsellers' if it means pandering to bad taste. Previously we have only published poetry in book form, mainly because we haven't received the kind of ms we'd like to publish in the novel.''
How to Contact: Submit outline/synopsis with 2-3 sample chapters. No simultaneous submissions; photocopied submissions OK. Reports in 6 weeks on mss.
Terms: Pays in 50 author's copies and 10-15% royalties. Advance: 50 copies of book. Book catalog for 6x9 SASE plus 38¢ postage.
Tips: ''Study the market you're aiming for and look to the people who have written the best things in that field as a guide. We are looking for work that is innovative in form and content. Don't waste your time or money sending us pop or hack type fiction. We will only consider work that we believe will have a significant cultural impact.''

AND BOOKS, 702 S. Michigan, South Bend, IN 46618. Editorial Director: Janos Szebedinsky. Estab. 1977. Publishes paperback originals. Number of titles: 20 in 1982. Sometimes comments on rejected mss.
Needs: Experimental, practical mystery, fantasy, occasional translations. ''No romance, please.''
How to Contact: Prefers submission of outline/synopsis and sample chapters with SASE before complete ms. Simultaneous and photocopied submissions OK. Reports in 4 weeks on mss.
Terms: Pays 5-10% royalties; no advance. Book catalog for legal-sized SASE plus 38¢ postage.
Tips: ''Satire and humor mixed with science fiction would be a welcome change. Remember, impatience is the pitfall of writers. We presently are publishing more non-fiction paperbacks but continue to look for good fiction.''

ANDREW MOUNTAIN PRESS, Box 14353, Hartford CT 06114. Editor: Candace Catlin Hall. Estab. 1979. Publishes paperback originals. Averages 3 total titles, 1 fiction title each year. Sometimes critiques rejected mss.
Needs: Juvenile (picture book). ''We don't want to see anything except children's picture books.'' Recently published: *The Furry Wind* (children's picture book).
How to Contact: Submit complete ms with SASE. Simultaneous and photocopied submissions OK. Reports in 2 months on mss.
Terms: Pays in author's copies. Free writer's guidelines for SASE.
Tips: ''Find out what sells—go to libraries and look through the books that the library has

bought—then try to find a suitable publisher. Children's books should not be moralistic—update your styles." Many mss are rejected because "submissions are outdated or just don't have a different twist."

ANGEL PRESS, PUBLISHERS, 171 Webster St., Monterey CA 93940. (408)372-1658. Editorial Director: André D'Angelo. Estab. 1962. Publishes hardcover and paperback originals. Number of titles: 1 in 1980, 2 in 1981. Encourages new writers. Sometimes comments on rejected mss.
Needs: Feminist, gay/lesbian, erotica, religious/inspirational, satire, controversial.
How to Contact: Query with SASE. Simultaneous and photocopied submissions OK. Reports in several months on mss.
Terms: Negotiates royalties. Free book catalog.
Tips: "All beginning writers should get professional criticism from knowledgeable editors before submitting a ms. A professional opinion carries a lot of weight in deciding what to publish. All submissions must be accompanied by a complete resume of the writer's writing background and an analysis of the potential market. Furthermore, we need to know what the author intends to do to promote sales: radio, shows, public appearances, etc."

ANGST WORLD LIBRARY, 1160 Forest Creek Rd., Selma OR 97538. Fiction Editor: Thomas Carlisle. Estab. 1974. Publishes paperback originals. Averages 1-2 total titles, 1-2 fiction titles each year. Seldom critiques rejected mss.
Needs: Experimental, fantasy, horror, literary, psychic/supernatural, science fiction, suspense/mystery. "Very limited needs. We would like to see short story or novella length pieces dealing with phenomenological existentialism *a la* Colin Wilson." No sword and sorcery science fiction or space opera. Recently published *The Twenty-Fifth Hour*, by Lawrence Russell (speculative science fiction).
How to Contact: Submit outline/synopsis and 1 sample chapter with SASE. Simultaneous and photocopied submissions OK. Reports in 1-2 months on mss.
Terms: Pays in 10 author's copies. "First edition of 250-500 copies is paid by author's copies or token royalty. Additional editions vary." Book catalog for #10 SAE and 1 first class stamp.
Tips: "Attempt to convey new ideas within a traditional format that communicates to the literate reader."

ANSUDA PUBLICATIONS, Box 158J, Harris IA 51345. Fiction Editor: Daniel Betz. Estab. 1978. Publishes paperback originals. Plans 1-2 first novels this year. Averages 3-5 total titles, 1 fiction title each year. Sometimes critiques rejected mss.
Needs: Fantasy, horror, literary, mainstream, psychic/supernatural, short story collections, suspense/mystery. "Interested mostly in fantasy, horror, psychic and supernatural. No romance, juvenile, experimental, translations or science fiction." Recently published: *Hor-Tasy*, edited by Daniel Betz (anthology of horror and fantasy stories).
How to Contact: Query first or submit outline/synopsis and 1-2 sample chapters. SASE always. Photocopied submissions OK. Reports in 1 day on queries, 1-4 weeks on mss.
Terms: Pays in royalties by arrangement and 2 author's copies. Writer's guidelines and book catalog for #10 SASE. Sample copy $2.95.

APPLE-WOOD BOOKS, INC., Box 2870, Cambridge MA 02139. (617)923-9337. Editorial Director: Phil Zuckerman. Estab. 1976. Publishes hardcover and paperback originals. Number of titles: 3 in 1981, 11 in 1982. Encourages new writers. Plans 6 novels for 1983. Sometimes comments on rejected mss.
Needs: Literary. "Could be in any category but must be literary." Recently published *The Bohemians*, by Alan Cheuse; *A Perpetual Surprise*, by Sheila Solomon Klass; and *Peter Leroy: A Serial Novel*, by Eric Kraft.
How to Contact: Query with SASE. Simultaneous and photocopied submissions OK. Reports in 2 weeks on queries, 3 months on mss.

Terms: Pays in 12 author's copies and 10-15% royalties. Book catalog for legal-sized SASE plus 38¢ postage.
Tips: "Major publishers publish very little serious fiction. We foresee more competition for publication, more genre books. Young writers should familiarize themselves with small, literary houses. Have patience. Enclose a cover letter."

APPLEZABA PRESS, Box 4134, Long Beach CA 90804. Editorial Director: Shelley Hellen. Estab. 1977. Publishes paperback originals. Number of titles: 1 in 1981.
Needs: Contemporary, literary, experimental, faction, feminist, gay/lesbian, erotica, fantasy, humor/satire, translations, short story collections. No gothic, romance, confession, inspirational. Recently published *The Cure*, by Gerald Locklin (satire).
How to Contact: Submit complete ms with SASE. No simultaneous submissions; photocopied submissions OK. Reports in 2 months.
Terms: Pays in author's copies and 10-15% royalties; no advance. Free book catalog.
Tips: "Write legibly. Cover letter with previous publications, etc. is OK, but I'm put off by the type of letter that goes to the effect: 'If you publish this ms, the both of us will get rich,' etc. Also, we have been receiving material that is satirical, black humor almost slapstick. We publish only book length material."

ARIADNE PRESS, 4817 Tallahassee Ave., Rockville MD 20853. President: Carol F. Hoover. Estab. 1976. Publishes hardcover originals. Number of titles: 1 in 1981. "Primarily interested in first novels, new writers."
Needs: Contemporary, literary, adventure, mystery, spy, historical, war, women's, feminist, humor/satire. "No short stories, only novels." Recently published *Lead Me to the Exit*, by Ellen Moore (a woman's changing role); and *The Rudelstein Affair*, by Michael Marsh (cloak-and-dagger spoof).
How to Contact: Query with SASE. Simultaneous and photocopied submissions OK. Reports in 2 weeks on queries, 1 month on mss.
Terms: Pays 10% in royalties; no advance.
Tips: "Try major publishers first. This is a shoestring operation, producing some 1,200 copies/book. Our aim is to publish first-rate, readable fiction which has not been accepted by major markets. It helps if the writer has the capacity and energy to publicize his own book and/or assist with distribution. We do receive quite a few manuscripts with a writing style of good quality. But the problem of organizing a plot which expresses the book's major themes through its characters, who develop the logic of their own actions, has usually not been solved."

AUGUST HOUSE, PUBLISHERS, INC., Imprint includes Parkhurst/Little Rock, 1010 W. Third St., Little Rock AR 72201. (501)376-4516. Fiction Editor: J. Wink. Estab. 1978. Publishes hardcover and paperback originals and paperback reprints. Encourages new writers from Arkansas exclusively. Plans 1 first novel per year. Averages 12 total titles, 4 fiction titles each year. Occasionally critiques mss for $14/hour.
Needs: Contemporary, fantasy, historical (Arkansas), humor/satire, juvenile (fantasy), religious/inspirational, short story collections, women's. Novels are directed to Arkansas readers: strictly regional emphasis. "We want important new fiction."
How to Contact: Submit outline/synopsis and 4 sample chapters with SASE. Simultaneous and photocopied submissions OK. "We report by December 1st of each year."
Terms: Pays in royalties of 4% minimum, 10% maximum. Advance is negotiable. Subsidy publishes 7-12 books/year. Writer's guidelines for # 10 SAE and 1 first class stamp. Book catalog for 6x9 SAE and 2 first class stamps.
Tips: "We want more comical novels."

AUTOLYCUS PRESS, Subsidiary of Norfolk-Hall, Ltd., Box 21644/Southwest Station, St. Louis MO 63109. (314)647-4363. Editor: Christine Keller. Estab. 1964. Publishes hardcover and paperback originals and reprints. Plans five first novels this year (professional writers preferred).

Averages 5 total titles, 2 fiction titles each year. Publishes also in German and Japanese. Occasionally critiques book-length mss for $50 average.

Needs: Adventure, contemporary, fantasy, historical, humor/satire, juvenile (fantasy, spy/adventure, contemporary), suspense/mystery, young adult (historical). "Open market for original contemporary and adventure novels—five to ten per year." No experimental, avant garde. Recently published *Hemingsteen*, by Michael Murphy (literary novel); *H. Beford Jones*, by H. Bedford Jones (autobiography) and *Cyclops at the Ceremonial*, by Vincent Starrett (fiction reprint).

How to Contact: Query with SASE. Simultaneous and photocopied submissions OK. Reports in 3 weeks on queries (and mss).

Terms: Pays in royalties of 12% minimum, 15% maximum; advance negotiable; 10 author's copies; depends on grant/award money. "Subsidy publishing will be acceptable. Negotiable with author if saleable property. Larger royalty if subsidy publication. Individual arrangement with author depending on book." Writer's guidelines for 9x12 SASE.

Tips: "Write exactly what you think is yours and no one else's, in your own way, without direct imitation." Special awards given for superior works; average $500.

AVANT BOOKS, 3737 5th Ave., Suite 203, San Diego CA 92103. Editor: Michael Gosney. Estab. 1976. Publishes paperback originals. Averages 4-6 total titles, 2 fiction titles each year. Sometimes critiques rejected mss; charges $150-250 for detailed critique.

Needs: Contemporary, juvenile (contemporary), literary, religious/inspirational, science fiction. "We are looking for contemporary literature dealing with spiritual-transformational, ecological, and progressive social themes." Recently published: *Deva*, by Michael Tobias (mountaineering adventure in Tibetan Himalayas; spiritual/mystical overtones; highly anthropological and ecological).

How to Contact: Query first with SASE. Simultaneous and photocopied submissions OK. Reports in 2-4 weeks on queries; 2-3 months on mss.

Terms: Pays in royalties of 6% minimum, 10% maximum. "Subsidy publishes selected works only." Free book catalog.

BANDANNA BOOKS, 209 W. De la Guerra, Santa Barbara CA 93101. Editorial Director: Sasha Newborn. Estab. 1981. Publishes hardcover and paperback originals.

Needs: Autobiography. Recently published *First-Person Intense*, by S. Newborn (anthology of autobiography); *Autobiographies* by R. Kostelanetz.

How to Contact: Query or submit outline/synopsis and 1 sample chapter. SASE for query, ms. No simultaneous submissions; photocopied submissions OK. Reports in 3 weeks on queries, 1 month on mss.

Terms: Pays 8% maximum royalties and in author's copies. "Other arrangements negotiable." Subsidy publishes 20% of total books. "We have published with academic sponsorship as a co-publishing arrangement." Book catalog for SASE.

Tips: "Watch German films to get an idea of personal realism Bandanna is after."

LeBEACON PRESSE, Subsidiaries include M'godolim Press, Gormezano Reference Publications, 2921 E. Madison St., Suite 7 FWM, Seattle WA 98122. (206)322-1431. Publisher/Fiction Editor: Keith S. Gormezano. Estab. 1977. Publishes paperback originals and reprints. Averages 5-7 total titles, 3-5 fiction titles each year. Critiques mss for $25/100 pages or 25¢/page.

Needs: Adventure, comics, erotica, ethnic, humor/satire, literary, science fiction, short story collections, suspense/mystery, translations, young adult (fantasy/science fiction, problem novels/13-16 years, spy/adventure). Recently published: *Cousins*, by Shabetai Ben-Israel (war/love/historical); *Mongrel Harmony*, by David Repp (short fiction collection) and *Man Who Turned into a Woman*, by K.S. Gormezano (science fiction).

How to Contact: Query first with SASE. Simultaneous and photocopied submissions OK. Reports in 3 months on queries; 4 months on mss.

Terms: Pays in royalties of 5% minimum, 25% maximum; varied number of author's copies; depends on grant/award money. Subsidy publishes 10% of books. "We subsidy publish only when

we feel the work merits publication and money sources are 'dry.' For persons who wish to self publish, we will assign an ISBN upon request and forward orders at 10% of sale to them."
Tips: "Read at least one new novel a week and keep an eye on small press field." LeBeacon Presse Awards in fiction, novel, collection of short stories.

BENINDA BOOKS, Box 9251, Canton OH 44711. Editorial Director: George P. Argiry. Estab. 1977. Publishes paperback originals. Number of titles planned: undecided.
Needs: Adventure, mystery, western.
How to Contact: Query with SASE. No simultaneous or photocopied submissions. Reports in 2 weeks.
Terms: Pays 10% maximum in royalties; no advance. Free book catalog.

BERKELEY POETS WORKSHOP AND PRESS, Box 459, Berkeley CA 94701. Fiction Editor: Bruce Boston. Estab. 1969. Publishes paperback originals. Averages 3 total titles, 1 fiction title each year. Sometimes critiques rejected mss.
Needs: Short stories to 5,000 words only. Contemporary, experimental, fantasy, humor/satire, literary, mainstream, short story collections—must publish in magazine—*Berkeley Poets Cooperative*—first, in order to be accepted for publication.
How to Contact: Submit short stories with SASE. Photocopied submissions OK. Reports in 1 month on mss.
Terms: Pay depends on grant/award money; 2 author's copies. Free book catalog.
Tips: *Berkeley Poets Cooperative* magazine awards prizes for short stories.

BICENTENNIAL ERA ENTERPRISES, INC., Box 1148, Scappoose, OR 97056. Contact: Cathy Lee. Estab. 1978. Number of titles: 1 in 1981.
Needs: Adventure, mystery, spy. "No low class, poorly written, dumb, sex junk."
Terms: No advance.

THE BIELER PRESS, Box 3856, St. Paul MN 55165. (612)292-9936. Contact: Gerald Lange. Estab. 1975. Publishes hardcover and paperback originals. Number of titles: 4 in 1981; 6 in 1982.
Needs: Contemporary, literary. Recently published *Everything That Has Been Shall Be Again; the Reincarnation Fables of John Gilgun*(hardcover and paperback original).
How to Contact: Query with SASE. Simultaneous and photocopied submissions OK. Reports in 1 week on queries, irregularly on mss. Send non-returnable ms and SASE for response.
Terms: Pays 10% in author's copies (original), 10% in royalties (reprint); no advance. Free book catalog.
Tips: "Be committed to your work, not your publishing credits."

BILINGUAL PRESS, Subsidiary includes Bilingual Review/Press, Dept. Foreign Languages, Eastern Michigan University, Ypsilanti MI 48197. (313)487-0042. Editor: Gary Keller. Estab. 1974. Publishes hardcover and paperback originals. Plans 4 first novels this year. Averages 15 total titles, 10 fiction titles each year. Publishes also in Spanish. Sometimes critiques rejected mss.
Needs: Ethnic, historical, literary, short story collections, translations. US Hispanic themes only. "We will publish up to 12-15 good novels per year on US Hispanic life if the material is available." Recently published: *Not by the Sword*, by Nash Candelaria (historical novel, New Mexico, 19th century); *First Encounters*, by Sabine Ulibarri´ (short stories about contact between Anglos and Chicanos).
How to Contact: Query first with SASE. Simultaneous and photocopied submissions OK. Reports in 4 weeks on queries.
Terms: Pays in standard royalty of a 10% with an average of $300 advance. Subsidy publishes less than 10% of total books. "We occasionally subsidy publish a scholarly book. We never subsidy publish fiction, poetry or any books in the trade market." Free book catalog.
Tips: "A strong market is developing for US Hispanic fiction."

BKMK PRESS, UMKC, 107 Cockefair Hall, 5100 Rockhill Rd., Kansas City MO 64110. (816)276-1305. Editor-in-Chief: Dan Jaffe. Estab. 1971. Publishes paperback originals. Averages 6 total titles; 1 fiction title each year.
Needs: Contemporary, ethnic, experimental, historical, literary, translations. "We are new to fiction publishing but we plan to print one collection or anthology of short stories per year."
How to Contact: Query first with SASE. Reports in 2 weeks on queries.
Terms: Pays in royalties (approximately 10%, adjustable by contract). Book catalog free on request.

THE BLACKHOLE SCHOOL OF POETHNICS, Box 555, Port Jefferson NY 11777. Editorial Director: Grinley Nash. Estab. 1978. Publishes various forms of books.
Needs: "Minimal, having to do with what wasn't known and perhaps now is and will change life for everything but humans." Recently published *Aid to El Salvador*, by Richard Elman (broadside); *Spam*, by Jim Tyack and Ray Freed (64 pp. 5½x4¼; *The Cows Are Chewing Their Barns to Pieces*, by Graham Everett (broadside).
How to Contact: Submit outline/synopsis with SASE. No simultaneous submissions. Photocopied submissions OK "if they're vital to the ms." Reports "when we want."
Terms: Pays "a share after bills"; no advance.
Tips: "Verbosity is a trend today. Avoid great expectations."

BOOKS FOR ALL TIMES, INC., Box 2, Alexandria VA 22313. Publisher/Editor: Joe David. Estab. 1981. Publishes hardcover and paperback originals. "No plans for new writers at present." Averages 1 fiction title to date. Occasionally critiques rejected mss.
Needs: Contemporary, literary, short story collections. "No novels at the moment; hopeful, though, of someday soon publishing a collection of quality short stories. No popular fiction or material easily published by the major or minor houses specializing in mindless entertainment. Only interested in stories of the Victor Hugo or Sinclair Lewis quality." Recently published: *The Fire Within*, by Joe David (literary).
How to Contact: Query first with SASE. Simultaneous and photocopied submission OK. Reports in 1 month on queries.
Terms: Pays negotiable advance. "Publishing/payment arrangement will depend on plans for the book." Book catalog free on request.
Tips: Interested in "controversial, honest books which satisfy the reader's curiosity to know. *The Fire Within*, for example, does quite well despite the ignoring it's getting from the established press and establishment, because it delivers answers and entertains at the same time."

BROKEN WHISKER STUDIO, 711 S. Dearborn, Loft 505, Chicago IL 60605. Editorial Director: Joan H. Lee. Estab. 1976. Publishes paperback originals. Number of titles: 3 in 1981. Encourages new writers. Sometimes comments on rejected mss, "if we especially like a work, but can't use it, for example."
Needs: Contemporary, literary, experimental.
How to Contact: Submit complete ms with SASE. No simultaneous submissions; photocopied submissions OK. Reports in 1 month on mss.
Terms: Pays in author's copies and royalties. "We use a negotiable contract." No advances.
Tips: "We publish *short* fiction that is no more than 150 pages. Novellas, short stories, poetry, juveniles. We use art work, are interested in combinations (syntheses) of visual and verbal. Interested in material for chapbooks, broadsides, and poemcards. Rejections are because of poor writing (style, storytelling, charactization, tone, etc)."

BUCKSKIN PUBLICATIONS, Box 7, Sunset Route, Bonita AZ 85643. Managing Editor: Thomas Ryan Nelson. Estab. 1981. Publishes paperback originals. Plans 6 first novels this year. Averages 24 total fiction titles each year. Occasionally critiques rejected mss.

Needs: Fantasy, science fiction, short story collections. "We want *only* previously unpublished fantasy and science fiction!"
How to Contact: Submit complete ms only with SASE. Photocopied submissions OK. Reports in 2-3 months on mss.
Terms: Pays in royalties of 10% minimum, 15% maximum. No advances. Book catalog for $5.
Tips: "Learn the language, develop style, proof copy, and provide sharp, clean copy."

J.S. CAIRNS, 15 Brinkburn St., Sunderland, England SR4-7RG. Secretary: J.S. Cairns. Estab. 1941. Publishes paperback originals. Averages 1 total title each year.
Needs: Recently published: *Memory of Tomorrow*, by Marc Fingal (science fiction).
How to Contact: Query first with IRC. Reports in 2 months on queries.
Terms: Publishing arrangements are collective; cooperative; self-publishers with plans to expand. Manual for $2.
Tips: "If unpublished, produce your own first or at least, self-publish a short story. The cost can be trivial."

CALAMUS BOOKS, Box 689, Cooper Station, New York NY 10276. Imprint includes Gay Presses of New York. Editorial Director: Larry Mitchell. Estab. 1977. Publishes paperback originals. Number of titles: 2 in 1981, 4 in 1982.
Needs: Gay/lesbian. "We will publish any type of fiction as long as it is gay/lesbian." Recently published *Moritz*, by Bob Herron.
How to Contact: Query or submit complete ms. SASE for query and ms. Simultaneous and photocopied submissions OK. Reports in 6 weeks.
Terms: Pays in 20 author's copies and 7-8% royalties. Offers $200 advance. Free book catalog.

CARNIVAL PRESS, Box 19087, Minneapolis MN 55419. (612)823-3614. Editorial Consultants: Carol A. Marron and Susan Talanda. Estab. 1981. Number of titles: 3 limited edition in 1981; 3 trade edition in 1982; 14 limited edition planned for 1983. Encourages new writers. Sometimes comments on rejected mss.
Needs: Juvenile: enduring, universal tales, ethnic children's fiction (preferably from ethnic authors), suitable for both trade edition paperbacks with an international audience and deluxe limited edition printings. Also, books of high "spiritual" nature for children and their families. "No adult or adolescent fiction." Recently published *Ceremony—In the Circle of Life*, by White Deer of Autumn; *The Day the Gypsies Came to Town*, by Audrey Nelson Masterson; and *Mother Told Me So*, by Carol A. Marron (all limited editions for 1981; limited edition trade hardbound books for 1982; will be released in paperback trade editions for Spring, 1983)
How to Contact: Query with SASE. Simultaneous and photocopied submissions OK. Reports in 1 month.
Terms: Pays set cash amount for first-time authors; royalties with advance for previously published authors. In first instance, press purchases *all* rights.
Tips: "The children's market is difficult to write for, but most authors think it's a snap. Each word is important and each scene must further the action of the story. Strongly and critically edit your work. Children's fiction for our "All Ages, Interests" audience must be less than 3,000 words. Remember that our books will feature illustrations that will also help tell your story, so do not overdo details, descriptions. Each book ms should shoot for 15 or 14 printed pages of text (200 words maximum per page), each page being opposite a full-color illustration. Submissions self-edited to this format will be better received than others that are too wordy or do not give thought to an illustrated layout. Avoid condescending attitudes toward both children and adult characters. Don't introduce unnecessary characters into the story. Keep the conflict clearly upfront for young readers. When dialogue can tell the story, please use it. Avoid using a narrative that tells the story passively without letting dialogue and action do the job. And even with 'message' stories, your tale has to be entertaining. Before submitting mss to us, test your story out on children and adults. Children will be your most honest critics, but mss must appeal to *every* member of the family! We've observed a shift to fantasy and a disturbing lack of submissions dealing with 'real' children

Close-up

Carol Marron
Carnival Press

Reading bedtime stories to her own children (now ages six to twelve) sparked Carrol Marron's interest in writing and publishing. In 1976 she began attending classes in children's literature at the University of Minnesota, and by 1979 she had founded the Children's Writers' Guild in Minneapolis. Marron enjoys writing when she has time and has had one picture book published; *Mother Told Me So* is now in hardback and will come out in paperback this spring.

But the giant step came in 1980. Thanks to a private financial backer, Marron started Carnival Press, a small press specializing in children's picture books. At first Carnival sold deluxe limited editions to private collectors, but Marron wanted to get their books into the mainstream of trade book publishing and thus into the hands of more children, so the press has adopted a quality paperback format. She says, "In today's hard economic times, I think the challenge for small press publishers is to make alliances in the marketplace and explore new methods of distribution."

From the beginning Carnival Press has been committed to encouraging talented new authors and illustrators. "I don't like the term 'slush pile,' " declares Marron. "Many of our stories come from unsolicited manuscripts and I treat every submission with respect."

Promising stories are passed along for written reports and publishing decisions among the three reader/editors who comprise the editorial staff. Marron works directly with the authors if rewrites are necessary, then matches them with illustrators. This year she expects to use nationally known artists for the first time. Local authors and illustrators are apt to find themselves involved in production, and Marron takes care of the mostly regional promotion and distribution herself. By spring 1983 Carnival Press will have a total of seven paperbacks and three hardbacks in print, and in the future they will continue only with paperbacks.

As a small independent press, Carnival may take more risks, but strives for the same literary standards the larger presses achieve. Marron says the quality of Carnival's relationship with authors during the editing process has to do with individual personalities: "The tone of a cover letter can influence our decision to publish or reject if the author seems unusually cooperative or somewhat inflexible."

Carol Marron further advises writers "to carefully examine their work to see if it is of *use to a child*. Authors should acknowledge a child's need for love, acceptance, fun and adventure. Although a story may reflect an author's philosophy of life, it should not preach it. I recommend filling stories with a strong dose of humor and action by using characters who *do* things in a variety of situations." Favorite subjects for Carnival's preschool and primary-grade audience are realistically portrayed children with a variety of physical and emotional circumstances; humorous stories; and authentic folk tales.

—Catherine Cooper

in 'real life' settings. We'd like to see more of that latter type of story, as well as tales showing children in other lands, cultures, and backgrounds. We are looking for the Cadillac of children's fiction only—by well-established children's authors and very promising new talent. Since our production costs are very high, first-time authors must allow us to purchase all rights—we are taking a major risk in these cases.''

CARPENTER PRESS, Rt. 4, Pomeroy OH 45769. Editorial Director: Robert Fox. Estab. 1973. Publishes paperback originals. Number of titles: 4 in 1981; 1 in 1982.
Needs: Contemporary, literary, experimental, science fiction, fantasy. "Literary rather than genre science fiction and fantasy." Recently published *Seviathan*, by Hugh Fox; and *Special Offer*, by Jerry Bumpu (fantasy). "Do not plan to publish more than three books/year including chapbooks, and this depends upon funding, which is erratic."
How to Contact: Query with SASE. Unsolicited mss are returned unopened. Simultaneous and photocopied submissions OK. Reports promptly.
Terms: Pays in author's copies or 10% royalties. "Terms vary according to contract." No advance. Free book catalog.
Tips: "Don't try to impress us with whom you've studied or where you've published. Read as much as you can so you're not unwittingly repeating what's already been done. I look for freshness and originality rather than superlative technique. I wouldn't say that I favor experimental over traditional writing. Rather, I'm interested in seeing how recent experimentation is tying tradition to the future, and to the work of writers in other countries. In the next few years, I see an increase in the publishing of small press fiction, and an increase in sales, because of greater awareness by the reading public. Our books should be read before submitting."

THE CENTER FOR STUDY OF MULTIPLE BIRTHS, 333 E. Superior St., Suite 463-5, Chicago IL 60611. Executive Director: Donald Keith. Estab. 1977. Publishes hardcover and paperback originals. Encourages new writers. Sometimes comments on rejected mss.
Needs: "Will only consider mss related to twins, triplets or other multiples. Do not send anything that is not related. None will be returned or acknowledged."
How to Contact: Query with SASE. Simultaneous and photocopied submissions OK. Reports in 6 weeks.
Terms: Pays 10-15% royalties; no advance. Book catalog for legal-sized SASE.
Tips: "Do not send unless it has been queried first. Do not query unless it's about our subject! Do your homework. Edit the work before you send it out. Send neat and readable material. Unsolicited mss in other fields will be disposed of and unanswered."

CHALLENGE PRESS, 1107 Lexington Ave., Dayton OH 45407. (513)275-8637. Imprint includes *Confrontation/CHANGE Review*. Editor: F.M. Finney. Estab. 1976. Publishes hardcover originals and reprints. Number of titles: 2 in 1981, 8 in 1982.
Needs: Literary, mystery, historical, ethnic (black). "No historical-Southern fiction".
How to Contact: Query with SASE. Simultaneous and photocopied submissions OK. Reports in 2 weeks on queries, 6 weeks on mss. Will not accept unsolicited mss until mid-1983.
Terms: Pays 15-40% royalties and by outright purchase of $1,000 maximum; no advance. Book catalog for 7x10 SASE.
Tips: "We are a small operation; therefore do not expect a 'quick' reply. We are reasonable and encourage simultaneous submissions. We expect a shift to two extremes—the historical novel and science fiction for young adults."

CHAPMAN, 52 Bath St., Edinburgh, Scotland EH15 1HF. Imprints include Lothlorien. Editorial Director: Joy M. Hendry. Estab. 1970. Number of titles: 3 in 1981.
Needs: Contemporary, literary, experimental. "No novels."
How to Contact: Query or submit complete ms. SAE and IRC for query, mss. Reports in 2 weeks.
Terms: Pays 5 pounds/printed page on publication.

CHARISMA PRESS, 459 River Rd., Box 263, Andover MA 01810. Editorial Director: Fr. Lucius Annese. Publishes hardcover and paperback originals and reprints. Number of titles: 1 in 1982.
Needs: Literary. "Ours is a public purpose. We publish books by members of Charisma Press. For nonmembers we help writers to write step-by-step, but we do not publish non-members. For this purpose we have Charisma Press Institute consisting of two parts, the *basics* and the *advanced*. The texts we use are *Writing Skills* and *Write and Publish* both by the Director of Charisma Press, Fr. Lucius Annese. Persons interested in this educational service may contact us. No irreligious, uninspiring, unedifying material considered."
How to Contact: Query with SASE.
Terms: "We do not pay." Additional information for SASE. Free book catalog.
Tips: "Avoid inconsistencies, prejudice, and unreality. Realism and nature, direct and simple, are the current formulas. Be compact and let each word count. I encourage writers." Charges for services either by attendance or correspondence through Charisma Institute.

CHTHON PRESS, 10 Mark Vincent Dr., Westford MA 01886. Imprints include Nonesuch Publications and Spindle City Editions. Publisher: Paul J.J. Payack. Estab. 1973. Publishes paperback originals.
Needs: Experimental, science fiction, metafiction only. Recently published *CPU Wars*, by Charles Andres (paperback).
How to Contact: "By invitation only." Simultaneous and photocopied submissions OK. Reports in 6 weeks.
Terms: Pays by standard royalty contract. Free book catalog.
Tips: "Find your 'voice' and once you've found it write and write and write. But this is only half the task. It is the author's duty to make sure his work is available to the populace. Therefore, submit your work to every publisher you can think of and view rejections simply as part of the publication process."

COFFEE BREAK PRESS, Box 103, Burley WA 98322. (206)857-4329. Estab. 1977. Publishes paperback originals. Plans 1-2 first novels, new collections of short stories. Averages 5 fiction titles each year.
Needs: Juvenile (color a story—tells a complete story—for children up to 6 years). "Prefer something dealing with humor of any kind." No pornography. Recently published: *Niddy Noddy the Noodle Maker*, by Virginia Maas; *The Summer the Flowers Had No Scent* (4th edition), by D.M. Nicoldi; and *Earthen Pots and a Stone Wall*, by Cora G. Chose.
How to Contact: Submit outline/synopsis and 3 sample chapters or complete ms for shorter mss with SASE. Photocopied submissions OK. Reports in 2 weeks on queries; 3-4 weeks on mss.
Terms: Pays in negotiable royalties.

CREATIVE WITH WORDS PUBLICATIONS, 24665 Cabrillo St., Carmel CA 93923. Editor-in-Chief: Brigitta Geltrich. Estab. 1975. Publishes paperback originals. Publishes anthologies of new writers. Averages 2-3 total titles each year. Occasionally critiques rejected mss for $5, short poems; $10, short stories; $20 for longer stories, folklore items.
Needs: Humor/satire, juvenile (animal, easy-to-read, fantasy), short story collections. Needs short stories appealing to children; 'tales' of folklore nature, appealing to all ages."
How to Contact: Query first; submit complete ms with SASE. Photocopied submissions OK. Reports in 4 weeks on queries; 2 months on mss.
Terms: Pays in author's copies; payment depends on grant/award money—"still under consideration." Writer's guidelines for SASE.

CROSS-CULTURAL COMMUNICATIONS, 239 Wynsum Ave., Merrick NY 11566. (516)868-5635. Editorial Director: Stanley H. Barkan. Estab. 1971. Publishes hardcover and paperback originals. Number of titles: 6 chapbooks in 1981.
Needs: Contemporary, literary, experimental, ethnic, humor/satire, juvenile and young adult

folktales, translations. "Main interests: bilingual short stories and children's folktales, parts of novels of authors of other cultures, translations; some American fiction. No fiction that is not directed toward other cultures." Recently published *New Worlds from the Lowlands*, edited by Mannul Van Loggem; and *No Telephone to Heaven*, by Joseph Bruchac (novel of Native American in Ghana).

How to Contact: Query with SASE. "Note: Original language ms should accompany translations." Simultaneous and photocopied submissions "of good quality" OK. Reports in 1 month.

Terms: Pays "sometimes" 10-25% in royalties and "occasionally" by outright purchase, in author's copies—"10% of run for chapbook series," and "by arrangement for other publications." No advance. Book catalog for 5½x8½ SASE plus 37¢ postage.

Tips: "Write because you want to or you must; satisfy yourself. If you've done the best you can in that subject, style, and circumstance, then you've succeeded. Authentic creative expression should be your goal. You will find a publisher and an audience eventually. Generally, we have a greater interest in nonfiction-novels and translations. Short stories and excerpts from novels written in one of the traditional neglected languages are preferred—with the original version (i.e., bilingual). Our kinderbook series will soon be in production with a similar bilingual emphasis, especially for folktales, fairy tales, and fables."

THE CROSSING PRESS, 17 W. Main St., Trumansburg NY 14886. Editor: Elaine Gill. Publishes paperback and hardcover originals. Estab. 1966.
Needs: Literary, contemporary, women's, feminist, gay/lesbian.
How to Contact: Query with SASE. Reports in 1 month. Free book catalog.
Terms: Pays 7½-10% royalties.

CURBSTONE PRESS, 321 Jackson St., Willimantic CT 06226. Imprints include Augustinus/ Curbstone. Co-Directors: Judy Doyle, Alexander Taylor. Estab. 1975. Number of titles: 16 in 1982.
Needs: Contemporary, literary, experimental, faction, historical, women's, feminist, gay/lesbian, ethnic, translations. Recently published *Centralia Dead March*, by T. Churchill (documentary novel); *Anna (1) Anna*, by Klans Ritbjerg (Danish-novel); *Complete Freedom*, by Tove Ditlersen (collection of short stories translated from Danish).
How to Contact: Submit outline/synopsis and sample chapters with SASE or submit through agent. No simultaneous submissions; photocopied submissions OK. Reports in 6 weeks on mss.
Terms: Pays in author's copies (10%); no advance. Free book catalog.
Tips: "Our authors have usually established a reputation in magazines. If an author has not published individual pieces in literary magazines or journals, he would be well advised to do so before submitting work to us. We are especially interested in socially engaged work or works expressing the struggle for equality and human rights. We also publish translations of contemporary world authors."

DEINOTATION-7 PRESS, Box 194, Susquehanna PA 18847. Author/Publisher: Al Stella. Estab. 1978. Publishes paperback originals. Number of titles: 2 in 1981.
Needs: Contemporary.
How to Contact: Submit through agent only. Simultaneous and photocopied submissions OK. Reports in quite awhile on mss.
Terms: Pays in appropriate amount of author's copies. No advance. Subsidy publishes all books, "cost plus percentage." Book catalog with # 10 SASE and 26¢ postage.
Tips: "You gotta hang in there. The writer can avoid pitfalls by keeping in mind the deep, underlying purpose of Deinotation-7 Press."

DIANA'S, Subsidiary includes Diana's Bimonthly Press, 71 Elmgrove Ave., Providence RI 02906. (401)274-5417. Editor: Tom Ahern. Estab. 1971. Publishes paperback originals. Plans 1 first novel this year. Averages 3 total titles, 2 fiction titles each year. Sometimes critiques rejected mss.

Needs: Experimental, literary. No mainstream. Recently published: *Equilibrium and the Rotary Disc*, by Robert Cumming (illustrated); *Okupant X*, by Gary Panter (illustrated).
How to Contact: Submit outline/synopsis and sample chapters with SASE. Simultaneous and photocopied submissions OK. Reports in 1 week on mss.
Terms: Pays by outright purchase, $50-100 or 50 author's copies. Free book catalog.

DILLON PRESS, INC., 500 South 3rd St., Minneapolis MN 55415. (612)333-2691. Editor: Terry Hopkins. Estab. 1961. Publishes hardcover originals. Averages 20 total titles, 4-5 fiction titles each year.
Needs: Juvenile—5th grade reading level. ''We would like to do a series (6 to 8 titles) of fiction novels for young adults in mystery, horror/occult, science fiction. We are also looking for engaging stories about lifestyles, problems, experiences of today's young people. No folktales or picture books.''
How to Contact: Submit complete ms with SASE. Simultaneous and photocopied submissions OK. Reports in 6-8 weeks on mss.
Terms: Pays in royalties of 5% minimum, 10% maximum. Book catalog for 9x11 SASE.

DIMENSIONIST PRESS, 5931 Stanton Ave., Highland CA 92346. (714)862-4521. Editor: Arnold Arias. Estab. 1978. Publishes paperback originals. Number of titles: 1 in 1981, 1 in 1982.
Needs: Literary, experimental, psychic/supernatural, science fiction, fantasy, juvenile and easy-to-read.
How to Contact: Query and send complete ms with SASE. Simultaneous and photocopied submissions OK. Reports in 2 weeks on queries and mss.
Terms: Negotiates terms with author. No advance.
Tips: ''Dimensionist Press represents a new movement in the arts, *Dimensionism*. A Dimensionist strives to evoke or describe a visionary-mystical experience or future world or extra-dimensional realm in art, music, or literature.''

THE DRAGONSBREATH PRESS, R1, Sister Bay WI 54234. Editor: Fred Johnson. Estab. 1973. Publishes paperback and hardback originals. Number of titles: 2 in 1980, 0 in 1981.
Needs: Contemporary, literary, experimental, erotica, science fiction, fantasy, and humor/satire. ''*No novels*, but rather single short stories.''
How to Contact: Query and when requested send complete ms with SASE. Simultaneous and photocopied submissions OK. Reports in 1 month on queries, 2 months on mss. ''Always include a cover letter.''
Terms: Negotiates terms with author. No advance. ''Since we are a small press, we prefer to work cooperatively, sharing the work and expenses between the author and the press.''
Tips: ''This is a small press working with the book as an art form producing handmade limited-edition books combining original artwork with original writing. Since we work with hand-set type and have limited time and money we are not interested in novels, but prefer shorter writing suited to handwork and illustrating. We are not a typical publishing house; books would have limited distribution, mainly to art and book collectors.''

DREAM GARDEN PRESS, 1199 Iola Ave., Salt Lake City UT 84104. (801)355-2154. Editor: Marc Brown. Estab. 1980. Publishes hardcover and paperback originals and paperback reprints. Plans 1 first novel this year. Average 6 total titles, 1-2 fiction titles each year. Occasionally critiques rejected mss.
Needs: Contemporary, experimental, literary, western. ''We're interested in the offbeat and the unusual. We don't want to see your novel if you're convinced it's destined to be a 'blockbuster.' '' Recently published: *The Leather Throne*, by Owen Ulph (western—''not Louis L'Amour'').
How to Contact: Query first. Simultaneous and photocopied submissions OK. Reports in 2-4 weeks on queries.
Terms: Pays in royalties.

JUR EDITIONS, INC., Box 449, Chester Springs PA 19425. (215)458-5005. Associate ⌐ or: Kristin Dufour. Estab. 1954. Publishes hardcover and paperback originals and hardcover and paperback reprints. Sometimes critiques rejected mss.
Needs: Contemporary, experimental, literary, short story collections, translations, women's. Recently published: *The Knife*, by Peadar O'Donnell (historical).
How to Contact: Submit outline/synopsis and 1-2 sample chapters with SASE. Simultaneous and photocopied submissions OK. Reports in 4-6 weeks on mss.
Terms: Negotiable. Free book catalog.

E&E PUBLISHING, Box 312, Junction City OR 97448. Editor: Richard L. Evans. Estab. 1981. Publishes paperback originals and reprints. Plans to publish 50% new writers. Averages 5 total titles, 1-2 fiction titles each year. Occasionally critiques rejected mss. "In special circumstances charges $10/1,000 words plus postage for critique."
Needs: Adventure, contemporary, erotica (nothing pornographic), experimental, fiction, fantasy, historical, humor/satire, juvenile (sports, spy/adventure), religious/inspirational, science fiction, short story collections, suspense/mystery, war, western, young adult (fantasy/science fiction, sports, spy/adventure). "Books should be not over 60,000 words. We do accept or encourage short stories for our anthologies. We would like to begin a line of humorous fiction." No experimental or overly erotic.
How to Contact: Submit outline/synopsis and complete ms with SASE. Simultaneous and photocopied submissions OK. Reports in 2 months on mss.
Terms: Pays in royalties of 6% minimum, 15% maximum; outright purchase; author's copies or honorarium depends on particulr project. Subsidy publishes 5% of books. Writer pays for production. Publisher matches those funds on advertising and distribution.
Tips: Offers $100 for best short story (4,000 words or less) used in an anthlogy (yearly).

EAST EAGLE PRESS, Subsidiary of East Eagle Company, Box 812, Huron SD 57350. (605)352-5875. Publisher: Patrick Haley. Estab. 1981. Plans 2 children books this year. Averages 2 total fiction titles each year. Occasionally critiques rejected mss.
Needs: Juvenile—any form. "East Eagle Press publishes children's literature. We are interested in finely crafted stories which will challenge, teach, entertain and (if we're real lucky) honestly touch readers. I am not interest in cute, little nothings. I am not interested in pompous condescension."
How to Contact: Submit outline/synopsis and 1 sample chapter or complete ms (depending on length) with SASE. Simultaneous and photocopied submissions OK. Reports in 4-6 weeks on mss.
Terms: Pays in royalties of 10%.

THE ECCO PRESS, 18 W. 30th St., New York NY 10001. (212)685-8240. Associate Editor: Megan Ratner. Editor: Daniel Halpern. Estab. 1970. Publishes hardcover and paperback originals and hardcover and paperback reprints. Plans 1 first novel this year. Averages 10-12 total titles, 4 fiction titles each year. Occasionally critiques rejected mss.
Needs: Literary, short story collections. "We can publish possibly one or two novels a year." No science fiction, romantic novels, western (cowboy) fiction. Recently published: *In the Garden of the North American Martyrs*, by Tobias Wolfe (short story collection); *The Catherine Wheel*, by Jean Stafford (reprint novel) and *The Delicate Prey*, by Paul Bowles (reprint short story).
How to Contact: Query first especially on novels with SASE. Photocopied submissions OK. Reports in 1 week on queries; 6-8 weeks on mss.
Terms: Pays in royalties of 5% minimum; 10% maximum; advance is negotiable. Writer's guidelines for SASE. Book catalog free on request.

EXPANDED MEDIA EDITION, Aloys Shulte Str. 15, 5300 Bonn, West Germany. Fiction Editor: Pociao. Estab. 1969. Publishes paperback originals. Plans 1 first novel this year. Averages 2 total titles, 2 fiction titles each year. Publishes also in German. Occasionally critiques rejected mss.

Needs: Contemporary, experimental, literary. No horror.
How to Contact: Query first with IRC. Simultaneous and photocopied submisions OK. Reports in 1 week on queries; 4 weeks on mss.
Terms: Pays in royalties of 8% minimum, 10% maximum; in 10 author's copies. Book catalog for IRC.

FABLEWAVES PRESS, Box 7874, Van Nuys CA 91409. (213)785-9042. Fiction Editor: Claude Lanoux. Publishes paperback originals. Plans 1 first novel this year. Averages 3 total titles, 3 fiction titles each year. Occasionally critiques rejected mss.
Needs: Experimental, fantasy, humor/satire, literary, mainstream, science fiction, short story collections. "No specific needs, except well-crafted novels that reflect the follies of our time. No pro-war, pro-wealth, pro-power, pro-materialistic visions." Recently published: *Intrepid Visions*, by Jacques Carrié (bizarrely imaginative short stories).
How to Contact: Query first with SASE. All unsolicited manuscripts are returned unopened. Reports in 6 weeks on queries, 16 weeks on mss.
Terms: Pays in royalties of 6% minimum.
Tips: "Unless lucky, it'll take years of hard work/dedication to get anywhere; develop your own voice, do your thing but keep in touch with the mainstream."

FANTOME PRESS, 720 N. Park Ave., Warren OH 44483. Imprint includes *Journal Fantome*. Editor/Publisher: C.M. James. Estab. 1976. Publishes limited edition folios.
Needs: Gothic, erotica, science fiction and fantasy. "No other subjects accepted." Very short prose and prose poems only. Recently published *Antarktos*, by H.P. Lovecraft; *The Riddle*, by Joseph Payne Brennan; and *When Chaugnar Wakes* by Frank Belknap Long.
How to Contact: Query and send complete ms with SASE. Simultaneous and photocopied submissions OK. Reports in 6 weeks on queries and mss.
Terms: Negotiates terms with author. No advance. Free book catalog with SASE and 20¢ postage.
Tips: "Avoid sending material outside of our genre."

FICTION COLLECTIVE, INC., c/o Department of English, Brooklyn College, Brooklyn, NY 11210. Co-Directors: Thomas Glynn, Harold Jaffe, Mark Leyner, and Curtis White. Estab. 1974. "We publish hardcover and paperback originals. We encourage new writers of contemporary and experimental fiction. The Collective is primarily interested in new fiction and all that term implies." Currently has 35 titles in print.
Needs: Contemporary, literary and experimental. Recently published *My Father More or Less*, by Jonathan Baumbach; *Coming Close*, by B.H. Friedman; *Winnebago Mysteries*, by Moira Crone; *Mourning Crazy Horse*, by Harold Jaffe.
How to Contact: Query with SASE. Simultaneous and photocopied submissions OK. Reports in 1 month on queries, 5 months on mss. Send queries to Fiction Collective Manuscript Central, Department of English, Illinois State University, Normal, Illinois 61761.
Terms: "The Collective is a non-profit writers cooperative. The Collective makes editorial decisions. Books are published with assistance from NEA and NYSCA. If a manuscript is accepted for publication, then the author shares in editorial decisions." No advance. Free book catalog.

W.D. FIRESTONE PRESS, Publisher/Editor: W.D. Firestone. Estab. 1979. Publishes hardcover and paperback originals. Averages 2 total titles, 2 fiction titles each year. Sometimes critiques rejected mss.
Needs: Fantasy, horror, science fiction, short story collections. Especially needs fantasy. Recently published: *Summer Wine*, by H.L. Prosser (fantasy short fiction collection).
How to Contact: Query first with SASE. All unsolicited manuscripts are returned unopened. Simultaneous and photocopied submissions OK. Reports in 1 month on queries; 2 months on mss.
Terms: Pays in 60 author's copies.
Tips: "Tell a story with a good plot and well-developed characters. We see a trend toward fantasy and sword and sorcery work."

FJORD PRESS, Box 615, Corte Madera CA 94925. (415)924-9566 or 549-1910. Editor-in-Chief: Steven T. Murray. Senior Editor: Susan Doran. Estab. 1981. Publishes paperback originals and reprints. Averages 3-6 total titles, 3-6 fiction titles each year.
Needs: Adventure, contemporary, ethnic, experimental, fantasy, feminist/lesbian, gay, historical (general), horror, literary, mainstream, science fiction, short story collections, suspense/mystery, war, women's—*translations only*, no American material. Interested in "translations of modern or contemporary European novels that have not been done in English before. No original American fiction." Recently published: *Fitzcarraldo*, by Werner Herzog; *Evening Light*, by Stephan Hermlin (East German memoirs), and *Stolen Spring*, by Hans Scherfig (Danish novel).
How to Contact: Query first with SASE. Photocopied submissions OK. Reports in 3 weeks on queries; 3 months on mss.
Terms: Pays in royalties of 1% minimum, 7.5% maximum (for public domain works) and author's copies. Advance is negotiable. "We try to arrange a suitable mixture of advance/royalties/copies with translators. Advances are usually small." Book list for legal size SAE with 1 first class stamp.

FLY BY NIGHT, Box 921, Huntington NY 11743. Fiction Editor: John Pages. Estab. 1979. Publishes paperback originals. Averages 3 total titles, 3 fiction titles each year. Sometimes critiques rejected mss.
Needs: Experimental, literary.
How to Contact: Query first with SASE. Simultaneous and photocopied submissions OK. Reports in 1 week on queries; 4 weeks on mss.
Terms: Pays in 5 author's copies. Free book catalog on request when available.

FLYING BUTTRESS PUBLICATIONS, Box 254, Endicott NY 13760. Fiction Editor: T. Nantier. Estab. 1976. Publishes hardcover and paperback originals. Averages 1-3 total titles, 1-3 fiction titles each year. Sometimes critiques rejected mss.
Needs: Comics, fantasy, horror, humor/satire, science fiction, suspense/mystery, young adult (fantasy/science fiction, spy/adventure). Especially interested in graphic novels (comics in book form) in series form preferably. No overly esoteric type fiction.
How to Contact: Submit outline/synopsis and 1-2 sample chapters with SASE. Simultaneous and photocopied submissions OK. Reports in 3-4 weeks on mss.
Terms: Pays in royalties of 8% minimum, 12% maximum. Advance is negotiable. Book catalog for large SAE with 1 first class stamp.
Tips: "Graphic albums are a very successful artform in Europe and will establish themselves in this country as well. Comics are considerably more than what most people think."

FOLDER EDITIONS, 103-26 68th Rd., Forest Hills NY 11375. (212)275-3839. Associate Editor: Perry Aldan. Editorial Director: Dr. Daisy Aldan. Fiction Editor: Diana Cohen. Estab. 1959. Publishes hardback and paperback originals. Number of titles: 1 in 1981; 2 in 1982.
Needs: Contemporary, literary, women's, fantasy and translations. No obscene erotica, horror, violence, crime, sport or science fiction. Recently published *A Golden Story*, by Daisy Aldan (novella) and *The Fall of Antichrist*, by Albert Steffen (play translated by Dora Baker).
How to Contact: Query with SASE. Photocopied submissions OK; no simultaneous submissions. Reports in 1 week on queries and mss.
Terms: Pays in 10 free author's copies. "We are a small press. If we get a grant, we will pay the author."
Tips: "There is a big market for books of superficial sensationalism, violence and sex. We exist to counteract this, to influence once more the taste of readers for good literature. Do not debase your art, your dignity, or in other words, the word, for money. Have a sense of responsibility for what you write and for the welfare of the world. Make sure there are no errors in spelling, grammar, etc. Avoid obscenities, clichés. Ask yourself if what you are writing will add to or detract from the reader's experience of writing as an art. We are interested only in quality literature."

FROG IN THE WELL, 430 Oakdale Rd., East Palo Alto CA 94303. (415)323-1237. Fiction Editor: Susan Hester. Estab. 1980. Publishes paperback originals. Averages 2-3 total titles, 1-3 fiction titles each year. Sometimes critiques rejected mss.
Needs: Feminist/lesbian, short story collections (about women), women's.
How to Contact: Submit outline/synopsis and 3 sample chapters with SASE. Simultaneous (if noted) and photocopied submissions OK. Reports in 2-3 months on mss.
Terms: Pays in royalties (50% of profits); 12 author's copies. Free book catalog on request.
Tips: "Write well—write from personal experience. Develop your own style."

GAY PRESSES OF NEW YORK, Box 294, New York NY 10014. (212)255-4713 or 691-9066. Co-Publishers: Terry Helbing, Larry Mitchell and Felice Picano. Publishes paperback originals. Plans 1 first novel this year. Averages 2 total fiction titles each year.
Needs: Feminist/lesbian, gay, literary. Recently published: *Torch Song Trilogy*, by Harvey Fierstein (play) and *Voltaire Smile*, by Ron Harvie (short stories).
How to Contact: Query first; submit outline/synopsis and sample chapters. Simultaneous and photocopied submissions OK. Reports in 3 weeks on queries.
Terms: Pays in royalties of 6% minimum, 10% maximum. Book catalog free on request.

GAY SUNSHINE PRESS, Box 40397, San Francisco CA 94140. (415)824-3184. Imprint includes *Gay Sunshine Journal*. Editor: Winston Leyland. Estab. 1975. Publishes hardcover and paperback originals. Number of titles: 7 in 1981; 7 in 1982; 7 planned for 1983.
Needs: Literary, experimental, gay and translations. "We desire fiction on gay themes of *high* literary quality and prefer writers who have already had work published in literary magazines." Recently published: *A Thirsty Evil*, Short Stories by Gore Vidal.
How to Contact: Query with SASE. Reports in 2 weeks on queries, 1 month on mss.
Terms: Negotiates terms with author.
Tips: "Before submitting a ms to a publisher, ask competent people in your own city for an appraisal of the literary quality of your work. No sophomoric writing. Avoid sending in a ragged ms."

GRAPHIC IMAGE PUBLICATIONS, Box 1740, LaJolla CA 92038. (618)457-0344. Managing Editor: Susan Crow. Estab. 1981. Publishes paperback originals and reprints. Plans 2-3 first novels this year. Averages 4-5 total titles, 2-3 fiction titles each year. Occasionally critiques rejected mss.
Needs: Erotica, fantasy, contemporary romance, juvenile (animal, easy-to-read, fantasy, picture book), literary, mainstream, science fiction, suspense/mystery. "Would like to receive 3 to 4 submissions on juvenile, suspense/mystery and science fiction." Recently published *Night Vision*, by Eric Edwin Hahn (suspense/mystery).
How to Contact: Query first; submit outline/synopsis and 3-4 sample chapters with SASE. Simultaneous and photocopied submissions OK. Reports in 6-8 weeks on queries; 12-14 weeks on mss.
Terms: Pays in royalties of 5% minimum; 15% maximum; negotiates advance; or outright purchase. "Would consider subsidy publishing if the author has experience and background to make it worthwhile." Writer's guidelines for # 10 SASE.
Tips: "Be confident of your work and be aggressive when looking for a publisher (send queries)."

GRIFFON HOUSE PUBLICATIONS, Box 81, Whitestone NY 11357. (212)767-8380. President: Frank Grande. Estab. 1976. Publishes paperback originals and reprints.
Needs: Contemporary, literary, experimental, ethnic (open) and translations.
How to Contact: Query with SASE. No simultaneous submissions; photocopied submissions OK. Reports in 1 month on queries, 6 weeks on mss.
Terms: Pays in 6 free author's copies. No advance.

GUERNICA EDITIONS, Box 633, Station N.D.G., Montreal, Quebec, Canada H4A 3R1. Imprint includes *The Guernica Review*. President and Poetry Editor: Antonio D'Alfonso. Fiction Editor: Umberto Claudio. Estab. 1978. Publishes hardcover and paperback originals and reprints. Sometimes comments on rejected mss.
Needs: Contemporary, literary, romance, confession, women's, feminist, gay/lesbian, erotica, psychic/supernatural, religious/inspirational, humor/satire, juvenile and young adult and translations.
How to Contact: Query with SASE. No simultaneous submissions; photocopied submissions OK. Reports in 2 weeks on queries, 6 weeks on mss.
Terms: Pays 2-3 author's copies. "We will be paying in the near future." No advance. Free book catalog.
Tips: "Have perseverance, intelligence, courage. *Guernica* was established for writers who have not been published in the way they thought they should have been. We want writers who know the value of their work. We will accept any writer who has been published in magazines but who has not been published in book form."

HARIAN CREATIVE PRESS BOOKS, 47 Hyde Blvd., Ballston Spa NY 12020. Imprints include The Harian Press, Barba-Cue Special and *What's Cooking?* Serials; Creative Romances and Cosmic Read. President/Executive Editor: Dr. Harry Barba. Editor, Creative Romances and Cosmic Read: Marian Andrea. European office: Greg Barba. Estab. 1967. Publishes hardcover and paperback originals. Number of titles: 4 in 1982. "We publish first fiction and nonfiction writers initially in *Harian Creative Awards* (6 in 1981). Comments on rejected mss. Entry fee required. Cost depends on genre and length."
Needs: Contemporary, romance, science fiction, fantasy, translations, and "socially functional". No obscenity, pornography for its own sake, or violence. Recently published *The Day The World Went Sane*, by Harry Barba (science fiction); and *Harian Creative Awards I*, edited by Harry Barba.
How to Contact: Query or submit outline/synopsis and sample chapters (2-3). SASE always. Simultaneous and photocopied submissions OK. Reports in 1 month on queries, 6 weeks on ms.
Terms: Terms are negotiated; no advance. "Except for Harian Creative Awards, we publish co-operatively. Only mss meeting our regular standards are so published. Terms are negotiated on basis of market needs, current cost of production, and quality and depth of market penetration desired by writer." Free book catalog with 9x11 SASE.
Tips: "Keep a good job and write when you can find the time. Writing is a salubrious act. The benefits are not just monetary; they are emotional and intellectual. But money is also important. We look for functionally suitable style—manner married to matter."

HERITAGE PRESS, Box 18625, Baltimore MD 21216. (301)383-9330. President: Wilbert L. Walker. Estab. 1979. Publishes hardcover originals. Averages 2 total titles, 1-2 fiction titles each year.
Needs: Ethnic (black). Interested in "fiction that presents a balanced portrayal of the black experience in America, from the black perspective. No fiction not dealing with blacks, or that which views blacks as inferior. Recently published: *Stalemate at Panmunjon*, by Wilbert L. Walker (the Korean War).
How to Contact: Query first with SASE. Simultaneous and photocopied submissions OK. Reports in 2 weeks on queries, 2 months on mss.
Terms: "We plan to subsidy publish only those works that meet our standards for approval. No more than 1 or 2 a year. Payment for publication is based on individual arrangement with author." Book catalog free on request.
Tips: "Write what you know about. No one else can know and feel what it is like to be black in America better than one who has experienced our dichotomy on race." Would like to see new ideas with broad appeal.

HIBISCUS PRESS, Box 22248, Sacramento CA 95822. Editor-in-Chief: Margaret Wensrich. Estab. 1972. Publishes paperback originals. Plans to publish first novels. Averages 1-2 total titles,

1 fiction title each year. Occasionally critiques mss. Fee depends on length. Query first with SASE. "All queries must have a SASE for an answer."
How to Contact: Query letter first with SASE. Reports in 2-3 weeks on queries.
Terms: Has co-op publishing agreement. Terms mutually agreeable.
Tips: "Keep at it. Small presses nurture the writers of the future. Publish self, if you believe in what you are doing."

LAWRENCE HILL & CO., INC., 520 Riverside Ave., Westport CT 06880. (203)226-9392. Publisher: Lawrence Hill. Estab. 1973. Publishes hardcover and paperback originals and reprints. Averages 12-15 total titles, 2-3 fiction titles each year. Occasionally critiques rejected mss.
Needs: Literary, translations. No genres (in general): romance, science fiction (in particular). Recently published: *To the Honorable Miss S . . .* , by B. Traven (short stories); *Chirundu*, by E. Mphaele (African-anglophone); and *King Albert*, by F. Bebey (African-franophone in translations).
How to Contact: Query first with SASE. Simultaneous and photocopied submissions OK. Reports in 2 weeks on queries.
Terms: Pays in royalties. Book catalog for # 10 SASE.

HYENA EDITIONS, Box 121, Water Mill NY 11976. Fiction Editor: Ché Wax. Publishes pamphlets. Averages 10 fiction titles each year.
Needs: Absurdist texts and erotic fiction. "Especially interested in erotic fiction by women for our series: Modern Eros Editions." Recently published: *Etiquette of Flatulence*, by Opal Louis Nations (absurdist); *Expurgations*, by Derek Pell (experimental texts); and *Fairy Tales*, by Sheila Pinder (erotic stories).
How to Contact: Query first with SASE. All unsolicited manuscripts are returned unopened. Reports in 3 weeks on queries.
Terms: Pays in 25 author's copies.

ILLUMINATIONS PRESS, 2110 9th St., Apt. B, Berkeley CA 94710. (415)849-2102. Publisher: N. Moser. Estab. 1965. Publishes paperback originals occasionally. Encourages new writers. Sometimes comments on rejected mss.
Needs: Contemporary, literary, experimental and humor/satire. Material dealing with nature and mysticism (using nature images, in other words) for possible anthology in '82-3.
How to Contact: Query with SASE. Simultaneous and photocopied submissions OK. Reports in 1 month on queries, 6 months on mss.
Terms: Pays 1 or more author's copies usually. No advance. Free book catalog with $1.95 postage.
Tips: "Keep language simple. Don't try to change the world in fiction. Write what you know and feel for sure. Avoid excessively complicated language or poor characterizations. I think there will be a return to clarity and the narrative. Be sure to query first, prior to sending a fiction ms."

IN BETWEEN BOOKS, Box T, Sausalito CA 94965. (415)331-2423. Contact: Karla Andersdatter. Estab. 1973. Publishes paperback originals.
Needs: Fantasy. Open to most children's subjects if queried first. Recently published *Marissa The Tooth Fairy*, by Karla Andersdatter (children's fantasy), and *Follow the Blue Butterfly*.
How to Contact: Query with SASE. No simultaneous submissions. Photocopied submissions OK. Reports in 6 weeks on queries. "Manuscripts sent without query will be burned!"
Terms: After first printing, pays 10% in royalties. Negotiable author's copies. No advance. Free book catalog.
Tips: "Golden Books has taken over. Commercialism is rampant. I like quality and a fresh, unique style. Write on two levels so adults get the 'message' too. Read a lot. Avoid cutsey-wootsey, goodie-goodie 'fantasies.' "

I-74 Press, Box 2223, Chapel Hill NC 27514. (919)968-1149. Editor/Publisher: Robert Fromberg. Fiction Editor: Becky Fromberg. Estab. 1980. Publishes paperback originals. Plans 1 first novel or story collection this year. Averages 3-4 total titles, 3-4 fiction titles each year. Sometimes critiques rejected mss.

Needs: Experimental, literary, short story collections. "Reading serious fiction (novels, novellas, story collections) whose style is something other than strictly traditional. No commercial/mainstream/political fiction." Recently published: *A Reader of New American Fiction* (collection of contemporary stories and parts of novels) and *OONO*, by Patricia Eakins (chapbook).

How to Contact: Query first, then submit complete mss. SASE always. Photocopied submissions OK. Reports in 1 week on queries; 1 month on mss.

Terms: Pays in royalties of 10% minimum or in author's copies (5-10% of press run). "Royalites or copies, by arrangement." Free book catalog on request.

Tips: "Please ignore trends, the what-would-sell approach. We look for quality work, whether marketable or not. We've noticed a trend toward traditional modes and style. We lean toward a more experimental/exploratory approach."

JELM MOUNTAIN PUBLISHING, 209 Park St., Laramie WY 82070. (307)742-8053. Imprint includes Jelm Mountain Press. Editor: Jean Jones. Estab. 1976. Publishes paperback originals, some hardcovers. Number of titles: 1 in 1981, 4 in 1982, 4-6 planned for 1983. Encourages new writers. Plans 2 first novels for '83. Sometimes comments on rejected ms; "charges only when critique or comment is requested by author." Fee variable.

Needs: Historical, western and fantasy. Recently published *Pachee Goyo: History and Legends from the Shoshone*, by Rupert Weeks; and *Wyoming Sun*, by Edward Bryant (science fiction fantasy).

How to Contact: Query and submit outline/synopsis and sample chapters with SASE. Simultaneous and photocopied submissions OK. Reports in 2 week on queries, 4 weeks on mss.

Terms: No advance. Subsidy publishes 50% of total books; ⅓ up front. Free book catalog with SASE.

Tips: "Be serious, learn the fundamentals of writing, keep your mind on the story and not on how popular or rich it will make you. Our editor prefers an up-beat approach—meeting life's challenges! We major in Wyoming literature/regional materials with historical authenticity. Our press is small enough to give writers, especially novices, a lot of attention, but we hope they are willing to help by being able to pay for extra services."

JOHNSTON GREEN AND COMPANY (PUBLISHERS) LIMITED, (formerly JCR Green Publisher Ltd.), Box 1, Portree, Isle of Skye, Scotland 1V51 9BT. Imprints include Aquila Publishing and Club Leabhar. Managing Director: JCR Green. Estab. 1968. Publishes hardcover and paperback originals. Number of titles: 15 in 1981; 25 in 1982; 50 planned for 1982.

Needs: Contemporary, literary, experimental, adventure, mystery, spy, historical, erotica, psychic/supernatural, science fiction, fantasy, horror, humor/satire, translations and short stories. No romance, westerns, gothic, feminist, war, confession, women's, gay/lesbian, ethnic, religious/inspirational or juvenile/young adult. Recently published *In Search of Jasper McDoom*, by Stephen Wade (short stories), *The Miserable Child And Her Father*, by Dinah Brooke, (literary novel, hardback) and *The Raven Waits*, by June Oldham (hardcover historical novel).

How to Contact: Query and send complete ms with SAE or IRC. No simultaneous submissions, photocopied submissions OK. Reports in 1 month on queries, 6 weeks on mss.

Terms: Pays 10-15% in royalties and in short chapbook copies. No advance. Free book catalog with 9x6 SASE and 4 International Reply Coupons.

Tips: Mss rejected "simply because they are not good enough. We require highest quality work, of a contemporary character. Most of the mss we require to be 'out of the ordinary run of the mill' in both characterization and literary style. The great majority of work we receive is bloody awful. However we believe that there is a lot to be said for American fiction as it stands today, being very interesting to us."

ANNE JOHNSTON/THE MOORLANDS PRESS, 11 Novi Lane, Leek, Staffordshire, England ST13 6NS. Editor: J.C.R. Green. Estab. 1982. Publishes hardcover and paperback originals

and reprints. ''We encourage new writers, and plan 10 fiction titles in 1983.'' Averages 40 total titles, 10-15 fiction titles (projected) each year. Occasionally critiques rejected mss; payment negotiable with editor.
Needs: Contemporary, erotica, experimental, faction, fantasy, literary, mianstream, psychic/supernatural, science fiction short story collections, translations. ''We are completely open to suggestions, being a new imprint. However both the owner and editor work for other publishers (the owner is also an agent) and we require well written work in the categories mentioned only.''
How to Contact: Query first with synopsis with IRC. Simultaneous and photocopied submissions OK. Reports in 4 weeks on queries.
Terms: Pays in royalties of 10% minimum, 15% maximum, advance for agented ms; 10 (paperback) and 5 (hardback) author's copies; depends on grant/award money. ''Prepared to consider subsidy publication.'' Writer's guidelines for 9x6 SAE and 4 IRCs. Book catalog for 9x6 SAE and 4 IRCs.

JUMP RIVER PRESS, INC., 810 Vernon Ave. # 4, Madison WI 53714 (608)221-9402. Fiction Editor: Mark Bruner. Estab. 1979. Publishes paperback originals. Plans 2 first novels this year. Averages 6 total titles, 2 fiction titles each year.
Needs: Adventure, contemporary, erotica, ethnic, experimental, historical (general), horror, juvenile (historical), literary, mainstream, short story collections, translations, young adult (historical). Interested in folklore/historical novels. No religious fiction.
How to Contact: Query first with SASE. Photocopied submissions OK. Reports in 2 weeks on queries; 1 month on mss.
Terms: Pays in royalties of 10% minimum.

KAWABATA PRESS, Imprint includes Sepia Magazine, Knill Cross House, HR Anderton Rd., Millbrook, NR Toppoint, Cornwall, England. Fiction Editor: C. Webb. Estab. 1977. Publishes paperback originals. No first novels planned this year, but new writers encouraged. Averages 6-8 total titles, 1 fiction title each year. Occasionally critiques rejected mss.
Needs: Contemporary, experimental, humor/satire, literary, short story collections. Nothing traditional, adventure, science fiction, romance, historical, detective, etc. Recently published: *Best Bitter*, by C.D. Webb (short stories).
How to Contact: Query first with IRC. Simultaneous and photocopied submissions OK. Reports in 1 week on queries.
Terms: Pays in royalties of 10% minimum; 4 author's copies. Book catalog free on request.
Tips: ''I'm only a very small press and rarely can afford to publish novels—but none sell at all well. If the writer is serious, be prepared never to be published—if he writes in 'genre' send his work to the reptile houses.''

KIDS CAN PRESS, 585½ Bloor St., West, Toronto, Ontario, Canada M6G 1K5. (416)534-3141. Fiction Editor: Ricky Englander. Estab. 1973. Publishes Canadian authored paperback originals. Plans 4 first novels this year. Averages 6 total titles, 6 fiction titles each year.
Needs: Juvenile (easy-to-read, historical, picture book, spy/adventure, contemporary), young adult (easy-to-read, historical, problem novels, sports, spy/adventure). No anthropomorphisized animals.
How to Contact: Submit entire ms with SASE. Simultaneous and photocopied submissions OK. Reports in 2 months on mss.
Terms: Pays in royalties of 5% minimum, 10% maximum. Advance is negotiable. ''Can offer subsidies through Ontario Arts Council to Ontarians only.'' Book catalog free on request.
Tips: ''Canadian citizens or landed immigrants only, please.''

LAKES & PRAIRIES PRESS, 6334 N. Sheridan Rd. 4-D, Chicago, IL 60660. Editor: Edward Haggard. Publishes trade and paperback books. Estab. 1974.
Needs: Literary, contemporary, feminist, young adult, serialized and condensed novels.

How to Contact: Query. SASE for query, ms. Reports in 3 weeks on queries, 2 months on mss.
Terms: Pays in author's copies.
Tips: "Lakes & Prairies Press is a spin-off small book press from *Lakes & Prairies, A Journal of Writings*, which is no longer published. The first book appeared in fall 1980 and is a volume of poetry. We are devoted to the publication of short stories and short novels. We are not interested in writing of a strictly commercial/slick intent and inspiration. That is not to say we are indifferent to quality prose that may also have commercial appeal; such work is perfectly acceptable."

LAME JOHNNY PRESS, Star Rte. 3, Box 9A, Hermosa SD 57744. Editorial Director: Linda M. Hasselstrom. Estab. 1970. Publishes hardcover and paperback originals and paperback reprints. Encourages new authors. Usually comments on rejected mss.
Needs: Historical, contemporary fiction about the West, Middle West, Great Plains. Also publishes originally researched work about the region. "I accept on quality, not quantity. I want fiction of and for Great Plains, no gothic, romance, fantasy, and especially no so-called 'contemporary' explorations of the author's navel and psyche." Recently published *The Indian Maiden's Captivity* and *The Heart of the Country*, by E.R. Zietlow (western historical fiction).
How to Contact: Query. No simultaneous submissions; photocopied submissions OK. Reports in 1 month on queries, usually 1 month on mss.
Terms: Pays 10% of print run in author's copies and 30-50% in royalties. No advance. "Lame Johnny is a cooperative press—author must contribute cash and possibly work to the production of his/her book. Arrangement varies with author's financial situation, and mine. Often require author pay all actual printing costs; editing, publicity, etc., shared." Book catalog for legal-sized SASE with 38¢ postage.
Tips: "Write what you know. Avoid self-analysis. More self-contemplation is evident in style today. Publication of novel depends on quality of writing primarily; degree of identification with my region."

LAPIS EDUCATIONAL ASSOCIATION, INC., 18420 Klimm Avenue, Homewood IL 60430. Editorial Director: Karen Degenhart. Estab. 1977.
Needs: Contemporary, literary, religious/inspirational, psychology. "Jungian psychology focus only. We very rarely publish fiction."
How to Contact: Query. SASE for query, ms. Simultaneous and photocopied submissions OK. Reports in 2 weeks on queries, "indefinite" on mss.
Terms: "We do not pay. Authors must be fee paying members of this association to be published but may join after submitting ms. Members pay a $10 yearly fee if they are selected to be published. Don't have to join to submit ms." No advance. Free book catalog.

LAUGHING BEAR PRESS, Box 23478, San Jose CA 95153. Imprint includes *Laughing Bear* magazine (irregularly published). Editor: Tom Person. Estab. 1976. Publishes paperback originals. Encourages new writers. Plans 1 first novel for '83. Sometimes comments on rejected mss if requested.
Needs: Literary, experimental, mystery, spy, western, gothic, science fiction, fantasy, horror. "Not interested in anything over 50,000 words at this time. Styles are open, but I lean away from religious, confession, or psychic material."
How to Contact: Query with SASE. Simultaneous and photocopied submissions OK. Reports in 2 weeks on queries, 1 month on mss. "We use little unsolicited material."
Terms: Pays in at least 10 author's copies.
Tips: "First learn to write a sentence that is a story in itself; then move out to the one-page story, the short story, the serial, and finally the novel. Read the best—and the worst. Become a storyteller before you try to write a story, and listen to your voice in the telling. I think there is a strong trend back toward the detective, gothic, and western story. But with new twists. A familiar story form can act as a solid base for innovation. The reader has a familiar skeleton for reference. Laughing Bear Press has published mostly poetry in the past, but as I am becoming more involved in writing fiction myself, we will become more involved in publishing it."

LIBRARY RESEARCH ASSOCIATES, Rt. 5, Box 41, Dunderberg Rd., Monroe NY 10950. Editorial Director: Matilda A. Gocek. Estab. 1968. Publishes hardcover and paperback originals. Number of titles: 2 in 1981. Encourages new writers. Plans 1 first novel for '82.
Needs: Historical of New York State only. Recently published *By Faith Alone*, by Doris Crofut (hardcover trade).
How to Contact: Submit outline/synopsis and sample chapters with SASE. No simultaneous submissions; photocopied submissions OK. Reports in 6 weeks.
Terms: Pays in royalties; no advance. Subsidy publishes 10% of total books. Book catalog for legal-sized SASE with 20¢ postage.
Tips: "There is a gradual return to a good story line less dependent upon violence and explicit sex. I am looking to develop a line of fiction titles based on actual events or people in New York State. Fictionalized biographies based on fact would be welcomed, particularly of women in New York, any period. Do not ask me to evaluate your work as a matter of course. Do not cost me more than my time to read the material."

LINTEL, Box 34 St. George, Staten Island NY 10301. Editorial Director: Walter James Miller. Estab. 1977. Publishes hardcover and paperback originals. Number of titles: 2 in 1982, 5 planned for 1983. Sometimes comments on rejected mss.
Needs: Experimental, short fiction, poetry. Recently published *The Mountain*, by Rebecca Rass (experimental/fantasy).
How to Contact: Query with SASE. Simultaneous and photocopied submissions OK. Reports in 1 month on queries, 8 weeks on mss.
Terms: Negotiated. No advance. Free book catalog.
Tips: "*Lintel* is devoted to the kinds of literary art that will never make The Literary Guild or even the Book-of-the-Week Club: literature concerned with the advancement of literary art."

LLEWELLYN PUBLICATIONS, Box 43383, St. Paul MN 55164-0383. (612)291-1970. President: Carl L. Weschcke. Estab. 1901. Publishes hardcover and paperback originals. Averages 6-10 total titles each year, occasionally 1 fiction title.
Needs: Psychic/supernatural. "No fiction written by people with no real knowledge of the occult or parapsychology—no devil worship, demon possession, cultish junk."
How to Contact: Query first with SASE. Photocopied submissions OK. Reports in 1-4 weeks on queries, 1-4 weeks on mss.
Terms: Pays in royalties of 10% minimum; 10 author's copies free and more at 40% discount. Subsidy publishing "rare—but if done, author pays all production costs, we pay all distribution costs, and share proceeds 50/50." Book catalog for 50¢.
Tips: "We see a trend towards interest in genuine psychic phenomena, practical control of it, and awareness of human need for psychic/spirtual development."

LORIEN HOUSE, Box 1112, Black Mountain NC 28711. (704)669-6211. Contact: D. Wilson. Estab. 1969. Encourages new writers. Plans 2 first novels for 1983. Sometimes comments on rejected mss.
Needs: Experimental, fantasy, humor/satire. "No emphasized sex or horror."
How to Contact: Query or submit complete ms. SASE for query, ms. Simultaneous and photocopied submissions OK. Reports in 1 week on queries, 2 weeks on mss.
Terms: Co-op publication. Writer and publisher split all costs, then income is split the same percentage. Subsidy publishes 1 book every 2 years. No advance. Free book catalog.
Tips: "Before sending, have 5 people read your ms, including at least two strangers, for honest opinions. I don't want to hear how great the piece is; I just want to know the category, approach and specific story line in a query. My publishing firm is small. Emphasis began on poetry, shifted to solar energy to pay the bills. Fiction is difficult selling for a small press, but I do want a crack at what is out there."

LOS TRES OSOS, Subsidiary of Walnut Press, 6036 N. 10th Way, Phoenix AZ 85014. (602)265-7765. Director: Janice Davis. Estab. 1978. Publishes paperback originals. First novels are not encouraged. Averages 4 total titles, 4 fiction titles each year. Occasionally critiques rejected mss.

Needs: Juvenile (easy-to-read, picture book, bilingual). Needs material for 'Reading is fundamental' program.

How to Contact: Query first. Simultaneous submissions OK. Reports in 2 weeks on queries.

Terms: Pays honorarium—negotiates for outright purchase by individual arrangement with author depending on book.

LOST ROADS PUBLISHERS, Box 310, Eureka Springs AR 72632. Editors: C.D. Wright, Forest Gander. Estab. 1977. Publishes paperback originals and reprints. Plans 1 first collection of short fiction this year. Averages 1-6 total titles each year. Publishes also in Spanish; translation from the Dutch. Sometimes critiques rejected mss.

Needs: Contemporary, ethnic, experimental, feminist/lesbian, literary, short story collections, translations, women's.

How to Contact: Query first with SASE. Simultaneous and photocopied submissions OK. Reports in 3 weeks on queries; 3 months on mss.

Terms: Pays in royalties of 10% minimum (on subsequent editions not first edition); 25-50 author's copies; $50-300 depending on grant award. Book catalog for SASE.

LOW-TECH PRESS, 30-73 47th St., Long Island City NY 11103. (212)721-0946. Publisher: Ron Kolm. Estab. 1981. Publishes paperback originals. "We publish new writers, but only in anthologies—no novels planned in the future." Averages 2 total titles each year. Occasionally critiques rejected mss "if the ms is good."

Needs: Contemporary, experimental, satire, literary, mainstream, short story collections.

How to Contact: Query first with SASE. Reports in 1 week on queries.

Terms: Pays in author's copies (depending on size of printing).

M.O.P. PRESS, Rt. 24, Box 53c, Fort Myers FL 33908. (813)482-0802. Editorial Director: Shirley Aycock. Estab. 1978. Publishes chapbooks. Number of titles: 5 in 1981; 12 in 1982. Encourages new writers. Sometimes comments on rejected mss.

Needs: "Practically anything except erotica, juvenile." Recently published *Winging It*, by M.O.P./sra (chapbook, poetry). "Would like to do at least one 'long' short story or novelette this year. So far have had no requests."

How to Contact: Query first with SASE "for lengthy ms." No simultaneous submissions; photocopied submissions OK. Reports "as soon as possible. This might be as long as 6 weeks if involved in printing when received."

Terms: "We do not pay. Order blank and/or printing quotes for SASE."

Tips: "We will consider and provide quote for printing for authors who would wish to self-publish prose. M.O.P. operation is limited to about 50 pages, sufficient for novelette, short story or poetry, chapbook style only."

MAFDET PRESS, Publisher/Editor: W.D. Firestone. Estab. 1970. Publishes hardcover and paperback originals. Averages 2 total titles, 2 fiction titles each year. Sometimes critiques rejected mss.

Needs: Literary, short story collections. No mainstream.

How to Contact: Query first with SASE. All unsolicited mss are returned unopened. Simultaneous and photocopied submissions OK. Reports in 1 month on queries; 2 months on mss.

Terms: Pays in 60 author's copies.

Tips: "Know your English grammar. Tell a story with a good plot and well-developed characters. We see a trend towards fantasy, and sword and sorcery work."

MAINESPRING PRESS of Maine Writers Workshop, Imprint includes *Letters* Magazine, Box 82, Stonington ME 04681. (207)367-2484. Fiction Editor: Helen Nash. Estab. 1969. Contributors include: R. Buckminster Fuller, E.B. White, Carlos Baker, Kay Boyle, Richard Eberhart, etc. Averages 1 fiction title each year.

Needs: Adventure, contemporary, faction, historical, humor/satire, literary, science-fiction, young adult (fantasy/science fiction, historical). No pornography, non-ethic.

How to Contact: Query first or submit 25 pages with large SASE. Reports in 1 week on queries.

Terms: Pays in royalties of 10% minimum, 15% maximum; author's copies or an honorarium. Free sample copy with large SASE.

Tips: "Write endlessly, then rework."

MAIZE PRESS, Box 8251, San Diego CA 92102. (714)455-1128. Managing Editor: Xelina. Estab. 1971. Publishes paperback originals and reprints. Plans 3 first novels this year. Averages 2-3 total titles, 2 fiction titles each year. Occasionally critiques rejected mss.

Needs: Erotica, ethnic, experimental, juvenile (contemporary), literary, women's. No science fiction. Recently published: *There Are No Madmen Here*, by Gina Valdes (nonfiction); *Old Faces and New Wine*, by Alejandro Morales (fiction); *Bleeding Hearts and Smiling Faces*, by Lin Romero (prose/poetry); and *Cronicas Diagolicas*, de Jorgellica, edited by Juan Rodriquez (prose collection).

How to Contact: Query first or submit complete ms with SASE. Photocopied submissions OK. Reports in 3 weeks on queries; 3 months on mss.

Terms: Pays in author's copies. Writer's guidelines free.

Tips: "Social realism is essential."

MARS HILL ASSOCIATES, 9 E. 10th St., Suite 227, Holland MI 49423. (616)396-3006. Editor: Leonard George Goss. Estab. 1981. Publishes hardcover and paperback originals. Plans 2-3 first novels this year. Sometimes critiques rejected mss.

Needs: Fantasy, psychic/supernatural, religious/inspirational, science fiction. Publishes 3 or 4 novels each year—"we need novels with the qualities of classical fantasy or true myth; imaginative fiction along the lines of Tolkien, C.S. Lewis, or Charles Williams. Another category: historical sagas of biblical characters recreating Old Testament or New Testament times and customs; contemporary sagas of Christian people today, with warts and all."

How to Contact: Submit outline/synopsis and 2-3 sample chapters with SASE. Simultaneous (if notified and given time-table) and photocopied submissions OK. Reports in 4-6 weeks on mss.

Terms: Pays in royalties of 7% minimum, 15% maximum. "We would consider subsidy publishing. However, this is not our mainstay."

Tips: "Mars Hill Associates is a new publishing venture, begun in 1981. We propose to publish broadly in the category of fiction. We seek original works of fiction informed by the larger Christian worldview, and are especially interested in the genre of fantasy in both lighter stories and more psychological novels."

MASTERS PUBLICATIONS, Box 1332, Brooklyn NY 11201. (212)596-1598. Imprints include Real Life Books, Transition Books. Editorial Director: Jim Masters. Estab. 1976. Publishes paperback originals. Number of titles: 5 in 1980; 7 in 1981. Encourages new writers. Comments on rejected mss for $20.

Needs: Juvenile (ages 5-10). "Especially stories about children with handicaps, or children who are moving, starting school, new sibling, etc. No adult trade fiction." Recently published *Starting School* and *New Baby*, by Dr. Gil Martin (activity books).

How to Contact: Submit complete ms or outline/synopsis and sample chapters. SASE always. Simultaneous and photocopied submissions OK. Reports in 6 months.

Terms: Pays 5-15% royalties or by outright purchase. Also pays in 10 author's copies; nominal advance.

Tips: "Persist. Don't expect a reply overnight!"

METIS PRESS, INC., Box 25187, Chicago IL 60625. Editorial Director: Chris Johnson. Estab. 1976. Publishes paperback originals. Number of titles: 1 in 1981; 3 in 1982. Encourag ers. Sometimes comments on rejected mss.

Needs: Women's, feminist, gay/lesbian. Especially needs novels with lesbian content. Recently published *The Secret Witch*, by Linda J. Stem (children's); *Shedevils*, by Barbara Sheen (women's short stories); *Wild Women Don't Get the Blues*, by Barbara Emrys (lesbian short stories); *Hurting and Healing and Talking it Over*, by Arny Christine Straayer (lesbian short stories).
How to Contact: Query or submit complete ms. SASE with query, ms. Simultaneous and photocopied submissions OK. Reports in 6 weeks on queries, 3 months on mss.
Terms: Pays in royalties, by outright purchase and in author's copies; no advance. Free book catalog.

MICAH PUBLICATIONS, Imprints include Echad and Whole Global Anthology Series, 255 Humphrey St., Marblehead MA 01945. (617)631-7601. Literary and General Editor: Roberta Kalechofsky. Estab. 1975. Publishes paperback originals and reprints. Averages 3 total titles, 2 fiction titles each year. Sometimes critiques rejected mss.
Needs: Historical (specific), literary, religious, short story collections, translations. Recently published: *The Book of Tziril*, by Bess Waldman (family chronicle).
How to Contact: Submit outline/synopsis and sample chapters (about 40 pages) with SASE. Simultaneous and photocopied submissions OK. Reports in 3 months on mss.
Terms: Pays in royalties of 50% minimum and 15 author's copies. "Our arrangements are flexible, and subject to specific requirements of each book or what kind of cooperation the author can make towards advertising, printing (production) or distributing his/her work. We do not accept money or subsidies of any kind, but we will accept work—for instance, if the author can typeset his ms or do art work for it, and we fully expect him or her to undertake a portion of the work in trying to sell, advertise or promote the book—in return for which our royalties are high." Book catalog free on request.
Tips: "Practice a sterner discipline in fighting the market mentality, the illusions of quick fame— and the corrupting need for media publicity."

MOLE PUBLISHING CO., Rt. 1, Box 618, Bonners Ferry ID 83805. (208)267-7349. President: Mike Oehler. Estab. 1978. Publishes hardcover and paperback originals. "We would be willing to publish new writers. Averages 1/2 title each year. Occasionally critiques rejected mss.
Needs: Experimental, literary. "We are looking for novels specifically dealing with 'back to the land movement.' Homesteading, redneck vs. long-hair conflict, environmental decay, homesteaders vs. authorities, suvivalists, etc. This is a field which we believe has not been covered."
How to Contact: Submit outline/synopsis and 2 sample chapters with SASE. Simultaneous and photocopied submissions OK. Reports in 2 months on mss.
Terms: Negotiable. Self-publishers with plans to expand.

MORNING STAR PRESS, Poplar Hill Rd., West Whately, via RFD Haydenville MA 01039. Imprints include *The Phoenix*, American Novelists Cooperative, American Poets Cooperative. Editorial Director: James Cooney. Estab. 1938. Publishes hardcover and paperback originals. Encourages new writers. Plans 2 or more first novels for '82. Sometimes comments on rejected mss.
Needs: All forms of literature, novels, stories, travel books, diaries. "No exclusions except works which do not intrinsically espouse human rights and democracy."
How to Contact: Query or submit complete ms. SASE always. Simultaneous and photocopied submissions OK. Reports in 2 weeks on queries, 1 month on mss.
Terms: Pays 25% royalties; no advance.
Tips: "Whatever you write, do it out of belief and love; whenever you are discouraged, read and re-read the unabridged letters of Vincent Van Gogh, one of the world's obscure great writers."

MOSAIC PRESS, 358 Oliver Rd., Cincinnati OH 45215. (513)761-5977. Publisher: Miriam Irwin. Estab. 1977. Publishes hardcover originals of miniatures. Plans to publish 5 new authors this year. Averages 18-24 total titles, 2 fiction titles each year. Sometimes critiques rejected mss.
Needs: Comics, historical, humor/satire, juvenile (animal, historical, picture book, sports), literary, religious/inspirational, young adult (historical, sports). "Our books are short (2,500 words

maximum). No fantasy, science fiction or occult.'' Recently published: *The Invisible Dog*, by Rochelle Dubois (stray dog story).
How to Contact: Query first or submit complete ms. SASE always. Simultaneous and photocopied submissions OK. Reports in 2 weeks on queries; 2 weeks on mss.
Terms: Pays in outright purchase of $50 and 5 author's copies. ''We also do subsidy publishing of private editions. Negotiable arrangements.'' Writer's guidelines $4; book catalog $3.

MOSAIC PRESS/VALLEY EDITIONS, Box 1032, Oakville, Ontario, Canada L6J 5E9. (416)844-0963. Contact: Editorial Director. Estab. 1975. Publishes hardcover and paperback originals. Number of titles: 2 in 1980; 3 in 1981.
Needs: Literary only.
How to Contact: Query with SAE and IRC. No simultaneous submissions; photocopied submissions OK. Reports in 2 weeks on queries, 3 months on mss.
Terms: Pays 10% royalties; no advance. Free book catalog.

MOUNTAIN STATE PRESS, University of Charleston, 2300 MacCorkle Ave. SE, Charleston WV 25304. (304)346-9471, Ext. 259. Contact: Editorial Director. Estab. 1978. Publishes hardcover and paperback originals and reprints. Number of titles: 4 in 1980; 7 in 1981; 10 planned for 1982. ''We were established to publish new writers. We plan to do 4 first novels in 1982.'' Sometimes comments on rejected mss.
Needs: ''We publish only material about Appalachia or material in *all* categories by Appalachian residents. No racist or sexist material. Literary quality is our basic criterion. We need upbeat Appalachian-setting fiction. We will be needing 4-8 strong novels in the next two years, and will also consider collections of short fiction, whether reprint or original.'' Recently published *As I Remember It*, by Stanley Eskew (autobiographical Appalachian fiction); *A Tree Full of Stars*, by Davis Grubb (children's Christmas novel); *Tale of the Elk*, by W.E.R. Byrne (anecdotes about the Elk River region of WV).
How to Contact: Query or submit complete ms. SASE for query, ms. Simultaneous, if so indicated, and photocopied submissions OK. Reports in 1 week on queries, 1 month on mss.
Terms: Pays 10-30% royalties and by outright purchase; sometimes offers advance. Book catalog for legal-sized SASE with 20¢ postage.
Tips: ''Study fiction writing techniques, and keep at it with a vengeance. Appalachian fiction is a steadily growing market. We want economical style; believable, sharply drawn characters; strong, suspenseful plots; upbeat themes; no preaching. Book length mss only.''

THE NAIAD PRESS, INC., Box 10543, Tallahassee FL 32302. (904)539-9322. Imprints include Labrys Books, Pagoda Publications and Volute Books. Editorial Director: Barbara Grier. Estab. 1973. Number of titles: 8 in 1981; 10 in 1982; plans 16 in 1983.
Needs: Feminist, lesbian. Recently published *Outlander*, by Jane Rule; *Black Lesbians*, by J.R. Roberts and *Mrs. Porter's Letters*, by Vicki P. McConnell (lesbian mystery, first of the Nyla Wade series).
How to Contact: Query. SASE for query, ms. No simultaneous submissions; photocopied submissions OK ''but we prefer original mss.'' Reports in 1 week on queries, 2 months on mss.
Terms: Pays 15% royalties; no advance. Book catalog for legal-sized SASE.
Tips: ''Work hard, pretend that your book will be read fifty years from today and try not to be an object of mirth at that remove. We publish lesbian/feminist fiction primarily and prefer honest work (i.e., positive, upbeat lesbian characters). Lesbian content must be accurate . . . a lot of earlier lesbian novels were less than honest. No breast beating or complaining.'' New imprint will publish reprints and original fiction.

NEW BEDFORD PRESS, Subsidiary of Anacre Industries, Inc., 5800 W. Century Blvd., Division 91502, Los Angeles CA 90009. (213)837-2961. Imprint includes Bedpress Books. Editorial Director: Saul Burnstein. Fiction Editor: Mary Bloom. Estab. 1978. Publishes hardcover and paperback originals and paperback reprints. Plans 2 first novels this year. Averages 3 total titles, 3 fiction titles each year. Occasionally critiques rejected ms.

Needs: Adventure, contemporary, faction, juvenile (spy/adventure). "We want to see novels with good characterizations, good universal plots that the average reader could identify with." No westerns, science fiction, gothic, war or feminist. Recently published *A Card for the Players*, by Jefferson (gambling).

How to Contact: Query first with SASE. All unsolicited manuscripts are returned unopened. Simultaneous and photocopied submissions OK. Reports in 1 week on queries, 1 month on mss.

Terms: Pays in royalties of 5% minimum, 15% maximum; $2,500-3,500 in advance and pays in 50 author's copies.

Tips: "We have success with fiction that can be easily adapted to film and television. The worldwide audience always identifies with a good, solid story. Go to the movies. If you liked the picture, chances are ten to one it had a solid story. That's what made all those old movies classics."

NEW READERS PRESS, Subsidiary of Laubach Literacy International, Imprint includes Sundown Books, Box 131, Syracuse NY 13210. Editorial Director: Caroline Blakely. Estab. 1964. Publishes paperback originals. Plans 1-2 first novels this year. Averages 4-5 total titles; 4-5 fiction titles each year. Occasionally critiques rejected mss.

Needs: Adventure, gothic/historical or contemporary romance, suspense/mystery, young adult (easy-to-read, problem novels). Needs "5 to 10 short easy-to-read novels emphasizing character development, rather than slam-bam action. No stereotyped or written to formula novels." Recently published: *The Other Side of Yellow*, by Jessie Redding Hull (problem novel); *Ben's Gift*, by Cynthia Barnett (novel about handicapped person); and *Out of the Rough*, by Dorothy Kayser French (teenage problem novel with a sports setting).

How to Contact: Query first or submit outline/synopsis and sample chapters with SASE "if author knows the kind of fiction we publish." Simultaneous and photocopied submissions OK. Reports in 2 weeks on queries; 2 months on mss.

Terms: Pays in royalties of 6% minimum; advance of $200 average.

Tips: "Market is catching on for easy-to-read short novels for adults or teenagers emphasizing character development. Reviews have been excellent. We hope to get some acceptable mystery and romantic novels."

NEW RIVERS PRESS, 1602 Selby Ave., St. Paul MN 55104. Editorial Director: C.W. Truesdale. Fiction Editors: C.W. Truesdale and Roger Blakely. Estab. 1968. Number of fiction titles: 2 in 1981; 2 or 3 in 1982.

Needs: Contemporary, literary, experimental, historical (especially personal), translations. "No popular fantasy/romance. Nothing pious, polemical (unless very good other redeeming qualities). We are interested in only quality literature and always have been (though our concentration in the past has been poetry)."

How to Contact: Query. SASE for query, ms. No simultaneous submissions; reluctantly accepts photocopied submissions. Reports in 1 month on queries, within 2 months of query approval on mss.

Terms: Pays in 100 author's copies; no advance. Free book catalog.

Tips: "We are not really concerned with trends. We read for quality, which experience has taught can be very eclectic and can come sometimes from out of nowhere. We are interested in publishing short fiction (as well as poetry and translations) because it is and has been a great American indigenous form and is almost completely ignored by the commercial houses. The worst thing a writer can do, except for writing badly, is to say too much about his work—overselling it. This puts us off and is likely to make objective evaluation more difficult. Find a *real* subject, something that belongs to you and not what you think or surmise that you should be doing by current standards and fads. Be very patient with yourself in writing, take time, exercise care and craft, and be patient with getting published. A great deal of good energy is wasted by young (and old) writers crying ov⸺ ⸺ctions."

ED PRESS, 1665 Euclid Ave., Berkeley, CA 94709. (415)540-7576. Editor: Helen ⸺tab. 1971. Publishes paperback originals and reprints in Spanish/English and Chinese/

English. Number of titles: 1 in 1981, 2 in 1982. Encourages new writers. Sometimes comments on rejected mss.

Needs: Feminist, gay/lesbian, ethnic, juvenile (easy-to-read, fantasy, historical, contemporary) and young adult (historical, problem novels, easy-to-read teen). "No adult fiction that is not for children." Recently published *Silas and the Mad-Sad People*, by Amber Jayanti.

How to Contact: Query or submit complete ms. SASE always. Simultaneous and photocopied submissions OK. Reports in 2 weeks on queries, 1 month on mss.

Terms: Pays in royalties and by outright purchase; no advance. Book catalog and writer's guidelines for legal-sized SASE.

Tips: "As we are a feminist collective publishing antiracist, antisexist books, we discourage writers from sending us 'apolitical animal-type stories' whose intent is to avoid rather than confront issues. We publish children's books free from stereotyping with content that is relative to today's happenings, stories with active female characters who take responsibility for their lives, stories that challenge assumptions about the inferiority of women and Third World peoples." Rejects mss that are "trite or trivial."

THE NEW SOUTH COMPANY, Box Z 4918, Los Angeles CA 90024-0918. (213)208-6122. Editor: Nancy Stone. Estab. 1976. Publishes hardcover and paperback originals and paperback reprints. Averages 1-2 total titles each year. Occasionally critiques mss for $50.

Needs: Literary. "We want to publish one good novel in 1982." Recently published: *Moments of Light*, by Fred Chappell (short stories).

How to Contact: Query first; then submit complete ms. SASE always. Simultaneous and photocopied submissions OK. Reports in 3 weeks on queries; 5 weeks on mss.

Terms: Pays in royalties of 6% minimum, 12% maximum.

Tips: "Know the language and how it is used; don't take short cuts; don't imitate. We have seen poorly written, dull stuff masquerading as experimental. Something—a lack of discipline, a distorted attitude about success, perhaps—is draining the power and originality from fiction."

NORTH POINT PRESS, 850 Talbot Ave., Berkeley CA 94706. (415)527-6260. Editor-in-Chief: Jack Shoemaker. Assistant Editor: Thomas Christensen. Estab. 1980. Publishes hardcover and paperback originals and hardcover and paperback reprints. Averages 24 total titles, 6 fiction titles each year.

Needs: Contemporary, experimental, literary, short story collections, translations. Especially needs serious and experimental. No "genre" fictions written for a "market." Recently published *Crystal Vision*, by Gilbert Sorrentino; *Eclogues*, by Guy Davenport; and *Blue Boy*, by Jean Giono (translation). Chances for fiction not good.

How to Contact: Query first with SASE. Photocopied submissions OK. Reports in 2 months on queries; 6 months on mss.

Terms: Royalty payment varies; advance negotiable.

OMMATION PRESS, 5548 N. Sawyer, Chicago IL 60625. Imprints include *Mati Magazine*, *Ditto Rations Chapbook Series*, *Offset Offshoot Series*, *Salome: A Literary Dance Magazine*, *Dialogues on Dance Series*. Editorial Director: E. Mihopoulos. Estab. 1975. Number of book titles: 2 in 1981; 10 in 1982. Encourages new writers. Rarely comments on rejected mss.

Needs: Contemporary, literary, experimental, feminist, prose poetry. "For *Salome: A Literary Dance Magazine* Dialogues on Dance Series, dance-related fiction; for *Mati's* Offset Offshoot Series, poetry mss that include prose poems." Recently published *Songs for Isadora*, by Linda W. Wagner; *The Dancer's Muse*, by Karren L. Alenier.

How to Contact: Submit complete ms with SASE. Simultaneous, if so indicated, and photocopied submissions OK. Reports in 1 month.

Terms: Pays in 50 author's copies (and $100 honorarium if grant money available). Book catalog for legal-sized SASE.

OUTCROWD. 3 Pleasant Villas, 189 Kent Street, Mereworth, Maidstone, Kent, United Kingdom ME18 5QN. (0622)36436. Editorial Director: Rob Earl. Estab. 1976. Publishes paperback originals. Number of titles: 5 in 1979, 5 in 1980.

Needs: Contemporary, humor/satire. "I suggest a hit or miss approach by writers. I'll consider most things on their merits." Recently published *VING 1, Gasunda 3, Uncle Nasty's Extra Special, Codex Bandito 1 — 5*, by various authors (paperback pamphlets).

How to Contact: Query with SASE. Simultaneous and photocopied submissions OK. Reports in 6 weeks.

Terms: Pays in author's copies.

Tips: "Keep trying, but give up if the writing is a chore. I haven't received a lot of mss lately. Don't expect wonders, but by all means contact us. I won't ask for money. But I am only a small press, very anarchic in my approach to publishing.

PACIFIC ARTS AND LETTERS, Subsidiaries include Alps Monthly, Peace & Pieces Books, Box 99394, San Francisco CA 94109. (415)771-3431. Fiction Editor: Rev. Maurice Custodio. Estab. 1970. Publishes hardcover and paperback originals and paperback reprints. Established writers only. Averages 2-4 total titles, 1 fiction title each year.

Needs: Humor/satire, literary. Needs "short novels/novellas in sharp social satire style. For a tax-deductible contribution of $150 we mention fiction authors and books on our TV program in San Francisco and our video programs at the Bay Area Small Press Bookfairs. SASE required for application and information." Recently published: *Today's Outstanding Writers*, by Richard Morris, et. al. and *The 69 Days of Easter*, by Todd S.J. Lawson (humor/satire).

How to Contact: Query first with SASE. Photocopied submissions OK. Reports in 3 weeks on queries.

Terms: Pays honorarium ("we are non-profit"). Note: Authors must be *Alps Monthly* subscribers to submit manuscripts. "Under exceptional circumstances and for $25,000-75,000 tax-deductible donation fee, we will publish and promote 5,000 to 20,000 copies of a fiction book by well-known public figure or movie star. Individual arrangement with author." Writer's guidelines for SASE and 3 first class stamps. Book catalog for SASE and 3 first class stamps.

Tips: "Fiction is in danger of existential death; the emergence of the marriage of nonfiction and fiction in creative writing may save it. Write realistic, 'Twilight Zone' fiction and hope for the best. Bizarre fiction and romance novels seem to be most in demand today. Well-constructed or involved fiction (unfortunately) is on the wane."

PAN PACIFIC PUBLICATIONS, Box 2190, Brisbane, Qld, Australia 4000. Tel. (07)2273538. Publication and Public Relations Officer: Ms. V. Cartlidge. Estab. 1977. Publishes paperback originals. Averages varied number of total titles, varied number of fiction titles each year.

Needs: Psychic/supernatural, religious/inspirational. Needs spiritual novels. Recently published: *The Vicar*, by D.C. Jefferies (spiritual novel).

How to Contact: Submit outline/synopsis and sample chapters. Simultaneous and photocopied submissions OK. Reports in 4 weeks on mss.

Terms: Pays in royalties of 10% maximum.

Tips: "Keep trying! Polish well before submitting."

PANJANDRUM BOOKS, Imprint includes Panjandrum Press, Inc., 5428 Hermitage Ave., North Hollywood CA 91607. (213)477-8771. Editor: Dennis Koran. Estab. 1971. Publishes paperback originals. Averages 4-5 total titles, 1 fiction title each year. Occasionally critiques rejected mss.

Needs: Contemporary, experimental, fantasy, literary, science fiction, translations. "We are *highly* selective." Recently published: *Fighting Men*, by Willard Manus (contemporary war novel with social message); *Tres Inmensas Novelas*, by Vicente Hudobo and H. Arp (Translation); and *Four Texts* by Antonin Artaud (translation).

How to Contact: Query first with return postcard or SASE for reply. Photocopied submissions OK. Reports in 2 weeks on queries.

Terms: Pays in royalties of 6% minimum, 10% maximum; advance is negotiable; 10 author's copies. Book catalog for 75¢ with 6x9 SASE and 2 first class stamps.

PARABLE PRESS, 136 Gray St., Amherst MA 01002. (413)253-5634. Publisher/Managing Editor: Bethany Strong. Estab. 1975. Publishes hardcover and paperback originals. Averages 3 total titles, 2 fiction titles each year. Occasionally critiques rejected mss on request.
Needs: Contemporary, historical, humor/satire, juvenile (historical), young adult (historical, problem novels). ''Overstocked at present.''
Tips: ''We treat each project as special and individual. Whether or not a book is a 'first' for the author is not considered significant. Each work is considered on its own merit and how it fits in with our ideals.''

PARKHURST PRESS, Box 143, Laguna Beach CA 92652. (714)494-3092. Editor: Lynne Thorpe. Estab. 1981. Publishes paperback originals. Plans for first novels very limited this year. Averages 1 total title, 1 fiction title each year.
Needs: Fantasy, feminist, humor/satire. Recently published *Alida—*, by Edna MacBrayne (erotic).
How to Contact: Query first with SASE. All unsolicited manuscripts are returned unopened. Photocopied submissions OK. Reports in 2 weeks on queries; 4 weeks on mss.
Terms: Negotiates author's copies and royalties. Prefer individual arrangement with author. ''Cooperative or collective would be considered.''
Tips: ''Read, write, study, follow your instincts, and produce well crafted work. We foresee a growing demand for and support of publishers who produce quality work that is relevant, entertaining, and thought-provoking.''

PASCAL PUBLISHERS, 21 Sunnyside Ave., Wellesley MA 02181. (617)235-4278. Contact: J. Greene. Estab. 1980. Publishes paperback originals. Averages 1-2 total titles, 1-2 fiction titles each year. Occasionally critiques rejected mss.
Needs: Juvenile (historical, picture book, Jewish topics). Needs story books for young readers with Jewish content. No adult material. Recently published: *The Hanukah Tooth*, by Jacqueline Greene (picture book) and *A Classroom Hanukah* (story/project book).
How to Contact: Query first with SASE. Simultaneous and photocopied submissions OK. Reports in 3 weeks on queries.
Terms: Pays in royalties or in outright purchase. ''We would consider joint venture with author under special circumstances.'' Book catalog free on request.

PAYCOCK PRESS, Box 57206, Washington DC 20037. Imprint includes *Gargoyle Magazine*. Editor/Publisher: Richard Peabody, Jr. Estab. 1976. Publishes paperback originals and reprints. Number of titles: 2 in 1981; 2 in 1982; 2 planned for 1983. Encourages new writers. Sometimes comments on rejected mss. Publishes fiction and poetry volumes.
Needs: Contemporary, literary, experimental, humor/satire and translations. ''No tedious academic resume-conscious writing or NEA-funded minimalism. We'd be interested in a good first novel that deals with the musical changes of the past few years.'' Recently published *The Love Letter Hack*, by Michael Brondoli (contemporary/literary) and *Natural History*, by George Myers, Jr. (poems and stories).
How to Contact: Query with SASE. No simultaneous submissions; photocopied submissions OK. Reports in 1 week on queries, 1 month on mss.
Terms: Pays in author's copies 10% of print run plus 50% of all sales ''after/if we break even on book.'' No advance.
Tips: ''Keep trying. Many good writers simply quit. Many mediocre writers keep writing, eventually get published, and become better writers. If the big magazines won't publish you, try the small magazines, try the local newspaper. Don't think about writing—do it. Always read your fiction aloud. If you think something is *silly*, no doubt we'd be embarrassed too. Write the kind of stories you'd like to read and can't seem to find. We are more concerned with *how* a novelist says what he/she says, than with *what* he/she says. However, we are particularly interested in fiction which underscores our collective humanity. I sense a drift away from the Pynchonesque style of the last few years, away from 'mandarin narcissism,' and a return to what John Gardner and John Fowles have been espousing as 'moral fiction,' e.g.: imaginative ideas conveyed in real life terms.

Maybe a return to slice-of-life stories would be a good idea for the '80s. We're pretty open-minded. We like verbal tension we can believe in. Try to write about what you know. Don't try to bluff us.''

PEACE PRESS, INC., 3828 Willat Ave., Culver City CA 90230. (213)838-7387. Editor: R. Reuben. Estab. 1972. Publishes hardcover and paperback originals and hardcover and paperback reprints. Averages 8 total titles, 0-2 fiction titles each year. Sometimes critiques rejected mss.
Needs: Contemporary, fiction, feminist/lesbian, gay, humor/satire, translations, women's. Recently published: *The Woman Who Slept With Men to Take the War Out of Them*, by Deena Metzger (feminist).
How to Contact: Query first, then submit outline/synopsis and sample chapters. SASE always. Simultaneous submissions OK. Reports in 2 months on queries, mss.
Terms: Pays in royalties; advance. Book catalog free on request.

PENTAGRAM, Box 379, Markesan WI 53946. Fiction Editor: Michael Tarachow. Estab. 1974. Publishes hardcover and paperback originals. Plans 1 first novel this year. "Fiction *is* published, but poetry is the main emphasis here.'' Averages 3-7 total titles, 0-2 fiction titles each year.
Needs: Adventure, erotica, experimental, literary. "We're committed for next 2 years; writers should *always* query with SASE before sending actual mss.'' Recently published: *Anacoluthon*, by Tom Bridwell; *The Master*, by Tom Clark; and *A Man in Stir*, by Theodore Enslin.
How to Contact: Query first with SASE. Reports in 1-2 weeks on queries.
Terms: Payment arrangements variable. Book catalog free on request.

PEPPERMINT PRESS, 204 Stibbard Ave., Toronto, Ontario, Canada M4P 2C3. Imprints include Abraxas and Aura Publications. Publisher: Richard Miller.
Needs: "Our publishing program for the next five years has been established. Consequently, we will not be accepting any new material for another 2 or 3 years.''

PERIVALE PRESS, 13830 Erwin St., Van Nuys CA 91401. (213)785-4671. President: Lawrence P. Spingarn. Estab. 1968. Number of titles: 1 in 1981; 3 in 1982. Encourages new writers. Sometimes comments on rejected mss.
Needs: Contemporary, literary, experimental, western, women's, feminist, ethnic (any), erotica, and translations. No adventure, mystery, spy, historical, war, gothic, romance, confession, gay/lesbian, psychic, religious, science fiction, horror or juvenile. Novellas up to 125 pp. in typescript; no limitation on genres or styles. Publishes one per year. Recently published *Rice Powder*, by Sergio Galindo (novella of Mexico); and *Mountainhouse*, by Pat McDermid.
How to Contact: Query with SASE. Simultaneous and photocopied submissions OK. Reports in 1 week on queries, 10 weeks on mss.
Terms: Pays 10-15% in royalties. No advance. Subsidy publishes 20% of total books. Author pays cost of printing and gets contract which stipulates that this amount, usually about $1,000, will be returned from sales within 18 months. Free book catalog with SASE and 20¢ postage.
Tips: "Place stories first, even in literary magazines, before submitting ms to publisher. Novels should appeal to a college-educated audience. We foresee the publication of more serious novels of a less sensational kind in the next few years. On translated work, get clearance from original publisher before submitting. Writer should consider a subsidy plan whereby his investment is returned through sales; he should also agree to making personal appearances (lectures, TV shows, etc.) if we offer contract.''

PERSEPHONE PRESS, Box 7222, Watertown MA 02172. (617)924-0336. Publishers: Pat McGloin and Gloria Z. Greenfield. Estab. 1976. Publishes paperback originals and reprints. Number of titles: 5 in 1981; 5 planned for 1982. Encourages new writers. Plans 1 first novel for '82. Sometimes comments on rejected mss.
Needs: Woman-identified pioneering work and translations also about women. "We are always interested in seeing good quality lesbian novels.'' No heterosexual romance. Recently published

This Bridge Called My Back: Writings by Radical Women of Color Editors, Cherrie Moraga and Gloria Anzaldua; *Choices: A Novel about Lesbian Love*, by Nancy Toder; *Claiming An Identity They Taught Me To Despise*, by Michelle Clief; *Lifetime Guarantee: A Journey through Loss and Survival*, by Alice Bloch.

How to Contact: Query with SASE. No simultaneous submissions; photocopied submissions OK. Reports in 1 month on queries.

Terms: Receives 50% profit. No advance. Free book catalog.

Tips: "Get involved in writing groups and start publishing short stories in journals. Do not send ms without first sending query and receiving response. Make sure ms is clean and in orderly fashion. Should not have any sexist, homophobic, racist or anti-Jewish material in it. Persephone Press is dedicated to fostering lesbian-feminist sensibility through the publication of innovative and provocative writings by women."

PHEASANT RUN PUBLICATIONS, Box 14043, St. Louis MO 63178. (314)291-3439. Fiction Editor: Janis Torrey. Estab. 1981. Publishes hardcover and paperback originals. Plans 5 first novels this year. Averages 2 total titles, 2 fiction titles each year. Publishes also in German and Spanish. Occasionally critiques rejected mss.

Needs: Adventure, erotica, experimental, fantasy, historical, horror, literary, psychic/supernatural. Needs intellectual fiction with emphasis on experimentation. No romance, western or youth. Recently published: *Reign of the Madman: The Birdcatcher*, by Walter Schenck (experimental/psychological).

How to Contact: Query first with SASE. Simultaneous and photocopied submissions OK. Reports in 1 week on queries, 4 weeks on mss.

Terms: Pays in royalties of 10% minimum, 12% maximum.

Tips: "Be independent, but be prepared for disappointments."

PHUNN PUBLISHERS, Box 201, Wild Rose WI 54984. (414)622-3251. Imprints include Lambscroft Books. Senior Editor: Jeri Bross. Estab. 1976. Publishes hardcover and paperbook originals and reprints. Plans 4-8 first novels this year. Occasionally comments on rejected mss.

Needs: Adventure, fantasy, historical romance, historical, humor/satire, juvenile (animal, easy-to-read, fantasy, historical, sports, spy/adventure, contemporary, inspirational, science fiction, short story collections, suspense/mystery, war, western, women's, young adult (easy-to-read, fantasy/science fiction, historical, problem novels, sports, spy/adventure). "We especially invite works of never before published authors. No pornography, gay/lesbian; or derogatory ethnic attitudes." Recently published: *Tomorrow is a River*, by Peggy Hanson Dopp and Barbara Fitz Vroman (historical romance novel); and *From the Top of a Secret Tree*, by Pearl Dopp (autobiography).

How to Contact: Query first; submit complete ms with SASE. Simultaneous and photocopied submissions OK. Reports in 1-3 weeks on queries; 1-3 months on mss.

Terms: Pays in royalties of 8% minimum; 15% maximum. "Open to subsidy publishing. Also cooperative publishing and individual arrangement with author depending on book." Writer's guidelines for # 10 SASE and 2 first class stamps.

Tips: "Don't give up. Be alert to small presses and co-op publishing, especially for your first. But be aware that distribution is the challenge for any book! Value and learn from your rejections. Our submissions show that regardless of what the major publishing houses are accepting, there are many writers who shun the neurotic and pornographic and have good positive manuscripts worthy of consideration."

PIG IRON PRESS, Box 237, Youngstown OH 44501. (216)744-2258. Editor: Jim Villani. Fiction Editor: Rose Sayre. Estab. 1973. Publishes paperback originals. Plans 1 first novel this year. Averages 2 total titles, 1 fiction title each year.

Needs: Comics, contemporary, experimental, fantasy, humor/satire, literary, science fiction, war (Viet Nam). "Need only short fiction for anthologies as per categories." Recently p *Going Public*, by John King (experimental).

How to Contact: Submit outline/synopsis and 3 sample chapters with SASE. Photocopied submissions OK. Reports in 4 weeks on queries; 3 months on mss.
Terms: Pays in royalties of 10% minimum; 10% maximum. Writer's guidelines for # 10 SASE. Book catalog free on request.

PIKESTAFF PUBLICATIONS, INC., Box 127, Normal IL 61761. (309)452-4831. Imprints include The Pikestaff Press: Pikestaff Fiction Chapbooks; *The Pikestaff Forum*, general literary magazine. Editorial Directors: James R. Scrimgeour and Robert D. Sutherland. Estab. 1977. Publishes hardcover and paperback originals. Number of titles: 2 in 1981. Encourages new writers. Sometimes comments on rejected mss.
Needs: Contemporary, literary and experimental. "No slick formula writing written with an eye to the commercial mass-market or pure entertainment that does not provide insights into the human condition. Not interested in heroic fantasy (dungeons & dragons, swords & sorcery); science-fiction of the space-opera variety; westerns; mysteries; love-romance; gothic adventure; or pornography (sexploitation)."
How to Contact: Query or submit outline/synopsis and sample chapters (1-2 chapters). SASE always. No simultaneous or photocopied submissions. Reports in 1 month on queries, 3 months on mss.
Terms: Negotiates terms with author.
Tips: "Explore the possibilities of self-publication; there are many how-to books on the market that explain the ropes. One advantage is the control you can maintain over the shape and appearance of the final product—and you're not subject to editorial whim. Always be honest and play fair with your editors; don't be afraid to assert yourself. Yet be willing to learn. Don't be superficial with your writing. Develop your craft. Have fictional characters we can really *care* about; we are tired of disembodied characters wandering about in their heads unable to relate to other people or the world about them. Avoid too much TELLING; let the reader participate by leaving something for him or her to do. Yet avoid vagueness, opaqueness, personal or 'private' symbolisms and allusions."

PLAIN WRAPPER PRESS, Via Carlo Cattaneo 6, Verona, Italy 37121. Tel. (045)38-9-43. Printer/Publisher: Gabriel Rummonds. Estab. 1966. Publishes hardcover and paperback originals. Publishes new writers, "but most of our authors are well-established." Averages 4-5 total titles, 1-2 fiction titles each year. Also publishes in Italian and Spanish with English translations. Occasionally critiques rejected mss.
Needs: Contemporary, experimental, fantasy, literary, short stories, translations. "All pieces must be short—under 6,000 words. We do not publish novels—short pieces only. No ethnic, political." Recently published short stories by Italo Calvino, Anthony Burgess, Luigi Santucci.
How to Contact: Query first. Photocopied submissions OK. Reports in 2 weeks on queries.
Terms: Pays in outright purchase of $200 minimum; $400 maximum per 1,000 words. "We do accept some commissions." Writer's guidelines free. Book catalog free on request.
Tips: "Our books are all hand-printed limited editions, usually fewer than 150 copies per title. No reprints."

THE PRAIRIE PUBLISHING COMPANY, Box 264, Station C, Winnipeg, Manitoba, Canada R3M 3S7. (204)885-6496. Publisher: Ralph Watkins. Estab. 1969.
How to Contact: Query with SASE. No simultaneous submissions; photocopied submissions OK. Reports in 1 month on queries, 6 weeks on mss.
Terms: Pays 10% in royalties. No advance. Free book catalog.
Tips: "Do not be discouraged by rejections."

PRESS GANG PUBLISHERS, 603 Powell St., Vancouver, British Columbia, Canada V6A 1H2. (604)253-1224. Estab. 1972. Publishes hardcover and paperback originals. Number of titles: 1 in 1980; 3 in 1981. Sometimes comments on rejected mss.
Needs: Non-sexist children's books; novels for adolescents or adults, with a feminist perspec-

tive. Recently published *Common Ground; Stories by Women* (anthology).

How to Contact: Query if in doubt, submit complete ms or submit outline/synopsis and sample chapters with SAE and IRC. Simultaneous and photocopied submissions OK (but we must be told). Reports in 3 weeks on queries, 3 months on mss.

Terms: Pays 5-10% in royalties. Terms vary and are negotiated indvidually. No advance Free book catalog.

Tips: "We seek to produce books for as general an audience as possible, but with a particular focus on women and feminists. Mss with many American places named are given low priority. Sexist or racist material not considered."

PRESSED CURTAINS, 4 Bower St., Maidstone, Kent, England ME16 8SD. Tel. (0622)63681. Subsidiary includes Curtains Magazine. Editor: Paul Buck. Estab. 1971. Publishes paperback originals. Publishes new writers in magazine first. Averages 6 total titles, 4 fiction titles each year. Publishes also in French. Occasionally critiques rejected mss.

Needs: Contemporary, erotica, experimental, literary, translations. "The needs are set by the writers—the more suitable fiction I receive, the more I'll publish." Recently published: *Lust*, by Paul Buck (textual); *A Tale*, by Andrew Benjamin (textual); and *Memories of the Pale*, by Bernard Noël (translation).

How to Contact: Photocopied submissions OK.

Terms: Pays in royalties; in author's copies or honorarium. "Each book is arranged with author. Being extremely literary and experimental, payment is not prime concern for publisher or writer." Book catalog free on request.

PRESSWORKS PUBLISHING, INC., Box 190441, Dallas TX 75219. (214)749-1044. President: Anne Dickson. Estab. 1981. Publishes hardcover and paperback originals and reprints. Averages 10 total titles, 6 fiction titles each year.

Needs: Historical, humor/satire, literary, short story collections, western. Recently published: *MSS*, edited by John Gardner (collection of stories); *The First Geo Mills*, by Stanley Elkin (short story); and *Presents*, by Donald Barthelme (short story).

How to Contact: Submit outline/synopsis and 3 sample chapters with SASE. Simultaneous and photocopied submissions OK. Reports in 2-3 months on queries; 3-4 months on mss.

Terms: Pays in royalties of 10% minimum; 15% maximum; in outright purchase of $900 minimum; $2,500 maximum. Writer's guidelines for SASE. Book catalog free on request.

PRO ACTIVE PRESS, 1190 Miller Ave., Berkeley CA 94708. (415)549-0839. Editor: Jim Craig. Estab. 1973. Publishes hardcover and paperback originals. Plans 1-2 first novels this year. Averages 1 total title each year.

Needs: Utopian. "Only Utopian novels that clearly show ways to move out of the Reagan era into a future that is good for everyone. Nothing involving the supernatural, occult, psychic, or spirtual realms. No horror stories. Nothing dependent upon future technology."

How to Contact: Query first with SASE. Simultaneous and photocopied submissions OK. Reports in 2 weeks on queries; 2 months on mss.

Terms: Pays in royalties. Writer's guidelines for # 10 SASE.

PROZA PRESS, Box 410, 2400 AK Alphen a/d Rijn, Holland. Publisher: Robert Lyng. Estab. 1976. Publishes paperback originals. No first novels planned, but short stories, plays, etc. Averages 4 total titles, 2-3 fiction titles each year. Also publishes some Dutch and German. Occasionally critiques rejected mss.

Needs: Contemporary, experimental, fantasy, horror, humor/satire, literary, short story collections, suspense/mystery, translations. "Will consider doing 2 shorter novels in 1983-1984." Recently published *The Elizabeth Augustine Reader*, by E. Augustine (collection short stories and plays); and *American Garbage*, by P. McGivern (short stories).

How to Contact: Simultaneous and photocopied submissions OK. SAE and IRC. Reports in 4 weeks on queries and mss.

Terms: Pays in royalties of 10% minimum, 15% maximum; up to 50 author's copies. Subsidy publishes 1 title per year—sometimes more. Author pays only actual production cost. Author receives minimum 30 free copies plus 12½% sales. Writer's guidelines for IRC ($1.50 postage).
Tips: "Keep violence to the absolute minimum required by your subject. Humor is extremely beneficial, if not silly or slapstick. Pay close attention to characterization. Details (well-selected) are more effective than a slow dialogue. Literature *can* be entertaining. The trend toward 'self analysis' fiction is still too strong. This usually produces flat, 2-dimensional characters and situations. Too much fiction has stereotyped 'hero' or 'anti-hero.' "

THE PUBLISHING WARD, INC., 725 Breakwater Dr., Fort Collins CO 80525. (303)226-5107. Editor: Dan S. Ward. Estab. 1982. Publishes hardcover and paperback (limited) originals. Plans 1-2 first novels this year. Averages 4-6 total titles; 4-6 fiction titles each year.
Needs: Historical, humor/satire, science fiction. Needs "futuristic science fiction with realistic characters and well-researched historical novels. No fantasy. Recently published *Dawn, The Chosen*, by D.S. Ward (science fiction/romance).
How to Contact: Submit complete ms with SASE. Simultaneous and photocopied (good) submissions OK. Reports in 6 weeks on mss.
Terms: Pays in royalties of 10% minimum, 15% maximum.
Tips: "More need for good novels to fill cable TV/movie channels."

PUCKERBRUSH PRESS, 76 Main St., Orono ME 04473. (207)866-4868. Publisher/Editor: Constance Hunting. Estab. 1970. Publishes paperback originals and reprints. Number of titles: 2 in 1981, 4 in 1982. Sometimes comments on rejected mss.
Needs: Literary. No other category considered. In novels, looking for "truly new" material, "but usually publish short story collections." Recently published *A Stranger Here, Myself*, by Thelma Nason (short stories); and *)The Police Know Everything—Downeast Stories*, by Sanford Phippen; and *The Rocking Horse Stories*; by Douglas Young.
How to Contact: Submit outline/synopsis and sample chapters (2) with SASE. Simultaneous and photocopied submissions OK. Reports in 6 weeks on mss.
Terms: Pays 10% maximum in royalties and 10 free author's copies. No advance.
Tips: "There's less experimental subject matter, more satire; style is cleaner and revision is in. Read to find out how it's done; then do your *own* writing."

QUALITY PUBLICATIONS, INC., Box 2633, Lakewood OH 44107, Executive Editor: Gary S. Skeens. Estab. 1978. Publishes paperback originals. Averages 6 total titles, 3 fiction titles each year. Occasionally critiques rejected mss.
Needs: Adventure, contemporary, faction, historical, short story collections, western. No low quality or pornographic mss or mss lacking characterization, plot, etc. Recently published *As Any Mountain of Its Snows*, by Joseph Davey (short story collections).
How to Contact: Query first; submit outline/synopsis and 4 sample chapters with SASE. Simultaneous and photocopied submissions OK. Reports in 2 weeks on queries, 6 weeks on mss.
Terms: Pays in royalties of 10% minimum, 20% maximum. Payment "depends on the book; discussion with individual authors." Writer's guidelines free. Book catalog free on request.
Tips: "Be honest. Have good characterization, plot, write from the gut and make the reader feel . . . I mean, really feel. Most of all, *write*. I think there will be a rise in experiential fiction as well as urban or street fiction, work that people can truly feel; and, the literary quality will not lessen, but rise." Not accepting mss until late 1983.

QUINTESSENCE PUBLICATIONS, 356 Bunker Hill Mine Rd., Amador City CA 95601. (209)267-5470. Publisher: Marlan Beilke. Estab. 1976. Publishes hardcover and paperback originals.
Needs: Literary.
How to Contact: Query with SASE. Simultaneous and photocopied submissions OK. Reports in 2 weeks on queries, 1 month on mss.

Terms: Open to negotiation; no advance. "We will subsidy print/publish. Usual arrangement: Typesetting: 1/2; Final proofs: 1/4; Delivery: 1/4." Free book catalog with SASE and postage for 2 oz. weight.

Tips: "Quality must be paramount throughout. Miracles occur as a result of sweat. We've noticed increased interest in the writing by/of/about Jack London and Robinson Jeffers. We print/publish strictly letterpress editions—handset and linotype exclusively. We prefer subsidy publishing for those who seek letterpress printing."

RACCOON BOOKS, Suite 401, Mid-Memphis Tower, 1407 Union, Memphis TN 38104. (901)357-5441. Managing Editor: Phyllis A. Tickle. Editor: David Spicer. Estab. 1975. Publishes hardcover and paperback originals and reprints. Number of titles: 3 in 1981. Encourages new writers. Sometimes comments on rejected mss.

Needs: Contemporary, literary and experimental. Prefers short short stories and novellas.

How to Contact: Submit complete ms with SASE. Simultaneous and photocopied submissions OK. Reporting depends on the quality of the mss.

Terms: Negotiates terms; no advance.

RIVERSEDGE PRESS, INC., Box 1547, Edinburg TX 78539. Contact: Editor. Estab. 1977. Encourages new writers. Sometimes comments on rejected mss.

Needs: Contemporary, literary, experimental, fiction, historical, feminist, ethnic (Chicano), translations and the Southwest. No book-length fiction. "We use short stories and short story collections."

How to Contact: Simultaneous and photocopied submissions OK. Reports in 1 month on queries, 8 weeks on mss.

Terms: Pays from 2-15 author's copies; no advance.

Tips: "Since we publish primarily short fiction, I think our type of publication is a good training ground for ideas which might be incorporated into longer fiction later. Pedantic, moralizing, and sexist views are not welcome. Nor is extreme erotica. I am always looking for fiction which suggests that moments of satisfaction with the human condition are indeed still possible even in this 'worst of all possible worlds.' Obviously as long as people do not *all* engage in mass suicide, there is something to be said for life and humanity. Say it, in fresh ways."

ROSSEL BOOKS, 44 Dunbow Dr., Chappaqua NY 10514. (914)238-8954. President: Seymour Rossel. Estab. 1981. Publishes hardcover and paperback originals and paperback reprints. Averages 5 total titles, 1 fiction title each year. Occasionally critiques rejected mss.

Needs: Juvenile (easy-to-read, historical, picture book, spy/adventure, contemporary), young adult (easy-to-read, fantasy/science fiction, historical, problem novels, spy/adventure). "We seek fiction manuscripts for young adults and juveniles only; must have Judaic content, since we specialize in Jewish publishing." No adult fiction. "Our first fiction title will be published in 1983. It is a mystery/adventure for young adults concerned with anti-Semitism on Long Island."

How to Contact: Query first; submit outlines/synopsis and 2 sample chapters with SASE. Simultaneous and photocopied submissions OK. Reports in 2 weeks on queries; 1 month on mss.

Terms: Pays in negotiable royalties; negotiates advance. Book catalog for # 10 SASE and 37¢ postage.

Tips: "We will publish more fiction, as we expand our line."

S & S PRESS, Box 5931, Austin TX 78763. Imprint includes Black Rose Books. Publisher: D.W. Skrabanek. Estab. 1978. Publishes paperback originals. Averages 2-3 total titles, 0-1 fiction title each year. Sometimes critiques rejected mss.

Needs: Horror, humor/satire. No love stories, etc. "We publish fiction with very specific slants. For example, our next fiction/poetry publication will be an anthology of macabre/horror literature." Recently published: *Kitty Torture*, by D.S. Phantom and Bosco da Gama. "Ms length to 100 pages, usually much shorter, 24-48 pages."

How to Contact: Query first with SASE. Photocopied submissions OK. Reports in 4 weeks on queries; 6-8 weeks on mss.

Terms: Pays in 1-2 author's copies. "We are basically self-publishers, but we have published works by other authors and plan to continue doing so."

ST. LUKE'S PRESS, INC., Suite 401, Mid-Memphis Tower, 1407 Union, Memphis TN 38104. Managing Editor: Dr. Robert Eason. Senior Editor: Phyllis Tickle. Estab. 1975. Publishes hardcover and paperback originals. Averages 3 total titles each year. Occasionally critiques rejected mss.
Needs: Literary, psychic/supernatural, translations, women's. No religious, gothic or gay.
How to Contact: Submit outline/synopsis and 3 sample chapters with SASE. Simultaneous and photocopied submissions OK. Reports in 4 weeks on mss.
Terms: Pays "according to circumstances. Individual arrangements with author depending on book, etc." Free book catalog on request.

SALT LICK PRESS, Box 1064, Quincy IL 62301. Imprint includes Lucky Heart Books. Publisher/Editor: James Haining. Estab. 1969. Publishes paperback originals. Encourages new writers. Plans 1 first novel for '82. Sometimes comments on rejected mss.
Needs: Contemporary, literary, experimental, fiction, women's, feminist, gay/lesbian, ethnic, erotica, psychic/supernatural, science fiction, fantasy, horror, humor/satire and translations. Recently published *A Quincy History*, by James Haining; *Lovers/Killers*, by Robert Trammel; *Next Services*, by Michalea Moore; *New Icons*, by Peggy Davis; *Peter Rabbit's Trick*, by David Searcy; and *Boccherini's Minuet* (2nd Ed.); by Gerald Burns.
How to Contact: Submit complete ms with SASE. No simultaneous submissions, photocopied submissions OK. Reports in 1 month on mss.
Terms: Pays in author's copies; no advance.

SAMISDAT, Box 129, Richford VT 05476. Imprint includes *Samisdat Magazine*. Editor/Publisher: Merritt Clifton. Estab. 1973. Publishes paperback originals. Number of titles: 2 in 1981; 1 planned for 1982. Encourages new writers. "Over 60% of our titles are first books—about 1 first novel per year." Sometimes comments on rejected mss.
Needs: Recently published *How He Got The Mule*, by Doug Odom (2 short stories & poem); *The Green Chain*, by Everett Whealdon (novel); and *Betrayal*, by Merritt Clifton (novella).
How to Contact: Query or submit complete ms. SASE always. Reports in 1 week on queries, time varies on mss.
Terms: No advance. Free book catalog with SASE
Tips: "We do not wish to see *any* book-length ms submissions from anyone who has not already either published in our quarterly magazine, *Samisdat*, or at least subscribed for about a year to find out who we are and what we're doing. We are not a 'market' engaged in handling books as commodities and are equipped to read only about one novel submission per month over and above our magazine submission load. Submissions are getting much slicker, with a lot less guts to them. This is precisely the opposite of what we're after. Our regular magazine contributors are providing all the book-length material we can handle right now. Read the magazine. Submit stories or poems or chapters to it. When familiar with us, and to our subscribers, query about an appropriate book ms. We don't publish books except as special issues of the magazine, and blind submissions stand absolutely no chance of acceptance at all. Submissions from people who've taken the trouble to understand us, on the other hand, have a pretty good batting average—if they're something within our technical capabilities to begin with. Our author payments for books are a paradox: At this writing, we've published exactly 115 titles over the past 9 years, about 85% of which have earned the authors a profit. On the other hand, we've relatively seldom issued royalty checks—maybe 15 or 20 in all this time, and all for small amounts. We're also paradoxical in our modus operandi: Authors cover our cash expenses (this comes to about a third of the total publishing cost—we're supplying equipment and labor) in exchange for half of the press run, but we make no money from authors and if we don't promote a book successfully, we still lose."

SCHOOL OF LIVING PRESS, RD. 7, York PA 17402. (717)755-2666. Editor: Mildred J. Loomis. Estab. 1936. Publishes paperback originals.

Close-up

Alta
Shameless Hussy Press

When Alta began her small press 14 years ago, few approved of her so-called unorthodox publishing plans. Regardless, Alta continued to publish only the books she loved, and reaffirmed what many people said about her by calling her publishing venture the Shameless Hussy Press.

Alta ("it's easier to remember one name") might be symbolic in Spanish or short for altruism. In her one-woman publishing struggle she has maintained a "high" level of courage and conviction, and the campaign has been "difficult," "arduous."

Her ideals, of course, don't pay the rent on her two-bedroom house, the office setting for the Shameless Hussy Press. Over the years to keep the press going, Alta has had to borrow money and/or rely on occasional grants; she also works part-time doing bookkeeping and typing term papers. But she reserves special time during her long week for her own writing, which she has done in one form or another for 36 years, or ever since she was able to print her ABC's legibly. Essays, poetry and novels comprise the 30 books she has written, and 11 have been published by various small presses, including her collection of poetry, *I Am Not a Practicing Angel*.

Alta's publishing pursuits began in 1969 after a discouraging attempt to put together a women's anthology for a women's conference. Finding very little material, Alta realized the need to publish women writers, their pertinent subjects—and some of her own work.

"At first I did everything myself, including the printing," she says. Now with the help of a part-time assistant, she mainly handles the editorial responsibilities—the reading and selecting of manuscripts and their preparation for the printer. There have been some very lean years, she admits, except for a period when two of her books (*The Haunted Pool*, by George Sand and *For Colored Girls Who Have Consid-*

ered Suicide, by Ntozake Shange) were on bestseller lists, thanks to prodigious promotion and distribution, two of the most difficult aspects of a small press.

Alta publishes three books a year, and has represented noted feminist authors: Shange, Susan Griffin, Joyce Carol Thomas, Mitsuye Yamada. Five of her authors have been male, but with subjects either "of extreme consciousness of the feminist movement or ones that bypass the problem."

Understandably, the SHP publisher does not accept kindly the public's current romance with romantic fiction with themes she finds so contrary to the subjects she espouses. Romantic novels, she says are "really damaging, unreal, and lack the values of self-questioning," a regressive change from the fiction of a few years ago which helped women escape their confining roles.

But life is cyclical, says the SHP editor with optimism. Of her publishing objectives, she intends to "keep going. . . . My work so far has been good. I've worked hard. I can't ask any more of myself than that."

To other writers, she advises: Believe in yourself; believe in your work. There has always been a small audience for great books—and there always will be. And don't allow yourself to think there is a stigma to small press or self-publishing.

Needs: "We work only with titles that either fictionally or nonfictionally deal with human, decentralist social change. Titles for the future in planning stages."
How to Contact: Simultaneous and photocopied submissions OK. Reports in 1 week on queries, 1 month on mss.
Terms: Pays in 5 author's copies; no advance. Free brochure with SASE.
Comments: "We see a larger public interest in social change. Keep at it. Be clear, brief and illustrate with specifics. Avoid long treatises; be sure of researched facts."

SECOND COMING PRESS, Box 31249, San Francisco CA 94131. (415)647-3679. Imprint includes Second Coming. Editor/Publisher: A.D. Winans. Estab. 1972. Publishes hardcover and paperback originals. Plans 1 first novel this year. Averages 4-6 total titles, 1-2 fiction titles each year. Occasionally critiques rejected mss.
Needs: Contemporary, fantasy, humor/satire, literary, science fiction, short story collections. "Not accepting material until Summer, 1983." Recently published: *Skinny Dynamite*, by Jack Micheline (short story collection).
How to Contact: "Send sample chapter or two with outline." Simultaneous and photocopied submissions OK. Reports in 2-4 weeks on mss.
Terms: Pays in author's copies (10% print run). Book catalog available Spring '83.

SEED CENTER, Box 658, Garberville CA 95440. (707)986-7575. Editor: Sura Thurman. Estab. 1972. Publishes paperback originals and reprints. Sometimes comments on rejected mss.
Needs: Contemporary, literary, women's, psychic/supernatural, religious/inspirational, science fiction, fantasy, humor/satire and juvenile and young adult.
How to Contact: Query with SASE. Reports in 2 weeks on queries, 1-3 months on mss.
Terms: Pays 8-15% in royalties; no advance. Free book catalog.

SEVEN BUFFALOES PRESS, Box 249, Big Timber MT 59011. Editor/Publisher: Art Cuelho. Estab. 1975. Publishes paperback originals. Plans 1-2 first novels this year. Averages 4-5 total titles, 3-4 fiction titles each year.
Needs: Contemporary, short story collections, "rural, American Hobo, Okies, American Indian, Southern Appalachia, Arkansas, and The Ozarks. Not currently accepting unsolicited mss (1983). Query about mss first. Wants farm and ranch based stories . . . novels. Recently published *Birthright*, by Richard Dokey (collection of rural farm short stories).
How to Contact: Query first with SASE. Photocopied submissions OK. Reports in 1 week on queries; 2 weeks on mss.
Terms: Pays in royalties of 10% minimum; 15% on second edition or in author's copies (10% of edition). No advance. Free writer's guidelines and book catalog for SASE.
Tips: "There's too much influence from T.V. and Hollywood; media writing I call it. We need to get back to the people; to those who built and are still building this nation with sweat, bood, and brains. More people are into it for the money; instead of for the good writing that is still to be cranked out by isolated writers. Remember, I was a writer for 20 years before I became a publisher."

SHAMELESS HUSSY PRESS, Box 3092, Berkeley, CA 94703. (415)548-7800. Publisher: Alta. Estab. 1969. Number of titles: 4 in 1981.
Needs: Contemporary, literary, experimental, adventure, mystery, spy, historical, western, women's, feminist, ethnic, science fiction, fantasy, humor/satire, juvenile and young adult. "Our specialty is women's and feminist." Recently published *The Wise Queen*, by K. Simon (children's fiction).
How to Contact: Submit outline/synopsis and sample chapters. SASE for query and ms. Simultaneous and photocopied submissions OK. Reports in 6 weeks.
Terms: Pays in author's copies; no advance. Free book catalog.
Tips: "Publish yourself."

THE SMITH, 5 Beekman St., New York NY 10038. Editor: Harry Smith. Fiction Editor: Nancy Hallinan. Managing Editor: Tom Tolnay. Estab. 1964. Publishes paperback originals. Number of titles: 1 in 1981; 1 in 1982.
Needs: Experimental, literary, some science fiction, women's. Fiction with artistic merit; not confined but receptive to avant garde.Recently published *Stranger From Home*, by Elizabeth Leonie Simpson (novel); *The Dooming Eye*, by Peter Edlev; and *Traffic*, by Tom Smith.
How to Contact: Submit short outline and/or single chapter with SASE.
Terms: Pays by outright purchase of $1,000 maximum; no advance. Free book catalog.

S.O.S. BOOKS, 1821 Kalorama Rd., NW, Washington DC 20009. Fiction Editor: Richard Flynn. Estab. 1982. Publishes paperback originals. "We hope to publish at least two first books in 1983." Averages 2 total titles each year. Occasionally critiques rejected mss. "There is no charge for a critique, but there is a reading fee for every ms."
Needs: Experimental, literary, mainstream, short story collection. "We are primarily interested in manuscripts of fiction or poetry of approximately 48-80 typed pages, but will consider short novels. At this point, we expect our first fiction title to be a collection of short stories. We are not interested in genre fiction or in poorly written fiction with no literary merit."
How to Contact: Submit complete ms accompanied by $5 reading fee with SASE. Simultaneous and photocopied submissions OK. Reports in 2 weeks on queries; 2 months on mss.
Terms: Pays in 50 author's copies; honorarium or standard royalties (no advance). "The author chooses his method of compensation from among these three." Writer's guidelines for SASE.

SPECTRE PRESS, 61 Abbey Rd., Heathfield, Fareham, Hampshire, England PO15 5HN. Tel. TICHFIELD 45524. Publisher/Editor: Jon Harvey. Estab. 1976. Publishes hardcover and paperback originals. Plans 2 first novels this year. Averages 3-4 total titles, 3-4 fiction titles each year. Occasionally critiques rejected mss.
Needs: Comics, fantasy, horror, juvenile (fantasy), psychic/supernatural, science fiction, short story collections, young adult (fantasy/science fiction). Needs "original works in fantasy/horror/science fantasy. We quote no numbers as, being a small press, we are limited in resources. Novels may either be published in book form or serialized—if possible—in our house journal, *Spectral*." No psychedelic or hard science fiction. Recently published *Man Who Lifted the Mountain*, by Manoj Das (Indian fairy story); and *Ghoul Warning and Other Omens*, by Brian Lumley (fantasy/horror/science fiction poetry).
How to Contact: Submit outline/synopsis and sample chapters with IRCs. Photocopied submissions OK. Reports in 6 weeks on queries; 2 months on mss.
Terms: Pays negotiable advance; author's copies—10 for novels, 2 for short stories. Pays approximately 1¢ per word, but this is variable with the length of the work. Negotiable with authors. Writer's guidelines for SASE. Book catalog free on request.
Tips: "Be neat and tidy in your submissions. Always enclose a cover letter. Always enclose the cost of return postage and *never* in US stamps."

SPIRITUAL FICTION PUBLICATIONS, 5 Garber Hill Rd., Blauvelt NY 10913. (914)359-9292. Editor-in-Chief: Bernard J. Garber. Fiction Editor: Michael Miller. Averages 4-5 titles each year. Subsidiary of: Garber Communications, Inc.
Needs: Spiritual fiction or spiritual/esoteric fiction. No science fiction. Recently published or reprinted: *Zanoni: A Rosicrucian Tale*, by Edward Bulwer-Lytton; *A Romance of Two Worlds*, by Marie Corelli; and*Seraphita* by Balzac.
How to Contact: Query first or send 2-3 page outline, plus 10-15 pages of sample chapter. SASE with query, ms. Photocopied submissions OK. Reports in 2 weeks on queries; 2 months on mss.
Tips: "Read what we have published." Categories include: occult, historical, inspirational, science, religious, psychic and supernatural.

STATION HILL PRESS, Barrytown NY 12507. (914)758-5840. Imprints include Open and Cordella Books. Publishers: Gearze Quasha, Susan Quasha. Managing Editor: Michele Martin.

small press

Estab. 1978. Publishes paperback and cloth originals. Averages 15-25 total titles, 1-4 fiction titles each year.

Needs: Contemporary, experimental, literary, translations, new age. "We are interested in 2-3 short- to medium-length novels by gifted writers." Recently published: *Death Sentence* and *Madness of the Day*, by Maurice Blanchot (novellas) and *Ann Margret Loves You*, by Franz Kamin (short fiction collection); and *Great Expectations*, by Kathy Acker (novel).

How to Contact: Query first with SASE. Simultaneous and photocopied submissions OK. Reports in 4-6 weeks on queries; 3 weeks to 3 months on mss.

Terms: Pays in author's copies (10% of print run or by standard royalty, depending on the nature of the material). Subsidy publishes 25% of books. "Co-venture arrangements are possible with higher royalty." Book catalog free on request.

STORY PRESS, Box 10040, Chicago IL 60610. (312)442-7295. Editor: Richard Meade. Editorial Director: Laura Meade. Estab. 1978. Publishes hardcover and paperback originals. Number of titles: 2 in 1981. Encourages new writers. Sometimes comments on rejected mss.

Needs: Contemporary, literary, women's and ethnic. "We are a literary press and are not interested in most kinds of popular fiction. We publish only collections of stories." Recently published *The Monkey Puzzle Tree*, by Florence Cohen (short stories); *Squid Soup*, by Michael Mooney (short fiction); and *August Heat*, by Richard Dokey (short stories).

How to Contact: Query with SASE. Simultaneous and photocopied submissions OK. Reports in 2 weeks on queries, 3 months on mss.

Terms: Pays in author's copies (10% of the press run); no advance. Writer's guidelines for SASE. Free book catalog.

Advice: "Write and begin submitting to small magazines. Don't send chapters of novels or poorly prepared mss."

Tips: "We notice movement toward interior landscapes away from fiction with a clear narrative line. In the next few years "we foresee fewer outlets for literary fiction, especially short stories. We try to keep open an outlet for serious short fiction, promoting our titles extensively."

SUN & MOON PRESS, 4330 Hartwick Rd., College Pk MD 20740. (301)864-6921. Subsidiary includes Contemporary Literature Series. Editor-in-Chief: Douglas Messerli. Estab. 1979. Publishes hardcover and paperback originals and reprints. Plans 4 first novels in 1983. Averages 12 total titles, 6 fiction titles each year. Occasionally critiques if quality ms.

Needs: Contemporary, experimental, feminist/lesbian, gay, literary, mainstream, short story collections, translations, women's. Needs "contemporary tending toward experimental fiction." Recently published *The Contemporary American Fiction*, edited by Douglas Messerli; *The Relation of My Imprisonment*, by Russell Banks; and *Wier and Pouce*, by Steve Katz.

How to Contact: Submit complete ms with SASE. Photocopied submissions OK. Reports in 3 months on mss.

Terms: Pays in royalties of 10%. Writer's guidelines for SASE. Book catalog for 8 1/2x11 SASE and 20¢ postage.

SUREY BOOKS, (formerly Surree Limited, Inc.), 9465 Mission Park Place, Santee CA 92071. Editor: Pete Dixon. Publishes paperback originals. Prints approximately 90 titles annually. Encourages new writers. Occasionally comments on rejected mss.

Needs: Contemporary, gay male erotica, hetero. In the next few years, plans "48 novels, 3/4 gay (male), 1/4 hetero."

How to Contact: Submit outline/synopsis and sample chapters (1-2) with SASE.

Terms: Pays by outright purchase; no advance, up to six months till publication/pay.

Tips: "There's an increased openness and forthright treatment of all subject matter, and a willingness of major publishers to put out 'outre' material. Study the specific market and publisher you wish to submit to; gear your efforts to their individual formats."

SWIFTWATER BOOKS, Box 22026, Tampa FL 33622. Contact: Editorial Department. Estab. 1978. Publishes hardcover and paperback originals and reprints. Averages 30 total titles each year.
Needs: Gay, science fiction. "We have not published any fiction so far, but are prepared to consider material in these two categories *only*."
How to Contact: Send complete ms only with SASE. Simultaneous and photocopied ("preferred to avoid risk of loss or damage") submissions OK. Reports in 2-3 months on mss.
Terms: Pays in royalties, amount varies but generally follows industry standard; negotiates outright purchase.
Tips: "We are primarily nonfiction book packagers, but have an ability to reach science fiction and gay fiction markets."

THISTLEDOWN PRESS (POETRY PUBLISHER), 668 E. Place, Saskatoon, Saskatchewan, Canada S7J 2Z5. Editor-in-Chief: Mr. P. O'Rourke. Estab. 1975. Publishes hardcover and paperback originals. Occasionally critiques rejected mss.
Needs: Literary. Fiction needs limited—"we are basically a poetry press planning a move into fiction. We *only* want to see short stories."
How to Contact: Query first with SASE. Photocopied submissions OK. Reports in 2 months on queries.
Terms: Pays in royalties of 10% maximum. Writer's guidelines free. Book catalog free on request.

THREE TREES PRESS, Box 70, Postal Station "V", Toronto, Ontario, Canada M6R 3A4. (416)762-2121. Publisher: W. Horak. Estab. 1976. Publishes hardcover and paperback originals. Averages 9 total titles, 6 fiction titles each year.
Needs: Juvenile (fantasy, picture book, contemporary), science fiction, young adult (fantasy/science fiction).
How to Contact: Submit outline/synopsis and sample chapters with IRCs. Photocopied submissions OK. Reports in 2 months on mss.
Terms: Pays in royalties of 10% maximum. Writer's guidelines and book catalog for IRCs.
Tips: "Only Canadian citizens or residents need apply. Stress on flair and imagination."

THUNDER CITY PRESS, Box 11126, Birmingham AL 35202. Imprint includes *Thunder Mountain Review*. Editorial Director: Steven Ford Brown. Estab. 1975. Publishes paperback originals. Number of titles: 2 in 1981.
Needs: Contemporary, literary, experimental, translations. "Always looking for the next great American novel."
How to Contact: Query. SASE for query, ms. No simultaneous submissions; photocopied submissions OK. Reports in 2 weeks on queries, 1 month on mss.
Terms: Pays in author's copies (10%) and royalties "after we break even"; no advance. Book catalog for SASE.
Tips: "There is a place for good fiction writers in publishing today. There is so much poor writing being passed off as good fiction. We see an increased emphasis on fiction in translations especially from Latin America. I publish very little fiction at present but plan to expand in the future."

TIDE BOOK PUBLISHING COMPANY, Box 268, Manchester MA 01944. Subsidiary of Tide Media. President: Rose Safran. Estab. 1979. Publishes paperback originals. Average 1 title each year. Occasionally critiques rejected mss.
Needs: Adventure, contemporary, contemporary romance, historical, humor/satire, literary, mainstream, women's. Needs women's novels with a social service thrust; contemporary. No gothic, trash.
How to Contact: Query first; submit outline synopsis and 1-2 sample chapters with SASE. Simultaneous submissions OK. Reports in 1 month on queries and mss.

Terms: Pays in 100 author's copies. Considering cost plus subsidy arrangements—will advertise.

TREACLE PRESS, Box 638, New Paltz NY 12561. Editor: Bruce McPherson. Estab. 1973. Publishes hardcover and paperback originals. Number of titles: 5 in 1981. Encourages new writers. Sometimes comments on rejected mss.
Needs: Literary, experimental, feminist and translations. Recently published *Likely Stories: A Collection of Untraditional Fiction*; *The Best Laugh Last*, by John B. Rosenman; *The Menaced Assassin*, by Ascher/Straus.
How to Contact: Query with SASE. No unsolicited mss. No simultaneous submissions; photocopied submissions OK. Reports in 2 weeks on queries, 1-10 weeks on mss.
Terms: Pays 6-12% in royalties; varied amount of free author's copies. Free book catalog with SASE.
Tips: "We are interested in serious literary fiction with particular emphasis on experimental works. Most writers haven't taken trouble (or pleasure) to find out what we publish. If they did we would have fewer submissions in first place, and those would be of higher quality."

TRIPLE 'P' PUBLICATIONS INTERNATIONAL, Box 8776, Kennedy Station, Boston MA 02114. (617)437-1856. Subsidiaries include *Persuasion Magazine* and *The Kiosk Newsletter*. Editorial Manager: Eugene FPC de Mesne. Fiction Editor: Monica Selwyn-Jones. Estab. 1974. Publishes hardcover and paperback originals. Plans 2 first novels this year. Average 3-4 total titles, 3-4 fiction titles each year.
Needs: Adventure, fantasy, horror, historical, literary, psychic/supernatural, science fiction, short story collections. Needs "the unusual, bizarre, suspense story, with defineable characters, and tight plots, set in different periods of history. No melodramas. We do *not* want fiction that conforms to life, but rather, fiction that gives the reader an unusual view of human struggle and coping with situations that arise. No pat solutions or trite romance mush will be considered. Also, no religion or political harangues, please." Recently published *Enter Babylon* (sub-culture NYC); *Not Until Midnight* (bi-sexual exposé); and *Chose and Chosen* (psychological exposé) all written by Julian Ocean.
How to Contact: Query to editorial manager with SASE, brief outline, business-like letter only. Simultaneous and photocopied submissions OK. Reports in 4-6 weeks on queries.
Terms: Negotiates advance.
Tips: Wants to see "unusual slants on the human experience, with well-developed characters the reader can identify with, and plots that are not only believeable but remain with the reader long after he has finished the story. Be sure you have something saleable, otherwise you will waste a lot of valuable time. Know how to tell your story."

TURNSTONE PRESS, St. John's College, University of Manitoba, Winnipeg, Manitoba, Canada R3T 2M5. (204)474-9860. Estab. 1976. Publishes paperback originals. Plans 1 first novel this year. Averages 15 total titles. Occasionally critiques rejected ms.
Needs: Experimental, literary. "We have just started to consider and publish fiction, and will be doing only 2-3 a year. Interested in new work exploring new narrative/fiction forms."
How to Contact: Query first with SAE and IRC. Photocopied submissions OK. Reports in 1 week on queries; 2 months on mss.
Terms: "Like most Canadian literary presses, we depend heavily on government grants which are not available for books by non-Canadians." Pays in royalties of 10%; 10 (complimentary) author's copies. Book catalog free on request.

TYPOGRAPHEUM, Bennington Rd., Francestown NH 03043. Contact: R.T. Risk. Estab. 1976. Publishes hardcover originals. Averages 2 total titles each year. Occasionally critiques rejected mss.
Needs: Literary.
How to Contact: Query first.
Terms: Pays by individual arrangement with author.

UNDERWHICH EDITIONS, Box 262, Adelaide St. Stn., Toronto, Ontario, Canada M5C 2J4. (416)961-4247. Subsidiaries include Kontakte, Ganglia, Gronk and Wild Press. Imprints include Experimental and Literary Art. Contact: Editor/Publisher. Estab. 1979. Publishes hardcover and paperback originals. Averages 12 total titles, 1 fiction title each year.
Needs: Comics, contemporary, erotica, experimental. Must be "highly experimental or innovative in terms of style, structure, etc."
How to Contact: Query first with SAE and IRC. Reports in 3 weeks on queries; 2 months on mss.
Terms: Pays in 20 author's copies. "Arrangements: 1) editor finances book; author only receives copies. 2) editor and author finance book; profits are shared re percentage of investment. 3) author finances book; receives all profits from book." Book catalog free on request.
Tips: "Don't write standard format fiction. Explore new *forms*. We see fiction becoming more popular, more trendy, less literary, less intelligent. More consumer-entertainment oriented and less artistic, having less lasting quality."

UNDERWOOD/MILLER, 239 N. 4th St., Columbia PA 17512. (717)684-2925. Publisher: Chuck Miller. Estab. 1976. Publishes hardcover originals and reprints. Averages 12 total titles, 10 fiction titles each year.
Needs: Fantasy, horror, science fiction. Recently published *Lost Moons*, by Jack Vance (science fiction short story collections); and *Golden Fire*, by Stephen R. Donaldson (fantasy novel).
How to Contact: Query first with SASE. Simultaneous and photocopied submissions OK. Reports on queries in 2 weeks.
Terms: Pays in royalties of 10% minimum; negotiable advance. Book catalog free on request.

THE UNIVERSITY OF ARKANSAS PRESS, 201 Ozark St., Fayetteville AR 72701. (501)575-3246. Director: Miller Williams. Estab. 1980. Publishes hardcover and paperback originals. Plans "1 first novel or book of short fiction" this year. Averages 6-10 total titles, 1 fiction title each year.
Needs: Literary, mainstream, short story collections, translations. Recently published *In the Land of Dreamy Dreams*, by Ellen Gilchrist (short fiction).
How to Contact: Query first with SASE. Simultaneous and photocopied submissions OK "if very clean." Reports in 2 weeks on queries.
Terms: Pays in royalties of 10%; 10 author's copies. Writer's guidelines free for 6x9 SASE. Book catalog free for letter SAE and 1 first class stamp.
Tips: "University presses are going to publish an increasing percentage of the good fiction."

UNIVERSITY OF ILLINOIS PRESS, Box 5081, Station A, Champaign IL 61820. (217)333-0950. Fiction Editor: Ann Lawry Weir. Estab. 1918. Publishes paperback originals ("simultaneous publication"). Number of titles: 4 per year. Encourages new writers who have journal publications. Sometimes comments on rejected mss.
Needs: Contemporary, literary, experimental. "No novels." Recently published *Pastoral*, by Susan Engberg; *Babaru*, by B. Wongar; and *Canyons of Grace* by Levi S. Peterson.
How to Contact: Query or submit complete ms. SASE for query, ms. Simultaneous and photocopied submissions OK. Reports in 1 week on queries, 2-4 months on mss.
Terms: Pays "10% of net of first 10,000 cloth copies sold; 15% thereafter; 7½% net on first 10,000 paperback; 10% thereafter." No advance. Free book catalog.
Tips: "We do not publish novels and we have no outlet for individual short stories. We publish collections of short fiction by authors who've usually established their credentials by being accepted for publication in periodicals, generally literary periodicals. But 5 recently published books are by authors who have had no previous book publications."

SHERRY URIE, West Glover VT 05875. Editorial Director and Fiction Editor: Sherry Urie. Estab. 1974. Publishes paperback originals and reprints. Number of titles: 3 in 1981. Sometimes comments on rejected mss.

Needs: Contemporary, literary, mystery, historical, women's, religious/inspirational. "New England settings. We will consider all types of fiction." Recently published *Green Mountain Farm*, by Elliott Merrick (Vermont adventures).
How to Contact: Submit complete ms with SASE. Simultaneous and photocopied submissions OK. Reports in 1 month on mss.
Terms: Pays by individual arrangement; no advance. "Would consider subsidy publishing by individual arrangement." Book catalog for 35¢.

VÉHICULE PRESS, Box 125, Station "La Cité", Montreal, Quebec, Canada H2W 2M9. Publisher/Editor: Simon Dardick. Estab. 1973. Publishes hardcover and paperback originals. Plans 1 first novel this year. Averages 7 total titles, 1 fiction title "starting in '82." Interested in translation from French (Quebec).
Needs: Humor/satire, juvenile, short story collections, suspense/mystery, translations, women's. No romance or formula writing. "Fiction published to date has included": *Trouble on Happy Lane*, by Eric Martin, (mystery satire); *The Growth of Human Ideas*, by Peter Payack, (humorous/philosophical stories); and *The Bequest* by Jerry Wexler (short stories).
How to Contact: Query first; or submit complete ms with SASE ("essential"). Simultaneous and photocopied submissions OK "if notified of such . . . " Reports in 2 weeks on queries, 2 months on mss.
Terms: Pays in royalties of 10% minimum; 15% maximum "depends on press run and sales." Pays in author's copies (10% of run "only if author wants this arrangement.") "Translators of fiction can receive Canada Council funding which publisher applies for. Some Council money is also available for assistance to writers for specific projects." Free book catalog.

WEST END PRESS, Box 7232, Minneapolis MN 55407. Imprint includes Worker Writer Series. Publisher: John Crawford. Estab. 1976. Publishes paperback originals. Plans 1 first novel this year. Averages 4 total titles, 1 fiction title each year. Occasionally critiques rejected mss.
Needs: No special categories. "Clear accounts of working-class experience, or related social themes (ethnic, feminist) set in home, workplace, etc." No "detective, science fiction, CIA or FBI-oriented, thrillers, or hippies, adolescent adults speculating on lost opportunities in the '60s. Recently published *The Smile* (1980), by Harry Bernstein (naturalistic); *Ransack* (1980), by Mike Henson (city life); and *The Girl* (1978), by Meridel LeSueur (city life).
How to Contact: Query first; submit outline/synopsis and sample chapters with SASE. Reports in 2 weeks on queries.
Terms: Pays in royalties of 5% minimum; 7½% maximum; 10-15% of print run in author's copies. Subsidy publishes "occasionally. Must be demonstrably helpful to our Worker Writer imprint." Book catalog free on request.
Tips: "Write cleary so people can understand you. Dramatize, don't narrate. We see too much melodramatic 'space age' stuff, more dealing with nuclear holocaust, social chaos, etc. There is modest but steady interest in our line. Progressive literature does not suffer during a depression."

JOHN WESTBURG, 1745 Madison St., Fennimore WI 53809. (608)822-6237. Subsidiaries include Westburg Associates Publishers, John Westburg and Associates, and *The North American Mentor Magazine*. Editorial Director: John Westburg. Estab. 1964. Number of titles: 1 in 1981. Sometimes publishes in French, Spanish and German.
Needs: Contemporary, literary, experimental, adventure, historical, western, war, science fiction, fantasy, humor/satire. "We desire writing that is in good taste, for mature readers of above average education. Short stories should have action, plot, significance, depth of thought amd should be elevating rather than depressing; tragedy is welcome provided there is a true tragic flaw in the protagonist; character should be depicted in the action rather than by description. Sustained wit without sarcasm or humiliation would be welcome. Propaganda pieces, whether racial, religious, or political, are not wanted. No vulgarity, no obscenity, no blasphemy, no pornography, no 'ethnic' whatsoever that debases any nationality or race, no anti-Caucasian racism, no religious works presenting ideas of 'true' believers, no ugliness or shoddiness in human behavior, no vilifi-

cation, etc. The only fiction stories that we published last year were short fiction stories in the *North American Mentor Magazine*.

How to Contact: Submit complete ms with SASE. "Post office will not accept prepaid postage by metered machines. Must include return postage." Reports in 3-6 months.

Terms: Pays in 1 author's copy; no advance. Book catalog for SASE.

Tips: "Be sure to read your ms carefully again and again before you put it in the mail. Good writing does require rereading, rewriting, and revision after revision to put it in finest order. A great deal of illiteracy, anti-values, anti-humanism, and cheap vulgarity seem to be current in most submissions to us. I hope this is not a trend. *The North American Mentor Magazine* is a noncommercial literary and humanities quarterly supported entirely by subsidies and subscriptions and donations. All staff are volunteer and unpaid. We have limited record-keeping facilities. Therefore, owing to the complexity of the new copyright laws, we must obtain all rights to the work we publish in order to keep the record-keeping categories to a bare minimum. However, we readily give permission to the author to publish elsewhere any of his work that we publish."

WILSON BROTHERS PUBLICATIONS, Box 712, Yakima WA 98907. (509)457-8275. Editorial Director: Robert S. Wilson. Estab. 1978. Publishes paperback originals. "We are an extremely small firm. We have published a series entitled *Trolley Trails Through the West* and a travelog entitled *Rambling Through British Columbia*. We also offer custom publishing for other authors, any type of work whether fiction or nonfiction on a limited basis. Thus far our production in that line has been nonfiction. We produce only soft cover books, usually 8½x11 though can also produce 5½x8½. Our services include editing, production of the book, and advice to the author about advertising and marketing. We do not buy mss for our own use. Author *pays entire cost* of production and books are his when completed, shipped to destination of his choice."

How to Contact: Query or submit complete ms. SASE for query, ms. No simultaneous submissions; photocopied submissions OK. Reports in 1 week on queries, 2 weeks (usually) on mss.

WIM PUBLICATIONS, Box 5037, Inglewood CA 90310 and Box 367, College Corner OH 45003. (513)523-5994. Editorial Director: S.Diane Bogus. Estab. 1979. Publishes paperback originals and hardcover. Number of titles: 1 in 1981; 2 in 1982; 2 planned for 1983.

Needs: Feminist, gay/lesbian. No abstract experimental or plotless work.

How to Contact: Query with SASE or call. All unsolicited mss are returned unopened. Simultaneous and photocopied submissions OK. Reports in 2-4 weeks.

Terms: "We do not pay royalties on books. We are a small press which likes its authors to help with promotion of books." Free book catalog.

Tips: "Trust that there *is* a publisher for your work. Work at getting better. Associate with writers. Read. Operate professionally. There's a trend towards documentary type fiction, more first person, more present time narratives/settings."

WOLFHOUND PRESS, 68 Mountjoy Sq., Dublin, Ireland. Publisher: Seamus Cashman. Production Editor: Mary Paul Keane. Estab. 1974. Publishes hardcover and paperback originals and hardcover reprints. Plans 3 first novels this year. Publishes also in Dutch and French. Occasionally critiques rejected mss.

Needs: Contemporary, experimental, juvenile, literary, short story collections. Recently published *Voyovic*, by Quinn (short stories); *Pupil*, by Monk Gibbon (autobiographical moments of love); and *Kelly*, by Michael Mullen (fantasy).

How to Contact: Query first; submit outline/synopsis and 3 sample chapters with SASE. Simultaneous and photocopied submissions OK. Reports in 2 months on queries; 3 months on mss.

Terms: Pays in royalties of 5% minimum, 10% maximum; negotiates advance; 6 author's copies. Book catalog free on request.

WOMEN'S EDUCATIONAL PRESS, 16 Baldwin St., Toronto, Ontario, Canada M5T IL2. (416)598-0082. Contact: Lois Pike. Estab. 1972. Publishes paperback originals. Averages 5 titles, 1 fiction title each year. Sometimes critiques rejected mss.

Needs: Canadian writers only. Contemporary, experimental, women's, feminist, gay/lesbian, fantasy, juvenile and young adult. Recently published *The True Story of Ida Johnson*, by Sharon Riis; *Dragonhunt*, by Frances Duncan (experimental feminist fiction) and *Quilt*, by Donna E. Smyth.
How to Contact: Query or submit complete ms. SAE, IRC always. Simultaneous and photocopied submissions OK. Reports in 3 months.
Terms: Pays in negotiated royalties. Writer's guidelines for IRC, SAE; book catalog free on request.
Tips: "We're looking for novels dealing with women's concerns, social change, and radical perspectives on the experiences of women in Canada." Canadian authors only or landed immigrants.

WOODSONG GRAPHICS, Box 231, New Hope PA 18938. (215)794-8321. Editor: Ellen Bordner. Estab. 1977. Publishes paperback originals. Averages 1-5 total titles each year. Sometimes critiques rejected mss.
Needs: Adventure, contemporary, ethnic, experimental, fantasy, gothic/historical, contemporary romance, historical (general), humor/satire, juvenile (animal, easy-to-read, fantasy, historical, picture book, sports, spy/adventure, contemporary), literary, mainstream, psychic/supernatural, religious/inspirational, science fiction, suspense/mystery, war, western, women's, young adult (easy-to-read/teen, fantasy/science fiction, historical, problem novels, sports, spy/adventure). "We are just beginning to explore this field." No deviant sex of any kind or pornography.
How to Contact: Query first or submit complete ms. SASE always. Simultaneous and photocopied submissions OK. Reports in 2 weeks on queries, 6 weeks on mss.
Terms: Pays in royalties of 15% maximum; negotiates advance. "We have not subsidy published, but will consider it if appropriate. Arrangements will depend totally on the author and manuscript."

WORD BEAT PRESS, Box 10509, Tallahassee FL 32302. Editor: Allen Woodman. Estab. 1982. Publishes paperback originals. "Hope to publish 3 short story collections a year." Occasionally critiques rejected mss.
Needs: Short story collections. Seeks novellas to publish. "We plan on publishing a series of perfect bound fiction chapbooks."
How to Contact: Query first with SASE. Photocopied submissions OK. Reports in 3 weeks on queries.
Terms: Pays in royalties of 10% minimum; advance of $100 average; 10 author's copies. "We are interested in short story chapbooks of between 40 to 90 typed, double-spaced manuscript pages. We plan on paying authors $100 and 10 copies for first 300 copies printed, and on a royalty basis for each additional printing. Most mss will be selected from the yearly competition. Book catalog for SASE. Offers Word Beat Press Fiction Chapbook Award.

YORK PRESS, Box 1172, Fredericton, N.B., Canada E3B 5C8. (506)455-6501. Editorial Director: Dr. S. Elkhadem. Estab. 1975. Publishes hardcover and paperback originals. Publishes in English exclusively. Number of titles: 16 in 1982; 4 planned for 1983.
Needs: Contemporary, experimental, translations by established writers. "No mss written mainly for entertainment; i.e. those without literary or artistic merit." Recently published *Modern Egyptian Short Stories* and *Three Contemporary Egyptian Novels*, translated and edited by Saad El-Gabalawy.
How to Contact: Query with SAE, IRC. No simultaneous submissions; photocopied submissions OK. Reports in 1 week on queries, 1 month on mss.
Terms: Pays 5-10% in royalties; no advance. Free book catalog.
Tips: "We are devoted to the promotion of scholarly publications; areas of special interest in-
    neral and comparative literature, literary criticism, and creative writing of an experimen-
    ."

ZEPHYR PRESS, 13 Robinson St., Somerville MA 02145. Subsidiary of Aspect, Inc. Fiction Editor: Ronna Johnson. Managing Editor: Ed Hogan. Estab. 1980. Publishes hardcover and paperback originals. Averages 2-3 total titles, 0-2 fiction titles each year. $12 reading fee for all mss submitted; written critique with all responses.

Needs: Contemporary, ethnic, experimental, feminist/lesbian, gay, historical, humor/satire, literary, mainstream, science fiction, short story collections, women's. "We in general seek fiction or short stories by younger or less-established writers, a continuation of our interests as editors of the now defunct *Aspect* magazine." Recently published *I Brake for Delmore Schwartz*, by Richard Grayson (short stories).

How to Contact: Query first with SASE recommended. Reports in 2-4 weeks on queries.

Terms: Pays in author's copies of 10% of print (1st edition); 20% royalties on publisher's net (subsequent editions, if any). "There can be some flexibility of terms, based on mutual arrangements, if desired by author and publisher." Book catalog for SASE and 2 first class stamps.

Tips: "Get lots of feedback in a constructive atmosphere (writing classes, formal or informal workshops or writers' groups) before deciding your ms has reached publishability."

> 66 *Nothing you write, if you hope to be any good, will ever come out as you first hoped.*
> —**Lillian Hellman** 99

Commercial publishers

In the commercial book publishing industry, 1982 was a tumultous year. Book sales, in general, were down, and costs and interest rates were up. Publishers and imprints merged, consolidated or phased out their lines, and large houses published fewer books. The publishing watchword was—and is—"caution."

Nevertheless the general tone is hopefulness. Publishing experts say the antidote to this economic gloom and doom is developing new or improved creative marketing strategies. Publishing houses are also beginning to look toward increased use of new technology, innovative book formats, additional imprints or lines targeted to special audiences and the reprinting of old books (mostly classic fiction).

This is a shakedown period, according to Oscar Dystel, former president and consultant to Bantam Books. ". . . When it's over fewer companies will be left," he says, "and they'll be publishing a wider variety of material." Donald Fine, president and publisher of Arbor House, predicts more good books, "even experimental books of genuine quality, and an end to this "imitative hysteria" (in subjects and category lines).

Editors like Aaron Asher, executive editor of Harper and Row, believe publishing is still an individual "piecework trade." He says, "I choose books that interest me, which leaves me no worse off than those editors who seize upon what they conceive to be a hot market trend. Uncertainty is very much a part of the business—the nice part." Thus even if fiction is having its problems in a troubled industry, the good or ambitious books usually win out, as per *The White Hotel*, by D.M. Thomas, and other novels.

Love for romance

Sometimes thought to be a endangered species, literary fiction (as opposed to light commercial fiction) is now represented in new imprints begun within the last year. Bantam, Avon, and Penguin Books now strive to preserve and perpetuate literary excellence with careful selection of titles and special marketing tactics. Along with this increased interest in serious fiction, more original novels are published in paperback, a developing trend within the industry which affords more publishing opportunities for novelists. In

1982, according to Betty Lee Fox, *Library Journal* reviewed 216 first novels, 25 of which were paperbacks, many more this year than ever before.

Library Journal's annual first novelist tally generally does not include those first works in category lines, which serve as an excellent entry into publishing—particularly in romantic fiction. Today romance, as termed by one trade magazine, is "the backbone of the publishing industry," and accounts for about 40% of all paperbacks sold. At least seven new lines with major publishers have appeared within the year, and although interest in Regencies and gothics has declined, contemporary romances dominate bookstore racks. Now there are romances for women readers of all ages, stories involving all types of protagonists: teen girls, minority and ethnic women, gays, married couples with problems, and mature women. Rules and guidelines determine story evolvement, and each line has its own formula. So great is the interest in romance fiction to service its 20 million insatiable readers that Waldenbooks has created a romance book club and editors actively scout conferences and magazines for new writers for more books. The field is wide open, but competition is keen. Silhouette Books receives as many as 500 unsolicited manuscripts a month.

Next to women's romances, horror and the occult are the most read genres. On the heels of V.C. Andrews' popular and gripping teen stories and Stephen King's chillers, new young adult horror lines are capturing the attention of young readers. Sales in this young adult group have escalated tremendously since 1980 for several reasons: the luck publishers have had in finding manuscripts "with irresistible quality" that youngsters want to read and the special treatment bookstores have given these titles.

Serious about series

In 1982 children's books sold better than in preceding years. Two new mystery lines plus the Choose Your Adventure and Which Way series enjoy current popularity, thanks to highly-directed distribution to responsive children's groups.

The mystery business is better than ever, says one bookseller; in fact, the mystery may be entering its second "Golden Age" according to one prediction. An emerging set of young American readers with an addiction to mysteries accounts for the steady-to-growing interest. To satisfy the demands, publishers are reissuing mystery classics and setting up special lines and prizes. The genre remains healthy; and generally, once a mystery reader, always a mystery reader.

Science fiction, however, usually appeals to the under-25 crowd, and demographics show a gradual decrease in this age group. Editors of lines in several major houses still maintain that science fiction is "going strong" and has broader appeal: More women are SF readers *and* writers; several SF books were on the bestseller lists last year; and science fiction romances are expected soon.

Poor attendance at the annual Western Writers Association demonstrates that western fiction is on the downslide, or at least in the process of change. New adult westerns with the hero showing affection for someone beside his horse replace the old style western which is primarily monopolized by Louis L'Amour and a few others. Western fiction advances are low and publishing opportunities limited; the authors of the new adult style are often pseudonyms for the old style authors. In the action/adventure lines, like Warner's Men of Action series, a constant broad-based readership is expected.

Editors of erotic novels seek "sex in the superlative," material described as a cross between men's magazines and women's romances. The depressing economic climate begets escape fiction—which erotica is—and publishers are jumping on the bandwagon with new erotica lines.

Collected short stories generally do not provide an avenue for the publication of unknown writers, except in the small press. But well-known writers such as Alice Walker, Ann Beattie, Isaac B. Singer, Margaret Atwood and several others, published collections in 1982, a fact which in itself helps preserve an art form, sometimes believed to be a dying breed.

The current recession partially contributes to the continued interest in category/genre fiction versus general mainstream fiction. If people are uneasy about the economy, they are likely to look for either self-help books or light, entertaining fiction. (Suggestions for specialized markets can be found in the category index under the subject heading.)

In mainstream/general fiction, editors note recurring accepted subjects also. Anxiety is the subject of the '80s, what sex was to the '60s or politics to the '30s. Novels reflect current themes and center on failed marriages, putting one's life together, women in careers and relationships. Honest, contemporary issues form the story, but as one publishing house editor says, "It takes a very good writer to faithfully recreate the world around him," as Ann Beattie and John Cheever have recently done.

Persistent pursuit

Fewer opportunities may exist for the mainstream or serious writer of fiction, but changes in the field may open in the future. Paperback publishing is gaining greater credibility with publishers, retailers and book critics, who in the past have disdained softcover novels. And more original paperpack novels and creative marketing strategies will bring better and more books to the reading public, which increases each year. Also, publishing houses are aware of the concerns of the writer. All houses could save money *not* accepting unsolicited manuscripts but as an editor at Macmillan says, "Any author should be able to reach us," and there's the constant hope that the next literary great will be discovered in the slush pile.

Readable, high quality writing is what all editors look for. "If we like the book, if it speaks to us, and we think it would speak to others, if it is eloquent," editors will respond to it. Not to be ignored, however, are the current trends and changes within the commercial world—subjects and styles in favor, taboos to be avoided. Categories undergo changes within themselves as readers become more interested and sophisticated and the subject expands.

To stay on top of these changes, spend time in the library or bookstore where current releases and new lines are displayed. Study the titles and styles and read as many books in your subject as possible. Read also two highly informative publications: *Publishers Weekly* and *Library Journal*, whose quarterly issues feature essays by first novelists that reveal which houses are receptive to beginning novelists.

Regardless of your subject or theme, observe the general recommendations that editors offer:

● Write about what you know best. But stay away from autobiographical themes. A story must attract thousands, not hundreds, and have universal appeal, with relevant themes, action, incidents, and narrative of interest to a large readership.

● Spend every spare minute writing your manuscript. Your hours at the typewriter or word processor—writing and rewriting—will pay off in the end.

● Prepare your outline/proposal or query as requested carefully; this is your method of selling the book. Make it original in form and content—and send no outline or letter photocopies.

● Before submitting a manuscript, proposal or query, *study* the following listings closely and *use* the information they provide.

● Be persistent in your pursuit of a publisher. Remember the example of first novelist Robert Olen, whose highly acclaimed novel *Alley of Eden* was rejected 20 times before Horizon Press published it in 1982.

A & P BOOKS, Box 6639, Oakland CA 94603. Division of Atlantic & Pacific Commerce Co., Inc. President: E.H. Mikkelsen. Editor: Dee Lillegard. Estab. 1974. Publishes hardcover and paperback originals. Encourages new writers. Sometimes comments on rejected mss.
Needs: Juvenile and young adult: sports, animal, historical. Also, "recreation-education-entertainment combined."
How to Contact: Submit outline/synopsis and sample chapters. Simultaneous and photocopied submissions OK. Reports within 1 month with SASE.
Terms: Pays in royalties and by outright purchase; also offers advance.
Tips: 'We are alarmed at the generally low reading ability of young people across the country and have seen a trend in other publishing houses toward accomodating this lower level. We do not see ourselves following that trend."

ACADEMY CHICAGO, 425 N. Michigan Ave., Chicago IL 60611. Editor: Anita Miller. Estab. 1975. Publishes hardcover originals and paperback and hardback reprints. Number of titles: 6 in 1981; 1 in 1982. Plans 3 in 1983. Encourages new writers. Plans 1 first novel in '82. Sometimes comments on rejected mss.
Needs: Mystery, feminist and translations. No experimental, religious, romance, or children's. "Mysteries interest us especially.".
How to Contact: Query and/or submit outline/synopsis with SASE. No simultaneous submissions; photocopied submissions OK. Reports in 2 weeks on queries, 6 weeks on mss.
Terms: Pays 7-15% in royalties; no advance.
Tips: "Fiction is hard to sell. We think it needs a special appeal, mystery, women, etc. We used to accept multiple submissions but will not any more."

ACE CHARTER BOOKS, Berkley Publishing Group, 200 Madison Ave., New York NY 10016. (212)689-9200. Estab. 1977. Publishes paperback originals and reprints. Number of titles: 60 in 1981.
Needs: General mass market fiction; suspense a la Ludlum and Stephen King. No other genres. Recently published *The Evil*, by Hugh B. Cave (occult); *The Hollow Men*, by Sean Flannery (espionage); *Bushido*, by Beresford Osborne (suspense).
How to Contact: Send partial or complete ms. Prefers partial or complete outline/synopsis. SASE. "All submissions—unsolicited—will be rejected from this point forward." Simultaneous and photocopied submissions OK. Reports in 1 month on queries, 2 months on mss.
Terms: Negotiates contract and pays ½ in advance, ½ on delivery of original ms. Reprints: Pays ½ when agreement signed and ½ on publication. Book catalog for SASE.
Tips: "Be thorough in queries and synopses/outlines."

ACE/TEMPO BOOKS, Division of Berkley Publishing Group, 200 Madison Ave., New York NY 10016. (212)686-9820. Senior Editor: Kathy O'Hehir. Publishes paperback originals and reprints. Encourages new writers. Plans 6 first novels in '83. Rarely comments on rejected mss.
Needs: Contemporary romance; science fiction, suspense, occult, women's. "First love romance stories for young adults." Recently published *The Keeping Days Series*, by Norma Johnston. Publishes 2 titles/month under *The Caprice Romance Series*.
How to Contact: Submit outline/synopsis and sample chapters (3) with SASE. Simultaneous and photocopied submissions OK. Reports in 3 months on queries and mss.
Terms: Advance and royalty rates vary. Free book catalog with 9x11 SASE.
Tips: "Librarians and educators are looking for contemporary romances for young adults. Be aware of publishing trends. Study the formula of various genres or create a story within a contemporary framework. Since we are looking specifically for romances—first love stories—the writer

comm. publishers

should realize the difference between problem novels and romances."

ALCHEMY BOOKS, 681 Market St. # 755, San Francisco CA 94105. (415)362-2708. Editor-in-Chief: D. Mark Pittard. Managing Editor: Kenneth Park Cameron. Estab. 1975. Publishes hardcover originals. Total number of titles: 35 in 1981.
Needs: Contemporary, literary, science fiction, political, historical, humor/satire, fantasy, easy-to-read, animal, children's. "Alchemy Books is looking for current subjects which relate to today's concerns. Thoughtful and important books with emotional content; also those which are just for fun." Recently published: *The Unworthy Ones*, by B. Palmer; *Sensual Americans*, by V. Ashford; and *The Olympians*, by R. Tompkins.
How to Contact: Query and submit complete ms with SASE. Simultaneous and photocopied submissions OK. Reports in 2 weeks on queries, 3-4 months on mss.
Terms: Regular royalty schedule. No advance.
Tips: "Our program calls on the author to participate fully and vigorously in the promotion of his work."

ARBOR HOUSE PUBLISHING COMPANY, 235 E. 45th St., New York NY 10017. Imprint includes Priam Books. Editorial Director: Arnold Ehrlich. Publisher: Donald I. Fine. Estab. 1969. Publishes hardcover originals and Priam trade paperbacks. Number of titles: 63 in 1981; 63 in 1982.
Needs: Subjects open. Recently published *Murder in the Supreme Court*, by Margaret Truman; *Eight Million Ways to Die*, by Lawrence Block; *Cat Chaser*, by Elmore Leonard; and *Unacceptable Losses*, by Irvin Shaw.
How to Contact: Submit through agent. Simultaneous and photocopied submissions OK (but does not prefer them).
Terms: Pays in negotiable royalties; offers advance. Free book catalog.

ARCHWAY PAPERBACKS, 1230 Avenue of the Americas, New York NY 10020. (212)246-2121. Subsidiary of Pocketbooks. Imprint includes Which Way Adventure Stories (for 8-12 year olds). Assistant Editor: Regina Dahlgren. Publishes paperback originals.
Needs: Animal stories, contemporary romance, young adult (girls' novels, suspense/adventure, adventure). Recently published Which Way Series; Follow Your Heart Romances.
How to Contact: Query first; submit outline/synopsis and sample chapters with SASE.
Tips: "Look at previously published novels in Archway/Which Way series. Clearly present ideas in typed ms."

ATLANTIC MONTHLY PRESS, 8 Arlington St., Boston MA 02116. (617)536-9500. Imprint is Atlantic-Little, Brown. Editor: Melanie Kroupa. Publishes hardcover quality paperback originals. Number of titles: 12 in 1981; 16 in 1982.
Needs: Juvenile: sports, animal, mystery/adventure, realistic contemporary fiction, picture books and easy-to-read. Recently published: *The Darkangel*, by Meredith Ann Pierce; *IOU's*, by Ouida Sebestyen; and *Blissful Joy and the SATs: A Multiple Choice Romance*, by Shelia Greenwald.
How to Contact: Submit complete ms or submit through agent (but not necessary) with SASE. No simultaneous submissions; photocopied submissions OK. Reports in 1 month on mss.
Terms: Pays variable advances and royalties.
Tips: "Today there is interest in young adult romance. Books for young adults should show superior story telling with strong characterization and convincing action and plot development."

AUGSBURG PUBLISHING HOUSE, Box 1209, Minneapolis MN 55440. (612)330-3432. Editor: Roland Seboldt. Estab. 1850. Publishes paperback originals. Number of titles: 4 in 1981; 3 in 1982.
Needs: Religious/inspirational short stories for young readers (grades 8-12); for young teens 12-14, youth 14-17, adults. Recently published: *Who Am I Lord*, by Betty Steele Everett (short story

devotions for girls); *How Do I Make Up My Mind Lord*, by Robert Kelly (short story devotions for boys); *Change in the Wind*, by Phyllis Reynolds Naylor (short stories for teenagers).
How to Contact: Query or submit complete ms or submit outline/synopsis and sample chapters with SASE. Simultaneous and photocopied submissions OK. Reports in 6 weeks on queries.
Terms: Pays 10% in royalties and offers $500 advance. Free book catalog with SASE.
Tips: "We are looking for short stories with life related problems and Christian themes."

AVALON BOOKS, 22 E. 60th St., New York NY 10022. Imprint of Thomas Bouregy & Co., Inc. Editor: Rita Brenig. Publishes hardcover originals. Number of titles: 60 in 1981; 60 planned for 1983. Recently published: *The Maple Princess*, by Susan Kirby (romance); *Web of Haefen*, by Juaneta Tyree Osborne (gothic), and *Putman's Ranch War*, by Wayne C. Lee (western).
Needs: "We want well-plotted, fast-moving, romances, gothics, westerns, and nurse-romances, all of about 50,000 words."
How to Contact: Send one-page outline with SASE or submit complete ms with SASE. Do not telephone. Reports in 12 weeks on mss.
Terms: Offers $400 advance which is applied against sales of the first 3,500 copies of the book.
Tips: "We like the writers to focus on the plot, drama, and characters, not the background."

AVON BOOKS, Camelot Books, Children's Book Imprint. 959 8th Ave., New York NY 10019. (212)262-7454. Editorial Editor: Jean Feiwel. Estab. 1967. Publishes paperback originals and reprints. Number of titles: 36 in 1981.
Needs: Contemporary, fiction, adventure, mystery, western: animal, fantasy/science fiction and easy-to-read picture books. No historical. Recently published: *Irma & Jerry*, by George Selden (fiction); A Hippopotamus Ate The Teacher, by Mike Thaler (picture book).
How to Contact: Query or submit outline/synopsis and sample chapters (3) with SASE. Simultaneous and photocopied submissions OK. Reports in 8 weeks on queries and mss.
Terms: Pays 4-10% in royalties; offers $1,500-5,000 in advance. Free book catalog with SASE.

A & W PUBLISHERS, INC., 95 Madison Ave., New York NY 10016. (212)725-4970. Imprints include A & W Visual Library and Galahad Books. Executive Editor: Carolyn Trager. Fiction Editor: Ruth Pollack. Estab. 1972. Publishes hardcover and paperback originals and reprints. Number of fiction titles: 2 in 1981; 6 in 1982.
Needs: Open to most all subjects. No juvenile.
How to Contact: Query or submit complete ms or submit outline/synopsis and sample chapters (3) or submit through agent. Simultaneous and photocopied submissions OK. Reports in 2 weeks on queries, 6 weeks on mss.

BAKER BOOK HOUSE, CO., Box 6287, Grand Rapids MI 49506. (616)676-9185. Editor: Dan Van't Kerkhoff. Publishes paperback originals. Encourages new writers. Plans 4 first novels for 1983.
Needs: Juvenile (ages 10-16). Looking for mystery, historical, adventure for preteens and young teens. Recently published: *Killer Dog*, by Sett Lassock; *Big Foot and the Timberland Mystery*, by Margaret Scariano; and *A Summer's Growth*, by Lucille Travis.
How to Contact: Submit complete ms with SASE. Simultaneous and photocopied submissions OK. Reports in 1 month on mss.
Terms: Publishes on royalty basis; no advance. Free book catalog for SASE.
Tips: Publishes novels which "fill the need for a wholesome Christian fiction for young people."

BALLANTINE BOOKS, 201 E. 50th St., New York NY 10022. Subsidiary of Random House. Senior Editor: Pam Strickler. Publishes paperback originals (general fiction, mass-market). Averages over 120 total titles each year.
Needs: Gothic/historical, contemporary romance, historical, women's. The above categories can be submitted unsolicited to Pam Strickler, others to the house must be agented.
How to Contact: Submit outline/synopsis and 100 pages (for longer works) with SASE. Photo-

copied submissions OK. Reports in 2 months on queries; 4-5 months on mss.
Terms: Pays in royalties and advance.

BANTAM BOOKS, INC., 666 5th Ave., New York NY 10103. (212)765-6500. Imprints include Skylark, New Age, Circle of Love, Windstone and Sweet Dreams. Estab. 1945. Publishes paperback originals and reprints and hardcovers. Number of titles: 500 in 1981; 500 in 1982; 600 planned for 1983.
Needs: Contemporary, literary, adventure, mystery, spy, historical, western, war, gothic, romance, women's, feminist, gay/lesbian, ethnic, psychic/supernatural, religious/inspirational, science fiction, fantasy, horror, humor/satire and young adult. Recently published: *Washington*, by Dana Fuller Ross (fiction); *The Road to Gandolfo*, by Robert Ludlum (suspense); and *No Time For Tears*, by Cynthia Freeman.
How to Contact: submit through agent. No unsolicited material accepted. Simultaneous and photocopied submissions OK. Reports on queries as soon as possible.
Terms: Individually negotiated; offers advance.

BEAUFORT BOOKS, INC., 9 E. 40th St., New York NY 10016. (212)685-8588. Estab. 1980. Publishes hardcover and trade paperback originals. Number of titles: 15 in 1980; 35 in 1981. Sometimes comments on rejected mss.
Needs: Contemporary, faction, adventure, women's, humor/satire and young adult: sports, animal, spy/adventure, fantasy. Five young adult novels needed each year for next year. Recently published: *Made for TV*, by Breen; and *The Girl in the Grass*, by Roth (young adult).
How to Contact: Submit complete ms with SASE. No simultaneous submissions; photocopied submissions OK. Reports in 6 weeks on mss.
Terms: Royalties vary with individual; advance also varies with each author.

BERKLEY/ACE SCIENCE FICTION, (formerly Ace Science Fiction), Berkley Publishing Group, 200 Madison Ave., New York NY 10016. Imprints include Ace Books, Charter and Tempo. Editor: Susan Allison. Estab. 1948. Publishes paperback originals and reprints. Number ot titles: 15/month.
Needs: Science fiction and fantasy. No other genre accepted. No short stories. Recently published: *Systemic Shock*, by Dean Ing (science fiction); *Tomoe Gozen*, by Jessica Amanda Salmonson (fantasy); *Elsewhere* (fantasy anthology).
How to Contact: Submit outline/synopsis and sample chapters (3) with SASE. No simultaneous submissions; photocopied submissions OK. Reports in 3 months minimum on mss. "Queries answered immediately if SASE enclosed."
Terms: Pays 6-8% in royalties; advance $2,500 minimum. Free book catalog.
Tips: "Good science fiction and fantasy is almost *always* written by people who have read and loved a lot of it. We are looking for knowledgable science or magic, as well as sympathetic characters with recognizable motivation. We need both fantasy and science fiction. In science fiction, we are looking for solid, well-plotted sf: good action adventure, well-researched hard science with good characterization, and books that emphasize characterization without sacrificing plot. In fantasy, again, we are looking for all types of work, from high fantasy to sword and sorcery." Submit fantasy to Terri Windling, science fiction to Susan Allison, Beth Meacham, Melissa Ann Singer.

BETHANY HOUSE PUBLISHERS, (formerly Bethany Fellowship, Inc.), 6820 Auto Club Rd., Minneapolis MN 55438. (612)944-2121. Editor: Carol Johnson. Estab. 1956. Publishes paperback originals. Number of titles: 5 in 1980; 5 in 1981.
Needs: Religious/inspirational, adventure, mystery, romantic, historical, gothic, juvenile. Recently published: *Once Upon a Summer*, by Janette Oke (prairie romance); and *Love's Secret Storn*, by Lenora Pruner (gothic).
How to Contact: Query or submit outline/synopsis and sample chapters (2-3) with SASE. Simultaneous and photocopied submissions OK. Reports in 1 month on queries, 6 weeks on ms.
Terms: Pays in royalties; no advance. Free book catalog with 8 1/2x11 SASE and $2 postage.

JOHN F BLAIR, PUBLISHER, 1406 Plaza Dr., Winston-Salem NC 27103. (919)768-1374. Editor: E.J. Friedenberg. Editor-in-Chief: John F. Blair. Estab. 1954. Publishes hardcover originals and paperback originals. Number of titles: 3 in 1981; 6 in 1982; 6-8 planned for 1983. Encourages new writers. Plans first novel for '83. Sometimes comments on rejected mss.
Needs: Contemporary, literary, experimental, feminist, ethnic, humor/satire and young adult. Basically likes regional material dealing with Southeastern US. No confession or erotica. "We do not limit our consideration of manuscripts to those representing specific genres or styles. Our primary concern is that anything we publish be of high literary quality." Recently published: *Tales of the South Carolina Low Country*, by Nancy Rhyne (regional folklore); and *Banners Over Terre d'Or*, by Gay Weeks Neale (juvenile fiction).
How to Contact: Query or submit through agent with SASE. Simultaneous and photocopied submissions OK. Reports in 2-3 weeks on queries, 12 weeks on mss.
Terms: Pays 10% standard royalties, 7% on paperback royalties. Royalties can go as high as 15% by special arrangement. Free book catalog.
Tips: "We are not interested in books for the very young. Currently we are saturated with historical novels. We are primarily interested in serious adult novels of high literary quality."

THE BOBBS-MERRILL COMPANY, INC., 630 3rd Ave., New York NY 10017. Publisher: Grace G. Shaw. Publishes hardcover originals. Number of titles: 4 in 1980; none in 1981. Needs: Contemporary, faction, historical, war and women's. "We do not want any young people's books or juveniles.' Recently published *Dancehall*, by Bernard Connors.
How to Contact: Query with SASE or submit through agent. No simultaneous submissions; photocopied submissions OK.
Terms: Each arrangement is on an individual basis; offers advance.
Tips: "Subject matter is less literary and more commercial. If the writer wishes to be published, he should study the bestseller lists and read the books on them. I'm sorry to say, however, that the chances of publishing a literary novel in the fine publishing tradition of old are very slim. Literary/ serious novels rarely sell in large numbers and few publishers can afford to subsidize them. The best procedure is to write a short, factual query. A letter of this sort rather than a flowery statement that tries to impress has a better chance of creating interest. Writers should be advised not to call a week after submission and ask to speak to the editor. After a month, it makes sense to write a follow-up query."

BOOKCRAFT, INC., 1848 W. 2300 South, Salt Lake City UT 84119. Editor: George Bickerstaff. Publishes hardcover originals. Number of titles: 2 in 1981; 3 in 1982, 2 planned for 1983. Encourages new writers. "We are always open for creative, fresh ideas. We expect to publish several novels in 1983."
Needs: Contemporary, historical, western, romance, women's, and religious/inspirational. Recently published: *Seeker of the Gentle Heart*, by Blaine Yorgason and Brenton Yorgason (western/historical); *Corker*, by Anya Barteman (romance); and *The Awakening*, by Richard M. Eyre (adventure).
How to Contact: Query or submit outline/synopsis and sample chapters with SASE. No simultaneous submissions; photocopied submissions OK. Reports in 2 months on both queries and mss.
Terms: Pays royalties; no advance. Free book catalog.
Tips: "Read our fiction. Our market is the membership of The Church of Jesus Christ of Latter-day Saints (Mormons), and all stories must be related to the background, doctrines or practices of that church. No preaching, but tone should be fresh, positive, and motivational. No anti-Mormon works. Copy of information for authors supplied on request."

BOREALIS PRESS, 9 Ashburn Dr., Ottawa, Ontario, Canada K2E 6N4. Imprint includes *Journal of Canadian Poetry*. Editor: Frank Tierney. Fiction Editor: Glenn Clever. Estab. 1970. Publishes hardcover and paperback originals and reprints. Average number of titles: 20.
Needs: Contemporary, literary, adventure, historical, juvenile and young adult. "Must have a Canadian content or author; otherwise query first." Recently published: *Tale Spinner in a Spruce*

Tipi, by Evalyn Gantreau (Cree Indian tales); and *Way and Ginger*, by Jack Howard (humor).
How to Contact: Submit complete ms with SASE (Canadian postage or International Reply Coupons). No simultaneous submissions; photocopied submissions OK. Reports in 2 weeks on queries, 8-10 weeks on mss.
Terms: Pays 10% in royalties and 3 free author's copies; no advance. Free book catalog with SASE or IRC.
Tips: "Have your work professionally edited. We generally publish only material with a Canadian content or by a Canadian writer."

MARION BOYARS PUBLISHERS INC., 99 Main St., Salem NH 03079. Send all mss and mail to 18 Brewer St., London, England W1R 4AS. Fiction Editor: Marion Boyars. Estab. 1960 (England); 1979 (USA). Publishes hardcover and paperback originals and hardcover and paperback reprints. Plans 1 first novel this year. Averages 30 total titles, 10-12 fiction titles each year.
Needs: Contemporary, ethnic, experimental, feminist/lesbian, literary, science fiction, short story collections, translations, women's, young adult (problem novels). Looking for "first class fiction." No pulp. Recently published: *The Interceptor Pilot*, by Kenneth Gangemi; *Jules and Jum*, by Henri-Pierre Roche; and *The Egghead Republic*, by Arno Schmidt.
How to Contact: Query first, then submit complete ms with SASE. Photocopied submissions OK. Reports in 3 weeks on queries; 6 weeks on mss.
Terms: Pays in royalties ("standard terms"); negotiates advance. Book catalog free on request.
Tips: "We publish only good literature."

BRADBURY PRESS, INC., 2 Overhill Rd., Scarsdale NY 10583. (914)472-5100. Editor: Richard Jackson. Publishes juvenile hardcover originals. Number of titles: 18 in 1981; 20 in 1982. Encourages new writers. Seldom comments on rejected mss.
Needs: Contemporary, adventure, science fiction, romance (realistic), humor/satire, juvenile and young adult. "Also, stories about real kids with realistic dialogue." No fantasy or religious material. Recently published: *Tiger Eyes*, by J. Blume; *The Gift of the Sacred Dog*, by P. Goble; and *Tunnel Vision*, by F. Arrick.
How to Contact: Query first. Send complete ms with SASE. No simultaneous submissions; photocopied submissions OK. Reports in 3 months on mss.
Terms: Pays 10% or 5% to author and 5% to artist on retail price; advance negotiable. Free book catalog for 69¢ postage.

GEORGE BRAZILLER, INC., One Park Ave., New York NY 10016. (212)889-0909. Managing Editor: Keith Goldsmith. Estab. 1955. Publishes hardcover originals and paperback reprints. Plans 1 first novel this year. Averages 25 total titles, 6 fiction titles each year. Occasionally critiques rejected mss.
Needs: Experimental, feminist, literary, short story collections, translations. Recently published *The Replay*, by Michael Curtin (literary/humor); *Child's Play*, by David Malouf (novellas); and *A Weekend with Claude*, by Beryl Bainbridge (literary/feminist).
How to Contact: Query first with SASE. Photocopied submissions OK. Reports in 2 weeks on queries.
Terms: Negotiates advance. Book catalog free on request.

BROADMAN PRESS, 127 9th Ave. N., Nashville TN 37234. (615)251-2433. Editorial Director: Thomas L. Clark. Publishes hardcover and paperback originals. Average number of titles: 5.
Needs: Adventure, historical, religious/inspirational, humor/satire, juvenile and young adult. Will accept no other genre. Recently published: *Ahaz*, by Constance Head (Biblical fiction); *Joey's Ghost Pumpkin*, by Fern P. Dooley (juvenile); and *The Secret Dream*, by Muriel F. Blackwell (juvenile).
How to Contact: Query but decision is not made until ms is reviewed. No simultaneous submissions; photocopied submissions OK. Reports in 2 months on queries and mss.
Terms: Pays 10% in royalties; no advance. Free book catalog.

CHARLES RIVER BOOKS, 1 Thompson Sq., Charlestown MA 02129. Senior Editor: B. Comjean. Editorial Director: Dennis Campbell. Estab. 1978. Publishes hardcover and paperback originals and hardcover reprints.
Needs: Open to all categories. Recently published *The Time of the Leonids*, by Christine Bruckner (novel); *The Green Line*, by Tom Molloy (novel); and *The Loss of Heaven*, by Jack Warner (novel).
How to Contact: Query. Simultaneous and photocopied submissions OK. Reports in 6 weeks.
Terms: Pays 7½x12% royalties; "modest" advance. Book catalog for 8½x11 SASE.
Tips: Most mss have "very limited appeal".

CHILDRENS PRESS, Division of Regensteiner Publishing Enterprises, Inc., 1224 W. Van Buren, Chicago IL 60607. (312)666-4200. Editorial Director: Fran Dyra. Estab. 1946. Publishes hardcover originals. Plans 8-10 first novels this year. Averages 125-150 total titles; 40 fiction titles each year.
Needs: Juvenile (animal, easy-to-read, fantasy, historical, picture book, sports, spy/adventure, contemporary, nonfiction). Recently published *Henry & Melinda*, by Silky Sullivan (2nd grade sports story); *J.P. Landers: Solve a Mystery*, by Marian Lee (3rd grade mystery series); and *Please, Wind*, by Carol Greene (1st grade beginning reader).
How to Contact: Query first if long mss (more than 5 mss pages or series idea); submit outline/synopsis and sample chapters or complete ms with SASE. Simultaneous submissions and photocopied submissions OK. Reports in 6-8 weeks on queries; 6-8 weeks on mss.
Terms: Pays occasionally in royalties of 5% minimum; negotiates advance; and generally pays in outright purchase of $500 minimum; 6 author's copies. Occasionally subsidy publishes; offers 50% subsidiary rights. Writer's guidelines free; book catalog free on request.
Tips: "Have patience and determination. Know the market needs of publisher by looking at public library and seeing what types of product publisher distributes."

THE CHILD'S WORLD, INC., Box 989, Elgin IL 60120. President: Jane Buerger. Estab. 1968. Publishes hardcover and paperback originals. Number of titles: approximately 50 per year.
Needs: Juvenile: sports, animal, spy/adventure, historical, fantasy/science fiction, easy-to-read. "All of our titles are for the juvenile market. Most are only 32 pages." Recently published the *Word Bird* Series, by Jane Moncure (beginning reading series); *The Healthkin* Series, by Jane Moncure; and *What Is It*, by Jane Buerger and Jane Moncure (values series).
How to Contact: Submit complete ms or submit outline/synopsis with SASE. Simultaneous and photocopied submissions OK. Reports in 1 month on queries.
Terms: Pays by outright purchase of $400-$700; no advance. Free book catalog.
Tips: "Avoid sending material for high school and adult age groups."

CLARION BOOKS, TICKNOR & FIELDS: A HOUGHTON MIFFLIN COMPANY, 52 Vanderbilt Ave., New York NY 10017. (212)972-1190. Editor/Publisher: James C. Giblin. Estab. 1965 "as the children's book division of Seabury Press; 1979 as a new children's book imprint of Houghton Mifflin Company." Publishes hardcover originals, and paperback reprints from its own backlist. Number of titles: 22 in 1981; 28 in 1982, 30 planned in 1983. Encourages new writers. Plans 2 first novels for '83. Comments on rejected mss "only if we're encouraging a revision."
Needs: Juvenile and young adult: sports, animal, adventure, fantasy/science fiction, easy-to-read, humorous contemporary stories for ages 8-12 and 10-14; "fresh, personal stories that capture our attention, and that we think young readers would enjoy." Recently published *I'll Always Remember You . . . Maybe*, by Stella Pevsner (contemporary young adult novel); *The Climb*, by Carol Carrick (picture book adventure); *Hey, Remember Fat Glenda?*, by Lila Perl (humorous school and family story).
How to Contact: Query on mss of more than 50 pages. SASE for query, ms. Reluctantly considers simultaneous submissions; photocopied submissions OK. Reports in 2 weeks on queries, 8 weeks on mss.

Terms: Pays 5% royalties on picture books; 10% on older books; offers $1,500-$2,000 advances. Free book catalog.

Tips: "It's a truism, but I really believe that the best novels come out of the author's self-knowledge of his or her own experience and background. Don't send us imitations of other writers' successes. We've noticed a return to lighter stories from the heavier problem novels of recent years."

CLARKE, IRWIN & CO. LTD., 791 St. Clair Ave. W., Toronto, Ontario, Canada M6C 1B8. Editorial Director: John Pearce. Estab. 1930. Publishes hardcover and paperback originals. Number of titles: 15 in 1982; 25 planned for 1983.

Needs: Contemporary, literary, adventure, mystery, spy, historical, war, women's, fantasy, humor/satire, juvenile and young adult: sports, animal, spy/adventure, historical, fantasy/science fiction. Specializes in Canadian subjects. Recently published *Famous Last Words*, by Timothy Findley (adult); *Murder on Location*, by Howard Engel (adult mystery); *Hunter in the Dark*, by Monica Hughes (young adult).

How to Contact: Query, submit outline synopsis and sample chapters or submit through agent. Simultaneous and photocopied submissions OK. Reports in 1 week on queries, 1 month on mss.

Terms: Pays in royalties; offers advance.

COKER PUBLISHING HOUSE, Box 27842, Houston TX 77007. (713)861-4882. Editorial Director and Fiction Editor: G.L. Webb. Estab. 1978. Publishes paperback originals. Number of titles: 10 in 1980; 10 in 1981.

Needs: Literary, experimental, fantasy. "We will also consider quality fiction (analytical and insightful) in the existential traditon of Nietzsche, Dostoevsky, Hesse, Camus, and Sartre; works similar in style and quality to Kosinsky, Wheelis, and Gardner. No romance or horror." Recently published *Bondage*, by W.L. Garrison.

How to Contact: Submit outline/synopsis and sample chapters with SASE. Simultaneous and photocopied submissions OK. Reports in 2 weeks on queries, 6 weeks on mss.

Terms: Pays in author's copies and by negotiation; no advance.

Tips: "First, one should only write if he has something to say. Second, one should write to please oneself as opposed to what is presently in vogue in fiction."

COLUMBIA PUBLISHING COMPANY, INC., Frenchtown NJ 08825. (201)996-2141. President: Bernard Rabb. Estab. 1973. Publishes hardcover originals. Number of titles: 3 in 1980; 3 in 1981. "We encourage new writers; but have no first novels under contract." Sometimes comments on rejected mss.

Needs: Literary, experimental, historical, translations. Recently published *Cousin Drewey*, by John L. Sinclair (Southwest literary novel); *Don Juan*, by Gonzalo Torrente Ballester (literature).

How to Contact: Submit complete ms with SASE. Simultaneous and photocopied submissions OK. Reports in 6 months.

Terms: Pays in royalties; offers advance.

Tips: "Do *not* send us romantic novels, science fiction novels, spy novels, parables which will instruct the world to change its ways, gothic novels, shoot-'em-up westerns or the like. Thoughtful writers, serious writers, and writers with vision, sensitivity, and style are always welcome. If the writer thinks his work will be a blockbuster bestseller and will be a movie at MGM, chances are the work is not for us. But if the work is intended for the smaller audience of literate readers, then we would like to consider it for publication."

CONCORDIA PUBLISHING HOUSE, 3558 S. Jefferson Ave., St. Louis MO 63118. (314)664-7000. Contact: Children's Books Dept. Estab. 1869. Number of titles: 15 in 1981. Encourages new writers. Rarely comments on rejected mss.

Needs: Religious/inspirational fiction "is all that we will consider." Recently published *God, Why* series: *God, Why Is She the Way She Is?*, by Linda Jacobs Ware; *God, Why Did He Die?*, by Anne Harler; *God, Why Am I So Miserable?*, by Mildred H. Arthur; *God, When Will I Ever Belong?*, by Katherine D. Marko; *I Am*, by J. Marxhausen (all children's fiction). New titles in this

series will be released in 1982. Haley Adventure Series, by Aleda Renken, 1981, four titles.
How to Contact: Query or submit outline/synopsis. SASE for query, ms. Simultaneous and photocopied submissions OK. Reports in 2 weeks on queries, 6 weeks on mss.
Terms: Pays 5-10% in royalties and 6 author's copies; offers $300 average advance.
Tips: "We publish very little *adult* fiction. Except for a few series which are well established, we are cutting back on fiction. Our market looks to us for a different kind of book. Need in the marketplace; well written book with *series* potential, like Haley Adventure stories."

DAVID C. COOK PUBLISHING COMPANY, 850 N. Grove, Elgin IL 60120. (312)741-2400. Imprints include Chariot Books, Making Choices Series, PennyPincher Series, and Bible Adventure Series. Managing Editor: Janet Hoover Thoma. Estab. 1875. Publishes hardcover and paperback originals. Number of fiction titles: 12 in 1981; 14 planned for 1982, 10 planned for 1983. Encourages new writers.
Needs: Contemporary, religious/inspirational, women's, juvenile and young adult: sports, animal, spy/adventure, historical, biblical, fantasy/science fiction, picture book, easy-to-read. Recently published *The Babe and the Lamb*, by Ray and Sally Cioni; *The Cereal Box Adventures*, by Barbara Bartholomew (part of the Making Choices Series); and *The Claw and the Spider Web*, by Valerie Riddix (part of PennyPincher Series).
How to Contact: Query with SASE. All unsolicited manuscripts are returned unopened. Simultaneous and photocopied submissions OK. Reports in 3 months on queries.
Terms: Pays 7-15% on an escalating clause ("depending on whether it is trade, mass market or cloth") in royalties and 10 author's copies; offers advance. Free writer's guidelines with SASE.
Tips: "Two areas of interest are: (1) the Chariot Bible Adventure Series for teens and historical fiction for adults. The Chariot Biblical novel should fit the young teen audience, and should feature a character who appears in the Bible as a young person. Then, in 25,000 to 45,000 words, it should follow the character's growth in his/her understanding of self and God, in the context of Bible events and culture. For this age group, action is more important than extensive cultural information. Chariot Books includes Making Choices books, which are reader participation novels, and PennyPincher books, novels about sports, adventure, romance, school life or fantasy. (2) The adult historical fiction, which is Biblically based, should bring alive in a credible fashion events and/or characters that figure in the flow of the Biblical narrative, though they need not be major events or characters. The piece may be a romance, family saga, or follow another format as long as these points are kept in mind: A) it must be as accurate, where it touches local color, as the best scholarship allows; B) the story line must be interesting and not preachy; C) the thrust of the story must be consistent with Biblical doctrine; D) it must be good literature. We anticipate more of a demand for fiction in the Christian market with more quality material being offered. We also anticipate that a broader range of styles and subject matter will be considered acceptable."

CROSSWAY BOOKS, Division of Good News Publishers, 9825 W. Roosevelt Rd., Westchester IL 60153. (312)345-7474. Editorial Director: Jan P. Dennis. Estab. 1938. Publishes hardcover and paperback originals. Plans 2-3 first novels this year. Averages 20-25 total titles, 4-5 fiction titles each year. Critiques rejected mss.
Needs: Contemporary, fantasy, juvenile (fantasy), literary, religious/inspirational, science fiction, short story collections, young adult (fantasy/science fiction). "All fiction published by Crossway Books must be written from the perspective of historic orthodox Christianity. It need not be *explicitly* Christian, but it must understand and view the world through Christian principle. For example, our book *Alpha Centauri* takes place in a pre-Christian era, but Christian themes (e.g., sin, forgiveness, sacrifice, redemption) are present. We will publish as many novels in the next two or so years as we can find, as long as they meet these criteria. We are *anxious* to discover and nurture Christian novelists." No sentimental, didactic, "inspirational" religious fiction; heavy-handed allegorical or derivative (of C.S. Lewis or J.R.R. Tolkien) fantasy; Biblical or "end times" fiction. Recently published: *Alpha Centauri*, by Robert Siegel (fantasy/young adult); *Whalesong*, by Robert Siegel (fantasy/adult/young adult) and *The Wheels of Heaven*, by David E. Lawrence (science fiction).

How to Contact: Submit complete ms with SASE; also accepts phone calls. Reports in 3 weeks to 4 months on mss.

Terms: Pays in royalties and negotiates advance. Book catalog free on request.

Tips: "Christian novelists—you must get your writing *up to standard*. The major reason novels informed by a Christian perspective do not have more presence in the market is because they are inferior. Sad but true. I believe Crossway can successfully publish and market *quality* Christian novelists. Also read John Gardner's *On Moral Fiction*. The market for fantasy/science fiction continues to expand (and genre fiction in general). There are more attempts lately at Christian science fiction and fantasy, though they generally fail from didacticism or from being overly derivative."

CROWELL AND LIPPINCOTT JUNIOR BOOKS, 10 E. 53rd St., New York NY 10022. (212)593-7044. See: Harper & Row Junior Books Group.

CROWN PUBLISHERS, INC., 1 Park Ave., New York NY 10016. (212)532-9200. Editorial Director Children's Book Dept.: Marci McGill. Publishes hardcover originals. "Occasionally publish paperbacks simultaneously with hardcover but no original paperbacks." Number of titles: 20 in 1981. Encourages new writers. Sometimes comments on rejected mss.

Needs: Humor/satire, juvenile and young adult: sports, animal, spy/adventure, fantasy/science fiction, realistic fiction, easy-to-read, ethnic (all). Recently published *Journey to the Planets*, by Patricia Lauber; *War Without Friends*, by Evert Hartman; and *Ben's Lucky Hat*, by Hans-Eric Hellberg. "We would like more fiction in all age groups (7-9 ages) (8-10 ages) 12-up. Humorous, realistic, science fiction, adventure stories & mysteries."

How to Contact: Complete ms for fiction and picture books. No simultaneous submissions; photocopied submissions OK. Reports "within six to eight weeks."

Terms: Pays "advance against royalty." Free book catalog.

Tips: Novels must have "strong emotional content—the reader is able to care about the characters and what happens to them. Write about what you know."

DANDELION PRESS, 184 5th Ave., New York NY 10010. (212)929-0090. Subsidiary of Merchandise Dynamics, Inc. Vice President: H. Cohen. Estab. 1979. Publishes hardcover and paperback originals and reprints. Averages 25 total titles; 20 fiction titles each year.

Needs: Adventure, faction, fantasy, gothic/historical, contemporary romance, historical, horror, humor/satire, juvenile, mainstream, psychic/supernatural, science fiction, suspense/mystery, war, western, women's, young adult.

How to Contact: Query first. Simultaneous submissions OK. Reports in 2 weeks on queries.

Terms: Pays in outright purchase and author's copies.

DAW BOOKS, INC., 1633 Broadway, New York NY 10019. Imprint includes DAW Books. Assistant Editor: Betsy Wollheim. Estab. 1971. Publishes paperback originals. Plans 2 first novels this year. Averages 60 total titles, 60 fiction titles each year. Occasionally critiques rejected mss.

Needs: Fantasy, science fiction.

How to Contact: Submit complete ms with SASE. Reports in 6 weeks on mss.

Terms: Pays in royalties or in advance.

DELACORTE JUVENILE, 1 Dag Hammerskjold Plaza, New York NY 10017. See Dell Publishing Co., Inc. "We prefer query letters with detailed synopses or novel length contemporary fiction only. No picture books." For ages 9 and up. "Will, regretably, no longer consider unsolicited material at this time."

DELACORTE PRESS, 1 Dag Hammerskjold Plaza, New York NY 10017. See Dell Publishing Co., Inc.

L PUBLISHING CO., INC., 1 Dag Hammerskjold Plaza, New York NY 10017. Imprints le Delacorte Press, Delacorte Juvenile, Delta, Dell, Laurel-Leaf, Yearling, Purse. Estab.

1922. Publishes hardcover and paperback originals and paperback reprints.

Needs: See below for individual imprint requirements.

How to Contact: General guidelines for unagented submissions. Reports in 3 months. Photocopied and simultaneous submissions OK. Please adhere strictly to the following procedures: 1. Send *only* a 4 page synopsis or outline with a cover letter stating previous work published or relevant experience. Enclose SASE. 2. *Do not* send ms, sample chapters or artwork. 3. *Do not* register, certify or insure your letter. Dell is comprised of several imprints, each with its own editorial department. Please review carefully the following information and direct your submissions to the appropriate department. Your envelope must be marked: Attention: (One of the following names of imprints), Editorial Department—Proposal.

DELACORTE: Publishes in hardcover; looks for top-notch commercial fiction. Recently published *Eden Burning*, by Belva Plain; *Crossings*, by Danielle Steel. 50 titles/year.

DELTA: Publishes in trade paperback; rarely publishes original fiction; looks for useful, substantial guides (nonfiction). 20 titles/year.

DELL: Publishes mass-market paperbacks; rarely publishes original nonfiction; looks for family sagas, historical romances, sexy modern romances, adventure and suspense thrillers, psychic/supernatural, horror, war novels. Especially interested in submissions for Candlelight Ecstasy Romances. Not currently publishing original mysteries, westerns, or science ficton. 300 titles/year.

DELACORTE JUVENILE: Publishes in hardcover for children and young adults, grades K-12. 20 titles/year. "We prefer complete mss for fiction."

LAUREL-LEAF: Publishes originals and reprints in paperback for young adults, grades 7-12. 50 titles/year.

YEARLING: Publishes originals and reprints in paperback for children, grades K-6. 50 titles/year.

PURSE: Publishes miniature paperbacks about 60 pages in length on topics of consumer interest. No fiction.

Terms: Pays 6-15% in royalties; offers advance. Book catalog for 8½x11 SASE plus $1.30 postage (Attention: Customer Service).

Tips: "Don't get your hopes up. Query first only with 4 page synopsis plus SASE. Study the paperback racks in your local drugstore. We encourage all authors to seek agents."

DELTA PRESS, 1 Dag Hammerskjold Plaza, New York NY 10017. See Dell Publishing Co., Inc.

THE DIAL PRESS, 1 Dag Hammarskjold Plaza, New York NY 10017. Editorial Director: J. Jurjevics. Estab. 1924. Publishes hardcover and trade paperback originals. Number of titles: averages 70-75.

Needs: Contemporary, literary, adventure, mystery, spy, historical, western, women's, feminist, psychic/supernatural.

How to Contact: Query, submit outline/synopsis and about 3 sample chapters of book ("*first three chapters—not middle of book*") or submit through agent. SASE return of ms. Simultaneous and photocopied submissions OK if legible. Reports in 6 weeks on queries, 6 weeks on mss.

Terms: Pays in royalties; offers advance. Free book catalog with SASE.

DODD, MEAD & COMPANY, INC., 79 Madison Ave., New York NY 10016. (212)685-6464. Fiction Editors: Allen Klots, Margaret Norton. Estab. 1839. Publishes hardcover originals and hardcover and paperback reprints. Number of titles: averages 125.

Needs: Contemporary, literary, adventure, mystery, spy, historical, war, gothic, women's, ethnic, religious/inspirational, humor/satire, juvenile and young adult: sports, animal, spy/adventure, historical, fantasy, and easy-to-read. Recently published *The Prisoner's Wife*, by Jack Holland; *Dog in the Manger*, by Ursula Curtis; *Sheiks and Adders*, by Michael Innes; *The Fateful Summer*, by Velda Johnston (mysteries).

How to Contact: Query or submit outline/synopsis and sample chapters. Complete ms for mysteries. SASE for query, ms. "Reluctantly" considers simultaneous submissions. Photocopied submissions OK. Reports in 1 month.

Terms: Pays in royalties; offers advance. Free book catalog with SASE.

TOM DOHERTY ASSOCIATES, 8-10 W. 36th St., New York NY 10018. (212)564-0150. Imprint includes TOR Books. Fiction Editor: Harriet McDougal. Managing Editor: Katya Pendill. Science Fiction Editor: Jim Baen. Estab. 1980. Publishes paperback originals and reprints. Plans 12 first novels this year. Averages 75 total titles, 60 fiction titles each year. Occasionally critiques rejected mss.
Needs: Fantasy, horror, psychic/supernatural, occult. Recently published: *Of Women & Their Elegance*, by Norman Mailer (fiction); *Wells of Hell*, by Graham Masterton; *Misfire*, by Jonathan Evans (suspense fiction); and *Test of Fire*, by Ben Bovn (science fiction).
How to Contact: Query first with SASE, then submit outline/synopsis with 3 sample chapters with SASE. Photocopied submissions OK. Reports in 4 weeks on queries; 6 weeks on mss.
Terms: Pays in royalties; advance is negotiable.

DOUBLEDAY AND CO., INC., 245 Park Ave., New York NY 10017. (212)953-4561. Imprint includes Dolphin Press. Executive Editors: Lisa Drew, Kate Medina. Estab. 1897. Publishes hardcover originals. Averages 150 total titles each year.
Needs: Will consider all genres except confession and erotica. Recently published *The Almighty*, by Irving Wallace; *Woman of Substance*, by Barbara Taylor Bradford; and *Stepping, Three Women at the Water's Edge, Bodies and Souls*, by Nancy Thayer.
How to Contact: Query. All unsolicited mss are returned unopened. Simultaneous and photocopied submissions OK. Reports in "up to 2½ months on queries and mss.
Terms: Pays in royalties; offers advance.
Tips: "Your letter of inquiry should be addressed to Editorial Department. First sentence should tell us whether the book is a novel, mystery or whatever and what the book's about in a clear and straightforward description. Summarize plot and background and give a sketch of major characters. If you have already been published, give us details at the end of your letter along with credentials or experience that qualify you to write your book."

DOUBLEDAY CANADA, 105 Bond St., Toronto, Ontario, Canada M5B 1Y3. (416)977-7891. Senior Editor: Janet Turnbull. Submissions should be sent Attn: Trade Editorial Dept. Publishes hardcover and trade paperback originals and reprints. Number of titles: 11 in 1982.
Needs: Contemporary, literary, faction, adventure, mystery, spy, historical, war, confession, women's, feminist, ethnic, psychic/supernatural, humor/satire, translations. "Encourage Canadian content or Canadian writers." Recently published *The Favorite*, by L.R. Wright.
How to Contact: Submit outline/synopsis, brief character sketches and 2-3 chapters along with brief biography. Photocopied submissions OK. Reports in 2 months.
Terms: Pays in royalties; offers advance. Free book catalog.
Tips: "It helps if the author tells who his potential market is."

E.P. DUTTON PUBLISHERS, 2 Park Ave., New York NY 10016. Imprint inlcudes Henry Robbins Books and Joan Kahn Books. Editor-in-Chief: Joseph Kanon. Juvenile: Ann Durrell. Paperback and Artbook Editor: Cy Nelson. Publishes hardcover and paperback originals and paperback reprints in the Obelisk line and Starlight Teen Romance. Encourages new writers. Plans 1-2 first novels for '83. Sometimes comments on rejected mss.
Needs: Contemporary, experimental, humor/satire, literary, juvenile, suspense/mystery, war, women's, young adult and translations. No gothics, historicals, romance, or poetry. Recently published *Bloodmoor Romance*, by Joyce Carol Oates; *Camia*, by Tristan Trevis; *Tzili*; the *Story of a Life*, by Aharon Appelfeld and *Hotel New Hampshire*, by John Irving.
How to Contact: Temporarily not accepting unsolicited mss. Writers may send a query letter. Reports in 8 weeks on queries.
Terms: Rates vary individually; offers advance. Free writer's guidelines for SASE with 18¢ postage; free book catalog for SASE with 72¢ postage.
Tips: "Do not overlook literary magazines and journals. They are often receptive and have more time to supply feedback."

EAKIN PUBLICATIONS, Box 23066, Austin TX 78735. (512)756-6911. Imprint includes Nortex. Editor: Edwin M. Eakin. Estab. 1978. Publishes hardcover and paperback originals.
Needs: Juvenile. Specifically needs historical fiction for school market, juveniles set in Texas for Texas gradeschoolers. Recently published *Davy Crockett, The Untold Story*, by Frank A. Driskill; *Jane Long, Mother of Texas*, by Catherine Gonzalez; and *Texas—Yesterday and Today*, by Sibyl Hancock and Fay Venable.
How to Contact: Query or submit outline/synopsis and sample chapters. Simultaneous and photocopied submissions OK. Reports in 3 months on queries.
Terms: Pays 10-15% in royalties; no advance. Free book catalog on request.

EDC PUBLISHING, 8141 E. 44th St., Tulsa OK 74145. (800)331-4418. Subsidiary of Educational Development Corporation. General Manager: Richard L. Howard. Publises hardcover and paperback originals and reprints. Encourages new writers. Averages 30 total titles, 10 fiction titles each year. Publishes also in Spanish, French, German. Occasionally critiques rejected ms.
Needs: Juvenile (animal, easy-to-read, fantasy, historical, picture book, sports, spy/adventure, contemporary), young adult (easy-to-read, fantasy/scence fiction, sports, spy/adventure). Recently published *Ulysses*, by Homer—Retold by Webb & Amery (classic); *Robinson Crusoe*, by Defoe (classic); and *King Arthur*, by Wilkies (classic).
How to Contact: Query first; submit outline/synopsis and 1 sample chapter. Simultaneous and photocopied submissions OK. Reports in 2 weeks on queries; 2 months on mss.
Terms: Pays in outright purchase. Writer's guidelines free; book catalog free on request.

EMC PUBLISHING, 300 York Ave., St. Paul MN 55101. (612)771-1555. Editor: Rosemary Barry. Estab. 1956. Publishes hardcover and paperback originals. Averages 40 total titles, 10 fiction titles each year.
Needs: Juvenile (animal, easy-to-read, sports, contemporary), young adult (easy-to-read, problem novels, sports). "We sell to the school market; therefore, our needs for the next year are very limited. No adult fiction, no religious orientation."
How to Contact: Query first with SASE. All unsolicited mss are returned unopened. Photocopied submissions OK. Reports in 1 month on queries.
Terms: Pays in royalties; changes depending on project. Catalog for 8½x11 SASE and 2 first class stamps.

PAUL S. ERIKSSON, PUBLISHER, Battell Bldg., Middlebury VT 05753. (802)388-7303. Editor: Paul S. Eriksson. Estab. 1960. Publishes hardcover and paperback originals. Number of titles: 5 in 1981.
Needs: Mainstream. Recently published *Deadly Dream*, by Theodore S. Drachman, MD (medical mystery).
How to Contact: Submit outline/synopsis and sample chapters. No simultaneous submissions; photocopied submissions OK.
Terms: Pays 10-15% in royalties; advance offered if necessary. Free book catalog.
Tips: "We do very little fiction."

EVEREST HOUSE, PUBLISHERS, 33 West 60 Street, New York NY 10023. Senior Editor: Evans Marshall. Estab. 1977. Publishes hardcover and trade paperback originals. Number of titles: about 40 titles/year.
Needs: High quality fiction aimed at hardcover market. Recently published *The Rose Exterminator*, by William Carney and *The Celebrant*, by Eric Rolfe Greenbury.
How to Contact: Query with outline and sample chapters. No complete mss please. Reports within 2 months on queries. SASE must accompany submission.
Terms: Pays standard royalties; offers varied advance.

FARRAR, STRAUS & GIROUX, 19 Union Sq. W., New York NY 10003. Imprints include Hill & Wang and Octagon. Children's Books Editor-in-Chief: Stephen Roxburgh. Number of titles: 30 in 1981.

Needs: Juvenile and young adult. Recently published *Jake and Honeybunch Go to Heaven*, story and illustrations by Margot Zemach (picture book); *Annie on My Mind*, by Nancy Garden (contemporary young adult novel); and *The Green Book*, by Jill Paton Walsh with illustrations by Lloyd Bloom (children's novel).
How to Contact: Submit outline/synopsis and sample chapters (3). No simultaneous submissions, photocopied submissions OK. Reports in 1 month on queries, 8 weeks on mss.
Terms: Pays in royalties; offers advance. Free book catalog with SASE.

FAWCETT, Division of Random House/Ballantine, 201 E. 50th St., New York NY 10022. (212)751-2600. Imprints include Crest, Gold Medal. Senior Editor: Michaela Hamilton. Executive Editor: Leona Nevier. Estab. 1955. Publishes paperback orginals. Prints 160 titles annually. Encourages new writers. Plans 8 first novels for 1983.
Needs: Historical, suspense, occult, men's adventure and particularly women's. Recently published *The Velvet Thorn*, by Angela Alexie; *The Revengers*, by Donald Hamilton; and *Virginia Clay*, by Meredith Rier.
How to Contact: Query with SASE. Send outline and sample chapters for adult mass market. If ms is requested, simultaneous and photocopied submissions OK. Reports in 1 month on queries, 2 months on mss.
Terms: Pays usual advance and royalties.

THE FIRST EAST COAST THEATRE & PUBLISHING CO., INC., Box A244, Village Station, New York NY 10014. Imprint includes First East Coast. Editor: Paul Boccio. Fiction Editors: Paul and Karen Boccio. Estab. 1979. Publishes paperback originals. Published 2 titles in 1981.
Needs: "Our company will not consider the 'fashion' novel. We are interested in promoting serious material; that is, fiction written in a strong, individual style, demonstrating a unique and new voice."
How to Contact: Query or submit outline/synopis and sample chapters (5) with SASE. Simultaneous and photocopied submissions OK. Reports in 2 weeks on queries, 1 month on mss.
Terms: Pays 7-12% in royalties; offers $1,000 in advance.
Tips: Mss are rejected because "many are poorly written. But we also receive 'misdirected' works; e.g., 'fashion' and romance novels when we advertise specifically that we are not interested in these. Writers should know to whom they are sending their work. We believe there is a desire to read contemporary novels which deal honestly with contemporary life. It takes a good writer to faithfully recreate the world around him in the present."

✓**FLARE BOOKS**, Young Adult Book Imprint of Avon Books, 959 8th Ave., New York NY 10019. (212)262-7454. Editorial Director: Jean Feiwel. Publishes paperback originals and reprints. Averages 36 total titles each year.
Needs: Contemporary, experimental, humor, mainstream, mystery, and suspense for readers 12-20. Recently published: *Breaking Up*, by Norma Klein; *Taking Terri Mueller*, by Norma Fox Mazer; *The Battle Off Midway Island*, by Theodore Island; *Justice and Her Brothers*, by Virginia Hamilton; and *The Pigeon*, by Jay Bennett.
How to Contact: Query or submit outline/synopsis and 3 sample chapters with SASE. Simultaneous and photocopied submissions OK. Reports in 6-8 weeks queries and mss.
Terms: Pays a 6-10% royalty and the advance averages $1,500-5,000.

BERNARD GEIS ASSOCIATES, INC, 128 E. 56th St., New York NY 10022. (212)752-1975. Editorial Director: Judith Shafran. Estab. 1958. Publishes hardcover and paperback originals. Plans 5-10 first novels this year. Averages 12-15 total titles, 10 fiction titles each year.
Needs: Adventure, contemporary, faction, horror, literary, mainstream, psychic/supernatural, suspense/mystery. Recently published *The Cardinal Sins*, by Andrew M. Greeley (contemporary); *Thy Brother's Wife*, by Andrew M. Greeley (contemporary); and *Cathedral*, by Nelson De M⁽ᵉ⁾le (suspense).

How to Contact: Submit outline/synopsis and 3 sample chapters. Photocopied submissions OK. Reports in approximately 4 weeks on queries; 6 weeks on mss.

DAVID R. GODINE, PUBLISHER, INC., 306 Dartmouth St., Boston MA 02116. (617)536-761. Imprint includes Nonpareil Books. Editorial Director: William B. Goodman; Manuscript Submissions: Deanne Smeltzer; Juvenile Ms Submissions: Sarah Saint-Onge. Estab. 1970. Publishes hardcover and paperback originals and reprints. Number of titles: 28 in 1983. Encourages new writers "but we've never published a first novel, only first collections of short stories." Comments on rejected mss "if of particular interest."
Needs: Contemporary, literary, mystery, historical, ethnic, humor/satire, juvenile, young adult. Recently published *Finding A Girl in America*, by Andre Dubus (short stories); and *The State of Ireland*, by Benedict Kiely (short stories); and *Obason*, by Joy Kogawa.
How to Contact: Query with outline synopsis. Simultaneous and photocopied submissions OK.
Terms: Pays 5-10% in royalties; offers $500-1,000 in advance. Occasionally subsidy publishes, "but only if a book is exceptionally fine, yet too expensive for us to produce on our own—color photography, for example." Free book catalog.
Tips: "Though we don't do a lot of fiction (probably no more than 2 novels a season), we are planning more. Use tactful perseverance, but not pushiness, or demands for answers to queries."

GOSPEL LIGHT PUBLICATIONS, 2300 Knoll Dr., Ventura CA 93003. (805)644-9721. Subsidiaries include Regal Books, Vision House. Imprints includes Galaxy Books and Cricket Books. Senior Editor: Donald E. Pugh. Fiction Editor: Carol Brown. Estab. 1933. Publishes hardcover and paperback originals. Plans 1-2 first novels this year. Averages 40 total titles, 5-7 fiction (including young adult) titles each year. Occasionally critiques rejected mss.
Needs: Fantasy, juvenile (fantasy, adventure, contemporary), religious/inspirational, young adult (fantasy, problem novels, adventure). "We are looking for Christian fiction to sell to an evangelical market. We want it to be exciting reading, teach something and be well written. It need not have an explicit Christian message in it; we steer away from anything to 'preachy'. No charismatic; prophetic/end times; typical Christian testimonies; anything promoting loose morals (no explicit sex, etc.)." Recently published *Night of Fire, Days of Rain*, by Bob Zoller (juvenile adventure); *Diabolus Seeks Revenge*, by Tom Finley (juvenile fantasy/adventure); and *Our Family Got a Stepparent*, by Carolyn Phillips (juvenile problem solving).
How to Contact: Query first with SASE. Simultaneous and photocopied submissions OK. Reports in 4 weeks on queries; 8-12 weeks on mss.
Terms: Pays in royalties of 10% maximum; 10 author's copies. Writer's guidelines free for # 10 SASE; book catalog for 9x12 SAE and 2 first class stamps.
Tips: "We are just starting to branch into adult novels. The market for good Christian reading (clean, fast-paced, well-written) is tremendous. We have done very little adult fiction in the past because no one seems to be able to write Christian fiction and have it be good from a literary standpoint. We are trying to fill this gap. Be persistent in trying to get something published if it's good!"

GREAT WESTERN PUBLISHING CO., INC., 416 Magnolia, Glendale CA 91204. (213)246-7470. Vice President: Michael Scheer. Fiction Editor: John Sanbourn. Estab. 1979. Publishes hardcover and paperback originals and paperback reprints. Plans 10 first novels this year. Averages 80 total titles, varied amount of fiction titles each year. Occasionally critiques rejected mss.
Needs: Adventure, contemporary, ethnic, fantasy, gothic/historical, contemporary romance, historical, humor/satire, psychic/supernatural, religious/inspirational, science fiction, suspense/mystery, war, western, young adult (spy/adventure). "We are interested in all categories except pornography and children's fiction." Recently published *A Question of Judgment*, by Terence Mix and Victor Rosen (mystery/thriller); *Change of Heart*, by Earl Jones (adventure); and *Rings of Dhone*, by Joseph Martin (science fiction).
How to Contact: Submit complete ms with SASE. Simultaneous and photocopied submissions OK. Reports in 2 months on mss.

comm. publishers

Terms: Negotiates advance; pays in 75 author's copies. Book catalog free on request.

GREEN TIGER PRESS, 1061 India St., San Diego CA 92101. Imprints include Star & Elephant, Circling Suns. Editor: Harold Darling. Editorial Assistant: Helen Neumeyer. Estab. 1971. Publishes hardcover and paperback originals and reprints. Number of titles: 6 in 1980; 18 in 1981. Encourages new writers. Sometimes comments on rejected mss.
Needs: Experimental. Specific interest in imaginative fiction for children lending itself to illustration. "We are publishers of illustrated picture books. Our work tends to be imaginative or poetic in flavor, somewhat anachronistic in sentiment, and soldily visual in focus." Recently published *The Teddy Bear's ABC's*, by Laura Rinkle Johnson, illustrations by Margaret Landers Sanford (reprint of 1907 book redesigned and colored); and *Emily and the Shadow Shop*, by Cooper Edens, illustrations by Patrick Dowers.
How to Contact: Query or submit complete ms or outline/synopsis and sample chapters or submit through agent. Simultaneous and photocopied submissions OK. Reports in 2 weeks on queries, 6-8 weeks on mss.
Terms: A variety of arrangements is possible depending upon the capacity in which a given work is used; offers advance. Star and Elephant Catalogue $1; The Green Tigers Compendium $3.95 and $2 postage.
Tips: "Read voraciously. Even bad books can provide much by way of negative example." The types of novels published are determined by "our inner beliefs and needs matched with our understanding of the curiosity and hungers of the reading pubic."

GREENLEAF CLASSICS, INC., Box 20194, San Diego CA 92120. Editorial Director: Douglas Saito. Acquisitions Editor: Ralph Vaughan. Estab. 1961. Publishes paperback originals. Prints 360 titles annually.
Needs: Erotica. No science fiction, fantasy, mysteries, satire, memoirs, period pieces or occult themes.
How to Contact: Query (requesting guidelines) or submit complete ms or outline/synopsis and sample chapters (3) with SASE. No simultaneous submissions. Reports in 1 week on queries, 2 weeks on mss.
Terms: Pays by outright purchase $400; no advance.
Tips: "Don't waste time submitting until you've received our guidelines. Send SASE for writer's guidelines."

✓**GREENWILLOW BOOKS**, Division of Wm. Morrow & Co., 105 Madison Ave., New York NY 10016. (212)889-3050, ext. 214. Editor-in-Chief: Susan Hirschman. Estab. 1975. Publishes hardcover originals. Number of titles: 60 annually.
Needs: Juvenile and young adult: sports, animal, spy/adventure, historical, fantasy/science fiction and easy-to-read. Primarily picture books, easy readers, and some young-adult novels. Recently published *On Market Street*, by Arnold and Anita Lobel (picture alphabet book); *The House On the Hill*, by Mildred Masters (a first novel); and *The Blue Sword*, by Robin McKinley (fantasy).
How to Contact: Submit complete ms or outline/synopsis and sample chapters (2-3) or submit through agent with SASE. No simultaneous submissions; photocopied submissions OK. Reports in 2 weeks on queries, 6 weeks on mss.
Terms: Royalty and advance. Free book catalog.

GROVE PRESS, INC., 196 W. Houston St., New York NY 10014. Imprints include Evergreen, Black Cat and Outrider. Editorial Director: Barney Rosset. Estab. 1952. Publishes hardcover and paperback originals and reprints. Number of titles: averages 50/year.
Needs: Contemporary, literary, experimental, mystery, spy, historical, feminist, gay/lesbian, ethnic, erotica, science fiction, humor/satire, translations and investigative journalism.
How to Contact: Submit outline/synopsis and sample chapters (2) or submit through agent. Must have SASE. Simultaneous and photocopied submissions OK. Reports in 1 month on queries mss.

Terms: Pays in royalties and offers advance. Free book catalog.

HARCOURT BRACE JOVANOVICH, 1250 6th Ave., San Diego CA 92101. Imprint includes Voyager paperbacks, Let-Me-Read, and Sports Star. Manager: Maria Modugno. Senior Editor: Kathleen Krull. Editorial Assistant: Paula Bryant. Publishes hardcover originals and reprints. Number of titles: 20-25 per year, including several first novels. Actively seeking new writers. Sometimes comments on rejected mss "if it shows real promise on the part of the author."
Needs: "We are looking for honestly approached and thoughtfully written mss with high appeal for children and young adults: contemporary fiction, sports, animals, spy-adventure, historical, fantasy/science fiction, easy-to-read, humor. We especially need books for early readers and material with potential for bookstore sales." Recently published *A Visit to William Blake's Inn*, by Nancy Willard; *The People in Pineapple Place*, by Anne Lindbergh; *You Shouldn't Have to Say Goodbye*, by Patricia Hermes; and *Strega Nona's Magic Lessons*, by Tomie de Paola.
How to Contact: Submit complete ms for picture books or outline/synopsis and sample chapters (2-4) for novels. No phone calls. No simultaneous submissions; photocopied submissions OK. Send SASE. Please do not send originals of art; photocopies preferred. Reports in 2 weeks on queries, 6-8 weeks on mss.
Terms: Varies according to individual book. Send for free catalog.

HARLE HOUSE, 133 S. Heights, Houston TX 77007. (713)869-9092. Imprint includes Larksdale. Publisher: J. Goodman. Fiction Editor: Glenda Kachelmeier. Estab. 1978. Publishes paperback originals. Plans 6 first novels this year. Averages 12 total titles, 6 fiction titles each year. Occasionally critiques rejected mss for $50.
Needs: Adventure, contemporary romance, historical, juvenile (easy-to-read, historical), mainstream, religious/inspirational, young adult (easy-to-read, historical). No "science fiction, western, or anything smutty." Recently published *Twice the Heartache*, by Judy Campbell (mainstream/inspirational).
How to Contact: Submit complete ms with SASE. Simultaneous (if stated) and photocopied submissions OK. Reports in 2 months on queries; 4 months on mss.
Terms: "Standard Author's Guild payment." Book catalog for 8½x11 SASE and 3 first class stamps.

HARLEQUIN ENTERPRISES, LTD., 225 Duncan Mill Rd., Don Mills, Ontario, Canada M3B 3K9. (416)445-5860. Imprints include Harlequin Romances, Harlequin Presents, Harlequin American Romances, Gold Eagle, Superromances. Editor: George Glay. Estab. 1949. Publishes paperback originals and reprints. Number of titles: averages 200/year.
Needs: Romance and heroic adventure. Will accept nothing that is not related to the desired categories.
How to Contact: Send outline and first 50 pages (2 or 3 chapters) or submit through agent with IRC and SASE. Absolutely no simultaneous submissions, photocopied submissions OK. Reports in 1 month on queries; 6 weeks on ms.
Terms: Offers royalties, advance.
Tips: "The quickest route to success is to follow directions for submissions: query first. Before sending a ms, read as many Harlequin Romances as you can get your hands on. It's very important to study the style and do your homework first."

HARMONY BOOKS, Division of Crown Publishers, 1 Park Ave., New York NY 10016. (212)532-9200. Editor: Peter H. Shriver. Publishes hardcover originals. Number of titles: 2 in 1981.
Needs: Contemporary, literary. Recently published *The Royal Game and Other Stories*, by Stefan Zweig (short stories); and *Hitchhiker's Guide to the Galaxy*, by Douglas Adams (science fiction).
How to Contact: Query with SASE. Simultaneous and photocopied submissions OK. Reports in 6 weeks on query.
Terms: Advance given varies.
Tips: "Be sure and send query letter first."

✓**HARPER & ROW JUNIOR BOOKS GROUP**, 10 E. 53rd St., New York NY 10022. (212)593-7044. Imprints include Harper & Row Junior Books, including Charlotte Zolotow Books; T.Y. Crowell and Lippincott Junior Books. Publisher: Elizabeth Gordon. Editors: Charlotte Zolotow, Nina Ignatowicz, Lucille Schultz, Marilyn Kriney, Barbara Fenton, Laura Geringer. Publishes hardcover originals and paperback reprints. Number of titles: *Harper—Cloth*: 65 in 1981, 65 in 1982; *Harper—Trophy* (paperback): 16 in 1981, 16 in 1982; *Crowell*: 34 in 1981, 36 in 1982; *Lippincott*: 17 in 1981, 16 in 1982.
Needs: Picture books, easy-to-read, middle-grade, teen-age and young adult novels; fiction, fantasy, animal, sports, spy/adventure, historical, science fiction, problem novels, contemporary. Recently published: Harper, *Happy Winter*, by Karen Gundersheimer (ages 4-8); *The Two-Thousand Pound Goldfish*, by Betsy Byars (ages 10 up); Harper/Charlotte Zolotow Books: *Summerboy*, by Robert Lipsyte (ages 12 up); *Summer Switch*, by Mary Rodgers (ages 10 up); Crowell: *Avocado Baby*, by John Burningham (ages 3-6); Lippincott: *Ghosts of Departure Point*, by Eve Bunting (ages 11 up); *The Secret Life of Hardware*, by Vicki Cobb (ages 10 up).
How to Contact: Query; submit complete ms; submit outline/synopsis and sample chapters; submit through agent. SASE for query, ms. Please identify simultaneous submissions; photocopied submissions OK. Reports in 2-3 months.
Terms: Average 10% in royalties. Royalties on picture books shared with illustrators. Offers advance. Book catalog for self-addressed label.
Tip: "Write from your own experience and the child you once were. Read widely in the field of adult and children's literature. Realize that writing for children is a difficult challenge."

HARPER & ROW PUBLISHERS, INC., 10 E. 53rd St., New York NY 10022. (212)593-7000. Publisher & Editorial Director: Edward L. Burlingame. Managing Editor: Katharine Kirkland. Estab. 1817. Publishes hardcover originals. Plans 6-8 first novels for '83.
Needs: Harper & Row will review only manuscripts and proposals submitted by agents or those works submitted upon recommendation of someone known by one of Harper's editors. Recently published *The Dean's December*, by Saul Bellow; *Cinnamon Skin*, by John D. MacDonald; and *Southern Discomfort*, by Rita Mae Brown.

HARVEY HOUSE PUBLISHERS, 20 Waterside Plaza, New York NY 10010. Publisher: L.F. Reeves. Publishes hardcover originals.
Needs: Juvenile and young adult. "We prefer realistic fiction about contemporary problems. No science fiction, romance, fantasy, talking animals or rehashed fairy tales." Recently published *Hot Wire*, by Butterworth.
How to Contact: Simultaneous and photocopied submissions OK, if so informed. Reports in 6 weeks on queries and mss.
Terms: Pays royalties based on wholesale and retail price; offers advance depending on the ms.

HERALD PRESS, Division of Mennonite Publishing House, 616 Walnut Ave., Scottdale PA 15683. (412)887-8500. Editor: Paul M. Schrock. Publishes hardcover and paperback originals. Number of fiction titles: 4-6 per year. Encourages new writers. Plans 2 first novels for '82.
Needs: Religious/inspirational, juvenile and young adult. Recently published *The Weight*, by Joel Kauffmann (young adult); *River of Glass*, by Wilfred Martens (historical); and *Mystery at Indian Rocks*, by Ruth Nulton Moore (juvenile).
How to Contact: Query or submit outline/synopsis and sample chapters (2) with SASE. No simultaneous submissions; photocopied submissions OK. Reports in 2 weeks on queries, 6 weeks on mss.
Terms: Pays 10-15% in royalties; 12 free author's copies; no advance. Book catalog 65¢.
Tips "We are happy to respond to book proposals from Christian authors of adult and juvenile fiction."

HIGHWAY BOOK SHOP, Highway 11N, Cobalt, Ontario, Canada P0J 1C0. (705)679-8375. Editor: Paul McDowell. Estab. 1970. Publishes paperback originals. Plans 3 first novels this year.

Averages 20 total titles, 3-5 fiction titles each year. "We are planning to develop a series in French." Critiques rejected mss.

Needs: Adventure, contemporary, ethnic, fantasy, gothic/historical, contemporary romance, historical (general), humor/satire, juvenile (animal, easy-to-read, fantasy, historical, picture book, spy/adventure, contemporary), religious/inspirational, short story collections, suspense/ mystery, war. Especially wants "stories emphasizing northern Ontario themes or those of interest to Canadians nationwide." No erotica, gay/lesbian, translation. Recently published: *The Saint and the Warrior*, by Crawford E. Dewar (historical); *Treasure for Tony*, by Lyn Cook (children's contemporary) and *Hume*, by R.R. Robinson (contemporary, town politics, S. Ontario, 1930s).

How to Contact: Query first, then submit outline/synopsis and 2 sample chapters with SASE. Reports in 3 weeks on queries; 3 months on mss.

Terms: Pays in royalties of 10% minimum, 15% maximum (for exceptional work) and in author's copies ("10 free copies across the board"). Book catalog free on request.

Tips: "Novels pegged to contemporary concerns seem to do the best. *Treasure for Tony* and *Hume* both seem to be doing well because of this. Historical novels may also do well if they're fast-moving. We tend to stick to regional novels or Canadiana."

HOLIDAY HOUSE, INC., 18 E. 53rd St., New York NY 10022. (212)688-0085. Editor: Margery Cuyler. Estab. 1935. Publishes hardcover originals. Number of titles: 30 in 1980. Encourages new writers.

Needs: Contemporary, literary, adventure, romance, science fiction, humor, animal stories. Recently published *Doris Fein: Murder Is No Joke*, by T. Ernesto Bethancourt (thriller); *The Secret Window*, by Betty Ren Wright (fiction); and *Judge Benjamin: Superdog*, by Judith Whitejack McInerney (humor). "We're not in a position to be too encouraging, as our list is tight, but we're always open to good 'family' novels and humor."

How to Contact: Query first on picture books or submit outline/synopsis and sample chapters (3). Simultaneous and photocopied submissions OK. Reports in 1 week on queries, 1 month on mss.

Terms: Advance and royalties are flexible, depending upon whether the book is illustrated. Free book catalog with SASE.

Tips: "This appears to be a decade in which publishers are interested in reviving the type of good, solid story that was popular in the '50s. Certainly, there's a trend toward humor, formula series, romance and religion. Problem novels seem to be out."

HOLLOWAY HOUSE PUBLISHING, 8060 Melrose, Los Angeles CA 90046. (213)653-8060. Executive Editor: Robert Leighton. Associate Editor: Leslie Gersicoff. Estab. 1961. Publishes paperback originals and reprints. Number of titles: averages 25/year.

Needs: Contemporary, adventure, ethnic, sports and biographies, black romances. "Black novels. Must be action packed—aimed at an adult market. No 'this is my story' treatments. Plots should be well-developed, characters easily identified and action graphically depicted with realistic dialogue, authentic slang, and current 'street' language." Recently published *Black Angels*, by Stanley Hobbs; *Sugar Man*, by Thomas Shaw; and *Sunday Hell*, by Butch Holmes.

How to Contact: Query with SASE. Simultaneous and photocopied submissions OK, only excellent copies. Reports in 2 weeks on queries, 6 weeks on mss.

Terms: Pays standard rate on royalties; offers advance. Free book catalog with business size SASE.

Tips: "Too many writers assume that because they have worked on a book, someone should read it. Follow guidelines; query letters are usually uninformative, necessitating a letter to query the 'author's query.' A query letter should contain information enough to intrigue the editor. Query letters reading . . .'and I'd appreciate your reading my book,' with no description, direction or outline are most often ignored. A ms will be reviewed upon arrival. If it is unacceptable for any of the above reasons, it will be returned promptly. If it is accepted for consideration, please allow at least six weeks for a decision."

HORIZON PRESS PUBLISHERS, LTD., 156 5th Ave., New York NY 10010. (212)924-9225. Imprints distributed include The Smith, Foolscap Press. Editor: Ben Raeburn. Estab. 1950. Publishes hardcover and paperback originals. Number of titles: 27 in 1981. Recently published *Against the Stream*, by James Hanley; *The Alleys of Eden*, *Sun Dogs*, by Robert Olen Butler; and *Conversations: A Kind of Fiction*, by James K. Feibleman.
How to Contact: Query. Reports in 2 weeks on queries, 3 months on mss.
Terms: Standard royalties. Free book catalog with SASE.

HOUGHTON MIFFLIN COMPANY, 2 Park St., Boston MA 02107. (617)725-5000. Subsidiaries include J.P. Tarcher Inc., Ticknor and Fields Inc. Managing Editor: Linda Glick. Publishes hardcover and paperback originals and paperback reprints. Plans 1 first novel this year. Averages 150 (includes childrens) total titles, 60 fiction titles each year.
Needs: Adventure, contemporary, fantasy, contemporary romance, historical, literary, mainstream, science fiction, suspense/mystery, war, women's. No religious, gothic, occult or westerns. Recently published *The Legacy*, by Howard Fast (generational); *Mosquito Coast*, by Paul Theroux (mainstream/literary); and *Shoeless Joe*, by W.P. Kinsella (literary).
How to Contact: Query first; submit outline/synopsis and 3 sample chapters with SASE. Simultaneous and photocopied submissions OK. Reports in 4 weeks on queries; 4-6 weeks on mss.
Terms: Pays in royalties of 10-12-15%; pays advance.

ICARUS PRESS, Box 1225, South Bend IN 46624. (219)233-6020. President: Bruce Fingerhut. Estab. 1977. Number of titles: 15 in 1982 (2 fiction).
Needs: Contemporary, literary, historical, war, translations. No western, romance, erotica.
How to Contact: Query or submit outline/synopsis and sample chapters. SASE for query. Photocopied and simultaneous submissions OK, if so indicated. Reports in 3 weeks on queries; may take as long as 2 months on mss.
Terms: Pays 12-18% of net in royalties; offers "modest" advance. Free book catalog.
Tips: "We are treading lightly to start. We'll do one work of comedy by an established Soviet emigre writer and a specialized dossier-mystery. We shall then sit back and see whether we are successful in marketing fiction (both from our author's and our own point of view) before embarking on a crash program."

IDEALS PUBLISHING CORP., 11315 Watertown Plank Rd., Milwaukee WI 53226. (414)771-2700. Imprint includes "Good Friends" Juveniles. V.P. Publishing: James A. Kuse. Estab. 1947. Number of titles: 2 in 1982.
Needs: Juvenile: animal, easy-to-read. No adult fiction or any other subjects or categories.
How to Contact: Submit complete ms with SASE. No simultaneous submissions, photocopied submissions OK. Reports in 6 weeks on mss.
Terms: Varies; offers variable advance.
Tips: "Know the publisher's books before submitting."

INDIANA UNIVERSITY PRESS, 10th and Morton Sts., Bloomington IN 47405. (812)337-4203. Director: John Gallman. Estab. 1950. Publishes hardcover and paperback originals and reprints. "First two novels published fall 1982. Have published translations. Little by little publishing more original fiction. We hope to do 3-5 novels per year." Encourages new writers.
Needs: "Serious, quality, novel-length fiction. We hope to establish ourselves as a major publisher of important fiction by American writers, the kinds of books which will not readily be taken by commercial publishers because they do not look toward a specific audience or necessarily offer the right kind of 'entertainment.' The word *serious* implies an effort on the part of the writer to offer insights about character, society, the structure of thought, the nature of the universe. We will not be disappointed if our books are also entertaining, and we are not looking for any particular style or approach: narrative stories are welcome, as are complex constructions in the manner of Thomas Pynchon or John Barth. There is no particular criterion with regard to length. All that matters is quality. We want our books to be distinctive, distinguished, special. And we would prefer works that are unself-conscious about either self or art." Recent published: *Twofold Vibration*, by

Raymond Federman; and *Oxherding Tale*, by Charles Johnson.

How to Contact: Query first describing ms. "The next step in consideration would be to see a sample chapter. As the third step, we would ask to see the entire work." All unsolicited mss are returned unopened. No simultaneous submissions; photocopied submissions OK. Reports in 2 weeks on queries.

Terms: Pays 6-10% of list price in royalties; occasional small advance. Some subsidy publishing (waiver of royalties or nonrefundable cash grant). Free writer's guidelines and book catalog for SASE.

Tips: "Absolutely do not want simultaneous submissions. Follow guidelines."

ISLAND PRESS, Star Rt. 1, Box 38, Covelo CA 95428. Senior Editor: Barbara Dean. Estab. 1978. Publishes paperback originals; very little fiction.

Needs: "We are interested only in the unusual fiction that would merge with our primarily non-fiction list; fiction dealing with environmental consciousness or with human experience leading to personal/spiritual growth. No gothic, science fiction, romance, confession, etc." Recently published *The Christmas Coat* (story of a family discovering itself); *No Substitute for Madness*, by R. Jones (vignettes from the experiences of an unusual teacher); *The Search for Goodbye-To-Rains*, by P. McHugh (young man's odyssey across America to find himself).

How to Contact: Query or submit outline/synopsis and sample chapters. SASE for ms. Simultaneous and photocopied submissions OK. Reports in 3 months.

Terms: Pays 10-15% in royalties; $500-$1,500 advance. Book catalog for SASE.

ALFRED A. KNOPF, 201 E. 50th St., New York NY 10022. Senior Editor: Ashbel Green. Estab. 1915. Publishes hardcover originals. Number of titles: 42 in 1981, 33 in 1982.

Needs: Contemporary, literary, mystery, spy. No western, gothic, romance, erotica, religious, science fiction. Recently published *Midnight Clear*, by William Wharton; *Dinner at the Homesick Restaurant*, by Anne Tyler; and *Rabbis and Wives*, by Chaim Grade (contemporary).

How to Contact: Submit complete ms with SASE. Simultaneous and photocopied submissions OK. Reports in 1 month on mss.

Terms: Pays 10-15% in royalties; offers advance.

Tips: Publishes book length fiction of literary merit by known and unknown writers.

KNOPF AND PANTHEON BOOKS FOR YOUNG READERS, 201 E. 50th St., New York NY 10022. Subsidiary includes Random House, Inc. Send mss: Wanda Basset, manuscript reader. Fiction Editor: Pat Ross. Publishes hardcover and paperback originals. Averages 40-50 total titles, approximately 30 fiction titles each year.

Needs: Adventure, contemporary, fantasy, horror, humor/satire, juvenile (animal, easy-to-read, fantasy, historical, picture book, sports, spy/adventure, contemporary), supernatural, science fiction, suspense/mystery, young adult (fantasy/science fiction, historical, sports, spy/adventure). "Young adult novels, picture books, middle-group novels, books for Capers series—a new series of original paperback books aimed at an average fourth-grade reading level offering a variety of high-motivational stories including mysteries, adventures, fantasies, science fiction stories, and hilarious escapades. Manuscript length is approximately 9,000 to 11,000 words." Recently published: *Notes for Another Life*, by Sue Ellen Bridgers, (young adult noel); *The Secret Life of the Underwear Champ*, by Betty Miles, (Capers) and *Who Stole the Wizard of Oz?* (Capers).

How to Contact: Query with outline/synopsis and 2 sample chapters with SASE. Simultaneous and photocopied submissions OK. Reports in 6-8 weeks on mss.

Terms: Free writer's guidelines and book catalog for 9x12 SASE.

LARKSDALE PRESS, 133 S. Heights Blvd., Houston TX 77007. (713)869-9092. Imprints include Linolean Press (religious). Publisher: James F. Goodman. Editor-in-Chief: Nancy Buquoi Adleman. Estab. 1978. Publishes hardcover and paperback originals. Number of titles: 3 in 1980; 12 in 1981.

Needs: No special categories desired. Recently published *Officer in Trouble*, by James Viner

(police fiction in its second printing) and *The Last Grey Wolf*, by Tom Townsend.
How to Contact: Query or submit complete ms to Brad Sagstetter, Managing Editor. SASE for query, ms. Photocopied and simultaneous submissions OK, if so indicated. Reports in 1 month on queries, 4 months on mss. "Mss SASE *must* include envelope."
Terms: Pays in royalties; no advance. Book catalog for SASE.
Tips: "We are primarily interested in novels with a purpose, a philosophy, and a moral position. Offensive language, illicit sex, immoral conduct by hero or heroine is out. Letter of transmittal must tell us what it's about and the purpose of the book.

SEYMOUR LAWRENCE INC., Co-publisher with E.P. Dutton, 61 Beacon St., Boston MA 02108. (617)227-1719. Publisher/President: Seymour Lawrence. Publishes hardcover and paperback originals. Number of titles: 16 in 1981; 15 in 1982.
Needs: Adult fiction. Recently published *Deadeye Dick*, by Kurt Vonnegut; *Neighbors*, by Thomas Berger; and *Under the Apple Tree*, by Dan Wakefield.
How to Contact: Submit outline/synopsis and sample chapters with SASE.
Terms: Pays in royalties of 10% to 5,000 copies; 12½% to 10,000; 15% thereafter on hardcover books.

LESTER AND ORPEN DENNYS LTD., 78 Sullivan St., Toronto, Ontario, Canada M5T 1C1. (416)593-9602. Imprint includes International Fiction List. Editor: Gena K. Gorrell. Publishes hardcover originals and reprints. Encourages new writers. Plan 3 first novels for '83. Sometimes comments briefly on rejected mss "if warranted."
Needs: Contemporary, literary, experimental, faction, adventure, mystery, spy, historical, war, women's, feminist, science fiction, fantasy, horror, humor/satire, translations, art. Recently published *Alter Ego*, by Patrick Watson (psychological thriller); *The Trial of Adolph Hitler*, by Philippe Van Rjndt (historical suspense); *Canada 1984*, by Murray Soupcoff (humor/satire); *Ways of Escape*, by Graham Greene (autobiography).
How to Contact: Prefers partial submissions on specialized topics. Send enough material so company can judge work. Simultaneous and photocopied submissions OK. Reports in 2 weeks on queries, 8 weeks on mss.
Terms: Pays in royalties; offers advance. Free book catalog.
Tips: "The trend seems to be away from literary fiction, but we encourage the literary novel as art form."

LIBRA PUBLISHERS, INC., 391 Willets Rd., Roslyn Heights, LI, NY 11577. (516)484-4950. President: William Kroll. Estab. 1960. Publishes hardcover originals. Number of titles: 4 in 1980.
Needs: All categories considered. Recently published *Please Stand By-Your Mother's Missing*, by Tallman & Gilsenan (satire of women's movements); *Billie Is Black*, by S. Forman (adventures of black slave escapees in old West); *The Gentle Losers*, by F. Gerber (WWII experiences of Dutch under German occupation).
How to Contact: Prefers submission of complete ms but queries OK. SASE for query, ms. Simultaneous and photocopied submissions OK. Reports in 1 week on queries, 2 weeks on mss.
Terms: Pays 10-15% in royalties; no advance. Free book catalog.
Tips: "Have persistence. We prefer finished copy rather than drafts."

LIPPINCOTT JUNIOR BOOKS, 10 E. 53rd St., New York NY 10022. (212)593-7044. See Harper & Row Junior Books Group.

LITTLE, BROWN & CO., 34 Beacon St., Boston MA 02106. Editorial Department, Trade Division; Children's Book: Betsy Isele, Editor.
Needs: Fiction, sports books, juveniles.
Terms: Pays on royalty basis.

Close-up

Carolyn Nichols
Bantam/Loveswept

The poster in Carolyn Nichols' modern office on Fifth Avenue says what 20 million readers of romance novels have said for years: "Look, Love Is Here to Stay and That's Enough." Large publishers have had to agree—and editors like Carolyn Nichols, senior editor at Bantam, are setting up romance series to comply with the current demands.

Nichols is responsible for much of the evolution of the romance field. In 1980 she created Berkley/Jove Publishing Group's highly successful Second Chance at Love, romances involving mature women. This line in turn has spawned similar series at other publishing houses, including her own new romance line, Loveswept, at Bantam.

Months of planning go into the development of a project like Loveswept. Nichols speaks in the vernacular about her series: Like a baby, it generally takes about nine months to get a romantic novel out, but the search for authors, the planning and preparation, "the getting pregnant process," may take longer. Nichols is launching Loveswept, literally *her* baby, by late spring 1983.

Loveswept romances are page turners. Nichols stresses, with lots of plot that flows and develops in accordance with the age and situation of the heroine, who generally falls into one of three groups:

1. The 18-23 year-old woman may be finishing school or starting an entry level job. "Mr. Wonderful should appear as close to page one as possible," and the loss of virginity may occur, usually near the middle of the book.

2. The 24-35 year-old heroine is in full bloom, involved in a compelling career or interesting hobby. She is not necessarily naive or inexperienced; she is nice, assertive, spunky—but not hard, and has all sorts of obstacles appropriate to her age to overcome before the happily-ever-after ending.

3. Ms. 35-45 year-old may be like Carolyn Nichols herself: an attractive, ambitious, winning executive of a major corporation. She will be a single woman, maybe a widow or divorcee, with difficult but not insurmountable problems with Mr. W.

In general, says Ms. Nichols, a former writer of seven romance novels, "all stories must be believable but not necessarily realistic," light and escapist, and "they should tap into the fantasies of women." Children are occasionally successful in a story; but a "24-year old executive does not ring true."

It's safest to send a letter first asking about an idea for a setting, an occupation, plot twist, Loveswept's editor stresses. Then if requested, send three sample chapters or the manuscript with a cover letter. "The real test is not how you sell yourself in a letter—but how you write the book. . . . Give your best effort creatively and technically. Strive for quality. Great romances will always sell."

Keeping on top of market changes is imperative. To save time before starting a manuscript, Nichols advises: Write or telephone someone in the romance department of a publishing house—a secretary, editorial assistant, but *not* the senior editor—and inquire about recommended titles reflecting current trends. Read selectively, study the individual style, and check back every four to six months.

How to Contact: Submissions only from authors who have previously published a book or have published in professional or literary journals, newspapers or magazines. Query first.

LODESTAR BOOKS, (formerly Elsevier/Nelson Books), a Division of E.P. Dutton, Inc., 2 Park Ave., New York NY 10016. (212)725-1818. Editorial Director: Virginia Buckley. Publishes hardcover fiction for young adults, ages 10-14, ages 8-12. No picture books. Number of titles: 25-30 annually, 12-15 fiction titles annually.
Needs: Contemporary and humorous for ages 8-12. Adventure, juvenile (fantasy, sports, spy/adventure, contemporary), young adult (fantasy/science fiction, probem novels, sports, spy/adventure). Recently published: *The Barracuda Gang*, by Malcolm Bosse (young adult novel); *The Case of the Cop Catchers*, by Terrance Dicks (mystery); *Hello, Mr. Chips*, by Ann Bishop (humor).
How to Contact: Query first or submit complete ms with SASE. Simultaneous and photocopied submissions OK. Reports in 3 months.
Terms: Pays 7½-15% in royalties; offers negotiable advance. Writer's guidelines for SASE and one first class stamp. Book catalog for 9x12 SASE and 88¢ postage.
Tips: "Know the market, work closely with editor, read other books, polish your manuscript."

LOVESWEPT, 666 5th Ave., New York NY 10103. (212)765-6500. Subsidiaries include Seal Books (Canada) and Transworld/Corgi (UK). Senior Editor: Carolyn Nichols. Editorial Assistant: Susan Koenig. Estab. 1982 (imprint). Publishes paperback originals. Plans several first novels this year. Averages 40+ total titles each year. Occasionally critiques rejected mss.
Needs: Contemporary romance. "Contemporary romance, highly sensual, believable primary characters, fresh and vibrant approaches to plot. No gothics, regencies, suspense. Check with editorial assistant for trend-setting titles recommended by the editors."
How to Contact: Query first with SASE; submit outline/synopsis and 3 samples chapters if published; send complete ms if unpublished with SASE. Photocopied submissions OK. Reports in 4-5 weeks on queries; 1½-2 months on mss.
Terms: Pays in royalties of 6%; negotiates advance.
Tips: "Use and/or devise new twists and approaches to the genre and be highly sensual."

MACMILLAN OF CANADA, A Division of Gage Publishing Limited, 146 Front Street West, Suite 685, Toronto, Ontario, Canada H5J 1G2. (416)597-1060. Publisher: Douglas M. Gibson. Editor-in-Chief: Anne Holloway. Publishes in English exclusively. Estab. 1905. Publishes hardcover and quality paperback originals. Number of titles: 23 in 1981. Encourages new writers. Plans 1 first novel for '82. Comments on rejected mss "only if there is considerable merit."
Needs: Quality fiction for discriminating market, preferably with Canadian theme, setting or author. Recently published *The Rebel Angels*, by Robertson Davies (literary novel by well known Canadian author); *Home Truths*, by Mavis Gallant (literary; short stories); *Final Decree*, by George Jonas (first novel); *A Woman Called Scylla*, by David Gurr (thriller).
How to Contact: Submit first three chapters with brief outline and resume. SASE for return of ms. Simultaneous and photocopied submissions acceptable. Replies within 3 months.
Terms: Negotiable.
Tips: Will publish "between five and ten novels yearly." Looks for "literary quality; interesting stories."

MACMILLAN PUBLISHING CO., INC., 866 3rd Ave., New York NY 10022. (212)935-2000. "Address juvenile mss to Children's Book Dept. No adult mss accepted." Imprints include Collier Books, The Free Press. Publishes hardcover juvenile originals and hardcover and paperback reprints. Number of juvenile titles: 21 in 1981; 42 in 1982; 35 in 1983. Recently published: *Beyond the Divide*, by Kathryn Sasky; *Me and My Kitten*, by Nicole Rubel; and *Beastly Riddles*, by Joseph Low.
Needs: Will consider all juvenile categories. Future lists very full.

How to Contact: Query, submit outline/synopsis and sample chapters, submit complete ms or submit through agent. Photocopied submissions OK. Reports in 6 weeks.
Terms: Pays in royalties; offers advance. Free book catalog.

MADRONA PUBLISHERS, INC., 2116 Western Ave., Seattle WA (206)624-6840. President: Daniel J. Levant. Editorial Director: Sara Levant. Publishes hardcover and paperback originals and paperback reprints. Encourages new writers. Plans 2 first novels for '82.
Needs: Contemporary. "We are always interested in quality fiction; our need is simply for the best manuscripts we can get."
How to Contact: Query with SASE. Simultaneous and photocopied submissions OK. Reports in 6 weeks.
Terms: Pays 7½-15% royalties; offers modest advances. Free book catalog.

MANYLAND BOOKS, INC., 84-39 90th St., Woodhaven NY 11421. (212)441-6768. Editorial Director: Stepas Zobarskas. Estab. 1961. Publishes hardcover and paperback originals. Number of titles: 5 in 1981. Encourages new writers. Plans at least 1 first novel for '82.
Needs: Literary, experimental, adventure, spy, historical, war, ethnic (all), erotica, religious/inspirational, translations. Recently published *The House of a Stranger*, by Gerald E. Baily; *Prague Diptych*, by Marija Petrovska; *Anna Marinkovich*, by Edward Ifkovic (novels).
How to Contact: Submit complete ms with SASE. Photocopied submissions OK. Reports in 2 months.
Terms: "Open for negotiations." No advance. Subsidy publishes 25% of total books. Usual arrangement is "an advance-prepaid purchase order from 700 to 1,000 copies." Free book catalog.

RICHARD MAREK PUBLISHERS, St. Martin's/Marek, 175 Fifth Ave., New York NY 10010. (212)674-5151. Publisher: Richard Marek. Estab. 1981. Publishes hardcover originals. Number of titles: 25 in 1982.
Needs: Will consider all categories.
How to Contact: Query or submit through agent. SASE for query, ms. Simultaneous and photocopied submissions OK. Reports in 3 months on queries, 12 months on mss.
Terms: Pays in royalties; offers advance. Free book catalog.

MARGARET K. McELDERRY BOOKS/ATHENEUM PUBLISHERS, 597 5th Ave., New York NY 10017. (212)486-2665. Editorial Director: Margaret K. McElderry. Division estab. 1971. Publishes hardcover originals and paperback editions of some titles as in Aladdin Books. Number of titles: 30 in 1981; 29 in 1982.
Needs: All categories for juvenile and young adult: picture books, contemporary, literary, experimental, adventure, mystery, science fiction, fantasy. Recently published *The Huntsman*, by Douglas Hill (science fiction) and *Footsfall*, by Elizabeth Harlan (contemporary realism).
How to Contact: Query or submit complete ms. SASE for query, ms. Simultaneous submissions OK only if so indicated (and preferably *not*); no photocopied submissions. Reports in 1 week on queries, 1 month on mss.
Terms: Pays in royalties; offers advance. Free book catalog.
Tips: "Fantasy and science fiction still riding high. We swing away from contemporary problem novels for young readers except when outstanding."

MILLER BOOKS, 2908 W. Valley Blvd., Alhambra CA 91803. (213)284-7607. Imprint includes San Gabriel Valley Magazine. Editorial Director: Joseph Miller. Estab. 1962. Publishes hardcover originals and paperbacks. Number of titles: 4 in 1981. Encourages new writers.
Needs: Considers all categories except erotica and religious. Especially needs western and political novels. Recently published *Headless Horseman*, by Henry Boye (fiction).
How to Contact: Submit complete ms. SASE for query, ms. Simultaneous and photocopied submissions OK. Reports in 2 weeks on mss.
Terms: Pays 10-15% royalties; no advance. "Private books paid by author." Subsidy publishes

"private books—mostly about families or poetry." Free book catalog.
Tips: "Write something original that is not about someone of stature. Do not send good reporting; this should be sent to our magazine. Write positive, not depressing or negative stories."

MOODY PRESS, 2101 W. Howard St., Chicago IL 60645. (312)973-7800. Address fiction to: Ella K. Lindvall, Managing Editor. Estab. 1894. Publishes hardcover and paperback originals and hardcover and paperback reprints. Number of fiction titles: 20 in 1982; 18 planned for 1983.
Needs: Contemporary, historical, western, religious/inspirational, young adult adventure. "No erotica, gay, psychic, fantasy, or other categories which would offend Christians." Recently published *Heather's Choice*, by Carol Gift Page (teen); *Mystery at McGeehan Ranch*, by Sandy Dengler (preteen); and *Shannon*, by Jerry B. Jenkins (adult mystery).
How to Contact: Submit outline/synopsis and sample chapters with biographical sketch of author. SASE for query, ms. No simultaneous submissions; photocopied submissions OK. Reports in 1 week on queries, 8 weeks on mss.
Terms: "No comment." No advance. Book catalog for 8½x11 SASE plus 97¢ postage.
Tips: "Study books on fiction writing. Read the fiction your chosen publishing house has in print. Plot before you write. Keep the reader in mind—how do you want the story to affect him? Don't submit a first or second draft. Rewrite. We publish to teach and/or evangelize, not just entertain, and seek books which are not only religious in nature, but are clearly Biblically based, and in which the Christian message is central to the plot, not subordinate to it."

WILLIAM MORROW AND COMPANY, INC., 105 Madison Ave., New York NY 10016. Imprints include Quill, Perigord, Greenwillow Books, Lothrop, Lee & Shepard and Fielding Publications (travel books), and Morrow Jr. Books. Editor-in-Chief: Hillel Black. Editorial Director: James D. Landis. Estab. 1926. Plans to publish approximately 250 total hardcover and paperback editions in 1983, of which approximately one third will be fiction.
Needs: "Morrow accepts only the highest quality submissions in" contemporary, literary, experimental, adventure, mystery, spy, historical, war, romance, women's, feminist, gay/lesbian, science fiction, horror, humor/satire, translations. Juvenile and young adult divisions are separate. Recently published *Master of the Game*, by Sidney Sheldon; *Indecent Exposure*, by David McClintick; and *The Man from St. Petersburg*, by Ken Follett.
How to Contact: Submit through agent. All unsolicited mss are returned unopened. "We will only accept queries, proposals, or mss when submitted through a literary agent." Simultaneous and photocopied submissions OK. Reports in 2 months.
Terms: Pays in royalties; offers advance. Free book catalog.
Tips: "The Morrow divisions of Morrow Junior Books, Greenwillow Books, and Lothrop, Lee and Shepard handle juvenile books."

MOTT MEDIA, INC., PUBLISHERS, 1000 East Huron St., Milford MI 48042. (313)685-8773. Imprint includes Mott Media. Trade Editor: Leonard George Goss. Estab. 1974. Publishes hardcover and paperback originals and paperback reprints. Plans 2-3 first novels this year. Averages 25 total titles each year. Critiques rejected mss.
Needs: Juvenile (fantasy, historical), religious/inspirational, women's. Especially needs religious, historical Biblical characters, futuristic narrative. First fiction title published in spring/summer season of 1982.
How to Contact: Submit outline/synopsis with 3 sample chapters. Simultaneous and photocopied submissions OK. Reports in 3 weeks on queries.
Terms: Pays in royalties of 7% minimum, 15% maximum. Book catalog free on request.
Tips: "For Christian publishers, this may well prove the decade for fiction. Trend is toward science fiction/futuristic (a la Charles Williams, etc.)."

MOUNTAINEERS BOOKS, 715 Pike St., Seattle WA 98101. (206)682-4636. Editorial Director: John Pollock. Estab. 1906. Publishes hardcover and paperback originals and hardcover and paperback reprints all in the mountaineering field. May publish fiction in 1983 or 1984.

Needs: Adventure, humor/satire. "Might consider well done mss but only on mountaineering theme. It could be humorous and/or for juvenile audience." No mystery.
How to Contact: Query with SASE. Simultaneous ("depending on circumstances") and photocopied submissions OK. Reports in 2 months.
Terms: Pays 10-15% royalties "based on wholesale or retail price; occasionally offers advance. Free book catalog.
Tips: "We are interested in receiving more fiction, but it must be good and it must be about mountaineering."

NEW AMERICAN LIBRARY, 1633 Broadway, New York NY 10019. (212)397-8000 Imprints include Signet, Mentor, Signet Classic, Plume, DAW, Meridian, and NAL Hardcover. Fiction Editor: Ms. Pat Taylor. Estab. 1948. Publishes hardcover and paperback originals and paperback reprints. Number of titles: 150 in 1981; 175 in 1982.
Needs: Contemporary, adventure, mystery, spy, historical, war, romance, confession, women's, psychic/supernatural, science fiction, horror, regency romance, series. "No short stories." Recently published *Fever*, by Naden Cook; *Cujo*, by Stephen King; and *Tar Baby*, by Toni Morrison.
How to Contact: Submit complete ms or submit outline/synopsis and sample chapters with SASE or submit through agent. Simultaneous and photocopied submissions OK. Reports in 3 months.
Terms: Pays in royalties and author's copies; offers advance. Free book catalog.

NEW READERS PRESS, Box 131, Syracuse NY 13210. (315)422-9121. Subsidiary of Laubach Literacy International. Subsidiary includes Sundown. Assistant Editorial Director: Kay Koschnick. Fiction Editors: Wendy Stein and Sheila Tucker. Estab. 1963. Publishes paperback originals. Plans 2-3 first novels this year. Averages 15-20 total titles, 3-4 fiction titles each year. Occasionally critiques rejected mss.
Needs: Adventure, contemporary romance, young adult (easy-to-read, historical, problem novels, romance, spy/adventure), easy-to-read (adult). "Short novels (not more than 15,000 words) written at 3rd-4th grade reading level but of interest to adults or teenagers." Recently published *In and Out the Windows*, by Harriette Coret (problem); *Along the Gold Rush Trail*, by Gail Kenna (adventure); and *Freedom Side*, by Marcie Stadelhofen (historical).
How to Contact: Query first; submit outline/synopsis and 2-3 sample chapters or complete ms with SASE. Simultaneous and photocopied submissions OK. Reports in 2 weeks on queries; 3 months on mss.
Terms: Pays in royalties of 6% minimum; in advance of $200 average; in addition, 10 author's copies. Writer's guidelines free; book catalog free on request.

W.W. NORTON & COMPANY, INC., 500 5th Ave., New York NY 10110. (212)354-5500. For unsolicited mss contact: Sterling Lawrence. Estab. 1924. Publishes hardcover originals. Number of titles: 178 in 1982; plans undetermined for 1983. Sometimes comments on rejected mss.
Needs: Contemporary, adventure, mystery, spy, historical, western, war, women's, feminist, humor/satire, translations. No occult, science fiction, religious, gothic, romances, experimental, faction, confession, erotica, psychic/supernatural, fantasy, horror, juvenile and young adult. Recently published *A Private Life*, by Cynthia Propper Seton (contemporary); *Night Rituals by Michael Jahn (mystery); A Change of Scene*, by Elizabeth Cullinan (contemporary); *Almost Famous*, by David Small (contemporary); *Love Is Not Enough*, by Bob Shanks (contemporary); *Ugly Girl*, by Barbara Rex (historical); *Anger*, by May Sarton (contemporary); *Cool Repentance*, by Antonia Fraser (mystery); *The Great Hotel Robbery*, by John Minahan (adventure).
How to Contact: Submit outline/synopsis and sample chapters. Simultaneous and photocopied submissions OK. Reports in 4-6 weeks on queries and mss. Return of material not guaranteed unless return postage is enclosed.
Terms: Pays 10% of catalog retail price on first 5,000 copies; 12½ on next 5,000; 15% thereafter

in addition to 25 author's copies; offers advance. Free book catalog.
Tips: "Read the masters. To paraphrase Eliot, the minor writer borrows, the major writer *steals*. And parenthetically makes it his own. Then, get an agent. Unagented mss have a very hard time of it. Chances are, if your book is good and you have no agent, you will eventually succeed. But the road to success would be easier and shorter if you had an agent backing the book. We are interested in a more literary rather than commercial style."

√ **OAK TREE PUBLICATIONS, INC.**, 11175 Flintkote Ave., San Diego CA 92121. (714)457-3200. Editor: Gary Williams. Publishes hardcover and paperback originals. Encourages new writers. Rarely comments on rejected mss.
Needs: Juvenile and young adult. No picture books. Open to contemporary themes, subjects for juvenile (up to 12) and young adult. "Prefer story with role model, positive message." Recently published *Baseball Becky*, by Michael Dessert; and *Daniel Webster Jackson and the Wrongway Railway*, by Robert Walker.
How to Contact: Query or submit complete ms with SASE. Simultaneous and photocopied submissions OK.
Terms: Pays 10-15% in royalties; offers variable advance. Free book catalog with 9x12 SASE.
Tips: "We look for a well-written story with new subject slant. We usually need at least 30,000 words. Generally prefer not to pay large advance, especially for first-time author. We would like books that either parents or children will relate to."

ODDO PUBLISHING CO., Box 68, Beauregard Blvd., Fayetteville GA 30214. (404)461-7627. Managing Editor: Charles W. Oddo. Publishes hardcover and paperback originals.
Needs: Short children's supplementary readers. "We do not publish novels." Recently published *Bobby Bear Meets Cousin Boo*, by Marilue: *Bobby Bear & the Blizzard*, *Bobby Bear Goes to the Beach*, *Timmy Tiger & the Butterfly Net*, *Timmy Tiger & the Masked Bandit*, by Kay D. Oana.
How to Contact: Submit complete ms with SASE. Reports in 3-4 months on mss.
Terms: Pays in royalties for special mss only. "We judge all mss independently and pay by outright purchase accordingly." Send 50¢ for book catalog and postage cost.
Tips: "Mss must be easy to read, general with current themes. Must be easily coordinated to illustrations. No stories of grandmother long ago, no romance, permissive or immoral words or statements."

THE PAN AMERICAN PUBLISHING COMPANY, Box 1505, Las Vegas NM 87701. Imprint includes Shield Books. Editor-in-Chief: Rose Calles. Fiction Editor: Rita Vargas. Estab. 1934. Publishes hardcover and paperback originals and reprints. Number of titles: 4 in 1981; 6 in 1982. Encourages new writers. 3 first novels in '82. Sometimes comments on rejected mss.
Needs: Mystery, historical, romance, psychic/supernatural, science fiction, fantasy, horror, and southwestern historical fiction. No gay/lesbian or erotica. Recently published *The Legend of La Llorona*, by Ray John de Aragon (horror); *City of Candy & Streets of Ice Cream*, by R. John de Aragon (easy-to-read); and *The Gypsum Throne*, by Barbara Revell Ely (historical fiction).
How to Contact: Query with SASE. Simultaneous and photocopied submissions OK. Reports in 4-6 weeks on queries.
Terms: Pays 10% in royalties; no advance. Free book catalog with SASE.
Tips: "The fiction market is a highly competitive one. However, new writers continue to be published year after year. We see that the audience for southwestern historical fiction is growing rapidly and will continue to do so for the next few years. Perhaps the new author should keep this in mind while considering the writing of a book with general appeal."

PARENTS MAGAZINE PRESS, 685 3rd Ave., New York NY 10017. (212)878-8612. Editorial Director: Stephanie Calmenson. Publishes hardcover originals. Number of titles: 14 in 1981. Rarely comments on rejected mss.
Needs: Juvenile: easy-to-read text for what are essentially picture books. No other categories are

acceptable. Recently published *But No Elephants*, by Jerry Smath (picture storybook); *Sand Cake*, by Frank Asch (picture storybook); and *Detective Bob and The Great Ape Escape*, by David Harrison, pictures by Ned Delaney (picture storybook).

How to Contact: Submit complete picture book ms with SASE. No simultaneous submissions. Reports in 6-8 weeks.

Terms: Flat fee for book club editon; royalty for trade and library editions.

Tips: "We are looking primarily for humorous stories of 400-600 words for our 48 page books, which are illustrated in bright, full color, and designed to *entertain* young children, age 3-8."

PARKER BROTHERS CHILDREN'S BOOKS, 50 Dunham Rd., Beverly MA 01915. (617)927-7600. Subsidary of General Mills. Editor: John G. Keller. Estab. 1883. Publishes hardcover originals. Averages 10-15 total titles; 10-15 fiction titles each year. Occasionally critiques rejected mss.

Needs: Juvenile (animal, easy-to-read, picture book). "We want to see ideas for themes/characters around which we can build a series of books in different formats." Will begin publishing in 1983 with 6-9 picture books.

How to Contact: Query first with SASE. Simultaneous and photocopied submissions OK. Reports in 2 weeks on queries; 4 weeks on mss.

Terms: Pays in outright purchase of $2,500 minimum, $5,000 maximum.

PELICAN PUBLISHING COMPANY, 1101 Monroe St., Gretna LA 70053 Editor: Frumie Selchen. Editorial Director: James Calhoun. Estab. 1928. Publishes hardcover reprints and originals. Number of titles: 26 in 1982. Comments on rejected mss "infrequently."

Needs: Contemporary, literary, experimental, mystery, historical, war, ethnic, religious/inspirational, humor/satire, juvenile and young adult. No sex or violence.

How to Contact: Query or submit complete ms or outline/synopsis and sample chapters (3-5) with SASE. No simultaneous submissions, photocopied submissions OK. Reports in 2 weeks on queries; varies on mss.

Terms: Pays 10% in royalties; 10 free author's copies; advance only under special conditions. Free list of titles with SASE.

PERSEA BOOKS, INC., 225 Lafayette St., New York NY 10012. Fiction Editor: Karen Braziller. Estab. 1974. Publishes hardcover and paperback originals and paperback reprints. Plans 1 first novel this year. Averages 6 total titles, 2 fiction titles each year. Occasionally critiques rejected mss.

Needs: Experimental, literary, translations. Recently published *The Rock Pool*, by Cyril Connolly (satire/reprint); and *A Meditation*, by Juan Benet (translation/experimental).

How to Contact: Query first with SASE. Simultaneous and photocopied submissions OK. Reports in 2 weeks on queries.

Terms: Pays in royalties and advance. Book catalog free on request.

PHILOMEL BOOKS, 51 Madison Ave., New York NY 10010. (212)689-9200. Subsidiary includes The Putnam Publishing Group. Associate Fiction Editors: Joan Knight and Linda Falken. Publishes hardcover originals and paperback reprints. Averages 30 total titles each year. "Critiques only if we feel there is some reason to from our point of view."

Needs: Juvenile (animal, easy-to-read, fantasy, historical, picture book, sports, spy/adventure, contemporary), young adult (easy-to-read, fantasy/science fiction, historical, problem novels, sports, spy/adventure).

How to Contact: Query first with SASE. Photocopied submissions OK. Reports in 2 weeks on queries; 6 weeks on mss.

Terms: Payment "arrangement varies."

Tips: "Philomel is devoted to children's and 'young adult' books. We do fiction and nonfiction, picturebooks and some paperbacks. All are high quality, and suited for both bookstores and for the institutional market. Our new books are also definitely 'up market.' We are quite filled for some time to come, so cannot be too encouraging about new projects, but our door is never entirely closed.''

PINNACLE BOOKS, INC., 1430 Broadway, New York NY 10018. Editorial Director: Patrick O'Connor. Publishes paperback originals and reprints. Number of titles: averages 180/year. Encourages new writers. Plans 60 first novels for '82. Rarely comments on rejected mss.
Needs: Contemporary, mystery, war, women's, horror, and international intrigue. No pornography or hard core. Recently published *Once A Catholic*, by Robert Byrne (historical/romance); *Six Gun Samurai*, by Patrick Lee (men's adventure); *The Devil's Breath*, by Robert Irvine (supernatural); and *Scandals*, by Barney Leason (contemporary).
How to Contact: Query or submit outline/synopsis and sample chapters (4) with SASE. Simultaneous and photocopied submissions OK. Reports in 6-8 weeks on queries, 6-8 weeks on mss.
Terms: Contracts and terms standard and competitive. Free book catalog with 4x9½ SASE.
Tips: ''Keep abreast of current trends. Read bestsellers and try to see why they sell. Secure an agent to do your submitting. If you don't have an agent, use the query form with SASE before submitting a ms. Request specific 'tip sheets' from a publisher before submitting anything. Follow each publisher's method of submission exactly to avoid confusion, delay and problem. No telephone calls, please.''

PLATT & MUNK, Division of Grosset & Dunlap, 51 Madison Ave., New York NY 10010. Senior Editor: Teresa Kennedy. Publishes hardcover and paperback originals and reprints.
Needs: Juvenile and young adult: sports, animal, spy/adventure, fantasy/science fiction and easy-to-read. Recently published *Once Upon a Car*, illustrated by Kathy Mitchell; *Ghosts and Goblins*, by Tim Kirk; and *Who's Coming to Tuck Me In*, by Carolyn Ryan.
How to Contact: Query first with sample chapter; submit complete ms with SASE. Simultaneous and photocopied submissions OK. Reports in 5 weeks on mss.
Terms: Pays by outright purchase of $1,000-$3,500; no advance.

POCKET BOOKS, Division of Simon & Schuster, 1230 Avenue of the Americas, New York NY 10020. (212)246-2121. Editor-in-Chief: Marty Asher. Publishes paperback originals and reprints. Number of titles: averages 250/year.
Needs: Contemporary, literary, faction, adventure, mystery, spy, historical, western, war, gothic, romance, women's, feminist, ethnic, erotica, psychic/supernatural, science fiction, fantasy, horror, and humor/satire. Recently published *Hotel New Hampshire*, by John Irving; and *White Hotel*, by D.M. Thomas.
How to Contact: Query with SASE. Reports in 6 months on queries.
Terms: Pays in royalties; by outright purchase; and offers advance. Free book catalog.
Comments: ''We are not interested in increasing the number of queries, only the quality of fiction.''

POSEIDON PRESS, 1230 Avenue of the Americas, New York NY 10020. (212)246-2121. Distributed by Simon & Schuster. Editor-in-Chief: Ann E. Patty. Estab. 1981. Publishes hardcover originals. ''Since our list is small, we encourage with reservations. We will be doing 2 first novels in 1982.'' Averages 10-12 total titles, 6-8 fiction titles each year. Does ''not critique rejected ms by unsolicited authors unless work merits it.''
How to Contact: Submit outline/synopsis and 1 sample chapter (small no more than 30 pages). Photocopied submissions OK. Reports in 1½ months on queries; 2 months on mss.
Terms: Payment varies; discussed according to content of book.

CLARKSON N. POTTER, INC., 1 Park Ave., New York NY 10016. (212)532-9200. Distributed by Crown Publishers, Inc.. Editorial Director: Carol Southern. Director of Operations: Michael Fragnito. Number of titles: 40 in 1981.
Needs: Contemporary, literary, adventure, historical, juvenile, women's, humor/satire. No lurid romance.

How to Contact: Query or submit outline/synopsis and sample chapters or submit through agent. Simultaneous and photocopied submissions OK. Reports in 3 weeks on queries, 4 weeks on mss.
Terms: Pays 8-12% in royalties on hardcover; 6-7½% in royalties on paperback; offers $2,500 up in advance. Free book catalog with SASE.
Tips: "Don't submit until proposal or ms is as good as you can make it."

PRENTICE-HALL, Children's Book Department, Englewood Cliffs NJ 07632. Editor-in-Chief: Barbara Francis. Publishes hardcover originals and paperback reprints. Number of titles: averages 30-35 children's hardcover books and 20 children's reprint paperbacks/year. Encourages new writers. Sometimes comments on rejected mss.
Needs: Juvenile and young adult: picture books, humor, mystery, non-gimmicky science fiction, imaginative nonfiction. Recently published *Voyage of the Lucky Dragon*, by Jack Bennett (novel); *The Bank Holdup*, by Wolfgang Ecke (mystery); *Happy Birthday, Moon*, by Frank Asch; and *Dig to Disaster* (A Miss Mallard Mystery), by Robert Quackenbush (mystery/fantasy).
How to Contact: Query first. Submit outline/synopsis and sample chapters ("if multi-published author with established reputation") or complete ms ("if new unpublished writer") with SASE. Simultaneous and photocopied submissions OK. Reports in 4 weeks on queries, 6-8 weeks on mss.
Terms: Pays in royalties; offers average advance. Free book catalog with SASE.
Tips: "New emphasis on contemporary young adult novels. Will continue with high caliber picture books. Also interested in easy-to-read and good historical fiction"

PRINCETON LOVE ROMANCES, 685 Rt. 202, Morristown NJ 07960. (201)539-6990. Subsidiary of Princeton Productions. Editor: M. Meacham. Estab. 1982. Publishes recorded cassettes. "We need 100-200 new stories." Averages 100-200 fiction titles each year.
Needs: Contemporary, contemporary romances, short story collections. "We expect to need several hundred stories—9,000 words or more." No fantasy, science fiction or horror.
How to Contact: Query first asking for writer's guidelines; then send complete ms. Simultaneous and photocopied submissions OK. Reports in 2 weeks for guidelines; 2 months on mss.
Terms: Pays in outright purchase of $250 minimum. Tape recorder rights only. Printing rights revert to author.
Tips: "Keep in mind that we record narrated stories on 60-minute cassettes to be played rather than read. A successful writer will also understand the difference between sex and romance for our readers."

QUANTUM UNIVERSE SPECIAL EDITIONS, Box 6821, Silver Spring MD 20906. Subsidiary of Quantum Universe Productions. Imprint includes QUP Quality Paperbacks/Special Editions. Editor: Carl R. Dietrich. Estab. 1982. Publishes hardcover and paperback originals and reprints. Plans 3 first novels this year. Averages 25 total titles, 20 fiction titles each year. Occasionally critiques rejected mss.
Needs: Fantasy, horror, humor/satire, psychic/supernatural, science fiction, young adult (fantasy/science fiction). "Primarily social science fiction, future history novels, science fiction and fiction humor. No hazy, surrealistic plots or unimaginative rewrites of favorite authors."
How to Contact: Submit outline/synopsis and 3 sample chapters with SASE. Simultaneous and photocopied submissions OK. Reports in 1 week on queries; 2 weeks on mss.
Terms: Pays in royalties of 5% minimum, 10% maximum; 2 author's copies. Subsidy publishes by individual arrangement. Writer's guidelines for SASE and 2 first class stamps.
Tips: "Look around you. Read. History is an excellent source of material. Realistic dialogue and motivation are a *must*! We find that hard times are a plus for escapism. The burgeoning interest in high technology has created a whole new science fiction market."

RAND MCNALLY & COMPANY, Juvenile Division, Box 7600, Chicago IL 60680. (312)67-9100. Senior Editor: Dorothy Haas. Estab. 1856.

Needs: Juvenile: sports. No juvenile novels or adult fiction. "Fiction to us means a picture book only, or a word book which shows preschool words with inventive illustrations to make the book appealing." Recently published *The Incredible Invention of Alexander Woodmouse*, by Pamela Sampson; and *The Visit*, by Joan Esley.
How to Contact: No query necessary on picture books. SASE with mss. No simultaneous submissions; photocopied submissions OK. Reports in 3 months on mss.
Terms: Pays in royalties and by outright purchase. Book catalog with 9x11 ½ SASE.

RANDOM HOUSE, INC., 201 E. 50th St., New York NY 10022. Imprints include Vintage Books, Knopf, Pantheon, Ballantine, Modern Library, Fawcett. Publishes hardcover and paperback originals. Number of titles: averages 80/year. Encourages new writers. Rarely comments on rejected mss.
Needs: Adventure, contemporary, historical, literary, mainstream, short story collections, suspense/mystery, women's. "We publish fiction of the highest standards." Authors include James Michner, Robert Ludlum, Truman Capote.
How to Contact: Query with SASE. Simultaneous and photocopied submissions OK. Reports in 3 weeks on queries, 2 months on mss.
Terms: Payment as per standard minimum book contracts. Free writer's guidelines.

RANDOM HOUSE, INC./Juvenile Division, 201 E. 50th St., New York NY 10022. (212)751-2600. Managing Editor: Penny Seiden. Publishes hardcover and paperback originals. Number of titles: 124 in 1981, 160 in 1982.
Needs: Juvenile.
How to Contact: "At present, we are only reviewing mss from published authors and agents."
Tips: "Usually most of work is generated in-house, or freelancers are commissioned for flat fee."

RED DEMBNER ENTERPRISES, CORP., 1841 Broadway, New York NY 10023. (212)265-1250. Imprint includes Dembner Books. Editor: S. Arthur Dembner. Senior Editor: Anna Dembner. Publishes hardcover originals. Encourages new writers.
Needs: Contemporary, adventure, mystery/suspense and historical. "We are prepared to publish a limited number of well-written, non-sensational works of fiction." Recently published *Like Father*, by D. Black (novel); and *Search in Gomorah*, by Daniel Panger.
How to Contact: Submit outline/synopsis and sample chapters with SASE. Simultaneous and photocopied submissions OK.
Terms: Offers negotiable advance.

RESOURCE PUBLICATIONS, Box 444, Saratoga CA 95070. (408)252-4195. Publisher: William Burns. Publishes paperback originals.
Needs: Religious/inspirational/educational. "Religious fiction should be useable for sermons or classroom religious education. Material is intended to be shown to pros in the field for analogy or demonstration in teaching." Recently published *Winter Dreams and Other Such Friendly Dragons*, by Joseph Juknialis; *In Season and Out*, by Bruce Clanton (illustrated short stories); and *Parables for Little People*, by Larry Castaznola, S.J.
How to Contact: Submit complete ms with SASE. No simultaneous submissions; photocopied submissions OK. Reports in 2 months on mss.
Terms: Pays 8% in royalties; no advance.
Tips: "Seeks authors who wish to make a commitment to their work by purchasing a supply of copies from the first press run." Does not use much fiction; prefers very short fantasy stories.

ST. MARTIN'S PRESS, 175 5th Ave., New York NY 10010. (212)674-5151. President: Thomas. J. McCormack. Publishes hardcover and paperback originals. Number of titles: 164 in 1980, "the most by any American publisher.".
Needs: Contemporary, literary, experimental, faction, adventure, mystery, spy, historical,

Close-up

Thomas McCormack
St. Martin's Press

Thomas McCormack is an optimist. Contrary to the opinions of many doomsaying publishers about today's tight market, McCormack, the president of St. Martin's Press, says, "I would guess that the chances of getting a book published now are greater than ever before—and that includes paperback originals and hardcover titles."

McCormack's optimism is reflected in the annual number of novels published by St. Martin's, almost one-half of their total published books and "the most fiction published by an American publisher." In his 13 years as president of St. Martin's he has seen, in general, little change in the publishing climate. There may be no more interest in fiction today, but no less than in previous years either.

St. Martin's takes pride in producing first novelists, a special group whom they shepherd along for more (and often bigger, breakthrough) books in the future. It is St. Martin's form of investment, an endorsement in fiction. By 1982 St. Martin's Press had published about 32 times more fiction than in 1970. Their publishing philosophy is power in accumulation—not printing a few blockbusters or bestsellers. "We don't get rich on any single book, but with many we pay the rent. . . . We are a prosperous house," says McCormack.

To share production costs, St. Martin's publishes some of their books jointly with London publishers. Thus they are able to support mid-list, middle range books with smaller printings (about 5,000-25,000 copies). Last year this lower Manhattan publishing house published 33 first novels, most with just a few thousand copies and often at the 7½% royalty rate. The lower-than-average royalty may mean the difference between a new writer getting published or not at all.

St. Martin's receives as many as 2,500 manuscripts a year plus a similar number of fiction and nonfiction queries and proposals. A proposal telling about the book, a cover letter, and at least ten pages of text is the preferred method of submission. Very few submissions go beyond the first reading—only about two percent—but if the writer is not disqualified there, an editor will ask for the entire manuscript. When one of a half-dozen assistants gives a project the go-ahead, it is sent along to the in-house editor most comfortable with that subject.

McCormack states reasons for rejection: the characters are unreal/synthetic or not appealing and likable; the plot goes nowhere, and nothing happens to the characters; or the dialogue is wooden and meaningless. Unfortunately, there are so many ways that fiction can fail that McCormack says, "it's always a lovely pleasure when something comes in and it gets through the whole minefield—the many areas an author could go wrong but didn't."

Besides his considerable administrative duties, McCormack continues to edit occasional or special books. He has spent years studying the physiology of fiction—what makes it work, what makes it fail or be slightly off, what might remedy the problem: the nuts and bolts, the mechanics so necessary for an editor of fiction. "A publisher or an editor can't be just a book technician," the president explains. "If he can't 'groove' with books the way the common reader does, then he doesn't belong in the business. He has to be able to get excited and say 'That's great!' "

Even after 24 years in the business, Tom McCormack still demonstrates that excitement and enthusiasm, and says, "there's nothing like finding a special book, that rare gem in the manuscript pile, one that's destined to take off." For author *and* editor, it's a gratifying process.

western, war, gothic, romance, confession, women's, feminist, gay/lesbian, ethnic, erotica, psychic/supernatural, religious/inspirational, science fiction, fantasy, horror and humor/satire. No plays, children's literature or short fiction. Recently published *Jade: A Novel of China*, by Pat Bair; *Sassafras, Cypress and Indigo*, by Ntozake Shange; and *Northern Exposure*, by Michael Killan (international political intrigue).

How to Contact: Query or submit complete ms with SASE. Simultaneous and photocopied submissions OK. Reports in 2-3 weeks on queries, 4-6 weeks on mss.

Terms: Pays standard advance and royalties.

ST. PAUL EDITIONS, 50 St. Paul's Ave., Boston MA 02130. (617)522-8911. Editorial Staff Member: Sister Mary Anne. Estab. 1932. Publishes hardcover and paperback originals. Averages 50 total titles, 4-5 children's fiction titles each year. Publishes also in Spanish and Italian.

Needs: Juvenile (animal, easy-to-read, historical, sports, religious/inspirational). "Stories with a lesson or moral to them. Also stories which explain a religious truth or virtue." Recently published *Where's Grandma?*, by Daughters of St. Paul (story to help children accept death of a loved one); *Little Lost Lamb*, by Geri Berger (Good Shepherd theme); and *Legend of Little White Hood*, by B. Battistella (Christmas legend).

How to Contact: Submit complete ms with SASE. Simultaneous and photocopied submissions OK. Reports in 2-3 months on mss.

Terms: Pays in author's copies (negotiable with author). Children's book list free on request.

Tips: "Books submitted with artwork preferred."

SCHOLASTIC-TAB PUBLICATIONS, 123 Newkirk Rd., Richmond Hill, Ontario, Canada L4C 3G5. (416)883-5300. Imprints include North Winds Press; Scholastic Magazines, New York; Scholastic Publications, London; Ashton Scholastic, Australia. Managing Director: W.C. McMaster. Editorial Director: F.C.L. Muller. Publishes hardcover and paperback originals and reprints. Also publishes in French. Number of new titles: 36 in 1981; 44 in 1982. Encourages new writers. Plans about 5 first novels for '82. Sometimes comments on rejected mss.

Needs: Juvenile: mystery, sports, animal, spy/adventure, fantasy/science fiction and easy-to-read. Canadian authors only will be considered. Recently published *Beware the Fish!*, by Gordon Korman (humor); *Strange Creatures From the Time of the Dinosaurs*, by Erna Rowe and Alan Daniel (juvenile); and *The Toothpaste Genie*, by Frances Duncan (juvenile).

How to Contact: Query or submit complete ms or outline/synopsis and sample chapters (3). Simultaneous and photocopied submissions OK (would like to know if it is a multiple submission). Reports in 2 weeks on queries; 2 months on mss.

Terms: Usually pays in royalties; offers varied advance. Free book catalog.

Tips: "We're still interested in 'maturing' or young adult mss, but also want more in the areas of mystery, adventure, fantasy. We usually consider only full-length materials, for grades K-12. Preschool titles or read-aloud titles may not be suitable; 'thin' stories with 'cute' characters aren't suitable at all. We want books young readers will turn to independently. If a book is well-written and compelling enough to be selected and enjoyed by a child, we seriously consider it."

CHARLES SCRIBNER'S SONS, 597 5th Ave., New York NY 10017. Director of Trade Publishing: Jacek K. Galazka. Fiction Editors: Laurie G. Schieffelin, Susanne Kirk, Michael Pietsch. Estab. 1846. Publishes hardcover originals and paperback reprints of its own titles. Number of titles: 60 in 1981; 65 planned for 1982. Seldom comments on rejected mss.

Needs: Contemporary, adventure, mystery, spy, women's, feminist, science fiction, horror, humor/satire, juvenile and young adult. Recently published *A Novel Called Heritage*, by Margaret Mitchell Dukore; *The Skull Beneath the Skin*, by P.D. James (mystery); and *The Way to St. Ives*, by Sonia Gernes.

How to Contact: Submit outline/synopsis and sample chapters (2) with SASE or submit through agent. Reports in 2 weeks on queries, 1 month on mss.

Terms: Pays in royalties; offers advance.

Tips: Two literary prizes offered. (See editor close-up p. 601.)

CHARLES SCRIBNER'S SONS, BOOKS FOR YOUNG READERS, 597 Fifth Ave., New York NY 10017. (212)486-4035. Director: Clare Costello. Managing Editor: David Toberisky. Publishes hardcover originals. Averages 20-25 total titles, 8-13 fiction titles each year. Critiques some rejected mss.
Needs: Juvenile (animal, easy-to-read, fantasy, historical, picture book, sports, spy/adventure, contemporary, ethnic, science fiction), young adult (fantasy/science fiction, romance, historical, problem novels, sports, spy/adventure). Recently published: *The Avenger*, by Margaret Hodges (young adult historical); *Philo Potts*, by Mildred Ames (junenile, contemporary); and *Tin Can Tucker*, by Lynn Hall (young adult western).
How to Contact: Submit complete ms with SASE. Simultaneous and photocopied submissions OK. Reports in 6-8 months on mss.
Terms: Pays in royalties of 10% minimum, 12½% maximum; negotiates advance ($2,500 average amount); in 10 author's copies. Book catalog free on request.
Tips: "Stories about contemporary children, their problems and experiences" are doing well for us in today's market.

SEAL BOOKS, McCLELLAND AND STEWART-BANTAM LTD., 60 St. Clair Ave. E., # 601, Toronto, Ontario, Canada M4T 1N5. (416)922-4970. Editor: Tanya Long. Estab. 1977. Publishes paperback originals and reprints. Plans 7 first novels this year. Averages 40 titles, 30 fiction titles each year. Critiques rejected mss.
Needs: Adventure, contemporary, faction, fantasy, gothic/historical or contemporary romance, historical (general), horror, humor/satire, juvenile (fantasy, historical, spy/adventure, contemporary), mainstream, psychic/supernatural, science fiction, suspense/mystery, war, western, women's, young adult (fantasy/science fiction, historical, problem novels, spy/adventure). Wants to see novels by Canadian authors suitable for the mass market. Nothing highly experimental. Recently published: *Patriots*, by Robert E. Wall (historical); *Destinies*, by Charlotte Vale Allen (mainstream); and *Bodily Harm*, by Margaret Atwood..
How to Contact: Query first; submit outline/synopis and 3-4 sample chapters or submit complete ms if available. Simultaneous and photocopied submissions OK. Reports in 2 weeks on queries; 6 weeks on mss.
Terms: Pays in royalties; offers advance.
Tips: Sponsors Seal Books First Novel Award, annual competition.

SEAVIEW BOOKS, Division of Playboy Press, 747 3rd Ave., New York NY 10017. Editor: Charles Sopkin. Publishes hardcover reprints and originals. Number of titles: 60 in 1980; 70 in 1981; 70 in 1982.
Needs: Contemporary, literary, faction, historical, women's, feminist, ethnic, psychic/supernatural and western. Recently published *Circles of Time* (historical), *Umbertina*, by Helen Barolini (ethnic); and *A Certain Slant of Light*, by Margaret Bonauno (contemporary).
How to Contact: Query or submit outline/synopsis and sample chapters (2-3) with SASE. Simultaneous and photocopied submissions OK. Reports in 1 month on queries and mss.
Terms: Pays standard rate of 10% or $5,000 in royalties; offers advance.

SECOND CHANCE AT LOVE, 200 Madison Ave., New York NY 10016. (212)686-9820. Subsidiary of Berkley/Jove Publishing Group. Senior Editor: Ellen Edwards. Estab. 1981. Publishes paperback originals. Plans "many" first novels. Averages 72 total titles each year with plans to expand with a new line to be launched by 1983. Critiques rejected ms.
Needs: Contemporary romance. No gothic, suspense, mystery or historicals. Recently published: *The Golden Touch*, by Robin James; *Torn Asunder*, by Ann Cristy; *Satin and Steel*, by Jaclyn Conlee (contemporary romances).
How to Contact: Submit outline/synopsis and 2 sample chapters if published romance writer or complete manuscript if unpublished with SASE. Photocopied submissions OK. Reports in 1 month on queries; 2 months on mss.
Terms: Advance against royalties. Free writer's guidelines and book catalog with SASE.

Tips: "Study the books published in the line along with our guidelines and *target* submissions to our needs."

SIERRA CLUB BOOKS, 530 Bush St., San Francisco CA 94108. (415)981-8634. Subsidiary includes Sierra Club. Editor-in-Chief: D. Moses. Estab. 1892. Publishes hardcover and paperback originals and paperback reprints. Plans 1 first novel this year. Averages 15-20 titles, 1-2 fiction titles each year.
Needs: Contemporary, juvenile (contemporary conservation, environment).
How to Contact: Query only with SASE. "We publish virtually no fiction. We will only deal with queries; we are not staffed to deal with mss." Simultaneous and photocopied submissions OK. Reports in 2 weeks on queries.
Terms: Pays in royalties. Free book catalog for SASE.

SIGNET, 1633 Broadway, New York NY 10019. (212)397-8000. Imprints include Rapture Romances, New American Library, Inc. Submissions Editor: Ms. Pat Taylor. Estab. 1948. Publishes hardcover and paperback originals and paperback reprints. Encourages new writers. Averages 120 + fiction titles each year. Occasionally critiques rejected mss.
Needs: Comics, contemporary, contemporary romance, horror, humor/satire, women's, young adult (problem novels). "We are not particularly keen to receive unsolicited regular original novels at this time." No literary novels or any type not suited to mass market paperback distribution.
How to Contact: Query first with SASE; submit outline/synopsis and 3 sample chapters through agent. Simultaneous and photocopied submissions OK. Reports in 3 weeks on queries; 8-10 weeks on mss.
Terms: Royalties "vary according to author's experience and previous credits. Our advances and royalties are in line with the major established paperback houses." Writer's guidelines free. Book catalog free on request.
Tips: "Study the books which are being published, the authors who are most successful, and get a true picture of the marketplace. An agent is a big help. Horror novels, children in jeopardy, hard-hitting novels of contemporary life, novels which could lend themselves to series are doing well in todays market. We notice that authors are not writing with as much care. Style is lacking. Subject matter is too familiar and plots often confusing."

SILHOUETTE BOOKS, Simon & Schuster Bldg., 1230 Avenue of the Americas, New York NY 10020. (212)586-6151. Imprints includes: Silhouette Romances, First Love from Silhouette, Silhouette Special Edition, Silhouette Desire. Editor: Karen Solem. Senior Editor: Alicia Condon, Editor: Mary Clare Susen, Editor: Leslie J. Wainger; First Love from Silhouette: Senior Editor: Nancy Jackson. Assistant Editor: Leslie J. Wainger. Estab. 1979. Publishes paperback originals. Number of titles: 51 in 1980; 82 in 1981; 198 planned for '82; 252 planned for 1983. Sometimes comments on rejected mss.
Needs: Contemporary romance, adult and young adult. No historical. Recently published *Intimate Strangers*, by Brooke Hastings; *Corporate Affair*, by Stephanie James; and *The Second Time*, by Janet Dailey.
How to Contact: Submit complete ms with SASE. No simultaneous submissions; photocopied submissions OK. Reports in 6 weeks on mss.
Terms: Pays in royalties; offers advance (negotiation on an individual basis).
Tips: "Request our tip-sheet and study our published books before submitting to make sure that the submission is a potential Silhouette. Authors should never send the only copy of a ms as we are not responsible for loss of or damage to submissions."

SIMON & PIERRE PUBLISHING COMPANY LIMITED, Box 280, Adelaide St. Postal Stn., Toronto, Ontario, Canada M5C 2J4. Imprint includes Bastet Books, Canplay Series. Editor: Marian M. Wilson. Estab. 1972. Publishes hardcover and paperback originals. Number of titles: averages 4/year.
Needs: Contemporary, literary, adventure, mystery, spy, historical, humor/satire, juvenile,

young adult and translations. No romance, erotica or horror. Recently published *Zoom*, by Andrew Brycht (contemporary); *Pressure Point*, by Jack H. Crisp (mystery/spy/adventure); and *La Sagouine*, by Antonine Maillet (historical).

How to Contact: Query or submit complete ms or submit outline/synopsis and sample chapter or submit through agent with SASE. Simultaneous and photocopied submissions OK. Reports in 1 month on queries, 3 months on mss.

Terms: Pays in royalties; no advance. Free book catalog.

Tips: "There's a greater interest in lifestyles evident today in fiction. We prefer Canadian authors. Include with submissions: professional resume listing previous publications, detailed outline of proposed work and sample chapters."

GIBBS M. SMITH, INC., (formerly Peregrine Smith, Inc.), Box 667, Layton UT 84041. (801)376-9800. Imprint includes Peregrine Smith Books. Editor: G.M. Smith. Fiction Editor: Buckley Jeppson. Estab. 1970. Publishes hardcover and paperback originals. Number of titles: 0 in 1981, 2 in 1982.

Needs: Contemporary, literary and historical. No children's, young adult or romance categories. Recently published *Trout Madness*, by Robert Traver (fishing stores).

How to Contact: Query with SASE. No simultaneous submissions. Reports in 2-6 weeks on queries.

Terms: Negotiable royalties; no advance. Free book catalog with 6x9 SASE.

Tips: Mss rejected because "they are not literary enough, too common or mainstream."

SONICA PRESS, Box 42720, Los Angeles CA 90042. (213)666-7197. Fiction Editor: Dorthea Atwater or Peter Hay. Estab. 1979. Publishes hardcover originals. Plans 1 first novel this year. Averages 4-6 total titles, 2 fiction titles each year. Occasionally critiques rejected mss.

Needs: Contemporary, faction, fantasy, historical (general), humor/satire, mainstream, science fiction, suspense/mystery, translations. No romance, horror or juvenile. Recently published: *Spacewater Blues*, by Homer Weiner (1st novel; science fiction/fantasy, in the style of Vonnegut and Tom Robbins.).

How to Contact: Query first with SASE; submit outline/synopsis and 2 sample chapters. All unsolicited manuscripts are returned unopened. Simultaneous and photocopied submissions OK. Reports in 2 weeks on queries; 6 weeks on mss.

Terms: "Depends on individual deal. Standard royalties policy (10% minimum; 15% maximum). Negotiates advance (ranges from $50-1,500). Free book list for # 10 SASE.

Tips: "Don't write manuscript before getting good grounding in basic writing skills and classical novel elements."

STANDARD PUBLISHING, 8121 Hamilton Ave., Cincinnati OH 45231. (513)931-4050. Director: Marjorie Miller. Estab. 1866. Publishes hardcover and paperback originals and reprints. Number of titles: averages 10/year. Sometimes comments on rejected mss.

Needs: Religious/inspirational and easy-to-read. "Should have some relation to moral values or Biblical concepts and principles." Recently published *Three Ring Inferno*, by Daryle Courtney (teen adventure); *What Happens in Spring?*, by Sandra Brooks (children's); and *Andro, the Star of Bethlehem*, by Anne Claire (children's).

How to Contact: Query or submit outline/synopsis and sample chapters (2-3) with SASE. Simultaneous and photocopied submissions OK. Reports in 2 months on queries, 12 weeks on mss.

Terms: Pays varied royalties and by outright purchase; offers varied advance. Free book catalog with SASE.

STEIN AND DAY PUBLISHERS, Scarborough House, Briarcliff Manor NY 10510. (914)762-2151. Imprints include Stein and Day Books, Scarborough Books, Day Books. President: Sol Stein. Vice President/Editor: Patricia Day. Executive Editor: Benton M. Arnovitz. Estab. 1962. Publishes fiction for the general reader. Number of titles: 73 in 1980; 100 in 1981.

Needs: Fiction. No westerns or romance. Recently published *Touch the Devil*, by Jack Higgins

comm. publishers

(fiction); *The Gaza Intercept*, by E. Howard Hunt; and *Reclining Nude*, by Claudia Riess.
How to Contact: *Must* send query letter first with SASE; no unsolicited mss. Reports as soon as possible.
Terms: Standard.

STEMMER HOUSE PUBLISHERS, INC., 2627 Caves Rd., Owings Mills MD 21117. (301)363-3690. Imprint includes International Design Library, Stemmer House Story-to-Color. Editor: Barbara Holdridge. Publishes hardcover and paperback originals and reprints. Number of titles: averages 1/year. Encourages new writers.
Needs: Contemporary, literary, historical, war, ethnic, fantasy, juvenile and young adult. No detective or science fiction. Recently published *On the Verge*, by Dikkon Eberhart (contemporary); *Dark Places, Deep Regions*, by Margaret Sutherland (contemporary); and *The Rhapsody in Blue of Mickey Klein* (1940's).
How to Contact: Query or submit complete ms or outline/synopsis and sample chapters (3) or submit through agent (not necessary) with SASE. Simultaneous and photocopied submissions OK. Reports in 2 weeks on queries, 6 weeks on mss depending on backlog.
Terms: Pays 5-10% in royalties; offers small advance. Free book catalog.
Tips: "Trend today seems to be less literate work. Write to be read 50 years from today. Don't tell us how good the novel is. Perfect your grammar and spelling. Most writers seem to have read the latest paperback and swear to write something 'just as good'—but it's most often not even an improvement."

SUN BOOKS/SUN PUBLISHING, CO., Box 4383, Albuquerque NM 87196. Editor: Skip Whitson. Estab. 1973. Publishes paperback originals and reprints. Number of titles: 62 in 1981, over 100 in 1982.
Needs: Manuscripts on the "Coming Earth Changes" are our only current interests. Recently published *Rolling Thunder: The Coming Earth Changes*, by J.R. Jochmans.
How to Contact: Query with SASE. Simultaneous and photocopied submissions OK. Reports in 3 months on queries.
Terms: Pays 8% of retail price in royalties and by outright purchase depending on book. Will also subsidy publish; with advance. Free book list with SASE.
Tips: "We have noticed a growth in science-oriented fiction and "earth changes" books in the last few years. However, be prepared to print your own book. Because of the competitive market, some publishers find it risky to publish unpublished authors, so it is often difficult breaking in."

SWEET DREAMS, 133 5th Ave., New York NY 10003. (212)420-1555. Editor: Eve Becker. Estab. 1981. Publishes paperback originals. Plans approximately 30 new titles.
Needs: Young adult romance. Recently published: *P.S. I Love You*, by Barbara Conklin; *The Popularity Plan*, by Rosemary Vernon; and *Little Sister*, by Yvonne Greene (young adult romance novels).
How to Contact: Query first with SASE. Simultaneous and photocopied submissions OK. Reports in 2 weeks on queries; 1 month on mss.
Terms: Negotiated. Free writer's guidelines for SASE.

TANDEM PRESS PUBLISHERS, Box 237, Tannersville PA 18372. (717)629-2250. Editor: Judith Keith. Fiction Editor: Elisa Fitzgerald. Estab. 1969. Publishes hardcover and sells rights for paperback originals. Number of titles: averages 4/year. Encourages new writers. Sometimes comments on rejected mss.
Needs: Contemporary, contemporary romance, espionage, mystery, historical, gothic, romance and women's. "We give all submissions a read." Recently published *Desires of thy Heart*, by Joan C. Cruz (historical romance); *Lucetta*, by Elinor Jones (historical romance); *Tamara*, by E. Jones (historical romance); and *Night Jasmine*, by Mary Lou Widmer (contemporary romance).
How to Contact: Query with SASE. No simultaneous submissions; photocopied submissions OK. Reports in 2 weeks on queries, 1 month on ms.

Terms: Pays in royalties; offers varied advance.

Tips: "Historical romance is difficult to sell in hardcover or in paperback because the market is glutted. Contemporary romance is in demand. Mysteries, too, are difficult if written by a total unknown. As a small publisher we find it best to sell works by new authors as original paperbacks for smaller advances so as to establish a track record for them. The market is paradoxical. Hardcover sales are way down as are paperbacks. The average shelf-life of middle list paperback books is 13 days. Whatever the author receives upfront as an advance against royalties is what he essentially will earn on that particular work as returns are enormous. Concentrate on good contemporary romance because the greatest number of paperback and hardcover book buyers are women. Write your query letters with care as we often determine the quality of the writing by the letters we receive. And, once the ms is submitted, please wait to hear from us; if it is something we want, we will call you. Always include phone numbers with submissions. While the hardcover fiction market is depressed there is a good market in paperbacks, television and movies. Many times materials we receive are weak as potential books, but we then work with the author to develop the story with the possibility of selling the idea for television or movies. In this case we act as agent."

TAPESTRY ROMANCES, 1230 Avenue of the Americas, New York NY 10020. (212)246-2121. Subsidiary of Simon & Schuster. Editor: Kate Duffy. Estab. 1982. Publishes paperback originals. Averages 24 fiction titles (2 per month; approximately 85,000 words each) each year. Rejected mss are just returned.

Needs: Historical, romance. Recently published *Marielle*, by Edna Halliday; and *Defiant Love*, by Maura Seger.

How to Contact: Query first; submit outline/synopsis and 3 sample chapters with SASE. Simultaneous and photocopied submissions OK. Reports in 3-6 months on queries and mss.

Terms: Pays in royalties and advance.

Tips: Read published Tapestry novels for examples.

TEXAS MONTHLY PRESS, Box 1569, Austin TX 78767. (512)476-7085. Subsidiary of Mediatex, Inc. Editorial Assistant: Candi Vernon. Fiction Editor: Barbara Reavis. Estab. 1978. Publishes hardcover and paperback originals and reprints (60,000 word minimum). Plans 3 first novels this year. Averages 22 total titles, 2-3 fiction titles ("would like more") each year. Occasionally critiques rejected mss.

Needs: Contemporary, ethnic, faction, historical, humor/satire, literary, mainstream, suspense/mystery, western. "Books must reflect some facet of life in Texas or the Southeast. A southwestern setting alone is not enough—must be intrinsically regional. We hope to publish at least two original works of fiction each year." No experimental, gothic, historical romance, short stories." Recently published *A Family Likeness*, by Janis Stout (generational saga depicting the evolution of country girls into city women); *The Power Exchange*, by Alan Erwin (political intrigue); and *The Gay Place*, by William Brammer (political drama recounting LBJ's heyday—faction).

How to Contact: Query first; submit oultine/synopsis and 3 sample chapters with SASE. Simultaneous and photocopied submissions OK. Reports in 2 weeks on queries; 1 month on mss.

Terms: Pays in royalties of 5% minimum; 12½% maximum—"varies; standard range for hard- and soft-cover." Negotiates advance. Book catalog free on request.

Tips: "We are making a concerted effort to find more quality fiction. It is our goal to offer writers of fiction a publishing option outside of New York." Frank Wardlaw prize for literary excellence awarded annually to the author of the best work about Texas or Southwest. Preference is given to previously unrecognized authors. $1,000 honorarium and publication. Deadline Sept. 1.

THORNDIKE PRESS, One Mile Rd., Thorndike ME 04986. (207)948-2962. Senior Editor: Timothy A. Loeb. Estab. 1977. Publishes hardcover and paperback originals and reprints. Number of titles: 25 in 1981, 100 total in 1982. Encourages new writers. Plans 2-3 first novels for '83. Sometimes comments briefly on rejected mss.

Needs: Contemporary, humor/satire, quality fiction, regional history and lifestyle, nature and outdoors. "We are not publishing children's fiction or young adult material, nor are we interested in books out of the mainstream, such as feminist or gay, for example.'' Recently published *Polly Hill*, by Clifford S. Reynolds; *Champagne and A Gardener*, by B.J. Morrison (mystery); and *Stories Told in the Kitchen*, by Kendall Morse (humor).

How to Contact: Query or submit complete ms or outline/synopsis and sample chapters (3-4) with SASE. Simultaneous and photocopied submissions OK. Reports in 2 weeks on queries, 1 month on ms.

Terms: Pays 5-10% in royalties; by outright purchase $100-$1,000; offers $500-1,500 advance. Free book catalog.

Tips: "Know your market before mailing submissions. Those titles not appropriate to our line are rejected automatically. If a writer wants to be successful, he should know the product line of the firm he is submitting to and work within that framework. A little research beforehand will pay dividends in time and money saved." Most over-the-transom material is "best labelled mass market. We look for quality fiction of high literary value, plus regional fiction/mysteries."

TICKNOR & FIELDS, Affiliate of Houghton-Mifflin, 383 Orange St., New Haven CT and 52 Vanderbilt Ave., New York NY 10017. Editors: James Raimes, Elisabeth Scharlatt. Estab. 1979. Publishes hardcover originals.

Needs: Open to all categories but only to "the best there is. We are very fussy."

How to Contact: No unsolicited mss accepted. No simultaneous submissions (unless very special); photocopied submissions OK. Reports in 7 weeks on ms.

Terms: Pays standard amount of royalties. Offers advance depending on the book. Free book catalog with SASE and 1st class stamps.

TIMELY BOOKS, Box 267, New Milford CT 06776. Editor-in-Chief: Yvonne MacManus. Estab. 1978. Publishes 5½x8½ trade paperbacks. Number of titles: 2 in 1981; 2 in 1982. One original mss to date, but interested in more. Encourages new writers. Sometimes comments on rejected mss.

Needs: Feminist and lesbian only, at this time. Recently published *The Cruise*, by Paula Christian (lesbian fiction).

How to Contact: Query with SASE. No simultaneous submissions; photocopied submissions OK. Reports in 6 weeks or less on queries.

Terms: Pays 6-10% in royalties; no advance.

Tips: "Dissect bestsellers, scene by scene, to see what makes them 'work.' Read. Sloppy mss and cute letters are a total turnoff. We wish to publish quality, professional mss of interest to feminists and the lesbian community—fiction or nonfiction. No erotica or poetry. Our books are *by women*, for women."

TIMES BOOKS, 3 Park Ave., New York NY 10016. (212)725-2050. President and Publisher: Joseph T. Consolino. Vice-President and Editor-in-Chief: Jonathan Segal. Vice-President and Senior Editor: Edward T. Chase. Vice-President and Director of Subsidiary Rights: A. Randle Robinson. Vice President, Production and Administration: Hugh G. Howard. Publishes hardcover and paperback originals. Total number of titles: 40 in 1981; 40 in 1982; 40 planned for 1983.

Needs: Recently published *Princess*, by Robert Lacey; *China*, by Fox Butterfield.

How to Contact: Does not accept unsolicited mss.

Terms: Pays royalties; free book catalog.

TIMESCAPE BOOKS, 1230 Avenue of the Americas, New York NY 10020. (212)246-2121. Subsidiary of Pocket Books. Director of Science Fiction: David Hartwell. Publishes paperback originals and reprints. Averages 3 originals, 1 reissue/month.

Needs: Science fiction.

How to Contact: Query first; submit outline/synopsis and sample chapters with SASE.

Terms: Pays in royalties and advance.

Tips: "Be a science fiction reader first."

TOR BOOKS, 8 W. 36th St., New York NY 10018. Managing Editor: Katya Pendill. Fiction Editor: Harriet McDougal. Science Fiction Editor: Jim Bacon. Estab. 1980. Publishes paperback originals and reprints. Averages 75 total titles, 75 fiction titles each year.
Needs: Adventure, comics, fantasy, horror, mainstream, science ficton, suspense, young adult (fantasy/science fiction). No romance. Recently published *Brimstone*, by Robert Duncan (intrigue); *Wells of Hell*, by Graham Masterton (horror); and *Anansi*, by Niven & Barnes (science fiction).
How to Contact: Submit outline/synopsis and sample chapters and complete ms with SASE. Photocopied submissions OK.
Terms: Pays in royalties and advance. Book catalog free on request.

UNIVERSITY OF MISSOURI PRESS, Box 7088, Columbia MO 65205-7088. (314)882-7641. Associate Director: Susan McGregor Kelpe. Publishes hardcover and paperback originals. Number of titles: averages 2-3/year.
Needs: Contemporary, literary, adventure, war, feminist, ethnic, and humor/satire. No novels.
How to Contact: No simultaneous submissions; photocopied submissions OK. Submissions accepted February and March of odd-numbered years only.
Terms: Competition for publication only. Free book catalog.
Tips: "Publishes short fiction in Breakthrough Series, not to exceed 35,000 words."

VANGUARD PRESS, INC., 424 Madison Ave., New York NY 10017. (212)753-3906. Editor: Bernice Woll. Estab. 1926. Publishes hardcover originals. Number of titles: averages 15-20/year.
Needs: Contemporary, literary, faction, adventure, mystery, spy, war, humor/satire, juvenile and young adult. Recently published *Green Island*, by Michael Schmidt (short stories); and *The Fence*, by Bruce McGinnis (novel).
How to Contact: Query or submit outline/synopsis and sample chapters (3) with SASE. Advise if simultaneous submissions; photocopied submissions OK. Reports in 2-4 weeks on queries, 8-12 weeks on mss.
Terms: Pays in royalties; offers advance, amount depending on book.
Tips: "We're always interested in new writers."

VESTA PUBLICATIONS, LTD., Box 1641, Cornwall, Ontario, Canada K0H 5V6. (613)932-2135. Editor: Stephen Gill. Estab. 1974. Publishes hardcover and paperback originals. Number of titles: 10 in 1981. Encourages new writers. Seldom comments on rejected mss.
Needs: Literary, experimental, historical, war, gothic, romance, ethnic, religious, science fiction, juvenile, young adult and translations. Recently published *Immigrant*, by Stephen Gill; *Corey*, by Norma Linder; *The House on Dorchester Street*, by Ronald J. Corke.
How to Contact: Query with SASE. Simultaneous and photocopied submissions OK. Reports in 1 week on both queries and mss.
Terms: Pays 10-12% in royalties; no advance. Subsidy publishes 5% of total books. "We ask the writer to pay half of our publishing cost. In many cases it is even less than half." Free book catalog.
Tips: "Today there is a more simple, straightforward style. Never give up and keep writing for every possible media."

VIKING PENGUIN, INC., 625 Madison Ave., New York NY 10022. Imprints include Viking Junior Books, Studio Books. Estab. 1925. Number of fiction titles: averages 40/year.
Needs: "All categories are open; quality fiction, in general."
How to Contact: Submit complete ms through agent or through intermediary to specific editor. Simultaneous and photocopied submissions OK. Reports in 6 weeks on ms.
Terms: Amount and type of advance payment and royalty scale depend on the individual situation. Free book catalog.

comm. publishers

VIRAGO PRESS, Ely House, 37 Dover St., London W1X 4HS, England. Imprints include Virago Modern Classics. Fiction Editors: Carmen Callil and Ursula Owen. Estab. 1973 and 1976. Publishes hardcover and paperback originals and paperback reprints. Plans 3 first novels this year. Averages 50 total titles, 30 fiction titles each year. Occasionally critiques rejected mss.
Needs: Contemporary, fantasy, feminist/lesbian, humor/satire, literary, mainstream, religious/inspirational, science fiction, short story collections, translations, women's. Looking for new young writers. No rubbish. Recently published *The Sheltered Life*, by Ellen Glasgow (classic reprint); *Amateur Passions*, by Lorna Tracy (short stories); and *Tea & Tranquilizers*, by Diane Harpwood (domestic novel).
How to Contact: Query first; submit outline/synopsis and 2 sample chapters with SASE. Simultaneous submissions OK. Reports in 1 month; 2-3 months on mss.
Terms: Pays in royalties of 5% minimum, 10% maximum; advance of $15,000 average or negotiable; 6-8 author's copies. Book catalog free on request.

WALKER AND COMPANY, 720 5th Ave., New York NY 10019. Imprint includes Walker Educational Book Co. (WEBCO). Editor-in-Chief: Richard K. Winslow. Adult Trade Editor: Ruth Cavin. Publishes hardcover originals and reprints. Number of titles: averages 40/year. Sometimes comments on rejected mss.
Needs: Mystery ('whodunits'), romance (Regency), westerns. Science fiction and horror hardcover juvenile and young adult only. Recently published *Lovers' Vows*, by Joan Smith and *The Tynedale Daughters*, by Norma Lee Clare (regencies); *Nothing to do with the Case*, by Elizabeth Lemarch and *Murder in Fancy Dress*, by Laurie Mantell (mysteries); *The Scarlet Hills*, by Harry Beck (western).
How to Contact: Query or submit complete ms or outline synopis and sample chapters (2) with SASE or submit through agent. No simultaneous submissions; photocopied submissions OK. Reports in 1 month on queries, 6 weeks on mss.
Terms: Negotiable. Free book catalog with 6x9 SASE.
Tips: Mss "must be absolutely superlative to 'make it' in bad market. We can't afford to publish marginal projects. In historical romances, gothics are out. In mysteries there's a return to the conventional whodunit, the English type of police procedural or 'country house' kind of murder mystery, as opposed to violent, overtly sexual, tough private eye stories. There is an upsurge of interest in good, well-written westerns.''

FREDERICK WARNE AND CO., INC., 2 Park Ave., New York NY 10016. Editor: Jonathan J. Lanman. Parent company started in 1881 in England. Publishes hardcover originals. Number of titles: averages 10/year. Encourages new writers. 3-4 first novels for '82. Sometimes comments on rejected mss.
Needs: Juvenile and young adult: sports, animal, spy/adventure, historical and fantasy/science fiction. Recently published *Where the Buffaloes Begin*, by Olaf Baker, illustrated by Stephen Gammell (picture book); *The Night Journey*, by Kathryn Lasky (young adult); and *Johnny Stands*, by Harry W. Paige (middle grade).
How to Contact: Query with letter only or submit through agent. No simultaneous submissions. Reports in 1 week on queries, 10 weeks on ms.
Terms: Pays 5-10% in royalties; offers varied advance. Free book catalog.

WARNER BOOKS, 75 Rockefeller Plaza, New York NY 10019. Editor-in-Chief: Bernard W. Shir-Cliff. Estab. 1970. Publishes hardcover and paperback originals. Number of titles: averages 150/year.
Needs: "Buys mss on individual merit, not by category; wants to see all categories." Recently published *Chances*, by Jackie Collins; *Officers' Wives*, by Thomas Fleming; and *Cardinal Sins*, by Andrew Greeley.
How to Contact: Query with detailed letter or detailed outline, enough for editor to tell quickly if book is in area desired; also include writing credentials. Simultaneous and photocopied submissions OK. Reports in 1 day to 5 weeks on queries.

Terms: Pays 6-10% in royalties; offers advance. Free book catalog with standard SASE.
Tips: ''We want to see strong contemporary fiction.''

WASHINGTON SQUARE PRESS, 1230 Avenue of the Americas, New York NY 10020. (212)246-2121. Subsidiary includes Pocket Books (Simon & Schuster). Fiction Editors: John Thornton and Marnie Hagmann. Publishes paperback originals and reprints. Averages 34 total titles, ''roughly half'' fiction titles each year.
Needs: Adventure, contemporary, ethnic, experimental, historical (general), horror, humor/satire, literary, mainstream, psychic/supernatural, religious/inspirational, short story collections, suspense/mystery, translations, war, women's. Recently published: *Sister Wolf*, by Arin Arenberg; *Badenheim 1939*, Aharon Appelfeld, *Jack in the Box*, by William Kottwinkle.
How to Contact: Query through agent only; then submit outline/synopsis and 2-3 sample chapters. Simultaneous and photocopied submissions OK. Reporting time is ''quite variable, from 2 weeks to several months.''
Terms: Pays in royalties of 6% minimum; 10% maximum; advance is negotiable. Free book catalog.
Tips: ''It's hard to find really exciting literary works which also match our specific mass-market situation.'' WSP is a paperback category line; and publishes literary fiction and serious nonfiction.

WESTERN PUBLISHING COMPANY, INC., 850 3rd Ave., New York NY 10022. Imprint includes Golden Books. Juvenile Editorial Director: Janet Campbell. Estab. 1909. Publishes hardcover and paperback originals. Number of titles: averages 100/year.
Needs: Adventure, mystery, humor and juvenile: sports, animal, spy/adventure, and easy-to-read. Recently published *The Curious Little Kitten*, by Linda Hayward; *The Mouse Family's New Home*, by Edith Kunhardt; and *The First Day of School*, by Patricia Relf.
How to Contact: Send a query letter with a description of the story and SASE. Unsolicited mss are returned unread.
Terms: Pays by outright purchase or royalty.

THE WESTMINSTER PRESS (CHILDREN'S BOOK EDITORIAL), 925 Chestnut St., Philadelphia PA 19107. (215)928-2723 or 928-2724. Subsidiary of United Presbyterian Church USA. Editor: Barbara S. Bates. Estab. 1839. Publishes hardcover originals. Averages 10-12 total titles, 1-2 fiction titles each season.
Needs: Adventure, contemporary, juvenile (contemporary), young adult. ''Stories with terrific suspense and/or emotional impact and well-written.'' No historical or period novels. Recently published *Pass Me a Pine Cone*, by P.A. Wood (young adult); *Countdown at 37 Pinecrest Drive*, by SusAn Fleming (juvenile humor); and *Timequake*, by Robert C. Lee (science fiction).
How to Contact: Submit outline/synopsis and sample chapters with SASE. Photocopied submissions OK. Reports in 3 weeks on queries; 2 months on mss.
Terms: Pays in royalties of 5% minimum, 10% maximum; negotiates advance. Book catalog for SASE.
Tips: ''Fiction must by powerful enough to lure reader from TV.''

ALBERT WHITMAN & CO., 5747 W. Howard, Niles IL 60648. Editor: Kathleen Tucker. Publishes hardcover originals. Number of titles: averages 20 year.
Needs: Juvenile only. ''We like to see true-to-life, humorous and upbeat novels and mysteries for middle-grade children. We also want simple picture book mss for very young children; fantasies and realistic stories are both accepted. No young adult novels or alphabet books.'' Recently published *Poppy and the Outdoors Cat*, by Dorothy Haas (novel); *City Trucks*, by Robert Quackenbush (picture book); *A Pet for Duck and Bear*, by Judy Delton; *Daddy's New Baby*, by Judith Vigna; and *Deadline for Danger*, by Mary Blount Christian.
How to Contact: Submit complete ms of picture book or outline/synopsis and sample chapters of novel with SASE. Photocopied submissions OK. Reports in 2 months.

Terms: Pays varied royalties and by outright purchase; also offers advance. Free book catalog with SASE.

WINSTON-DEREK PUBLISHERS, Box 90883, Nashville TN 37209. (615)356-7384. Imprint: Scythe Books, and the Althea Bantree Mystery. Senior Editor: Marjorie Staton. Estab. 1979. Publishes hardcover and paperback originals and reprints. Plans 3 first novels this year. Averages 15-20 total titles, 7-9 fiction titles each year. Occasionally critiques rejected mss.
Needs: Ethnic, lesbian, gay, gothic or contemporary romance, historical, juvenile (historical), religious/inspirational, short story collections, suspense/mystery, young adult (easy-to-read, historical). "Must be 50,000-65,000 words or less. Novels strong with human interest. Characters overcoming a weakness or working through a difficulty. Prefer plots related to a historical event but not necessary. No science fiction, explicit eroticism, minorities in conflict without working out a solution to the problem. Down play on religious ideal and values." Recently published *Night Woods*, by Darlene Goodenow (mystery suspense); *The Golden Circle*, by David Collins (historical); *Strange Paradox*, by James W. Winston (Americana) and *The Imperfect Poodle*, by Sister Sandra Smithson (Allegory).
How to Contact: Submit outline/synopsis and 3-4 sample chapters with SASE. Simultaneous and photocopied submissions OK. Reports in 4 weeks on queries; 6 weeks on mss. Must query first. Do not send complete manuscript.
Terms: Pays in royalties of 10% minimum, 15% maximum; negotiates advance. Writer's guidelines free for # 10 SASE. Book catalog free on request.
Tips: "Stay in the mainstream of writing. The public is reading serene and comtemplative literature. Problem solving is saleable." Offers $500 award for the best short story published annually in the *Winston-Derek Anthology of Short Fiction*.

WOLFHOUND PRESS, 68 Mountjoy Sq., Dublin, Ireland. Production Editor: Mary Paul Keane. Estab. 1974. Publishes hardcover and paperback originals and hardcover reprints. Plans 3 first novels this year. Publishes also in Dutch and French. Occasionally critiques rejected mss.
Needs: Contemporary, experimental, juvenile, literary, short story collections. Recently published *Voyovic*, by Quinn (short stories); *Pupil*, by Monk Gibbon (autobiographical moments of love); and *Kelly*, by Michael Mullen (fantasy).
How to Contact: Query first; submit outline/synopsis and 3 sample chapters with SASE. Simultaneous and photocopied submissions OK. Reports in 2 months on queries; 3 months on mss.
Terms: Pays in royalties of 5% minimum, 10% maximum; negotiates advance; 6 author's copies. Book catalog free on request.

YEARLING, 1 Dag Hammerskjold Plaza, New York NY 10017. See Dell Publishing Co., Inc. Publishes originals and reprints for children grades K-6. Most interested in humorous upbeat novels, mysteries and family stories, 60 titles a year. "Will, regrettably, no longer consider unsolicited material at this time."

ZEBRA BOOKS, 475 Park Ave. S, New York NY 10016. (212)889-2299. President: Roberta Grossman. Executive Editor: Leslie Gelbman. Estab. 1975. Publishes hardcover reprints and paperback originals. Number of titles: 130 in 1980; 150 in 1981; 160 in 1982.
Needs: Contemporary, adventure, historical, war, gothic, romance, confession, women's, erotica, psychic/supernatural, and horror. "Romantic suspense, no! Gothic, yes!." Recently published *The Sword of Hachiman*, by Lynn Guest (a novel of early Japan); *Brazen Ecstasy*, by Janelle Taylor (historical romance); *The Pleasure Dome*, by Judith Leaderman; and *Savage Rapture*, by Sylvie F. Sommerfield (historical).
How to Contact: Query or submit complete ms or outline/synopsis and sample chapters with SASE. Simultaneous and photocopied submissions OK. Reports in 3 months on queries and mss.
Terms: Pays 4-8% in royalties; offers $500 and up. Free book catalog.
Tips: "Put aside your literary ideals, be commercial. Work fast and on assignment. Keep your cover letter simple and to the point. Too many times, 'cutesy' letters about category or content turn

us off some fine mss. More involved family and historical sagas. But please do research. We buy many unsolicited mss, but we're slow readers. Have patience. We generate most of our fiction in-house, rarely to unsolicited or agent-sponsored fiction.''

CHARLOTTE ZOLOTOW BOOKS, 10 East 53 St., New York NY 10022. (212)593-7044. See Harper & Row Junior Books Group.

> ❝ *Success: That's more fantasy than anything I ever write. But I was determined to write. I went to the library and checked out writing books, and I studied them. I was dedicated.*
>
> **—Jean Auel** ❞

Contests and awards

Bernard Malamud began to think seriously about a career in writing after he won a *Scholastic Magazine* essay contest as a senior in high school.

Contests and awards have helped launch the careers of many novelists and short story writers. Often a training ground for unknowns, competition can provide beneficial exposure and publicity, which in turn may lead to readings, interest from publishers or agents, scholarships, or invitations to writers' workshops and conferences. Awards, and sometimes just the entry itself, provide "writer credibility" for the beginner, and recognition and reputation later in publishing circles.

Magazine and publishing editors realize the value of contests and awards; winners help sell their books and magazines. Since *Redbook* began its Young Writers' Contest in 1976, the issues with the winning stories have been consistent big newsstand sellers. Editors also realize how hard it is for fiction writers to break into print; for example, the Pushcart Prize honors deserving manuscripts that commercial houses are unwilling to publish.

Awards for fiction felt the economic crunch in 1982, and several discontinued their events or cut back on the number of prizes or the amount of the award because of lack of funds. Nevertheless other magazines and publishing houses stepped in to offer additional opportunities in fiction competition. There are contests for every type and ability of fiction writer, recognition for unpublished and published short stories and novels of all lengths and subjects, on state, regional, national and international levels. The rewards range from simple inclusion in a small magazine or an honorarium for a beginner to a prestigious international award or sizable book contract for the highly qualified professional novelist.

If planning to enter a contest, treat and prepare your entry as you would for publication in a magazine or with a publisher. Be sure to *study* the entire listing and its specifications for eligibility: age, nationality, geographical location and fiction subject matter.

Unless the contest states that the entry will not be returned, a SASE or an international reply coupon (IRC) is necessary for all correspondence, including the request for an entry blank.

Again we have divided the contests and awards into two sections: those that encourage submissions by an individual and those that invite published work from publishers and organizations.

Contests and awards by individual submission

The following is a list of magazines, publishers and organizations that accept published or unpublished manuscripts or entries of short stories or novels submitted by an individual:

AGA KHAN PRIZE, *Paris Review*, 541 E. 72nd St., New York NY 10021. Contact: George Plimpton, editor. Annual award.
Purpose: To promote younger and lesser known writers.
Requirements: Unpublished submissions with SASE. Deadline entry: May 1 to June 1. Award judged by the editors.
Award: $500.
Information: Unpublished short story (1,000-10,000 words). Translations acceptable but should be accompanied by a copy of the original text. Contest/award rules and entry forms available with SASE. Receives approximately 1,000 entries.

AHNENE PUBLICATIONS POETRY AND PROSE CONTEST, Box 456, Mayville, Ontario, Canada K0C 1T0. Contact: M. Williams, president. Estab. 1982. Annual award.
Purpose: "To foster unknown writers and poets."
Requirements: Unpublished and previously published submissions "if rights have reverted to author."
Award: $30 top prize in each category; $85 in grand prizes in two categories (total of $500).
Information: Judged by Ahnene Publications. "Categories are modified each year. Deadlines explained to possible entrants. Write for information." Entry fee: $1/poem or prose piece.
Information: "Writers outside Canada must include an IRC or 35¢ in coin." Looking for "quality, conciseness of thought, ideas originally expressed; closely adhering to categories. All winners to be published each January."

ALBERTA NEW NOVELIST COMPETITION, Alberta Culture in cooperation with General Publishing Co. Ltd. of Toronto, 12 Floor, CN Tower, Edmonton, Alberta, Canada T5J 0K5. Contact: John Patrick Gillese, Director. Estab. 1972. Biannual award.
Purpose: To encourage the development of fiction writers living in the province of Alberta.
Requirements: The competition is open to any writer who has never before had a novel published and who is a resident of the province of Alberta. Deadline entry: Dec. 31. No SASE is necessary. Brochures and further information available.
Award: $4,000. Of this, $2,500 is an outright award given by Alberta Culture and $1,500 is an advance against royalties given by General Publishing Co. Ltd.
Information: Length may range from 60,000-100,000 words. Novels in adult category only of highest literary quality.

THE ALBERTA WRITING FOR YOUNG PEOPLE COMPETITION, Alberta Culture in cooperation with Clarke Irwin Company Ltd., 12 Floor, CN Tower, Edmonton, Alberta, Canada T5J 0K5. Contact: John Patrick Gillese, Director. Estab. 1980. Biannual award.

awards

Purpose: The competition is designed to direct Alberta's writers to the challenging world of writing for juveniles.
Requirements: Unpublished submissions. Deadline entry: Dec. 31. The competition brochure and/or further information will be sent, upon request.
Award: There is a $2,500 prize; an outright award of $1,500 from Alberta Culture and a $1,000 advance against royalties from Clarke Irwin.
Information: "We are looking for the best publishable manuscript—fiction or nonfiction—written for young readers. There are 2 categories: book mss for young adults (up to age 16) averaging 40,000 words in length; and book mss suitable for younger readers (8-12 years) running between 12,000 and 20,000 words."

THE NELSON ALGREN AWARD, *Chicago* Magazine, 3 Illinois Center, 303 E. Wacker Dr., Chicago IL 60601. (312)565-5000. Contact: Christine Newman, literary editor/articles editor. Estab. 1981. Annual award.
Purpose: "To recognize an outstanding, unpublished short story (between 2,500 and 10,000 words in length)."
Requirements: Unpublished submissions.
Award: $5,000 plus publication of the winning story in *Chicago* Magazine.
Information: Judged by writers. "There are three rounds of reading—by first readers, second readers, and final judges." Entry deadline: Entries are accepted from October 15th-January 15th. No entry fee. "A poster bearing the rules of the contest will be sent to writers who inquire." Receives more than 2,000 submissions. Looking for: "The task, as Nelson Algren wrote in an introduction to *The Neon Wilderness*, 'is to reveal the way things are with us; be it horrors or joys.' "
Results of Awards: "Our first winner has received many inquiries from agents and film companies and she says that she is writing more than ever."

SHERWOOD ANDERSON SHORT FICTION PRIZE, *Mid-America Review*, Dept. of English, Bowling Green State University, Bowling Green, OH 43403. (419)372-2725. Contact: Robert Early, editor. Estab. 1981. Annual award.
Purpose: "To encourage the writer of quality short fiction."
Requirements: Unpublished material.
Award: $200.
Information: Judged by a fiction writer of national reputation. No deadline. No entry fee. "Winners are selected from stories published by the magazine, so submission for publication is the first step." Looking for quality. Receives "around 300 entries."

ARIZONA QUARTERLY BEST SHORT STORY, University of Arizona, Tuscon AZ 85721. Contact: Albert Gegenheimer, editor. Annual award.
Purpose: To recognize the best short story of the year from the magazine as chosen by the editorial board.
Award: Bound copy of the year's volume and appropriate certificate plus award money which may vary from year to year.

ARTISTS FOUNDATION, ARTISTS FELLOWSHIPS, Artists Foundation, Inc., 110 Broad St., Boston MA 02110. Contact: Susan B. Walton, Acting Director. Estab. 1975. Annual award.
Purpose: To encourage artists to live and work in Massachusetts.
Requirements: All manuscripts are to be typed so there will be no indication of whether work has been previously published or not. For Massachusetts residents only, over 18, and not enrolled as students. All work to be completed within the last five years; does not need to be published. Deadline entry: October 1. Contest/award rules and entry form available with SASE.
Award: $5,000.
Information: Looking for artistic excellence. Work is judged anonymously by a panel of professional, working writers who are from out of state. Receives 300-375 entries. "Many of our award

writers have gone on to win NEA awards, Guggenheim, Fulbright, Grolier, PEN, CAPS, Winship, National Book Award, Lamont, Yaddo.''

ASF/PEN TRANSLATION PRIZE, American-Scandinavian Foundation, 127 E. 73rd St., New York NY 10021. Contact: Richard Jones and Kate Daniels. Estab. 1980. Annual award. Specified years for fiction. 1983 is next fiction prize.
Purpose: To encourage the translation and publication of the best of contemporary Scandinavian poetry and fiction and to make it available to a wider American audience.
Requirements: Previously published in the original Scandinavian language. Original authors should have been born within the past 100 years. Deadline entry: February 15. Contest/award rules and entry forms available with SASE.
Award: $500 and publication in *Scandinavian Review*.
Information: Looking for high quality both as fiction and as translation. Receives approximately 75 entries.

THE ATHENAEUM LITERARY AWARD, The Athenaeum of Philadelphia, 219 S. 6th St., Philadelphia PA 19106. Contact: Literary Award Committee. Estab. 1950. Annual award.
Purpose: To recognize and encourage outstanding literary achievement in Philadelphia and its vicinity.
Requirements: Previously published submissions from the preceding year. Deadline entry: December. Nominations shall be made in writing to the Literary Award Committee by the author, the publisher, or a member of the Athenaeum accompanied by a copy of the book. Award judged by committee appointed by Board of Directors.
Award: A bronze medal bearing the name of the award, the seal of the Athenaeum, the title of the book, the name of the author, and the year.
Information: Looking for significance and importance to the general public as well as literary excellence. The Athenaeum Literary Award is granted for a work of general literature, not exclusively for fiction. Juvenile fiction is not included. Receives approximately 50 entries.

ATLANTIC FIRSTS, *Atlantic Monthly*, 8 Arlington St., Boston MA 02146. Contact: Fiction Editor. Estab. 1940 (approximately).
Purpose: To encourage submission of original fiction to *The Atlantic*, and honor unusual accomplishments.
Requirements: Unpublished submission. No deadline entry date. Awards given periodically at the discretion of the editor. Contest/award rules and entry forms available with SASE.
Award: $1,000 first prize; $750 second prize.
Information: Judged on strong story line, characterization, sophisticated use of language and distinctiveness. Receives approximately 10,000 entries.

AURA CREATIVE WRITING, *AURA* Literary/Arts Review, 117 Campbell Hall, University Station, Birmingham AL 35294. (205)934-3216. Contact: Laurie Youngers, editor. Estab. 1979. Annual award.
Purpose: "To encourage creative writing by the students of our University and to award them the opportunity to see their work in print."
Requirements: Unpublished submissions.
Award: Cash awards in three categories, one of which is short fiction. First, second and third places awarded (money depends on what is available)."
Information: Judged by "writer outside the University system, if possible. In the past it has been one of our Writers-in-Residence. Also, the editorial staff has some imput." Deadline varies. "Sometimes we run the contest in the spring, then the next year in the fall, and the reverse." No entry fee. "The entries are restricted to the students at our University. Notices are posted, and given to the writing teachers." Looking for "clean story lines, good characterizations." Receives 20-25 entries.

THE AUTHOR AWARDS, Sabia Enterprises (a non-profit venture), Box 89, Gwynedd Valley PA 19437. Contact: Joan Robinson Sabia, director. Estab. 1982. Annual award.
Purpose: "The Author Awards are sponsored by Sabia Enterprises as a non-profit venture to reward writers for doing what they do best."
Requirements: "The works may or may not have been published during the year of the contest. However, works published before are not eligible."
Award: Prizes vary. 1982: First Prize $75, Second Prize $25, as many as 4 Honorable Mentions.
Information: Judging will be done by consultation. Entry deadline: Nov. 1. No entry fee. Looking for "fiction which entertains while moving the reader to a deeper understanding or questioning of the world. Any subject. Any form. One entry/author." Does not receive enough entries. "This is the second year of the award and it is designed to help writers financially and emotionally."

AVON FLARE NOVEL COMPETITION FOR TEENAGERS, Avon Books, 959 8th Ave., New York NY 10019. (212)262-7454. Contact: Jean Feiwel, editorial director. Estab. 1982.
Purpose: "To seek out teenaged writers."
Requirements: "Unpublished writers must be between 13-18 years of age."
Award: $5,000 advance, 6% royalty; contract under Avon's standard terms.
Information: Judged by editors of Flare. Entry deadline: September 30, 1983. No entry fee. Entry forms or rules for SASE. Looking for "contemporary novels for teenagers, about teenagers. This is the first time, and I don't know if we'll be doing it again."

AWP AWARD SERIES IN SHORT FICTION, The Associated Writing Programs, c/o Old Dominion University, Norfolk VA 23508. Contact: Kate McCune, publication and distribution. Estab. 1977. Annual award.
Purpose: The AWP Award Series was established in cooperation with several university presses in order to make quality short fiction available to a wide audience.
Requirements: Unpublished submissions. Deadline entry: December 31. Awards judged by distinguished writers in each genre. "Hortense Calisher, John Irving, Joyce Carol Oates, Stanley Elkin, Wallace Stegner, Gail Godwin, and Raymond Carver have been past judges in our Short Fiction and Novel Series." Contest/award rules and entry forms available with SASE.
Award: The winning manuscript in short fiction is published by the University of Missouri Press. The winning author is invited to read at the AWP Annual Meeting, a reading that carries a $1,000 honorarium.
Information: No bias other than quality. $5 submission fee with ms. Receives approximately 250 entries in short fiction contest.

AWP AWARD SERIES IN THE NOVEL, The Associated Writing Programs, c/o Old Dominion University, Norfolk VA 23508. Contact: Kate McCune, publication and distribution. Estab. 1979. Annual award.
Purpose: The AWP Award Series was established in cooperation with several university presses in order to publish and make fine fiction available to a wide audience.
Requirements: Unpublished submissions in book form. Deadline entry: December 31. Awards judged by distinguished writers in each genre. "Hortense Calisher, John Irving, Joyce Carol Oates, Stanley Elkin, Wallace Stegner, Gail Godwin and Raymond Carver have been past judges in our Short Fiction and Novel Series." Contest/award rules and entry forms available with SASE.
Award: The winning novel ms is published by the State University of New York Press. The winning author is invited to read at the AWP Annual Meeting, a reading that carries a $1,000 honorarium. In addition, AWP tries to place mss of finalists (from 3-8 in each genre) with participating presses.
Information: Looking for quality. $5 submission fee with ms. Receives approximately 200 entries in novel series.

EMILY CLARK BALCH AWARDS, *The Virginia Quarterly Review*, 1 West Range, Charlottesville VA 22903. Contact: Staige D. Blackford, editor. Estab. 1957. Annual award.

Purpose: To recognize distinguished short fiction by American writers.
Requirements: Stories published in *The Virginia Quarterly Review* during the calendar year. No unsolicited stories considered. Submit a story to *VQR* for consideration.
Award: $500.
Information: Looking for originality.

ALTHEA BANTREE MYSTERY, Winston-Derek Publishers, Box 90883, Nashville TN 37209. (615)356-7384. Contact: Marjoris Staton, chief editor. Estab. 1979. Annual award.
Purpose: "To perpetuate the American Mystery of the Edgar Allen Poe genre."
Requirements: Unpublished material.
Award: $500 writers workshop grant.
Information: Judged by an editorial committee. Entry deadline: December 31. No entry fee. Entry forms or rules for SASE. Looking for "plot, style, originality, suspense, intrigue, and most of all, logicality." Receives 150-200 entries.

THE BERKELEY MONTHLY SHORT FICTION COMPETITION, *The Berkeley Monthly*, 910 Parker St., Berkeley CA 94710. (415)848-7900. Contact: Adele Framer, editor. Estab. 1982. Annual award.
Purpose: "To encourage the writing and reading of short fiction."
Requirements: Unpublished submissions.
Award: 1st prize: $100 and publication; 2nd: $50 and publication; 3rd: $25 and publication; up to 4 honorable mentions.
Information: Judged by a panel of writers and editors. Entry deadline: October 15. No entry fee. "Send a neatly-typed double-spaced ms, with a one-paragraph biography of the writer, a signed statement to the effect that the story is original and unpublished, and a SASE for return." Looking for "memorable images and lucid technique. If we get enough response of good quality, this will be an annual event. I wish to bring *The Monthly* to the attention of dedicated fiction writers."

IRMA SIMONTON BLACK CHILDREN'S BOOK AWARD, Bank Street College, 610 W. 112th St., New York NY 10025. (212)663-7200, ext. 254. Contact: Williams Hooks, publications director. Estab. 1971. Annual award.
Purpose: "To honor the young children's book published in the preceeding year judged the most outstanding in text as well as in art."
Requirements: Previously published submissions. "Must be published the year preceeding the May award."
Award: Press luncheon at Harvard Club, a scroll, and seals by Maurice Sendak for attaching to award book's run."
Information: Judged by "a college-wide committee who chooses 5 books, which are judged by children in 5 different kinds of schools. The winner is the one the majority of children choose." Entry deadline: January 15. No entry fee. "Write to address above. Usually publishers submit books they want considered, but individuals can too. No entries are returned." Looking for "the finest text possible, which reflects interests and developmental levels of young children, as well as fine art." Receives about 200 entries.

BLACK WARRIOR REVIEW LITERARY AWARDS, *Black Warrior Review*, Box 2936, University of Alabama, University AL 35486-2936. (205)348-5526. Contact: Dev Hathaway, Editor.
Requirements: Unpublished material.
Purpose: "To recognize the work of fiction judged the best in each volume year of the *BWR*."
Award: $500.
Information: Judged by "an outside judge whose name is not revealed until the award has been announced. In the past the judges have included Raymond Carver, Mark Costello, and William Goyen." Manuscripts read year round. No entry fees; "just SASE." Looking for "distinctive literary quality." Receives approximately 750 entries.

BOSTON GLOBE-HORN BOOK AWARDS, *Boston Globe* Newspaper, *Horn Book* Magazine, Promotion Department, 135 Morrissey Blvd., Boston MA 02107. Contact: Stephanie Loer, children's book editor. Estab. 1967. Annual award.
Purpose: "To honor most outstanding fiction, illustration and nonfiction books published within the US."
Requirements: Previously published material from July 1-June 30 of following year. Submit by April 1.
Award: $200 first prize in each category; silver plate for the 3 honor books in each category.
Information: Judged by judges picked annually; usually children's librarians or critics. Entry deadline: April 1. No entry fee. Entry forms or rules for SASE. Contact: Stephanie Loer at above address. Looking for "outstanding writing, plot, characterization, etc." Receives approximately 400-500 books for fiction, illustration and non-fiction.

CANADA COUNCIL TRANSLATION PRIZES, The Canada Council/Conseil des Arts des Canada, 255 Albert St., Box 1047, Ottawa, Ontario, Canada K1P 5V8. (613)237-3400. Contact: Senior English Writer. Two annual awards.
Purpose: "To recognize the 2 works judged to be best of the translations published in the preceding year (one in English, one in French)."
Requirements: Previously published submissions from the preceding year.
Awards: 2 prizes each worth $5,000.
Information: Judged by the council. Books are eligible providing that they have been written and translated by Canadians or by persons who have resided as immigrants for five years in Canada.

CANADIAN AUTHORS ASSOCIATION AWARD (PROSE FICTION), Canadian Authors Association, Suite 412, 131 Bloor St. W., Toronto, Ontario, Canada M5S 1R1. (416)923-9360. Contact: Chairman, Awards Committee. Estab. 1975. Annual award.
Purpose: "To honor writing that achieves literary excellence without sacrificing popular appeal."
Requirements: Submissions must be published during the previous calendar year.
Award: $5,000 plus silver medal.
Information: Judged by a panel of three judges. Entry deadline: December 31 of calendar year. No entry fee. Entry forms or rules for SASE. Restricted to a full-length novel. Author must be Canadian or Canadian landed immigrant.

CCL STUDENT WRITING CONTEST, Conference on Christianity and Literature, Department of English, Calvin College, Grand Rapids MI 49506. (616)949-4000. Contact: John H. Timmerman, editor. Estab. 1974. Annual award.
Purpose: "To recognize excellence in undergraduate writing."
Requirements: Unpublished submissions.
Award: $50, $30, and $15 awarded in book certificates.
Information: "Judges assigned annually." Entry deadline: March 1. No entry fee. Entry forms or rules for SASE. Looking for "excellence in artistic achievement and reflection of writer's Christian premises." Competition is announced annually in the journal *Christianity and Literature*. Receives about 200 entries.

CENTER FOR THE STUDY OF CHRISTIAN VALUES IN LITERATURE WRITING CONTEST, A-279 JKBA, Brigham Young University, Provo UT 84602. (801)378-2274. Contact: Marilyn Arnold, center director and editor of journal *Literature and Belief*. Estab. 1980. Annual award.
Purpose: "To encourage the writing of quality literature that represents Christian values and themes."
Requirements: Unpublished submissions.
Awards: Non-student—1st $200; 2nd $125; 3rd $75; honorable mention $25; Student—1st $100; 2nd $75; 3rd $50; and honorable mention $25.

Information: Judged by Center for the Study of Christian Values in Literature board members and creative writing faculty at BYU. Entry deadline: March 15. No entry fee. Entry forms or rules for SASE. "The Center is interested in literature that achieves a meaningful blend of artistic form and moral content. Therefore all entries should be well developed expressions of the writer's Christian commitment and moral conviction." Receives about 800 entries.

CHATELAINE FICTION COMPETITION, *Chatelaine Magazine*, 481 University Ave., Toronto, Ontario, Canada M5W 1A7. Contact: Barbara West, fiction editor.
Purpose: To encourage Canadian authors to write short fiction.
Requirements: Canadian writers only may enter contest. Awards judged by editors. Check magazine or write for rules. SASE. Deadline: February 28.
Award: 1st prize: $5,000; 2nd prize: $2,500; 3rd prize: $1,500. All three stories published in *Chatelaine*. A number of runners-up are bought at normal fiction rates.
Information: "Preferably story should entertain or enlighten the reader while illuminating some aspect of being a woman in Canada today." Receives 3,000+ entries.

CHICAGO FOUNDATION FOR LITERATURE AWARD, Friends of Literature, 3415 Pratt, Lincolnwood IL 60645. (312)677-9218. Contact: James Friend, president. Estab. 1931. Annual award.
Purpose: "To honor Chicago area writers or those who in their life or career have had some connection with Chicago."
Requirements: Previously published submissions published during the calendar year preceding the presentation of the award.
Award: A check for $500 and hand embossed plaque.
Information: Judged by the Board of Directors serving as a book committee with the possible advice of the Advisory Council. Entry deadline: January 15. No entry fee. Entry forms or rules for SASE. "We are generally looking for quality writing, preferably by a young or new author, with a sense of prose style and serious purpose. In addition to the Chicago Foundation for Literature award(s) several other sponsored or memorial awards in varying amounts are frequently given but these may vary from year to year. They are usually open to either fiction or nonfiction." Receives about 20-30 entries.

CHIRICÚ FICTION AWARD, *Chiricú*, Indiana University, 849 Ballantine Hall, Bloomington IN 47405. (812)337-8577. Contact: Omar S. Castañeda, editor-in-chief. Estab. 1980. Annual award offered when money is available.
Purpose: "To encourage submissions to the magazine."
Requirements: Unpublished submissions only.
Award: $20-50.
Information: Judged by the editorial staff. Entry deadline: March. No entry fee. "All submissions are automatically entered into the competition." Looking for "high quality writing. We hope to see better and better material."

THE CHRISTOPHER AWARD, The Christophers, 12 E. 48th St., New York NY 10017. Contact: Ms. Peggy Flanagan, awards coordinator. Estab. 1949. Annual award.
Purpose: "To encourage creative people to continue to produce works which 'affirm the highest values of the human spirit' in adult and children's books."
Requirements: Published submissions only. "Award judged by a grass roots panel and a final panel of experts. Juvenile works are 'children tested.' "
Information: Examples of books awarded: *All Together Now*, by Sue Ellen Bridgers (ages 12 and up); *Frederick's Alligator*, by Esther Allen Peterson (ages 5-8); *What Happened in Hamelin*, by Gloria Skurzynski (ages 9-12). Receives 400-500 adult book entries and about 200 children's works—fiction and nonfiction.

CLEVELAND MAGAZINE FICTION CONTEST, *Cleveland Magazine*, 1621 Euclid Ave., Cleveland OH 44122. Contact: Michael D. Roberts, editor. Estab. 1977. Annual award.

awards

Requirements: Unpublished submissions only. Award judged by editorial staff. Deadline entry: Nov. 1.
Information: "Story must be set in Greater Cleveland and contain a little of the true flavor of the area. The short story is not to exceed 10,000 words." Receives 100-150 entries.

COOKE COUNTY COLLEGE SHORT STORY CONTEST (NON-STUDENT), Cooke County College, Box 815, Gainesville TX 76240. Contact: Joseph Colin Murphey, director of creative writing. Estab. 1970. Annual award.
Purpose: "To promote interest in creative writing and to become acquainted with talented writers in the area or elsewhere."
Requirements: Unpublished submissions only. Deadline entry: "about the end of March. Contest Awards Day is held around April 25th." Entry form or rules for SASE.
Award: Certificate of award. First prize, $30; second, $20; third, $10 plus publication in the college literary magazine of the winners.
Information: Looking for "short stories that have a plot, well-developed characters and themes that are subtle but universal, meaningful and profound."

CONNECTICUT WRITERS LEAGUE ANNUAL WRITING CONTEST, Box 78, Farmington CT 06032. (203)677-0740. Contact: Maryland Lincoln, publications director. Estab. 1982. Annual award.
Purpose: "To encourage writing. Winners are published in the annual publication, *The Connecticut Writer*, produced by the Connecticut Writers League."
Requirements: Unpublished submissions.
Award: "1982 prizes were $50 for 1st place in poetry, non-fiction and fiction; 2nd place, $5 each in above categories."
Information: "A contest committee screens the manuscripts; final selections are made by judges outside the Connecticut Writers League. In 1982, we ran the contest from Feb. to July. Interested persons should send for guidelines in the spring." Entry fee: $2. Looking for "a good story. Our first year drew 388 entries from all over the country. The winners were quite pleased. A party for the publication was planned also."

CROSSCURRENTS THIRD ANNUAL FICTION AWARDS, *Crosscurrents*, 2200 Glastonbury Rd., Westlake Village CA 91361. Contact: Linda Brown Michelson, editor. Estab. 1981. Annual Award.
Purpose: "To encourage excellence."
Requirements: Unpublished submissions only. Deadline entry: Sept. 30. Entry form or rules for SASE. Contest rules will be available after May 15, 1983.
Information: Looking for "craft and substance."

FARM WIFE NEWS WRITING CONTEST, *Farm Wife News* Magazine, Box 643, Milwaukee WI 53201. (414)423-0100. Contact: Ruth C. Benedict, managing editor. Estab. 1971. "No frequency established yet, but we plan to have other contests, as soon as volume of worthy entries from past contest is published."
Purpose: "To honor, entertain, elevate and inform farm and ranch women writers who have something to say about their particular lifestyle and concerns."
Requirements: Unpublished submissions.
Awards: To be announced.
Information: Judged by local writers (i.e., greater Milwaukee area) with expertise in the field of their division. Entry deadline: write or check magazine. No entry fee. Only subscribers of *Farm Wife News* may enter. Entry blanks and rules published in the magazine. Looking for stories with "new experiences, new perceptions about farm women, ranch women, agriculture in America, philosophies for personal living—pretty much open. Expressive thoughts on this very special way of life." "3,500 entries total in our first contest (in all divisions). I would estimate higher response in future contests."

FLARE, Maclean-Hunter Ltd., 481 University Ave., Toronto, Canada M5W 1A7. Contact: Julie Beddoes, associate editor.
Purpose: To award Canadian authors of short fiction.
Requirements: Open to Canadian writers and landed immigrants of Canada only, who have not published fiction in a national magazine excepting literary or college publications. Awards judged by editors and honorary judges.
Information: Check the magazine (September issue) for entry information. Receives approximately 300 entries.

FOCUS PROSE CONTEST, *Focus: A Journal for Lesbians*, 1151 Mass Ave., Cambridge MA 02138. (617)259-0063. Contact: *Focus* editorial staff. Estab. 1976. Annual award.
Purpose: "To encourage lesbian writers of prose (essays, fiction, biography)."
Requirements: Unpublished submissions.
Award: $35.
Information: Judged by *Focus* editorial staff. Entry deadline: first week in August. No entry fee. "Write directly and enclose SASE; but 'rules' are very simple: prose." Looking for "relevance to audience, quality writing, good style and structure. We are particularly interested in encouraging new writers. This year the quality was quite good." Receives about 30 entries.

FRIENDS OF AMERICAN WRITERS AWARD, Friends of American Writers, 755 N. Merrill, Park Ridge IL 60068. Contact: Jane Lederer, chairman of award committee (for award in adult literature). Contact: Joyce McCarron, 55 Indian Hill Rd., Winnetka IL 60093 (for 2 awards in juvenile literature). Estab. 1922. Annual award.
Purpose: "To encourage good writing standards among comparatively new authors with Midwest backgrounds or by those who write about that locale."
Requirements: "A book must have been publihed during the calendar year to be considered and be received by December 1 of that year. No poetry." Judged by committee.
Award: Adult fiction: First place $1,200; 2nd: $750. Juvenile awards: First place: $500; 2nd: $350.
Information: Looking for "writing that shows promise by an author with fewer than 4 books published." Receives 35-40 entries.

CARLOS FUENTES FICTION AWARD, *Columbia: A Magazine of Poetry & Prose*, 404 Dodge, Columbia University, New York NY 10027. Contact: Trudy Dittmar, fiction editor. Estab. 1978. Annual award.
Purpose: "To recognize and promote talented writing."
Requirements: Unpublished submissions only. Deadline entry: February. Judged by Fiction Board of about 15. Entry form or rules for SASE.
Award: $100 for best fiction piece in each issue.
Information: Looking for "originality, talent, and ability to move the reader." Receives approximately 100 entries.

GOLDEN HEART AWARD, Romance Writers of America, 5206 F.M. 1960 West, Suite 207, Houston TX 77069. (713)440-6885. Contact: Patricia Hudgins, executive secretary; Bobbie Jolly, president. Estab. 1981. Annual award.
Purpose: "To give recognition and attention to the unpublished writer."
Requirements: Unpublished submissions. Author must be unsold in romance genre.
Award: Golden heart with a 14 kt. gold necklace.
Information: Judged by "agents and editors, those who serve as staff for that year's conference." Entry deadline: "not firm yet." Entry fee and requirement to attend under consideration. Method of submission being revised by special awards committee.

GOLDEN KITE, Society of Children's Book Writers, Box 296, Mar Vista Station, Los Angeles CA 90066. Contact: Sue Alexander, chairperson. Estab. 1973. Annual award.

Purpose: "To recognize outstanding works of fiction, nonfiction and picture-illustration for children created by members of the Society of Children's Book Writers and published in the award year."

Requirements: Published submissions during January-December of publication year. Deadline entry: December 15. Awards judged by a panel of 5 (different every year): 3 writers, 1 editor, 1 librarian. Rules for SASE.

Award: Statuette and plaque.

Information: Looking for quality material for children. Individual "must be member of the SCBW to submit books." Receives 150-250 entries.

GOLDEN MEDALLION, Romance Writers of America, 5206 FM 1960 West, Suite 207, Houston TX 77069. (713)440-6885. Contact: Patricia Hudgins, executive secretary. Estab. 1982. Annual award.

Purpose: "To recognize best of works published preceeding year in romantic fiction in several categories."

Requirements: Previously published submissions. "1982 awards were for works published in 1981."

Award: "A specially designed medallion and a presentation box with facsimile of medallion and etched bronze plate."

Information: Deadline to be announced. Request issue of publication that contains rules with $1.25 or SASE (large envelope) with 71¢ postage. Looking for "the best representatives of published works—in each category of romantic fiction. Strong storyline characterization. Absolutely pleased with the quality of writing received."

GOVERNOR GENERAL LITERARY AWARDS, Canada Council, 255 Albert St., Ottawa, Ontario, Canada K1P 5V8. Contact: Senior English Writer. Estab. 1937. Eight annual awards.

Purpose: "To honor the Canadian writers of 4 English-language and 4 French-language works published during the preceding year. Awards are given in the fields of fiction, nonfiction, poetry, and drama."

Requirements: All Canadian books in these 4 categories published in the preceding year are considered. No entry forms are required.

Award: $5,000 each award.

Information: "All books in the 4 fields are considered by one of 8 juries of Canadian experts in literature (4 for French language works, 4 for English language)." Looking for excellence. In nonfiction approximately 200 books are considered annually; in the other categories 50-100.

GREAT PLAINS STORY TELLING & POETRY READING CONTEST, 106 Navajo, Council Bluffs IA 51501. (712)366-1136. Contact: Robert Everhart, director. Estab. 1976. Annual award.

Purpose: "To provide an outlet for writers to present not only their works, but also to provide a large audience for their presentation live by the writer."

Requirements: Previously published or unpublished submissions.

Award: 1st prize $75; 2nd prize $50; 3rd prize $25; 4th prize $15; and 5th prize $10. Trophies to the top three.

Information: Judged by previous year's winner plus two other competent persons in the field. Entry deadline: day of contest, which takes place over Labor Day Weekend. Entry fee: $4. Entry forms or rules for SASE. Judged on "how well story relates to a pioneer theme, and if it is a traditional fictional story." Receives about 20-25 entries.

GULFSHORE LIFE'S ANNUAL FICTION CONTEST, *Gulfshore Life Magazine*, 3620 Tamiami Trail N., Naples FL 33940. Contact: Molly J Burns, editor. Estab. 1979. Annual award.

Purpose: "To encourage writers and to offer our readers outstanding fiction."

Requirements: Unpublished submissions only. Deadline entry: March 1. Award judged by editorial staff. Entry form or rules for SASE.

Award: Prizes of cash or merchandise.
Information: "Story must have a Florida setting. No more than one entry per person. Submissions must not exceed 3,500 words. Open to all writers. All entries must be previously unpublished." Receives approximately 200 entries.

HARIAN CREATIVE FICTION AWARDS, Harian Creative Press & The Workshop Under the Sky, Box 189, Ballston Spa, NY 12020. Contact: Dr. Harry Barba, publisher and executive director. Contest offered "when warranted by quality of submissions."
Purpose: "To encourage socially functional writing, socially functional literature, writing that communicates a 'moral' texture without being preachy; writing strong in characterization and plot and written in a functionally suitable style, all of which leaves the reader a little higher up as a connected human being, concerned, compassionate and resolution-oriented."
Requirements: Entry fee varies depending on genre (fiction, poetry, plays, etc.) and length. Award judged by publisher and others. $500 first prize; $300 second; several $100 Merit Awards.
Information: Write for entry rules. Receives approximately 1,500 entries.

DRUE HEINZ LITERATURE PRIZE, The Howard Heinz Endowment and the University of Pittsburgh Press, University of Pittsburgh Press, 127 North Bellefield Ave., Pittsburgh PA 15260. (412)624-4110. Estab. 1980. Annual award.
Purpose: "To support the writer of short fiction at a time when the economics of commercial publishing make it more and more difficult for the serious literary artists working in the short story and novella to find publication."
Requirements: Unpublished submissions.
Award: $5,000 and publication by the University of Pittsburgh Press.
Information: Judged by an initial screening panel and a final judge. Entry deadline: August 31. Submissions will be received only during the months of July and August. No entry fee. Entry forms or rules for SASE. "Submissions should consist of a manuscript of short stories, one or more novellas, or a combination of one or more novellas and short stories." Receives about 260 entries. "This is only the third year of the prize."

HIGHLIGHTS FOR CHILDREN, 803 Church St., Honesdale PA 18431. Contact: Constance McAllister, fiction editor.
Purpose: "To honor quality stories of adventure and mystery for children 12 and under."
Requirements: 900 words or less. No entry form necessary. To be submitted by Feb. 1 to "Fiction for Children" at address above.
Award: $750, divided among three winning stories.
Information: No violence or crime. Winners announced by March 31. Non-winning entries returned after deadline. "Please provide SASE."

THEODORE HOEPTNER AWARD, *Southern Humanities Review*, 9092 Haley Center, Auburn AL 36830. Contact: David K. Jeffrey or Barbara A. Mowat, co-editors. Estab. 1970. Annual award.
Purpose: "To reward the author of the best essay or short story published in the *SHR* each year."
Requirements: Unpublished submissions to the magazine only. Award judged by editors and editorial board.
Award: $100.
Information: Receives several hundred entries.

HONENBERG AWARD, *Memphis State Review*, Dept. of English, Memphis State University, Memphis TN 38152. (901)454-2668. Contact: William Page, editor. Estab. 1982. Annual award.
Purpose: "To encourage writing of outstanding merit."
Requirements: Unpublished submissions.
Award: $100.
Information: Judged by a review panel. No entry fee. For entry submit fiction for publication in *Memphis State Review*.

INDIANA REVIEW FICTION AWARD, *Indiana Review*, 316 N. Jordan, Bloomington IN 47405. (812)337-3439. Contact: Clint McCown, editor. Estab. 1981. Annual award.
Purpose: "To encourage, locate and publish stories that are moving, interesting or innovative in conception, and to reward outstanding literary writers with publication and a small sum."
Requirements: All fiction published in *Indiana Review* will automatically be considered for the award, which will carry a cash value of at least $100. Looking for "quality of language, command of voice, ability to move the reader *fairly*, awareness of a world outside the living room, innovation in technique: all these things in harmony."

INKY TRAILS FICTION OF THE YEAR AWARD, Inky Trails Publications, Box 345, Middleton ID 83644. Contact: Pearl L. Kirk, editor/publisher. Annual award.
Purpose: "To help a new writer get started to reach the better publications."
Requirements: Unpublished submissions only. "If used for magazine we will use those published. If ms is published we give credit for first printing." Deadline entry: February 15. Award judged by qualified persons, e.g., teachers or fiction writers in Idaho. Entry form or rules for SASE. $3 entry fee.
Award: $15 and $10. "If there are enough entries we may raise award money."
Information: "Any subject except science fiction, horror and sexual natures. Keep it clean. For under 14 years: romance, war, love, history, personal, western, mystery, adventure, humor, juvenile, young adult, religion."

INTERNATIONAL IMITATION HEMINGWAY COMPETITION, Harry's Bar & American Grill, 2020 Avenue of the Stars, Los Angeles CA 90067. Contact: Mark S. Grody, chairman, Grody/Tellem Communications, Inc., 9100 Sepulveda Blvd., Suite 200, Los Angeles CA 90045. Estab. 1977. Annual award.
Purpose: "To select the best entry under the guideline, Write one really good page of really 'bad' Hemingway'; i.e., select the best 'Imitation Hemingway' entry."
Requirements: Unpublished submissions.
Award: "Dinner for two at Harry's Bar & American Grill in Florence, Italy plus the round-trip plane fare for two. If the winner is from Europe, he/she comes to Los Angeles."
Information: Judged by "a distinguished panel of literary/Hemingway experts; panel may change annually. Past judges have included: Jack Hemingway, son of Ernest; authors Ray Bradbury, George Plimpton, Barnaby Conrad; syndicated columnist Jack Smith. Entry deadline: February 15. No entry fee. Send SASE for official entry blank to Harry's Bar & American Grill, 2020 Avenue of the Stars, Los Angeles, CA 90067; or, enter on a plain piece of paper." Looking for "great imitation. Some entries will be funny; the best entries will be *very* funny." Receives about 2,500 entries from all over the world. "Generally, the entries have been excellent." Winner to be announced early April. "All entries must mention Harry's—nicely."

INTERNATIONAL READING ASSOCIATION CHILDREN'S BOOK AWARD, IRA/Institute for Reading Research, 800 Barksdale Rd., Box 8139, Newark DE 19711. (302)731-1600. Contact: Mr Sam Sebesta, Miller Hall, University of Washington, Seattle WA 98105. Estab. 1975. Annual award.
Purpose: "To encourage an author who shows unusual promise in the field of children's books. The award is given for an author's first or second book."
Requirements: Previously published submissions. Submissions must be published during the calendar year prior to the year in which the award is given.
Award: $1,000 stipend.
Information: Judged by a special subcommittee of the International Reading Association. Entry deadline: December 1. No entry fee. Contest/award rules and awards flyer for SASE. To enter the contest, the author or publisher should send seven copies of the book to Mr. Sam Sebesta at the above address. Looking for quality of writing and appeal to young readers.

IOWA SCHOOL OF LETTERS AWARD FOR SHORT FICTION, Iowa Writers' Workshop, Iowa School of Letters/English-Philosophy Building/The University of Iowa, Iowa City IA

52242. Contact: Connie Brothers. Estab. 1969. Annual award.

Purpose: "To encourage writers in short fiction (a literary genre largely neglected by commercial publishers)."

Requirements: Deadline entry: September 30. Entries must be submitted between August 1 and September 30. Rules for SASE.

Award: "$1,000 plus publication of the winning collection by University of Iowa Press the following fall, and a visit to the University of Iowa Campus to be honored at a reception.

Information: "Iowa Writers' Workshop does initial screening of entries; finalists (about 5) sent to a judge for final selection. A different well-known writer is chosen each year as judge." Receives 250-300 entries. Previous award winners state it gave them the beginnings of an audience, placed their work before important people in a position to give them an upward boost, and seven of them have published 1-3 books each since receiving the award."

JOSEPH HENRY JACKSON AWARD, The San Francisco Foundation, 425 California # 1602, San Francisco CA 94104. Contact: Susan Kelly, assistant coordinator. Estab. 1957. Annual award.

Purpose: "To award the author of an unpublished, partly completed book-length work of fiction, nonfiction, short story, or poetry."

Requirements: Unpublished submissions only. Applicant must be resident of Northern California or Nevada for 3 consecutive years immediately prior to the date for which submission is being made. Age of applicant must be 20 through 35. Deadline entry: January 15. Entry form and rules for SASE.

Award: $2,000 and award certificate.

JESSE H. JONES AWARD, Texas Institute of Letters, Box 8594, Waco TX 76710. Contact: J. Edward Weems, secretary/treasurer. Estab. 1948. Annual award.

Purpose: "To recognize the best work of fiction by a Texan or about Texas."

Requirements: Award judged by a jury of Texas Institute of Letters members. Entry form or rules for SASE.

Information: Deadline: Nov. 1. Receives approximately 30 entries.

KANSAS QUARTERLY/KANSAS ARTS COMMISSION AWARDS, *Kansas Quarterly*, 106 Denison Hall, Kansas State University, Manhattan KS 66506. Contact: The editors. Estab. 1972. Annual awards.

Purpose: "To reward and recognize the best fiction published in *Kansas Quarterly* during the year from authors anywhere in the US or abroad."

Requirements: "Anyone who submits unpublished material which is then accepted for publication becomes eligible for the awards." No deadline; material simply may be submitted for consideration at any time. To submit fiction for consideration, send it in with SASE.

Award: Recognition and monetary sums of $300, $200, $100, $50.

Information: Looking for "the best that is available. Ours are not 'contests'; they are monetary awards and recognition given by persons of national literary stature. Judges have included William Inge, John Cheever, John Gardner, Kay Boyle, Anne Tyler, William Gass, David Madden, George Garrett."

JACK KEROUAC ANNUAL FICTION PRIZE, *Magic Changes*, 553 W. Oakdale, # 317, Chicago IL 60657. Contact: John Sennett, editor. Estab. 1979. Annual award.

Purpose: "To encourage writers to write the finest fiction."

Requirements: Unpublished submissions only. No deadline. Award judged by editors. Entry form or rules for SASE.

Award: First, second and third cash prizes are a percentage of entry fees. Entry fee: $2.

Information: Looking for short stories, short fiction. Winning entries published in *Magic Changes*. Receives 15-20 entries.

LA REINA PRESS CREATIVE WRITING AWARDS, La Reina Press/*Live Writers!*, Box 8182, Cincinnati OH 45208. Contact: Lupé A. González, publisher. Estab. 1982. Annual award.

Purpose: "To recognize upcoming American authors."
Requirements: "A majority should be unpublished—50/50 is acceptable."
Award: "The award for First Place Fiction is publication and distribution of entry by La Reina Press plus 50 author's copies. Two Honorable Mentions will have portions of their entries published in *Live Writers!* a literary magazine and 3 author's copies."
Information: "Different judges are chosen every year. Judges are authors of novels and short fiction." Entry deadline: Nov. 15. Entry fee: $5 "to help defray the costs of publishing, etc." Entry forms or rules for SASE. Looking for "well-written stories, believable characters, dialogue and events."

LA REINA PRESS ESCRITORES LATINO AWARDS, La Reina Press/*Live Writers!*, Box 8182, Cincinnati OH 45208. Contact: Lupé A. González, publisher. Estab. 1982. Annual award.
Purpose: "To recognize the literary contributions made by Latino writers in the US depicting the Latino viewpoint with English/Spanish and English work."
Requirements: "A majority should be unpublished—50/50 is acceptable."
Award: "The award for First Place Fiction is publication and distribution of entry by La Reina Press plus 50 author's copies. Two Honorable Mentions will have portions of their entries published in *Live Writers!* a literary magazine and 3 author's copies."
Information: "The publisher of La Reina is the judge, but other Latino authors will be asked to judge in the future." Entry deadline: Nov. 15. Entry fee: $5 "to help defray the costs of publishing, etc." Entry forms or rules for SASE. "We are looking for well-written stories that give insight into the lives of Latinos in the US, stories of our history, etc. The quality of Latino literature can be seen in the work of Rudolfo Anaya and Estela Portillo Trambley."

LOGAN LITERARY AWARDS, *Pennsylvania Review*, 532 N. 25th St., Pennside PA 19606. (215)779-5269. Contact: David M. Hinrichs, editor-in-chief. Annual award.
Purpose: "To single out and reward superlative work."
Requirements: Previously published submissions "Must be published in magazine during given year of award."
Award: $50 cash prize to best short story, poem and article submissions.
Information: Judged by the editorial staff. "Acceptance for publication is the sole requirement for entry." No entry fee. Contact *Pennsylvania Review* for entry information. "Our sole bias is toward superlative writing. We emphasize craftsmanship. We seek fiction that achieves a balance between form and content. We have no preference between what might be termed experimental or mainstream." Length: 1,000 to 5,000 words.

LOUISIANA LITERARY AWARD, Louisiana Library Association (LLA), Box 131, Baton Rouge LA 70821. (504)342-4928. Contact: Chair, Louisiana Literary Award Committee. Estab. 1948. Annual award.
Purpose: "To promote interest in books related to Louisiana and to encourage their production."
Requirements: Previously published submissions. Submissions are to be previously published during the calendar year prior to presentation of the award. (The award is presented in March or April.)
Award: Bronze medallion.
Information: Judged by a committee of six members of the Louisiana Library Association, appointed to serve three-year overlapping terms. Entry deadline: publication by December 31. No entry fee. "All Louisiana-related books which committee members can locate are considered, whether submitted or not. Interested parties may correspond with the committee chair at the address above. All books considered *must* be on subject(s) related to Louisiana. Works of fiction are evaluated according to literary merit, style and technique, and interest (locale, development of characters, plot, etc.). The Louisiana Literary Award also is open to works of nonfiction. Each year, there may be a fiction *and/or* nonfiction award. Most often, however, there is only one award recipient, and he or she is the author of a work of nonfiction." Receives about 150-200 entries (including nonfiction).

CANDACE LOVE FELLOWSHIP, International Black Writers, *Black Writers News*, 4019 S. Vincennes, Chicago IL 60653. (312)624-3184. Contact: Alice C. Browning, founder director. Estab. 1970. Annual award.
Purpose: "To help a writer complete a novel or a book of short stories."
Requirements: Unpublished submissions.
Award: $500-1,000, "we hope."
Information: Judged by a committee of novelists and short story writers. Entry deadline: March. Entry fee: $25. Entry forms or rules for SASE. Looking for "characters coming alive, good climax, material which holds the interest of the reader." Receives 10-25 or more entries.

MADEMOISELLE FICTION WRITERS COMPETITION, *Mademoiselle Magazine*, 350 Madison Ave., New York NY 10017. Contact: fiction editor.
Requirements: Each entry must be accompanied by self-addressed stamped envelope and 3x5 card with name, age, home address. Award judged by editors.
Award: 1st prize: $750 plus publication of winning story in a future issue of *Mademoiselle*; 2nd prize: $300 cash prize.
Information: Open to all writers 18-30. Entries will not be returned unless accompanied by SASE. Receives 800-1,000 entries. "Agents have contacted us about winners."

MAELSTROM REVIEW BEST SHORT STORY OF THE YEAR, 34 Winter St., Portland ME 04102. Contact: Leo Mallman, editor.
Purpose: To recognize the best short story of the year published in the *Maelstrom Review*.
Requirements: Unpublished submissions. Award judged by editors, contributing editors, and patrons of *MR*.
Information: "No entry rules, suggest sample issue, $2. Mss become eligible once accepted for publication in *Maelstrom Review*." Receives 30-50 entries each contest.

MASSACHUSETTS ARTISTS FELLOWSHIP, Artists Foundation—Artists Fellowship Program, 110 Broad St., Boston MA 02110. (617)482-8100. Contact: Lucine Folgueras, director. Estab. 1975. Annual award.
Purpose: "To reward outstanding Massachusetts artists and to encourage them to live and create within the Commonwealth."
Requirements: Previously published or unpublished submissions. All work must have been created within the last five years.
Award: $5,000 in unrestricted funds.
Information: Judged by out-of-state artists (writers) who are peers in their fields. Entry deadline: October 1. No entry fee. "Entry forms are available upon request, however, it is not necessary to enclose an SASE. Our forms will not fit in a business-size envelope and we do not require envelopes to be mailed. All work is judged anonymously and is looked at only for artistic merit. The panelists are looking for good work. We receive about 400 applicants each year."

THE MCCLELLAND AND STEWART AWARDS FOR FICTION, National Magazine Awards Foundation, 44 Eglinton Ave. W., Suite 501, Toronto, Ontario, Canada M4R 1A1. (416)922-3184. Estab. 1977. Annual award.
Purpose: "To honor excellence in Canadian magazine writing."
Requirements: Submissions must be previously published work appearing in the calendar year previous to that in which the award is issued."
Award: 1st $1,000 and 2nd $500.
Information: Judged by a panel of independent judges who are picked each year by the directors of the Foundation. Entry deadline: Early January—exact day differs slightly from year to year. Entry fee: $10. Entry forms or rules for SASE. Receives about 100 entries. "This contest is open only to Canadian citizens or landed immigrants whose work has appeared in Canadian magazines."

THE JOHN H. MCGINNIS MEMORIAL AWARD, *Southwest Review*, SMU Press, Southern Methodist University, Dallas TX 75275. Contact: Charlotte T. Whaley, senior editor. Estab.

1962. Biannual award. (One year for fiction and the next for nonfiction).
Requirements: Previously published submissions in the *Southwest Review* within a two-year period prior to the announcement of the award. Award judged by the editors.
Award: $1,000.
Information: "Looking for stories of character development or psychological penetration rather than those depending chiefly on plot. The John H. McGinnis Memorial Award is given each year for material—alternately fiction and nonfiction—that has been published in the *Southwest Review* in the previous two years. Thus, stories are not submitted directly for the award, but simply for publication in the magazine. From among those published in each two-year period, then, the judges select what they feel to be the best story for the McGinnis award."

THE VICKY METCALF AWARD, Canadian Authors Association, Suite 412, 131 Bloor St. W., Toronto, Ontario, Canada M5S 1R1. (416)923-9360. Contact: Chairwoman, Headquarters Committee. Estab. 1963. Annual award.
Purpose: "The prize is given solely to stimulate writing for children, written by Canadians, for a *number* of strictly children's books—fiction, nonfiction or even picture books. No set formula."
Requirements: Previously published submissions. "No limitation on when the first ones were published."
Award: $1,000.
Information: Judged by a panel including previous winners, who are not eligible again. Entry deadline: Dec. 31. No entry fee. "Nominations may be made by any individual or association by letter *in triplicate* listing the published works of the nominee. While there is no set formula the books are usually considered in regard to their inspirational value for children. Since the award is for a number of books (for a while the number was seven or over), the number of nominees varies considerably from year to year."

VICKY METCALF SHORT STORY AWARD, Canadian Authors Association, Suite 412, 131 Bloor St. W., Toronto, Ontario, Canada M5S 1R1. (416)923-9360. Contact: Betty Dyck, committee chairwoman or Ginny Sumodi, secretary.
Purpose: "To promote Canadian authors of children's literature (open only to Canadian citizens)."
Requirements: Previously published submissions. Submissions must be previously published during previous calendar year in Canadian children's magazine or anthology.
Award: $500 and $1,000 (Canadian) 2 awards.
Information: Judged by panel of children's librarians and writers. Entry deadline: Dec. 31. No entry fee. Entry forms or rules for SASE. Looking for "books for ages 7-17 with originality, literary quality."

MINNESOTA VOICES PROJECT, New Rivers Press, 1602 Selby Ave., St. Paul MN 55104. Contact: C.W. Truesdale, editor/publisher. Estab. 1981. Annual award.
Purpose: "To publish and foster recognition of regional writers of fiction—short novels and poetry."
Requirements: Unpublished submissions.
Awards: $500 to each author published in the series plus "a generous royalty agreement if book goes into second printing."
Information: Judged by panel of professional writers and teachers of writing and contemporary literature. Entry deadline: March 1. No entry fee. SASE for guidelines. Send two copies of each ms of 125-200 pages; restricted to writers from Minnesota, Wisconsin, North and South Dakota and Iowa. 1981 competition: 1 of 4 books published were short fiction; 1982 competition: 2 of 4 books were short fiction.

MS MAGAZINE COLLEGE FICTION CONTEST, Ms. Foundation, 119 W. 40th St., New York NY 10018. Contact: College Fiction Editor.
Award: Electric typewriter plus publication in annual college issue (September).

Information: Contest announced annually in February or March issue. Full or part-time students of all ages enrolled in a degree course are eligible.

MYTHOPOEIC FANTASY AWARD (The "Aslan Award"), The Mythopoeic Society, Box 4671, Whittier CA 90607. Contact: Christine S. Lowentrout, award chairman. Estab. 1970. Annual award.

Purpose: "To present a literary award to a fantasy/science fiction writer for his contribution to the field of fantasy literature."

Requirements: Previously published submissions. Submissions are to be previously published during the year prior.

Award: Bronze trophy of a lion, special honors at the annual Mythopoeic Conference. Many publishers note the award on book jacket.

Information: Judged by society members nominated. The top 5 nominees are read by a committee of at least 11 people, and voted upon. Entry deadline: July. No entry fee. Entry forms or rules for SASE. Write to Correspondence Secretary: Lisa Cowan, Box 5276, Orange CA 92667. Looking for the best (and most popular) fantasy fiction of the year. Members may nominate up to 5 books. "This is an honorary award, similar to the 'Hugo' award for Best Science Fiction book of the year." For published authors only.

NATIONAL WRITERS CLUB ANNUAL BOOK CONTEST, National Writers Club, 1450 S. Havana, Aurora CO 80012. (303)751-7844. Contact: Donald E. Bower, director. Estab. 1974. Annual award.

Purpose: To encourage and recognize writing by freelancers in the field of the novel.

Requirements: Unpublished submissions. Deadline entry: July 1. Award judged by successful writers. Contest/award rules and entry forms available with SASE. Charges $20 for entry fee.

Award: $1,000 in prizes; $400 first prize.

Information: Looking for originality of idea, and freshness of writing. Receives approximately 300 entries. "Four out of last five winners have been published."

NATIONAL WRITERS CLUB ANNUAL SHORT STORY CONTEST, National Writers Club, 1450 S. Havana, Aurora CO 80012. (303)751-7844. Contact: Donald E. Bower, director. Estab. 1940. Annual award.

Purpose: To encourage and recognize writing by freelancers in the short story field.

Requirements: Unpublished submissions. Award judged by professional writers. Write for rule sheet. Charges $10 for entry fee.

Information: Receives approximately 300 entries.

NATIONAL YOUTH WRITING COMPETITION, Interlochen Arts Academy, Interlochen MI 49643. Contact: Karen Galbraith. Estab. 1976. Annual award.

Purpose: To identify and encourage young writers.

Requirements: Contest is open to students in grades nine to twelve. Deadline entry: December 15. Panel of judges varies from year to year—usually guest writers on campus. Contest/award rules and entry forms available with SASE.

Award: First prize $100; second prize $50; and third prize $25 with publication in the *Interlochen Review*. Charges $4 for entry fee.

Information: Receives approximately 5,000 entries.

NEW JERSEY AUTHOR AWARDS, New Jersey Institute of Technology, 323 High St., Newark NJ 07102. (201)889-7336. Contact: Dr. Herman A. Estrin, professor of English. Estab. 1960. Annual award.

Purpose: "To recognize New Jersey writers."

Requirements: Previousy published submissions.

Awards: Citation inscribed with the author's name and his work.

Information: Entry deadline: October. No entry fee. Entry forms or rules for SASE. Receives about 50 entries. Those honored include Harriet Adams, Mary Mapes Dodge, Phillip Roth, Belva Plain, and many other contemporary writers of New Jersey.

NIGHTSUN LITERATURE AND ART CONTEST, *Nightsun*, Frostburg State College, Dept. of Philosophy, Frostburg MD 21532. (301)689-4249. Contact: Jorn K. Bramann, editor. Estab. 1980. Annual award.
Purpose: "To honor the 3 best contributions to each issue of *Nightsun*, whether fiction or other."
Requirements: Unpublished submissions.
Award: 1st prize: $50 in cash; 2nd and 3rd prize: free subscription to *Nightsun* (for author or friend).
Information: Judged by the editors of *Nightsun*. Entry deadline: September 1. Entry fee: $6.80, the price of a one year subscription. (No fee, if work is solicited.) Looking for "high quality. *Sometimes* particularly desirable themes will be announced in preceding issue of *Nightsun*." Received about 250 entries last year.

FRANK O'CONNOR FICTION AWARD, *Descant*, Department of English, Texas Christian University, Fort Worth TX 76129. (817)921-7240. Contact: Betsy Colquitt, editor. Estab. 1979 with *Descant*; earlier awarded through *Quartet*. Annual award.
Purpose: To honor achievement in short fiction.
Requirements: Submissions must be published in the magazine during its current volume.
Award: $100 prize.
Information: Judge selected by the editorial staff of the magazine. No entry fee. "12 to 15 stories are published annually in *Descant*. Winning story is selected from this group."

THE SCOTT O'DELL AWARD FOR HISTORICAL FICTION, Scott O'Dell (personal donation), c/o Houghton Mifflin, 2 Park St., Boston MA 02107. (617)725-5000. Contact: Mrs. Zena Sutherland, professor, 1100 E. 57 St., Chicago, Il 60637. Estab. 1981. Annual award.
Purpose: "To encourage the writing of good historical fiction about the New World (Canada, South and Central America, and the United States) for children and young people."
Requirements: Previously published submissions during the year preceding that year in which the award is given. To be written in English by a US citizen set in New World (Canada, Central or South America and the US).
Award: $5,000.
Information: Judged by the advisory committee of the *Bulletin of the Center for Children's Books*, at the University of Chicago. Entry deadline: December 31. No entry fee. Entry forms or rules for SASE. Looking for "accuracy in historical details, and all the standard literary criteria for excellence: style, setting, characterization, etc."

THE JULIAN OCEAN LITERATURE AWARD, Triple "P" Publications International, Box 8776, Kennedy Station, Boston MA 02114. (617)437-1856. Contact: Eugene F.P.C. de Mesne, editorial manager. Estab. 1979. Annual award, named after Julian Ocean, publisher, author, poet, critic, book designer and artist.
Purpose: "To further new talent; to promote art and publishing; to give incentive to artists and writers who would like to compete for an award; to give fiction a broader scope and presentation."
Requirements: Unpublished submissions.
Award: $20 prize money and a large certificate, plus recognition via National Writers Club, COSMEP Newsletter and Support Services Newsletter (winners announced in these publications).
Information: Judged by "5 persons unknown to each other, in various parts of the United States. Each judge is then free to make his/her judging independently." Entry deadline: December 31. Entry fee: $1. SASE is a *must* for entry forms; rules sent on request. "No taboos. Only requirement for entry is excellence and professionalism in presentation, development and theme. Entrants should be aware we are open to new ideas and fictional slants. In 1981, our second year:

received 5,613 entries; in 1982, our third year: we anticipate over 5,000 entries. Judges have mentioned it is difficult to choose the winners with so much good material coming in.''

OHIOANA BOOK AWARD, Ohioana Library Association, 1105 Ohio Departments Bldg., 65 S. Front St., Columbus OH 43215. Contact: James P. Barry, director. Estab. 1929. Annual award (only if the judges believe a book of sufficiently high quality has been submitted).
Purpose: To bring recognition to outstanding books by Ohioans or about Ohio.
Requirements: "Books to be submitted on or before publication date, in two copies. Each spring a jury considers all books received since the previous jury. Award judged by a jury, selected each year from librarians, book reviewers, and other knowledgeable people. No entry forms, etc., are needed. We will be glad to answer letters asking specific questions."
Award: Certificate and medal.
Information: "Books must be by an Ohioan (defined as a person born in Ohio or who has lived there for a total of at least 5 years), or about Ohio or the state's people. The submission must be of high quality." Receives 350-450 entries.

THE OKANAGAN SHORT FICTION AWARD, *Canadian Author & Bookman*, 131 Bloor St. W., Suite 412, Toronto, Ontario, Canada M5S 1R1. Contact: Geoff Hancock, fiction editor. Estab. 1979. Award offered 4 times a year.
Purpose: To present good fiction "in which the writing surpasses all else" to an appreciative literary readership, and in turn help Canadian writers retain an interest in good fiction.
Requirements: Unpublished submissions. Entries are invited in each issue of our quarterly *CA&B*. Writers are asked to submit mss only. Sample copy $1; guideline printed in the magazine. "Our award regulations stipulate that writers must be Canadian, stories must not have been previously published, and be under 3500 words. Mss should be typed double-spaced on 8 ½x11 bond. SASE requested. Award is made possible through a Capital Trust Fund (donor anonymous) and, it is hoped, will continue in perpetuity." Award judged by fiction editor.
Award: $125 to each author whose story is accepted for publication.
Information: Looking for superior writing ability, stories with good plot, movement, dialogue and characterization. Receives approximately 100 entries/month.

ONTARIO ARTS COUNCIL GRANTS TO WRITERS, Ontario Arts Council, 970 Copeland, North Bay, Ontario, Canada P1B 3E4. (416)961-1660. Contact: Steven Stevanovic, editor. Estab. 1977. Contest/award offered when money is available.
Purpose: "To encourage quality writing."
Requirements: Unpublished submissions. Recommended by a publishing house or magazine editor.
Award: Cash; varies up to $5,000.
Information: Judged by the editors of *Nebula* magazine. No entry deadline or entry fee. "Simply submit material for possble publication. All eligible contributors are considered." Looking for quality. Receives about 200 entries.

OZARK WRITERS AND ARTISTS GUILD, Box 411, Siloam Springs AK 72761. Contact: Maggie Smith, director. Estab. 1935. Annual award.
Purpose: "To encourage writers in both poetry and prose."
Requirements: Unpublished submissions.
Award: 1st prize, $25; 2 honorable mentions, $15 and $10.
Information: "Judges vary, but for the most part are doctors, professors, teachers at John Brown University, University of Arkansas, etc." Entry deadline: June 15, 1982. Entry fee: $4 for 4 entries. Send SASE for contest sheet.

PACIFIC NORTHWEST WRITERS CONFERENCE, 1811 NE. 199th St., Seattle WA 98155. (206)364-1293. Contact: Amos Wood. Annual award.
Purpose: "To encourage writers."

Requirements: Unpublished submissions.
Award: $250 first prize; $150 second prize; $100 third prize.
Information: Judged by qualified writers. Entry deadline: April 15. Entry fee: $5 (entrant must be a member of PNWC). Entry forms or rules for SASE. Looking for adult short fiction (not to exceed 4,000 words, may be any type: short story, confession, etc.); juvenile short fiction (not to exceed 4,000 words); and novel (first chapter and maximum five-page synopsis required, plus any additional chapters or excerpts, total not to exceed 10,000 words). Receives "around 500 entries."

PAN-AMERICAN INTERNATIONAL LITERARY AWARD, Pan-American Publishing Company, Box 1505, Las Vegas NM 87701. (505)454-0132. Contact: Rose Calles, editor-in-chief. Estab. 1978. Annual award.
Purpose: "To provide another avenue for previously unpublished writers to have their works published plus receive a cash award."
Requirements: Unpublished submissions.
Award: "The winning entry will be published and distributed by Pan-American Publishing. The winning author will receive a $250 cash award and a minimum of 10% royalties; second-place winner a $100 cash award; third $50."
Information: Judged by a panel of editors. Entry deadline: December 31. Entry fee: $25. "Entry fee shall help to defray expense of hiring additional readers. Editors will judge submissions selected by the readers." Entry forms or rules for SASE. Looking for "well-developed plots with plenty of protagonist and antagonist action." Receives about 100 entries.

WILLIAM PEDEN PRIZE IN FICTION, *The Missouri Review*, 231 Arts & Sciences, University of Missouri, Columbia MO 65211. (314)882-2339. Contact: Speer Morgan, editor. Estab. 1981. Annual award.
Purpose: "To honor the best short story published in *The Missouri Review* each year."
Requirements: Previously published in *The Missouri Review*. Submissions are to be previously published in the volume year for which the prize is awarded.
Award: $500 cash.
Requirements: Judged by a single independent judge of reputation. No deadline or entry fee. No rules; all fiction published in *MR* automatically become contestants. "We like ficton with some slight quirk in character, plot, or incident."

JAMES D. PHELAN AWARD, The San Francisco Foundation, 500 Washington St., 8th Floor, San Francisco CA 94111. Contact: Susan Kelly, assistant coordinator. Estab. 1935. Annual award.
Purpose: To award the author of an unpublished work-in-progress of fiction, (novel or short story), nonfictional prose, poetry or drama.
Requirements: Unpublished submissions. Applicant must have been born in the state of California and be 20-35 years old. Deadline entry: January 15. Contest/award rules and entry forms available from above address.
Award: $2,000 and a certificate.

PIERIAN PRESS EDITORS' PRIZE, Box A5, Brandon University, Brandon, Manitoba, Canada R7A 6A9. Contact: R.W. Brockway, chief editor. Quarterly award.
Purpose: To encourage and reward effective writing of good quality.
Requirements: Unpublished submissions. All material accepted for publication automatically entered.
Award: 1st prize $25, and 2nd prize a short story anthology. "Prizes are awarded on the basis of the best of published stories per issue plus one or two book prizes for runners-up. Since we have limited resources, we feel we can compensate our writers best by giving what we have to the most deserving rather than pay a derisory sum to all of our fiction writers per issue; also the prize enables us to commend the fine writer."
Information: Looking for well-developed plot, effective writing and imaginative themes.

EDGAR ALLAN POE AWARDS, Mystery Writers of America, Inc., 150 5th Ave., New York NY 10011. Contact: Gloria Amoury, executive secretary. Estab. 1945. Annual award.
Purpose: To enhance the prestige of the mystery.
Requirements: Previously published submissions in the calendar year. Deadline entry: December 31. Each award committee operates differently. Contact above address for specifics.
Award: Ceramic bust of Poe. Awards for: Best Mystery Novel, Best First Novel, Best Softcover Original Novel, Best Short Story and Best Juvenile Novel.
Information: Looking for excellence.

KATHERINE ANNE PORTER PRIZE FOR FICTION, *Nimrod*, Arts and Humanities Council, 2210 S. Main St., Tulsa OK 74114. Annual award.
Requirements: Accepts mss for consideration beginning December 1. Deadline for submissions, March.
Award: $500 first prize and $250 second prize. Winning entries wll be published in either the Fall/Winter 1982 or Spring/Summer 1983 issue of *Nimrod*. Winners will be brought to Tulsa for a reading and the presentation of the prize.
Requirements: Only one submission per author (2 photocopies). No minimum length; 7,500 word maximum. No previously published works, works accepted for publication or dual submissions are eligible. *Nimrod* requires first refusal rights on all submissions. *Nimrod* editors read each manuscript and a final judge chooses from the 20 selected finalists. In the past, fiction judges have included: Alison Lurie, Charles Johnson, and R.V. Cassill. Author's name must not appear on the manuscript. Submission should be accompanied by a cover sheet containing the title of the work and the author's name and address. The title of the work, however, should also appear on the first page of the manuscript. "CONTEST ENTRY" should be clearly indicated on both the outer envelope and the cover sheet. Manuscripts should be typed and fiction manuscripts should be double-spaced. All entries not officially accepted for publication will be released to their authors within six weeks after the contest results are announced. Contest winners will be announced in June. Manuscripts will not be returned. Send SASE for further information.
Information: All potential contest participants are asked to purchase a copy of *Nimrod* (at the reduced rate of $4.50 per copy) in order to familiarize themelves with our magazine. Receives approximately 450 entries.

SIR WALTER RALEIGH AWARD, North Carolina Literary & Historical Association, 109 E. Jones St., Raleigh NC 27611. (919)733-7305. Contact: Becky Myer, assistant secretary-treasurer. Annual award.
Purpose: To stimulate among the people of the state an interest in their own literature.
Requirements: Previously published submissions only by North Carolina authors. It must be an original work published during the twelve months ending June 30 of the year for which the award is given. Entry Deadline: July 15. Award judged by a panel of five judges including the current president of the North Carolina Literary and Historical Association. The other four judges are chosen by the English and history departments of different North Carolina colleges and universities or selected by the president and secretary. Contest/award rules and entry forms available with SASE.
Award: Statuette of Sir Walter Raleigh.
Information: Looking for creative and imaginative quality, excellence of style and universality of appeal.

REDBOOK'S YOUNG WRITERS' CONTEST, *Redbook*, 230 Park Ave., New York NY 10169. (212)850-9375. Contact: Mimi Jones, associate fiction editor. Estab. 1976. Annual award.
Purpose: "To reward the achievements of young, unpublished short story writers and to acquaint them with the most effective ways to submit their work professionally."
Requirements: Unpublished submissions. Open to men and women 18-28 years. See March, April or May 1983 *Redbook* for complete rules or send SASE, starting in Feb. 1983 for rules sheet.
Award: 1st prize: $1,000, plus $1,000 for publication in *Redbook* Magazine; 2nd prize: $500; three 3rd prizes: $250 each.

awards

Information: Judged by the editors of *Redbook* Magazine. Entry deadline: May 31, 1983. No entry fee. Looking for "literary excellence. There are no restrictions with regard to subject matter; any eligible story that succeeds on its own terms will be given full consideration." Received about 5,000 entries in 1982. "Extremely pleased with quality of writing received. Two prize winners in previous contests have expanded their contest stories into novels and had them published: Caroline Leavitt's *Meeting Rozzy Halfway* was brought out by Seaview Books in January, 1981, and Joseph Monninger's *The Family Man* will be published by Atheneum. Seven former finalists in the contest went on to publish short stories in *Redbook*, and several others have placed their work with other magazines."

SAN JOSE STUDIES BEST STORY AWARD, Bill Casey Memorial Fund, 125 S. 7th St., San Jose CA 95192. Contact: Selma Burkom.
Purpose: To recognize the author of the best story (or essay or poem) appearing in a previous volume of *San Jose Studies*.
Requirements: Award judged by the trustees of the journal.
Award: $100. Winning author to receive a year's complimentary subscription to the journal.

SAXIFRAGE PRIZE, Saxifrage, Inc., 1402 Burning Tree Dr., Chapel Hill NC 27514. Contact: Roger Sauls. Estab. 1980. Biannual award.
Purpose: To recognize the best book of short stories published by a small press or university press during the eligibility period.
Requirements: Submit work published within 2 years prior to entry period of January 1—May 1 of odd numbered years.
Award: $2,000 to author, $500 to publisher.

SCIENCE FICTION/FANTASY SHORT STORY CONTEST, Science Fiction Writers of Earth, Box 12293, Fort Worth TX 76116. (817)451-8674. Contact: Gilbert Gordon Reis, acting president (SFWOE). Estab. 1980. Annual award.
Purpose: "To promote the art of science fiction/fantasy short story writing."
Requirements: Unpublished submissions by unpublished authors.
Award: 1st prize, $100; 2nd prize, $50; and 3rd prize, $25.
Information: "A nominating committee (from SFWOE members) will select the best stories. A panel of independent judges (from science fiction editors and authors) determines the winner from the nominated stories." Entry deadline: Each October 30th contest closes; winners awarded in January of the following year. Entry fee: $5; $2 for second entry ($5 includes a year's membership in SFWOE). Entry forms/rules for business size SASE. Looking for "well written science fiction or fantasy from 2,000 to 7,500 words." A moderate number of entries is received. "Any monies left from entry fees used to increase next year's awards. The quality of stories has been very poor to almost good. There's plenty of room for *good* stories to win contest."

SEAL BOOKS FIRST NOVEL COMPETITION, Seal Books, 60 St. Clair Ave. E., Suite 601, Toronto, Ontario, Canada M4T 1N5. Contact: Editor. Estab. 1977.
Requirements: Unpublished submissions. Deadline entry: December 31. Contest/award rules and entry forms available with SASE. Applicant must be either a Canadian citizen or a Canadian landed immigrant.
Award: $50,000 of which $10,000 is an outright prize and $40,000 a nonreturnable advance against earnings plus a contract with Seal Books (the mass market imprint of McClelland & Stewart-Bantam Ltd.) that will guarantee publication of novel first in hard bound edition, then as paperback.
Information: Mss to be not less than 60,000 words. Must be double-spaced on white paper, submitted in English under author's own name. Receives 300-400 entries.

THE SEATON AWARDS, *Kansas Quarterly*, 106 Denison Hall, Kansas State University, KS 66506. Contact: Editors. Estab. 1980. Annual awards.

Purpose: To reward and recognize the best fiction published in *KQ* during the year from authors native to or resident in Kansas.

Requirements: Submissions must be unpublished. Anyone who submits unpublished material which is then accepted for publication becomes eligible for the awards. Seaton Awards are specifically for Kansas natives or Kansas residents. No deadline. Material simply may be submitted for consideration at any time with SASE.

Award: Recognition and monetary sums of $200, $150, $100 and $50.

Information: Looking for the best that is available. "Ours are not contests. We give monetary awards and recognition by Kansas writers with national literary stature. Judges have included Kennth S. Davis, Michael Heffernan."

SEVENTEEN FICTION CONTEST FOR TEENS, *Seventeen Magazine*, 850 3rd Ave., New York NY 10022. Contact: Dawn Raffel.

Purpose: To honor best short fiction by a teenage writer.

Requirements: Rules are found in the April issue. Contest for 13-19 year olds. Award judged by a panel of *Seventeen*'s editors.

Award: $500 first place; $300 second place; $200 third place; $50 to 6 honorable mentions.

Information: Receives approximately 1,500 entries.

SOUTHERN REVIEW/LOUISIANA STATE UNIVERSITY ANNUAL SHORT FICTION AWARD, *Southern Review*, Drawer D, University Station, Baton Rouge LA 70893. (504)388-5108. Contact: Donald E. Stanford, chairman SR/LSU Short Fiction Award Committee. Estab. 1980. Annual award.

Purpose: "To encourage publication of good fiction."

Requirements: Previously published submissions published during each calendar year.

Award: $500 to author. Consideration as a text in introduction to fiction courses at LSU.

Information: Judged by an award committee chaired by Donald E. Stanford, editor *Southern Review* and an outside referee. Deadline soon after close of each calendar year. No entry fee. No rules except the book of short stories must be published by an American publisher. Looking for "style, sense of craft, plot, in-depth characters." Receives 20-40 books a year.

ANNUAL SPITBALL FICTION CONTEST, *Spitball* Poetry Magazine, 231 E. 7th St., Covington KY 41011. (606)261-3024. Contact: Mike Shannon, editor. Estab. 1981. Annual award.

Purpose: "To attract high quality baseball ficton to publish in our magazine."

Requirements: Previously published submissions.

Award: Publishing in *Spitball*, copies of issue story appears in, and merchandise prizes (baseball-related).

Information: Judged by the editors of *Spitball*. Entry deadline: August 31. No entry fee. Entry forms or rules for SASE. "We have no preference in style, as long as subject is baseball. (Reading our fiction issue would probably help the writer unfamiliar with baseball fiction.)"

SPUR AWARD CONTEST, Western Writers of America, Meridan Rd., Victor MT 59875. Contact: Rex Bundy, WWA Secretary-Treasurer. Estab. 1952. Annual award.

Purpose: To encourage excellence in western writing.

Requirements: Previously published submissions. Entries are accepted only from the current calendar year for each year's award; that is, books can only be entered in the year they are published. Deadline entry: December 31. Award judged by a panel of experienced authors appointed by the current Spur Awards Chairman. A panel consists of three judges, each individually evaluating submissions; total points determine winners. Contest/award rules and entry forms available with SASE.

Award: A wooden plaque shaped like a W with a golden spur attached. "No money is awarded in Spur categories; however, a special $500 Medicine Pipe Bearer Award, funded by a WWA member, is offered in the Best First Western Novel competition. First novels may be entered in both Spur and Medicine Pipe Bearer competition."

Information: "Books must be of the traditional or historical western theme, set anywhere west of the Mississippi River before the 20th century, ideally from 1850 to 1900." Received 47 novels in 1980. Beginning with the 1981 competition, a Spur is awarded for Best Historical Fiction, Best Juvenile Fiction and Best Short Fiction works. "Past award winners include such names as Nelson Nye, Jeanne Williams, Elmer Kelton, Wayne Barton and others too numerous to list."

STORY TIME SHORT-STORY CONTEST, *Rhyme Time/Story Time*, Box 2377, Coeur d'Alene ID 83814. (208)667-7511. Contact: Linda Hutton, editor. Estab. 1982. Annual award.
Purpose: "To encourage short-story writers."
Requirements: Unpublished submissions.
Award: $10 first prize; $7.50 second prize; $5 third prize.
Information: Judged by staff of *Rhyme Time/Story Time*, Idaho Writers' League and North Idaho College Department of English. Entry deadline: August 15, 1983. Entry fee: $2. Looking for "tightly written plot and well-developed characters." Receives approximately 50-60 entries.

SUN DOG AWARDS, *Sun Dog*/Florida State University English Department, 406 William Bldg., Florida State University, Tallahassee FL 32306. Contact: Allen Woodman, or Joe Taylor, editors. Estab. 1982.
Purpose: "$100 is awarded to the best fiction piece in every issue of *Sun Dog*. All regular submissions are considered for the contest. Submissions accepted year round."
Requirements: Unpublished submissions only. Must be typed and include SASE.
Award: $100 and publication.
Information: Judged by independent judges. Entries accepted year round. "Send us your best work. Stories should be under 30 pages. We receive about 300 submissions an issue. Agents and other editors often write us for addresses of writers appearing in our issues. We encourage writers to read our magazine first. Sample copies are $3."

TAMPA MAGAZINE SHORT STORY CONTEST, 4100 W. Kennedy Blvd., Tampa FL 33609. (813)872-7449. Contact: Bob Casterline, articles editor. Annual award.
Requirements: Unpublished submissions.
Award: $300, publication in March issue.
Information: Entry deadline: November 30. No entry fee. Entry forms or rules for SASE. Story to "focus on Tampa Bay area to tell reader about character of Tampa and its environs." Looking for "high-quality, stylish fiction."

TRANSLATION CENTER AWARD, The Translation Center, 307A Mathematics Bldg., Columbia University, New York NY 10027. Contact: Diane G. H. Cook, executive director. Annual award.
Purpose: "For outstanding translation of a substantial part of a booklength *literary* work."
Award: $500.
Information: Judged by awards committee. Entry deadline: January 15. No entry fee. Entry forms or rules for SASE. "Competitions are sponsored annually to encourage excellence in individual works and the development of new translators."

UNIVERSITY OF MISSOURI BREAKTHROUGH COMPETITION, 200 Lewis Hall, Columbia MO 65211. Contact: Susan E. Kelpe, associate director. Biannual competition/annual award.
Requirements: Entry fee is $7.50. Mss are read only in odd numbered years. Award judged by professional writer or critic.
Award: Publication in series.
Information: Looking for fiction, 96-124 pages. "In the past, most entries have been academics. Judges are professional writers." Receives approximately 325 entries.

JAMES F. VICTORIN MEMORIAL AWARD, Dialogue Publications, Inc., 3100 Oak Park Ave., Berwyn IL 60402. (312)749-1908. Contact: Mrs. Annette Victorin, editor of fiction and poetry. Estab. 1972. Annual award.

Purpose: "To recognize best short story published in *Dialogue* during previous year."
Requirements: Previously published submissions in *Dialogue*.
Award: $100.
Information: Judged by Mrs. A. Victorin and her literary colleagues. No entry fee. Publication of any story constitutes entry. ONLY BLIND OR VISUALLY HANDICAPPED ENTRANTS ARE ELIGIBLE. Receives 10-12 entries.

EDWARD LEWIS WALLANT MEMORIAL BOOK AWARD, 3 Brighton Rd., West Hartford CT 06117. Sponsored by Dr. and Mrs. Irving Waltman in cooperation with the Hartford Jewish Community Center. Contact: Mrs. Irving Waltman. Estab. 1963. Annual award.
Purpose: Memorial to Edward Lewis Wallant which offers incentive and encouragement to beginning writers.
Requirements: Previously published submissions the year before the award is conferred in the spring. Books may be submitted for consideration to Dr. Lothar Kahn, one of the permanent judges. Address: Central Conn. State College, New Britain, CT.
Award: $250 plus award certificate.
Information: "Looking for creative work of fiction by an American Jew which has significance for the American Jew. The novel (or collection of short stories) should preferably bear a kinship to the writing of Wallant. The award will seek out the writer who has not yet achieved literary prominence when published."

FRANK WARDLAW PRIZE, Texas Monthly Press, Box 1569, Austin TX 78767. Contact: Barbara Reavis, senior editor. Estab. 1980. Annual award.
Purpose: "To encourage literary excellence in Texas publishing, and to honor previously unrecognized Texas writers."
Requirements: Unpublished submissions.
Award: $1,000 honorarium and publication/royalty contract.
Information: Judged by Texas Monthly Press editorial board. Entry deadline: June 1, every year. No entry fee. Material must be Texas related, original; 60,000 word minimum. Receives approximatey 100 entries.

WESTERN HERITAGE AWARDS, National Cowboy Hall of Fame, 1700 NE 63rd St., Oklahoma City OK 73111. (405)478-2250. Contact: Marsi Thompson, public relations director. Estab. 1961. Annual award.
Purpose: "To honor outstanding quality in literature."
Requirements: Previously published submissions. Submissions are to be published during the previous calendar year.
Award: The Wrangler, a replica of a C.M. Russell Bronze.
Information: Judged by a panel. Entry deadline: January 31. No entry fee. Entry forms or rules for SASE. Looking for "stories that best capture the spirit of the West." Receives about 200 entries.

WORD BEAT PRESS FICTION CHAPBOOK COMPETITION, Word Beat Press, Box 10509, Tallahassee FL 32302. Contact: Allen Woodman, editor. Estab. 1982. Annual award.
Purpose: "To publish quality fiction chapbooks."
Requirements: "Stories previously published may be included, but credit must be given."
Award: $100 and 10 copies of publication. All finalists, not just winner, will be considered for publication.
Information: "Janet Burroway, poet and novelist, is the judge for 1983; Eve Shelnutt is judge for 1984. Each year a different nationally recognized author will judge." Entry deadline: March 15. Entry fee: $5. Entry forms or rules for SASE. Looking for "40 to 90 typed, double-spaced, manuscript pages of fiction. This can be any number of short stories or short-shorts. We will also consider novellas."

WQ EDITORS' PRIZE, *Cross-Canada Writers' Quarterly*, Box 277, Station F, Toronto, Ontario, Canada M4Y 2L7. Contact: Ted Plantos, editor. Estab. 1981. Annual award.

Purpose: "To encourage and publicize the best in new Canadian fiction writing."
Requirements: Unpublished submissions.
Award: Cash award plus publication of the 1st and 2nd prize winner in *Cross-Canada Writers' Quarterly*.
Information: Judged by a panel of magazine editors. Entry deadline: variable. "We plan the award to coincide with a particular issue of the magazine, which can vary from year to year. Details are announced in a preceding issue. Entry fee will vary from contest to contest, since we hold the event annually only. However, the fee is nominal." Details are also announced in a preceding issue of the magazine. The competition is *limited to subscribers*. "Stories must demonstrate good handling of characterization, setting, plot and dialogue. Theme and approach should be fresh and original."

WRITER'S DIGEST ANNUAL WRITING COMPETITION (Short Story Division), *Writer's Digest*, WD Writing Competition, 9933 Alliance Rd., Cincinnati OH 45242. (513)984-0717.
Requirements: Unpublished submissions. Deadline entry: Midnight June 1. All entries must be original, unpublished, and not previously submitted to a *Writer's Digest* contest. Short story: 2,000 words maximum, one entry only. Entry form must accompany ms. No acknowledgment will be made of receipt of mss nor will mss be returned. Enclosure of SASE will disqualify entry.
Award: Cash ($500), electric typewriters, plaques, and certificates of recognition. Names of Grand Prize winner and top 100 winners are announced in the October issue of *Writer's Digest*.
Information: Send SASE to *WD* Writing Competition for rules and entry form.

YOUNG AMBASSADOR CONTEST, *Young Ambassador* Magazine, Box 82808, Lincoln NE 68501. (402)474-4567. Contact: David Lambert, managing editor. Annual contest.
Purpose: "To give teens (up to 17 years) an opportunity to use their talents and compete with their peers."
Requirements: Submissions must be original and previously unpublished. "Story must have spiritual emphasis. Up to 1,800 words."
Award: "Payment for story comparable to our payment for regular freelance fiction."
Information: Judged by *Young Ambassador* staff members. Entry deadline: April 15. No entry fee. Entry forms or rules for SASE. Contest rules for 1983 in the October 1982 issue. Number of entries varies; sometimes 100-200. "Some mss are very good; some are not. Only young people through age 17 are eligible."

Contests and awards by invitation only

We have listed the following awards as incentive and interest to the individual writer, but they are exclusively *by invitation*. Current published work by authors is submitted by publishers or agents to these specialized contests. If you feel that your work will meet the requirements of a special competition, we suggest that you ask your publisher or agent to enter your material.

JANE ADDAMS CHILDREN'S BOOK AWARD, Jane Addams Peace Association and The Women's International League for Peace & Freedom, 1213 Race St., Philadelphia PA 19107. Contact: Annette C. Blank, 5477 Cedonia Ave., Baltimore MD 21206. Estab. 1953. Annual award.
Purpose: The award is made for a book that promotes the cause of peace, social justice, and world community.
Requirements: Published submissions. Announcement of the award is made Sept. 6 for a book published the previous year. Books submitted may be translated or published in English in other countries.

Award: A hand illuminated scroll; seals are placed on the book jacket by the publisher. Honor scrolls are awarded to books that merit this recognition.
Information: Choices are made by a national committee of people from various sections of the country concerned with children's books and their social values. Receives approximately 75 entries. "Quality has varied from very poor to excellent—books for very young children and from 6-9 need improving."

AMERICAN ACADEMY AND INSTITUTE OF ARTS AND LETTERS LITERARY AWARDS, 633 W. 155th St., New York NY 10032. Contact: Lydia Kaim, assistant to the executive director. Annual awards.
Purpose: To honor authors for excellence in literature and encourage them in their creative work.
Requirements: Previously published in book form. Selection is by the Academy Institute. *Applications not accepted.*
Award: Prizes vary. $5,000 in 1981 to winners (4 for fiction). Special awards include: 1) Richard Hinda Rosenthal Foundation Award: $3,000 for "an American work of literary fiction published during the preceding 12 months;" 2) Sue Kaufman Prize for First Fiction: $1,000 and 3) William Dean Howells Medal for Fiction (every 5 years). Award of Merit Medal for the Novel (every 5 years). The Harold D. Vursell Memorial Award: $5,000 to single out recent writing in book form that merits recognition for the quality of its prose style. The Morton Dauwen Zabel award: $2,500 for a writer of fiction of progressive, original and experimental tendencies (every 3 years).

THE AMERICAN BOOK AWARDS, Association of American Publishers, 1 Park Ave., New York NY 10016. Contact: Joan Cunliffe. (212)689-8920. Annual award.
Purpose: To honor distinguished hardcover and paperback books in fiction; children's books, first novel, general nonfiction, autobiography/biography, history, science, translation, poetry and original paperback.
Requirements: Previously published books. Deadline entry: August 15. Awards judged by 11-member panel: 3 authors, 2 critics, 2 editors/publishers, 2 libraries, 2 booksellers. In translation only—a special 5-member panel.
Award: $1,000 for each category, and a Louise Nevelson sculpture.
Information: Selections are submitted by publishers only. Receives over 1,300 entries.

LEBARON R. BARKER FICTION AWARD, Doubleday & Company, Inc., 245 Park Ave., New York NY 10017. Contact: Sally Arteseros, senior editor. Estab. 1973. Awarded at the discretion of the judges.
Purpose: To acknowledge and reward growth and development of fiction writers. In memory of LeBaron R. Barker, Jr., distinguished Doubleday editor.
Award: $2,500 prize.
Information: This award is given only to a novel published by Doubleday & Company. Authors cannot make submissions for the award. The award is given to a novel which represents a "giant step forward" for the author, a "distinct advance in the author's craftsmanship and approach to the art of fiction."

BOOKS IN CANADA AWARD FOR FIRST NOVELS, Books in Canada, 366 Adelaide St. E, Toronto, Ontario, Canada M5A 3X9. (416)363-5426. Contact: Michael Smith, editor. Estab. 1976. Annual award.
Purpose: "To promote and recognize Canadian writing."
Requirements: Published submissions from the previous calendar year.
Award: $1,000.
Information: Judged by a panel of 4 critics and novelists plus chairman from Books in Canada. No entry fee. Submissions are made by publishers. Contest is restricted to first novels in English published in Canada in the previous calendar year. Awards are announced in the April issue of Books in Canada each year, with comments by judges, etc.

BRANDEIS UNIVERSITY CREATIVE ARTS AWARDS, Commission Office, Irving 104, Brandeis University, Waltham MA 02254. (617)647-2296. Contact: Molly J. Dubis, executive secretary. Estab. 1957. Award offered every third year.
Purpose: "To recognize proven talent who have created a distinguished body of work and have been recognized as leaders in their art form or show impressive ability, artistic breakthrough for younger artists."
Requirements: No applications accepted. Jury decisions only.
Award: $2,500 plus citation/medal.
Information: Judged by professional jurors chosen by the Creative Arts Awards commission. No applications accepted.

JOHN W. CAMPBELL AWARD, World Science Fiction Convention, c/o Howard DeVore, 4705 Weddel St., Dearborn Heights MI 48125.
Purpose: To award the best new writer in science fiction.
Requirements: Previously published submissions in the field of science fiction or fantasy.
Award: Award is associated with the Hugo Science Fiction Achievement Awards.
Information: Members of the World Science Fiction Convention *nominate* contestants by ballot. Writers may not nominate their own work.

CANADA COUNCIL CHILDREN'S LITERATURE PRIZES, Canada Council, 255 Albert St., Ottawa, Ontario, Canada K1P 5V8. Contact: Senior English Writer. Estab. 1975. Four annual awards (two for text; two for illustrations).
Purpose: "To honor the Canadian writers and illustrators of books for young people published during the preceding year."
Requirements: "All Canadian books for children published during the preceding year are considered by two independent juries of Canadian experts in children's literature (one for English-language works, one for French-language works). No entry forms are required."
Award: $5,000 each.
Information: Judged on excellence. "In recent years there have been from 50-100 of these books."

CANADIAN FICTION MAGAZINE CONTRIBUTOR'S PRIZE, *Canadian Fiction Magazine*, Box 946, Station F, Toronto, Canada M4Y 2N9. Contact: Geoffrey Hancock, editor-in-chief. Estab. 1975. Annual award.
Purpose: To celebrate the best story published in either French or English during the preceding year.
Requirements: Unpublished submissions only. All manuscripts published in *CFM* are eligible. Judged by editor-in-chief. Deadline: August 15.
Award: $250, public announcement, photograph. Prize winners are often republished in Best Canadian or American short story anthologies.
Information: "Looking for contemporary creative writing of the highest possible literary standards. Previous winners include Leon Rooke, Ann Copeland, John Metcalf, W.P. Kinsella, Mavis Gallant, David Sharpe, Keath Fraser and Guy Vanderhaeghe." Receives approximately 1,200 entries.

CANADIAN LIBRARY ASSOCIATION BOOK OF THE YEAR FOR CHILDREN AWARD, 151 Sparks St., Ottawa, Ontario, Canada K1P 5E3. Estab. 1947. Annual award.
Purpose: "To encourage the writing and publishing of children's books in Canada."
Requirements: Published submissions during the calendar year preceeding the announcement of the award.
Award: Specially designed and engraved medals presented at annual banquet.
Information: Judged by a national committee of professionally qualified children's librarians who select titles and judge the winners.

CHILD STUDY CHILDREN'S BOOK AWARD, Child Study Children's Book Award, Committee at Bank St. College, 610 W. 112th St., New York NY 10025. Contact: Josette Frank, executive editor. Estab. 1943. Annual award.
Purpose: "To honor a book for children or young people which deals realistically with problems in their world. It may concern universal, personal or emotional problems."
Requirements: Only books sent by publishers for review are considered. No personal submissions. Books must be published within current calendar year. Our committee consists of volunteers who meet all year. It includes librarians, teachers, administrators, writers, illustrators, parents, students, etc.
Award: Certificate. Cash prize.

DOROTHY CANFIELD FISHER AWARD, Vermont Congress of Parents and Teachers and Vermont Department of Libraries, 41 Kingsland Terrace, Burlington VT 05401. Contact: Virginia Golodetz, Chairperson. Estab. 1957. Annual award.
Purpose: "To encourage Vermont school children to become enthusiastic and discriminating readers and to honor the memory of one of Vermont's most distinguished and beloved literary figures."
Requirements: "Publishers send the committee review copies of books to consider. Only books of the current publishing year can be considered for next year's award. Master list of titles is drawn up in late February or March each year. Children vote each year in the Spring and the award is given before the school year ends."
Award: Illuminated scroll.
Information: Judged by a committee of eight librarians, teachers and parents. Submissions must be "written by living American authors, be suitable for children in grades 4-8, and have literary merit. Can be nonfiction also." Receives about 600 entries.

GREAT LAKES COLLEGES ASSOCIATION NEW WRITERS AWARDS, Great Lakes Colleges Association, Wabash College, Crawfordsville IN 47933. Contact: Donald W. Baker, director. Estab. 1969. Annual award.
Purpose: "To recognize good young writers, promote and encourage interest in good literature."
Requirements: Submissions previously published "during the year preceding each year's February 28 deadline for entry, or the following spring." Award judged by critics and writers in residence at Great Lakes Colleges Association colleges and universities. Entry form or rules for SASE.
Award: "Invited tour of up to twelve Great Lakes Colleges (usually 7 or 8) with honoraria and expenses paid."
Information: Looking for "quality. Entries in fiction (there is also a poetry section) must be novels or volumes of short stories already published, and must be submitted (four copies) *by publishers only*—but this may include privately published books." Number of entries varies; 27 volumes of fiction last year.

ERNEST HEMINGWAY FOUNDATION AWARD, PEN American Center, 47 5th Ave., New York NY 10003. Contact: John Morrone, coordinator of programs. Estab. 1976. Annual award.
Purpose: "To give beginning writers recognition and encouragement and to stimulate interest in first novels among publishers and readers."
Requirements: Submissions previously published during calendar year under consideration. Deadline entry: December 31. Entry form or rules for SASE.
Award: $7,500.
Information: "The Ernest Hemingway Foundation Award is given to an American author of the best first-published booklength work of fiction published by an established publishing house in the US each calendar year."

awards

THE 'HUGO' AWARD (Science Fiction Achievement Award), The World Science Fiction Convention, c/o Howard DeVore, 4705 Weddel St., Dearborn Heights MI 48125. Temporary; address changes each year.
Purpose: "To recognize the best writing in various categories related to science fiction and fantasy."
Requirements: The award is voted on by ballot by the members of the World Science Fiction Convention from previously published material of professional publications. Writers may not nominate their own work.
Award: Metal spaceship 15 inches high. "Winning the award almost always results in reprints of the original material and increased payment. Winning a 'Hugo' in the novel category frequently results in additional payment of $10,000-$20,000 from future publishers."
Information: "Some titles in the novel category have remained in print almost continuously for some 20 years and are frequently reprinted in foreign editions."

IRISH AMERICAN CULTURAL INSTITUTE FICTION AWARD, Irish American Cultural Institute, 683 Osceola Ave., St. Paul MN 55105. Contact: President. Estab. 1980. Biannual award.
Purpose: "To stimulate writing about Irish-American life. The first award will be made in 1982."
Requirements: Previously published material. Deadline entry: June 30 each biennium. "The book will be chosen from published books dealing with Irish-Americans in the late 18th century colonies or states. It will be the responsibility of publishers to submit their nominations (in the form of published books—proof copy acceptable if the work has not yet 'hit the streets')."
Award: $5,000 outright.
Information: "The Irish American Cultural Institute is a public foundation that already makes annual literary awards in Ireland. This new fiction award will be the first made in the US specifically for an Irish-related novel. Looking for excellence of writing and insightful understanding of the Irish-American life of the period."

JANET HEIDINGER KAFKA PRIZE IN FICTION BY AMERICAN WOMEN, University of Rochester: Annual Writers Workshop & Department of English, University College, University of Rochester, Rochester NY 14627. Contact: Mrs. Rita Julian, assistant dean. Estab. 1976. Annual award.
Purpose: "The prize will be awarded (no more than once a year) to a woman citizen of the US who has written the best book-length published work of prose fiction, whether novel, short stories, or experimental writing."
Requirements: Previously published material during the calendar year in which it is submitted. Deadline entry: December 31. Entry forms are distributed to publishers. Entries evaluated by 5 jurors. "Works written primarily for children and vanity house publication will not be considered. Mss must be submitted by the publishers."
Information: Looking for "literary quality." Receives 40-50 entries.

ROBERT F. KENNEDY BOOK AWARDS, 4014 49th St. NW, Washington DC 20016. (202)362-0515. Contact: Ms. Coates Redmon. Endowed by Arthur Schlesinger, Jr., from proceeds of his biography, *Robert Kennedy and His Times*. Annual award.
Purpose: To award the author of a book that best honors the causes that concerned Robert F. Kennedy.
Requirements: Previously published submissions during the calendar year. Deadline: December 31. The 2nd Annual RFK Book Awards contest was judged by Patt Derian, John Bartlow Martin, Louis Martin and Budd Schulberg (for books published in 1981). The winners: a double first prize to Peter S. Prescott for *The Child Savers* (Knopf) and Janet Sharp Hermann for *The Pursuit of a Dream* (Oxford).
Award: $2,500 cash prize is awarded in the spring.
Information: Looking for "a work of literary merit in fact or fiction that shows compassion for

the poor or powerless or those suffering from injustice. In the first year of contest, 105 entries were received.''

LOS ANGELES TIMES BOOK PRIZES, *L.A. Times*, Book Review, Times Mirror Square, Los Angeles CA 90053. (213)972-7777. Contact: Art Seidenbaum, book editor. Estab. 1980. Annual award.
Purpose: ''To recognize finest books published each year.''
Requirements: Previously published submissions between September 1 to September 1.
Award: $1,000 cash prize plus a handmade, leather-bound version of the winning book.
Information: Judged by anonymous judges outside the newspaper. Entry is by nomination by 80 reviewers: publishers, editors; writers are not invited to enter. No entry fee. Looking for excellence.

NATIONAL JEWISH BOOK AWARDS, JWB Jewish Book Council, 15 E. 26th St., New York NY 10010. Contact: Ruth Frank, director. Annual award.
Purpose: ''To promote greater awareness of Jewish-American literary creativity.''
Requirements: Previously published submissions in English only by a US or Canadian author/translator. Submissions must be during the calendar year. Award judged by authors/scholars. Awards announced in spring.
Award: $500 to the author/translator plus citation to publisher. Awards include Children's Literature William (Zev) Frank Memorial Award (this award will be given to the author of a children's book on a Jewish theme); Children's Picture Book Marcia and Louis Posner Award (this award will be given to the author and illustrator of a children's book on a Jewish theme in which the illustrations are an intrinsic part of the text); William and Janice Epstein Award for Jewish Fiction (this award will be given to the author of a book of fiction of Jewish interest, either a novel or a collection of short stories); and The Workmen's Circle Yiddish Literature Award (this award will be given to the author of a book of literary merit in the Yiddish language, works of fiction, poetry, essays and memoirs are eligible).

NATIONAL MAGAZINE AWARD, Fiction category. Sponsored by the American Society of Magazine Editors, administered by the Columbia Graduate School of Journalism, Room 706, Columbia University, New York NY 10027. Annual award.
Purpose: To encourage imagination and innovation along with editorial responsibility and integrity.
Requirements: Must be published in a magazine in the calendar year previous to award date (e.g., published in 1982 for April 1983 award date). Receives approximately 70 entries for fiction. Entries must be submitted through the editor of the magazine in which story has been published.
Award: Winning magazine will receive a silver plaque and reproduction of Alexander Calder's stabile ''Elephant.'' Certificates to authors.

NATIONAL MEDAL FOR LITERATURE, The American Book Awards, 1 Park Ave., New York NY 10016. Contact: Joan Cunliffe. Annual award.
Purpose: ''Prestigious literary award conferred on a living American writer for his or her continuing contribution to American letters.''
Award: $15,000 and a bronze medal.
Information: Award is endowed by the Guinzburg Fund, in memory of Harold K. Guinzburg, founder of The Viking Press. Recipients include Eudora Welty, Thornton Wilder, Conrad Aiken, E.B. White, and others. Candidates nominated by special committee.

NEBULA AWARD, Science Fiction Writers of America, 68 Countryside Apts., Hackettstown NJ 07840.
Purpose: To honor outstanding writing in science fiction and fantasy.
Requirements: Previously published work (science fiction and fantasy of various lengths).
Award: Lucite trophies designed by Judith Blish.

awards

Information: Recommendations, nominations, and final ballot casting are all done by active members of Science Fiction Writers of America, Inc. "On the average there are between 150 and 200 works of various lengths (short story, novella, novelette, and novel) recommended. Only 5 or 6 in each category make the final ballot."

THE NENE AWARD, Hawaii Association of School Librarians and Children's and Youth Section, Hawaii Library Association, Liliha Library, 1515 Liliha St., Honolulu HI 96817. Contact: Mrs. Miriam Sato, chairperson (chairperson changes annually). Estab. 1964. Annual award.
Purpose: "To help the children of Hawaii become acquainted with the best contemporary writers of fiction for children; to become aware of the qualities that make a good book; to choose the best rather than the mediocre; and to honor an author whose book has been enjoyed by the children of Hawaii."
Award: Koa plaque.
Information: Judged by the children of Hawaii. No entry fee. The Nene Committee chooses the entries for each year. Looking for the best of children's fiction which is also enjoyed by the children. "Beverly Cleary has been awarded the prize 5 times; her books are constantly read."

NEUSTADT INTERNATIONAL PRIZE FOR LITERATURE, *World Literature Today*, 110 Monnet Hall, University of Oklahoma, Norman OK 73019. Contact: Dr. Ivar Ivask, director. Estab. 1970. Biennial award.
Purpose: To recognize distinguished and continuing achievement in fiction, poetry, or drama.
Award: $25,000, an eagle feather cast in silver, an award certificate and a special issue of *WLT*.
Information: "We are looking for outstanding accomplishment in world literature. The Neustadt Prize is not open to application. Nominations are made only by members of the international jury, which changes for each award. Jury meetings are held in February of even-numbered years. Unsolicited manuscripts, whether published or unpublished, cannot be considered. Previous laureates: Elizabeth Bishop (USA), 1976; Czeslaw Milosz (Poland/USA), 1978; and Josef Skvorecký (Czechoslovakia/Canada), 1980; Octavio Paz (Mexico), 1982."

JOHN NEWBERY AWARD, American Library Association (ALA) Awards and Citations Program, Association for Library Services to Children, 50 E. Huron St., Chicago IL 60611. Annual award.
Requirements: Entry restricted to US citizen-resident. Nomination by ALA members only.
Award: Medal.

NOBEL PRIZE FOR LITERATURE, Swedish Academy, Kallagrand 4, Borshuset, 11129 Stockholm, Sweden. Estab. 1901. Annual award.
Requirements: Entries restricted; nomination by Swedish academy.
Award: Gold medal, diploma and 725,000 kroner to author of international reputation for total literary output.
Information: Considered the most prestigious literary award.

PEN AMERICAN CENTER AWARDS, 47 5th Ave., New York NY 10003. Annual award.
Requirements: Previously published submissions. Decisions for all prizes are made by a panel of judges appointed by the Executive Board of PEN.
Award: Awards include: Ernest Hemingway Foundation Award, $7,500; PEN Translation Prize: $1,000 annually; PEN Writing Awards for Prisoners: a total of $525 is awarded annually for fiction, poetry, nonfiction; and The PEN Faulkner Award: $5,000. (See separate listings.)

THE PEN FAULKNER AWARD, c/o Folger Shakespear Library, 201 E. Capitol St. SE, Washington DC 20003. Attention: Jean Nordhous. American Center, 47 5th Ave., New York NY 10003. (212)255-1977. Estab. 1980. Annual award.
Purpose: "To award the most distinguished book length work of fiction published by an American writer. First award presented April 18, 1981."

Requirements: Published submissions only. Publishers submit four copies of eligible titles published the preceding year. No juvenile. Authors must be American citizens or permanent residents of the US. Book award judged by three writers chosen by the Trustees of the Award.
Award: $5,000.
Information: This new annual award which "reflects the truly national character of our literary talent" is judged by a panel of writers' peers. Receives approximately 250 entries.

MAXWELL PERKINS PRIZE, Charles Scribner's Sons, 597 5th Ave., New York NY 10017. (212)486-2888.
Purpose: "To find talented writers never before published and encourage beginning authors. Given to a first work of fiction about the American experience."
Requirements: Unpublished submissions.
Award: $10,000—$5,000 against royalties, $5,000 cash prize.
Information: Entry deadline: September 30. No entry fee. Looking for "American or US resident writing on some aspect of American life." No unsolicited material accepted. Must enter via agent or invitation from a Scribner editor.

PLAYBOY'S ANNUAL AWARDS, *Playboy Magazine*, 919 N. Michigan Ave., Chicago IL 60611. Estab. 1956. Annual award.
Purpose: To acknowledge and award *Playboy* contributors.
Requirements: Winners are selected by the magazine staff. Only material published in the magazine during the calendar year is considered. This is not an open competition.
Award: $1000 and a medallion.

PRESIDENT'S AWARD, *The Ohio Journal*, Ohio State University Dept. of English, 164 W. 17th Ave., Columbus OH 43210. Contact: William Allen, editor. Estab. 1978. Annual award.
Purpose: To acknowledge and compensate the most outstanding fiction and poetry contribution of the year published in *The Ohio Journal*.
Requirements: Previously published submissions in *The Ohio Journal*. Deadline entry: August 15. Submit fiction to be considered for publication. All published fiction is automatically entered. "Various famous authors judge our competition; most recently, Mike Curtis of *The Atlantic Monthly*." Guidelines available. Sample copy of magazine, $2.
Award: $100.
Information: Looking for outstanding fiction.

PRIZE STORIES: THE O. HENRY AWARDS, Doubleday & Company, Inc., 245 Park Avenue, New York NY 10017. Contact: Sally Arteseros, senior editor. Estab. 1919. Annual award.
Purpose: To honor the memory of O. Henry with a sampling of outstanding short stories and to make these stories better known to the public. These awards are published by Doubleday every spring.
Requirements: Previously published submissions. "All selections are made by the editor of the volume, William Abrahams. No stories may be submitted. Mr. Abrahams reads several hundred magazines (all listed in the back of the volume) to select the 20 or so finest (published) American stories."

PULITZER PRIZE IN FICTION, Columbia University, Graduate School of Journalism, 702 Journalism Bldg., New York NY 10027. Contact: Robert C. Christopher. Estab. 1917 by Joseph Pulitzer. Annual award.
Purpose: For distinguished fiction published in book form during the year by an American author, preferably dealing with American life.
Requirements: 4 copies of the book, entry form, biography and photo of author. Open to American authors. Deadline entry: November 1.
Award: $1,000.
Information: Over 500 books for five categories: fiction, history, biography, poetry, nonfiction.

PUSHCART PRIZE, Pushcart Press, Box 380, Wainscott NY 11975. Contact: Bill Henderson, editor. Annual award.
Purpose: To publish and recognize the best of small press literary work.
Requirements: Previously published submissions; books or short stories on any subject or short self-contained sections. Must have been published during the current calendar year. Deadline: Oct. 15. Nomination by small press publishers/editors only. Award judged by 150 editors.
Award: Publication in *Pushcart Prize: Best of the Small Presses* plus $100 to lead story.

REGINA MEDAL AWARD, Catholic Library Association, 461 W. Lancaster Ave., Haverford PA 19041. Contact: Matthew R. Wilt, executive director. Estab. 1959. Annual award.
Purpose: To honor a continued distinguished contribution to children's literature.
Award: Silver medal. Award given during Easter week.
Information: Looking for excellence. Selection by a special committee; nominees are suggested by the Catholic Library Association Membership.

SCRIBNER CRIME NOVEL AWARD, Charles Scribner's Sons, 597 5th Ave., New York NY 10017. (212)986-2888.
Purpose: "To find talented writers never before published and encourage beginning authors." Award given to a first mystery.
Requirements: Unpublished submissions. "No unsolicited material accepted. Must enter via agent or invitation from a Scribner editor."
Award: $7,500—$5,000 as an advance against royalties; $2,500 cash prize.
Information: Entry deadline: September 30. No entry fee. Contestant must be American or permanent US resident. "Ms must be of classic detection, historical reconstructions, fictionalized 'true crime,' espionage, police procedurals, private-eye. No supernatural, pastiche, or parody of an established character in fiction."

CHARLIE MAY SIMON BOOK AWARD, Arkansas Department of Education, Elementary Council, Arch Ford Bldg., Capitol Mall, Division of Instruction, Room 301B, Little Rock AR 72201. (501)371-1861. Contact: Joseph R. Foster, coordinator of elementary education. Estab. 1971. Annual award.
Purpose: "To encourage reading by children in quality children's literature."
Requirements: Previously published submissions.
Award: Medalion.
Information: Judged by children in grades four, five and six in Arkansas elementary schools. Entry deadline: Dec. 31. No entry fee. "The committee doesn't accept requests from authors. They will look at booklists of books produced during the previous year and check recommendations from the following sources; *Booklist, Bulletin of the Center for Children's Books, Children's Catalog, Elementary School Library Journal, Hornbook, Library of Congress Children's Books, School Library Journal*. Most authors receiving this award have been established writers."

THE KENNETH B. SMILEN/PRESENT TENSE LITERARY AWARD, *Present Tense Magazine*, 165 E. 56th St., New York NY 10022. (212)751-4000. Contact: Murray Polner, editor. Estab. 1980. Annual award.
Purpose: "To encourage the flourishing of Jewish literary and intellectual life by stimulating the writing of significant, serious works with Jewish themes."
Requirements: Submissions are to be previously published during the year immediately preceding the granting of awards.
Award: $1,000 for seven categories, one of which is for fiction.
Information: Judged by 3 eminent writers, chosen each year. Entry deadline: December 31. No entry fee. Nominations may only be made by the publisher. Receives 200-300 entries.

MARK TWAIN AWARD, Missouri Association of School Librarians. Contact: Phillip A. Sadler, Mark Twain Award chairperson, Central Missouri State University, Warrensburg MO 64093. Estab. 1970. Annual award.

Close-up

Susanne Kirk
Scribner Crime Novel Award,
Maxwell Perkins Prize

Susanne Kirk spent nine years in Hong Kong, Viet Nam and Japan as a foreign correspondent and editor. She returned to New York and a new job at Scribners eight years ago "to settle down."

Settling down, as she described her job in her office overlooking Fifth Avenue, means a daily agenda of reading manuscripts and queries, editing her assigned titles, meeting and working with her authors, thinking up new ideas for books, reading magazines to find new writers, and helping to judge the manuscripts for the two new Scribner prizes: the Maxwell Perkins Prize for First Novels and the Scribner Crime Novel Award.

The senior editor says, "we do actively search for mysteries and first novels here at Scribners," the historic publishing house of such literary greats as Hemingway, Faulkner, Wolfe and Maxwell Perkins. Hence the reasons for initiating in 1982 the two awards which brought in about 1,500 manuscripts that first year. Such overwhelming response required revised rules the second year; manuscripts now *must* be agented or submitted by invitation of Scribner editors.

For years mysteries have been a staple at Scribners. Entries for the Crime Novel Award may include: thrillers, spy novels, murder mysteries, private eye/detective/investigator stories, true crime, and police procedurals. The novels can repeat a theme, but, advises Kirk, they must be intricately plotted, demonstrate original, likable characters and build good suspense.

New Scribner's authors are signed on from the competition—and also via queries, the preferred form of contact. A query should be no more than two pages, freshly-typed and well-written with good syntax, style and no misspellings. A sloppily prepared query suggests that the manuscript will also contain mistakes and be time-consuming to edit.

Kirk's other recommendations about queries: Get to the point; a few lines about the novel will suffice. "State your writing qualifications—background and publishing experience, etc.—to make you stand out from the next person. . . . Be truthful, and try *not* to oversell, be presumptuous or let your ego get in the way." Also, it helps to suggest the book's audience.

At Scribners, queries not only prompt a faster response (than a manuscript) but they are more likely to be referred to the right editor with that particular expertise. Once the query is okayed, editors will ask for sample chapters. The final decision to publish is made by Charles Scribner Jr., chairman of the company.

"There's often great distance between liking a query and actually publishing the novel," states Kirk. Only about five percent of the queries responded to positively will result in a published author. Thus it's important, Kirk stresses, to be realistic. Understand that the market is difficult. Before submitting your manuscript, read the market books, go to the bookstores to see what is selling, and analyze the publisher thoroughly to be sure it is interested in your kind of book.

awards

Purpose: To introduce children to the best of current literature for children and to stimulate reading.
Requirements: Previously published submissions. A committee selects the books nominated for the award; children throughout the state vote to choose a winner from the committee's list. Books must be published two years prior to nomination for the award list. Publishers may send books they wish to nominate for the list to the chairperson.
Award: A bronze bust of Mark Twain, created by Barbara Shanklin, a Missouri sculptor.
Information: 1) Books should be of interest to children in grades 3 through 8; 2) written by an author living in the US; 3) of literary value which may enrich children's personal lives.

HAROLD D. VURSELL MEMORIAL AWARD, American Academy and Institute of Arts and Letters, 633 W. 155th St., New York NY 10032. (212)368-5900. Estab. 1978. Annual award.
Purpose: "To single out recent writing in book form that merits recognition for the quality of its prose style. It may be given for a work of fiction, biography, history, criticism, belles lettres, memoir, journal or a work of translation."
Requirements: Previously published submissions.
Award: $5,000.
Information: Judged by a 7-member jury composed of members of the Department of Literature of the American Academy and Institute of Arts and Letters. **No applications accepted**.

MAJORIE PEABODY WAITE AWARD, American Academy and Institute of Arts and Letters, 633 W. 155th St., New York NY 10032. (212)368-5900. Estab. 1956. Awarded every third year to a writer.
Purpose: "Conferred to an older person for continuing achievement and integrity in his art, given in rotation to an artist, a composer and a writer."
Requirements: Previously published submissions.
Award: $1,500.
Information: Judged by a 7-member jury composed of members of the Department of Literature of the American Academy and Institute of Arts and Letters. **No applications accepted**.

WILLIAM ALLEN WHITE CHILDREN'S BOOK AWARD, Emporia State University, 1200 Commercial, Emporia KS 66801. Contact: Mary E. Bogan, executive secretary. Estab. 1952. Annual award.
Purpose: To honor the memory of one of the state's most distinguished citizens by encouraging the boys and girls of Kansas to read and enjoy good books.
Requirements: "We do not accept submissions from authors or publishers."
Award: Bronze medal.
Information: The White Award Book Selection Committee looks for excellence of literary quality in fiction, poetry and nonfiction appropriate for 4th through 8th graders. All nominations to the annual White Award master list must be made by a member of the White Award Book Selection Committee.

LAURA INGALLS WILDER AWARD, American Library Association/Association for Library Service to Children, 50 E. Huron St., Chicago IL 60611. Award offered every 3 years.
Purpose: "To honor a significant body of work for children for illustration, fiction or nonfiction."
Award: Bronze Medal.
Information: Voted on by members of Association for Library Service to Children.

MORTON DAUWEN ZABEL AWARD, American Academy and Institute of Arts and Letters, 633 W. 155th St., New York NY 10032. (212)368-5900. Estab. 1969. Awarded annually.
Purpose: "To honor writers of progressive, original and experimental tendencies."
Requirements: Previously published submissions.
Award: $2,500.

Information: Judged by 7-member jury composed of members of the Department of Literature of the American Academy and Institute of Arts and Letters (Department of Literature). Individual submissions not accepted.

> 66 *Art is not difficult because it wishes to be difficult, rather because it wishes to be art. However much the writer might long to be in his work, simple, honest, straightforward, these virtues are no longer available to him. He discovers that in being simple, honest, straightforward, nothing much happens: He speaks the unspeakable, whereas we are looking for the as-yet-unspeakable, the as-yet unspoken.*
> **—Donald Barthelme** 99

Agents east

by Jean M. Fredette

As little boys and girls, literary agents probably once aspired to be great writers, editors, lawyers, actors. Most likely *anything* but what they are today—and undoubtedly not one ever said, "When I grow up, I'm going to be an agent."

Agenting is seldom if ever planned; it happens. There are no preparatory schools or programs in universities, and in New York no license or certification is required. Circumstances, contacts, literary interests and experience dictate an agent's career choice.

"Anyone can hang up a shingle and announce, 'I'm a literary agent,' " says Peter Skolnik of Sanford J. Greenburger Associates and former president of the Independent Literary Agents Association (ILAA), "politicians, garment workers, delicatessen owners—it's an open field." Abe Lastfogel, former chairman of the William Morris Agency, concurs: "The easiest thing in the world to become and the hardest thing to remain, is an agent."

Particularly in the current economy. To be an agent today means rolling with the publishing punches and adapting to the mercurial and fluid business trends which decide the kind and number of books sold: the Pac-Man-like publishing conglomerate takeovers and the consolidation of smaller companies and imprints; the editor chess game of who-went-with-which-publishing house and who-got-checkmated; and the new and improved video and cable technologies which involve more complicated author rights to consider. To succeed—even survive—an agent must have a memory of silicon software. Not to mention high levels of energy, motivation and enthusiasm to get through the long frenetic days.

Jean Fredette was assistant editor for the first edition of Fiction Writer's Market *in 1981 and is currently the editor. She has contributed to* Writer's Digest, Writer's Yearbook, *local and foreign publications.*

Connecting with clients

In times like these, what keeps an agent going? How does an agency function? What made him/her get into the business in the first place? To answer these questions and others, *Fiction Writer's Market* talked to literary agents in New York from four reputable, well-known agencies of different sizes, those recommended by writers, publishers, editors and their peers.

Business styles and background vary greatly, but there are certain aspects of agenting about which all agents agree. The two particular kicks in the business are selling something for a person who has never sold before, and selling something nobody wants, which can happen in a trendy marketplace on the 20th or even 40th try. More basically, agents hope for a big book, a promising author, an unknown whose literary life they can help copyright into bestsellerdom, a long fruitful career, or at least a first sale with potential.

"I'm not really happy unless I can launch a new and important writer every six months," says Al Zuckerman, head of Writers House and current president of ILAA. New talent is the lifeblood of the entire publishing industry because even blockbuster novelists do die eventually. The process often starts in the literary agency.

There's a "crying hunger" for a good book, but it's *quality* all agents demand. Ninety-nine percent of the material, estimates one New York agent, is *not* quality. Writers can't get an agent, Zuckerman goes on to say, "because they can't write a good book—or one in tune with the marketplace." If a listing in a market or reference book states that the agency is taking on new clients, and a writer receives a returned manuscript stamped with "Sorry—not taking new clients at this time," that statement, or an equivalent, means quite euphemistically several things: that the subject is not appropriate, the writing is amateurish, the story is poorly constructed, the theme is unoriginal or overworked, the material is simply not right for the agent, or a variety of reasons. Such a response is a genteel form of rejection.

How do agents connect with good clients? There is often an active search: speaking or appearing at writers conferences, scouting publications, attending national and international book fairs. Or writers are referred by clients, editors, publishers. Occasionally successful author/agent relationships evolve from inquiries that have come in cold, but very seldom is there a bond resulting from an unsolicited manuscript, a submission policy generally *not* encouraged. Entrée is only possible with professionally prepared correspondence, neatly typed and error-free, or rejection is inevitable. There are seldom second chances with agents.

Agent research

Agents themselves admit that getting an agent is tough. But so is the entire publishing process, and it may be even more difficult getting an editor without an agent's help. Not all publishers read slush piles, the unsolicited (over-the-transom) manuscripts because the process requires the hiring-on of extra help to sort through and read the material. The few rare good works readers find do not justify the expense. That's where the agent comes in. She/he (more often she: It's about three-to-one, women to men in the industry) will read the material, evaluate the market potential for the manuscript and plan a subsequent plan or strategy for selling the work, thus leaving the writer more creative time to write.

For the unpublished writer, finding a reputable agent is an even taller order, although as Bill Adler, agent and author of *Inside Publishing*, says, there has never, to his knowledge, been a literary agent scandal. Most authors' representatives are ethical and act professionally. "Reputable" by one definition can mean those agents which do not charge the unpublished writer a fee before publication (a reading fee, a marketing fee, a filing fee, etc.), a practice which neither the SAR (Society of Authors' Representatives) nor the ILAA condones. An agent's income, they collectively feel, is exclusively dependent on income *earned* from the writer.

How do writers find agents? First, with a little research. *Literary Market Place*, "the yellow pages of the American publishing industry," offers the most complete list of agencies and agents (over 270); and SAR (40 E. 49th St., New York NY 10017) and ILAA (21 W. 26th St., New York NY 10010) furnish their membership lists on request with *SASE*. *Writer's Market* and *Fiction Writer's Market* both provide addresses and market information about agencies not requiring pre-publication fees.

About half of the total number of agencies employ written contracts (versus verbal agreements); and 77% (as polled by the Authors Guild in 1981) find the 10% commission a manageable fee, if the editing of proposal or manuscript is not extensive. Most all agents edit work to a certain degree before the sale, a few continue the process during publication. Some follow trends exclusively, others stand by their convictions of merit. Most all seek new clients, and not a few charge reading fees.

There are the agent psychologists, the handholders, the mother confessors, the contract/rights specialists, the reserved, the conservative, and those with hype and flash.

Diversity and individuality mean a style of their own.

The Roslyn Targ Literary Agency

In New York agenting/publishing circles, Roslyn Targ's jaunty hat is as well known in the '80s as Hedda Hopper's was in the Hollywood '40s. Targ wears a lot of hats—out of the office and inside as well. As the sole agent in the Roslyn Targ Literary Agency, she is also a lawyer, an editor, a psychologist, a salesperson and a diplomat, the responsibilities an agent's role includes. But that is her choice. "I want to stay small," says Targ from her office on West 57th Street. "I'm not interested in becoming part of a conglomerate. . . . I'm a very definite person, and I know how I like to run things."

Targ's four-room office is almost Kafkaesque in setting with its floor to ceiling books and boxed manuscripts ("There are more in the storage room"). Interspersed are framed letters, photos from literary luminaries, posters, paintings, testimonial memorabilia to the 12 successful years Targ has had her agency under her own name.

The agency itself goes back to the mid-forties when Franz Horch, a Jewish refugee from Vienna, saw the need for more translation of American books into foreign languages. He set up shop, contacted famous American authors and established a considerable clientele (Thurber, E.B. White, John Dos Passos, Edna Ferber), whose royalties from foreign rights today provide a stable backlist for the agency. Targ, or Roz as she is called, has broadened that base tremendously with her own acquisitions, but she is still known as "the *grande dame* of foreign rights," a title she can rightfully employ when she conducts business from her desk in her large, imposing rattan peacock chair, the main focal point in her office.

Roslyn Targ went to work for Horch after graduation from Hunter College with a degree in economics. She became Horch's "girl Friday," assimilated her employer's experience over the years and combined a fine-tuned business acumen, her love of books and writers and dramatic flair for her own business.

"The excitement for me really is to find that unknown writer and to connect that writer with the right editor and publisher," says Targ. She speaks in superlatives of

Glennita Miller, one of her new young novelists, who debuts in early 1983 with *Keepers of the Kingdom*, a big novel about Africa that earned a hefty five-figure advance, an extraordinary sum for a first novel. Targ subsequently followed the sale through with the subsidiary and foreign rights, tasks she likes to do herself, that is, handle all the rights after the initial sale.

Glennita Miller's book is one of the rare over-the-ransom (query) success stories. Targ realized from the first page that the author was a born storyteller. "I'm not hungry," she admits, but she continues to seek new talent in fiction and nonfiction to add to her already sizable client list. She continually scans magazines and newspapers for articles and stories by gifted writers, those with possible potential for future books, and she follows up with a phone call to the publication to ascertain the status of the writer (Does he/she already have an agent?). Contacts and meetings at the annual Frankfurt Book Fair in October produce new clients, American and foreign. By July Targ had a full appointment book for that week of the conference with editors and publishers (British, French, Dutch, etc.).

Targ encourages queries ("with SASE, of course") *about the subject first*. Then, if interested, she will give the go-ahead to send on a few chapters or the entire manuscript. Unsolicited manuscripts are generally *not* successful, and an approach via phone is fairly taboo. Of course, *all* correspondence, letters, queries, she urges, should be representative of the professional work that is to follow.

Establishing personal relationships with her authors, the primary objective for Targ, is achieved by correspondence and phone calls, much of the day's work. Chemistry is terribly important, she stresses. "Next to the parent, lover, wife, husband, I think the agent is the most important element in the author's life. That chemistry better be right."

Finding an equally compatible editor for the author is also on order—or just keeping up with the current revolving door trend at publishing houses. "My God, you need a scorecard," Targ says of the editor turnover in the city. The frequent business lunch "away from the stilted office setting," most often at the nearby Russian Tearoom where Targ has her own table, is where she keeps tab on editor changes, personal interests and subject choices, material she stores in her mental archives for future sales. Evening cocktail and publishing parties are also information centers for news, trends, auctions, etc. Informal social events provide the opportunities to get to know publishers and editors— "from the chairman of the board down to the junior editor." Her submissions are based on total knowledge of the publishing house.

Beyond the initial shaping of the manuscript once the book/project is sold to a publisher, Targ generally leaves the editing to the contracted editor and intercedes only if called upon. She keeps touch with her authors regularly during all phases of writing with a quick phone call or a personal note to inquire about their book ideas, projects in action.

Like all businesses today, agenting is more involved, more of a science. Placing the novel is more complex and time-consuming than in recent years, Targ has found, because of the conglomerate bureaucracy, department specialization and resulting red tape. Tight-fisted publishers are slow to release advance money or royalty checks, and sometimes getting money from a foreign publisher is easier than from one down the street. The entire process is long, drawn out and frustrating—and waiting for a client's money requires many more hours of letter-writing, phone calls, maybe even a mailgram, or a business lunch to cajole stubborn editors into action.

Trends do govern decisions—and it's not just what's selling in the bookstores, says Targ. An agent must constantly be in touch with editors to find out what future trends they may see, particularly in nonfiction. In selling the book, the agent has to consider the timing of the project, the type of subject or treatment, the publication time involved (sometimes 24 months), what big authors or books at various houses are already contracted. Thus a writer in search of an agent should not submit the entire manuscript, but send a comprehensive outline plus one chapter if the author has no track record.

Once there is interest in the book from an editor, the negotiating begins. Knowing how far you can negotiate—that's where experience comes in,'' says Targ. Publishing company policies differ and it's important to know them all. Targ leaves the fine points in the contract to her assistant, one of her two staff members. A contract is drawn up to spell out what is good for the author, and what the obligations are for each.

Rising rents (tripled since 1974), spiraling phone and postage rates, the economic realities of business, have forced the agency's usual 10% commission to 15% sometimes, depending on the extent of the work, the amount of preparation before the manuscript is submitted to an editor. Of reading fees, Targ says, "I simply don't believe in them. If I don't want to take something on, I just won't do it." Her decision is usually made on the basis of the first 30 pages.

During the long full day—from her early morning exercises, through the morning mountain of mail, the myriad phone calls and meetings, to her midnight reading sessions—does Roslyn Targ give time to her new young writers? Yes, she vows, as much time as to the established ones. She is conscientious about returning all her calls, "to maintain that valued personal touch."

"How can I be in such a business?" she asks, and then answers. "I love it—with all its problems, and God knows there are plenty of problems. Especially now. I can't conceive of doing anything else."

Writers House

Writers House looks more like the setting of a Dickensian novel than the office of a literary agency. This noble building in lower Manhattan was once a counting house for the Astor family in the late 19th century, and is now a model of restored Victoriana. Even old Mr. Astor himself would nod approvingly at the period replicas, the patterned wood floors, the marble fireplaces.

Al Zuckerman, founder and president of the agency, is pleased himself—with his restoration project and with the rapid development of his business. In eight years, Writers House has earned a fine reputation in the publishing industry, and his staff, which now numbers 11, is growing.

It's 9 a.m. and Zuckerman is in his almost-ballroom-sized office. He sits at his massive mahogany desk with a cup of coffee and a Danish while he sorts through memos and mail. A so-called "routine day" is split 50-50 between agenting and managerial duties. But today is a little different. Ken Follett, Zuckerman's principal client, is coming in this morning from England to work on his new book: a nonfiction thriller set in Iran, with *The Bull and the Peacock* as its working title. At 9:30, Follett comes into the room unannounced. "Good morning," he booms, and his clipped British tones echo off the high ceiling. After some chatting and joking around, Zuckerman shows Follett to a conference room, where the two will spend the day editing the manuscript. Zuckerman enjoys editing and dissecting a book, but agents that edit are rare; few agents have the time or skill to edit work personally.

Al Zuckerman's comprehensive background in the media prepared him for his agent role. He attended the Yale School of Drama and stayed on to teach playwriting—

which is, he insists, the best apprenticeship for writers. "Playwriting, if studied serious-ly, is excellent preparation for novel-writing." The principles of dramatic construction—pace, action, excitement, dramatic focus, good characters, facile dia-logue—are techniques that novelists can and should acquire.

Zuckerman went on to write screenplays, soap operas, and finally *Head of the House*, a Jewish Godfather novel. While writing *Head of the House*, he decided *he* could be an agent. "I had been represented by agents as a dramatic writer and novelist, and I thought I knew more about writing than most of them." His confidence paid off; Writers House now represents about 200 writers.

Other Writers House agents also "grow up organically"; each begins as a secretary under Zuckerman's tutelage. This leads to one WH style, and "not a disparate collection of individuals," and that in turn leads to an unusual in-House cohesiveness and coopera-tion. Writers House is more like a home.

Merrilee Heifetz, in the adjacent office, is the most recent graduate of Zuckerman's informal school of agenting. She is talking on the phone, which is how she spends much of her day.

Writers looking for an agent should send "an intelligent query letter," with a syn-opsis and sample chapters, "something small I can get to," Heifetz says after she hangs up. She stresses the importance of presenting a professional package to potential buyers, whether the "buyer" is an agent or an editor. Thus, she follows her employer's tenets: the more complete the proposal/package, the better the chances for editor acceptance. What is a "complete proposal/package"? A thoroughly edited proposal, including an outline and sample chapters, presented with the aid of an artist or printer to give the editor ideas about how the final book could look.

WH represents about an equal number of fiction and nonfiction books, yet earns about 80% of its fees from fiction. One Ken Follett novel, for example, can bring in as much as 200 nonfiction books. WH charges a 10% commission—15% or 20% on books that need extensive editing.

Zuckerman believes strongly that writers should know what types of books are sell-ing. He says that, for instance, there's little publishing action for male action novels, ex-cluding those by Follett, Robert Ludlum and a handful of other thriller/action/suspense writers. In fact, says Zuckerman, *The Guns of Navarone* would not sell today. In gener-al, agents recommend that, to find out what sells today, writers scout bookstores, talk to librarians and bookstore owners, read trade magazines and books (including *Publishers Weekly*, *Library Journal*, *The New York Times*, *Writer's Digest*), or call an *assistant* to a book editor at a large publishing house to discuss the market.

And the writer's knowledge should go far beyond awareness of market trends. No book will sell easily, Zuckerman says, if its author hasn't gotten out into the world and out of "small-town" thinking. "A writer can't expect to write a big book if he hasn't somehow lived a big life," Zuckerman says. "He can't do it without life experience."

The Sterling Lord Agency

As the name might imply, Sterling Lord, Inc., is an agency of dignity and respecta-bility. Its address in the Madison Avenue high-rent district is as lofty as its name. Yet, the objectives of the agency are basic and down to earth.

Thirty-five years ago, Sterling Lord founded the agency, which now employs six agents who represent a sizable list of authors: from the novelists with the household names, to the lawyers, politicians and media personalities, to the not-so-well-known librarian heroes of serious literature. Among Lord's clients are Erica Jong, Ben Bradlee, F. Lee Bailey, Howard Fast, Jimmy Breslin, Arthur Koestler and Dick Schaap.

The Sterling Lord office complex reflects the agency's style. The decor of the modern interior is as conservative and low-key as the business style of the agents themselves. The staff strives to avoid the hype and publicity often associated with this high-visibility business. Only recently did Lord agents decide to appear at or speak at writers conferences and publishing-related functions.

Pat Berens, former assistant to Sterling Lord and now vice-president of the company, is in her office preparing her speech for a writers conference at the University of Rochester. She looks forward to the weekend and to spreading her enthusiasm for and interest in books. "I'm really a frustrated schoolteacher," she says, "and I *love* talking about the business."

Berens's entry into agenting was, like those of many other agents, "by accident." Studying for her doctorate in reformation history, she went to work as Sterling Lord's assistant when she found the job market in her field discouraging and tight. Lord was "a wonderful teacher," and within a year Berens was selling books on her own. She gradually developed her own list of clients, decided not to go back to school, and has since trained several of her own assistants in the Lord tradition.

For Pat Berens, it has been ten years of learning—and gaining respect and understanding for the writer's plight. "It is terribly difficult to write *anything*," she says. Even the much-maligned romances. She tells of an acquaintance, a woman who wanted Berens to read her romance manuscript. Berens consented and eventually sold the book. The woman's bridge club members decided that they would each follow suit and write a romance novel. They sent the manuscripts to Berens and they were amateurish, "horrible . . . . Any book is tough to write, if done well . . . . If someone says to me, 'I could do that easily,' I say, 'Try it!' "

Sterling Lord agents seek quality on every level, and generally decisions are not affected by market trends. If, for instance, an unusual literary novel comes in, Berens may approach a reputable small press or a university press, markets most agents won't pursue. Occasionally, a book Berens believes in can't be sold anywhere. "It happens—and it's heartbreaking." On the other hand, she once sold a book on the 22nd submission, "and the book made money."

Following trends and fads is not a foolproof marketing strategy, Berens insists. Generational novels, for example, may not be *au courant*—until someone comes out with a bestseller. Then everyone wants one, and the editors "run in packs," she says. "I want to sell a book on its merit, not the fad of the moment. And I'm not interested in an editor who won't take something not in vogue. It shows a lack of imagination." She admits that the economy has restrained editors, who must choose books carefully, but writing survived the Depression, and it will survive the recession. This is a difficult time in publishing, Lord agents agree, but it has always been difficult for first novels and serious work. The problem today, Berens explains, is that writers' expectations are too high. They read about the $500,000 advances and are disappointed to receive $7,500. "Take the offer," she advises. "Get published and get established."

Most of Berens's clients were referred to her by editors, other clients, or contacts from workshops or conferences like the one she is about to attend. Occasionally she has sold manuscripts she has received cold, but she prefers query letters that describe the work and present some personal data about the author. Mention any contacts if you can; for example, say something like, "I enjoyed meeting you (hearing you speak) at the writers conference," etc. And a query addressed to a specific agent has much more appeal that a "Dear Agent" letter.

Once the author is signed on, the agency draws up a contract, called a representative agreement, that explains the responsibilities and expectations of author and agent. Each agent handles his/her own legal agreements, unless there are problems, which are either sorted out through employee consultations or with the Sterling Lord lawyer. The Lord commission remains at 10% "because most writers don't make that much money."

As Pat Berens collects her speech notes and prepares to leave for a business lunch, she concludes that writing must be a *compulsion*—and that that feeling must be apparent in the manuscript or proposal. "The writer must feel that what he has to say is so very important that it *has* to be put on paper . . . . The real writer *can't not* write."

The William Morris Agency

The William Morris Agency was founded in 1898 in a small office on 14th Street, New York's entertainment center of that era. Today there are offices in New York, Beverly Hills, Nashville, London, Rome and Munich and more than 1,500 writers, performers, directors, producers, a clientele that resembles the guest list to the Emmy, Oscar and Pulitzer Prize Awards; even Rodney Dangerfield gets respect at William Morris. In 84 years, at the consistent agent commission of 10%, that's no small change—and a lot of entertainment.

The agency, probably the largest talent empire in the world, is structured on the professional ethics and integrity of old William Morris years ago, who insisted on a special kinship with his clients, a policy which prompted the playwright Abe Burrows to say once that he no longer minded paying commissions to his W.M. agent because "it's like sending money home to mother."

Mother, however, does not live in such a large house. The physical enormity of the office in New York—four floors of the towering MGM Building—plus the agency's awesome track record can be mind-boggling to the rookie, regardless of talent. A few years ago, a new client, a starlet, was heard to say that if they couldn't find Patty Hearst, she was probably inside the William Morris Agency.

For writers, happily, the entire agenting process seems much less complex. Although the literary department is in the modern MGM maze, it is quite separate and in "its own little world." Longtime receptionist Toddy Armhaus, a name synonymous with the William Morris Literary Department, greets all writers, the new and established alike, many of whom "just sit and chat." Her storehouse of anecdotes and stories about famous writers ("all very, very nice") might fill her own book someday. She has loved her 40 years of working for "some of the most wonderful people in the world"—including Owen Laster, the literary department chief and vice president of the company.

Owen Laster occupies a large modern corner office. It's a sparsely furnished but beautifully decorated and comfortable room lined with windows overlooking the east side of mid-Manhattan, and the many books that Laster has personally been involved with. Neat and organized, it's a setting befitting the department head, especially when he meets with writers, producers and directors on major book and property deals. Owen Laster himself, a sort of Ivy League Jack Nicholson, is relaxed and casual as he leans back in his chair and rests a foot on the coffee table.

He explains. In the literary department there are currently seven agents ("an eclectic group") and one assistant agent plus secretaries and bookkeepers. Each has his/her own responsibilities, that is, selling books to publishers and, if possible, the subsequent ancillary rights. Despite the size of the agency—or the department—it is, in the tradition of old Mr. Morris, a "very one-on-one (and sometimes two-on-one) relationship." Agents in a company of this size have the advantage of utilizing the special departments for foreign rights, movie rights and other legal matters (contracts), job areas that free the agents to work with their "approximately 400 clients."

"It's been a rough two years," Laster says realistically, "but I am optimistic because business tends to be cyclical." Rough does not preclude success, however: During the week of Feb. 22, 1981 there were six William Morris agented (hardcover) books (plus two paperbacks) on the bestseller list, and individual W.M.A. books have appeared fairly regularly since.

Laster sees a drift away from fiction in a sagging economy, but the really big sellers will always be fiction. The agenting pleasure for Laster—the icing on the cake—is not a million dollar deal as one might expect, but perhaps a $5,000, $10,000 initial advance for a talented writer who will go on to financial and/or literary acclaim.

In spite of his considerable executive duties (and about 80 phone calls a day), Owen Laster maintains his own client list, primarily novelists, "whose properties better lend themselves to film, TV or stage adaptation." When a special manuscript or book with potential subsidiary rights comes in, Laster invites his colleagues plus motion picture or TV agents, directors or producers from down the hall to his office to discuss the business possibilities. The contacts are right there in the building; proximity is an asset, a time-saver, Laster believes. "It's one-stop shopping."

The W.M.A. Literary Department tries very hard to keep an open policy in obtaining clients, but "a lot depends on the approach of the talent." The best method is a recommendation from a client or editor; and the worst, or least effective, besides a phone call, is a Dear Mr. Morris letter. Morris Sr. died in 1932 and Morris Jr. retired in 1952.

Agents generally stay with William Morris, perhaps because of its training program and opportunities for advancement. College graduates, men *and* women, start in the mail room or as secretaries. When Owen Laster graduated from Syracuse University 20 years ago, he was downstairs, too. He worked his way up as an assistant to a TV agent, and then moved to the literary department in 1967. He became department head in 1974.

Michael Carlisle, Laster's young assistant, who shortcut the usual hierarchical process, was hired into the department on his Paris law experience in international trade and his family background in publishing. Agenting combines his three interests: books, working with people and business. Today he's an agent in his own right, and while assisting Laster, he sometimes shares and even inherits his employer's clients.

Carlisle is actively building his "stable of writers" and he's very intense and conscientious about it. And caring. He interrupts his work to speak on the phone with a woman from Texas, a writer with whom he has earnestly corresponded in great detail and encouragement in his efforts to develop a fruitful relationship. He makes editorial suggestions and changes for her manuscript—a part of the necessary getting-to-know-you pre-contract procedure.

Another example of the tradition of developing agents within the company is illustrated by Robert Gottlieb, who began his career right out of college. Now at 29, he represents over 50 authors who work in both fiction and nonfiction. As an agent, Gottlieb believes that many elements make up his craft, but most important is servicing his clients and working for their individual careers. From his large and comfortable office, he shares the ups and downs of his writers, protecting them so that the business world does not interfere with their creative lives. Gottlieb adds, "In a world of 'bigger is better' an agent has his job cut out for him as the 'bottom line' plays an ever-growing role in how publishers view the book business."

Foreign rights is an area of enormous importance to the agency and its clients. Pam Bernstein, who joined the foreign rights division of the company four years ago as a trainee, heads that section. She also handles her own writers. In an office lined with W.M.A. books, she deals with the world by international telex. Having just returned from the Frankfurt (Germany) Book Fair, she states: "Each year I travel to Frankfurt to renew my contacts with the foreign publishers. It's a matter of knowing which books will travel and how a particular market reacts to our authors."

Bernstein, who reads all her colleague's books, believes strongly in working with her co-agents in the different countries, following up on their assessment of how an author should be published. As for her own clients, her main interest is fiction plus a non-fiction specialty in women's issues.

In their author pursuits, the William Morris agents read voraciously—magazines, newspapers, books, particularly in their subjects of special interest. They also spend untold hours reading hundreds of queries and manuscripts with no agent specification. Rotating every two weeks the agents read the material that comes in; they respond to the author, return the manuscript if necessary, and/or pass on potential clients to fellow agents if the subject is not individually appropriate. Understandably the volume of queries is considerable; thus unsolicited manuscripts are not accepted.

Dedication—that's the name of the agenting game. "It's wonderful to help ideas, information and creative projects meet wth a receptive audience," says Owen Laster. "And to be involved in that process is an exciting profession."

> " The indispensable characteristic of a good writer is a style marked by lucidity.
> —*Hemingway* "

Agents who handle fiction

Many writers—among them, novelists John Updike and Joseph Wambaugh—prefer not to have an agent. They do their own deal-making, hire an attorney for contract review, and keep the 10% for domestic sales—or, increasingly, the 15%—for themselves. Others find an agent invaluable and cannot function in the manuscript-marketing world without one. Still others cannot find an agent at all. They lack the credits, the contacts . . . whatever it takes to get an agent's sincere attentions.

Getting an agent

If you are hunting for an agent, the search won't be easy. But if you have good ideas (preferably book-length ones), and if you are persistent, the search can be successful. The most direct approach is to contact an agent by mail with a brief query letter (not to exceed two single-spaced typewritten pages) in which you describe your work, yourself, and your publishing history. For fiction, the first few chapters in order (up to 50 typed double-spaced pages) will tell an agent whether the book is no or go; sending divided chapters from the same book to several agents simultaneously is confusing and a waste of time. Your letter should be personalized—not a photocopied form letter with the agent's name typed in; and *always include SASE* with enough postage for a reply plus return of materials. If you don't hear from an agent within six weeks, send a polite note asking if the material has been received—and include a photocopy of your original query plus materials and another SASE. If you hear nothing within four months, send a note withdrawing the material—and contact another agent using the same method, immediately.

Agents and the market today

Literary agencies generally come in three sizes: small (handling up to 60 clients), medium (up to 100), and large (over 100). An agent should not be measured by the number of clients, or even by the number of sales made in a given time period, but rather by the number of deals and dollars that really account for writing success. Agents work for *additional* sales of your manuscripts. No good agent will be satisfied selling your novel to a hardcover publisher, for instance; he'll invest some time in selling it to a paperback house, to a movie producer, to a newspaper syndicate for serialization, to a book club, to a foreign publisher. To do this, the agent exercises energy, ideas, connections and business experience the writer probably doesn't have.

Most agents do not handle magazine articles, short stories, poetry, or essays. There is not enough revenue generated from such sales to make them worth an agent's time. Most writers develop their own rapport with the people who edit such publications and sell to them directly. Later, when a writer is doing books, his agent may handle such small sales—as a professional courtesy, not an income maker. If you are writing genre fiction—such as mysteries, science fiction or romances—you may have to get a couple of book sales behind you before an agent will handle your work. Most publishers who do genre fiction are generally receptive to hearing from authors directly anyway.

The fee-charging agent

The responsibilities of agents are many; what they *cannot*, do is: sell unsalable work; teach a beginner how to write salable copy; act as editor of the writer's work; solve the author's personal problems or lend money; be available outside of office hours except by appointment; or perform the functions of press agent, social secretary or travel agent. In other words, having an agent is *not* the final solution to your writing problems. An agent can aid and simplify your career, but ultimately your career is in your hands.

Some agents charge fees, claiming that reading new material consumes so much time that might otherwise be spent selling books, they have to charge the fee or stop reading unsolicited material altogether. Here are some questions to ask about reading fees:

Is it a one-time fee, or will you have to pay again on subsequent submissions?

Will you have to pay the fee again when resubmitting a revised manuscript?

Will the fee be refunded if the agent decides to represent you?

Will the agent waive the fee if you have already had work published, or if you have particular expertise in the area you are writing about?

What do you get for the fee? Just a reading, or some criticism and analysis?

Agents may offer suggestions on how a book might be rewritten to be made salable, but under no circumstances do legitimate agents charge a fee for editing your manuscript. *Editing should be done by editors—after the book is sold.*

Remember, though, that most agents *don't* charge a reading fee, and you should try to work with those agents first.

The pseudo-agent

Do not confuse true literary agents with other individuals or "agencies" that advertise as "consultants" offering manuscript criticism or "literary services" for a fee that may cover a critique, an edit, or a rewrite of your manuscript. Ask anyone who claims to be an "agent," or who uses agent-like phrasing ("We like your manuscript and we think it is marketable—of course, some revisions will be necessary to make it professionally acceptable," etc.) when discussing a fee of any sort, to give you a list of *recent* book sales. If an agent type has not sold three books to established publishing houses in the previous year, he is probably out of the publishing market midstream. Make sure you can afford such literary services offered you. Fees may range from several hundred to several *thousand* dollars—and there is no guarantee that the arrangement will result in a sale to recoup your investment. Such firms and individuals may make their profits from reading and criticism and editing fees—not from sales to publishers.

Contract considerations

Be careful, too, in signing any contract with an agent. Many legitimate agents conduct business with a handshake, believing that a contract will neither solidify a good relationship nor help a bad one. They want to be free to drop (or add) clients as relationships develop. Other agents—and many pseudo-agents—require a contract that should be studied carefully with an attorney before signing. Know what rights the agent is handling for your material, and check that no charges are made for services that you do not fully understand and agree to. Some agencies charge for criticism or impose a "marketing fee" for office overhead, etc. If you pay such a fee, you are entitled to see any correspondence that such a marketing endeavor would produce.

Legitimate agents will discuss marketing problems a manuscript might be having. If you have any doubts about where (or whether) your manuscript is being marketed, ask to see the mail between your agent and the publishers he claims to be showing your work to. If you have paid a marketing fee, it is illegal for the agent to withhold a prepaid service longer than three months—unless the customer is allowed to cancel the order and get a refund. An agent who breaks this law can be sued by the writer. Thorough research and careful selection of an agent will help you avoid the complications and problems that sometimes beset an inexperienced writer.

Attention . . .

We have listed agents here who have advised us that they charge no reading fees or prepublication fees at all. If you find in your dealings with any of them that additional fees of any kind are required, please advise us and we will review the situation. Some agents, not listed here, ask beginning, untested, unpublished writers to pay a one-time fee, a "marketing fee," a processing fee, revision fee, or whatever. Our feeling is that the agent who is sincerely interested in developing and representing an author should be willing to do the initial work necessary—that is, going through manuscripts and searching for the diamond in the slush pile. There should be no profit from the submissions of hopefuls who might get a rejection slip and a quick trip to nowhere in the publishing game.

CAROLE ABEL, LITERARY AGENT, 160 W. 87th St., New York NY 10024. (212)724-1168. Contact: Carole Abel. Novels only. Send outline/proposal. Also reviews nonfiction (50/50 fiction to nonfiction). Presently accepting new clients. Agent's commission: 15%. Member of I.L.A.A.

DOMINICK ABEL LITERARY AGENCY, INC., 498 West End Ave., 12C, New York NY 10024. (212)877-0710. Novels only. Query or send outline/proposal with SASE. Also reviews nonfiction (20-80% fiction to nonfiction). Occasionally accepts new clients. Agent's commission: 10%. Member of I.L.A.A.

EDWARD J. ACTON, INC., 825 3rd Ave., New York NY 10022. (212)675-5400. Contact: Edward J. Acton. Novels only. Send outline plus sample chapters. Also reviews nonfiction (50-50 fiction to nonfiction). Presently accepting new clients. Interested in new/beginning novelists. Agent's commission: 15%. Members of I.L.A.A. Send all mss to Asher Jason, V.P.

ADAMS, RAY & ROSENBERG, INC., 9200 Sunset Blvd., Los Angeles CA 90069. (213)278-3000. Contact: Shelly Wile. Novels only. Send entire ms. Also reviews nonfiction (80% fiction-20% nonfiction). Not interested in new/beginning novelists. Agent's commission: 10%. "Will accept ms submissions from new people only if they are recommended by established authors or editors of my acquaintance.''

MAXWELL ALEY ASSOCIATES, 720 E. Hyman, Aspen CO 81611. (212)679-5378. Contact: Maxwell Aley or Elizabeth Aley. Novels only. Query with sample chapters with SASE. Also reviews nonfiction (50/50 fiction to nonfiction). Reviews fiction "occasionally if good." Presently accepting new clients "but rarely." Rarely interested in new/beginning novelists. Writer must demonstrate 1 or 2 substantial sales. Agent's commission: 10%. Member of I.L.A.A. Specializes in westerns, but not restricted. Reviews also stage, screen and TV plays.

JAMES ALLEN, LITERARY AGENT, 538 E. Harford St., Milford PA 18337. (717)296-7266. Contact: James Allen. Novels only. Prefers "genre fiction more than mainstream, especially science fiction and fantasy." Query, then send entire ms, "if I've expressed interest in seeing it." Also reviews nonfiction (50/50 fiction to nonfiction). Presently accepting new clients "on a *very* limited basis, preferably already-published authors." Agent's commission: 10%.

ALLEN & YANOW LITERARY AGENCY, Box 5158, Santa Cruz CA 95063. (408)427-1293. Contact: Mort Yanow. Novels and short story collections. "No genre." Send outline plus sample chapters; or entire ms. Also reviews nonfiction (50/50 fiction to nonfiction). Presently accepting new clients. Agent's commission: 10%.

MARCIA AMSTERDAM AGENCY, 41 W. 82nd St., New York NY 10024. (212)873-4945. Send outline plus first three chapters. Also reviews nonfiction. Presently accepting new clients. Interested in new/beginning novelists. Agent's commission: 10% domestic rights.

JULIAN BACH LITERARY AGENCY, 747 3rd Ave., New York NY 10017. (212)753-2605. Query. Presently accepting new clients. Member of S.A.R.

BILL BERGER ASSOCIATES, 444 E. 58th St., New York NY 10022. (212)486-9588. Novels only. Query; send outline/proposal or outline plus sample chapters with SASE. Also reviews nonfiction. Presently accepting previously published clients. Writer must demonstrate a minimum number of sales. Agent's commission: 10%. Member of S.A.R.

RON BERNSTEIN, 119 W. 57th St., New York NY 10019. (212)265-0750. Contact: Victoria Wisdom. Novels and screenplays only. Area of specialization: screenplays. Query only. Also reviews nonfiction (2-1 fiction to nonfiction). Presently accepting new clients "but not unsolicited material." Writer must demonstrate a minimum number of sales. Agent's commission: 10%. Member of I.L.A.A.

BOLDT & BOLDT LITERARY AGENCY, Box 9262, San Jose CA 95117. (408)374-5492. Contact: D. Boldt. Novels only. Area of specialization: Only adult-oriented romantic fiction and women's historical romantic fiction. Query; then send outline/proposal; or 3 sample chapters. Presently accepting new clients. Interested in new/beginning novelists. Agent's commission: 10% (15% on foreign sales to $100,000; then 10%). "Enclose SASE with *all* submissions as mss that arrive without SASE cannot be automatically returned."

BEVERLY BOND LITERARY AGENT, 1725 Wroxton Court, Houston TX 77005. (713)524-4974. Novels only. Query letter first with SASE. Prefers entire ms to sample chapters. Also reviews nonfiction (75/25 fiction to nonfiction). Presently accepting new clients. Interested in new/beginning novelists. Agent's commission: 10%.

GEORGES BORCHARDT INC., 136 E. 57th St., New York NY 10022. (212)753-5785. Novels; nonfiction. Query; "but only if recommended by someone we know." (3/1 nonfiction to fiction). Presently accepting new clients but very few. Interested in new/beginning novelists. Agent's commission: 10%. Member of S.A.R.

BARBARA BOVA LITERARY AGENCY, 32 Gramercy Park S., New York NY 10003. (212)982-6616. Novels only. No science fiction. Send outline/proposal with SASE. Also reviews nonfiction (50/50). Selectively accepting new clients. Agent's commission: 10%.

✓ **BRADFORD AND ASSOCIATES**, 2111 M 30th St., # 1073, Boulder CO 80301. (303)449-1128. Contact: D. Bradford. Novels only. Send outline plus sample chapters. Also reviews nonfiction (1/15 fiction to nonfiction). Presently accepting new clients. Interested in new/beginning novelists. Agent's commission: 15%. Wants "SASE, no originals, only copies, bio not resume, and author's view of selling strengths."

BRANDT & BRANDT, 1501 Broadway, New York NY 10036. (212)840-5760. Contact: Carl Brandt. "Send letter on background and what you are currently doing." Interested in new/beginning novelists. Agent's commission: 10%. Member of S.A.R.

BRISK, RUBIN, STEINBERG, 838 Michigan, Evanston IL 60202. (312)864-7222. Contact: M. Steinberg. Novels only. Send outline plus sample chapters. Also reviews nonfiction (40/60 fiction to nonfiction). Presently accepting new clients. Interested in new/beginning novelists. Agent's commission: 15%.

CURTIS BROWN ASSOCIATES LTD., Subsidiary of Curtis Brown, Ltd., New York, 575 Madison Ave., New York NY 10022. (212)755-4200. No unsolicited material. Query. Presently accepting new clients. Interested in new/beginning novelists. Agent's commission: 10%. Member of S.A.R.

NED BROWN INC., 407 N. Maple Dr., Beverly Hills CA 90210. East Coast: Lorna Brown, Vice-President, Ned Brown Inc., 139 Charter Oak Dr., New Canaan CT 06840. (203)966-2437. Novels only. Send entire manuscript. Also reviews nonfiction. Presently accepting new clients "only if published commercially or recommended by another author or client." Agent's commission: 10%.

PEMA BROWNE LTD., 185 E. 85th St., New York NY 10028. (212)369-1925. Contact: Perry J. Browne. Fiction and nonfiction. Area of specialization: romance, science fiction, men's, adventure, etc. Send entire manuscript. Also reviews nonfiction (50/50). Presently accepting new clients. Interested in new/beginning novelists. Agent's commission: 15%.

SHIRLEY BURKE AGENCY, 370 E. 76th St., P-704, New York NY 10021. (212)861-2309. Contact: Shirley Burke. Novels. Query; send outline/proposal. Also nonfiction. "Not accepting new clients unless the material asked for is more than acceptable." Interested in new/beginning novelists. Agent's commission: 15%.

✓ **MARIA CARVAINIS AGENCY**, 235 West End Ave., New York NY 10023. (212)580-1559. Novels and short story collections. "I handle all kinds of fiction from serious to commercial." Query with SASE. Also reviews nonfiction (40% fiction and 60% nonfiction, "although this is always in flux.") Presently accepting new clients. Interested in new/beginning novelists. Agent's commission: 15%. "I am a signatory to the Writers Guild of America, East Inc. and member-at-large of the Authors Guild Inc. and the Author's League of America, Inc."

HY COHEN LITERARY AGENCY, 111 W. 57th St., New York NY 10019. (212)757-5237. Fiction and nonfiction. Send sample chapters with SASE. Agent's commission: 10%.

SHIRLEY COLLIER AGENCY, 1127 Stradella Rd., Los Angeles CA 90077. (213)270-4500. Contact: Shirley Collier. Novels and biography. Prefers "good writing; no smut." Query first with SASE. Also reviews nonfiction (10/1 fiction to nonfiction). Not presently accepting new clients. Interested in new/beginning novelists. Writer must demonstrate a minimum number of sales to three top magazines. Agent's commission: 10%.

MOLLY MALONE COOK LITERARY AGENCY, INC., Box 338, Provincetown MA 02657. (617)487-1931. Novels, novelettes, short story collections. Query. Also reviews nonfiction (50/50 fiction to nonfiction). Presently accepting new clients.

COSAY, WERNER ASSOCIATES, INC., 9744 Wilshire Blvd., Los Angeles CA 90212. (213)550-1535. Novels only. Query; send outline/proposal or outline plus sample chapters. Also reviews nonfiction (3/1 fiction to nonfiction). Presently accepting new clients. Agent's commission: 10%.

GLENN COWLEY MANAGEMENT, 60 W. 10th St., New York NY 10011. (212)473-2082. Novels only. Send outline plus sample chapters with SASE. Also reviews nonfiction (50/50). Presently accepting new clients. Interested in new/beginning novelists. Agent's commission: 15%.

LIZ DARHANSOFF LITERARY AGENCY, 1220 Park Ave., New York NY 10028. (212)534-2479. Novels only. Query; send outline/proposal or outline plus sample chapters. Also reviews nonfiction. Presently accepting new clients. Interested in new/beginning novelists. Agent's commission: 10%. Member of I.L.A.A.

JOAN DAVES, 59 E. 54th St., New York NY 10022. (212)759-6250. Fiction and nonfiction. Query "with good information about the writer." Presently accepting new clients "but rarely." Interested in new/beginning novelists. Writer must demonstrate some prior credits or professional experience to be accepted as client. Agent's commission: 10% domestic. Member of S.A.R.

DIXIE LEE DAVIDSON LTD., 1052 Howard St., Omaha NE 68102. (402)346-6065. Contact: Dixie Lee Davidson. Novels only. Query. Also reviews nonfiction (20%-80% fiction to nonfiction). Presently accepting new clients. Interested in new/beginning novelists. Agent's commission: 10%.

ANITA DIAMANT: THE WRITERS' WORKSHOP, INC., 51 E. 42 St., New York NY 10017. (212)687-1122. Novels and nonfiction. Send outline/proposal. Presently accepting new clients. Interested in new/beginning novelists. Agent's commission: 10%. Member of S.A.R.

CANDIDA DONADIO & ASSOCIATES, INC., 111 W. 57th St., New York NY 10019.

ALYSS DORESE AGENCY, 41 W. 82nd St., New York NY 10024. (212)580-2855. Novels and short story collections. Query or send outline/proposal. Also reviews nonfiction (2 to 1 fiction to nonfiction). Presently accepting new clients. Interested in new/beginning novelists. Agent's commission: 10%. Member of Writers Guild.

JOSEPH ELDER AGENCY, 150 W. 87th St., # 6D, New York NY 10024. Novels only. "Must query first, include SASE." Also reviews nonfiction (75/25 fiction to nonfiction). Presently accepting new clients but very selectively. Interested in new/beginning novelists "but rarely take one on." Writer need not demonstrate a number of sales "but it's very rare to take on a new client with no track record." Agent's commission: 10%. Member of I.L.A.A.

ANN ELMO AGENCY INC., 60 E. 42nd St., New York NY 10165. (212)661-2880. Novels, short stories, plays. Query. Also reviews nonfiction. Accepts only published writers. Writer must demonstrate a minimum number of sales for acceptance. Agent's commission: 10%. Member of S.A.R.

BARTHOLD FLES, LITERARY AGENT, 501 Fifth Ave., New York NY 10017. (212)687-7248. Novels and short story collections. Juveniles: intermediate and teenage only. No picture books. Send outline plus sample chapters. Also reviews nonfiction (one to one—of sales). Presently accepting new clients. Interested in new/beginning novelists. Writer preferably demonstrates a minimum number of sales for acceptance. Agent's commission: 10%; 20% British rights and translations.

THE FOLEY AGENCY, 34 E. 38th St., New York NY 10016. (212)686-6930. Contact: Joan or Joe Foley. Novels. Query first with SASE. Also reviews nonfiction (40-60 fiction to nonfiction). Presently accepting some new clients. Agent's commission: 10%.

JAY GARON-BROOKE ASSOCIATES, 415 Central Park West, New York NY 10025. (212)866-3654. Contact: Jay Garon. Novels only. Area of specialization: "Whatever is selling at a given time; right now contemporary romances." Query first; send entire ms. Also reviews nonfiction. Presently accepting new clients with credits. Agent's commission: 15% domestic; 30% foreign sales.

FRANCES GOLDIN, LITERARY AGENT, 305 E. 11th St., New York NY 10003. (212)777-0047. Novels only. "I don't handle fiction which is racist, sexist, ageist or pornographic." Query; or send outline/proposal. Also reviews nonfiction (1-5 fiction to nonfiction). Presently accepting new clients "but extremely selective." Interested in new/beginning novelists. Agent's commission: "varies, depending on who the author is and what the property is." Member of I.L.A.A.

GOODMAN ASSOCIATES, 500 West End Ave., New York NY 10024. (212)873-4806. General adult fiction and nonfiction. No science fiction or children's books. Written query. Presently accepting new clients. Interested in new/beginning novelists. Agent's commission: 15% domestic; 20% foreign. Member of I.L.A.A.

IRENE GOODMAN LITERARY AGENCY, 134 W. 81st St., New York NY 10024. (212)874-7463. Novels only. Area of specialization: romances; commercial mass market. Send outline plus sample chapters. No reply without SASE. Also reviews nonfiction ("about half and half"). Presently accepting new clients. Interested in new/beginning novelists. Agent's commission: 15%. Member of I.L.A.A.

SANFORD J. GREENBURGER ASSOCIATES, 825 3rd Ave., New York NY 10022. (212)753-8581. Contact: Lucy Stille. Novels only. Also reviews nonfiction (60/40 fiction to nonfiction). Presently accepting new clients. Interested in new/beginning novelists. Agent's commission: 15%. Member of I.L.A.A.

REECE HALSEY AGENCY, 8733 Sunset Blvd., Los Angeles CA. (213)OL2-2409. Novels only. Query only with SASE. Also reviews nonfiction ("no set ratio"). Not presently accepting new clients. Interested in new/beginning novelists. Agent's commission: 10%.

HEACOCK ASSOCIATES, INC., 1523 6th St., Suite # 14, Santa Monica CA (213)451-8523 or (213)393-6227. Contact: James B. Heacock. Novels only. Area of specialization: category romances and mainstream. Query; submit outline plus sample chapters (20 to 30 pages). Must include SASE. Also reviews nonfiction (20/80 fiction to nonfiction). Presently accepting new clients. Interested in new/beginning novelists. Agent's commission: 10% if published and 15% for first timers; 20% on foreign translations. Member of I.L.A.A.

SHIRLEY HECTOR AGENCY, 29 W. 46th St., New York NY 10036. (212)719-2482.

HEINLE & HEINLE ENTERPRISES, 29 Lexington Rd., Concord MA 01742. (617)369-4858. Contact: Beverly D. Heinle. Novels only. Prefers New England area writers. Query; then submit outline/proposal or outline plus sample chapters. Also reviews nonfiction (40/60 fiction to nonfiction). Presently accepting new clients. Interested in new/beginning novelists. Agent's commission: 10%.

Close-up

Peter Skolnik
Sanford J. Greenburger Associates

A literary agent today wears many hats. He must be an editor, a salesman, a lawyer, a psychologist and a diplomat. Add boundless energy and enthusiasm and you have Peter Skolnik.

Skolnik brings a rich and varied background to his eight years of agenting at Sanford J. Greenburger Associates. His degrees in English Literature and Fine Arts from Harvard and Columbia respectively, and his work as a director and producer in the theater, film and TV give him a valuable perspective on the other side of the negotiating table. And special empathy for the writer, as well. Skolnik is also the author of two nonfiction books.

Although he handles fiction and nonfiction, Skolnik generally finds fiction more "emotionally satisfying," especially if he can be instrumental in shaping the career of a promising new novelist with more than one book to write. His typical client list might include 35-40 writers whose books, manuscripts or ideas may be in a quiescent or active stage: a book idea, a proposal, an unedited manuscript or one actually out on submission. At any given time, the agent may be actively working on 10-15 projects.

Ten and twelve hour days are not uncommon in the agenting business. Long frenetic days for Peter Skolnik might include an occasional work breakfast, "a lot of lunch" where much of the business with editors and publishers takes place, office work with authors, reading and responding to proposals, telephone calls, meetings, contract and subsidiary rights negotiations, a publisher's party, and/or the inevitable reading of manuscripts at home in the evening.

At Sanford J. Greenburger, query letters rather than unsolicited manuscripts are encouraged. Skolnik is building up his already substantial client list extremely cautiously, but he too, welcomes inquiries (or queries), letters which describe the project in just enough detail to explain the subject. Although he has found good writers over the transom from time to time, most new clients are via referrals from clients, agents, or editors.

Today, because of economic problems and resulting constrictions in the marketplace, selling a book to a publisher is difficult. Skolnik, the former president of ILAA (Independent Literary Agents Association), urges writers *not* to expect miracles. An agent works almost exclusively on speculation; he reads the material for no pay and receives money only when the manuscript is sold. Thus it is in the agent's best interest to place a book for a client, and if he believes in a project he does work hard to sell it.

Skolnik offers this advice: Before beginning a book—or spending months, even years on a novel—ask yourself who would want to read your book and why. "So often," he says, "you know when you read material that the writers have absolutely no idea what is selling in the bookstores today. They're not reading novels with a critical eye—asking why they're working, how they're constructed, what's making the reader turn the page or what techniques are used to give characterization, pace or tension. Nor have would-be-writers read the acknowledged successful masters in their field/genre. Without this type of study, it's like trying to put on a play without ever having been to one."

agents

FREDERICK HILL ASSOCIATES, 2237 Union St., San Francisco CA 94123. (415)921-2910. Contact: Frederick Hill. Novels and young adult fiction. No juveniles. Query. Also reviews nonfiction (roughly 50-50). Presently accepting new clients. Interested in new/beginning novelists. Agent's commission: 10%.

KAREN HITZIG AGENCY, 34 Gramercy Park E., New York NY 10003. (212)260-3776. Novels only. Send outline plus sample chapters with SASE. Also reviews nonfiction (50/50). Presently accepting new clients. Interested in new/beginning novelists. Agent's commission: 10%. "All inquiries and manuscripts must include SASE in order to receive a reply."

HUTTO MANAGEMENT, 405 W. 23rd St., New York NY 10011. Novels only. Query. Also reviews nonfiction. Interested in new/beginning novelists. Agent's commission: 10%. Member of S.A.R. Accepts new clients by recommendation only.

INTERNATIONAL CREATIVE MANAGEMENT, 40 W. 57th St., New York NY 10019. (212)556-5600. Contact: Maggie Curran. Novels and novelettes. Query preferred; send outline plus sample chapters. Also reviews nonfiction. Presently accepting new clients. Interested in new/beginning novelists. Agent's commission: 10%; 15% British; 20% foreign. Unsolicited mss will not be accepted. Member of S.A.R.

JCA LITERARY AGENCY, INC., 242 W. 27th St., New York NY 10001. (212)807-0888. Not presently accepting new clients. Agent's commission: 10%. Member of S.A.R.

J&S LITERARY SERVICES, 128 2nd Place, Brooklyn NY 11231. (212)237-2339. Contact: Steve Blackwelder. Novels only. Query with SASE. Also reviews nonfiction (5/1 fiction to nonfiction). Presently accepting new clients. Interested in new/beginning novelists. Agent's commission: 10%; 20% foreign.

J DE S ASSOCIATES, Shagbark Rd., Wilson Point, S. Norwalk CT 06854. (203)838-7571. Fiction and nonfiction. Send outline and sample chapters. Presently accepting new clients. Agent's commission: 15%.

JET LITERARY ASSOCIATES, INC., 124 E. 84th St., Suite 4A, New York NY 10028. (212)879-2578. Novels only. Query. Also reviews nonfiction (50/50 fiction to nonfiction). Presently accepting new clients on a selective basis. Agent's commission: 15%.

KIDDE, HOYT & PICARD, 335 E. 51st St., New York NY 10022. (212)755-9461. Novels only. Area of specialization: straight fiction or romance. Query; send outline/proposal. Also reviews nonfiction. Presently accepting some new clients. Interested in new/beginning novelists who have been published with shorter work at least. Agent's commission: 10%.

DANIEL P. KING, LITERARY AGENT, 5125 N. Cumberland Blvd., Whitefish Bay WI 53217. (414)964-2903. TELEX 724389. Contact: Daniel P. King. Novels, novelettes, short stories, short story collections. Area of specialization: mystery and crime. Query; then submit outline/proposal. Also reviews nonfiction (80% fiction; 20% nonfiction). Presently accepting new clients. Interested in new/beginning novelists. Agent's commission: 10%; 20% foreign.

HARVEY KLINGER, INC., 301 W. 53 St., New York NY 10019. (212)581-7068. Novels only. Query. Also reviews nonfiction (50-50 fiction and nonfiction). Presently accepting new clients. Interested in new/beginning novelists. Agent's commission: 15%.

LUCY KROLL AGENCY, 390 West End Ave., New York NY 10024. (212)877-0627. Novels only. Query with SASE. Also reviews nonfiction (25%-75% fiction to nonfiction). Not presently accepting new clients. Writer must demonstrate a minimum number of sales for acceptance. Agent's commission: 10%. Member of S.A.R.

BILL KRUGER LITERARY SERVICES, 1308 Canterbury Rd. N., St. Petersburg FL 33710. (813)381-5348. Contact: William F. Kruger. Novels, novelettes, short story collections. Query; submit outline plus 3 sample chapters. Also reviews nonfiction (3 to 1 fiction to nonfiction). Presently accepting new clients. Interested in new/beginning novelists. Agent's commission: 10% published writers, 15% nonpublished writers. "With nonpublished writers we request SASE until a sale is made; then it's on me."

PETER LAMPACK AGENCY, INC., 551 5th Ave., Suite 2015, New York NY 10017. (212)687-9106. Novels, novelettes, motion pictures, television properties. Written query only. Also reviews nonfiction (60/40 fiction to nonfiction). Presently accepting new clients. Interested in new/beginning novelists. Agent's commission: 15% US and Canada; 20% foreign rights.

MICHAEL LARSEN/ELIZABETH POMADA LITERARY AGENTS, 1029 Jones St., San Francisco CA 94109. Novels only. Query; send outline/proposal. "Outline plus 3 sample chapters with SASE is best; I ask people to send 50 pages plus an outline." Also reviews nonfiction (E. Pomada does 90% fiction to 10% nonfiction, M. Larsen is just the reverse: 10% fiction to 90% nonfiction). Presently accepting new clients. Interested in new/beginning novelists. Agent's commission: 15% the first $75,000 per year in author income; 10% thereafter. Member of I.L.A.A.

ELIZABETH LAY, LITERARY AGENT, 4321 Gilbert St., Oakland CA 94611. (415)652-0556. Novels only. Query. Also reviews nonfiction (50-50 fiction to nonfiction). Presently accepting new clients. Interested in new/beginning novelists. Agent's commission: 10%; 20% UK and translations.

LENNIGER LITERARY AGENCY, 104 E. 40th, New York NY 10016. (212)661-9393. Novels only. "No unsolicited mss, please." Also reviews nonfiction (60 fiction; 40 nonfiction). Presently accepting new clients. New clients by invitation. Agent's commission: 10%.

ELLEN LEVINE LITERARY AGENCY INC., Suite 906, 370 Lexington Ave., New York NY 10017. (212)889-0620. Novels and nonfiction books. Query first; then outline (or sample chapters) if invited as a result of query. Approximately 60-40% fiction/nonfiction. Presently accepting new clients if previously published. Agent's commission: 10%. Member of S.A.R and I.L.A.A.

THE STERLING LORD AGENCY INC., 660 Madison Ave., New York NY 10021. (212)PL1-2533. Contact: Patricia Berens. Novels, nonfiction. Query first. Presently accepting new clients. Agent's commission: 10%. Member of S.A.R.

BARBARA LOWENSTEIN ASSOCIATES, INC., 250 W. 57th St., New York NY 10107. (212)586-3825. Contact: Barbara Lowenstein. Fiction and nonfiction. Send outline plus 2 sample chapters. Presently accepting new clients. Has an agent specializing in category romance. Agent's commission: 15%. Member of I.L.A.A. Must include SASE with all submissions.

DONALD MacCAMPBELL INC., 12 E. 41st St., New York NY 10017. (212)683-5580. Novels only. Area of specialization: women's fiction. Query or send entire manuscript if encouraged on basis of query. Presently accepting new clients. No unsolicited mss. Agent's commission: 10% plus 5% on first sale. "Unpublished novelists must offer the agency first look at the top copy (no Xerox) of a complete manuscript along with a SASE for possible return."

ELAINE MARKSON LITERARY AGENCY, 44 Greenwich Ave., New York NY 10011. (212)243-8480. Query letter first. *Do not* send unsolicited mss. "Authors should write to us (*don't call*) and we will respond." Also reviews nonfiction (about 20 to 1 fiction to nonfiction). Presently accepting new clients. ("Very rarely, but we do accept clients if we are very impressed with their potential.") Interested in new/beginning novelists. Agent's commission: 10%. Member of I.L.A.A.

MARGARET McBRIDE LITERARY AGENCY, 4875 N. Harbor Dr., San Diego CA 92106. (714)225-0280. Fiction and nonfiction for adult mainstream market. Prefers query letter first; outline/proposal second; outline plus sample chapters third. No unsolicited mss. Presently accepting new clients only if material seems highly marketable. Interested in new/beginning novelists only if the writer has a well defined premise and outline. Agent's commission: 15%. Member of I.L.A.A.

RENATE BOHNE McCARTER, 823 Park Ave., New York NY 10021. Novels only. Send outline plus sample chapters. Also reviews nonfiction (specializing in anthropology and archeology). Not presently accepting new clients. Interested in new/beginning novelists. Agent's commission: 10%.

MARTHA MILLARD LITERARY AGENCY, 357 W. 19th St., New York NY 10001. (212)924-2087. Novels only. Query plus return postage. Also reviews nonfiction (50-50 fiction to nonfiction). Presently accepts new clients. Not interested in new/beginning novelists. Agent's commission: 10%. Member of I.L.A.A. "Always query, if asked to submit material; always include return postage. List any published credits in query letter."

ROBERT P. MILLS, LTD., 333 5th Ave., New York NY 10016. (212)655-6575. Query only. Also reviews nonfiction (65-35 fiction to nonfiction). Presently accepting new clients. Agent's commission: 10%. Member of S.A.R.

HOWARD MOOREPARK, 444 E. 82nd St., New York NY 10028. (212)737-3961. Novels only. Send outline plus sample chapters or entire manuscript. Also reviews nonfiction. Presently accepting new clients. Agent's commission: 10-15%.

HOWARD MORHAIM LITERARY AGENCY, 501 5th Ave., New York NY 10017. (212)370-1585. Novels only. Query. Also reviews nonfiction (70/30 fiction to nonfiction). Presently accepting new clients. Interested in new/beginning novelists. Agent's commission: 10%. Member of I.L.A.A.

WILLIAM MORRIS AGENCY, INC., 1350 Avenue of the Americas, New York NY 10019. (212)586-5100. Send outline plus sample chapters, not entire manuscript. Reviews fiction and nonfiction. Occasionally accepts new clients. Agent's commission: 10%. Member of S.A.R.

HENRY MORRISON INC., 58 W. 10th St., New York NY 10011. (212)260-7600. Novels only. Query. Also reviews nonfiction and screenplays. Presently accepting new clients. Interested in new/beginning novelists. Agent's commission: 15%.

MULTIMEDIA PRODUCT DEVELOPMENT, INC., 410 S. Michigan Ave., # 828, Chicago IL 60605. (312)922-3063. Contact: Jane Jordan Browne. Novels only. Query with SASE. Also reviews nonfiction (75% nonfiction; 25% fiction). Presently accepting new clients. Agent's commission: 10%; for published writers; 15% for first novelists.

JEAN V. NAGGAR LITERARY AGENCY, 336 E. 73rd St., New York NY 10021. (212)794-1082. Novels only. Query with SASE. Also reviews nonfiction. Presently accepting new clients on a selective basis. Interested in some new/beginning novelists. Agent's commission: 15% domestic; 20% foreign/new authors. Member of I.L.A.A.

CHARLES NEIGHBORS, INC., 240 Waverly Place, New York NY 10014. (212)924-8296. Novels only. Send outline plus sample chapters. Also reviews nonfiction (about 2 to 1 fiction to nonfiction). Presently accepting new clients. Interested in new/beginning novelists. Writer must demonstrate at least one sale for acceptance. Agent's commission: 10%. Member of I.L.A.A.

MARY NOVIK LITERARY AGENT, 5519 Deerhorn Lane, North Vancouver, British Columbia, Canada V7R 4S8. Novels only. Area of specialization: romance. "Query letter with outline best." Presently accepting new clients. Agent's commission: 10%. "Information about agency available if SASE or IRC sent (Canadian postage only)."

HAROLD OBER ASSOCIATES, INC., 40 E. 49th St., New York NY 10017. (212)759-8600. Novels only. Reads all kinds, category and mainstream. Query first. Also reviews nonfiction (about 75-25 fiction to nonfiction). "Our specialty is really fiction." Presently accepting new clients but very limited numbers. (Represents British agencies also.) Interested in new/beginning novelists if query letter is appealing. Agent's commission: 10% US; 15% British; 20% other foreign. Member of S.A.R.

FIFI OSCARD ASSOCIATES, 19 W. 44th St., New York NY 10036. 764-1100. Contact: Ivy Fischer Stone. Novels and nonfiction. Presently accepting new clients. Query first. Writer must demonstrate a minimum number of sales for acceptance. Agent's commission: 10%. Member of S.A.R.

RAY PEEKNER LITERARY AGENCY, 3210 S. 7th St., Milwaukee WI 53215. Contact: Ray Peekner. Novels only. Query. Also reviews nonfiction (50/50 fiction to nonfiction). Not presently accepting new clients. Agent's commission: 10%.

RODNEY PELTER, LITERARY AGENT, 129 E. 61st St., New York NY 10021. (212)838-3432. Contact: Rodney Pelter. Novels and nonfiction in general. Query with SASE and résumé or send outline plus first 150 pages with SASE and résumé. Presently accepting new clients. Interested in new/beginning novelists. Agent's commission "varies, depending on size of the advance and is graduated in accordance with total earnings of each book."

SIDNEY PORCELAIN, Box 69, Brigantine NJ 08203. (609)266-0795. Novels, novelettes and short stories. Query. Also reviews nonfiction. Presently accepting new clients. Interested in new/beginning novelists. Agent's commission: 10%.

JULIAN PORTMAN AGENCY, 1680 N. Vine St., Suite 507, Hollywood CA 90028. (213)463-8154. Novels and novelettes. Query; send outline plus sample chapters. Also reviews nonfiction (50/50 fiction to nonfiction). Presently accepting new clients. Interested in new/beginning novelists. Agent's commission: 15%. Recently opened new branch office: Julian Portman Agency, 9106 Samostet Trail, Skokie IL 60076.

CLARKSON N. POTTER, 2 Westwood Rd., Jamestown RI 02835. (401)423-1720. Query or send outline/proposal. Also reviews nonfiction. Presently accepting new clients. Agent's commission: 10%.

FROMMER PRICE INC., 185 E. 85th St., New York NY 10028. (212)289-0589. Contact: Diana Price. Adult novels only. Area of specialization: mainstream/literary fiction; no category. Query; send outline/proposal or outline plus sample chapters. Also reviews nonfiction (30/70 fiction to nonfiction). Presently accepting new clients. Interested in new/beginning novelists. Agent's commission: 15%.

THE AARON M. PRIEST LITERARY AGENCY INC., 344 E. 51st St., New York NY 10022. (212)685-3860. Adult trade only. Send outline plus sample chapters with SASE. Also reviews nonfiction (75% fiction). Presently accepting new clients. Interested in new/beginning novelists. Agent's commission: 10% (foreign mailing and copying charged to author).

PAUL R. REYNOLDS, INC., 12 E. 41st St., New York NY 10017. (212)689-8711. Contact: J. Hawkins. Novels, short stories and short story collections, periodicals, foreign rights and juvenile. Send outline. Also reviews nonfiction. Presently accepting new clients. Interested in new/beginning novelists. Agent's commission: 10%. Member of S.A.R.

ROBBINS & COVEY ASSOCIATES, 2 Dag Hammarskjold Plaza, 866 2nd Ave., Suite 403, New York NY 10017. (212)223-0720; Los Angeles address: 10000 Santa Monica Blvd., 3rd Floor, Century City CA 90067. (213)203-0800. Novels and short story collections. Query first with SASE. "No unsolicited mss accepted. Only accept material from previously published or referred writers." Also reviews nonfiction (1 to 3 fiction to nonfiction). Presently accepting new clients. Interested in new/beginning novelists. Agent's commission: 15%.

MARIE RODELL-FRANCES COLLIN LITERARY AGENCY, 110 W. 40th St., New York NY 10018. Novels only. Area of specialization: general adult trade books. Query with SASE. Also reviews nonfiction (50-50 fiction to nonfiction). Agent's commission: 10%; 20% overseas. Member of S.A.R.

ROSENSTONE/WENDER, 3 E. 48th St., New York NY 10017. (212)832-8330. Novels, novelettes, short stories, short story collections. Query. Does not accept unsolicited mss. Also reviews nonfiction (50/50 fiction to nonfiction). Presently accepting new clients. Interested in new/beginning novelists. Agent's commission: 10%. Member of S.A.R.

ELEANOR MERRYMAN ROSZEL, 1710 Bolton St., Baltimore MD 21217. (301)669-8326. Contact: E.M. Roszel. Novels only. Query. Also reviews nonfiction "about half and half" (fiction and nonfiction). Presently accepting new clients. Interested in new/beginning novelists. Agent's commission: 10%. "Queries and unsolicited mss should come with SASE; otherwise I shall not respond."

JANE ROTROSEN AGENCY, 226 E. 32nd St., New York NY 10016. (212)889-7133. Novels only. Query. Also reviews nonfiction (60-40 fiction to nonfiction). Presently accepting new clients. Interested in new/beginning novelists. Agent's commission: 15%. Member of I.L.A.A.

RUSSELL & VOLKENING, INC., 551 5th Ave., New York NY 10017. (212)682-5341. Novels, novelettes and short stories. Send outline plus 50 pages with SASE. Also reviews nonfiction (80% fiction—20% nonfiction). Presently accepting new clients. Interested in new/beginning novelists. Agent's commission: 10%. Member of S.A.R.

RAPHAEL SAGALYN, INC., LITERARY AGENCY, 1120 19th St., NW, Suite 801, Washington DC 20036. Member of I.L.A.A. "I am not accepting/encouraging unsolicited mss now."

JOHN SCHAFFNER ASSOCIATES, INC., 425 E. 51st St., New York NY 10022. Query only. Presently accepting few new clients. Agent's commission: 10%. Member of S.A.R.

ARTHUR SCHWARTZ, 435 Riverside Dr., New York NY 10025. Novels only. Area of specialization: Commercially-oriented fiction (i.e., frank, realistic sex), adult-oriented romantic fiction, family sagas, women's historical romantic fiction. No "Harlequin" type books. Query. ("Do not register, certify or insure; retain original mss for your file. Enclose ms-size SASE."). Also reviews nonfiction (1-2 fiction to nonfiction). Presently accepting new clients. Interested in new/beginning novelists. Agent's commission: 12½%. Member of I.L.A.A.

FRANCES SCHWARTZ LITERARY AGENCY, 60 E. 42nd St., Suite 413, New York NY 10017. (212)661-2881. Fiction and nonfiction. Query with SASE. Presently accepting new clients.

JAMES SELIGMANN AGENCY, 280 Madison Ave., New York NY 10016. (212)679-3383. Novels and novelettes. No mysteries, science fiction, fantasy or suspense. Query; send outline/proposal or outline with sample chapters. Also reviews nonfiction (50/50 fiction to nonfiction).

Presently accepting new clients. Interested in new/beginning novelists. Agent's commission: 15%. Member of S.A.R.

BOBBE SIEGEL, RIGHTS REPRESENTATIVE, 41 W. 83rd St., New York NY 10024. (212)877-4985. Contact: Bobbe Siegel. Novels only. Query; or send outline plus sample chapters or entire ms. Also reviews nonfiction (65% fiction to 35% nonfiction). Presently accepting new clients. Interested in new/beginning novelists. Agent's commission: 15%.

ROSALIE SIEGEL, AUTHOR'S AGENT, 111 Murphy Dr., Pennington NJ 08534. (609)737-1007. Novels, novelettes, short stories, and "short story collections only by clients I already represent." Area of specialization: preferably quality fiction—*not* romance or gothic. Query or send entire manuscript, "if I ask to see it." Also reviews nonfiction (75-25 fiction to nonfiction). Agent's commission: 10%. Member of I.L.A.A.

ELYSE SOMMER, INC., Author's Representative. (516)295-0046, 962 Allen Lane, Box E, Woodmere LI NY 11598. Novels only. Area of specialization: contemporary bestseller types, family sagas. No science fiction; futuristic books. Send outline plus 2 sample chapters with SASE. Entire manuscript should be available. Also reviews nonfiction (1-4 fiction to nonfiction). Presently accepting new clients. Interested in new/beginning novelists. Agent's commission: 10-15%. Member of I.L.A.A.

SPADE & ARCHER, Bear Flag Inn, 2814 I St., Sacramento CA 95816. Contact: Robert Henry West. Mystery/detective fiction only. Send outline/proposal or sample chapters. Also reviews nonfiction (1-5 fiction to nonfiction). Presently accepting new clients. Interested in new/beginning novelists. Agent's commission: 15%.

PHILIP G. SPITZER LITERARY AGENCY, 111-25 76th Ave., Forest Hills NY 11375. (212)263-7592. Novels only. Query. Also reviews nonfiction (50-50 fiction to nonfiction). Seldom accepts new clients. Agent's commission: 10%. Member of S.A.R.

RENÉE SPODHEIM ASSOCIATES, 698 West End Ave., New York NY 10025. (212)222-4083. Book-length only. Send outline plus sample chapters. Also interested in nonfiction. Presently accepting new clients. Interested in new/beginning novelists. Agent's commission: 15%.

CHARLES M. STERN ASSOCIATES, Box 32742, San Antonio TX 78216. (512)349-6141. Novels, nonfiction and how-to. Send query with SASE and/or send outline/proposal. Presently accepting new clients. Interested in new/beginning novelists/writers. Agent's commission: 10% published authors; 15% unpublished authors.

GLORIA STERN AGENCY, 1230 Park Ave., New York NY 10028. (212)289-7698. Area of specialization: serious material suitable for original hardcover novel. Send outline/proposal and writer's background and SASE for answer. Also reviews nonfiction (20-80% fiction to nonfiction). Presently accepting few new clients (1/month). "Must have had articles or short stories published, have some writing background." Interested in new/beginning novelists. Agent's commission: 10-15%. Member of I.L.A.A.

LARRY STERNIG LITERARY AGENCY, 742 Robertson St., Milwaukee WI 53213. Not presently accepting new clients.

JO STEWART AGENCY, 201 E. 66th St., New York NY 10021. (212)879-1301. Novels and nonfiction. Presently accepting new clients. Interested in new/beginning novelists. Agent's commission: 15%. Member of S.A.R.

GUNTHER STUHLMANN AUTHOR'S REPRESENTATIVE, Box 276, Becket MA 01223. Novels and nonfiction books (no unsolicited mss). Area of specialization: high quality; no SF/detection/adventure. Query with SASE. Presently accepting new clients but "very few, usually upon recommendation." Interested in new/beginning novelists "if extremely talented." Agent's commission: 10% US and Canada; 15% Britain and Commonwealth; 20% elsewhere.

ALFONSO TAFOYA, 655 6th Ave., # 212, New York NY 10010. (212)929-1090. Novels and short story collections. No genre fiction. Query. Also reviews nonfiction (50/50 fiction to nonfiction). Presently accepting new clients. Agent's commission: 15%. Member of I.L.A.A.

ROSLYN TARG LITERARY AGENCY, INC., 250 W. 57th St., New York NY 10107. (212)582-4210. Novels only. Query with SASE. Also reviews nonfiction. Presently accepting new clients. Interested in new/beginning novelists. Agent's commission: 15% "on all new unpublished authors I take on." Member of S.A.R. and I.L.A.A.

TEAL & WATT LITERARY AGENCY, 2036 Vista Del Rosa, Fullerton CA 92631. (714)738-8333. Contact: Patricia Teal. Novels only. Area of specialization: sub-specialty; romance novels. Send outline plus 3 sample chapters. Also reviews nonfiction (2-1 fiction to nonfiction). Presently accepting new clients. Interested in new/beginning novelists. Agent's commission: 10%.

SUSAN URSTADT INC., 125 E. 84th St., New York NY 10028. (212)744-6605. No science fiction, romance or occult. Send outline/proposal. Also reviews nonfiction (25/75 fiction to nonfiction). Presently accepting new clients. Interested in new/beginning novelists "if very good." Agent's commission: 10%. Member of I.L.A.A.

AUSTIN WAHL AGENCY, LTD., 332 S. Michigan Ave., Suite 1823, Chicago IL 60604. (312)922-3329. Novels, novelettes and short stories. Send outline/proposal plus information on author's background and where manuscript may have been submitted previously. Also reviews nonfiction (75% fiction—25% nonfiction). Presently accepting new clients "only on a very selective basis." Interested in new/beginning novelists "only if the manuscript has real market potential. We do prefer the author to have some publication credits." Agent's commission: 10-15%.

JOHN A. WARE LITERARY AGENCY, 392 Central Park West, New York NY 10025. (212)866-4733. Novels only; prefer query letter first. Outline plus 2-3 sample chapters or entire manuscript. Also reviews nonfiction (approximately 50-50 fiction to nonfiction). Presently accepting new clients. Interested in new/beginning novelists. Agent's commission: 10%.

CHERRY WEINER LITERARY AGENCY, 1734 Church St., Rahway NJ 07065. (201)574-0358. Only full-length manuscripts marketed. Query; or send outline/proposal. Also reviews nonfiction (85% fiction). Agent's commission: 15%.

WRITERS & ARTISTS AGENCY, 162 W. 56th St., New York NY 10019. (212)246-9029. Novels and short stories. Query only. Also reviews nonfiction. Agent's commission: 10%. Member of S.A.R.

WRITERS HOUSE, INC., 21 W. 26th St., New York NY 10010. Novels only. Area of specialization: romance, saga, spy thrillers, young adult, among others. Send outline plus 3 sample chapters and background. Also reviews nonfiction (75% fiction). Presently accepting new clients. Interested in new novelists "who already have published short fiction, or a novel or two." Member of I.L.A.A.

WRITERS' PRODUCTIONS, Box 418, Riverdale Station, The Bronx NY 10471. (212)796-5501. Contact: David L. Meth. Novels, novelettes, short stories, short story collections. Send outline plus sample chapters. Reviews "much more fiction." Presently accepting new clients. Interested in new/beginning novelists. Agent's commission: 10%. "Send a sample of 25-50 pages only, with a SASE for return of the ms. Clean, professional copies only. No phone calls, please."

SUSAN ZECKENDORF ASSOC., INC., 171 W. 57th St., New York NY 10019. (212)245-2928. Contact: Susan Zeckendorf. Query; send outline/proposal or outline plus sample chapters. Reviews nonfiction (25% fiction). Presently accepting new clients. Agent's commission: 10%. Member of I.L.A.A.

GEORGE ZIEGLER, 160 E. 97th St., New York NY 10029. Novels only. Area of specialization: non-category novels. Query; send outline plus 1 sample chapter with SASE. No phone calls. Also reviews nonfiction (50/50). Presently accepting new clients. Interested in new/beginning novelists. Agent's commission: 15%.

> 66 *. . . for fiction, imaginative work that is, is not dropped like a pebble upon the ground, as science may be; fiction is like a spider's web, attached ever so lightly perhaps, but still attached to life at all four corners.*
>
> *—Virginia Woolf* 99

agents

Category index

The category index is an alphabetized list of subjects containing the magazines and publishers that buy or accept specific categories of fiction. The four sections—literary/little magazines, commercial periodicals, small press and commercial publishers—are represented individually.

If you are seeking a market for your science fiction short story, for example, check the literary/little magazine section and/or the commercial periodical section under science fiction. After you have selected a possible market, refer to the market index for the correct page number. Then find the listing, and read it *carefully*.

This index is one method of connecting you with the proper market, but it is not to be used exclusively. Many magazines or presses are very general in their specifications and do not choose to be listed by categories. In the literary/little section there are no markets listed with needs for contemporary short stories because the great majority of these publications publish this type of fiction.

Literary/Little Magazines

Adventure. Amazon; Argonaut; Ball State Univ. Forum; Beacon Review; Berkeley Monthly Mag.; Black Jack; Blueline; Broomstick; California Horse Review; California Quarterly; Callaloo; Canadian Author & Bookman; Cedar Rock; Channel X; Coffee Break; Constellations; Cumberlands; Cut Bank; Deadspawn; De Colores Journal; Disabled Writers' Quarterly; Dreamweaver Mag.; Earth's Daughters; Earthwise Quarterly; Event; Fantasy Book; Fighting Woman; Freedom's Heart; Galactic Discourse; Green Feather; Hob Nob; Icelandic Canadian; Inky Trails Pub.; Kaleidoscope; Little Apple; Magical Blend; Menomonie Review; M'Godolim; Montana Review; Negative Capability; New Arts Review; New England Sampler; New Oregon Review; Newcomers Lit. Mag.; Nimrod; Novalis; Octomi; Origins; Other Side of Paradise; Owlflight; Pacific Rim Review; Paradox; PDSA Club; Persons; Phantasm; Potboiler; Proof Rock; Prorodeo Sports; Pteranodon Mag; Pub; Pulpsmith; Quantum Universe Mag.; Queen's

Quarterly; Reflect; Salome: Lit. Dance Mag.; Second Growth: Appalachian Nature & Culture; Sojourner; Space and Time; Stardate; Stardust; Street Mag.; Time to Pause; Tule River Times; Unknowns; Villager; Virginia Quarterly Review; Women: Journal of Liberation; Wyrd.

Canada. Ahnene Pub.; Alchemist; Antigonish Review; Black Cat Mystery Mag.; Canadian Author & Bookman; Capilano Review; Cross-Canada Writers' Quarterly; C.S.P. World News; Descant; Disabled Writers' Quarterly; Dreamweaver Mag.; Event; Fiddlehead; Fireweed; Grain; Green's Mag.; Guernica Review; Hysteria; Icelandic Canadian; Impulse Mag.; Malahat Review; Matrix; Moosehead Review; Nebula Mag.; Northward Journal; Origins; Pierian Spring; Potboiler; Prism Int.; Quarry; Queen's Quarterly; Room of One's Own; Stardust; Univ. of Windsor Review; Wascana Review; Waves; Wee Giant; West Coast Review; Whetstone; Wot; Word Loom; Writ.

Confession. Ball State Univ. Forum; California Quarterly; Confrontations; Critique; Double Harness Mag.; Global Tapestry Journal; Scree; Some Other Mag.; Spitball; Street Mag.

Erotica. Artful Dodge; Bellingham Review; Bogg; Bread & Roses; California Quarterly; Caprice; Chiricu; Clifton Mag.; Cut Bank; Day Tonight/Night Today; Double Harness Mag.; Dreamweaver Mag.; Earth's Daughters; Erotic Fiction Quarterly; Exit; Fat Tuesday; Foreign Artists, Poets and Authors Review; Gay Chicago Mag.; Global Tapestry Journal; Grain; High Rock Review; Hysteria; Kindred Spirit; Ludds Mill; Magic Changes; Maize, Notebooks of Xicano Art and Lit.; Montana Review; Moorlands Review; New Heat; New Oregon Review; Newcomers Lit. Mag.; Novalis; Occident; Overtone Series; Owlflight; Pawn Review; Phantasm; Potboiler; Proof Rock; Rapscallion's Dream; Samisdat; Scree; Some Other Mag.; Sou'wester; Stardust; Total Abandon Modern Arts Mag.; Uroboros; Willow Springs; Yellow Silk.

Ethnic. Amazon; Another Chicago Mag.; Areito; Artful Dodge; Ball State Univ. Forum; Bellingham Review; Bibliophilos; Black Jack; Black Scholar; Bread & Roses; Bridge; Broomstick; California Quarterly; Callaloo; Caprice; Celery; Chelsea; Chiricu; Clifton Mag.; Colonnades; Conditions; Confrontation/Change Review; Constellations; Cut Bank; Day Tonight/Night Today; De Colores Journal; Earth's Daughters; Earthwise Quarterly; Epoch Mag.; Fireweed; Foreign Artists, Poets and Authors Review; Helicon Nine; High Rock Review; Hysteria; Icelandic Canadian; Inside Out; Japanophile; Jewish Currents Mag.; Latin American Lit. Review; Laurel Review; Little Apple; Live Writers!; Luna; Maize, Notebooks of Xicano Art and Lit.; Menomonie Review; Metamorfosis; Midstream—Monthly Jewish Review; Midwest Arts & Lit.; Montana Review; Negative Capability; New America; New Arts Review; New Heat; Newcomers Lit. Mag.; Nimrod; Northward Journal; Obsidian; Okike; Origins; Overtone Series; Owlflight; Pacific Quarterly Moana; Pale Fire Review; Phantasm; Puerto Del Sol; Pulp; Rapscallion's Dream; Reflect; Revista; San Jose Studies; Scree; Second Growth: Appalachian Nature & Culture; Sez; Sing Heavenly Muse!; Sojourner; Source; South Carolina Review; South Dakota Review; Sou'wester; Street Mag.; Sun Tracks; Syracuse Scholar; Touchstone; Unicorn; Universal Black Writer Mag.; Valley Grapevine; Virginia Quarterly Review; Western Humanities Review; Word Loom; Writers Forum; Xavier Univ. Review; Yellow Silk.

Experimental. Ahnene Pub.; Akros Review; Another Chicago Mag.; Antioch Review; Artful Dodge; Backspace; Ball State Univ. Forum; Berkeley Monthly Mag.; Berkeley Poets Co-op.; Bibliophilos; Black Warrior Review; Bloodroot; Dogg; Dottomfish Mag.; Bread & Roses; Brown Review; Buff; Cache Review; California Quarterly; Calliope; Capilano Review; Caprice; Celery; Channel X; Chicago Review; Chiricu; Colorado State Review; Conjunctions; Constellations; Corona; Cosmic Circus; Crosstown Rag; Cut Bank; Day Tonight/Night Today; Deadspawn; Disabled Writers' Quarterly; Dog River Review; Earth's Daughters; Fat Tuesday; Fireweed; Gallery Works; Gargoyle Mag.; Georgia Review; Grain; Granta; Great River Review; Greensboro Review; Grimoire; Hecate; Helicon Nine; High Rock Review; Hysteria; Impulse Mag.; Indian Lit.; Indiana Review; Inside Out; Kaleidoscope; Kindred Spirit; Konglomerati; Kudos; Linq; Lionhead; Little Apple; Loonfeather; Ludds Mills; Luna; Madison Review; Menomonie Review; Metro; Mississippi Review; Montana Review; Moorlands Review; Nebo; Negative Capability; Nepgan Review; New Heat; New Renaissance; Nexus; Nightsun; Nimrod; Northwest Review; Novalis; Octomi; Okike; Origins; Outermost; Overtone Series; Owlflight; Pacific Rim Review; Pale Fire Review; Partisan Review; Pennsylvania Review; Pikestaff Forum;

Portland Review; Potboiler; Proof Rock; Ptolemy/Browns Mills Review; Puerto Del Sol; Pulp; Quarry; Queen's Quarterly; Rapscallion's Dream; Reflect; Revista; Scree; Sepia; Slick; Smackwarm; Sojourner; Sou'wester; Spitball; Stardate; Stardust; Street Bagel; Street Mag.; Syracuse Scholar; Taylor One-Shot; Total Abandon Modern Arts Mag.; Touchstone; Undinal Songs; Uroboros; West Coast Review; Whetstone; Wisconsin Academy Review; Wisconsin Review; Wolfsong; Word Loom; Writers Forum; Wyrd; Xavier Review; Yellow Silk.

Fantasy. AFTA; Ahnene Pub.; Akros Review; Antithesis; Argonaut; Artful Dodge; Aurora; Ball State Univ. Forum; Beacon Review; Bellingham Review; Berkeley Poets Co-op; Bibliophilos; Bloodrake; Both Sides Now; Box 749; Bread & Roses; Brown Review; Cache Review; California Quarterly; Canadian Author & Bookman; Caprice; Cedar Rock; Channel X; Chicago Review; Chiricu; Clifton Mag.; Coffee Break; Confrontation/Change Review; Constellations; Corona; Cosmic Circus; Crosstown Rag; Cumberlands; Cut Bank; Cygnus Chronicles; Dark Horizons; Deadspawn; De Colores Journal; Disabled Writers' Quarterly; Dog River Review; Dreamweaver Mag.; Earth's Daughters; Earthwise Quarterly; Eerie Country; Empire; Event; Exit; Fantasy Book; Fantasy Macabre; Fantasy Tales; Fighting Woman News; Fireweed; Floating Island; Freedom's Heart; Fruition; Galactic Discourse; Global Tapestry Journal; Golden Isis; Gothic; Granta; Grimoire; Helicon Nine; Hob-Nob; Hor-Tasy; Hysteria; Inky Trails Pub.; Inlet; Journal Fantome; Kadath; Kaleidoscope; Kalliope Journal of Women's Arts; Kayak; Kindred Spirit; Konglomerati; Little Apple; Living Color; Luna; Magic Changes; Magical Blend; Memphis State Review; Mendocino Review; Menomonie Review; M'Godolim; Midwest Arts & Lit.; Mississippi Review; Moorlands Review; Mythellany; Naked Singularity; Negative Capability; Nepgan Review; New England Sampler; New Laurel Review; New Oregon Review; Nexus; North American Mentor Mag.; North Country Anvil; Novalis; Octomi; Origins; Other Side of Paradise; Outermost; Owlflight; Pale Fire Review; Pandora (FL); Paradox; Parsec Fanzine; PDSA Club News; Persons; Piedmont Literary Review; Pig Iron; Portland Review; Potboiler; Primavera; Proof Rock; Prop; Pteranodon Mag.; Pub; Pulpsmith; Quantum Universe Mag.; Quarry; Owen's Quarterly; Rampant Guinea Pig; Rapscallion's Dream; Reflect; Riverside Quarterly; Salome: Literary Dance Mag.; Sands; Sing Heavenly Muse!; Slick; Smackwarm; Sojourner; Southern Humanities Review; Sou'wester; Space and Time; Stardate; Stardust; Street Mag.; Syracuse Scholar; Taylor One-Shot; Threshold of Fantasy; Time to Pause; Touchstone; Undinal Songs; Unicorn; Unknowns; Virginia Quarterly Review; Weirdbook; Wolfsong; Women: Journal of Liberation; Words Lost; Wyrd; Xavier Review; Yellow Silk.

Feminist or Lesbian. AFTA; Amazon; Another Chicago Mag.; Artful Dodge; Aura; Aurora; Ball State Univ. Forum; Bare Wires; Bellingham Review; Bloodroot; Both Sides Now; Bread & Roses; Broadsheet Mag.; Broomstick; California Quarterly; Calliope; Canadian Author & Bookman; Chiricu; Clifton Mag.; Conditions; Day Tonight/Night Today; De Colores Journal; Disabled Writers' Quarterly; Double Harness Mag.; Dreamweaver Mag.; Earth's Daughters; Event; Feminist Studies; Fighting Woman News; Focus: Journal for Lesbians; Galactic Discourse; Gay Chicago Mag.; Granta; Harvard Advocate; Hecate; Heresies; Home Planet News; Hysteria; Inside Out; Jam To-day; Kindred Spirit; Lesbian Voices; Letters Mag. (NY); Linq; Live Writers!; Ludds Mills; Luna; Mati; Menomonie Review; Nexus; Nightsun; Occident; Other Side of Paradise; Overtone Series; Owlflight; Pale Fire Review; Pandora (FL and NJ); Persons; Phantasm; Plainswoman; Portland Review; Primavera; RFD; Room of One's Own; Salome: Literary Dance Mag.; Samisdat; Sez; Sing Heavenly Muse!; Sojourner; Source; Sou'wester; Stardust; 13th Moon; Virginia Quarterly Review; Willow Springs; Women: Journal of Liberation; Word Loom; Yellow Silk.

Foreign (excluding Canada). Antigruppo; Aquarius; Broadsheet Mag.; Busy Bees' News; Caprice; Chandrabhaga; Compass Poetry & Prose; Cygnus Chronicler; Dark Horizons; Double Harness Mag.; Encounter; Fantasy Tales; Foresight; Global Tapestry Journal; Granta; Hecate; Impegno; Indian Lit.; Ins & Outs; Iron Mag.; Kadath; Kudos; Kunapipi; Linq; Ludds Mill; Moorlands Review; Nepgan Review; New Arts Review; Okike; Outcrowd; Pacific Quarterly Moana; PDSA Club; Prospice; Sepia; Smoke; Stand; Start Mag.; Stony Thursday Book; Together.

Gay. AFTA; Amazon; Another Chicago Mag.; Artful Dodge; Aurora; Bare Wires; Bellingham Review; Both Sides Now; Bread & Roses; California Quarterly; Caprice; Chiricu; Clifton Mag.;

Corona; Cosmic Circus; Day Tonight/Night Today; Disabled Writers' Quarterly; Double Harness Mag.; Dreamweaver Mag.; Event; Feminist Studies; Fireweed; Galactic Discourse; Gay Chicago Mag.; Granta; Harvard Advocate; Hecate; Home Planet News; Hysteria; Inside Out; Kindred Spirit; Letters Mag. (NY); Linq; Ludds Mill; Menomonie Review; M'Godolim; Occident; Overtone Series; Owlflight; Phantasm; Portland Review; Primavera; Samisdat; Sez; Sojourner; Source; Sou'wester; 13th Moon; Willow Springs; Yellow Silk.

Historical. Amazon; Antigruppo; Areito; Ball State Univ. Forum; Berkeley Monthly Mag.; Bibliophilos; Blueline; Cache Review; Constellations; Critique; Cut Bank; Fireweed; Four Winds; Freedom's Heart; Fruition; Gorham; Helicon Nine; Jewish Currents; Linq; Luna; Mendocino Review; Metro; Montana Review; New Arts Review; New Oregon Review; Newcomers Lit. Mag.; Overtone Series; Owlflight; PDSA Club News; Persons; Phoebe; Pilgrim Way; Portland Review; Ptolemy/Browns Mills Review; Quantum Universe Mag.; Queen's Quarterly; Reflect; Sojourner; Spitball; Street Mag.; Syracuse Scholar; Touchstone; Tule River Times; Unknowns; The Villager; Wisconsin Academy Review; Word Loom; Xavier Review.

Horror. AFTA; Ahnene Pub.; Antithesis; Argonaut; Beacon Review; Bellingham Review; Bibliophilos; Black Cat Mystery; Bloodrake; Cache Review; Canadian Author & Bookman; Clifton Mag.; Coffee Break; Cosmic Circus; Dark Horizon; Deadspawn; Disabled Writers' Quarterly; Dreamweaver Mag.; Eerie Country; Eldritch Tales; Fantasy Book; Fantasy Macabre; Fantasy Tales; Golden Iris; Gothic; Grimoire; Hor-Tasy; Journal Fantome; Kadath; Little Apple; Living Color; M'Godolim; Moorlands Review; Naked Singularity; Nepgan Review; New Arts Review; New Heat; New Oregon Review Newcomers Lit. Mag.; North Country Anvil; Novalis; Other Side of Paradise; Outermost; Owlflight; Paradox; Potboiler; Pub; Pulpsmith; Quantum Universe Mag.; Rapscallion's Dream; Space and Time; Spiderweb; Stardate; Street Mag.; Taylor One-Shot; Threshold of Fantasy; Undinal Songs; Weirdbook; Words Lost; Wyrd.

Humor. AFTA; Ahnene Pub.; Akros Review; Amazon; Another Chicago Mag.; Antigruppo; Antithesis; Aquarius; Aurora; Backspace; Ball State Univ. Forum; Bare Wires; Beacon Review; Bellingham Review; Berkeley Monthly Mag.; Berkeley Poets Co-op; Bibliophilos; Black Jack; Blueline; Bogg; Both Sides Now; Box 749; Breath of People; Brown Review; Bug Tar; Cache Review; California Pelican; California Quarterly; Calliope; Canadian Author & Bookman; Caprice; Celery; Channel X; Chicago Review; Chiricu; Clifton Mag.; Coffee Break; Colonnades; Confrontations; Constellations; Corona; Cosmic Circus; Crosstown Rag; Cumberlands; Cut Bank; Day Tonight/Night Today; Deadspawn; De Colores Journal; Disabled Writers' Quarterly; Dog River Review; Double Harness Mag.; Dreamweaver Mag.; Earth's Daughters; Earthwise Quarterly; Eureka Review; Event; Fat Tuesday; Fireweed; Forms; Freedom's Heart; Gargoyle; Golden Isis; Helicon Nine; Hob-Nob; Home Planet; Icelandic Canadian; Indian Lit.; Inky Trails Pub.; Inlet; Inside Out; Iron Mag.; Jewish Currents Mag.; Kaleidoscope; Karamu; Kindred Spirit; Laurel Review; Letters Mag. (NY); Linq; Little Apple; Live Writers!; Living Color; Luna; Maize; Notebooks of Xicano Art and Lit.; Mendocino Review; Menomonie Review; Metamorfosis; M'Godolim; Micropsychology Newsletter; Midwest Arts & Lit.; Mississippi Review; Moorlands Review; Mythellany; New Arts Review; New England Sampler; New Heat; New Oregon Review; New Renaissance; Newcomers Lit. Mag.; Nexus; Nit & Wit; North Country Anvil; Octomi; Origins; Other Side of Paradise; Outcrowd; Outermost; Owlflight; Pacific Quarterly Moana; Pale Fire Review; Pandora (FL and NJ); Pawn Review; PDSA Club News; Pennsylvania Review; Persons; Phantasm; Phoebe; George Mason Review; Piedmont Literary Review; Portland Review; Potboiler; Poultry; Prairie Schooner; Primavera; Proof Rock; Prorodeo Sports; Pteranodon Mag.; Ptolemy/Browns Mills Review; Pulpsmith; Quantum Universe Mag.; Queen's Quarterly; Rampant Guinea Pig; Rapscallion's Dream; Reflect; Salome: Lit. Dance Mag.; Samisdat; San Jose Studies; San Juan Horseshoe; Scholia Satyrica; Second Coming; Second Growth; Appalachian Nature & Culture; Sepia; Signals; Sing Heavenly Muse!; Slick; Smackwarm; Sojourner; South Carolina Review; Southern Humanities Review; Space and Time; Stardate; Stardust; Stony Thursday Book; Story Quarterly; Street Bagel; Syracuse Scholar; Taylor One-Shot; Threshold of Fantasy; Time to Pause; Touchstone; Tule River Times; Uncle Mag.; Unicorn; Unknowns; Uroboros; Villager; Virginia Quarterly Review; Wascana Review; Western Humanities Review; William and Mary Review; Wisconsin Academy Review; Wolfsong; Women: Journal of Liberation; Word Loom; Wyrd; Yellow Silk.

Juvenile. Amazon; Black Scholar; Breath of People; Busy Bees' News; De Colores Journal; Fruition; Inky Trails Pub.; Linq; Mendocino Review; Mythellany; PDSA Club News; Pilgrim Way; Sojourner; Stone Soup; Time to Pause; Together.

Men's. Aura; Ball State Univ. Forum; Beacon Review; Black Scholar; California Quarterly; Calliope; Canadian Author & Bookman; Coffee Break; Cottonwood Review; Cumberlands; Cut Bank; De Colores Journal; Double Harness Mag.; Inside Out; Kindred Spirit; Letters Mag. (NY); Maize; Menomonie Review; Montana Review; Moorlands Review; New America; New Heat; New Oregon Review; Notebooks of Xicano Art and Lit.; Occident; Pacific Rim Review; Phantasm; Prorodeo Sports; Rapscallion's Dream; Reflect; San Jose Studies; Sez; Signals; Street Bagel; Virginia Quarterly Review.

Mystery/Spy/Suspense. AFTA; Amazon; Argonaut; Ball State Univ. Forum; Beacon Review; Bellingham Review; Bibliophilos; Black Cat Mystery Mag.; Cache Review; California Quarterly; Canadian Author & Bookman; Coffee Break; Constellations; Crosstown Rag; Cumberlands; Deadspawn; De Colores Journal; Disabled Writers' Quarterly; Dreamweaver Mag.; Earthwise Quarterly; Exit; Fantasy Macabre; Foreign Artists, Poets and Authors Review; Galactic Discourse; Golden Isis; Hob-Nob; Inky Trails Pub.; Inside Out; Joint Endeavor; Kaleidoscope; Letters Mag. (Maine); Little Apple; Live Writers; Mendocino Review; M'Godolim; Moorlands Review; Mystery Time; Negative Capability; Nepgan Review; New Arts Review; New England Sampler; New Heat; New Oregon Review; Newcomers Lit. Mag.; Origins; Owlflight; Pale Fire Review; PDSA Club News; Phantasm; Potboiler; Prorodeo Sports; Pteranodon Mag.; Pub; Pulpsmith; Salome: Lit. Dance Mag.; Sing Heavenly Muse!; Sojourner; Spiderweb; Spitball; Stardate; Street Mag.; Taylor One-Shot; Tempest; Time to Pause; Touchstone; Tule River Times; Unknowns; Villager; Wisconsin Academy Review; Women: Journal of Liberation.

Prose Poem. Ahnene Pub.; Akros Review; Antaeus; Antithesis; Aquarius; Artful Dodge; Ball State Univ. Forum; Barnwood; Berkeley Poets Co-op; Bibliophilos; Black Warrior Review; Blueline; Bogg; Bottomfish Mag.; Cache Review; California Quarterly; Celery; Chandrabhaga; Chiricu; Condition; Corona; Cut Bank; Day Tonight/Night Today; Disabled Writers' Quarterly; Dog River Review; Earth's Daughters; Fat Tuesday; Fruition; Galactic Discourse; Gallery Works; Grain; Grimoire; Hecate; Helicon Nine; High Rock Review; Indian Lit.; Indiana Review; Inside Out; Jewish Currents Mag.; Joint Endeavor; Journal Fantome; Kaleidoscope; Kindred Spirit; Kudos; Linq; Little Apple; Luna; Madison Review; Mendocino Review; Menomonie Review; Metamorfosis; Metro; Micropsychology Newsletter; Montana Review; Moorlands Review; Nebo; Negative Capability; New Heat; Newcomers Lit. Mag.; Nexus; Nightsun; Nimrod; Octomi; Okike; Origins; Other Side of Paradise; Outermost; Overtone Series; Owlflight; Pale Fire Review; Partisan Review; Pennsylvania Review; Portland Review; Proof Rock; Puerto Del Sol; Rapscallion's Dream; Rhino; Salome: Lit. Dance Mag.; Sands; Scree; Sepia; Smoke; Sojourner; Street Bagel; Street Mag.; Syracuse Scholar; Taylor One-Shot; Touchstone; Undinal Songs; Unicorn; Unknowns; Webster Review; West Coast Review; Willow Springs; Wolfsong; Word Loom; Wyrd; Xavier Review; Yellow Silk.

Psychic/Supernatural. AFTA; Amazon; Anthithesis; Argonaut; Ball State Univ. Forum; Bellingham Review; Bibliophilos; Black Cat Mystery Mag.; Both Sides Now; Bread & Roses; California Quarterly; Cedar Rock; Coffee Break; Cosmic Circus; Critique; Cumberlands; Dark Horizons; De Colores Journal; Disabled Writers' Quarterly; Dreamweaver Mag.; Earthwise Quarterly; Eerie Country; Fantasy Book; Fantasy Macabre; Fantasy Tales; Floating Island; Foresight; Galactic Discourse; Golden Isis; Gothic; Grimoire; High Rock Review; Hob-Nob; Inky Trails Pub.; Kadath; Kaleidoscope; Kindred Spirit; Little Apple; Luna; Magic Changes; Magical Blend; Midwest Arts & Lit.; Moorlands Review; Naked Singularity; Negative Capability; Nepgan Review; New Arts Review; New England Sampler; New Heat; New Oregon Review; Novalis; Outermost; Owlflight; Pale Fire Review; Portland Review; Proof Rock; Pub; Quantum Universe Mag.; Rapscallion's Dream; Reflect; Samisdat; Shadows Of; Slick; Stardate; Stardust; Street Mag.; Threshold of Fantasy; Time to Pause; Undinal Songs; Weirdbook; Wyrd.

Religious/Inspirational. Ahnene Pub.; Ball State Univ. Forum; Both Sides Now; California Quarterly; Critique; Disabled Writers' Quarterly; Earth's Daughters; Fellowship in Prayer;

Forms; Hob-Nob; Inky Trails Pub.; Kaleidoscope; M'Godolim; Midstream—Monthly Jewish Review; Midwest Arts & Literature; New England Sampler; Pilgrim Way; Rapscallion's Dream; Street Mag.; Studia Mystica; Time to Pause; Together; Xavier Review.

Romance (Contemporary). Ahnene Pub.; Ball State Univ. Forum; Blow; California Quarterly; Canadian Author & Bookman; Coffee Break; Constellations; Crosstown Rag; De Colores Journal; Earthwise Quarterly; Hob-Nob; Inky Trails Pub.; Kaleidoscope; Negative Capability; New Heat; PDSA Club News; Proof Rock; Pteranodon Mag.; Salome: Lit. Dance Mag.; Sojourner; Stardate; Street Mag.; Time to Pause; Unicorn; Virginia Quarterly Review.

Romance (Gothic/Historical). Ball State Univ. Forum; Bellingham Review; Bibliophilos; Canadian Author & Bookman; Confrontations; Constellations; Double Harness Magazine; Dreamweaver Mag.; Earthwise Quarterly; Eerie Country; Gothic; Karamu; Negative Capability; New England Sampler; Pteranodon Mag.; Samisdat; Sojourner; Undinal Songs; Weirdbook.

Science Fiction. Abbey; AFTA; Amazon; Antithesis; Argonaut; Artful Dodge; Aura; Aurora; Ball State Univ. Forum; Beacon Review; Bellingham Review; Beyond Fiction; Bibliophilos; Bloodrake; Bogg; Cache Review; California Quarterly; Canadian Author & Bookman; Cedar Rock; Chicago Review; Chiricu; Clifton Mag.; Coffee Break; Confrontations; Constellations; Cosmic Circus; Critique; Crosstown Rag; Cygnus Chronicler; Day Tonight/Night Today; Deadspawn; De Colores Journal; Disabled Writers' Quarterly; Dreamweaver Mag.; Earthwise Quarterly; Empire; Eureka Review; Event; Exit; Fantasy Book; Fighting Woman News; Floating Island; Foreign Artists, Poets and Authors Review; Freedom's Heart; Galactic Discourse; Global Tapestry Journal; Golden Isis; Hob-Nob; Home Planet News; Hysteria; Inlet; Iron Mag.; Jam Today; Kaleidoscope; Kalliope; Journal of Women's Arts; Kindred Spirit; Konglomerati; Letters Mag. (NY and Maine); Linq; Little Apple; Live Writers!; Ludds Mill; Luna; Magic Changes; Mati; Memphis State Review; Mendocino Review; Menomonie Review; M'Godolim; Midwest Arts & Lit.; Moorlands Review; Moosehead Review; Naked Singularity; Nebo; Nepgan Review; New Arts Review; New Heat; New England Sampler; New Heat; New Oregon Review; Newscribes; Nexus; Nimrod; North American Mentor Mag.; Octomi; Origins; Other Side of Paradise; Outermost; Owlflight; Pale Fire Review; Pandora (FL); Paradox; Parsec Fanzine; Pawn Review; Persons; Piedmont Lit. Review; Portland Review; Potboiler; Primavera; Pteranodon Mag.; Pulpsmith; Quantum Universe Mag.; Quarry; Queen's Quarterly; Rampant Guinea Pig; Rapscallion's Dream; Red Cedar Review; Reflect; Riverside Quarterly; Salome: Lit. Dance Mag.; Samisdat; Second Coming; Slick; Sojourner; Space and Time; Stardate; Stardust; Syracuse Scholar; Taylor One-Shot; Tempest; Threshold of Fantasy; Unicorn; Unknowns; Wisconsin Academy Review; Words Lost; Wyrd; Yellow Silk.

Serialized, Condensed or Excerpted Novels. Antaeus; Anthithesis; Aquarius; Artful Dodge; Aurora; Ball State Univ. Forum; Bellingham Review; Bibliophilos; Black Jack; Buff; Cache Review; California Horse Review; California Quarterly; Chiricu; Day Tonight/Night Today; De Colores Journal; Disabled Writers' Quarterly; Double Harness Mag.; Fantasy Book; Fat Tuesday; Fireweed; Global Tapestry Journal; Granta; High Rock Review; Hob-Nob; Inside Out; Kaleidoscope; Kudos; Little Apple; Loonfeather; Ludds Mill; Memphis State Review; Mendocino Review; Metamorfosis; Montana Review; Naked Singularity; Nepgan Review; New Arts Review; Newcomers Lit. Mag.; Octomi; Okike; Origins; Overtone Series; Pacific Rim Review; Pale File Review; PDSA Club News; Phoenix; Pikestaff Forum; Pub; Puerto Del Sol; Pulp; Quantam Universe Mag.; Quarry; Salome: Lit. Dance Mag.; South Dakota Review; Stardate; Stony Thursday Book; Story Quarterly; Street Mag.; Syracuse Scholar; Time to Pause; Tule River Times; Unknowns; Virginia Quarterly Review; Webster Review; West Coast Review; Western Humanities Review; Word Loom; Writ Mag.; Xavier Review.

Translations. Akros Review; Another Chicago Mag.; Antaeus; Antigonish Review; Antigruppo; Antioch Review; Arizona Quarterly; Artful Dodge; Aurora; Backspace; Ball State Univ. Forum; Barat Review; Beacon Review; Bellingham Review; Bibliophilos; Box 749; Bread & Roses; Cache Review; California Quarterly; Chandrabhaga; Chariton Review; Chiricu; Colorado State Review; Columbia: Mag. of Poetry & Prose; Conditions; Confrontation; Conjunctions; Constellations; Critique; Croton Review; Cut Bank; De Colores Journal; Denver Quarterly; Descant; Dimension; Disabled Writers' Quarterly; Dog River Review; Double Harness Mag.; Dreamweaver

Mag.; Earthwise Quarterly; Exit; Fighting Woman News; Fireweed; Forms; Gargoyle; Global Tapestry; Gothic; Granta; Harvard Advocate; Helicon Nine; High Rock Review; Home Planet; Icelandic Canadian; Inside Out; Iron Mag.; Jewish Currents Mag.; Kindred Spirit; Kudos; Letters Mag. (NY); Little Apple; Mati; M'Godolim; Midwest Arts & Lit.; Mississippi Review; Montana Review; Moorlands Review; Moosehead Review; Negative Capability; Nepgan Review; New Arts Review; New Heat; New Laurel Review; New Orleans Review; New Renaissance; Nimrod; Nit & Wit; Northwest Review; Occident; Octomi; Okike; Origins; Overtone Series; Owlflight; Pacific Quarterly Moana; Parabola; Partisan Review; Pawn Review; Phantasm; Portland Review; Prairie Schooner; Prism Int.; Proof Rock; Prospice; Ptolemy/Browns Mills Review; Puerto Del Sol; Pulp; Quarry; Quarterly West; Revista; Salome: Lit. Dance Mag.; Sands; Sepia; Slick; Snowy Egret; Sojourner; Some Other Mag.; South Dakota Review; Sou'wester; Stand; Stony Thursday Book; Street Mag.; Syracuse Scholar; Thunder Mountain Review; Total Abandon Modern Arts Mag.; Touchstone; Translation; Triquarterly; Virginia Quarterly Review; Webster Review; Westbranch; West Coast Review; Western Humanities Review; Willow Springs; Writ Magazine; Word Loom; Xavier Review; Yale Literary Mag.; Yellow Silk.

War. Berkeley Monthly Mag.; Pacific Rim Review.

Western. Ball State Univ. Forum; Beacon Review; Berkeley Monthly Mag.; Black Jack; California Horse Review; California Quarterly; Canadian Author & Bookman; Coffee Break; Colorado State Review; Constellations; Cut Bank; De Colores Journal; Dreamweaver Mag.; Earthwise Quarterly; Four Winds; Green Feather; Inky Trails Pub.; New Arts Review; Owlflight; Phantasm; Prorodeo Sports; Pteranodon Mag.; Pulpsmith; Samisdat; San Juan Horseshoe; Scree; Sojourner; Street Mag.; Time to Pause; Tule River Times; Unknowns; Valley Grapevine; Writers Forum.

Women's. AFTA; Ahnene Pub.; Amazon; Aura; Aurora; Ball State Univ. Forum; Barat Review; Bare Wires; Beacon Review; Berkeley Monthly Mag.; Black Scholar; Bread & Roses; Broadsheet Mag.; Broomstick; California Quarterly; Calliope; Canadian Author & Bookman; Chiricu; Coffee Break; Colorado State Review; Conditions; Constellations; Cottonwood Review; Cumberlands; Cut Bank; Day Tonight/Night Today; De Colores Journal; Double Harness Mag.; Earth's Daughters; Feminist Studies; Galactic Discourse; Helicon Nine; Heresies; Inside Out; Jewish Currents Mag.; Kalliope; Letters Mag. (NY); Little Apple; Maize; Montana Review; Negative Capability; New America; New Heat; Notebooks of Xicano Art and Lit.; Menomonie Review; Occident; Okike; Overtone Series; Pacific Rim Review; Pale Fire Review; Pandora (FL and NJ); PDSA Club News; Phantasm; Plainswoman; Proof Rock; Queen's Quarterly; Reflect; Room of One's Own; Salome: Lit. Dance Mag.; San Jose Studies; Sez; Signals; Sing Heavenly Muse!; Sojourner; Source; Story Quarterly; Street Bagel; Virginia Quarterly Review; Wisconsin Academy Review; Women: Journal of Liberation; Xavier Review.

Young Adult. Bibliophilos; Black Scholar; Channel X; Constellations; De Colores Journal; Foreign Artists, Poets and Authors Review; Helicon Nine; Hob-Nob; Inky Trails Pub.; Inside Out; Kaleidoscope; Mythellany; Negative Capability; New England Sampler; New Heat; Other Side of Paradise; PDSA Club News; Persons; Portland Review; Purple Cow; Sojourner; Stone Soup; Street Mag.; Time to Pause; Unknowns.

Commercial Periodicals

Adventure. Ahoy; Alaska Outdoors; Alive!; Amazing Sci. Fi. Stories; American Squaredance; Augusta Spectator; Autobuff; Bird Talk; Birmingham Settlement Mag.; Boys' Life; Bread; Bronze Thrills; Buffalo Spree; Butterfat; Canadian Skater; Cavalier; Chatelaine; Chesapeake Bay; Chic; Christian Adventure; Christian Life; Clubhouse; Coastal Journals; Cobblestone; Color Computer; Corvette Fever; Cosmopolitan; Crusader; Currents; Dash; Dialogue; Discoveries; Easyriders; Ebony Jr!; Essence; Family Radio & TV Mag.; Friend; Gent; Gentleman's Companion; Gospel Carrier; Hang Gliding Mag.; Hi-Call; High Adventure; Highwire; Hustler; Inside Running; Jack & Jill; Junior Trails; Lighted Pathway; Messenger of Sacred Heart; Ms

Mag.; New Age; New Alaskan; New Eng. Senior Citizen News; Nugget; Oracle; Penthouse; Playboy; Players; Pockets; Prestige; Prime Times; Ranger Rick's Nature Mag.; Read; Road King; Running Times; San Gabriel Valley; Sat. Evening Post; Seventeen; Spirit; Stag; Straight; Student; Touch; Trailer Boats; Trails; Venture; Western People; Western Producer; Wisconsin Restaurateur; Working For Boys; Wyo. Rural Elec. News; Young Judean.

Canada. Ahoy; Butterfat Mag.; Canadian Skater; Chatelaine; Chickadee; Deaf Canadian; Elite; Farm & Forest; Flare; Living Message; Messenger of Sacred Heart; Our Family; Reader's Choice; Western People.

Confession. American Squaredance; Bronze Thrills; Crusader; Friday of Jewish Exponent; Hers; Jive; National Supermarket Shopper; Secrets; Student.

Contemporary/Mainstream. Atlantic Monthly; Augusta Spectator; Bird Talk; Birmingham Settlement Mags; Boston Monthly; Boston Review; Boys' Life; Buffalo Spree Mag.; Chatelaine; Chicago; Clubhouse; Color Computer; Contact High; Cosmopolitan; Darling; Dialogue; Ebony Jr!; Electricity; Elite; Esquire; Face-to-Face; Fair Lady; Family Circle; Farm Wife News; First Class; Friday of Jewish Exponent; Friend; Gent; Gentleman's Companion; Good Housekeeping; Greek Accent; Harper's; Highwire; Home Life; Inside; Inside Running; Insight; Junior Trails; Lighted Pathway; Living & Loving; Living Message; Lutheran Journal; Mademoiselle; Mature Living; McCall's; Moment; Ms Mag.; New Age; New Eng. Senior Citizen News; New Satirist; Nugget; Other Side; Oui Mag.; Penthouse; Pioneer Woman; Playboy; Pockets; Prestige; Prime Times; Racquetball Illustrated; Reader's Choice; Redbook; Running Times; St. Anthony Messenger; St. Joseph's Messenger & Advocate of Blind; San Gabriel Valley Mag.; Seventeen; Straight; Student Surgical Technologist; Teens Today; Today's Christian Woman; Trailer Boats Mag.; Trails; Virtue; Western People; Wisconsin Restaurateur; Woman's Day; Woman's World; Working Mother; Young Judean; Young Miss.

Erotica. Beaver; Beef; Cavalier; Chic; Electricity; Elite; Gallery; Gem; Gent; Harvey for Loving People; Hustler; Men; Nugget; Penthouse; Penthouse (UK); Pillow Talk; Players; Prime Times; Rapport; Running Times; Stag; Swank.

Ethnic. Alive!; American Mizrachi Woman; Ararat; Attenzione; Baltimore Jewish Times; B'nai B'rith Int.; Jewish Monthly; Boston Review; Bronze Thrills; Buffalo Spree; Butterfat; Chicago; Clubhouse; Crusader; Ebony Jr!; Family Circle; Friday of Jewish Exponent; Greek Accent; Hadassah; Hers; Highwire; Inside; Inside Kung Fu; Mademoiselle; Moment; Ms Mag.; New Eng. Senior Citizen News; Other Side; Pioneer Woman; Pockets; Prestige; Prime Times; Scandinavian Review; Scholastic Scope; Seventeen; Stories; Student; Teens Today; Touch; World Over; Wyo. Rural Elec. News; Young Judean.

Experimental. Augusta Spectator; Birmingham Settlement; Boston Review; Essence; Hang Gliding Mag.; New Age; New Satirist; The Other Side; Players; Runner; Rod Serling's Twilight Zone.

Fantasy. Amazing Sci. Fi. Stories; American Squaredance; Ares; Autobuff; Bird Talk; Birmingham Settlement Mags; Bronze Thrills; Campus Life; Chesapeake Bay; Color Computer; Corvette Fever; Ebony Jr!; Electricity; Elite; Essence; Gallery; Gentleman's Companion; Hang Gliding Mag.; Highwire; Inside Running; Isaac Asimov's Sci. Fi. Mag.; Men; Ms Mag.; National Doll World; National Supermarket Shopper; New Satirist; Omni; Oracle; Other Side; Oui Mag.; Playboy; Players; Pockets; Prestige; Ranger Rick's Nature; Read; Road King; Running Times; Rod Serling's Twilight Zone; Seventeen; Trailer Boats; Trails; Woman's Day; Young Judean.

Feminist or Lesbian. Bronze Thrills; Buffalo Spree; Harvey for Loving People; Highwire; Mademoiselle; Ms Mag.; New Age; Playgirl; Prime Times; Woman's Day.

Foreign (excluding Canada). Birmingham Settlement Mags; Darling; Dolly Magazine; Fair Lady; Family Radio & TV Mag.; Hers; Island Mag.; It Mag.; Living & Loving; Mother; My Weekly; Penthouse (UK); Reality; Your Family.

Gay. Bronze Thrills; Contact High; Fair Lady; Highwire; Mademoiselle; Ms Mag.; New Age; Other Side; Redbook; Runner; Seventeen.

Historical. American Squaredance; Baltimore Jewish Times; Butterfat; Chesapeake Bay; Christian Adventure; Clubhouse; Coastal Journals; Cobblestone; Currents; Daughters of Sarah; Friday of Jewish Exponent; Gentleman's Companion; Gospel Carrier; Hang Gliding Mag.; High Adventure; Inside Running; Lighted Pathway; Moment; New Eng. Senior Citizen News; Players; Pockets; Prestige; Romantic Times; Running Times; Stories; Wyo. Rural Elec. News; Young Judean.

Horror. Cavalier; Gallery; Gent; Gentleman's Companion; Hang Gliding Mag.; Highwire Mag.; Inside Running; Nugget; Penthouse; Playboy; Rod Serling's Twilight Zone.

Humor. Alive!; Amazing Sci. Fi. Stories; American Squaredance; Augusta Spectator; Autobuff; Baltimore Jewish Times; Bird Talk; B'nai B'rith Int.; Jewish Monthly; Boston Monthly; Boston Review; Boys' Life; Beef; Buffalo Spree; Campus Life; Chatelaine; Chesapeake Bay Mag.; Chicago; Color Computer; Contact High; Corvette Fever; Darling; Dash; Dialogue; Ebony Jr!; Electricity; Elite; Essence; Family Circle; Farm Wife News; Fine Line Productions; First Class; Friday of Jewish Exponent; Friend; Gallery; Gambling Scene West; Gem; Gent; Golf Journal; Greek Accent; Hang Gliding Mag.; Harper's; Hi-Call; Highwire Mag.; Home Life; Ideals; Inside; Inside Running; Jack & Jill; Lighted Pathway; Living Message; Mature Living; McCall's; Men; Messenger of Sacred Heart; Ms Mag.; My Weekly; National Doll World; National Forum; Phi Kappa Phi Journal; The National Supermarket Shopper; New Age; New Alaskan; New Eng. Senior Citizen News; New Satirist; Nugget; One Mag.; Oracle; Other Side; Oui; Penthouse (UK); Playboy Mag.; Players; Prestige; Prime Times; Racquetball Illustrated; Ranger Rick's Nature Mag.; Rapport; Reader's Choice; Reality; Road King; Road Rider; Runner; Running Times; St. Joseph's Messenger & Advocate of the Blind; San Gabriel Valley Mag.; Sat. Evening Post; Seventeen; Sprint; Stag; Stories; Straight; Sunshine Mag.; Surgical Technologist; Swank; 'Teen Mag.; Teens Today; Trailer Boats Mag.; Trails; Venture; Virtue; Vista; Western People; Western Producer; Wisconsin Restaurateur; Woman's Day; Working For Boys; Wyo. Rural Elec. News; Young Judean; Your Family.

Juvenile. Action; Ahoy; Bible in Life Friends; Bird Talk; Chickadee; Child Life; Children's Digest; Children's Playmate; Church Herald; Clubhouse; Cricket; Crusader; Dash; Discoveries; Ebony Jr!; Family; Farm & Forest; Friend; Highlights for Children; Humpty Dumpty's; Ideals; Jack & Jill; Junior Trails; Lighted Pathway; Ms Mag.; My Friend; Pockets; Pony Ride; R-A-D-A-R; Ranger Rick's Nature Mag.; Secrets; Story Friends; Sunshine; Surprises; Teens Today; Touch; Trails; Turtle Mag.; Venture; Western Producer; The Wisconsin Restaurateur; Woman's Day; Wonder Time; Working For Boys; Working Mother; Young Crusader; Young Judean.

Men's. Autobuff; Buff; Buffalo Spree; Cavalier; Chicago; Contact High; Dialogue; Easyriders; Elite; Gem; Gent; Gentleman's Companion; Hers; Highwire; Hustler; Ideals; Lookout; Lutheran Journal; Mademoiselle; Men; Nugget; Oui; Penthouse; Penthouse (UK); Playboy; Prime Times; Road King; Stag; Sunshine; Surgical Technologist; Swank; Western Producer; Wisconsin Restaurateur; Wyo. Rural Elec. News.

Mystery/Spy/Suspense. Ahoy; Alfred Hitchcock's Mystery Mag.; Augusta Spectator; Boys' Life; Buffalo Spree; Chatelaine; Chesapeake Bay; Christian Adventure; Clubhouse; Cosmopolitan; Dialogue; Discoveries; Ebony Jr!; Ellery Queen's Mystery Mag.; Fair Lady; Family Circle; Gent; Gospel Carrier; Greek Accent; Hang Gliding Mag.; Hi-Call; High Adventure; Highwire; Inside Running; Jack & Jill; Men; Messenger of the Sacred Heart; Mike Shayne Mystery Mag.; Mother; Ms Mag.; National Forum; Phi Kappa Phi Journal; National Supermarket Shopper; New Eng. Senior Citizen News; Nugget; Other Side; Oui; Playboy; Pockets; Prestige; Prime Times; Ranger Rick's Nature Mag.; Read; Road King; Sat. Evening Post; Rod Serling's Twilight Zone Mag.; Seventeen; Straight; Surgical Technologist; 'Teen Mag.; Trailer Boats Mag.; Trails; Western Producer; Wisconsin Restaurateur; Woman's World; Young Judean.

Prose Poem. Bird Talk; Boston Monthly; Butterfat; Campus Life; Currents; The Family; Friday of Jewish Exponent; My Friend; National Forum: Phi Kappa Phi Journal; One Mag.; Prestige Mag.; Sat. Evening Post.

Psychic/Supernatural. Bronze Thrills; Color Computer; Currents; Dialogue; Essence; Gent; Hers; Highwire Mag.; Ideals; Messenger of Sacred Heart; National Doll World; New Age; Nugget; Oracle; Penthouse; Prestige Mag.; Rod Serling's Twilight Zone; Stag; Stories.

Religious/Inspirational. Alive!; Alive Now!; Bible in Life Friends; Bible in Life Stories; Bird Talk; Brigade Leader; Charisma; Christian Adventure; Christian Life; Christian Living for Senior Highs; Church Herald; Church Musician; Clubhouse; Columbia; Contact High; Crusader; Dash; Daughters of Sarah; Discoveries; Evangel; Face-to-Face; Family; Family Circle; Friday of the Jewish Exponent; Friend; Gospel Carrier; Hi-Call; High Adventure; His Mag.; Home Life; Ideals; In Touch; Insight; Junior Trails; Lighted Pathway; Liguorian; Live; Living With Teenagers; Lookout; Lutheran Journal; Mature Living; Mature Years; Messenger of Sacred Heart; Modern Liturgy; Moment Mag.; My Friend; National Doll World; New Age; One Mag.; Our Family; Pockets; Prestige Mag.; Queen of All Hearts; Reader's Choice; Reality; St. Anthony Messenger; St. Joseph's Messenger & Advocate of the Blind; San Gabriel Valley Mag.; Sat. Evening Post; Seek; Seventeen; Sprint; Story Friends; Straight; Student; Sunday Digest; Sunshine Mag.; Surgical Technologist; Surprises; Teens Today; Today's Christian Woman; Touch; Trails; Venture; Virtue; Vista; Woman's Day; Wonder Times; Working For Boys; World Over; Young Ambassador; Young & Alive; Young Judean.

Romance (Contemporary). Affaire de Coeur; Augusta Spectator; Bronze Thrills; Chatelaine; Cosmopolitan; Darling; Essence; Fair Lady; Family Circle; Family Radio & TV Mag.; First Class; Good Housekeeping; Hi-Call; Messenger of Sacred Heart; Mother; My Weekly; National Supermarket Shopper; Playgirl; Prestige; Prime Times; Rapport; Reader's Choice; Romantic Times; St. Joseph's Messenger & Advocate of the Blind; Seventeen; Straight; 'Teen Mag.; Teens Today; Trails; Woman's World; Young Miss; Your Family.

Romance (Gothic). Affaire de Coeur; Fair Lady; Good Housekeeping; Romantic Times; Sat. Evening Post.

Science Fiction. Amazing Sci. Fi. Stories; American Squaredance; Analog Sci. Fi./Sci. Fact; Ares; Boys' Life; Campus Life; Cavalier; Color Computer; Crusader; Currents; Ebony Jr!; Fair Lady; Gallery Mag.; Gent; Hang Gliding Mag.; Inside Running; Isaac Asimov's Sci. Fi. Mag.; Jack & Jill; Men; Messenger of Sacred Heart; Ms Mag.; National Forum; Phi Kappa Phi Journal; Nugget; Omni; Oracle; Penthouse; Playboy; Players; Ranger Rick's Nature Mag.; Read; Road King; Running Times; Sat. Evening Post; Rod Serling's Twilight Zone Mag.; Seventeen; Surgical Technologist; Trailer Boats Mag.; Trails; Wisconsin Restaurateur; Young Judean.

Serialized, Condensed or Excerpted Novels. Amazing Sci. Fi. Stories; Analog Sci. Fi./Sci. Fact; B'nai B'rith Int. Jewish Monthly; Boston Review; Bronze Thrills; Campus Life; Capper's Weekly; Chicago; Darling; Ebony Jr!; Essence; Fair Lady; Friday of Jewish Exponent; Inside Running; Mademoiselle; McCall's; Moment; My Weekly; National Forum; Phi Kappa Phi Journal; New Age; New Satirist; Oracle; Penthouse; Playgirl; Prestige; Redbook; Romantic Times; Runner; Stories; Virtue; Western People; Western Producer.

Translations. Boston Monthly; Boston Review; Friday of Jewish Exponent; Greek Accent; Inside, Moment Mag.; New Age; Romantic Times; Runner; Scandinavian Review; Stories; World Over; Young Judean.

Western. American Squaredance; Boys' Life; Clubhouse; Dialogue; Ebony Jr!; Gentleman's Companion; Hi-Call; High Adventure; Messenger of Sacred Heart; New Eng. Senior Citizen News; Penthouse; Playboy; Road King; San Gabriel Valley Mag.; Sat. Evening Post; Seventeen; Western Producer; Wisconsin Restaurateur; Wyo. Rural Elec. News.

Women's. Birmingham Settlement Mags; Buffalo Spree; Chicago; Christian Life; Contact High; Cosmopolitan; Daughters of Sarah; Deaf Canadian; Dialogue; Electricity; Esquire; Fair Lady; Family Circle; Family Radio & TV Mag.; Flare; Good Housekeeping; Hers; Highwire; Ideals; Lady's Circle; Lookout; Lutheran Journal; Mademoiselle; McCall's; Mother; Ms Mag.; My Weekly; National Supermarket Shopper; Pioneer Woman; Playgirl; Prestige; Prime Times;

Reader's Choice; Reality; Redbook; Secrets; Stories; Sunshine; Today's Christian Woman; Virtue; Western Producer; Wisconsin Restaurateur; Woman's Day; Working Mother; Wyo. Rural Elec. News; Your Family.

Young Adult. Alive!; Boys' Life; Campus Life; Canadian Skater; Christian Adventure; Christian Living for Senior Highs; Church Herald; Cobblestone; Co-ed; Electricity; Farm & Forest; Gospel Carrier; Hers; Hi-Call; Highwire; His; Home Life; Insight; Lighted Pathway; Liguorian; Lookout; Lutheran Journal; One Mag.; Pony Ride Mag.; Prestige; Read; Reader's Choice; Reality; Scholastic Scope; Seventeen; Sprint; 'Teen Mag.; Teens Today; Trails; Venture; Wisconsin Restaurateur; Young & Alive; Young Miss.

Small Press

Adventure. Acheron Press; Agape; Ariadne Press; Autolycus Press; Le Beacon Presse; Beninda Books; Bicentennial Enterprises; E&E Pub.; Fjord Press; Johnston Green and Co.; Jump River Press; Mainespring Press; Pentagram; Pheasant Run Pub.; Phunn Pub.; Quality Pub.; Shameless Hussy Press; Tide Book Pub.; Triple 'P' Pub.; Woodsong Graphics.

Canada. Guernica Editions; Kids Can Press; Peppermint Press; Prairie Pub.; Press Gang Pub.; Thistledown Press; Three Trees Press; Turnstone Press; Underwhich Editions; Vehicule Press; Women's Educational Press; York Press.

Contemporary/Mainstream. Acheron Press; Agape; Ansuda Pub.; Applezaba Press; Ariadne Press; Autolycus Press; Avant Books; Berkeley Poets Workshop; Bieler Press; BKMK Press; Books For All Times; Broken Whisper Studio; Carpenter Press; Chapman; Cross-Cultural Comm.; Crossing Press; Deinotation-7 Press; Dragonsbreath Press; Dream Garden Press; Dufour Editions; E&E Pub.; Expanded Media Editions; Fablewaves Press; Fiction Collective; Fjord Press; Folder Editions; Griffon House Pub.; Guernica Editions; Harian Creative Press Books; Anne Johnston/Moorlands Press; Johnston Green and Co.; Jump River Press; Kawabata Press; Lame Johnny Press; Lapis Educational Assoc.; Lost Roads Pub.; Low-Tech Press; Mainespring Press; New Rivers Press; North Point Press; Panjandrum Books; Paycock Press; Peace Press; Pig Iron Press; Pikestaff Pub.; Plain Wrapper Press; Pressed Curtains; Proza Press; Quality Pub.; Raccoon Books; Second Coming Press; Seed Center; Seven Buffaloes Press; Shameless Hussy Press; S.O.S. Books; Station Hill Press; Story Press; Sun & Moon Press; Surey Books; Thunder City Press; Tide Book Pub.; Underwhich Editions; Univ. of Illinois Press; Sherry Urie; Woodsong Graphics; Wolfhound Press; York Press; Zephyr Press.

Erotica. Allegany Mountain Press; Angel Press; Applezaba Press; Le Beacon Presse; E&E Pub.; Fantome Press; Guernica Editions; Anne Johnston/Moorlands Press; Jump River Press; Maize Press; Pentagram; Perivale Press; Pheasant Run Pub.; Pressed Curtains; Surey Books; Underwhich Editions.

Ethnic. Akiba Press; Le Beacon Presse; Bilingual Press; BKMK Press; Challenge Press; Cross-Cultural Comm.; Dufour Editions; Fjord Press; Griffon House Pub.; Lost Roads Pub.; Maize Press; New Seed Press; Perivale Press; Seven Buffaloes Press; Shameless Hussy Press; Story Press; Woodsong Graphics; Zephyr Press.

Experimental. Acheron Press; Allegany Mountain Press; And Books; Angst World Library; Applezaba Press; Berkeley Poets Workshop; BKMK Press; Broken Whisper Studio; Carpenter Press; Chthon Press; Cross-Cultural Comm.; Diana's; Dimensionist Press; Dragonsbreath Press; Dream Garden Press; Dufour Editions; E&E Pub.; Expanded Media Editions; Fablewaves Press; Fiction Collective; Fjord Press; Fly By Night; Gay Sunshine Press; Griffon House Pub.; I-74 Press; Anne Johnston/Moorlands Press; Johnston Green and Co.; Jump River Press; Kawabata Press; Laughing Bear Press; Lintel; Lorien House; Lost Roads Pub.; Low-Tech Press; Maize Press; Mole Pub.; New Rivers Press; North Point Press; Panjandrum Books; Paycock Press; Pentagram; Pheasant Run Pub.; Pikestaff Pub.; Pig Iron Press; Plain Wrapper Press; Pressed Curtains; Proza Press; Raccoon Books; School of Living Press; Shameless

Hussy Press; The Smith; S.O.S. Books; Station Hill Press; Sun & Moon Press; Thunder City Press; Treacle Press; Underwhich Editions; Univ. of Illinois Press; Woodsong Graphics; Wolfhound Press; York Press; Zephyr Press.

Fantasy. And Books; Angst World Library; Ansuda Pub.; Applezaba Press; Autolycus Press; Berkeley Poets Workshop; Buckskin Pub.; Carpenter Press; Dimensionist Press; Dragonsbreath Press; E&E Pub.; Fablewaves Press; Fantome Press; W.D. Firestone Press; Fjord Press; Flying Buttress Pub.; Folder Editions; Harian Creative Press; Jelm Mountain Pub.; Anne Johnston/Moorlands Press; Johnston Green and Co.; Laughing Bear Press; Lorien House; Mars Hill Assoc.; Panjandrum Books; Parkhurst Press; Perivale Press; Pheasant Run Pub.; Phunn Pub.; Pig Iron Press; Plain Wrapper Press; Proza Press; Second Coming Press; Shameless Hussy Press; Spectre Press; Triple 'P' Pub.; Underwood/Miller; Woodsong Graphics.

Feminist or Lesbian. Angel Press; Applezaba Press; Ariadne Press; Calamus Books; Crossing Press; Fjord Press; Frog in the Well; Gay Sunshine Press; Guernica Editions; Lost Roads Pub.; Metis Press; Naiad Press; New Seed Press; Peace Press; Sun & Moon Press; Surey Books; Wim Pub.; Zephyr Press.

Foreign. J.S. Cairns; Chapman; Expanded Media Editions; Anne Johnston/Moorlands Press; Kawabata Press; Pan Pacific Pub.; Plain Wrapper Press; Pressed Curtains; Proza Press; Spectre Press; Wolfhound Press.

Gay. Angel Press; Appelzaba Press; Calamus Books; Crossing Press; Fjord Press; Frog in the Well; Guernica Editions; Lost Roads Pub.; Metis Press; Naiad Press; New Seed Press; Parkhurst Press; Peace Press; Perivale Press; Persephone Press; Press Gang Pub.; Shameless Hussy Press; Sun & Moon Press; Swiftwater Books; Treacle Press; Wim Pub.; Zephyr Press.

Historical. Akiba Press; Ariadne Press; Autolycus Press; Bilingual Press; BKMK Press; Challenge Press; E&E Pub.; Fjord Press; Jelm Mountain Pub.; Jump River Press; Lame Johnny Press; Library Research Assoc.; Mainspring; Micah Pub.; Mosaic Press; New Rivers Press; Pheasant Run Pub.; Phunn Pub.; Pressworks Pub.; Quality Pub.; Shameless Hussy Press; Triple 'P' Pub.; Sherry Urie; Woodsong Graphics; Zephyr Press.

Horror. Angst World Library; Ansuda Pub.; W.D. Firestone Press; Fjord Press; Flying Buttress Pub.; Johnston Green and Co.; Jump River Press; Laughing Bear Press; Pheasant Run Pub.; Proza Press; S&S Press; Spectre Press; Triple 'P' Pub.; Underwood/Miller.

Humor. Allegany Mountain Press; Angel Press; Applezaba Press; Ariadne Press; Autolycus Press; Le Beacon Press; Berkeley Poets Workshop; Creative With Words Pub.; Cross-Cultural Comm.; Dragonsbreath Press; E&E Pub.; Fablewaves Press; Flying Buttress Pub.; Guernica Editions; Johnston Green and Co.; Kawabata Press; Lorien House; Low-Tech Press; Mainspring Press; Mosaic Press; Pacific Arts and Letters; Parkhurst Press; Paycock Press; Peace Press; Phunn Pub.; Pig Iron Press; Pressworks Pub.; Proza Press; S&S Press; Second Coming Press; Shameless Hussy Press; Tide Book Pub.; Vehicule Press; Woodsong Graphics; Zephyr Press.

Juvenile. Acheron Press; Agape; Andrew Mountain Press; Autolycus Press; Avant Books; Carnival Press; Coffee Break Press; Creative With Words Pub.; Cross-Cultural Comm.; Dillon Press; Dimensionist Press; E&E Pub.; East Eagle Press; Guernica Editions; In Between Books; Jump River Press; Kids Can Press; Los Tres Osos; Maize Press; Masters Pub.; Mosaic Press; New Seed Press; Parents Without Partners; Pascal Pub.; Phunn Pub.; Press Gang Pub.; Rossel Books; Shameless Hussy Press; Spectre Press; Three Trees Press; Vehicule Press; Woodsong Graphics; Wolfhound Press.

Mystery/Spy/Suspense. Acheron Press; And Books; Angst World Library; Anusda Pub.; Ariadne Press; Autolycus Press; Le Beacon Presse; Beninda Books; Bicentennial Era Enterprises; Challenge Press; E&E Pub.; Fjord Press; Flying Buttress Pub.; Johnston Green and Co.; Laughing Bear Press; Phunn Pub.; Proza Press; Shameless Hussy Press; Sherry Urie; Vehicule Press; Woodsong Graphics.

Commercial Publishers

Adventure. Avon Books; Bantam Books; Beaufort Books; Bethany House Pub.; Borealis Press; Bradbury Press; Broadman Press; Clarke, Irwin & Co.; Dandelion Press; Dale Pub. Co.; Dial Press; Dodd, Mead & Co.; Doubleday Canada; Fawcett; Bernard Geis Assoc.; David R. Godine, Pub.; Great Western Pub.; Harle House; Harlequin Ent.; Highway Book Shop; Holiday House; Holloway House Pub.; Houghton Mifflin Co.; Knopf & Pantheon Books for Young Readers; Lester & Orpen Dennys; Lodestar Books; Manyland Books; Moody Press; Wm. Morrow & Co.; Mountaineers Books; New American Library; New Readers Press; W.W. Norton & Co.; Pocket Books; Clarkson N. Potter; Random House; Red Dembner Ent.; St. Martins Press; Chas. Scribner's Sons; Seal Books; McClelland & Stewart-Bantam; Simon & Pierre Pub. Co.; Tor Books; Univ. of Missouri Press; Western Pub. Co.; Zebra Books.

Canada. Borealis Press; Clarke, Irwin & Co.; Doubleday Canada; Highway Book Shop; Lester & Orpen Dennys; Macmillan of Canada; Seal Books; McClelland & Stewart-Bantam Ltd.; Simon & Pierce Pub.; Vesta Pub.

Confession. Doubleday Canada; New American Library; St. Martin's Press; Zebra Books.

Contemporary/Mainstream. Ace/Tempo Books; Alchemy Books; Avon Books; Bantam Books; Beaufort Books; John F. Blair, Pub.; Bobbs-Merrill Co.; Bookcraft; Marion Boyars Pub.; Bradbury Press, Inc.; Clarke, Irwin & Co.; David C. Cook, Pub.; Crossway Books; Dandelion Press; Dial Press; Dodd, Mead & Co.; Doubleday Canada; E.P. Dutton Pub.; Paul S. Eriksson, Pub.; Bernard Geis Assoc.; David R. Godine, Pub.; Great Western Pub.; Grove Press; Harle House; Harmony Books; Highway Book Shop; Holiday House; Holloway House; Houghton Mifflin; Icarus Press; Alfred A. Knopf; Knopf & Pantheon Books for Young Readers; Lester & Orpen Dennys; Lodester Books; Madrona Pub.; Moody Press; New American Library; W.W. Norton & Co.; Pan American Pub. Co.; Pelican Pub. Co.; Pinnacle Books; Pocket Books; Clarkson N. Potter; Princeton Love Romances; Random House; Red Dembner Enterprises; St. Martin's Press; Chas. Scribner's Sons; Seal Books, McClelland & Stewart-Bantam; Sierra Club Books; Signet, Simon & Pierre Pub. Co.; Gibbs M. Smith; Sonica Press; Stemmer House Pub.; Tandem Press Pub.; Texas Monthly Press; Thorndike Press; Tor Books; Univ. of Missouri Press; Virago Press; Wolfhound Press; Zebra Books.

Erotica. Greenleaf Classics; Grove Press; Manyland Books; Pocket Books; St. Martin's Press; Zebra Books.

Ethnic. Bantam Books; John F. Blair, Pub.; Marion Boyars Pub.; Crown Pub.; Doubleday Canada; David R. Godine, Pub.; Great Western Pub.; Grove Press; Highway Book Shop; Holloway House; Manyland Books; Pelican Pub.; Pocket Books; Stemmer House; Texas Monthly Press; Univ. of Missouri Press; Vista Pub.; Winston-Derek Pub.

Experimental. Avalon Books; John F. Blair, Pub.; Marion Boyars Pub.; George Braziller; Columbia Pub. Co.; E.P. Dutton Pub.; Green Tiger Press; Grove Press; Lester & Orpen Dennys; Manyland Books; Wm. Morrow & Co.; Pelican Pub. Co.; Persea Books; St. Martin's Press; Vesta Pub.; Wolfhound Press.

Fantasy. Ace Science Fiction; Alchemy Books; Bantam Books; Beaufort Books; Clarke, Irwin Co.; Crossway Books; Crown Pub.; Daw Books; Tom Doherty Assoc.; Gospel Light Pub.; Great Western Pub.; Highway Book Shop; Houghton Mifflin Co.; Knopf & Pantheon Books for Young Readers; Pan American Pub. Co.; Pocket Books; Quantum Universe Special Editions; St. Martin's Press; Seal Books, McClelland & Stewart-Bantam; Sonica Press; Stemmer House Pub.; Tor Books; Virago Press.

Feminist or Lesbian. Academy Chicago; Bantam Books; Dial Press; Grove Press; Wm. Morrow & Co.; St. Martin's Press; Timely Books; Winston-Derek Pub.

Gay. Bantam Books; John F. Blair, Pub.; Marion Boyars Pub.; George Braziller; Doubleday Canada; Grove Press; Wm. Morrow & Co.; W.W. Norton & Co.; St. Martin's Press; Chas. Scribner's Sons; Timely Books; Univ. of Missouri Press; Virago Press; Winston-Derek Pub.

Historical. Alchemy Books; Ballantine Books; Bantam Books; Bethany House Pub.; Bobbs-Merrill Co.; Bookcraft, Inc.; Borealis Press; Broadman Press; Clarke, Irwin & Co.; Columbia Pub. Co.; Dandelion Press; Dell Pub. Co.; Dial Press; Dodd, Mead & Co.; Doubleday Canada; Fawcett; David R. Godine, Pub.; Great Western Pub. Co.; Grove Press; Harle House; Harequin Ent.; Highway Book Shop; Icarus Press; Manyland Books; Moody Press; Wm. Morrow & Co.; New American Library; W.W. Norton & Co.; Pan American Pub. Co.; Pelican Pub. Co.; Pocket Books; Clarkson N. Potter; Random Houe; Red Dembner, Ent.; St. Martin's Press; Simon & Pierre Pub.; Gibbs M. Smith; Sonica Press; Stemmer House Pub.; Tandem Press Pub.; Texas Monthly Press; Thorndike Press; Vesta Pub.; Winston-Derek Pub.; Zebra Books.

Horror. Ace Charter Books; Bantam Books; Dandelion Press; Dell Pub.; Tom Doherty Assoc.; Bernard Geis Assoc.; David R. Godine, Pub.; Knopf & Pantheon Books for Young Readers; Lester & Orpen Dennys; Wm. Morrow & Co.; New American Library; Pan American Pub. Co.; Pinnacle Books; Pocket Books; Quantum Universe Special Editions; St. Martin's Press; Signet; Tor Books; Walker & Co.; Zebra Books.

Humor. Alchemy Books; Bantam Books; Beaufort Books; John F. Blair, Pub.; Bradbury Press; Broadman Press; Clarke, Irwin & Co.; Crown Pub.; Dandelion Press; Dodd, Mead & Co.; Doubleday Canada; E.P. Dutton Pub.; David R. Godine, Pub.; Great Western Pub.; Grove Press; Highway Book Shop; Holiday House; Knopf & Pantheon Books for Young Readers; Lester & Orpen Dennys; Lodestar Books; Wm. Morrow & Co.; Mountaineers Books; W.W. Norton & Co.; Pelican Pub. Co.; Pocket Books; Clarkson N. Potter; Quantum Universe Special Editions; St. Martin's Press; Chas. Scribner's Sons; Signet; Simon & Pierre Pub. Co.; Sonica Press; Texas Monthly Press; Thorndike Press; Univ. of Missouri Press; Virago Press; Western Pub. Co.

Juvenile. A&P Books; Alchemy Books; Archway Paperbacks; Atlantic Monthly Press; Baker Book House; Bethany House Pub.; Borealis Press; Bradbury Press; Broadman Press; Children's Press; Child's World; Clarion Books, Ticknor & Fields; Clarke, Irwin & Co.; David C. Cook Pub. Co.; Crossway Books; Crown Pub.; Dandelion Press; Dodd, Mead & Co.; E.P. Dutton Pub.; Eakin Pub.; EDC Pub.; EMC Pub.; Farrar, Straus & Giroux; David R. Godive, Pub.; Gospel Light Pub.; Green Tiger Press; Harcourt Brace Jovanovich; Harle House; Harper & Row Jr. Books; Herald Press; Highway Book Shop; Houghton Mifflin Co.; Ideals Pub.; Knopf & Pantheon Books for Young Readers; Little, Brown & Co.; Lodestar Books; Macmillan Pub.; Margaret K. McElderry Books/Atheneum Pub.; Moody Press; Mott Media; Oak Tree Pub.; Oddo Pub.; Parents Mag. Press; Parker Bros. Children's Books; Pelican Pub. Co.; Philomel Books; Platt & Munk; Clarkson N. Potter; Prentice-Hall; Rand McNally & Co.; Random House; St. Paul Editions; Scholastic-Tab Pub.; Chas. Scribner's Sons; Chas. Scribner's Sons, Books for Young Readers; Sierra Club Books; Silhouette Books; Simon & Pierre Pub.; Standard Pub.; Stemmer House Pub.; Vesta Pub; Walker & Co.; Fred. Warne & Co.; Western Pub. Co.; Westminster Press; Albert Whitman & Co.; Winston-Derek Pub.; Wolfhound Press.

Mystery/Spy/Suspense. Academy Chicago; Ace Charter Books; Ace/Tempo Books; Avon Books; Bantam Books; Bethany House Pub.; Clarke, Irwin & Co.; Crown Pub.; Dandelion Press; Dell Pub. Co.; Dial Press; Dodd, Mead & Co.; Doubleday Canada; E.P. Dutton Pub.; Fawcett; Bernard Geis Assoc.; David R. Godine, Pub.; Great Western Pub.; Grove Press; Harlequin Ent.; Highway Book Shop; Houghton Mifflin Co.; Alfred A. Knopf; Knopf & Pantheon Books for Young Readers; Lester & Orpen Dennys; Manyland Books; Wm. Morrow & Co.; New American Library; W.W. Norton & Co.; Pan American Pub. Co.; Pelican Pub. Co.; Pinnacle Books; Pocket Books; Random House; Red Dembner Ent.; St. Martin's Press; Chas. Scribner's Sons; Seal Books, McClelland & Stewart-Bantam; Simon & Pierre Pub. Co.; Sonica Press; Tandem Press Pub.; Texas Monthly Press; Thorndike Press; Walker & Co.; Western Pub. Co.; Winston-Derek Pub.

Psychic/Supernatural. Bantam Books; Dandelion Press; Dell Pub. Co.; Tom Doherty Assoc.; Doubleday Canada; Bernard Geis Assoc.; Great Western Pub.; Knopf & Pantheon Books for

Young Readers; Pan American Pub. Co.; Pocket Books; Quantum Universe Special Editions; St. Martin's Press; Seal Books, McClelland & Stewart-Bantam; Zebra Books.

Religious/Inspirational. Augsburg Pub. House; Bantam Books; Bethany House Pub.; Bookcraft; Broadman Press; Concordia Pub. House; David C. Cook Pub.; Crossway Books; Dial Press; Dodd, Mead & Co.; Gospel Light Pub.; Great Western Pub.; Harle Houe; Herald Press; Highway Book Shop; Manyland Books; Moody Press; Mott Media Pub.; New American Library; Pelican Pub. Co.; St. Martin's Press; Standard Pub.; Vesta Publications; Virago Press; Winston-Derek Pub.

Romance (Contemporary). Archway Paperbacks; Avalon Books; Ballantine Books; Bantam Books; Bookcraft; Bradbury Press; Dell Pub. Co.; Harle House; Harlequin Ent.; Highway Book Shop; Holiday House; Holiday House Pub.; Loveswept; Wm. Morrow & Co., Inc.; Pocket Books; Princeton Love Romances; St. Martin's Press; Second Chance at Love; Signet; Silhouette Books; Sweet Dreams; Tandem Press Pub.; Vesta Pub.; Walker & Co.

Romance (Gothic/Historical). Ballantine Books; Bantam Books; Bethany House Pub.; Dandelion Press; Dodd, Mead & Co.; Great Western Pub.; Highway Book Shop; Houghton Mifflin Co.; Loveswept; New Readers Press; Pocket Books; Seal Books, McClelland & Stewart-Bantam; Tandem Press Pub.; Tapestry Romances; Vesta Pub.; Winston-Derek Pub.; Zebra Books.

Science Fiction. Ace Science Fiction; Ace/Tempo Books; Alchemy Books; Bantam Books; Marion Boyars Pub.; Bradbury Press; Crossway Books; Dandelion Press; Daw Books; Tom Doherty Assoc.; Great Western Pub.; Grove Press; Holiday House; Houghton Mifflin Co.; Knopf & Pantheon Books for Young Readers; Wm. Morrow & Co.; New American Library; Pan American Pub. Co.; Pocket Books; Quantum Universe Special Editions; St. Martin's Press; Chas. Scribner's Sons; Seal Books, McClelland & Stewart-Bantam; Sonica Press; Timescape Books; Tor Books; Vesta Pub.; Virago Press; Walker & Co.

Short Story Collections. Marion Boyars Pub.; George Braziller; Crossway Books; Highway Book Shop; Princeton Love Romances; Random House; Virago Press; Winston-Derek Pub.; Wolfhound Press.

Translations. Academy Chicago; Marion Boyars Pub.; George Braziller; Columbia Pub.; Doubleday Canada; E.P. Dutton Pub.; Grove Press; Icarus Press; Lester & Orpen Dennys; Manyland Books; Wm. Morrow & Co.; W.W. Norton & Co.; Pelican Pub.; Persea Books; Chas. Scribner's Sons; Simon & Pierre Pub. Co.; Sonica Press; Vesta Pub.; Virago Press.

War. Bantam Books; Bobbs-Merrill Co.; Clarke, Irwin & Co.; Dandelion Press; Dell Pub. Co.; Dodd, Mead & Co.; Doubleday Canada; E.P. Dutton Pub.; Great Western Pub.; Houghton Mifflin Co.; Icarus Press; Manyland Books; Wm. Morrow & Co.; New American Library; W.W. Norton & Co.; Pelican Pub. Co.; Pinnacle Books; Pocket Books; St. Martin's Press; Stemmer House; Univ. of Missouri Press; Vesta Pub.; Zebra Books.

Western. Avalon Books; Avon Books; Bantam Books; Bookcraft, Inc.; Dandelion Press; Dial Press; Great Western Pub.; Moody Press; W.W. Norton & Co.; Pocket Books; St. Martin's Press; Seal Books, McClelland & Stewart-Bantam; Texas Monthly Press; Walker & Co.

Women's. Ace/Tempo Books; Ballantine Books; Bantam Books; Beaufort Books; Bobbs-Merrill Co.; Bookcraft; Marion Boyars Pub.; Clarke, Irwin & Co.; David C. Cook Pub.; Dandelion Press; Dial Press; Dodd, Mead & Co.; Doubleday Canada; E.P. Dutton Pub.; Fawcett; Houghton Mifflin Co.; Wm. Morrow & Co.; Mott Media; New American Library; W.W. Norton & Co.; Pinnacle Books; Pocket Books; Clarkson N. Potter; Random House; St. Martin's Press; Seal Books, McClelland & Stewart-Bantam Ltd.; Signet; Tandem Press Pub.; Virago Press; Zebra Books.

Young Adult. A&P Books; Ace/Tempo Books; Archway Paperbacks; Atlantic Monthly Press; Augsburg Pub. House; Bantam Books; Beaufort Books; John F. Blair, Pub.; Borealis Press; Marion Boyars Pub.; Bradbury Press; Broadman Press; Clarion Books, Ticknor & Fields; Clark, Irwin & Co.; David C. Cook Pub.; Crossway Books; Crocon Pub.; Dandelion Press; Dell Pub.

Co.; Dodd, Mead & Co.; E.P. Dutton Pub.; EDC Pub.; EMC Pub.; Farrar, Straus & Giroux; Flare Books; David R. Godine, Pub.; Gospel Light Pub.; Great Western Pub. Co.; Harcourt Brace Jovanovich; Harle House; Harper & Row Jr. Books Group; Herald Press; Knopf & Pantheon Books for Young Readers; Little, Brown & Co.; Lodestar Books; Margaret K. McElderry Books/ Atheneum Pub.; Moody Press; New Readers Press; Oak Tree Pub.; Pelican Pub. Co.; Philomel Books; Platt & Munk; Prentice-Hall; Quantum Universe Special Editions; Chas. Scribner's Sons; Chas. Scribner's Sons, Books for Young Readers; Seal Books, McClelland & Stewart-Bantam; Signet; Simon & Pierre Pub.; Stemmer House Pub.; Sweet Dreams; Tor Books; Vesta Pub.; Walker & Co.; Fred. Warne & Co.; Westminster Press; Winston-Derek Pub.

Index

E

H

I

T

Other Writer's Digest Books

General Writing Books
  Beginning Writer's Answer Book, edited by Polking, et al $9.95
  How to Get Started in Writing, by Peggy Teeters $10.95
  Law and the Writer, edited by Polking and Meranus (paper) $7.95
  Make Every Word Count, by Gary Provost (paper) $6.95
  Teach Yourself to Write, by Evelyn Stenbock $12.95
  Treasury of Tips for Writers, edited by Marvin Weisbord (paper) $6.95
  Writer's Encyclopedia, edited by Kirk Polking $19.95
  Writer's Market, $18.95
  Writer's Resource Guide, edited by Bernadine Clark $16.95
  Writing for the Joy of It, by Leonard Knott $11.95
Magazine/News Writing
  Craft of Interviewing, by John Brady $9.95
  Magazine Writing: The Inside Angle, by Art Spikol $12.95
  Newsthinking: The Secret of Great Newswriting, by Bob Baker $11.95
  Stalking the Feature Story, by William Ruehlmann $9.95
  Write On Target, by Connie Emerson $12.95
  Writing and Selling Non-Fiction, by Hayes B. Jacobs $12.95
Fiction Writing
  Fiction Writer's Help Book, by Maxine Rock $12.95
  Fiction Writer's Market, edited by Jean Fredette $17.95
  Handbook of Short Story Writing, edited by Dickson and Smythe (paper) $6.95
  How to Write Best-Selling Fiction, by Dean R. Koontz $13.95
  How to Write Short Stories that Sell, by Louise Boggess $9.95
  One Way to Write Your Novel, by Dick Perry (paper) $6.95
  Writing Romance Fiction—For Love and Money, by Helene Schellenberg Barnhart $14.95
  Writing the Novel: From Plot to Print, by Lawrence Block $10.95
Special Interest Writing Books
  Children's Picture Book: How to Write It, How to Sell It, by Ellen E.M. Roberts $17.95
  Complete Book of Scriptwriting, by J. Michael Straczynski $14.95
  How to Make Money Writing . . . Fillers, by Connie Emerson $12.95
  How to Write and Sell Your Personal Experiences, by Lois Duncan $10.95
  How to Write & Sell (Your Sense of) Humor, by Gene Perret $12.95
  How to Write "How-To" Books and Articles, by Raymond Hull (paper) $8.95
  Mystery Writer's Handbook, edited by Lawrence Treat (paper) $8.95
  Poet's Handbook, by Judson Jerome $11.95
  TV Scriptwriter's Handbook, by Alfred Brenner $12.95
  Travel Writer's Handbook, by Louise Purwin Zobel $13.95
  Writing and Selling Science Fiction, Compiled by The Science Fiction Writers of America (paper) $7.95
  Writing for Children & Teenagers, by Wyndham/Madison $10.95
  Writing to Inspire, by Gentz, Roddy, et al $14.95
The Writing Business
  Complete Handbook for Freelance Writers, by Kay Cassill $14.95
  How You Can Make $20,000 a Year Writing, by Nancy Edmonds Hanson (paper) $6.95
  Jobs for Writers, edited by Kirk Polking $11.95
  Writer's Survival Guide: How to Cope with Rejection, Success, and 99 Other Hang-Ups of the Writing Life, by Jean and Veryl Rosenbaum $12.95

To order directly from the publisher, include $1.50 postage and handling for 1 book and 50¢ for each additional book. Allow 30 days for delivery.

Writer's Digest Books, Department B
9933 Alliance Road, Cincinnati OH 45242
Prices subject to change without notice.

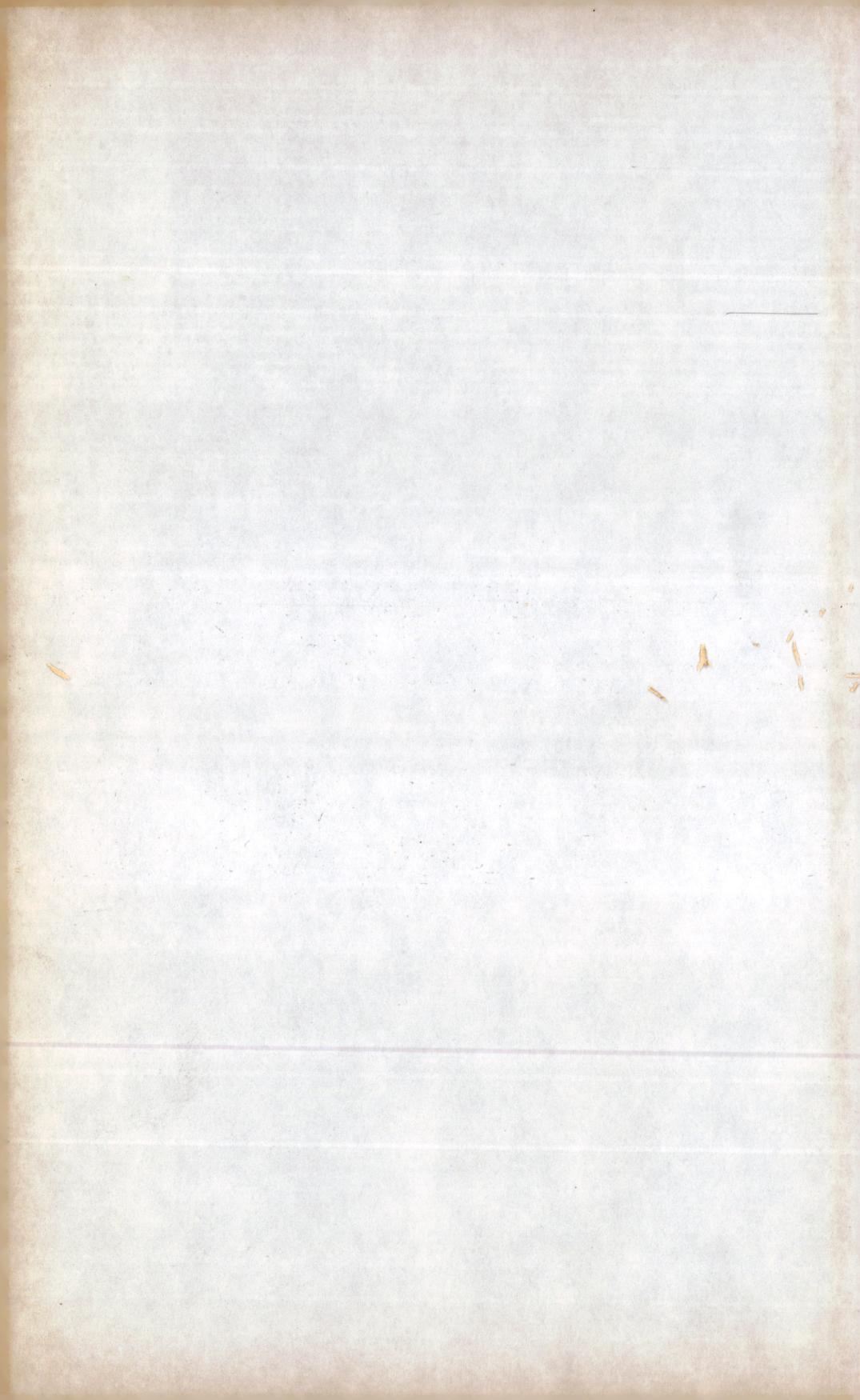